The FILE FORMATS Handbook

The FILE FORMATS Handbook

Günter Born

INTERNATIONAL THOMSON COMPUTER PRESS

I(T)P An International Thomson Publishing Company

London • New York • Bonn • Johannesburg • Boston • Madrid • Melbourne • Mexico City
Paris • Singapore • Tokyo • Toronto • Albany, NY • Belmont, CA • Cincinnati, OH • Detroit, MI

The File Formats Handbook

I(T)P A division of International Thomson Publishing Inc.
The ITP logo is a trademark under licence

British Library Cataloguing-in-Publication Data
A catalogue record for this book is available from the British Library

First printed 1995
Reprinted 1995
Printed in the UK by Clays Ltd, St Ives plc

ISBN 1-85032-117-5

International Thomson Computer Press
Berkshire House
High Holborn
London WC1V 7AA
UK

International Thomson Computer Press
20 Park Plaza
14th Floor
Boston MA 02116
USA

`http://www.thomson.com/itcp.html`

Imprints of International Thomson Publishing

Table of contents

Preface

In the beginning, mankind shared a common language. One day, the proud people of Babylon decided to build a huge tower. As punishment for their hubris, God smote them with confusion. Since that time, a multitude of languages has existed. This is the story of the Tower of Babel. Back in the good old days, there was only one file format. This was used by a single computer, the ENIAC. As time went by, people with different ideas built new towers (of computers). Thus, computers now use a multitude of different file formats....

In 1987 and 1988 I became involved in projects that required the exchange of data between spreadsheets, databases and the software that I was developing. Whilst working on these projects, I came across expressions such as DIF format, SYLK format and SDF format. At that time, detailed information about these formats was not available. A survey of the existing literature produced no results, simply because there was no published information. And so at the beginning of 1989, my editor, Georg Weiherer, and I came to the conclusion that a definitive text on file formats was badly needed. I took on this challenge. At that time I could not have foreseen the amount of trouble that this idea would cause me!

During the next two years, I collected all available information on the subject. This proved to be extremely difficult and frustrating. Many companies refused to release any information about the structure and contents of their file formats. Some companies ignored my queries, while others tried to use their legal advisers to discourage me from pursuing the project. But to be fair, I should mention that companies like WordPerfect, Lotus, Microsoft, Micrografx and GSS supported me by providing the required information.

After two long and painful years, the first edition of my file formats book was released for the German market. The book became a standard and, so far, several revised and extended editions have been released. The book will also be published in Russian.

My intention was to translate the book into English, to allow more programmers access to the information. Historically, however, translation has tended to be a one-way system, as many an

English language book has been rendered into other languages, but seldom the reverse. So it took some years for my project to see the light of day in English. I began to write the English version of the book in 1993. In the autumn of that year I met Bob Bolick of International Thomson Publishing, who agreed to publish the book. It took another year for me to complete the English version and include all the planned extensions.

Now the book is ready and I would like to thank my family for their patience, inspiration and support during the past year. My thanks also go to Bob Bolick, for deciding to go ahead with the project and to my editors Jonathan Simpson and Liz Israel for their cooperation and patience. Last but not least, I wish to thank the many reviewers who read the manuscript and helped to improve its clarity and simplicity.

I hope that this book will be a valid and helpful reference for everyone concerned with file formats. Collating the different file formats for publication has been a huge and sometimes frustrating task, both from a logistical and commercial viewpoint. Notwithstanding the difficulties, I would like to continue to improve future editions of this book; and for this I'm going to need all the help I can get. If you can help me, please send any comments or suggestions to me at the following address:

International Thomson Publishing Europe
Berkshire House
168-173 High Holborn
London WCIV 7AA
United Kingdom
E-mail (Internet): jonathan.simpson@ITPUK.CO.UK

This book is dedicated to all those involved in file formats, who would like to overcome the 'Tower of Babel' syndrome.

Günter Born

Introduction

***Word** processing, databases, spreadsheets, graphics, multimedia and so on are of growing importance for many people, and there are a huge number of programs available to carry out these tasks. The problem is, how do you exchange data created by one program with another program? Data exchange between programs from several vendors, or sometimes between programs from the same vendor, is quite often impossible. Many programs use their own vendor-specific file formats. Newer software for Windows or UNIX comes with import and export filters for different file formats, but not all formats are supported. To make your own software compatible with other file formats, information about the internal structure of these formats is needed. Unfortunately, most of the information about file formats is either confidential, not well documented, or not available for public use. This book puts an end to this situation and describes file formats for different platforms (DOS/Windows, OS/2, UNIX, Mac, Atari, Amiga). The goal is to support developers, consultants and users with a vendor- and product-independent reference for file formats.*

The book is divided into several parts:

Part 1

This part describes various dBASE compatible formats. The applications covered are dBASE, Clipper and FoxPro.

Part 2

This part deals with formats used by a number of spreadsheet programs. The formats used by LOTUS 1-2-3 and EXCEL are described, together with the specifications of data exchange formats such as DIFF, SYLK and so on.

Part 3

In the area of word processing, the number of formats is huge. This part describes the formats for MS-WORD, WordPerfect and AMI PRO. Program-independent formats such as Microsoft's Rich Text Format (RTF) and the SGML standard are also discussed.

Part 4

Storing and exchanging graphics data is one of the most important areas. Part 4 describes the most popular formats for graphics, animation and multimedia.

Part 5

Since the release of Windows 3.0 the formats used by this software have become more and more popular. This part describes formats such as BMP, WMF, WRI, CRD and so on. The OS/2 BMP formats are also discussed.

Part 6

Part 6 describes sound formats, including the formats for the Sound Blaster and Adlib cards as well as the MIDI file format.

Part 7

Many output devices use PostScript, HP-GL/2 or PCL commands. This part deals with the formats of these commands.

Appendices

The appendices contain additional information about conversion programs and a summary of several file formats.

PART 1

Database file formats

File formats discussed in Part 1

dBASE *is one of the most successful database programs in the PC sector. The first version of the program (dBASE II), whose file formats were partly published by Ashton Tate, was launched in 1983; the most recent version is dBASE V.*

Part 1 *deals with dBASE, Clipper and FoxPro file formats and with data exchange using the SDF format.*

1

File formats in dBASE II

Although *more recent versions of the program, in the form of dBASE III and IV, are available, dBASE II format is still used. The file formats of this early version are therefore described briefly below.*

1.1 dBASE II – Format of DBF files

dBASE II stores data in files with the suffix `.DBF`. These files have been structured in such a way that both data and the definitions of that data can be stored. Each DBF file therefore consists of three parts: the header, the field descriptions and the actual data records (Figure 1.1).

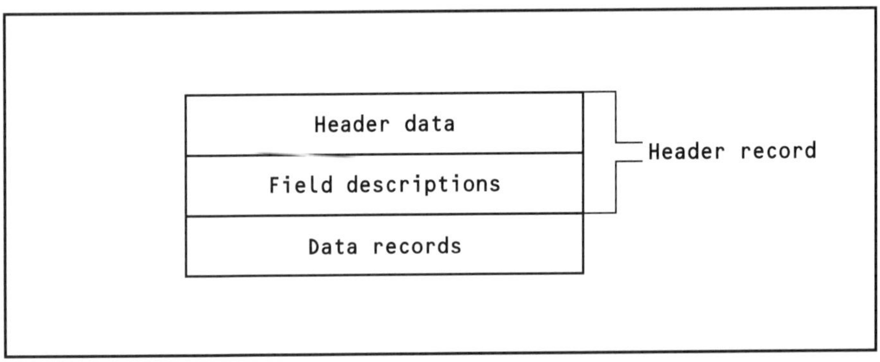

Figure 1.1
dBASE DBF file structure

The header record, which contains the header and the field descriptions, is 520 bytes in length and is structured as shown in Table 1.1:

Offset	Bytes	Remarks
00H	1	dBASE version number 02H dBASE II DBF file
01H	2	Number of data records (0-FFFFH)
03H	3	Date of last write access Binary format (DDMMYY)
06H	2	Record length in bytes (up to 1000)
08H-207H	16*n	16 bytes per field description; n is a maximum of 32
16*N+9	1	End of header marker (0DH)

Table 1.1 Format of a DBF header in dBASE II

The header occupies bytes 0 to 7. The first byte always contains the value 02H, which indicates a file created by dBASE II. Later versions of dBASE contain different identifiers. Bytes 1 and 2 contain the number of data records in the file. This value includes data records that have been marked for deletion but not yet removed with pack (this will be discussed in greater detail later). Up to 65535 data records can be stored using dBASE II.

dBASE II stores the date of the last write access in bytes 3 to 5. One byte each is used to represent the day, the month and the year. For example, the hex-values 0FH 07H 59H represent 15 July 1989.

The length of the data record is stored in bytes 6 and 7. The maximum record length allowed by dBASE II is 1000 bytes, and each record can be divided into a maximum of 32 fields. In general, the field limit is reached before the record length limit.

The header is followed by the descriptions of the data fields. A maximum of thirty-two 16-byte entries, each containing the name, type, length and other data relating to a field, are allocated. The layout of a field description is shown in Table 1.2:

Offset	Bytes	Remarks
00H	11	Field name (ASCIIZ string)
0BH	1	Field type (in ASCII)
0CH	1	Field length in bytes (binary 0 up to FFH)
0DH	2	Field data address in memory
0FH	1	Number of decimal places in field

Table 1.2 DBF field description

in dBASE II

The first 11 bytes are allocated to the field name, which is stored as an ASCIIZ string (*ASCII Zero String*). If the name is shorter than 11 characters, the remaining bytes should be set to 00H. In case of an undefined name, all bytes are set to 00H.

The *field type* is stored in byte 11 (0BH), and is one of the ASCII characters C, N or L. The ASCII characters that may appear in the actual data fields are shown in Table 1.3.

Char	Field type	ASCII characters
C	Character	ASCII character
N	Numeric	– . 0...9
L	Logical	YyNnTtFf 20H

Table 1.3 Field types in dBASE II

The length of the field is stored in byte 12 (0CH). For strings, the length is the maximum length of the text in this field. Logical fields always have a length of 1. With decimal numbers and integers, the length indicates the maximum field width. The number of decimal places, including the decimal point, is stored in byte 15 (0FH). (With dBASE II, decimal accuracy of calculation is limited to 10 places.)

The *data address* in bytes 13–14 (0DH–0EH) is used internally by dBASE II and is of no interest to other programs.

The *field descriptions* occupy bytes 8–519 (08H–207H). If all 32 fields are defined, the character 0DH (CR, Carriage return), which indicates the end of the field definitions, appears in byte 520 (208H). If fewer than 32 fields are defined, the character 0DH is positioned after the last field description used, and the remaining bytes up to and including byte 520 are filled with zero (00H).

The header record is followed by the data records. These records each have the same structure, shown in Figure 1.2:

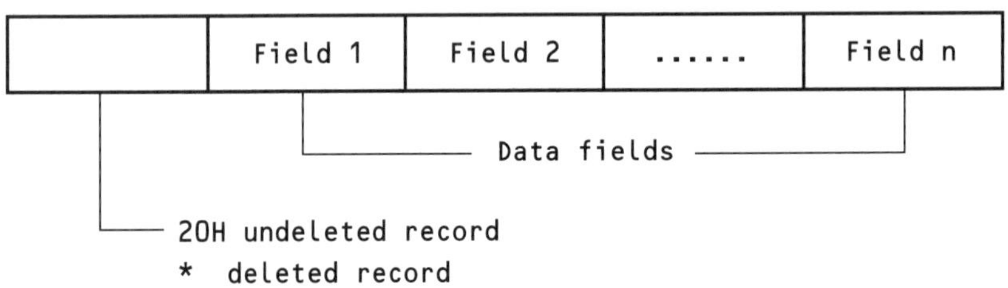

Figure 1.2 Structure of a dBASE II data record

The first byte of each record indicates whether it is valid (undeleted) or deleted. All valid records contain the value 20H (blank) in this byte. A command of the type append blank automatically puts this value in the first byte, since it is implemented simply by adding a record containing blank characters at the end of the file. As soon as a record is deleted by the user, dBASE II overwrites the first byte with the character *. In a subsequent pack operation, this record will be removed from the database. If the user wishes to retrieve (undelete) a deleted record, dBASE simply overwrites the * entry with a blank. Table 1.4 indicates the structure of the DBF file shown in Figure 1.3 as a memory dump.

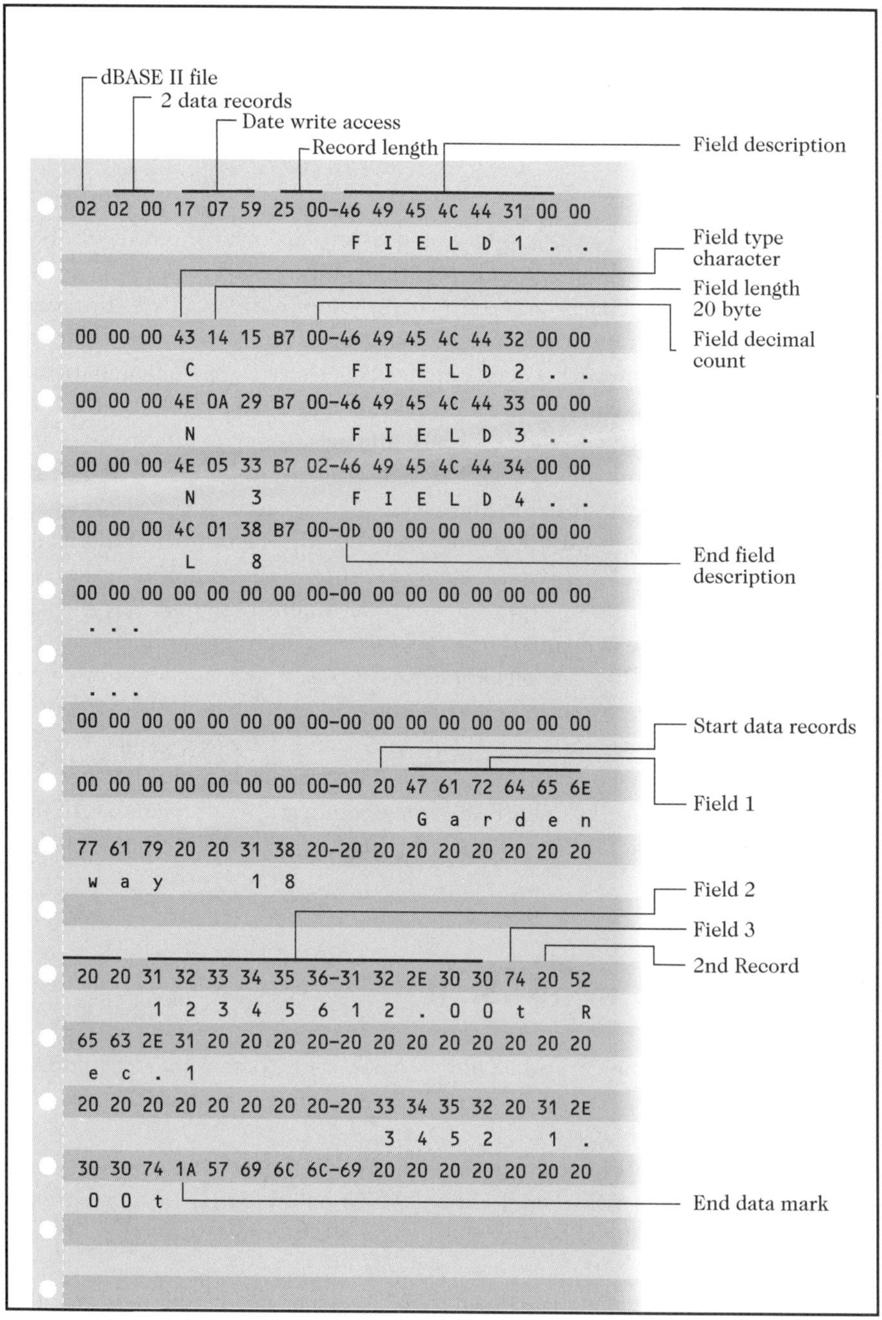

Figure 1.3
`TEST.DBF`
memory dump

Name	Type	Length	Decimals
Field1	C	020	
Field2	N	010	
Field3	N	005	2
Field4	L	001	

Table 1.4 Structure of the DBF file `TEST.DBF`

The configuration of the database on the DOS file system is of particular interest. dBASE II initially creates the header record. Then the program begins to load the actual data. Every `append blank` adds a record containing *n* blank characters to the file, where *n* corresponds to the record length calculated from the field definitions. Next, the blank characters are overwritten by the actual field data. There are no field separators between data fields because the field boundaries are described exactly in the field descriptions. Only the first byte is administered by dBASE II. As stated above, the value `20H` (blank) indicates valid records, while an asterisk (*) indicates entries released for deletion. However, the records marked for deletion are still in the database, and this fact is reflected in the number of records stored in the header. The records marked * are only removed after a `pack` operation, in which dBASE simply searches through all the records and moves the valid entries up so that the deleted records are overwritten. The end of the valid data area is always indicated by the byte `1AH`. However, the size of a DBF file is not altered by the `pack` operation although – according to the user's manual – the records have been removed.

The explanation is that dBASE II retains the deleted records at the end of the file. They can no longer be addressed by dBASE II because the byte `1AH` at the end of the valid data effectively indicates the end of the file. However, appropriate auxiliary tools can be used to display the data and possibly even to reconstruct it. The size of the file is not reduced to the correct value until the database is copied into a second database by the dBASE `copy` command. In the context of data protection, this feature is clearly not without importance. In effect, data can only be deleted by using the commands `pack` and `copy`.

1.2 Index file structure in dBASE II

The database uses its own index files – known as `.NDX` *files* – to access the data via a key. In dBASE II, they support both index-sequential access and sequential search. Figure 1.4 shows the structure of these files.

The file starts with an *anchor node*, which contains a pointer to the following nodes containing the key data. These nodes are followed by the *data nodes*, in which pointers to the data records in the DBF file are stored. The NDX files have a fixed 512-byte record structure, the first record acting as the anchor node. The structure of the anchor node is shown in Table 1.5.

The pointer in bytes 2–3 indicates which node is being used as a root node. Additional pointers are used to navigate through the file. Pointers are also used to locate the next free entry when new records are being added. For example, the address of the next free node is shown in bytes 4–5, and other pointers are stored in the individual key records.

Bytes 6 and 7 indicate the size of a key, although the significance of this parameter is not always absolutely clear. The records containing the actual keys have a fixed length of 512 bytes, and *n* keys can be stored in each node. The maximum number of keys per node is stored in byte 8.

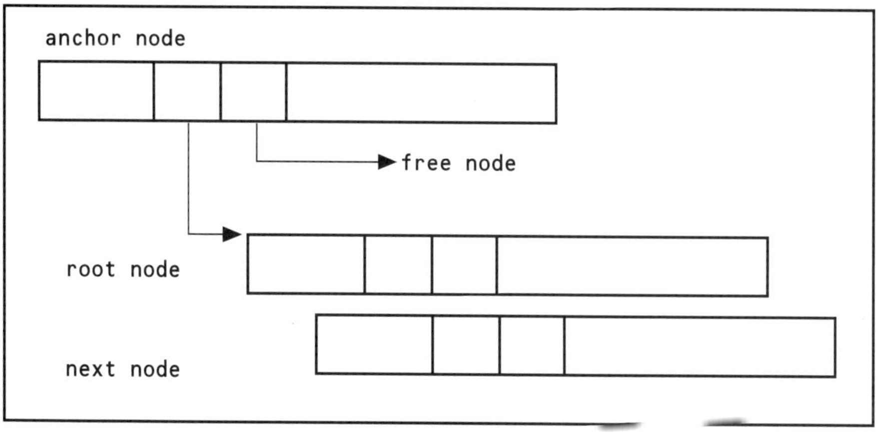

Figure 1.4 Structure of an NDX file in dBASE II

Offset	Bytes	Remarks
00H	2	Reserved
02H	2	Pointer to root node
04H	2	Pointer to next free node
06H	1	Key length in bytes + 2 (Key_Length)
07H	1	Size of key entry = 2 + 2 + bytes in key expression
08H	1	Maximum number of keys per node
09H	1	Numeric key flag = 00H if character key, otherwise it is a numeric key
0AH-6EH	100	Key expression as ASCIIZ string (maximum 100 bytes)
6FH-1FFH		Unused

Table 1.5 Format of an NDX anchor node in dBase II

The key type is stored in byte 9. A value of 00H indicates a character key; any other value indicates a numeric key.

The last entry in the anchor node is an ASCIIZ string containing the key expression, whose maximum length is 100 bytes. Shorter key expressions are padded with the value 00H. Bytes 110–511 (6EH–1FFH) of the anchor node are not used in dBASE II NDX files.

Table 1.6 shows the format of nodes containing keys.

The first byte of a key node contains the number of keys in the node. Thus, each node can contain a different number of keys; the maximum number, however, is determined by the value of byte 8 of the anchor node. The remainder of the node contains *n* key records. The structure of these records is shown in Table 1.7.

Offset	Bytes	Remarks
00H	1	Number of keys in node
01H-1FFH	510	Array of key records

Table 1.6 Key node format (dBASE II NDX file)

Bytes	Remarks
0-1	Pointer to following key (lower level)
2-3	Record number in DBF File
4-n	Key expression (ASCII text)

Table 1.7 Key record format (dBASE II NDX file)

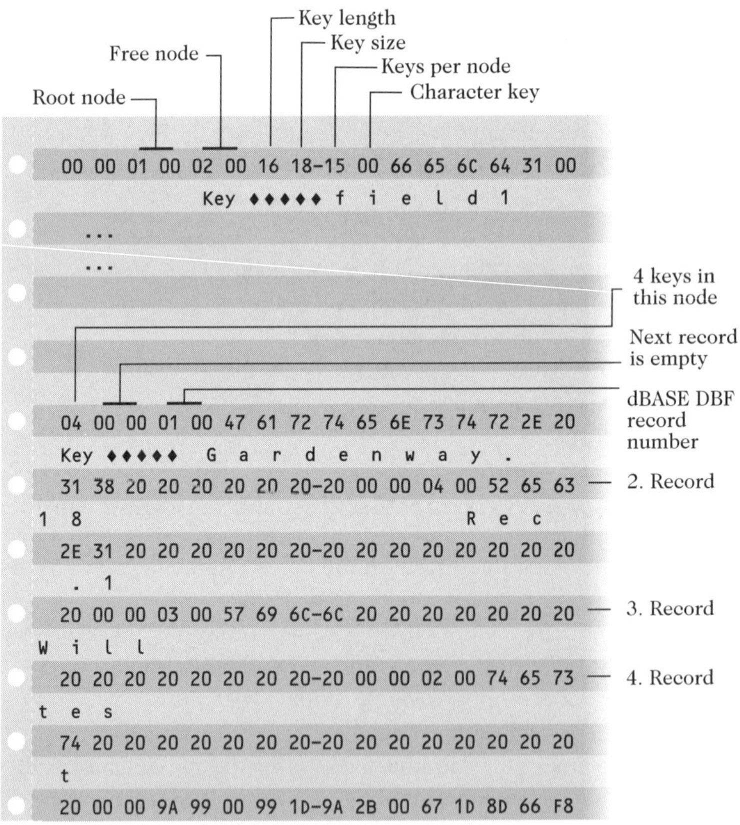

Figure 1.5 Part of a dBASE II NDX file memory dump

In the first word, there is a pointer to the following key record. The second word contains a pointer to the associated data record in the DBF file. The remainder of the record contains the relevant key expression in ASCII characters.

Further information can be obtained from actual NDX files with a dump program (for example, debug).

1.3 MEM file format in dBASE II

dBASE II enables the contents of the currently defined variables to be stored in a special file, the MEM file. New variables can then be defined, or existing values overwritten. 'Original values' which have been overwritten in this way can be recovered from the MEM file, if necessary. The internal structure of a MEM file is as follows:

Bytes	Remarks
`0-10`	Variable name (ASCIIZ string)
`11`	Variable type
	`C3H` Character variable
	`CEH` Numeric variable
	`CCH` Logical variable
`12`	Length of the stored value
`13-14`	Unknown
`15`	'`E`' marks the start of a definition
`16`	Number of decimals
`17-18`	Zero bytes
`19-n`	Value of the variable

Table 1.8 The format of a MEM file in dBASE II

Character variables are stored as ASCIIZ strings. If the text is shorter than the length of the field, the leading positions are filled with zero bytes. With logical variables, dBASE II reserves 17 bytes for the value, but only uses the last byte to store the value `00H` (false) or `01H` (true). Numeric values are coded in an internal dBASE II notation. The end of the valid data in a MEM file (`EOF`) is indicated by a byte containing `1AH`.

The above information was obtained by means of reverse engineering. It is therefore quite possible that certain bytes have other meanings in addition to those listed.

2

File formats in dBASE III

Ashton Tate *developed dBASE III and dBASE III+ as successors to dBASE II. Internally, the file formats are practically identical; consequently, only the file structure of dBASE III+ will be described here.*

2.1 DBF file format in dBASE III and dBASE III+

The structure of these files is based on that of dBASE II, although the capacity of the newer versions is considerably enhanced. The following table indicates the differences between the two versions:

Parameter	dBASE II	dBASE III
Records	65535	1 billion
Record length	1000	4000
Fields per record	32	128
Length of character field	256	256
Length of logical field	1	1
Decimal places in numeric field	10	15
Data field	–	8
Memo field	–	10

Table 2.1 Differences between dBASE II and dBASE III (+)

In dBASE III, every DBF file consists of a *header field description* and *data* (*see* Figure 1.1).

The length of the header record, comprising the header and field descriptions, depends on the version of the program and the number of fields defined. This structure is shown in Table 2.2:

Offset	Bytes	Remarks
00H	1	dBASE version 02H dBASE II DBF file 03H dBASE III DBF file 83H dBASE III DBF memo file
01H	3	Date of last write access (binary format YYMMDD)
04H	4	Number of data records
08H	2	Header length in bytes
0AH	2	Record length in bytes
0CH	20	Reserved
20H	32*N	32 bytes per field containing the field description
32 * N+1	1	0DH header end

Table 2.2 The format of a DBF header in dBASE III

As with dBASE II, the information is stored in a mixture of ASCII and binary formats.

The first byte is used to identify the dBASE version. For dBASE II it is 02H. From dBASE III onwards, the value stored in the lower nibble (bits 0...3) is 3H. The highest bit (7) indicates whether there are memo fields in the file. If there are, a DBT file containing the memo texts is associated with the DBF file, and the byte thus contains the code 83H. In all other cases, the value in the first byte is 03H. If dBASE discovers any other value it will refuse access, since the file cannot be a DBF file.

The next field is three bytes long and contains the date of the last write access coded in binary form. The format used is YYMMDD – the year is stored first.

The next field comprises 4 bytes which indicate the number of data records in the DBF file. These bytes are interpreted as an unsigned 32-bit number. The Intel convention on memory allocation (lowest byte of the number assigned to the lowest address) applies. The number of records includes both valid records and those already marked for deletion.

Bytes 8–9 contain an unsigned 16-bit number giving the length of the header in bytes. This information is significant because the DBF file can contain a variable number of field descriptions (*see below*).

Bytes 10–11 (0AH–0BH)contain the length of a data record in bytes, as an unsigned 16-bit number. This value is always one more than the sum of the individual field lengths. This is because the first byte of a data record is always reserved for marking deleted records.

From byte 12 (0CH), there is a 20 byte reserved area for internal use. In the network version, 13 bytes in this area are used (but not documented). The 20 reserved bytes ensure that the header occupies exactly 32 bytes.

Information on the structure of the data records follows the header, as with dBASE II. Here too, there are individual field descriptions, but from dBASE III onwards, up to 128 fields can be defined. For every field in the database, there is a 32-byte record whose format is shown in Table 2.3:

Offset	Bytes	Remarks
00H	11	Field name in ASCII
0BH	1	Field type in ASCII (C, N, L, D, M)
0CH	4	Field data address in memory
10H	1	Field length in bytes (binary)
11H	1	Decimal count field
12H	2	Reserved
14H	1	ID working area
15H	2	Reserved
17H	1	Set fields flag
18H	8	Reserved

Table 2.3 DBF field description in dBASE III

The first 11 bytes of the field description contain the *field name*, as an ASCIIZ string. In this respect, dBASE shows clear resemblance to the C programming language, which also terminates character strings with a zero byte. If the field name does not require all 11 characters, the remaining bytes are set to 00H.

The next byte contains the ASCII character indicating the *field type*. Table 2.4 shows the valid field types from dBASE III onwards. By contrast with dBASE II, date and memo fields are now included.

Character	Field type	Characters
C	Character	ASCII
N	Numeric	– 0...9
L	Logical	YyNnTtFf ?
D	Date	YYYYMMDD
M	Memo	DBT block number

Table 2.4 Coding for field types in dBASE III

Bytes 12–15 (0CH–0FH) are used internally by dBASE for storing the field address. This address is of no significance to the user.

The *field length* is given in binary in byte 16 (10H). The maximum number of characters per field is therefore 255. This length is only used for character fields; for numeric fields, the value indicates the number of decimal places including the decimal point (however, the calculation accuracy for numbers in dBASE III is still limited to 15 places). For memo fields, the field length is always 10 bytes, as it contains the block number of the memo text stored in the associated DBT file. Further details are given in the description of the DBT format. Logical fields have a length of 1 byte, while 8 bytes are reserved for date fields.

With numeric fields, byte 17 (11H) specifies the *number of places after the decimal point*. For all other field types, this byte has the value 00H. It is important to note that the number of places after the decimal point is always smaller than the field length.

The remaining 14 bytes are reserved for internal purposes. They simply need to be skipped in order to reach the next field description. The `set fields` byte is of no relevance, since dBASE clearly uses this entry only in memory.

Each defined field in the data structure has its own 32-byte field description record in the header of the DBF file. The end of the field descriptions is indicated by the character 0DH.

As in dBASE II, the actual *data records* in dBASE III and dBASE III+ are appended to the field description section. The record length is stored in the file header, as explained above. A data record is stored in pure ASCII format without field separators, which considerably simplifies the import and export of data using the SDF option.

Data in character fields is represented by a sequence of ASCII characters. If the text is shorter than the length specified in the field definition, blank characters (code = 20H) are assigned to the remaining bytes.

Numeric values are also stored as ASCII strings. The number of character positions is specified in the field description, as is the number of places after the decimal point, where relevant. It should be noted that the decimal point is included in this value and that one digit is therefore 'lost'. If the number is smaller than the field length provided, the number is right-justified within the fields and the leading zeros are replaced by blanks (20H) (for example " 999.99").

Logical values are represented in one byte, using the characters F or T.

The date field contains the date as an 8-character ASCII string in the format YYYYMMDD.

A memo field contains a 10-byte number specifying the block in the DBT file that contains the associated text. Leading zeros are replaced by blanks. If the field contains 10 blank characters, then no text record exists in the associated DBT file.

Furthermore, all fields, regardless of their type, can be processed as ASCII text.

As soon as a new record is added to the file by the command `append blank`, dBASE fills this record with blanks. The first byte in the record is used to mark deleted data, and since a blank is stored there for new records, these cannot be deleted. Only if the first byte contains the character * will the record be removed from the DBF file when the next `pack` command is given. This means that `delete` operations are very fast and it also enables reasonably trouble-free `undelete` operations. Records handled in this way do, however, remain in the database, and it is quite likely that several hundred such records, none of which is valid, may be retained. Access without using an index is naturally very slow because all records (deleted and undeleted) must be read. The remedy for this weakness is to use `pack` to remove deleted records from the DBF file as often as possible. Records marked for deletion are overwritten by subsequent valid records and the entry in the header is reduced to the number of undeleted records.

The *end of the valid data* in the file is indicated by the character 1AH. It is important to realize that this EOF marking is managed not by DOS but by dBASE. Since the `pack` operation does not alter the size of the DBF file, there will still be deleted records behind the EOF marker. Appropriate tools can be used to restore these. The dBASE command `copy file to` transfers only valid records into another file, thereby reducing the length of the file. Figure 1.7 shows an extract from a DBF file in dBASE III as a hex-dump.

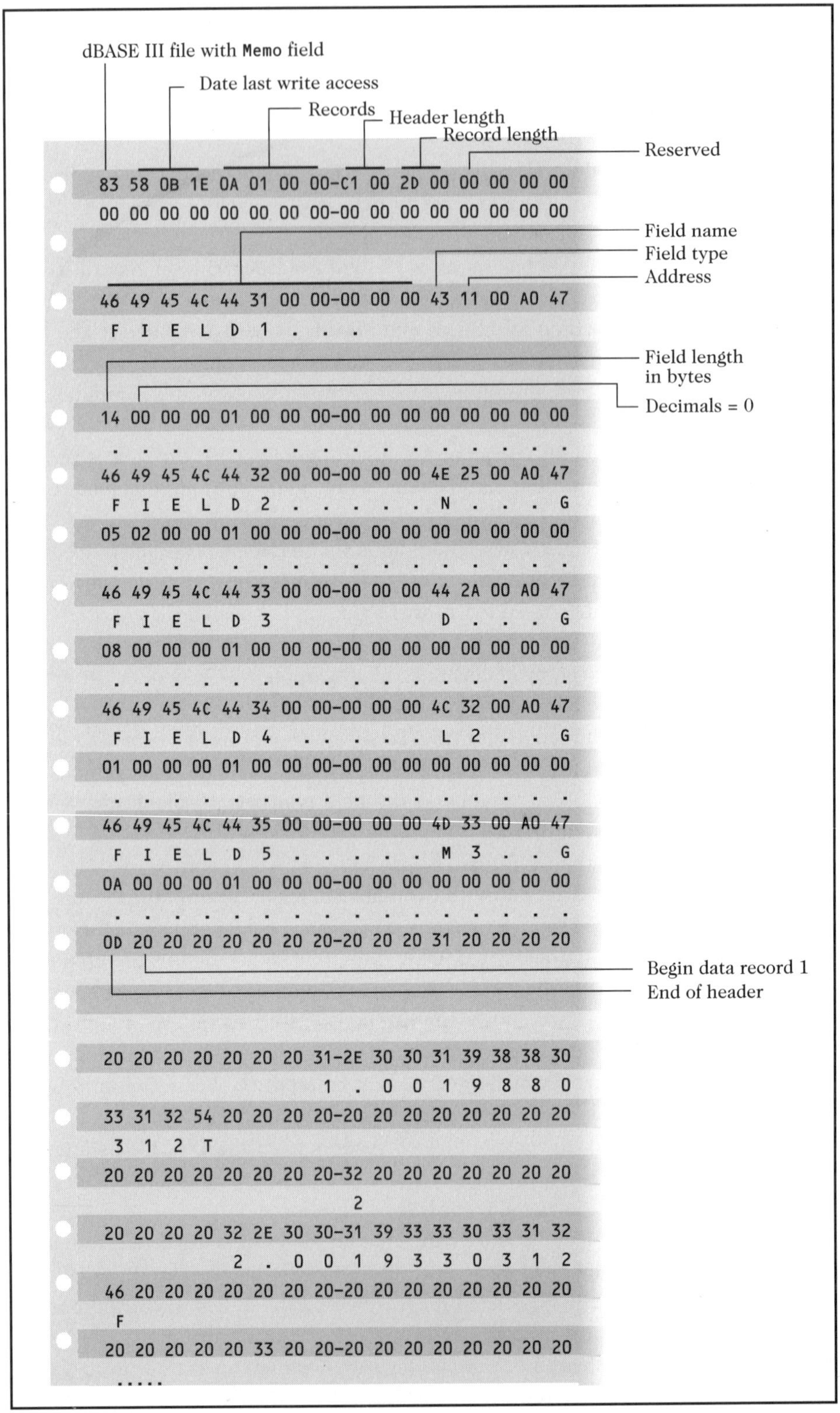

Figure 2.1 Memory dump of a dBASE III file (TEST.DBF)

2.2 Index file structure (NDX) in dBASE III

dBASE uses its own index files (NDX) to enable access to data via keys. dBASE NDX files use a modified B-tree structure for the management of index data. (There are, however, a number of differences from the clipper NTX structure).

2.2.1 Structure of the NDX header

The NDX file is divided into pages each comprising 512 bytes. The first page is used as a header and is followed by the index pages. The structure of the header is shown in Table 2.5.

Offset	Bytes	Remarks
00H	4	`Start_key_page` (root page)
04H	4	`Total_pages`
08H	4	Reserved
0CH	2	`Index_key_len`
0EH	2	`Max_keys_page`
10H	2	`NDX_key_type`
12H	4	`Size_key_record`
16H	1	Reserved
17H	1	`Unique_flag`
18H	488	`Key_name`

Table 2.5 Format of the dBASE NDX header

The 512-byte header describes the structure of the index pages and contains a pointer to the root of the B-tree.

The `Start_key_page` field (offset `00H`) contains the record number (4 bytes) of the `root_page`. This is the first page (root) of the B-tree. To determine the offset in bytes, multiply the value by the record length of 512 bytes.

Because the DOS file system is limited to 4-byte offset pointers, the (theoretical) value of `7FFFFFH` (corresponding to 8388607 pages) is the largest usable number. In practice, this limit is never reached when using DOS because of the restricted capacity of the hard disk.

During the structuring of the index pages, the B-tree is frequently `re-sorted`. If the record number of the start page (root of the B-tree) changes, the record number of the start page in the header must be updated.

The number of 512-byte pages in the NDX file is stored in the 4-byte field `Total_pages` (offset `04H`). The `Index_key_len` field (offset `0CH`) specifies the length of the key on which the NDX file is based, in bytes.

The maximum number of keys that can be stored in one 512-byte page is given in Max_keys_page (offset 0EH) and is determined by the length of the key. The actual number of entries in a page is stored at the start of the page (*see* Section 2.2.2: The structure of index pages).

The type of index is stored in the NDX_key_type field (offset 10H). Numeric keys (code = 01H) or alphanumeric keys (code = 00H) may be used. How keys are represented in the pages of the tree depends on the type of key involved. Numeric indices and indices based on the date are entered as floating-point numbers in IEEE format (8 bytes). Alphanumeric indices are stored as ASCII strings. If the string is shorter than the length of the key, it is padded (to the right) by blanks.

The length of a key record in bytes is stored in the Size_key_rec field (offset 12H). This field dictates the distance between two key entries in the index page (*see* Section 2.2.2: The structure of index pages).

The byte field unique (offset 17H) acts as a flag. If the flag contains the value 1, the index was created with the option unique on. The value 0 indicates that the index was created with unique off.

At offset 18H (24 decimal), there is a 488-byte area which is used to extend the page to 512 bytes. The name of the key is stored in this filler area as an ASCIIZ string. This string is given when the index file is defined (set index on ...).

2.2.2 The structure of index pages

The NDX header is followed by *n* 512-byte index pages. The number *n* is defined in the header at offset 04H. The keys to the associated data records in the DBF file are stored in the index pages. The structure of an index page is given in Table 2.6.

The first 4 bytes of an index page (the Key_record_page field) contain the number of key entries in the page. If the page is empty, the value 00H 00H 00H 00H is shown.

Offset	Bytes	Remarks
00H	4	Key_record_page
04H	4	Left_page_num_1
08H	4	DBF_rec_num_1
0CH	Len	Key_data_1 (key)
..H	4	Left_page_num_2
..H	4	DBF_rec_num_2
..H	Len	Key_data_1 (key)
		....
..H	4	Left_page_num_n
..H	4	DBF_rec_num_n
..H	Len	Key_data_n (key)

Table 2.6 Structure of a dBASE NDX index page

This is followed by n entries containing the key values, where n is the value given in Key_record_page. Each key entry consists of a data structure containing the fields Left_page_num, DBF_rec_num and Key_data.

Left_page_num contains a pointer to the page located to the left of the current key in the B-tree (*see* Figure 2.2). This index page contains all the keys that in the sort sequence are smaller than or the same size as the key required. The pointers to these pages are stored as record numbers, that is, the page offset is calculated by multiplying the record number by the record length of 512 bytes. (In clipper NTX files, by contrast, absolute record addresses are used.)

DBF_rec_num contains the record number of the associated DBF file data. Within the nodes of the B-tree, this 4-byte entry is set to 0, which indicates that there is another index page in which the actual key is stored. Reference to the DBF record is not made until the leaf of the tree is reached, where the field contains the relevant record number. To determine the offset of the data (in bytes), multiply the record number by the length of the record from the DBF header (offset 0AH) (*see* Table 2.2).

The actual key is stored in Key_data. The length of this field is determined by the length of the index field (offset 12H in the header of the NDX file). With ASCII fields in the index, spaces to the right are filled with blanks. Numeric indices and the date index are stored as 8-byte IEEE floating-point numbers. A schematic representation is given in Figure 2.2.

By contrast with the NTX files (clippers), the individual pages do not have a pointer field containing pointers to the following keys. The entries in the index pages should themselves be interpreted as references to other index pages. This is shown schematically by the keys indicated in Figure 2.2. The entry:

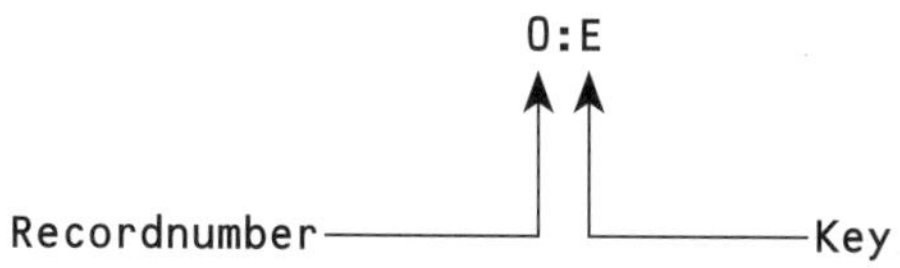

in a page consists of a number, which should be interpreted as a record number in the DBF file. If the value is 0, there is a reference to another index page. If 3:E is indicated, the required expression E is stored in the third DBF record. The text after the colon indicates the actual key. The example given in Figure 2.2 is restricted to one letter here for reasons of space. (Please note also that the colon has been used in the above figure only for illustration. In the NDX file, the data structure described in Table 2.6 exists for every entry.)

The entry 0:E thus means that another index page exists where all keys that in the sort sequence are less than or equal to the required expression are stored. This index page is the left-hand branch (viewed from the node) of the B-tree and may, in its turn, refer to other pages. However, if the required key is larger than the current value in Key_data_n, the next entry Key_data_n+1 of the current index page must be examined according to the procedure described above. If the last entry in the page is reached without the key being found and without branching to a subsequent page, then there is no entry in the index file.

The structure of the index pages means that the search for the key is carried out sequentially, which is not the most efficient method. Furthermore, dBASE cannot reuse empty pages in an NDX file. In this respect, the clipper NTX structure presented below is considerably more efficient.

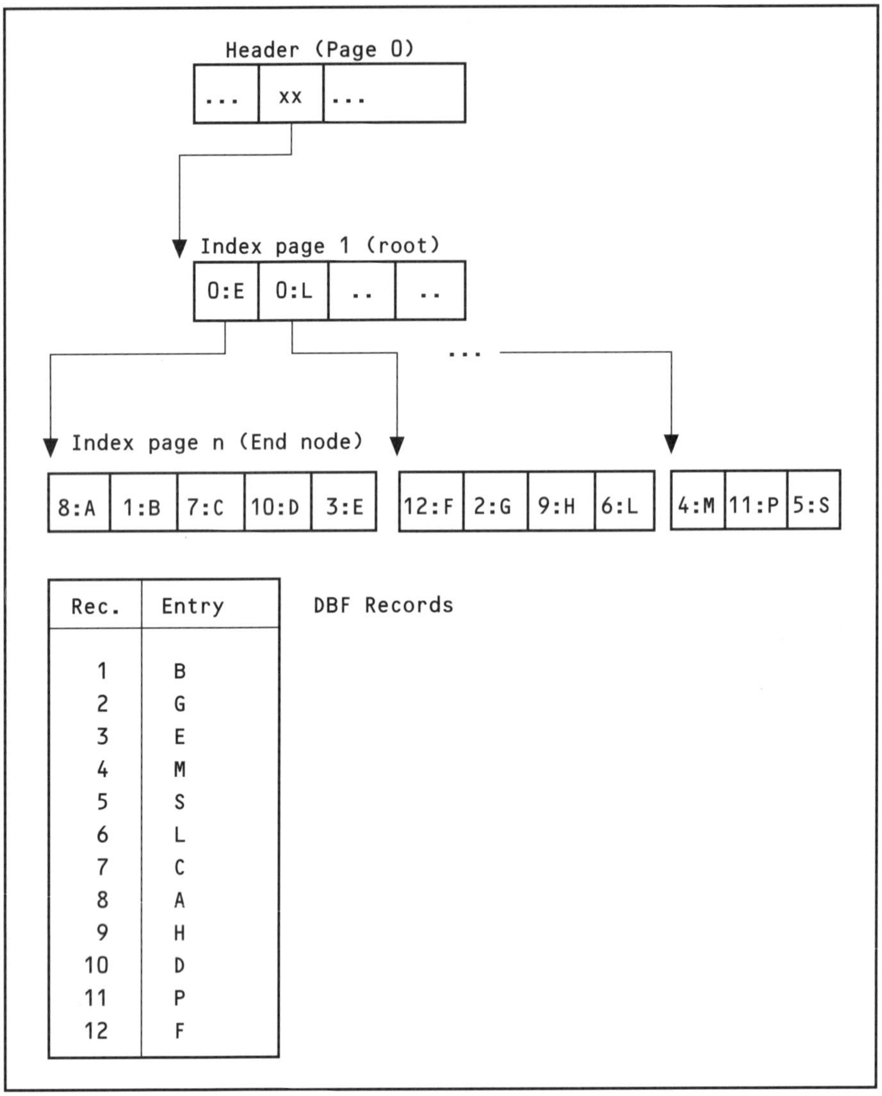

Figure 2.2
Structure of an NDX B-tree

2.3 Clipper index file format (NTX)

For dBASE III users, the company Computer Associated offers its own compiler which converts programs into executable code. For reasons of performance, developers have defined another (more efficient) index file structure (NTX), alongside the dBASE NDX index structure.

These NTX files consist of n pages each containing 1024 bytes. The first page contains the NTX header, while the remaining pages store the keys and the pointers of the B-tree.

2.3.1 The structure of the NTX header

The header of the NTX file is also 1024 bytes long. Its format is shown in Table 2.7:

Offset	Bytes	Remarks
00H	2	Clipper signature (`sign`)
02H	2	Compiler version (`version`)
04H	4	Pointer to root node
08H	4	Pointer to first empty page
0CH	2	Item size
0EH	2	Key size
10H	2	Key decimals
12H	2	Maximum items
14H	2	Half page size
16H	256	Key expression (ASCIIZ)
272H	1	Unique flag

Table 2.7
The NTX header

The 2-byte `sign` field contains the signature `0003H` for valid clipper 87 index files and `0006H` for clipper 5.x files. Because of the data storage method, the byte sequence in the file is `03H 00H` for clipper 87 and `06H 00H` for clipper 5.x.

The version number of the clipper compiler is entered in the `version` field (offset `02H`). This indicates the software version that created the index.

The `root node` field (offset `04H`) contains a 4-byte pointer which indicates the offset (in bytes) from the start of the field to the beginning of the first index page. The index keys are stored from this index page onwards.

Empty index pages are managed using the `empty page` field (offset `08H`). A clipper index file consists of individual pages of 1024 bytes each. The first page containing the header information is followed by the pages containing index entries. However, a number of pages within the index file may be empty and these pages are kept in a linked list. The 4-byte pointer `empty page` defines the offset (in bytes) from the beginning of the file to the first empty page. The first 4 bytes of an empty page contain a pointer to the next empty page. The end of this list is indicated by the value `00H 00H 00H 00H` in the first four bytes of the page. If the `empty page` field contains `0`, there are no empty pages available. (Note: this technique enables unused pages to be used again. dBASE does not acknowledge this form of memory management, and empty pages can therefore no longer be used. An empty page arises when all the index entries for a page have been deleted from the database.)

The `item size` field takes 2 bytes and defines the size of a key entry in an index page. The value is determined according to the formula:

```
item size = index_key_len + 2*4 bytes
```

Two pointers (page, record number) of 4 bytes each are added to the memory requirement for the actual index. The resulting value is the step size needed to gain access to the individual entries in an index page.

The word `key size` (offset `0EH`) defines the size of the actual key from which the index was structured. For example, if the key field contains 10 characters (`C*10`), `key size` is also set to the value `10`. This value is 8 bytes smaller than the value in the field `item size`.

The `key dec` field (offset `10H`) contains 2 bytes indicating the number of decimal places for numeric keys. It is not used for alphanumeric keys.

The index page is managed using the `max key` field (offset `12H`). For each index page, *n* index entries (key expressions + associated pointers) can be stored. The number of entries depends on the index length, since the page contains 1024 bytes. The 2-byte field `max key` indicates the maximum number of index entries per page.

The 2-byte field `half page` specifies the number of key expressions per page divided by 2. This value determines the minimum number of entries to be stored in one page of the B-tree. This information is important when structuring the B-tree, because it should be a balanced tree if possible.

The following field `key expr` (offset `16H`) contains the key expression as an ASCIIZ string. A maximum length of 256 characters is allowed. The string ends with the character `00H`.

`Unique` is a byte flag defined as a Boolean (offset `272H`), which indicates the status of the `Unique flag` when the index was created. The value `1` defines `UNIQUE ON`; `0` indicates `UNIQUE OFF`.

The remainder of the 1024-byte header is reserved for filler bytes.

2.3.2 The structure of the index page

The NTX header is followed by the index pages. Each 1024-byte page contains a number of entries (keys), which refer to the data records of the DBF files. Table 2.8 shows the structure of an index page.

Offset	Bytes	Remarks
`00H`	2	Number of items `(count-1)`
`02H`	$x * 2$	Pointer fields `(ref[maxitem+1])` to next *n* entries (items)
`xxH`		*n* key records (items) containing:
	4	Offset of left page
	4	Record number
	n	Key

Table 2.8 Structure of an NTX index page

The first field in the index page occupies 2 bytes. This field contains the number of occupied entries –1 in the page (items). This value must lie between `half page` and `max item`. Only the first index page may contain values between `1` and `max item`.

From offset `02H` onwards, there is a number of 2-byte fields containing pointers to the key records (items) in the page. In accordance with Table 2.8, key records consist of 3 fields (page, record number, key). The meaning of these fields will be described below. `max item+1` words are reserved for the pointers, and (`count+1`) words used. The value `0` in a pointer field indicates that there is no associated key record in the page. A positive value denotes the offset from the beginning of the page to the key record within the page.

The pointer fields are followed by the actual key records (items). The number of items is stored in the first word (`count+1`) of the index page. Each key record (item) consists of three fields (page, record number, key). The first field `page` contains a 4-byte pointer to the logically preceding index page (the offset in bytes from the start of the file). The `record number` field may contain a 4-byte pointer to the data record of the DBF file (offset in bytes from the start of the DBF file to the data record). The `key` field, which holds the key, is of variable length. Its actual length is defined in the header of the NTX file in the `key size` field (offset `0EH`).

When comparing the search expression with the entry in the `key` field, three situations may arise:

- The search expression matches the key. In this case, the record number (offset in bytes) of the DBF file is located in the `record number` field.
- The search expression comes logically before the key. In this case, the search must be continued in another node of the tree. The `page` field indicates the 4-byte offset in the NTX file of the next (logically preceding) index page. All the entries in the index pages of a tree section addressed by `page` are less than the current index in the field `key`.
- The search expression comes logically after the key. Here, `page` cannot be used, because it refers to preceding nodes. Instead, access to the next key record must be gained (via the pointer field at the start of the index page). This record must then be analyzed according to the rules described above.

If the end of the page is reached without the key agreeing, the index file does not contain the search expression. This method enables a very rapid search of the B-tree to be made.

The `key` field contains the key of the relevant data record in the form of an ASCII string. This also applies to numeric keys. The length is defined in the header of the NTX file, in the `key size` field. A date index (such as 1 December 1991) is stored as an 8-byte string of characters (`19911201`). Numeric index values are also treated as strings (because DBF fields are also stored as strings). The number of places after the decimal point is defined by the `key dec` field in the NTX header. It should, however, be noted that the decimal point is included in the key (for example, `999.99`), that is, the number of decimal places is 1 less than defined in `key size`. If the numbers are smaller than the size of the `key` field, preceeding positions are filled with blanks. These details are shown graphically in Figure 2.3.

All pages are 1024 bytes long. At the start of a page, there is a pointer field indicating the entries in the index page. These entries contain the key expressions (for example, `A`, `E`, `L` and so on) and the pointers to subsequent pages. One pointer also refers directly to the associated data record in the DBF file. To take an example, the entry `3:E` means that the third record in the DBF file is associated with the key E. The number 3 is thus the record number of the DBF file. The logically preceding page contains all the keys that come before E in the sort sequence. (The index in this example is restricted to 1 character.) All keys greater than E are located either in one of the following entries in the page, or in the following pages. This index page structure is considerably more efficient than the NDX pages of dBASE III.

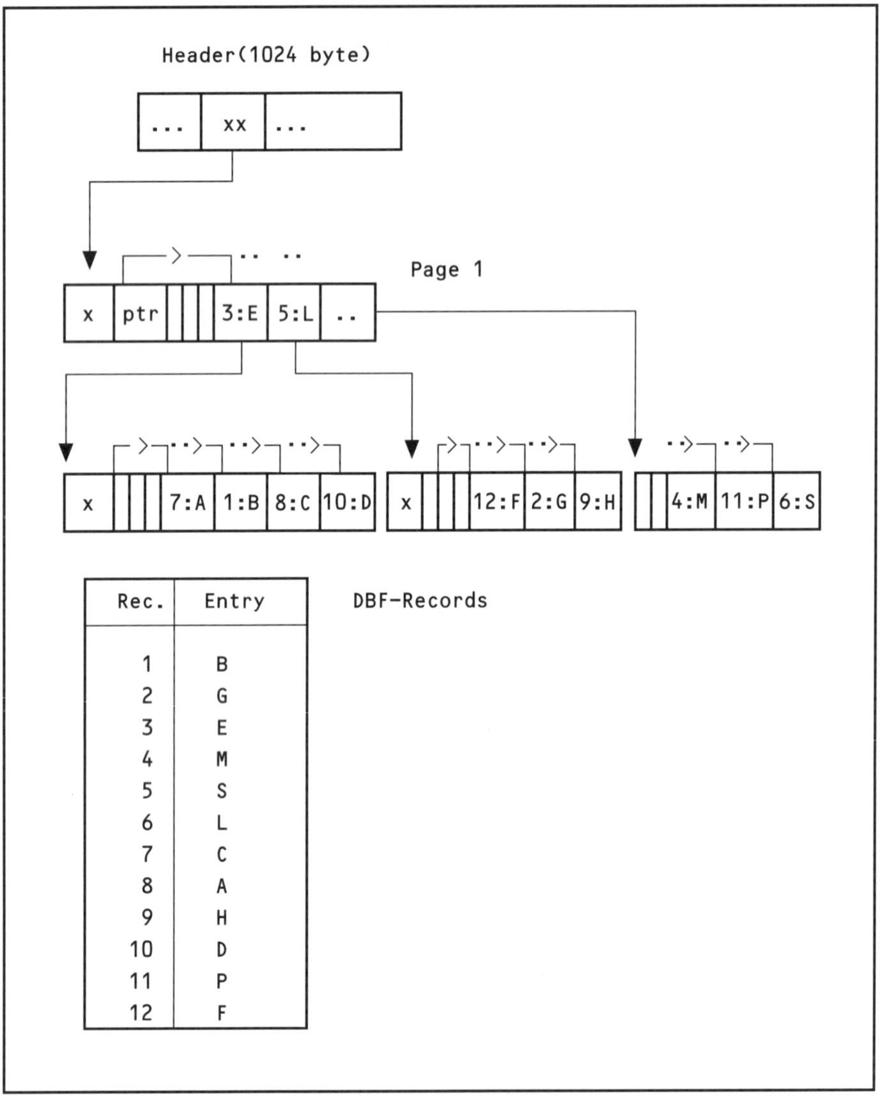

Figure 2.3
Structure of an NTX B-tree

2.4 MEM file format in dBASE III

In dBASE III and dBASE III+, it is possible to save the current variables in a file. For each variable stored, the file contains a record consisting of a 32-byte header, followed by the contents of the variable. The header is structured as shown in Table 2.9:

Bytes	Remarks
1-11	Variable name (ASCIIZ string)
12	Variable type
13-16	4 filler bytes (unused)
17	Variable length in bytes
18	Valid decimal places
19-32	Filler bytes (unused)
32-n	Variable value

Table 2.9 Format of a dBASE III MEM file

The first 11 bytes contain the name of the variable as an ASCIIZ string, that is, the last byte is terminated with `00H`. This is followed by the type of the variable, which must be one of the following:

```
C = Character
D = Date
L = Logical
N = Numeric
```

The variable type field contains the ASCII code for the type (for example, `C = 43H`), and the highest bit is always set. The following value for the character C is thus derived:

```
C =>43H OR 80H => C3H
```

and stored as the code for the variable type. The same process is applied to the other variable types. The next 4 bytes are not used; they act as filler bytes. The length of the variable is stored at offset `17 (11H)` and the number of places after the decimal point (for numeric values) at offset `18` (`12H`). The remaining 14 bytes of the header are unused. These are followed by *n* bytes containing the value of the variable. Character variables are stored as ASCIIZ strings. If the text is shorter than the field reserved, the trailing positions are filled with zero bytes. For logical variables, dBASE III reserves 1 byte for the value, which contains either `00H` (false) or `01H` (true). For numerical values, coding is carried out according to a notation internal to dBASE III (8-byte floating-point number). Date variables are also treated as floating-point numbers. The end of the valid records (`EOF`) is indicated by the code `1AH`.

2.5 DBT files in dBASE III (Memo files)

Memo files to accommodate text were first introduced in dBASE III. In the actual database files (DBF files), there is just one field containing a pointer to the memo file or to a block of text within the file (Figure 2.4).

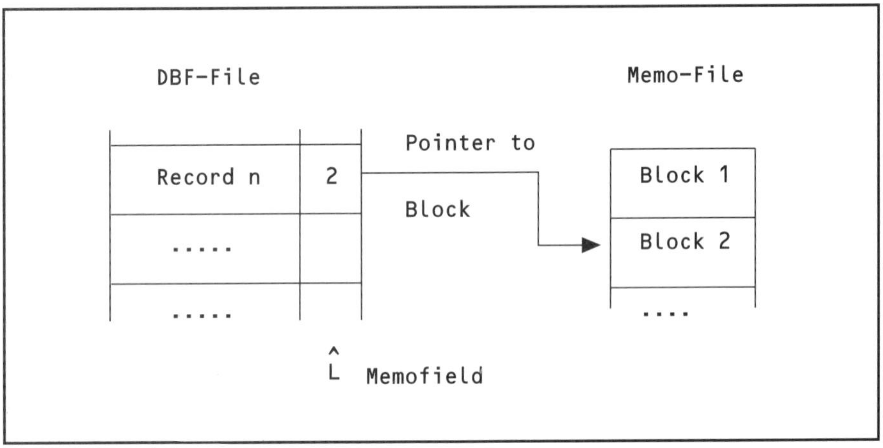

Figure 2.4 Block reference in a memo file

The pointer in the memo field of the DBF file is not visible to the user. If there is no text block for this record, the DBF file will contain a blank entry in the memo field. Otherwise, the field will contain a 10-byte pointer, which is interpreted as an ASCII number. dBASE III opens a second file alongside the DBF file; it has the same name but the DBT extension. The texts of the relevant memo fields are stored here. The memo file consists of 512-byte blocks. Only the first 4 bytes of the header records are used, and they indicate the next free block in the memo file (Figure 2.5). It can be seen from Figure 2.5 that the pointer at the head of the memo file always points to the end of the file.

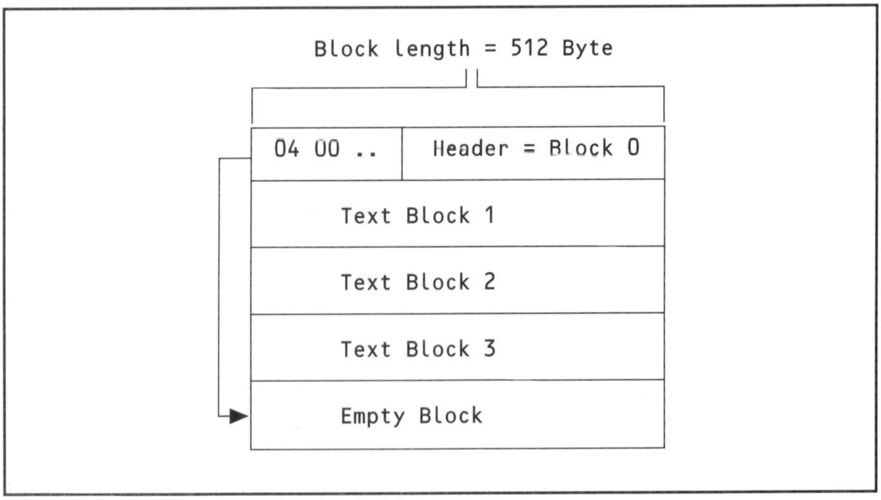

Figure 2.5 Block structure in a memo file

If new text is to be stored in a memo field, dBASE reads the header pointer of the memo file and stores the value in the corresponding memo field of the DBF file. The pointer in the memo field of the DBF file thus specifies the 512-byte DBT block from which the associated text begins. The text is then simply appended to the end of the memo file. If the text is longer than 512 bytes, a multiple of this number is added. The end of the text is indicated by two bytes with the code 1AH. If necessary, the remainder of the block is filled with filler bytes. The header pointer is adjusted to point to the next free block.

A serious weakness in memo file management becomes evident if alterations to memo texts are carried out, because the altered text is simply added to the end of the file and the new pointer stored in the memo field of the DBF file. The old text is retained in the memo file – but without a pointer, which means that it can no longer be found. Also, this method increases the size of the memo file considerably, if frequent text alterations are made. The only way out of this dilemma is to use the dBASE III command COPY..., which enables unused texts to be removed from the memo file.

2.6 FRM files in dBASE III

In dBASE III, report formats can be stored in FRM files, which are described briefly below. The data structure of one FRM file is shown in Table 2.10.

The 2-byte sign field contains the signature 0002H for valid FRM files. Because of the data storage method, the byte sequence in the file is 02H 00H.

The expressions for the reports are stored in their own data area, the exp_area in the file. This is simply a 1440-byte text string. The texts may be static texts or formulas containing variables and so on. Formulas are evaluated by dBASE at run time. There is a pointer in the 2-byte exp_end field (offset 02H) indicating the first free character in the expressions area (exp_area).

Offset	Bytes	Remarks
00H	2	Signature (sign)
02H	2	Pointer to end of expressions (exp_end)
04H	55*2	Length of expressions (exp_length[55])
72H	55*2	Expression indices (exp_index[55])
E0H	1440	String containing expressions (exp_area)
680H	25*x	Data structure 25 : FRM_FIELD:
	2	width
	2	pad1
	1	pad2
	1	total
	2	dec
	2	exp_contents

Table 2.10 Structure of an FRM file (*continues over...*)

Databases

Offset	Bytes	Remarks
7ACH	2	title_exp_num
7AEH	2	grp_on_exp_num
7B0H	2	sub_on_exp_num
7B2H	2	grp_head_exp_num
7B4H	2	sub_head_exp_num
7B6H	2	page_width
7B8H	2	line_per_page
7BAH	2	left_margin
7BCH	2	right_margin
7BEH	2	num_of_cols
800H	1	dbl_space
801H	1	summary
802H	1	eject
803H	1	plus_bytes
804H	2	sign2

Table 2.10 Structure of an FRM file (*cont.*)

The field `exp_length[55]` is made up of 55 2-byte entries and contains the length in bytes of every expression within the text area.

The field `exp_index[55]` contains, for each expression, a pointer to the beginning of the expression text. This field implicitly indicates the sequence of expressions to be evaluated.

The field containing these indices is followed by a 1440 byte area in which the actual expressions (static texts or rules for calculation) are stored as texts. The end of the occupied area is indicated in the field `exp_end` (offset `02H`). The beginning of each individual expression and its length in bytes is stored in the two fields `exp_index[]` and `exp_length[]`.

The expressions area is followed by a data structure of 25 elements which is known as the `FRM_FIELD[25]`. This data structure contains one entry for each field used in the report. However, the first field (index `0`) remains unused. Each element of `FRM_FIELD` contains the following variables:

width

This 2-byte variable defines the field width (number of characters) in which the field value is to be printed.

pad1, pad2

These variables are used as fill patterns; `pad1` occupies 2 bytes, while `pad2` consists of 1 byte.

total

This field defines whether a numeric field is to be output as a total (`Y` or `N`).

dec

With numeric fields, this variable indicates the number of decimal places.

exp_contents

Some outputs may be the result of a calculation. The `exp_contents` field contains the number of the corresponding expression.

exp_header

This variable contains the number of the text string (from the expressions field) that is associated with the field.

This concludes the description of the elements of the `FRM_FIELD`. The following comments relate to file-structure entries.

The 2-byte field `title_exp_num` contains the number of the expression for the title line of the report. This expression is a simple string.

The 2-byte field `grp_on_exp_num` contains the number of the `GROUP ON` expression. The 2-byte field `sub_on_exp_num` contains the number of the `SUB GROUP ON` expression. The 2-byte field `grp_head_exp_num` contains the number of the `GROUP ON` header text (stored as an expression). The 2-byte field `sub_head_exp_num` contains the number of the `SUB GROUP ON` header text (stored as an expression).

The following five fields each occupy 2 bytes and relate to the formatting of the printed page. The number of characters per line (page width) is given by the `page_width` field. This is followed by `line_per_page` which defines the number of lines on each printed page. The `left_margin` and `right_margin` fields specify the width of the left margin and right margin respectively (in characters). The `num_of_cols` field indicates the number of columns in the report. This also corresponds to the number of fields used in the expression.

The next four fields, which have only one byte each, deal with control of the output. The `dbl_space` field is used to select whether characters are to be double-spaced or not: `double spacing` mode is switched on if there is a `Y` in this field, and off if there is an `N`. In the `summary` field, `Y` indicates that the total is to be positioned below the output column `N` and that no total is required.

The `eject` field defines whether a page-feed is required after outputting a group: `Y` indicates carry out a page-feed; `N` cancels the page-feed.

The `plus_bytes` field is not used prior to version III+. From dBASE III+, it contains three bits which control the output of a report:

Bit 0:	Page-feed before the report
Bit 1:	Page-feed after the report
Bit 2:	Simple report without page-feed (plain report)

The option is switched on if the relevant bit is set to 1. The end of the file is indicated by a word containing the signature `0002H` (byte sequence `02H 00H`).

2.7 LBL files in dBASE III

In dBASE III, format instructions for labels can be stored in LBL files. The data structure of an LBL file is shown in Table 2.1.

Offset	Bytes	Remarks
00H	1	Signature (sign)
01H	60	Remarks
3DH	2	Height
3FH	2	Width
41H	2	Left margin
43H	2	Label line
45H	2	Label space
47H	2	Label across
49H	16*60	Label text (info[16][60])
409H	1	Signature 2 (sign2)

Table 2.11 Structure of an LBL file

The 1-byte sign field contains the signature 02H for valid LBL files. This is followed by a comment text of up to 60 characters which specifies the predefined size of the label. This text is usually filled with blanks.

The height field contains the number of lines in the label, while the width field defines the print width of the individual lines of the label. The number of blanks for the left margin of the label is indicated in left_margin.

The following parameters control the printer when printing out one sheet containing several labels. The label_line field defines the space (in lines) between each row of labels. The label_space parameter defines the number of blanks between individual labels on one line. This number is important for controlling the print header at the start of the next label (to the right). The label_across parameter indicates how many labels are to be printed in each row on the printed page.

An area containing the text of the label begins at offset 49H. The label may contain 16 lines of text, with 60 characters per line. The text area is thus arranged as a field containing 16 strings of 60 characters. The expressions required to produce the printed line are contained in these strings.

The file is terminated at offset 409H with a second signature 02H (1 byte).

2.8 Format of the file DBPRINT.PTB

Printer compatibility represents rather a problem when using dBASE III. The user is often faced with the difficulty of printing special characters or accents. In dBASE III+, a certain amount of assistance is provided by the file DBPRINT.PTB; however, the structure and function of this file are largely undocumented. The following paragraphs take a closer look at this file (Table 2.2):

Byte	Code	Meaning
1	00	Header – start of record
2	xx	First code byte (dBase character)
3	xx	Second code byte (printer code) optional

Table 2.12
Record structure of DBPRINT.PTB

The contents of this file are used to adapt the connected printer to the characters to be printed. This is always necessary if, for example, the printer is not directly compatible with the character set of a PC running MS-DOS. In such cases, it is not usually possible to print out special characters and accents. Instead of the German umlaut Ä, a square bracket [will be printed; the German letter ß does not exist at all. The reason for this problem is that all characters above ASCII 128 in the ASCII table are not standardized. It is thus quite possible for the computer to send the correct code for the character ß to the printer and also to represent it correctly on screen, because the code corresponds with the computer's character set. However, a differently configured printer will output its own character in response to the code received. In order to be able to represent a character to which a different code is ascribed in the printer's character table, the dBASE character must be converted into this code via a translation table. Such a translation table is stored in the file DBPRINT.PTB. If this file is available at the start of dBASE III+, it will be loaded and used for recoding printer commands.

As a rule, the file consists of several bytes which are stored in records of variable length. Each record begins with a 1-byte header which specifies the *record type*. Two different header types are permissible:

Header	Remark
00H	Data record: 2–3 bytes (including the header)
08H	Comment record: *n* bytes

Table 2.13
Header types

If another header (00H or 08H) appears in the file, the current record is terminated. The end of the file is indicated by a blank record (00H 00H). The file generally starts with the header 08H, followed by a comment text with notes on printer compatibility (*see* Figure 2.6).

The comment text is followed by the actual records containing the printer codes, according to the structure shown in Table 2.2. The ASCII code for the character to be converted is stored in the second byte (for example, the value 41H for replacement of the letter A). The ASCII code for the replacement letter is given in the third byte. For example, if the value 40H is entered, dBASE will output the letter with the code 40H (@) on the printer.

If one of the characters to be printed is not included in the printer character set or is to be omitted in the printout, its code must be included in the table. A record containing only the header and the second byte is stored for this character. Since the third byte is missing, dBASE suppresses the character in the printer output.

Entries can be removed from `DBPRINT.PTB` very simply by placing the value `08H` in the header byte instead of `00H`. dBASE will interpret this entry as a comment. Subsequent re-activation can be effected by altering the header byte.

Comment with printer name

```
08 45 70 73 6F 6E 20 46 58 20 47 65 72 6D 61 6E
 .  E  p  s  o  n     F  X     G  e  r  m  a  n
00 A0 61 00 82 65 00 A1 69 00 A2 6F 00 A3 75 00
 .  .  a  .  .  e  .  .  i  .  .  o  .  .  u  .
85 61 08 60 00 8A 65 08 60 00 8D 69 08 60 00 95
 .  a  .  '  .  .  e  .  '  .  .  i  .  '  .  .
6F 08 60 00 97 75 08 60 00 83 61 08 5E 00 88 65
 o  .  '  .  .  u  .  '  .  .  a  .  ^  .  .  e
08 5E 00 8C 69 08 5E 00 93 6F 08 5E 00 96 75 08
 .  ^  .  .  i  .  ^  .  .  o  .  ^  .  .  u  .
5E 00 84 84 00 89 65 00 8B 69 00 94 94 00 81 81
 ^  .  .  .  .  .  e  .  .  i  .  .  .  .  .  .
```

Figure 2.6 Memory dump of the file `DBPRINT.PTB`

3

File formats in dBASE IV

The *natural successor to dBASE III+ developed by Ashton Tate was dBASE IV which removes many of the limitations of its predecessors. The structure of DBF files in this program version are described below.*

3.1 DBF file format in dBASE IV

The structure of these files is based on that of dBASE III, although the performance of this version has been enhanced. As in the older versions, each DBF file consists of three parts: the header, field descriptions and the actual data.

The length of the header record containing the header and field descriptions depends on the configuration of the program. For example, in network versions, the header requires a larger number of bytes. The structure is shown in Table 3.1.

As in dBASE III, this information is stored as a mixture of ASCII and binary formats.

The first byte is used to identify the dBASE version. In dBASE II, the value entered here is `02H`; from dBASE III onwards the value `3H` is contained in the lower nibble (bits `0`...`3`), and the highest bit (`7`) indicates whether the file contains memo fields. If it does, a DBF file containing the memo texts is associated with the DBF file, and the byte accordingly contains the code `83H`. In all other cases, the value in the first byte is `03H`.

! **I have information that some dBASE versions write the code for `7BH` for DBF files with memo fields. In this cases, the version is set to `1`.**

However, there are indications that dBASE IV versions may use the value `7BH` for DBF files with memo fields. In such cases the value `01H` is used as the version number.

The next field consists of 3 bytes containing the date of the last write access coded in binary form with the format YYMMDD – the year (`0...99`) is thus placed in the first byte.

The following 4-byte field contains the number of data records in the DBF file. These 4 bytes are interpreted as an unsigned 32-bit number, based on the normal Intel conventions on memory allocation (lowest value byte of the number at the lowest address). The number of records includes those already marked for deletion.

Offset	Bytes	Remarks
00H	1	dBASE version
		Bit 0–2 dBASE version
		Bit 3 Memo field indicator
		Bit 4–6 Reserved for SQL
		Bit 7 Flag for dBASE III+ memo files
01H	3	Date of last write access
		(Binary format YYMMDD)
04H	4	Number of records in DBF file
08H	2	Header length in bytes
0AH	2	Record length in bytes
0CH	2	Reserved
0EH	1	Transaction flag
0FH	1	Encryption flag
10H	12	Reserved
1CH	1	Working index flag
		01H = MDX file
		00H = No multi-key index
1DH	3	Reserved
20H	32*N	32-byte description for each field
32 * (N+1)	1	Header end (0DH)

Table 3.1 Format of a dBASE IV DBF header

The next field is an unsigned 16-bit number giving the length of the header in bytes. The header contains 32 bytes plus *n* 32-byte records containing field descriptions plus a terminating byte, coded 0DH. This header length was adopted from dBASE III+.

The length of a data record is stored in bytes 10–11 (0AH–0BH) as an unsigned 16-bit number. This number is always one more than the sum of the field lengths, because one byte is reserved at the start of a data record to mark deleted records.

From byte 12 (0CH), there is a 20-byte area reserved for internal use. At offset 14 (0EH), for example, there is a flag indicating the success or failure of a transaction. The flag remains set if there are incomplete transactions. The command BEGIN TRANSACTION sets the value of the flag to 01H. The END TRANSACTION and ROLLBACK commands unset the flag. The status of this flag can be checked using the dBASE IV function ISMARKED().

Byte 15 (0FH) indicates whether the data within the file has been encrypted by dBASE. The value 0 indicates unencrypted data, while 1 indicates that data has been stored in encrypted form.

However, resetting the value from 1 to 0 does not decode this data; this can only be carried out by dBASE itself. Encryption is only possible with dBASE IV.

Byte 28 (1CH), which is reserved in dBASE III, is used in version IV to indicate multi-key index files. If this type of file has been set up by dBASE, the byte contains the value 01H. Otherwise the value is set to 00H.

Information on the structure of the data records follows the header, as with dBASE III. Here, too, there are individual field descriptions, with a maximum of 255 fields available in dBASE IV. For every field in the database, there is a 32-byte record, whose format is shown in Table 3.2:

Offset	Bytes	Remarks
00H	11	Field name (ASCII characters)
0BH	1	Field type (in ASCII C, N, F, L, D, M)
0CH	4	Field data address in memory
10H	1	Field length in bytes
11H	1	Decimal places (in bytes)
12H	2	Reserved for multi-user access
14H	1	ID for working areas
15H	10	Reserved
1FH	1	Working index flag 01H MDX with subindex

Table 3.2 DBF field description in dBASE IV

The first 11 bytes of the field description contain the field name (10 characters + 00H), which is stored as ASCIIZ text. In this respect, dBASE relies heavily on the C language, which also terminates character strings with a zero byte. If the field name does not extend to 11 characters, the remaining bytes are filled with 00H.

The next byte contains the ASCII character for the field type (Table 3.3 shows the coding for the valid field types for dBASE IV). Compared with dBASE III+, dBASE IV offers an extended floating-point format (F).

The field type is followed by 4 bytes, which are used internally by dBASE to store the field address. This value is of no importance for external purposes.

The field length is stored in binary in byte 16 (10H). One field can contain a maximum of 255 characters; however, this can only be exploited by character fields (which in any case are a maximum of 154 characters). For numeric fields, this value specifies the number of decimal places, including the decimal point.

From version IV onwards, dBASE offers two options for representing floating-point numbers:

- With the new F-format, the data is processed internally in a floating-point representation using binary arithmetic; this leads to greater precision.
- As an alternative, the data can be represented in decimal in the N-format which is already familiar from dBASE II. Precision in this case is limited to approximately 15 places.

Character	Field type	Characters
`C`	Character	ASCII-characters
`N`	Numeric 1	– 0...9
`F`	Numeric 2	– 0...9
`L`	Logical	YyNnTtFf ?
`D`	Date	YYYYMMDD
`M`	Memo	DBT block number

Table 3.3 Coding field types in dBASE IV

For memo fields, the field length is always 10 bytes, in order to store the block number of the memo text held in the associated DBT file (further details are given in the description of the DBT format). The length of logical fields is 1, and 8 bytes are reserved for a date field.

For numeric fields, byte `17 (11H)` specifies the number of places after the decimal point. For all other types of field, this byte has the value `00H`. The important factor is that the number of decimal places is always smaller than the field length.

The remaining 14 bytes are reserved for internal purposes. They should merely be skipped in order to access to the next field description. The `set fields` byte is also of no further relevance, since dBASE IV uses this entry only in memory.

Every defined field in the data structure has its own 32-byte field description record in the header of the DBF file. In dBASE IV, up to 255 fields per record can be defined, with a record length of up to 4000 bytes. The last field description in the header is terminated by the character `0DH` (carriage return). If not all fields are defined, this character is located after the last field definition.

Like dBASE III, the data records in dBASE IV are appended to the definition section. The record length is stored in the file header, as explained above. A data record is stored in pure ASCII format without field separators, which considerably simplifies the import and export of data using the `SDF` option. All fields can be processed as ASCII text, regardless of their type.

As soon as a new record is added to the file by the command `APPEND BLANK`, dBASE fills this record with blanks. The first byte in the record is used to mark deleted data, and since a blank is entered even for new records, these cannot be deleted. Only if the first byte contains the character `*` will the record be removed from the DBF file when the next `PACK` command is given. This means that `DELETE` operations are very fast, and it also enables reasonably trouble-free `UNDELETE` operations. Records handled in this way do, however, remain in the database, and it is quite likely that several hundred such records – none of which is valid – may be retained. Access without using an index is naturally very slow because all records (deleted and undeleted) must be read. The remedy for this weakness is to use `PACK` to remove deleted records from the DBF file as often as possible. Records marked for deletion are overwritten by subsequent valid records, and the entry in the header is reduced to the number of undeleted records.

The end of the valid data area is indicated by the character `1AH`. In contrast to earlier dBASE versions, dBASE IV also alters the physical size of the file. After this operation, the DOS `EOF` marker is positioned directly after the character `1AH`, and the deleted records are finally removed.

Figure 3.1 shows an extract from a DBF file in dBASE IV represented as a hex-dump.

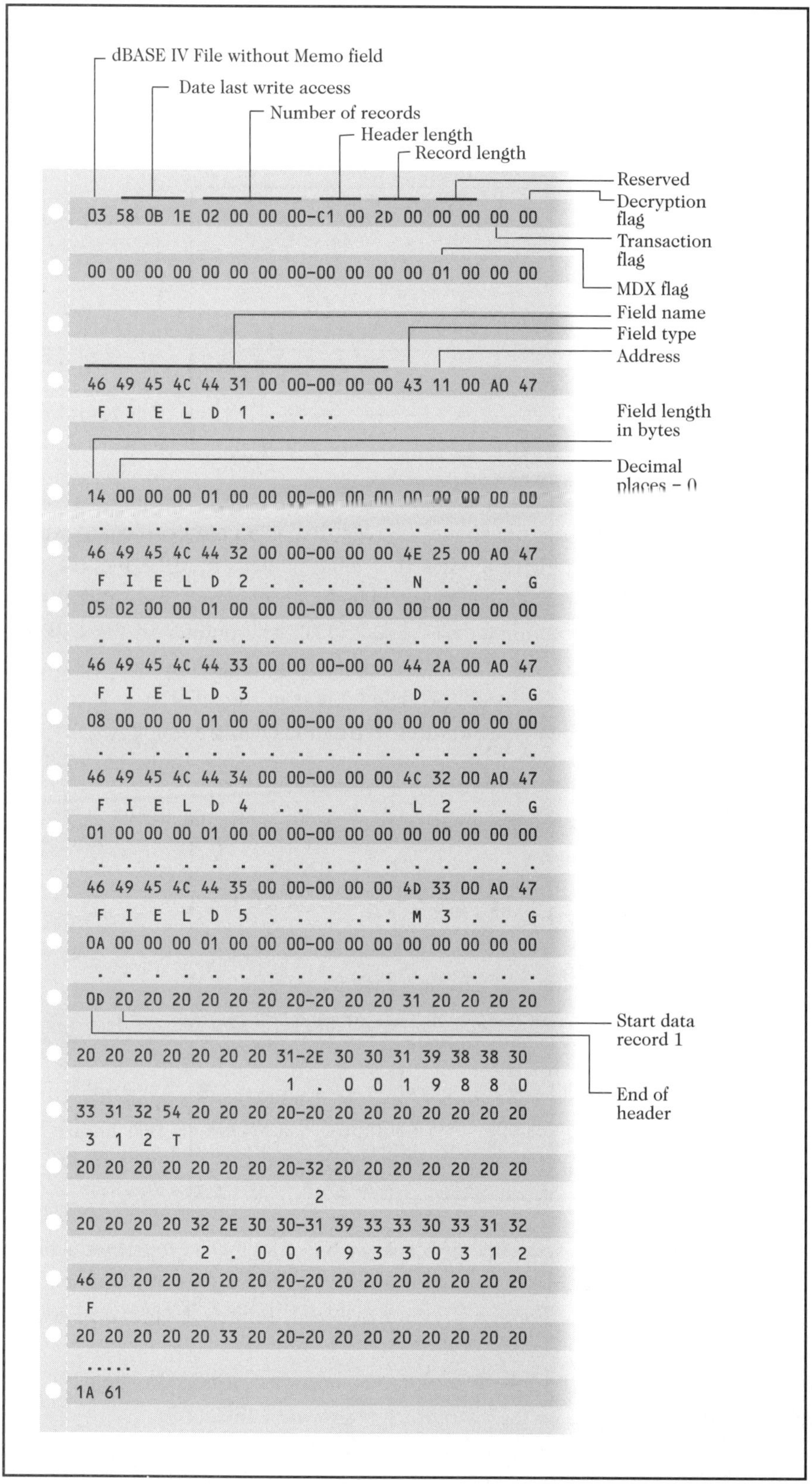

Figure 3.1 Dump of a dBASE IV file (`TEST.DBF`)

3.2 DBT file format in dBASE IV

Memo files are used to store texts. In the database files themselves (DBF files), there is only one field containing a pointer to the actual memo file. The structure is as follows:

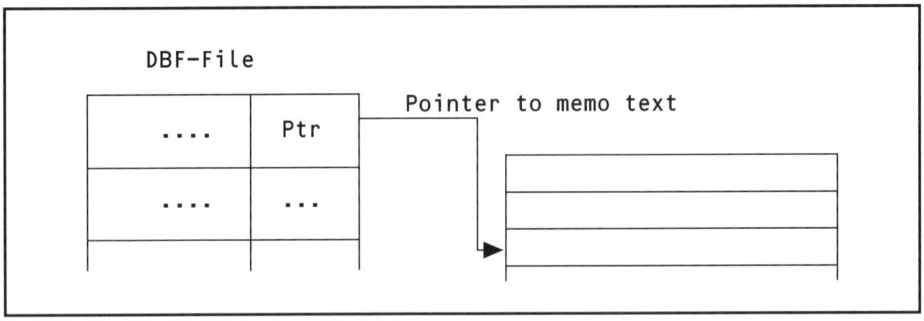

Figure 3.2 Pointers to memo text in a DBT file

The value of each MEMO field in the DBF file should be regarded as a pointer (block number) to an entry in the associated DBT file. The DBT file has the same name as the DBF file; the only difference is in its extension. DBT files are subdivided into blocks on n bytes; in dBASE IV, the block length can be determined with the command `SET BLOCKSIZE`. The pointer in the DBF file indicates the offset in blocks in the DBT file. If no text is stored in the memo file, the associated field in the DBF file will contain 10 blanks. In dBASE IV, deleted text in the MEMO file is released and can be reused. The structure of the file is based on dBASE III and is defined as follows:

Offset	Bytes	Remarks
00H	4	Pointer to first free block
04H	4	Unused
08H	8	DBF file name (no extension)
10H	1	Flag: 03H dBASE III Header, else 00H
11H	3	Reserved
14H	2	Block length in bytes
16H	n	Fill bytes 00H to end of block

Table 3.4 DBT header (block 0) in dBASE IV

The DBT file consists of a continuous sequence of blocks n bytes long. The length of a block can be defined using `SET BLOCKSIZE TO` and is stored in block 0 in bytes 14–15H. It should be noted, however, that dBASE III DBT files are given the block length 1 (for reasons of compatibility).

Block 0 is followed by n blocks of fixed length, which may be occupied or free. Occupied blocks are addressed by entries in the DBF database; their structure is shown in Table 3.5.

The length of the memo field data is stored in the block at offset 04H, thereby dispensing with the end marker (1AH) used in dBASE III. In the text, sections are terminated with the codes 0DH and 0AH. Line-breaks are indicated by 8DH and 0AH.

Offset	Bytes	Remarks
00H	4	Reserved (FFH FFH 08H 00H)
04H	4	Length of memo field entry in bytes
08H	*n*	Memo field

Table 3.5
Header of a used DBT block (dBASE IV)

In block 0, there is a pointer at offset 00H to the first free block of the DBT file. In dBASE IV, free DBT blocks can be reused. The free blocks are therefore managed by means of a pointer structure (*see* Table 3.6).

The number of the first free block and the length of a block can be found starting from the DBT header.

Offset	Bytes	Remarks
00H	4	Pointer to next free block
04H	4	Pointer to next used block
08H	*n*	Filler bytes to end of block

Table 3.6
Empty DBT block chaining (dBASE IV)

4

File formats in FoxPro

The *database program FoxPro is based on the dBASE DBF file format, but also has a number of extensions which will be considered below.*

4.1 FoxPro format of DBF files

In FoxPro, the following versions are available:

- FoxPro 1.0
- FoxPro 2.0
- FoxBase+
- FoxPro 2.5 and FoxPro for Windows 2.5a/2.6

The structure of FoxPro DBF files is based on that of dBASE III DBF files. As shown in Figure 4.1, each DBF file consists of three parts: the header, the field definition and the actual data.

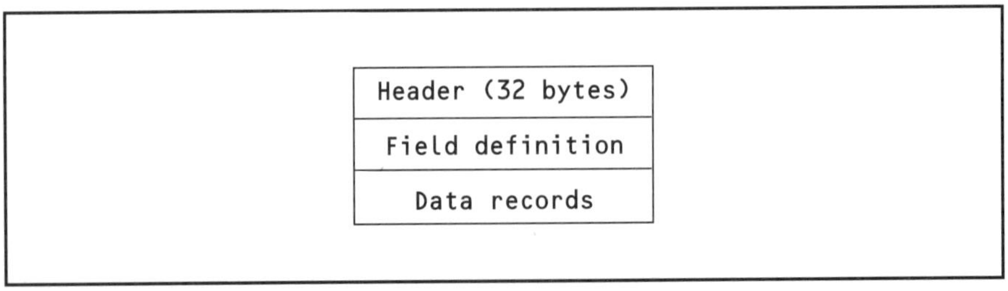

Figure 4.1 Structure of a FoxPro DBF file

The data in the file is stored in a mixture of ASCII text and binary format. The header consists of binary data, while the data records are stored as pure ASCII text.

4.1.1 The DBF header

The header always contains 32 bytes. Its structure is shown in Table 4.1.

Offset	Bytes	Remarks	
00H	1	Version DBF file	
		03H	dBASE III+/FoxBase+ without memo fields
		03H	dBASE IV / FoxPro 2.x without memo fields
		83H	dBASE III+/FoxBase+ with memo fields
		8BH	dBASE IV with memo fields
		F5H	FoxPro with memo fields
01H	3	Date of last change (binary format YYMMDD)	
04H	4	Number of data records in file	
08H	2	Pointer to first record (offset in bytes)	
0AH	2	Record length (including delete byte)	
0CH-1FH	20	Reserved	
20H	32*N	32 bytes per field description	
32*(N+1)	1	End of header (0DH)	

Table 4.1 Format of a FoxPro DBF header

The first byte is used to identify the version of the program that produced the DBF file. In dBASE III, the value 03H is stored here. The highest bit (7) is used by dBASE III to indicate whether the file contains memo fields. In FoxBase+, the same notation has been adopted. The same applies to FoxPro files that do not contain memo fields. However, if a FoxPro DBF file contains memo fields, FoxPro enters the signature F5H in the first byte. In this case, associated with the DBF file is an FPT file containing memo texts (or graphic data). If FoxPro finds any value other than those listed in Table 4.1, it will refuse access, because the file cannot be a DBF file.

The next three bytes contain the date of the last write access (in the format YYMMDD). The first byte contains the year (0 .. 99).

The 4-byte field at offset 4 contains the number of data records in the DBF file. This value is interpreted as an unsigned 32-bit number, to which the Intel conventions on memory allocation apply (lowest byte number at the lowest address). The value includes all records, even those already marked for deletion.

The next field is an unsigned 16-bit number containing the length of the header in bytes. The length of the header varies in accordance with the variable number of field descriptions that can be contained in a DBF file (*see below*). The length of the header represents a pointer (offset in bytes) to the first data record.

The length of a data record is stored at offset 10 (0AH) as an unsigned 16-bit number. This value includes the first byte (blank, or * if the record is marked for deletion) and must correspond to the sum of the individual field lengths +1.

At offset 12 (0CH) there is a reserved area of 20 bytes provided for internal management. For example, dBASE IV uses this area for network management. FoxPro 2.5a (for Windows) stores the code for the code page used in the byte at offset 31 (1FH). Thus, the contents of text and data fields can be represented using different character sets in FoxPro. Furthermore, sorting is also based on the relevant code page. The coding has not been officially documented, but Table 4.2 presents a list of codes used so far.

Code	Code page	Remark
01H	437	US MS-DOS
02H	850	International MS-DOS
03H	1251	Russian Windows
	1252	Windows ANSI-Codes
64H	852	EE MS-DOS
65H	866	Russian MS-DOS
66H	865	Nordic MS-DOS

Table 4.2
Code pages in FoxPro 2.5a

In FoxPro versions 2.5b and 2.6, additional code pages are supported. However, the coding for these code pages is not currently known.

4.1.2 Field description

The field descriptions follow at offset 32 (20H). These are based on the parameters from dBASE III, but new field types have been introduced. Each field definition contains 32 bytes and, in FoxPro, 255 fields are permitted. The structure of the field description is shown in Table 4.3.

Offset	Bytes	Remarks
00H	11	Field name in ASCII
0BH	1	Field type in ASCII (C,N,L,M,G,D,F,P)
0CH	4	Field position in record
10H	1	Field length in bytes (binary)
11H	1	Places after decimal point (in bytes)
12H–1FH	14	Reserved

Table 4.3
FoxPro DBF field description

The first 11 bytes of the field definition contain the field name as ASCIIZ text, that is, the name is always terminated with a zero byte 00H. If the field name is shorter than 10 characters, the remaining bytes are filled 00H.

The ASCII character for the field type is stored in the next byte. Table 4.4 shows the coding of valid field types for FoxPro 2.x. In comparison with dBASE III, there are additional object fields, floating-point fields and picture fields.

Character	Field type	Characters
C	Character	ASCII characters
N	Numeric	- 0..9
L	Logical	YyNnTtFf ?
M	Memo field	DBT block number
G	Object	FPT block number
D	Date	YYYYMMDD
F	Floating point no.	0 .. 9
P	Picture	FPT block number

Table 4.4 FoxPro 2.x field types

As well as these supplementary field types, a field description in FoxPro differs in another respect from dBASE. While dBASE saves the internal data addresses of the field at offset 12 (0CH), FoxPro stores the position of the field in the data record. As a result, the sequence of field descriptions no longer needs to agree with the sequence of fields in the data record. Furthermore, the bytes from offset 18 (12H) onwards are reserved. The field length is stored in binary in one byte at offset 16 (10H). Each field can thus contain a maximum of 255 characters. This length is only fully exploited in the case of character fields. With numeric fields, this value indicates the number of places including the decimal point. However, numbers can only be processed to an accuracy of approximately 15 places in FoxPro. Memo fields, object fields and graphic fields always have a field length of 10 bytes, because in these cases they contain the block number of the data stored in the associated FPT file (or DBT file in FoxPro 1.0). Further details are given in the description of FPT and DBT formats. Logical fields have a length of 1, while 8 bytes are reserved for date fields. For numeric fields, the following byte at offset 17 (11H) specifies the number of places after the decimal point. With all other types of field, this byte has the value 00H. It is important to note that the number of places after the decimal point is always smaller than the field length.

Every defined field in the data structure has its own 32-byte field description record in the header of the DBF file. The end of the field description area is indicated by the character 0DH.

4.1.3 DBF data records

The data records are appended after the field descriptions, as with dBASE. The record length is determined by the length of the relevant fields and is indicated in the header of the file. This value is always 1 more than the sum of the field lengths, because one byte is reserved for deletion marking. The data is stored in pure ASCII format without field separators. An undeleted record always contains a blank character (code `20H`) in the first byte, while records marked as deleted contain the character `*` (code `2AH`) in this position. This makes the import or export of ASCII data (for example, using the SDF option) very simple.

If a new record is added to the file with the `APPEND BLANK` command, FoxPro will fill this record with blanks. Since there is a blank in the first byte in the record, the record cannot be deleted. Only if the first byte contains the character `*`, the record will be removed from the DBF file when the next `PACK` command is given. This means that very rapid `DELETE` operations are possible, and also enables trouble-free `UNDELETE` operations.

The end of the valid data area is indicated by the character `1AH`. This `EOF` indicator is managed by FoxPro and not by DOS.

4.2 The structure of a FoxBase+ DBT file (memo file)

Memo data in FoxBase+ is stored in DBT files. The structure of these files was derived from dBASE III, and they are less efficient than FoxPro memo files (FPT). These are described in the following section. In the DBF file, in the relevant field of the data record, there is only one pointer to the block of the memo file (*see* Figure 4.2).

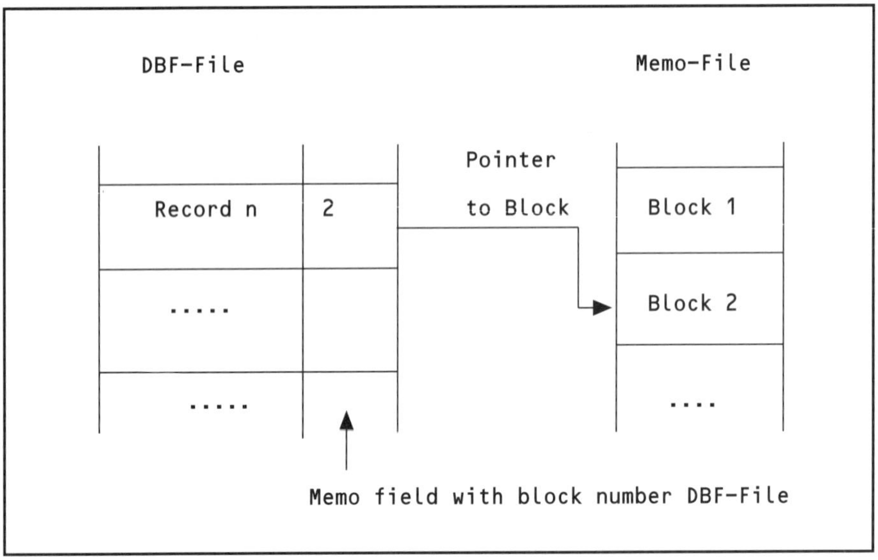

Figure 4.2 Pointer to a memo block within a memo field

The pointer in the memo field of the DBF file is invisible to the user. If there is no text block for this record, the memo field will be blank.

The FoxBase+ memo file consists of 512-byte blocks. The first 2 bytes of the first block contain the number of the next free block in the memo file (Figure 4.3).

The offset to the start of the free block is calculated as:

```
Offset := Block number * 512
```

It should be noted that the block number is in Intel format (low byte first). If a new text is to be stored in a memo field, FoxBase+ reads the header pointer of the memo file and stores the value in the appropriate memo field of the DBF file. The text is simply appended to the end of the memo file. Then the number of the next free block is calculated and stored in the header of the memo file.

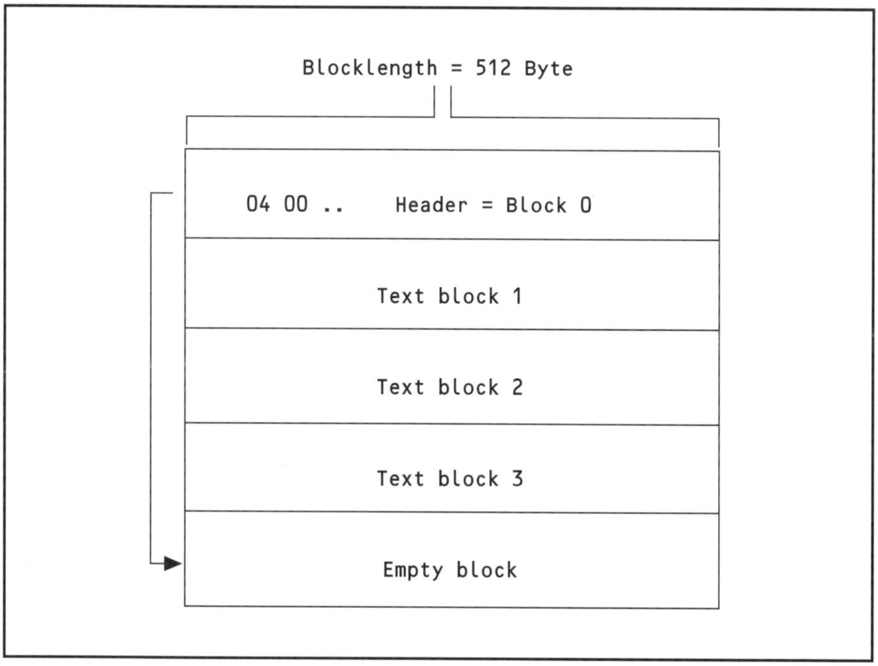

Figure 4.3 Block structure of a FoxBase+ memo file

Changes to MEMO texts are simply added to the end of the memo file and the new pointer entered in the memo field of the DBF file. Thus, the old text is retained in the memo file. This has the effect of seriously increasing the size of memo files, if texts are frequently altered. The only means of ensuring that unused texts are removed from the memo file is to issue a `COPY` command.

If a text is longer than 512 bytes, FoxBase+ simply uses another 512-byte block. This process is repeated until every byte of the text has been stored. The pointer in the DBF file points to the start of the first block of the relevant text. The end of the text is indicated by the character `1AH`. Any remaining bytes up to the end of the 512-byte block remain undefined.

4.3 The structure of FoxPro FPT files (object files and memo files)

From FoxPro 2.0 onwards, FPT files are available for memo texts and binary data (graphics). FoxPro 2.5 additionally enables objects to be stored in FPT files. The data may represent the object itself or merely a reference to the associated object (application with data).
In FoxPro 2.x, the FPT files have a unified structure and consist of a data header and n data blocks. The length of the data header is fixed at 512 bytes. The remainder of the file is subdivided into blocks of fixed length. The block length is preset to 512 bytes, but can be altered using the command `SET BLOCKSIZE`.

4.3.1 The header of an FPT file

The structure of the data header is shown in Table 4.5.

Offset	Bytes	Remarks
00H	4	Position of first free block
04H	2	Unused
06H	2	Block size in bytes
08H	504	Unused
...		
1FFH		

Table 4.5
Header of a FoxPro FPT file

The first 4 bytes contain an offset pointer to the first free byte of the memo file. The pointer is stored in Motorola format (low byte last) rather than in Intel format. The offset 2000H is thus stored as the byte sequence 00H 00H 20H 00H. The next two bytes at offset 04H are unused. The block size in bytes is stored at offset 06H. This value is read as a hexadecimal number from left to right (02H 00H corresponds to 200H). The value is used to define the length of the following data blocks and is set via the FoxPro command SET BLOCKSIZE. The remaining bytes in the first block are unused.

4.3.2 The data area of the FPT file

The data blocks containing the memo texts or object data start at offset 512 (200H). The data blocks are of a fixed length which is stored at offset 06H in the header of the FPT file. Each block must start on an even address boundary. The position of the start of the block can be calculated by multiplying the block number (from the DBF file) by the block size (from the header of the FPT file):

```
Offset block := block number * block size
```

If there is no entry for a record, the DBF file for this record will have a blank entry in the memo field or object field. Otherwise there will be a 10-byte block number, which is interpreted as an ASCII number. Figure 4.4 shows extracts from a hex-dump of an FPT file.

The data (memo fields, graphics, objects and so on) is transferred as records to the individual data blocks. Each record always begins at the start of a block and therefore on an even address boundary. It is entirely possible for the record to occupy more than one block. It is, however, important that the following record begins at the start of the next block. In this case, any remaining bytes up to the end of the block remain undefined. The structure of a data record is shown in Table 4.6.

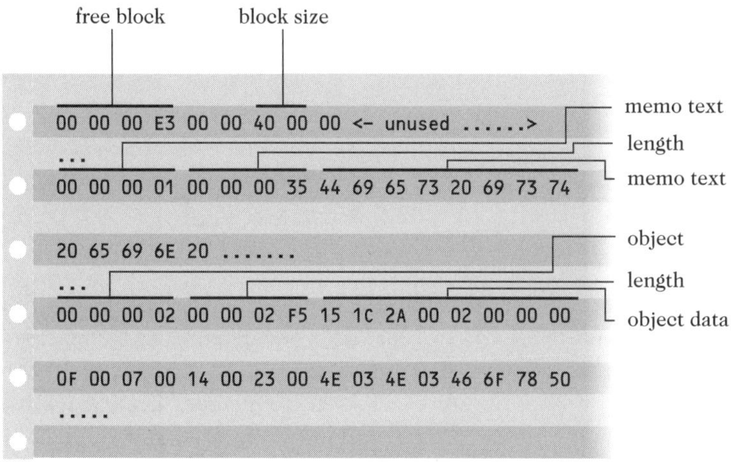

Figure 4.4 Dump of an FPT file

Offset	Bytes	Remarks
00H	4	Record type 0: Picture 1: Memo 2: Object
04H	4	Length of memo field in bytes
08H..n	*n*	Memo text with *n* bytes

Table 4.6 Structure of a data block

The first 4 bytes contain the data type. A distinction is made between text (memo) and binary data (graphics or object). For text the code 1 is entered. It should be noted that the values are preset as hexadecimal numbers in Motorola format (for example, 00H 00H 00H 01H for the code 1). In the data area, ASCII or ANSI texts are used. If the code 0 appears (00H 00H 00H 00H), the data area contains the binary data for a picture. In my experience, this is only possible on a Macintosh, because FoxPro uses the object field type on DOS machines. However, as far as I can determine, the code 2 (00H 00H 00H 02H) is used for objects. This may involve a picture, a sound or an embedded object. The structure of the data area, which is dictated by the linked application object (Excel Table, Paintbrush Picture and so on), is not documented.

The length of the data area is stored at offset 04H as a 4-byte pointer. This value should also be read from left to right as a hexadecimal number.

The data area, which may be of variable length, follows at offset 08H. This data area may encompass several blocks of the FPT file. The area between the end of the data and the end of the final block remains undefined, because the following record must be located on a block boundary. With memo fields, FoxPro sometimes enters the memo field code here.

4.4 The structure of uncompressed IDX index files

FoxPro supports a number of different index files:

- Uncompressed IDX files
- Compressed (compact) IDX files
- Multi-index CDX files

The structure of uncompressed IDX files is dealt with below.

Uncompressed index files (IDX) have a tree structure. The keys (index entries) are distributed across various index nodes, starting from the start (or root) node (*see* Figure 4.5). The leaves of the tree (end nodes) thus contain references to the actual data records. To search for a record in the tree, the tree must have a unique path from the start node to the end node. The entries at each node are then successively compared with the search expression. If the search key is smaller than the key in the node (for example, search expression = `F`, entry = `G`), the search has to be continued in the next lowest node. For example, if a search is being carried out for the expression `K` in the tree, the following operations must be implemented:

- Compare the expression `K` with the first entry `F` in the start node.
- Since the search expression is larger than the entry, the next entry must be analyzed.
- This entry is also smaller than the search expression.
- Since there are no more entries, the search expression is not present in the tree.

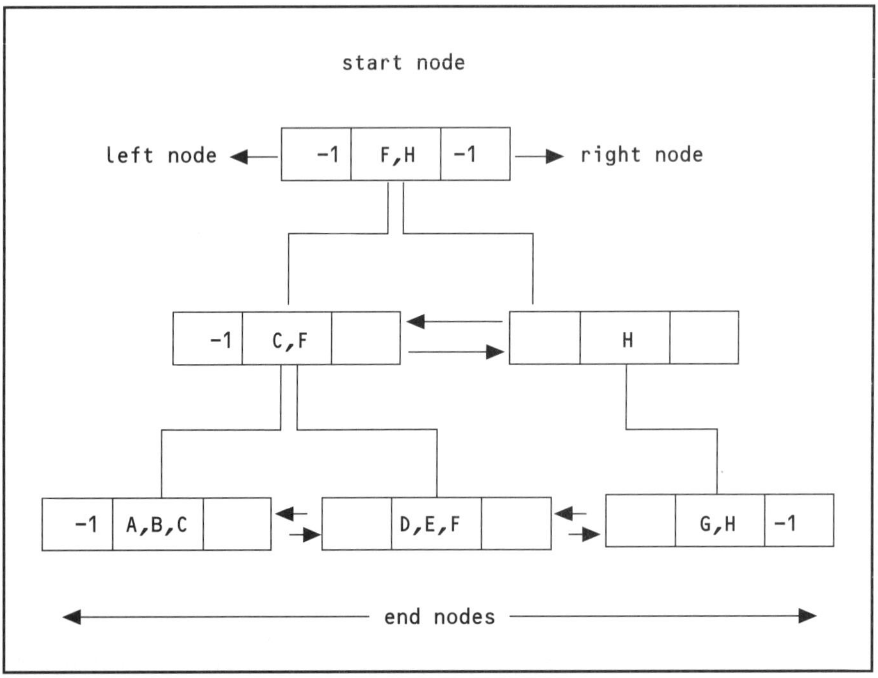

Figure 4.5 Tree structure of IDX files

However, if the letter C is being searched for, the result of the first comparison will be that the search expression is smaller than the entry. The search will branch off to the next lowest node in the relevant section of the tree. Here, the first comparison scores a hit, because the entry is the same as the search expression. A branch is now made to the next lowest node (end node). On the third access to the data, the search expression is the same as the entry, and the record number is available to the database.

Searching via the index tree enables rapid access to the data in the database. To optimize the search procedures within the tree, each node has another two pointers to the directly neighboring nodes on the same level. This means that when searching through index areas, it is not necessary to go back to the various branching points of the tree. If the neighboring node does not exist, the pointer will indicate the value –1 (FFFF FFFFH).

I should like to follow these initial considerations with an explanation of the structure of the index file. The index file consists of a header and an unlimited number of nodes. The header and the individual nodes are always 512 bytes long.

4.4.1 The header of the IDX file

The header of an uncompressed IDX file contains all the information on the start node, the current file size, the length of the key and so on. The structure of the header is shown in Table 4.7.

Offset	Bytes	Remarks
00H	4	Pointer to start node
04H	4	Pointer to free node list (-1 no free nodes)
08H	4	Pointer to file end
0CH	2	Key expression length in bytes
0EH	1	Index options 1: Unique index 8: Index with FOR clause
0FH	1	Index signature (not used)
10H	220	Key expression (ASCII string)
ECH	220	FOR expression (ASCII string)
1C8H	56	Unused

Table 4.7 IDX header record

The first 4 bytes contain a pointer (in Intel format) to the start node. This value is the offset from the start of the file to the beginning of the start node and it must be a multiple of 512 bytes.

When processing the index file, new entries are added to the node and existing entries are deleted. Thus, individual nodes may possibly have no entries. At offset 4, there is therefore a pointer to the list of free index nodes. The pointer should be interpreted as an unsigned number in Intel format. If there is no list of blank index nodes, the pointer will contain –1 (FFFF FFFFH).

FoxPro indicates the size of the index file at offset 8. The word at offset 12 (0CH) defines the length of the key expression in bytes.

FoxPro can set up an index file via a unique key. Alternatively, search areas can be indicated via a FOR clause. These two search options use different search expressions. For this reason, the byte at offset 14 (0EH) indicates the relevant index option. The value 1 shows that the index has been structured via a unique key, while 9 shows that the index was produced via a FOR clause.

The byte at offset 15 (0FH) is provided for index coding, but this is not used with uncompressed IDX files. The key expression for unique indices is stored at offset 16 (10H) onwards. FoxPro converts numeric index fields into character strings, thereby enabling the same search and sort algorithms to be used. Numeric values are converted into an IEEE format, then into Intel format and, in the case of negative values, converted to the absolute value. This value is then used as the key, which may comprise up to 220 characters.

The file may also be structured on the basis of a FOR expression. In this option, the FOR expression is stored at offset 236 (ECH) onwards with a maximum length of 220 characters.

The remaining bytes from offset 456 (1C8H) to 511 (1FFH) are unused.

4.4.2 The structure of the node records

The header record is followed by the individual nodes, each of which is 512 bytes long. Each of these data records contains an attribute, the number of keys stored, the pointers to the neighboring nodes and the actual index entries. Table 4.8 shows the structure of an index node.

Offset	Bytes	Remarks
00H	2	Node attribute 0: Index node 1: Start node 2: End node
02H	2	Key entries
04H	4	Pointer to left node (same level, -1 no node)
08H	4	Pointer to right node (same level, -1 no node)
0CH	500	Area for key entries; each entry contains the key and a 4-byte pointer

Table 4.8 Structure of an uncompressed index node in an IDX file

The first two bytes contain the attribute of the relevant node. The value can also be formed from the sum of the individual attributes (0: index node, 1: start node, 2: end node). The number is stored in Intel format (for example, 03H 00H).

The number of key entries in the node is stored at offset 2. This value is also stored in Intel format. It is followed by the pointers to the neighboring nodes at the same level. Each of these pointers occupies 4 bytes and is stored in Intel format. If there is no neighboring node, FoxPro will enter the value –1 (FFFF FFFFH). The pointer to the left node begins at offset 4 and the pointer to the right node at offset 8.

The 500 bytes from offset 12 (0CH) to the end of the node contain the index entries. Each entry consists of an actual key expression followed by a 4-byte pointer (*see* Figure 4.6).

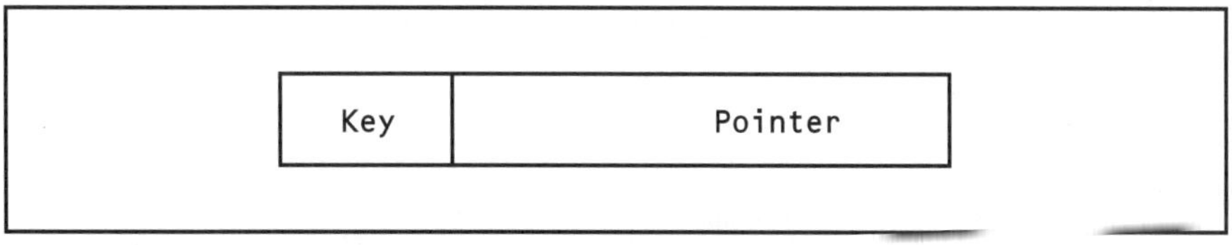

Figure 4.6 Structure of a key entry

The length of the key entry is contained in the header record. This key entry is followed by a 4-byte pointer in Motorola format (high byte first). The interpretation of this pointer depends on the attribute of the node. If an end node is involved (attribute 2 or 3), the pointer contains the data record number for the DBF file. With start and index nodes (attribute 0 or 1), the pointer defines the offset of the next lowest node containing the section for the tree (*see* Figure 1.4). The combination of key and pointer occurs n times within the node. The value of n is stored at offset 2 at the start of the node and must be between 0 and 100 (1-byte key and 4-byte pointer). If $n = 0$, there is a blank node. The list of blank nodes is maintained via the pointer in the header of the index file.

4.5 The structure of a compact IDX index file

FoxPro also offers the possibility of storing the contents of an IDX file in compressed form. This reduces the file size and accelerates search access. When packing, double letters in the index are compressed. However, the compact IDX files do have a somewhat modified structure, which is also used in multi-index files (CDX).

4.5.1 The header of a compact IDX file

The header record of a compact index file is 1024 bytes in length and is structured as shown in Table 4.9.

The first 4 bytes define the pointer to the start node, stored in Intel format. The next 4-byte pointer at offset 4 refers to the start of the free index node list. The value is stored in Intel format and contains the number -1 (FFFF FFFFH) if there is no list.

The 4 bytes at offset 8 are reserved for internal purposes. They are followed at offset 12 (0CH) by a value in Intel format containing the length of the key expression.

The index options are stored in the byte at offset 14 (0EH). For compact index files the option 32 (20H) is also defined. As soon as this bit is set, FoxPro recognizes a compact index file. The value 64 (40H) is used to indicate CDX files.

Offset	Bytes	Remarks
00H	4	Pointer to start node
04H	4	Pointer to free node list (-1 no free node list)
08H	4	Reserved for internal use
0CH	2	Key length in bytes
0EH	1	Index options 1: Unique index 8: Index with FOR clause 32: Compact index file 64: CDX index file
0FH	1	Index signature
10H–1F5H	485	Reserved (internal use)
1F6H	2	Sort direction 0: ascending 1: descending
1F8H	2	Reserved (internal use)
1FAH	2	Length of all FOR expressions
1FCH	2	Reserved (internal use)
1FEH	2	Length of all key expressions
200H	512	All key entries

Table 4.9 Header of a compact IDX file

The byte at offset 15 (0FH) contains an index code, whose meaning is not clear. The bytes from offset 16 (10H) to 501 (1F5H) are reserved for internal purposes. The word at offset 502 (1F6H) defines the sequence of index sorting:

0: ascending
1: descending

and is stored according to the Intel convention.

The word at offset 504 (1F8H) is reserved for internal purposes. At offset 506 (1FAH), there is a word in Intel format containing the length of all FOR expressions in the index file. For IDX files, this length is related to a FOR expression. The word at offset 508 (1FCH) is reserved.

At offset 510 (1FEH), there is a word in Intel format containing the length of all key expressions. For IDX files, there is only one key. At offset 512 (200H), there is a 512-byte area containing the actual index expression. With multi-index files, several key expressions can be stored here.

4.5.2 The structure of node records

The header record is followed by the index nodes. Each node comprises 512 bytes. However, it is also possible to compress index data within the index node. Index nodes are therefore subdivided into:

- internal index nodes
- external index nodes

Internal index nodes contain the information in uncompressed form (*see* Table 4.10).

Offset	Bytes	Remarks
00H	2	Node attribute 0: Index node 1: Start node 2: End node
02H	2	Number of key entries
04H	4	Pointer to left node (same level, -1 no node)
08H	4	Pointer to right node (same level, -1 no node)
0CH	500	Area for key entries; each entry contains the key and a 4-byte pointer

Table 4.10 Internal index node structure

This structure corresponds to the structure of the nodes in uncompressed index files. Here, too, the first word contains the attribute of the index node (0: index node, 1: start node, 2: end node). This is followed by a word in Intel format containing the number of keys stored in the node. Starting at offset 4, there are two 4-byte pointers to the nodes to the left and right, respectively, on the same level. Non-existent nodes are indicated by –1. All the values from offset 12 (0CH) onwards are stored in Intel format.

The area from offset 12 (0CH) to offset 511 (1FFH) is devoted to key entries. The key index and the data record number are always contained in the node. The entry occurs *n* times.

A modified structure has been introduced for nodes with compressed index data (*see* Table 4.11).

With external index nodes, the first 12 bytes are the same as for uncompressed index files. At offset 12 (0CH), there is a word in Intel format indicating the free space in the node. FoxPro administers the area containing the index entries from offset 24 (18H) to 511 (1FFH) as shown below:

- compressed index values are entered at the start of the area
- the actual index is entered at the end of the area

This enables new indices to be inserted at the end of the area. Masks for the compressed data begin at offset 14. The 4-byte field at offset 14 (0EH) defines a binary mask for the data record number. This data record number must be ANDed with the mask in order to add the record to the database. In this way, records consisting of fewer than 4 bytes can be stored, which saves space in memory.

Offset	Bytes	Remarks
00H	2	Node attribute 0: Index node 1: Start node 2: End node
02H	2	Number of key entries
04H	4	Pointer to left node (same level, -1 no node)
08H	4	Pointer to right node (same level, -1 no node)
0CH	2	Free space in node
0EH	4	Mask for data record number
12H	1	Mask for double characters
13H	1	Mask for following characters
14H	1	Bits in record number
15H	1	Bits in double characters
16H	1	Bits in following characters
17H	1	Bytes per record number, double characters and following characters
18H	488	Area for key entries and information

Table 4.11 The structure of an external index node

The bytes at offsets 18 (12H) and 19 (13H) define masks for the compressed characters of the index. The individual bits must be ANDed with these masks in order to calculate the original index value.

The byte at offset 20 (14H) defines how many bits are used within an entry to represent the record number (for example, 16 or 32). The byte at offset 21 (15H) defines the number of bits used for the representation of double characters in the index. The number of bits for following characters is indicated at offset 22 (16H). The number of bytes for the record number, the number of double characters and the number of following characters are indicated in the byte at offset 23. The value 3 indicates that every entry in the area from offset 24 (18H) to 511 (1FFH) comprises 3 bytes. These three bytes are subdivided into bit sequences for the record number, the number of double characters and the number of following characters. However, the means by which the compression of characters is carried out is not documented.

4.6 The format of multi-index files (CDX)

FoxPro enables index files that can accommodate several indices to be produced. These index files are always stored in compressed form. The structure is identical to that of compact IDX files. The index option in the header (offset 14) contains the value 64 for a multi-index file. The end node points to the index key of the multi-index file. For each index key within the index file, there is an individual index tree which has the same structure as a compact IDX file.

This information was obtained from the FoxPro programming manual. However, some aspects of index files are not covered.

4.7 The structure of a FoxPro 1.0 label file (LBX)

In FoxPro 1.0 data for labels is stored in LBX files, the structure of which is shown in Table 4.12.

Offset	Bytes	Remarks
00H	1	Version 03H for FoxPro 1.0 LBX file
01H	60	Comment (ASCII string)
3DH	2	Lines in label
3FH	2	Width of left margin
41H	2	Label width
43H	2	Number of labels per row
45H	2	Space between labels (blanks)
57H	2	Number of blank lines between rows of labels
59H	2	Length of label text (in characters)
4BH	*n*	Label text, 0DH = line separator

Table 4.12 FoxPro 1.0 LBX structure

The data is stored in Intel format. The text containing the label data is stored at offset 75 (4BH) onwards as an ASCII string, individual lines being separated by the character 0DH. The length of the ASCII string is indicated in the word at offset 73 (49H). The remaining entries in the table define the output format (width, height, columns and so on) of the labels.

In FoxPro 2.0 and later, label data is stored in DBF files. The report generator then generates a working file from this data. The same applies to report and mask files. The structure of DBF files is described in the FoxPro documentation.

5

Data exchange using the SDF format

The preceding sections have been devoted to describing the internal structure of dBASE files. In terms of systems programming it is clearly important to gain direct access to these structures. In many other cases, however, it is sufficient if the data from dBASE is available in ASCII format or can be read in ASCII format – for example, for data exchanging with LOTUS 1-2-3, Multiplan, Word and so on.

By using the `SDF` option (*System Data Format*) with the `copy to` command, dBASE II, dBASE III, dBASE III+ and dBASE IV can be used to convert databases into ASCII files. The syntax for the command is shown below:

```
COPY TO <File> [Fields] [FOR/WHILE] [SDF] [DELIMITED With BLANK/<Delimiter>]
```

The parameters shown in square brackets are optional. In principle, the `COPY` command is used to copy a database opened with `USE` into a file marked `<File>`. The `fields` parameter enables specific fields of the database to be selected for the copying operation. Other conditions relating to the selection of data records can be formulated using the `FOR/WHILE` option. Up to this point, a normal dBASE database is produced; however, as soon as the `SDF` option appears, dBASE will create an ASCII file from the data in the DBF file. The instruction shown below creates the ASCII file `ASCII.TXT`, the records being terminated with the Return character:

```
COPY TO ASCII.TXT SDF
```

The data used in this example must have the following structure (Table 5.1):

Name	Type	Length	Decimals
Field1	C	20	
Field2	N	10	
Field3	N	5	2
Field4	L	1	

Table 5.1 Field format of a dBASE file

The fields are set up with the originally defined lengths. If any value is shorter than the field length, dBASE fills the remaining positions with blanks. The ASCII records will then have the structure shown in Figure 5.1.

In this way, individual, fixed-length fields can be read record by record. This format is particularly suitable for use with text-processing programs, because their output already has a tabular structure.

```
       Field 1             Field 2       Field 3      Field 4
<  20 Characters    > < 10 Char. >  < 5 Char.>    < 1 Char.>

  This is Field 1       10000          1.23           T
  This is record 2      3234           0.98           F
  List price            3              0.00           T
  Waiting room 122      1233           1.98           F
         .               .              .             .
```

Figure 5.1 Output format with the `SDF` option

5.1 The DELIMITED option

Since the formatting described above is not always desirable for input/output, it is possible to define *field delimiters* in the data conversion process. This is achieved by selecting the following option:

```
DELIMITED WITH ...
```

This parameter instructs dBASE to output delimiters between the fields or to use the characters defined as delimiting characters.

The following instruction creates an ASCII file named `HALLO.TXT`, in which the fields of the DBF file are separated by a comma:

```
APPEND FROM <File> [FOR/WHILE] [SDF] DELIMITED WITH BLANK/<Delimiter>]
```

As shown in Figure 5.2, texts are also placed in inverted commas:

```
7000,'Stuttgart','Waldstr.',13
8000,'Munich','Station',5
5000,'Cologne','Kalkstr.',10
```

Figure 5.2 Data output using the `DELIMITED` option

In addition to normal delimiters, *blanks*, *semicolons* or *inverted commas* can also be used as delimiters. The first of the two instructions shown below, for example, exchanges the inverted commas in Figure 5.2 for single inverted commas; the second instruction produces output texts separated by semicolons:

```
COPY TO HALLO.TXT  DELIMITED WITH '
COPY TO HALLO.TXT  DELIMITED WITH ;
```

A blank used as a delimiter can be problematic, because it is not always clear whether the blank is marking the end of a field or is intended to be a component of a text field. In addition, numbers from numeric and text fields can no longer be distinguished.

Conversely, there is another command for converting ASCII files into DBF files:

```
APPEND FROM <File> [FOR/WHILE][SDF][DELIMITED...]
```

The ASCII file must be formatted in such a way that the data is compatible with dBASE fields.

5.2 Import/export of external formats

From dBASE III+ onwards, it is possible to interchange data directly with other standard products using the following file formats:

- DIF (Data Interchange Format), for example Visicalc
- SYLK (Symbolic Link Format), for example Multiplan
- WKS, for example LOTUS 1-2-3 format

The general form of the `COPY` command is shown below:

```
COPY TO <File>
   FIELDS <Fieldlist>
   FOR/WHILE <Condition>
   TYPE <Type>
```

One of the options `DIF`, `SYLK` or `WKS` should be given as the file type. dBASE III+ will then create the relevant file in the format required.

External formats can be read in by dBASE III using `APPEND`. The command is:

```
APPEND FROM <File> [FOR/WHILE] [SDF] [DELIMITED]
```

However, if a text file is to be read into a dBASE file, it must fulfill certain requirements:

- The structure of the text must exactly match the structure of the database.
- Every record must be terminated by `CR/LF` (Carriage Return or Line Feed).
- The number, sequence and length of fields within each line must agree with the database definition. If the field length of the text is shorter than defined in the database, the transfer will be carried out, but dBASE will truncate longer text fields, ignoring excess characters to the right.
- Numeric fields are set to `0` in the database if no value is specified. This enables various possibilities for data exchange with external programs. Further details are given in the user manuals for the relevant version of dBASE.

5.3 The structure of a CSV file

Many programs permit the exchange of data in the form of ASCII text; the values are represented as Comma Separated Values (CSV).

These files are structured very simply:

- The file is built up line by line as an ASCII string.
- The individual values are separated by commas.
- Texts are framed in inverted commas (').

Furthermore, three header lines are available for the definition of field names and data types. A brief example from the Timeline product (Symantec), which contains data in CSV format, is given below:

```
-110,5
-120,'Person','Price','Process','Units','Balance'
-130,1,2,6,6,5
-900,'Brown',150,'Resource','$ per hour','No'
-900,'Moore',100,'Resource','$ per hour','Yes'
-900,'Miller',250,'Resource','$ per hour','No'
-900,'Smith',150,'Resource','$ per hour','No'
```

The structure is very simple. In the first column, there is a negative number, which (specifically for Timeline) describes the following data in the record. The value –900 indicates useful data, while smaller values indicate definitions. The number 5 in the first line specifies that all the following lines have 5 columns. The second line gives the names of the data fields (columns) to be exported. These names are enclosed in inverted commas and separated by commas. The third line contains 5 numbers which define the data type of each column. The structure of these field types is shown below:

Type	Remark
1	Text
2	Numeric values (positive or negative) With decimal point
3	Integers without decimals (signs allowed)
4	Cardinal values (no sign, no decimals)
5	Logical values (Yes or No)
6	Enumeration
7,9	Date field (start date)
8,10	Date field (end date)

Table 5.2 Field types

This representation is also specific to Timeline.

The data records (indicated by –900) start in the fourth line. All values are separated by commas. Text must be enclosed in inverted commas ('), and if inverted commas appear in the text, they must be doubled. The data sequence corresponds to the field names in the file header. Within a date field, commas may exceptionally appear (for example, 1988, 12, 31, 9, 0 = 31 December 1988, 9:00).

In the case of alphanumeric fields, the fixed field width can be exceeded, and the text will be truncated on the right. If the text is shorter than the defined column width, this will be ignored. The field is not padded with spaces. Boolean fields contain the entries Yes or No and are not influenced by the column width. Data in numeric fields are neither truncated nor padded; complete values are presented.

It should, however, be noted that these definitions are software dependent. The data for other CSV files may be coded differently.

PART 2

Spreadsheet formats

File formats discussed in Part 2

Spreadsheets *use their own formats to store calculation tables. A distinction is made between the internal representation of data and the exchange of this data between various standard programs in DIF, SYLK and SDI format.*

The *various formats are described in this part.*

6

LOTUS 1-2-3 WKS/WK1 file format

Millions *of copies of the spreadsheet program LOTUS 1-2-3 are now in use. The contents of the calculation tables produced by this program, including data and calculation formulas, can all be stored in files. Depending on the version of LOTUS (1.0, 1.A, 2.01, 2.2 or 3.0), these files have the extension* `.WKS`, `.WK1` *or* `.WK3`. *This chapter discusses the internal structure of the WKS/WK1 format, which is not widely understood.*

6.1 WKS/WK1 formats in LOTUS 1-2-3 (up to version 2.01)

Both LOTUS 1-2-3 and the spreadsheet program Symphony store data and calculation formulas in what are known as *binary files*. Texts from the spreadsheets are stored in the binary file in ASCII format. Depending on the version of the program used, these files have the extension WKS or WK1. Although there are some differences between the files in different versions of LOTUS, they all share a common record structure, which is also used by Symphony:

```
<Record type> <Record length> <Data>
```

The significance of the individual fields is as follows:

- The 2-byte *record type* field defines the record type and determines the structure of the following data field. For records containing data, this record type can be interpreted as an opcode for calculations or for the structure of the spreadsheet. Both terms (*record type/opcode*) are thus used synonymously. However, the *record type* field is stored in the Intel format (little endian); the opcodes vary according to the version of LOTUS.
- The 2-byte *record length* field specifies the length of the following data field in bytes. The least significant byte (LSB) is stored first.

- The length of the *data* field depends on the field type. Values, calculation formulas, definitions of the structure of the spreadsheet and so on, are all stored in this field.

In interpreting a LOTUS or Symphony file of this structure, the individual records can easily be recognized. Only certain opcodes, which are all upwardly compatible, vary between versions. Further details of the format described here are given in the spreadsheet shown in Figure 6.1.

```
                    Test Spread Sheet
                    =================

Product                 Price      Disc.     Net
--------------------------------------------------
Diskettes 5 1/4         15         10        13.5
Paper                   25         7.8       23.05
Files                   3.5        5         3.325
--------------------------------------------------
Sum                     43.5                 39.875
   Formula
A1: '
C1: 'Test Spread Sheet
C2: '==================
A4: 'Product
C4: 'Price
D4: 'Disc.
E4: 'Net
A5: '___________________________
A6: 'Diskettes 5 1/4
C6: 15
D6: 10
E6: +C6*(100-D6)/100
A7: 'Paper
C7: 25
D7: 7.8
E7: +C7*(100-D7)/100
A8: 'Files
C8: 3.5
D8: 5
E8: +C8*(100-D8)/100
A9: '___________________________
A10: 'Sum
C10: @SUM(C6..C8)
E10: @SUM(E6..E8)
```

Figure 6.1 Test spreadsheet

The contents of this spreadsheet have been stored as a WK1 file and extracts are listed as a hex-dump in Figure 6.2.

Even without knowing the meaning of individual opcodes, the record structure is easily recognized. The text that appears in the spreadsheet is stored directly in ASCII strings.

The columns and rows of the spreadsheet are shown in Figure 6.3.

Rows and columns are given letters and numbers only for the convenience of the user. Internally, LOTUS and Symphony use 16-bit row and column numbers. Each field position can be unambiguously identified by two numbers. This numbering is also used within the file.

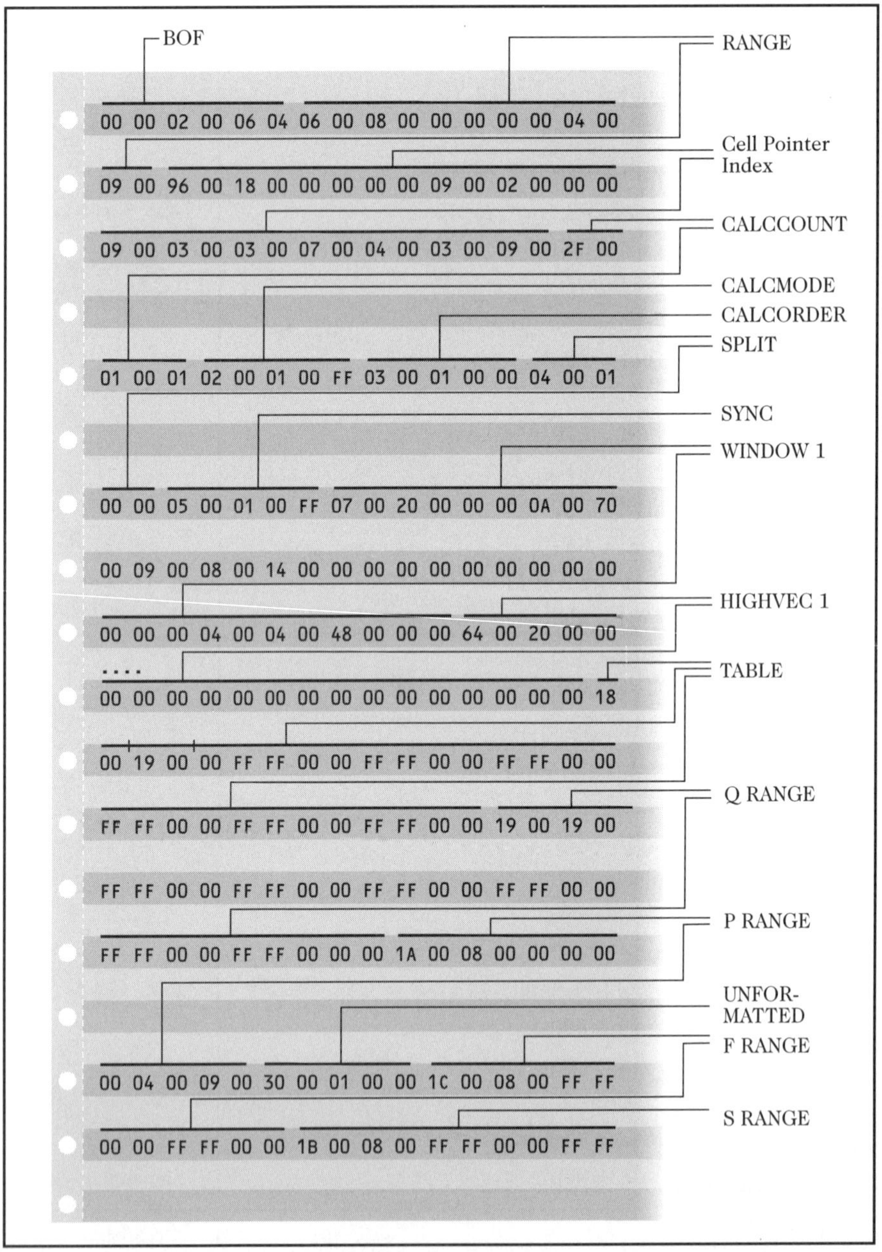

Figure 6.2 **WK1 file hex-dump (*continues over...*)**

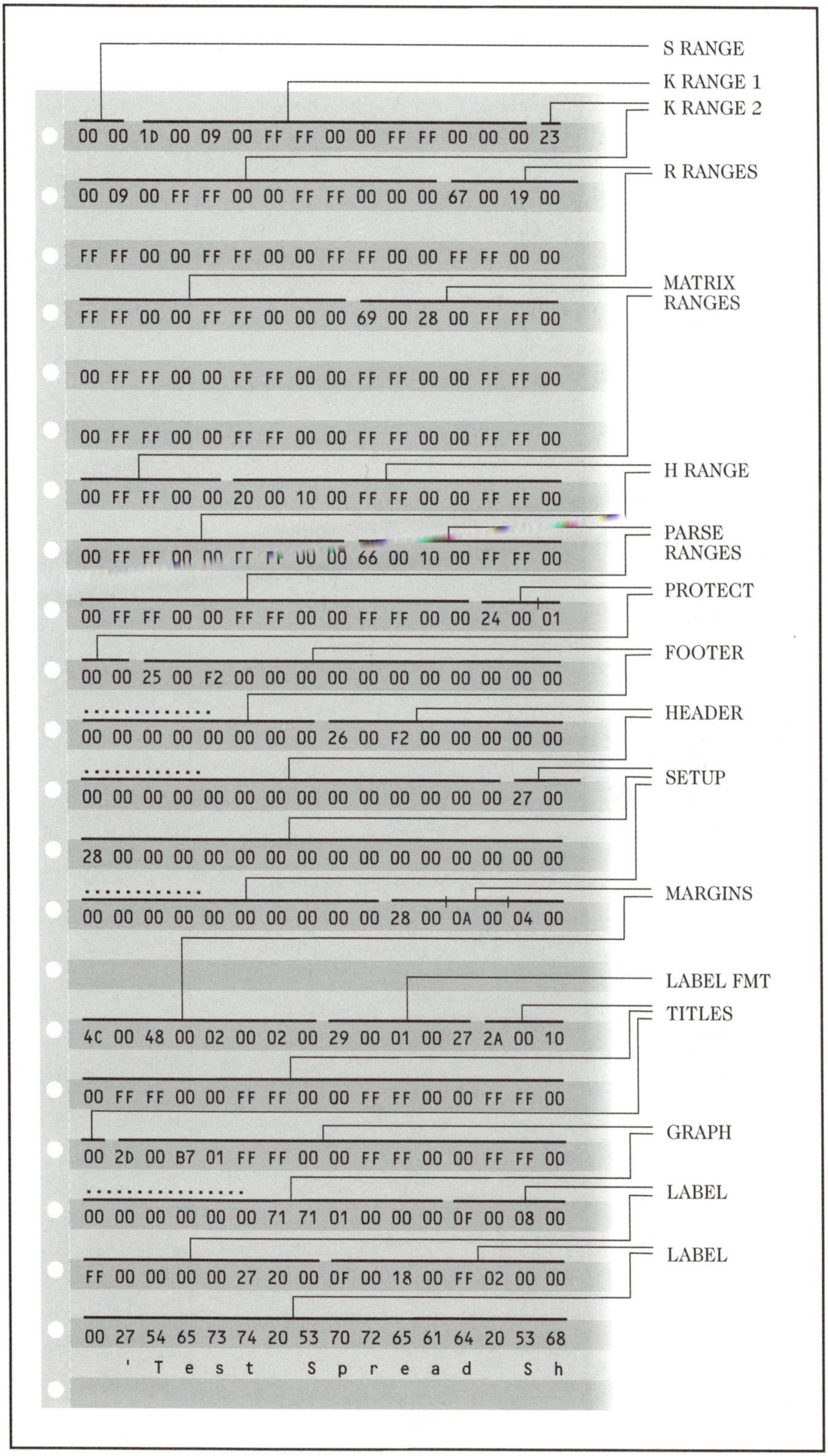

Figure 6.2 WK1 file hex-dump (*cont.*)

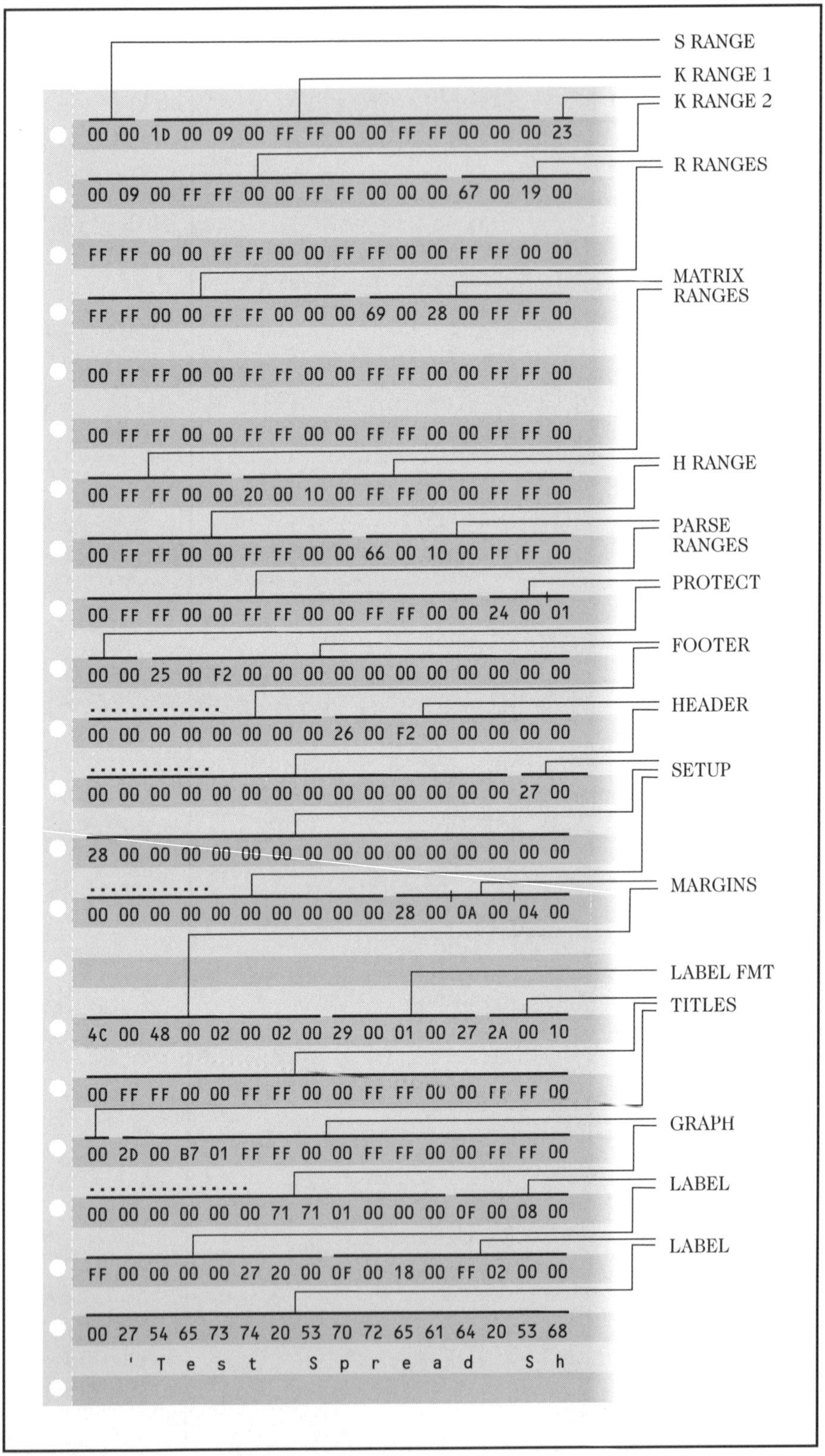

Figure 6.2 WK1 file hex-dump (*cont.*)

Spreadsheets

```
0B 05 64 00 0C 03 0F 00 0D 00 FF 00 00 07 00 27

46 69 6C 65 73 20 00 0E 00 0D 00 FF 02 00 07 00
 F  i  l  e  s
00 00 00 00 00 00 0C 40 0D 00 07 00 FF 03 00 07

00 05 00 10 00 24 00 FF 04 00 07 00 9A 99 99 99

99 99 0A 40 15 00 01 FE BF 00 80 05 64 00 01 FF

BF 00 80 0A 04 0B 05 64 00 0C 03 0F 00 32 00 FF

00 00 08 00 27 2D 2D 2D 2D 2D 2D 2D 2D 2D 2D 2D
             '  -  -  -  -  -  -  -  -  -  -  -
.........

00 0F 00 0C 00 FF 00 00 09 00 27 53 75 6D 20 20
                                 '  S  u  m
00 10 00 1B 00 FF 02 00 09 00 00 00 00 00 00 C0

45 40 0C 00 02 00 80 FC BF 00 80 FE BF 50 01 03

10 00 1B 00 FF 04 00 09 00 00 00 00 00 00 F0 43
                                                   EOF
40 0C 00 02 00 80 FC BF 00 80 FE BF 50 01 03 01

00 00 00
```

Figure 6.2
WK1 file hex-dump (*cont.*)

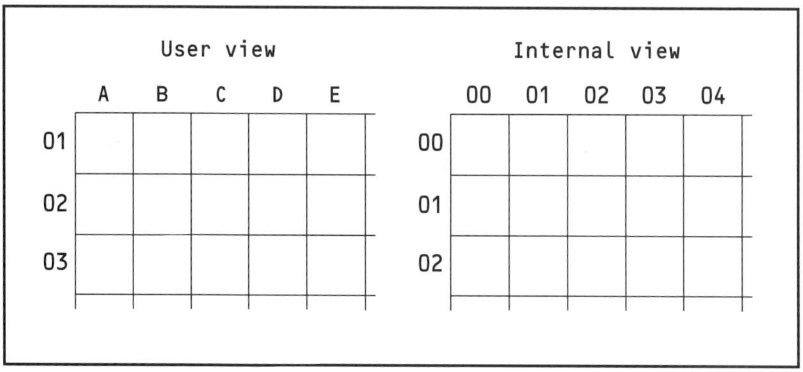

Figure 6.3
Column and row numbers

6.2 Record types in Lotus 1-2-3 (versions 1.1 to 2.01)

The record types (opcodes) that occur in WKS files, which are used by both LOTUS and Symphony, are presented below together with the relevant data structures. Each opcode occupies two bytes, the LSB (least significant byte) being stored first. Later versions of the program always contain the same opcodes, but a number of new record types have been added.

6.2.1 BOF (Opcode 0000H)

This field type marks the beginning of a valid WKS/WK1 file. The record is structured as follows:

Offset	Bytes	Remark
00H	2	Opcode BOF = 0000H
02H	2	Length = 0002H
04H	2	Version number of file format 0404H 1-2-3 WKS format version 1.A 0405H Symphony file 1.0 0406H 1-2-3 WK1 format version 2.01 and Symphony 1.1

Table 6.1 LOTUS WKS record structure (Opcode 0000H)

The 2-byte data field contains the version of the file format. More recent versions of LOTUS and Symphony continue this numbering system.

6.2.2 EOF (Opcode 0001H)

This record indicates the end of a WKS or WK1 file. The record is structured as follows:

Offset	Bytes	Remark
00H	2	Opcode EOF = 0001H
02H	2	Length = 0000H

Table 6.2 LOTUS WKS record structure (Opcode 0001H)

The record is only 4 bytes long. There is no data field.

6.2.3 CALC_MODE (Opcode 0002H)

In LOTUS, the user can specify whether recalculation of results is to be carried out automatically after every entry (default setting) or only after a MANUAL request. The calculation mode is stored in a record whose structure is as follows:

Offset	Bytes	Remark
00H	2	Opcode CALC_MODE = 0002H
02H	2	Length = 0001H
04H	1	Calculation mode
		00H = Manual recalculation
		FFH = Automatic recalculation

Table 6.3
LOTUS WKS record structure (Opcode 0002H)

By default, the data byte contains the value FFH for automatic recalculation after every entry.

6.2.4 CALC_ORDER (Opcode 0003H)

Each time results are calculated it is possible to select the sequence in which the formulas in the spreadsheet are to be used. This sequence is saved in a record with the following structure:

Offset	Bytes	Remark
00H	2	Opcode CALC_ORDER = 0003H
02H	2	Length = 0001H
04H	1	Recalculation order
		00H = Natural recalculation order
		01H = By column
		FFH = By row

Table 6.4
LOTUS WKS record structure (Opcode 0003H)

In case of calculation by column (code 01H), only the formulas in the relevant column are processed. LOTUS then begins calculation of the next column.

6.2.5 WINDOW_SPLIT (Opcode 0004H)

LOTUS enables the screen to be split into two halves (horizontal/vertical). A code byte specifying the mode is stored in a record structured as follows:

Offset	Bytes	Remark
00H	2	Opcode Window_Split = 0004H
02H	2	Length = 0001H
04H	1	Split window
		00H = No split
		01H = Vertical split
		FFH = Horizontal split

Table 6.5 LOTUS WKS record structure (Opcode 0004H)

By default, the value 00H is stored in the data field. The codes 01H and FFH appear only when the screen is divided (*split*).

6.2.6 CURSOR_SYNC (Opcode 0005H)

This field type specifies whether the synchronization of cursor movements within a window is switched on or off. The structure of the record is shown below:

Offset	Bytes	Remark
00H	2	Opcode CURSOR_SYNC = 0005H
02H	2	Length = 0001H
04H	1	Code
		00H = Windows not synchronized
		FFH = Windows synchronized

Table 6.6 LOTUS WKS record structure (Opcode 0005H)

The one-byte data field contains the appropriate code.

6.2.7 SAVE_RANGE (Opcode 0006H)

In LOTUS, this record specifies the RANGE of cells to be stored in the file; as a rule, the whole spreadsheet is saved. The following structure applies:

Offset	Bytes	Remark
00H	2	Opcode SAVE_RANGE = 0006H
02H	2	Length = 0008H
04H	2	Start column
06H	2	Start row
08H	2	End column
0AH	2	End row

Table 6.7
LOTUS WKS record structure (Opcode 0006H)

The top left corner (row/column) and the bottom right corner are specified in the data field. If the file has been opened via the `file save` command, all the fields in the spreadsheet will be saved in the file. With `file Xtract`, only the cells in the section specified will be saved. In this case, the section coordinates are entered in the data field. It should be noted that LOTUS defines the column and row addresses as 16-bit numbers (the LSB being stored first). Empty fields at the end of a column or row are not taken into account when the cells are stored. If there is no data in the area described as the `range`, LOTUS sets the value of the start column in the data field to `-1`. The `06H` record type is generally located directly after the `BOF` record. This should be particularly noted if WKS or WK1 files are created by external programs.

6.2.8 WINDOW1 (Opcode 0007H)

Two windows can be defined in LOTUS. The setting of the first window (`WINDOW1`) is stored under opcode `07H`. The record structure is shown in Table 6.8.

The information in the `Offset` column is in hexadecimal notation. All 16-bit values have the `LSB` in the first byte. Record length varies between different versions of LOTUS. LOTUS 1.A creates WKS files with a `WINDOW1` data range of 31 bytes (`1FH`); the record length of WK1 `WINDOW1` records from LOTUS 2.01 onwards is 32 bytes (`20H`). However, as far as I can determine, the bytes at offset `22` and `23` are unused and set to `00H` in all versions.

In the first two words, LOTUS stores the current position of the cursor in the worksheet. One byte at offset `08H` describes the cell format in the worksheet. The structure of this byte is shown in Figure 6.4. The most significant bit indicates whether the cells within the window are *write-protected*, and is coded as shown in Table 6.9a.

Offset	Bytes	Remark
00H	2	Opcode WINDOW1 = 0007H
02H	2	Length = 001FH (WKS files)
		0020H (WK1 files)
04H	2	Current cursor column
06H	2	Current cursor row
08H	1	Cell format byte
09H	1	Unused (00H)
0AH	2	Column width
0CH	2	Number of columns (on screen)
0EH	2	Number of rows (on screen)
10H	2	Leftmost column
12H	2	Top row
14H	2	Number of title columns
16H	2	Number of title rows
18H	2	Left column title
1AH	2	Top row title
1CH	2	Border width column
1EH	2	Border width row
20H	2	Windows width
22H	2	Unused (00H 00H)

Table 6.8 LOTUS WKS record structure (Opcode 0007H)

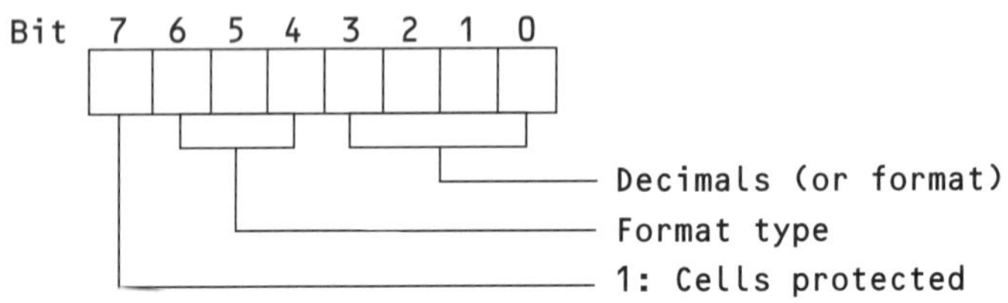

Figure 6.4 LOTUS coding of the cell format byte

Bit 7	Function
1	Protected
0	Unprotected

Table 6.9a LOTUS coding of bit 7 of the cell format byte

Bits 4–6 contain three-figure binary numbers indicating the type of format to be used for presenting the values. The formats available are shown below:

Bits 6 5 4	Format
000	Fixed
001	Scientific notation
010	Currency
011	Percent
100	Comma
101	Free
110	Free
111	Special format

Table 6.9b
LOTUS coding of bits 4–6 of the cell format byte

For format types 0–6, the remaining bits 0–3 specify the number of decimal places (between 0 and 15). Format type 7 represents a special format which is defined in bits 0–3 (Table 6.10).

Bits 3 2 1 0	Format
0000	+/–
0001	General format
0010	Date format: day, month, year
0011	Date format: day, month
0100	Date format: month, year
0101	Text formats
0110	Unused
0111	Unused
1000	Unused
1001	Unused
1010	Unused
1011	Unused
1100	Unused
1101	Unused
1110	Unused
1111	Standard

Table 6.10
Coding of special formats in LOTUS

The remaining words contain additional information on the screen window, such as column width, number of columns on screen and so on.

6.2.9 COLUMN_WIDTH_1 (Opcode 0008H)

In LOTUS, this record specifies the width of a column in window 1. The structure of the record is shown below.

Offset	Bytes	Remark
00H	2	Opcode COLUMN_WIDTH_1 = 0008H
02H	2	Length = 0003H
04H	2	Column number (16 bits)
06H	1	Column width

Table 6.11 LOTUS WKS record structure (Opcode 0008H)

In the WINDOW1 data record, there is already an entry for the column width. However, this value applies to all the columns in the spreadsheet, while record 08H is used to indicate the widths of individual columns. The relevant column number (LSB first) is defined in the first word. The following byte indicates the width of the column in characters.

The record type is only used if individual columns deviate from the global definition.

6.2.10 WINDOW2 (Opcode 0009H)

In LOTUS, this record saves the setting for the second window. The same record structure applies as for WINDOW1 (Opcode 07H).

6.2.11 COLUMN_WIDTH_2 (Opcode 000AH)

If a WINDOW2 has been saved, it is possible to enter the column widths individually. These definitions are saved in the COLUMN_WIDTH_2 record type (Opcode 0AH), which has the same structure as the COLUMN_WIDTH_1 record type (Opcode 08H).

6.2.12 NAME (Opcode 000BH)

This record can be used to store the name of a RANGE in LOTUS 1-2-3. The structure is shown in Table 6.12.

A name can be allocated to each RANGE. This name may be up to 16 characters long and is stored as an ASCIIZ string (text terminated by 00H) starting in the first data byte. This is followed by the start and end coordinates of the range. A separate record is required for every range.

Offset	Bytes	Remark
00H	2	Opcode NAME = 000BH
02H	2	Length = 0018H (24 bytes)
04H	6	ASCIIZ string containing the name
14H	2	Start column of range
16H	2	Start row of range
18H	2	End column of range
1AH	2	End row of range

Table 6.12 LOTUS WKS record structure (Opcode 000BH)

6.2.13 BLANK (Opcode 000CH)

Normally, LOTUS does not store blank cells. This means that protected or formatted blank cells are actually lost when the file is saved. Record type 0CH saves this type of cell. It has the following structure:

Offset	Bytes	Remark
00H	2	Opcode BLANK = 000CH
02H	2	Length = 0005H
04H	1	Format byte
05H	2	Column number
07H	2	Row number

Table 6.13 LOTUS WKS record structure (Opcode 000CH)

In the first data byte, LOTUS stores the format coding (shown in Table 6.9 under the WINDOW1 record). This is followed by two words containing the coordinates for the cell.

6.2.14 INTEGER (Opcode 000DH)

Directly entered *integers* are transferred from the spreadsheet to the file. The record is structured as shown in Table 6.14.

This record has 7 data bytes. The first byte contains the *number format*. The coding is shown in Table 6.9 (*see* WINDOW1). The following two words indicate the position of the cell containing the integer value. This is followed by a 16-bit word containing the integer value itself. The highest bit indicates whether the number is *positive* (bit = 0) or *negative* (bit = 1). This allows a range of values for integers between -32768 and +32767.

Spreadsheets

Offset	Bytes	Remark
00H	2	Opcode INTEGER = 000DH
02H	2	Length = 0007H
04H	1	Format byte
05H	2	Column number
07H	2	Row number
09H	2	Integer value

Table 6.14 LOTUS WKS record structure (Opcode 000DH)

6.2.15 NUMBER (Opcode 000EH)

LOTUS uses this record type to save floating point numbers. The structure is shown below:

Offset	Bytes	Remark
00H	2	Opcode NUMBER = 000EH
02H	2	Length = 000DH (13 data bytes)
04H	1	Format byte
05H	2	Column number
07H	2	Row number
09H	8	64-bit IEEE floating long real

Table 6.15 LOTUS WKS record structure (Opcode 000EH)

Offset	Bytes	Remark
00H	1	Sign 0 = positive -1 = negative (-1 = FFH) 2 = Range byte 3 = String byte
01H	2	Exponent: signed integer
03H	8	64-bit unsigned fraction

Table 6.16 LOTUS 1-2-3 floating point number

The record has 13 data bytes, the format of the number being defined in the first byte. The relevant coding is given in Table 6.9 (*see* WINDOW1). The position of the cell containing the floating point value (*real value*) is indicated in the next two words. These, in turn, are followed by 8 bytes in which the value is stored as a 64-bit IEEE floating point number. This representation corresponds to the coding of the 8087 format. Internally, LOTUS uses its own representation, in which 11 bytes are used for storing the floating point number (Table 6.16). The first byte contains a value that specifies how the next number is to be interpreted. Codes 2 and 3 are used to indicate range and string values.

If the cell contains the value ERR, LOTUS 1-2-3 will fill the 11 bytes as shown in Table 6.17. The first byte is set to 0, and the exponent word to 0FFFH. The 8 bytes of the mantissa are set to 0. The same applies to the code NA (*not available*), except that the first byte is set to the value -1.

Offset	Value
00H	ERR = 0; NA = -1
01H-02H	2047 = 0FFFH
03H-10H	8*0

Table 6.17 Internal representation for ERR and NA in LOTUS 1-2-3

6.2.16 LABEL (Opcode 000FH)

Fixed texts within a spreadsheet are stored as labels by LOTUS. In the WKS/WK1 files, there is a special record type for storing texts. It is structured as shown below:

Offset	Bytes	Remark
00H	2	Opcode LABEL = 000FH
02H	2	Length = 00xxH (variable up to 245 bytes)
04H	1	Format byte
05H	2	Column number
07H	2	Row number
09H	5-240	ASCIIZ string containing LABEL text

Table 6.18 LOTUS WKS record structure (Opcode 000FH)

Figure 6.2 shows examples of labels containing text constants (for example, *Test Spreadsheet*). The length of the data record is dictated by the length of the label text. The format byte is coded as shown in Table 6.9.

This is followed by two words containing the column and row numbers. The actual text begins at offset 09H. It must be terminated by a null byte (00H) and may have a maximum length of 240 bytes. The length of the field itself may vary between 5 and 245 bytes. The byte at offset 09H always contains one of the following control characters:

Character	Remark
|	Printer command string 'Parse Lineformat'
\	Repeating character
'	Align left
"	Align right
^	Centered

Table 6.19
Printer control character in a label field

The character \ in LOTUS introduces repetitions. However, it is not clear to me when this character is used because it does not occur in the text labels in the test sample.

6.2.17 FORMULA (Opcode 0010H)

In LOTUS and Symphony, a cell may contain a calculation formula. The formula is stored in a record with the opcode `10H`, structured as follows:

Offset	Bytes	Remark
00H	2	Opcode FORMULA = 0010H
02H	2	Length = xxxxH (variable up to 2064 bytes)
04H	1	Format byte
05H	2	Column number
07H	2	Row number
09H	8	Result 64-bit IEEE long real
11H	2	Length of the formula in bytes
13H	15-2048	Formula code (maximum 2048 bytes)

Table 6.20
LOTUS WKS record structure (Opcode 0010H)

The cell format byte is stored in the first data byte, coded as shown in Table 6.9. This is followed by the coordinates for the cell as two 16-bit values. The result of the calculation formula is stored at offset `09H`, as an 8-byte IEEE double-precision floating point number. The length of the formula in bytes is stored in the following word. The data field ends with the formula code. The length of the data field varies between 30 and 2064 bytes, and the formula occupies between 15 and 2048 bytes. LOTUS and Symphony convert a formula into inverse parenthesis-free (Polish) notation. Each entry in this formula is represented by its own function code and an associated data field:

```
Code,Data field,.....,Code,Data field
```

The one-byte code specifies the type of the operator (variable, constant, brackets, addition and so on), and is followed by the data for this operator. The relevant coding is shown in Table 6.21.

Code	Bytes	Remark
00H	1	Constant
	8	64-bit long real
01H	1	Variable
	2	Column number (LSB first)
	2	Row number (LSB first)
02H	1	Range
	2	Start column
	2	Start row
	2	End column
	2	End row
03H	1	End of formula code (return)
04H	1	Parentheses
05H	1	Integer constant
	2	16-bit integer value
06H	1	String constant
	x	ASCIIZ string (variable length)
07H	1	–
08H	1	Unary -
09H	1	Addition +
0AH	1	Subtraction -
0BH	1	Multiplication *
0CH	1	Division /
0DH	1	Exponentiation ^
0EH	1	Equals =
0FH	1	Not equal <>
10H	1	Less than or equal <=
11H	1	Greater than or equal >=
12H	1	Less than <
13H	1	Greater than >
14H	1	AND
15H	1	OR
16H	1	NOT
17H	1	Unary +

Table 6.21 Opcodes in a LOTUS formula (*continues over...*)

Code	Bytes	Remark
18H-1EH	1	–
1FH	1	@NA (Not applicable)
20H	1	@ERR (Error)
21H	1	@ABS (Absolute value)
22H	1	@INT (Integer value)
23H	1	@SQRT (Square root)
24H	1	@LOG (Base 10)
25H	1	@LN (Natural log)
26H	1	@PI (Constant pi)
27H	1	@SIN (Sine)
28H	1	@COS (Cosine)
29H	1	@TAN (Tangent)
2AH	1	@ATAN2 (Arctangent 4th quadrant)
2BH	1	@ATAN (Arctangent 2nd quadrant)
2CH	1	@ASIN (Arcsine)
2DH	1	@ACOS (Arccosine)
2EH	1	@EXP (Exponential)
2FH	1	@MOD(X,Y) (Modulus)
30H	1	@CHOOSE
31H	1	@ISNA(x) (x=NA THEN 1)
32H	1	@ISERR(x) (x=ERR THEN 1)
33H	1	@FALSE (Return 0)
34H	1	@TRUE (Return 1)
35H	1	@RAND (Random number 0...1)
36H	1	@DATE (Days since 1.1.1900)
37H	1	@TODAY (Serial date number)
38H	1	@PMT (Payment)
39H	1	@PV (Present value)
3AH	1	@FV (Future value)
3BH	1	@IF (Boolean)
3CH	1	@DAY (Day of month)
3DH	1	@MONTH
3EH	1	@YEAR
3FH	1	@ROUND
40H	1	@TIME
41H	1	@HOUR
42H	1	@MINUTE
43H	1	@SECOND
44H	1	@ISNUMBER
45H	1	@ISSTRING
46H	1	@LENGTH

Table 6.21 Opcodes in a LOTUS formula (*cont.*)

Code	Bytes	Remark
47H	1	@VALUE
48H	1	@FIXED
49H	1	@MID
4AH	1	@CHR
4BH	1	@ASCII
4CH	1	@FIND
4DH	1	@DATEVALUE
4EH	1	@TIMEVALUE
4FH	1	@CELLPOINTER
50H	1	@SUM (Range | cell | constant)
51H	1	@AVG (Range | cell | constant)
52H	1	@CNT (Range | cell | constant)
53H	1	@MIN (Range | cell | constant)
54H	1	@MAX (Range | cell | constant)
55H	1	@VLOOKUP (X,Range,OFFSET)
56H	1	@NPV (Int, Range)
57H	1	@VAR (Range)
58H	1	@STD (Range)
59H	1	@IRR (Guess,Range)
5AH	1	@HLOOKUP (X,Range,Offset)
5BH	1	DSUM (Database function)
5CH	1	AVG (Database function)
5DH	1	DCNT (Database function)
5EH	1	DMIN (Database function)
5FH	1	DMAX (Database function)
60H	1	DVAR (Database function)
61H	1	DSTD (Database function)
62H	1	@INDEX
63H	1	@COLS
64H	1	@ROWS
65H	1	@REPEAT
66H	1	@UPPER
67H	1	@LOWER
68H	1	@LEFT
69H	1	@RIGHT
6AH	1	@REPLACE
6BH	1	@PROPER
6CH	1	@CELL
6DH	1	@TRIM
6EH	1	@CLEAN

Table 6.21 Opcodes in a LOTUS formula (*cont.*)

Spreadsheets

Code	Bytes	Remark
71H	1	@STREQ
72H	1	@CALL
73H	1	-
74H	1	@RATE
75H	1	@TERM
76H	1	@CTERM
77H	1	@SLN
78H	1	@SOY
79H	1	@DDB
7AH-9BH	1	-
9CH	1	@AAFSTART
CEH	1	@AAFUNKOWN (1-2-3, V 2.0)
FFH	1	@AAFEND (1-2-3, V 2.0)

Table 6.21 Opcodes in a LOTUS formula (*cont.*)

6.2.18 TABLE (Opcode 0018H)

This data record is used for storing LOTUS tables. It has the following structure:

Offset	**Bytes**	**Remark**
00H	2	Opcode LABEL = 0018H
02H	2	Length = 0019H (25 bytes)
04H	1	0 = No table 1 = Table 1 2 = Table 2
05H	2	Table range start column
07H	2	Table range start row
09H	2	Table range end column
0BH	2	Table range end row
0DH	2	Input cell 1 start column
0FH	2	Input cell 1 start row
11H	2	Input cell 1 end column
13H	2	Input cell 1 end row
15H	2	Input cell 2 start column
17H	2	Input cell 2 start row
19H	2	Input cell 2 end column
1BH	2	Input cell 2 end row

Table 6.22 LOTUS WKS record structure (Opcode 0018H)

Two data tables are stored in LOTUS, but the exact meaning of the data structure is not known.

6.2.19 QUERY_RANGE (Opcode 0019H)

This data record is used to store data from a QUERY range. The format of the data record is as follows:

Offset	Bytes	Remark
00H	2	Opcode QUERY_RANGE = 0019H
02H	2	Length = 0019H (25 bytes)
04H	2	Input range start column
06H	2	Input range start row
08H	2	Input range end column
0AH	2	Input range end row
0CH	2	Output range start column
0EH	2	Output range start row
10H	2	Output range end column
12H	2	Output range end row
14H	2	Criteria start column
16H	2	Criteria start row
18H	2	Criteria end column
1AH	2	Criteria end row
1CH	1	Command code
		0 : No command
		1 : Find command
		2 : Extract command
		3 : Delete command
		4 : Unique command

Table 6.23 LOTUS WKS record structure (Opcode 0019H)

Further information on the record structure is not available.

6.2.20 PRINT_RANGE (Opcode 001AH)

This data record is used to store data from a PRINT range. The record is structured as shown in Table 6.24.

This record contains the coordinates of a spreadsheet extract to be printed. Every cell shown in the window will be printed when the print command is issued.

Offset	Bytes	Remark
00H	2	Opcode PRINT_RANGE = 001AH
02H	2	Length = 0008H
04H	2	Start column
06H	2	Start row
08H	2	End column
0AH	2	End row

Table 6.24 LOTUS WKS record structure (Opcode 001AH)

6.2.21 SORT_RANGE (Opcode 001BH)

This data record is used to store the data from a SORT range. The format is shown in Table 6.25.

The record contains the coordinates of a spreadsheet area to be sorted.

Offset	Bytes	Remark
00H	2	Opcode SORT_RANGE = 001BH
02H	2	Length = 0008H
04H	2	Start column
06H	2	Start row
08H	2	End column
0AH	2	End row

Table 6.25 LOTUS WKS record structure (Opcode 001BH)

6.2.22 FILL_RANGE (Opcode 001CH)

This data record is used for storing the data within a FILL range. The record is structured as follows:

Offset	Bytes	Remark
00H	2	Opcode FILL_RANGE = 001CH
02H	2	Length = 0008H
04H	2	Start column
06H	2	Start row
08H	2	End column
0AH	2	End row

Table 6.26 LOTUS WKS record structure (Opcode 001CH)

The record contains the coordinates of a section of the spreadsheet that is to be filled with data.

6.2.23 KEY_RANGE1 (Opcode 001DH)

This data record is used to store the data within a SORT KEY range. The record is structured as follows:

Offset	Bytes	Remark
00H	2	Opcode KEY_RANGE1 = 001DH
02H	2	Length = 0009H
04H	2	Start column
06H	2	Start row
08H	2	End column
0AH	2	End row
0CH	1	Search order 00H: descending FFH: ascending

Table 6.27 LOTUS WKS record structure (Opcode 001DH)

In this data record, a section of the spreadsheet is defined. The cells within this section are sorted according to the *primary key*, in ascending or descending order.

6.2.24 H_RANGE (Opcode 0020H)

This data record is used to store the internal data within a range (*distribution* range). The format of the record is as follows:

Offset	Bytes	Remark
00H	2	Opcode H_RANGE = 0020H
02H	2	Length = 0010H (16 bytes)
04H	2	Value range start column
06H	2	Value range start row
08H	2	Value range end column
0AH	2	Value range end row
0CH	2	Binary range start column
0EH	2	Binary range start row
10H	2	Binary range end column
12H	2	Binary range end row

Table 6.28 LOTUS WKS record structure (Opcode 0020H)

The exact meaning of this data record is not known.

Spreadsheets

6.2.25 KEY_RANGE2 (Opcode 0023H)

This data record is used to store a KEY2 range. The format of the record is shown below:

Offset	Bytes	Remark
00H	2	Opcode KEY_RANGE2 = 0023H
02H	2	Length = 0009H
04H	2	Start column
06H	2	Start row
08H	2	End column
0AH	2	End row
0CH	1	Search order 00H: descending FFH: ascending

Table 6.29 LOTUS WKS record structure (Opcode 0023H)

A section of the spreadsheet is defined in this record. The cells in this section are sorted according to the *secondary key*.

6.2.26 PROTECT (Opcode 0024H)

LOTUS indicates in this record whether the worksheet is protected or not.

Offset	Bytes	Remark
00H	2	Opcode PROTECT = 0024H
02H	2	Length = 0001H
04H	1	Code 00H: Protection off 01H: Protection on

Table 6.30 LOTUS WKS record structure (Opcode 0024H)

The one-byte data field indicates whether the cells of the worksheet are write-protected or not.

6.2.27 FOOTER (Opcode 0025H)

LOTUS uses this record to store the footer which will appear on the printout. The structure is as follows:

Offset	Bytes	Remark
00H	2	Opcode FOOTER = 0025H
02H	2	Length = 00F2H (variable up to 242 bytes)
04H	0-241	ASCIIZ string containing the footer

Table 6.31 LOTUS WKS record structure (Opcode 0025H)

At offset 4, there is an ASCIIZ string containing the text of the footer. The entry may be blank or contain up to 241 characters, (the text must always be terminated by a null byte).

6.2.28 HEADER (Opcode 0026H)

In this record, LOTUS stores the header which will appear on the printout.

At offset 4, there is an ASCIIZ string containing the text of the header. The entry may be blank or contain up to 241 characters (the text must always be terminated by a null byte).

Offset	Bytes	Remark
00H	2	Opcode HEADER = 0026H
02H	2	Length = 00F2H (variable up to 242 bytes)
04H	0-241	ASCIIZ string containing header

Table 6.32 LOTUS WKS record structure (Opcode 0026H)

6.2.29 SETUP (Opcode 0027H)

A *set-up* text can be defined for each printer used. This text is sent to the printer before printing starts. The text is saved in a record structured as follows:

Offset	Bytes	Remark
00H	2	Opcode SETUP = 0027H
02H	2	Length = 0028H (40 bytes)
04H	40	ASCIIZ string containing the set-up text

Table 6.33 LOTUS WKS record structure (Opcode 0027H)

The definition may be blank or contain up to 39 characters.

6.2.30 MARGINS (Opcode 0028H)

Offset	Bytes	Remark
00H	2	Opcode MARGINS = 0028H
02H	2	Length = 000AH
04H	2	Left margin
06H	2	Right margin
08H	2	Page length
0AH	2	Top margin
0CH	2	Bottom margin

Table 6.34 LOTUS WKS record structure (Opcode 0028H)

In this record, LOTUS stores information on the *margins* which will appear on the printout. This information can be used to align the printed document.

6.2.31 LABEL_FORMAT (Opcode 0029H)

In this record, LOTUS stores details of label alignment. The relevant coding is shown in the following table:

Offset	Bytes	Remark
00H	2	Opcode LABEL_FORMAT = 0029H
02H	2	Length = 0001H
04H	1	Alignment
		27H Left
		22H Right
		5EH Centered

Table 6.35 LOTUS WKS record structure (Opcode 0029H)

Labels are printed left-justified, right-justified or centered, according to the code byte.

6.2.32 TITLES (Opcode 002AH)

This data record is used to store margin dimensions. Fields are selected using the *titles* command. However, the precise meaning of this definition is not known.

Offset	Bytes	Remark
00H	2	Opcode TITLES = 002AH
02H	2	Length = 0010H (16 bytes)
04H	2	Row margin start column
06H	2	Row margin start row
08H	2	Row margin end column
0AH	2	Row margin end row
0CH	2	Column margin start column
0EH	2	Column margin start row
10H	2	Column margin end column
12H	2	Column margin end row

Table 6.36 LOTUS WKS record structure (Opcode 002AH)

6.2.33 GRAPH (Opcode 002DH)

LOTUS stores the definitions required to produce graphs in this data record.

Offset	Bytes	Remark	
00 / 00H	2	Opcode GRAPH = 002DH	
02 / 02H	2	Length = 01B5H (437 bytes)	
04 / 04H	2	X Range	Start column
06 / 06H	2		Start row
08 / 08H	2		End column
10 / 0AH	2		End row
12 / 0CH	2	A Range	Start column
14 / 0EH	2		Start row
16 / 10H	2		End column
18 / 12H	2		End row
20 / 14H	2	B Range	Start column
22 / 16H	2		Start row
24 / 18H	2		End column
26 / 1AH	2		End row
28 / 1CH	2	C Range	Start column
30 / 1EH	2		Start row
32 / 20H	2		End column
34 / 22H	2		End row
36 / 24H	2	D Range	Start column
38 / 26H	2		Start row
40 / 28H	2		End column
42 / 2AH	2		End row
44 / 2CH	2	E Range	Start column
46 / 2EH	2		Start row
48 / 30H	2		End column
50 / 32H	2		End row
52 / 34H	2	F Range	Start column
54 / 36H	2		Start row
56 / 38H	2		End column
58 / 3AH	2		End row
60 / 3CH	2	A Labels	Start column
62 / 3EH	2		Start row
64 / 40H	2		End column
66 / 42H	2		End row
68 / 44H	2	B Labels	Start column
70 / 46H	2		Start row
72 / 48H	2		End column
74 / 4AH	2		End row
76 / 4CH	2	C Labels	Start column
78 / 4EH	2		Start row
80 / 50H	2		End column
82 / 52H	2		End row

Table 6.37 LOTUS WKS record structure (Opcode 002DH) (*continues over...*)

Offset	Bytes	Remark	
84 / 54H	2	D Labels	Start column
86 / 56H	2		Start row
88 / 58H	2		End column
90 / 5AH	2		End row
92 / 5CH	2	E Labels	Start column
94 / 5EH	2		Start row
96 / 60H	2		End column
98 / 62H	2		End row
100/ 64H	2	F Labels	Start column
102/ 66H	2		Start row
104/ 68H	2		End column
106/ 6AH	2		End row
108/ 6CH	1	Graph type	00H = XY-graph
			01H = Bar graph
			02H = Pie chart
			04H = Lines
			05H = Stacked bars
109/ 6DH	1	Grid type	00H = None
			01H = Horizontal
			02H = Vertical
			03H = Both
110/ 6EH	1	Color	00H = Black and white
			FFH = Color
111/ 6FH	1	A Range line format	
			00H = No lines
			01H = Line
			02H = Symbol
			03H = Line + Symbol
112/ 70H	1	B Range line format	
			00H = No lines
			01H = Line
			02H = Symbol
			03H = Line + Symbol
113/ 71H	1	C Range line format	
			00H = No lines
			01H = Line
			02H = Symbol
			03H = Line + Symbol

Table 6.37 LOTUS WKS record structure (Opcode 002DH) (*cont.*)

Spreadsheets

Offset	Bytes	Remark
114/ 72H	1	D Range Line format 00H = No lines 01H = Line 02H = Symbol 03H = Line + Symbol
115/ 73H	1	E Range line format 00H = No lines 01H = Line 02H = Symbol 03H = Line + Symbol
116/ 74H	1	F Range Line format 00H = No lines 01H = Line 02H = Symbol 03H = Line + Symbol
117/ 75H	1	A Range data label alignment 00H = Center 01H = Right 02H = Below 03H = Left 04H = Above
118/ 76H	1	B Range data label alignment 00H = Center 01H = Right 02H = Below 03H = Left 04H = Above
119/ 77H	1	C Range data label alignment 00H = Center 01H = Right 02H = Below 03H = Left 04H = Above
120/ 78H	1	D Range data label alignment 00H = Center 01H = Right 02H = Below 03H = Left 04H = Above

Table 6.37 LOTUS WKS record structure (Opcode 002DH) (*cont.*)

Offset	Bytes	Remark	
121/ 79H	1	E Range data label alignment	
			00H = Center
			01H = Right
			02H = Below
			03H = Left
			04H = Above
122/ 7AH	1	F Range data label alignment	
			00H = Center
			01H = Right
			02H = Below
			03H = Left
			04H = Above
123/ 7BH	1	Scale	00H = Automatic
			FFH = Manual
124/ 7CH	8	X-axis lower limit	
			64-bit IEEE float
132/ 84H	8	X-axis upper limit	
			64-bit IEEE float
140/ 8CH	1	Y-scale	00H = Automatic
			FFH = Manual
141/ 8DH	8	Y-axis lower limit	
			64-bit IEEE float
149/ 95H	8	Y-axis upper limit	
			64-bit IEEE float
157/ 9DH	40	Text first title (40 characters)	
197/ C5H	40	Text second title (40 characters)	
237/ EDH	40	Text X-axis (40 characters)	
277/115H	40	Text Y-axis (40 characters)	
317/13DH	20	Legend A-axis (20 characters)	
337/151H	20	Legend B-axis (20 characters)	
357/165H	20	Legend C-axis (20 characters)	
377/179H	20	Legend D-axis (20 characters)	
397/18DH	20	Legend E-axis (20 characters)	
417/1A1H	20	Legend F-axis (20 characters)	
437/1B5H	1	X format (text)	
438/1B6H	1	Y format (text)	
439/1B7H	2	Skip factor	

Table 6.37 LOTUS WKS record structure (Opcode 002DH) (*cont.*)

This table contains all the information required to create a graph in LOTUS format.

6.2.34 NAMED_GRAPH (Opcode 002EH)

LOTUS uses this record to store the definitions of a current graph, if the graph has a name.

Offset	Bytes	Remark	
00 / 00H	2	Opcode NAMED_GRAPH = 002EH	
02 / 02H	2	Length = 01C5H (453 bytes)	
04 / 04H	16	Name (ASCIIZ string)	
04 / 04H	2	X Range	Start column
06 / 06H	2		Start row
07 / 08H	2		End column
10 / 0AH	2		End row
12 / 0CH	2	A Range	Start column
14 / 0EH	2		Start row
16 / 10H	2		End column
18 / 12H	2		End row
20 / 14H	2	B Range	Start column
22 / 16H	2		Start row
24 / 18H	2		End column
26 / 1AH	2		End row
28 / 1CH	2	C Range	Start column
30 / 1EH	2		Start row
32 / 20H	2		End column
34 / 22H	2		End row
36 / 24H	2	D Range	Start column
38 / 26H	2		Start row
40 / 28H	2		End column
42 / 2AH	2		End row
44 / 2CH	2	E Range	Start column
46 / 2EH	2		Start row
48 / 30H	2		End column
50 / 32H	2		End row
52 / 34H	2	F Range	Start column
54 / 36H	2		Start row
56 / 38H	2		End column
58 / 3AH	2		End row

Table 6.38 LOTUS WKS record structure (Opcode 002EH) (*continues over...*)

Offset	Bytes	Remark	
60 / 3CH	2	A Labels	Start column
62 / 3EH	2		Start row
64 / 40H	2		End column
66 / 42H	2		End row
68 / 44H	2	B Labels	Start column
70 / 46H	2		Start row
72 / 48H	2		End column
74 / 4AH	2		End row
76 / 4CH	2	C Labels	Start column
78 / 4EH	2		Start row
80 / 50H	2		End column
82 / 52H	2		End row
84 / 54H	2	D Labels	Start column
86 / 56H	2		Start row
88 / 58H	2		End column
90 / 5AH	2		End row
92 / 5CH	2	E Labels	Start column
94 / 5EH	2		Start row
96 / 60H	2		End column
98 / 62H	2		End row
100/ 64H	2	F Labels	start column
102/ 66H	2		start row
104/ 68H	2		end column
106/ 6AH	2		end row
108/ 6CH	1	Graph type	
			00H = XY-graph
			01H = Bar graph
			02H = Pie chart
			04H = Lines
			05H = Stacked bars
109/ 6DH	1	Grid type	00H = None
			01H = Horizontal
			02H = Vertical
			03H = Both
110/ 6EH	1	Color	00H = Black and white
			FFH = Color
111/ 6FH	1	A Range line format	
			00H = No lines
			01H = Line
			02H = Symbol
			03H = Line + Symbol

Table 6.38 LOTUS WKS record structure (Opcode 002EH) (*cont.*)

Offset	Bytes	Remark
112/ 70H	1	B Range line format
		00H = No lines
		01H = Line
		02H = Symbol
		03H = Line + Symbol
113/ 71H	1	C Range line format
		00H = No lines
		01H = Line
		02H = Symbol
		03H = Line + Symbol
114/ 72H	1	D Range Line format
		00H = No lines
		01H = Line
		02H = Symbol
		03H = Line + Symbol
115/ 73H	1	E Range line format
		00H = No lines
		01H = Line
		02H = Symbol
		03H = Line + Symbol
116/ 74H	1	F Range Line format
		00H = No lines
		01H = Line
		02H = Symbol
		03H = Line + Symbol
117/ 75H	1	A Range data label alignment
		00H = Center
		01H – Right
		02H = Below
		03H = Left
		04H = Above
118/ 76H	1	B Range data label alignment
		00H = Center
		01H = Right
		02H = Below
		03H = Left
		04H = Above

Table 6.38
LOTUS WKS record structure (Opcode 002EH) (*cont.*)

Offset	Bytes	Remark
119/ 77H	1	C Range data label alignment 00H = Center 01H = Right 02H = Below 03H = Left 04H = Above
120/ 78H	1	D Range data label alignment 00H = Center 01H = Right 02H = Below 03H = Left 04H = Above
121/ 79H	1	E Range data label alignment 00H= Center 01H = Right 02H = Below 03H = Left 04H = Above
122/ 7AH	1	F Range data label alignment 00H = Center 01H = Right 02H = Below 03H = Left 04H = Above
123/ 7BH	1	Scale 00H = Automatic FFH = Manual
124/ 7CH	8	X-axis lower limit 64-bit IEEE float
132/ 84H	8	X-axis upper limit 64-bit IEEE float
140/ 8CH	1	Y-scale 00H = Automatic FFH = Manual
141/ 8DH	8	Y-axis lower limit 64-bit IEEE float

Table 6.38 LOTUS WKS record structure (Opcode 002EH) (*cont.*)

Spreadsheets

Offset	Bytes	Remark
149/ 95H	8	Y-axis upper limit 64-bit IEEE float
157/ 9DH	40	Text first title (40 characters)
197/ C5H	40	Text second title (40 characters)
237/ EDH	40	Text X-axis (40 characters)
277/115H	40	Text Y-axis (40 characters)
317/13DH	20	Legend A-axis (20 characters)
337/151H	20	Legend B-axis (20 characters)
357/165H	20	Legend C-axis (20 characters)
377/179H	20	Legend D-axis (20 characters)
397/18DH	20	Legend E-axis (20 characters)
417/1A1H	20	Legend F-axis (20 characters)
437/1B5H	1	X format (text)
438/1B6H	1	Y format (text)
439/1B7H	2	Skip factor

Table 6.38 LOTUS WKS record structure (Opcode 002EH) (*cont.*)

This table contains all the information required to create a graph in LOTUS format, including its name. The structure is therefore identical to Table 6.37 except for the additional field containing the 16-character name.

6.2.35 CALC_COUNT (Opcode 002FH)

In this record, LOTUS stores information on how often a calculation (*iteration*) is to be carried out.

Offset	**Bytes**	**Remark**
00H	2	Opcode CALC_COUNT = 002FH
02H	2	Length = 0001H
04H	1	Iteration counter

Table 6.39 LOTUS WKS record structure (Opcode 002FH)

6.2.36 UNFORMATTED (Opcode 0030H)

This record contains information on whether the printed document is to be formatted or not.

Offset	Bytes	Remark
00H	2	Opcode UNFORMATTED = 0030H
02H	2	Length = 0001H
04H	1	Format code:
		00H = Formatted
		01H = Unformatted

Table 6.40 LOTUS WKS record structure (Opcode 0030H)

The default setting is unformatted.

6.2.37 CURSOR_WINDOW_1_2 (Opcode 0031H)

This data record defines the window of the spreadsheet (Window 1 or Window 2) in which the cursor is currently located. The record is structured as follows:

Offset	Bytes	Remark
00H	2	Opcode CURSOR_WINDOW_1_2 = 0031H
02H	2	Length = 0001H
04H	1	Format code:
		01H = Cursor in WINDOW 1
		02H = Cursor in WINDOW 2

Table 6.41 LOTUS WKS record structure (Opcode 0031H)

This information is only relevant if the screen is in split-screen mode, that is, if it is divided into sections.

6.2.38 WKS_PASSWORD (Opcode 004BH)

This record is used for decoding an encrypted worksheet. The record type is supported in LOTUS 1-2-3 from version 2.0 onwards and in Symphony.

Offset	Bytes	Remark
00H	2	Opcode WKS_PASSWORD = 004BH
02H	2	Length = 0004H
04H	4	Password

Table 6.42 LOTUS WKS record structure (Opcode 004BH)

The precise meaning of this record is not known.

6.2.39 HIDDEN_VECTOR1 (Opcode 0064H)

Offset	Bytes	Remark
00H	2	Opcode HIDDEN_VECTOR1 = 0064H
02H	2	Length = 0020H (32 bytes)
04H	32	Bit field

Table 6.43 LOTUS WKS record structure (Opcode 0064H)

This data record contains 32 bytes, representing 256 individual bits. One column of the worksheet is assigned to each bit. A *hidden* column is involved if the bit is set to 1, that is, the column is not visible. The bit field is arranged so that the LSB is stored first. Bit 0 in byte 0 relates to the first column. This function is available from LOTUS 1-2-3, version 2.0 onwards. If the screen is split, the bits relate only to the columns in WINDOW 1.

6.2.40 HIDDEN_VECTOR2 (Opcode 0065H)

This data record also contains 32 bytes representing 256 individual bits. By contrast with the HIDDEN_VECTOR1 record described above, one column of the worksheet that appears in WINDOW 2 is allocated to each bit. If a bit is set to 1, a *hidden* column is involved, that is, the column is not visible.

Offset	Bytes	Remark
00H	2	Opcode HIDDEN_VECTOR2 = 0065H
02H	2	Length = 0020H (32 bytes)
04H	32	Bit field

Table 6.44
LOTUS WKS record structure (Opcode 0065H)

The bit field is arranged so that the LSB is stored first. Bit 0 in byte 0 refers to the first column. The function is available from LOTUS 1-2-3, version 2.0 onwards. The values are valid only if the screen is in split mode, that is, divided into sections.

6.2.41 PARSE_RANGES (Opcode 0066H)

This record contains 16 bytes, which are used from version 2.0 of LOTUS 1-2-3 onwards. The following format applies:

Offset	Bytes	Remark
00H	2	Opcode PARSE_RANGES = 0066H
02H	2	Length = 0010H (16 bytes)
04H	2	Parse input range start column
06H	2	Start row
08H	2	End column
0AH	2	End row
0CH	2	Parse output range start column
0EH	2	Start row
10H	2	End column
12H	2	End row

Table 6.45
LOTUS WKS record structure (Opcode 0066H)

The exact meaning of this record is not known.

6.2.42 REGRESS_RANGES (Opcode 0067H)

This record contains 25 data bytes, which are used from version 2.0 of LOTUS 1-2-3 onwards. The record defines the data range for the evaluation of linear regressions.

Offset	Bytes	Remark
00H	2	Opcode REGRESS_RANGES = 0067H
02H	2	Length = 0019H (25 bytes)
		Linear regression range
04H	2	Start column
06H	2	Start row
08H	2	End column
0AH	2	End row
		Dependent variable range
0CH	2	Start column
0EH	2	Start row
10H	2	End column
12H	2	End row
		Output range
14H	2	Start column
16H	2	Start row
18H	2	End column
1AH	2	End row
1CH	1	Zero intercept flag
		0 = Zero intercept
		-1 = Intercept at origin (FFH)

Table 6.46 LOTUS WKS record structure (Opcode 0067H)

6.2.43 MATRIX_RANGES (Opcode 0069H)

This record contains 40 data bytes, which are used from version 2.0 of LOTUS 1-2-3 onwards. The following format applies:

Offset	Bytes	Remark
00H	2	Opcode MATRIX_RANGES = 0069H
02H	2	Length = 0028H (40 bytes)
		Matrix inversion source
04H	2	Start column
06H	2	Start row
08H	2	End column
0AH	2	End row

Table 6.47 LOTUS WKS record structure (Opcode 0069H) (*continues over...*)

Offset	Bytes	Remark
		Matrix inversion destination
0CH	2	Start column
0EH	2	Start row
10H	2	End column
12H	2	End row
		Matrix multicand range
14H	2	Start column
16H	2	Start row
18H	2	End column
1AH	2	End row
		Matrix multiplier range
1CH	2	Start column
1EH	2	Start row
20H	2	End column
22H	2	End row
		Matrix product range
24H	2	Start column
26H	2	Start row
28H	2	End column
2AH	2	End row

Table 6.47 LOTUS WKS record structure (Opcode 0069H) (*cont.*)

This record defines the data range for matrix calculations.

6.2.44 CELL_PTR_INDEX (Opcode 0096H)

From LOTUS 1-2-3, version 2.0, this record contains the *cell pointer index*, which is structured as shown in Table 6.48. The record contains a list of columns with active cells. The exact meaning of this record is not known.

In version 2.2, LOTUS 1-2-3 uses the same record structure as in version 2.01. A number of new functions are introduced, but their structure is not known at present.

Offset	Bytes	Remark
00H	2	Opcode CELL_PTR_INDEX = 0096H
02H	2	Length = 0006H
04H	2	Column number (integer)
06H	2	Row number of lowest active cell
08H	2	Row number of highest active cell

Table 6.48 LOTUS WKS record structure (Opcode 0096H)

7

LOTUS 1-2-3 WK3 record

Lotus *1-2-3 version 3.x provides many extensions (for example, three dimensional tables) which the file format must reflect. Lotus 1-2-3 uses WK3 files for the calculation sheet and additional files for worksheet formatting.*

7.1 Lotus 1-2-3 WK3 File Format

LOTUS 1-2-3 version 3.x uses an extended format to store the new record types. The structure of this format is similar to the older WK1 format. Each record contains a header and a stream of data bytes (Figure 7.1).

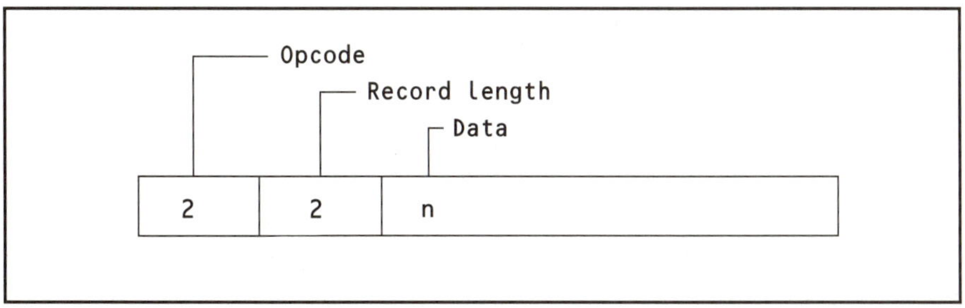

Figure 7.1
Structure of WK3 records

The first word contains the opcode used to identify the record type. The next word defines the length of the following data area. The various data records will be discussed in the following pages.

> **!** **All values in WK3 format are stored according to the Intel convention. The offset column in the tables always contains hexadecimal values. Other values are defined as decimal values.**

LOTUS 1-2-3 stores the records in a predefined order in the WK3 file. Figure 7.2 shows a hex-dump of a WK3 file.

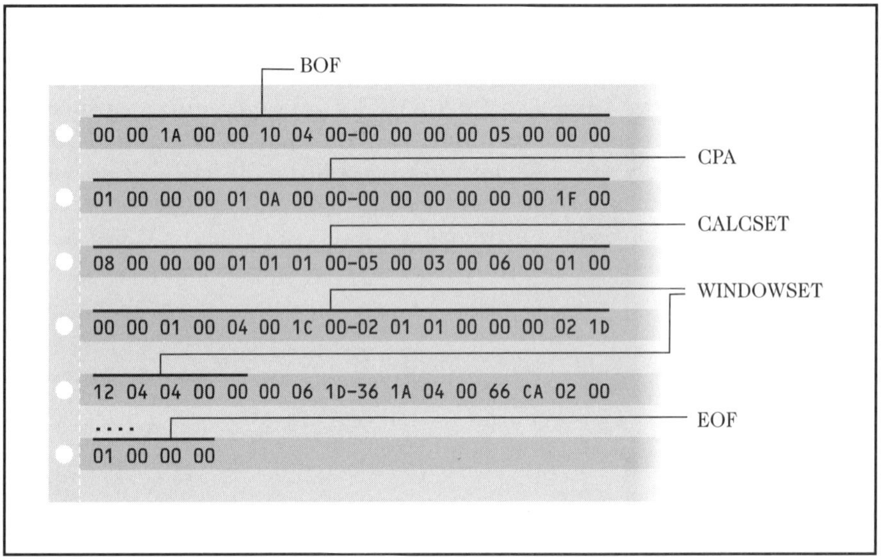

Figure 7.2 Hex-dump of a WK3 file

From LOTUS 1-2-3 version 3.0 onwards, it has been possible to divide the calculation table into several worksheets. This structure must be recognized when the cells are being addressed. The following pages describe the structure of WK3 data records.

Worksheets are numbered from 0 (sheet A) to 256. The column range is 0 to 255, and the row range 0 (Row 1) to 65535.

7.1.1 BOF (Opcode 0000H)

This *beginning of file* record contains the WK3 file signature and some information about the active worksheet range. Its structure is as follows:

Offset	Bytes	Field description
00H	2	Opcode BOF = 0000H (version 3.x)
02H	2	Length = 26 (001AH)
04H	2	File revision code (1000H)
06H	2	File revision subcode (0004H)
08H	4	Active worksheet range start 2-byte row 1-byte worksheet 1-byte column
0CH	4	Active worksheet range end 2-byte row 1-byte worksheet 1-byte column
10H	2	Counter
12H	2	Reserved (00H 00H)
14H	1	LMBCS group number for the table
15H	1	Flag field
16H	8	Start of range/End of range lead byte Table

Table 7.1
LOTUS WKS record structure (Opcode 0096H)

Spreadsheets

The BOF record contains 26 bytes and is longer than in WK1 format. The first two bytes define a signature (version code). LOTUS products use the signatures shown in Table 7.2.

Code	Version
0404	LOTUS 1-2-3 version 1A (WKS)
0406	LOTUS 1-2-3 version 2.0 to 2.2 (WK1)
1000	LOTUS 1-2-3 version 3.0 (WK3)
0600	LOTUS 1-2-3/J (WJ1)
8007	LOTUS 1-2-3 version 2.0 (FRM)
0405	Symphony 1.0/1.01 (WRK)
0406	Symphony 1.1/1.2/2.0 (WR1)

Table 7.2
Version codes for LOTUS products

LOTUS 1-2-3 version 3 defines the file revision subcode (offset 06H) as 0004H.

The two 4-byte values (offset 8) use the data type CELLCOORD and define the beginning (start of range) and the end (end of range) of the active worksheet.

The word at offset 16 (10H) contains a counter which is set to 0 when the file is created. Each write access to the file increments the counter by 1. The counter will wrap around when it overflows.

The word at offset 18 (12H) is reserved and is set to 00 00.

7.1.1.1 Multibyte Character Set (LMBCS)

The byte at offset 14H contains the LMBCS group number. LOTUS uses several character codes within one worksheet (ASCII, special characters, German umlaut, Japanese Kanji characters, and so on). These character sets are defined in the specifications for the *LOTUS Multibyte Character Set* (LMBCS).134

- Code 00H is defined as a string terminator.
- All characters between 1 and 31 start a multibyte character sequence.
- Character codes between 32 and 128 define the US ASCII character set.
- The codes between 129 and 255 are used for optimized local character sets.

All strings that start with a code between 1 and 31, refer to LMBCS tables. These tables are grouped from 1 to 31, like DOS code.

- The group numbers from 1 to 23 are used for country-specific character sets.
- Groups with numbers from 1 to 15 always contain two bytes (1-byte code group, 1-byte character code).
- Group 1 defines the IBM code page 850 (Latin alphabet languages).
- Group 2 defines the IBM code page 851 (Greek alphabet and mathematical symbols).
- Group 5 defines Cyrillic fonts.
- Groups 6 to 15 are undefined.
- Groups 16 to 23 are used for three-byte character codes (1-byte code group, 2-byte character code). Group 16 represents the Japanese Kanji characters.
- Groups 19 to 23 are undefined.
- Groups 24 to 31 are defined for applications.

The LMBCS tables contain 1-byte characters (US ASCII character set) and 2-byte codes (international character set). A character code between 31 and 128 should be treated as an ASCII character. If the character is preceded by a group byte, the character code defines the code in the table.

To optimize foreign languages, the codes between 128 and 255 are reserved for country-specific characters. This code group is stored in a separate record.

The byte at offset 20 (14H) in the BOF record defines the LMBCS group number. Offset 21 (15H) contains a flag byte (*see* Table 7.3).

Bits	Description
01H	File was not saved with full IEEE 10-byte floating point precision
02H	Automatic reservation requested
04H	Group mode turned on
08H	Recalculation flag
F0H	Precision bits

Table 7.3 Coding for the flag byte

If bit 4 (value 08H) is set, LOTUS 1-2-3 will not recalculate after reading the file. If the flag is off, 1-2-3 will recalculate all formulas while reading the file. If the bit is set but the *precision bits* are different from those on the executing platform, 1-2-3 will recalculate all the formulas. Only LOTUS 1-2-3 can set this bit. The precision bits allow access to files created by LOTUS products on other system platforms. This setting is calculated using the formula:

```
18 - significant decimals
```

LOTUS 1-2-3 version 3.0 uses 18 decimals (all four bits are set to 0). LOTUS 1-2-3/J uses only 15 decimals (the bits are set to 3).

The 8 bytes at offset 22 (16H) define two pointers to the start and the end of the LMBCS table, respectively.

! **This record type is also used in LOTUS 1-2-3 FRM files, but the signature and the content are different.**

7.1.2 EOF (Opcode 0001H)

Offset	Bytes	File description
00H	2	Opcode EOF = 0001H (version 3.x)
02H	2	Length = 0 (0000H)

Table 7.4 LOTUS WK3 record structure (Opcode 0001H)

This record has no data fields and the length field is set to zero. The record indicates the logical end of a LOTUS 1-2-3 file type (WK1, WKS, WK3, FRM, and so on). Data after this record is ignored by a reader.

7.1.3 PASSWORD (Opcode 0002H)

This record indicates an encrypted WK3 file. Table 7.5 defines the record structure:

Offset	Bytes	Field description
00H	2	Opcode PASSWORD = 0002H (version 3.x)
02H	2	Length = 16 (0010H)
04H	16	Encrypted password

Table 7.5 LOTUS WK3 record structure (Opcode 0002H)

The data area is a string containing the encrypted password.

7.1.4 CALCSET (Opcode 0003H)

Table 7.6 defines the structure of the CALCSET record. This record defines the method and order of calculation and is a combination of the WK1 record types 2 and 3.

Offset	Bytes	Field description
00H	2	Opcode CALCSET = 0003H (version 3.x)
02H	2	Length = 6 (0006H)
04H	2	Autocalc flag 0: Manual 1: Automatic (default)
06H	2	Calculation order 0 = Natural order 1 = Column-wise order 2 = Row-wise order
08H	2	Iteration Count (1–50)

Table 7.6 LOTUS WK3 record structure (Opcode 0003H)

If the *autocalc flag* is set to manual, 1-2-3 will recalculate the formula only after the user presses the CALC button. In automatic mode, the recalculation will be carried out every time an entry has been changed since the last recalculation.

If the calculation order is set to natural, before recalculation, LOTUS 1-2-3 will first recalculate any formulas on which it depends. Column-wise calculation starts with cell A:A1 in the first active file. Row-wise calculation starts in cell A:A1 in the first active file and processes the other cells row by row. The last word contains the iteration counter (1–50).

7.1.5 WINDOWSET (Opcode 0004H)

This record contains information about the windows (1–3) setting at the time the file is saved. The record structure is shown in Table 7.7.

This record must be stored in a WK3 file. The first byte (offset 4) defines the number of windows displayed. The next byte indicates the synchronization of the windows. The byte at offset 6 defines the number of the current window. If a window was stored in zoomed mode, the flag at offset 07H is set to 1. The window offset is computed from the top (window 1) to the bottom (window 3).

The description of the active windows 1 to 3 starts at offset 8 (08H). This description contains the number of columns per row, the window height in characters, the window width in characters, and the left and top edge of the window in characters. The data for windows 2 and 3 are optional. The WK3 file contains only one WINDOWSET record.

Offset	Bytes	Field description
00H	2	Opcode WINDOWSET = 0004H (version 3.x)
02H	2	Length = 28 (001CH)
04H	1	Number of displayed windows
05H	1	Windows synchronization mode 0: Unsynchronized 1: Synchronized
06H	1	Current window (value 1, 2 or 3) In perspective mode values are: 0 = Front 1 = Middle 2 = Back In vertical mode values are: 1 = Left 2 = Right In vertical mode values are: 1 = Top 2 = Bottom

Table 7.7 LOTUS WK3 record structure (Opcode 0004H) (*continues over...*)

Offset	Bytes	Field description
07H	1	Window zoomed 0 = No 1 = Yes
08H	2	Window 1 worksheet offset
0AH	1	Window 1 column count (per row)
0BH	1	Window 1 screen row count (number of columns in one row)
0CH	1	Window 1 screen column count (in chars)
0DH	1	Window 1 left edge screen column (in chars)
0EH	1	Window 1 top edge screen row (in chars)
0FH	1	Reserved
10H	2	Window 2 worksheet offset (optional)
12H	1	Window 2 cell column count (optional)
13H	1	Window 2 screen row count (optional)
14H	1	Window 2 screen column count (optional)
15H	1	Window 2 left edge screen row (optional)
16H	1	Window 2 top edge screen row (optional)
17H	1	Reserved
18H	2	Window 3 worksheet offset (optional)
1AH	1	Window 3 cell columns count (optional)
1BH	1	Window 3 screen row count (optional)
1CH	1	Window 3 screen column count (optional)
1DH	1	Window 3 left edge screen column (optional)
1EH	1	Window 3 top edge screen row (optional)
1FH	1	Reserved

Table 7.7 LOTUS WK3 record structure (Opcode 0004H) (*cont.*)

7.1.6 SHEETCELLPTR (Opcode 0005H)

This record defines a cell pointer, the origin of the window and title information for a worksheet on which the cell pointer has been moved.

Offset	Bytes	Field description
00H	2	Opcode SHEETCELLPTR = 0005H (version 3.x)
02H	2	Length = 16 (0010H)
04H	1	Worksheet offset
05H	1	Window 2 (horizontal/vertical) flag

Table 7.8 LOTUS WK3 record structure (Opcode 0005H) (*continues over...*)

Offset	Bytes	Field description
		0: not Window 2 1: Window 2
06H	2	Reserved
08H	2	Row of cell pointer
0AH	1	Column of cell pointer
0BH	1	Window origin (leftmost column)
0CH	2	Window origin (topmost row)
0EH	2	Topmost row that held a title row
10H	1	Leftmost column that held a title column
11H	1	Number of title columns
12H	2	Number of title rows

Table 7.8 LOTUS WK3 record structure (Opcode 0005H) (*cont.*)

The first data byte defines the worksheet offset. The next byte flags the orientation of the windows (horizontal/vertical). The entries at offsets 08H and 0AH define a cell pointer (row word, column byte). The next two entries define the origin of the window: leftmost column (byte) and topmost row (word). The entries at offsets 0EH and 10H describe the title of a worksheet. This definition is not valid if the number of title columns is set to zero. This record is only needed if a cell pointer has been moved (from the home position). In a WK3 file multiple entries are allowed.

7.1.7 SHEETLAYOUT (Opcode 0006H)

Table 7.9 describes the sheet layout record, which contains information about the default column width.

LOTUS 1-2-3 uses this default value for all cells that do not have their own cell width definition. The word at offset 8 defines the default column width in characters. This record is not mandatory in a WK3 file, but there can be more than one.

Offset	**Bytes**	**Field description**
00H	2	Opcode SHEETLAYOUT = 0006H (version 3.x)
02H	2	Length = 5 (0005H)
04H	1	Worksheet offset
05H	1	Window 2 (horizontal/vertical) flag 0: Not window 2 1: Window 2
06H	2	Reserved
08H	1	Default column width

Table 7.9 LOTUS WK3 record structure (Opcode 0006H)

Spreadsheets

7.1.8 COLUMNWIDTH (Opcode 0007H)

This record defines the column width of cells that differ from the default column width in the SHEETLAYOUT record. The record has a variable length and contains information on a per worksheet basis as follows:

Offset	Bytes	Field description
00H	2	Opcode COLUMNWIDTH = 0007H (version 3.x)
02H	2	Length = 6–516 bytes, step width 2
04H	1	Worksheet offset
05H	1	Window 2 flag 0: Not window 2 1: Window 2
06H	2	Reserved
08H	1	First column offset (start at 0)
09H	1	First column width
0AH	1	Next column offset (optional)
0BH	1	Next column width (optional)
0CH	1	and so on...

Table 7.10 LOTUS WK3 record structure (Opcode 0007H)

Each column set to a width other than the default value results in a two-byte entry in this record (offset, column width). A WK3 file can contain multiple COLUMNWIDTH records. The number of entries should be calculated as: No. = (length – 4)/2.

7.1.9 HIDDENCOLUMN (Opcode 0008H)

This record has a variable length and contains information about hidden columns in a worksheet. Its structure is defined in Table 7.11.

Offset	Bytes	Field description
00H	2	Opcode HIDDENCOLUMN = 0008H (version 3.x)
02H	2	Length = 5–260 bytes, step width 1
04H	1	Worksheet offset

Table 7.11 LOTUS WK3 record structure (Opcode 0008H) (*continues over...*)

Offset	Bytes	Field description
05H	1	Window 2 (horizontal/vertical) flag 0: Not window 2 1: Window 2
06H	2	Reserved
08H	1	Offset of first hidden column
09H	1	Offset of second hidden column
0AH	1	and so on...

Table 7.11 LOTUS WK3 record structure (Opcode 0008H) (*cont.*)

This record indicates the hidden columns in a particular worksheet. Each worksheet defines its own record. The number of hidden columns can be determined from the length of the record body (No. = record length – 4). The first column specified in a window must be visible. The column offsets are calculated from 0.

7.1.10 USERRANGE (Opcode 0009H)

This record is optional and stores details of user-defined, named ranges (Table 7.12).

Offset	**Bytes**	**Field description**
00H	2	Opcode USERRANGE = 0009H (version 3.x)
02H	2	Length = 26–539 bytes, step width 1
04H	2	Range type 0: Regular user range 1: Unknown user range
06H	16	User range name (LMBCS characters)
16H	4	Upper left corner (as cell coordinates) 2-byte row 1-byte worksheet 1-byte column
1AH	4	Lower right corner (as cell coordinates) 2-byte row 1-byte worksheet 1-byte column
1EH	*n*	Note for the user range (up to 513 chars)

Table 7.12 LOTUS WK3 record structure (Opcode 0009H)

The coordinates of the user range (offsets 16H, 1AH) are not defined if the range type is 1 (unknown). If a note is defined, the string will be stored as an LMBCS sequence (maximum 513 bytes including a 00H terminator). A WK3 file may contain multiple records.

7.1.11 SYSTEMRANGE (Opcode 000AH)

This record is optional and contains information about system ranges.

Offset	Bytes	Field description
00H	2	Opcode SYSTEMRANGE = 000AH (version 3.x)
02H	2	Length = variable
04H	2	Range type 0: Coordinate pair 1: Range alias
06H	16	Name of system range
16H	4	Upper left corner 2-byte row 1-byte worksheet 1-byte column or range alias, if range type is 1
1AH	4	Lower right corner 2-byte row 1-byte worksheet 1-byte column

Table 7.13 LOTUS WK3 record structure (Opcode 000AH)

Cell coordinates will be defined if the range type is set to 0. Otherwise the data at offset 16H is a range alias. This is an LMBCS string (drive:\path\file.wk3 rangename+00H) up to 513 characters long.

7.1.12 ZEROFORCE (Opcode 000BH)

This record is optional and defines the *force zero intercept flag* for /Data Regression. The structure is defined in Table 7.14.

Offset	Bytes	Field description
00H	2	Opcode ZEROFORCE = 000BH (version 3.x)
02H	2	Length = 1 (0001H)
04H	1	Force Zero Intercept Flag 0: Do not force zero intercept 1: Force zero intercept

Table 7.14 LOTUS WK3 record structure (Opcode 000BH)

Only one record per file is allowed.

7.1.13 SORTKEYDIR (Opcode 000CH)

This (optional) record contains the /Data Sort key directions.

Offset	Bytes	Field description
00H	2	Opcode SORTKEYDIR = 000CH (version 3.x)
02H	2	Length = 4–510 bytes, step width 2
04H	*n**2	1. Sort direction (1 byte) 0: Ascending 1: Descending FFH: Unused 2. Reserved (1 byte) Repeated 2-byte entries for Sort directions

Table 7.15 LOTUS WK3 record structure (Opcode 000CH)

The record contains one entry for each sort key. If there is no /Data Sort key defined, there will be no SORTKEYDIR record in the file. Each /Data Sort key is stored in a 2-byte entry within the SORTKEYDIR record. Only one record is allowed in each file.

7.1.14 FILESEAL (Opcode 000DH)

This record describes the /File Admin Seal password. The record structure is defined in Table 7.16.

Offset	Bytes	Field description
00H	2	Opcode FILESEAL = 000DH (version 3.x)
02H	2	Length = 18 (12H)
04H	16	Password (LMBCS string, 15 characters)
14H	2	Seal type 0: File sealed 1: Reservation setting sealed

Table 7.16
LOTUS WK3
record structure
(Opcode 000DH)

The password is stored as a string (maximum 15 LMBCS characters, zero terminated). Only one record is allowed in each file.

7.1.15 DATAFILLNUMS (Opcode 000EH)

This optional record contains the start, step and stop values for /Data Fill areas in a worksheet.

These values fill a range with data. The start, step, and end values are 10-byte real numbers, whose structure is shown in Figure 7.3.

Offset	Bytes	Field description
00H	2	Opcode DATAFILLNUMS = 000EH (version 3.x)
02H	2	Length = 32 (20H)
04H	10	Start value TREAL
0EH	10	Step value TREAL
18H	10	End value TREAL
22H	2	Step type 1 = Numeric 2 = Year 4 = Quarter 8 = Month 16 = Week 32 = Day 64 = Hour 128 = Minute 256 = Second

Table 7.17
LOTUS WK3
record structure
(Opcode 000EH)

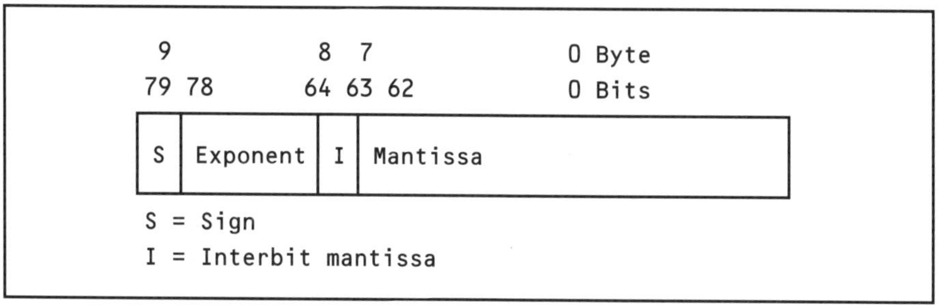

Figure 7.3 Coding of `TREAL` number

The exponent contains a `BIAS` of `3FFFH`. The value 0.0 must have exponent = `0`, S = `0` or `1` and I = `0`. Values not equal to 0.0 produce an exponent greater than zero and I = `1`. `TREAL` numbers can contain special values (*see* Table 7.18).

Type	Bytes 9–8	Bytes 7–0
Number	0-FFFEH	Value
Blank	FFFFH	0
ERR	FFFFH	7 = C0H, 6-0 = 0
NA	FFFFH	7 = D0H, 6-0 = 0
String	FFFFH	7 = E0H, 6-0 = blank

Table 7.18 Coding for special values

7.1.16 PRINTMAIN (Opcode 000FH)

This record is only present if a print expression is defined.

Offset	Bytes	Field description
00H	2	Opcode `PRINTMAIN` = 000EH (version 3.x)
02H	2	Length = 86 (56H)
04H	1	ID-Number print setting worksheet 1 = Current print settings 2-255 = Named print settings
05H	16	Print settings name LMBCS string (null terminated, maximum 15 chars)
15H	16	Driver suite name LMBCS string (null terminated, maximum 15 chars)

Table 7.19 LOTUS WK3 record structure (Opcode `000FH`) (*continues over...*)

Offset	Bytes	Field description
25H	16	Link suit name LMBCS string (null terminated maximum 15 chars)
35H	1	Line space 0 = Standard 1 = Compressed
36H	1	Format flag 0 = Unformatted 1 = Formatted
37H	1	Orientation 0 = Portrait 1 = Landscape
38H	1	Automatic linefeed 0 = No (default) 1 = Yes
39H	1	Wait flag 0 = No wait 1 = Wait
3AH	1	Range font type 0 = Default font 1 = Regular serif 2 = Bold serif 3 = Italic serif 4 = Bold italic serif 5 = Regular sans serif 6 = Bold sans serif 7 = Italic sans serif 8 = Bold italic sans serif
3BH	1	Header font type (*see* range font)
3CH	1	Border font type (*see* range font)
3DH	1	Frame font type (*see* range font)
3EH	1	Range color 0 = Default 1 = White 2 = Red 3 = Green 4 = Blue 5 = Yellow 6 = Magenta 7 = Cyan 8 = Purple

Table 7.19 LOTUS WK3 record structure (Opcode 000FH) (*cont.*)

Offset	Bytes	Field description
3FH	1	Blank header printing flag 0 = Suppress blank header 1 = Print blank header
40H	1	Character spacing 0 = Standard 1 = Compressed 2 = Expanded
41H	1	Reserved
42H	1	Priority (Background print) 0 = Default 1 = High 2 = Low
43H	1	Frame flag 0 = No frame 1 = Print frame
44H	1	Image size 0 = Margin fill 1 = Length fill 2 = Reshape
45H	1	GO type 0 = None 1 = Range 2 = Image 3 = Sample test page
46H	1	Image rotation 0 = No 1 = Yes
47H	1	Reserved
48H	1	Format type 0 = As displayed 1 = Cell formulas
49H	1	Image density 0 = High quality 1 = Draft quality
4AH	2	Left margin
4CH	2	Right margin
4EH	2	Top margin
50H	2	Bottom margin
52H	2	Image height (1–1000)
54H	2	Image width (1–1000)
56H	2	Page length in lines

Table 7.19 LOTUS WK3 record structure (Opcode 000FH) (*cont.*)

Offset	Bytes	Field description
56H	2	Page length in lines
58H	2	Baud rate (serial printer)
		0 = 4800 (standard)
		1 = 110
		2 = 150
		3 = 300
		4 = 600
		5 = 1200
		6 = 2400
		7 = 4800
		8 = 9600
		9 = 19200

Table 7.19 LOTUS WK3 record structure (Opcode 000FH) (*cont.*)

This record is optional and occurs for each print expression in a worksheet.

7.1.17 PRINTSTRING (Opcode 0010H)

This record is optional, but it must follow a PRINTMAIN record. The PRINTSTRING record contains all the print settings in variable length strings.

The print string is a sequence of LMBCS characters occupying up to 512 bytes, terminated by an additional null byte (00H).

Offset	**Bytes**	**Field description**
00H	2	Opcode PRINTSTRING = 0010H (version 3.x)
02H	2	Length = 3–315, step width 1
04H	1	ID number print setting worksheet
05H	1	String type
		0 = Header
		1 = Footer
		2 = Setup
		3 = Image name
06H	*n*	PRINT string

Table 7.20 LOTUS WK3 record structure (Opcode 0010H)

7.1.18 GRAPHMAIN (Opcode 0011H)

This record is optional and contains all fixed length settings for a graph.

Offset	Bytes	Field description
00H	2	Opcode GRAPHMAIN = 0011H (version 3.x)
02H	2	Length = 178
04H	1	ID number graph settings worksheet
05H	16	Name graph settings (LMBCS, 0 terminated)
15H	3	1,2,3 text field font types 0 = Default font 1 = Regular serif 2 = Bold serif 3 = Italic serif 4 = Bold italic serif 5 = Regular sans serif 6 = Bold sans serif 7 = Italic sans serif 8 = Bold italic sans serif
18H	7	Color values (A–F range) 0 = Default 1 = White 2 = Red 3 = Green 4 = Blue 5 = Yellow 6 = Magenta 7 = Cyan 8 = Purple FEH = Hide FFH = Use associated system range
1FH	6	Hatch values (A–F range) 0 = Default 1 = Solid 2 = Fine crosshatch 3 = Diagonal triple 4 = Diagonal double 5 = Coarse crosshatch 6 = Diagonal double 7 = Diagonal single 8 = Hollow FFH = Use associated system range

Table 7.21 LOTUS WK3 record structure (Opcode 0011H) (*continues over...*)

Spreadsheets

Offset	Bytes	Field description
25H	6	1-2-3/M extended file name (1st part, LMBCS)
2BH	3	1.,2.,3. text field with text size 0 = Default 1 = Smallest to 9 = Largest
2EH	1	Grid type 0 = None 1 = Horizontal 2 = Vertical 3 = Both
2FH	1	Color flag 0 = Use color if possible 1 = Do not use color 2 = Use color
30H	1	Graph type 0 = Line 1 = Bar 2 = XY 3 = Stacked bar 4 = Pie 5 = High-low-close-open 6 = Reserved 7 = Mixed 8 = Reserved 9 = Graph type extended
31H	3	Scale generation (X-, Y-, 2Y-axes) 0 = Automatic FFH = Manual
34H	3	Exponent generation (X-, Y-, 2Y-axes) 0 = Automatic FFH = Manual
37H	3	Indicator generation (X-, Y-, 2Y-axes) 0 = Display indicator 1 = Do not display indicator FFH = Display manually entered indicator
3AH	3	Scale types (X-, Y-, 2Y-axes) 0 = Standard 1 = Logarithmic

Table 7.21 LOTUS WK3 record structure (Opcode 0011H) (*cont.*)

Offset	Bytes	Field description
3DH	3	Width generation offsets (X-, Y-, 2Y-axes) 0 = Automatic FFH = Manual
40H	6	Axis type (A–F range) 1 = Y-axis 2 = 2Y-axis
46H	6	Line formats (A–F range) 0 = Lines and symbols 1 = Lines 2 = Symbols 3 = Neither lines nor symbols 4 = Area
4CH	6	Label formats (A–F range) 0 = Center 1 = Right 2 = Below 3 = Left 4 = Above
52H	1	Horizontal Grid flag 0 = Display Y-axis grid lines 1 = Display 2Y-axis grid lines 2 = Display Y- and 2Y-axis grid lines
53H	1	Rotation flag 0 = Vertical 1 = Horizontal
54H	1	Autograph flag 0 = Permanent ranges 1 = Autograph ranges
55H	1	Percentage flag 0 = No graph data ranges as % 1 = Data graph as % of all ranges
56H	1	Stacked flag 0 = Not stacked 1 = Stack
57H	2	Reserved

Table 7.21 LOTUS WK3 record structure (Opcode 0011H) (*cont.*)

Spreadsheets

Offset	Bytes	Field description
59H	3	Text colors (X-, Y-, 2Y-axes) 0 = Default 1 = White 2 = Red 3 = Green 4 = Blue 5 = Yellow 6 = Magenta 7 = Cyan 8 = Purple FEH = Hide
5CH	2	Skip factor for x-range (1–8192)
5EH	6	Label width 1–50 (X-, Y-, 2Y-axes)
64H	2	Graph name setting range extender field values from 0000H to FFFFH
66H	2	2nd part 1-2-3/M extended file name (LMBCS)
68H	6	Exponents (X-, Y-, 2Y-axes)
6EH	12	Formats (X-, Y-, 2Y-axes)
7AH	30	Scale minima (X-, Y-, 2Y-axes) as TREAL
98H	30	Scale maxima (X-, Y-, 2Y-axes) as TREAL

Table 7.21 LOTUS WK3 record structure (Opcode 0011H) (*cont.*)

The structure of TREAL is defined in Figure 7.3. Variable length settings are stored in GRAPHSTRING records. A WK3 file may contain multiple GRAPHMAIN records. The *text field font type* is one byte long. There are three bytes defined at offset 15H for the first, second and third font type of a text field.

The six bytes at offset 25H define the first part of the 1-2-3/M extended file name, coded as LMBCS characters. If this field does not contain a null terminator, the second part of the name is defined in a word at offset 66H.

The exponents at offset 68H are coded as one word for each axis. The format description (offset 6EH) for the axes contains three entries of four bytes each. Figure 7.4 shows the coding of these bytes.

7.1.19 GRAPHSTRING (Opcode 0012H)

This (optional) record contains all graph settings with variable length strings.

Offset	Bytes	Field description
00H	2	Opcode GRAPHSTRING = 0012H (version 3.x)
02H	2	Length = 4–515, step width 1
04H	1	ID-Number graph settings worksheet 0 = No ID FFH = ID
05H	1	Graph string type code 0 = Data Range A legend 1 = Data Range B legend 2 = Data Range C legend 3 = Data Range D legend 4 = Data Range E legend 5 = Data Range F legend 6 = X-axis indicator 7 = Y-axis indicator 8 = 2Y-axis indicator 9 = X-axis title 10 = Y-axis title 11 = 2Y-axis title 12 = Graph title 13 = Graph subtitle 14 = Graph note 15 = Graph subnote
06H	*n*	Graph string, LMBCS (maximum 513 chars)

Table 7.22 LOTUS WK3 record structure (Opcode 0012H)

Spreadsheets

This record must follow the associated GRAPHMAIN record. A graph string is stored as a variable length LMBCS string with a null terminator (00H). A WK3 file may contain multiple records.

7.1.20 FORMAT (Opcode 0013H)

This record stores cell and global formatting information in WK3 files.

Offset	Bytes	Field description
00H	2	Opcode FORMAT = 0013H (version 3.x)
02H	2	Length = 4–1028
04H	1	Worksheet number
05H	1	Subtype (always 0)
06H	2	Row
08H	*n*	Array of format records (up to 1024 chars)

Table 7.23 LOTUS WK3 record structure (Opcode 0013H)

The format description is grouped separately from other cell information. This allows information to be compressed within the format records. This format compression is carried out in two ways:

- Sequences of identical, formatted cells in a row are compressed by run length encoding (4-byte format descriptor, 1-byte repeat counter). Trailing sequences of default formatted cells in a row are dropped.
- If a row of cell formats is identical to a previous row in the worksheet, it is represented by a reference to the earlier row (using the DUPFMT record subtype).

Any row of cells with default formatting (0FFH) is omitted. Rows are scanned and broken down into sequences of identical formatted cells.

- A single cell format description requires four bytes and the high bit (R) of the format value is zero (single cell indicator).
- A multiple cell format description requires five bytes, the four-byte format descriptor with the high bit (R) set to one, followed by a repeat count byte.

A format descriptor (FRMT string) uses four bytes and has the structure shown in Figure 7.4. This format record is the same as for 1-2-3, Release 2.01. Within the WK3 file, there are three types of format record:

- the FORMAT record describing a row format (subtype 0);
- the GBLFMT record describing the global format for the worksheet (subtype 1);
- the DUPFMT record to duplicate a FORMAT record for a different row of a worksheet (subtype 2).

```
31    30-11                  10 9 8 7  6-4    3-0

| R | reserved              | H | P | n | p |  Typ  |  NN  |

P = Protection
H = Highlighted
p = Number in brackets()
n = Color of cell contents if number is negative
R = Repeat count follows, if bit is set to 1
```

Figure 7.4 Format of a 4-byte `FRMT` string

These records are differentiated by their subtype byte (second byte in the data area). The records must be written in ascending cell order, row by row. A WK3 file may contain multiple records.

7.1.21 GBLFMT (Opcode 0013H)

This record has the same opcode as the `FORMAT` record. It describes the global format of the worksheet. This record type is not mandatory. Multiple records may be stored in a file.

Offset	Bytes	Field description
00H	2	Opcode `GBLFMT` = 0013H (version 3.x)
02H	2	Length = 12–525
04H	1	Worksheet number
05H	1	Subtype = 1
06H	2	Reserved (must be 0000H)
08H	4	Global format record (`FRMT`)
0CH	2	/Worksheet Global Label prefix character code
0EH	2	Global zero suppression flag 0 = Display zeros 1 = Suppress zeros
10H	*n*	Global zero string (up to 513 LMBCS chars)

Table 7.24 LOTUS WK3 record structure (Opcode 0013H)

The global format is stored in four bytes (*see* Figure 7.4). Valid entries for the `/Worksheet Global Label` prefix character code are:

34 = "
39 = '
94 = ^

If the *global zero suppression flag* is set to 0, the record length is reduced to 12 bytes. If this flag is set to 1, a variable length LMBCS string (containing the global zero string) will follow. The minimum length is 2 bytes (1 character and the 00 terminator).

7.1.22 DUPFMT (Opcode 0013H)

This record is used to define a duplicated format for a row of cells. The format description must exist in a previous record.

Offset	Bytes	Field description
00H	2	Opcode DUPFMT = 0013H (version 3.x)
02H	2	Length = 8
04H	1	Worksheet number
05H	1	Subtype = 2
06H	2	Row
08H	2	Worksheet in a file containing the row format
0AH	2	Row in a file containing the row format

Table 7.25 LOTUS WK3 record structure (Opcode 0013H)

This record type is used to duplicate rows in a worksheet that have the same format as preceding rows.

7.1.23 ERRCELL (Opcode 0014H)

This record defines a cell of type 'ERR', resulting from a `/Range Value` operation (where the value was ERR), or a subsequent `/Copy` or `/Move` of another ERRCELL.

Offset	Bytes	Field description
00H	2	Opcode ERRCELL = 0014H (version 3.x)
02H	2	Length = 4
04H	4	Cell coordinates 2-byte row 1-byte worksheet 1-byte column

Table 7.26 LOTUS WK3 record structure (Opcode 0014H)

The cell is (numerically) identical to a formula cell containing the entry +@ERR. The advantage of the ERRCELL record is that it is more efficient in use. The record type is optional, and a file may contain multiple records.

7.1.24 NACELL (Opcode 0015H)

This record defines a cell of type 'NA', resulting from a /Range Value operation (where the value was NA), or a subsequent /Copy or /Move of another NACELL.

Offset	Bytes	Field description
00H	2	Opcode NACELL = 0015H (version 3.x)
02H	2	Length = 4
04H	4	Cell coordinates 2-byte row 1-byte worksheet 1-byte column

Table 7.27 LOTUS WK3 record structure (Opcode 0015H)

The cell is (numerically) identical to a formula cell containing the entry +@NA. The advantage of the NACELL record is that it is more efficient in use. The record type is optional, and a file may contain multiple records.

7.1.25 LABELCELL (Opcode 0016H)

This record defines a label.

Offset	Bytes	Field description
00H	2	Opcode LABELCELL = 16H (version 3.0)
02H	2	Length = 6–518, step length 1
04H	2	Row number
06H	1	Worksheet number
07H	1	Column number
08H	*n*	Label as an LMBCS string

Table 7.28 LOTUS WK3 record structure (Opcode 0016H)

There is a label record for every cell in the worksheet that contains a label entry. The label string contains LMBCS characters (maximum 512) terminated by a zero byte (00H).

7.1.26 NUMBERCELL (Opcode 0017H)

This record type defines a cell that contains a number that is not represented in the small number format.

Offset	Bytes	Field description
00H	2	Opcode NUMBERCELL = 17H (version 3.0)
02H	2	Length = 14
04H	2	Row number
06H	1	Worksheet number
07H	1	Column number
08H	10	Cell value as a TREAL number

Table 7.29 LOTUS WK3 record structure (Opcode 0017H)

This record can be used for numbers that could be saved in the SNUM format (the translate utility uses this format). The format of a TREAL value is shown in Figure 7.3.

7.1.27 SMALLNUMCELL (Opcode 0018H)

This record type defines a cell containing an integer value stored in the small number format in a WK3 file.

Offset	Bytes	Field description
00H	2	Opcode SMALLNUMCELL = 18H (version 3.0)
02H	2	Length = 6
04H	2	Row number
06H	1	Worksheet number
07H	1	Column number
08H	2	Cell value as a small number

Table 7.30
LOTUS WK3 record structure (Opcode 0018H)

The integer value (–16384 to 16383) is stored as a word at offset 08H. Bit 0 is always 0, bits 1 to 15 contain a signed integer.

7.1.28 FORMULACELL (Opcode 0019H)

This record describes a cell containing a formula.

Offset	Bytes	Field description
00H	2	Opcode FORMULACELL = 19H (version 3.0)
02H	2	Length = 14–2048, step width 1
04H	2	Row number
06H	1	Worksheet number
07H	1	Column number
08H	10	Formula value as a TREAL number
12H	*n*	Formula token stream (*n* opcodes)

Table 7.31
LOTUS WK3 record structure (Opcode 0019H)

The formula token stream contains a sequence of operators and their operands. The last byte in the token stream is the *end of formula opcode* (03H). Table 7.32 shows the operators defined for a WK3 file. The operators from code 1FH to 6FH are the same as the WK1 operators.

LOTUS and Symphony present formulas in parenthesis-free (Polish) notation. Each entry starts with a formula code byte, followed by the operands:

```
formula code, operands,.....,formula code, operands
```

The formula code defines the operator type (variable, constant, bracket, +, and so on). This operator is followed by zero, one or multiple bytes containing the operand values.

Code	Bytes	Formula
00H	11	Constant + 1 TREAL argument
01H	6	Cell reference +
		RELBITS (1 byte)
		bit 0=1: Column 0 is relative
		1=1: Row 0 is relative
		2=1: Sheet 0 is relative
		3=1: Column 1 is relative
		4=1: Row 1 is relative
		5=1: Sheet 1 is relative
		CELLCOORDINATES (4 bytes)
		2-byte row
		1-byte worksheet
		2-byte column
02H	10	Range + RELBITS + 2
		* CELLCOORDINATES
03H	1	End of formula record (Return)
04H	1	Parentheses (no arguments)
05H	3	Integer constant (16-bit SNUM)
06H	1	String constant (LMBCS); the string
		follows in a FORMULASTRING record
07H	4	Named range reference
		with range name
08H	1	Absolute named range
09H	5	ERR range reference + 4 bytes garbage
0AH	6	ERR cell reference + 5 bytes garbage
0BH	11	ERR constant + 10 bytes garbage
0CH	1	dBASE field reference
0DH	1	dBASE field placeholder
0EH	1	Unary -
0FH	1	Plus +

Table 7.32 Opcodes in a LOTUS formula (*continues over...*)

Code	Bytes	Formula
00H	11	Constant + 1 TREAL argument
01H	6	Cell reference + RELBITS (1 byte) bit 0=1: Column 0 is relative 1=1: Row 0 is relative 2=1: Sheet 0 is relative 3=1: Column 1 is relative 4=1: Row 1 is relative 5=1: Sheet 1 is relative CELLCOORDINATES (4 bytes) 2-byte row 1-byte worksheet 2-byte column
02H	10	Range + RELBITS + 2 * CELLCOORDINATES
03H	1	End of formula record (Return)
04H	1	Parentheses (no arguments)
05H	3	Integer constant (16-bit SNUM)
06H	1	String constant (LMBCS); the string follows in a FORMULASTRING record
07H	4	Named range reference with range name
08H	1	Absolute named range
09H	5	ERR range reference + 4 bytes garbage
0AH	6	ERR cell reference + 5 bytes garbage
0BH	11	ERR constant + 10 bytes garbage
0CH	1	dBASE field reference
0DH	1	dBASE field placeholder
0EH	1	Unary -
0FH	1	Plus +
10H	1	Minus -
11H	1	Multiply *
12H	1	Division /
13H	1	Power ^
14H	1	Equals =
15H	1	Not equal <
16H	1	Less than or equal <=
17H	1	Greater than or equal >=
18H	1	Less than <
19H	1	Greater than >

Table 7.32
Opcodes in a LOTUS formula (*cont.*)

Code	Bytes	Formula
1AH	1	AND
1BH	1	OR
1CH	1	NOT
1DH	1	Unary + (not for recalculation)
1EH	1	& (Concatenate)
1FH	1	@NA (Not applicable)
20H	1	@ERR (Error)
21H	1	@ABS (Absolute value)
22H	1	@INT (Integer value)
23H	1	@SQRT (Square root)
24H	1	@LOG (Logarithm base 10)
25H	1	@LN (Logarithm natural)
26H	1	@PI (Constant pi)
27H	1	@SIN (Sine)
28H	1	@COS (Cosine)
29H	1	@TAN (Tangent)
2AH	1	@ATAN2 (Arctangent 4th quadrant)
2BH	1	@ATAN (Arctangent 2nd quadrant)
2CH	1	@ASIN (Arcsine)
2DH	1	@ACOS (Arccosine)
2EH	1	@EXP (Exponentiation)
2FH	1	@MOD(X,Y) (Modulus function)
30H	1	@CHOOSE (+ 2 variable)
31H	1	@ISNA(x) (x=NA THEN 1)
32H	1	@ISERR(x) (x=ERR THEN 1)
33H	1	@FALSE (Return 0)
34H	1	@TRUE (Return 1)
35H	1	@RAND (Random number 0..1)
36H	1	@DATE (Days since 1.1.1900)
37H	1	@TODAY
38H	1	@PMT (Payment)
39H	1	@PV (Present value)
3AH	1	@FV (Future value)
3BH	1	@IF
3CH	1	@DAY (Day of month)
3DH	1	@MONTH
3EH	1	@YEAR
3FH	1	@ROUND
40H	1	@TIME
41H	1	@HOUR

Table 7.32 Opcodes in a LOTUS formula (*cont.*)

Code	Bytes	Formula
42H	1	@MINUTE
43H	1	@SECOND
44H	1	@ISNUMBER
45H	1	@ISSTRING
46H	1	@LENGTH
47H	1	@VALUE
48H	1	@FIXED
49H	1	@MID
4AH	1	@CHR
4BH	1	@ASCII
4CH	1	@FIND
4DH	1	@DATEVALUE
4EH	1	@TIMEVALUE
4FH	1	@CELLPOINTER
50H	1	@SUM (Range | Cell | Constant)
51H	1	@AVG (Range | Cell | Constant)
52H	1	@CNT (Range | Cell | Constant)
53H	1	@MIN (Range | Cell | Constant)
54H	1	@MAX (Range | Cell | Constant)
55H	1	@VLOOKUP (X,Range,OFFSET)
56H	1	@NPV (Int,Range)
57H	1	@VAR (Range)
58H	1	@STD (Range)
59H	1	@IRR (Guess,Range)
5AH	1	@HLOOCKUP (X,Range,Offset)
5BH	1	DSUM (Database function, 3 arguments)
5CH	1	AVG (Database function)
5DH	1	DCNT (Database function)
5EH	1	DMIN (Database function)
5FH	1	DMAX (Database function)
60H	1	DVAR (Database function)
61H	1	DSTD (Database function)
62H	1	@INDEX
63H	1	@COLS
64H	1	@ROWS
65H	1	@REPEAT
66H	1	@UPPER
67H	1	@LOWER
68H	1	@LEFT
69H	1	@RIGHT

Table 7.32 Opcodes in a LOTUS formula (*cont.*)

Code	Bytes	Formula
6AH	1	@REPLACE
6BH	1	@PROPER
6CH	1	@CELL
6DH	1	@TRIM
6EH	1	@CLEAN
6FH	1	@S
70H	1	@N
71H	1	@EXTRACT
72H	1	–
73H	1	@@
74H	1	@RATE
75H	1	@TERM
76H	1	@CTERM
77H	1	@SLN
78H	1	@SYD
79H	1	@DDB
7AH	1	@SPLfunc
		new opcodes
7BH	1	@SHEETS
7CH	1	@INFO
7DH	1	@SUMPRODUCT
7EH	1	@ISRANGE
7FH	1	@DGET
80H	1	@DQUERY
81H	1	@COORD
82H	1	–
83H	1	@TODAY
84H	1	@VDB
85H	1	@DVARS
86H	1	@DSTDS
87H	1	@VARS
88H	1	@STDS
89H	1	@D360
8AH	1	–
8BH	1	@ISAPP (Add-in)
8CH	1	@ISAAF (Add-in)
		Japanese (nihon) @functions
8DH	1	@WEEKDAY

Table 7.32 Opcodes in a LOTUS formula (*cont.*)

Table 7.32 Opcodes in a LOTUS formula (*cont.*)

Code	Bytes	Formula
8EH	1	@DATEDIF
8FH	1	@RANK
90H	1	@NUMBERSTRING
91H	1	@DATESTRING
92H	1	@DECIMAL
93H	1	@HEX
94H	1	@DB
95H	1	@PMTI
96H	1	@SPI
97H	1	@FULLP
98H	1	@HALFP
99H	1	@PUREAVG
9AH	1	@PURECOUNT
9BH	1	@PUREMAX
9CH	1	@PUREMIN
9DH	1	@PURESTD
9EH	1	@PUREVAR
9FH	1	@PURESTDS
A0H	1	@PUREVARS
A1H	1	@PMT2
A1H	1	@PMT2
A2H	1	@PV2
A3H	1	@FV2
A4H	1	@TERM2
		Add-in @funct. *for WK1, created in 1-2-3 release 3*
9CH	1	_
9DH	1	R2_SHEETS
9EH	1	R2_INFO
9FH	1	R2_SUMPRODUCT
A0H	1	R2_ISRANGE
A1H	1	R2_DGET
A2H	1	R2_DQUERY
A3H	1	R2_COORD
A4H	1	R2_VDB
A5H	1	R2_DVARS
A6H	1	R2_DSTDS
A7H	1	R2_VARS
A8H	1	R2_STDS
A9H	1	R2_D360

Code	Bytes	Formula
AAH	1	_
ABH	1	R2_ISAPP
ACH	1	R2_ISAAF
ADH	1	R2_WEEKDAY
AEH	1	R2_DATEDIF
AFH	1	R2_RANK
B0H	1	R2_DGET
B1H	1	R2_DATESTR
B2H	1	R2_DECIMAL
B3H	1	R2_HEX
B4H	1	R2_DB
B5H	1	R2_PMTI
B6H	1	R2_SPI
B7H	1	R2_FULLP
B8H	1	R2_HALP
B9H	1	R2_PUREAVG
BAH	1	R2_PURECOUNT
BBH	1	R2_PUREMAX
BCH	1	R2_PUREMIN
BDH	1	R2_PURESTD
BEH	1	R2_PUREVAR
BFH	1	R2_PURESTDS
C0H	1	R2_PUREVARS
C1H	1	R2_PMT2
C2H	1	R2_PV2
C3H	1	R2_FV2
C4H	1	R2_TERM2
C5H	1	R2_DSUMDIFF
C6H	1	R2_DAVGDIFF
C7H	1	R2_DCOUNTDIFF
C8H	1	R2_DMINDIFF
C9H	1	R2_DMAXDIFF
CAH	1	R2_DVARDIFF
CBH	1	R2_DSTDDIFF
CCH	1	R2_INDEXDIFF

Table 7.32 Opcodes in a LOTUS formula (*cont.*)

The formula type (number, ERR, NA, string) is encoded in the formula value field. If the formula type is STRING, the next record in the file must contain a FORMULASTRING. The string formula type does not define a value for the TREAL value field (offset 08H).

7.1.29 FORMULASTRING (Opcode 001AH)

This record follows a `FORMULACELL` record that specifies a string formula. The record contains the string value of the previous record.

Offset	Bytes	Field description
00H	2	Opcode `FORMULASTRING = 1AH` (version 3.0)
02H	2	Length = 5–517, step width 1
04H	2	Row number
06H	1	Worksheet number
07H	1	Column number
08H	*n*	LMBCS string value (up to 513 characters)

Table 7.33 LOTUS WK3 record structure (Opcode 001AH)

The LMBCS string value contains up to 512 characters and a terminator (00H). A WK3 file may contain more than one such record.

7.1.30 XFORMAT (Opcode 001BH)

This is a variable length record of up to 2048 bytes. The contents of this extended format record have not yet been defined.

7.1.31 DTLABELMISC (Opcode 001CH)

This record is optional and contains miscellaneous information for `/Data Table` commands.

Offset	Bytes	Field description
00H	2	Opcode `DTLABELMISC = 1CH` (version 3.0)
02H	2	Length = 6
04H	2	Type of the last /Data Table command 0 = No command 1 = /Data Table 1 2 = /Data Table 2 3 = /Data Table 3 4 = /Data Table Legend
06H	4	LMBCS label fill character

Table 7.34 LOTUS WK3 record structure (Opcode 001CH)

Spreadsheets

This record allows a user to execute the last /Data Table command by pressing the TABLE key [F8]. In a WK3 file, only one such record is allowed.

7.1.32 DTLABELCELL (Opcode 001DH)

This record contains the description of the /Data Table input cell list.

Offset	Bytes	Field description
00H	2	Opcode DTLABELCELL = 1DH (version 3.0)
02H	2	Length = variable
04H	2	Type of cell 0 = Down 1 = Across 2 = Page/worksheet
06H	2	Cell count or continuation flag (N)

Table 7.35 LOTUS WK3 record structure (Opcode 001DH)

If the value in the word at offset 06H is greater than 0, it represents the cell count. This record is optional, and several records may occur in a file.

7.1.33 GRAPHWINDOW (Opcode 001EH)

This record indicates a graph (hot graph) which is currently displayed.

Offset	Bytes	Field description
00H	2	Opcode GRAPHWINDOW = 1EH (version 3.0)
02H	2	Length = 1
04H	1	Flag 0 = No graph window is present 1 = Graph window is present

Table 7.36 LOTUS WK3 record structure (Opcode 001EH)

This record defines what is known as a 'hot graph'. This graph will change each time a new value is entered in the worksheet. Only one record is allowed in a file.

7.1.34 CPA (Opcode 001FH)

This record contains a cell pointer array, which is used to pre-allocate the cell pointer index.

Offset	Bytes	Field description
00H	2	Opcode CPA = 1FH (version 3.0)
02H	2	Length = variable 8–132
04H	1	Worksheet number 0–255
05H	1	Column number 0–255
06H	1	Number of entries 1–32
07H	1	Reserved
08H	*n*	Repeated number of entries: 2-byte row start 2-byte row end

Table 7.37 LOTUS WK3 record structure (Opcode 001FH)

7.1.35 LPLAUTO (Opcode 0020H)

This record defines bits for auto-invoke and key assignments.

The file descriptor defines the drive, path and name of the file to be loaded. This descriptor is a null-terminated LMBCS string up to 130 characters long. There is only one bit defined in the bit field at offset 04H. All other bits are reserved.

Offset	Bytes	Field description
00H	2	Opcode LPLAUTO = 20H (version 3.0)
02H	2	Length = variable 8–132
04H	2	Bit field (value 8000H = Auto-invoke)
06H	*n*	File descriptor

Table 7.38 LOTUS WK3 record structure (Opcode 0020H)

7.1.36 QUERY (Opcode 0021H)

This optional record contains information for the `/Data Query` command and is stored (only once) in the WK3 file.

Offset	Bytes	Field description
00H	2	Opcode QUERY = 21H (version 3.0)
02H	2	Length = 1
04H	1	Last /Data Query type 0 = No command 1 = Find 2 = Extract 3 = Delete 4 = Unique 5 = Modify

Table 7.39 LOTUS WK3 record structure (Opcode 0021H)

The record allows the user to execute the last `/Data Query` command again, by pressing the QUERY [F7] key.

7.1.37 HIDDENSHEET (Opcode 0022H)

This record indicates all hidden worksheets in the WK3 file.

Offset	Bytes	Field description
00H	2	Opcode HIDDENSHEET = 22H (version 3.0)
02H	2	Length = variable 1–255
04H	1	Worksheet offset of first hidden worksheet
05H	1	Worksheet offset of next hidden worksheet
		....

Table 7.40 LOTUS WK3 record structure (Opcode 0022H)

The record is optional and may occur only once in a file. This results in a maximum of 255 entries for the worksheet offsets in the record. Each entry defines the offset from the first worksheet in the file. The offset value starts from 0.

7.2 LOTUS 1-2-3 FRM file format

LOTUS 1-2-3 version 3.x creates FRM files parallel to the WK3 files. The FRM files begin with a BOF record (26 bytes long), which has a different signature (00H 00H 1AH 00H 01H 80H 01H 00H....). The file is terminated by an EOF record (code 01H 00H). In the file, there are several records with structures similar to the WK3 file. The record structure for the FONTNAME record is shown in Table 7.41.

Offset	Bytes	Field description
00H	2	Opcode FONTNAME = AEH (version 3.0)
02H	2	Length = variable
04H	1	Entry number (1 to *n*)
05H	*n*	Font name (LMBCS string + 00H)

Table 7.41 LOTUS FRM record structure (Opcode 00AEH)

The meaning of the other record types is unknown.

8

LOTUS 1-2-3 PIC format

LOTUS graphs can be stored in PIC files and then printed using PRINTGRAPH *or imported into external programs. LOTUS stores all the data in PIC formats as vectors. There is also information in the file on which fonts (and font sizes) to use. Figure 8.1 shows the contents of a PIC file as a hex-dump.*

8.1 File header

A PIC file starts with a 17-byte header, which always contains the signature `01 00 00 00` in the first 4 bytes. The meaning of the remaining bytes is not known, but the sequence of bytes shown in Figure 8.1 occurs in all PIC files.

8.2 Record descriptions

The header is followed by several records of differing lengths. The record type is specified by the first byte (opcode). Table 8.1 gives a list of possible record types.

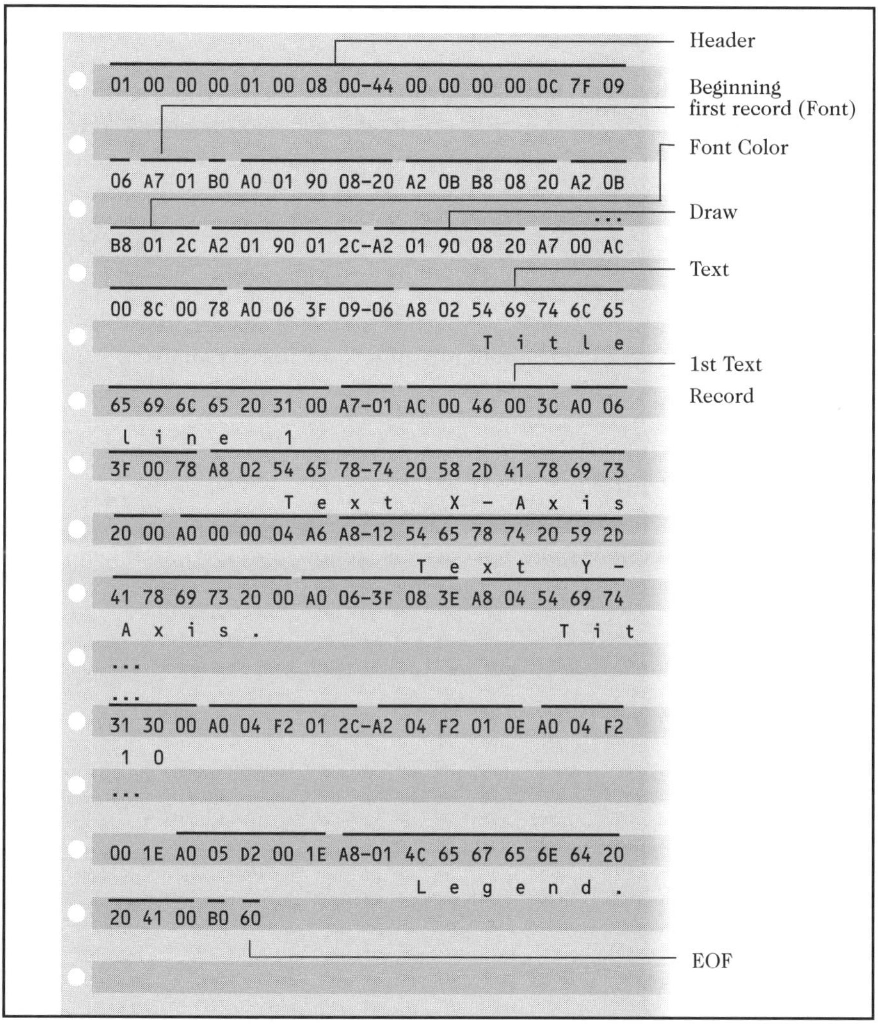

Figure 8.1 Dump of a PIC file

Type	Remark
`30H`	`FILL` (x1,y1) .. (xn,yn) draws a filled polygon
`60H-6FH`	`EOF-Mark` (End of file, 1 byte)
`A0H`	`MOVE x,y` (5 bytes)
`A2H`	`DRAW x,y` (5 bytes)
`A7H`	`FONT n` (2 bytes)
`A8H`	`TEXT` (variable length ASCIIZ string) Byte 2 specifies the subtype for text orientation `<A8><Subtype><ASCIIZ string>`
`ACH`	`SIZE n,m` (5 bytes)
`B0H-BFH`	`COLOR` (coding lower 4 bits)
`D0H`	`FILLO` (x1,y1) .. (xn,yn)

Table 8.1 Records in LOTUS PIC files

8.2.1 FILL (x1,y1)...(xn,yn) (Opcode 30H)

The `FILL` command draws a filled polygon in the color currently set. The polygon has no outline. An indefinite number of coordinate pairs (x,y) may be specified. Each coordinate is represented as a 16-bit value. The opcode is followed by a byte showing the number of coordinate pairs (starting with `0`).

8.2.2 END OF FILE (Codes 60H to 6FH)

The end of the PIC file is indicated by one byte containing the `EOF` code. The numbers permitted as `EOF` codes are `60H` to `6FH`, the most frequently used being `60H`.

8.2.3 MOVE (X,Y) (Opcode A0H)

This record consists of 5 bytes and contains the opcode `A0H`, followed by two 16-bit numbers indicating the X and Y coordinates for the new point. The cursor is moved to the appropriate point without a line being drawn.

8.2.4 DRAW (X,Y) (Opcode A2H)

This record also consists of 5 bytes and contains the opcode `A2H` followed by two 16-bit numbers indicating the X and Y coordinates for the new point. The cursor is moved from the present position to the appropriate point, and a line (1 pixel wide) is drawn in the color currently set. The new point then becomes the current coordinate.

8.2.5 FONT n (Opcode A7H)

This record occupies 2 bytes and defines the font to be used. The first byte contains the opcode `A7H`, the second byte the definition of the font. The relevant coding is shown below:

`0` = Type face 1
`1` = Type face 2

Additional values have not yet been implemented.

8.2.6 TEXT xxxx (Opcode A8H)

This record begins with the opcode A8H and is of variable length. The opcode is followed by a byte defining the direction of the text. The upper 4 bits specify the direction of the output (D); the position (P) is indicated in the lower 4 bits. The options shown in Table 8.2 apply to these bits.

Value	Remark
-	Bits 4–7 (direction)
0	Horizontal (left to right)
1	Vertical (top to bottom)
2	Horizontal (right to left)
3	Vertical (bottom to top)
-	Bits 0–3 (position)
0	Center drawing rectangle
1	Center left
2	Center upper
3	Center right
4	Center lower
5	Left upper corner
6	Right upper corner
7	Left lower corner
8	Right lower corner

Table 8.2 Coding text alignment

The following points relate to the positioning of the text. The text is output at the current cursor position. It can be assumed that the text will be framed in a rectangle which can only be positioned relative to the current coordinate point. The text is also moved relative to the current coordinate point. The code 0 positions the text so that its center is on the current coordinate point.

The opcode A8H and the byte containing the direction and position bits is followed by the text. This is stored as an ASCIIZ string, that is, the last byte is followed by the terminator code 00H. The length of the text may not exceed 64 kbytes, a restriction which is rarely met in practice. The text is output at the current position in the direction indicated. The color and font settings also affect the output of the text.

8.2.7 SIZE n,m (Opcode ACH)

This record determines the size of the characters. The opcode ACH is followed by two 16-bit numbers which indicate the dimensions of a rectangle with the coordinates (0,0) and (n,m). Within the character fonts, the size of the individual characters is fixed. The SIZE command influences the scaling of the characters via the parameters (n,m), that is, the characters are enlarged accordingly.

8.2.8 COLOR (Opcode BxH)

This 1-byte record is used to set the current color. The color is coded in the lower 4 bits. There are 16 colors available, represented by the opcodes B0H to BFH. The actual color is then processed for output via PRINTGRAPH.

8.2.9 FILLO (x1,y1)..(xn,yn) (Opcode D0H)

This is another record that produces a filled polygon. However, in this case the polygon is highlighted with a border in the color selected. Several pairs of coordinates (X,Y) can be given, represented as 16-bit numbers. The number of coordinates is stored in the second byte, after the opcode.

Very simple drawings can be produced using this file type. All the coordinate data within the PIC file takes the form of 16-bit numbers. The data refers to a virtual, rectangular, Cartesian coordinate system with 3200 points in the X-direction and 2311 points in the Y-direction. PRINTGRAPH adapts these coordinates to the coordinate system of the output device. The zero-point (origin) of the coordinate system is located at the bottom left-hand corner. The values for the coordinates are not stored according to the Intel convention: the high byte of a coordinate value is stored first. The number 0FH 00H thus becomes the byte sequence 3F 00H in the file. (This number is normally stored as 00H 3FH.)

9

LOTUS Symphony format

***Symphony** is an extension of the LOTUS 1-2-3 spreadsheet program and is also distributed by LOTUS Development. As in the case of LOTUS 1-2-3, the contents of the spreadsheets, including data and calculation formulas, can be stored in files. Depending on the version of the program (1.1, 2.0), these data can be stored in a format which complies very precisely with the LOTUS specifications. Symphony uses binary formats to store the data and calculation formulas, while texts from the spreadsheets are stored in ASCII format.*

The record structure is the same as in LOTUS 1-2-3:

```
<Record Type> <Record Length> <Data>
```

This structure is retained throughout the various versions. The meaning of the individual fields is given below:

- The `record type` field is two bytes long and – as the name suggests – contains information on the record type. This determines the structure of the following data field. For records that contain data, this record type can be interpreted as an opcode specifying calculation instructions or the structure of the spreadsheet. The terms *record type* and *opcode* are therefore treated synonymously. In the `record type` field, the lowest byte is stored in the first byte of the file. The opcodes vary according to the different versions of Symphony.
- The `record length` field occupies two bytes and specifies the length of the following data field in bytes. The LSB is stored first.

- The `data` field is of variable length, depending on the field type. This field contains values, calculation formulas, definitions for the structure of the spreadsheet, and so on.

Depending on the version of the program, the file extension is either WKS (Symphony version 1.0) or WK1 (version 2.0). A hex-dump of the WK1 file is not given here, because its structure is very similar to the LOTUS file. The same applies to the way the file is mapped onto the spreadsheet. Rows and columns are only provided with letters and numbers at the user interface; internally, LOTUS/Symphony operate with 16-bit row and column numbers. Each cell position can thus be unambiguously identified by two numbers. This numbering system is also used in the file.

9.1 Record types in Symphony

The various types of record (*opcodes*) that appear in the WKS files are presented below together with their data structures. Many of the opcodes are also used in LOTUS 1-2-3. However, in later versions, new opcodes have been added. Each opcode consists of two bytes, where the low byte (LSB) is stored first.

9.1.1 BOF (Opcode 0000H)

This record marks the beginning of a valid WKS/WK1 file. The record is structured as follows:

Offset	Bytes	Remark
00H	2	Opcode BOF = 0000H
02H	2	Length = 0002H
04H	2	Version number file format 0404H 1-2-3 WKS format in version 1 0405H Symphony file 0406H 1-2-3 file in WK1 format version 2.0 and Symphony 1.1

Table 9.1 Symphony record structure (Opcode 0000H)

The data field contains two bytes which indicate the version code of the data format. More recent versions of Symphony continue this numbering system.

9.1.2 EOF (Opcode 0001H)

This record indicates the end of a WKS or WK1 file. The record is structured as follows:

Offset	Bytes	Remark
00H	2	Opcode EOF = 0001H
02H	2	Length = 0000H

Table 9.2 Symphony record structure (Opcode 0001H)

The record is only 4 bytes long, and the data field is omitted.

9.1.3 CALC_MODE (Opcode 0002H)

In Symphony, the user can determine whether the results are to be recalculated automatically after each entry (default setting) or only after a specific command. The calculation mode is stored in this record, which is structured as follows:

Offset	Bytes	Remark
00H	2	Opcode CALC_MODE = 0002H
02H	2	Length = 0001H
04H	2	Recalculation mode 00H = Manual FFH = Automatic

Table 9.3 Symphony record structure (Opcode 0002H)

The default value for the data byte is FFH, for automatic recalculation after every entry.

9.1.4 CALC_ORDER (Opcode 0003H)

Each time the results are calculated, the sequence in which the formulas are to be processed can be specified. The order is stored in a record structured as follows:

Offset	Bytes	Remark
00H	2	Opcode CALC_ORDER Opcode = 0003H
02H	2	Length = 0001H
04H	2	Calculation order 00H = Natural 01H = Column FFH = Row

Table 9.4 Symphony record structure (Opcode 0003H)

For calculation by column (code 01), only the formulas in the relevant column are processed. Symphony then begins calculating the formulas in the next column.

9.1.5 RANGE (Opcode 0006H)

In Symphony, this record is used to specify the RANGE of cells to be stored in the file. The whole spreadsheet is usually saved. The record is structured as shown below:

Offset	Bytes	Remark
00H	2	Opcode RANGE = 0006H
02H	2	Length = 0008H
04H	2	Start column
06H	2	Start row
08H	2	End column
0AH	2	End row

Table 9.5 Symphony record structure (Opcode 0006H)

In the data field, the top left corner (row/column) and the bottom right corner are stored. If the file was created using the `File-save` command, all the fields in the spreadsheet will be in the file. If `File-Xtract` was used, only the cells in the specified extract will be stored, and the coordinates for this extract will be stored in the data field. It should be noted that Symphony stores the column and row addresses in the form of 16-bit numbers. The LSB is stored first. In storing the cells, blank fields at the end of a column or row are not taken into account. If there are no data in the range specified, Symphony will set the value of the start column to –1. The 06H record type generally comes immediately after the BOF record. This should be remembered if WKS or WK1 files are created by external programs.

9.1.6 COLUMN_WIDTH_1 (Opcode 0008H)

This record is used in Symphony to define the width of the columns in the window described in the next record. The structure is described below:

Offset	Bytes	Remark
00H	2	Opcode COLUMN_WIDTH_1 = 0008H
02H	2	Length = 0003H
04H	2	Column number (16 bits)
06H	1	Column width

Table 9.6 Symphony record structure (Opcode 0008H)

The relevant column number (LSB first) is shown in the first word. The following byte indicates the width of the column in characters.

9.1.7 BLANK (Opcode 000CH)

Normally, Symphony does not store blank cells, so the information in protected or formatted blank cells would be lost during the storage process. The record type 0CH, which saves these cells, is provided to avoid this problem. The following structure applies:

Offset	Bytes	Remark
00H	2	Opcode BLANK = 000CH
02H	2	Length = 0005H
04H	1	Format byte
05H	2	Column number
07H	2	Row number

Table 9.7 Symphony record structure (Opcode 000CH)

In the first data byte, Symphony stores the cell format coding:

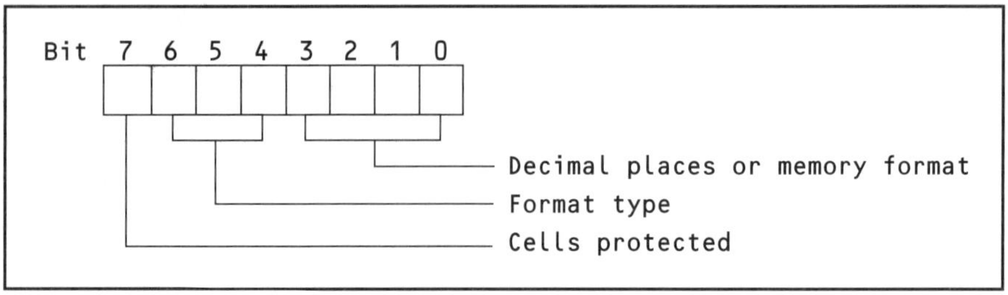

Figure 9.1
Cell format
in Symphony

Bit 7 indicates whether the cells within the window are *write-protected* and is coded as follows:

Bit 7	Function
1	Protected
0	Unprotected

Table 9.8a
Coding formats

Bits 4–6 contain a binary number indicating the format to be used for presenting the value. The following formats are available:

Bits 6 5 4	Format
000	Fixed
001	Scientific notation
010	Currency
011	Percent
100	Comma
101	Free
110	Free
111	Special format

Table 9.8b
Coding formats

For format types 0–6, the remaining bits 0–3 specify the number of decimal places (between 0 and 15). Format type 7 represents a special format, which is further specified in bits 0–3.

Bits 3210	Format
0000	+/–
0001	General format
0010	Date format: day, month, year
0011	Date format: day, month
0100	Date format: month, year
0101	Text format
0110	Hidden
0111	Date + hours, minutes, seconds
1000	Date + hours, minutes
1001	Date, international 1
1010	Date, international 2
1011	Time, international 1
1100	Time, international 2
1101	Unused
1110	Unused
1111	Standard

Table 9.9 Coding for special formats in Symphony

This is followed by two words containing the cell coordinates. The record is only created if protected cells are present.

9.1.8 INTEGER (Opcode 000DH)

Directly entered whole numbers (*integers*) are transferred from the spreadsheet to the file. In Symphony, the record is structured as follows:

Offset	Bytes	Remark
00H	2	Opcode INTEGER = 000DH
02H	2	Length = 0007H
04H	1	Format byte
05H	2	Column number
07H	2	Row number
09H	2	Integer value

Table 9.10 Symphony record structure (Opcode 000DH)

The record contains 7 data bytes, the format of the number being stored in the first byte. (The coding is listed in Table 9.9.) The following two words describe the position of the cell containing the integer value. This is followed by a 16-bit word containing the value. The most significant bit indicates whether the value is positive or negative (bit = 1). An integer value between –32768 and +32767 can be stored in one cell.

9.1.9 NUMBER (Opcode 000EH)

Symphony stores floating point numbers in this record, whose structure is shown below:

Offset	Bytes	Remark
00H	2	Opcode NUMBER = 000EH
02H	2	Length = 000DH (13 bytes)
04H	1	Format byte
05H	2	Column number
07H	2	Row number
09H	8	64-bit IEEE floating-point value

Table 9.11 Symphony record structure (Opcode 000EH)

The record contains 13 data bytes, with the format of the floating point number in the first byte. (The coding is listed in Table 9.8) The next two words describe the position of the cell containing the floating point number. These fields are followed by 8 bytes in which the value is stored as a 64-bit IEEE floating point number. This representation corresponds to the coding of the 8087 format. Internally, Symphony uses its own representation, in which 11 bytes are used for the storage of floating point numbers. As shown in Table 9.12, the first byte contains a value which specifies the interpretation of the following number. Range and string values are indicated by the codes 2 and 3.

Offset	Bytes	Remark
00H	1	Sign 0 = Positive value FFH = Negative value 2 = Range byte 3 = String byte
01H	2	Exponent (signed integer)
03H	8	64-bit unsigned fraction

Table 9.12 LOTUS Symphony floating point representation

If the value ERR is present in the cell, Symphony will set the 11 bytes to the values shown in Table 9.13.

The value ERR contains the signature 0 in the first byte, while the exponent word contains 0FFFH. The 8 bytes of the mantissa are set to 0. The same applies to the code NA (*not available*), except that the first byte is set to the value -1. The remaining bytes are coded as shown in Table 9.13.

Offset	Value
00H	ERR = 0; NA = -1
01H-02H	2047 = 0FFFH
03H-10H	8 * 0

Table 9.13 Internal representation of the ERR and NA values in Symphony

9.1.10 LABEL (Opcode 000FH)

Symphony stores fixed passages of text from a spreadsheet in the form of labels. In the WKS/WK1 file, there is a special record type for storing text. Its structure is shown below:

Offset	Bytes	Remark
00H	2	Opcode LABEL = 000FH
02H	2	Length = 00xxH (variable up to 240 bytes)
04H	1	Format byte
05H	2	Column number
07H	2	Row number
09H	5-240	ASCIIZ string (LABEL text)

Table 9.14 Symphony record structure (Opcode 000FH)

An example of labels is shown in Figure 6.2, in the text constants (for example in Test Spreadsheet). The length of the data record depends on the length of the label text.

The first data byte contains the format byte, coded as shown in Table 9.8. This is followed by two words giving the column and row numbers. The text begins at offset 09H and must be terminated by a null byte (00H). The string may have a maximum length of 240 bytes. The length of the field is between 5 and 240 bytes. The byte at offset 09H always contains one of the following control characters:

Character	Remark
\	Repeater
'	Left-aligned text
"	Right-aligned text
^	Text centered

Table 9.15 Control characters in a Symphony LABEL record

The character \ is used in Symphony to introduce repetitions. However, exactly when this character is used is not clear, because it does not occur in the text labels in the test sample.

9.1.11 FORMULA (Opcode 0010H)

In addition to numeric values, a Symphony cell may also contain a calculation formula. This formula is stored in a record with the opcode 10H, which is structured as follows:

Offset	Bytes	Remark
00H	2	Opcode FORMULA = 0010H
02H	2	Length = xxxxH (variable up to 2064 bytes)
04H	1	Format byte
05H	2	Column number
07H	2	Row number
09H	8	Result as 64-bit IEEE long real
11H	2	Length formula in bytes
13H	15-2063	Formula opcodes (maximum 2048 bytes)

Table 9.16 Symphony record structure (Opcode 0010H)

The first data byte contains the cell format coded as shown in Table 9.8

This is followed by the coordinates for the cell in the form of two 16-bit values. At offset 09H, the result of the calculation formula is defined as an 8-byte IEEE double precision floating point number. The length of the formula in bytes is stored in the following word. The last part of the data field contains the formula code. The length of the data record varies between 23 and 2064 bytes, and the length of the formula is between 15 and 2048 bytes. Both LOTUS and Symphony convert a formula into inverse parenthesis-free (Polish) notation. Every entry in this formula is represented by its own function code and an associated data field:

```
Code,Data field,.....,Code,Data field
```

The code comprises one byte and specifies the operator type (variable, constant, brackets, addition, and so on). It is followed by the data for this operator. In this context, the coding is as follows:

Code	Bytes	Remark
00H	1	Constant
	8	64-bit long real value
01H	1	Variable
	2	Column number (LSB first)
	2	Row number (LSB first)
02H	1	Range
	2	Start column number (LSB first)
	2	Start row number (LSB first)
	2	End column number (LSB first)
	2	End row number (LSB first)
03H	1	End of formula
04H	1	Parenthesis
05H	1	Integer constant
	2	(16-bit integer value)
06H	1	String constant
	x	(variable length ASCIIZ string)
07H	1	-
08H	1	Negation (unary minus)
09H	1	Addition +
0AH	1	Subtraction -
0BH	1	Multiplication *
0CH	1	Division /
0DH	1	Exponential function ^
0EH	1	Equal =
0FH	1	Not equal <>
10H	1	Less than or equal <=
11H	1	Greater than or equal >=
12H	1	Less than <
13H	1	Greater than >
14H	1	AND
15H	1	OR
16H	1	NOT

Table 9.17 Opcodes within a Symphony formula (*continues over...*)

Code	Bytes	Remark
17H	1	unary +
18H-1EH	1	-
1FH	1	@NA (Not applicable)
20H	1	@ERR (Error)
21H	1	@ABS (Absolute)
22H	1	@INT (Integer)
23H	1	@SQRT (Square root)
24H	1	@LOG (Logarithm base 10)
25H	1	@LN (Natural logarithm)
26H	1	@PI (Constant pi)
27H	1	@SIN (Sine)
28H	1	@COS (Cosine)
29H	1	@TAN (Tangent)
2AH	1	@ATAN2 (Arctangent 4th quadrant)
2BH	1	@ATAN (Arctangent 2nd quadrant)
2CH	1	@ASIN (Arcsine)
2DH	1	@ACOS (Arccosine)
2EH	1	@EXP (Exponential function)
2FH	1	@MOD(X,Y) (Modulus)
30H	1	@CHOOSE
31H	1	@ISNA(x) (x=NA then 1)
32H	1	@ISERR(x) (x=ERR then 1)
33H	1	@FALSE (Return 0)
34H	1	@TRUE (Return 1)
35H	1	@RAND (Random number 0..1)
36H	1	@DATE (Days since 1.1.1990)
37H	1	@TODAY (Date)
38H	1	@PMT (Payment)
39H	1	@PV (Present value)
3AH	1	@FV (Future value)
3BH	1	@IF
3CH	1	@DAY (Day of month)
3DH	1	@MONTH
3EH	1	@YEAR
3FH	1	@ROUND
40H	1	@TIME
41H	1	@HOUR
42H	1	@MINUTE

Table 9.17 Opcodes within a Symphony formula (*cont.*)

Code	Bytes	Remark
44H	1	@ISNUMBER
45H	1	@ISSTRING
46H	1	@LENGTH
47H	1	@VALUE
48H	1	@FIXED
49H	1	@MID (Mean value)
4AH	1	@CHR
4BH	1	@ASCII
4CH	1	@FIND
4DH	1	@DATEVALUE
4EH	1	@TIMEVALUE
4FH	1	@CELLPOINTER
50H	1	@SUM (Range | cell | constant)
51H	1	@AVG (Range | cell | constant)
52H	1	@CNT (Range | cell | constant)
53H	1	@MIN (Range | cell | constant)
54H	1	@MAX (Range | cell | constant)
55H	1	@VLOOKUP (X,Range,OFFSET)
56H	1	@NPV (Int, Range)
57H	1	@VAR (Range)
58H	1	@STD (Range)
59H	1	@IRR (Guess,Range)
5AH	1	@HLOOKUP (X,Range,Offset)
5BH	1	DSUM (Database function)
5CH	1	AVG (Database function)
5DH	1	DCNT (Database function)
5EH	1	DMIN (Database function)
5FH	1	DMAX (Database function)
60H	1	DVAR (Database function)
61H	1	DSTD (Database function)
62H	1	@INDEX
63H	1	@COLS
64H	1	@ROWS
65H	1	@REPEAT
66H	1	@UPPER
67H	1	@LOWER
68H	1	@LEFT
69H	1	@RIGHT

Table 9.17 Opcodes within a Symphony formula (*cont.*)

Spreadsheets

Code	Bytes	Remark
6AH	1	@REPLACE
6BH	1	@PROPER
6CH	1	@CELL
6DH	1	@TRIM
6EH	1	@CLEAN
6FH	1	@S
70H	1	@V
71H	1	@STREQ
72H	1	@CALL
73H	1	@APP (Symphony 1.0)
		@INDIRECT (Symphony 1.1)
74H	1	@RATE
75H	1	@TERM
76H	1	@CTERM
77H	1	@SLN
78H	1	@SOY
79H	1	@DDB
7AH-9BH	1	-
9CH	1	@AAFSTART
CEH	1	-
FFH	1	@AAFMAX (Symphony 1.1)

Table 9.17 Opcodes within a Symphony formula (*cont.*)

9.1.12 TABLE (Opcode 0018H)

This data record is used to store Symphony data tables, and has the the following structure:

Offset	**Bytes**	**Remark**
00H	2	Opcode TABLE = 0018H
02H	2	Length = 0019H (25 bytes)
04H	1	0 = No table
		1 = Table 1
		2 = Table 2

Table 9.18 Symphony record structure (Opcode 0018H) *(continues over...)*

Offset	Bytes	Remark
05H	2	Table range start column number
07H	2	Table range start row number
09H	2	Table range end column number
0BH	2	Table range end row number
0DH	2	Input cell 1 start column
0FH	2	Input cell 1 start row
11H	2	Input cell 1 end column
13H	2	Input cell 1 end row
15H	2	Input cell 2 start column
17H	2	Input cell 2 start row
19H	2	Input cell 2 end column
1BH	2	Input cell 2 end row

Table 9.18 Symphony record structure (Opcode 0018H) *(cont.)*

In Symphony, the record specifies the position of the `if...then` tables. The exact meaning of this data structure is not known.

9.1.13 PRINT_RANGE (Opcode 001AH)

From Symphony 1.1 onwards, this data record is used to store the data from a `PRINT` range. The record is structured as follows:

Offset	**Bytes**	**Remark**
00H	2	Opcode PRINT_RANGE = 001AH
02H	2	Length = 0008H
04H	2	Start column
06H	2	Start row
08H	2	End column
0AH	2	End row

Table 9.19 Symphony record structure (Opcode 001AH)

The record contains the coordinates of a section of the spreadsheet which is to be printed out. All the cells within the window are printed when the print command is given.

9.1.14 FILL_RANGE (Opcode 001CH)

This record is used to store the data from a `fill-range`, that is, the coordinates of a section of spreadsheet which is to be filled with data. The format is as follows:

Offset	Bytes	Remark
00H	2	Opcode FILL_RANGE = 001CH
02H	2	Length = 0008H
04H	2	Start column
06H	2	Start row
08H	2	End column
0AH	2	End row

Table 9.20 Symphony record structure (Opcode 001CH)

9.1.15 HRANGE (Opcode 0020H)

This record is used to store the internal data from a range in Symphony. The record is structured as shown in Table 9.21 below.

The exact meaning of this record is not known.

Offset	Bytes	Remark
00H	2	Opcode HRANGE = 0020H
02H	2	Length = 0010H (16 bytes)
04H	2	Value range start column
06H	2	Value range start row
08H	2	Value range end column
0AH	2	Value range end row
0CH	2	Binary range start column
0EH	2	Binary range start row
10H	2	Binary range end column
12H	2	Binary range end row

Table 9.21 Symphony record structure (Opcode 0020H)

9.1.16 PROTECT (Opcode 0024H)

Symphony uses this data record to indicate whether the cells of a worksheet are protected or not. Only one byte is stored, which is coded as shown below.

Offset	Bytes	Remark
00H	2	Opcode PROTECT = 0024H
02H	2	Length = 0001H
04H	1	Protection 0: Off 1: On

Table 9.22 Symphony record structure (Opcode 0024H)

9.1.17 LABEL_FORMAT (Opcode 0029H)

Symphony uses this data record to note how labels are aligned. The following coding applies:

Offset	Bytes	Remark
00H	2	Opcode LABEL_FORMAT = 0029H
02H	2	Length = 0001H
04H	1	Label alignment 27H Left 22H Right 5EH Centered

Table 9.23 Symphony record structure (Opcode 0029H)

Labels can be left-justified, right-justified or centered.

9.1.18 CALC_COUNT (Opcode 002FH)

This data record specifies how often a calculation (*iteration*) is to be carried out.

Offset	Bytes	Remark
00H	2	Opcode CALC_COUNT = 002FH
02H	2	Length = 0001H
04H	1	Iteration counter

Table 9.24 Symphony record structure (Opcode 002FH)

9.1.19 WINDOW (Opcode 0032H)

This data record contains information on the structure of the window.

Offset	Bytes	Remark
00/ 00H	2	Opcode WINDOW = 0032H
02/ 02H	2	Length = 0090H (144 bytes)
04/ 04H	16	Window name (ASCII string)
20/ 14H	2	Cursor column
22/ 16H	2	Cursor row
24/ 18H	1	Format byte
25/ 19H	1	Unused
26/ 1AH	2	Column width
28/ 1CH	2	Number of columns
30/ 1EH	2	Number of rows
32/ 20H	2	Start row of non-title area
34/ 22H	2	Start column of non-title area
36/ 24H	2	Number of title columns
38/ 26H	2	Number of title rows
40/ 28H	2	Title left column
42/ 2AH	2	Title top row
44/ 2CH	2	HOME position column
46/ 2EH	2	HOME position row
48/ 30H	2	Number of screen columns
50/ 32H	2	Number of screen rows
52/ 34H	1	Hidden status
		00H = hidden
		FFH = not hidden
53/ 35H	1	Previous windows
		00H = SHEET
		01H = DOC
		02H = GRAPH
		03H = COMM
		04H = FORM
		05H = APPLICATION
54/ 36H	1	Border display
		00H = Cell
		FFH = No cell

Table 9.25 Symphony record structure (Opcode 0032H) (*continues over...*)

Offset	Bytes	Remark
55/ 37H	1	Border lines display
		00H = Display lines
		FFH = No lines
56/ 38H	2	Window range start column
58/ 3AH	2	Window range start row
60/ 3CH	2	Window range end column
62/ 3EH	2	Window range end row
64/ 40H	2	Offset
66/ 42H	1	Insert mode flag
		00H = Insert off
		Other = Insert on
67/ 43H	16	Graph name
83/ 53H	1	Window type
		00H = SHEET
		01H = DOC
		02H = GRAPH
		03H = COMM
		04H = FORM
		05H = APPLICATION
84/ 54H	1	Auto display mode flag
		61H = ('a') Auto display on
		Other values: Manual display
85/ 55H	1	Forms filter
		00H = Filter active
		Other: No filter
86/ 56H	16	Associated form name
102/66H	2	FORMS current record number
104/68H	1	Space display flag
		00H = No spaces
		Other: Display spaces
105/69H	1	Number of spaces
		01H = 1 space
		02H = 2 spaces
		03H = 3 spaces
106/6AH	1	Text alignment
		'l' = Left (code 6CH)
		'r' = Right (code 72H)
		'c' = Centered (code 63H)
		'e' = Even position (code 65H)

Table 9.25 Symphony record structure (Opcode 0032H) (*cont.*)

Spreadsheets

Offset	Bytes	Remark
107/6BH	2	Right margin FFH = Default 00H-FEH: User defined
109/6DH	2	Left margin FFH = Default 00H-F0H: Left margin
111/6FH	2	TAB interval
113/71H	1	Return display mode 00H = Soft carriage return Other: Hard return
114/72H	1	Auto justify 00H = Off Else = On
115/73H	16	Application name
131/83H	17	Reserved

Table 9.25 Symphony record structure (Opcode 0032H) (*cont.*)

The contents of the individual fields within this record are based on the functions of Symphony.

9.1.20 STRING (Opcode 0033H)

Offset	**Bytes**	**Remark**
00H	2	Opcode STRING = 0033H
02H	2	Length = 00xxH (variable)
04H	1	Format code
05H	2	Column number
07H	2	Row number
09H	xx	ASCIIZ string, variable length

Table 9.26 Symphony record structure (Opcode 0033H)

This data record is used to store the result of a string function. The cell format is stored in the first data byte, coded as shown in Table 9.8. The next two fields contain the cell coordinates. These are followed by the string, terminated by a null byte (00H). The length of the string may be variable.

9.1.21 LOCK_PASSWORD (Opcode 0037H)

This data record contains a password which is used to lock write-access to certain defined cells.

Offset	Bytes	Remark
00H	2	Opcode LOCK_PASSWORD = 0037H
02H	2	Length = 0004H
04H	4	Password

Table 9.27 Symphony record structure (Opcode 0037H)

9.1.22 LOCKED (Opcode 0038H)

This data record contains the lock flag, which indicates the write-protection status.

Offset	Bytes	Remark
00H	2	Opcode LOCKED = 0038H
02H	2	Length = 0001H
04H	1	Lock flag 0 = Lock off 1 = Lock on

Table 9.28 Symphony record structure (Opcode 0038H)

When the flag is set, Symphony locks write-access to certain cells. These cells can then only be accessed by giving the correct password.

9.1.23 QUERY (Opcode 003CH)

This data record describes the settings for the QUERY command.

Offset	Bytes	Remark
00 / 00H	2	Opcode QUERY = 003CH
02 / 02H	2	Length = 007FH (127 bytes)
04 / 04H	16	Name (ASCIIZ string)

Table 9.29 Symphony record structure (Opcode 003CH) *(continues over...)*

Offset	Bytes	Remark
20 / 14H	2	Input range start column
22 / 16H	2	Start row
24 / 18H	2	End column
26 / 1AH	2	End row
28 / 1CH	2	Output range start column
30 / 1EH	2	Start row
32 / 20H	2	End column
34 / 22H	2	End row
36 / 24H	2	Criteria range start column
38 / 26H	2	Start row
40 / 28H	2	End column
42 / 2AH	2	End row
44 / 2CH	2	Form entry start column
46 / 2EH	2	Start row
48 / 30H	2	End column
50 / 32H	2	End row
52 / 34H	2	Form definition range start column
54 / 36H	2	Start row
56 / 38H	2	End column
58 / 3AH	2	End row
60 / 3CH	2	Report output start column
62 / 3EH	2	Start row
64 / 40H	2	End column
66 / 42H	2	End row
68 / 44H	2	Report header start column
70 / 46H	2	Start row
72 / 48H	2	End column
74 / 4AH	2	End row
76 / 4CH	2	Report footer start column
78 / 4EH	2	Start row
80 / 50H	2	End column
82 / 52H	2	End row
84 / 54H	2	Table range start column
86 / 56H	2	Start row
88 / 58H	2	End column
90 / 5AH	2	End row
92 / 5CH	2	Input cell start column
94 / 5EH	2	Start row
96 / 60H	2	End column

Table 9.29 Symphony record structure (Opcode 003CH) (*cont.*)

Offset	Bytes	Remark
98 / 62H	2	End row
100/ 64H	2	1st Key range start column
102/ 66H	2	Start row
104/ 68H	2	End column
106/ 6AH	2	End row
108/ 6CH	2	2nd Key range start column
110/ 6EH	2	Start row
112/ 70H	2	End column
114/ 72H	2	End row
116/ 74H	2	3rd Key range start column
118/ 76H	2	Start row
120/ 78H	2	End column
122/ 7AH	2	End row
124/ 7CH	1	Last command
		00H = No command
		01H = Find
		02H = Extract
		03H = Delete
		04H = Unique
125/ 7DH	1	1st Key order
		00H = Descending
		FFH = Ascending
126/ 7EH	1	2nd Key order
		00H = Descending
		FFH = Ascending
127/ 7FH	1	3rd Key order
		00H = Descending
		FFH = Ascending
128/ 80H	1	Report records flag
		00H = Multiple records
		FFH = One record
129/ 81H	1	Records flag
		00H = Multiple records
		FFH = One record
130/ 82H	1	Marks
		00H = Yes
		FFH = No

Table 9.29 Symphony record structure (Opcode 003CH) (*cont.*)

9.1.24 QUERY_NAME (Opcode 003DH)

This data record is used to store the current QUERY name.

Offset	Bytes	Remark
00H	2	Opcode QUERY_NAME = 003DH
02H	2	Length = 0010H
04H	16	QUERY name (ASCIIZ string)

Table 9.30 Symphony record structure (Opcode 003DH)

9.1.25 PRINT (Opcode 003EH)

This data record contains the definitions for the PRINT record in Symphony.

Offset	Bytes	Remark
00 / 00H	2	Opcode PRINT = 003EH
02 / 02H	2	Length = 02A7H (679 bytes)
04 / 04H	16	Name (ASCIIZ string)
20 / 14H	2	Source range start column
22 / 16H	2	Start row
24 / 18H	2	End column
26 / 1AH	2	End row
28 / 1CH	2	Row border start column
30 / 1EH	2	Start row
32 / 20H	2	End column
34 / 22H	2	End row
36 / 24H	2	Column border start column
38 / 26H	2	Start row
40 / 28H	2	End column
42 / 2AH	2	End row
44 / 2CH	2	Destination range start column
46 / 2EH	2	Start row

Table 9.31 Symphony record structure (Opcode 003EH) (*continues over...*)

Offset	Bytes	Remark
48 / 30H	2	End column
50 / 32H	2	End row
52 / 34H	1	PRINT Format
		00H = As displayed
		Else: Formulas
53 / 35H	1	Page breaks
		00H = Yes
		Else = No
54 / 36H	1	Line spacing
55 / 37H	2	Left margin
57 / 39H	2	Right margin
59 / 3BH	2	Page length
61 / 3DH	2	Top of page
63 / 3FH	2	Bottom of page
65 / 41H	41	Set-up string (ASCIIZ string, 40 bytes)
106/ 6AH	241	Header (ASCIIZ string, 240 bytes)
347/15BH	241	Footer (ASCIIZ string, 240 bytes)
589/24DH	16	Source database name (ASCIIZ string)
605/25DH	1	Attribute
		00H = No
		Else = Yes
606/25EH	1	Space compression
		00H = No
		Else = Yes
607/25FH	1	Destination file name
		00H = Printer
		01H = File
		02H = Range
608/260H	2	Start page
610/262H	2	End page
612/264H	70	Destination file name (ASCIIZ string)
682/2AAH	1	Wait flag
		00H = No
		Else = Yes

Table 9.31 Symphony record structure (Opcode 003EH) (*cont.*)

Spreadsheets

9.1.26 PRINT_NAME (Opcode 003FH)

This data record is used to store the current name of the PRINT record.

Offset	Bytes	Remark
00H	2	Opcode PRINT_NAME = 003FH
02H	2	Length = 0010H
04H	16	ASCIIZ string with PRINT name

Table 9.32 Symphony record structure (Opcode 003FH)

9.1.27 GRAPH_2 (Opcode 0040H)

This data record describes the settings for the production of graphs in Symphony.

Offset	Bytes	Remark	
00 / 00H	2	Opcode GRAPH_2 = 0040H	
02 / 02H	2	Length = 01F3H (499 bytes)	
04 / 04H	16	Name (ASCIIZ string)	
20 / 14H	2	X Range	Start column
22 / 16H	2		Start row
24 / 18H	2		End column
26 / 1AH	2		End row
28 / 1CH	2	A Range	Start column
30 / 1EH	2		Start row
32 / 20H	2		End column
34 / 22H	2		End row
36 / 24H	2	B Range	Start column
38 / 26H	2		Start row
40 / 28H	2		End column
42 / 2AH	2		End row
44 / 2CH	2	C Range	Start column
46 / 2EH	2		Start row
48 / 30H	2		End column
50 / 32H	2		End row

Table 9.33 Symphony record structure (Opcode 0040H) (*continues over...*)

Offset	Bytes	Remark	
52 / 34H	2	D Range	Start column
54 / 36H	2		Start row
56 / 38H	2		End column
58 / 3AH	2		End row
60 / 3CH	2	E Range	Start column
62 / 3EH	2		Start row
64 / 40H	2		End column
66 / 42H	2		End row
68 / 44H	2	F Range	Start column
70 / 46H	2		Start row
72 / 48H	2		End column
74 / 4AH	2		End row
76 / 4CH	2	A Labels	Start column
78 / 4EH	2		Start row
80 / 50H	2		End column
82 / 52H	2		End row
84 / 54H	2	B Labels	Start column
86 / 56H	2		Start row
88 / 58H	2		End column
90 / 5AH	2		End row
92 / 5CH	2	C Labels	Start column
94 / 5EH	2		Start row
96 / 60H	2		End column
98 / 62H	2		End row
100/ 64H	2	D Labels	Start column
102/ 66H	2		Start row
104/ 68H	2		End column
106/ 6AH	2		End row
108/ 6CH	2	E Labels	Start column
110/ 6EH	2		Start row
112/ 70H	2		End column
114/ 72H	2		End row
116/ 74H	2	F Labels	Start column
118/ 76H	2		Start row
120/ 78H	2		End column
122/ 7AH	2		End row

Table 9.33 Symphony record structure (Opcode 0040H) (*cont.*)

Offset	Bytes	Remark
124/ 7CH	1	Graph type 00H = XY-graph 01H = Bar graph 02H = Pie chart 04H = Line 05H = Stacked bar
125/ 7DH	1	Grid type 00H = No grid 01H = Horizontal 02H = Vertical 03H = Both
126/ 7EH	1	Color 00H = Black and white FFH = Colors
127/ 7FH	1	A Range line format 00H = No lines 01H = Line 02H = Symbol 03H = Line + Symbol
128/ 80H	1	B Range line format 00H = No lines 01H = Line 02H = Symbol 03H = Line + Symbol
129/ 81H	1	C Range line format 00H = No lines 01H = Line 02H = Symbol 03H = Line + Symbol
130/ 82H	1	D Range line format 00H = No line 01H = Line 02H = Symbol 03H = Line + Symbol
131/ 83H	1	E Range line format 00H = No line 01H = Line 02H = Symbol 03H = Line + Symbol

Table 9.33 Symphony record structure (Opcode 0040H) (*cont.*)

Offset	Bytes	Remark
132/ 84H	1	F Range line format 00H = No line 01H = Line 02H = Symbol 03H = Line + Symbol
133/ 85H	1	A Range data label alignment 00H = Center 01H = Right 02H = Below 03H = Left 04H = Above
134/ 86H	1	B Range data label alignment 00H = Center 01H = Right 02H = Below 03H = Left 04H = Above
135/ 87H	1	C Range data label alignment 00H = Center 01H = Right 02H = Below 03H = Left 04H = Above
136/ 88H	1	D Range data label alignment 00H = Center 01H = Right 02H = Below 03H = Left 04H = Above
137/ 89H	1	E Range data label alignment 00H = Center 01H = Right 02H = Below 03H = Left 04H = Above
138/ 8AH	1	F Range data label alignment 00H = Center 01H = Right 02H = Below

Table 9.33 Symphony record structure (Opcode 0040H) (*cont.*)

Offset	Bytes	Remark
139/ 8BH	1	Scaling X-axis
		00H = Automatic
		FFH = Manual
140/ 8CH	8	X-Axis lower limit
		64-bit IEEE floating point
148/ 94H	8	X-Axis upper limit
		64-bit IEEE floating point
156/ 9CH	1	Scaling Y-Axis
		00H = Automatic
		FFH = Manual
157/ 9DH	8	Y-Axis lower limit
		64-bit IEEE floating point
165/ A5H	8	Y-Axis upper limit
		64-bit IEEE floating point
173/ ADH	40	Text first title (40 characters)
213/ D5H	40	Text second title (40 characters)
253/ FDH	40	Text X-Axis (40 characters)
293/125H	40	Text Y-Axis (40 characters)
333/14DH	20	Legend A-Axis (20 characters)
353/161H	20	Legend B-Axis (20 characters)
373/175H	20	Legend C-Axis (20 characters)
393/189H	20	Legend D-Axis (20 characters)
413/19DH	20	Legend E-Axis (20 characters)
433/1B1H	20	Legend F-Axis (20 characters)
53/1C5H	1	X-Format
454/1C6H	1	Y-Format
455/1C7H	2	Skip factor
457/1C9H	1	Scale factor X-Axis:
		00H = On
		FFH = Off
458/1CAH	1	Scale factor Y-Axis:
		00H = On
		FFH = Off

Table 9.33 Symphony record structure (Opcode 0040H) (*cont.*)

Offset	Bytes	Remark
459/1CBH	1	Suppress: 00H = On Else = Off
460/1CCH	8	Origin bar graph (IEEE floating-point)
468/1D4H	8	X linear scale (float)
476/1DCH	8	Y linear scale (float)
484/1E4H	1	X log scale
485/1E5H	1	Y log scale
486/1E6H	1	Color X graphic region (hue)
487/1E7H	1	Color A graphic region (hue)
488/1E8H	1	Color B graphic region (hue)
489/1E9H	1	Color C graphic region (hue)
490/1EAH	1	Color D graphic region (hue)
491/1EBH	1	Color E graphic region (hue)
492/1ECH	1	Color F graphic region (hue)
493/1EDH	2	Width Y-Axis
495/1EFH	8	Aspect

Table 9.33 Symphony record structure (Opcode 0040H) (*cont.*)

9.1.28 GRAPH_NAME (Opcode 0041H)

This data record contains the current name of the GRAPH record.

Offset	Bytes	Remark
00H	2	Opcode GRAPH_NAME = 0041H
02H	2	Length = 0010H
04H	16	GRAPH name (ASCIIZ string)

Table 9.34 Symphony record structure (Opcode 0041H)

Spreadsheets

9.1.29 ZOOM (Opcode 0042H)

ZOOM describes the original coordinates of an enlarged window.

Offset	Bytes	Remark
00H	2	Opcode ZOOM = 0042H
02H	2	Length = 0009H
04H	1	ZOOM Flag
		0 = ZOOM off
		1 = ZOOM on
05H	2	X-coordinate
07H	2	Y-coordinate
09H	2	Column depth
0BH	2	Row depth

Table 9.35 Symphony record structure (Opcode 0042H)

9.1.30 SYMPHONY_SPLIT (Opcode 0043H)

This data record is used to store the number of *split* windows. The structure of the record is shown below:

Offset	Bytes	Remark
00H	2	Opcode SYMPHONY_SPLIT = 0043H
02H	2	Length = 0002H
04H	2	Number of split windows

Table 9.36 Symphony record structure (Opcode 0043H)

9.1.31 NUMBER_SCREEN_ROWS (Opcode 0044H)

This data record determines the number of rows displayed on screen.

Offset	Bytes	Remark
00H	2	Opcode NUMBER_SCREEN_ROWS = 0044H
02H	2	Length = 0002H
04H	2	Rows on screen

Table 9.37 Symphony record structure (Opcode 0044H)

9.1.32 NUMBER_SCREEN_COLUMNS (Opcode 0045H)

This data record determines the number of columns displayed on screen.

Offset	Bytes	Remark
00H	2	Opcode NUMBER_SCREEN_COLUMNS = 0045H
02H	2	Length = 0002H
04H	2	Columns on screen

Table 9.38 Symphony record structure (Opcode 0045H)

9.1.33 RULER (Opcode 0046H)

This data record stores the ruler-range. The structure is as follows:

Offset	Bytes	Remark
00H	2	Opcode RULER = 0046H
02H	2	Length = 0019H (25 bytes)
04H	16	Name (ASCIIZ string)
14H	2	Range start column
16H	2	Range start row
18H	2	Range end column
1AH	2	Range end row
1CH	1	Range type 0 = Single cell 1 = Range

Table 9.39 Symphony record structure (Opcode 0046H)

The last byte specifies whether the data in the range field relates to a whole range or simply to a single cell.

9.1.34 NAMED_SHEET (Opcode 0047H)

In this data record, the coordinate for a named data range is stored. The structure is defined as shown in Table 9.40.

Offset	Bytes	Remark
00H	2	Opcode NAMED_SHEET = 0047H
02H	2	Length = 0019H (25 bytes)
04H	16	Name (ASCIIZ string)
14H	2	Range start column
16H	2	Range start row
18H	2	Range end column
1AH	2	Range end row
1CH	1	Range type
		0 = Single cell
		1 = Range

Table 9.40 Symphony record structure (Opcode 0047H)

The last byte specifies whether the data in the range field relates to a whole range or simply to a single cell.

9.1.35 AUTO_COMM (Opcode 0048H)

This data record contains the name of the communications file which is to be loaded automatically.

Offset	Bytes	Remark
00H	2	Opcode AUTO_COMM = 0048H
02H	2	Length = 0041H (65 bytes)
04H	65	Path name (ASCIIZ string)

Table 9.41 Symphony record structure (Opcode 0048H)

The file name, including drive and path name, must be specified in the ASCIIZ string. Symphony uses this file name to load the relevant communications file automatically.

9.1.36 AUTO_MACRO (Opcode 0049H)

This data record specifies a range that contains a macro. The macro is executed automatically.

Offset	Bytes	Remark
00H	2	Opcode AUTO_MACRO = 0049H
02H	2	Length = 0008H
04H	2	Start column
06H	2	Start row
08H	2	End column
0AH	2	End row

Table 9.42 Symphony record structure (Opcode 0049H)

9.1.37 PARSE (Opcode 004AH)

This data record contains the addresses for a range of cells containing information on the QUERY command.

Offset	Bytes	Remark
00H	2	Opcode PARSE = 004AH
02H	2	Length = 0010H (16 bytes)
04H	2	Parse range start column
06H	2	Parse range start row
08H	2	Parse range end column
0AH	2	Parse range end row
0CH	2	Review range start column
0EH	2	Review range start row
10H	2	Review range end column
12H	2	Review range end row

Table 9.43 Symphony record structure (Opcode 004AH)

9.1.38 WKS_PASSWORD (Opcode 004BH)

This data record is used for decoding an encrypted worksheet. The record type is supported from LOTUS 1-2-3, version 2.0 onwards and in Symphony, from version 1.1.

Offset	Bytes	Remark
00H	2	Opcode WKS_PASSWORD = 004BH
02H	2	Length = 0004H
04H	4	Password

Table 9.44 Symphony record structure (Opcode 004BH)

The precise meaning of this record is not known.

9.1.39 HIDDEN_VECTOR (Opcode 0064H)

This data record contains 32 bytes, representing 256 individual bits. One column of the work sheet is allocated to each bit. If the bit is set to 1, the column is *hidden*, that is, not visible.

Offset	Bytes	Remark
00H	2	Opcode HIDDEN_VECTOR = 0064H
02H	2	Length = 0020H (32 bytes)
04H	32	Bit field

Table 9.45 Symphony record structure (Opcode 0064H)

The bit field is arranged so that the lowest byte is stored first. Bit 0 in byte 0 thus corresponds to the first column. This function is only available from Symphony 1.1 onwards.

9.1.40 CELL_POINTER_INDEX (Opcode 0096H)

From Symphony version 1.1 onwards, this data record contains the `cell pointer index`. It is structured as follows:

Offset	Bytes	Remark
00H	2	Opcode CELL_POINTER_INDEX = 0096H
02H	2	Length = 0006H
04H	2	Column number (integer)
06H	2	Number of lowest row active cell
08H	2	Number of highest row active cell

Table 9.46 Symphony record structure (Opcode 0096H)

This record defines the range of active cells in a column. The exact meaning of this record is not known.

In later versions of Symphony, additional opcodes are defined. The contents of the corresponding records are, however, not yet known. It should be relatively simple to identify them on the basis of the above information. Since the opcodes are upwardly compatible, data can generally be read from future file versions.

10

Data Interchange Format (DIF)

The *exchange of data between LOTUS 1-2-3 /Symphony and external programs via WKS/WK1 files presents considerable problems. This is especially true if only the calculation data are required. Some years ago, LOTUS Development defined an ASCII format allowing data to be interchanged between various applications, regardless of the current program. This format is called* Data Interchange Format (DIF) *and currently represents a standard which is supported by many other products.*

DIF only enables the interchange of data in ASCII format between various applications. Program-specific information such as cell formats or calculation formulas is not transferable.

The idea of the DIF standard is based on the transfer of data from spreadsheet cells in records, by column or by row, in the form of ASCII text. In DIF, the columns are referred to as *vectors* and the rows as *tuples*. A DIF file is composed of two sections, as shown in Figure 10.1:

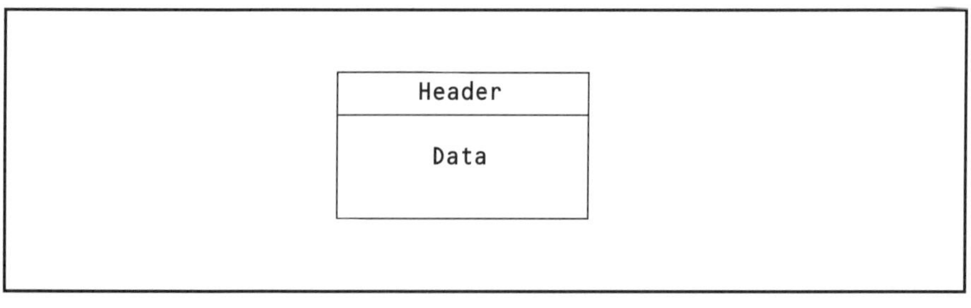

Figure 10.1
Structure of a DIF file

Before the actual data, there is a header containing information and definitions relating to the spreadsheet. The basic structures of the header and data records are described below.

10.1 The structure of the DIF header

The DIF header consists of at least four mandatory entries and various optional entries. Each header entry has the following format:

```
<Topic>
<Vector>,<Value>
"<String>"
```

The fields have been enclosed in angle brackets < > and have a special meaning.

`Topic` contains the keyword – a name with a maximum length of 32 upper-case letters – which specifies the record type. The following record types, at least, must occur in the header:

- TABLE
- VECTORS
- TUPLES
- DATA

Additional keywords for optional record types are presented on the following pages.

The `vector` field contains a numeric value, which specifies the interpretation of the subsequent data. The entry `0` indicates that the record relates to the complete table. All positive non-zero values specify the column to which the record relates. The numeric value in the next field must always be set to `0`, unless otherwise specified.

An optional text string can appear in the third line. If no text is to be transferred, two double inverted commas (`""` without any intervening space) appear in this position.

The four types of record `TABLE`, `VECTOR`, `TUPLES` and `DATA` are structured as follows.

10.1.1 TABLE

Information about the table is stored in this record. The format is as follows:

```
TABLE
0,<version>
"<Title>"
```

The `vector` field must be `0`, no other value is permitted. The version number in the next field must be set to `1`. An ASCII string, for example the name of the program to be produced, can be stored in the title line. If no text is entered, at least two double inverted commas with no spaces between them should be output to complete the record. Angle brackets (`<` and `>`), such as those used above for marking the fields, may not occur in the DIF file. A DIF file must start with a `TABLE` record type.

10.1.2 VECTORS

The next record in the DIF header specifies the number of *vectors* (columns) in the table. The format is as follows:

```
VECTORS
0,<Count>
""
```

In the `vector` field, the value `0` is compulsory, because the information relates to the whole table. The `count` field specifies the number of columns in the transferred table. The `text` field remains blank but its position must be indicated with two double inverted commas. A record of this type must not follow directly after the `TABLE` record. However, it is important that it is positioned before the first record containing vector definitions (for example, `LABELS`).

10.1.3 TUPLES

The number of *tuples* (rows) within a table is specified in a record whose format is as follows:

```
TUPLES
0,<Count>
""
```

The `vector` field must always contain the value `0`, because the record relates to the whole table. `Count` specifies the number of rows in the table. The `text` field remains blank but must be indicated by inverted commas.

10.1.4 DATA

This record type is also required in the DIF header. It marks the end of the header and is structured as shown below:

```
DATA
0,0
""
```

The record has a fixed structure as shown. It is followed by the records for the data section.

Figure 10.2 shows an example of the minimum required header for a DIF file.

```
TABLE               ; Header
0,1                 ; 0 = complete table, version 1
"Testdata"          ; Title
VECTORS             ; column definition
0,5                 ; 5 columns
""                  ; no text
TUPLES              ; row definition
0,10                ; 10 rows
""                  ; no text
DATA                ; End DIF Header
0,0
""
```

Figure 10.2 Example of a DIF header

The construction of this header is based on the data from the test spreadsheet shown in Figure 6.1. The comments (prefixed by a semicolon in the figure) do not belong to the DIF file and have been added by way of explanation.

The DIF format specification permits further optional record types (for example column headings), although these are not supported by all programs. For the sake of completeness, these record types are listed below.

10.1.5 LABEL

This record type enables a heading to be defined for one or more columns. The structure of the record is shown below:

```
LABEL
<Vector>,<Lines>
"<Text>"
```

The number of the relevant column is stored in the `vector` field. If the heading relates to several columns, the appropriate number of columns should be entered in the next field – otherwise, enter the value 1. The actual heading appears in the third line, enclosed in inverted commas.

10.1.6 COMMENT

This record can be used to store additional information (comment text) about a column. The structure is shown below:

```
COMMENT
<Vector>,<Lines>
"<Comment>"
```

The `vector` field contains the number of the relevant column; it is possible to specify several columns by placing the number of the last relevant column in `lines`. The comment is given in the third line enclosed in double inverted commas.

10.1.7 SIZE

This record type enables a fixed width in bytes to be specified for a column. The following structure applies:

```
SIZE
<Vector>,<Bytes>
""
```

The number of the relevant column is given in the `vector` field; the following field contains the length of the column in bytes. The `text` field remains blank.

10.1.8 PERIODICITY

When analyzing time sequences, information on the periodicity of the data is often required. This can be indicated using the optional record type shown below:

```
PERIODICITY
<Vector>,<Period>
""
```

The `vector` field contains the number of the column that holds the readings; the following field gives the time periods for these data. The `text` field remains blank.

10.1.9 MAJOR-START

When analyzing time sequences (for example, turnover figures), this record can be used to specify the first year to which the data refer:

```
MAJORSTART
<Vector>,<Start>
""
```

The `vector` field contains the number of the column that holds the data. The following `start` field contains the first year to which the data refer. The `text` field remains blank.

10.1.10 MINOR-START

This record type also enables time data to be specified for the data transferred.

```
MINORSTART
<Vector>,<Start>
""
```

The `vector` field contains the number of the column that holds the data. The following `start` field contains the first time value to which the data refer. This may be hours, minutes, months, and so on. The `text` field remains blank.

10.1.11 TRUE-LENGTH

Not all of the fields of a given column necessarily contain active values. The following record type is used particularly for cases in which the last fields of a column contain no significant data.

```
TRUELENGTH
<Vector>,<Length>
""
```

The `vector` field contains the number of the column that holds the data. The following `length` field indicates the number of rows containing significant data. The `text` field remains blank.

10.1.12 UNITS

This optional record type enables the transfer of units for the data of a particular column. The structure is shown below.

```
UNITS
<Vector>,0
"<Unit>"
```

The vector field contains the number of the column that contains the data. The value 0 should be entered in the following field. The unit is transferred as ASCII text within double inverted commas in the text field. If inverted commas occur in the text (for example, indicating inches), a second set of double inverted commas may be used (for example, "5 1/4"").

10.1.13 DISPLAY-UNITS

This record type is used to specify the name of a column. The column will then be displayed with the relevant name.

```
DISPLAYUNITS
<Vector>,0
"<Name>"
```

The vector field contains the number of the named column. In the third row, the name must be enclosed in double inverted commas. This text is independent of any unit which may be transferred.

This ends the description of optional record types. If a DIF file contains these record types, they can easily be skipped by the program reading it, which means that the supplementary information will be lost but the data can still be read.

10.2 The DIF data record structure

The header of a DIF file is terminated by a DATA record, to which the actual data records are appended. These records consist of two rows and have the following format:

```
<Type>,<Value>
<String>
```

The data type specifies how the following information is to be interpreted. A distinction is made between different types:

10.2.1 Special Data (-1)

This type indicates a special format which marks the beginning or end of the DIF data range. In both cases the `value` field contains the number `0`. The keywords `BOT` (Beginning of Tuple) or `EOD` (End of Data) appear in the second row. They do not need to be placed inside double inverted commas. The valid record structures are as follows:

```
-1,0
BOT
-1,0
EOD
```

The special type `BOT` marks the beginning of a row in the table. The record type `EOD` marks the end of the data in the DIF file. All the information after this record is skipped as comment. It is entirely possible for a file to have several `BOT` records; however, it should have only one `EOD` record.

10.2.2 Numeric Data (0)

Numeric data is transferred using this data type, according to the following record structure:

```
0,<Value>
<Value indicator>
```

The code for the record type is `0`. The value for the relevant cell is transferred in the following field as an ASCII string. In the next row, there is an indicator specifying the type of the value field. The following keywords are permitted for `value indicator`.

Indicator	Remark	Value
`V`	Value	Any
`NA`	Not available	0
`ERROR`	Error	0
`TRUE`	Logical constant	1
`FALSE`	Logical constant	0

Table 10.1
Value indicators in DIF files

In case of the indicators `NA` and `ERROR`, the `value` field must contain `0`. In all other cases, the value for the relevant cell is given in this field. For example, the value `10.5` can be transferred as follows:

```
0,10.5
V
```


10.2.3 String Data (1)

In addition to numeric data, texts and string constants frequently need to be transferred. To do this, `record type 1` must be used in the data field. Its structure is shown below:

```
1,0
"<String>"
```

With this record type, the value field must be `0`. The string constant is enclosed in double inverted commas and stored in the second line. The constant `Price`, shown in Figure 6.1, is transferred as DIF data with the following record:

```
1,0
"Price"
```

In DIF files, data is always output by row; the data within one row relates to successive columns. The beginning of a new row can be initiated at any time using the `BOT` (Beginning of Tuple) record. The next value will relate to the first column of the relevant row. The interchange always begins with row 1, column 1. As soon as all the columns of a row have been transferred, a `BOT` marker for a new row appears. When interpreting a DIF file, this sequence should always be observed, otherwise the results will appear as a transposed matrix (columns and rows inverted). As a rule, a record corresponding to every column and row specified in the header must be present in the data field. The end of the data range is indicated by `EOD`.

This concludes the description of the various data records in DIF files. Figure 10.3 shows the spreadsheet from Figure 6.1 as a DIF file:

```
TABLE                   ; Header
0,1
""
VECTORS
0,5
```

Figure 10.3 **Test spreadsheet as a DIF file** (*continues over...*)

```
""
TUPLES
0,10
""
DATA                    ; Header end
0,0
""
-1,0                    ; Beginning of 1st row
BOT                     ; Special data type (-1)
1,0
""
1,0
""
1,0                     ; Text constant (1)
'Test Spread Sheet'
1,0
""
1,0
""
-1,0                    ; Beginning of 2nd row
BOT
1,0
""
1,0
""
1,0
"----"
1,0
""
1,0
""
-1,0                    ; Beginning of 3rd row
BOT
1,0
""
1,0
""
1,0
""
1,0
""
1,0
""
-1,0                    ; Beginning of 4th row
BOT
1,0
"Product"
1,0
""
1,0
```

Figure 10.3
Test spreadsheet as a DIF file (*cont.*)

```
"Price"
1,0
"Disc."
1,0
"Net"
-1,0                    ; Beginning of 5th row
BOT
1,0
"----"
1,0
""
1,0
""
1,0
""
1,0
""-1,0                  ; Beginning of 6th row
BOT
1,0
"Diskettes 5 1/4"
1,0
""
0,15
V
0,10
V
0,1.350000000000000E+01
V
-1,0                    ; Beginning of 7th row
BOT
1,0
"Paper"
1,0
""
0,25                    ; Numerical value (0)
V
0,7.800000000000000E+00
V
0,2.305000000000000E+01
V
-1,0                    ; Beginning of 8th row
BOT
1,0
```

Figure 10.3 Test spreadsheet as a DIF file (*cont.*)

```
"Files"
1,0
""
0,3.500000000000000E+00
V
0,5
V
0,3.325000000000000E+00
V
-1,0                   ; Beginning of 9th row
BOT
1,0
"----------------"
1,0
""
1,0
""
1,0
""
1,0
""
-1,0                   ; Beginning of 10th row
BOT
1,0
"Sum"
1,0
""
0,4.350000000000000E+01
V
1,0
""
0,3.987500000000000E+01
V
-1,0                   ; End of data area
EOD
```

Figure 10.3 Test spreadsheet as a DIF file (*cont.*)

The comments (indicated by a preceding semicolon) do not belong to the DIF file; they have been added by way of explanation.

11

Super Data Interchange format (SDI)

Transferring *data in DIF files imposes a number of limitations in terms of the information transferred. For example, it may not be possible to create the formula contained in an individual cell or the corresponding format.*

The company *Computer Associates International* expanded the DIF definition for the product SuperCalc 3. The result is known as *Super Data Interchange* (SDI) format. In terms of its structure, an SDI file is based on a DIF file: it consists of a header followed by the data section. The keywords of the DIF definition have been adopted and expanded to include as a number of extra definitions, columns are referred to as *vectors* and rows as *tuples*.

In SuperCalc (version 2.0) the rows are numbered from 1 to 9999 and the column range is from 1 to 128. This numbering is reflected in the SDI format.

The records in the header and data section are of variable length, so that each row of an SDI file is terminated by `CR/LF` (*carriage return/line feed*). ASCII characters are used for the definition of character and column formats. Table 11.1 lists the format characters for this type of file:

Characters	Remark
`L`	Numeric values left-aligned
`R`	Numeric values right-aligned
`TL`	Text left-aligned
`TR`	Text right-aligned
`$`	Numeric values with 2 decimals and trailing zeros
`*`	Display numeric values as `*`, for example display `3` as `***`; `0` is displayed as a space
`I`	Display numeric values as integers
`G`	Standard format with best fit to cell width
`D`	Delete all formats and use standard format
`E`	Display with exponent

Table 11.1 Control codes in SDI format

11.1 The header of an SDI file

The SDI header consists of a minimum of two entries and various optional entries. Each entry in the header is structured as follows:

```
<Topic>
<Vector>,<Value>
""<String>""
```

The fields here have been enclosed in angle brackets `< >` and have a special meaning.

`Topic` contains the keyword specifying the record type. These keywords are names with a maximum length of 32 upper-case letters. The header of an SDI file must contain at least the `TABLE` and `DATA` records. Five additional, optional record types have been defined. By contrast with the record types in DIF files, these include `VECTORS` and `TUPLES`. The possible record types are:

- `TABLE`
- `VECTORS`
- `TUPLES`
- `GDISP-FORMAT`
- `COL-FORMAT`
- `ROW-FORMAT`
- `DATA`

The `VECTOR` field contains a numeric value, which specifies the interpretation of subsequent data. The entry `0` indicates that the record relates to the whole table. All positive non-zero values specify the column to which the record refers. The numeric value in the next field must always be set to `0`, unless otherwise specified.

In the third row, an optional text string may be inserted. If no text is transferred, two double inverted commas will be entered here (`""`, without any separating space between them).

The structure of the various record types is described below.

11.1.1 TABLE (mandatory)

This is the first record in an SDI file; it signals the beginning of the header. The format of the record is fixed, as shown below:

```
TABLE
0,1
""
```

Spreadsheets

The keyword `TABLE` must appear in upper-case; the second and third rows must be output with the parameters shown above. There must be no text between the inverted commas in the third row; the SDI format deviates from the DIF description in this respect.

11.1.2 VECTORS (optional)

This record type specifies the number of *vectors* (columns) in the table. The format is as follows:

```
VECTORS
0,<Count>
""
```

The `count` field specifies the number of columns in the table transferred. The `text` field remains blank and must be indicated by two double inverted commas.

11.1.3 TUPLES (optional)

This record type specifies the number of *tuples* (rows) in the table. The format is as follows:

```
TUPLES
0,<Count>
""
```

`Count` specifies the number of rows in the table. The `text` field remains blank and must be indicated by two double inverted commas.

11.1.4 GDISP-FORMAT (optional)

This record type is used for formatting the spreadsheet and has the following structure:

```
GDISP-FORMAT
<width>,0
<format string>
```

The record has no equivalent in the DIF format and is therefore structured somewhat differently. The `width` field specifies the global column width for the whole spreadsheet. In the third line, there is a string containing the formatting control character – the possible control characters are shown in Table 11.1. By contrast with the other record types, the text here must not be placed in inverted commas, for example:

```
GDISP-FORMAT
10,0
LTR$
```

The formula sets the column width for all cells in the spreadsheet to 10 characters. All numeric values are aligned with the left cell margin (`L`), while text must be right-justified (`TR`). All numeric values are output with two decimal places (`$`).

11.1.5 COL-FORMAT (optional)

In addition to the global format display (`GDISP-FORMAT`) for all cells in the spreadsheet, `COL-FORMAT` enables individual columns to have different formats; this can be repeated several times in one header. Each record is structured as follows:

```
COL-FORMAT
<col>,<width>
<format string>
```

The number of the relevant column is entered in the `col` field, and the width in characters in the following `width` field. The third row must contain a format string using the characters from Table 11.1. This string must not be enclosed in inverted commas.

11.1.6 ROW-FORMAT (optional)

This record type is used to specify the format of a row. The record consists of three lines with the following structure:

```
ROW-FORMAT
<row>,<width>
<format string>
```

The number of the relevant row is specified in the `row` field. The following `width` field defines the width of the individual cells. In the third row, there must be a format string using the characters from Table 11.1; the string must not be enclosed in inverted commas. This record type may appear in the header several times. The format of each row can thus be set in any way required.

Spreadsheets

11.1.7 DATA (mandatory)

This record type closes the SDI header and is mandatory. It indicates the beginning of the data section and is structured as follows:

```
DATA
0,0
""
```

Figure 11.1 shows an example of an SDI header.

The comments (preceded by semicolons) do not belong to the SDI file; they have been added by way of information.

```
TABLE      ; Header
0,1        ; 0 = complete table, version 1
""
COL-FORMAT ; Column definition
0,5        ; Column 0, 5-character width
""
DATA       ; End of SDI Header
0,0
""
```

Figure 11.1 Example of an SDI header

11.2 Data section of an SDI file

The data section begins after the `DATA` record. In this section, there must be an entry for every cell of the spreadsheet. Cell A1 of the table is transferred first. This is followed by cells B1 to X2 of the first row, each new row being started with the keyword `BOT`, a blank row (`CR/LF`) or some other form of separator (for example a semicolon).

The actual data records are structured as follows:

```
<Typ>,<Value>
<String>
```

The record type is stored in `typ`, as shown in Table 11.2:

Type	Remark
1	Text
0	Numeric value
-1	Data definition
-2	GOTO specification
-3	Input display format
-4	Calculation formula
-5	Repeat counter

Table 11.2 Record types for SDI data

Seven different data types are defined in SDI format; the meaning of the remaining fields depends on the data type. The relevant structures are described below:

11.2.1 Text Entry (Typ = 1)

This data type is used for the transfer of texts in SDI format. The structure is as follows:

```
1,<Value>
<String>
```

The last row contains the text to be transferred. However, if this contains only blanks, they must be enclosed in double inverted commas. The `value` field may contain `0` or `1`. These values specify how the subsequent text is to be interpreted. If the value is `0`, the following row will contain a regular text. This text is stored in the relevant cell. Value `1` specifies that the subsequent text is repeated in several cells. Information on the number of repetitions is stored in record type `-5` (*repeat count entry*).

11.2.2 Numeric Entry (Typ = 0)

In SDI, numeric values are transferred using this data type. The record is structured as follows:

```
0,<Value>
<Format>
```

The `value` field contains the number to be transferred. The format indicator in the second row determines the representation in the relevant cell. The keywords shown in Table 11.3 are permitted in this field, in accordance with the DIF definition.

Indicator	Remark	Value
V	Value	All
NA	Not available	0
ERROR	Error	0
NULL	Cell unused	0

Table 11.3 Format for a numeric value in SDI files.

Valid numeric values are indicated by the letter `V`; the `value` field contains the numeric value as an ASCII string. With the format `NA` (*not available*) there is no numeric value available, and the relevant field contains the entry `0`. The same applies to the `NULL` and `ERROR` formats. The sample shown in Figure 11.2 contains some SDI data records:

```
00,13.000     ; valid value 13.0
V
0,0           ; value not available
NA
0,0           ; cell unused
NULL
0,0           ; wrong value
ERROR
```

Figure 11.2 Data records in SDI format

The comments do not belong to the SDI format; they have been added by way of explanation.

11.2.3 Data Definition Entry (Typ = –1)

This record type is used to indicate a new row (*Beginning of Tuple*) or the end (*End of Data*) of the data section. The following variations are permitted:

```
-1,0    ; row start
BOT
-1,0    ; end of data area
EOD
```

The keyword BOT (*Beginning of Tuple*) appears before the first data record for a new row in the spreadsheet. This is particularly useful if there are only blank cells at the end of a row. The keyword EOD (*End of Data*) marks the end of the data section. This record may be followed by further entries, but these will be ignored. The value field must contain 0.

11.2.4 Origin Specifier (GOTO) (Typ = –2)

This record type enables individual cells to be addressed. The record consists of two rows with the following structure:

```
-2,0
<String>
```

The field for the numeric values should always contain the value 0. The following row contains the cell coordinates in this format:

```
Column:Row
```

The values are separated by a colon. The cell with the coordinates Column = 10, Row = 3 would thus be addressed with the following record:

```
-2,0
10:3
```

In SuperCalc 3, the values for the column numbers may be between 1 and 128 and the row numbers between 1 and 9999. This record type enables the position of the next cell to be specified directly, which enables unoccupied cells to be skipped.

11.2.5 Level Display Formatting Entry (Typ = –3)

This data type enables the format of the preceding cell to be referenced. The record structure is as follows:

```
-3,0
<Format-String>
```


The characters shown in Table 11.1 are allowed as a `format-string`, where several characters may be combined. The format instruction for the preceding row should be adopted – if there is no preceding row, the SDI parser will issue an error message.

11.2.6 Formula Entry (Typ = –4)

SuperCalc can also read in formulas using the SDI format. The record structure is shown below:

```
-4,0
<Formula>
```

A valid calculation formula must be transferred in the formula field.

11.2.7 Repeat Count Entry (Typ = –5)

This record type uses the repetition factor which was ignored in a `Text Entry` record (Section 11.2.1), where string repetitions could be specified.

```
-5,<repetition factor>
<string format>
```

The repetition factor relates to the string in the preceding cell. Only the control character `R` may appear in the string format field. The text in the preceding cell will be copied into the following cells *n* times.

12

Standard Interface format (SIF)

***In** earlier versions of Open Access, an additional format was defined for the transfer of data; this transfers the contents of the spreadsheet as an ASCII file.*

As in the case of DIF and SDI, each element of the spreadsheet is transferred to its own cell. The first row in the file contains a number indicating the row number in the spreadsheet. Each item of information is separated by a comma, while the semicolon is used to mark the end of a spreadsheet row. Texts are enclosed in apostrophes (single inverted commas). Figure 12.1 shows the spreadsheet from Figure 6.1 in SIF format.

```
10
' ',
' ',
'Test Spread Sheet';
' ',
' ',
'================';
' '

'Product',
' ',
'Price',
'Disc.',
'Net';
'----------------';
'Diskettes 5 1/4',
15.00,
10.00,
13.50;
```

Figure 12.1 Output of a Test Spreadsheet as a SIF file (*continues over...*)

```
'Paper',
' ',
25.0,
7.80,
23.50;
'Files',
' ',
3.50,
5.00,
3.325;
'-------------------';
'Sum',
' ',
43.50,
' ',
39.875;
```

Figure 12.1 Output of a test spreadsheet as a SIF file (*cont.*)

The spreadsheet transferred in this way contains 10 rows terminated by semicolons. This is specified in the first row of the SIF file, which is then followed by the individual records.

13

Symbolic Link Format (SYLK)

***For** Multiplan, Excel and Chart, Microsoft has defined its own format for exchanging data with external programs. This format is known as Symbolic Link Format (SYLK). Not just data, but all the information required for the definition of a spreadsheet can be transferred.*

SYLK has a row-oriented record structure, where each record is terminated by `CR/LF`. The following basic structure applies to all records:

```
<Record type><Field type><Fields>
```

Each record contains several items of information and is thus divided into individual fields. Angle brackets (`<` and `>`) have been used here to distinguish the individual fields, but they should not be entered in the data records themselves. The character `#` is used below as a space marker for blank characters (`20H`).

The first entry indicates the `record type` of the record. This type specifies the structure and the meaning of the following fields and consists of one or two upper-case letters (for example `ID`, `F`, `B`, `C` and so on).

The second entry is optional and describes the `field type`. With certain record types, it is used to select various sub-functions. A semicolon is always placed before the field type as a separator. Further details are given in the description of record types.

Depending on the record type, these two entries are followed by additional fields containing data.

13.1 Record descriptions

13.1.1 ID Record (ID)

The first record within a SYLK file is the ID record type which is structured as follows:

```
<Record type>;<Field type><Field>
    ID       ;P           <Name>
```

The field type is predefined as ;P. This is followed by the name of the program that created the file in the form of an ASCII string. A valid SYLK ID record is shown below:

```
ID;PdBASE II CR/LF
```

The field type P may be omitted, in which case any text that follows the semicolon is considered to be comment.

The second field type (;N) occurs in Multiplan and Excel; it indicates that ;N protection is to be used for the cells instead of ;P protection.

The field type ;E is only defined for Excel and indicates that NE records are present as redundant formulas to support external references directly.

13.1.2 Format Record (F)

This record type describes the formatting of a cell or of the complete spreadsheet. Within the record, various field types are permitted. The individual variations are shown below:

13.1.2.1 Cell Coordinates (;Xn;Yn)

The first field type enables an individual cell to be addressed; all further definitions will then relate to this cell. The record has the following format:

```
<Record type><Field type>
    F          ;Xn;Yn
```

The column number of the relevant field is indicated after the character X, while the number following the letter Y specifies the row number. The cell A10 can be addressed using the following record:

```
F;X10;Y1
```

It should be noted that the letters used for addressing a row (A=1) are converted to numbers and that each field type in SYLK format is introduced by a semicolon.

13.1.2.2 Cell Format (;F<c1>#<n>#<c2>)

This field type enables the format of the cell to be indicated. The record itself is structured as follows:

```
<Record type> <Field type> <Fields>
    F            ;F         <c1>#<n>#<c2>
```

The character `#` is used as a place-holder for a blank (`20H`). The first `F` is the record type, while `;F` defines the format type *Cell format*. The field type is followed by several fields which are enclosed in angle brackets (`<` and `>`). The field `<c1>` contains one of the format control characters shown in Table 13.1, as an indication of the cell format of the spreadsheet.

Character	Remark
`D`	Default
`C`	Continuous
`E`	Exponent
`F`	Fixed
`I`	Integer
`G`	General
`$`	Currency $xxx.xx
`*`	Bar graph

Table 13.1 Format control characters in the `<c1>` field of an `F` format

The format control character `C` is used to produce a *continuous cross-cell display* in which the data may, if necessary, extend beyond the cell margins. Texts and values are not cut short. The letter `E` indicates representation in scientific exponential notation, while `F` indicates fixed representation. `I` is used for integer values. `G` selects the display format of the spreadsheet program in such a way that the display fits into the cell in the best possible manner (standard representation). SYLK selects currency representation by means of `$`; each value is preceded by the character `$` and the numbers have only two decimal places. The character `*` is used for the transmission of data in bar-graph form; each asterisk represents one unit.

The field `<n>` contains a value which specifies the number of *digits* per cell. The last field `<c2>` indicates how the display is to be arranged within the cell (*see* Table 13.2).

Character	Remark
D	Default
C	Center
G	General
L	Left-aligned
R	Right-aligned

Table 13.2 Format control codes in the <c2> field for text alignment

The effect of the command depends on the preceding record. If this contains the cell coordinates (F;Xn;Yn), the format code refers to the specified cell. With the record (F;Rn;Cn), the code relates to the complete row or column.

13.1.2.3 Row/column formatting (;Rn;Cn)

This field type specifies the columns and rows to which the subsequent format record refers. The structure is as follows:

```
<Recordtype><Fieldtype>
    F        ;Rn;Cn
```

The letter R specifies a row, whose number appears immediately after it. The letter C specifies a column. This field type can be used for the definition of complete rows or columns.

13.1.2.4 Default Format (;D<c1>#<n>#<c2>#<c3>)

In a similar way to the F format, this field type enables the standard format for cells to be defined. The record is structured as shown below:

```
<Recordtype> <Fieldtype> <Fields>
    F          ;D          <c1>#<n>#<c2>#<c3>
```

The character # is used as a place-holder for a blank (20H). The first F is the record type, while ;D defines the *default format*. The field type is followed by several fields which are enclosed in angle brackets (< and >). The contents of c1 and c2 are the same as for the F format. The <c3> field contains the standard width of the columns.

13.1.2.5 Comma Format (;K)

This field type indicates that numbers are to be displayed with commas. The record is structured as follows:

```
<Recordtype> <Fieldtype>
    F          ;K
```

The semicolon belongs to the field type.

13.1.2.6 Formula Format (;E)

This field type specifies the formula option, which enables Multiplan to read formulas. The following structure applies:

```
<Recordtype><Fieldtype>
    F         ;E
```

The semicolon belongs to the field type.

13.1.2.7 Width Format (;W<c1>#<c2>#<c3>)

This field type enables the width of several columns of the spreadsheet to be indicated. The record is structured as shown below:

```
<Recordtype> <Fieldtype> <Fields>
    F          ;W          <c1>#<c2>#<c3>
```

The character `#` is used as a place-holder for a blank (`20H`). The first `F` marks the record type, while `;W` indicates the field type for the width definition. The `c1` field specifies the first column to which the format applies; `c2` indicates the last column. The width of the column in characters is given in `c3`.

13.1.2.8 Font Format (;N)

This field type is only implemented in EXCEL and defines the font to be used:

```
F;N Font_Id Size
```

The font name and font size must be defined as parameters.

13.1.2.9 Picture Format (;P)

This format also exists only in EXCEL; it refers to an EXCEL picture which is stored in an `FP` record. The following syntax applies:

```
F;P Index
```

The index indicates the picture number in the FP record.

13.1.2.10 Style Format (;Sx)

This field type defines how the character font is to be used. The character x is used as a placeholder for one of the following letters:

I	Italic
D	Bold
T	Gridlines Top
L	Left
B	Bottom
R	Right

If F;SI is entered, the type faces will be displayed in italics. The format exists only in EXCEL.

13.1.2.11 Header Format (;H)

In EXCEL, this format specifies that the headings for columns and rows are to be suppressed (F;H).

13.1.2.12 Grid Format (;G)

This format is available only in EXCEL. As soon as the record F;G appears, the grid lines in the display are suppressed.

13.1.3 Boundary Record (B)

This record type defines the number of columns and rows in the spreadsheet. The structure is shown below:

```
<Recordtype> <Fieldtype> <Fields>
    B           ;X;Y
```

The field type Y specifies the number of rows; the relevant value is placed immediately after the field type. X specifies the number of columns; the number is placed after this field type.

13.1.4 Cell Format Record (C)

This record specifies how numeric or textual values are to be represented. For example, it indicates whether a cell is to be protected. Within the record, several field types are permitted. These are described in detail below:

13.1.4.1 Cell Coordinates (;Xn;Yn)

The first field type enables an individual cell to be addressed, to which all other definitions apply. The format of the record is as follows:

```
<Recordtype><Fieldtype>
    C       ;Xn;Yn
```

`X` is followed by the column number of the relevant field, while the number after the letter `Y` specifies the row number. The structure corresponds to the `F` format.

13.1.4.2 Cell Value (;K)

This field type is used for transferring the value of a numeric cell – data, text or logical values can be specified. The value is placed after the field type `K` and text must be enclosed in double inverted commas.

```
<Recordtype><Fieldtype>
    C         ;K"Turnover"
    C         ;K12345.45
```

The logical constants `false` and `true` also are placed in inverted commas; the value `ERROR` must be preceded by the character `#`.

13.1.4.3 Protected (;P)

The field type `P` activates the protection of the current cell. A *protected* cell cannot be modified.

13.1.4.4 Not Protected (;N)

If this field type occurs, the cell is not locked or write-protected.

13.1.4.5 Expression (;E<expr.>)

Using SYLK, calculation formulas can be transferred. The field type E enables the transfer of such formulas. The record is structured as follows:

```
<Recordtype> <Fieldtype> <Fields>
    C           ;E          <expr.>
```

The field type ;E is followed by a valid Multiplan calculation formula in ASCII text.

13.1.4.6 Row/column addressing (;Rn;Cn)

This field type enables rows and columns to be specified, which are referred to by the following record (S;..). The record is structured as follows:

```
<Recordtype><Fieldtype>
    F;Rn;Cn
```

The letter R specifies a row, followed directly by its number. The letter C addresses a column.

13.1.4.7 Shared Expression-Value (;S)

This record type indicates that the formula for this cell is to be collected from another cell. The coordinates are taken from the preceding ;Rn;Cn record. If the ;S-type occurs, no E (Expression) may be used in the same sequence. The field types ;D or ;G must precede the ;Rn;Cn record.

13.1.4.8 Shared Expression (;D)

This field type indicates a cell whose calculation formula is used by another cell (*see also* E format).

13.1.4.9 Shared Values (;G)

This field type indicates a cell whose value is shared by another cell (*see also* K format). In this case, the E format may not be used simultaneously.

13.1.4.10 Cell Hidden (;H)

This field type only occurs in EXCEL and indicates that the contents of a cell are not displayed (that is, they are hidden). If this attribute is set for all cells, the whole spreadsheet is protected.

13.1.4.11 Expression Matrix (;M)

This field type also is implemented only in EXCEL; it contains the expressions of a matrix. The dimensions of the matrix relate to the data in the `;T` record (top left corner) and the `;R` and `;C` records (bottom right corner). If the `;M` field type occurs, the `;K` field type is ignored. In this case no `;E` field is written either.

13.1.4.12 Table Reference (;T)

In EXCEL, this field type indicates the coordinates of the top left corner of a table (*see* Expression Matrix). The bottom right corner of the table is defined via `;R` and `;C`. The format of the record is as follows:

```
C;Tx,y
```

where `x` and `y` define the column and row numbers.

13.1.4.13 Inside a Matrix (;I)

This format also is supported only by EXCEL; it defines values within a table. When using this record type, the dimensions of the table must be defined beforehand with `;T` and `;R;C`. As soon as an `;I` field occurs, all records with the `;K` type are ignored, and no `;E` records are displayed.

13.1.5 Picture Record (P)

This record type is only supported by EXCEL and precedes all `F` records. The record has only one entry for a picture. The format is as shown below:

```
P Picture
```

An EXCEL picture is defined in the picture range.

13.1.6 Name Record (NN)

This record type specifies the range (window) from a spreadsheet (for example, Multiplan) which is to be allocated to a name. The range can then be addressed via the name; two field types are necessary for this description.

Spreadsheets

13.1.6.1 Name (;N<Name>)

The first field type defines the name of the range. The format of this record is as follows:

```
<Recordtype><Fieldtype>
    NN        ;N<Name>
```

The name of the range appears directly after the character `N` as an ASCII string.

13.1.6.2 Range (;E<Range>)

The corresponding range specified by defining the corner points should be transferred in a second field type.

```
<Recordtype><Fieldtype>
  NN      ;E<Range>
```

The definitions for the section to which the name is allocated are contained in the `range` field. An example of this type of range is shown below:

```
Rn11:n12Cn13:n14,Rn21:n22Cn23:n24,....
```

`R` stands for row and `C` stands for column. The four numbers `Rn11:n12Cn13:n14` therefore indicate a range in the worksheet.

13.1.6.3 Macro (;G)

This record type is only used with EXCEL; it describes the name of a macro to be executed. The relevant syntax is as follows:

```
NN;G ch1 ch2
```

`ch1` represents the name of the macro and `ch2` represents the command key. With Macintosh computers, only the first letter is used.

13.1.6.4 Ordinary Name (;K)

This record type is used in Multiplan 2.0 to indicate the names of unused commands and alias names. The format is as follows:

```
NN;K ch1 ch2
```

`ch1` represents the command and `ch2` represents the alias name.

13.1.6.5 Usable Function (;F)

This record type is available in EXCEL; it is used to indicate a usable function. The record has no parameters (for example, `NN;F`).

13.1.7 Options Record (O)

This record was introduced in the more recent versions of SYLK in order to transfer global options. The record has several field types.

13.1.7.1 Iteration Count (;A)

This field type defines whether an iteration is switched on. The structure of the record is as follows:

```
O;A cIter numDelta
```

The parameter `cIter` indicates whether the iteration is set. The step size for the iteration is contained in `numDelta`. This field type is used only in EXCEL.

13.1.7.2 Completion Test (;C)

This field type is used only in the more recent versions of SYLK; it carries out a completion test on the current cell. The record has no other parameters.

13.1.7.3 Protected (;P)

If this record (`O;P`) occurs in a SYLK file, the spreadsheet is protected (no password).

13.1.7.4 A1-Mode (;L)

This record type is used only in EXCEL; it indicates that A1 mode references should be used.

13.1.7.5 Manual Recalc (;M)

This record type is used only in EXCEL; it indicates that a manual recalculation is to be carried out. The record has no parameters.

13.1.7.6 Precision (;R)

In EXCEL, this record type indicates that the resolution is to be used in accordance with the formatting. The record has no further parameters.

13.1.7.7 Executable Macro (;E)

This record type refers to EXCEL files and marks an executable macro SYLK file. The record type should precede a `;G` field or an `;F` field. The same applies to the `C` record, which may also contain macro definitions.

13.1.8 Name Link (NE)

This record type enables a connection to another inactive spreadsheet (external table) to be specified. Three field types are permitted.

13.1.8.1 Name (;F<Name>)

The first field type defines the file name of the corresponding (source) spreadsheet.

```
<Recordtype><Fieldtype>
    NE        ;F<Name>
```

The character `F` is followed directly by the file name as an ASCII string.

13.1.8.2 Source Range (;S)

The corresponding range in the source spreadsheet should be indicated in a second field type.

```
<Recordtype><Fieldtype>
    NE        ;S<Range>
```

The range definitions are contained in the `range` field.

13.1.8.3 Range (;E)

The corresponding range, specified by defining the corner points in the target spreadsheet, should be given in the third field type.

```
<Recordtype><Fieldtype>
    NE       ;E<Range>
```

The range definitions are contained in the `range` field.

13.1.9 File substitution (NU)

This record type enables one file name to be substituted for another. The name is replaced in two stages.

13.1.9.1 File Name (;L<Name>)

The first field type defines the name of the file to be substituted.

```
<Recordtype><Fieldtype>
    NU       ;L<Name>
```

The character `L` is followed directly by the file name as an ASCII string.

13.1.9.2 Substitute Name (;F<Name>)

The name of the replacement file should be indicated in the second field type.

```
<Recordtype><Fieldtype>
    NU       ;F<Name>
```

13.1.10 Window (W)

This record type enables windows from the spreadsheet to be defined. The following field types apply:

13.1.10.1 Window Number (;N)

The first field type defines the number of the corresponding window.

```
<Recordtype><Fieldtype>
     W     ;Nx
```

The character `N` is followed by the window number.

13.1.10.2 Coordinates (;A y x)

The coordinates for the top left corner of the window given in the `;N` field type must be given in the second field type:

```
<Recordtype><Fieldtype>
   W       ;A y x
```

The letters `y` and `x` represent the coordinates of the cell in the top left corner.

13.1.10.3 Bordered Flag (;B)

If this field type is used, the window will be provided with a border.

13.1.10.4 Split Window (;ST)

This field type enables the window to be subdivided using a title. The following record format applies:

```
<Recordtype><Fieldtype>
   W       ;ST cy cx
```

The character `cy` specifies the number of rows in the window, while `cx` specifies the cursor position in the new window.

13.1.10.5 Split window, horizontal (;SH)

This field type enables the window to be split into two horizontal halves. The following record format applies:

```
<Recordtype><Fieldtype>
    W       ;SH 1cy cx
```

The character cy specifies the number of rows in the window. If the value 1 is placed before it, the range cannot be displayed completely in the window, but it can be scrolled. The position of the cursor in the new window is indicated in cx.

13.1.10.6 Split window, vertical (;SV)

This field type enables the window to be split into two vertical halves. The following record format applies:

```
<Recordtype><Fieldtype>
    W       ;SV cy 1cx
```

The character cy specifies the number of rows in the window. The position of the cursor in the new window is indicated in cx. If the value 1 is placed in front of it, the window can be scrolled.

13.1.10.7 Colors (;C)

This record type determines the colors for the foreground, background and borders. The structure is shown below.

```
;C n1 n2 n3
```

These parameters are defined as follows:

n1 = Color of foreground
n2 = Color of background
n3 = Color of borders

This color coding applies only to DOS, used with IBM computers or compatibles.

13.1.10.8 MAC R-Type (;R)

This record type is produced only on Macintosh machines using Multiplan.

The structure is as follows:

```
;R n1 n2 ... n14
```

The individual parameters are defined as follows:

`n1 .. n8`	Title freeze information
`n9 .. n12`	Scroll bar information
`n13 .. n14`	Split bar information

More detailed information on the meaning of these parameters is not available.

13.1.11 External Link Record (NL)

This record is only used by CHART for external communication (links). The following field types are available:

13.1.11.1 Destination Index (;C)

This field type defines an index for an external link. The following format applies:

```
;C n
```

The parameter `n` specifies the index number for the link.

13.1.11.2 Dependent Area Name (;D)

This field type indicates an area with dependent variables (dependent variable source area). The format is as follows:

```
;D expr
```

The entry `expr` defines either the name or an index for the area.

13.1.11.3 Dependent Area (;E)

This expression is used to indicate the dimensions of an area for a dependent name. The following format applies:

```
;E[RC] n
```

`R` and `C` define the relative rows and columns of the area, while `n` indicates the index.

13.1.1.4 Independent Area Name (;I)

This field type refers to a name or an index for independent (source) variables. The following format applies:

```
;I expr
```

`expr` is used to define either the name or an index for this range.

13.1.11.5 Independent Area (;J)

This expression is used to indicate the dimensions of an area for an independent name. The following format applies:

```
;J[RC] n
```

`R` and `C` define the relative rows and columns of the area, while `n` indicates the index.

13.1.11.6 File Name (;F)

This field type indicates the file name of the source area. The following format applies:

```
;F Filename
```

The `file name` parameter must contain a valid file name.

13.1.14 End of SYLK (E)

This record type indicates the end of the SYLK file. A number of rules apply to the structure of a SYLK file:

- The first record must be an `ID` record.
- The file must close with an `E` record.
- All record and field codes must be entered in upper-case letters.
- Record and field type are separated by a semicolon.
- Each record must be terminated by `CR/LF`.
- There must be no `CR/LF` characters within a record or field.

- D and G records always relate to the last C command.
- When using NE records, the file name must be defined beforehand using NU.
- The dimensions and subdivision of the window must be defined in logically ascending sequence.

The first cell of a spreadsheet is always at the top left corner (1,1). Field coordinates are indicated by the letters X (column) and Y (row). Texts must be enclosed in double inverted commas, while numeric values are transferred as fixed-point numbers or with exponents. The size and format of the table must be defined before the data transfer (B record). Data can generally be transferred using the record type C.

Figure 13.1 shows the test spreadsheet from Figure 6.1 in SYLK format.


```
ID;DEMO.SYLK
B;Y5;X10
F;W1 15
F;W2 2
F;W3 10
F;W4 10
F;W5 11
C;Y1;X3;K"Test Spread Sheet"
C;Y2;X3;K"================="
C;Y4;X1;K"Product"
C;Y4;X3;K"Price"
C;Y4;X4;K"Disc."
C;Y4;X5;K"Net"
C;Y5;X1;K"---------------"
C;Y6;X1;K"Diskettes 5 1/4"
C;Y6;X3;K15.00
C;Y6;X4;K10.00
C;Y6;X5;K13.50
C;Y7;X1;K"Paper"
C;Y7;X3;K25.00
C;Y7;X4;K7.80
```

Figure 13.1 Test spreadsheet (SYLK format) (*continues over...*)

```
C;Y7;X5;K23.05
C;Y8;X1;K"Files"
C;Y8;X3;K3.50
C;Y8;X4;K5.00
C;Y8;X5;K3.325
C;Y9;X1;K"-------------"
C;Y10;X1;K"Sum"
C;Y10;X3;K43.50
C;Y10;X5;K39.875
E
```

Figure 13.1
Test spreadsheet (SYLK format) (*cont.*)

The first line contains a comment which is not evaluated. The following rows containing the F;W records specify the column widths. These are followed by the C records, which contain the data and text. For clarity, the X and Y coordinates for each cell have been given in the C record, which is not strictly necessary in the SYLK definition. The file is terminated with the E record.

14

SYLK format extensions for CHART

For *the CHART program, Microsoft has defined a number of extensions to the SYLK format. These are described briefly below.*

14.1 Pseudo-records

These represent information which is contained within a text variable (quoted value) in the C record in a normal SYLK file. Microsoft uses these records in CHART in order to code information which is not to be altered by Multiplan.

The entries are structured in normal record format:

```
'<Recordtype>;<Fieldtype><Field>'
```

The first two letters of the name of the program that created the record are always taken as the record type.

14.1.1 Field types

14.1.1.1 Type of Data (;Ttyp)

This field type specifies the data type in one column. The record structure is as follows:

```
'xx;Ttyp'
```

The following letters may appear in `typ`:

`A`	Text alphanumeric
`D`	Date as text
`N`	Numeric value
`S`	CHART sequence

The letters `xx` are used as place-holders for the record type. However, further information is not available.

14.1.1.2 Text Align (;Atext or ;Btext)

These are two different field types which define how the texts are to be aligned.

`'xx;Atext'`	Text after string
`'xx;Btext'`	Text before string

The exact meaning of this record type is not clear.

14.1.1.3 Highlighted data entry point (;Cn)

This field type specifies an index for entry fields which are visibly highlighted when in entry mode (*see below*). The record is structured as follows:

```
'xx;Cn'
```

The relevant index value is contained in `n`.

14.1.1.4 Displayed Time (;Dn)

This field type indicates the unit for the time axis for a sequence of data which is to be displayed (or printed).

```
'xx;Dn'
```

The index n is coded as follows:

1	Year
2	Quarter
4	Month
8	Day
16	Weekday

The relevant scaling is then written into the time axis.

14.1.1.5 Display Entry Mode (;En)

This field type defines an index to a name in the top line of the screen. The record format is as follows:

```
'xx;En'
```

The parameter n is the number of the name. In entry mode, entries can then be made in this field.

14.1.1.6 Format (;F)

This field type defines the format of data sequences. The record format is as follows:

```
'xx;Fn'
```

The parameter n defines the index for the format of the data sequence. The following coding applies:

0	Short
1	Medium
2	Long

The exact meaning of these formats is not known.

14.1.1.7 Scaling (;G or ;H)

These field types define the scaling factors in units. The format is as follows:

`'xx;Gnum'`	for the value category (category, or X-axis)
`'xx;Hnum'`	for scaling the values (Y-axis)

The scaling factor is contained in `num`.

14.1.1.8 Included (;I)

This field type is defined as `included for plotting`. However, its meaning is not altogether clear.

14.1.1.9 Edited (;J)

This field type is defined as `edited`; its meaning is also unclear.

14.1.1.10 Linked (;L)

This field type defines the order of a series of values. The format is as follows:

```
'xx;Ln'
```

The record occurs in conjunction with a series of values. If several series of values occur in the `SYLK` file, the parameter `n` indicates the order of the associated value series. The value series are then stored in the `SYLK` file in the order indicated.

14.1.1.11 Type (;M)

This field type defines the type of calculation for a result value which relates to a series of values. The format:

```
'xx;Mn'
```

contains the parameter `n` which represents the following types of calculation:

Code	Type
0	Average
1	Cumulative sum
2	Difference
3	Growth
4	Link to external file
5	Percent
6	Statistics
7	Trend
8	Copy
9	Entry
10	Copy from external file

Table 14.1
Calculation type

The exact meaning of these individual functions is not currently known.

14.1.1.12 Name (;N)

This field type defines a name for the series of values (title for the series). The format is as follows:

```
'xx;Ntext'
```

The appropriate title (name) is shown in `text`.

14.1.1.13 Origin (;O)

This field type defines the origin of a data series. The format is as follows:

```
'xx;Otext'
```

The appropriate title (name) is shown in `text`.

14.1.1.14 Period (;P)

This field type indicates the period for a series of times or values. The format is as follows:

```
'xx;Pn'
```

n defines the spacing between individual values (for example, daily values recorded each hour, $n = 1$).

14.1.1.15 Dependent (;R)

This field type visibly highlights the values dependent on the entry. The record has no other parameters.

14.1.1.16 Start Value (;S)

This field type defines a start value:

```
'xx;Sn'
```

for a series of dates or values. The start value is given in the parameter n.

14.1.1.17 Time Unit (;U)

This field type defines the time unit for the series of values which relate to a date. The format:

```
'xx;Un'
```

contains an index in the parameter n with the following coding:

Code	Time Unit
1	Year
2	Quarter
3	Month
8	Day
16	Weekday

Table 14.2
Time unit

This time unit can be used for presenting the values.

In addition to these pseudo-records, CHART has a series of extensions for describing a graphic display. These records will be described briefly below. All of these record types begin with the letter G. Records describing an extensive graphic object can be followed by other records containing additional information. The sequence of the records is therefore important. The preceding records describe the context for the subsequent data records.

14.2 GS record

The syntax of this record is as follows:

```
GS; In ;F1 ;Rn ;Cn ;Mn ;Nn
```

The record describes the complete worksheet. The F1 field contains flags, the first of which indicates that only one character is used (0 or 1). In the record, the F is followed by a 0 or a 1. A 1 signifies:

Show borders field in split command

With the entry 0, borders are not shown. The number of rows is defined in Rn and the number of columns in Cn. The parameters Mn and Nn indicate the width and height of the worksheet in units of $\frac{1}{1440}$ of an inch.

It is entirely possible for a SYLK file to contain several GS records. However, each GS record must be followed immediately by GC records. The number of such records is indicated in the parameter In.

14.3 GC record

The syntax of the record is as follows:

```
GC; F6 ;Tn; Xn ;Cn ;On ;Gn ;Nn ;Ln ;En ;Un ;Rn ;An ;Dn ;Sn
```

and it describes a graphic display. The record must be followed by the records listed below:

```
GM, GL, GF, GX, GD, GN, GA (;An times), GA, GA, GE (;Sn times), GE
```

The parameter F6 represents a flag field with 6 entries which can be set to 0 or 1 (for example, F011001). The following coding applies to the individual positions:

1	Legend defined
2	100% chart (format type)
3	Three-dimensional (stacked) chart
4	Bar graph or column graph (1 = display bar or column as bar graph else display column)
5	Chart series or points in category
6	Auto series assignment

Table 14.3
Position order

The parameter ;Tn indicates the type of graph:

Code	Type
1	Bar graph or column
2	Line
3	Pie
4	Area
5	Scatter

Table 14.4
Graph type

The parameter ;On indicates the spacing within the bar graph as a percentage. In the case of clusters, the parameter Gn indicates the intervening space as a percentage. The starting angle for a pie chart is indicated in Nn.

The parameter ;An defines how many GA records containing labels are to follow. An additional two GA records for the Master Series and the Master Value labels must also follow.

The parameter ;Dn defines the number of value series to be displayed.

The parameter ;Sn specifies how many GE records containing the points of a data series are to follow. Another GE record containing the points of the master series must also follow.

The meaning of these records is shown below:

GM	Graphic position
GL	Link to other diagrams
GF	Frame of a diagram
Gx	Axis description
GD	Legend description
GN	Length of dropdown lines
GA	Labels
GZ	Defines value series
GE	Defines value series with deviation from master series

Table 14.5
Meaning of
Gx records

The structure of these records is described on the following pages.

14.3.1 GL record

The syntax of this record is shown below:

```
GL ;Rn ;Sn ;F4
```

The record describes the links between individual fields and the format information. The individual parameters are coded as follows:

;R	'Link to chart #' field in format link command; diagrams are numbered
;S	Box number as specified in 'in box #' field
;F	4 flags with the following meanings: 1. Link height 2. Link width 3. Link value axis 4. Link category axis

Table 14.6
GL record

However, the exact meaning of the individual parameters is not known at present.

14.3.2 GE record

The syntax of this record is as follows:

```
GE ;Pn ;Cn ;In ;Mn ;F7 ;En
```

This must be followed by a GN record giving a description of the borders. The record describes a series of points in a diagram (pie chart or single curve in one diagram). The meaning of the individual parameters is as follows:

;P	Pattern
;C	Color points
;I	Point or point row
;M	Symbol
;F	7 flags
;E	Exploded pie

Table 14.7
GE record

With pie charts, the parameter ;E indicates a value, as a percentage, which determines how far apart the segments are to be moved (exploded presentation).

The pattern is referred to as an index between 0 and 15; the following patterns are defined:

Code	Pattern
0	Clear
1	Solid
2	Dense
3	Medium
4	Sparse
5	White
6	!!
7	==
8	\\
9	//
10	++
11	XX
12	Dark \\
13	Light \\
14	Dark //
15	Light //

Table 14.8 Pattern definition

The color is coded as a byte value; the individual bits indicate the intensity of the basic color. The following coding applies:

Bits 0,1:	Proportion of blue
2,3,4:	Proportion of green
5,6,7:	Proportion of red

The form of the symbol for the representation of the curve is defined using an index between 0 and 9. The following coding applies:

Code	Symbol
0	No symbol
1	. (point)
2	+
3	*
4	o
5	x
6	–
7	• (filled)
8	Empty rectangle
9	Filled rectangle

Table 14.9 Symbol form

The value for the flags contains seven characters coded as follows:

Code	Flag
1.	`Auto marker style`
2.	`-`
3.	`Auto color`
4.	`Auto pattern`
5.	`Show series/point label`
6.	`Show value label`
7.	`Show value label in percent`

Table 14.10
Flag code

The option is switched on if the character in the relevant position is set to `1`.

14.3.3 GA record

This record describes the labels (lettering) in a diagram; the syntax is as follows:

```
GA ;Ttext ;F4 ;An ;Vn ;S2
```

This record must be followed by the records shown below in Table 14.11. The meaning of the individual parameters of the `GA` record is shown in Table 14.12.

`GP`	Relative position of label
`GT`	Other text attributes
`GW`	Label with arrow
`GP`	Relative position of arrow head
`GF`	Frame of a label
`GM`	Absolute position of arrow head

Table 14.11
`GA` record

`;T`	Text for object (if AutoText <> 1)
`;F`	4 flags
`;A`	Align
`;V`	Vertical align
`;S`	2 flags

Table 14.12
`GA` record parameter

The flags indicated in the parameter F are coded as follows:

1.	Label deleted
2.	–
3.	Autotext (0 = text in alpha command)
4.	Vertical alignment

Table 14.13
Flag coding

The value for the ;A command defines the following text alignments:

0	Center
1	Left
2	Right

Table 14.14
Text alignment

For vertical alignment (;V), the following formats are defined:

0	Bottom
1	Center
2	Top

Table 14.15
Vertical text alignment

The parameter ;S defines the two flags:

1	show key
2	show value

I do not currently have access to detailed information on the effect of these parameters.

14.3.4 GP record

This record describes the relative position of a label or an arrow. The following syntax applies:

```
GP ;Mn ;F2 ;On ;Yn ;Xn
```

The individual parameters should be interpreted as follows:

;M	Distance in 1/1440 inches
;F	2 flags
;O	Label type
;Y	Field for curve/point
;X	Category field

Table 14.16
GP record

The flags define two switches:

1	Set, if 'label for' field is free
2	AutoText flag

The type of label in the parameter ;O is defined as follows:

1	Title text
2	Category X-axis
3	Value Y-axis
4	Series/point

Table 14.17
Label type

14.3.5 GD record

This record describes the legend of a diagram and has the following format:

```
GD ;Tn ;Sn ;F1
```

The record must be followed by:

GT	Legend text
GF	Legend frame

The contents of the individual parameters of the GD record are defined as follows:

;T	Legend type
;S	Spacing field
;F	Auto legend

Table 14.18
Text alignment

The type of legend defines the position of the lettering:

0	Bottom
1	Corner
2	Top
3	Vertical

Table 14.19
Legend position

The distance between different objects is set in the spacing parameter, as follows:

0	Close
1	Medium
2	Open

Table 14.20
Object distance

14.3.6 GW record

This record type describes an arrow which is allocated to an axis label. The syntax is as follows:

```
GW ;Tn ;Sn ;F1
```

The parameters of the GW record are as follows:

;T	Header field
;S	Size of header text
;F	Flag (1 = Open field)

Table 14.21 GW record parameters

The parameter ;T specifies how the header line is to be set out:

0	Narrow
1	Medium
2	Wide

Table 14.22 Header line

The parameter ;S defines the size of the header text:

0	Off
1	Small
2	Medium
3	Large

Table 14.23 Header text size

This must be followed by a GN record describing the attributes of the arrow shaft.

14.3.7 GX record

This record consists only of the letters GX and has no parameters. It introduces the description of the axes, that is, it must be followed by the record types:

GY	Style for category axis
GX	Style for value axis
GR	Value axis range
GI	Category axis range
GF	Frame plot area

14.3.8 GY record

This record describes the style for category axis and has the following syntax:

```
GY ;Jn ;Nn ;Tn ;F1 ;Mn ;Dn ;On
```

The meaning of the parameters is as follows:

;J	Major tick marks
;N	Minor tick marks
;T	Labels for tick marks
;F	Auto label distance
;M	Label distance (in 1⁄1440 inch)
;O	Font type
;D	Distance

Table 14.24
GY record

The coding for the ;J and ;N parameters (tick marks) is:

0	None
1	Inside
2	Outside
3	Cross

Table 14.25
Tick marks

The following applies to the parameter `;T` (labels for tick marks):

0	None
1	Axis
2	Low
3	High

Table 14.26
Labels for tick marks

The `GY` record must be followed by:

GT	Thickness label and text attributes
GN	Line style axis
GN	Major line style
GN	Minor line style

14.3.9 GI record

This record describes the axis (category) to which the values relate (usually time or X-axis). It is structured as follows:

```
GI ;Cn ;F3 ;In
```

The meaning of the parameters is:

;C	Category (group) number (at which other axes cross)
;F	3 flags
;I	Number of (value) groups per section

Table 14.27
`GI` record parameters

The following applies to the flags:

1.	Crossing between points
2.	Crossing after last category
3.	Reverse data sequence

Table 14.28
`GI` record flags

The GI record must be followed by a GR record, defining the range of the independent variables (in case of interrupted diagrams).

14.3.10 GR record

This record describes the range (scaling) of an axis and is structured as follows:

```
GR ;In ;An ;Jn ;Nn ;Cn ;F7
```

The n values are given either as decimal numbers or in exponential form. The meaning of the individual parameters is as follows:

;I	Minimum
;A	Maximum
;J	Interval 1 (major)
;N	Interval 2 (minor)
;C	Cross axis
;F	7 flags

Table 14.29 GR record parameters

The coding for the flags is as follows:

;I	Auto minimum
;A	Auto maximum
;J	Auto interval 1 (major)
;N	Auto interval 2 (minor)
;C	Auto cross axis
;F	–

Table 14.30 GR record flags

The exact meaning of these flags is not clear.

14.3.11 GF record

This record describes the frame of a diagram and is structured as follows:

```
GF ;Cn ;Pn ;F4 ;Rn
```

The individual parameters should be interpreted as follows:

;C	Background color
;P	Background pattern
;F	4 flags
;R	Frame type

Table 14.31
GF record parameters

The coding for the color and the pattern has already been described above (see GE record). For the flags, the following coding applies:

1.	Auto position
2.	Auto size
3.	Auto color
4.	Auto pattern

Table 14.32
GF record flags

The following definitions apply to the frame type:

0	Normal
1	Bevel
2	Double
3	Round
4	Shadow

Table 14.33
Frame type

The GF record must be followed by:

GN	Line definition for margin
GM	Position of bottom left corner
GM	Size of frame (top right corner)

14.3.12 GT record

This record type describes the text attributes and has the following syntax:

```
GT ;Cn ;On ;Sn ;F2
```

The meaning of the individual parameters is as follows:

;C	Color
;O	Font
;S	Font size in $^1/_{1440}$ inch
;F	2 flags

Table 14.34
GT record parameters

The flags relate to:

1. Auto font
2. Auto color

The coding for color has been described above; however, the coding for fonts is somewhat more complex. A value between 0 and 255 is given; this defines both the font type and the style of typeface. The style is subdivided as follows:

0-63	Normal
64-127	Italic
128-191	Bold
192-255	Bold italic

Table 14.35
Font styles

Within these four ranges, various fonts are available, as shown below in Table 14.36. For example, code 1 produces the font Modern B in normal style, while code 65 produces the same font in italic style.

Modern A	–	Modern P
Roman A	–	Roman P
Script A	–	Script H
Decor A	–	Decor H
Foreign A	–	Foreign H
Symbol A	–	Symbol H

Table 14.36 Fonts

14.3.13 GN record

This record describes line attributes and has the following format:

```
GN ;Cn ;Pn ;Wn ;F2
```

The meaning of these parameters is:

;C	Color
;P	Pattern
;W	Weight
;F	2 flags

Table 14.36 GN record parameters

The flags relate to:

1. Auto color
2. Auto pattern

The codings for color and pattern have been described above. The parameter `Weight` defines the thickness of the line:

0	Light
1	Medium
2	Heavy

Table 14.38 Line thickness

14.3.14 GM record

This record type defines spacing in terms of pairs of coordinates which can be interpreted as point coordinates or sides of a rectangle. The record is structured as follows:

```
GM ;Yn ;Xn
```

The parameters:

;Y	Vertical spacing in 1/1440 inch
;X	Horizontal spacing in 1/1440 inch

should be interpreted as relative coordinate data.

14.3.15 GZ record

This record type defines a number for a (value) series in a diagram. The record has only one field:

```
GZ ;In
```

which indicates the number of the series to be adopted in the diagram.

This ends the description of the SYLK extensions for CHART. It has not been possible to present all the information to the level of detail I would have liked. This is partly because very little information on these extensions (some of it inaccurate) was available to me. Furthermore, there was no CHART package available at the time of writing to test the individual records. However, I have included the text as it stands in the hope that it may be of use to some readers.

15

Excel binary interchange format (BIFF)

This *format is used in Microsoft EXCEL for Windows and for Macintosh (and OS/2). Like LOTUS 1-2-3, a BIFF file contains a series of variable length records. These records store information (formulas, cell values, labels, and so on) about the spreadsheet. The following section describes the structure of these records.*

15.1 The BIFF record structure in versions 2.0–4.0

All BIFF versions (2.0 - 4.0) use the same record structure, shown in Table 15.1. The length of a BIFF record depends on the record type.

Offset	Bytes	Remarks
00H	2	Record type
02H	2	Record length
04H	*n*	Record data

Table 15.1 BIFF record structure

The following general points should be noted:

- The first 16-bit field defines the record type. Most of the record types are upwardly compatible. If a record structure changes, the value 200H is added to the record type for BIFF3, while 400H is added for BIFF4. The BOF record changes from 09H 00H 04H 00H 07H 00H 01H 00H in BIFF2 to

09H 02H 06H 00H 00H 00H 01H 00H 6AH 04H in BIFF3. In BIFF4 the BOF record has the signature 09H 04H....

- The second 16-bit field defines the length of the following data area in bytes. The maximum length of a BIFF record is 2084 bytes (2080 data bytes + record type + record length). Objects with more than 2080 data bytes are split into a parent record and several continuation records.
- EXCEL BIFF files are exchangeable across Windows (Intel 80x86) and Macintosh (Motorola 68xx0) platforms. These microprocessor families use different internal representations to store 16-bit words. EXCEL writes a BIFF file in the Intel format (low byte first). A Mac BIFF reader/writer must swap the bytes of each word and the words themselves in a 32-bit value. The data series 0209H 0070H 0000H 0010H A3F0H is stored as 09H 02H 70H 00H 00H 00H 10H 00H F0H A3H in the BIFF file.
- Some fields or bits in the record descriptions are marked as reserved. A program may not use these bits. If a reserved value is given as 0, this value must be stored in the record.
- Cell numbering starts with 0 (not with 1). Cell A1 is defined as row number 00H and column number 00H. Cell B3 maps onto row number 02H, column number 01H.
- Undefined or unused cells are not stored in a BIFF file, to save space.

15.2 Record types in BIFF2–BIFF4

Table 15.2 lists the record types for BIFF2–BIFF4. The length of the data area may differ between versions.

BIFF2	BIFF3	BIFF4	Record
00H	200H	200H	DIMENSIONS
01H	201H	201H	BLANK
02H	-	-	INTEGER
03H	203H	203H	NUMBER
04H	204H	204H	LABEL
05H	205H	205H	BOOLERR
06H	206H	406H	FORMULA
07H	207H	207H	STRING
08H	208H	208H	ROW
09H	209H	409H	BOF
0AH	0AH	0AH	EOF
0BH	20BH	40BH	INDEX
0CH	0CH	0CH	CALCCOUNT

Table 15.2 BIFF records (version 2.0–4.0) (*continues over...*)

BIFF2	BIFF3	BIFF4	Record
0DH	0DH	0DH	CALCMODE
0EH	0EH	0EH	PRECISION
0FH	0FH	0FH	REFMODE
10H	10H	10H	DELTA
11H	11H	11H	ITERATION
12H	12H	12H	PROTECT
13H	13H	13H	PASSWORD
14H	14H	14H	HEADER
15H	15H	15H	FOOTER
16H	16H	16H	EXTERNCOUNT
17H	17H	17H	EXTERNSHEET
18H	218H	218H	NAME
19H	19H	19H	WINDOWPROTECT
1AH	1AH	1AH	VERTICALPAGEBREAKS
1BH	1BH	1BH	HORIZONTALPAGEBREAKS
1CH	1CH	1CH	NOTE
1DH	1DH	1DH	SELECTION
1EH	1EH	1EH	FORMAT
1FH	-	-	FORMATCOUNT
20H	-	-	COLUMNDEFAULT
21H	221H	221H	ARRAY
22H	22H	22H	1904
32H	223H	223H	EXTERNNAME
24H	-	-	COLWIDTH
25H	225H	225H	DEFAULTROWHEIGHT
26H	26H	26H	LEFTMARGIN
27H	27H	27H	RIGHTMARGIN
28H	28H	28H	TOPMARGIN
29H	29H	29H	BOTTOMMARGIN
2AH	2AH	2AH	PRINTHEADERS
2BH	2BH	2BH	PRINTGRIDLINES
2FH	2FH	2FH	FILEPASS
31H	231H	231H	FONT
32H	-	-	FONT2
36H	236H	236H	TABLE
37H	-	-	TABLE2
3CH	3CH	3CH	CONTINUE
3DH	3DH	3DH	WINDOW1
3EH	23EH	23EH	WINDOW2
40H	40H	40H	BACKUP

Table 15.2
BIFF records (version 2.0–4.0) (*cont.*)

BIFF2	BIFF3	BIFF4	Record
41H	41H	41H	PANE
42H	42H	42H	CODEPAGE
43H	243H	443H	XF
44H	-	-	EFONT
4DH	4DH	4DH	PLS
50H	50H	50H	DCON
51H	51H	51H	DCONREF
52H	52H	52H	DCONNAME
55H	55H	55H	DEFCOLWIDTH
	56H	56H	BUILTINFMTCOUNT
	59H	59H	XCT
	5AH	5AH	CRN
	5BH	5BH	FILESHARING
	5CH	5CH	WRITEACCESS
	5DH	5DH	OBJ
	5EH	5EH	UNCALCED
	5FH	5FH	SAVERECALC
	60H	60H	TEMPLATE
	61H	61H	INTL
	63H	63H	OBJPROTECT
	7DH	7DH	COLINFO
	27EH	27EH	RK
	7FH	7FH	IMDATA
	80H	80H	GUTS
	81H	81H	WSBOOL
	82H	82H	GRIDSET
	83H	83H	HCENTER
	84H	84H	VCENTER
	86H	86H	WRITEPROT
	87H	87H	ADDIN
	88H	88H	EDG
	89H	89H	PUB
	8BH	8BH	LH
	8CH	8CH	COUNTRY
	8DH	8DH	HIDEOBJ
	91H	91H	SUB
	92H	92H	PALETTE
	93H	93H	STYLE
	94H	94H	LHRECORD

Table 15.2
BIFF records (version 2.0–4.0) (*cont.*)

BIFF2	BIFF3	BIFF4	Record
	95H	95H	LHNGRAPH
		96H	SOUND
		97H	SYNC
		98H	LPR
		99H	STNDARDWIDTH
		9AH	FNGROUNAME
		9CH	FNGROUPCOUNT
		A0H	SCL
		A1H	SETUP
		A2H	FNPROTO
		A9H	COORDLIST
		ABH	GCW

Table 15.2 BIFF records (version 2.0–4.0) (*cont.*)

A BIFF file starts with a `BOF` record and terminates with an `EOF` record. The other records in a BIFF file appear in a predefined order. Table 15.3 shows the record order in a BIFF3 file.

Type	Remarks
209H	`BOF` record, extended in BIFF 3
86H*	`WRITEPROT` (Document is write-protected)
2FH	`FILEPASS` (Password protection)
60H*	`TEMPLATE` (Document is a template)
87H*	`ADDIN` (Document is a macro)
5CH*	`WRITEACCESS` (Access user name)
5BH*	`FILESHARING` (File sharing and encryption)
5EH*	`UNCALCED` (Recalculation status)
20BH	`INDEX` (Index record)
61H*	`INTL` (Document is an international macro)
42H	`CODEPAGE` (Code page)
0CH	`CALCOUNT` (Iteration counter)
0DH	`CALCMODE` (Calculation mode)
0EH	`PRECISION`
0FH	`REFMODE` (Reference mode)
10H	`DELTA` (Interation step width)
11H	`ITERATION` (Iteration mode)
22H	`1904` (Date system)

Table 15.3 BIFF records (version 3.0) (*continues over...*)

Type	Remarks
2AH	PRINT HEADERS
2BH	PRINT GRIDLINES
5FH*	SAVERECALC (Recalculate before storing)
82H*	GRIDSET
83H*	HCENTER (Center horizontal)
84H*	VCENTER (Center vertical)
80H*	GUTS (Row and column gutter)
225H	DEFAULT ROW HEIGHT
8CH*	COUNTRY (Index to country code)
8DH*	HIDEOBJ (Object hide status)
81H*	WSBOOL (Boolean status)
1BH	HORIZONTAL PAGE BREAKS
1AH	VERTICAL PAGE BREAKS
231H	FONT
14H	HEADER
15H	FOOTER
26H	LEFT MARGIN
27H	RIGHT MARGIN
28H	TOP MARGIN
29H	BOTTOM MARGIN
4DH	PLS (Environment-specific print information)
40H	BACKUP
16H	EXTERNCOUNT (Number of external references)
17H	EXTERNSHEET (External sheets)
223H	EXTERNNAME (External name)
59H*	XCT (Counter CRN records)
5AH*	CRN
56H	BUILTINFMTCOUNT (Built-in format counter)
1EH	FORMAT (Number format)
218H	NAME
12H	PROTECT (Protected cells)
19H	WINDOW PROTECT (Protected window)
63H*	OBJPROTECT (Protected object)
13H	PASSWORD
243H	XF (Extended cell format)
93H*	STYLE
92H*	PALETTE
55H	DEFCOLWIDTH (Default column width)
7DH*	COLINFO (Column format)
200H	DIMENSIONS (Table size)

Table 15.3
BIFF records (version 3.0) (*cont.*)

Type	Remarks
208H	ROW
27EH*	RK (Cell with an RK number)
201H	BLANK (Blank cell)
203H	NUMBER (Cell with a number value)
204H	LABEL (Cell with a label)
205H	BOOLERR (Cell with a boolean/ERR value)
206H	FORMULA (Formula cell)
221H	ARRAY (Formula in a array)
3CH	CONTINUE (Continue record)
207H	STRING (Text in a formula)
236H	TABLE (Input per DATA TABLE)
5DH*	OBJ (Object description)
7FH*	IMDATA (Image data)
1CH	NOTE
50H	DCON (Consolidation data check)
51H	DCONREF (Reference data check)
52H	DCONNAME (Name reference)
3DH	WINDOW1
23EH	WINDOW2
41H	PANE
1DH	SELECTION
94H*	LHRECORD (Lotus help)
95H*	LHNGRAPH (Lotus help graph)
88H*	EDG
89H*	PUB
91H*	SUB
0AH	EOF

Table 15.3 BIFF records (version 3.0) (*cont.*)

Records marked * were introduced in BIFF3. Record types greater than 200H were changed in BIFF3. The following sections describe the records in BIFF2–BIFF4.

15.2.1 ADDIN – Add In Macro (record type 87H, version 3.0–4.0)

A BIFF file can contain macros from a worksheet. This record type notifies the reader that *Add In Macros* are stored in the file. The ADDIN record consist only of four bytes (record type and length) and must follow the BOF record.

15.2.2 ARRAY – Array-Entered Formula (record type 21H, version 2.0–4.0)

This record type was defined in BIFF2 and has the opcode 21H. The record describes a formula, entered in an array record. This record must follow a FORMULA record. The parsed formula is stored in an internal format (*see* the FORMULA record, Section 15.2.42). In BIFF2 the record has the following format:

Offset	Bytes	Remarks
00H	2	Record type (21H 00H)
02H	2	Record length in bytes
04H	2	First row of the array
06H	2	Last row of the array
08H	1	First column of the array
09H	1	Last column of the array
0AH	1	Recalculation flag
		>0: required recalculation
0BH	1	Length of parsed expression
0CH	*n*	Parsed expression

Table 15.4 BIFF record type 21H (version 2.0)

In BIFF3/BIFF4 a modified structure with opcode 221H is used:

Offset	Bytes	Remarks
00H	2	Record type (21H 02H)
02H	2	Record length in bytes
04H	2	First row of the array
06H	2	Last row of the array
08H	1	First column of the array
09H	1	Last column of the array
0AH	2	Option flag
0CH	2	Expression length
0EH	*n*	Parsed expression

Table 15.5 BIFF record type 221H (version 3.0/4.0)

From BIFF3, the expression can contain more than 255 bytes. The option flag is modified as follows:

Bit	Remarks
0	1: Recalculation always required
1	1: Recalculation when file is opened (ignored in BIFF3)

Table 15.6
Option flag

All other bits are unused.

15.2.3 BACKUP – Save Backup Version (record type 40H, version 2.0–4.0)

This record specifies whether or not EXCEL should save a backup version of a file. The record structure is used in all BIFF versions.

Offset	Bytes	Remarks
00H	2	Record type (40H 00H)
02H	2	Record length in bytes
04H	2	1 = Save Backup Version

Table 15.7
BIFF record
type 40H
(version 3.0/4.0)

A value of 1 will store a BACKUP in a BIFF file.

15.2.4 BLANK – Blank Cell (record type 01H, version 2.0–4.0)

This record describes an empty cell. BIFF2 uses the following structure:

Offset	Bytes	Remarks
00H	2	Record type (01H 00H)
02H	2	Record length in bytes
04H	2	Row number (starts from 0)
06H	2	Column number (starts from 0)
08H	3	Cell attributes

Table 15.8
BIFF record
type 01H
(version 3.0)

The row and column numbering starts from 0. Table 15.8 shows the cell attributes used in BIFF2.

Offset	Bit	Remarks
00H	7	1: Cell is hidden
	6	1: Cell is locked
	5-0	XF record index
01H	7-6	FONT record index
	5-0	FORMAT record index
02H	7	1: Cell is shadowed
	6	1: Cell has bottom border
	5	1: Cell has top border
	4	1: Cell has right border
	3	1: Cell has left border
	2-0	Alignment: 0 = General 1 = Left 2 = Centered 3 = Right 4 = Fill

Table 15.9 Coding of cell attribute flag in BIFF2

In BIFF3 and BIFF4 a pointer to an XF record is stored instead of the cell attribute flag. The BLANK record has opcode 201H in these versions.

Offset	Bytes	Remarks
00H	2	Record type (01H 02H)
02H	2	Record length in bytes
04H	2	Row number (starts from 0)
06H	2	Column number (starts from 0)
08H	2	Index to an XF record containing the cell format

Table 15.10 BIFF record type 201H (version 3.0/4.0)

The row and column numbering starts from 0.

Spreadsheets

15.2.5 BOF – Beginning of File (record type 09H, version 2.0–4.0)

This is the first record in a BIFF file and identifies the BIFF version. In BIFF2 the following record structure is used:

Offset	Bytes	Remarks
00H	2	Record type (09H 00H)
02H	2	Record length in bytes
04H	2	Version number
06H	2	Document type (dt) 10H: Worksheet (.XLS) 20H: Chart (.XLC) 40H: Macro sheet (.XLM)

Table 15.11 BIFF record type 09H (version 2.0)

In BIFF3 and BIFF4 an extended record structure is used (Code 209H and 409H).

Offset	Bytes	Remarks
00H	2	Record type (09H 02H or 09H 04H)
02H	2	Record length in bytes
04H	2	Version number
06H	2	Document type (dt) 10H: Worksheet (.XLS) 20H: Chart (.XLC) 40H: Macro sheet (.XLM) 100H: Workspace/workbook (.XLW)
08H	2	Reserved (00H 00H)

Table 15.12 BIFF record type 209H (version 3.0/4.0)

The version number is always 0 in BIFF3. The high byte of the version number is used in Multiplan documents as a flag byte:

0100H	File contains a Multiplan document
FE00H	Reserved

Table 15.13 Coding of the version field

The document type field (dt) specifies the type of the BIFF file (BIFF2, BIFF3 and so on). The last word in the record is used for internal purposes and should be ignored by a BIFF reader. Excel uses different extensions (XLS, XLC, XLM) for the BIFF files. The last word in the record must be set to 0.

15.2.6 BOOLERR – Cell with Err value (record type 05H)

This record describes a cell containing a boolean constant or an ERR value. The record structure is defined in BIFF2 as:

Offset	Bytes	Remarks
00H	2	Record type (05H 00H)
02H	2	Record length in bytes
04H	2	Row number (starts from 0)
06H	2	Column number (starts from 0)
08H	3	Cell attribute
0BH	1	Boolean value or ERR value
0CH	1	Type flag

Table 15.14 BIFF record type 05H (version 2.0)

The coding of the cell attribute is shown in the BLANK record (Section 15.2.4). In BIFF3 and BIFF4 the record is one byte shorter. The cell attribute field (offset 08H) is replaced by the XF record index. The cell attributes are stored in the XF record.

Offset	Bytes	Remarks
00H	2	Record type (05H 02H)
02H	2	Record length in bytes
04H	2	Row number (starts from 0)
06H	2	Column number (starts from 0)
08H	2	Index to an XF record containing the cell format
0AH	1	Boolean or ERR value (bBoolErr)
0BH	1	Type

Table 15.15 BIFF record type 0205H (version 3.0/4.0)

This record describes a boolean constant or an error value in a cell. The field type depends on the value at offset 0BH (0 = boolean, 1 = error). The value is stored in the byte at offset 0AH. Error values are defined as:

Value	Error type
00H	#Null!
07H	#DIV/0!
0FH	#VALUE!
17H	#REF!
1DH	#NAME?
24H	#NUM!
2AH	#N/A

Table 15.16 Coding of the error value

Boolean values are defined as 0 for false and 1 for true.

15.2.7 BOTTOMMARGIN – Bottom Margin Setting (record type 29H, version 2.0–4.0)

This record defines the bottom margin in inches.

Offset	Bytes	Remarks
00H	2	Record type (29H 00H)
02H	2	Record length in bytes
04H	8	Bottom margin

Table 15.17

BIFF record type 29H (version 2.0–4.0)

The bottom margin value is stored as an 8-byte IEEE floating point value.

15.2.8 BUILTINFMTCOUNT – Number of Format Records (record type 56H, version 3.0–4.0)

This record type is defined from BIFF3 and stores the number of format records.

Offset	Bytes	Remarks
00H	2	Record type (56H 00H)
02H	2	Record length in bytes
04H	2	Number of format records

Table 15.18

BIFF record type 56H (version 3.0–4.0)

BIFF2 files use the FORMATCOUNT record for this purpose.

15.2.9 CALCCOUNT – Iteration Count (record type 0CH, version 2.0–4.0)

This record is used in BIFF2–BIFF4 to store the maximum iterations option from the calculation dialog box.

Offset	Bytes	Remarks
00H	2	Record type (0CH 00H)
02H	2	Record length in bytes
04H	2	Iteration counter

Table 15.19 BIFF record type 0CH (version 2.0–4.0)

15.2.10 CALCMODE – Calculation Mode (record type 0DH, version 2.0–4.0)

This record stores the calculation mode defined in the calculation dialog box.

Offset	Bytes	Remarks
00H	2	Record type (0DH 00H)
02H	2	Record length in bytes
04H	2	Calculation mode: 0 = manual 1 = automatic −1 = automatic, except tables

Table 15.20 BIFF record type 0DH (version 2.0–4.0)

15.2.11 CODEPAGE – Code Page for File (record type 42H, version 2.0–4.0)

This record has the same structure in all EXCEL versions.

Offset	Bytes	Remarks
00H	2	Record type (42H 00H)
02H	2	Record length in bytes
04H	2	Code page

Table 15.21 BIFF record type 42H (version 2.0–4.0)

The record stores information about the code page used for the sheet. The code pages are defined in Table 15.22.

Code	Remarks
01B5H	437 IBM PC Multiplan
	850 Presentation Manager
8000H	Macintosh
8001H	ANSI (Windows) BIFF2 and BIFF3
04E4H	ANSI (Windows) BIFF4

Table 15.22 Code pages used in EXCEL

EXCEL 4.0 uses the code 04E4H for the Windows code page.

15.2.12 COLINFO – Column Format (record type 7DH, version 3.0–4.0)

This record defines the format for a range of columns.

Offset	Bytes	Remarks
00H	2	Record type (7DH 00H)
02H	2	Record length in bytes
04H	2	First formatted column
06H	2	Last formatted column
08H	2	Column width in 1/256 of the character width
0AH	2	Index to the XF record
0CH	2	Options low byte Bit 0: 1 Column range is hidden 1-7: Unused
0DH		Options high byte Bit 0-2: Outline level column range 3: Reserved (must be 0) 4: 1 Column range collapsed in outlining 5-7: Reserved (must be 0)
0EH	1	Reserved (must be 0)

Table 15.23 BIFF record type 7DH (version 3.0–4.0)

This record formats a range of columns. In BIFF2 the `COLWIDTH` record is used for this purpose. In BIFF3 the `COLWIDTH` record is obsolete and the standard width of the cells is stored in a `DEFCOLWIDTH` record. In BIFF4 the `STANDARDWIDTH` record is used to store the cell width.

15.2.13 COLUMNDEFAULT – Standard Cell Attributes (record type 20H, version 2.0)

This record type is used in BIFF2 to store the standard cell attributes.

Offset	Bytes	Remarks
00H	2	Record type (20H 00H)
02H	2	Record length in bytes
04H	2	First column with standard format
06H	2	Last column with standard format
08H	*n*	Field with standard cell attributes

Table 15.24 BIFF record type 20H (version 2.0)

The coding of the cell attributes is defined in the `BLANK` record (*see* Section 15.2.4).

15.2.14 COLWIDTH – Column Width (record type 24H, version 2.0)

This record type is used only in BIFF2 and defines the standard cell width.

Offset	Bytes	Remarks
00H	2	Record type (24H 00H)
02H	2	Record length in bytes
04H	1	First column in a range
05H	1	Last column in a range
06H	2	Column width in $\frac{1}{256}$ of the character width

Table 15.25 BIFF record type 24H (version 2.0)

The column width is defined in $\frac{1}{256}$ of a character width. In BIFF3 the `COLINFO` record is used to store this information.

15.2.15 CONTINUE – Continue Record (record type 3CH, version 2.0–4.0)

The maximum length of a BIFF record is 2084 bytes (including the header). If a data area is longer than 2080 bytes, it is stored in a parent record and several `CONTINUE` records.

Offset	Bytes	Remarks
00H	2	Record type (3CH 00H)
02H	2	Record length in bytes
04H	*n*	Data

Table 15.26 BIFF record type 3CH (version 2.0–4.0)

The interpretation of the data depends on the previous parent record.

15.2.16 COORDLIST – Polygon Coordinates (record type A9H, version 4.0)

This record type is defined from BIFF4 and is used to store the vertex coordinates of a polygon.

Offset	Bytes	Remarks
00H	2	Record type (A9H 00H)
02H	2	Record length in bytes
04H	*n*	Data

Table 15.27 BIFF record type A9H (version 4.0)

The coordinates are stored as X,Y pairs (unsigned integer words). The coordinates define a bounding box of 4000 by 4000 points.

15.2.17 COUNTRY – Country Settings (record type 8CH, version 3.0–4.0)

The COUNTRY record defines the standard country code or the settings from WIN.INI.

Offset	Bytes	Remarks
00H	2	Record type (8CH 00H)
02H	2	Record length in bytes
04H	2	Standard country code (iCountryDef)
06H	2	WIN.INI country code (iCountryIni)

Table 15.28 BIFF record type 8CH (version 3.0–4.0)

The default settings are defined by the EXCEL version that writes the document. The US version uses the entry 1. The field iCountryIni contains the WIN.INI settings for the country. The index is calculated from the international telephone country code (1 = USA, 49 = Germany, 32 = Belgium, 44 = GB, and so on).

15.2.18 CRN – Record Count (record type 5AH, version 3.0–4.0)

The CRN record describes non-resident formula operands in BIFF3/BIFF4.

Offset	Bytes	Remarks
00H	2	Record type (5AH 00H)
02H	2	Record length in bytes
04H	1	Last column of non-resident operand
05H	1	First column of non-resident operand
06H	2	Row of non-resident operand
04H	x	Operand structure

Table 15.29 BIFF record type 5AH (version 3.0–4.0)

Spreadsheets

The operand structure depends on the stored values.

Cell operand is a number

Offset	Bytes	Remarks
00H	1	01H indicates a number
01H	8	8-byte IEEE value

Table 15.30 Operand structure for numbers

Cell operand is a string

Offset	Bytes	Remarks
00H	1	02H indicates a string
01H	1	String length in bytes
21H	*x*	String

Table 15.31 Operand structure for strings

Cell operand is a logical variable

Offset	Bytes	Remarks
00H	1	04H indicates a logical value
01H	2	1 = true, 0 = false
03H	6	Unused

Table 15.32 Operand structure for logical values

Cell operand is an ERROR value

Offset	Bytes	Remarks
00H	1	10H indicates an ERROR value
01H	2	Error number
03H	6	Unused

Table 15.33 Operand structure for ERROR values

For example, a formula's data are defined as:

```
=SUM(EXT.XLS!A1:A3)
```

The data are stored in the external file `EXT.XLS`. The formula creates a `CRN` record with the cell description (`A1:A3`). If a formula contains several rows or independent ranges, a `CRN` record is created for each item. If several formulas use the same range, only one `CRN` record is created.

15.2.19 DCON – Data Consolidation (record type 50H, version 2.0–4.0)

This record stores information from the *Consolidation* dialog box, and is used in all BIFF versions.

Offset	Bytes	Remarks
00H	2	Record type (50H 00H)
02H	2	Record length in bytes
04H	2	Index to the consolidate function
06H	2	1 = Left column option is on
08H	2	1 = Top row option is on
06H	2	1 = Create links to source Data option is on

Table 15.34 BIFF record type 50H (version 3.0–4.0)

Offset 04H contains an index to the data consolidation function.

Value	Function
0	AVERAGE
1	COUNT
2	COUNTA
3	MAX
4	MIN
5	PRODUCT
6	STDEV
7	STDEVP
8	SUM
9	VAR
10	VARP

Table 15.35 Consolidation function indices

15.2.20 DCONNAME – Data Consolidation Named Reference (record type 52H, version 2.0–4.0)

This record stores a named range, which should be consolidated:

Offset	Bytes	Remarks
00H	2	Record type (52H 00H)
02H	2	Record length in bytes
04H	1	Length of range name source data
05H	*n*	Range name source data
xxH	1	Length of document name
xxH	*n*	Document name

Table 15.36 BIFF record type 52H (version 2.0–4.0)

15.2.21 DCONREF – Data Consolidation Reference (record type 51H, version 2.0–4.0)

This record describes a cell range which should be consolidated, and is used in all BIFF versions.

Offset	Bytes	Remarks
00H	2	Record type (51H 00H)
02H	2	Record length in bytes
04H	2	First row of source data
06H	2	Last row of source data
08H	1	First column of source data
09H	1	Last column of source data
0AH	1	Length of document name
0BH	*n*	Document name

Table 15.37 BIFF record type 51H (version 2.0–4.0)

The *document name* field contains the name in an encoded format (*see* EXTRNSHEET record, Section 15.2.31).

15.2.22 DEFAULTROWHEIGHT – Default Row Height (record type 25H, version 2.0–4.0)

This record is available in all BIFF versions and defines the default cell height. The record structure in BIFF2 is shown in the following table:

Offset	Bytes	Remarks
00H	2	Record type (25H 00H)
02H	2	Record length in bytes
04H	2	Default cell height

Table 15.38 BIFF record type 25H (version 2.0)

The cell height is defined in 1/20 point. In BIFF3 and BIFF4 a modified record structure is used, which has the opcode 225H.

Offset	Bytes	Remarks
00H	2	Record type (25H 02H)
02H	2	Record length in bytes
04H	2	Option flag
06H	2	Default cell height

Table 15.39 BIFF record type 225H (version 3.0–4.0)

The options are defined as a bitfield:

Offset	Bit	Remarks
00H	0	1: Font and row height not compatible
	1	1: Row height is 0
	2	1: Thick border above row
	3	1: Thick border below row
	4–7	Unused
01H	0–7	Unused

Table 15.40 Coding of the option field

15.2.23 DEFCOLWIDTH – Default Column Width (record type 55H, version 2.0–4.0)

This record defines the default column width.

Offset	Bytes	Remarks
00H	2	Record type (55H 00H)
02H	2	Record length in bytes
04H	2	Default column width

Table 15.41 BIFF record type 55H (version 2.0–4.0)

The cell width is defined in characters. This value is valid for all cells that are not explicitly formatted. The record structure is used in all BIFF versions.

15.2.24 DELTA – Iteration Increment (record type 10H, version 2.0–4.0)

This record type is used in all BIFF versions:

Offset	Bytes	Remarks
00H	2	Record type (10H 00H)
02H	2	Record length in bytes
04H	8	Maximum iteration increment

Table 15.42 BIFF record type 10H (version 2.0–4.0)

The maximum iteration increment is stored as an IEEE 8-byte floating point number. The value is set in the calculation option in EXCEL.

15.2.25 DIMENSIONS – Table Size (record type 00H, version 2.0–4.0)

The record describes the table size. In BIFF2 the following structure is defined:

Offset	Bytes	Remarks
00H	2	Record type (00H 00H)
02H	2	Record length in bytes
04H	2	First defined row of the document
06H	2	Last defined row of the document
08H	2	First defined column of the document
0AH	2	Last defined column of the document

Table 15.43 BIFF record type 00H (version 2.0)

Note that the current cell numbers are always 1 more than the values in the record (row A is row 0, column 1 is column 0). In BIFF3 and BIFF4 the record contains an additional reserved word.

Offset	Bytes	Remarks
00H	2	Record type (00H 02H)
02H	2	Record length in bytes
04H	2	First defined row of the document
06H	2	Last defined row of the document
08H	2	First defined column of the document
0AH	2	Last defined column of the document
0CH	2	Reserved (0000H)

Table 15.44 BIFF record type 200H (version 3.0–4.0)

The reserved word must be set to 0.

15.2.26 EDG – Edition Globals (record type 88H, version 3.0–4.0)

This record is used from BIFF3 and contains information for the Publisher (Macintosh). EXCEL ignores this record under Windows.

Offset	Bytes	Remarks
00H	2	Record type (88H 00H)
02H	2	Record length in bytes
04H	4	Count of section records created +1
08H	2	Count of PUB records in file
0AH	2	Reserved (0000H)

Table 15.45 BIFF record type 88H (version 3.0–4.0)

15.2.27 EFONT – Extended Font (record type 45H, version 2.0)

This record type is used only in EXCEL 2.0.

Offset	Bytes	Remarks
00H	2	Record type (45H 00H)
02H	2	Record length in bytes
04H	4	Index to color table
		0 Black
		1 White
		2 Red
		3 Green
		4 Blue
		5 Yellow
		6 Magenta
		7 Cyan

Table 15.46 BIFF record type 45H (version 2.0)

BIFF3 stores the color information in the FONT record.

15.2.28 EOF – End of File (record type 0AH, version 2.0–4.0)

This record type terminates all EXCEL files and is used in all BIFF versions.

Offset	Bytes	Remarks
00H	2	Record type (0AH 00H)
02H	2	Record length in bytes

Table 15.47 BIFF record type 0AH (version 2.0–4.0)

The record contains no data and must be the last record in the file.

15.2.29 EXTERNCOUNT – Number of External References (record type 16H, version 2.0–4.0)

If EXCEL uses external documents, this record appears in the file.

Offset	Bytes	Remarks
00H	2	Record type (16H 00H)
02H	2	Record length in bytes
04H	2	Number of external documents

Table 15.48 BIFF record type 16H (version 2.0–4.0)

The number of references includes external work sheets and DDE links. If the links are of the same type, (.XLS) only one value is used in the counter. The record is used in all BIFF versions.

15.2.30 EXTERNNAME – External Reference Name (record type 23H)

This record contains the name of an external reference (document). In BIFF2 the following record structure is used:

Offset	Bytes	Remarks
00H	2	Record type (23H 00H)
02H	2	Record length in bytes
04H	1	Length of name
05H	x	Reference name

Table 15.49 BIFF record type 23H (version 2.0)

This record must follow an EXTERNSHEET record. An external reference in Windows is a macro, a worksheet or a Windows DDE link. If the name is longer than 255 characters, it will be continued in as many CONTINUE records as required. From BIFF3 an extended record structure is used:

Offset	Bytes	Remarks
00H	2	Record type (23H 02H)
02H	2	Record length in bytes
04H	2	Option flags
		Bit 0: 1 Built-in name
		1-2: Reserved (0)
		3-15: Unused
06H	1	Length of name
07H	x	Reference name

Table 15.50 BIFF record type 223H (version 3.0–4.0)

15.2.31 EXTERNSHEET – External Reference (record type 17H, version 2.0–4.0)

This record defines the name of an external document.

Offset	Bytes	Remarks
00H	2	Record type (17H 00H)
02H	2	Record length in bytes
04H	1	Length of name
05H	x	Document filename

Table 15.51 BIFF record type 17H (version 2.0–4.0)

For each external document a record is written to the BIFF file. The number of records is equal to the value in the `EXTERNCOUNT` record. The order of the `EXTERNSHEET` records in a BIFF file should not be changed. All document names are stored as ASCII strings. Whenever possible, the filenames are encoded to make BIFF files exchangeable across different platforms. Encoded filenames are identified by the first character in the name:

Code	Filetype
0	Reference to an empty sheet name
1	Encoded filename
2	External reference, self-referential
3	DDE link

Table 15.52 Type of an external reference

If the first character is `00H`, the reference points to an empty sheet (for example, `=!$A$1`). The code `02H` indicates a self-referential external reference (for example, `SALES:XLS` contains the formula `=SALES.XLS!$A$1`).

The code `01H` in the first character indicates an encoded filename, which is used to make the name less system-dependent. The following table shows the codes used to encode the filename:

01H	The next byte represents an MS-DOS drive letter. On the Macintosh, one-character drive names are not used. Instead of code `01H`, the value `05H` is used.
02H	The source document is on the same drive as the dependent document.
03H	The source document is in a subdirectory of the current directory. The subdirectory name precedes the code, and the filename follows the code.
04H	The source document is in the parent directory.
05H	Defines a LongVolume on the Macintosh. This code is followed by a drive name.
06H	The source document is in the EXCEL start-up directory.
07H	The source document is in the alternate start-up directory.
08H	The source document is in the library directory.
09H	The source document is included in a workbook.

The code `02H` indicates an external filename which is on the same drive as the dependent document.

15.2.32 FILEPASS – Password Protected File (record type 2FH, version 2.0–4.0)

This record type is used in EXCEL files if the contents are saved with a password. The record must follow the BOF record. All records after the FILEPASS record are encrypted.

Offset	Bytes	Remarks
00H	2	Record type (2FH 00H)
02H	2	Record length in bytes
04H	2	Password

Table 15.53 BIFF record type 2FH (version 2.0–4.0)

EXCEL uses a second record type (PASSWORD) to protect the document.

15.2.33 FILESHARING – File Sharing and Password (record type 5BH, version 3.0–4.0)

This record stores information, from the *Save as* command. Also, the record contains the encrypted access passwords.

Offset	Bytes	Remarks
00H	2	Record type (5BH 00H)
02H	2	Record length in bytes
04H	2	ReadOnlyRec option flag
06H	2	Encrypted password
08H	1	Length of name
09H	x	User name

Table 15.54 BIFF record type 5BH (version 3.0–4.0)

The word at offset 04H defines a flag which is set to 1 if the *Read Only Recommended* option is set during the *Save as* operation. The next word contains an encrypted password. If its value is 0, the file is written without access protection. The following bytes define the user name and its length.

15.2.34 FNGROUPCOUNT – Built-in Function Group (record type 9CH, version 4.0)

This record type is used from BIFF4 and defines the number of built-in functions (Financial, Mathematical, Date, Time and so on) in the file.

Offset	Bytes	Remarks
00H	2	Record type (9CH 00H)
02H	2	Record length in bytes
04H	2	Number of built-in functions

Table 15.55 BIFF record type 9CH (version 4.0)

The word at offset 04H defines the number of built-in functions.

15.2.35 FNGROUPNAME – Function Group Name (record type 9AH, version 4.0)

This record is defined from BIFF4 and defines the name of a custom function created by a REGISTER() or DEFINE.NAME macro.

Offset	Bytes	Remarks
00H	2	Record type (9AH 00H)
02H	2	Record length in bytes
04H	1	Length of name
05H	*n*	Name of custom function group

Table 15.56 BIFF record type 9AH (version 4.0)

The word at offset 04H defines the length of the following name.

15.2.36 FNPROTO – Function Prototype (record type A2H, version 4.0)

This record is also defined from BIFF4 and contains the prototype functions.

Offset	Bytes	Remarks
00H	2	Record type (A2H 00H)
02H	2	Record length in bytes
04H	2	Size of prototype data array
06H	*n*	Array of function prototypes

Table 15.57 BIFF record type A2H (version 4.0)

The field at offset 06H has the following data structure for each entry:

Offset	Bytes	Remarks
00H	1	1: Name is a function or a command in a macrosheet
01H	1	Index to function group
02H	1	Length of argument list
03H	1	Length of name
04H	*n*	Function name
xxH	*n*	Argument list

Table 15.58 Function prototype data structure

15.2.37 FONT – Font Description (record type 31H, version 2.0–4.0)

This record contains the font description. BIFF2 uses the following record structure:

Offset	Bytes	Remarks
00H	4	Record type (31H 00H)
02H	2	Record length in bytes

Table 15.59 BIFF record type 31H (version 2.0) (*continues over...*)

Offset	Bytes	Remarks
04H	2	Font height
06H	2	Font attribute
		Bit 0–7: Reserved (0)
		8: 1 Bold
		9: 1 Italic
		10: 1 Underline
		11: 1 Strikeout
		12–15: Reserved (0)
08H	1	Length of font name
09H	x	Font name

Table 15.59 BIFF record type 31H (version 2.0) (cont.)

All reserved bits in the font attribute flag must be set to 0. In BIFF3 and BIFF4 an extended structure is used to store additional color information (BIFF2 has its own record for this purpose). The font can be changed with an XF record. The font height is defined in ¹⁄₂₀ point.

Offset	Bytes	Remarks
00H	2	Record type (31H 02H)
02H	2	Record length in bytes
04H	2	Font height
06H	2	Font attributes
		Bit 0: 1 Bold
		1: 1 Italic
		2: 1 Underline
		3: 1 Strikeout
		4: 1 Outline
		5: 1 Shadow
		6–7: 0 reserved
		8–F: 0 unused
08H	2	Index in color palette
0AH	1	Length of font name
0BH	x	Font name

Table 15.60 BIFF record type 231H (version 3.0–4.0)

Fonts are numbered from 0 to n and are specified in the font record. The font index in an XF record is used to change the font in a document. The *Outline* and *Shadow* attributes are valid only for the Macintosh.

Spreadsheets

15.2.38 FONT2 – Additional Font Information (record type 32H, version 2.0)

This record type is only used in EXCEL 2.0 and defines additional font information for the FONT record.

15.2.39 FOOTER – Print Footer on each Page (record type 15H, version 2.0–4.0)

This record defines a text sequence for the footer printed on each page.

Offset	Bytes	Remarks
00H	4	Record type (15H 00H)
02H	2	Record length in bytes
04H	1	Length of text string (in bytes)
05H	x	Footer text string

Table 15.61 BIFF record type 15H (version 2.0–4.0)

The text must be defined in the *Footer* Dialog Box.

15.2.40 FORMAT – Number Format (record type 1EH, version 2.0–4.0)

This record type defines the format for values in the document. BIFF versions 2.0 and 3.0 use the following record structure:

Offset	Bytes	Remarks
00H	2	Record type (1EH 00H)
02H	2	Record length in bytes
04H	1	Length of format string
05H	x	Format string for numbers

Table 15.62 BIFF record type 1EH (version 2.0–3.0)

In BIFF4 a modified record structure is used:

Offset	Bytes	Remarks
00H	2	Record type (1EH 04H)
02H	2	Record length in bytes
04H	2	Format index code
06H	1	Length of format string
07H	x	Format string for numbers

Table 15.63 BIFF record type 41EH (version 4.0)

The format index code is used for internal purposes in EXCEL. All FORMAT records should be stored together in a BIFF file and their order should not be changed. New format definitions should be appended to the end of the list.

15.2.41 FORMATCOUNT – Number of Built-in Format Records (record type 1FH, version 2.0)

This record type is used only in BIFF2 and defines the number of format records in a document.

Offset	Bytes	Remarks
00H	2	Record type (1FH 00H)
02H	2	Record length in bytes
04H	2	Number of format records

Table 15.64 BIFF record type 1FH (version 2.0)

The structure of the FORMAT record is described in Section 15.2.40 above.

15.2.42 FORMULA – Cell Formula (record type 06H, version 2.0–4.0)

A cell containing a formula is described in this record type. In BIFF2 the following structure is used:

Offset	Bytes	Remarks
00H	2	Record type (06H 00H)
02H	2	Record length in bytes

Table 15.65 BIFF record type 06H (version 2.0) *(continues over...)*

Offset	Bytes	Remarks
04H	2	Row number (starts from 0)
06H	2	Column number (starts from 0)
08H	3	Cell attributes
0BH	8	Current value of formula
13H	1	Recalculation flag Bit 0: Always calculate formula 1: Calculate formula if file opened 2–15: Unused
14H	1	Length of parsed expression
15H	*n*	Parsed expression

Table 15.65 BIFF record type 06H (version 2.0) (*cont.*)

The cell attributes are defined in the BLANK record (*see* Section 15.2.4). In BIFF3 and BIFF4 the record structure is changed (*see* Table 15.66). In BIFF4 the opcode 406H is used.

Offset	**Bytes**	**Remarks**
00H	4	Record type (06H 02H)
02H	2	Record length in bytes
04H	2	Row number (starts from 0)
06H	2	Column number (starts from 0)
08H	2	Index to XF record (containing cell format)
0AH	8	Current value of formula
12H	1	Recalulation flag Bit 0: Always calculate formula 1: Calculate formula if file open 2–15 : Unused
14H	2	Length of parsed expression
16H	*n*	Parsed expression

Table 15.66 BIFF record type 206H and 406H (version 3.0–4.0)

The formula is stored as a parsed expression in the FORMULA record. The formula result is stored as an 8-byte IEEE number. Boolean or ERROR values are stored as encoded 8-byte values (the last word contains the value FFFFH). Boolean values are stored as:

Bytes	Remarks
1	Type boolean (always 1)
1	Reserved (0)
1	Boolean value
3	Reserved (0)
2	Always FFFFH

Table 15.67 Coding of boolean values in a FORMULA record

An ERROR value is stored as:

Bytes	Remarks
1	Type error (always 2)
1	Reserved (0)
1	ERROR value
3	Reserved (0)
2	Always FFFFH

Table 15.68 Coding of an ERROR value in a FORMULA record

A result string is stored in the record as:

Bytes	Remarks
1	Type string (always 0)
5	Reserved (0)
2	Always FFFFH

Table 15.69 Coding of a string result

The string itself is not stored in the FORMULA record; it is appended in a STRING record.

At offset 22H (BIFF3/BIFF4) the parsed string representing the formula is stored. EXCEL uses reverse Polish notation to represent a formula. A formula is a sequence of tokens, where tokens are operands and operators. Each *token* consists of a *token type*, followed by the value. The token type is always a byte between 01H and 7FH. The values from 80H to FFH are reserved. Tokens that consist only of a token type are valid. Other tokens are followed by several bytes containing the token value. The following table defines some token types:

12H	Unary plus (+)
13H	Unary minus (–)
14H	Percent (%)
	Two operand tokens
03H	Addition
04H	Subtraction
05H	Multiplication
06H	Division
07H	Exponentiation (Exponent = 2)
08H	Concatenation
09H	Less than
0AH	Less than or equal
0BH	Equal
0CH	Greater than or equal
0DH	Greater than
0EH	Not equal
0FH	Intersection (space operator)
10H	Union (comma operator)
11H	Range (bounding rectangle)
	Constant tokens
16H	Missing argument
17H	String (1-byte length + string)
1CH	Error value (1-byte)
1DH	Boolean 0 = false, 1 = true
1EH	Integer (2-byte unsigned)
1FH	Number (8-byte IEEE-Float)

Table 15.70 Coding of simple tokens

EXCEL uses additional tokens to describe operands. These token structures are more complex and are described below.

15.2.42.1 Array constant (Opcode 20H)

Offset	Bytes	Remarks
00H	1	Opcode 20H
01H	6	Reserved in BIFF2
	7	Reserved in BIFF3/4
..H	1	Number of entries
..H	2	Number of rows in the array constant
..H	*n*	Array values

Table 15.71 Array constant (20H)

The array values are coded as:

Bytes	Remarks
1	01H IEEE value follows
8	8-byte IEEE value
1	02H String value follows
1	String length
n	String

Table 15.72 Coding of an array element

15.2.42.2 Name-Operand (Opcode 23H)

This token defines a named reference and has the following structure:

Offset	Bytes	Remarks
00H	2	Index to the reference
02H	5	Reserved in BIFF2
	8	Reserved in BIFF3/4

Table 15.73 Structure of a name operand

The index points to a table containing the external reference names (EXTERNNAME).

15.2.42.3 Cell Reference (Opcode 24H)

This token defines a reference to a single cell:

Offset	Bytes	Remarks
00H	2	Bit 0-13: Row number Bit 14 : 1 Column relative Bit 15 : 1 Row relative
02H	1	Column

Table 15.74 Structure of a cell reference operand

The column and row numbers are relative or absolute, depending on bits 14 and 15 of the first word.

15.2.42.4 Area Reference (Opcode 25H)

A range of several cells is defined by this token:

Offset	Bytes	Remarks
00H	2	Bit 0–13: Number of first row Bit 14 = 1 Column relative Bit 15 = 1 Row relative
02H	2	Bit 0–13: Number of last row Bit 14 = 1 Column relative Bit 15 = 1 Row relative
04H	1	First column
05H	1	Last column

Table 15.75 Structure of an area reference operand

Relative and absolute row and column numbers are allowed.

15.2.42.5 Constant Reference Subexpression (Opcode 26H)

This token defines a reference to an operand.

Offset	Bytes	Remarks
00H	4	Reserved
04H	2	Expression length
06H	2	Number of rectangles to follow
		Array of rectangles:
	2	First row
	2	Last row
	1	First column
	1	Last column

Table 15.76 Structure of a constant reference subexpression-operand

Each entry is 6 bytes long and defines a rectangle of cells. If the data cannot fit into one record, `CONTINUE` records are used.

15.2.42.6 Erroneous Constant Reference Subexpression (Opcode 27H)

This token has the following structure:

Offset	Byte	Remarks
00H	3	Reserved in BIFF2
	4	Reserved in BIFF3/BIFF4
	1	Expression length (BIFF2)
	2	Expression length (BIFF3/BIFF4)

Table 15.77 Structure of an erroneous constant reference subexpression-operand

The subexpressions follow in a Deleted Cell Reference or Deleted Area Reference token.

15.2.42.7 Deleted Cell Reference (Opcode 2AH)

This reference is the result of a change in the worksheet (delete, move, and so on). The opcode byte is followed by three reserved bytes.

15.2.42.8 Deleted Area Reference (Opcode 2BH)

This reference describes a deleted area in a worksheet. The opcode byte is followed by six reserved bytes.

15.2.42.9 Cell Reference within a Name (Opcode 2CH)

This reference occurs only within a parsed expression in a `NAME` record and defines a reference to a single cell. The opcode is followed by the following structure:

Offset	Bytes	Remarks
00H	2	Row Bit 15: 1 = Row relative 0 = Row absolute Bit 14: 1 = Column relative 0 = Column absolute Bit 0-13: Row
02H	1	Column

Table 15.78 Structure of a cell reference within a `NAME` operand

15.2.42.10 Area Reference within a Name (Opcode 2CH)

This reference occurs only within a parsed expression in a NAME record and defines a reference to a range. The opcode is followed by the following structure:

Offset	Bytes	Remarks
00H	2	First row Bit 15: 1 = Row relative 0 = Row absolute Bit 14: 1 = Column relative 0 = Column absolute Bit 0-13: Row
02H	2	Last Row
04H	1	First Column
05H	1	Last Column

Table 15.79 Structure of an area reference within a NAME operand

The coding of the first and last row in a word is similar. The two most significant bits are used to define a relative or absolute address. Bits 0-13 are used for the row number. The column number is coded in one byte. The information about relative/absolute addressing is obtained from bit 14 of the row number.

Control Tokens

An EXCEL expression can contain further tokens to control the data area:

15.2.42.11 Array Formula (Opcode 01H)

This token defines an array which contains the formula. The token is used only in FORMULA records. The following structure appears after the opcode byte:

Offset	Bytes	Remarks
00H	2	Row number of upper left corner
02H	1	Column number of upper left corner

Table 15.80 Array Formula

From BIFF3 the column number is stored in a word instead of a byte.

15.2.42.12 Data Table (Opcode 02H)

This token indicates a data table in a worksheet and is used only in FORMULA records. The token is the only token in a formula and has the following structure:

Offset	Bytes	Remarks
00H	2	Row number of upper left corner
02H	1	Column number of upper left corner

Table 15.81 Data Table

From BIFF3 the column number is stored in a word.

15.2.42.13 Parenthesis (Opcode 15H)

This opcode defines a pair of parentheses in an expression.

15.2.42.14 Special Attributes (Opcode 19H)

This opcode is used for different purposes. Depending on the BIFF version, the opcode byte precedes the following structures:

Offset	Bytes	Remarks
		BIFF2
00H	1	Option flag
01H	1	Data byte
		BIFF3 and BIFF4
00H	1	Option flag
01H	2	Data word
		BIFF4 if Bit 6 in option flag is 1
00H	1	Option flag
01H	1	Spacing attribute
02H	2	Number of spaces

Table 15.82 Special Attributes

The option flag is a bit field containing the following flags:

Bit	Remarks
0	1: Formula contains volatile functions
1	1: Implement optimized IF function
2	1: Implement optimized CHOOSE function
3	1: Jump to another position in the expression
4	1: Implement optimized SUM function
5	1: Formula is a BASIC style assignment
6	1: Macro formula contains spaces after the equal sign (BIFF3, BIFF4)
7	Unused

Table 15.83 Coding of the option flags

15.2.42.15 External Reference (Opcode 1AH)

This token has the following structure:

Offset	Bytes	Remarks
00H	4	Reserved in BIFF2
	6	Reserved in BIFF3, BIFF4
..H	2	Index to worksheet
..H	1	Reserved (0)

Table 15.84 External Reference

15.2.42.16 End External Reference (Opcode 1BH)

This token has the following structure:

Offset	Bytes	Remarks
00H	3	Reserved in BIFF2
	4	Reserved in BIFF3, BIFF4

Table 15.85 End External Reference

15.2.42.17 Incomplete Constant Reference Subexpression (Opcode 28H)

This token has the following structure:

Offset	Bytes	Remarks
00H	3	Reserved in BIFF2
	4	Reserved in BIFF3, BIFF4
..H	1	Length of reference in BIFF2
	2	Length of reference in BIFF3, BIFF4

Table 15.86 Incomplete Constant Reference Subexpression

15.2.42.18 Reference Subexpression

EXCEL uses several opcodes for subexpressions:

Opcode	Function
29H	Variable Reference Subexpression
2EH	Reference Subexpression (only in a NAME record)
2FH	Incomplete Reference Subexpression within a NAME record

Table 15.87 Opcodes for Reference Subexpressions

The opcode byte is followed by:

Offset	Byte	Remarks
00H	1	Length of reference in BIFF2
	2	Length of reference in BIFF3, BIFF4

Table 15.88 Reference Subexpression Structure

Function operators

EXCEL expressions may contain operators for functions. In BIFF the following operators are used.

15.2.42.19 Function Operator (Opcode 21H)

This operator follows a function with a fixed number of arguments. The opcode is followed by a byte (BIFF2) or a word (BIFF3, BIFF4) containing a function index.

15.2.42.20 Variable Argument Function Operator (Opcode 22H)

This operator indicates a function with a variable number of arguments. The opcode is followed by:

Offset	Bytes	Remarks
00H	1	Bit 0–6: Number of arguments Bit 7–1: Function prompts the user
01H	1	Index of the function (BIFF2)
	2	Bit 0–14: Index (BIFF3, BIFF4) Bit 15: Function is command-equivalent

Table 15.89 Variable Argument Function

15.2.42.21 Command-Equivalent Function Operator (Opcode 38H)

A command-equivalent function is followed by the number of arguments and a function index:

Offset	Bytes	Remarks
00H	1	Number of arguments
01H	1	Index to the function

Table 15.90 Command-Equivalent Function

All other opcodes are reserved for future extensions.

15.2.43 GCW – Global Column Width Flags (record type ABH, version 4.0)

This record is defined from BIFF4 and has the following structure:

Offset	Bytes	Remarks
00H	2	Record type (ABH 00H)
02H	2	Record length in bytes
04H	2	Length of the following structure
06H	2	Global column width flag (A-P)
08H	2	Global column width flag (Q-AF)
..		...
..H	2	Global column width flag (IG-IV)

Table 15.91 BIFF record type ABH (version 4.0)

The record defines a field containing 256 flag bits. Each bit represents a column in a worksheet. If the bit is set, the column uses the standard width. If the bit is 0, the column width is defined in a STANDARDWIDTH record.

The *Global Column Width Flag* word is defined as a bit field. Each bit defines a column (Bit 0 = 1st column, Bit 1 = 2nd column, and so on).

15.2.44 GRIDSET – State Change of Gridlines Option (record type 82H, version 3.0–4.0)

The record defines the grid state and signals new user settings.

Offset	Bytes	Remarks
00H	4	Record type (82H 00H)
02H	2	Record length in bytes
04H	2	1 = Changed settings

Table 15.92 BIFF record type 82H (version 3.0–4.0)

The settings are available in the page setup dialog box.

Spreadsheets

Spreadsheets

15.2.45 GUTS – Size of Row and Column Gutter (record type 80H, version 3.0–4.0)

This record defines the row and column gutters:

Offset	Bytes	Remarks
00H	2	Record type (80H 00H)
02H	2	Record length in bytes
04H	2	Row gutter-left border
06H	2	Column gutter-top border
08H	2	Maximum outline level-row gutter
0AH	2	Maximum outline level-column gutter

Table 15.93 BIFF record type 80H (version 3.0–4.0)

The gutter is measured in screen units (pixels).

15.2.46 HCENTER – Horizontal Center between Margins (record type 83H, version 3.0–4.0)

This record type is defined from BIFF3 and sets the option to center a sheet between the left and right margins during printing.

Offset	Bytes	Remarks
00H	2	Record type (83H 00H)
02H	2	Record length in bytes
04H	2	1 = Center printout

Table 15.94 BIFF record type 83H (version 3.0–4.0)

15.2.47 HEADER – Print Header (record type 14H, version 2.0–4.0)

This record defines the header string for a document.

Offset	Bytes	Remarks
00H	2	Record type (14H 00H)
02H	2	Record length in bytes
04H	1	Length of header string
05H	*n*	Header string

Table 15.95
BIFF record type 14H (version 2.0–4.0)

15.2.48 HIDEOBJ – Object Display Options (record type 8DH, version 2.0–4.0)

This record stores information about object visibility.

Offset	Bytes	Remarks
00H	2	Record type (8DH 00H)
02H	2	Record length in bytes
04H	2	Display options 0: Show all options on 1: Place-holder option on 2: Hide option on

Table 15.96
BIFF record type 8DH (version 2.0–4.0)

15.2.49 HORIZONTAL PAGE BREAKS – Explicit Row Page Breaks (record type 1BH, version 2.0–4.0)

This record contains a list of explicit row page breaks.

Offset	Bytes	Remarks
00H	2	Record type (1BH 00H)
02H	2	Record length in bytes
04H	2	Number of page breaks
06H	*n**2	Array of row numbers

Table 15.97

BIFF record type 1BH (version 2.0–4.0)

The array (offset 06H) contains the 2-byte row numbers where page breaks occur, in ascending order.

15.2.50 IMDATA – Image Data (record type 7FH, version 3.0–4.0)

This record type defines a complete bitmap picture.

Offset	Bytes	Remarks
00H	2	Record type (7FH 00H)
02H	2	Record length in bytes
04H	2	Image format 02H: Windows Metafile Mac PICT 09H: Windows Bitmap 0EH: Special format
06H	2	Environment 1: Windows 2: Macintosh
08H	4	Length of data area in bytes
0CH	*n*	Data area

Table 15.98 BIFF record type 7FH (version 3.0–4.0)

If a Windows Bitmap image is stored, the data area begins with a BMP header (BITMAPCOREINFO), followed by a Bitmap structure (*see* BMP description in Part 4).

If an image is stored in an application-dependent format, offset 04H contains the value 0EH. EXCEL ignores the image data in this case.

15.2.51 INDEX – Index (record type 0BH, version 2.0–4.0)

This record appears in each BIFF file and describes an index. BIFF version 2.0 uses the following structure:

Offset	Bytes	Remarks
00H	2	Record type (0BH 00H)
02H	2	Record length in bytes
04H	4	Absolute file position of the first NAME record
08H	2	First row in the document
0AH	2	Last row in the document
0CH	*x*	Array of absolute file positions

Table 15.99 BIFF record type 0BH (version 2.0)

From BIFF3 an extended record structure is used:

Offset	Bytes	Remarks
00H	2	Record type (0BH 02H)
02H	2	Record length in bytes
04H	4	Offset of the first NAME record
08H	2	First row in the document
0AH	2	Last row in the document
0CH	4	Offset of XF record
10H	*x*	Array of absolute file positions

Table 15.100 BIFF record type 20BH (version 3.0–4.0)

The record contains pointers (offset in bytes) to other records. The field at offset 04H defines a pointer to the start of the first NAME record. The next two fields define the first and last row in a worksheet used by the formula. The row numbers begin with 0 and the value for the last row will be counted +1.

Offset 0CH (BIFF3, BIFF4) contains a pointer to the start of the first XF record. The structure ends with an array of 4-byte pointers which define the offset of the ROW records. If all the ROW records are stored together, there is only one entry in the BIFF file.

15.2.52 INTEGER – Cell Value Integer (record type 02H, version 2.0)

This record defines an integer value in BIFF2.

Offset	Bytes	Remarks
00H	2	Record type (02H 00H)
02H	2	Record length in bytes
04H	2	Row number (starts from 0)
06H	2	Column number (starts from 0)
08H	3	Cell attributes
0BH	2	Integer value

Table 15.101 BIFF record type 02H (version 2.0)

The row and column numbers start from 0. The cell value is stored as an unsigned integer. The structure of the cell attributes is defined in the BLANK record (*see* Section 15.2.4). The record is used only in BIFF2. From BIFF3 EXCEL stores integer values in RK records.

15.2.53 INTL – International Macro Sheet (record type 61H, version 3.0–4.0)

This record signals that a macro is stored as an *international macro sheet* in a BIFF file.

Offset	Bytes	Remarks
00H	2	Record type (61H 00H)
02H	2	Record length in bytes
04H	2	Reserved (00H 00H)

Table 15.102 BIFF record type 61H (version 3.0–4.0)

15.2.54 ITERATION – Iteration Mode (record type 11H, version 2.0–4.0)

The record sets the iteration mode:

Offset	Bytes	Remarks
00H	2	Record type (11H 00H)
02H	2	Record length in bytes
04H	2	1 = Iteration On

Table 15.103 BIFF record type 11H (version 2.0–4.0)

A value of 1 switches the iteration mode to On.

15.2.55 IXFE – Index Extended Format Record (record type 44H, version 2.0)

In BIFF2 this record is used to define an index to an XF record.

Offset	Bytes	Remarks
00H	2	Record type (44H 00H)
02H	2	Record length in bytes
04H	2	Index to the XF record

Table 15.104 BIFF record type 44H (version 2.0)

15.2.56 LABEL – Cell Value String (record type 04H, version 2.0–4.0)

A label is defined with this record type. BIFF2 uses the following structure:

Offset	Bytes	Remarks
00H	4	Record type (04H 00H)
02H	2	Record length in bytes
04H	2	Row number (starts from 0)
06H	2	Column number (starts from 0)
08H	3	Cell attributes
0BH	1	Length of text string
0CH	*x*	Text string

Table 15.105 BIFF record type 04H (version 2.0)

Spreadsheets

For information about the cell attributes see the BLANK record (Section 15.2.4). BIFF3 and higher use the following structure:

Offset	Bytes	Remarks
00H	2	Record type (04H 02H)
02H	2	Record length in bytes
04H	2	Row number (starts from 0)
06H	2	Column number (starts from 0)
08H	2	Index to the XF record containing the cell format
0AH	2	Length of the text string
0CH	*x*	Text string

Table 15.106 BIFF record type 204H (version 3.0–4.0)

The row and column numbers start from 0. The label text is stored in a string with a maximum length of 255 bytes.

Spreadsheets

15.2.57 LEFTMARGIN – Left Margin Measurement (record type 26H, version 2.0–4.0)

This record defines the left margin in inches.

Offset	Bytes	Remarks
00H	2	Record type (26H 00H)
02H	2	Record length in bytes
04H	8	Left margin (8-byte IEEE floating point)

Table 15.107 BIFF record type 26H (version 2.0–4.0)

15.2.58 LH – Alternate Menu Key Flag (record type 8BH, version 3.0–4.0)

This record is defined from BIFF3 and specifies the alternate menu key flag for LOTUS 1-2-3 Help.

Offset	Bytes	Remarks
00H	2	Record type (8BH 00H)
02H	2	Record length in bytes
04H	2	Alternate menu key flag 1: LOTUS 1-2-3 Help 0: EXCEL Menu bar

Table 15.108 BIFF record type 8BH (version 3.0–4.0)

15.2.59 LHNGRAPH – Named Graph Information (record type 95H, version 3.0–4.0)

From BIFF3, this record specifies a graph (the structure is similar to the LOTUS WKS-NGRAPH record). The first 13 bytes contain integer values. These values flag all valid X-references A–F and valid data labels A–F.

15.2.60 LHRECORD – .WKx File Conversion Info (record type 94H, version 3.0–4.0)

This record is defined from BIFF3 and is used during import/export of LOTUS WKS, WK1 and WK3 files.

Offset	Bytes	Remarks
00H	2	Record type (94H 00H)
02H	2	Record length in bytes
04H	2	Sub-record type
06H	2	Length of data record
08H	*n*	Data record

Table 15.109 BIFF record type 94H (version 3.0–4.0)

The following sub-record types are defined:

Code	Type
01H	Reserved
02H	Header string for the /GRAPH SAVE PRINT Help command
03H	Footer string for the /GRAPH SAVE PRINT Help command
04H	Left border for the /GRAPH SAVE PRINT command (IEEE value)
05H	Right border for the /GRAPH SAVE PRINT command (IEEE value)
06H	Top border for the /GRAPH SAVE PRINT command (IEEE value)
07H	Bottom border for the /GRAPH SAVE PRINT command (IEEE value)
08H	Current /Graph View Data (*see* LOTUS WKS GRAPH record, Section 6.2.33)
09H	Global column width (Integer)
0AH	Reserved
0BH	Table type 0: None (standard) 1: Table 1 2: Table 2
0CH	Reserved

Table 15.110 Coding of sub-records

15.2.61 LPR – Sheet Print with LINE.PRINT (record type 98H)

This record is used in BIFF4 if a `LINE.PRINT` macro is used to print a sheet.

Offset	Bytes	Remarks
00H	2	Record type (98H 00H)
02H	2	Record length in bytes
04H	2	Option flag
06H	2	Left border (in character)
08H	2	Right border (in character)
0AH	2	Top border (in character)
0CH	2	Bottom border (in character)
0EH	2	Lines per page
10H	1	Length of setup string
11H	*n*	Printer setup string

Table 15.111 BIFF record type 98H (version 4.0)

The option flag is a bit field with the following structure:

Bit	Remarks
0	1: Alert user after printing each sheet
1	1: Print header/footer
2	1: Carriage return at end of page

Table 15.112 Coding of option flag

15.2.62 NAME – Document name (record type 18H, version 2.0–4.0)

This record contains the document name. In BIFF2 the following structure is used:

Offset	Bytes	Remarks
00H	2	Record type (18H 02H)
02H	2	Record length in bytes

Table 15.113 BIFF record type 18H (version 2.0) (*continues over...*)

Offset	Bytes	Remarks
04H	1	Name attributes 1
05H	1	Name attributes 2
06H	1	Keyboard shortcut
07H	1	Length of name text
08H	2	Length of name definition
0AH	*x*	Name text
..H	*x*	Parsed expression for the name's definition
..H	1	Length of name definition

Table 15.113 BIFF record type 18H (version 2.0) (*cont.*)

The name attributes 1 field is coded in BIFF2 as:

Bit	Remarks
0	Reserved (must be 0)
1	1: Name is a function or a command in a macro sheet
2	1: Name contains a complex function
3-7	Reserved (must be 0)

Table 15.114 Code name attributes 1

The name attributes 2 field is defined only if bit 1 in name attribute 1 is set:

Bit	Remarks
0	1: Name of a macro function
1	1: Name of a macro command
2-7	Reserved (must be 0)

Table 15.115 Code name attributes 2

In BIFF3 the following record structure is used:

Offset	Bytes	Remarks
00H	2	Record type (18H 02H)
02H	2	Record length in bytes
04H	2	Name attributes
06H	1	Keyboard shortcut
07H	1	Length of name text
08H	2	Length of name definition
0AH	*x*	Name text
..H	*x*	Parsed expression of name's definition

Table 15.116 BIFF record type 218H (version 3.0)

The attribute word is defined as follows:

Bit	Remarks
0	1: Name is hidden
1	1: Name is a function
2	1: Name is a command
3	1: Name is a command or a function in a macro
4	1: The name contains a complex function
5	1: Name is a built-in name
6-15	Unused

Table 15.117 Coding of the attribute word

If bit 4 in the attribute word is set, the name contains a complex function (TREND, MINVERSE, and so on) that returns an array, or it is a user-defined function, or it contains a row/column function.

BIFF4 uses the following record structure:

Offset	Bytes	Remarks
00H	2	Record type (18H 02H)
02H	2	Record length in bytes
04H	2	Name attributes

Table 15.118 BIFF record type 218H (version 4.0) (*continues over...*)

Offset	Bytes	Remarks
06H	1	Keyboard shortcut
07H	1	Length of name text
08H	2	Length of name definition
0AH	x	Name text
..H	x	Parsed expression with name's definition

Table 15.118 BIFF record type 218H (version 4.0) (*cont.*)

The attribute word is defined as follows:

Bit	**Remarks**
0	1: Name is hidden
1	1: Name is a function
2	1: Name is a command
3	1: Name is a command or a function in a macro
4	1: Name contains a complex function
5	1: Name is a built-in name
6-11	Index in function group
12-15	Unused

Table 15.119 Coding of attribute word in BIFF4

The parsed expression for a name is stored in the internal EXCEL format for formulas. All NAME records should be stored together.

Built-in function names appear in BIFF2 as ASCII text. From BIFF3 the BIFF structure contains only a byte giving the function name code.

Code	**Function name**
00H	Consolidate_Area
01H	Auto_Open
02H	Auto_Close
03H	Extract
04H	Database

Table 15.120 Coding of built-in function names (*continues over...*)

Code	Function name
05H	Criteria
06H	Print_Area
07H	Print_Table
08H	Recorder
09H	Data_Form
0AH	Auto_Activate
0BH	Auto_Deactivate
0CH	Sheet_Title

Table 15.120 Coding of built-in function names (*cont.*)

15.2.63 NOTE – Note Associated with a Cell (record type 1CH, version 2.0–4.0)

This record contains notes entered for a cell.

Offset	Bytes	Remarks
00H	2	Record type (1CH 00H)
02H	2	Record length in bytes
04H	2	Row
06H	2	Column
08H	2	Length of note text (in bytes)
0AH	*n*	Note text

Table 15.121 BIFF record type 1C280 280z (version 2.0–4.0)

The row and column numbers start from 0. If a note contains more than 2048 characters, it is split between a parent record and several child NOTE records. The first NOTE record has the structure described in the table above. Offset 08H defines the length of the complete note. The other NOTE records have the following structure:

Offset	Bytes	Remarks
00H	2	Record type (1CH 00H)
02H	2	Record length in bytes
04H	2	FFFFH
06H	2	Reserved (0000H)
08H	2	Length of this section of note text (bytes)
0AH	*n*	Note text (section)

Table 15.122 NOTE child record

15.2.64 NUMBER – Cell Value Float (record type 03H, version 2.0–4.0)

An 8-byte floating point value is stored in this record. In BIFF2 the record has the following structure:

Offset	Bytes	Remarks
00H	2	Record type (03H 00H)
02H	2	Record length in bytes
04H	2	Row number (starts from 0)
06H	2	Column number (starts from 0)
08H	3	Cell attributes
0BH	8	IEEE number

Table 15.123 BIFF record type 03H (version 2.0)

The row and column numbers start from 0. The cell attributes are described for the BLANK record (Section 15.2.4). The value is stored as an 8-byte floating point number. In BIFF3 and BIFF4 the following structure is used:

Offset	Bytes	Remarks
00H	4	Record type (03H 02H)
02H	2	Record length in bytes
04H	2	Row number (starts from 0)
06H	2	Column number (starts from 0)
08H	2	Index to an XF record
0AH	8	IEEE floating point value

Table 15.124 BIFF record type 203H (version 2.0)

The record is one byte shorter than in BIFF2 because the cell attribute (3 bytes) is replaced by the index to an XF record (2 bytes).

15.2.65 OBJ – Object Description (record type 5DH, version 3.0–4.0)

Objects (Line, Rectangle, Oval, Arc, Text, Image, Polygon, Group and Button) are described with an OBJ record. The first 34 bytes in a record are the same for all object types.

Offset	Bytes	Remarks
00H	2	Record type (5DH 00H)
02H	2	Record length in bytes
04H	4	Number of objects (begin with 1)
08H	2	Object type 0: Group 1: Line 2: Rectangle 3: Oval 4: Arc 5: Chart 6: Text 7: Button 8: Picture 9: Polygon (BIFF4 only)
0AH	2	Object ID number
0CH	2	Option flag
0EH	2	Column containing top left corner of object's bounding box
10H	2	X position of top left corner of bounding box in 1/1024 of the cell width
12H	2	Row containing top left corner of the object's bounding box
14H	2	Y position of top left corner of the object's bounding box
16H	2	Column containing bottom left corner of the object's bounding box
18H	2	X position of bottom right corner of the object's bounding box in 1/1024 of the cell width
1AH	2	Row containing bottom right corner of the object bounding box
1CH	2	Y position of bottom right corner of the object's bounding box
1EH	2	Length of ASCIIZ string containing a macro reference
20H	2	Unused

Table 15.125 BIFF record type 5DH (version 2.0–4.0)

The bounding box coordinates are defined relative to the left and upper border of the underlying cell. The option flag is coded for all objects as follows:

Bit	Remarks
0	1: Object is hidden
1	1: Object is visible
2-7	Unused
8	1: Object is selected
9	1: Object moves and varies in size with cells
10	1: Object moves with cells
11	0: Reserved
12	1: Object is locked when sheet is protected
13-14	Reserved
15	1: Object is part of a group

Table 15.126 Coding of option flag

The entries after offset 34 (22H) depend on the object type.

15.2.65.1 Line Object

A line object uses the following structure:

Offset	Bytes	Remarks
22H	1	Index to color palette
23H	1	Line style
		0: Solid
		1: Dashed
		2: Dotted
		3: Dash-dot
		4: Dash-dot-dot
		5: Unused
		6: Dark gray
		7: Medium gray
		8: Light gray

Table 15.127 Line Object (*continues over...*)

Spreadsheets

Offset	Bytes	Remarks
24H	1	Line weight
		0: Hairline
		1: Single
		2: Double
		3: Thick
25H	1	Bit 0 = 1: Automatic option On
26H	2	Line end
28H	1	Quadrant index
		0: Top left/bottom right
		1: Top right/bottom left
		2: Bottom right/top left
		3: Bottom left/top right
29H	1	Unused

Table 15.127 Line Object (*cont.*)

The index to the color palette is between 08H and 17H. The value 18H defines the color *Auto*. The line end is defined in the word at offset 28H:

Bit	Line end
0–3	Arrowhead style
	0: None
	1: Open
	2: Filled
4–7	Arrowhead width
	0: Narrow
	1: Medium
	2: Wide
8–11	Arrowhead length
	0: Short
	1: Medium
	2: Long
12–15	Unused

Table 15.128 Attributes for arrowhead

15.2.65.2 Rectangle Object

If the object is a rectangle, the bytes after offset 22H are defined as follows:

Offset	Bytes	Remarks
22H	1	Index to background color palette
23H	1	Index to foreground color palette
24H	1	Fill pattern
		0: White
		1-4: Grayscale
		0EH,0FH: Grayscale
		05H-0CH: Hatch
		10H-12H: Vertical/horizontal hatch
25H	1	Automatic fill option 1= On
26H	1	Index in color palette for line color
27H	1	Line style (see Line Object)
28H	1	Line weight (see Line Object)
29H	1	1: Automatic border On
2AH	2	Frame style

Table 15.129 Rectangle Object

The index to the color palette defines values between 08H and 17H. The code 18H defines the color *Auto*. The line style codes are defined above (line object). The frame style contains 16 bits and is defined at offset 2AH:

Bit	Frame style
0	1: Rounded corners
1	1: Rectangle shadowed
2–9	Diameter of rounded corners
10–15	Unused

Table 15.130 Frame style for rectangles

The fill pattern is between 00H and 12H and is defined as the fill pattern in the EXCEL select list for frames.

Spreadsheets

15.2.65.3 Oval Object

If the object is an oval, the record uses the following structure for the entries after offset 34 (22H):

Offset	Bytes	Remarks
22H	1	Index to background color palette
23H	1	Index to foreground color palette
24H	1	Fill pattern (*see* Rectangle Object)
25H	1	Automatic fill option 1: On
26H	1	Line color index to color palette
27H	1	Line type (*see* Line Object)
28H	1	Line weight (*see* Line Object)
29H	1	1: Automatic border On
2AH	2	Frame style

Table 15.131 Oval Object

The index into the color palette is between 08H and 17H. The entry 18H defines the color *Auto*. The codes for the line type are as defined for the line object (*see above*).

The frame style (offset 2AH) is defined as:

Bit	Frame style
0	Unused
1	1: Shadowed
2–9	Unused
10–15	Unused

Table 15.132 Frame style for ovals

15.2.65.4 Arc Object

Arc objects have the following structure for entries after offset 34 (22H):

Offset	Bytes	Remarks
22H	1	Index to background color palette
23H	1	Index to foreground color palette
24H	1	Fill pattern (*see* Rectangle Object)
25H	1	Automatic fill option 1: On

Table 15.133 Arc Object (*continues over..*)

Offset	Bytes	Remarks
26H	1	Line color index to color palette
27H	1	Line type (*see* Line Object)
28H	1	Line weight (*see* Line Object)
29H	1	1: Automatic border On
2AH	1	Quadrant index: 0: Upper right 1: Upper left 2: Lower left 3: Lower right
2BH	1	Reserved (0)

Table 15.133 Arc Object (*cont.*)

The color palette index is between 08H and 17H. The entry 18H is used for the color *Auto*. The line style coding is shown in the line object definition.

15.2.65.5 Chart Object

A chart object has the following structure for entries after offset 34 (22H):

Offset	**Bytes**	**Remarks**
22H	1	Index to background color palette
23H	1	Index to foreground color palette
24H	1	Fill pattern (*see* Rectangle Object)
25H	1	Automatic fill option 1: On
26H	1	Line color index to color palette
27H	1	Line type (*see* Line Object)
28H	1	Line weight (*see* Line Object)
29H	1	1: Automatic border On
2AH	2	Frame style (*see* Rectangle Object)
2CH	2	Reserved (must be set to 0)
2EH	16	Reserved (must be set to 0)

Table 15.134 Chart Object

The index for the color palette has the same values as in other objects. The chart object record is followed by an embedded CHART BIFF file. The CHART file begins with a BOF record and ends with an EOF record (the chart record structure is defined in the EXCEL 4 SDK).

15.2.65.6 Text Object

If an OBJ record contains a text object, the following structure is used for entries after offset 34 (22H):

Offset	Bytes	Remarks
22H	1	Index to background color palette
23H	1	Index to foreground color palette
24H	1	Fill pattern (*see* Rectangle Object)
25H	1	Automatic fill option 1: On
26H	1	Line color index to color palette
27H	1	Line type (*see* Line Object)
28H	1	Line weight (*see* Line Object)
29H	1	1: Automatic border On
2AH	2	Frame style (*see* Rectangle Object)
2CH	2	Object text length
2EH	2	Reserved
30H	2	Length of all TXORUNS structures in the record
32H	2	Index to FONT record, if offset 30H = 0, else reserved
34H	2	Reserved
36H	2	Option flag
38H	2	Orientation flag 0: Left to right 1: Top down, character upright 2: Rotate 90 degrees counterclockwise 3: Rotate 90 degrees clockwise
3AH	8	Reserved (last field if text object is empty)
42H	*n*	Object text
..H	8	TXORUNS structure
..H	8	TXORUNS structure

Table 15.135
Text Object

The index to the color palette is between 08H and 17H. The entry 18H defines the color *Auto*. The codes for the line type are as defined for the line object. The word at offset 32H is only valid if the entry in the previous word is 0 (no text object).

The TXORUNS structure contains information about the format of the text object. The TXORUNS structure is used for each change in the text format.

Offset	Bytes	Remarks
0	2	Index to 1st character in new format
2	2	Index to FONT record
4	4	Reserved

Table 15.136 The TXORUNS structure

A text object contains at least two TXORUNS structures. The first word (index to the 1st character) is set to the length of the text object (offset 2CH). The index to the FONT record is set to 0.

The option flag (offset 36H) defines the text orientation:

Bit	Remarks
0	Unused
1-3	Horizontal text alignment 0: Left 1: Centered 2: Right
4-6	Vertical text alignment 0: Left 1: Centered 2: Right
7	1: Autotext size On
8	Unused
9	1: Lock text On
10-15	Unused

Table 15.137 Coding of Option flag

15.2.65.7 Button Object

An OBJ record for a button definition uses the same structure as a text object for the entries after offset 34 (22H).

Offset	Bytes	Remarks
22H	1	1BH: Button
23H	1	1BH: Button

Table 15.138 Button Object (*continues over...*)

Offset	Bytes	Remarks
24H	1	01H: Button
25H	1	01H: Button
26H	1	18H: Button
27H	1	00H: Button
28H	1	00H: Button
29H	1	01H: Button
2AH	2	50H: Button
2CH	2	Length of button name
2EH	2	Reserved
30H	2	Length of all TXORUNS structures in the record
32H	2	Index to FONT record, if offset 30H = 0, else reserved
34H	2	Reserved
36H	2	Option flag (*see* Text Object)
38H	2	Orientation flag 0: Left to right 1: Top down, text upright 2: Rotate 90 degrees counterclockwise 3: Rotate 90 degrees clockwise
3AH	8	Reserved (last field if empty button)
42H	*n*	Button name
..H	8	TXORUNS structure
..H	8	TXORUNS structure

Table 15.138 Button Object (*cont.*)

All entries are used for the button object.

15.2.65.8 Picture Object

If a picture is included in an OBJ record, the following structure is used after offset 34 (22H):

Offset	Bytes	Remarks
22H	1	Index to background color palette
23H	1	Index to foreground color palette
24H	1	Fill pattern (*see* Rectangle Object)

Table 15.139 Picture Object (*continues over...*)

Offset	Bytes	Remarks
25H	1	Automatic fill option 1: On
26H	1	Line color index to color palette
27H	1	Line style (*see* Line Object)
28H	1	Line weight (*see* Line Object)
29H	1	1: Automatic border On
2AH	2	Frame style (*see* Rectangle Object)
2CH	2	Image format 00H: Text format 01H: No image data 02H: Windows Metafile or Mac PICT 09H: Windows Bitmap
2EH	4	Reserved
32H	2	Length of FMLA structure
34H	2	Reserved
36H	2	Option flag
2EH	*n*	FMLA structure

Table 15.139 Picture object (*cont.*)

The option flag has the following bit structure:

Bit	Remarks
0	0: Picture sized manually
1	1: Reference in FMLA structure is a DDE reference
2-15	Unused (0)

Table 15.140 Coding of option flag in a picture object

The FMLA data structure contains a reference which is used by EXCEL to build the image.

Offset	Bytes	Field
00H	2	Length
02H	4	Reserved
06H	*n*	Parsed expression

Table 15.141 FMLA data structure

The length of the structure (in bytes) is defined in the first word. At offset 06H a parsed expression in internal EXCEL format follows (*see* FORMULA record, Section 15.2.42).

15.2.65.9 Group Object

It is possible to group different objects in EXCEL. This information is stored in a group object with the following structure after offset 34 (22H):

Offset	Bytes	Remarks
22H	4	Reserved
26H	2	ID-number of the object that follows the last object of this group
28H	16	Reserved

Table 15.142
Group Object

15.2.65.10 Polygon Object

EXCEL stores a polygon description in an OBJ record. The OBJ record has the following structure for entries after offset 34 (22H):

Offset	Bytes	Remarks
22H	1	Index to background color palette
23H	1	Index to foreground color palette
24H	1	Fill pattern (*see* Rectangle Object)
25H	1	Automatic fill option 1: On
26H	1	Line color index to color palette
27H	1	Line style (*see* Line Object)
28H	1	Line weight (*see* Line Object)
29H	1	1: Automatic border On
2AH	2	Frame style (*see* Rectangle Object)
2CH	2	1: Polygon closed
2EH	10	Reserved
36H	2	Number of vertex coordinates
38H	8	Reserved

Table 15.143
Polygon Object

The vertex coordinates are saved in a COORDLIST record.

15.2.66 OBJPROTECT – Protect Object (record type 63H, version 3.0–4.0)

This record stores an option from the *Options Protect Document* dialog box.

Offset	Bytes	Remarks
00H	2	Record type (63H 00H)
02H	2	Record length in bytes
04H	2	1 = Object is protected

Table 15.144 BIFF record type 63H (version 3.0–4.0)

15.2.67 PALETTE – Color Palette Definition (record type 92H, version 3.0–4.0)

This record defines a color palette.

Offset	Bytes	Remarks
00H	2	Record type (92H 00H)
02H	2	Record length in bytes
04H	2	Number of entries
06H	4	First palette color
0AH	4	Second palette color
0EH	4	....

Table 15.145 BIFF record type 92H (version 3.0–4.0)

The palette entries are stored as 4-byte codes. The first three bytes define the color (red, green, blue). The fourth byte is empty. If the standard palette is used, the BIFF file contains no COLOR records. In EXCEL 3.0 the palette defines 16 colors.

15.2.68 PANE – Number of Panes and Position (record type 41H, version 2.0–4.0)

This record defines the number of panes and their position.

Offset	Bytes	Remarks
00H	2	Record type (41H 00H)
02H	2	Record length in bytes
04H	2	Horizontal position of split (0 = none)
06H	2	Vertical position of split (0 = none)
08H	2	Top row visible in bottom pane
0AH	2	Leftmost visible column in right pane
0CH	2	Number of the active pane

Table 15.146 BIFF record type 41H (version 2.0–4.0)

The position of the horizontal and vertical split is defined in $\frac{1}{20}$ point. The active pane is defined in the last word:

Value	Active pane
0	Lower right
1	Upper right
2	Lower left
3	Upper left

Table 15.147 Coding the active pane

A `WINDOWS2` record is used if the document window associated with a pane has frozen panes. If there is a vertical split, the first word defines the number of visible rows in the upper pane. If there is a horizontal split, the second word defines the number of visible columns in the left pane.

15.2.69 PASSWORD – Password Protection (record type 13H, version 2.0–4.0)

This record contains the encrypted password.

Offset	Bytes	Remarks
00H	2	Record type (13H 00H)
02H	2	Record length in bytes
04H	2	Encrypted password

Table 15.148 BIFF record type 13H (version 2.0–4.0)

The password is set in the *Protect Document* option.

15.2.70 PLS – Environment-Specific Print Record (record type 4DH, version 4DH)

The PLS record is used on the Macintosh to store environment-specific print information.

Offset	Bytes	Remarks
00H	2	Record type (4DH 00H)
02H	2	Record length in bytes
04H	2	Operating system
		0 = Microsoft Windows
		1 = Macintosh
		2 = OS/2
06H	n	TPRINT structure

Table 15.149 BIFF record type 4DH (version 2.0–4.0 Macintosh)

This record type is used in BIFF2 only, on the Macintosh. From BIFF3 this record can also be used under Windows with the following structure:

Offset	Bytes	Remarks
00H	2	Record type (4DH 00H)
02H	2	Record length in bytes
04H	2	Operating environment
		0 = Microsoft Windows
		1 = Macintosh
06H	2	Orientation
		1: Portrait
		2: Landscape
08H	2	Paper size
0AH	2	Scale factor (Windows DEVMODE)

Table 15.150 BIFF record type 4DH (version 3.0 Windows)

In BIFF4 additional information was added for Windows:

Spreadsheets

Spreadsheets

Offset	Bytes	Remarks
00H	2	Record type (4DH 00H)
02H	2	Record length in bytes
04H	2	Environment 0 = Microsoft Windows 1 = Macintosh
06H	2	Orientation 1: Portrait 2: Landscape
08H	2	Paper size
0AH	2	Scale factor
0CH	2	Printer resolution
0EH	2	Y-resolution of printer

Table 15.151 BIFF record type 4DH (version 4.0 Windows)

The paper size, scaling and resolution depend on the Windows DEVMODE data structure.

15.2.71 PRECISION – Precision (record type 0EH, version 2.0–4.0)

This record stores the *Precision As Displayed* option.

Offset	Bytes	Remarks
00H	4	Record type (0EH 00H)
02H	2	Record length in bytes
04H	2	0: Precision as displayed option selected

Table 15.152 BIFF record type 0EH (version 2.0–4.0)

15.2.72 PRINTGRIDLINES – Print Grid Lines (record type 2BH, version 2.0–4.0)

This record stores the *Gridline* option.

Offset	Bytes	Remarks
00H	2	Record type (2BH 00H)
02H	2	Record length in bytes
04H	2	1: Print gridlines

Table 15.153 BIFF record type 2BH (version 2.0–4.0)

15.2.73 PRINTHEADERS – Print Row/Column Header (record type 2AH, version 2.0–4.0)

The record contains a flag for the row and column heading option from the page setup box.

Offset	Bytes	Remarks
00H	2	Record type (2AH 00H)
02H	2	Record length in bytes
04H	2	1: Print row and column heading

Table 15.154 BIFF record type 2AH (version 2.0–4.0)

15.2.74 PROTECT – Cells protected (record type 12H, version 2.0–4.0)

The record stores the *Protect Document* option.

Offset	Bytes	Remarks
00H	2	Record type (12H 00H)
02H	2	Record length in bytes
04H	2	1 = Document is protected

Table 15.155 BIFF record type 12H (version 2.0–4.0)

15.2.75 PUB – Publisher (record type 89H, version 3.0–4.0)

This record type is used for the Macintosh only and stores information for Mac-Publisher.

Offset	Bytes	Remarks
00H	2	Record type (89H 00H)
02H	2	Record length in bytes
04H	2	Option flag
06H	6	Reference structure
0CH	36	Section record associated with the publisher area
30H	*n*	Contents of the alias pointed to by the section record

Table 15.156 BIFF record type 89H (version 3.0–4.0)

The option flag uses the following bits:

Bit	Remarks
0	1: Published appearance is shown when printed
1	1: Published size is shown when printed
2–15	Unused

Table 15.157 Coding of the option flag

In Windows this record must be skipped. The data area is stored after offset 30H.

15.2.76 REFMODE – Reference Mode (record type 0FH, version 2.0–4.0)

This record stores the reference mode set in the *Workspace* option.

Offset	Bytes	Remarks
00H	2	Record type (0FH 00H)
02H	2	Record length in bytes
04H	2	Reference mode: 0 = R1C1 Mode 1 = A1 Mode

Table 15.158 BIFF record type 0FH (version 2.0–4.0)

15.2.77 RIGHTMARGIN – Right Margin Definition (record type 27H, version 2.0–4.0)

This record defines the right margin of a printout in inches.

Offset	Bytes	Remarks
00H	2	Record type (27H 00H)
02H	2	Record length in bytes
04H	8	Right margin (IEEE value)

Table 15.159 BIFF record type 27H (version 2.0–4.0)

15.2.78 RK – Cell With RK Number (record type 27EH, version 3.0–4.0)

This record contains a cell value in an internal number format (RK).

Offset	Bytes	Remarks
00H	2	Record type (7EH 02H)
02H	2	Record length in bytes
04H	2	Row number (starts from 0)
06H	2	Columns number (starts from 0)
08H	2	Index to an XF record containing the cell format
0AH	4	4-byte RK number

Table 15.160 BIFF record type 27EH (version 3.0–4.0)

EXCEL stores data in an internal 32-bit format to save space. An RK number is either a 30-bit integer or the most significant 30 bits of an IEEE number. The two LSB (bit 0 and bit 1) are always reserved for the RK field. This field encodes the RK type:

Code	Priority	RK type
0	1	IEEE number
1	3	IEEE number * 100
2	2	Integer number
3	4	Integer number * 100

Table 15.161 Coding RK types

In an IEEE number (RK type 0, 1) the MSB defines the sign. Bits 20–30 define the exponent and the mantissa is stored in bits 2-10. Bits 0 and 1 are used to encode the RK type.

An integer value (RK type 2, 3) uses bits 2-31 for the value. Bits 0 and 1 are used for the RK type.

EXCEL first tries to store a value in an RK record. The column *Priority* (Table 15.161) defines the priority for coding a number. If EXCEL cannot store a number in the RK format, a NUMBER record is used to store the number in IEEE floating point format. The INTEGER record type is obsolete from BIFF3.

15.2.79 ROW – Row Description (record type 08H, version 2.0–4.0)

This record contains information about the cell size. In BIFF2 the following structure is used:

Offset	Bytes	Remarks
00H	2	Record type (08H 00H)
02H	2	Record length in bytes
04H	2	Row number
06H	2	First defined column of a row
08H	2	Last defined column of a row +1
0AH	2	Row height
0CH	2	Reserved (should be 0)
0EH	1	1: Row has standard cell attributes
0FH	2	Relative file offset to cell records for the row
11H	3	Standard cell attributes
14H	2	XF record index number

Table 15.162 BIFF record type 08H (version 2.0)

The cell attributes are described in the BLANK record (*see* Section 15.2.4). From BIFF3 a modified structure is used:

Offset	Bytes	Remarks
00H	2	Record type (08H 02H)
02H	2	Record length in bytes
04H	2	Row number

Table 15.163 BIFF record type 208H (version 3.0–4.0) (*continues over...*)

Offset	Bytes	Remarks
06H	2	First defined column of a row
08H	2	Last defined column of a row +1
0AH	2	Row height
0CH	2	Reserved (should be 0)
0EH	2	Relative file offset to the first cell record of the row
10H	2	Option flag
12H	2	Index to XF record

Table 15.163 BIFF record type 208H (version 3.0–4.0) (*cont.*)

The word at offset 12H only contains a valid index to an XF record if bit 7 in the option flag is set. The word at offset 0CH is used internally and should be set to 0. The cell numbering starts at 0.

The following table shows the coding of the option flag:

Bit	**Remarks**
0-2	Index to outline level row
3	Reserved
4	1: Row collapsed in outline
5	1: Row height is set to 0
6	1: Font and row height incompatible
7	1: Row formatted, even if contains all blank cells
8-15	Reserved

Table 15.164 Coding of option flag

The row height is defined in 1/20 point. If bit 15 in the row height is set, the standard row height is used. The lower bits contain the original row height in 1/20 point.

15.2.80 SAVERECALC – Recalculate before Save (record type 5FH, version 3.0–4.0)

This record stores a flag which organizes the recalculation of a worksheet.

Offset	**Bytes**	**Remarks**
00H	2	Record type (5FH 00H)
02H	2	Record length in bytes
04H	2	1: Recalculate before save

Table 15.165 BIFF record type 5FH (version 3.0–4.0)

Spreadsheets

15.2.81 SCL – Window Zoom Magnification (record type A0H, version 4.0)

This record type is used in BIFF4 to store a zoom factor.

Offset	Bytes	Remarks
00H	2	Record type (A0H 00H)
02H	2	Record length in bytes
04H	2	Numerator of reduced fraction
06H	2	Denominator of reduced fraction

Table 15.166 BIFF record type A0H (version 4.0)

The magnification is stored as a reduced fraction (75% = 3/4). Without an SCL record the magnification is set to 100%.

15.2.82 SELECTION – Current Selection (record type 1DH, version 2.0–4.0)

This record defines the selected cell in a split window.

Offset	Bytes	Remarks
00H	2	Record type (1DH 00H)
02H	2	Record length in bytes
04H	1	Pane number
05H	2	Row number of the active cell
07H	2	Column number of the active cell
09H	2	Reference number of the active cell
0BH	2	Number of entries in the following field
0DH	*n*	Array of references

Table 15.167 BIFF record type 1DH (version 2.0–4.0)

The byte at offset 04H defines which pane is used:

Number	Pane
0	Bottom right
1	Top right
2	Bottom left
3	Top left

Table 15.168 Coding of the pane number

If the window is not split, the code 3 is stored. The index to the reference array starts from 0. The reference field has the following structure:

Offset	Bytes	Remarks
0	2	First row of the reference
2	2	Last row of the reference
4	1	First column of the reference
5	1	Last column of the reference

Table 15.169 Structure of the reference array

If a selection exceeds the record length, several SELECTION records are used.

15.2.83 SETUP – Page Setup (record type A1H, version 4.0)

This record contains the page setup parameters.

Offset	Bytes	Remarks
00H	2	Record type (A1H 00H)
02H	2	Record length in bytes
04H	2	Paper size
06H	2	Scale factor
08H	2	First page number
0AH	2	Fit to width
0CH	2	Fit to height
0EH	2	Option flag

Table 15.170 BIFF record type A1H (version 4.0)

The structure of the option flag is as follows:

Bit	Remarks
0	Print over, then down
1	0: Landscape, 1: Portrait
2	1: Paper size, scale and orientation are not initialized
2	Black and white cells
3–15	Unused

Table 15.171 Coding of the option flag

15.2.84 SOUND – Sound Note (record type 96H, version 4.0)

This record is used to store a sound note.

Offset	Bytes	Remarks
00H	2	Record type (96H 00H)
02H	2	Record length in bytes
04H	2	4257H Sound signature
06H	2	Environment 1: Windows 2: Macintosh
08H	2	Length of sound data
0AH	*n*	Sound data

Table 15.172 BIFF record type 96H (version 4.0)

15.2.85 STANDARDWIDTH – Standard Column Width (record type 99H, version 4.0)

This record is defined from BIFF4 and contains the standard cell width.

Offset	Bytes	Remarks
00H	2	Record type (99H 00H)
02H	2	Record length in bytes
04H	2	Standard cell width

Table 15.173 BIFF record type 99H (version 4.0)

The value is defined in $\frac{1}{256}$ of the character width.

15.2.86 STRING – String Value of a Formula (record type 07H, version 2.0–4.0)

If a formula has a string result, this result is stored in the STRING record following the FORMULA record. BIFF2 uses the following record structure:

Offset	Bytes	Remarks
00H	2	Record type (07H 00H)
02H	2	Record length in bytes
04H	1	String length in bytes
05H	*n*	String

Table 15.174 BIFF record type 07H (version 2.0)

From BIFF3 the field for the string length is stored in a word:

Offset	Bytes	Remarks
00H	2	Record type (07H 02H)
02H	2	Record length in bytes
04H	2	String length in bytes
06H	*n*	String

Table 15.175 BIFF record type 207H (version 3.0–4.0)

A STRING record can follow an ARRAY record, if the formula is entered as an element in the array (field).

15.2.87 STYLE – Style Info (record type 293H, version 3.0–4.0)

Each style in a worksheet is saved in a STYLE record.

Offset	Bytes	Remarks
00H	2	Record type (93H 02H)
02H	2	Record length in bytes
04H	2	Style flag
06H	1	Internal style number or the length of the name of a user-defined style
07H	*n*	1-byte level outline style or style name

Table 15.176 BIFF record type 293H (version 3.0–4.0)

The coding of the *style flag* is shown in the following table:

Bit	Remarks
0-11	Index to the XF record
12-14	Unused
15	0: User-defined style 1: Built-in style

Table 15.177
Style flag

If bit 15 in the style flag is set, the style is user-defined. In this case the length of the style name is defined in the word at offset 06H, followed by the name. Otherwise a style number is specified. This number is coded as follows:

Number	Style
0	Normal
1	RowLevel_n
2	ColumnLevel_n
3	Comma
4	Currency
5	Percent

Table 15.178
Coding of the style number

The outline styles RowLevel_n and ColumnLevel_n are defined by codes 1 and 2. These styles are associated with level code n-1.

15.2.88 SUB – Subscriber (record type 91H, version 3.0–4.0)

This record type is used only for the Macintosh Publisher.

Offset	Bytes	Remarks
00H	2	Record type (91H 00H)
02H	2	Record length in bytes
04H	6	Reference structure

Table 15.179
BIFF record type 91H (version 3.0–4.0) (*continues over...*)

Offset	Bytes	Remarks
0AH	2	Number of rows in SUB range
0CH	2	Number of columns in SUB range
0EH	2	Option flag
10H	2	Size of alias range
12H	36	Section record
36H	*n*	Alias range
..H	*n*	String containing a path to the Publisher + 00H

Table 15.179 BIFF record type 91H (version 3.0–4.0)

The option flag has the following structure:

Bit	Remarks
0	Reserved
1	1: Description in object layer
2-15	Reserved

Table 15.180 Coding of option flag

15.2.89 SYNC – Sync Window (record type 97H, version 4.0)

This record type stores the scroll position, if the Sync option for horizontal or vertical split windows is set.

Offset	Bytes	Remarks
00H	2	Record type (97H 00H)
02H	2	Record length in bytes
04H	2	Row index to upper left row heading
06H	2	Column index to upper left column heading

Table 15.181 BIFF record type 97H (version 4.0)

15.2.90 TABLE – Data Table (record type 36H, version 3.0–4.0)

A data table (defined with a /TABLE command) is stored in this record type. BIFF2 uses the following structure:

Offset	Bytes	Remarks
00H	2	Record type (36H 00H)
02H	2	Record length in bytes
04H	2	First row of the table
06H	2	Last row of the table
08H	1	First column of the table
09H	1	Last column of the table
0AH	1	Recalculation flag 0: Table is calculated >1: Table needs recalculation
0BH	1	Flag 0: Column input table 1: Row input table
0CH	2	Row input cell
0EH	2	Column input cell

Table 15.182 BIFF record type 36H (version 2.0)

In BIFF2 the record describes a one-input data table. The TABLE2 record is used for a two-input data table.

From BIFF3 the following structure is used:

Offset	Bytes	Remarks
00H	2	Record type (36H 02H)
02H	2	Record length in bytes
04H	2	First row of the table
06H	2	Last row of the table
08H	1	First column of the table
09H	1	Last column of the table
0AH	2	Option flag
0CH	2	Row of the row input cell
0EH	2	Column of the row input cell
10H	2	Row of the column input cell
12H	2	Column of the column input cell

Table 15.183 BIFF record type 97H (version 3.0–4.0)

The option flag contains 2 bytes and is defined as:

Bit	Remarks
0	Always calculate formula
1	Calculate formula if file is opened
2	0: Input cell is a column input cell
	1: Input cell is a row input cell
3	0: One-input data table
	1: Two-input data table
4-15	Reserved

Table 15.184 Coding option flag

The area in which the table is entered is defined from offset 04H to 09H. This area is the inner part of the table and excludes the outer columns or rows with input values or table formats.

15.2.91 TABLE2 – Data Table 2 (record type 37H, version 2.0)

This record type is used to store two-input data tables (X,Y) in BIFF2.

Offset	Bytes	Remarks
00H	2	Record type (37H 00H)
02H	2	Record length in bytes
04H	2	First row in table
06H	2	Last row in table
08H	1	First column in table
09H	1	Last column in table
0AH	1	Recalculation flag
		0: Table calculated
		x: Table needs recalculation
0BH	1	Reserved (must be 0)
0CH	2	Row of row input cell
0EH	2	Column of row input cell
10H	2	Row of column input cell
12H	2	Column of column input cell

Table 15.185 BIFF record type 37H (version 2.0)

15.2.92 TEMPLATE – Document is a Template (record type 60H, version 3.0–4.0)

If this record occurs, the file is a template. The record consists only of the opcode and the record length (60H 00H) and must follow the BOF record.

15.2.93 TOPMARGIN – Top Margin Settings (record type 28H, version 2.0–4.0)

This record defines the top margin in inches for printer output.

Offset	Bytes	Remarks
00H	2	Record type (28H 00H)
02H	2	Record length in bytes
04H	8	Upper margin in inches (IEEE floating point)

Table 15.186 BIFF record type 28H (version 2.0–4.0)

The margin is defined in the *File Page Setup* command dialog box and is stored as an 8-byte IEEE floating point value.

15.2.94 UNCALCULATED – Recalculation Status (record type 5EH, version 3.0–4.0)

If this record is present, the *calculation* message was visible in the status bar when EXCEL saved the file.

Offset	Bytes	Remarks
00H	2	Record type (5EH 00H)
02H	2	Record length in bytes
04H	4	Reserved (must be 0)

Table 15.187 BIFF record type 5EH (version 3.0–4.0)

This occurs if a sheet is set to manual recalculation and the user changes the content of a cell. The results are not valid until a recalculation is done.

15.2.95 VCENTER – Center Vertical (record type 84H, version 3.0–4.0)

This record centers a printed sheet between the top and bottom margins.

Offset	Bytes	Remarks
00H	2	Record type (84H 00H)
02H	2	Record length in bytes
04H	2	1: Center output

Table 15.188 BIFF record type 84H (version 3.0–4.0)

15.2.96 VERTICALPAGEBREAKS – Column Page Breaks (record type 1AH, version 2.0–4.0)

This record contains a list of page breaks for columns.

Offset	Bytes	Remarks
00H	2	Record type (1AH 00H)
02H	2	Record length in bytes
04H	2	Number of page breaks
06H	*n**2	Field containing column numbers

Table 15.189 BIFF record type 1AH (version 2.0–4.0)

Offset 06H defines an array of 2-byte values, giving the column numbers where page breaks occur, in ascending order.

15.2.97 WINDOW1 – Windows Information (record type 3DH, version 2.0–4.0)

This record defines basic information for an EXCEL window.

Offset	Bytes	Remarks
00H	2	Record type (3DH 00H)
02H	2	Record length in bytes
04H	2	Horizontal window position
06H	2	Vertical window position
08H	2	Window width
0AH	2	Window height
0CH	1	1: Window is hidden

Table 15.190 BIFF record type 3DH (version 2.0–4.0)

The window coordinates and its size in 1/20 point are defined.

15.2.98 WINDOW2 – Windows Information (record type 3EH, version 2.0–4.0)

This record defines additional information for EXCEL windows. In BIFF2 the following structure is used:

Offset	Bytes	Remarks
00H	2	Record type (3EH 00H)
02H	2	Record length in bytes
04H	1	1: Window should display formulas
05H	1	1: Window should display gridlines
06H	1	1: Window should display row and column headings
07H	1	1: Panes in the windows should be frozen
08H	1	1: Window should display zero values
09H	2	Top row visible in the window
0BH	2	Leftmost column visible in the window
0DH	1	1: Draw column/row headings and gridlines in the windows default foreground color
0EH	4	Color grids and row/column heading

Table 15.191 BIFF record type 3EH (version 2.0)

From BIFF3 the following record structure is used:

Offset	Bytes	Remarks
00H	2	Record type (3EH 02H)
02H	2	Record length in bytes
04H	2	Option flag
06H	2	Top row visible in the window
08H	2	Leftmost column visible in the window
0AH	2	Color row/column heading and gridlines

Table 15.192 BIFF record type 23EH (version 3.0–4.0)

The option flag is defined as:

Bit	Remarks
0	0: Window should display formulas 1: Window should display gridlines
1	1: Display gridlines
2	1: Window should display row/column headings
3	1: Panes in the window are frozen
4	1: Window should display zero values
5	0: Color definition at offset 0AH 1: Standard color
6	1: Arabic EXCEL version
7	1: Display outline symbols
8–15	Reserved

Table 15.193 Coding of option flag

15.2.99 WINDOWPROTECT – Windows are protected (record type 19H, version 2.0–4.0)

This record stores the *Protect Document* option.

Offset	Bytes	Remarks
00H	2	Record type (19H 00H)
02H	2	Record length in bytes
04H	2	1 = Document windows protected

Table 15.194 BIFF record type 19H (version 2.0–4.0)

15.2.100 WRITEACCESS – User Name (record type 5CH, version 3.0–4.0)

The user name entered during installation is stored in this record.

Offset	Bytes	Remarks
00H	2	Record type (5CH 00H)
02H	2	Record length in bytes
04H	1	Name length
05H	x	User name

Table 15.195 BIFF record type 5CH (version 3.0–4.0)

The name is padded to a length of 31 bytes with blanks (20H).

15.2.101 WRITEPROT – Document Write-Protected (record type 86H, version 3.0–4.0)

This record contains no data and signals that the worksheet is write protected. All other information is stored in the FILESHARING record (Section 15.2.33).

15.2.102 WSBOOL – Workspace Info (record type 81H, version 3.0–4.0)

This record defines additional information for the worksheet area. BIFF3 uses the following structure:

Offset	Bytes	Remarks
00H	2	Record type (81H 00H)
02H	2	Record length in bytes
04H	2	Option flag

Table 15.196 BIFF record type 81H (version 3.0)

The option flag has the following structure:

Bit	Remarks
0	1: Auto page break visible
1–4	Unused

Table 15.197 Coding of option flag (*continues over...*)

Bit	Remarks
5	0: Auto Styles to Outline
6	1: Summary Rows Below Option On
7	1: Summary Columns to Right On
8	1: Fit to Page Option On
9	1: Save External Link Values Off
10–11	1: Outline Symbols displayed
12–15	Unused

Table 15.197 Coding of option flag (*cont.*)

The information stored in the flag comes from several option boxes.
In BIFF4 the same record structure is used, but the option flag is extended:

Bit	**Remarks**
0	1: Auto Page Break visible
1–4	Unused
5	0: Auto Styles to Outline
6	1: Summary Rows Below Option On
7	1: Summary Columns to Right On
8	1: Fit to Page Option On
9	1: Save External Link Values Off
10–11	1: Outline Symbols displayed
12–13	1: Sync Vertical Option On
	2: Sync Horizontal Option On
	3: Both Sync Options On
14	1: Alternate Expression Option On
15	1: Alternate Formula Entry Option On

Table 15.198 Coding of option flag in BIFF4

15.2.103 XCT – CRN Record Count (record type 59H, version 3.0–4.0)

This record stores the number of `CRN` records in a BIFF file.

Offset	Bytes	Remarks
00H	2	Record type (59H 00H)
02H	2	Record length in bytes
04H	2	Number of CRN records

Table 15.199 BIFF record type 59H (version 3.0–4.0)

The CRN records follow the XCT record.

15.2.104 XF – Extended Cell Format (record type 43H, version 2.0–4.0)

This record defines data for the extended EXCEL cell format. In BIFF2 the following record structure is used:

Offset	Bytes	Remarks
00H	2	Record type (43H 00H)
02H	2	Record length in bytes
04H	1	Index to FONT record
05H	1	Gridline codes (for Kanji EXCEL)
06H	1	Flags Bit 0-5: Index in FORMAT record 6 = 1 Cell is locked 7 = 1 Cell is hidden
07H	2	Alignment flag Bit 0-2: 0 General 1 Left 2 Center 3 Right 4 Fill Bit 3=1 Cell has left border Bit 4=1 Cell has right border Bit 5=1 Cell has top border Bit 6=1 Cell has bottom border Bit 7=1 Cell is shadowed

Table 15.200 BIFF record type 243H (version 2.0)

In BIFF3 a modified structure is used:

Offset	Bytes	Remarks
00H	2	Record type (43H 02H)
02H	2	Record length in bytes
04H	1	Index to the FONT record
05H	1	Index to the FORMAT record
06H	2	Flags
		Bit 0: 1 Cell is locked
		1: 1 Cell is hidden
		2: 1 For style XF
		3-9: Unused
		10: 1 Number check box is Off
		11: 1 Font check box is Off
		12: 1 Alignment check box is Off
		13: 1 Border check box is Off
		14: 1 Pattern check box is Off
		15: 1 Protection check box is Off
08H	2	Alignment Flag
		Bit 0-2:
		0 General
		1 Left
		2 Center
		3 Right
		4 Fill
		5 Justify
		6 Center across selection
		Bit 3: 1 Text wrap in cell
		4-15: Index to XF record
0AH	2	Flags
		Bit 0-5: Fill pattern
		6-10: Index to foreground color palette
		11-15: Index to background color palette

Table 15.201 BIFF record type 243H (version 3.0) (*continues over...*)

Spreadsheets

Offset	Bytes	Remarks
0CH	2	Flags Bit 0-2: Frame type (top line) 0 No frame 1 Normal line 2 Medium thick line 3 Dash (-----) 4 Dash short 5 Thick line 6 Double line 7 Dotted Bit 3-7: Index to color palette top frame Bit 8-10: Frame type (left border) Bit 11-15: Index in color palette left frame
0EH	2	Flags Bit 0-2: Frame type (bottom line) Bit 3-7: Index to color palette bottom frame Bit 8-10: Frame type (right border) Bit 11-15: Index to color palette right frame

Table 15.201 BIFF record type 243H (version 3.0) (*cont.*)

BIFF4 uses a modified structure:

Offset	**Bytes**	**Remarks**
00H	2	Record type (43H 04H)
02H	2	Record length in bytes
04H	1	Index to the FONT record
05H	1	Index to the FORMAT record
06H	2	Flags Bit 0: 1 Cell is locked 1: 1 Cell is hidden 2: 0 Cell XF 1 Style XF 3: Alternate Key Option Off 4-15: XF Index

Table 2.202 BIFF record type 443H (version 4.0) (*continues over...*)

Offset	Bytes	Remarks
08H	2	Alignment flag Bit 0-2: 0 General 1 Left 2 Center 3 Right 4 Fill Bit 3: 1 Wrap text in cell Bit 4-5: Vertical alignment 0 Top 1 Center 2 Bottom Bit 6-7: Text orientation 0 No rotation 1 Top to bottom (letters upright) 2 Rotate 90 degrees counterclockwise 3 Rotate 90 degrees clockwise Bit 8-9: Unused The following bits signal a changed option compared to the parent XF record: Bit 10: Index FORMAT record Bit 11: Index FONT record Bit 12: Alignment or text wrap field Bit 13: Border line field Bit 14: Pattern field Bit 15: Hidden or locked field
0AH	2	Flags Bit 0-5: Fill pattern 6-10: Index to color palette foreground 11-15: Index to color palette background
0CH	2	Flags Bit 0-2: Frame type (upper line) 0 No frame 1 Normal line 2 Medium thick line 3 Dashed (-----) 4 Dashed short

Table 15.202 BIFF record type 443H (version 4.0) (*cont.*)

Spreadsheets

Offset	Bytes	Remarks	
		5 Thick line	
		6 Double line	
		7 Dotted	
		Bit 3–7:	Index to color palette top frame
		Bit 8–10:	Frame type (left side)
		Bit 11–15:	Index to color palette left frame
0EH	2	Flags	
		Bit 0–2:	Frame type (bottom line)
		Bit 3–7:	Index to color palette bottom frame
		Bit 8–10:	Frame type (right side)
		Bit 11–15:	Index to color palette right frame

Table 15.202 BIFF record type 443H (version 4.0) (*cont.*)

The record extends the format description for one or several cell records in a BIFF file.

15.2.105 STYLE XF Record (record type 243H, version 3.0)

Style XF records have the following structure in BIFF3:

Offset	**Bytes**	**Remarks**
00H	2	Record type (43H 02H)
02H	2	Record length in bytes
04H	1	Index to FONT record
05H	1	Index to FORMAT record
06H	2	Flags
		Bit 0: 1 Cell is locked
		1: 1 Cell is hidden
		2: 0 For cell XF
		1 For style XF
		3–9: Unused
		10: 1 Number option Off

Table 15.203 BIFF record type 243H Style XF record (version 3.0) (*continues over...*)

Offset	Bytes	Remarks
		11: 1 Font Option Off 12: 1 Alignment option is Off 13: 1 Border option is Off 14: 1 Pattern option is Off 15: 1 Protection option is Off
08H	2	Alignment flag horizontal Bit 0-2: 0 General 1 Left 2 Center 3 Right 4 Fill Bit 3: 1 Textwrap in cell 4-15: FFF0H
0AH	2	Flags Bit 0-5: Fill pattern 6-10: Index to color palette foreground 11-15: Index to color palette background
0CH	2	Flags Bit 0-2: Frame type (top line) 0 No frame 1 Normal line 2 Medium thick line 3 Dashed (-----) 4 Dashed short 5 Thick line 6 Double line 7 Dotted Bit 3-7: Index to color palette top frame Bit 8-10: Frame type (left side) Bit 11-15: Index to color palette left frame
0EH	2	Flags Bit 0-2: Frame type (bottom line) Bit 3-7: Index to color palette bottom frame Bit 8-10: Frame type (right side) Bit 11-15: Index to color palette right frame

Table 15.203 BIFF record type 243H Style XF record (version 3.0) (*cont.*)

Spreadsheets

In BIFF4 the style XF record has the following structure:

Offset	Bytes	Remarks
00H	2	Record type (43H 04H)
02H	2	Record length in bytes
04H	1	Index to the FONT record
05H	1	Index to the FORMAT record
06H	2	Flags Bit 0: 1 Cell is locked 1: 1 Cell is hidden 2: 0 Cell XF 1 Style XF 3: Alternate Key Option Off 4-15: FFF0H
08H	2	Alignment flag Bit 0-2: 0 General 1 Left 2 Center 3 Right 4 Fill 5 Justify 6 Center across selection Bit 3: 1 Wrap text in cell Bit 4-5: Vertical alignment 0 Top 1 Center 2 Bottom Bit 6-7: Text orientation 0 No rotation 1 Top to bottom (letters upright) 2 Rotate 90 degrees counterclockwise 3 Rotate 90 degrees clockwise Bit 8-9: Unused Bit 10: Number option Off Bit 11: Font option Off Bit 12: Alignment option Off Bit 13: Border option Off Bit 14: Pattern option Off Bit 15: Protect option Off
0AH	2	Flags Bit 0-5: Fill pattern 6-10: Index to color palette forerground 11-15: Index to color palette background

Table 15.204 BIFF record type 443H (version 4.0) (*cont.*)

Offset	Bytes	Remarks	
0CH	2	Flags	
		Bit 0–2: Frame type (top line)	
		0 No frame	
		1 Normal line	
		2 Medium thick line	
		3 Dashed (-----)	
		4 Dashed short	
		5 Thick line	
		6 Double line	
		7 Dotted	
		Bit 3–7:	Index to color palette top frame
		Bit 8–10:	Frame type (left side)
		Bit 11–15:	Index to color palette left frame
0EH	2	Flags	
		Bit 0–2:	Frame type (bottom line)
		Bit 3–7:	Index to color palette bottom frame
		Bit 8–10:	Frame type (right side)
		Bit 11–15:	Index to color palette right frame

Table 15.204 BIFF record type 443H (version 4.0) (*cont.*)

15.2.106 1904 – 1904 Date Format (record type 22H, version 2.0–4.0)

This record type defines the date system used in the EXCEL document.

Offset	Bytes	Remarks
00H	2	Record type (11H 00H)
02H	2	Record length in bytes
04H	2	1 = 1904 Use date system

Table 15.205 BIFF record type 11H (version 2.0–4.0)

The date system is defined in EXCEL with the *Calculation* option.

! Note that additional records are defined for charts and workbooks (*see* Microsoft EXCEL 4 SDK). Microsoft EXCEL 5.0 uses a different file structure (*see* EXCEL 5 SDK).

PART 3

Word processing formats

File formats discussed in Part 3

Texts *produced by word processing programs are very rarely stored in ASCII code. It is much more likely that information on text formatting and various other control characters will be stored in the same file as the text. Every word processing program thus has its own format and, unfortunately, only very few companies are willing to publicize their internal file structures.*

Part 3 *describes the structure of text files used by some of the more well-known and widely distributed programs such as MS-Word, WordPerfect and WordStar.*

16

MS-Word format

MS-Word for DOS was one of the most popular word processing programs. This chapter describes the file format for Word 4.0/5.0 files.

In versions 3.0, 4.0 and 5.0 of Word from Microsoft, a mixed ASCII/binary format is used for the text files. These files are divided into three parts:

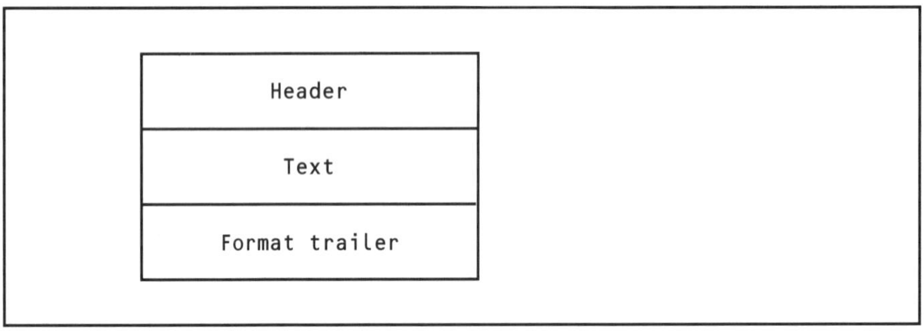

Figure 16.1
Structure of an MS-Word file

The data is stored in the file in 128-byte blocks. Some internal pointers take the form of block numbers from which the offset to the first byte of the relevant block can be calculated, using the following formula:

```
Offset = Block number * 80H
```

Figure 16.2 shows a sample text produced using Word:

Soft hyphenation	Soft hy-phen-ation	Alt -
Hyphenation 2	Hyphen-ation	Ctrl -
Paragraph block text		
Bold on	**Bold text**	Alt B
Normal on	Normal text	Alt Spacebar
Italics on	*Italic text*	Alt I
Underline on	Underlined text	Alt U
Underline double	Double-underlined text	Alt D
Small Capitals	SMALL CAPITALS	Alt K
Strike out	~~Strike out text~~	Alt D
Superscript	Superscript text	Alt H
Subscript	Subscript text	Alt T
Hidden	Hidden text	Alt G
Centered	Centered text	Alt Z
Left aligned	Left-aligned text	Alt L
Right aligned	Right-aligned text	Alt R
Indent left 1.5 cm	Indented text	Alt M
Indent right	Indented text	Alt V
Indent variable		Alt O
Standard paragraph		
Indent for 1st line negative; all other lines of a paragraph are indented left.		
Double line spacing		Alt 2
Capital	CAPITALS	Alt +

Figure 16.2 Text samples using MS-Word 4.0

If a block is not completely filled with data, the remainder of the block is undefined. The first block (block 0) of an MS-Word file contains an 128-byte header defining certain items of control information. This is followed by the blocks containing the actual text. With very few exceptions, these do not contain control codes. If there is no text, these blocks are omitted. The trailer consists of a number of blocks containing the format information for the text. A hex-dump of the corresponding Word file is shown in Figure 16.2.

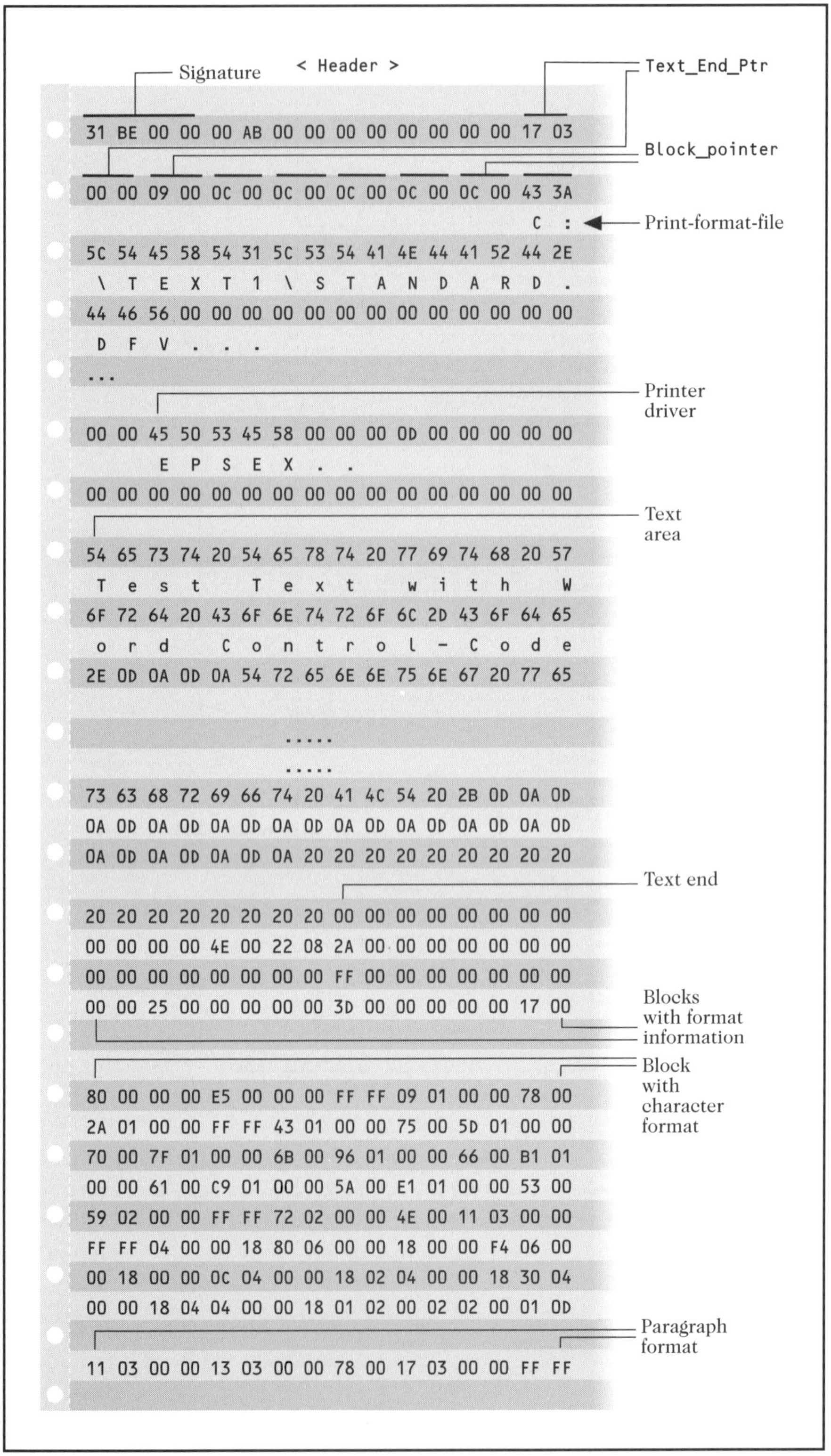

Figure 16.3 Hex-dump of an MS-Word 4.0 file (*continues over...*)

```
2A 01 00 00 FF FF 43 01 00 00 75 00 5D 01 00 00
70 00 7F 01 00 00 6B 00 96 01 00 00 66 00 B1 01
00 00 61 00 C9 01 00 00 5A 00 E1 01 00 00 53 00
59 02 00 00 FF FF 72 02 00 00 4E 00 11 03 00 00
FF FF 04 00 00 18 80 06 00 00 18 00 00 F4 06 00
00 18 00 00 0C 04 00 00 18 02 04 00 00 18 30 04
00 00 18 04 04 00 00 18 01 02 00 02 02 00 01 02
                                                  Section format block 1
80 00 00 00 A3 00 00 00 FF FF A5 00 00 00 FF FF
BD 00 00 00 FF FF D3 00 00 00 FF FF E5 00 00 00
78 00 09 01 00 00 78 00 2A 01 00 00 78 00 43 01
00 00 78 00 5D 01 00 00 78 00 7F 01 00 00 78 00
96 01 00 00 78 00 B1 01 00 00 78 00 C9 01 00 00
78 00 E1 01 00 00 78 00 F6 01 00 00 6F 00 0C 02
                                                  Pointer next block
00 00 66 00 0C 04 00 00 18 02 08 3C 01 1E 00 00
00 C5 02 08 3C 03 1E 00 00 00 C5 02 02 3C 03 10
                                                  Next block
0C 02 00 00 22 02 00 00 72 00 3A 02 00 00 69 00
59 02 00 00 67 00 72 02 00 00 67 00 8F 02 00 00
59 00 9F 02 00 00 FF FF A1 02 00 00 FF FF BD 02
00 00 4E 00 BF 02 00 00 FF FF DE 02 00 00 41 00
96 01 00 00 78 0C 3C 00 1E 00 00 00 00 00 00 00
E0 01 0A 3C 00 1E 00 00 00 C5 02 3B FD 0D 3C 00
1E 00 00 00 00 00 00 00 F0 00 F0 01 3C 08 3C 02
1E 00 00 00 C5 02 08 3C 00 1E 00 00 00 C5 02 0A
DE 02 00 00 FF 02 00 00 6E 00 01 03 00 00 6E 00
03 03 00 00 6E 00 05 03 00 00 6E 00 07 03 00 00
6E 00 09 03 00 00 6E 00 0B 03 00 00 6E 00 0D 03
00 00 6E 00 0F 03 00 00 6E 00 11 03 00 00 65 00
13 03 00 00 5C 00 15 03 00 00 59 00 17 03 00 00
FF FF 18 03 00 00 FF FF 00 C5 02 3B FD 02 3C 03
08 3C 03 1E 00 00 00 C5 02 08 3C 01 1E 00 00 00
C5 02 0C 3C 00 1E 00 00 00 00 00 00 00 E0 01 0E
                                                  Info-block
12 00 13 00 14 00 15 00 16 00 17 00 18 00 20 00
28 00 00 00 00 00 00 00 31 2E 31 2E 39 30 20 20
 (                       1  .  1  .  9  0
31 2E 31 2E 39 30 20 20 97 02 00 00 00 00 00 00
 1  .  1  .  9  0
00 00 00 00 00 00 00 00 00 00 00 00 00 00 00 00
00 00 00 00 00 00 00 00 00 00 00 00 00 00 00 00
```

Figure 16.3 Hex-dump of an MS-Word 4.0 file (*cont.*)

Word processing

Various types of pointer are used in the file:

- File pointers (*4 bytes*), which indicate the absolute position of a byte as an offset from the start of the file.
- Text pointers (*4 bytes*), which specify the relative position (from the start of the text) to a character in the text area. These pointers can be converted to file pointers by adding 80H.
- Block pointers (*2 bytes*), which point to a block. A block pointer is the number of a block within the file and can be converted into a file pointer by multiplying by 80H.

The structure of the three sections of the Word file (header, text, formats) is described below.

16.1 Word headers (versions 3.0, 4.0, 5.0)

As shown in Figure 16.3, Word contains the header information in the first 128 bytes (block 0). The *first 4 bytes* of the file always contain the hex codes 31H BEH 00H 00H. It is assumed that Word uses these bytes as a signature for formatted files. Table 16.1 shows a detailed breakdown of the header.

Offset	Bytes	Field description
00H	4	Word signature 31H BEH 00H 00H
04H	8	Reserved (00H ABH 00H 00H 00H 00H 00H 00H)
0EH	4	Pointer to End-of-text (1st character after text)
12H	2	Block pointer to the block containing the paragraph format
14H	2	Block pointer to the block containing the footnote table
16H	2	Block pointer to the block containing the section formats
18H	2	Block pointer to the block containing the nation table
1AH	2	Block pointer to the block containing the table of page breaks

Table 16.1 Format of a Word 4.0/5.0 header (*continues over...*)

Offset	Bytes	Field description
1CH	2	Block pointer to the block containing file manager information (author, date, and so on)
1EH	66	File name of print format, ASCII string
60H	2	Flag (reserved for Windows Write)
62H	8	Name of the printer driver, ASCII string
6AH	2	Number of blocks used in the file
6CH	2	Bit field for corrected text areas
6EH	18	Reserved (in version 4.0 always 00H); after version 5.0 used for unknown code

Table 16.1 Format of a Word 4.0/5.0 header (*cont.*)

The bytes column is in decimal. At offset 0EH, there is a 4-byte pointer (*file pointer*) to the first unused character after the text. The value is interpreted as an offset from the start of the file to the relevant byte. The number of characters in the text can be calculated by subtracting the number 80H (length of block 0). The following 6 words contain 2-byte pointers which are interpreted as *block numbers*. Information on the format of the text is contained in the specified blocks. A file pointer to the first byte of the block can be calculated by multiplying the block number by 80H. (The structure of format blocks is described below).

The *path, including the drive and file name,* for the print format template is stored at offset 1EH. This text is an ASCIIZ string, that is, the last character is 00H. In MS-DOS, the path is limited to 65 characters, which explains why 66 characters are reserved in the header. Unused bytes must be set to 00H. At offset 62H, there is an 8-byte field containing the name of the printer driver. If the name is shorter than 8 characters, the remaining bytes must be set to 00H. The drive, the path and the driver extension are not specified.

The field at offset 6AH indicates the *number of blocks* containing useful information. A Word file may contain additional blocks, but these are usually filled with null bytes and are ignored.

The word at offset 6CH is interpreted as a 16-bit *field*. It is used to store the format coding for corrected areas of text and generally contains the value 00H 00H, but when a text is modified using the command FORMAT/correction, Word stores the selected settings in the individual bits shown in Table 16.2.

Up to version 4.0, bits 6 to 15 are unused. From Word 5.0 onwards, bits 6 and 7 are used, but their exact meaning is not known. The remaining 18 bytes in the header are reserved and contain the value 00H in version 4.0. From version 5.0, a number of pointers are found in this position, but the significance of these is unknown.

Bit	Field description
0	Format bar: 1 = Yes, 0 = No
3-1	Inserted text
	000 = Underline
	001 = Large capitals
	010 = Normal
	011 = Bold
	100 = —
	101 = —
	110 = Underline double
	111 = —
5-4	Position of correction bar
	00 = No bar
	01 = Left
	10 = Right
	11 = Alternate (left, right)
15-6	Reserved (until version 4.0, unknown in 5.0)

Table 16.2 Coding for FORMAT/ Corrections in Word 4.0

16.2 The Word text area

In versions 3.0 to 5.0 of Word, the first byte containing text stored in ASCII format begins at offset 80H. This text may extend over several blocks. In the last text block, the area from the last valid text character to the end of the block is undefined. The end of the text is indicated in the header (offset 0EH). If Word stores a blank text window, the text block is omitted, and immediately the format information follows the header.

The text contains only a small number of control characters. Table 16.3 lists some of these codes.

Codes 1–5 are used to mark text blocks created by Word. Footnotes are only marked in the text if the user does not indicate footnote markers. If a footnote is allocated an automatic administration number, Word will store this footnote as normal text and information on formatting the footnotes is stored in a separate block in the trailer.

The characters CR/LF (*carriage return/line feed*) indicate the end of a paragraph in Word. It is therefore possible to import ASCII files into Word, because many editors place a CR/LF after every line. However, all Word paragraph commands will then be applied to individual lines, because Word will interpret them as paragraphs. It may therefore be necessary to remove the CR/LF characters at the end of individual lines.

Word uses the ASCII code 31 (1FH) to mark possible hyphenation points. The value 255 (FFH) is used to protect the space between words in terms of hyphenation.

Code	Field description
01H	Text block page
02H	Text block print date
03H	Text block print time
04H	Reserved
05H	Footnote without a footnote marker
09H	Tabulator
0BH	Line feed
0CH	Form feed
0D,0AH	CR/LF as paragraph end
1FH	Hyphenation conditional
C4H	Hyphenation protected
FFH	Space protected

Table 16.3 Interpretation of control codes in Word 4.0/5.0

16.3 Format area in Word

The last text block is followed by an area in which Word stores text formatting information. A number of distinct regions can be distinguished:

- Blocks containing character formats
- Blocks containing paragraph formats
- Blocks containing the footnote table
- Blocks containing section formats
- Blocks containing the section table
- Blocks containing the page break table
- Blocks containing file management information

Each of these regions may extend over several 128-byte blocks. The numbers of the first block in each region except the first are stored in the header, starting at offset 12H.

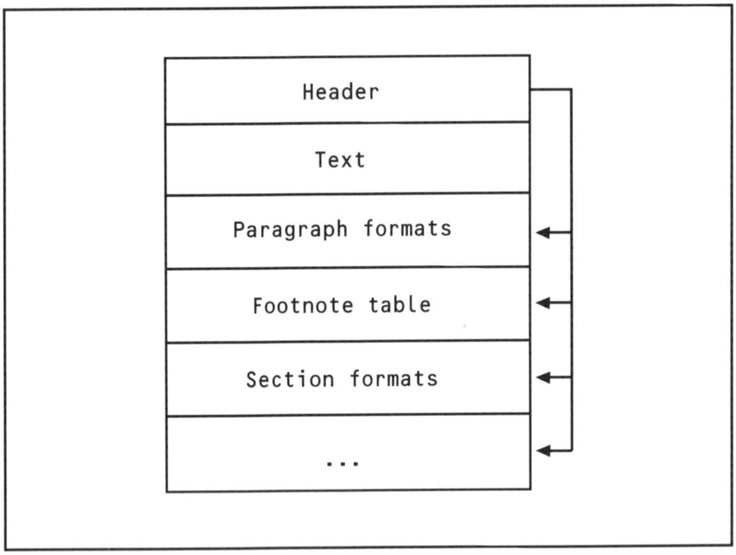

Figure 16.4
Pointers to format regions

16.3.1 Character formats

The first block after the text contains character formats. Word does not define a specific pointer to this block in the header, because its position can be determined by means of the text pointer at offset 0EH. If there is no text area, the description of character formats begins in block 1. Word uses a very sophisticated technique for storing the character formats. The number of possible combinations for formatting a line (bold, italic, and so on) is predetermined from the start and Word stores these format specifications in a table. Then all that is required is to note how the individual sections of text are to be formatted, as shown in Figure 16.5.

The text shown in Figure 16.5 is to be given the character formats normal, **bold** and *italic* as shown in the format table. Whenever bold appears in the text, the program merely refers to the appropriate entry in this table. A pointer marks the start of the bold text. The next format specification cancels the bold. This process is used in Versions 3.0, 4.0 and 5.0. The details shown below relate to Word 4.0 but, to a great extent, they also apply to version 5.0.

The block containing the character formats is structured as shown in Table 16.4. In the first four bytes, there is an offset pointer to the first character in the text to which the format applies. Since this character is always located in block 1, the pointer has the value 00H 00H 00H 80H, but in MS-DOS, the lowest byte is stored first (80H 00H 00H 00H). At offset 04H, there is a pointer table containing two pointers for each format area:

- a text pointer to the first character in a different format,
- a pointer to the format definition in the format table.

The 4-byte text pointer specifies the offset address of the first character to which the format indicated by the second pointer`no longer applies. This text pointer also acts as a start pointer for the new format specification. The next word in the data structure is the pointer to the format definition in the format table at the end of the block. This value is interpreted as an offset from the first text pointer (offset 04H) to the format entry in the format table (Figure 16.6).

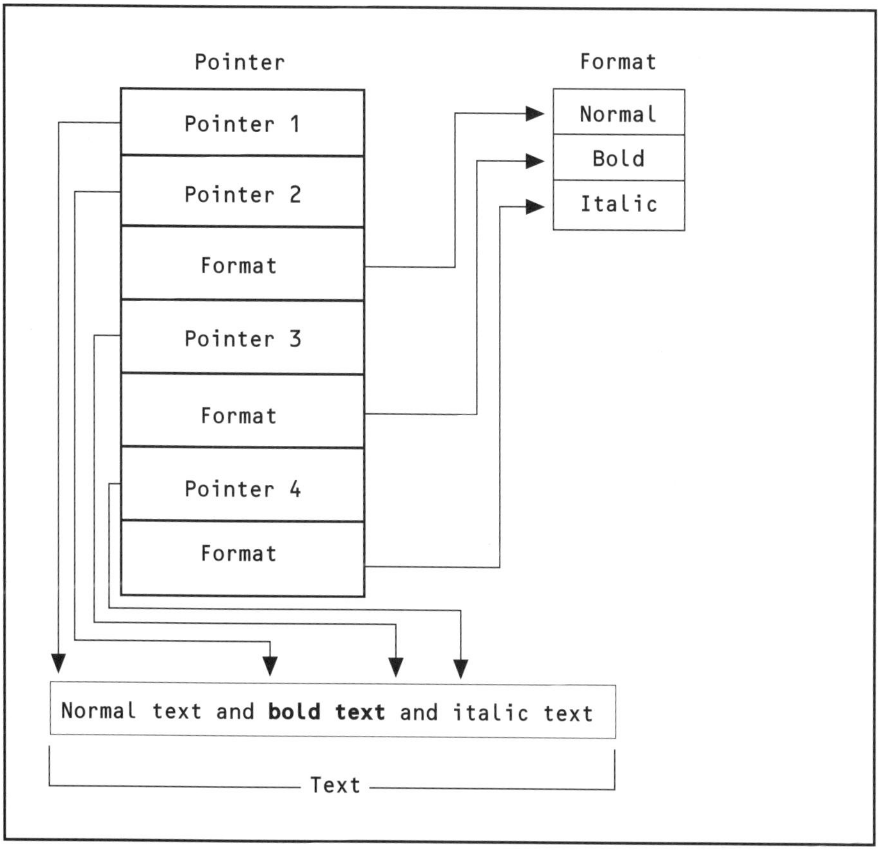

Figure 16.5
Text formats

Offset	Bytes	Field description
00H	4	Pointer to the 1st character in the 1st format
Beginning of table containing text and format pointers:		
04H	4	Pointer to 1st char in 2nd format
08H	2	Pointer to format table for 1st format
0AH	4	Pointer to 1st char in different format than 2nd format
08H	2	Pointer to format table for 2nd format
...	..	....
Beginning of format table		
...	...	....
7EH	...	Last format entry
7FH	1	Number of text areas to be formatted

Table 16.4
Structure of a character format block

Since the number of sections to be formatted varies during word processing, Word begins structuring the format table from the end of the block (that is, the last entry at offset 07EH is the first format in the table). Word stores each new format definition before the previous entry. The number of text areas to be formatted, and thus also the number of valid text pointers (excluding the start pointer), is stored at the end of the block (offset 7FH). The structure of the format table is described in more detail below.

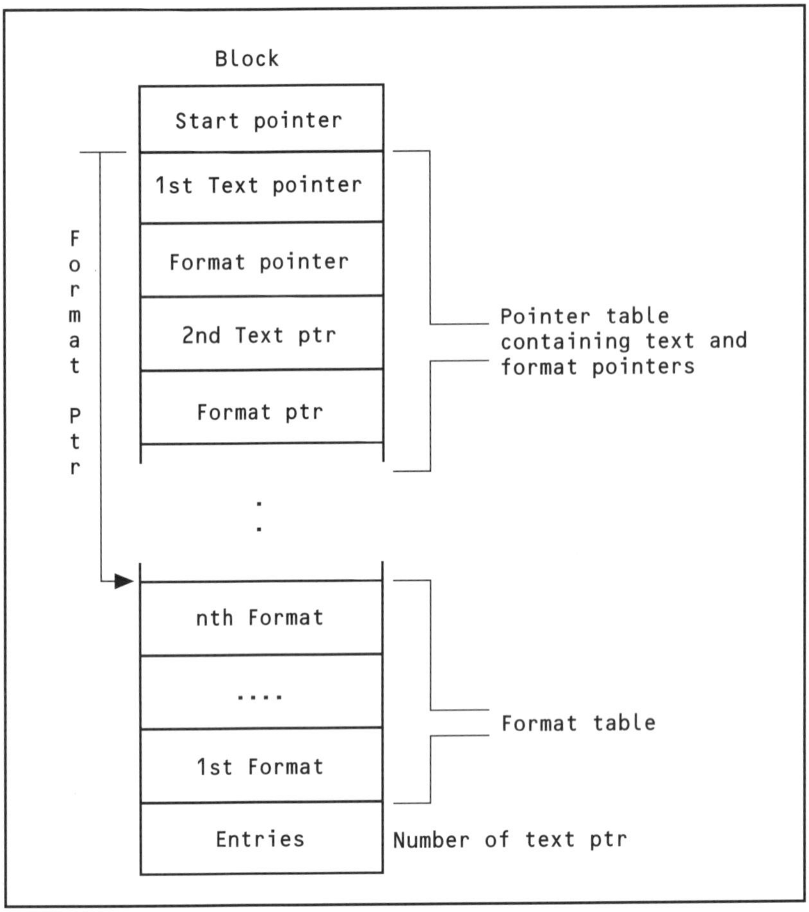

Figure 16.6 Position of the table containing the format descriptions

With longer texts, the number of text and format pointers may exceed the space available in the pointer table, which will cause the table to overflow. Word then creates a new block for character formats and stores information on the existence of this additional block in the last text pointer – if the value of this pointer is the same as the start address of the next block, an additional block is involved. As soon as an additional block is required, Word copies the contents of the current (last) block into memory and sets the number of entries (last byte) to zero. The start pointer is set to the value of the last valid text pointer in the preceding block. Thus the copy contains all the information from the preceding block, and Word fills up the new table with text and format pointers as required.

In the pointer table, a 2-byte format pointer is allocated to every 4-byte text pointer. This indicates the offset from the first text pointer to the relevant format definition at the end of the block. If 4 is added to this value, the result is the offset from the start of the block. If the format pointer contains FFFFH, the text is to be displayed in standard format. For example, the format pointer after the last valid text pointer may contain this value in order to switch back to standard format. If the formatted text exceeds a block, the value FFFFH is stored in the following block. Table 16.5 shows the structure of each entry in the format table.

Offset	Bytes	Field description
00H	1	Number of following bytes for this entry
01H	1	Coding print template: Bit 0 = 1: char formatted with a template, Bits 1–7 define the modes (*see* Table 16.6)
02H	1	Format code (*see* Figure 16.8)
03H	1	Font size in ½ point
04H	1	Character attribute (*see* Table 16.7)
05H	1	Reserved
06H	1	Character position (Superscript, subscript, and so on)
07H–0AH	4	Reserved

Table 16.5 Structure of a format table entry

A format generally consists of several bytes. The first byte indicates the number of following bytes in the definition. The minimum length of a format definition is 2 bytes (1 length byte, 1 format byte). However, if only one of the later bytes (for example, the character position) is required, all the intervening fields must also be stored, even though they are not used.

The second byte of the character format specifies the appropriate variant of the print format template, which describes how the text characters are to be formatted. Figure 16.7 shows the coding of the second byte.

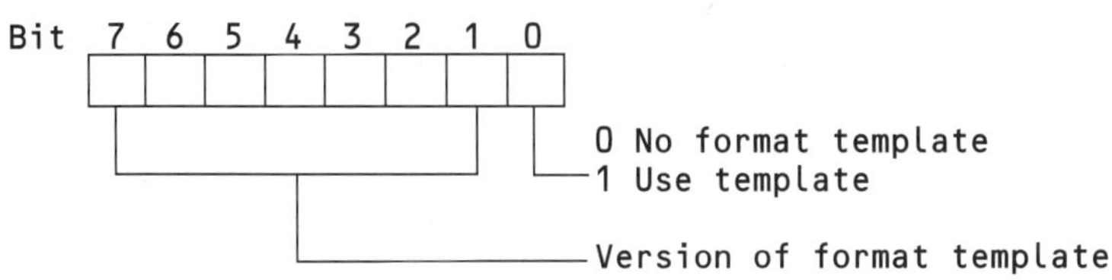

Figure 16.7 Definition of a (format) template

If the lowest bit (bit 0) is set, the remaining bits will contain the variant of the print format template required. Table 16.7 shows some of the templates given in the Word manual:

Code	Field description
0	Standard character
1–12	Template number 1–12
13	Footnote reference
14–18	Template number 13–17
19	Number of pages
20–27	Template number 18–25
28	Short information
29	Line numbers
30–64	Unused

Table 16.6 Various (format) templates

Additional information on this subject can be found in the standard Word documentation. Word stores information on the format structure (bold, italic, font number) in the third byte (if present). The coding is shown in Figure 16.8.

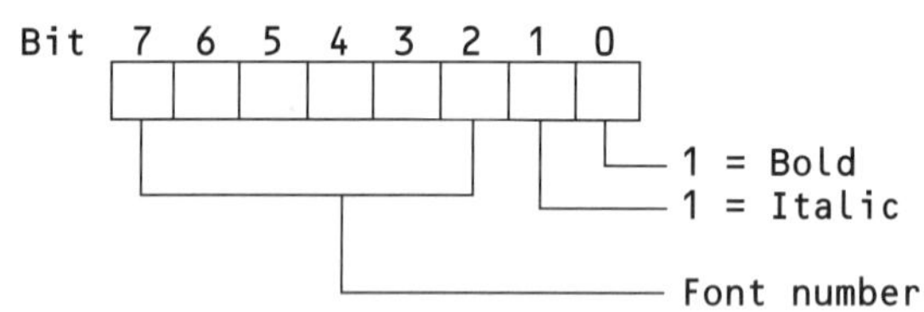

Figure 16.8 Font format coding

Bits 0 and 1 determine the typeface style (bold, italic), while the remaining bits are used for the font number. The allocation of font and font number depends on the printer driver.

The fourth byte specifies the font size in ½ points. The remaining character attributes are stored in the fifth byte. The coding is shown in Table 16.7.

So far, the byte at offset 05H has remained *reserved*. The same applies to the bytes at offsets 07H–0AH. The byte at offset 06H indicates whether a character is to be raised (superscript) or lowered (subscript).

If byte 7 is not equal to 0, bit 7 defines how the character is formatted.

Bits	Field description
0	1 = Underline
1	1 = Strike out
2	1 = Strike out double
3	1 = Insert character in correction mode
4-5	Character size
	00: Normal
	01: Large capitals
	10: —
	11: Capitals
6	Special characters (page, date, and so on)
7	Characters hidden

Table 16.7 Character format attributes

Byte 7	Description
00H	Character normal
01-7FH	Superscript characters
80-FFH	Subscript characters

Table 16.7 Character format attributes

16.3.2 Paragraph format block

In the header, at offset 12H, there is a pointer to the block containing the paragraph formatting details. The structure of this block is the same as that of the character format block. The start pointer (4 bytes) specifies the first character of the first paragraph, which is generally the start of the text. The pointer table then begins with a text pointer (4 bytes) and the offset (2 bytes) indicating the relevant format information. The text pointer points to the next paragraph; the format information offset relates to the first text pointer (the underlying structure is shown in Table 16.4). The last byte in the block indicates the number of valid entries (text pointers). If the last valid text pointer is the same as the start address of the next block, a following block containing additional paragraph formats is involved.

However, the structure defining the paragraph formats is somewhat different from the character format structure. The number of following bytes is stored in the first byte. Table 16.8 gives the structure of a paragraph format definition.

Offset	Bytes	Field description
00H	1	Number of following bytes for this entry
01H	1	Coding format template: Bit 0 = 1: Format template is used to format this paragraph Bits 1–7 define the template number (*see* Table 16.9)
02H	1	Paragraph attribute (*see* Table 16.10)
03H	1	Number of standard paragraph format (usually code 30 *see* Table 16.9)
04H	1	Heading level and representation (*see* Figure 16.8)
05H	2	Right indent in $1/20$ point
07H	2	Left indent in $1/20$ point
09H	2	Left indent of first line in $1/20$ point
0BH	2	Line spacing in $1/20$ point
0DH	2	Heading space in $1/20$ point
0FH	2	End space in $1/20$ point
11H	1	Header/footer and frame details
12H	4	Position of lines round header/footer
13H	4	Reserved (00H)
17H	80	Table of tab descriptions

Table 16.8
Paragraph format in Word 4.0/5.0

Code	Field description codes in bits 1–7
30	Standard format paragraph
31–38	Paragraph format templates 1–8
39	Paragraph footnote text
40–87	Paragraph format templates 9–56
88–94	Paragraph heading levels 1–7
95–98	Paragraph index levels 1–7
99–102	Paragraph table levels 1–7
103	Paragraph header/footer

Table 16.9
Format templates for paragraphs

The byte at offset 01H specifies the variant of the print format template. As in Figure 16.7, the value 1 in bit 0 indicates that the paragraph is to be formatted with a print format template. In case of retrospective direct formatting, this bit is zeroed, while the remaining bits containing the variant code are retained. The code in bits 1 to 7 indicates the variant of the print format template for paragraph formatting as shown in Table 16.9.

The next byte at offset 02H defines the attribute relating to the alignment of the paragraph (left, right, and so on). Table 16.10 shows the coding for these attributes.

Bit	Field description
0–1	Paragraph align 00 = Left 01 = Centered 10 = Right 11 = Block
2	Paragraph on same page
3	Next paragraph to same page
4	Use two columns for paragraph
5–7	Reserved

Table 16.10 Coding of paragraph attributes

The standard format is initially used for every paragraph. In case of retrospective direct formatting of a particular paragraph, Word stores the information on the paragraph print format in the byte at offset 03H (*see* Table 16.9).

The byte at offset 04H specifies the classification level of the paragraph and whether the paragraph is to be hidden. The coding of this byte is shown in Figure 16.9:

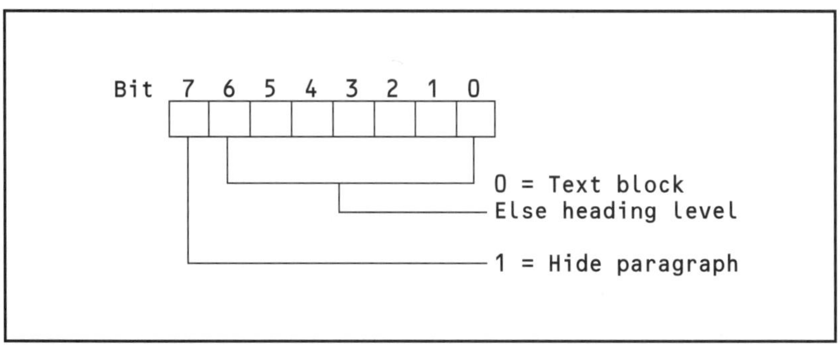

Figure 16.9 Coding heading levels

The next 6 bytes indicate the settings for indent, line spacing, and so on in 1/20 point units (*see* Table 16.8). At offset 11H, header/footer and frame information is stored. The coding of this byte is shown in Table 16.11.

If bits 4 and 5 contain the value 10, the sides of the frame will be displayed as single lines. The byte at offset 12H specifies the position of these lines (Figure 16.10).

Bit	Field description
0	0 = Header
	1 = Footer
1	1 = Header/Footer on odd pages
2	1 = Header/Footer on even pages
3	1 = Header/Footer on 1st page
4–5	Frame type
	00 = No frame
	01 = Frame
	10 = Define frame with lines
	11 = —
6–7	Frame lines
	00 = Single frame
	01 = Double frame
	10 = Single frame bold
	11 = —

Table 16.11 Coding of frame attributes

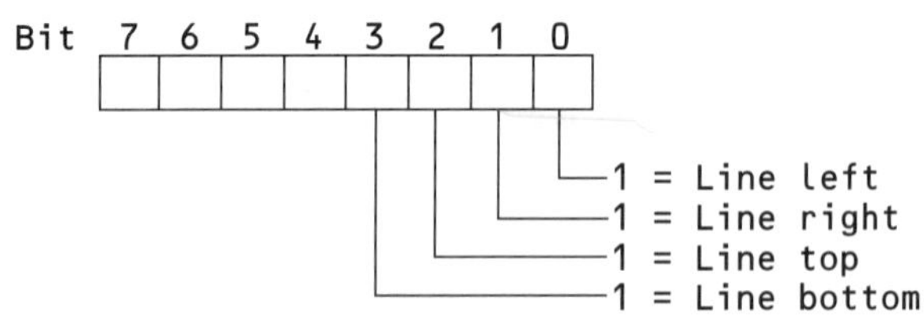

Figure 16.10 Coding of a frame composed of lines

The last part of a paragraph format definition (at offset 17H) contains any references to tabulators in the text. Four bytes are provided for each entry, and the format of these entries is shown in Table 16.12.

The last entry in the tabulator table is not necessarily 4 bytes long; it may contain between 2 and 4 bytes, because the number of directly formatted tabs can be calculated from the length byte at offset 00H.

Offset	Field description
00H	Indent in 1/20 points from left margin
02H	Tab attributes
	Bits 0–2: Alignment
	000 = Left
	001 = Centered
	010 = Right
	011 = ?
	100 = ?
	101 = ?
	110 = ?
	111 = ?
	Bits 3–5: Fill characters
	000 = Space
	001 = .
	010 = -
	011 = _
	Bits 6–7: Reserved
03H	Reserved (00H 00H)

Table 16.12 Coding of tab format

16.3.3 Format of the footnote block

Word stores footnotes and the associated references as normal ASCII strings in the text area. To facilitate the management of footnote numbering in the printout, the program creates a separate block for format information; the block number is stored in the pointer at offset 14H in the header. This footnote block does not always exist. If the value of the pointer in the header is the same as that of the pointer to the section format information (offset 16H), there is no footnote information. Otherwise, the block contains a table in which all the footnotes are described. Table 16.13 shows the structure.

The current number of footnotes + 1 present in the text is stored in the first word. The following word contains the maximum number of footnotes ever used in the text (that is, it includes any that have been deleted). Word uses this information to determine how much of the footnote description table (starting at offset 04H) has already been used. This is important, for example, if more than one block is used. For each footnote, a 4-byte text pointer to the position of the footnote reference and a pointer to the actual text of the footnote are stored. The first pair of pointers contains the start and end addresses of the last footnote text – which explains why the table indicates the number of footnotes + 1. Word uses the first two entries to determine the length of the last footnote text.

Offset	Bytes	Field description
00H	2	Number of footnotes in text + 1
02H	2	Number of footnotes in text + 1 (includes deleted footnotes)
Beginning of table containing footnote descriptions		
04H	4	Offset of footnote reference (from beginning of text)
08H	4	Offset of footnote text (from beginning of text)
...	...	.....

Table 16.13 Structure of a footnote block

16.3.4 Format of the section table block

In Word, a document can be divided into several sections. As soon as the user defines these sections, Word will create a block containing the section table and a block containing the section formats. The pointer in the header at offset 16H is the number of the block containing the section formats, while the number of the block containing the section table is stored at offset 18H. If the block numbers are the same as the block number in the pointer to the page break table (at offset 1AH), the section tables and format blocks do not exist. Otherwise, Word stores the relevant information for each section in these two blocks. The structure of the section table is shown in Table 16.14.

Offset	Bytes	Field description
00H	2	Number of sections
02H	2	Maximum number of sections
Beginning of table containing the section and format pointers		
04H	4	Offset of 1st character after this section
08H	2	Reserved
0AH	2	Offset to format description in the section format block
...	...	.....

Table 16.14 Structure of a block with a section table

The first word contains the total *number* of sections present; the following word indicates the maximum number of sections created so far. In this way, Word can determine the extent to which this table has already been structured. The actual section table begins at offset 04H. This table contains three entries for each section. The first pointer marks the end of a section, and the last entry is interpreted as a pointer to the associated format description, stored as the offset from the start of the section format block to the format description. The middle (second) entry is presumably not used in Word 4.0.

16.3.5 Format of the section format block

The number of the block containing the section formats is stored in the header, at offset 16H. Each section format has the following structure:

Offset	Bytes	Field description
00H	1	Number of following bytes in this entry
01H	1	Coding format template Bit 0 = 1: a format template is used to format this section; Bits 1–7 define the template (*see* Table 16.15)
02H	1	Attribute section (*see* Table 16.16)
03H	2	Page length in 1/20 point
05H	2	Page width in 1/20 point
07H	2	1st page number or FFFFH for continuous page numbering
09H	2	Upper border in 1/20 point
0BH	2	Length of text field in 1/20 point
0DH	2	Left border in 1/20 point
0FH	2	Text field width in 1/20 points
11H	1	Format section (line number and footnotes)
12H	1	Columns in section
13H	2	Distance of header from top in 1/20 point
15H	2	Distance of footer from top in 1/20 point
17H	2	Distance between columns in 1/20 point
19H	2	Gutter width in 1/20 point
1BH	2	Distance of page numbers from top border in 1/20 point

Table 16.15 **Structure of section format** (*continues over...*)

Word processing

Offset	Bytes	Field description
1DH	2	Distance of page numbers from left border in 1/20 point
1FH	2	Distance of line numbers from left border in 1/20 point
21H	2	Line numbers interval

Table 16.15 Structure of section format (*cont.*)

The coding of the print format template for a section is as follows: if bit 0 = 1, a print format template will be used. In this case, bits 1 to 7 contain the variant of the print format required as shown in Table 16.16.

Code	Field description
105	Standard format for a section
106–126	Section format templates 1–21

Table 16.16 Variants of print format templates for sections

Bit	Field description
0–2	Section change
	000 = Continuous
	001 = Column
	010 = Page
	011 = Even
	100 = Odd
3–5	Page number
	000 = Arabic numbers
	001 = Large Roman capitals
	010 = Small Roman capitals
	011 = Large capitals
	100 = Small capitals

Table 16.17 The coding of section attributes (*continues over...*)

Bit	Field description
6-7	Line numbers 00 = From beginning of page 01 = From beginning of section 10 = Continuous

Table 16.17 The coding of section attributes (*cont.*)

Information such as the format of line numbers and so on is stored in an attribute byte, at offset 02H, coded as shown in Table 16.17.

At offset 11H, there is another byte dealing with footnotes and line numbering. The relevant coding is shown in Figure 16.11.

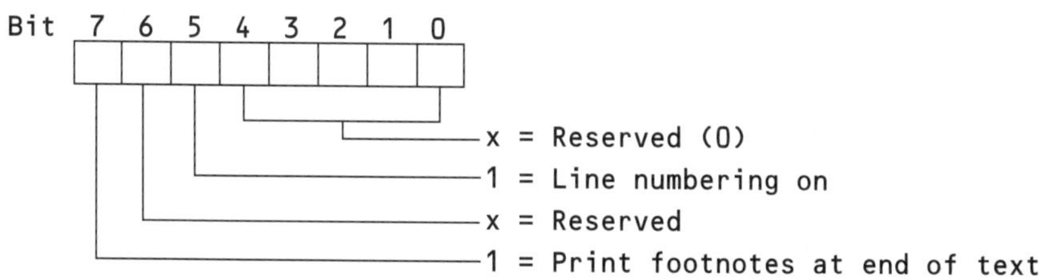

Figure 16.11 The coding for line numbering

16.3.6 Format of a page-break block

The number of the block containing details of page breaks is stored in the Word header, at offset 1AH. This block is not present if the entry is the same as the block numbers for other regions (offsets 16H, 18H, 1CH). Table 16.18 shows the format for page breaks.

The first word contains the number of page breaks. The table containing the locations of the page breaks begins at offset 04H.

Offset	Bytes	Field description
00H	2	Number of section with breaks
02H	2	Maximum number of page breaks

Table 16.18 Block containing details of page breaks (*continues over...*)

Offset	Bytes	Field description
Beginning of table containing page-break descriptions		
04H	4	Offset of 1st page break
08H	4	Offset of 2nd page break
...	...	.....

Table 16.18 Block containing details of page breaks (*cont.*)

16.3.7 File manager information block

The number of the block containing file manager information is stored at offset 1CH of the header, up to version 5.0 of Word. Word uses this information, for example, when searching through a text or when looking for a particular text. The structure of the block is shown in Table 16.19.

Dates are stored in the form month/day/year (for example, 01.23.90) in ASCII format and terminated with a null byte.

This information need not be present, and the fields can remain unused. In Word 5.0, unused entries in the block are overwritten with DCH.

Information on the internal memory structure has not been published by Microsoft. It is therefore possible that some of the details described in the above sections are not supported in all versions of Word.

Offset	**Bytes**	**Field description**
00H	2	Contains 12H 00H
...	...	
Beginning of file manager information		
12H	40	Document name (ASCIIZ string, maximum 40 chars)
3AH	12	Author's name (ASCIIZ string, maximum 12 chars)

Table 16.19 Structure of file manager information block (*continues over...*)

Offset	Bytes	Field description
46H	11	Reviser's name (ASCIIZ string, maximum 12 chars)
51H	14	Keyword (ASCIIZ string, maximum 14 chars)
5FH	10	Comment (ASCIIZ string, maximum 10 chars)
69H	9	version number (ASCIIZ string, max. 9 chars)
72H	8	Date of last change (MM/DD/YY) (ASCIIZ string)
79H	1	00H
7AH	8	Creation date (MM/DD/YY) (ASCIIZ string)
81H	1	00H
82H	4	Text size

Table 16.19 Structure of file manager information block (*cont.*)

16.4 Winword file format (1.0–6.0)

Winword 1.0, 2.0, 6.0 uses a similar format to Word for DOS to store text. Each DOC file consists of three sections (header, text, format) as described in Figure 16.1. The header and the internal format structure depend on the Winword version. The formats are backward compatible in each successive version. The header of a Winword file contains 384 (17FH) Bytes, followed by the text area. The text area stores the text in ANSI characters. The structure of a Winword header is shown in Table 16.20.

The complete structure of the Winword format is confidential and may not be published here. The information above is public and easy to identify. For further information about the Winword file format contact Microsoft. After signing a licence agreement, a copy of the specification is available.

Offset	Bytes	Remarks
00	2	Signature 9BH A5H (Winword 1.0) DBH A5H (Winword 2.0) D0H CFH (Winword 6.0)
02	2	version (Major)
04	2	version (Minor)
06	2	Language stamp
08	2	Next page number
0A	1	Flag
0B	1	Encryption (1 = Yes)
0C	6	Internal use
12	1	Platform 0: Windows 1: Mac
13	1	Reserved
14	2	Character set 0: ANSI 100H: Mac
16H	2	Internal character set
18H	4	Offset to 1st character in text area
1CH	4	Offset to text area end +1
20H	4	Offset to file end
...		Other file pointers

Table 16.20 Structure of a Winword header

17

WordStar format

WordStar, *which is produced by MicroPro, was one of the first word processing programs used with the IBM PC. The program was originally developed for the CP/M 80 operating system and subsequently transferred to MS-DOS. As a result, it retains many of the features of the earlier CP/M version. Although the performance of WordStar has been superseded to a large extent by Word and WordPerfect, it is included here because it is still very widely used. The following information relates to WordStar versions 2.2 to 6.x.*

WordStar files do not have header or trailer blocks containing format information. The program stores the text in ASCII format in its own file and inserts control data for formatting between the individual characters.

```
54 68 69 73 20 69 73 20 61 20 57 6F 72 64 53 74
 T  h  i  s     i  s     a     W  o  r  d  S  t
61 74 20 74 65 78 74 20 77 69 74 68 20 75 6D 6C
 a  r     t  e  x  t     w  i  t  h     u  m  l
61 75 74 73 20 1B 84 1C 1B E1 1C 0D 0A 0A 1A 1A
 a  u  t  s     ä     ß
0D 0A 0D 0A 1A 1A 1A 1A 1A 1A 1A 1A 1A 1A 1A 1A
.....
.....
```

Figure 17.1
Hex-dump of a WordStar text

The file itself is divided into 128-byte blocks. Any unused bytes in the last block are set to `1AH`, the normal DOS character for end of file.

Since WordStar originated in the CP/M era, it uses only 7 bits to represent data. Characters below `20H` and above `80H` are used as control codes (bold, underline, and so on).

The program distinguishes various groups of control codes. For example, some control characters act as toggles: the first occurence of the character switches a function on; the next occurence switches it off again (*see* Table 17.1).

Character	Code	Code description
^B	02H	Bold on/off
^D	04H	Double strike printing on/off
^I	09H	Tabulator (hard tab)
^J	0AH	LF-character
^K	0BH	Page offset header/footer
^L	0CH	Form feed
^S	13H	Underline on/off
^T	14H	Superscript on/off
^V	16H	Subscript on/off
^X	18H	Strikeout on/off
^Z	1AH	EOF-marker (end of text)
^[	1BH	ESC begin literal
^\	1CH	End literal
^]	1FH	Begin symmetrical sequence
^^	1EH	Soft hyphenation
^_	1FH	Soft hyphenation line end

Table 17.1 WordStar combination control codes

However, there are problems when using multinational character sets which use codes above 80H. This occurs, for example, with the German umlaut accent. WordStar sets the switch function (Table 17.1) for *literal* instructions. The special characters are then simply enclosed between the control codes 1BH and 1CH. With the code 1BH in front of a character, the next character will be printed *literally*. Code 1CH ends the *literal mode*, and the following characters are interpreted normally again. The German umlaut ä, for example, appears in the text as 1BH 84H 1CH. Without these brackets, WordStar will subtract the number 80H from the relevant character and use the code as a control command. Table 17.2 shows the control codes resulting from the umlauts.

This undesired conversion occurs, for example, when ASCII files are imported into WordStar.

In addition to the *paired* control codes mentioned above, WordStar also recognizes a number of control codes that generally occur on their own and have an immediate effect on the printed output (*see* Table 17.3).

A number of rules apply to the direct control codes above 80H. The 8th bit is set if the last character of a line contains a line break. A0H creates a phantom space. The combination 0DH,0AH is converted into 8DH,0AH (line break). The end of a paragraph is marked with what is known as a 'hard return' (0DH,0AH); the end of a page is marked with 0DH,8AH. The position of word-breaks is marked with a soft hyphen (code 1EH). At these points, the program can introduce a word-break. If these occur at the end of a line, the code 1FH is inserted as a separator.

Character	Code	Code description
ü	81H	01H = ^A
ä	84H	04H = ^D
Ä	8EH	0EH = ^N
ö	94H	14H = ^T
Ö	99H	19H = ^Y
Ü	9AH	1AH = ^Z
ß	E1H	61H = a

Table 17.2
Umlaut coding

Other control instructions occur in plain text within sections of text; these are known as *point commands*. As the name suggests, these instructions are introduced by a point (full-stop) followed by two letters.

Character	Code	Code description
^@	00H	Fix print position
^A	01H	Alternate font
^B	02H	Boldface type on/off
^C	03H	Print pause
^E	05H	Custom print control
^F	06H	Phantom space
^G	07H	Phantom rubout
^H	08H	Overprint previous character
^M	0DH	Carriage return
^N	0EH	Normal character width
^F	0FH	Binding space
^Q	11H	Custom print control
^R	12H	Custom print control
^U	15H	Reserved
^W	17H	Custom print control
^Y	19H	Italics on/off

Table 17.3
WordStar control codes

Up to version 3.0 of WordStar, it was necessary to specify parameters after these point commands as whole numbers. From WordStar 4.0, expressions are also allowed. In version 5.0, dimensions can be defined in inches. From version 5.5 (C), dimensions in points or in centimeters are also permitted. Data must be enclosed in single inverted commas (for example, `'CM'`), from version 5.5 (C). The commands in the following table are shown to aid understanding of the abbreviations:

Command	Remarks
.AV	Ask variable
.AW	Align and word wrap
.BN	Bin select (1 to 4)
.BP	Bidirectional print on/off
.CC	Conditional column break
.CO	Columns
.CP	Conditional page break
.CS	Clear screen and display message
.CV	Convert note type
.CW	Character width (in $1/120$ inch)
.DF	Data file to be merged into text format: CSV, DBF, WKS, and so on
.DM	Display a message
.E#	Set endnote value
.EI	End if
.EL	Else
.F#	Set footnote value
.FI	File insert (up to 7 levels)
.FM	Footer margin
.FO	Footer
.F1	Footer (following pages)
.F2	Second footer
.F3	Third footer
.GO	Go to top or bottom of document
.HE	Header
.H1	Header (following pages)
.H2	Second header
.H3	Third header
.HM	Header margin
.IF	If
.IG	Ignore (comment)
.IX	Index
.KR	Kerning

Table 17.3 WordStar commands (*continues over…*)

Command	Remarks
.L#	Line numbering
.LH	Line height (in 1/48 inch)
.LM	Left margin
.LQ	Letter quality on/off
.LS	Line spacing
.MA	Mathematical (store result of a calculation)
.MB	Bottom margin
.MT	Top margin
	Remarks
.OC	Centering on/off
.OJ	Output justification on/off
.OP	Omit page number
.P#	Paragraph number
.PA	Page break
.PC	Page column
.PE	Print endnotes
.PF	Paragraph realignment while printing
.PG	Number pages
.PL	Page length (in lines)
.PM	Paragraph margin
.PN	Page number
.PO	Page offset
.PR	Printer information
.PS	Proportional spacing on/off
.RM	Right margin
.RP	Repeat
.RR	Ruler
.RV	Read variable
.SR	Sub/superscript roll (in 1/48 inch)
.SV	Set variable
.TB	Tab stops
.TC	Table of contents .TC1 to .TC9
.UJ	Micro justify
.UL	Underline on/off
.XE .XQ	Custom print control, the hex sequence .XR .XW defines a control code
.XL	Form feed
.XX	Strikeout character

Table 17.3 WordStar commands (*cont.*)

17.1 Symmetrical code sequences

These code sequences were introduced from WordStar 5.0 onwards to provide functions that cannot be represented using point commands. All these sequences begin with the character 1DH and are structured as follows:

Offset	Byte	Field description
00H	1	1DH beginning of sequence
01H	2	Counter
03H	1	Sequence type
04H	*x*	Sequence data
..H	2	Counter
..H	1	1DH sequence end

Table 17.4 WordStar symmetrical code sequences

The number of characters in the sequence (minus 3) is stored in the word for the counter. All codes (including EOF 1AH) may appear in the sequence. The following symmetrical sequences are currently defined.

17.1.1 Header

17.1.1.1 Header Sequence (Type 00H)

This sequence defines the version and the name of the driver; it also contains a pointer to the style library within the file. The sequence is structured as follows:

Bytes	Field description
1	Header sequence (Type = 00H)
1	version number (BCD)
	50H = WordStar 5.0
	55H = WordStar 5.5
	60H = WordStar 6.0
9	Driver *n* (ASCIIZ string)
2	Reserved
4	Pointer to style library in file
107	Reserved

Table 17.5 WordStar header sequence

The complete record thus comprises 130 bytes including the frame consisting of 1DH ... 1DH.

17.1.2 Print Controls

These sequences contain the definitions for the printed output (colors and fonts).

17.1.2.1 Color Sequence (Type 01H)

This sequence defines a color and is structured as follows:

Bytes	Field description
1	Print control color (Type = 01H)
1	Color number (0 to 0FH)
1	Previous color in file
	Coding: 00H Black 01H Blue 02H Green 03H Cyan 04H Red 05H Magenta 06H Brown 07H Light gray 08H Dark gray 09H Light blue 0AH Light green 0BH Light cyan 0CH Light red 0DH Light magenta 0EH Yellow 0FH White to black

Table 17.6 WordStar color sequence

The sequence thus occupies 9 bytes.

17.1.2.2 Font Sequence (Type 02H)

This sequence defines the font and is structured as follows:

Bytes	Field description
1	Print control font (Type = 02H)
2	Font width in HMI (1/1800 inch)
2	Font height in VMI (1/1440 inch)
2	Type style
2	Previous font width in HMI (1/1800 inch)
2	Previous font height in VMI (1/1440 inch)
2	Previous type style

Table 17.7 WordStar font sequence

The word containing the type style is divided into individual bit fields (*see* Table 17.8):

Bit	Field description
15	Proportional flag
14	Letter quality flag
13–12	Symbol mapping bits
	00 = Code page 437
	01 = Code page 850
	10 = Mathematical character
	11 = Symbol font
11–10	Generic style bits
	00 = Sans serif font
	01 = Serif font
	10 = Script font
	11 = Display font
9	1 = Symmetrical sequence different from previous versions
8–0	Number of type style

Table 17.8 Coding type styles

The coding shown below currently applies to the numbering of fonts:

Number	Font
0	LinePrinter
1	Pica
2	Elite
3	Courier
4	Helv (also Helvetica, CG Triumvirate and Swiss)
5	Tms Rmn (also CG Times, Times Roman and Dutch)
6	Gothic (or number 130 Letter Gothic)
7	Script
8	Prestige (or number 48 Prestige Elite)
9	Caslon
10	Orator
11	Presentations
12	Helv Cond (also Swiss Condensed)
13	Serifa
14	Blippo
15	Windsor
16	Century (or number 23)
17	ZapfHumanist
18	Garamond
19	Cooper
20	Coronet
21	Broadway
22	Bodoni
23	Cntry Schlbk (or number 16)
24	Univ. Roman
25	Helv Outline
26	Peignot (also Exotic)
27	Clarendon
28	Stick
29	HP-GL Drafting
30	HP-GL Spline
31	Times
32	HPLJ Soft Font
33	Borders
34	Uncle Sam Open
35	Raphael
36	Uncial
37	Manhattan

Table 17.9 Font numbering (*continues over...*)

Number	Font
38	Dom Casual
39	Old English
40	Trium Condensed
41	Trium UltraComp
42	Trade ExtraCond
43	American Classic (also Amerigo)
44	Globe Gothic Outline
45	UniversCondensed (also Zurich Condensed)
46	Univers (also Zurich)
47	TmsRmnCond (Oki Laserline 6)
48	PrstElite (*see* also 8 Prestige)
49	Optima
50	Aachen (Postscript)
51	AmTypewriter
52	Avant Garde
53	Benguiat
54	Brush Script
55	Carta
56	Centennial
57	Cheltenham
58	FranklinGothic
59	FrstyleScrpt
60	FrizQuadrata
61	Futura
62	Galliard
63	Glypha
64	Goudy
65	Hobo
66	LubalinGraph
67	Lucida
68	LucidaMath
69	Machine
70	Melior (also Zapf Elliptical)
71	NewBaskrvlle (also Baskerville)
72	NewCntSchlbk
73	News Gothic (also Trade Gothic)
74	Palatino (also Zapf Calligraphic)
75	Park Avenue
76	Revue
77	Sonata

Table 17.9
Font numbering (*cont.*)

Number	Font
78	Stencil
79	Souvenir
80	TrmpMedievel (also Activa)
81	ZapfChancery
82	ZapfDingbats
83	Stone
84	CntryOldStyle
85	Corona
86	GoudyOldStyle
87	Excelsior
88	FuturaCondensed
89	HelvCompressed
90	HelvExtraCompressed
91	Helv Narrow
92	HelvUltraCompressed
93	KorinnaKursiv
94	Lucida Sans
95	Memphis
96	Stone Informal
97	Stone Sans
98	Stone Serif
99	Postscript
100	NPS Utility
101	NPS Draft
102	NPS Corr
103	NPS SansSer Qual
104	NPS Serif Qual
105	PS Utility
106	PS Draft
107	PS Corr
108	PS SansSer Qual
109	PS Serif Qual
110	Download
111	NPS ECS Qual (daisy wheel)
112	PS Plastic (daisy wheel)
113	PS Metal (daisy wheel)
114	CloisterBlack
115	Gill Sans (also Hammersmith)
116	Rockwell (also Slate)
117	Tiffany (ITC)

Table 17.9 Font numbering (*cont.*)

Number	Font
118	Clearface
119	Amelia
120	HandelGothic
121	OratorSC (Star *et al*)
122	Outline (Toshiba)
123	Bookman Light (Canon)
124	Humanist (Canon)
125	Swiss Narrow (Canon)
126	ZapfCalligraphic (Canon)
127	Spreadsheet (Quadlaser)
128	Broughm (Brother printers)
129	Anelia (Brother printers)
130	LtrGothic (Brother Definition)
131	Boldface (Boldface PS)
132	High Density (NEC)
133	High Speed (NEC)
134	Super Focus (NEC P2200)
135	Swiss Outline (Cordata)
136	Swiss Display (Cordata)
137	Momento Outline (Cordata)
138	Courier Italic (TI 855)
139	Text Light (Cordata)
140	Momento Heavy (Cordata)
141	BarCode
142	EAN/UPC
143	Math-7 (HPLJ)
144	Math-8 (HPLJ)
145	Swiss
146	Dutch
147	Trend (Nissho)
148	Holsatia (Qume Laser)
149	Serif (IBM Pageprinter)
150	Bandit (Cordata)
151	Bookman (Cordata)
152	Casual (Cordata)
153	Dot (Cordata)
154	EDP (Epson GQ3500)
155	ExtGraphics (Epson GQ3500)
156	Garland (Canon Laser)
157	PC Line

Table 17.9 Font numbering (*cont.*)

Number	Font
158	HP Line
159	Hamilton (QMS)
160	Korinna (Cordata)
161	LineDrw (QMS)
162	Modern
163	Momento (Cordata)
164	MX (Cordata)
165	PC (Cordata)
166	PI
167	Profile (Quadlaser)
168	Q-Fmt (QMS)
169	Rule (Cordata)
170	SB (Cordata)
171	Taylor (Cordata)
172	Text (Cordata)
173	APL
174	Artisan
175	Triumvirate
176	Chart
177	Classic
178	Data
179	Document
180	Emperor
181	Essay
182	Forms
183	*Facet*
184	Micro (also Microstyle, Eurostile)
185	OCR-A
186	OCR-B
187	Apollo (Blaser)
188	Math
189	Scientific
190	Sonoran (IBM Pageprinter)
191	Square 3
192	Symbol
193	Tempora
194	Title
195	Titan
196	Theme
197	TaxLineDraw

Table 17.9
Font numbering
(*cont.*)

Number	Font
198	Vintage
199	XCP
200	Eletto (Olivetti)
201	Est Elite (Olivetti)
202	Idea (Olivetti)
203	Italico (Olivetti)
204	Kent (Olivetti)
205	Mikron (Olivetti)
206	Notizia (Olivetti)
207	Roma (Olivetti)
208	Presentor (Olivetti)
209	Victoria (Olivetti)
210	Draft Italic (Olivetti)
211	PS Capita (Olivetti)
212	Qual Italic (Olivetti)
213	Antique Olive (also Provence)
214	Bauhaus (ITC)
215	Eras (ITC)
216	Mincho
217	SerifGothic (ITC)
218	Signet Roundhand
219	Souvenir Gothic
220	Stymie (ATF)
221	Bernhard Modern
222	Grand Ronde Script
223	Ondine (also Mermaid)
224	PT Barnum
225	Kaufmann
226	Bolt (ITC)
227	AntOliveCompact (also Provence Compact)
228	Garth Graphic
229	Ronda (ITC)
230	EngSchreibschrift
231	Flash
232	Gothic Outline (URW)
233	Akzidenz-Grotesk
234	TD Logos
235	Shannon
236	Oberon
237	Callisto

Table 17.9 Font numbering (*cont.*)

Number	Font
238	Charter
239	Plantin
240	Helvetica Black (PS)
241	Helvetica Light (PS)
242	Arnold Bocklin (PS)
243	Fette Fraktur (PS)
244	Greek (PS (Universal Greek))

Table 17.9 Font numbering (*cont.*)

The font numbers in Table 17.9 are in decimal notation. It should also be noted that the list of fonts is constantly being updated and so more fonts than those specified are actually supported.

> **!** **When compiling this list, I was amazed at how many font styles are currently in use in computer applications. Many of these fonts represent well-known font families such as Times, Helvetica, and so on but have had to be given different names because of license restrictions.**

17.1.3 Notes

The following sequences define footnotes and endnotes:

17.1.3.1 Footnote Sequence (Type 03H)

This sequence defines footnotes in the text and is structured as follows:

Bytes	Field description
1	Footnote (Type = 03H)
2	Line count of footnote text
2	Offset of footnote number TAG If bit 15 = 1: Other bits define the offset to an internal sequence with the footnote TAG 0: Footnote number to use
1	Unused
x	Text area for footnote

Table 17.10 Footnote sequence

If the footnote contains no tag, the sixth byte is used for the conversion flag. The text can contain another footnote sequence to display or print the tag associated with the note. The sequence uses the following structure:

Bytes	Field description
1	Footnote (Type = 03H)
2	Unused (line count assumed 1)
2	Footnote number
1	Conversion flag – normally 0, if .CV or .FV# then Bits 0–3: 4 Convert note to an endnote 6 Convert note to a comment Bits 4–7: Format type 0 Use symbols 1 Use upper case 2 Use lower case 3 Use numbers
x	Text area for footnote

Table 17.11 Internal footnote sequence

If the conversion flag is used, the lower 4 bits contain the conversion number of the footnote. If the value is set to 4, the footnote will be converted into an endnote. If the value = 6, the footnote will be converted into a comment. The format for the numbering (0 = symbols, 1 = capitals, 2 = lower case letters, 3 = numbers) is contained in the upper bits.

17.1.3.2 Endnote Sequence (Type 04H)

This sequence defines the endnotes in the text and is structured as follows:

Bytes	Field description
1	Endnote (Type = 04H)
2	Line count of endnote text
2	Offset of endnote TAG number Bit 15 = 1: The other bits define the offset to the internal sequence with the endnote TAG 0: Number endnote
1	Unused
x	Text area of endnote

Table 17.12 Endnote sequence

The text can contain another endnote sequence to display or print the tag associated with the note. The sequence uses the following structure:

Bytes	Field description
1	Endnote (Type = 04H)
2	Unused (line count assumed 1)
2	Endnote number
1	Conversion flag – normally 0, if .CV or .FV# then Bits 0–3: 3 Convert note to a footnote 6 Convert note to a comment Bits 4–7: Format type 0 Use symbols 1 Use upper case 2 Use lower case 3 Use numbers
x	Text area for endnote

Table 17.13 Internal endnote sequence

If the conversion flag is used, the lower 4 bits contain the conversion format. If the value is set to 4, the endnote will be converted into a footnote. If the value = 6, the endnote will be converted into a comment. The format for the numbering (0 = symbols, 1 = capitals, 2 = lower case letters, 3 = numbers) is contained in the upper bits.

17.1.3.3 Annotation (Type 05H)

This sequence defines annotations in the text and is structured as follows:

Bytes	Field description
1	Annotation (Type = 05H)
2	Line number of annotation
2	Offset of TAG annotation Bit 15 = 1: Other bits define the offset to an internal sequence with the TAG 0: Word is 0
1	Unused
x	Text area for annotation

Table 17.14a Annotation sequence

The text can contain another sequence of the same format. The structure of the sequence within the text area is defined below.

Bytes	Field description
1	Annotation (Type = 05H)
2	Unused (line count assumed 1)
2	Unused
x	Text area for endnote

Table 17.14b Text in an annotation sequence

17.1.3.4 Comment (Type 06H)

This sequence defines comments within the text and is structured as follows:

Bytes	Field description
1	Comment (Type = 06H)
2	Line count of comment
2	Unused
1	Conversion flag (0 or same as footnote)
x	Text area for comment

Table 17.15 Comment sequence

If the conversion flag is used, the same conditions apply as for the footnote. If the value of the lower 4 bits is set to 3, the comment will be converted into a footnote. If the value = 4, the comment will be converted into an endnote. The format for the numbering (0 = symbols, 1 = capitals, 2 = lower case letters, 3 = numbers) is contained in the upper bits. Comments do not contain any other internal sequences.

The codes 07H and 08H are reserved.

17.1.3.5 Tabs (Type 09H)

This sequence describes tabulators in the text and is structured as follows:

Bytes	Field description
1	Tabulator (Type = 09H)
2	Tabulator size in HMI
2	Absolute tabulator size in HMI
1	Tabulator type
1	Tabulator size in 1/10

Table 17.16
Tab sequence

The details of the dimensions of a tabulator are not completely clear at present. Various characters are used for different types of tab:

space	Hard tab
soft space	Soft tab
!	Center line tab
#	Decimal tab
[	Right-align line tab
. or *	Dot leader

Table 17.17
Tab types

These characters define the alignment of tabs. The code 0AH is reserved.

17.1.3.6 End of Page (Type 0BH)

This sequence should be ignored since it is used by the WordStar editor to display the page break.

17.1.3.7 Page Offset (Type 0CH)

This sequence is reserved for the printer driver and should not appear in a text document.

17.1.3.8 Paragraph Number (Type 0DH)

This sequence defines the numbering of paragraphs and is structured as shown in Table 17.18.

WordStar can implement paragraph numbering up to 8 levels. Numbering is managed using the sequence below.

Bytes	Field description
1	Paragraph number (Type = 0DH)
1	Level increase 0 stay at current level 1 move forward in a level (2 -> 2.1) >1 level moves forward from previous paragraph number
1	Level decrease 0 stay at current level 1 move forward in a level (2.1 -> 2) >1 level moves backward from previous paragraph number
1	Level number of current paragraph (1–*n*)
8*2	Level numbers; 8 words (1–8) each word defines a level number
31	ASCIIZ string containing the paragraph format

Table 17.18 Paragraph numbers

17.1.3.9 Index Entry (Type 0EH)

This record contains a text giving the relevant index entry.

17.1.3.10 Printer Control (Type 0FH)

This sequence stores control codes for driving the printer.

Bytes	Field description
1	Printer control (Type = 0FH)
2	Number of HMI this sequence uses
1	Number of characters for screen display
x	Display string
y	Printer control characters

Table 17.19 Printer controls

This sequence can be used to send text and control codes to the printer. The text can be displayed on screen. The printer characters follow the text for the screen display.

17.1.3.11 Graphic (Type 10H)

This sequence defines the file name of a graphic which is to be merged.

Bytes	Field description
1	Graphic (Type = 10H)
n	File name of graphic file

Table 17.20
Graphic

The length of the file name can be determined from the length of the sequence.

17.1.3.12 Paragraph Style (Type 11H)

This sequence describes the style of individual paragraphs.

Bytes	Field description
1	Paragraph style (Type 11H)
2	New paragraph style number
2	Previously selected paragraph style number
2	Previous paragraph modified style number
2	Previous previous selected for reverting

Table 17.21
Paragraph style

The phrase 'New paragraph style number' acts as an index to the document style library. The value defines the style selected by the user. The next entry is the index of the user's previously selected style. The 'Previous paragraph modified style number' is the style condition before the selection was made. Because the attributes and fonts may change, new temporary styles are created in the library. The phrase 'Previous previous selected for reverting' is the style selected by the user prior to the previous style. WordStar uses this to revert to the previous style.

The codes 12H to 14H are reserved.

17.1.3.13 Alternate Font Change (Type 15H)

This sequence occupies several bytes. One of the following values:

0 = Normal font
1 = Alternate font

is stored in the first byte. The remaining bytes contain an additional symmetrical sequence that defines the new font data (width, height, font number) and the previous font data (*see* Type 02H).

17.1.3.14 Truncation (Type 16H)

This sequence is only used if the characters of a symmetrical sequence do not fit into the main memory (RAM).

The remaining codes 17H to FFH are reserved.

17.2 Structure of a paragraph style library

The library containing various styles can be stored:

- in the file WSSTYLE.OVR
- as a copy in the edited file
- as a copy in a temporary file

A 32-bit offset to the relevant style can be stored in the header sequence (*see* Subsection 17.1.1.1). The value must refer to a 128-byte block containing what is known as the Master Index. The structure of this index is shown below:

Bytes	Field description
1	1AH EOF-mark
2	Next free 512-byte block Offset relative to index start
1	Object count (current 1)
	Beginning of Master Index
2	Number of index entries
2	Size of an object entry (102 = paragraph style)
4	Pointer to object index
	Beginning of object index
1	Number of index entries (14 = paragraph style)
4	Link to next index block relative to the start of the master index
24	Object name (left justified, padded with blanks)

Table 17.22 Master index (*continues over...*)

Bytes	Field description
	Beginning of object index
5	Internal use
4	Pointer to style definition
	Style definition
3*2	Font description (-1 = inherited)
4	Reserved
2	Left border in HMI (-2 = inherited)
2	Right border in HMI (-2 = inherited)
2	Paragraph limit in HMI (-2 = inherited)
2	Reserved
1	Number of regular tabs (0 = inherited)
1	Number of decimal tabs (0 = inherited)
32*2	Tab stops in HMI, regular tabs first
	(If 1st tab stop = -1, tabs are inherited)
2	Reserved
1	Justify flag
	0 No
	-1 Inherited from another font
	1 Left
	2 Centered
	3 Right
1	Word-wrap flag
	0 Off
	-1 Inherited from another font
	1 On
2	Line height in VMI (-1 = inherited)
1	Line spacing 1–9 (-1 = inherited)
2	Print attribute on
2	Print attribute off
1	Color (-1 = inherited)
6	Reserved

Table 17.22
Master index
(*cont.*)

If the print attribute bits in both words are set to `off`, the relevant attribute is adopted (inherited) from another font. The coding for the individual bits is shown in Table 17.23.

The coding for colors is described in Subsection 17.1.2.1.

Strikeout	000000000000001B
Doublestrike	000000000000010B
Underlining	000000000001000B
Subscript	000000000010000B
Superscript	000000000100000B
Bold	000000001000000B
Italics	000000010000000B

Table 17.23
Print attributes

18

WordPerfect format

The WordPerfect Corporation offers the very successful word processing program, WordPerfect, which operates not only on DOS PCs but also on DEC VAX computers and UNIX machines.

Versions 4.x/6.x of WordPerfect use a mixture of ASCII and binary format for storing text files. In version 4.x, format codes are embedded in the text; from version 5.0 the WPF files are divided into two parts as shown in Figure 18.1:

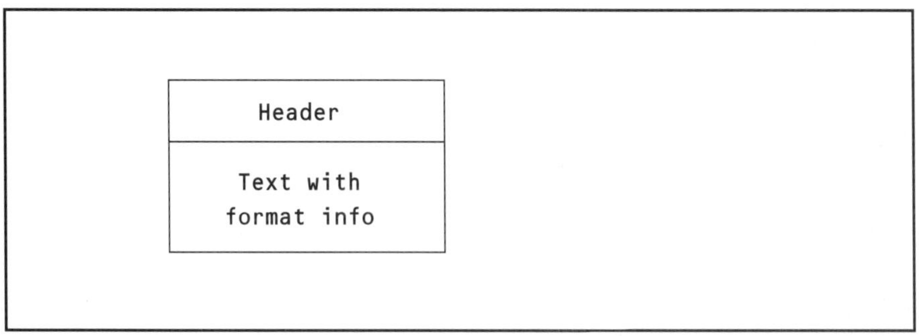

Figure 18.1 Structure of a WordPerfect file (version 5.0)

This chapter deals particularly with version 5.0. Figure 18.2 shows an extract from a WordPerfect file in the form of a hex-dump.

Signature -1 WPC
Offset beginning of text
Product type
File type
1st Index block

```
FF 57 50 43 E8 02 00 00 01 0A 00 00 00 00 00 00
   W  P  C
FB FF 05 00 32 00 AA 02 00 00 02 00 56 00 00 00
            2                       V
42 00 00 00 07 00 16 00 00 00 98 00 00 00 0C 00
B
57 00 00 00 AE 00 00 00 03 00 A5 01 00 00 05 01
W
00 00 00 00 FF FF 7A 00 4E 00 78 00 78 00 78 00
0A 00 01 00 00 00 00 00 F4 01 55 5E DB 01 78 00
14 1E 0C 17 8C 0A 00 00 00 04 11 40 C9 00 87 CF
01 00 01 00 FF FF FF FF FF FF FF FF FF FF FF FF
FF FF FF FF FF FF FF FF FF FF FF FF FF FF FF FF
FF FF FF FF FF FF FF FF 43 6F 75 72 69 65 72 20
                        C  o  u  r  i  e  r
31 30 70 74 20 31 30 20 50 69 74 63 68 00 00 00
1  0  p  t     1  0     P  i  t  c  h
00 00 00 00 00 00 00 00 00 00 00 00 00 00 00 00
00 00 00 00 00 00 00 00 00 00 00 00 00 00 00 00
00 00 00 00 00 00 00 00 00 00 00 00 00 00 00 00
00 00 00 00 00 00 00 00 00 00 00 00 00 00 00 00
11 00 00 00 00 D3 11 08 00 55 53 44 45 08 00 11
                           U  S  D  E
D3 D3 00 0C 00 2E 00 2C 00 2C 00 2E 00 0C 00 00
D3 D0 0B C5 00 90 33 D8 27 01 00 00 00 00 00 00
00 00 00 00 00 00 00 00 00 00 00 00 00 00 00 00
00 00 00 00 00 00 00 00 00 00 00 00 00 00 00 00
00 00 00 00 90 33 D8 27 01 08 53 74 61 6E 64 61
               3     '        S  t  a  n  d  a
72 64 00 00 00 00 00 00 00 00 00 00 00 00 00 00
r  d
00 00 00 00 00 00 00 00 00 00 00 00 00 00 00 00
00 00 00 00 D0 36 C2 26 01 00 00 00 00 00 00 00
00 00 00 00 00 00 00 00 00 00 00 00 00 00 00 00
00 00 00 00 00 00 00 00 00 00 00 00 00 00 00 00
00 00 00 D0 36 C2 26 01 00 53 74 61 6E 64 61 72
            6     &        S  t  a  n  d  a  r
64 00 00 00 00 00 00 00 00 00 00 00 00 00 00 00
d
```

Figure 18.2 Hex-dump of a WordPerfect file (*continues over...*)

```
00 00 00 00 00 00 00 00 00 00 00 00 00 00 00 00
00 00 00 00 03 08 C5 00 0B D0 D2 03 A0 00 00 01
C8 00 58 02 30 01 31 00 00 00 00 00 00 00 00 00
C3 05 C3 8D C4 05 C4 00 00 00 00 00 00 00 00 00
00 00 00 00 20 20 20 20 20 C3 05 C3 8D C4 05 C4
00 00 00 00 00 00 00 00 B0 04 B0 04 00 00 00 00
00 00 00 00 00 00 00 00 00 00 00 00 00 01 C8 00
58 02 30 01 31 00 00 00 00 00 00 00 00 00 C3 05
C3 8D C4 05 C4 00 00 00 00 00 00 00 00 00 00 00
00 00 C3 05 C3 8D C4 05 C4 00 8D C4 05 C4 00 00
00 00 00 00 00 00 B0 04 B0 04 00 00 00 00 00 00
00 00 00 00 00 00 00 00 00 00 A0 00 03 D2 D0 03
08 00 19 0A 0F 08 08 00 03 D0 D3 0B 0C 00 3C 00
                                                   2. Index block
90 01 50 00 C8 00 0C 00 0B D3 FB FF 05 00 32 00
00 00 00 00 09 00 02 00 00 00 DC 02 00 00 06 00
08 00 00 00 DE 02 00 00 08 00 02 00 00 00 E6 02
00 00 00 00 00 00 00 00 00 00 00 00 03 08 00 23
                                                   Header end
                                                   Begin text area
7C 00 3C 00 00 00 00 00 54 68 69 73 20 20 69 73
                         T  h  i  s        i  s
20 61 20 74 65 78 74 20 69 6E 20 57 6F 72 64 50
    a     t  e  x  t     i  n     W  o  r  d  P
65 72 66 65 63 74 2C 20 77 69 74 68 20 63 68 61
 e  r  f  e  c  t  ,     w  i  t  h     c  h  a
72 2E 20 20 C0 1E 01 C0 C0 3F 01 C0 C0 46 01 C0
 r  .           Ä           ö           Ü
0A C4 01 C4 C4 02 C4 C4 03 C4 C4 04 C4 0A
```

Figure 18.2 Hex-dump of a WordPerfect file (*cont.*)

Format information in the text is enclosed between special codes such as `C0H...C0H`.

18.1 WordPerfect header (version 5.0)

As can be seen from Figure 18.3, WordPerfect stores a header at the start of the file containing information about the contents of the file. The first 16 bytes contain an identification record which is used in all products manufactured by WordPerfect.

The first 4 bytes contain a signature which identifies the file as a WP text file. This is followed by a 4-byte pointer, indicating the offset from the start of the file to the first text character. The next byte indicates the type of product produced by the file. The byte at offset `09H` indicates the document type. The first 10 numbers are reserved for general purposes; the numbers above 10 are coded according to the product used (Table 18.1 shows the relevant codes). Version numbers, which come next, are always indicated by the value `0.0` in WordPerfect 5.0. In the *encryption flag*, the value `0` indicates an unencrypted file; other values are interpreted as keys. Table 18.1 contains a detailed description of the header:

Offset	Bytes	Field description
File ID header for all WPCORP products		
00H	4	WP signature -1,'WPC'
04H	4	Pointer to 1st text character
08H	1	Product type 1 WordPerfect 2 Shell 3 Notebook 4 Calculator 5 File manager 6 Calendar 7 Program editor 8 Macro editor 9 PlanPerfect 10 DataPerfect 11 Mail 12 Printer (PTR.EXE) 13 Scheduler 14 WordPerfect office
09H	1	File type 1 Macro file 2 Help file 3 Keyboard definition file 4 — ... 9 — 10 WP document 11 Dictionary file 12 Thesaurus file 13 Block 14 Rectangle block 15 Column block 16 Printer resource file (.PRS) 17 Setup file 18 Prefix information file 19 Printer resource file (.ALL) 20 Display resource file (.DRS) 21 Overlay file (WP.FIL) 22 WP graphic file (.WPG)

Table 18.1 Header prefix of a WP file (*continues over...*)

Offset	Bytes	Field description
		23 Hyphenation code module
		24 Hyphenation data module
		25 Macro resource file (MRS)
		26 Graphic driver (WPD)
		27 Hyphenation Lex module
0AH	1	Major version number
0BH	1	Minor version number
0CH	2	Encryption flag (0 = not encrypted)
0EH	2	Reserved (0)

Table 18.1
Header prefix of a WP file (*cont.*)

This 16-byte header is followed by one or more *index blocks* (WordPerfect 5.0) containing additional product-specific information. These index blocks contain indices and data.

Figure 18.3 shows the structure of the WordPerfect header version 5.0:

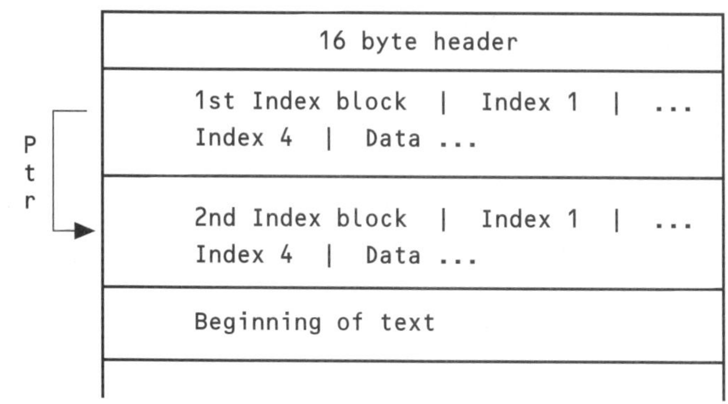

Figure 18.3
The headers and index blocks

The first 16 bytes of the ID header are followed by the header of the first index block; the length and contents of this header vary according to the particular file. The offset in Table 18.2 refers to the beginning of the index block. The value 10H should be added to the offsets in the first index block in order to calculate the offset from the start of the file.

The first word of the index block contains a signature identifying its type. For WP 5.0, this value is always FFFBH. The codes FFFCH to FFFEH are reserved so far. The signature FFFFH indicates a deleted index block which is still physically in the file. The number of indices in this block is stored at offset 02H. For WordPerfect 5.0, this value is always 5, because the block accommodates the header and 4 additional indices. The following word specifies the size of the index block in bytes. This is followed by a 4-byte pointer to the next index block in the file header. WordPerfect 5.0 is capable of creating several index blocks within the file header. The last index block of the series contains the value 00H 00H 00H 00H in this field.

Offset	Bytes	Field description
00H	2	Signature 0000H End of prefix area FFFBH Next header index block FFFCH Reserved (find next read) FFFDH Reserved (find first) FFFEH Reserved (matches any packet) FFFFH Deleted packet
02H	1	Number of indices (including the header) (for WP 5.0 always 5)
04H	1	Size of the index block
04H	4	File position of next index block
08H	2	Type of index 1
0AH	4	Length of data packet 1 in bytes
0EH	4	File position of data packet 1
12H	2	Type of index 2
14H	4	Length of data packet 2 in bytes
18H	4	File position of data packet 2
1CH	...	Index 3...4
...	...	Data for index block

Table 18.2 Format of an index block in the header

The header of the index block is followed by the headers of the 4 indices. These headers contain the type, length and address of the relevant data (Table 18.2 shows the corresponding data structures). The first word gives the type of the data block. The entry 00H here indicates the end of the index area. The appropriate coding is shown in Table 18.3:

Type	Field description
Packet types in a document block	
0000H	End of index area
0001H	Document summary
0002H	Reserved
0003H	Document standard values
0004H	Reserved
0005H	Reserved
0006H	Document flags
0007H	Font name string pool

Table 18.3 Index packet types (*continues over...*)

Type	Field description
0008H	Graphic image data
0009H	Format hash table
000AH	List of fonts used
000BH	Reserved
000CH	Document printer information
000DH	Reserved
...	
00FFH	Reserved
0100H	Style packets
...	
01FFH	Style packets
0200H	PS tables for fonts 0–FFH
...	
02FFH	Style packets
Packet types in SetUp-files	
0001H	Font list
0002H	Font string pool
0003H	PS table list
0004H	
...	
000FH	Reserved
0010H	Path names of Thesaurus/Dictionary
0011H	Screen type information
0012H	Miscellaneous (Backup time, etc.)
0013H	Ctrl and Alt key mappings
0014H	System default values
0015H	Reserved
0016H	Reserved
0017H	Miscellaneous (for SetUp)
0018H	Reserved
0019H	Reserved
001AH	Default printer selection
001BH	Printer selection list
001CH	Reserved
...	
001FH	Reserved
0020H	Screen attribute monochrome
0021H	Screen attribute CGA
0022H	Screen attribute PC 3270
0023H	Screen attribute EGA (italics)

Table 18.3 Index packet types (*cont.*)

Word processing

Type	Field description
0024H	Screen attribute EGA (underline)
0025H	Screen attribute EGA (small caps)
0026H	Screen attribute EGA (reserved)
...	
0029H	Screen attribute EGA (reserved)
002AH	Screen attribute Hercules RamFont (12 fonts)
002BH	Screen attribute Hercules RamFont (6 fonts)
002CH	Screen attribute Hercules RamFont Reserved
...	
002FH	"

Table 18.3 Index packet types (*cont.*)

The length of the data packet is stored in the next 4-byte field; this is followed by a 4-byte field containing the address of the data as an offset from the start of the file to the data area.

The packet type 0008H indicates graphic data within the file. This type of packet can appear only at the end of the last block. The value in the length field is always either 0 or 2; 0 indicates that there is no graphic data. Otherwise the data is located at the position given by the following pointer. The format of this data area is shown in Table 18.4.

The structure of the remaining data areas is not known. In addition to the codes mentioned, WordPerfect 5.0 already uses some of the codes marked as reserved.

Offset	Bytes	Field description
00H	2	Number of graphic images
02H	4	Size of first graphic image
...	...	...
...	4	Size of last graphic image
...	...	Data for first graphic image
...	...	...
...	...	Data for last graphic image

Table 18.4 Graphic image data packet

18.2 WordPerfect data areas

The text area consists of the actual ASCII characters and control codes positioned between these characters. In version 5.0, the text area begins after the header; the start of the text is indicated by a pointer at offset 04H. In version 4, there is no header, and the text area begins immediately at the start of the file.

Only the ASCII characters between 20H and 7FH are used to represent text. The codes 0–1FH are used for formatting as are codes 80H–FFH.

WordPerfect 5.0 distinguishes between 1-byte control codes and multi-byte codes – for example German umlauts are placed between C0H characters. Since the format codes for versions 4.0 and 5.0 are broadly similar, the following information applies to both versions. Deviations from this rule are indicated explicitly.

In the following text, various units of measurement are given for coordinates in WordPerfect protocols. The wpu unit (*WordPerfect unit*) represents $^1/_{1200}$ inch. The su (*screen unit*) represents 1 screen display column.

18.2.1 1-byte control codes from 00H to BFH

Codes lower than 20H are used for line feeds and tabs. In this respect, they correspond to the codes used generally in text files. The relevant coding is shown in Table 18.5.

Code	Version	Field description
01H	4.0/5.0	Reserved
02H	5.0	Page number printed here
03H	5.0	Merge codes C
04H	5.0	Merge codes D
05H	5.0	Merge codes E
06H	5.0	Merge codes F
07H	5.0	Merge codes G
08H	4.0/5.0	Reserved
09H	4.0	Hard tab (Reserved in 5.0)
0AH	4.0/5.0	Hard return
0BH	4.0/5.0	Soft new page
0CH	4.0/5.0	Hard new page in 4.0 Hard return in 5.0
0DH	4.0/5.0	Soft new line
0EH	5.0	Merge codes N
0FH	5.0	Merge codes O
10H	5.0	Merge codes P
11H	5.0	Merge codes Q
12H	5.0	Merge codes R
13H	5.0	Merge codes S
14H	5.0	Merge codes T
15H	5.0	Merge codes U
16H	5.0	Merge codes V
17H	5.0	Reserved
...	...	...
1FH	5.0	Reserved

Table 18.5 Control codes between 00H and 1FH

Version 4.0 uses only a few of the codes shown in Table 18.5. Merge files are not given a start code in version 4.0. The end is simply terminated with Ctrl R and Ret↵ (hard return).

The codes between 20H and 7FH represent the normal ASCII characters. Accents and special characters appear between the codes COH...COH, from version 5.0 onwards. Further details of this process are given in Subsection 18.2.2.

Table 18.6 gives the meaning of the control codes between 80H and BFH.

Version 4.0 defines the codes BCH (superscript), BDH (subscript), BEH (advance printer ½ line up) and BFH (advance printer ½ line down). Version 5.0 no longer uses these codes.

Code	Version	Field description
80H	4.0/5.0	Temporary (always deleted)
81H	4.0/5.0	Right justification on
82H	4.0/5.0	Right justification off
83H	4.0/5.0	End of centered/aligned text
84H	4.0	End of aligned text
	5.0	Reserved
85H	4.0	Temporary start point for a calculation formula
	5.0	Placeholder
86H	4.0/5.0	Center page top to bottom
87H	4.0/5.0	Columns on
88H	4.0/5.0	Columns off (at top of page)
89H	4.0	Tab right border
	5.0	Reserved in 5.0
8AH	4.0/5.0	Widow/Orphan on
8BH	4.0/5.0	Widow/Orphan off
8CH	4.0/5.0	Soft Page/Hard Return
8DH	4.0/5.0	Footnote/Endnote number
8EH	5.0	Figure number
8FH	5.0	Reserved
90H	4.0	Red line on
	5.0	Deletable return at end of line
91H	4.0	Red line off
	5.0	Deletable return at end of page
92H	4.0	Strikeout on
	5.0	End of page (deleted when forward formatted)
93H	4.0	Strikeout off
	5.0	Invisible return in line

Table 18.6 Single-byte functions (codes between 80H and BFH) *(continues over...)*

Code	Version	Field description
94H	4.0	Underline on
	5.0	Invisible return at end of line
95H	4.0	Underline off
	5.0	Invisible return at end of page
96H	4.0	Reverse video on
	5.0	Block on
97H	4.0	Reverse video off
	5.0	Block off
98H	4.0/5.0	Place holder (Table of Contents)
99H	4.0	Overwrite
	5.0	Reserved
9AH	4.0	Cancel hyphenation next word
	5.0	Cancel hyphenation
9BH	4.0/5.0	End of generated text
9CH	4.0	Bold on
	5.0	Reserved
9DH	4.0	Bold off
	5.0	Reserved
9EH	4.0/5.0	Hyphenation off
9FH	4.0/5.0	Hyphenation on
A0H	4.0/5.0	Hard space
A1H	4.0/5.0	Do sub-total
A2H	4.0/5.0	Sub-total entry
A3H	4.0/5.0	Do total
A4H	4.0/5.0	Total entry
A5H	4.0/5.0	Do grand total
A6H	4.0/5.0	Calculation column
A7H	4.0/5.0	Math on
A8H	4.0/5.0	Math off
A9H	4.0/5.0	Hard hyphen in line
AAH	4.0/5.0	Hard hyphen at end of line
ABH	4.0/5.0	Hard hyphen at end of page
ACH	4.0/5.0	Soft hyphen in line
ADH	4.0/5.0	Soft hyphen at end of line
AEH	4.0/5.0	Soft hyphen at end of page
AFH	4.0/5.0	Columns off at end of line
B0H	4.0/5.0	Columns off at end of page
B1H	5.0	Math negate
B2H	5.0	Reserved
...	...	....
BFH	5.0	Reserved

Table 18.6 Single-byte functions (codes between 80H and BFH) (*cont.*)

Word processing

18.2.2 Fixed-length multi-byte control codes from C0H to CFH

WordPerfect uses these control codes, for example, for representing special characters and accents. Since there are considerable differences in coding between Versions 4.0 and 5.0, the following description is limited to version 5.0.

18.2.2.1 Extended Character (code C0H)

Version 5.0 uses this control code to enclose characters above 80H. The format is as shown in Table 18.7.

Altogether, WordPerfect has 12 fonts, which must be taken into account in displaying special characters. The third byte in the record therefore indicates the number of the font.

Offset	Bytes	Field
00H	1	Extended character on (Code C0H)
01H	1	Character code
02H	1	Font number 1–12
03H	1	Extended character off

Table 18.7 Opcode C0H in version 5.0

18.2.2.2 Center, Align, Tab, Left Margin (code C1H)

In version 5.0, this record contains the following formatting information:

Offset	Bytes	Field
00H	1	Begin function (Code C1H)
01H	1	Flags Bits 7–6: 00 Tab 01 Align 10 Left margin release 11 Center Bit 5: 1 Center between margins, Flush right Bit 4: 1 for dot leader Bit 3: 0 align on alignment char 1 right justify/center tabs
02H	2	Old current column number (su)
04H	2	Absolute center/align/tab position (wpu)
06H	2	Position of start column (su)
08H	1	End function code

Table 18.8 Opcode C1H in version 5.0

18.2.2.3 Indent (code C2H)

This record is used for indented text in version 5.0:

Offset	Bytes	Field
00H	1	Begin function (Code C2H)
01H	1	Flags Bit 0: 0 left indent 1 left/right indent Bit 4: 1 dot leader
02H	2	Difference between new and old temporary margins (wpu)
04H	2	Old current column number (wpu)
06H	2	Absolute indent position (su)
08H	2	Start column position (wpu)
0AH	1	End function code

Table 18.9
Opcode C2H in version 5.0

18.2.2.4 Attributes On (code C3H)

This record switches the attributes on (version 5.0):

Offset	Bytes	Field
00H	1	Begin function (Code C3H)
01H	1	Attribute type 0: Extra large 1: Very large 2: Large 3: Small 4: Fine 5: Superscript 6: Subscript 7: Outline 8: Italics 9: Shadow 10: Red line 11: Double underline 12: Bold 13: Strikeout 14: Underline 15: Small capitals
02H	1	End function code

Table 18.10
Opcode C3H in version 5.0

18.2.2.5 Attributes Off (code C4H)

This record switches the attributes off (version 5.0).

Offset	Bytes	Field
00H	1	Begin function code (Code C4H)
01H	1	Attribute type
		0: Extra large
		1: Very large
		2: Large
		3: Small
		4: Fine
		5: Superscript
		6: Subscript
		7: Outline
		8: Italics
		9: Shadow
		10: Red line
		11: Double underline
		12: Bold
		13: Strikeout
		14: Underline
		15: Small capitals
02H	1	End function code

Table 18.11 Opcode C4H in version 5.0

18.2.2.6 Block Protect (code C5H)

In version 5.0, this record protects a block from revisions.

Offset	Bytes	Field
00H	1	Begin function code (Code C5H)
01H	1	0: Block protect on
		1: Block protect off
02H	2	Number of vertical wpu in block
04H	1	End function code

Table 18.12 Opcode C5H in version 5.0

18.2.2.7 End of indent (code C6H)

This record indicates the end of indented text in version 5.0.

Offset	Bytes	Field
00H	1	Begin function code (Code C6H)
01H	2	Old right temporary margin (wpu)
03H	2	Old left temporary margin (wpu)
05H	1	End function code

Table 18.13
Opcode C6H in version 5.0

18.2.2.8 Different display character when hyphenated (code C7H)

In version 5.0, this record defines the characters displayed in a hyphenation zone.

Offset	Bytes	Field
00H	1	Begin function code (Code C7H)
01H	1	Flags
		Bit 0: 1 word is hyphenated next to function
		Bit 1: 1 this function precedes hyphenation
		0 this function follows hyphenation
02H	2	Character when in line
04H	2	Character when hyphenated
06H	1	End function code

Table 18.14
Opcode C7H in version 5.0

The codes between C8H and CFH are reserved in version 5.0.

18.2.3 Variable length multi-byte control codes between D0H and FFH

WordPerfect uses these control codes to store format information. All records are symmetrical, so that the codes can be interpreted in both directions. The definitions given below are for version 5.0.

Word processing

18.2.3.1 Set lines per inch (code D0H, subcode 00H)

In version 5.0, WordPerfect uses this record to define the number of lines per inch. The function is a sub-function of code D0H.

Offset	Bytes	Field
00H	1	Set lines per inch (Code D0H)
01H	1	Sub-function code 00H
02H	2	Length word (value = 8)
04H	2	Old value of lines per inch
06H	2	New value of lines per inch
08H	2	Length word (value = 8)
0AH	1	Sub-function code 00H
0BH	1	End function code (Code D0H)

Table 18.15 Opcode D0H, 00H in version 5.0

18.2.3.2 Set left/right margin (code D0H, subcode 01H)

In version 5.0, WordPerfect uses this record to define the left and right margins.

Offset	Bytes	Field
00H	1	Set left/right margin (Code D0H)
01H	1	Sub-function code 01H
02H	2	Length word (value = 12)
04H	2	Old value for left margin (wpu)
06H	2	Old value for right margin (wpu)
08H	2	New value for left margin (wpu)
0AH	2	New value for right margin (wpu)
0CH	2	Length word (value = 12)
0EH	1	Sub-function code 01H
0FH	1	End function code (Code D0H)

Table 18.16 Opcode D0H, 01H in version 5.0

18.2.3.3 Set spacing (code D0H, subcode 02H)

In version 5.0, WordPerfect uses this record to define the line spacing. The spacing values occupy two bytes. The low byte defines the space in $1/256$ of the line height. The high byte defines the multiple of the line height.

Offset	Bytes	Field
00H	1	Set spacing (Code D0H)
01H	1	Sub-function code 02H
02H	2	Length word (value = 8)
04H	2	Old value for line spacing
06H	2	New value for line spacing
08H	2	Length word (value = 12)
0AH	1	Sub-function code 02H
0BH	1	End function code (Code D0H)

Table 18.17
Opcode D0H, 02H in version 5.0

18.2.3.4 Set hyphenation zone (code D0H, subcode 03H)

In WordPerfect 5.0, this record defines the hyphenation zone.

Offset	Bytes	Field
00H	1	Set hyphenation zone (Code D0H)
01H	1	Sub-function code 03H
02H	2	Length word (value = 8)
04H	1	Old value of left hyphenation zone
05H	1	Old value of right hyphenation zone
06H	1	New value of left hyphenation zone
07H	1	New value of right hyphenation zone
08H	2	Length word (value = 8)
0AH	1	Sub-function code 03H
0BH	1	End function code (Code D0H)

Table 18.18
Opcode D0H, 03H in version 5.0

The values of the hyphenation zone are defined as binary (0 to 255). These values will be recalculated as percentages (128/256 = 50%).

18.2.3.5 Set tabs (code D0H, subcode 04H)

This record defines the tab outputs. The 20 bytes containing the tab types store each tab code in 4 bits. Each byte stores two codes. All tab positions are defined in wpu (WordPerfect units).

Offset	Bytes	Field
00H	1	Set tabs (Code D0H)
01H	1	Sub-function code 04H
02H	2	Length word (value = 204)
04H	80	40 entries for old tab positions
58H	20	40 old tab types (1 nibble/tab)
		Coding for tab types
		0: Normal left justified
		1: Tab centered
		2: Tab right aligned
		3: Decimal aligned tab
		4: Left justified tab with dot leader
		5: —
		6: Right justified with dot leader
		7: Decimal aligned with dot leader
6CH	80	40 entries for new tab positions
C0H	20	40 old tab types (1 nibble/tab)
D4H	2	Length word (value = 204)
D6H	1	Sub-function code 04H
D7H	1	End function code (Code D0H)

Table 18.19
Opcode D0H, 04H
in version 5.0

18.2.3.6 Set top/bottom margin (code D0H, subcode 05H)

Offset	Bytes	Field
00H	1	Set top/bottom margin (Code D0H)
01H	1	Sub-function code 05H
02H	2	Length word (value = 12)
04H	2	Old value for top margin
06H	2	Old value for bottom margin
08H	2	New value for top margin
0AH	2	New value for bottom margin
0CH	2	Length word (value = 12)
0EH	1	Sub-function code 05H
0FH	1	End function code (Code D0H)

Table 18.20
Opcode D0H, 05H
in version 5.0

In version 5.0, WordPerfect uses this record to define the top and bottom margins. All values are defined in wpu.

18.2.3.7 Suppress page characteristics (code D0H, subcode 07H)

WordPerfect uses this record to define page formatting information (page numbering, header, and so on). The suppress code contains several bit fields. If the relevant bit is set, the line numbering and/or the header/footer will be suppressed.

Offset	Bytes	Field
00H	1	Suppress page characteristics (Code D0H)
01H	1	Sub-function code 07H
02H	2	Length word (value = 6)
04H	1	Old suppress code Coding: 1 = Suppress page numbering 2 = Suppress current page numbering and print page number at bottom center 4 = Suppress header A 8 = Suppress header B 10 = Suppress footer A 20 = Suppress footer B
05H	1	New suppress code
06H	2	Length word (value = 6)
08H	1	Sub-function code 07H
09H	1	End function code (Code D0H)

Table 18.21 Opcode D0H, 07H in version 5.0

18.2.3.8 Page number position (code D0H, subcode 08H)

This record type defines a new page number position.

Offset	Bytes	Field
00H	1	Page number position (Code D0H)
01H	1	Sub-function code 08H
02H	2	Length word (value = 10)

Table 18.22 Opcode D0H, 08H in version 5.0 (*continues over...*)

Offset	Bytes	Field
04H	1	Old position code (page number) Coding: 0 = None 1 = Top left 2 = Top center 3 = Top right 4 = Alternate top left/right 5 = Bottom left 6 = Bottom center 7 = Bottom right 8 = Alternate bottom left/right
05H	2	Old font size (wpu)
07H	1	New position code
08H	2	New font size (wpu)
0AH	2	Length word (value = 10)
0CH	1	Sub-function code 08H
0DH	1	End function code (Code D0H)

Table 18.22 Opcode D0H, 08H in version 5.0 (*cont.*)

18.2.3.9 Form (code D0H, subcode 0BH)

This record defines the text format.

Offset	**Bytes**	**Field**
00H	1	Form (Code D0H)
01H	1	Sub-function code 0BH
02H	2	Length word (value = 197)
04H	2	Old desired length
06H	2	Old desired width
08H	1	Old desired type
09H	1	Old desired type-name length

Table 18.23 Opcode D0H, 0BH in version 5.0 (*continues over...*)

Offset	Bytes	Field
0AH	41	Old desired type name
33H	2	Old effective length
35H	2	Old effective width
37H	1	Old effective type
38H	1	Old effective type name length
39H	41	Old effective type name
62H	1	Old effective orientation
		0 = Portrait, 1 = Landscape
63H	2	New desired length
65H	2	New desired width
67H	1	New desired type
68H	1	New desired type name length
69H	41	New desired type name
92H	2	New effective length
94H	2	New effective width
96H	1	New effective type
97H	1	New effective type name
98H	41	New effective type name length
C1H	1	New effective orientation
C2H	1	Matched form number
C3H	2	Matched form hash value
C5H	2	Length word (value = 197)
C7H	1	Sub-function code 0BH
C8H	1	End function code (Code D0H)

Table 18.23 Opcode D0H, 0BH in version 5.0 (*cont.*)

18.2.4 Font group sub-function (code D1H)

WordPerfect 5.0 uses this group of records to select the font and to define several other parameters. A subcode defines the function of each record.

18.2.4.1 Color (code D1H, subcode 00H)

This record defines the color of the text output. The colors are defined with 3-byte values. Each byte defines a value between 0 and FFH for the basic color (red, green, blue).

Offset	Bytes	Field
00H	1	Color (Code D1H)
01H	1	Sub-function code 00H
02H	2	Length word (value = 10)
04H	3	Old color as RGB with
		3 bytes (red, green, blue) 0–FFH
07H	3	New color as RGB
0AH	2	Length word (value = 10)
0CH	1	Sub-function code 00H
0DH	1	End function code (Code D1H)

Table 18.24 Opcode D1H, 00H in version 5.0

18.2.4.2 Font change (code D1H, subcode 01H)

WordPerfect 5.0 uses this record to define character sets. Some values are defined as WordPerfect Units (wpu, 1/1200 inch). The unit psu (Point Size Unit) is 1/10000 of the associated character point size. The *typeface descriptor* contains information on serif characters, grayscale, height, and so on. Each item of information is stored in a 3-byte data structure.

Offset	Bytes	Field
00H	1	Font change (Code D1H)
01H	1	Sub-function code 01H
02H	2	Length word (value = 32)
04H	1	Old font number
05H	24	New font description:
	2	Point size (in 3600ths)
	2	Optimum width (in wpu)
	2	Capital height (in psu)
	2	x height (in psu)
	2	Descender height (in psu)
	2	Italic adjustment (in psu +/–)
	3	Typeface descriptor
	1	Typeface definition flag
	1	Hash of typeface name
	1	Reserved (always 0)
	2	Hash of font name
	4	Character set completeness bits
		1 bit per character set in each word

Table 18.25 Opcode D1H, 01H in version 5.0 (*continues over...*)

Offset	Bytes	Field
1DH	1	Matched font
1EH	2	Matched font hash value
20H	2	Length word (value = 32)
22H	1	Sub-function code 01H
23H	1	End function code (Code D1H)

Table 18.25 Opcode D1H, 01H in version 5.0 (*cont.*)

In version 5.0, all other subcodes are undefined in function D1H.

18.2.5 Group definition sub-function (code D2H)

This group of records defines various parts of a document (columns, paragraphs, and so on).

18.2.5.1 Define mathematical columns (code D2H, subcode 00H)

This record defines columns containing calculation formula.

Offset	Bytes	Field
00H	1	Define math columns (Code D2H)
01H	1	Sub-function code 00H
02H	2	Length word (value = 212)
04H	24	Old math definition
1CH	20	Old calculation 0
30H	20	Old calculation 1
44H	20	Old calculation 2
58H	20	Old calculation 3
6CH	24	New math definition
84H	20	New calculation 0
98H	20	New calculation 1
ACH	20	New calculation 2
C0H	20	New calculation 3
D4H	2	Length word (value = 212)
D6H	1	Sub-function code 00H
D7H	1	End function code (Code D2H)

Table 18.26 Opcode D2H, 00H in version 5.0

18.2.5.2 Define columns (code D2H, subcode 01H)

This record defines columns in WordPerfect 5.0.

Offset	Bytes	Field
00H	1	Define Columns (Code D2H)
01H	1	Sub-function code 01H
02H	2	Length word (value = 198)
04H	1	Old number of columns
05H	24*2	Old left/right columns margins
35H	1	New number of columns Bit 0–4: columns 2–24 Bit 5: — Bit 6: 1 parallel columns Bit 7: 1 parallel columns with block protected
36H	48	New left/right column margins
66H	2	Length word (value = 198)
68H	1	Sub-function code 01H
69H	1	End function code (Code D2H)

Table 18.27 Opcode D2H, 01H in version 5.0

18.2.5.3 Paragraph number definition (code D2H, subcode 02H)

This record defines a new paragraph number as shown in Table 18.28.

The data structure at offset 2CH defines the punctuation characters in bytes 1 and 3. Byte 2 contains the code for paragraph numbering as shown in Table 18.29.

Offset	Bytes	Field
00H	1	Paragraph number definition (Code D2H)
01H	1	Sub-function code 02H
02H	2	Length word (value = 84)
04H	24	8 × 3-byte entries for old definitions
1CH	16	8 × 2-byte entries for old even numbers
2CH	24	8 × 3-byte entries with new definitions
44H	16	8 × 2-byte entries for new even numbers
54H	2	Length word (value = 84)
56H	1	Sub-function 02H
57H	1	End function code (Code D2H)

Table 18.28 Opcode D2H, 02H in version 5.0

Character	Numbering
I:	Uppercase Roman numerals
i:	Lowercase Roman numerals
A:	Capital letter
a:	Lower case letter
1:	Arabic numerals

Table 18.29 Paragraph numbering characters

Spaces are not included in paragraph numbers. If the first byte of an entry is 0, the second and third bytes will represent the character used for a bullet.

18.2.5.4 Footnote options (code D2H, subcode 03H)

WordPerfect 5.0 stores footnotes in this record.

Offset	Bytes	Field
00H	1	Footnote options (Code D2H)
01H	1	Sub-function code 03H
02H	2	Length word (value = 160)
04H	78	Old value
52H		New value (78 bytes)
	2	Spacing in footnotes
	2	Spacing between footnotes
	2	Number of footnotes kept together
	1	Flags Bits 0–1: 0 use numbers 1 use characters 2 use letters Bit 2: 1 numbering starts on each page Bit 3: 1 footnote continued mark Bit 4: 0 footnotes after text 1 footnotes at bottom of page Bits 6–5: 0 = no line separator 1 = 2 inch line 2 = line from left to right margin
	1	Number of chars used in place of footnote numbers

Table 18.30 Opcode D2H, 03H in version 5.0 (*continues over…*)

Offset	Bytes	Field
	5*2	Chars for footnote number (ASCII string, if $n < 5$)
	20	String for footnote number in text
	20	String for footnote number in note
	2	Left margin for footnotes (in wpu)
	2	Right margin for footnotes (in wpu)
	2	Lines/inch for footnotes
	2	Character width for footnotes (0 = auto)
	2	Space width in footnotes
	2	Minimum space for footnotes
	2	Maximum space for footnotes
	2	Attribute for footnotes
	3	Footnotes color
	1	Footnotes font
A0H	2	Length word (value = 160)
A2H	1	Sub-function code 03H
A3H	1	End function code (Code D2H)

Table 18.30 Opcode D2H, 03H in version 5.0 (*cont.*)

The fields containing old and new footnote settings have the same structure.

18.2.5.5 Endnote options (code D2H, subcode 04H)

WordPerfect 5.0 uses this record to store endnotes as shown in Table 18.31. This record structure is similar to the structure of the footnote options record. The fields for old and new endnote options have the same structure.

Offset	**Bytes**	**Field**
00H	1	Endnote options (Code D2H)
01H	1	Sub-function code 04H
02H	2	Length word (value = 160)
04H	78	Old value
52H		New value (78 bytes)
	2	Spacing in endnotes
	2	Spacing between endnotes
	2	Number of endnotes kept together

Table 18.31 Opcode D2H, 04H in version 5.0 (*continues over...*)

Offset	Bytes	Field
	1	Flags:
		Bits 1–0: 0 use numbers
		1 use characters
		2 use letters
	1	Number of chars in place of endnote numbers
	5*2	Chars used in place of endnote numbers (ASCII string, if $n < 5$)
	20	String for endnote numbers in text
	20	String for endnote numbers in note
	2	Left margin for endnotes (in wpu)
	2	Right margin for endnotes (in wpu)
	2	Lines/inch for endnotes
	2	Character width for endnotes (0 = auto)
	2	Space width in endnotes
	2	Minimum space for endnotes
	2	Maximum space for endnotes
	2	Attribute for endnotes
	3	Endnote text color
	1	Font for endnote text
A0H	2	Length word (value = 160)
A2H	1	Sub-function code 04H
A3H	1	End function code (Code D2H)

Table 18.31 Opcode D2H, 04H in version 5.0 (*cont.*)

18.2.5.6 Graph box options for figures (code D2H, subcode 05H)

This record is defined in WordPerfect 5.0 to store the graph box options for graphics in a document.

Offset	Bytes	Field
00H	1	Graph box options (Code D2H)
01H	1	Sub-function code 05H
02H	2	Length word (value = 128)
04H	62	Old values
42H		New values (62 bytes)
	1	Flags Bits 1–0: Numbering style figures level 1 1 Numbers 2 Upper case letters 3 Roman numerals (upper case) Bits 3–2: Numbering style figures level 2 0 Unused 1 Numbers 2 Use letters (lower case) 3 Roman numerals (lower case) Bit 4: 0 Position caption below window 1 Position caption above window Bit 5: 0 Position caption outside borders 1 Position caption inside borders
	1	Shading 0–100% (0 = no shade)
	2	Border styles 0 = none 1 = single 2 = double 3 = dashed 4 = dotted 5 = wide 6 = unused 7 = unused

Table 18.32 Opcode D2H, 05H in version 5.0 (*continues over...*)

Word processing

Offset	Bytes	Field
	2	Minimum offset from start of paragraph (in wpu)
	4*2	Spacing between border and text left, right, top, bottom (wpu)
	4*2	Spacing between border and picture left, right, top, bottom (wpu)
	20	Text figure number in caption
	2	Old figure number
	2	Line spacing for captions
	2	Lines/inch for captions
	2	Character width for captions (0 = auto)
	2	Space width for captions
	2	Minimum space for captions
	2	Maximum space for captions
	2	Attribute for captions
	3	Color for captions
	1	Font for captions
80H	2	Length word (value = 128)
82H	1	Sub-function code 05H
83H	1	End function code (Code D2H)

Table 18.32 Opcode D2H, 05H in version 5.0 (*cont.*)

18.2.5.7 Graph box options for tables (code D2H, subcode 06H)

This record stores the graph box options for tables. The structure is identical to the graph box record described above.

18.2.5.8 Graph box options for text boxes (code D2H, subcode 07H)

This record is used to store the graph box options for text blocks. The structure is identical to the graph box structure described above.

18.2.5.9 Graph box options for user-defined boxes (code D2H, subcode 08H)

This record is used to store the graph box options for user-defined text blocks. The structure is identical to the graph box structure described above.

18.2.6 Set group sub-functions (code D3H)

WordPerfect 5.0 uses this group of records to store control codes for text formatting. A subcode defines the function.

18.2.6.1 Set alignment character (code D3H, subcode 00H)

This record defines the characters for hyphenation and alignment.

Offset	Bytes	Field
00H	1	Set alignment character (Code D3H)
01H	1	Sub-function code 00H
02H	2	Length word (value = 12)
04H	2	Old alignment character
06H	2	Old hyphenation character
08H	2	New alignment character
0AH	2	New hyphenation character
0CH	2	Length word (value = 12)
0EH	1	Sub-function code 00H
0FH	1	End function code (Code D3H)

Table 18.33
Opcode D3H, 00H in version 5.0

18.2.6.2 Set underline mode (code D3H, subcode 01H)

WordPerfect 5.0 activates the underline function using this record.

Offset	Bytes	Field
00H	1	Set underline mode (Code D3H)
01H	1	Sub-function code 01H
02H	2	Length word (value = 6)
04H	1	Old definition
05H	1	New definition Bit 0 = 1: underline space Bit 1 = 1: underline tab, indents, and so on
06H	2	Length word (value = 6)
08H	1	Sub-function code 01H
09H	1	End function code (Code D3H)

Table 18.34
Opcode D3H, 01H in version 5.0

18.2.6.3 Set footnote number (code D3H, subcode 02H)

This record defines a new number for the next footnote.

Offset	Bytes	Field
00H	1	Set footnote number (Code D3H)
01H	1	Sub-function code 02H
02H	2	Length word (value = 8)
04H	2	Old number
06H	2	New number
08H	2	Length word (value = 8)
0AH	1	Sub-function 02H
0BH	1	End function code (Code D3H)

Table 18.35
Opcode D3H, 02H in version 5.0

18.2.6.4 Set endnote number (code D3H, subcode 03H)

This record defines a new number for the next endnote.

Offset	Bytes	Field
00H	1	Set endnote number (Code D3H)
01H	1	Sub-function code 03H
02H	2	Length word (value = 8)
04H	2	Old number
06H	2	New number
08H	2	Length word (value = 8)
0AH	1	Sub-function 03H
0BH	1	End function code (Code D3H)

Table 18.36
Opcode D3H, 03H in version 5.0

18.2.6.5 Set page number (code D3H, subcode 04H)

This function defines a new page number. If bit 15 in the word at offset 06H is set, the page numbers will be displayed in Roman numerals.

Offset	Bytes	Field
00H	1	Set page number (Code D3H)
01H	1	Sub-function code 04H
02H	2	Length word (value = 8)
04H	2	Old page number
06H	2	New page number
08H	2	Length word (value = 8)
0AH	1	Sub-function 02H
0BH	1	End function code (Code D3H)

Table 18.37 Opcode D3H, 04H in version 5.0

18.2.6.6 Line numbering (code D3H, subcode 05H)

In version 5.0, WordPerfect uses this record to store line numbers.

Offset	Bytes	Field
00H	1	Line numbering (Code D3H)
01H	1	Sub-function code 05H
02H	2	Length word (value = 14)
04H	1	Old spacing
05H	2	Old position
07H	2	Old starting number
09H	1	New spacing
		Bits 4–0: Spacing
		Line numbering (1–30)
		Bit 5: 1 new numbers on each page
		Bit 6: 1 number only text lines
		Bit 7: 1 numbering on
		0 numbering off
0AH	2	New position for line numbers (in wpu, left border to right border of line number)
0CH	2	New starting number
0EH	2	Length word (value = 14)
10H	1	Sub-function code 05H
11H	1	End function code (Code D3H)

Table 18.38 Opcode D3H, 05H in version 5.0

Word processing

18.2.6.7 Advance to page position (code D3H, subcode 06H)

In version 5.0, this record moves forward to a new page position.

Offset	Bytes	Field
00H	1	Advance to page position (Code D3H)
01H	1	Sub-function code 06H
02H	2	Length word (value = 9)
04H	1	Flags Bit 0: 0 relative 1 absolute Bit 1: 0 vertical 1 horizontal
05H	2	Old position (in wpu)
07H	2	New position (in wpu)
09H	2	Length word (value = 9)
0BH	1	Sub-function code 06H
0CH	1	End function code (Code D3H)

Table 18.39 Opcode D3H, 06H in version 5.0

18.2.6.8 Force odd/even page (code D3H, subcode 07H)

This record forces a new page on odd/even pages.

Offset	Bytes	Field
00H	1	Force odd/even page (Code D3H)
01H	1	Sub-function code 07H
02H	2	Length word (value = 7)
04H	2	Old page number
06H	1	Flags: 0 = even 1 = odd
07H	2	Length word (value = 7)
09H	1	Sub-function code 07H
0AH	1	End function code (Code D3H)

Table 18.40 Opcode D3H, 07H in version 5.0

18.2.6.9 Character/space width (code D3H, subcode 0AH)

WordPerfect stores the width of character spacing within this record.

Offset	Bytes	Field
00H	1	Character space width (Code D3H)
01H	1	Sub-function code 0AH
02H	2	Length word (value = 12)
04H	2	Old % of character width
06H	2	Old % of space width
08H	2	New % of character width
0AH	2	New % of space width
0CH	2	Length word (value = 12)
0EH	1	Sub-function code 0AH
0FH	1	End function code (Code D3H)

Table 18.41
Opcode D3H, 0AH
in version 5.0

Values are defined as a percentage of the character width.

18.2.6.10 Space expansion (code D3H, subcode 0BH)

WordPerfect can expand or compress a space to justify the right margin of a line. The parameters for space expansion are stored in this record.

Offset	Bytes	Field
00H	1	Space expansion (Code D3H)
01H	1	Sub-function code 0BH
02H	2	Length word (value = 12)
04H	2	Old minimum % of space width
06H	2	Old maximum % of space width
08H	2	New minimum % of space width
0AH	2	New maximum % of space width
0CH	2	Length word (value = 12)
0EH	1	Sub-function code 0BH
0FH	1	End function code (Code D3H)

Table 18.42
Opcode D3H, 0BH
in version 5.0

Values are defined as a percentage of the standard space width.

18.2.6.11 Set graph box number for figures (code D3H, subcode 0CH)

This record defines the numbers for figures.

Offset	Bytes	Field
00H	1	Figure number (Code D3H)
01H	1	Sub-function code 0CH
02H	2	Length word (value = 8)
04H	2	Old box number
06H	2	New box number
		Bits 4–0: 2nd level number
		Bits 15–5: 1st level number
08H	2	Length word (value = 8)
0AH	1	Sub-function code 0CH
0BH	1	End function code (Code D3H)

Table 18.43
Opcode D3H, 0CH in version 5.0

18.2.6.12 Set graph box number for tables (code D3H, subcode 0DH)

This record defines the table numbering options. The structure is identical to function 0CH.

18.2.6.13 Set graph box number for text boxes (code D3H, subcode 0EH)

This record defines the options for text blocks. The structure is identical to function 0CH.

18.2.6.14 Set graph box number for user-defined boxes (code D3H, subcode 0FH)

This record defines the options for user-defined text blocks. The structure is identical to function 0CH.

18.2.6.15 Set language (code D3H, subcode 11H)

This record defines the language for a text region.

Offset	Bytes	Field
00H	1	Set language (Code D3H)
01H	1	Sub-function code 11H
02H	2	Length word (value = 12)
04H	2	Old language 2-char ID (ASCII)

Table 18.44
Opcode D3H, 0CH in version 5.0
(continues over...)

Word processing

Offset	Bytes	Field
06H	2	New language 2-char ID (ASCII) US = American English DA = Danish NE = Dutch SU = Finnish FR = French DE = German IC = Icelandic IT = Italian NO = Norwegian PO = Portuguese ES = Spanish SV = Swedish UK = British English CA = Canadian French
08H	2	Length word (value = 8)
0AH	1	Sub-function code 11H
0BH	1	End function code (Code D3H)

Table 18.44 Opcode D3H, 11H in version 5.0 (*cont.*)

18.2.7 Format group sub-functions (code D4H)

WordPerfect version 5.0 uses this group of records to store format information. All records use code D4H together with a subcode.

18.2.7.1 End of page function (code D4H, subcode 00H)

This record defines the end of a page.

Offset	**Bytes**	**Field**
00H	1	End of page function (Code D4H)
01H	1	Sub-function code 00H
02H	2	Length word (variable)
04H	1	Group 0 marker
05H	1	Group 0 length (0BH)

Table 18.45 Opcode D4H, 00H in version 5.0 (*continues over...*)

Offset	Bytes	Field
06H	2	Number of formatter lines at end of page
08H	2	Actual page number of this page
0AH	2	Number of formatter lines used for footnotes
0CH	1	Number of pages used for footnotes
0DH	1	Number of footnotes on this page
0EH	1	Conditional end of page flag
0FH	1	Suppress code
10H	1	Center page top to bottom
11H	1	Group 1 marker (optional)
12H	1	Group 1 length (variable)
13H	...	Maximum number
...	*x*1	Maximum screen lines from Col ON for each column
...	2	Number of formatter lines for last column
...	2	Screen lines from Col ON for last line of last column
...	2	Screen lines column ON at top page
...	1	Group 2 marker (optional)
...	1	Group 2 length (variable)
...	1	Number of boxes formatter is tracking
...	*x*2	Formatter box table
...	2	Length word (variable)
...	1	Sub-function code 00H
...	1	End function code (Code D4H)

Table 18.45
Opcode D4H, 00H in version 5.0 (*cont.*)

x1 is calculated as (columns – 1) * 2 bytes, x2 is calculated as 14 * boxes.

18.2.7.2 End of line function (code D4H, subcode 01H)

WordPerfect 5.0 marks the end of a line with this record.

Offset	Bytes	Field
00H	1	End of line function (Code D4H)
01H	1	Sub-function code 01H
02H	2	Length word (variable)
04H	1	Group 0 marker (optional)
05H	1	Group 0 length (4)
06H	2	Maximum top shoulder height for line
08H	2	Maximum bottom shoulder height for line
0AH	2	Length word (variable)
0CH	1	Sub-function code 01H
0DH	1	End function code (Code D4H)

Table 18.46
Opcode D4H, 01H in version 5.0

18.2.7.3 Graph box information function (code D4H, subcode 02H)

This record defines some of the parameters for a graph box.

Offset	Bytes	Field
00H	1	Graph box information (Code D4H)
01H	1	Sub-function code 02H
02H	2	Length word (variable)
04H	1	Group 0 marker
05H	1	Group 0 length (14H)
06H	2	Old left margin (wpu)
08H	2	Old temporary left margin (wpu)
0AH	2	Old right margin (wpu)
0CH	2	Old temporary right margin (wpu)
0EH	2	Old number of formatter lines (wpu)
10H	2	New left margin (wpu)
12H	2	New temporary left margin (wpu)
14H	2	New right margin (wpu)
16H	2	New temporary right margin (wpu)
18H	2	New number of formatter lines (wpu)
1AH	1	Group 1 marker
1BH	1	Group 1 length (boxes * 8 bytes)

Table 18.47
Opcode D4H, 02H in version 5.0 (*continues over...*)

Offset	Bytes	Field
...	1	Flags Bit 0: 1 = top of box occurs on this line Bit 1: 1 = middle of box occurs on this line Bit 2: 1 = bottom of box occurs on this line Bits 5–3: box type 0 = figure 1 = table 2 = text box 3 = user-defined box
...	1	Box numbering mode
...	2	Box number Bits 4–0: level 2 number Bits 15–5: level 1 number
...	2	Box position left (wpu)
...	2	Box position right (wpu)
...	2	Length word (variable)
...	1	Sub-function code 02H
...	1	End function code (Code D4H)

Table 18.47 Opcode D4H, 02H in version 5.0 (*cont.*)

Each box in group 1 uses 8 bytes (including flag and box data). The record length is variable.

18.2.8 Header/footer group sub-functions (code D5H)

WordPerfect 5.0 uses this record to store control information for the header/footer of a page.

18.2.8.1 Header A (code D5H, subcode 00H)

This record defines the parameter for header A. The record stores the header text and the position of this text on the current page.

The *occurrence flag* defines the pages on which the header will be displayed. The value 0 suppresses the header display.

Offset	Bytes	Field
00H	1	Header A (Code D5H)
01H	1	Sub-function code 00H
02H	2	Length word (variable)
04H	1	Old occurrence flag
05H	2	Old number of formatter lines (in wpu)
07H	2	Old position of last header A function
09H	2	Old position of last header A function
0BH	1	New occurrence flag: 0 = never 1 = all pages 2 = odd pages 3 = even pages
0CH	2	New number of formatter lines (wpu)
0EH	2	New position of last header A function (Unused)
10H	2	New position of last header A function (Unused)
12H	2	Number of boxes inside header
14H	2	Formatter hash value
16H	*xx*	Header text as ASCII string
xxH	2	Length word (variable)
xxH	1	Sub-function code 00H
xxH	1	End function code (Code D5H)

Table 18.48 Opcode D5H, 00H in version 5.0

18.2.8.2 Header B (code D5H, subcode 01H)

WordPerfect permits the definition of a second header, B (for even pages), which is stored in this record. The structure of the record is identical to record D500H (Header A).

18.2.8.3 Footer A (code D5H, subcode 02H)

This record defines Footer A. The structure of the record is identical to that of the header definition (Code D500H).

18.2.8.4 Footer B (code D5H, subcode 03H)

This record stores a second Footer B. The structure is identical to record D500H (Header A).

18.2.9 Footnote/endnote group sub-functions (code D6H)

These records are used to define footnotes and endnotes in WordPerfect 5.0.

18.2.9.1 Footnote (code D6H, subcode 00H)

This record defines a footnote and stores the footnote text and the information about the numbering index. If bit 7 (flag) is clear, WordPerfect uses numbers. Otherwise letters (a,b,c...) will be used. The field length at offset 08H is calculated as page numbers * 2 (each page uses one word).

Offset	Bytes	Field
00H	1	Footnote (Code D6H)
01H	1	Sub-function code 00H
02H	2	Length word (variable)
04H	1	Flag Bit 7: 0 use numbers 1 use characters Bits 3–0: number or character if bit 7 = 1
05H	2	Footnote number or character
07H	1	Number of additional pages in footnote
08H	*x*1	Number of formatter lines for each page of footnote (in wpu)
xxH	2	Number of formatter lines on page (wpu)
xxH	2	Number of footnote lines on page (wpu)
xxH	2	Number of footnote pages on page (wpu)
xxH	2	Number of boxes inside footnote
xxH	2	Formatter hash value
xxH	*xx*	Text of footnote
xxH	2	Length word (variable)
xxH	1	Sub-function code 00H
xxH	1	End function code (Code D6H)

Table 18.49
Opcode D6H, 00H in version 5.0

18.2.9.2 Endnote (code D6H, subcode 01H)

This record stores the endnote text and the index information. If bit 7 (flag) is set, WordPerfect uses numbers. Otherwise letters are used. The record structure is similar to the footnote record.

Offset	Bytes	Field
00H	1	End note (Code D6H)
01H	1	Sub-function code 01H
02H	2	Length word (variable)
04H	1	Flag Bit 7: 0 use numbers 1 use characters Bits 3–0: number of characters if bit 7 = 1
05H	2	Endnote number or character
07H	2	Number of boxes inside endnote
09H	2	Formatter hash value
0BH	*xx*	Text of endnote
xxH	2	Length word (variable)
xxH	1	Sub-function code 01H
xxH	1	End function code (Code D6H)

Table 18.50 Opcode D6H, 01H in version 5.0

18.2.10 Generate group sub-functions (code D7H)

This record group stores text markers in a WordPerfect file.

18.2.10.1 Begin marked text (code D7H, subcode 00H)

This record defines the beginning of a text area.

Offset	Bytes	Field
00H	1	Begin marked text (D7H)
01H	1	Sub-function code 00H
02H	2	Length word (value = 5)
04H	1	Flag: Bits 7–4: 0 table of contents 1 list Bits 3–0: table of contents level number or list number
05H	2	Length word (value = 5)
07H	1	Sub-function code 00H
08H	1	End function code (Code D7H)

Table 18.51 Opcode D7H, 00H in version 5.0

18.2.10.2 End marked text (code D7H, subcode 01H)

This record defines the end of a text block.

Offset	Bytes	Field
00H	1	End marked text (D7H)
01H	1	Sub-function code 01H
02H	2	Length word (value = 5)
04H	1	Flag Bits 7–4: 0 table of contents 1 list Bits 3–0: table of contents level number, or list number
05H	2	Length word (value = 5)
07H	1	Sub-function code 01H
08H	1	End function code (Code D7H)

Table 18.52 Opcode D7H, 01H in version 5.0

18.2.10.3 Define marked text (code D7H, subcode 02H)

This record defines a marked text region.

Offset	Bytes	Field
00H	1	Define marked text (Code D7H)
01H	1	Sub-function code 02H
02H	2	Length word (variable)
04H	1	Flag Bits 7–4: 0 table of contents 1 index 2 list 3 table of authorities Bits 3–0: for table of contents = level number (0–4) for index: 0 = no concordance 1 = concordance for list: list number (0–4) for table of authorities (section number (0–15)

Table 18.53 Opcode D7H, 02H in version 5.0 (*continues over...*)

Word processing

Offset	Bytes	Field
05H	5	5 × definition of level or list for table of contents, index and lists: 0: no page numbers 1: page number after text with 2 preceeding blanks 2: page number after text in ( ) with 1 preceding space 3: page number flush right 4: page number flush right with preceding dot for table of authorities: Bit 0: 1 insert blank lines between authorities Bit 1: 1 dot before page number Bit 4: 1 underlining allowed
10H	...	Concordance file name (optional)
xxH	2	Length word (variable)
xxH	1	Sub-function code 02H
xxH	1	End function code (Code D7H)

Table 18.53 Opcode D7H, 02H in version 5.0 (*cont.*)

18.2.10.4 Index entry (code D7H, subcode 03H)

This record defines the entry for index numbering. The heading area and the subheading area are of variable lengths which are defined in the length word (sum of the lengths + 1). The areas are separated by a zero byte 00H.

Offset	Bytes	Field
00H	1	Index entry (Code D7H)
01H	1	Sub-function code 03H
02H	2	Length word (variable)
04H	xx	Heading (variable length)
xxH	1	Null separator (always 00H)
xxH	xx	Subheading
xxH	2	Length word (variable)
xxH	1	Sub-function code 03H
xxH	1	End function code (Code D7H)

Table 18.54 Opcode D7H, 03H in version 5.0

18.2.10.5 Table of authority entry (code D7H, subcode 04H)

This record defines a table of authorization entries. Section number 32 is for the short form only. All entries are separated by a null byte.

Offset	Bytes	Field
00H	1	Table of authority entry (Code D7H)
01H	1	Sub-function code 04H
02H	2	Length word (variable)
04H	1	Section number (0–15 or 32)
05H	x	Short form
xxH	1	Null separator (00H)
xxH	xx	Long form
xxH	2	Length word (variable)
xxH	1	Sub-function code 04H
xxH	1	End function code (Code D7H)

Table 18.55
Opcode D7H, 04H in version 5.0

18.2.10.6 Endnotes print here (code D7H, subcode 05H)

This record defines the position of endnotes.

Offset	Bytes	Field
00H	1	Endnotes print here (Code D7H)
01H	1	Sub-function code 05H
02H	2	Length word (value = 19)
04H	2	Column in old screen (su)
06H	1	Text lines to display
07H	2	Old number of formatter lines (wpu)
09H	2	Number of pages for endnotes
0BH	2	Number of formatter lines (wpu)
0DH	2	Position of last Endnote print here function
0FH	2	Position of last Endnote print here function
11H	2	Old number of endnotes to this point
13H	2	Length word (value = 19)
15H	1	Sub-function code 05H
16H	1	End function code (Code D7H)

Table 18.56
Opcode D7H, 05H in version 5.0

18.2.10.7 Save page information (code D7H, subcode 06H)

This record is only used during the generation of text. The record contains various parameters.

Offset	Bytes	Field
00H	1	Save page information (Code D7H)
01H	1	Sub-function code 06H
02H	2	Length word (value = 13)
04H	2	Number of formatter lines (wpu)
06H	2	Page number
08H	2	Page length of odd pages (wpu)
0AH	2	Page length of even pages (wpu)
0CH	2	Numbering mode 0 = numeric 1 = Arabic
0EH	2	Length word (value = 13)
10H	1	Sub-function code 06H
11H	1	End function code (Code D7H)

Table 18.57
Opcode D7H, 06H
in version 5.0

18.2.10.8 Auto reference definition (code D7H, subcode 07H)

This record stores text references.

Offset	Bytes	Field
00H	1	Auto reference definition (Code D7H)
01H	1	Sub-function code 07H
02H	2	Length word (variable)
04H	1	Reference type 0 : page number 1 : paragraph number 2 : footnote number 3 : endnote number 4 : figure number 5 : table number 6 : text box number 7 : U=user text box number
05H	*xx*	Tag ID text
xxH	1	Null separator (00H)

Table 18.58
Opcode D7H, 07H
in version 5.0
(*continues over...*)

Offset	Bytes	Field
xxH	*xx*	Text of referenced number
xxH	2	Length word (variable)
xxH	1	Sub-function code 07H
xxH	1	End function code (Code D7H)

Table 18.58 Opcode D7H, 07H in version 5.0 (*cont.*)

18.2.10.9 Auto reference tag (code D7H, subcode 08H)

This record stores auto reference tags in a WordPerfect file.

Offset	Bytes	Field
00H	1	Auto reference tag (Code D7H)
01H	1	Sub-function code 08H
02H	2	Length word (variable)
04H	*xx*	Tag ID text
xxH	1	Null terminator (00H)
xxH	2	Length word (variable)
xxH	1	Sub-function code 08H
xxH	1	End function code (Code D7H)

Table 18.59 Opcode D7H, 08H in version 5.0

18.2.10.10 Include sub-document (code D7H, subcode 09H)

If a sub-document is included in a document, this record defines the file name and other parameters.

Offset	Bytes	Field
00H	1	Include sub-document (Code D7H)
01H	1	Sub-function code 09H
02H	2	Length word (variable)
04H	2	Column in old screen (su)
06H	1	Number of text lines to display (wpu)
07H	*xx*	File name as ASCII string
xxH	2	Length word (variable)
xxH	1	Sub-function code 09H
xxH	1	End function code (Code D7H)

Table 18.60 Opcode D7H, 09H in version 5.0

18.2.10.11 Start of included sub-document (code D7H, subcode 0AH)

This record defines the start of the file included in a document.

Offset	Bytes	Field
00H	1	Start included sub-document (Code D7H)
01H	1	Sub-function code 0AH
02H	2	Length word (variable)
04H	2	Column in old screen (su)
06H	1	Number of lines to display (wpu)
07H	*xx*	File name as ASCIIZ string
xxH	*xx*	Password structure, if encrypted
xxH	2	Length word (variable)
xxH	1	Sub-function code 0AH
xxH	1	End function code (Code D7H)

Table 18.61 Opcode D7H, 0AH in version 5.0

18.2.10.12 End of included sub-document (code D7H, subcode 0BH)

This record marks the end of a sub-document inserted within a text.

Offset	Bytes	Field
00H	1	End included sub-document (Code D7H)
01H	1	Sub-function code 0BH
02H	2	Length word (variable)
04H	2	Column in old screen (su)
06H	1	Number of lines to display (wpu)
07H	*xx*	File name as ASCII string
xxH	2	Length word (variable)
xxH	1	Sub-function code 0BH
xxH	1	End function code (Code D7H)

Table 18.62 Opcode D7H, 0BH in version 5.0

18.2.11 Display group sub-functions (code D8H)

WordPerfect 5.0 uses the function code D8H to store additional information (date, paragraphs, and so on).

18.2.11.1 Date function (code D8H, subcode 00H)

This record contains a string field for date information.

Offset	Bytes	Field
00H	1	Date function (Code D8H)
01H	1	Sub-function code 00H
02H	2	Length word (variable)
04H	*xx*	Format string containing date
xxH	2	Length word (variable)
xxH	1	Sub-function code 00H
xxH	1	End function code (Code D8H)

Table 18.63
Opcode D8H, 00H
in version 5.0

Offset 04H marks the beginning of a variable length string containing the date information.

18.2.11.2 Paragraph number (code D8H, subcode 01H)

This record contains data on paragraph formatting.

Offset	Bytes	Field
00H	1	Paragraph number (Code D8H)
01H	1	Sub-function code 01H
02H	2	Length word (variable)
04H	1	New level number paragraph
		Bits 0–6: level number
		Bit 7 = 1: fixed level number
05H	16	8 words containing old level numbers
15H	*xx*	Format text mark (screen & printer)
xxH	2	Length word (variable)
xxH	1	Sub-function code 01H
xxH	1	End function code (Code D8H)

Table 18.64
Opcode D8H, 01H
in version 5.0

The byte at offset 04H defines the level number (bits 0–6). If bit 7 is set, a fixed level number is used. Offset 15H defines a variable length string containing the text format mark.

18.2.11.3 Overstrike (code D8H, subcode 02H)

This record switches the overstrike mode on.

Offset	Bytes	Field
00H	1	Overstrike (Code D8H)
01H	1	Sub-function code 02H
02H	2	Length word (variable)
04H	2	Maximum character width (su)
06H	*xx*	Overstruck characters
xxH	2	Length word (variable)
xxH	1	Sub-function code 02H
xxH	1	End function code (Code D8H)

Table 18.65
Opcode D8H, 02H
in version 5.0

18.2.12 Miscellaneous group (code D9H)

WordPerfect uses the function D9H to store miscellaneous information.

18.2.12.1 Embedded printer command (code D9H, subcode 00H)

This record contains control information for the printer.

The flag (offset 04H) indicates that a file name is used (flag = 1). In this case, the control codes are stored in this file. Otherwise control codes are stored within the record.

Offset	Bytes	Field
00H	1	Embedded printer command (Code D9H)
01H	1	Sub-function code 00H
02H	2	Length word (variable)
04H	1	Flag byte 0: command string 1: file name
05H	*xx*	Text string containing controls or file name
xxH	2	Length word (variable)
xxH	1	Sub-function code 00H
xxH	1	End function code (Code D9H)

Table 18.66
Opcode D9H, 00H
in version 5.0

18.2.12.2 Conditional end of page function (code D9H, subcode 01H)

This record marks paragraphs or regions of text where the lines are to be kept together.

Offset	Bytes	Field
00H	1	Conditional EOP function (Code D9H)
01H	1	Sub-function code 01H
02H	2	Length word (value = 5)
04H	1	Number of single spaced lines to be kept together
05H	2	Length word (value = 5)
07H	1	Sub-function code 01H
08H	1	End function code (Code D9H)

Table 18.67 Opcode D9H, 01H in version 5.0

WordPerfect uses this value to insert a page break if the number of lines cannot be kept together.

18.2.12.3 Comment (code D9H, subcode 02H)

This record stores a comment in a WordPerfect file.

Offset	Bytes	Field
00H	1	Comment (Code D9H)
01H	1	Sub-function code 02H
02H	2	Length word (variable)
04H	2	Old screen column (su)
06H	1	Number of text lines to display
07H	xx	Text string containing the comment
xxH	2	Length word (variable)
xxH	1	Sub-function code 02H
xxH	1	End function code (Code D9H)

Table 18.68 Opcode D9H, 02H in version 5.0

18.2.12.4 Kerning (code D9H, subcode 03H)

This record stores the kerning information and switches kerning on and off.

Offset	Bytes	Field
00H	1	Kerning (Code D9H)
01H	1	Sub-function code 03H
02H	2	Length word (value = 6)
04H	1	Old kerning value 0 = OFF 1 = ON
05H	1	New kerning value
06H	2	Length word (value = 6)
08H	1	Sub-function code 03H
09H	1	End function code (Code D9H)

Table 18.69 Opcode D9H, 03H in version 5.0

If the byte at offset 04H is set to 0, kerning is switched off.

18.2.13 Box group (code DAH)

The function code group DAH defines data for text boxes, figures, table borders, and so on.

18.2.13.1 Figure (code DAH, subcode 00H)

This record defines all the parameters for a box in which to insert graphics.

Offset	Bytes	Field
00H	1	Figure (Code DAH)
01H	1	Sub-function code 00H
02H	2	Length word (variable)
04H	2	Box number xx.xx Bits 15–5: number level 1 (xx.) Bits 4–0: number level 2 (.xx)
06H	1	Position and type flag Bits 1–0: box type 0 = paragraph 1 = page 2 = character (in-line)

Table 18.70 Opcode DAH, 00H in version 5.0 (*continues over...*)

Offset	Bytes	Field	
		Bits 4–2:	Position option
			0 = full page
			1 = top
			2 = middle
			3 = bottom
			4 = absolute
		Bit 5:	box bumped to next page
		Bits 7–6:	Reserved
07H	1	Alignment flags	
		Bits 1–0:	Alignment option
			0 = left
			1 = right
			2 = centered
			3 = left and right justified
		Bits 3–2:	Alignment with
			0 = margins
			1 = columns
			2 = absolute
		Bit 4:	scale width figure
		Bit 5:	scale height figure
		Bit 6:	reserved
		Bit 7:	0 = wrap text around
			1 = disable wrap text
08H	2	Box width (wpu)	
0AH	2	Box height (wpu)	
0CH	2	X position of box (wpu)	
0EH	2	Y position of box (wpu)	
10H	2	Outside left spacing between window and text (wpu)	
12H	2	Outside right spacing between window and text (wpu)	
14H	2	Outside top spacing between window and text (wpu)	
16H	2	Outside bottom spacing between window and text (wpu)	
18H	2	Inside left spacing between window and image (wpu)	
1AH	2	Inside right spacing between window and image (wpu)	

Table 18.70
Opcode DAH, 00H
in version 5.0
(*cont.*)

Offset	Bytes	Field
1CH	2	Inside top spacing between window and image (wpu)
1EH	2	Inside bottom spacing between window and image (wpu)
20H	2	Horizontal offset (wpu)
22H	2	Vertical offset (wpu)
24H	1	Column X for column alignment
25H	1	Column Y for column alignment
26H	2	Source image width (wpu)
28H	2	Source image height (wpu) for text boxes = number of format lines
2AH	2	Orientation Bit 15: 1 = mirror Bit 14: 1 = invert bits for monochrome bitmaps Bits 13–12: reserved Bits 11–0: rotation angle (0...360)
2CH	2	Width scale factor (100 = 100%)
2EH	2	Height scale factor (100 = 100%)
30H	2	X crop offset (wpu) for text boxes = formatter hash table
32H	2	Y crop offset (wpu) for text boxes = rotation 0 = 0 degrees 1 = 90 degrees 2 = 180 degrees 3 = 270 degrees
34H	1	Format type of box contents 0 = empty box 1 = reserved ... 15 = reserved 16 = WordPerfect text 17 = reserved ... 127 = reserved 128 = WPG format 129 = Lotus PIC format 130 = TIFF format

Table 18.70 Opcode DAH, 00H in version 5.0 (*cont.*)

Word processing

Offset	Bytes	Field
		131 = PC Paintbrush PCX format
		132 = Windows Paint (MSP) format
		133 = CGI Metafile (CGM) format
		134 = AutoCAD (DXF) format
		135 = reserved
		...
		137 = reserved
		138 = GEM Paint (IMG) format
		139 = HPGL format
		140 = reserved
		141 = PC Paint format
		142 = Mac Paint format
		143 = reserved
		144 = reserved
		145 = Dr. Halo II (PIC) format
		146 = reserved
		...
		255 = reserved
35H	21	ASCIIZ string containing file name
4AH	37	Reserved
6FH	2	Amount of extra space between caption and box (wpu)
71H	2	Image index number in graphics temporary file
73H	2	Number of formatter lines in caption (wpu)
75H	2	Formatter hash value for caption
77H	2	Length of caption in bytes
79H	xx	Text for caption
xxH	xx	Text for text box
xxH	2	Length word (variable)
xxH	1	Sub-function code 00H
xxH	1	End function code (Code DAH)

Table 18.70 Opcode DAH, 00H in version 5.0 (*cont.*)

Word processing

18.2.13.2 Table (code DAH, subcode 01H)

This record contains all the information for a table box in a text. The record structure is identical to a figure box (*see above*).

18.2.13.3 Text box (code DAH, subcode 02H)

This record contains all the information for a text box in a document. The record structure is identical to a figure box (*see above*).

18.2.13.4 User defined text box (code DAH, subcode 03H)

This record contains all the information for a user-defined text box in a document. The record structure is identical to a figure box (*see above*).

18.2.13.5 Horizontal line (code DAH, subcode 05H)

This record defines horizontal lines and their position in a text.

Offset	Bytes	Field
00H	1	Horizontal line (Code DAH)
01H	1	Sub-function code 05H
02H	2	Length word (value = 121)
04H	2	Reserved
06H	1	Vertical position flags Bits 1–0: reserved Bits 4–2: position option vertical lines 0 = full page 1 = top 2 = bottom 4 = absolute Bit 5: bump bit (always 0) Bits 7–6: reserved
07H	1	Alignment flags: Bits 2–0: Alignment option for horizontal lines 0 = left 1 = right 2 = centered

Table 18.71 Opcode DAH, 05H in version 5.0 (*continues over...*)

Offset	Bytes	Field
		3 = left and right justified
		4 = absolute for vertical lines
		0 = left margin
		1 = right margin
		2 = between columns x, x1
		3 = absolute position
		Bits 7–3: Reserved
08H	2	Width of line (wpu)
0AH	2	Height of line (wpu)
0CH	2	X position of line (wpu)
0EH	2	Y position of line (wpu)
10H	20	Reserved
24H	1	Shading (% black)
25H	1	Column x for vertical lines only
26H	4	Reserved
2AH	2	Constant = 0
2CH	2	Constant = 100
2EH	2	Constant = 100
30H	2	Constant = 0
32H	2	Constant = 0
34H	1	Constant = 0
35H	66	Reserved
77H	2	Constant = 0
79H	2	Length word (value = 121)
7BH	1	Sub-function code 05H
7CH	1	End function code (Code DAH)

Table 18.71 Opcode DAH, 05H in version 5.0 (*cont.*)

18.2.13.6 Vertical line (code DAH, subcode 06H)

This record defines vertical lines and their position in a text document. The structure is identical to the horizontal line record.

18.2.14 Style group (code DBH)

WordPerfect 5.0 uses function code DBH to store information on text documents.

18.2.14.1 Begin style ON (code DBH, subcode 00H)

This record marks the beginning of a style.

Offset	Bytes	Field
00H	1	Begin style ON (Code DBH)
01H	1	Sub-function code 00H
02H	2	Length word (variable)
04H	2	Old file position of Begin ON
06H	2	Old file position of Begin ON high part
08H	2	Old formatter hash value
0AH	1	Old hard return type code
0BH	1	Old unique style number
0CH	1	New hard return type code
0DH	1	New unique style number
0EH	2	Formatter hash value for text in style
10H	xx	Style name (maximum 21 bytes)
xxH	2	Length word (variable)
xxH	1	Sub-function code 00H
xxH	1	End function code (Code DBH)

Table 18.72 Opcode DBH, 00H in version 5.0

18.2.14.2 End style ON (code DBH, subcode 01H)

This record marks the end of a style.

Offset	Bytes	Field
00H	1	End style ON (Code DBH)
01H	1	Sub-function code 01H
02H	2	Length word (variable)
04H	2	Old file position of Begin ON
06H	2	Old file position of Begin ON high part
08H	2	Old formatter hash value at Begin
0AH	1	Old hard return type code
0BH	1	Old unique style number
0CH	2	New file position of Begin ON
0EH	2	New file position of Begin ON high part
10H	2	New formatter hash of old values
12H	1	New hard return type code
13H	1	New unique style number
14H	2	Formatter hash value for text in end style

Table 18.73 Opcode DBH, 01H in version 5.0 *(continues over...)*

Offset	Bytes	Field
10H	xx	Style name (maximum 21 bytes)
xxH	2	Length word (variable)
xxH	1	Sub-function code 01H
xxH	1	End function code (Code DBH)

Table 18.73
Opcode DBH, 01H in version 5.0 (*cont.*)

18.2.14.3 Global ON (code DBH, subcode 02H)

This record switches the global style on.

Offset	Bytes	Field
00H	1	Global ON (Code DBH)
01H	1	Sub-function code 02H
02H	2	Length word (variable)
04H	1	Unique style number
06H	2	Format hash value for text in style
08H	xx	Style name (maximum 21 bytes)
xxH	2	Length word (variable)
xxH	1	Sub-function code 02H
xxH	1	End function code (Code DBH)

Table 18.74
Opcode DBH, 02H in version 5.0

18.2.14.4 Style OFF (code DBH, subcode 03H)

This record marks the end of a global style region.

Offset	Bytes	Field
00H	1	Style OFF (Code DBH)
01H	1	Sub-function code 03H
02H	2	Length word (value = 5)
04H	1	Flag: 1 = text modified by format
05H	2	Length word (value = 5)
07H	1	Sub-function code 03H
08H	1	End function code (Code DBH)

Table 18.75
Opcode DBH, 03H in version 5.0

18.3 The WordPerfect 5.x/6.x format

WordPerfect defines a platform-independent format for all versions of the word processor. This format has been available since WordPerfect version 5.1. The format uses the version 5.0 record structure with several extensions. The differences are shown below. The format is used under DOS, VAX/VMS, UNIX, Windows, OS/2 and Macintosh.

18.4 WordPerfect Header (version 5.1+)

Figure 18.1 shows the WordPerfect header. The first 16 bytes define global information. This prefix is used by all WordPerfect products. Table 18.76 contains a description of the header structure.

Offset	Bytes	Field description
File ID Header for all WPCORP products		
00H	4	WP signature –1,'WPC'
04H	4	Pointer to 1st text character
08H	1	Product type 1 WordPerfect 2 Shell 3 Notebook 4 Calculator 5 File Manager 6 Calendar 7 Program Editor 8 Macro Editor 9 PlanPerfect 10 DataPerfect 11 Mail 12 Printer (PTR.EXE) 13 Scheduler 14 WordPerfect Office 15 DrawPerfect
09H	1	File type 1 Macro file 2 Help file 3 Keyboard definition file 4 — ... 9 — 10 WP document

Table 18.76 Header prefix of a WP file (version 5.1+) (*continues over...*)

Offset	Bytes	Field description
		11 Dictionary file
		12 Thesaurus file
		13 Block
		14 Rectangular block
		15 Column block
		16 Printer resource file (`.PRS`)
		17 Setup file
		18 Prefix information file
		19 Printer resource file (`.ALL`)
		20 Display resource file (`.DRS`)
		21 Overlay file (`WP.FIL`)
		22 WP graphic file (`.WPG`)
		23 Hyphenation code module
		24 Hyphenation data module
		25 Macro resource file (`.MRS`)
		26 Graphics screen driver (`WPD`)
		27 Hyphenation lex module
		28 Printer Q codes (VAX and DG)
		29 Spell code module - wordlist
		30 5.1 equation resource file (`WP.QRS`)
		31 VAX keyboard definition
		32 VAX `.SET`
		33 Spell code module - rules
		34 Dictionary - rules
		36 `.WPD` files
		37 Reserved
		...
		40 Reserved
		41 `WP51.INS` file (install options)
`0AH`	1	Main version number
`0BH`	1	Sub-version number
`0CH`	2	Encryption flag (0 = not encrypted)
`0EH`	2	Reserved (0)

Table 18.76 Header prefix of a WP file (version 5.1+) (*cont.*)

The type of the product that created the file is stored at offset 08H. In version 5.1 type 15 has been added for DrawPerfect. Future versions may have new product codes. In WordPerfect 5.1, version numbers always have the value 0.1. If the *encryption field* contains the value 0, the file is not encrypted, otherwise the value represents the encryption key.

This prefix is followed by a header trailer, already defined in WordPerfect 5.0 (*see above*). From version 5.1, the codes shown in Table 18.77 may also appear in the index block.

Type	Field description
WP 5.1 .SET file packet	
0001H	Reserved
0002H	Font string table
0003H	List PS tables
0004H	Font list
0005H	Serial/license number
0004H	Font string pool
0010H	Path name for Thesaurus
0011H	Information on screen type
0012H	Miscellaneous (backup time, and so on)
0013H	Ctrl- and Alt-key mappings
0014H	System initial values
0015H	Reserved
0016H	Reserved
0017H	Miscellaneous
0018H	Reserved
0019H	Reserved
001AH	Default printer
001BH	Selected printers
001CH	Print options
001DH	Default printer
001EH	Selected printers
001FH	Reserved
0020H	Screen attribute Monochrome
0021H	Screen attribute CGA
0022H	Screen attribute PC 3270
0023H	Screen attribute EGA (Italics)
0024H	Screen attribute EGA (Underline)
0025H	Screen attribute EGA (Small caps)
0026H	Screen attribute EGA (Reserved)
...	"
0029H	Screen attribute EGA (Reserved)
002AH	Screen attribute Hercules RamFont (12 fonts)

Table 18.77 Packet types in WP 5.1 index block (*continues over...*)

Type	Field description
002BH	Screen attribute Hercules RamFont (6 fonts)
002CH	Screen attribute Hercules RamFont
...	Reserved
002FH	Reserved
0030H	NEC 9801 PC
WP 5.1 packet types	
0050H	Reserved
0051H	Information on screen type
0052H	Miscellaneous (backup time, and so on)
0053H	[Ctrl]- and [Alt]-key mappings
0054H	Default printer
0055H	Miscellaneous
0056H	Print options
0057H	Font list
0058H	Serial/license number
0059H	Font string pool
005AH	WP default values
005BH	Reserved
005CH	Selected printers
005DH	PS table list
005EH	Auxiliary path name

Table 18.77 Packet types in WP 5.1 index block (*cont.*)

18.5 Text area in WordPerfect 5.1

The WordPerfect header is followed by the text area. The text includes 1-byte or multi-byte control codes containing the format descriptions. The 1-byte control codes use the same conventions as WordPerfect version 5.0. The differences are described below:

Some *single-byte functions* in the range 80H to BFH have been redefined (*see* Table 18.78).

Code	Field description
8CH	Hard/soft return
B2H	Outline OFF
99H	Dormant hard return

Table 18.78 New single-byte functions (5.1+)

18.5.1 Fixed-length multi-byte control codes (version 5.1+)

WordPerfect 5.1+ uses these control codes to describe German umlaut accents and special characters. There are several differences between version 5.0 and 5.1. Table 18.79 shows the unmodified opcodes (for a description of the record structure, *see* version 5.0, Subsection 18.2.2).

Opcode	Command
`C0H`	Extended character
`C2H`	Indent
`C4H`	Attribute Off
`C5H`	Block protect
`C6H`	End of indent
`C7H`	Different display character when hyphenated

Table 18.79 Unmodified multi-byte control characters

The structure of the new/modified version 5.1 records is described below.

18.5.1.1 Center, Align, Tab, Left Margin (code C1H)

In version 5.1, WordPerfect uses this record to store information on text alignment.

Offset	Bytes	Field
`00H`	1	Begin function code (Code `C1H`)
`01H`	1	Flags Bits 7–6: `00` tab `01` align `10` left margin release `11` center Bit 5: `1` center between 2 margins Bit 4: `1` dot leader Bit 3: `0` align on alignment character or center on column `1` right justified tabs Bit 2: `1` positioning within table cell

Table 18.80 Opcode `C1H` in version 5.1 (*continues over...*)

Offset	Bytes	Field
		Bit 1: 1 if type (tab, align, and so on) is hard
02H	2	Old current column number (su)
04H	2	Position of start column (0)
06H	2	Absolute center/align/tab position
08H	1	End function code (Code C1H)

Table 18.80 Opcode C1H in version 5.1 (*cont.*)

Flag bit 1 is new in version 5.1.

18.5.1.2 Attribute on (code C3H)

This record switches the following attributes on (version 5.1+):

Offset	**Bytes**	**Field**
00H	1	Begin function code (Code C3H)
01H	1	Attribute type 0: Extra large 1: Very large 2: Large 3: Small 4: Fine 5: Superscript 6: Subscript 7: Outline 8: Italics 9: Shadow 10: Red line 11: Double underline 12: Bold 13: Strikeout 14: Underline 15: Small capitals 16: Blink 17: Reverse video
02H	1	End function code (Code C3H)

Table 18.81 Opcode C3H in version 5.1

This record defines two new attribute types, 10 and 11, which are not included in version 5.0.

18.5.1.3 Attribute off (code C4H)

In WordPerfect 5.1, this record switches the attributes off.

Offset	Bytes	Field
00H	1	Begin function code (Code C4H)
01H	1	Attribute type 0: Extra large 1: Very large 2: Large 3: Small 4: Fine 5: Superscript 6: Subscript 7: Outline 8: Italics 9: Shadow 10: Red line 11: Double underline 12: Bold 13: Strikeout 14: Underline 15: Small capitals 16: Blink 17: Reverse video
02H	1	End function code (code C4H)

Table 18.82 Opcode C4H in version 5.1

The attribute types 10 and 11 are new in version 5.1.

18.5.2 Variable length multi-byte control codes (version 5.1)

WordPerfect uses multi-byte control codes to store format information within the text. Some records differ between versions 5.0 and 5.1. Table 18.83 lists the records with opcode D0H that are identical in both versions.

Subcode	Command
00H	Set lines per inch
01H	Set left/right margin
02H	Set spacing

Table 18.83 Unmodified opcodes D0H (version 5.1+) (*continues over...*)

Subcode	Command
03H	Set hyphenation zone
05H	Set top/bottom margin
08H	Page number position

Table 18.83 Unmodified opcodes D0H (version 5.1+) (*cont.*)

The following records are new or have been changed in WordPerfect 5.1.

18.5.2.1 Set tab (code D0H, subcode 04H)

This record defines the tab set margins.

Offset	Bytes	Field
00H	1	Set tabs (Code D0H)
01H	1	Sub-function code 04H
02H	2	Length word (value = 208)
04H	80	40 entries for old tab positions
54H	20	40 old tab types (1 nibble each)
		Bit 1: unused
		Bit 2: add dot leader
		Bits 3–4: coding for tab types
		0 : normal left-justified tab
		1 : tab centered
		2 : tab right aligned
		3 : decimal aligned tab
68H	80	40 entries for new tab positions
B8H	20	40 new tab types (1 nibble each)
CCH	2	Old "M" value
CEH	2	New "M" value
D0H	2	Length word (value = 208)
D2H	1	Sub-function 04H
D3H	1	End function code (Code D0H)

Table 18.84 Opcode D0H, 04H in version 5.1+

The 20 bytes containing the tab types define the code for each tab in a 4-bit nibble. Each byte defines two tab codes. Unused tab positions are set to 0.

18.5.2.2 Justification (code D0H, subcode 06H)

This record is new in version 5.1 and describes the justification of a text. The *decimal aligned* mode is only available in tables.

Offset	Bytes	Field
00H	1	Justification (Code D0H)
01H	1	Sub-function code 06H
02H	2	Length word (value = 6)
04H	1	Old justification mode
05H	1	New justification mode 0 : left 1 : full 2 : center 3 : right 4 : decimal aligned (in tables)
06H	2	Length word (value = 6)
08H	1	Sub-function code 06H
09H	1	End function code (Code D0H)

Table 18.85
Opcode D0H, 06H in version 5.1

18.5.2.3 Suppress page characteristics (code D0H, subcode 07H)

WordPerfect 5.1 stores information about a page (page number, header, and so on) in this record.

Offset	Bytes	Field
00H	1	Suppress page character (Code D0H)
01H	1	Sub-function code 07H
02H	2	Length word (value = 6)
04H	1	Old suppress code Code: 1 = suppress page numbering 2 = suppress current page numbering and print page number centered at bottom 4 = suppress header A 8 = suppress header B 10 = suppress footer A 20 = suppress footer B 80 = this code NOT at top of page
05H	1	New suppress code
06H	2	Length word (value = 6)
08H	1	Sub-function code 07H
09H	1	End function code (Code D0H)

Table 18.86
Opcode D0H, 07H in version 5.1+

18.5.2.4 Form (code D0H, subcode 0BH)

This record describes a form.

Offset	Bytes	Field
00H	1	Form (Code D0H)
01H	1	Sub-function code 0BH
02H	2	Length word (value = 290)
04H	2	Old desired length
06H	2	Old desired width
08H	1	Old desired type
09H	1	Old desired type name length
0AH	41	Old desired type name
33H	2	Old effective length
35H	2	Old effective width
37H	1	Old effective type
38H	1	Old effective type name length
39H	41	Old effective type name
62H	1	Old effective orientation
		0 = Portrait
		1 = Landscape
63H	2	New desired length
65H	2	New desired width
67H	1	New desired type
68H	1	New desired type name length
69H	41	New desired type name
92H	2	New effective length
94H	2	New effective width
96H	1	New effective type
97H	1	New effective type name length
98H	41	New effective type name
C1H	41	New effective orientation
EAH	1	Matched form number
EBH	2	Matched form hash value
EDH	2	Old left margin
EFH	2	Old right margin
F1H	2	Old top margin
F3H	2	Old bottom margin
F5H	1	Old flag indicating label form
F6H	2	Old page where label form is defined
F8H	1	Old number of rows per page
F9H	1	Old number of columns per page
FAH	2	Old left offset top left corner

Table 18.87 Opcode D0H, 0BH in version 5.1+ (*continues over...*)

Word processing

Offset	Bytes	Field
FCH	2	Old top offset top left corner
FEH	2	Old logical page width
100H	2	Old logical page length
102H	2	Old distance between label rows
104H	2	Old distance between label columns
106H	1	New flag indication label form
		Bit 0: 1 label form
		Bit 1: 1 label matched all others
107H	2	New page where label form is defined
109H	1	New number of rows per page
10AH	1	New number of columns per page
10BH	2	New left offset top left corner
10DH	2	New top offset top left corner
10FH	2	New logical page width
111H	2	New logical page length
113H	2	New distance between label rows
115H	2	New distance between label columns
117H	2	Label left margin
119H	2	Label right margin
11BH	2	Label top margin
11FH	2	Label bottom margin
121H	2	Length word (value = 290)
123H	1	Sub-function code 0BH
124H	1	End function code (Code D0H)

Table 18.87 Opcode D0H, 0BH in version 5.1+ (*cont.*)

18.5.3 Font selection sub-function (code D1H version 5.1)

WordPerfect version 5.1 uses the D1H records to select a font. A subcode defines the function. Only the function *Color* (Code D1H, Subcode 00H) is identical to version 5.0.

18.5.3.1 Font change (code D1H, subcode 01H)

In version 5.1 WordPerfect uses this record to select a font.

Offset	Bytes	Field
00H	1	Font change (Code D1H)
01H	1	Sub-function code 01H
02H	2	Length word (value = 35)
04H	1	Old font number
05H	24	New font description:
	2	Point size (in 3600ths)
	2	Optimum width (in wpu)
	2	Capitals height (in psu)
	2	x height (in psu)
	2	Descender height (in psu)
	2	Italic adjustment (in psu +/–)
	3	Typeface descriptor
	1	Typeface definition flag
	1	Hash of typeface name
	1	Reserved (always 0)
	2	Hash of font name
	4	Character set completeness bits 1 bit per font in each word
1DH	1	Matched font
1EH	2	Matched font hash value
20H	2	Point size
22H	2	Typeface flags
20H	2	Length word (value = 35)
22H	1	Sub-function code 01H
23H	1	End function code (Code D1H)

Table 18.88
Opcode D1H, 01H in version 5.1+

The record stores information on the character set used (for the printer). Some values are defined as WordPerfect Units (wpu, 1 wpu = 1/1200 inch). The *descender height* defines the distance between the character baseline and the lower extremity of characters like g, y, and so on. The unit psu (*point size unit*) is defined as 1/10000 of the font size (in points). The *typeface descriptor* is a data structure with information on serifs, character shapes, heights, and so on. The information is stored in a 3-byte data structure.

18.5.3.2 Color (DrawPerfect) (code D1H, subcode 02H)

In version 5.1, WordPerfect uses this record to obtain color information from DrawPerfect.

Offset	Bytes	Field
00H	1	Color DrawPerfect (Code D1H)
01H	1	Sub-function code 02H
02H	2	Length word (value = 6)
04H	1	Old print color (0-FFH)
05H	1	New print color (0-FFH)
06H	2	Length word (value = 6)
08H	1	Sub-function code 02H
09H	1	End function code (Code D1H)

Table 18.89
Opcode D1H, 02H in version 5.1

All other subcodes are reserved in version 5.1.

18.5.4 Group definition sub-functions (code D2H, version 5.1)

These records define parts of a document (tables, paragraphs, and so on) as groups. Some records use the same structure as version 5.0. Table 18.90 lists the records that have not been modified.

Code	Function
00H	Define math columns
01H	Define columns
03H	Footnote options
04H	Endnote options
05H	Graph box options for figures
06H	Graph box options for tables
07H	Graph box options for text boxes
08H	Graph box options for user-defined text boxes

Table 18.90
Unmodified records for function D2H (version 5.1+)

18.5.4.1 Paragraph number definition (code D2H, subcode 02H)

This record defines a new paragraph number.

Offset	Bytes	Field
00H	1	Paragraph number definition (Code D2H)
01H	1	Sub-function code 02H
02H	2	Length word (value = 140)
04H	24	8 × 3-byte entries containing old definitions
1CH	16	8 × 2-byte entries containing old level numbers
2CH	24	8 × 3-byte entries containing new definitions
44H	16	8 × 2-byte entries with new level numbers containing
54H	1	Old attach flag
55H	1	Old outline flag Bit 0 = 0enter key inserts paragraph number Bit 1 = 0tab to level of previous paragraph number
56H	18	Old outline style name
68H	1	New attach flag
69H	1	New outline flag
6AH	18	New outline style name
7CH	16	8 level numbers from previous definitions
8CH	2	Length word (value = 140)
8EH	1	Sub-function code 02H
8FH	1	End function code (Code D2H)

Table 18.91
Opcode D2H, 02H in version 5.1+

The data structure at offset 2CH defines the characters for chapter punctuation in the first and third bytes. The second byte defines paragraph numbering:

Notation	Numbering
I	Roman capitals
i	Lower case Roman
A	Capital letter
a	Lower case letter
1	Arabic

18.5.4.2 Graph box options for equations (code D2H, subcode 09H)

The *graph box options* enable new windows to be defined for equations. If a window is defined for an equation, all positions are relative to this window. The structure is identical to function `D2H`, `05H` in version 5.0.

18.5.4.3 Define tables (Table On) (code D2H, subcode 0BH)

This record is new to version 5.1 and defines a table.

Offset	Bytes	Field
00H	1	Define tables (Code D2H)
01H	1	Sub-function code 0BH
02H	2	Length word (value = variable)
04H	1	Flags Bits 0–2: table position options 0 = align with left margin 1 = align with right margin 2 = center between margins 3 = full (adjust column width) 4 = absolute offset from left margin Bits 3–4: — Bit 5: 0 minus signs 1 display negative results with parentheses Bit 6: 1 auto adjust column width Bit 7: 1 expand column width
05H	1	Shading (0–100%)
06H	2	Number of columns (maximum 32)
08H	2	Table number
0AH	2	Position left edge of table (wpu)
0CH	2	Left gutter space (wpu)
0EH	2	Right gutter space (wpu)
10H	2	Top gutter space (wpu)
12H	2	Bottom gutter space (wpu)
14H	2	Row number after header rows (0 = number header rows)

Table 18.92 Opcode D2H, 0BH in version 5.1+ (*continues over...*)

Offset	Bytes	Field
16H	2	Formatter lines at start of table
18H	2	Page number at start of table
1AH	2	Offset from left edge of paper
1CH	xx	Column widths (1 word/column) (in 1/1200)
xxH	xx	Column attributes (1 word/column)
xxH	xx	Column alignment (1 byte/column) Bits 0–2: horizontal alignment 0 = left 1 = justified (left, right) 2 = center 3 = flush right 4 = decimal align Bit 3: — Bits 4–7: number of characters to right of decimal alignment for cells
xxH	xx	New values to repeat old flag values (*see* offset 04H)
xxH	2	Null bytes (00H)
xxH	2	Length word (value = variable)
xxH	1	Sub-function code 0BH
xxH	1	End function code (Code D2H)

Table 18.92 Opcode D2H, 0BH in version 5.1+ (*cont.*)

18.5.4.4 Define link start (code D2H, subcode 0DH)

This function is new to version 5.1 and defines a link to another object.

Offset	Bytes	Field
00H	1	Define link start (Code D2H)
01H	1	Sub-function code 0DH
02H	2	Length word (value = variable)
04H	2	Old ufcur
06H	1	Number of lines of text to display
07H	1	Type (spreadsheet, text, ...)
08H	2	Date of file when last linked

Table 18.93 Opcode D2H, 0DH in version 5.1+ (*continues over...*)

Word processing

Offset	Bytes	Field
0AH	2	Time of file when last linked
0CH	2	Start column of range
0EH	2	Start row of range
10H	2	End column of range
12H	2	End row of range
14H	81	File name with length byte (maximum 81)
65H	21	Range name with length byte (maximum 21)
7AH	16	Range reference with length byte (maximum 16)
8AH	2	Length word (value = variable)
8CH	1	Sub-function code 0DH
8DH	1	End function code (Code D2H)

Table 18.93 Opcode D2H, 0DH in version 5.1+ (*cont.*)

18.5.4.5 Define link end (code D2H, subcode 0EH)

This function marks the end of a link and is defined from version 5.1 onwards.

Offset	**Bytes**	**Field**
00H	1	Define link end (Code D2H)
01H	1	Sub-function code 0EH
02H	2	Length word (value = variable)
04H	2	Old ufcur
06H	1	Number of lines of text to display
07H	2	Start column of range
09H	2	Start row of range
0BH	2	End column of range
0DH	2	End row of range
0FH	81	File name with length byte (maximum 81)
96H	2	Length word (value = variable)
98H	1	Sub-function code 0EH
99H	1	End function code (Code D2H)

Table 18.94 Opcode D2H, 0EH in version 5.1+

18.5.5 Set group sub-functions (code D3H, version 5.1)

In version 5.1, WordPerfect uses these records to store format information on the text. All functions use code D3H and a subcode. Table 18.95 lists the functions that are unchanged from version 5.0.

Code	Function
00H	Set alignment character
01H	Set underline mode
02H	Set footnote number
03H	Set endnote number
05H	Line numbering
06H	Advance to page position
07H	Force odd/even page
0AH	Character/space width
0BH	Space expansion
0CH	Set graph box number for figures
0DH	Set graph box number for tables
0EH	Set graph box number for text boxes
0FH	Set graph box number for user-defined boxes

Table 18.95 Function group D3H used from version 5.0 onwards

18.5.5.1 Set page number (code D3H, subcode 04H)

This record defines the page number and the format of the number.

Offset	Bytes	Field
00H	1	Set page number (Code D3H)
01H	1	Sub-function code 04H
02H	2	Length word (value = 10)
04H	2	Old page number
06H	2	New page number (bit 15 = Roman)
08H	1	Type of old page number
09H	1	Type of new page number
0AH	2	Length word (value = 10)
0CH	1	Sub-function code 02H
0DH	1	End function code (Code D3H)

Table 18.96 Opcode D3H, 04H in version 5.1

If bit 15 in the word at offset 06H is set, the page numbers are displayed as Roman numerals.

18.5.5.2 Character baseline in fixed line height (code D3H, subcode 08H)

This function was defined after WordPerfect version 5.0 (after June 1989); it defines the character baseline.

Offset	Bytes	Field
00H	1	Character baseline definition (Code D3H)
01H	1	Sub-function code 08H
02H	2	Length word (value = 6)
04H	1	Old definition
05H	1	New definition
06H	2	Length word (value = 6)
08H	1	Sub-function code 08H
09H	1	End function code (Code D3H)

Table 18.97 Opcode D3H, 07H in version 5.1

18.5.5.3 Set graph box number for equations (code D3H, subcode 10H)

This record is defined from version 5.1 onwards and stores equation numbers. The structure is identical to function D3H, 0CH in version 5.0.

18.5.5.4 Set language (code D3H, subcode 11H)

This record defines the language for a text area.

Offset	Bytes	Field
00H	1	Set language (Code D3H)
01H	1	Sub-function code 11H
02H	2	Length word (value = 12)
04H	2	Old language 2-character ID (ASCII)
06H	2	New language 2-character ID (ASCII) AF = Afrikaans CA = Catalan CZ = Czechoslovakian US = English US OZ = English Australia DK = Danish

Table 18.98 Opcode D3H, 11H in version 5.1 (*continues over...*)

Offset	Bytes	Field
		NL = Dutch
		SU = Finnish
		FR = French
		DE = German
		SD = Swiss
		GR = Greek
		IC = Icelandic
		IT = Italian
		NO = Norwegian
		PO = Portuguese
		BR = Portuguese Brazil
		SU = Russian
		ES = Spanish
		SV = Swedish
		UK = English UK
		CF = Canadian French
08H	2	Length word (value = 8)
0AH	1	Sub-function code 11H
0BH	1	End function code (Code D3H)

Table 18.98
Opcode D3H, 11H in version 5.1 (*cont.*)

18.5.5.5 Set page number style (code D3H, subcode 12H)

This record defines the style for a page number.

Offset	**Bytes**	**Field**
00H	1	Set page number style (Code D3H)
01H	1	Sub-function code 12H
02H	2	Length word (value = 64)
04H	30	Old page number style
22H	30	New page number style
40H	2	Length word (value = 64)
42H	1	Sub-function code 12H
43H	1	End function code (Code D3H)

Table 18.99
Opcode D3H, 12H in version 5.1

18.5.6 Format group sub-functions (code D4H, version 5.1)

WordPerfect defines this code from version 5.1 onwards to store format information. The function code is D4H together with a subcode.

18.5.6.1 End of page function (code D4H, subcode 00H)

This record defines the end of a page.

Offset	Bytes	Field
00H	1	End of page function (Code D4H)
01H	1	Sub-function code 00H
02H	2	Length word (variable)
04H	1	Group 0 marker
05H	1	Group 0 length (16H)
06H	2	Number of formatter lines at end of page
08H	2	Actual page number
0AH	2	Number of formatter lines used for footnotes
0CH	1	Number of pages used for footnotes
0DH	1	Number of footnotes on this page
0EH	1	Conditional end of page flag
0FH	1	Suppress code
10H	1	Center page top to bottom
11H	1	Page flags
12H	1	Page length
13H	1	Odd page size
14H	1	Even page size
15H	1	Odd top margin
16H	1	Even top margin
17H	1	Group 1 marker (optional)
18H	1	Group 1 length (variable)
19H	x1	Maximum number of formatter lines for each column
..H	x1	Maximum screen lines from column On for each column
..H	2	Starting formatter lines for last column
..H	2	Starting page for last column

Table 18.100 Opcode D4H, 00H in version 5.1+ (*continues over...*)

Offset	Bytes	Field
..H	2	Screen lines from column On for last line of last column
..H	2	Screen lines column On at top of page
..H	1	Suppress page state at column On
..H	2	Number of formatter lines used for footnotes at column On
..H	2	Number of pages used for footnotes at column On
..H	1	Group 2 marker (optional)
..H	1	Group 2 length (variable)
..H	1	Number of boxes formatter is tracking
..H	*x*2	Formatter box table
..H	2	Length word (variable)
..H	1	Sub-function code 00H
..H	1	End function code (Code D4H)

Table 18.100 Opcode D4H, 00H in version 5.1+ (*cont.*)

The value x1 is calculated as:

```
(lines - 1) * 2 bytes
```

The value x2 is calculated as:

```
14 * number of boxes
```

18.5.6.2 Beginning of line function (code D4H, subcode 01H)

In version 5.0, WordPerfect uses this record to mark the end of a line. From version 5.1, this record marks the beginning of a line.

Offset	Bytes	Field
00H	1	Beginning of line function (Code D4H)
01H	1	Sub-function code 01H
02H	2	Length word (variable)
04H	1	Group 0 marker
05H	1	Group 0 length (6)

Table 18.101 Opcode D4H, 01H in version 5.1+ (*continues over...*)

Offset	Bytes	Field
06H	2	Maximum top shoulder height for line
08H	2	Maximum bottom shoulder height for line
0AH	2	Old uflin (wpu)
0CH	1	Group 1 marker
0DH	1	Group 1 length (6)
0EH	2	Number of spaces on line
10H	2	Space adjustment (+/–)
12H	2	Justify margin (absolute)
14H	2	Length word (variable)
16H	1	Sub-function code 01H
17H	1	End function code (Code D4H)

Table 18.101 Opcode D4H, 01H in version 5.1+ (*cont.*)

This record is not required for third-party software, because WordPerfect generates the beginning of a line. Group 0 is only inserted if the maximum values are set differently from the current values. Group 1 is only inserted if *full justification* is required.

18.5.6.3 Graph box information function (code D4H, subcode 02H)

This record defines the parameters of a graph box.

Offset	**Bytes**	**Field**
00H	1	Graph box information (Code D4H)
01H	1	Sub-function code 02H
02H	2	Length word (variable)
04H	1	Group 0 marker
05H	1	Group 0 length (14H)
06H	2	Old left margin (wpu)
08H	2	Old temporary left margin (wpu)
0AH	2	Old right margin (wpu)
0CH	2	Old temporary right margin (wpu)
0EH	2	Old number formatter lines (wpu)
10H	2	New left margin (wpu)
12H	2	New temporary left margin (wpu)
14H	2	New right margin (wpu)
16H	2	New temporary right margin (wpu)
18H	2	Signed change in new number
1AH	1	Group 1 marker

Table 18.102 Opcode D4H, 02H in version 5.1+ (*continues over...*)

Offset	Bytes	Field
1BH	*xx*	Group 1 length (boxes * 8 bytes)
...	*xx*	Flags
		Bit 0: 1 = top of box is on this line
		Bit 1: 1 = middle of box is on this line
		Bit 2: 1 = bottom of box is on this line
		Bits 5–3: box type
		0 = figure
		1 = table
		2 = text box
		3 = user-defined box
		4 = equation box
...	1	Box numbering mode
...	2	Box number
		Bits 4–0: Level 2 number
		Bits 15–5: Level 1 number
...	2	Box position left (wpu)
...	2	Box position right (wpu)
...	2	Length word (variable)
...	1	Sub-function code 02H
...	1	End function code (Code D4H)

Table 18.102 Opcode D4H, 02H in version 5.1+ (*cont.*)

Each box in group 1 defines 8 bytes containing a flag and the box data. The record is of variable length.

18.5.6.4 Marker for repositioning (code D4H, subcode 03H)

The record defines a marker for the new position of a box.

Offset	**Bytes**	**Field**
00H	1	Marker repositioning (Code D4H)
01H	1	Sub-function code 03H
02H	2	Length word (value = 6)
04H	1	Mask of marker
05H	2	Length word (value = 6)
07H	1	Sub-function code 03H
08H	1	End function code (Code D4H)

Table 18.103 Opcode D4H, 03H in version 5.1

18.5.6.5 Function containing fixed text (code D4H, subcode 04H)

This record is defined from version 5.1 onwards; it defines fixed text, which is not displayed/edited.

Offset	Bytes	Field
00H	1	Fixed text (Code D4H)
01H	1	Sub-function code 04H
02H	2	Length word (variable)
04H	2	Hash value (reserved 0)
06H	*x*1	Text
xxH	2	Length word (variable)
xxH	1	Sub-function code 04H
xxH	1	End function code (Code D4H)

Table 18.104
Opcode D4H, 04H in version 5.1

18.5.6.6 Justification information (code D4H, subcode 05H)

This new record is inserted for justified text.

Offset	Bytes	Field
00H	1	Justification information (Code D4H)
01H	1	Sub-function code 05H
02H	2	Length word (value = 8)
04H	2	Start position (screen units)
06H	2	Start position (wpu)
08H	2	Length word (value = 8)
0AH	1	Sub-function code 05H
0BH	1	End function code (Code D4H)

Table 18.105
Opcode D4H, 05H in version 5.1

18.5.7 Header/footer group sub-functions (code D5H, version 5.1)

From version 5.1, WordPerfect uses the code D5H to store control information on the header/footer. The record structure is the same as in version 5.0.

18.5.8 Footnote/endnote group sub-functions (code D6H, version 5.1)

This record structure is defined from WordPerfect 5.0 onwards; it contains the footnotes/endnotes.

18.5.9 Generate group sub-functions (code D7H, version 5.1)

WordPerfect 5.1 uses this group to store text markers in a file. Table 18.106 lists the functions that are unchanged from version 5.0.

From version 5.1 onwards, the record `Auto reference definition` (Code `D7H`, Subcode `07H`) contains a new reference type (offset `04H`, code `8`: Equation box number).

Code	Function
00H	Begin marked text
01H	End marked text
02H	Define marked text
03H	Index entry
04H	Table of authority entry
05H	Endnotes print here
06H	Save page information
08H	Auto reference tag
09H	Include sub-document
0AH	Start of included sub-document
0BH	End of included sub-document

Table 18.106 Unmodified records D7H (version 5.1)

18.5.10 Display group sub-functions (code D8H, version 5.1)

This record group stores information about the text output (date, paragraphs, and so on). A new record type was defined for version 5.1.

18.5.11 Page number style insert (code D8H, subcode 03H)

This record stores information on the page number style. A variable length string containing the style for page numbering is stored at offset `04H`.

Bytes	Field	
00H	1	Page number style (Code D8H)
01H	1	Sub-function code 03H
02H	2	Length word (variable)
04H	xx	Style string
xxH	2	Length word (variable)
xxH	1	Sub-function code 03H
xxH	1	End function code (Code D8H)

Table 18.107 Opcode D8H, 00H in version 5.1

18.5.11 Miscellaneous group (code D9H, version 5.1)

This group contains several new records from version 5.1 onwards.

18.5.11.1 Outline ON (code D9H, subcode 04H)

This record stores control codes for paragraph numbering.

Offset	Bytes	Field
00H	1	Outline ON (Code D9H)
01H	1	Sub-function code 04H
02H	2	Length word (value = 20)
04H	16	Old level numbers for paragraph numbering
14H	2	Length word (value = 20)
16H	1	Sub-function code 04H
17H	1	End function code (Code D9H)

Table 18.108
Opcode D9H, 04H
in version 5.1

18.5.11.2 Leading adjustment (code D9H, subcode 05H)

This record contains information on the leading adjustment in a text.

Offset	Bytes	Field
00H	1	Leading adjustment (Code D9H)
01H	1	Sub-function code 05H
02H	2	Length word (value = 12)
04H	2	Old srt and HRr leading (1200)
06H	2	New srt and HRr leading (1200)
08H	2	Length word (value = 12)
0AH	1	Sub-function code 05H
0BH	1	End function code (Code D9H)

Table 18.109
Opcode D9H, 05H
in version 5.1

18.5.11.3 Kerning (code D9H, subcode 06H)

This record defines the kerning values.

Offset	Bytes	Field
00H	1	Kerning (Code D9H)
01H	1	Sub-function code 06H
02H	2	Length word (value = 6)
04H	2	Alter kerning value 100/kerning * (space width)
06H	2	Length word (value = 6)
08H	1	Sub-function code 06H
09H	1	End function code (Code D9H)

Table 18.110
Opcode D9H, 06H
in version 5.1

18.5.11.4 Kerning (code D9H, subcode 07H)

This record contains additional kerning options.

Offset	Bytes	Field
00H	1	Kerning (Code D9H)
01H	1	Sub-function code 07H
02H	2	Length word (variable)
04H	4	Product type, file type, main version, sub-version
08H	*xx*	Variable length information used for format conversion
06H	2	Length word (variable)
08H	1	Sub-function code 07H
09H	1	End function code (Code D9H)

Table 18.111
Opcode D9H, 07H
in version 5.1

18.5.12 Box group (code DAH, version 5.1)

This group (code DAH) defines the data for text boxes, frames, tables, and so on.

18.5.12.1 Figure (code DAH, subcode 00H)

This record defines all the parameters of a box for the insertion of pictures.

Offset	Bytes	Field
00H	1	Figure (Code DAH)
01H	1	Sub-function code 00H
02H	2	Length word (variable)
04H	2	Box number xx.xx Bits 15–5: number level 1 (xx.) Bits 4–0: number level 2 (.xx)
06H	1	Position and type flag Bits 1–0: Box type 0 = paragraph 1 = page 2 = character (in-line) Bits 4–2: Position option 0 = full page 1 = top 2 = middle 3 = bottom 4 = absolute Bit 5: Box bumped to next page Bit 6: 0 not offset 1 page offset appears after page definition on Bit 7: print equation flag 0 print as graphics 1 print as text
07H	1	Alignment flags: Bits 1–0: Alignment option 0 = left 1 = right 2 = centered 3 = left and right justified Bits 3–2: Alignment with 0 = margins 1 = columns 2 = absolute Bit 4: Scale width figure Bit 5: Scale height figure Bit 6: Reserved Bit 7: 0 = wrap text around 1 = disable wrap text

Table 18.112 Opcode DAH, 00H in version 5.1 *(continues over...)*

Offset	Bytes	Field
08H	2	Box width (wpu)
0AH	2	Box height (wpu)
0CH	2	X position of box (wpu)
0EH	2	Y position of box (wpu)
10H	2	Outside left spacing between window and text (wpu)
12H	2	Outside right spacing between window and text (wpu)
14H	2	Outside top spacing between window and text (wpu)
16H	2	Outside bottom spacing between window and text (wpu)
18H	2	Inside left spacing between window and text (wpu)
1AH	2	Inside right spacing between window and text (wpu)
1CH	2	Inside top spacing between window and text (wpu)
1EH	2	Inside bottom spacing between window and text (wpu)
20H	2	Horizontal offset (wpu)
22H	2	Vertical offset (wpu)
24H	1	Column X for column alignment
25H	1	Column Y for column alignment
26H	2	Source image width (wpu)
28H	2	Source image height (wpu) if text box = number of format lines
2AH	2	Orientation Bit 15: 1 = mirror Bit 14: 1 = invert bits for monochrome bitmaps Bits 13–12: reserved Bits 11–0: rotation angle (0...360)
2CH	2	Width scale factor (100 = 100%)
2EH	2	Height scale factor (100 = 100%)
30H	2	X crop offset (wpu) for text boxes = formatter hash value
32H	2	Y crop offset (wpu) for text boxes = rotation 0 = 0 degrees 1 = 90 degrees

Table 18.112 Opcode DAH, 00H in version 5.1 (*cont.*)

Offset	Bytes	Field
		2 = 180 degrees
		3 = 270 degrees
34H	1	Format type of box contents
		0 = empty box
		1 = reserved
		2 = graphics of disk
		3 = reserved
		...
		7 = reserved
		8 = equation text
		9 = reserved
		...
		14 = reserved
		15 = reserved
		16 = WordPerfect text
		17 = ASCII text
		18 = reserved
		...
		63 = reserved
		64 = internal table format
		65 = MathPlan 3.0 worksheet
		66 = Lotus 1-2-3 worksheet
		67 = DIF format
		68 = reserved
		...
		126 = reserved
		127 = reserved
		128 = WPG format
		129 = Lotus PIC format
		130 = TIFF format
		131 = PC Paintbrush PCX format
		132 = Windows Paint (MSP) format
		133 = CGI Metafile (CGM) format
		134 = AutoCAD (DXF) format
		135 = reserved

Table 18.112 Opcode DAH, 00H in version 5.1 (*cont.*)

Offset	Bytes	Field
		136 = reserved
		137 = MAC Paint file
		138 = HPGL format
		139 = Dr. Halo and Halo DPE format
		140 = PC Paint normal format
		141 = PC Paint BSAVE format
		142 = GEM IMG format
		143 = EPS files
		144 = PostScript files
		145 = reserved
		...
		255 = reserved
35H	21	ASCIIZ string containing file name
4AH	28	Reserved
66H	1	Justification flag for equation
		0 = center
		1 = left
		2 = right
67H	2	Absolute page number box appears on (defined page + bumped + page offset)
69H	1	Number of pages box is bumped from page it is defined on
6AH	1	Number of pages page type box is offset from page it is defined on
6BH	2	Desired width as entered by user (wpu)
6DH	2	Desired height as entered by user (wpu)
6FH	2	Amount of extra space between caption and box (wpu)
71H	2	Image index number in graphics temporary file
73H	2	Number of formatter lines in caption (wpu)
75H	2	Formatter hash value for caption
77H	2	Length of caption in bytes
79H	xx	Text for caption

Table 18.112
Opcode DAH, 00H in version 5.1 (*cont.*)

Offset	Bytes	Field
xxH	*xx*	Text for text box
xxH	2	Length word (variable)
xxH	1	Sub-function code 00H
xxH	1	End function code (Code DAH)

Table 18.112 Opcode DAH, 00H in version 5.1 (*cont.*)

18.5.12.2 Table (code DAH, subcode 01H)

This record contains the information for a table box and has the same structure as the picture box.

18.5.12.3 Text box (code DAH, subcode 02H)

This record contains the information for a text box and has the same structure as the picture box.

18.5.12.4 User-defined text box (code DAH, subcode 03H)

This record contains the information for a user-defined text box and has the same structure as the picture box.

18.5.12.5 Equation (code DAH, subcode 04H)

This record contains the information for an equation box and has the same structure as the picture box.

18.5.12.6 Horizontal line (code DAH, subcode 05H)

This record defines a horizontal line and its position.

Offset	Bytes	Field
00H	1	Horizontal line (Code DAH)
01H	1	Sub-function code 05H
02H	2	Length word (value = 121)
04H	2	Reserved

Table 18.113 Opcode DAH, 05H in version 5.1 (*continues over...*)

Offset	Bytes	Field	
06H	1	Vertical position flags	
		Bits 1–0:	reserved
		Bits 4–2:	position option
			for vertical lines
			0 = full page
			1 = top
			2 = middle
			3 = bottom
			4 = absolute
			for horizontal lines
			0 = baseline
			1 = —
			2 = —
			3 = —
			4 = absolute
		Bit 5:	bump bit (always 0)
		Bits 7–6:	reserved
07H	1	Alignment flags:	
		Bits 2–0:	Alignment option
			for horizontal lines
			0 = left
			1 = right
			2 = centered
			3 = left and right justified
			4 = absolute
			for vertical lines
			0 = left margin
			1 = right margin
			2 = between columns x, x1
			3 = absolute position
		Bits 7–3:	Reserved
08H	2	Width of line (wpu)	
0AH	2	Height of line (wpu)	
0CH	2	X-position of line (wpu)	
0EH	2	Y-position of line (wpu)	
10H	20	Reserved	
24H	1	Shading (% black)	

Table 18.113 Opcode DAH, 05H in version 5.1 (*cont.*)

Offset	Bytes	Field
25H	1	Column x for vertical lines only
26H	4	Reserved
2AH	2	Constant = 0
2CH	2	Constant = 100
2EH	2	Constant = 100
30H	2	Constant = 0
32H	2	Constant = 0
34H	1	Constant = 0
35H	50	Reserved
67H	2	Appearance page
69H	14	Reserved
77H	2	Constant = 0
79H	2	Length word (value = 121)
7BH	1	Sub-function code 05H
7CH	1	End function code (Code DAH)

Table 18.113 Opcode DAH, 05H in version 5.1 (*cont.*)

18.5.12.7 Vertical line (code DAH, subcode 06H)

This record is used to define a vertical line in the text. The structure is the same as for horizontal lines.

18.5.13 Style group (code DBH)

This function group (code DBH) stores information on the text format. The record structure is described in version 5.0 (*see* Subsection 18.2.14).

18.5.14 Table end of line codes group (code DCH, version 5.1)

These records are defined from version 5.1 onwards.

18.5.14.1 Beginning of column at EOL (code DCH, subcode 00H)

This record describes the beginning of a column.

Offset	Bytes	Field
00H	1	Beginning of column at EOL (Code DCH)
01H	1	Sub-function code 00H
02H	2	Length word (variable)
04H	1	Flags Bit 0: 1 use cell justification instead of column defaults Bit 1: 1 use cell attributes instead of column defaults Bits 2–3: vertical alignment cell 0 = top 1 = bottom 2 = center Bit 4: 1 = text type 0 = numerical type Bit 5: 1 cell has formula Bit 6: 1 cell is locked Bit 7: —
05H	1	Column number
06H	1	Column spanning information Bits 0–5: number of columns this cell spans Bit 7: 1 cell is continued from row above
07H	1	Row span information (number of rows/cell)
08H	2	Old maximum number of formatter lines for row (uflin) (wpu)
0AH	2	Old maximum screen lines for row (screen units)
0CH	2	Cell attributes
0EH	2	Cell justification Bits 0–2: horizontal justification 0 = left 1 = flush right 2 = centered 3 = left and right justified 4 = decimal align

Table 18.114 Opcode DCH, 00H in version 5.1 (*continues over...*)

Word processing

Offset	Bytes	Field
10H	*xx*	Variable length subgroup information
	1	Subgroup code
	xx	Subgroup length
xxH	2	Length word (value = 121)
xxH	1	Sub-function code 00H
xxH	1	End function code (Code DCH)

Table 18.114 Opcode DCH, 00H in version 5.1 (*cont.*)

Each group uses a variable length list for the *subgroup information*. If the length is set to 15, the group does not exist. The maximum length is restricted to 255 characters. In version 5.1 only group 1 (*cell formula*) is defined.

18.5.14.2 Beginning of row at EOL (code DCH, subcode 01H)

This record marks the beginning of a row.

Offset	Bytes	Field
00H	1	Beginning of row at EOL (Code DCH)
01H	1	Sub-function code 01H
02H	2	Length word (variable)
04H	1	Old row height flags: Bit 0: 0 single line text 1 multi-line text (wrap) Bit 1: 0 fixed height 1 auto height Bits 2–7: —
05H	2	Old row height (wpu)
07H	1	Old number of bytes of border information for this row (bit 7 = 1: 1 word per column, bit 7 = 0: 1 byte per column)
08H	*xx*	Old border information (number of columns * 2 bytes) Bits 0–2: for top border of cell Bits 3–5: for left border of cell

Table 18.115 Opcode DCH, 01H in version 5.1 (*continues over...*)

Offset	Bytes	Field
		Bits 6–7: —
		High byte:
		Bits 0–2: for bottom border of cell
		Bits 3–5: for right border of cell
		Bit 6: 1 if shaded cell
		Bit 7: 1 if this word is really a count word indication next style applies to number of words (number is stored in bits 0–14)
xxH	1	New row height flags
xxH	2	New row height (wpu)
xxH	1	New number of bytes of border information for this row (bit 7 = 1: 1 word per column, bit 7 = 0: 1 byte per column)
xxH	*xx*	New border information (number of columns * 2 bytes)
xxH	2	Old number of formatter lines at top of row (wpu)
xxH	2	Length word (variable)
xxH	1	Sub-function code 01H
xxH	1	End function code (Code DCH)

Table 18.115
Opcode DCH, 01H in version 5.1 (*cont.*)

18.5.14.3 Table Off at EOL (code DCH, subcode 02H)

This record is used to mark the end of a table.

Offset	**Bytes**	**Field**
00H	1	Table Off at EOL (Code DCH)
01H	1	Sub-function code 02H
02H	2	Length word (variable)
04H	1	Flags:
		Bits 0–1: old row height option
		Bits 2–7: —

Table 18.116
Opcode DCH, 02H in version 5.1 (*continues over...*)

Offset	Bytes	Field
05H	2	Old row height (wpu)
07H	1	Old number of bytes of border information for row
08H	*xx*	Old border information for row
xxH	1	Old number of rows
xxH	2	Old number of formatter lines at top of row (wpu)
xxH	2	Old size of header rows
xxH	2	Old number of columns
xxH	2	Length word (variable)
xxH	1	Sub-function code 02H
xxH	1	End function code (Code DCH)

Table 18.116 Opcode DCH, 02H in version 5.1 (*cont.*)

18.5.15 Table end of page codes group (code DDH, version 5.1)

This group of sub-functions is defined from version 5.1 onwards. The subcode 00H is free.

- Subcode 01H is used for the function *Beginning of row at end of page*. The record structure is identical to function DC01H.
- Subcode 02H is used for the function *Table off at end of page*. The record structure is identical to function DC02H.
- Subcode 03H is defined for the function *Beginning of row/hard page break* and has a structure identical to function DC01H.

18.5.16 Enhanced merge functions (code DEH, version 5.1)

This group is defined from version 5.1 onwards.

Offset	Bytes	Field
00H	1	Enhanced merge (Code DEH)
01H	1	Sub-function code xxH
02H	2	Length word (value = 4)
xxH	*xx*	Parameter of function
04H	2	Length word (value = 4)
xxH	1	Sub-function code xxH
xxH	1	End function code (Code DEH)

Table 18.117 Opcode DEH, xxH in version 5.1

The length word is set to 4 for most functions. Only sub-function DE34H has the value 6 for length. Table 18.118 shows the sub-functions that have been defined.

Subcode	Subfunction
20H	mrg_asgn (ASSIGN) var, expr
21H	mrg_bell (BELL)
22H	mrg_brk (BREAK)
23H	mrg_call (CALL) label
24H	mrg_cnclf (CANCEL OFF)
25H	mrg_cnclo (CANCEL ON)
26H	mrg_case (CASE) exp, case1, label.. (ELSE) label
27H	mrg_casec (CASE CALL) exp, case1, label.. (ELSE) label
28H	mrg_chnmo (CHAIN MACRO) macroname
29H	mrg_chnp (CHAIN PRIMARY) file name
2AH	mrg_chns (CHAIN SECONDARY) file
2BH	mrg_char (CHAR) var, message
2CH	mrg_comt (COMMENT) comment
2DH	mrg_cton (CTON) character
2EH	mrg_dateo (DATE) Old ^D
2FH	mrg_doc (DOCUMENT) file name
30H	mrg_else (ELSE)
31H	mrg_endfl (END FIELD) Old ^R
32H	mrg_endfor (END FOR)
33H	mrg_endif (END IF)
34H	mrg_endrec (END RECORD) Old ^E Number of fields in record (1 Word)
35H	mrg_endwhl (END WHILE)
36H	mrg_field (FIELD) field old ^F
37H	mrg_for (FOR) var, start, stop, step
38H	mrg_freach (FOR EACH) var, expr, expr...
39H	mrg_go (GO) label
3AH	mrg_if (IF) expr
3BH	mrg_ifb (IF BLANK) field
3CH	mrg_ifexst (IF EXISTS) var
3DH	mrg_notb (IF NOT BLANK) field
3EH	mrg_kybd (KEYBOARD) old ^C
3FH	mrg_label (LABEL) label
40H	mrg_local (LOCAL) var, expr
41H	mrg_look (LOOK) var
42H	mrg_mid (MID) expr, offset, count
43H	mrg_mrcmd (MRG CMND) codes (MRG CMND)

Table 18.118 Merge sub-functions (version 5.1) (*continues over...*)

Subcode	Subfunction
44H	mrg_nestm (NEST MACRO) macroname
45H	mrg_nestp (NEST PRIMARY) file name
46H	mrg_nests (NEST SECONDARY) file name
47H	mrg_next (NEXT)
48H	mrg_nextr (NEXT RECORD) Old ^N
49H	mrg_ntoc (NTOC) number
4AH	mrg_proc (PROCESS) codes (PROCESS)
4BH	mrg_oncan (ON CANCEL) action
4CH	mrg_onerr (ON ERROR) action
4DH	mrg_pagef (PAGE OFF)
4EH	mrg_pagen (PAGE ON)
4FH	mrg_prnt (PRINT) Old ^T
50H	mrg_prompt (PROMPT) message
51H	mrg_quit (QUIT) Old ^Q
52H	mrg_ret (RETURN)
53H	mrg_retcan (RETURN CANCEL)
54H	mrg_reterr (RETURN ERROR)
55H	mrg_rwrite (REWRITE) Old ^U
56H	mrg_stepf (Step OFF)
57H	mrg_stepo (Step ON)
58H	mrg_subp (SUBST PRIMARY) file name
59H	mrg_subs (SUBST SECONDARY) file
5AH	mrg_sys (SYSTEM) sysvar
5BH	mrg_text (TEXT) var, message
5CH	mrg_var (VARIABLE) var
5DH	mrg_wait (WAIT) 1/10
5EH	mrg_while (WHILE) expr
5FH	mrg_sprmt (STATUS PROMPT) message
60H	mrg_input (INPUT) message
61H	mrg_len (LEN) expr
62H	mrg_fldnm (FIELD NAME) name ...
63H	mrg_end end of merge command

Table 18.118 Merge subfunctions (version 5.1) (*cont.*)

18.5.17 Equation nested function group (code DFH, version 5.1)

The code `DFH` defines a new group of sub-functions in version 5.1. In this version only function `00H` is defined.

18.5.17.1 Equation nested function (code DFH, subcode 00H)

This record stores data for the output of equations.

Offset	Bytes	Field
00H	1	Equation nested function (Code DFH)
01H	1	Sub-function code 00H
02H	2	Length word (variable)
04H	2	Flags, bits 6–15 unused Bits 0–2: horizontal alignment 0 = left alignment 1 = right alignment 2 = center alignment Bits 3–5: vertical alignment 1 = top alignment 2 = center alignment 3 = bottom alignment
06H	2	Memory requirements of equation
08H	2	Offset of equation text from this location (0 in WP 5.1)
0AH	2	Equation base font size (graphic)
0CH	*xx*	Equation text
xxH	*xx*	Equation compact stream
xxH	2	Length word (variable)
xxH	1	Sub-function code 00H
xxH	1	End function code (Code DFH)

Table 18.119 Opcode `DFH`, `00H` in version 5.1

Word processing

18.5.18 Unknown function (code FEH, version 5.1)

18.5.18.1 Unknown function (code FEH, subcode FEH)

This function is used to mark unknown functions in a file.

Offset	Bytes	Field
00H	1	Unknown function (FEH)
01H	1	Sub-function code FEH
02H	*xx*	Variable length
xxH	1	Sub-function code FEH
xxH	1	End function code (Code FEH)

Table 18.120
Opcode FEH, FEH
in version 5.1

! The Wordperfect 6.x file format is backwardly compatible to earlier versions. A description is available from the vendor after signing a license agreement.

19

Rich Text format (RTF version 1.2)

This *format was defined by Microsoft as a method of encoding formatted text and graphics for ease of transfer between different applications. The RTF standard defines a format that can be used with different output devices, operating systems and environments. Most Microsoft products support the RTF definition. RTF is also the exchange format for the clipboard in Windows and for Word on different platforms (DOS, Windows, Macintosh).*

The Rich Text Format definition uses only the displayable characters of the ASCII, MAC and PC character sets to control the representation and formatting of a document. An RTF file consists of unformatted text, control words, control symbols and groups. The characters used can be coded as 7-bit ASCII characters, but in Word for Windows and Word for Macintosh, 8-bit characters should be used for data exchange. Figure 19.1 shows a section of an RTF document.

The document starts with the initial control sequences for the RTF reader. These control sequences are divided into *control words* and *control symbols*.

A *control word* is a specially formatted command (letter sequence) which starts with a *backslash* and ends with a *delimiter*:

```
\lettersequence <delimiter>
```

The `lettersequence` is made up of lower case alphabetic characters between a and z. All RTF keywords should be lower case. A delimiter marks the end of a control word, and can be one of the following characters:

- A *space*: in this case the space is part of the control word.
- A *digit* or a hyphen `-`: this indicates that a numeric parameter and a delimiter follows. Delimiters are spaces and other characters excluding a hyphen and digits. The range for the numeric value is –32767 to 32767. Word (DOS, Windows, Macintosh, OS/2) restricts the range to –31680 to 31680.

◆ All characters other than a letter or a digit. In this case the delimiting character terminates the control word and is not a part of it.

A *control symbol* consists of a backslash (\) followed by a single (non-alphabetic) character:

```
\control symbol
```

Only a few control symbols are defined. An RTF reader can skip unknown control symbols.

```
{\rtf1\pc
{\info{\revtim\mo06\dy05\yr1989}{\creatim\mo05\dy18\yr1989}
{\nofchars4912}}\deff0{\fonttbl{\f0\fmodern pica;}
{\f1\fmodern Courier;}{\f2\fmodern elite;}{\f3\fmodern
prestige;}
{\f4\fmodern lettergothic;}{\f5\fmodern gothicPS;}
{\f6\fmodern cubicPS;}{\f7\fmodern lineprinter;}
{\f8\fswiss Helvetica;}{\f9\fmodern avantgarde;}
{\f10\fmodern spartan;}{\f11\fmodern metro;}
{\f12\fmodern presentation;}{\f13\fmodern
APL;}{\f14\fmodern OCRA;}
{\f15\fmodern OCRB;}{\f16\froman boldPS;}{\f17\froman
emperorPS;}
{\f18\froman madaleine;}{\f19\froman zapf humanist;}
{\f20\froman classic;}{\f21\froman Roman f;}{\f22\froman
Roman g;}
{\f23\froman Roman h;}{\f24\froman timesroman;}{\f25\froman
century;}
{\f26\froman palantino;}{\f27\froman souvenir;}{\f28\froman
garamond;}
{\f29\froman caledonia;}{\f30\froman bodini;}{\f31\froman
university;}
{\f32\fscript script;}{\f33\fscript scriptPS;}{\f34\fscript
script c;}
{\f35\fscript script d;}{\f36\fscript commercial script;}
{\f37\fscript park avenue;}{\f38\fscript coronet;}
{\f39\fscript script h;}{\f40\fscript greek;}{\f41\froman
kana;}
{\f42\froman hebrew;}{\f43\froman Roman s;}{\f44\froman
russian;}
{\f45\froman Roman u;}{\f46\froman Roman v;}{\f47\froman
Roman w;}
{\f48\fdecor narrator;}{\f49\fdecor emphasis;}
{\f50\fdecor zapf chancery;}{\f51\fdecor decor d;}
```

Figure 19.1 Part of a Word RTF file (*continues over...*)

```
{\f52\fdecor old english;}{\f53\fdecor decor
f;}{\f54\fdecor decor g;}
{\f55\fdecor cooper black;}{\f56\ftech Symbol;}{\f57\ftech
linedraw;}
{\f58\ftech math7;}{\f59\ftech math8;}{\f60\ftech
bar3of9;}
{\f61\ftech EAN;}{\f62\ftech pcline;}{\f63\ftech tech h;}}
\ftnbj\ftnrestart \sectd \linex576\endnhere \pard \sl-240
\plain MICROSOFT WORD VERSION 5.0\par

This file provides you with information on certain
limitations on the conversion between texts which were
formatted in Word and texts which were formatted in RTF
(Rich Text Format). You will also be shown how you can
adapt the conversion of typefaces to your needs by
producing special files; these files are used in
conjunction with the conversion program. \par
```

Figure 19.1 Part of a Word RTF file (*cont.*)

A group consists of text and control words or control symbols enclosed in braces `{}`.

```
{  Begin group
}  End group
```

Each group specifies the text affected by the group and the different attributes and formats of that text. An RTF file can contain additional groups for fonts, styles, screen colors, pictures, footnotes, annotations, headers, and other character-formatting properties. If font, style, screen color and summary information are included, they must precede the first plain-text character in the document. If a group is not used it should be omitted.

If one of the following characters is used as an ASCII character in the text:

```
\ { }
```

a preceding backslash is required:

```
\\
\{
\}
```

This tells the RTF scanner that the following character is not a control code. Some codes are used for the print format without interpretation (Table 19.1).

Code	Field description
09H	Tabulator (\tab)
0AH	CR character
0CH	LF character

Table 19.1 Special characters in the RTF format

A CR/LF character in an RTF file will be skipped by the scanner. The character is used only to format the RTF file for printing. An RTF file should contain a CR/LF after 255 characters.

In a control word, the CR/LF character can have a special meaning (*see* the control word descriptions).

19.1 Destination control words

The following control words initialize the RTF reader and may occur only at the beginning of a file or group. All control words and parameters must be enclosed between braces:

```
{\rtf0\pc.......}
```

The following pages contain a short description of all destination control words.

\rtf <parameter>

This control word defines the header in the format \rtfN, where N is the version number (1 for RTF specification 1).

```
{\rtf0......}
```

This initial control word is followed by other control words.

\ansi, \pc, and so on.

The second control word in an RTF file is the specification of the character set used. The RTF specification supports different character sets.

The \pca control word is not implemented in all versions of Word. For exchanging text between different platforms, the \ansi code should be used.

Control	Character set
`\ansi`	ANSI (default)
`\mac`	Apple Macintosh
`\pc`	IBM PC with code page 437
`\pca`	IBM PC with code page 850

Table 19.2
Character coding

\fonttbl

This control word introduces the *font table group*. This group defines all the fonts available in the document and associates a name with a font number. For the font definition the following entries are defined:

- `\fnil`: Is used for unknown or default fonts. This is the default setting.
- `\froman`: This defines proportional spaced serif fonts from the *Roman* family (*Times Roman*, *Palatino*, and so on).
- `\fswiss`: With this control the fonts from the *Swiss* family (*Helvetica*, *Swiss*, and so on) are used.
- `\fmodern`: Defines fixed-pitch serif and sans serif fonts like *Pica*, *Elite* and *Courier*.
- `\fscript`: Associates script fonts (cursive, and so on) with a font number.
- `\fdecor`: Uses decorative fonts (*Old English*, *ITC Zapf Chancery*, and so on).
- `\ftech`: Defines technical, mathematical and symbol fonts (*Symbol*, and so on).
- `\bidi`: Defines bidirectional fonts for Arabic, Hebrew or other languages (*Miriam*, and so on).

A valid command to define a font table is:

```
{\fonttbl\f0\fnil default;}
{\f1\froman Roman h;}
{\f2\fswiss helvetica;}
```

The keyword `\fonttbl` is followed by the first font number `\f0`. After the font number, the definition of the font family (`\fnil` for default) is required. The next parameter indicates the font name (Roman h for the second font number `\f1`). The parameter `default` tells the reader to use the default font. The font name is terminated by a semicolon. The complete group is included in braces `{ }` (*see* Figure 19.1.)

The font definition is required before a `\stylesheet` control word or a text can occur. The standard font is defined by the control word `\deffn`.

\fcharset

The font table may be followed by a *character set* definition. This control word has a numeric parameter (\fcharsetN), which can be one of the following:

N	Character set
0	ANSI
2	Symbol
128	SHIFTJIS
161	Greek
162	Turkish
177	Hebrew
178	Arabic simplified
179	Arabic traditional
180	Arabic user
181	Hebrew user
204	Cyrillic
238	Eastern European
254	PC437
255	OEM

Table 19.3 Character sets

The control word \fcharset can be omitted.

\fprq

This control word defines the *font pitch request* in the parameter N (\fprqN).

N	Pitch
0	Default
1	Fixed
2	Variable

Table 19.4 Font pitch request

The control word is optional.

\cpg

A font may have a different character set from the characters used in a document. The *code page support* \cpgN control word defines the character set used. Valid values for \cpgN are:

N	Description
437	IBM standard character set
708	Arabic (ASMO 708)
709	Arabic (ASMO 449+, BCON V4)
710	Arabic (Transparent Arabic)
711	Arabic (Nafitha enhanced)
720	Arabic (Transparent ASMO)
819	Windows 3.1 (US and Europe)
850	IBM bilingual
852	Eastern European
860	Portuguese
862	Hebrew
864	Arabic
865	Norwegian
866	Soviet Union
932	Japanese
1250	Windows 3.1 (East Europe)
1251	Windows 3.1 (Soviet Union)

Table 19.5 Code page support

An RTF document must have an additional `\characterset` declaration (for example, `\ansi` or `\pc` and so on) for backward compatibility.

\fontemb

The control word `\fontemb` supports *font embedding* inside a font definition. An embedded font can be specified by a file name.

- `\ftnil`: This defines an unknown or default font type.
- `\fttruetype`: Defines a TrueType font type.

If a file name is specified, it is contained in the font table group.

\filetbl

The *file table* control word defines a list of files referenced in the document. The following control words are associated with the file table:

- `\file`: Marks the beginning of a file group. This is a destination control word.
- `\fidN`: The file ID number is referenced later in the document.
- `\frelativeN`: This control word defines the character position within the path (starting at 0), when the referenced file is relative to the path of the document file. This allows the reader to extract the complete path.

- `\fosnumN`: This control word is currently inserted for the Macintosh file system. `N` is an operating system-specific file number to identify the file (on the Macintosh it is the file ID).
- `\fvalidmac`: This defines the Macintosh file system.
- `\fvaliddos`: Defines the DOS file system.
- `\fvalidntfs`: Defines the NTFS file system.
- `\fvalidhpfs`: Defines the OS/2 HPFS file system.
- `\fnetwork`: Defines a network file system.

The `\fnetwork` control word may be used together with the other file source keywords.

\colortbl

This control word introduces the *color table group*, which defines screen and character colors. The colors in the tables are defined by three values for the colors red, green and blue. After the keyword `\colortbl` the RTF scanner searches for the definitions of the basic colors:

```
\red000
\green000
\blue000
```

The number `000` can be replaced by values between `0` and `255`.

```
{\colortbl\red128\green64\blue128;;\red0\green64\blue128;}
```

The definition of a color is terminated by a semicolon. Two semicolons will leave an entry in a table unmodified. The group is closed by a brace `}`. The parameter `\cfn` defines the foreground color (*n*=`0`, Standard). `\cbn` defines the background color (*n*=`0`, Standard).

\stylesheet

The *style sheet* control word marks the beginning of the style sheet group. This group contains definitions for the various styles used in the document:

- `\additive`: Used in a character style definition to indicate that style attributes should be applied in addition to current attributes.
- `\sbasedon000`: Defines the number of the style on which the current style is based.
- `\snext000`: Defines the next style associated with the current style.
- `\keycode`: This group is specified within the description of a style in the style sheet. The group defines key codes to activate a style `{\s0{\*\keycode \shift\ ctrl n}Normal;}`.
- `\alt`: Used to describe [Alt] short key codes for styles.

Word processing

- \shift: Used to describe [Shift] short key codes for styles.
- \ctrl: Used to describe [Ctrl] short key codes for styles.
- \fnN: Specifies a function key (N is function number 1 to 12) to be used as a short key for style.

A valid example of a style sheet definition is:

```
{\stylesheet{\s0\f3\fs20\qj Normal;}
{\s1\f3\fs30\b\qc Heading Level 3;}
```

The styles are numbered from 0 to n (\s0..). The first definition associates the style 0 (\s0) with the name Normal. Normal text will be displayed in font 3 (\f3), 10 point (\fs20). The parameter \qj indicates justified text. The second line defines style 1 with the name Heading Level 3. The font size is set to 15 point (\b for bold) and centered (\qc).

19.2 Revision and information group

\revtbl

This group consists of several subgroups to identify the author of a revision. If a revision conflict occurs, the sequence CurrentAuthor\'00\.... PreviousRevisionTime is inserted.

\info

The information group is introduced with the control word \info. This group contains information about the document (author, keyword, comments, and so on):

- \title: Defines the title of the document.
- \subject: Defines the subject of the document.
- \operator: This indicates the person who made the most recent change to the document.
- \author: This defines the author of the document.
- \keywords: This entry stores selected keywords for the document.
- \comment: Comments are ignored by the RTF reader.
- \doccomm: This contains comments, displayed in Word's edit summary information dialog box.
- \version: Defines a version number for the document.

The RTF writer adds the following additional information:

- \vern000: This is an internal version number.
- \creatim: Defines the time the document was created. This control word is followed by the date and time definition.

- \yr000: Year the document was created.
- \mo000: Month the document was created.
- \dy000: Day the document was created.
- \hr000: Hour the document was created.
- \min000: Minute the document was created.
- \sec000: Second the document was created.
- \revtim: This control word defines the time and date of the last revision.
- \printtim: Defines the date and time of the last printout.
- \buptim: Defines the date and time of the last backup.
- \edmins000: Defines the total time for editing.
- \nofpages000: Defines the number of pages in the document.
- \nofwords000: Defines the number of words in the document.
- \nofchars000: Indicates the number of characters counted in the document.
- \id000: This entry contains an internal ID number.

All control words without a numeric parameter describe a time and date in terms of \yr\mo \dy\hr\min\sec.

19.3 Document formatting properties

These control words specify the attributes (margins, footnote placements, and so on) of a document. The control words are inserted after the information group (if present) but before the plain text region, and are divided into several categories:

- Control words that format a complete text.
- Control words that influence the format of the current paragraph.
- Control words that are valid for the current text output.

The control words are listed below.

\deftabN

N defines the *default tab* width in twips (1 twip is equal to ⅟20 point or ⅟1440 inch). The value is 720.

\hyphhotzN

The parameter N defines the *hyphenation hot zone* in twips.

\hyphconsecN

N is the number of consecutive lines allowed to end in a hyphen (0 = no limit).

\hyphcaps

This control word toggles *hyphenation of capitalized words* (default is on; \hyphcaps 1 = on, \hyphcaps 0 = off).

\hyphauto

This control word toggles *automatic hyphenation* on or off (0 = off, 1 = on).

\linestartN

This control word sets the begin line number; 1 is the default value.

\fracwidth

This control word is used only for QuickDraw; it specifies that fractional character widths should be used.

***\nextfile**

This control word specifies the name of the next file to print or index. The file name must be included in braces.

***\template**

This control word defines the name of a template file. The name must be included in braces.

\makebackup

This control word specifies an automatic backup copy when the document is saved.

\defformat

This control word tells the RTF reader that the document should be saved in RTF format.

\psover

This control word prints PostScript over the text.

\doctemp

With Word for Windows, the document is a template. With Word for Macintosh, this document is a stationery file.

\deflangN

This control word defines the language (N) for the plain text. The possible properties are defined in the character-formatting properties area.

\fetN

N defines a footnote/endnote type (0 = no footnotes at all, 1 = endnotes only, 2 = footnotes and endnotes).

\ftnsep

This control word defines a character to separate footnotes from the document.

\ftnsepc

This control word defines a character to separate continued footnotes from the text document.

\ftncn

This control word is a marker for continued footnotes.

\aftnsep

This control word defines a text argument which separates endnotes from the document.

\aftnsepc

This control word defines a text argument which separates continued endnotes from the document.

\aftncn

The text argument is a marker for continued endnotes in the document.

\endnotes

All footnotes should be printed at the end of the section (default).

\enddoc

All footnotes should be printed at the end of the document.

\ftnbj

Footnotes are *bottom-justified* on the page.

\ftntj

Footnotes are *top-justified* on the page.

\aendnotes

Position an endnote at the end of a section (default).

\aenddoc

Position an endnote at the end of a document.

\aftnbj

Position an endnote at the bottom of a page.

\aftntj

Position an endnote beneath the text (top-justified).

\ftnstart000

This control word defines the start footnote number (default 1).

\aftnstart000

This control word defines the start endnote number (default 1).

\ftnrstp

This control word restarts footnote numbering at each page.

\fntrestart

Footnote numbering should restart at each section. (On the Macintosh the footnote numbering will restart on each page.)

\fntrstcont

Switch to continuous footnote numbering (default).

\afntrestart

Restart endnote numbering at each section.

\ftnnar

Footnote numbering – Arabic (1,2,3…)

\ftnnalc

Footnote numbering – Alphabetic (a,b,c…)

\ftnnauc

Footnote numbering – Alphabetic upper case (A,B,C...)

\ftnnrlc

Footnote numbering – Roman lower case (i,ii,iii...)

\ftnnruc

Footnote numbering – Roman upper case (I,II,III...)

\ftnnchi

Footnote numbering – Chicago manual of style (*,...)

\aftnnar

Endnote numbering – Arabic (1,2,3...)

\aftnnalc

Endnote numbering – Alphabetic (a,b,c...)

\aftnnauc

Endnote numbering – Alphabetic upper case (A,B,C...)

\aftnnrlc

Endnote numbering – Roman lower case (i,ii,iii...)

\aftnnruc

Endnote numbering – Roman upper case (I,II,III...)

\aftnnchi

Endnote numbering – Chicago manual of style (*,...)

\pgnstart000

This control word defines the page start number (default 1).

\paperw000

This control word defines the paper width in twips (1 twip is equal to $\frac{1}{20}$ point or $\frac{1}{1440}$ inch). The default value is 12240 twips.

`\paperh000`

This control word defines the paper height in twips (default 15840 twips).

`\pszN`

This control word is used to distinguish between paper sizes with identical dimensions in Windows NT. Values between `1` and `41` correspond to the defined paper sizes (in `DRIVINI.H`). Values greater than `41` correspond to user-defined paper sizes.

`\revprot`

The document is protected against revisions.

`\revison`

This control word turns revision marking on.

`\revpropN`

The argument `N` defines how the revised text should be displayed: `0` no properties shown, `1` bold, `2` italic, `3` underlined (default), `4` double-underlined.

`\revbarN`

Display vertical lines for altered text (`0` no marking, `1` left margin, `2` right margin, `3` outside (left/right).

`\annotprot`

The document is protected against annotations.

`\rtldoc`

The document will be formatted using Arabic pagination (right to left).

`\ltrdoc`

The document will have English-style pagination (default, left to right).

19.4 Section formatting

The next group of control words is used for formatting document sections:

`\sectd`

Reset to default section properties.

\endnhere

Endnotes are included in the section. The parameter 0 suppresses this option.

\binfsxnN

N is the printer bin used for the first page of the section.

\bindsxnN

N is the printer bin used for the pages of a section.

\dsN

This control word designates a section style.

\sectunlocked

The following section is unlocked for forms.

\sbknone

This control indicates no section break.

\sbkcol

A section break starts a new column.

\sbkpage

A section break starts a new page.

\sbkeven

A section break starts at an even page.

\sbkodd

A section break starts at an odd page.

\cols000

This control word defines the number of columns (default 1).

\colsx000

This control word defines the space between two columns in twips (default 720 twips).

\colno000

This control word defines the column number to be formatted (used in variable width columns).

\colsr000

This control word defines the space of the right column in twips. Used to specify formatting in variable-width columns.

\colw000

This control word defines the column width in twips.

\linebetcol

This control word defines the line between columns.

\linemod000

This control word defines the line number interval (default 1).

\linex000

This control word defines the distance from the line number to left text margin in twips (default 360 twips, automatic is 0).

\linestartsN

Begin line numbering with N.

\linerestart

Reset the line number to \linestartsN.

\lineppage

Line numbers restart on each page.

\linecont

Continue line numbers from preceding section.

\pgwsxnN

This control word defines the page width in twips.

\pghsxnN

This control word defines the page height in twips.

\marginlsxnN

This control word defines the left margin of a page in twips.

\marginrsxnN

This control word defines the right margin of a page in twips.

\margintsxyN

This control word defines the top margin in twips.

\marglN

This control word defines the left margin in twips (default 1800).

\margrN

This control word defines the right margin in twips (default 1800).

\margtN

This control word defines the top margin in twips (default 1440).

\margbN

This control word defines the bottom margin in twips (default 1440).

\facingp

This control word activates the odd/even headers and the gutters.

\gutter000

This control word defines the gutter width in twips (default is 0).

\margmirror

This control word switches margin definitions on left and right pages.

\landscape

This control word defines the orientation to be *landscape*. If the following parameter is 0, the orientation is reset to *portrait*.

\pgnstartsN

This control word sets the start page number (default 1).

\widowctl

This control word enables widow and orphan control. The parameter 0 disables the control.

\linkstyles

This control word updates document styles automatically, based on the template definitions.

\notabind

This is the first control word in the group of compatibility options (used in Word 6.0). This control word means 'do not add an automatic tab stop for hanging indents'.

\wraptrsp

Wrap trailing spaces onto the next line.

\prcolbl

Print all colors black on black-and-white printers.

\noextrasprl

Do not add extra space to line height (for raised/lowered characters).

\nocolbal

Do not balance columns.

\cvmme

Old escaped quotation marks (\") are treated as current style ("").

\sprstsp

This control word suppresses extra line spacing at the top of a page.

\sprsspbf

This control word suppresses space before a paragraph attribute, after a hard page or column break.

\otblrul

This control word combines table borders like Word for Macintosh 5.x.

\transmf

Metafiles are considered as transparent.

\swpbdr

This control word swaps the border on the right for odd-numbered pages.

\brkfrm

This control word shows hard page and column breaks in frames.

\formprot

This is the first control word of the forms formatting commands. This control word protects a document for forms.

\allprot

All areas in the document are protected.

\formshade

This control word flags a form shaded form field.

\formdisp

A document with a form drop down or check box is selected.

\printdata

The document has print form data only.

\margbsxnN

The parameter `N` defines the top margin of the page in twips. The value is reset with a `\sectd` command.

\guttersxnN

`N` defines the gutter width of a section in twips.

\indscpsxn

This control word defines the page orientation as landscape.

\titlepg

The first page has a special format.

\headery000

This control word defines the vertical header position in twips from the top of the page (default 720 twips).

\footery000

This control word defines the vertical footer position in twips from the bottom of the page (default 720 twips).

\pgnstartsN

This is the first control word in the group of page numbering control words. It defines the start page number (default = 1).

\pgncont

This control word specifies continuous page numbering (default).

\pgnrestart

This control word restarts the page number at `\pgnstarts000`.

\pgnx000

This control word defines the X-position of a page number in twips from the right margin (default 720 twips).

\pgny000

This control word defines the Y-position of the page number in twips from the top margin (default 720 twips).

\pgndec

Page numbers are in decimal format.

\pgnucrm

Page numbers are in *upper case Roman numerals*.

\pgnlcrm

Page numbers are in *lower case Roman numerals*.

\pgnucltr

Page numbers are in *upper case letters*.

\pgnlcltr

Page numbers are in *lower case letters*.

\pgnhnN

This control word indicates which heading level is used in the page number (0 = does not show heading level, 1–9 correspond to the heading levels).

\pgnhnsh

This control word defines the hyphen separator character.

\pgnhnsph

This control word defines the period separator character.

\pgnhnsc

This control word defines the colon separator character.

\pgnhnsm

This control word defines the em-dash separator character.

\pgnhnsn

This control word defines the en-dash separator character.

\pnseclvlN

This control word is used for multilevel lists; it sets the default numbering style.

\vertalt

The next control words specify the alignment of a text. `\vertalt` specifies *vertical align at top of page*.

\vertalc

This control word specifies *vertical align centered*.

\vertalj

This control word specifies *vertical justified*.

\vertalb

This control word specifies *vertical align at bottom*.

\rtlsect

Treat columns in this section from right to left.

\ltrsect

Treat columns in this section from left to right (default).

19.5 Headers and footers

These control words define headers and footers in a section. Each section may have its own header/footer.

\header

Headers should occur on all pages.

\headerl

The header appears on *left-hand* pages only.

\headerr

The header appears on *right-hand* pages only.

\headerf

This control word defines the *first page* header.

\footer

This control word displays a footer on all pages.

\footerl

This control word displays a footer on *left-hand* pages only.

\footerr

This control word displays a footer on *right-hand* pages only.

\footerf

This control word defines the footer for the *first page*.

19.6 Paragraph formatting properties

The next section describes the paragraph formatting control words.

\pard

This control word resets the RTF reader to the default paragraph properties.

\s000

This control word designates paragraph style. The style must be specified with the paragraph.

\hyphpar

This control word switches automatic hyphenation for the paragraph on or off (0 = off).

\intbl

This control word defines the paragraph as a part of a table.

\keep

This control word keeps the paragraph intact.

\nowidctlpar

This control word specifies no widow/orphan control.

\keepn

This control word keeps this paragraph with the next paragraph.

\levelN

This control word outlines level N of the paragraph.

\noline

This control word switches the line numbering off.

\sbys

This control word switches the *side by side* paragraph option on (0 switches off).

\pagebb

This control word sets *page break before paragraph* to on (0 switches the command off).

\ql

This control word specifies *quad left aligned* text.

\qr

This control word specifies *quad right aligned* text.

\qc

This control word specifies *quad centered* text.

`\qj`

This control word specifies *quad justified* text in a document.

`\fi000`

The first line is indented (default `0` twips).

`\li000`

Lines are left indented (default `0`).

`\ri000`

Lines are right indented (default `0`).

`\sb000`

This control word defines spaces before (default is `0`).

`\sa000`

This control word defines spaces after (default `0`).

`\sl000`

This control word defines the space between lines. `\sl000` switches *auto line mode* on.

`\slmultN`

This control word specifies line spacing in a multiple of single line spacing. (`0` = exactly, `1` = multiple).

`\subdocumentN`

This sub-document control word must be the only item in a paragraph and indicates that a sub-document should occur here. `N` is an index to the file table.

`\rtlpar`

This is a bidirectional control word and defines a paragraph with text displayed from left to right.

`\lttpar`

This is a bidirectional control word and defines a paragraph with text displayed from right to left (default).

19.7 Tabs formatting

The following control words are used to specify tabs in the document.

\tx000

This control word defines a tab position in twips from the left margin.

\tqr

This control word stands for *flush right tab*.

\tqc

This control word defines a *centered tab*.

\tqdec

This control word defines a *decimal aligned tab*.

\tldot

This control word defines a *tab leader dot*.

\tlhyphen

This control word defines a *tab leader hyphen*.

\tlul

This control word defines a *tab leader underline*.

\tlth

This control word defines the *tab leader thick line*.

\tb000

This control word defines a bar tab (*vertical tab*) position in twips from the left margin.

\tleq

This control word defines a *tab leader equals* sign.

19.8 Bullets and Numbering

This group of controls is used in bulleted or numbered paragraphs.

\pntext

This group precedes all numbered/bulleted paragraphs and contains the auto-generated text and formatting. It should precede the {*\pn..} to enable RTF readers to ignore the complete preceding group.

\pn

This control word turns the paragraph numbering on.

\pnlvlN

This control word sets the paragraph level (1–9).

\pnlvlblt

This is a bulleted paragraph (corresponds to level 11).

\pnlvlbody

This is simple paragraph numbering (corresponds to level 10).

\pnlvlcont

This is continued paragraph numbering, but the number is skipped (not displayed).

\pnnumonce

This control word numbers each cell only once in a table.

\pnacross

This control word numbers across rows (default across columns).

\pnhang

This control word marks a paragraph with a hanging indent.

\pnrestart

This control word restarts the numbering after each section break.

\pncard

This control word specifies cardinal numbering (One, Two, Three).

\pndec

This control word specifies decimal numbering (1, 2, 3).

\pnucltr

This control word specifies upper case alphabetic numbering (A, B, C).

\pnucrm

This control word specifies upper case Roman numbering (I, II, III).

\pnlcltr

This control word specifies lower case alphabetic numbering (a, b, c).

\pnlcrm

This control word specifies lower case Roman numbering (i, ii, iii).

\pnord

This control word specifies ordinal numbering (1st, 2nd, 3rd).

\pnordt

This control word specifies ordinal text numbering (First, Second, Third).

\pnb

This control word specifies bold numbering (from Word 6.0).

\pni

This control word specifies italic numbering (from Word 6.0).

\pncaps

This control word specifies all capitals numbering (from Word 6.0).

\pnscaps

This control word specifies small capitals numbering (from Word 6.0).

\pnul

This control word specifies continuous underlining (from Word 6.0).

\pnuld

This control word specifies dotted underlining.

\pnuld

This control word specifies double underlining.

\pnulnone

This control word turns underlining off.

\pnulw

This control word switches word underlining on.

\pnstrike

This control word specifies strike-through numbering.

\pncfN

This control word defines the font size (in half points) for numbering.

\pncfN

This control word specifies the foreground color (N is an index to a color table).

\pnfN

This control word specifies the font number for numbering.

\pnindentN

This control word specifies the minimum distance from the margin to the body of text.

\pnspN

This control word specifies the distance from the number to the body of text.

\pnprev

This control word is used for multilevel lists and includes information from the previous level to the current level (1, 1.1, 1.1.1, and so on).

\pnqc

This control word is used for centered numbering.

\pnql

This control word is used for left-justified numbering.

\pnqr

This control is word used for right-justified numbering.

\pnstartN

This control word defines the start value for paragraph numbering.

\pntxta

This control word specifies the text that follows the number (. for instance). This text is limited to 32 characters.

\pntxtb

This control word specifies the text before the number ((for instance). This text is limited to 32 characters.

19.9 Paragraph borders

This control word describes the paragraph borders.

\brdrt

This control word defines the top border.

\brdrb

This control word defines the bottom border.

\brdrl

This control word defines the left border.

\brdrr

This control word defines the right border.

\brdrbtw

This control word defines paragraphs with individual formatting within a single group of consecutive paragraphs (with identical border formatting).

\brdrbar

This control word defines the outside border (left/right for even/odd pages).

\box

This control word defines a border around the paragraph.

\brdrs

This control word specifies a single thickness border.

\brdrth

This control word specifies a double thickness border.

\brdsh

This control word specifies a shadowed border.

\brdrdb

This control word specifies a double border.

\brdrdot

This control word specifies a dotted border.

\brdrhair

This control word specifies a border with a hair line.

\brdrwN

This defines the width of a pen (in twips) used to draw the paragraph border line.

\brdrcfN

This control word defines the color (N is an index to a color table) of the border.

\brspN

This control word defines the space in twips between the border and the paragraph.

19.10 Paragraph shading

These control words define the shading of a paragraph.

\shadingN

This control word defines the paragraph shading (gray-level) in percent.

\bghoriz

This control word specifies a horizontal pattern drawn in the background of a paragraph.

\bgvert

This control word specifies a vertical pattern drawn in the background of a paragraph.

\bgfdiag

This control word specifies a forward diagonal pattern (\\\) drawn in the background of a paragraph.

\bgbdiag

This control word specifies a backward diagonal pattern (///) drawn in the background of a paragraph.

\bgcross

This control word specifies a cross background pattern for a paragraph.

\bgdkhoriz

This control word specifies a dark horizontal background pattern for a paragraph.

\bgdkvert

This control word specifies a dark vertical background pattern for a paragraph.

\bgdkfdiag

This control word specifies a dark forward diagonal pattern (\\\) for the background in a paragraph.

\bgdkbdiag

This control word specifies a dark backward diagonal pattern (///) drawn in the background of a paragraph.

\bgdkcross

This control word specifies a dark cross background pattern drawn in a paragraph.

\bgddkdcross

This control word specifies a dark diagonal cross background pattern for the paragraph.

\cfpatN

This control word specifies the color of the background pattern.

\cbpatN

This is the background color (`N`) of the background pattern.

19.11 Paragraph positioning

The following paragraph formatting control words specify the location of a paragraph on the page.

`\abswN`

This control word specifies absolute width of a frame in twips.

`\abshN`

This control word specifies the height of a frame in twips.

`\phmrg`

This control word specifies the margin as the horizontal reference frame.

`\phpg`

This control word specifies the page as the horizontal reference frame.

`\phcol`

This control word specifies the column as the horizontal reference frame (default if no horizontal frame is defined).

`\posxN`

This control word positions the frame `N` twips from the left edge of the reference frame.

`\posnegxN`

This control word positions as `\posxN`, but allows negative values.

`\posxc`

This control word centers the frame horizontally within the reference frame.

`\posxi`

This control word positions the paragraph horizontally inside the reference frame.

`\posxl`

This control word positions the paragraph to the left within the reference frame.

`\posxo`

This control word positions the paragraph horizontally outside the reference frame.

\posxr

This control word positions the paragraph to the right within the reference frame.

\posyN

This control word positions the paragraph `N` twips from the top edge of the reference frame.

\posnegyN

This control word is the same as `\posyN`, but allows negative values.

\posyil

This control word positions the paragraph vertically in line.

\posyt

This control word positions the paragraph at the top of the reference frame.

\posyc

This control word positions the paragraph vertically centered within the reference frame.

\posyb

This control word positions the paragraph at the bottom of the reference frame.

\pvmrg

This control word positions the reference frame vertically relative to the margin.

\pvpg

This control word positions the reference frame vertically relative to the page.

\nowrap

This control word belongs to the group of text wrapping commands. It prevents text from flowing around *absolute positioned objects* (APO).

\dxfrtextN

This control word defines the distance in twips of an absolute positioned paragraph from text.

\dfrmtxtxN

This control word defines the horizontal distance in twips from text on both sides of the frame.

\dfrmtxtyN

This control word defines the vertical distance in twips from text on both sides of the frame.

\dropcapliN

This control word defines the number of *lines to drop capital* which should be occupied (1–10).

\dropcaptN

This control word defines the *type of drop capital* (1 = in text drop cap, 2 = margin drop cap).

19.12 Table definitions

The RTF specification does not have a table group. Tables are specified as paragraph properties (a sequence of table rows; the rows are sequences of paragraphs partitioned into cells).

\trowd

This control word begins a table row and sets the default values.

\trgraphN

This control word defines half the space between the cells of a table row in twips.

\cellxN

This control word defines the right boundary of a table cell. This definition includes the (half) space between the cells.

\clmgf

This is the first cell (*cell merged first*) in a range of table cells to be merged.

\clmrg

This control word defines the contents of the table cell merged with a preceding cell.

\trql

This control word left-justifies a table row (but respects the containing columns).

\trqr

This control word right-justifies a table row (but respects the containing columns).

\trqc

This control word centers a table row (but respects the containing columns).

\trleftN

This control word defines the position of the left edge of the table.

\trrhN

This control word defines the height of a table row in twips.

\trhdr

This control word defines the table row header.

\trkeep

This table row cannot be split by a page break.

\rtlrow

Cells in this table row will have a right to left precedence.

\lttrow

Cells in this table row will have a left to right precedence (default).

\trbrdrt

Table row border top.

\trbrdrl

Table row border left.

\trbrdrb

Table row border bottom.

\trbrdrr

Table row border right.

\trbrdrh

Table row border horizontal.

\trbrdrv

Table row border vertical.

\cldrdrb

Bottom table cell border.

\clbrdrt

Top table cell border.

\clbrdrl

Left table cell border.

\clbrdrr

Right table cell border.

\clshdngN

This control word defines the shading of a table cell in percent.

\clbg...

These commands (\clbghoriz for instance) define the background pattern of a cell. The shading commands are defined in the paragraph formatting section (*see above*). The prefix bg (\bghoriz) is replaced by the prefix cl (\clhoriz).

19.13 Character formatting properties

The control words in this group define character formatting.

\plain

This control word resets the character formatting properties to default values.

\b

This control word writes the following text in bold. (Parameter 0 switches bold off.)

\caps

This control word writes the following text in capitals. (Parameter 0 switches the mode off.)

\deleted

This control word marks the text as deletion revision marked.

\dnN

This control word defines a subscript position in half points (default 6).

\sub

This control word subscripts text and shrinks point size (according to font size).

\nosupersub

This control word turns off superscripting or subscripting.

\expndN

This control word defines an expansion or compression factor (in quarter points) of the space between characters. Negative values stand for compression (default is 0).

\expndtwN

This control word defines an expansion or compression factor (in quarter points) of the space between characters in twips.

\kerningN

This control word defines the point size (in half points) above which to kern character pairs. (Parameter 0 switches kerning off.)

\f000

This control word defines the font number.

\fs000

This control word selects the font size in ½-points (default 24).

\i

The following text is *italic*. (Parameter 0 switches italic off.)

\outl

This control word defines outlined characters (\outl0 switches this option off).

\revised

The text has been modified since revision marking was turned on.

\revauthN

This control word defines an index to the revision table.

\revdttmN

This control word defines the time of the revision.

`\scaps`

This control word displays the text in SMALL CAPITALS (`\scaps0` switches the mode off).

`\shad`

The following text is shaded. Parameter `0` switches the mode off.

`\strike`

The following text is displayed with ~~strike-through~~ (the parameter `0` switches this mode off).

`\ul`

This control word specifies continuous underlining (`\ul0` switches underlining off).

`\ulw`

This control word switches underlining on for the following word.

`\uld`

This control word switches dotted underlining on.

`\uldb`

This control word specifies double underlining.

`\ulnone`

This control word switches underlining off.

`\up000`

This control word defines the *superscript* position in half points (default `6`).

`\super`

This control word superscripts text and shrinks the point size according to the font used.

`\v`

This control word defines a *hidden text* (`\v0` switches this mode off).

`\cf000`

This control word defines the foreground color (`000` is the index to the color table).

`\cb000`

This control word defines the background color (`000` is the index to the color table).

`\rtlch`

The characters in this text will be treated from right to left.

`\ltrch`

The characters in this text will be treated from left to right (default).

`\csN`

This control word defines a character style.

`\cchsN`

This control word indicates any character not belonging to the default document character set (Macintosh characters > `255`).

`\langN`

This control word applies a language to a character. `N` is the corresponding language.

ID	Language
400H	None
41CH	Albanian
401H	Arabic
421H	Bahasa
813H	Belgian Dutch (Flemish)
80CH	Belgian French (Walloon)
416H	Brazilian Portuguese
402H	Bulgarian
403H	Catalan
41AH	Serbo-Croat (Latin-script)
405H	Czech
406H	Danish
413H	Dutch
C09H	English Australia
809H	English UK

Table 19.6 Language support (*continues over...*)

ID	Language
409H	English US
40BH	Finnish
40CH	French
C0CH	French Canadian
407H	German
408H	Greek
40DH	Hebrew
40EH	Hungarian
40FH	Icelandic
410H	Italian
411H	Japanese (Nihon)
412H	Korean (Hongul)
414H	Norwegian (Bokmål)
814H	Norwegian (Nynorsk)
415H	Polish
816H	Portuguese
417H	Rhaeto-Romanic
418H	Romanian
419H	Russian
81AH	Serbo-Croat (Cyrillic)
804H	Chinese (simplified)
41BH	Slovak
40AH	Spanish (Castilian)
80AH	Spanish (Mexican)
41DH	Swedish
100CH	Swiss French
807H	Swiss German
810H	Swiss Italian
41EH	Thai
404H	Chinese (traditional)
41FH	Turkish
420H	Urdu

Table 19.6
Language support (*cont.*)

! **To read negative `\expnd` values from Word for Macintosh, the reader should use only the low-order six bits.**

The RTF definition uses property association control words. These control words contain a preceding letter a (`\ab`). The control word uses the same syntax as the character formatting control words (`\ab` for bold, `\ai` for italic, and so on). The character formatting control words are described above.

19.14 Special control words

The RTF format defines several special control words for special characters. If a special character control word is not recognized by the RTF reader, it will be ignored and the following text interpreted as plain text.

\chpgn

Current page number defines a new page number as in the header.

\chftn

Current footnote activates the automatic footnote numbering function.

\chdate

Current date defines the current date as in the header.

\chtime

Current time sets the current time as in the header.

\chatn

This control word defines an annotation reference.

\chftnsep

This control word anchors a character for a footnote separator.

\chftnsepc

This control word anchors a character for footnote continuation.

\chdpl

This control word specifies the current date in long format.

\chdpa

This control word specifies the current date in abbreviated format.

\|

This control word starts a formula text.

\:

This control word defines a sub-index.

*****

The RTF reader can ignore the text.

\\~

This control word defines a *fixed space* between two words.

\\-

This control word defines a *non-mandatory hyphen*.

_

This control word defines a *non-breaking hyphen*.

\\'hh

This control word defines a sequence of hexadecimal characters to represent a character.

\page

This control word forces a page break.

\line

This control word forces a line break (no paragraph break).

\par

This control word indicates the end of a paragraph. Can be exchanged with \10 or \13.

\sect

This control word defines the end of a section and paragraph.

\tab

This control word defines the tab character (equivalent to ASCII code 09H).

\cell

This control word defines the end of a table cell.

\row

This control word defines the end of a row in a table.

\column

This control word forces a column break.

\softpage

This control word inserts a non-mandatory page break.

\softcol

This control word inserts a non-mandatory column break.

\softline

This control word inserts a non-mandatory line break.

\softlheightN

This control word defines a non-mandatory line height (prefixed to each line).

\emdash

This control word specifies a long hyphen (em-dash).

\endash

This control word specifies a short hyphen (en-dash).

\emspace

This control word specifies a non-breaking space to the width of the character *m* in the current font.

\enspace

This control word specifies a non-breaking space to the width of the character *n* in the current font.

\bullet

This control word specifies a bullet character.

\lquote

This control word specifies a left single quotation mark.

\rquote

This control word specifies a right single quotation mark.

\ldblquote

This control word specifies a left double quotation mark.

\rdblquote

This control word specifies a right double quotation mark.

\zwj

Zero width joiner (used to ligate words).

\zwnj

Zero width non-joiner (unligate a word).

All 255 characters may be inserted without backslashes for a shorter RTF file. ASCII 9 is treated as a tab, ASCII 10 as a line feed and ASCII 13 as a carriage return. In Word for Windows the following (decimal) codes are defined: 149=`\bullet`, 150=`\endash`, 151=`\emdash`, 145=`\lquote`, 146=`\rquote`, 147=`\ldblquote`, 148=`\rdblquote`.

19.15 Picture control words

RTF files can include pictures from other applications (QuickDraw, Paintbrush, and so on). As a default setting, these pictures are stored in hexadecimal format, but binary format can be defined. Some measurements are in twips (1 twip is 1/20 th of a point).

\pic

This control word defines the picture and must be followed by the control words `brdr`, `shading`, `picttype`, `pictsize`, `metafileinfo` and `data`. The data area is defined as a string of hexadecimal values (default) or a binary sequence. In binary sequences no spaces between the control word and the data are allowed because the RTF reader would interpret these as delimiters. The following control words are optional and define the picture:

- `\pich000`: Defines the *picture height* in pixels. If this parameter is omitted, the height is calculated from the graphic.
- `\piw000`: Defines the *picture width* in pixels (*see* `\pich`).
- `\piwgoal000`: Defines the desired *picture width* in twips.
- `\pihgoal000`: Defines the desired *picture height* in twips.
- `\picscalex000`: Horizontal scaling, `N` is the scale in percent.
- `\picscaley000`: Vertical scaling, `N` is the scale in percent.
- `\picscaled`: This control word is used only with `\macpict` and scales the picture to fit within the specified frame.
- `\piccropt000`: Top cropping value in twips (default `0`). Positive values crop toward the center, negative values crop away from the center.
- `\piccropb000`: Bottom cropping value in twips (default `0`). Positive values crop toward the center, negative values crop away from the center.
- `\piccropl000`: Left cropping value in twips (default `0`). Positive values crop toward the center, negative values crop away from the center.
- `\piccropr000`: Right cropping value in twips (default `0`). Positive values crop toward the center, negative values crop away from the center.

- `\picscaley000`: Vertical scaling, `N` is the scale in percent.
- `\picbmp`: Specifies a metafile which contains bitmap data.
- `\picbppN`: Specifies the bits per pixel in a metafile bitmap (1, 4, 8, 24).
- `\binN`: Defines a picture with data in binary format. The parameter `N` (32 bits) defines the number of following bytes.

\macpict

This control word defines the picture as a QuickDraw picture.

\pmmetafileN

This control word defines an OS/2 metafile picture with type `N` as the picture source. The type is one of the following items:

N	Type
04H	PU_ARBITRARY
08H	PU_PELS
0CH	PU_LOMETRIC
10H	PU_HIMETRIC
14H	PU_LOENGLISH
18H	PU_HIENGLISH
1CH	PU_TWIPS

Table 19.7 PM metafile picture type

\wmetafileN

This control word defines a Windows metafile picture with type `N` as the picture source.

N	Type
1	MM_Text
2	MM_LOMETRIC
3	MM_HIMETRIC
4	MM_LOENGLISH
5	MM_HIENGLISH
6	MM_TWIPS
7	MM_ISOTROPIC
8	MM_ANISOTROPIC

Table 19.8 Windows metafile picture type

A space after the control word is not allowed; it is interpreted as a delimiter in binary format.

\dibitmapN

This control word defines a Windows device-dependent bitmap, where N is the type of the bitmap (0 = monochrome, color, and so on).

\wbitmapN

The source of the picture is a Windows device-independent bitmap. N is the type of the bitmap (default, 0 = monochrome).

19.16 Object control words

Microsoft OLE objects are described using control words from this group.

\object

This control word indicates the start of an object definition. This definition must be followed by the control words:

- \objemb: The object type is embedded.
- \objlink: The object type is linked.
- \objautlink: The object type is auto-linked.
- \objsub: This is a Mac Subscriber
- \objicemb: This is a Mac IC embedder.
- \linkself: The object is linked to another part of the same document.
- \objlock: Locks the object for updates.
- \objclass: Specifies the object class as a text argument.
- \objname: Defines the name of the object.
- \objtime: Describes the time of the last update of the object.

The following control words describe the object size and position:

- \objhN: Defines the object height.
- \objwN: Defines the object width.
- \objsetsize: Forces the object server to set the object to the dimensions defined by the client.
- \objalignN: Defines the align distance in twips from the left edge of the object to tab stop (used for equations).
- \objtransyN: Is the distance in twips the object should be moved vertically (y) from the baseline (used for equations).
- \objcroptN: Defines the top cropping distance in twips.

- \objcropbN: Defines the bottom cropping distance in twips.
- \objcroplN: Defines the left cropping distance in twips.
- \objcroprN: Defines the right cropping distance in twips.
- \objscalexN: Defines the horizontal scaling in percent.
- \objscaleyN: Defines the vertical scaling in percent.
- \objdata: Contains the data for the object.
- \objalias: Contains the object alias record (Macintosh publisher).
- \objsect: Contains the object section record alias record (Macintosh publisher).
- \rsltrtf: Forces result to RTF, if possible.
- \rsltpict: Forces result to Windows metafile or MacPict, if possible.
- \rsltbmp: Forces the result to be a bitmap, if possible.
- \rslttxt: Results in a plain text, if possible.
- \rsltmerge: Uses the formatting of the current result.
- \result: The result destination is optional in the object definition.

The Macintosh uses the control words \bkmkpub (Bookmark Publisher Object) and \pubauto (Publisher object automatic update).

19.17 Drawing objects control words

Drawing objects and drawing primitives use control words with \do... (Drawing objects), \dp... (Drawing primitive), \co... (Call out objects) and \fill... (Fill). These objects are described in the RTF specification, version 1.2.

19.18 Miscellaneous control words

The RTF specifications define several other control words for miscellaneous parts.

\footnote

This control word introduces a footnote.

\annotation

This control word introduces an annotation. If the annotation is associated with a bookmark, the control words {*\atrfstart N} {*\atrfend N} embed the bookmark. N is the name of the bookmark.

- \annotid: Defines the annotation ID.
- \atnauthor: Defines the annotation author.
- \atntime: Defines the time the annotation was created.

Some additional control words for annotation parameters are defined in the RTF specifications.

\field

This is a group to describe Word fields. The following control words are defined to describe field parameters:

- \flddirty: The field has been changed since the last update.
- \fldedit: Text has been edited since the last update.
- \fldlock: Field locked.
- \fldpriv: Result is not displayable.

\xe

The index group starts with \xe. It is followed by several control words:

- \xefN: Allows multiple indices within the same document.
- \bxe: Formats page numbers in cross-reference bold.
- \ixe: Formats page numbers in cross-reference italic.
- \txe text: Uses text argument instead of a page number.
- \rxe bookmark: Uses a text marker to define a range.

\toc

This control word defines the table of contents. The following control words are allowed for building up the table of contents:

- \tcfN: Compiles the table (N is mapped to A–Z, default is C).
- \tclN: Level number (default = 1).

19.19 Bookmark

The bookmark group contains only a few control words:

- `\*\bkmkstart`: Beginning of a bookmark.
- `\*\bkmkend`: End of a bookmark.

The `\bkmkcolN` is used to denote the first column of a table covered by a bookmark. `\bkmkcollN` denotes the last column.

20

Standard Generalized Markup Language (SGML)

The *file formats defined in the previous chapters are vendor-specific. To facilitate document exchange, the ISO Standard 8879 Standard Generalized Markup Language (SGML) was defined in 1986. The 1988 modified version is now available as a global standard for text exchange.*

20.1 Structure of an SGML file

SGML is a meta-language for describing text format. It contains elements for defining:

- the structure of a document
- the character set used
- parts of text used frequently
- external information used in the text
- techniques for the creation of layouts
- formatting commands

SGML is based on the ISO 646 7-bit character set, which ensures that document exchange is possible. All definitions, control commands and texts are written in plain text. The file is divided into an SGML declaration section and a section relating to the actual document. The declaration section contains information to initialize the SGML parser. This information is used by the SGML parser, and includes details of the character set, definitions of the scopes and syntax used and data on the amount of memory required for formatting. SGML definitions are enclosed in angle brackets <>. A declaration always begins with an exclamation mark followed by the keyword SGML. Figure 20.1 shows an extract from a valid SGML declaration:

```
<!SGML "ISO 8879-1986"
    Declaration for a Basic SGML Document
 CHARSET BASESET  "ISO 646-1983//CHARSET International
                  Reference Version (IRV)//ESC 2/5 4/0"

        DESCSET  0 9 UNUSED
                 9 2 9
                 11 2 UNUSED
 CAPACITY PUBLIC "ISO 8879-1986//CAPACITY Reference//EN"
 SCOPE    DOCUMENT
 SYNTAX   SHUNCHAR CONTROLS 0 1 2 3 4 5
                            127 255
          BASESET "ISO 646-1983//CHARSET International
                  Reference Version (IRV)//ESC 2/5 4/0"
          DESCSET 0 128 0
          FUNCTION RE    13
                   RS    10
                   SPACE 32
    ...
```

Figure 20.1
Part of an SGML declaration

A detailed definition is given in ISO Standard 8879.[1]

20.2 Structure of a document

The SGML declaration is followed by the actual text document, which comprises pure text and additional embedded control commands specifying the format of the text. Characters from the ISO 646 7-bit character set defined in the header are permitted for both text and control commands. There is an extension to this character set for multinational characters such as the German umlaut accent. The relevant character is preceded by and terminated by a semicolon or a blank. The coding for the German umlaut is shown in Table 20.1

`Ü`	Ü
`ü`	ü
`Ä`	Ä
`ä`	ä
`Ö`	Ö
`ö`	ö
`ß`	ß

Table 20.1
German umlaut coding in SGML

1 ***Information processing – Text and Office Systems.*** ISO 8879, Standard Generalized Markup Language (SGML)

A document in SGML notation is divided into three parts:

- the SGML *header* defining of the title
- the actual *text*
- the *appendix* containing the index, and so on.

The document must be structured hierarchically. To ensure exchangeability, the structures of a number of document types have been defined and published (*public*),[2] but it is possible to define new document types for private use (*private*).

Initially, the type of document (report, letter, book, and so on) is specified via an SGML declaration. This is followed by additional control commands giving information on the text format. Control commands in SGML always consist of letters and are enclosed between angle brackets <>. The end of each control command is indicated by repeating the same command, but with an oblique in front of it. Figure 20.2 shows an example in which a list is defined with the following sequence of commands:

```
<li> ...
 .......
</li>
```

```
<!DOCTYPE report PUBLIC"_">
<report>
<title>The SGML Standard
<author>Born Gunter
<p>SGML is a standardized language for the exchange of text
between different word processing programs and systems.
<p>SGML defines<li number=alpha>
<it>the structure of a document
<it>the character set used
<it>external information
<it>the text formats</li>
<h1>the document structure
<p>A <hp1>document</hp1> consists of nested
<ix>elements</ix>.
...
</report>
```

Figure 20.2
Part of an SGML document

2 Martin Bryan: ***SGML: An Author's Guide to the Standard Generalized Markup Language***
Addison Wesley, 1988, Wokingham, England, ISBN 0-201-17535-5

The following table lists some of the SGML commands:

Command	Description
`<abstract>`	Abstract of contents
`<acknowls>`	Acknowledgments
	`number` = number
	`id` = identifier for cross-reference
	`stitle` = short version title
`<adr>`	Address
`<appendix>`	Appendices to main body of text
	`number` = number
	`id` = identifier for cross-reference
	`stitle` = short version title
`<artwork>`	Space for insertion of artwork
	`sizex` = width of artwork
	`sizey` = depth of artwork
	`file` = name of artwork file
`<author>`	Author of publication
`<bibliog>`	Bibliography
	`number` = number
	`id` = identifier for cross-reference
	`stitle` = short version title
`<body>`	Main body of text
`<book>`	Defines a book
`<bt>`	Body of table
	`col` = number of columns
`<c>`	Cell of table row
	`straddle` = number of columns cell straddles
`<cit>`	Citation (reference to another publication)
	`id` = identifier for cross-reference
`<citref>`	Citation references
	`refid` = referred to identifier
	`page` = yes (add page number to reference)
`<colophon>`	Printer's colophon
`<copyright>`	Copyright details
`<date>`	Date of publication
`<dedicate>`	Dedication of book
`<details>`	Publication details

Table 20.2 Commands in SGML (*continues over...*)

Command	Description
<dd>	Definition of defined term
<ddhd>	Heading for definition column
	style = type style for heading
<docnum>	Number or other identifier of document
<dt>	Defined term
	id = identifier for cross-reference
<dthd>	Heading for defined terms column
	style = type style for heading
<editor>	Editor of publication
<eqn>	Equation
	type = type of notation used
<fig>	Figure
	id = identifier for cross-reference
	number = figure number (if fixed)
	frame = type of frame (box or rules)
	position = position in page (top, bottom, ...)
	type = column
	align = type of alignment (left, right, ...)
<figbody>	Body of figure
	form = runon
<figcap>	Caption for figure
<figdesc>	Description of figure
<figlist>	Position of list of figures
<figref>	Cross-reference to figure
	refid = referred to unique identifier
	pages = yes (add page number to reference)
<fn>	Footnote
	id = identifier for cross-reference
<fnref>	Cross-reference to footnote
	refid = referred to unique identifier
	pages = yes (add page number to reference)
<foreword>	Foreword
	number = number
	d = identifier for cross-reference
	stitle = short version of title
<from>	Defines the sender

Table 20.2 Commands in SGML (*cont.*)

Command	Description
<front>	Front matter of book
<ft>	Foot of table
	`col` = number of columns covered
<gd>	Definition of glossary term
	`source` = source of definition
	`see` = cross-reference to other definition
	`seealso` = link to further definition
<gdg>	Group of glossary definitions
	`number` = form of numbering required
<gl>	Glossary list
	`form` = compact (no space between entries)
	`termhi` = level of highlighting for terms
<glossary>	Start of glossary
	`number` = number
	`id` = identifier for cross-reference
	`stitle` = short version title
<gt>	Glossary term
	`id` = identifier for cross-reference
<h0>	Highest division of text
	`number` = number
	`id` = identifier for cross-reference
	`stitle` = short version title
<h0t>	Part title
<h1>	Main division of text
	`number` = number
	`id` = identifier for cross-reference
	`stitle` = short version title
<h1t>	Chapter title
<h2>	Section within main division of text
	`number` = number
	`id` = identifier for cross-reference
	`stitle` = short version title
<h1t>	Section title
<h3>	Subsection within main division of text
	`number` = number
	`id` = identifier for cross-reference
	`stitle` = short version title

Table 20.2 Commands in SGML (*cont.*)

Command	Description
<h3t>	Subsection title
<h4>	Sub-subsection within subsection of text
	number = number
	id = identifier for cross-reference
	stitle = short version title
<h4t>	Sub-subsection title
<h5>	Lowest level of numbered heading
	number = number
	id = identifier for cross-reference
	stitle = short version title
<h5t>	Low level title
<hc>	Heading for table columns
	cols = number of columns covered
<hd>	Other type of heading
	id = identifier for cross-reference
<hdref>	Cross-reference to heading
	refid = identifier for cross-reference
	page = yes (add page number)
<hp0>	Highlighted phrase, style 0
<hp1>	Highlighted phrase, style 1
<hp2>	Highlighted phrase, style 2
<hp3>	Highlighted phrase, style 3
<ht>	Heading of table
<index>	Position of index
<ISBN>	International Standard Book Number
	type = serial (ISBN number)
<it>	Item list
	id = identifier for cross-reference
<itref>	Cross-reference to item in list
	refid = referred to identifier
	pages = yes (add page number)
<ix>	Index entry
	id = identifier for cross-reference
	print = printed form of entry
	linkwith = listed under ...
	andwith = also listed under ...
	see = cross-reference to other definition

Table 20.2 Commands in SGML (*cont.*)

Command	Description
`<l>`	Line of text
	`position` = position
`<letter>`	Defines a letter
`<li>`	List
	`number` = type of numbering required
	`form` = compact (no space between entries)
`<LibCong>`	Library of Congress Cataloging in Publication data
`<lq>`	Long quotation
`<m>`	Defines a memo
`<name>`	Name of author/editor
`<note>`	Note
`<nt>`	Number of table
`<others>`	Other matter within preliminary pages
	`number` = number
	`id` = identifier for cross-reference
	`stitle` = short version title
`<p>`	Paragraph of text
`<poem>`	One or more poems
`<position>`	Position held by author
`<preface>`	Preface
	`number` = number
	`id` = identifier for cross-reference
	`stitle` = short version title
`<pt>`	Poem title
`<publishr>`	Publisher
`<q>`	Quotation within text
`<r>`	Row in table
`<report>`	Defines a report document
`<related>`	Related publications
`<subtitle>`	Subtitle of the document
`<table>`	Table within text
	`id` = identifier for cross-reference
	`cols` = maximum column numbers
	`tabs` = string with tab positions
`<tableref>`	Cross-reference to table
	`refid` = referred identifier to reference
	`pages` = yes (add page numbers)
`<terms>`	List of term definitions
	`style` = columns (terms and definitions)

Table 20.2 Commands in SGML (*cont.*)

Command	Description
<textbook>	Name of main document type
	`version` = version number or date
	`status` = status of document
	`security` = classification
<th>	Topic heading
<title>	Title of the document
	`htitle` = alternative form of half title
	`running` = alternative form of running headline
<titlep>	Title page
<tline>	Line within document title
<to>	Defines the receiver
<toc>	Position of table of contents
<top1>	First level topic
	`id` = identifier for cross-reference
<top2>	Second level topic
	`id` = identifier for cross-reference
<top3>	Third level topic
	`id` = identifier for cross-reference
<v>	Verse of poem
	`no` = number of verse
<xmp>	Example
	`style` = name of required format
	`keep` = number of lines kept on first page
	`form` = run on (ignore line ending in example)

Table 20.2 Commands in SGML (*cont.*)

A detailed description of the SGML specification is given in the ISO standard[3] and in Bryan.[4]

3 ***Information Processing – Text and Office Systems.*** ISO 8879, Standard Generalized Markup Language (SGML)
4 Martin Bryan: ***SGML: An Author's Guide to the Standard Generalized Markup Language*** Addison Wesley, 1988, Wokingham, England, ISBN 0-201-17535-5

21

AMI Pro version 3.0/4.0 file format

AMI Pro is a word processing program from Lotus. An AMI Pro document is stored in a file with the extension `.SAM`. To ensure that the file can be edited by a text editor, the contents of this file are held in 7-bit ASCII characters (with some exceptions).

The AMI Pro file format is compatible across several versions. In AMI Pro versions prior to 2.0, graphics included in documents are stored separately in `.Gxx` files, where `xx` stands for continuous numbers (`00`, `01`, `02`, and so on). From AMI Pro version 2.0, graphic data is stored at the end of a `.SAM` file. This section is marked by an `[embedded]` section header.

AMI Pro uses style sheets to format the document. The contents of these `.STY` files are identical to a `.SAM` file with the exception that there is no reference to a style sheet. An additional command `[newmac]` is used to specify a macro name. This macro is executed when the style sheet is opened.

21.1 The contents of a SAM file

All AMI Pro document files contain three sections:

- A structured section in the header defines all the information required to format the document.
- The structured section is followed by an unstructured section containing the main body of the text. This section includes headers, footers, notes, and so on.
- The last section is reserved for embedded data (pictures, equations, and so on).

The structured section at the beginning of the document is divided into parts, describing the components of the document (frames, layouts, styles, and so on).

- Each part begins with a keyword, embedded in brackets `[...]` (similar to the Windows init files).
- The `[...]` must be at the beginning of a line.
- The keyword is followed by a variable number of lines defining the data. These lines are indented by one or more tabs, to introduce a hierarchical structure to the text.
- Numeric fields in a line are defined as signed ASCII values.
- Dimensions and measurements are always in twips (1440 twips = 1 inch or 20 points).
- Flags and bitfields are stored as ASCII strings. To obtain the value of a bitfield, all the values should be added to produce the whole binary number.
- If a line contains bulleted text or a style name containing 8-bit characters, an escape sequence is used to preserve the 7-bit character of the file.

Details of these parts are defined in the next section.

21.2 Document section

All parts in this section have a keyword in the first line:

```
[keyword]
tab data line 1
tab data line 2
....
```

Table 21.1 The structure of an AMI Pro part

The following lines are indented by one or more tabs and contain the part data.

[encrypt]

This part is only present if the file is encrypted. The second line contains the *password*. In this case everything in the `.SAM` file is encrypted.

[ver]

This part indicates the version number of the software that created this file, and must precede the `[sty]` keyword. The line after the `[ver]` keyword contains the number of the AMI Pro file. This is not the version number of the software release; it is the version number of the file format used. AMI Pro 1.0 uses version 3.0, while AMI Pro 1.1 uses version 4.0 which is a superset of version 3.0. This chapter describes version 4.0 of the AMI Pro file format, making reference to the differences between this and the older versions.

[sty]

This part must follow a [ver] description and defines the name of the style sheet file for the document. If the file is a .STY file, the part is omitted. If the .SAM file was saved with the *Keep the format with document* option, the line after the keyword is blank. If this line is not present, the program displays an error message.

[files]

This part defines the names of additional files (imported graphics such as TIFF or PCX) used in the document. Imported files are defined with a full path, if they are stored on disk. Clipboard bitmaps are shown with the .Gxx extension. File names for drawings or DDE file links are also defined in this part.

[revision]

This part describes a flag, which is set to 1 if revision marking is on. If the line following the keyword contains a 0, there is no revision marking.

[recfiles]

This part describes a record file to merge with the document. The lines after the keyword describe the file name or the merge options. AMI Pro prints labels through merges (labels are treated as miniature pages filed on the label sheet). The lines after the keyword are in the following format:

Parameter	
Record file name (maximum 80 bytes)	
Description file (maximum 80 bytes)	
used only if the record file is not an AMI Pro file	
Flags (ASCII)	
1:	Merge Print
2:	Merge View Print
4:	Merge Save As
8:	With Conditions
16:	As Label
64:	New Wave Object
128:	New Wave Description Object
Units (1 = inch, 2 = centimeters, 3 = pica, 4 = points)	
Label Across (small number)	
Label Down (small number)	
First Down (<= 32 768 twips, 1 twip = 1/1440 inch)	
First Right (<= 32 768 twips)	

Table 21.2 [recfiles] data

All values are defined in ASCII characters.

[toc]

This part defines the *table of contents* and is only present in an AMI Pro file if the user has generated such a table in the document.

Parameter
Style for level one (name of the style used)
Style for level two
Style for level three
Separator for level one (string)
Separator for level two
Separator for level three
Flags
1: Use page number on level 1
2: Right-align level 1 number
4: Use page number on level 2
8: Right-align level 2 number
16: Use page number on level 3
32: Right-align level 3 number

Table 21.3
[toc] data

This part defines the options for regenerating the table of contents.

[master]

This part contains the master document information.

Parameter
Table of Contents name (maximum 78 characters)
Index name (maximum 78 characters)
Index flag (1 if separate rows for index)
Length of file list in bytes
Number of files
File list

Table 21.4
[master] data

This part appears in each master document.

[sequence]

This part describes a section sequence.

Parameter
Page number at which to start
Footnote number at which to start
Note number at which to start
Number of section sequences
Number of styles
For each section
Section number
Section name
For each style
Style number
Style name

Table 21.5 [sequence] data

This part will appear in each sub-document corresponding to a master document.

[desc]

This part specifies a document description containing several user-defined comments, the revision date, and other information.

Parameter
Description (maximum 120 characters)
User-defined field 1 (maximum 34 characters)
User-defined field 2 (maximum 34 characters)
User-defined field 3 (maximum 34 characters)
User-defined field 4 (maximum 34 characters)
Last revision date (in seconds since 1/1/1980, 12:00 a.m.)
Number of edits
Creation date (in seconds since 1/1/1980)
Edit time (total minutes to edit)
Number of pages in the file
Number of words in the file
Number of characters in the file
File size in Kbytes

Table 21.6 [desc] data (*continues over...*)

Parameter
Size of text (no longer used)
Keywords
Locked flag (if locked, the user name is given here, otherwise the field is empty {blank line})
Description field 5
Description field 6
Description field 7
Description field 8

Table 21.6
[desc] data
(*cont.*)

This data is used from version 4.0 (AMI Pro 1.1) onwards.

[book]

This part lists bookmarks in tables. Each bookmark is separated by spaces.

Parameter
Name of the bookmark
Number of the frame holding the table (user)
Row
Column

Table 21.7
[book] data

[prn]

This part contains the name of the printer for which the document is formatted. The name is the logical name listed in the Windows control panel. The driver name may also be listed (separated from the printer name by a comma).

Future versions of AMI Pro will use the driver name. If the line after [prn] is blank or if the part is missing from the file, AMI Pro uses the default printer from the Windows control panel.

[stpg]

This part is used in older versions and defines the first page number for the page numbering option. If the part is missing, AMI Pro starts with number 1. In version 4.0 the page number is stored in each page number mark.

[lang]

This part defines the language for the document. This definition is used for hyphenation and proofing.

Code	Language
1	American English
2	British English
3	French
4	Canadian French
5	Italian
6	Spanish
7	German
8	Dutch
9	Swedish
10	Norwegian
11	Danish
12	Portuguese
13	Finnish
14	Medical
15	Legal
16	Greek
17	Portuguese Brazil
18	Australian English
19	Polish
20	Russian

Table 21.8
Language coding

All values are in ASCII. If this part is omitted, AMI Pro uses American English.

[fopts]

This part defines the footnote options in AMI Pro and has the following structure:

Parameter	
Options flag	
	1: Gather at end of page
	2: Reset page number on each page
	4: Separator line
Start number (<= 9999)	
Separator line length (<= 32767 twips)	
Starting indent for footnotes (<= 32767 twips)	

Table 21.9
[fopts] data

[newmac]

This part only appears in style sheets and it designates the macro to be executed if the style sheet is opened.

Parameter
Macro name
Flag
0: Do not run the macro on open
1: Run the macro on open

Table 21.10
[newmac] data

[lnopts]

This part defines the line-numbering options in AMI Pro and has the following structure:

Parameter		
Options flag		
	1:	Number lines
	2:	Every line
	4:	Every odd line
	8:	Every fifth line
	16:	Reset each page
	32:	Every nth line
TAG name for formatting line numbers (<= 13 bytes)		
*n*th line distance		

Table 21.11
[lnopts] data

[docopts]

This part defines document options in AMI Pro. These options provide information which does not belong to the paragraph style or page layout (hyphenation, kerning, and so on).

Parameter	
Hyphenation hot zone (number of characters, maximum 9)	
Flags:	
1:	Kerning
2:	Widow/orphan control
4:	Background printing
8:	Background flowing
16:	Snap always
32:	Snap when open
64:	Snap never

Table 21.12
[docopts] data

These options apply to formatting throughout the document.

[tag]

The tag part defines the paragraph style.

Parameter
Tag name (maximum 13 characters)
Function key number (<=16, not 1 or 10)

Table 21.13
[tag] data

Each style sheet and each document without a style sheet is required to have one *body text*.

[fnt]

This part defines font information (typeface, font size, and so on).

Parameter
Typeface name (maximum 32 characters)
Size (in twips)
Color in standard RGB values
Black 0

Table 21.14
[fnt] data
(*continues over...*)

Parameter		
	Blue 16711680	
	Red 255	
	Magenta 16711935	
	Green 65280	
	Yellow 65535	
	Cyan 16776960	
	White 16777215	
Flags:		
	1:	Bold
	2:	Italic
	4:	Underline
	8:	Word underline
	16:	Capitals
	32:	Small capitals (Not in AMI Pro 1.0)
	64:	Double underline (Not in 1.0)
	128:	Strike through (Not in 1.0)
	256:	Superscript
	512:	Subscript
	1024:	All lower case
	2048:	Initial capitals
	4096:	First line bold
	16384:	Variable pitch
	32768:	Serif font

Table 21.14 [fnt] data (*cont.*)

Variable pitch and *serif font* are used when the exact font is not available. The colors are defined as valid RGB colors from Windows 3.0.

[algn]

This part contains alignment information and has the following structure:

Parameter		
Flags:		
	1:	Left align
	2:	Right align
	4:	Centered
	8:	Justify alignment

Table 21.15 [algn] data (*continues over...*)

Parameter	
16:	Indent both sides equally
256:	Hyphenation
512:	Indent tab
Align units (1: inch, 2: centimeters, 3: pica, 4: points)	
Indent all (<= 32767 twips)	
Indent first (<= 32767 twips)	
Indent rest (<= 32767 twips)	

Table 21.15 [algn] data (*cont.*)

Indent all applies from right and left if the flag *both sides* is set.

[spc]

This part defines the spacing between lines parameter.

Parameter	
Flags:	
1:	Single spacing
2:	1½ spacing
4:	Double spacing
8:	Custom spacing
16:	Add space always (applies to paragraph)
32:	Add space not at break (applies to paragraph)
Line spacing (<= 32767 twips)	
Spacing units (1,2,3,4)	
Paragraph above spacing (<= 32767 twips)	
Paragraph below spacing (<= 32767 twips)	
Paragraph spacing units (1: inch, 2: centimeters, 3: pica, 4: points)	
Line tightness (90, 100, 115)	

Table 21.16 [spc] data

The *add space* option is applied to the paragraph spacing, not to the line spacing. For *line tightness*, all values can be entered, but only three values are accepted.

[brk]

This part defines the page and column breaks.

Parameter	
Flags:	
1:	Page break before
2:	Page break after
4:	Page break within
8:	Keep with previous
16:	Keep with next
32:	Use tabs
64:	Next style
128:	Column break before
256:	Column break after

Table 21.17
[brk] data

The parameters for page breaks control paragraph formatting.

[line]

This part defines lines within a paragraph.

Parameter		
Flags:		
1:	Line above paragraph	
2:	Line below paragraph	
4:	Width of text line	
8:	Width of margin line	
16:	Custom line width	
Line length (<= 32 767 twips, if custom line)		
Length units (1: inch, 2: centimeters, 3: pica, 4: points)		
Line color (any valid Windows RGB value)		
	Black	0
	75% gray	12566463
	50% gray	8355711
	25% gray	4144949
	10% gray	1644825

Table 21.18
[line] data
(continues over...)

Parameter		
	Blue	16711680
	Red	255
	Magenta	16711935
	Green	65280
	Yellow	65535
	Cyan	16776960
	White	16777215
Reserved		
Line above style		
	1:	½ point
	2:	1 point
	3:	2 point
	4:	4 point
	5:	5 point
	6:	8 point
	7:	12 point
	8:	Double 1 pt–1 pt
	9:	Double 2 pt–2 pt
	10:	1 pt–2 pt–1pt
	11:	2 pt–1 pt
	12:	1 pt–2 pt
Line below style (same values)		
Line above spacing (<= 32767 twips)		
Line below spacing (<= 32767 twips)		
Line units (1: inch, 2: centimeters, 3: pica, 4: points)		

Table 21.18 [line] data (*cont.*)

The part defines the line style and the distance between the paragraph text and the line.

[spec]

Special characters (bullets, and so on.) used in the document are defined in this part.

Parameter
Unused (was bullet type in version 3.0)
Outline level (0–6 for numbering)
Bullet text (maximum 31 characters)
Unused

Table 21.19 [spec] data (*continues over...*)

Parameter	
Space units (1: inch, 2: centimeters, 3: pica, 4: points)	
Tab after flag (not used in 2.0)	
	0: Yes
	1: No
Bullet attributes	
Numbering flag	
	2: After lesser level
	4: After intervening level
	8: For legal (cumulative)

Table 21.19 [spec] data (*cont.*)

The bullet text may include the special characters below normal ANSI characters with (decimal) codes 8, 10–30. The *bullet attributes* are defined in the *Tag Font Flag*.

[nfmt]

This part defines the format of a numeric value in a table cell.

Parameter		
Alignment flag:		
	1:	Top of cell (not in AMI Pro 1.1)
	2:	Middle of cell (not in AMI Pro 1.1)
	4:	Bottom of cell (not in AMI Pro 1.1)
	8:	Use thousands separator
	16:	Use leading minus
	32:	Use trailing minus
	64:	Use parentheses for negative
	128:	Use red for negative
	256:	Use leading currency symbol
Cell format flag		
	1:	General
	2:	Fixed
	3:	Currency
	4:	Percent
Number of decimal places (maximum 15)		
Decimal symbol (1 character)		
Thousands separator (1 character)		
Currency symbol (3 characters)		
Next style name		

Table 21.20 [nfmt] data (*continues over...*)

Parameter
Number of tabs
For each tab one of the following elements:
type
offset in twips
Indent from right

Table 21.20
[nfmt] data
(*cont.*)

The tab type coding is the same as in the [frmlay] part.

[frm]

This part contains the frame description.

Parameter		
Page number (<= 32767)		
Flags:		
	1:	Bitmap (imported or clipboard)
	2:	Draw (not in AMI Pro 1.0)
	4:	Table (not in AMI Pro 1.0)
	8:	Internal use
	16:	Revision mark created
	32:	In a table cell
	64:	Opaque
	128:	Wrap around
	256:	Repeating
	512:	Text frame
The next bits are used only for frames containing text		
	1024:	Internal use (initialized to 0)
	2048:	Header
	4096:	Footer
	8192:	Odd page (not in AMI Pro 1.0)
	16384:	Internal use (initialized to 0)
	32768:	Imported
	65536:	Has line around frame
	121072:	No wrap beside

Table 21.21
[frm] data
(*continues over...*)

Parameter	
262144:	Metafile (not in AMI Pro 1.0)
524288:	Anchored (floating, not in AMI Pro 1.0)
1048576:	Page table (table file 0, not in AMI Pro 1.0)
2097152:	DDE frame (not used in AMI Pro 1.0)
4194394:	Even page repeat (not in AMI Pro 1.0)
8388608:	Grouped (not in AMI Pro 1.0)
16777216:	First frame in group (grouped field must be set, not used in AMI Pro 1.0)
33554432:	Last frame in group (grouped field must be set, not used in AMI Pro 1.0)
67208864:	Table of contents (table and page table must be set, not used in AMI Pro 1.0)
134217728:	Internal use (initialized to 0)
268435456:	New wave frame
536870912:	ISD frame
1073741824:	EPS frame
2114783648:	Revision mark deleted
Left offset (<= 32 767 twips)	
Top offset (<= 32 767 twips)	
Right offset (<= 32 767 twips)	
Bottom offset (<= 32 767 twips)	
Line around frame borders flag	
1:	All sides
2:	Left side
4:	Right side
8:	Top side
16:	Bottom side
Not used	
Border line position	
1:	Middle
2:	Inside
3:	Outside
4:	Close inside
5:	Close outside
Border line type (*see* Tag Line Style: Table 21.18)	

Table 21.21 `[frm]` data (*cont.*)

Parameter	
Shadow left (in twips)	
Shadow top (in twips)	
Shadow right (in twips)	
Shadow bottom (in twips)	
Rounded corners flag (% of width and height to round)	
Shadow color (RGB value)	
Border line color (*see* Tag Line Color: Table 21.18)	
Background color (*see* Tag Line Color: Table 21.18)	
If the frame is anchored:	ordinal number of anchor escape field in text
	desired indent in twips from column margin
	desired frame width in twips
If the frame is a DDE target:	application
	topic
	item

Table 21.21 [frm] data (*cont.*)

The shadow rectangle values are always non-negative. The specified amount of shadow should be displayed from the frame in each direction.

[frmmac]

This part contains the name of the macro to be run when the frame is selected.

[frmname]

This part contains the frame name (frame number) in ASCII.

[frmlay]

This part defines the layout of the (page) frame (width, margins, gutter, and so on) for the document.

Parameter
Length (<= 32 767 twips, to bottom of frame)
Width (<= 32 767 twips, frame right to frame left)
Not used
Left margin (<= 32 767 twips, from left of frame)
Bottom margin (<= 32 767 twips, from bottom of frame)

Table 21.22 [frmlay] data (*continues over...*)

Parameter
Margin units (1: inch, 2: centimeters, 3: pica, 4: points)
Top margin (<= 32767 twips, top of frame + top margin)
Right margin (<= 32767 twips, from right of frame)
Flags:
1: Column balance
2: Gutter line
4: —
Gutter line type (*see* Tag Line Above Style: Table 21.18)
Gutter color (*see* Tag Line Color: Table 21.18)
Not used
Not used
Not used
Number of columns (<= 32767)
For each column:
Left (offset from left of page, <= 32767 twips)
Right (offset from left of page, <= 32767 twips)
Number of tabs (<= 32767 tabs in this column)
For each tab in the column
Type Flag:
1: Left tab
2: Center tab
4: Numeric tab
16384: Leader hyphen
32768: Leader dot
49152: Leader underline
Offset from current column (<= 32767 twips)

Table 21.22 [frmlay] data (*cont.*)

The frame definition is followed by parts containing a description of the frame contents.

[txt]

This part follows a [frmlay] part if the frame is a text frame. The text is formatted according to the normal rules for text formatting. The *End Of Text* marker must be at the left margin of the file without tabs.

[btmap]

This part follows a frame structure, if the frame contains a bitmap. This part is not used in the version 2.0 specification.

Parameter
Bitmap type (set to 0, is used by Windows)
Width (in pixels, <= 32 767)
Height (in pixels, <= 32 767)
Width in bytes (rounded to whole number from width in pixels)
Bit planes (for color)
Bits/pixel (must be 1)
XOffset for cropping (–32 716 to 32 767 twips)
YOffset for cropping (–32 716 to 32 767 twips)
XSize of the image (scaling)
YSize of the frame (scaling)
XSize of the original bitmap
YSize of the original bitmap
Flags: 1: Original size 2: Fit in frame 4: Percentage 8: Custom size 16: Maintain aspect 32: Internal use (0) 64: Internal use (0) 128: Internal use (0) 256: Rotated 512: Internal use (0) 1024: EPS file 2048: Gray level TIFF file 4096: EPS with no display image
Units (1: inch, 2: centimeters, 3: pica, 4: points)
Name (duplicate for compatibility with older versions)
Path name (blank if pasted bitmap, path name if the graphic is an imported bitmap)
Image processing flag (not for AMI Pro 1.0): 1: Edge enhancements 2: Smooth edge 4: Negate 8: Brightness 16: Contrast

Table 21.23 [btmap] data (*continues over...*)

Parameter
— *remaining bits used internally*
Image processing brightness (0–255)
Image processing contrast (0–255)
Image processing gray level (2, 4, 6, 8 bits per sample)
Scaling percentage (1–page size%)
If the image is a drawing (not used in version 2.0)
Internal use
XSize of the original frame scaling use – Xsize of image
YSize of the original frame scaling use – Ysize of image
Units (1: inch, 2: centimeters, 3: pica, 4: points)
XSize of the image (for scaling)
YSize of the image (for scaling)
Scaling percentage (1-page size%)
If it is a NewWave object
Internal use (0)
Object reference number
View (given by NewWave)
Object opened (was in zoomed mode)
Opened (object is opened)

Table 21.23 [btmap] data (*cont.*)

[ISD]

This part follows a table structure, if the table contains an ISD (Image Structure Descriptor).

Parameter		
Source file name or `.Gxx` or `.Xxx`, where `xx` is a number		
Data format (file extension)		
Snapshot name (empty if no snapshot, use `.Gxx` or `.Xxx`)		
Scale flags:		
	1:	Original size
	2:	Fit in frame
	4:	Percentage
	8:	Custom size

Table 21.24 [isd] data (*continues over...*)

Parameter
Scale units (1: inch, 2: centimeters, 3: pica, 4: points)
Scale rectangle left (–32 757 to 32 767 twips)
Scale rectangle top (–32 757 to 32 767 twips)
Scale rectangle right (–32 757 to 32 767 twips)
Scale rectangle bottom (–32 757 to 32 767 twips)
Scale percent (only if scale in percent)
Rotation (clockwise in 1⁄10 degree)
Context size (library context size in words)
Context
Context format (context creator format)
Crop point X (in twips from left of frame, –32 767 to 32 767)
Crop point Y (in twips from top of frame, –32 767 to 32 767)
Filter context size
Filter context contents

Table 21.24 [isd] data (*cont.*)

[tbl]

This part follows a table structure. The following fields are on a single line, separated by spaces.

Parameter	
Number of rows (1–4000)	
Number of columns (2, initialized to 0)	
Default row height (<= 32 767 twips)	
Default gutter height (<= 32 767 twips)	
Default column width (<= 32 767 twips)	
Default gutter width (<= 32 767 twips)	
Flags:	
	1: Auto row grow
	2: Internal use (2, initialized to 0)
	4: If page table is centered
	8: Honor protection

Table 21.25 [tbl] data

The part describes a table.

[h]

This part follows a table structure and describes customized rows.

Parameter	
Row number (0 based)	
Height (<= 32767 twips)	
Gutter height (<= 32767 twips)	
Flags:	
1:	Contains connected cell
2:	Unique row height
4:	Unique gutter height
16:	Row is in heading
32:	Page break after row
64:	Created row with revision mark
128:	Deleted row with revision mark
Internal use (initialized to 0)	
Internal use (initialized to 0)	
Internal use (initialized to 0)	
...additional lines with the same fields	
[e] end of [h] record	

Table 21.26
[h] data

These seven fields are all on one line, separated by spaces. The part contains a line for each customized row and is terminated by the [e] keyword.

[w]

This part follows a table structure and describes customized columns.

Parameter	
Column number (0 based)	
Width (<= 32767 twips)	
Gutter width (<= 32767 twips)	
Flags:	
1:	Contains connected cell
2:	Unique cell width
4:	Unique gutter width

Table 21.27
[w] data
(continues over...)

Parameter	
16:	Columns in heading
32:	Page break after cell
64:	Created cell with revision mark
128:	Deleted cell with revision mark
Internal use (initialized to 0)	
...additional lines with the same fields	
[e] end of [w] record	

Table 21.27
[w] data
(*cont.*)

These fields are on one line, separated by spaces. The part contains a line for each customized column and is terminated by the [e] keyword.

[data]

This part contains cell data.

Parameter	
Row number (0 based)	
Column number (0 based)	
Flag 1	
1:	Internal use
2:	Internal use
4:	Internal use
8:	Left-aligned cell
16:	Right-aligned cell
24:	Center-aligned cell
32:	Justify cell
64:	Formula cell
128:	Part of a connected cell
256:	Top, left connected cells
512:	Cell with background shade
1024:	Internal use
2048:	Internal use
4096:	Internal use
Formula references in flags	
8192:	Invalid cell
16384:	Leader dots in this cell
32768:	Leader hyphen in this cell
49152:	Leader underline in this cell

Table 21.28
[data] data
(*continues over...*)

Word processing

Parameter	
Joined row information	
Joined column information	
Cell shade (1-based index to tag line colors, 1–8)	
Cell borders (word based on tag line style)	
	low four bits for left line
	next four bits for right line
	next four bits for top line
	next four bits for bottom line
Flag 2	
	1: cell contains text
Protect flag	
	1: cell is protected.

Table 21.28
[data] data
(*cont.*)

The joined row information contains the number of rows in a connected cell if it is the top left cell. For interior cells, this line contains the number of rows from the top row.

The joined column information contains the number of columns in the connected cell, if the cell is at the top left. For interior cells, the number of columns from the left column is specified.

[lay]

This part defines the page layout. AMI Pro uses only one page layout for a document.

Parameter		
Name of the layout (<= 13 characters, STANDARD for 1.0)		
Flags:		
	1:	Letter
	2:	Legal
	3:	A3
	4:	A4
	5:	A5
	6:	B5
	7:	Custom
	128:	Internal use
	256:	Landscape
	512:	Non-alternating
	1024:	Mirror-imaged
	2048:	2nd header
	4096:	2nd footer

Table 21.29
[lay] data

AMI Pro uses multiple styles for even/odd headers and footers and facing page layouts.

[rght]

This part contains information for the right page.

Parameter
Length (<= 32767 twips)
Width (<= 32767 twips)
Units for length and width (1: inch, 2: centimeters, 3: pica, 4: points)
Left margin (<= 32767 twips)
Bottom margin (<= 32767 twips)
Top margin (<= 32767 twips)
Right margin (<= 32767 twips)
Flags:
1: Columns balance
2: Gutter line
4: Page border line
Gutter line type
Gutter color
Page border type
Border units (1–4, see length units)
Border space (<= 32767 from text)
Number of columns (<= 32767)
For each column:
Left (offset from left of page, <= 32767 twips)
Right (offset from left of page, <= 32767 twips)
Number of tabs (tabs in this column, <= 32767 twips)
For each tab:
Type flag:
1: Left tab
2: Center tab
3: Right tab
4: Numeric tab
16384: Leader hyphen
32768: Leader dot
49152: Leader underline
Offset (in column, <= 32767 twips)

Table 21.30
[rght] data

The *gutter line type* uses the same bitfield for coding as the *line above style* in the [line] part. The type of the *gutter color* is the same as for the tag line color in the [line] part. The *page border type* uses the same code as the *line above style*.

[lft]

This part defines the information for the *left page* facing layout. It has the same structure as the right page layout (*see above*). In AMI Pro 1.0 this part is not used.

[hrght]

This part describes the *right header* and has the same structure as the text frame part (*see above*).

[frght]

This part describes the *right footer* and has the same structure as the text frame part (*see above*).

[hlft]

This part describes the *left header* and has the same structure as the text frame part (*see above*).

[flft]

This part describes the *left footer* and has the same structure as the text frame part (*see above*).

For version 1.0 there is no alternating left and right header/footer layout, so the right header/footer layout is used. The headers and footers have the same structure as a text frame, except that the keyword is `[lyfrm]` and the layout data is `[frmlay]` instead of `[lay]`.

[repfrm]

All repeating frames will be listed as `[repfrm]` with the flag bits set as repeating. The structure is the same as the headers and footers.

[l1]

This part defines the layout number of the first page.

Parameter
Number of layout used (<= 13 bytes)

Table 21.31
`[l1]` part

If the value in the field is greater than `0`, a layout is inserted at the beginning of the first page.

[pg]

This part defines some page hints for browsing quickly through the file. The format of these hints depends on the AMI Pro version and is not published.

[edoc]

This part defines the end of the document section. The document text begins after this section. If there is text in the document, this part must be present.

21.3 Text area

Text is stored in ASCII paragraphs after the document section. All character attributes and escape sequences are embedded in the paragraph text.

- The start of an escape sequence is a < sign and the end of an escape sequence is indicated by >.
- All characters in an escape sequence are enclosed between the characters <...>.
- If a < character appears as normal text, it must be doubled <<. If an escape sequence ends without a > character, the << and >> characters should be interpreted as escape delimiters (example: index page break escape sequence <:p<*!>>).

Paragraphs are followed by an empty line (except in the special case of an empty paragraph). Each paragraph may start with the style name of the paragraph. The style name begins with an @ character.

The (character is another special escape character. If this character occurs in the text, it is placed between the start and end escape characters <(>. The < character in the text is replaced with <;>.

There are two types of embedded escape in the text file. The first type deals with characters below 20H and above 80H. These characters are translated as follows when stored to the disk:

- If the character code is below 20H, a * followed by a value will be written to the disk. The character is the value written minus 20H.
- Character codes between 80H and BFH are represented by a / character followed by a value. The actual character code is the stored value minus 40H.
- If the character code is between C0H and FFH, the escape sequence is the \ character, followed by a value. The actual character code is the stored value minus 80H.

Using this coding results in the disk file containing only 7-bit ASCII codes.

Other embedded escapes are special codes used as character attributes or format information. The first of these has a start sequence (+ followed by the escape code). The end of the sequence is indicated by the – character followed by the escape code. Codes defined are shown in Table 21.32.

The semicolon (;) is a special escape sequence. This character should be translated into a single > sign in the document.

The other type of escape sequence always begins with a colon (:) followed by an escape code. Table 21.33 shows the escape codes defined.

Code	Remark
' '	Plain text (space)
!	Bold text
22H	Italic text
#	Underlined text
$	Word underlined text
%	Strike-through text
&	Superscript text
27H	Subscript text
(	Small capitals text
)	Double underlined
*	Protected text
+	All upper case
,	All lower case
-	Initial capitals
@	Left-aligned paragraph
A	Right-aligned paragraph
B	Centered paragraph
C	Justified paragraph
P	Trail (only in index page)
Q	Lead (only in index page)
R	Occurs in same paragraph (only index page)

Table 21.32 Escape codes starting with + in AMI Pro

Code	Remark
D	System date and style
P	Current page number and style
S	Line spacing
p	Page break
c	Column break
f	Text font change
R	Tab ruler

Table 21.33 Escape codes starting with : in AMI Pro (*continues over...*)

Code	Remark
`M`	Merge
`N`	Notes
`F`	Footnote
`H`	Header
`h`	Footer
`O`	Overstrike
`A`	Anchor
`t`	Table
`s`	Spelling
`v`	Revision marking for paragraph
`T`	Table of contents entry
`X`	Power field
`Z`	Bookmark
`d`	Add document description variable
`e`	DDE link
`n`	New Wave object
`r`	Insert last revision date
`k`	Insert creation time
`V`	Revision marking
`x`	Table footnote
`?`	Unknown

Table 21.33 Escape codes starting with : in AMI Pro (*cont.*)

The escape codes start a record containing fields and format codes. The following section describes the escape sequence syntax. Capital letters enclosed in brackets for example `[STYLE]`, indicate fields in the escape sequence and must be filled in.

21.2.1 Escape records

`<:D[STYLE]>`

This escape record defines the date, followed by the date style (letters from `a` to `l`). Table 21.34 defines the different formats.

Style	Format
`a`	8/1/94
`b`	June 3, 1995
`c`	2 October 1993

Table 21.34 Different date styles (*continues over...*)

Style	Format
d	Friday, May 1, 1994
e	August 2
f	Saturday August 2
g	8/2
h	8/2/1991
i	2nd August
j	2nd August 1994
k	1993 July 9
l	July, 1993

Table 21.34 Different date styles (*cont.*)

The letters `a`, `g` and `f` appear in lower case only. All other letters can appear in lower or upper case. Where applicable, the date order depends on the setting in the Windows control panel.

<:P[STYLE&PAGENUM],[PHYSICALPAGE],[PREFIX]>

This record defines the page numbering and style. The three fields are separated by commas. The first field contains two items of information. The first letter following the `P` defines the page number style:

Style	**Format**
1	Arabic numeral
I	Upper case roman numerals
i	Lower case roman numerals
A	Upper case letters
a	Lower case letters

Table 21.35 Page number style

The second part of the first field contains the first page number as an ASCII string. The second field contains the ASCII number of the physical page to start numbering. The third field contains an ASCII string (maximum 31 characters) which appears before the page number.

<:S+[SPACING]> or <:S->

This is the line spacing command. The command `<:S+xxxx>` turns the line spacing on. The pattern `xxxx` represents the ASCII number to set the amount of line spacing in twips.

Value	Spacing
0xffff	single line
0xfffe	1½ line
0xfffd	double line

Table 21.36
Values for line spacing

The command <:S-> turns the line spacing off.

<:p[FLAG]>

This command flags a page break escape, followed by a flag field. This field may be an escape sequence because some values are out of the ASCII character range (20H to 80H).

Value	Remark
0	Plain text
1	Index page
2	Table of contents
3	End notes
64	Page is vertically centered
128	Layout change with page break

Table 21.37
Page break flag

<:f[PTSIZE]<:f> or, [WINPITCH+FACE],[RED,GREEN,BLUE]>

This is the *font exchange* escape which takes two forms. If the <:f> string is used, the font reverts to its paragraph style settings. In other cases the escape string contains three fields separated by commas. The first field defines the font size in points (ASCII value). The second field defines the font pitch for Windows in the first character. The offset 20H is added to the value to shift the character into the ASCII code range. The following characters define the name of the type face. The last field contains three ASCII values, separated by commas; these define the font color mixed from red, green and blue (values between 0 and 255). If any of the three fields is omitted, the setting in the paragraph style applicable is used.

<:R> or <:R[COLS],[NUMTS1],[TABTYPE,OFFST],..,[NUMTS2]..>

This is the *tab ruler* escape which reverts the tab settings to the page layout (form <:R>). The second form defines new tab settings and contains several ASCII fields, separated by commas. The first field contains the number of columns. For each column, there is a field indicating the number of tab stops in that column. For each tab in the column there will be a structure containing two fields (TABTYPE, OFFST) which describe the tab settings.

Remark		
TABTYPE		
	1:	Left tab
	2:	Center tab
	3:	Right tab
	4:	Numeric tab
	16384:	Leader hyphen
	32768:	Leader dot
	49152:	Leader underline
OFFST (<= 32 767 twips)		

Table 21.38
Tab definition fields

The first four values in the TABTYPE field are mutually exclusive. The last three values are also mutually exclusive. The tab and the leader values can be added. The result is stored in the file as an integer value. Tabs with certain leaders are stored as negative numbers (–16 383 is –16 384 leader hyphen + 1 for left tab). The OFFST field defines the relative offset in twips from the beginning of a column to the tab position.

<:M[MERGEVARNAME]>

This is a *merge* escape, followed by the merge variable name.

<:N[EDITDATE]\n-Text-\n\n>

This escape defines a *note*, followed by a long ASCII number that represents the last edit date of this note. The next sequence defines a line feed followed by the text for this note. The text can span several paragraphs.

<:F\n-Text-\n\n>

This is a *footnote* escape, followed by the text (can span several paragraphs).

<:H[FLAG]-Text-\n\n>

The *header* and *footer* escapes (H, h) are followed by a flag which defines the type of the sequence:

Flag	Remark
1	Footer
2	Header
4	Odd page header/footer
8	Even page header/footer
16	Odd/even page header/footer

Table 21.39 The header/ footer flag

The first two values in Table 21.39 are mutually exclusive. The flag is followed by the header/ footer text string. This string can span several paragraphs and may include other escape sequences. The string cannot contain other header/footer strings or footnotes.

<:O+[OVERSTRIKECHAR]> or <:O->

The first form switches the *overstrike* mode on. The sequence contains a field specifying the overstrike character. The sequence `<:O->` switches the overstrike mode off.

<:t[FRAMENUM]> or <:A[FRAMENUM]>

These commands define a frame for tables (`<:t..>`) and for anchor escapes (`<:A..>`). The following field contains the zero-based ASCII number of the frame that it anchors.

<:X[TYPE],[FLAG],[FIELDTEXT]>

The fields escape (`X`) is made up of three parts.

- If the `X` escape sequence contains a text, the resulting text, which would appear in the document, will follow. The text ends with a trailing `X` escape sequence.
- The second `X` escape sequence is identical to the first with the exception that a tilde (˜) follows the `X`. This tilde marks the terminating escape sequence.

`TYPE` defines the type of the field:

Value	Remark
1	DDE field
2	Bookmark
3	General result field

Table 21.40 Field type (*continues over...*)

Value	Remark
4	Sequence field
5	Sets a global variable
6	Button field
7	Printer escape
8	Index entry
9	User-defined marker

Table 21.40 Field type

The field types `4`, `5`, `7` and `8` do not use the two-escape formats (there is no text to delimit). The `FLAG` field may contain the following entries:

Flag	**Remark**
0x1000	Auto evaluation field
0x2000	Locked
0x8000	Field is in main body

Table 21.41 Flag variables

The `FIELDTEXT` field is optional and contains the text. The structure is documented in the AMI Pro macro manual.

`<:Z[BOOKMARK]>`

This escape sequence defines a bookmark name.

`<:e[APPNAME],[TOPIC],[ITEM]>`

This is the DDE escape sequence and is made up of three parts (`:e[APPNAME],[TOPIC],[ITEM]` resultant text `:e`):

- The first sequence is written as `<:e>`, followed by the text that will appear in the document file.
- The next `<:e>` sequence designates the end of the text.

The third DDE escape sequence contains the application name, the topic and the item.

`<:d[FORMAT][DESCFIELD][NULL]>`

This is the document description field escape sequence. This sequence contains several parameters (file names, date, time, and so on) which are used to describe a document. The `FORMAT` field consists of only one byte containing the character a. The first byte in the DESCFIELD defines the following entries:

Value	Format
1	File name
2	Path
3	Style sheet name
4	Date created
5	Date last revised
6	Total number of revisions
7	Document description
8–15	User-defined fields
16–19	—
20	Time created
21	Time last revised
22	Total edit time
23	Number of pages
24	Number of words
25	Number of characters
26	Document size

Table 21.42 Code of the DESCFIELD

The entries in the field will be in the escape code format (to ensure that only ASCII codes appear). The NULL field contains 00H or <*>.

<:n[OBJREFNUM]>

This escape sequence defines a New Wave object, followed by an ASCII number giving the New Wave object reference number (double word).

<:k[FORMAT]>

The *creation date* escape sequence is followed by a format byte (*see* <d..> sequence).

<:b[NULL]>

The *creation time* escape sequence is followed by 00H or <*>. A resulting string is determined by the Windows control panel.

<:r[FORMAT]>

The *last revision date* escape sequence (r) is followed by this record. The FORMAT field is documented in the <:d..> escape sequence.

<:V[S or E][+ or -]>

The *revision marking* escape sequence (`V`) is followed by two bytes. The `S` marks the escape as the beginning of a revised text. The `E` character marks the end of a revised text. The second byte marks the revised text as inserted (`+`) or as deleted (`-`).

<:v[+ or -]>

The *paragraph revision marking* escape sequence (`v`) is followed by one byte. The `+` marks the revised text as inserted and the `-` as deleted.

<:x[FOOTNOTENUM],[FOOTNOTEROW]>

This escape sequence defines table footnotes and is followed by two ASCII numbers. The first number defines the footnote number. The second number is the row of the table in which the footnote will appear.

21.4 Embedded graphics

In versions 1.1 and 1.2 AMI Pro stores all its embedded objects in separate files. These files have the document name and the extensions `.G00`, `.G01`, and so on.

In release 2.0, AMI Pro appends all the object data to the end of the document file (after the text region). All AMI Pro versions treat a > which is not matched with a preceding < as the end of the document. The object data stored after this mark is in the native form (which means that this part does not consist of only 7-bit ASCII characters). AMI Pro also appends a final object directory after all the objects. The directory is written in ASCII with one line per object. Each line contains the object name and file type (numbering starts with 1), the file offset and length (0 is an external reference), and the file offset and length of the snapshot for the object (0 = none). The six fields are coded in ASCII, separated by spaces. Numbers are written in decimal notation. For external objects the path name is added at the end of the line.

In order to find a section, the directory seeks ten bytes from the end of the file and reads 8 ASCII hex digits, followed by a CR/LF. This number is the offset to the first ASCII line in the file. If that line starts with a `[`, it is a section title, which could be:

- `[embedded]` for the object directory
- `[glossary]` for a glossary index which is stored after the text region
- `[macro]` for a pcode macro which is also stored at the end of the file

To find the next (previous) section, the directory seeks 10 bytes before this line and repeats the search process. The search is complete if the 10 bytes read are not a hex ASCII sequence or if they do not point to a [character.

The file type for ISDs (Image Structure Descriptor) are shown in Table 21.43.

The file type can also be any 3 character extensions for external objects (`1.pcx 0 0 12334 1024 c:\pcx\pict1.pcx`).

For future compatibility, these structures will be retained but new fields may be added. If a reader finds an unknown command, it will be ignored and the reader will search for the next `[..]` keyword.

`.ole`	OLE link
`.bmp`	Windows bitmap
`.wmf`	Windows metafile
`.tex`	AMI equation
`.sdw`	AMI Draw or Chart
`.tgf`	AMI Image Processor (grayscale TIFF)

Table 21.43 File extensions for embedded objects

PART 4

Graphic formats

File formats discussed in Part 4

An extensive range of file formats has been developed for the storage of graphic data. In addition to GEM and Windows, the Paintbrush program has had a significant influence on the design of these formats, and the PCX format is now supported by many products. Since it is not possible to exchange graphics with manufacturer-specific formats, a number of companies decided to define a universal graphic format (TIFF). Part 4 describes the most important graphic formats for the PC, the Macintosh and other platforms.

22

ZSOFT Paintbrush format (PCX)

Paintbrush *is supplied with mouse drivers from Microsoft. This program was originally developed by ZSOFT and is used for creating and modifying graphics and pictures. The associated support program FRIEZE enables pictures from other applications such as LOTUS 1-2-3 to be imported. A special format, known as the PCX format, is used for storing graphic information. Since Paintbrush is so widely distributed, many programs support this format, including other graphics programs such as PC Paintbrush+ and Publishers Paintbrush and desktop publishing software such as Ventura Publisher (Xerox) and PC Pagemaker (Aldus). Graphics data read with a scanner is often stored in PCX format, to enable it to be incorporated into desktop publishing programs at a later stage.*

There is, however, a problem with describing the PCX format. Since the original definition for PC Paintbrush, five different versions have been introduced. This problem is particularly evident in the coding of color data and in storing bitmap character sets in font files. The initial versions of PC Paintbrush+ and Publishers Paintbrush were especially affected by these changes. However, ZSOFT now uses the original format, which is described below.

A graphic is divided into individual dots by means of rows and columns, as shown in Figure 22.1:

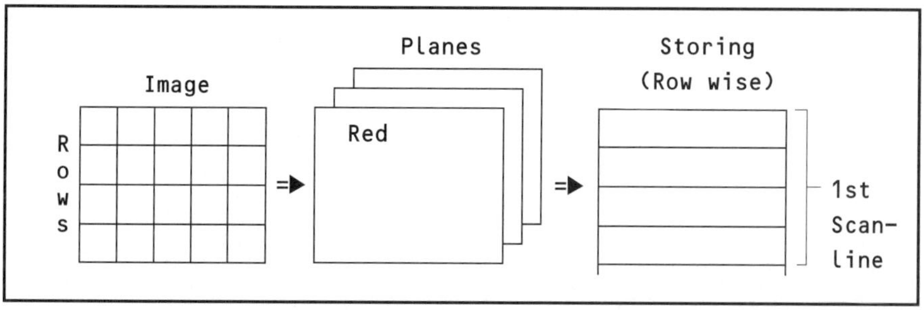

Figure 22.1
Image scan for PCX images

Each dot in the original image, addressed via row and column numbers, is referred to as a *pixel* (picture element). The whole image is created by stringing these pixels together row by row. With monochrome images, each pixel corresponds to one bit; if the bit is set, a dot will be created at the relevant position.

The whole process becomes more complex with the introduction of color. It is no longer possible to represent one pixel with one bit; the image is broken down into individual color *planes* (red, green, blue). The color representation of the image is then composed by adding these planes together. Unfortunately, the coding of this color information is dependent on the graphics card used. With EGA and VGA adapters, the color levels are generally called *bit planes*. As shown in Figure 22.1, a three-dimensional image representation can be achieved by breaking the original picture down into color planes. In PCX files, picture information is stored row by row. A complete row contains pixels from the relevant plane in the sequence plane 0 = blue, plane 1 = green, plane 2 = red, plane 3 = intensity. The resulting picture in the file is as follows:

Image row 0:	*n* bits color plane 0
	n bits color plane 1
	n bits color plane 2
	n bits color plane 3
Image row 1:	*n* bits color plane 0
	n bits color plane 1
	n bits color plane 2
	n bits color plane 3
Image row *n*:	*n* bits color plane 0
	n bits color plane 1
	n bits color plane 2
	n bits color plane 3

Figure 22.2
PCX color planes

Since the bits composed of graphic elements must be copied into the bytes of the file, the PCX format describes a rectangular image area consisting of *n* rows with *x* pixels in each row. The pixels are stored in words, so the number of bits (*x*) must be even and divisible by 16. If the image does not conform to this requirement, it may be necessary to leave individual bits unused at the end of the row. The same applies to the number of rows per image, which must be divisible by 8 or 16. It may be necessary to insert a number of blank rows at the bottom of the image. This principle is demonstrated in Figure 22.3:

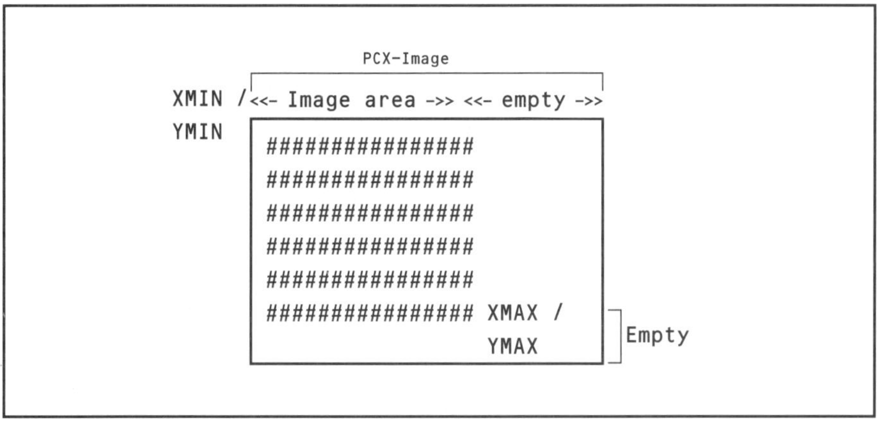

Figure 22.3 Mapping of a PCX image

The marked area (###) corresponds to the area of the original image, which is described by the coordinates (`XMIN,YMIN`) and (`XMAX,YMAX`). There may be empty bits at the right and bottom edges of the image.

22.1 Structure of the PCX header

In all versions, the header of a PCX file is structured uniformly and contains 128 bytes. This also applies to excerpts of images which are stored in PCC files. Table 22.1 shows the format of the PCX header.

Offset	Bytes	Remarks
00H	1	ID byte: 0AH = PCX file
01H	1	PCX file version
		0 = Version 2.5
		2 = Version 2.8 with palette
		3 = Version 2.8 without palette
		5 = Version 3.0
02H	1	Encoding flag
		0 = uncompressed
		1 = RLE compression
03H	1	Bits per pixel (per plane)
04H	8	Picture dimensions in words XMIN, YMIN, XMAX, YMAX
0CH	2	Horizontal pixel resolution in dpi (dots per inch)

Table 22.1 Structure of a PCX header (*continues over...*)

Offset	Bytes	Remarks
0EH	2	Vertical pixel resolution in dpi (dots per inch)
10H	48	Color map (palette) 16 × 3 bytes
40H	1	Reserved
41H	1	Color planes (maximum 4)
42H	2	Bytes per scan line (even)
44H	2	Palette data 1 = color – B/W 2 = grayscale
46H	58	Fill bytes

Table 22.1 Structure of a PCX header (*cont.*)

The first byte is used to identify a valid PCX file. ZSOFT established the value 10 (0AH) as a signature, and other manufacturers tend to follow this convention.

The second byte contains the Paintbrush version that created the file. The value 0 indicates version 2.5. From version 2.8 onwards it is possible to store the palette data in the PCX file. If this information is not present (for example in a B/W representation), the byte is set to 03H. For color graphics, the palette data is stored at offset 68, and the second byte contains 02H to indicate version 2.8 with palette data. From version 3.0, the byte contains 05H.

The third byte indicates whether the data in the PCX file is compressed. If the byte is 0, there is no compression. The value 1 indicates that the data has been compressed using the *Run Length Encoding* process (RLE). This is described in more detail below.

The number of bits per pixel (or *planes* per pixel) is shown at offset 3. However, this value does not take into account any color planes that may be present, and the number shown is generally 1.

A table containing 4 words (2 bytes each) begins at offset 04H. This table defines the dimensions of the image window (see also Figure 22.1). The coordinates of the upper left and lower right corner of the relevant section of the image are stored in the following sequence:

```
XMIN, YMIN    XMAX, YMAX
```

This is important in the case of image excerpts in which the coordinates need to be defined separately. The number of valid pixels per image often does not correspond exactly to the number of words. In this case, there will be empty bits at the right and lower edges of the image. When reading the PCX files, the invalid area can be masked.

The horizontal resolution (H_Res) of a pixel in dpi (dots per inch) is defined at offset 12 (0CH), while the vertical resolution (image height) in dpi is stored at offset 14 (0EH). Within the different versions of Paintbrush, there are several modifications, introduced to make the representation of the image device-independent. These values should therefore be treated with circumspection.

At offset 16 (10H), there is a 48 byte area for the color map. The definition of the individual colors for color graphics is contained here. The following information on color representation relates to the structure of this table. Any colors can be created by mixing or adding the three primary colors.

A color pixel can be represented by three bits, but this restricts the number of colors to $8 = 2^3$. The addition of one further bit, the *intensity bit*, gives 16 colors. A considerably finer gradation of colors is possible via color graphics adapters, and this has also had an influence on the storage of color information. The approach used by painters when they mix color is generally adopted, achieving different color tones by varying the intensity of the primary colors red, green and blue. The method used for color graphics cards is very similar. If the primary color is represented by a byte, its intensity can be varied through 255 shades. With three primary colors, three bytes per color are required. Thus three bytes would be required to represent the color of each individual pixel, which would demand a huge memory capacity. The problem is solved by storing the definition of the color in a table, so that only the table index has to be stored with the image data. For 16 colors, only 4 bits are needed, and for 255 shades, only 8 bits. The table in which the colors are defined is named after the artist's *palette*. How this palette is stored depends on the graphics card used.

22.1.1 CGA color palette information

With the standard CGA card from IBM (and other compatible cards), the storage of the color map is very complex. The 48 bytes in the header are subdivided into 16 groups of three bytes (triples). The first byte of each of the first two triples contains the data.

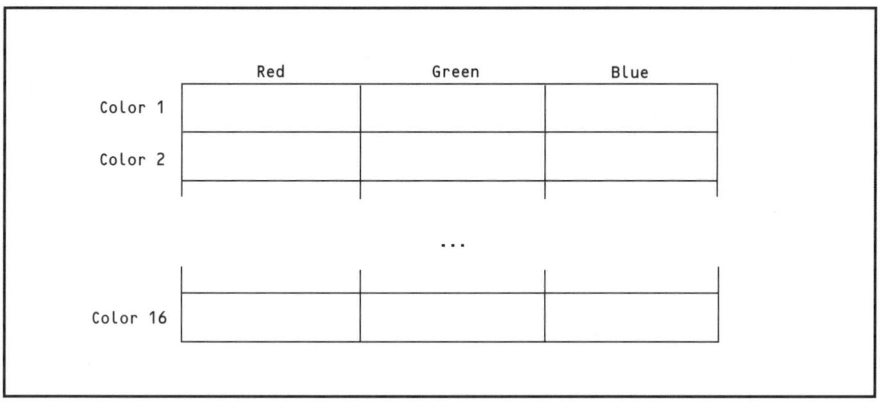

Figure 22.4
CGA color map

As a result, not all the bytes in a triple are used. With the CGA adapter, the background color is given in the first byte of the first triple (offset `16`, `10H`) and only the upper four bits are used. This enables the representation of 16 different colors. The upper three bits of the first byte of the second triple (offset `19`, `13H`) contain information on the foreground palette. The coding is as follows:

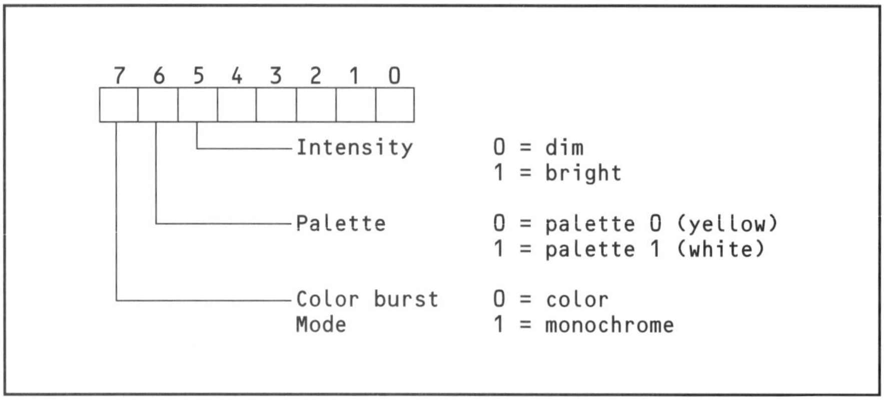

Figure 22.5 Coding of the second byte of the color map (CGA)

Information on the color (monochrome/color) is stored in bit 7. Bit 5 indicates the intensity of a pixel. One of the two CGA palettes can be selected using bit 6.

Palette	Colors
0	Green, Red, Brown (Yellow)
1	Cyan, Magenta, White

Table 22.2 CGA color palette

These three bits enable a total of 8 different combinations to be defined.

22.1.2 EGA/VGA 16 color palette

In standard EGA/VGA mode, only 16 colors are available. The color map is again divided into 16 triples of 3 bytes. Each primary color is allocated a byte in which the color intensity is stored. The values for one byte may lie between 0 and 255. This means that it is necessary to convert to the RGB palette of the adapter. With 16 colors, only the upper two bits per byte tend to be defined. With the IBM EGA adapter, four grades are possible for the RGB palette. The values stored in the three bytes should be divided by 64 before processing to give values of 0, 1, 2 or 3.

22.1.3 VGA 256 color palette

For each byte it is possible to code 256 different color grades. In order to support the VGA color mode, ZSOFT extended the color map, from version 3.0 onwards. Because the table in the header contains only 16 × 3 bytes, a special table containing 256 entries of 3 bytes each is appended to the end of the file. This table contains information on the color palette, which should be interpreted in the same way as the values of the (16 color) EGA palette (divide by 64). In the case of the VGA-BIOS palette, the bytes in the table should be divided by 4. If this mode is supported, the value 05H must be stored at offset 2 in the header (version 3.0). The last 769 bytes in the file can then be read into a buffer. If the signature 0CH is stored in the first byte of the buffer, there is valid information on the color palette in the following bytes.

This concludes the description of the *Color Map* field in the header.

The byte at offset 64 (40H) in the header is reserved for extensions.

The byte at offset 65 (41H) contains the number of color planes per pixel. At present, the maximum number of color planes is four (red, green, blue, intensity); for monochrome representation, this byte is set to 1.

At offset 66 (42H), there is a word indicating the number of bytes per image line. This number must always be even, because the image data is stored in words. If necessary, appropriate fill bits are used. For color images, the value in this byte corresponds to the row length of one color plane.

The word at offset 68 (44H) is not always used. It contains information on the interpretation of the palette values in the color map. The value 1 means that the data in the B/W or color graphic should be interpreted. If the value is 2, all points are stored as graylevels. If other values are entered here, the field is unused.

At the end of the header, from offset 70 (46H) onwards, there are an additional 58 unused bytes, making up the prescribed length of 128 bytes.

22.2 Coding of PCX data

The header is followed by the image data. Each picture is scanned row by row and broken down into its color planes (red, green, blue and intensity). Then, all the bits in the first row of the blue color plane are assembled into words and stored. Unused bits in the last word are filled with 0. The first row of the green color plane is stored next, followed by the red plane and the intensity plane. Only then can the processing of the second row of the blue color plane (for the second row of the images) be started. This is repeated until all rows have been stored. Any areas at the right and bottom edges of the image are filled with null bytes and must be masked when processing the image data.

! **The ZSOFT user's manual states that the sequence of color storage is red, green, blue. In fact, colors are stored in the file in the sequence blue, green, red.**

Information on the valid picture excerpt is stored in the PCX file header (XMIN, YMIN, XMAX, YMAX).

Figure 22.6 Original PC Paintbrush picture

For PCX files, there are now two methods of storing picture data in the file. In the first method, all bits are stored in uncompressed form, and a value other than 1 is stored at offset 02H in the header. Unfortunately, the memory requirement for this method is extremely high. Since many pixels are identical in pictures containing several uniform areas, it is clearly appropriate to compress the image data. Using the Run Length Encoding method, the value 1 is stored at offset 02H in the header, and the image data is compressed.

The RLE method simply means that identical bits are grouped together and their repetition rate is indicated. The coding is as follows:

- If the two upper bits (6, 7) are set (bit = 1), a compressed item of information is involved. Bits 0 to 5 are then interpreted as counters which indicate the repetition factor for the pattern stored in the following byte.
- If the two upper bits of a byte are not set (0), a pure data byte is involved and bits 0 to 7 can then be processed directly as image data. Thus when storing uncompressed bytes, care should be taken that the two upper bits are set to 0 in pixel sequence.

This compression has a number of consequences. Using the RLE method, up to 63 data bytes or 504 bits can be coded in 2 bytes, provided all bits have the same value (0 or 1). Sequences of pixels with alternating bits are grouped together by the byte and stored (in uncompressed form). In order to avoid confusion with RLE coding, data bytes with values greater than C0H must not be stored directly, and the compression method is used. For example, if an image row contains the bit pattern given by the following hex numbers:

FFH FFH FFH FFH 00H 00H 13H C9H

the RLE coding will be as follows:

C4H FFH C2H 00H 13H C1H C9H

Data byte 13H can be stored in uncompressed form. However, the value C9H brings about a conflict with RLE coding. The data byte C9H is therefore coded as an RLE sequence with the codes C1H C9H. In the case of pictures without repeating patterns, the compression procedure necessarily makes the file longer than it would be with pure, uncompressed storage of the image data, because bits 6 and 7 of a byte are not used. For this reason, PC Paintbrush can also store data in uncompressed form.

Figure 22.7 shows an extract from a PCX file. The original picture is shown in Figure 22.6. The information presented above enables the contents of a PCX file to be decoded relatively simply.

22.3 Format of the PC Paintbrush bitmap character

In PC Paintbrush, texts are inserted into the picture as bit patterns. The definition of the characters is stored in individual font files of a straightforward format (see Table 22.3).

The signature A0H is stored in the first byte, together with the font width in pixels. To determine the character width, subtract A0H from the value of the first byte.

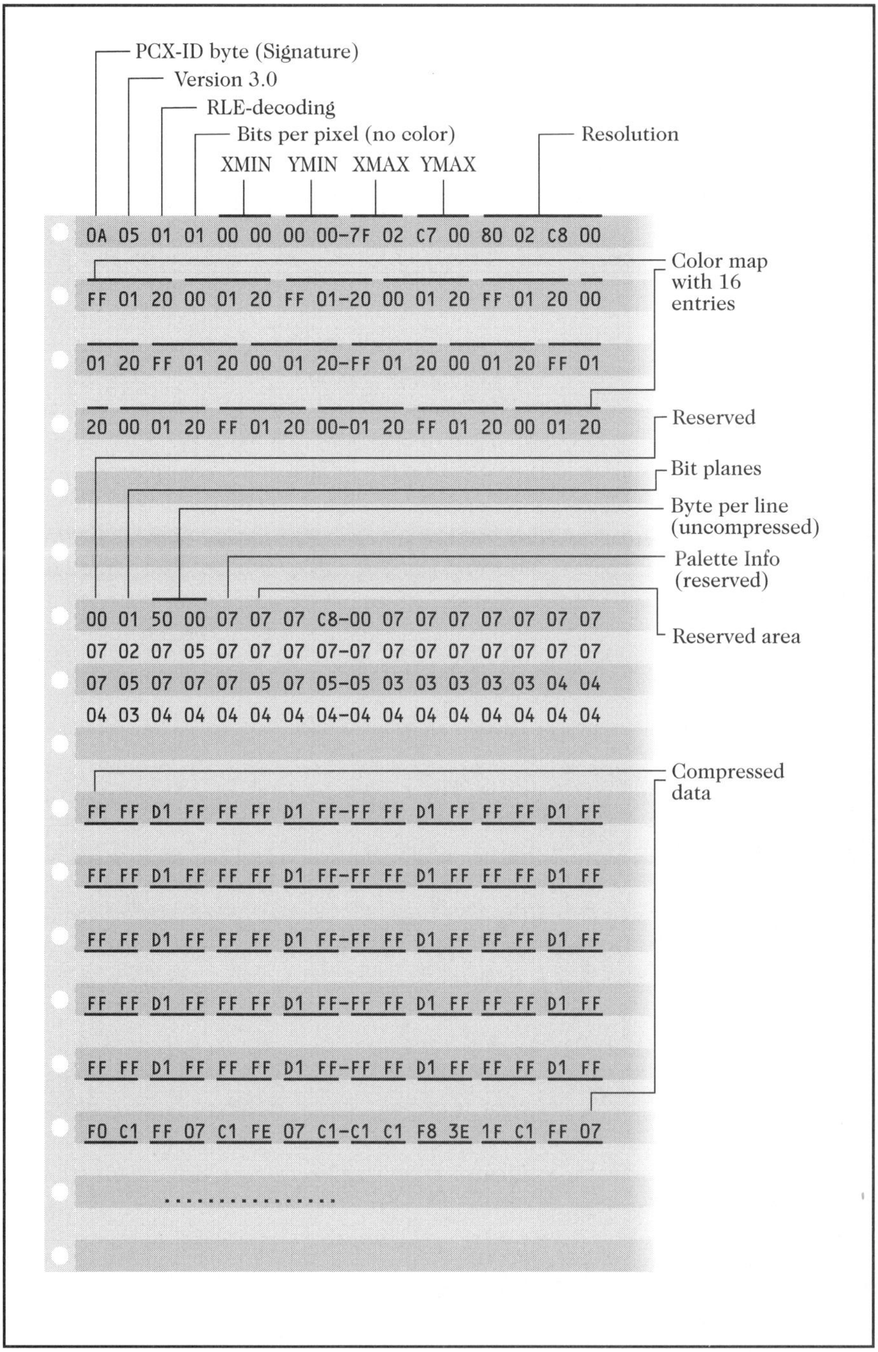

Figure 22.7 Hex dump of a PCX file

Byte	Remarks
1	A0H + font width in pixels
1	Character height in pixels
256	256 * (Character width + 1)
xxx	Character images

Table 22.3 Structure of a PCX character file

The *second byte* contains the height of a character matrix. This information is required because there are various font definitions with 5 × 7 or 9 × 14 pixels per character. A character matrix is broken down into individual rows. With a matrix in 5 × 7 format, 7 bytes are used for storage, while the 9 × 14 pixel representation uses 2 bytes per row and therefore needs 28 bytes per character. The individual characters are defined on the basis of the ASCII table and are stored at offset 258. Each character is left-justified in the character block. All characters in a font take up the same number of bytes. This data area with the character images is preceded by a field containing 256 entries in which the character width + 1 is stored. This is particularly important for user-created fonts, since these may occupy any size up to a maximum of 10 Kbytes. Figure 22.8 shows the hex dump of a 5 × 7 font:

Font width in pixels

Character height in pixels

256* (Character width + 1)

```
A5 07 01 01 01 01 01 01-01 01 01 01 01 01 01
01 01 01 01 01 01 01 01-01 01 01 01 01 01 01
01 01 06 02 04 06 06 06-06 03 03 03 06 06 03 06
03 06 06 04 06 06 06 06-06 06 06 03 03 05 06
05 06 06 06 06 06 06 06-06 06 06 04 06 06 06 06
06 06 06 06 06 06 06 06-06 06 06 06 04 06 04
06 06 03 06 05 05 05 05-05 05 05 04 05 05 05 06
06 05 05 06 05 05 06 05-06 06 06 06 05 02 05
06 06 01 01 01 01 01 01-01 01 01 01 01 01 01
01 01 01 01 01 01 01 01-01 01 01 01 01 01 01
01 01 01 01 01 01 01 01-01 01 01 01 01 01 01
01 01 01 01 01 01 01 01-01 01 01 01 01 01 01
01 01 01 01 01 01 01 01-01 01 01 01 01 01 01
01 01 01 01 01 01 01 01-01 01 01 01 01 01 01
01 01 01 01 01 01 01 01-01 01 01 01 01 01 01
01 01 01 01 01 01 01 01-01 01 01 01 01 01 01
01 01 00 00 00 00 00 00-00 00 00 00 00 00 00
```

Character definition

```
00 00 00 00 00 00 00 00-00 00 00 00 00 00 00
................
00 00 00 00 00 00 00 00-00 80 80 80 80 80 00 80
A0 A0 00 00 00 00 00 50-50 F8 50 F8 50 50 20 78
................
```

Figure 22.8 Hex dump of a 5× 7 character file

Graphics

This information enables customized character sets to be planned and included in PC Paintbrush.

22.4 CAPTURE File Format (SCR)

The program CAPTURE is supplied with MS-Word. The purpose of this program is to prepare screen shots for Word. The program recognizes two possible modes for screen shots.

- Text mode in which the screen is stored as ASCII text. In this case, the files have the extension `.LST`. The advantage of this mode is that the screen shot requires only a small amount of memory. The disadvantage is that the image attributes are lost. Also, it is not possible to store excerpts from the screen display.
- As an alternative, it is possible to store a text screen as a bitmap file. The text is then converted into a bitmap pattern and stored in a file with the extension `.SCR`. The same applies to screen shots in graphics mode. However, there are disadvantages. The conversion from text to bitmap takes a long time and the bitmap file requires a considerable amount of space on the disk. The advantage is that a bitmap file contains the attributes and the colors. It is therefore ideal for reconstructing a screen shot.

The only problem is that so far no programs support the Word SCR format. Even in Word, the files cannot be displayed; they can merely be printed.

However, a glance at the file structure shows a close resemblance to the format of the PCX file. The 128 byte header is structured similarly to the PCX format (see Table 22.1). The only differences are as follows:

- In PCX files, the first byte (offset `00H`) is set to `10` (`0AH`). An SCR file contains the value `205` in this byte (`CDH`). If this byte can be converted to the value `0AH` using a debugger (for example `DEBUG.COM`), the SCR file can be read and displayed with the Windows program Paintbrush.
- The second difference relates to screen shots. In PCX files, each row is terminated with a fill byte in order to reach the 16 bit limit. With the SCR format, this fill byte is not used; that is, a row will have the number of bytes per row defined in the header (offset `67`, `68`).
- Data is stored in the SCR file using RLE coding.

Given these facts, it is relatively easy to convert and display SCR files in the PCX format.

23

GEM Image format (IMG)

A number of GEM programs such as DR PAINT, DR DOODLE and Publishers Paintbrush use GEM IMG files for storing graphics. This is basically a pixel-oriented method of storing the screen window.

This window is divided into rows and columns of pixels as shown in Figure 23.1.

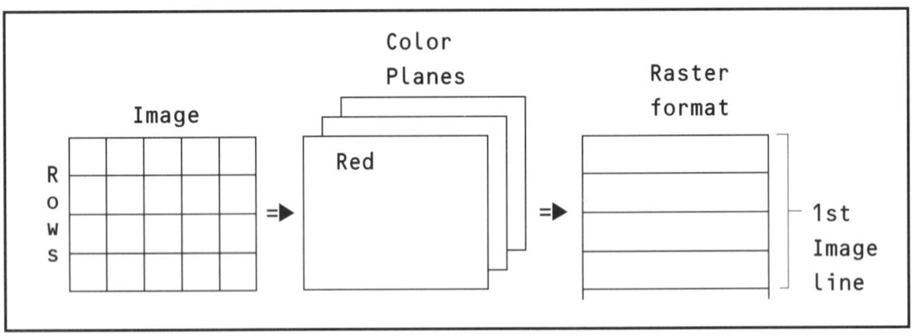

Figure 23.1
Image scan

Each element of the original image addressed by a row and column number is designated a pixel (*picture element*). The complete picture is formed by joining these pixels together. In black and white representation, each pixel corresponds to one bit, which may be set or unset. However, as a rule, color images are processed and stored. In this context, additional color information is assigned to each pixel, which can no longer be coded in one bit.

Depending on the coding used, the color of a pixel can generally be created from red, green, and blue together with information on intensity. This means that the actual image must be broken down into four partial images representing these three colors and the intensity. For example, a partial image in which all the pixels of the original image have a certain intensity of red may be produced. The same would apply to the partial image containing green taking account of pixels. By mixing the primary colors and the intensity bit, it is possible to reproduce the original picture in 16 colors.

The image is stored as a number of individual lines. For each line, the pixels of the individual color planes are recorded row by row. This means that the row containing all the red bits is stored first, then the row of green pixels, then the row of blue pixels and finally the intensity bits. Only when all this information has been stored can the next image line be processed. The process is shown schematically in Figure 23.1.

As mentioned in the discussion of other formats (PCX, TIFF, and so on), there are a number of difficulties connected with the memory requirements for this type of storage. A graphics screen with a resolution of 640 × 200 pixels needs 128,000 bits to store a B/W image. Here, each pixel is represented by one bit which is either set or unset. In the case of color graphics, each pixel (coded as described) requires four bits (red, green, blue, intensity). This requires four times the memory or 512 Kbits per image. To reduce the memory requirement, various data compression processes are used in IMG files. These are described below, together with the associated memory format. Figure 23.2 shows the basic structure of an IMG file:

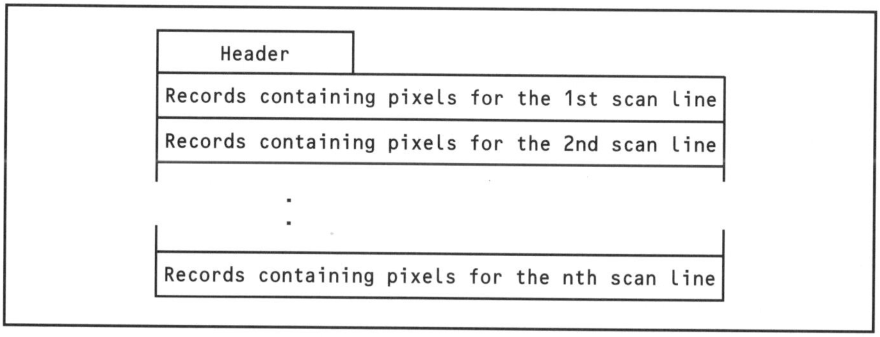

Figure 23.2 Record structure of an IMG file

The file consists of a header containing initialization data, followed by the actual image data in the relevant coding, divided into records of varying length depending on the method of compression.

23.1 IMG header

In the current versions of GEM (up to 2.x), the header consists of 8 words (16 bytes). This format allows the use of a standard color palette of 16 colors. Ventura Publisher uses an extended header with 9 words (18 bytes), to support a 256 color palette. Both headers are coded as follows:

Word	Coding
1	File version
2	Header length (in words)
3	Bits per pixel (color planes)
4	Pattern length
5	Pixel width (in micrometers)
6	Pixel height (in micrometers)
7	Length of scan line in pixels (image width)
8	Number of scan lines (pixel height)
9	Ventura Extension (Bit Image Flag)

Table 23.1 Structure of an IMG file header

! Important note: Header data is stored contrary to the usual Intel convention. The higher value byte in the word is stored at the lower byte address. When stored according to the Intel convention, the value FFH 03H is interpreted as 03H FFH. In the IMG header, this value is interpreted as FFH 03H. This should always be borne in mind when processing IMG files.

The first header entry indicates the version number of the GEM program that created the image. In versions up to 2.x, this is 00H 01H. This is followed by the field containing the header length. GEM stores the value 00H 08H here, at least up to version 2.x. However, Digital Research is keeping its options open regarding the length of the header. The extended Ventura Publisher header keeps 9 words. For this reason, applications programs should always read the header length to avoid problems with later GEM versions.

The third field contains the number of bits per pixel, which is relevant in the case of color graphics. The value 1 indicates monochrome, while values between 2 and 16 indicate color images.

This information is needed when storing and decoding image data in order to establish the number of color planes. The picture is stored line by line, each line containing the four rows of the pixel color planes. In GEM, the sequence of color planes is as follows:

Red, Green, Blue, Intensity

In the file, all the bits relating to the color red for the first line are stored first; these are followed by the bits for the green color plane, then the blue color plane and finally the intensity bits, all for the same line. Only then can the next image line be processed.

The fourth word determines the length of a pattern. This relates to the standard patterns (for example, a brick-wall pattern) which are available in graphics programs for filling areas. The information on the length of the pattern is required for the *Pattern Run* compression process. In many versions of GEM, this is fixed at 2 bytes; however, it may vary between 1 and 8.

The size of an individual pixel naturally depends on the properties of the device used. To enable the transfer and adaptation of existing pictures to other devices, the dimensions of a pixel are stored in the file header. The width of a pixel in micrometers is stored in field 5 and the pixel height in field 6. Using these parameters, it is generally possible to represent images independently of the device used. The entries must be appropriately adapted to the device that created the file.

Word 7 contains the number of pixels per image line (image width in pixels). This information is important because the image is stored by line/row. This field is therefore evaluated by various compression processes.

Word 8 contains the number of pixel rows in the IMG file. This value defines the image height in pixels.

Word 9 is only available if the header length (second entry) shows 9 words. Word 9 is used as a Bit Image Flag in Ventura Publisher. This flag controls the interpretation of multi-plane images as color or gray-scale images. If word 9 is present and the file contains more than 2 planes (word 3>2), the flag is valid. A value of 0 indicates color image data. A fixed color palette of 16 entries is used.

0: [3F,3F,3F]	1: [3F,00,00]	2: [00,3F,00]	3: [3F,3F,00]
4: [00,00,3F]	5: [3F,00,3F]	6: [00,3F,3F]	7: [2B,2B,2B]
8: [15,15,15]	9: [2B,00,00]	10: [00,2B,00]	11: [2B,2B,00]
12: [00,00,2B]	13: [2B,00,2B]	14: [00,2B,2B]	15: [00,00,00]

Table 23.2 GEM standard 16 color palette

The palette entries in the [] are hexvalues stored in the order red, green and blue. The value 1 in the Bit Image Flag (word 9) indicates a grayscale image. In this case, a fixed graylevel palette is used. The palette values for grayscales are defined as follows:

0:FF	1:7F	2:BF	3:3F	4:DF	5:5F	6:9F	7:1F	8:EF	9:6F
10:AF	11:2F	12:CF	13:4F	14:8F	15:0F	16:F7	17:77	18:B7	19:37
20:D7	21:57	22:97	23:17	24:E7	25:67	26:A7	27:27	28:C7	29:47
30:87	31:07	32:FB	33:7B	34:BB	35:3B	36:DB	37:5B	38:9B	39:1B
40:EB	41:6B	42:AB	43:2B	44:CB	45:4B	46:8B	47:0B	48:F3	49:73
50:B3	51:33	52:D3	53:53	54:93	55:13	56:E3	57:63	58:A3	59:23
60:C3	61:43	62:83	63:03	64:FD	65:7D	66:BD	67:3D	68:DD	69:5D
70:9D	71:1D	72:ED	73:6D	74:AD	75:2D	76:CD	77:4D	78:8D	79:0D
80:F5	81:75	82:B5	83:35	84:D5	85:55	86:95	87:15	88:E5	89:65
90:A5	91:25	92:C5	93:45	94:85	95:05	96:F9	97:79	98:B9	99:39
100:D9	101:59	102:99	103:19	104:E9	105:69	106:A9	107:29	108:C9	109:49
110:89	111:09	112:F1	113:71	114:B1	115:31	116:D1	117:51	118:91	119:11
120:E1	121:61	122:A1	123:21	124:C1	125:41	126:81	127:01	128:FE	129:7E
130:BE	131:3E	132:DE	133:5E	134:9E	135:1E	136:EE	137:6E	138:AE	139:2E
140:CE	141:4E	142:8E	143:0E	144:F6	145:76	146:B6	147:36	148:D6	149:56
150:96	151:16	152:E6	153:66	154:A6	155:26	156:C6	157:46	158:86	159:06
160:FA	161:7A	162:BA	163:3A	164:DA	165:5A	166:9A	167:1A	168:EA	169:6A
170:AA	171:2A	172:CA	173:4A	174:8A	175:0A	176:F2	177:72	178:B2	179:32
180:D2	181:52	182:92	183:12	184:E2	185:62	186:A2	187:22	188:C2	189:42
190:82	191:02	192:FC	193:7C	194:BC	195:3C	196:DC	197:5C	198:9C	199:1C

Table 23.3 GEM standard 256 grayscale palette (*continues over...*)

200:EC	201:6C	202:AC	203:2C	204:CC	205:4C	206:8C	207:0C	208:F4	209:74
210:B4	211:34	212:D4	213:54	214:94	215:14	216:E4	217:64	218:A4	219:24
220:C4	221:44	222:84	223:04	224:F8	225:78	226:B8	227:38	228:D8	229:58
230:98	231:18	232:E8	233:68	234:A8	235:28	236:C8	237:48	238:88	239:08
240:F0	241:70	242:B0	243:30	244:D0	245:50	246:90	247:10	248:E0	249:60
250:A0	251:20	252:C0	253:40	254:80	255:00				

Table 23.3 GEM standard 256 grayscale palette (*cont.*)

A value FF for index 0 means that all three entries (red, green, blue) use the same value (FFH,FFH,FFH). The grayscale palette is never stored in an IMG file. All palette values in Table 23.3 are given in hexadecimal.

23.2 Storage of IMG data

As mentioned above, GEM partitions an image into rows and columns, and each element in this matrix corresponds to one pixel. The images are stored line by line, the data from each color plane of the current line being stored in turn, in the case of color images. Only when the preceding line is complete will the next line be processed.

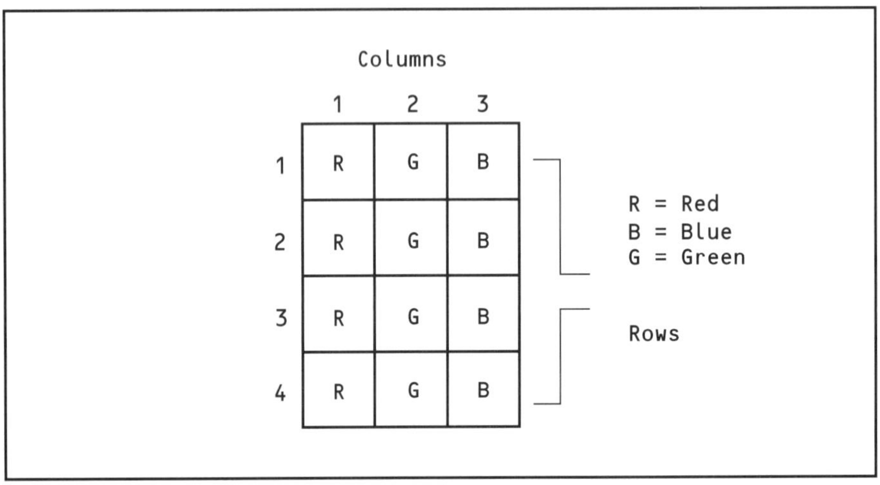

Figure 23.3 Pattern with red, green, blue

To store the pattern, 3 columns × 4 rows × 4 colors = 48 bits are required. The number of color bits is indicated in the header of an IMG file, and the pattern is scanned row by row before being stored in a file (Figure 23.4).

Using this information (Figures 23.4 and 23.5), the original picture can subsequently be reconstituted. The number of pixels per row is contained in the header of the IMG file (word 7).

The number of color bits per pixel is also shown in the header (word 3). If the value is 4, for example, every pixel is broken down into four color planes and stored.

Pixel 1st row (Red)	1	0	0
Pixel 1st row (Green)	0	1	0
Pixel 1st row (Blue)	0	0	1
Pixel 1st row (Int.)	0	0	0
		...	
Pixel 4th row (Red)	1	0	0
Pixel 4th row (Green)	0	1	0
Pixel 4th row (Blue)	0	0	1
Pixel 4th row (Int.)	0	0	0

Figure 23.4 Storing uncoded patterns

23.3 Image compression in IMG files

Even with a resolution of 640 × 300 pixels, the memory requirement for a picture is very high. If the resolution and quality of color are improved, it increases dramatically. For this reason, GEM uses various compression processes to reduce the volume of data:

- Solid Run
- Bit String
- Pattern Run
- Vertical Replication Count

The appropriate method is chosen for the various elements in the picture.

The header is followed by an area containing the image data, which is stored line by line, taking into account the color planes. The pixels are stored in records according to the following format:

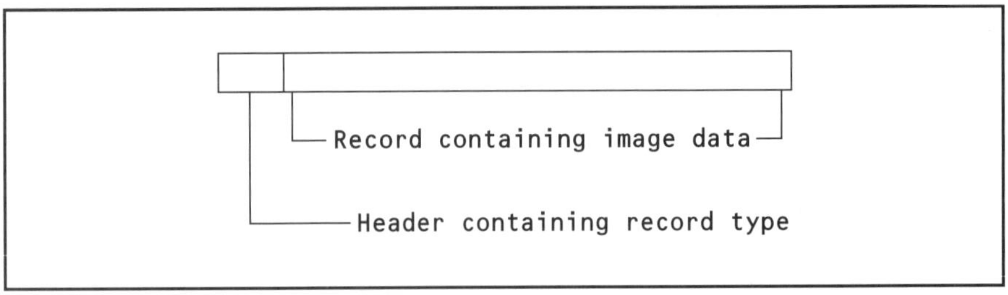

Figure 23.5
Record structure

The structure of the records varies according to the coding method used.

23.3.1 Pixel Coding

One obvious solution is to divide the individual pixels into their respective color planes and store them bit-wise. The four color bits per pixel and 640 pixels per row create the following memory demand per row:

640 pixels × 4 color planes / 8 bits = 320 bytes

Here, GEM attempts to save space in the memory by using appropriate coding.

23.3.2 Solid Run format

The simplest case is when several pixels within a line are identical. In breaking down the pixels into the individual bits of the color planes, there are often several consecutive bits with the same value (0 or 1). To represent this section, it is only necessary to indicate the value and the number of bits involved. If one byte is reserved as a repetition counter and bit 7 is used as a marker for *Solid Run*, the maximum number of bits represented is 127 per data byte. This constitutes a good level of compression. However, the specification goes one step further: bits with the same setting are taken in groups of 8 (1 byte). In *Solid Run* format, consecutive bytes with the same values are stored as shown in Figure 23.6:

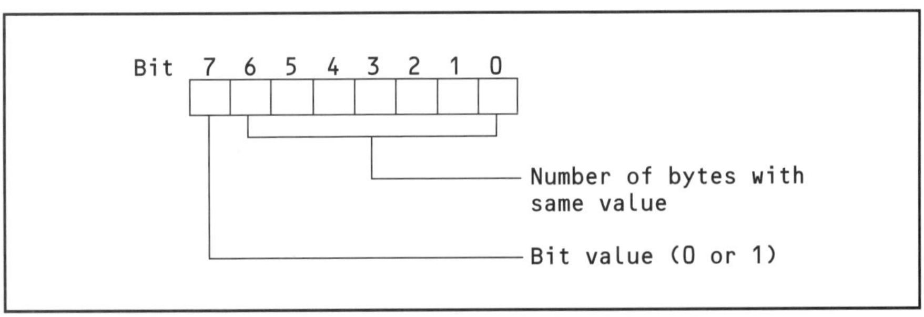

Figure 23.6
Solid run record format

The basis for this code is always one byte. The upper bit of this byte indicates the value of the compressed pixel (1 or 0). The remaining bits 0 to 6 indicate the number of compressed bytes. For instance, if there is a series of 320 bits with the value 1, this represents exactly 320/8 = 40 bytes. The same applies to series of bits containing the value 0. The following codes are therefore possible:

Bits = 0: 01H (1 byte or 8 bits)
...
7FH (127 bytes or 1016 bits)
Bits = 1: 81H (1 byte or 8 bits)
FFH (127 bytes or 1016 bits)

Entry 83H, for example, means that the following three bytes are represented with the value 1. This method enables a maximum of 127 similar bytes (corresponding to 7FH or FFH) to be compressed. The record is just one byte long and contains values between 01H and FFH.

The value 00H is not permitted as a count because it is meaningless and leads to conflicts with the header bytes in the *Bit String* (80H) and *Pattern Run* (00H) formats. A value of 80H is also invalid; it defines 0 repetitions of a byte of value FFH.

23.3.3 Bit String format

This format is used to represent uncompressible sections of an image. It enables non-repeatable patterns to be stored as a *bit string*. The bit string records are structured as shown in Figure 23.7:

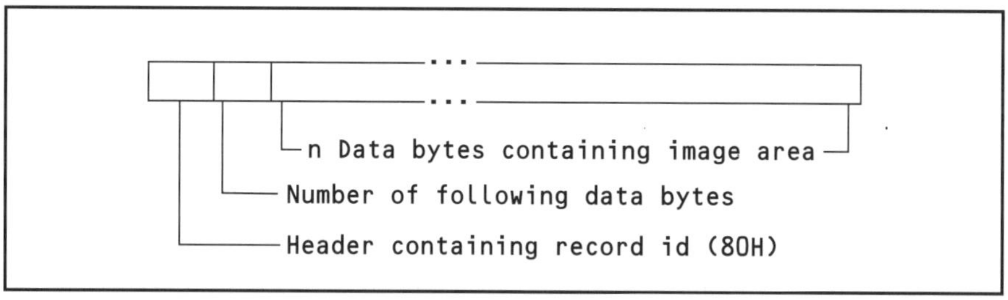

Figure 23.7 Bit String record format

The record begins with the code 80H in the first byte. The second byte indicates the number of following bytes containing the record data. The pixels are stored in these bytes as bit strings. Only an integer multiple of 8 can be stored as a pixel number. A maximum of 255 bytes (2040 bits) per record can be represented using the *Bit String* format. For longer patterns, a second record must be used. GEM only uses this format if no other coding method is possible.

Graphics

23.3.4 Pattern Run format

One other form of coding is used for the representation of patterns. Patterns used for filling areas and for backgrounds to pictures are generally supplied by the toolboxes of the graphics programs. They tend to have geometrical structures and can be represented using the format shown in Figure 23.8:

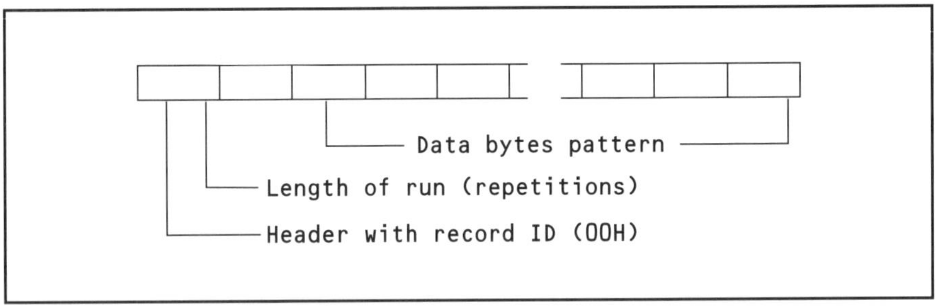

Figure 23.8 Pattern Run record format

The record begins with the value 00H as an identification code. This is followed by a byte indicating the repetition rate of the pattern. The value 5 indicates that the pattern should be created 5 times in consecutive bits in the relevant line. The remainder of the record contains the data bytes of the actual pattern. Each pixel of the pattern is represented by one data bit. It should be borne in mind that, here too, a pattern must consist of a number of pixels which is divisible by 8. In fact, GEM defines a fixed data length in IMG files for all patterns offered. This is stored in word 4 of the IMG header, and the value is usually limited to 2 bytes. A pattern must therefore be represented by $2 \times 8 = 16$ bits.

A pattern consisting of n bytes can be repeated up to 255 times in *Pattern Run* format, before a new record has to be created.

23.3.5 Vertical Replication Count format

The coding methods described so far relate to the representation of individual pixels in a string. However, images often contain identical lines. The top and bottom edges of a picture, for example, are often filled with the same color. In such cases, it is sufficient to describe this line once and copy it several times. *Vertical Replication Count* format was introduced to support this technique. It is only used when several consecutive image lines can be represented with the same coding. The image data is still coded using one of the formats described above (Pattern Run, Bit String, Solid Run). When using *Vertical Replication Count*, a second header, structured as shown in Figure 23.9, is placed before the header of the data record:

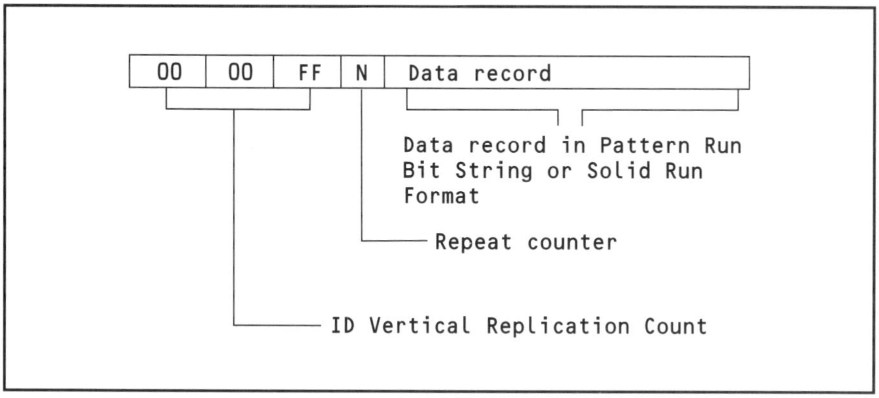

Figure 23.9 Vertical Replication Count record format

The record always begins with a four-byte header. The first three bytes contain the following signature:

`00H 00H FFH`

This code is not used by any other coding method and is employed only when several lines can be represented using *Vertical Replication Count*. The fourth byte contains the number of lines to be displayed. The entry `FEH` will cause the same line to be displayed 254 times. The maximum number of lines in the same representation is 255. The individual pixels are coded in accordance with the methods described above. When creating a picture in IMG format, all graphic objects (rectangles, circles, text) are represented in pixel format and stored in the formats described. Figure 23.10 shows a picture created with DR PAINT. It contains several objects, which have been stored in a file as pixel graphics. GEM even represents texts in individual pixels. As soon as a text is saved, the representational attributes (size, style) can no longer be changed. In black and white representation, the text GEM produces the following pixel pattern:

```
00111100   11111110   11000110 ┐
01100110   01100010   11101110 │
11000000   01100100   11111110 │
11001110   01111100   11111110 ├Pixel rows
01100110   01100100   11010110 │
00111110   01100010   11000110 │
00000000   00000000   00000000 ┘

   G          E          M
```

Figure 23.10 Bit pattern of the text GEM

Colored letters can be produced by mixing the primary colors (red, green, blue and intensity). In this case, the bits will be distributed across the four color planes. Superimposing the bits then produces one of the 16 possible colors for the relevant letters. When processing an IMG file, the various record formats are easy to recognize. Figure 23.11 shows an example of this type of file:

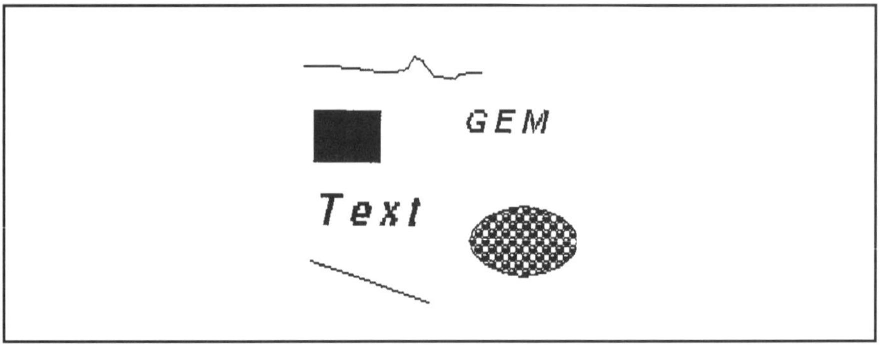

Figure 23.11 Original image in DR PAINT format

The IMG file can be displayed as a hex dump. A section of this display is shown in Figure 23.12

When constructing an image from the IMG file, each row of the corresponding color plane is produced separately, followed by the data for the next color plane of the same scan line. As soon as an image string is produced, it can be decided whether repetition using *Vertical Replication* count is possible.

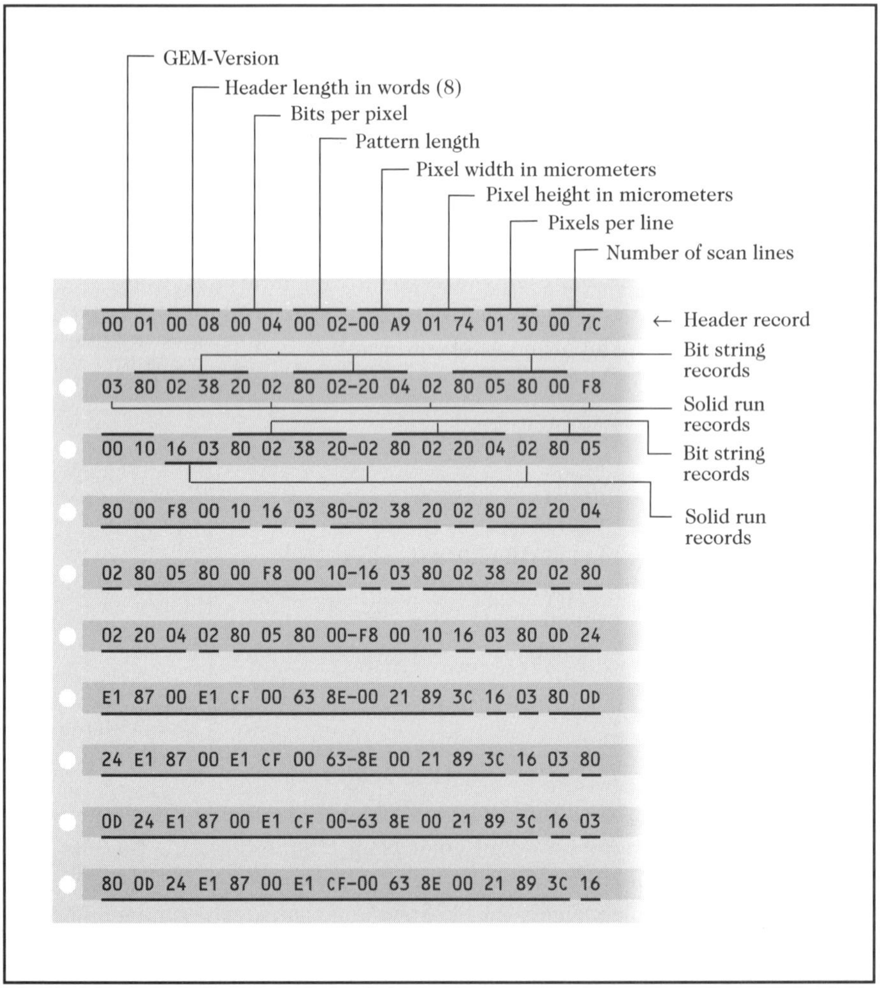

Figure 23.12 Hex dump of an IMG file (*continues over...*)

Graphics

```
03 80 0D 24 22 CC 00 23-04 00 B0 89 00 22 C6 10
16 03 80 0D 24 22 CC 00-23 04 00 B0 89 00 22 C6
10 16 03 80 0D 24 22 CC-00 23 04 00 B0 89 00 22
C6 10 16 03 80 0D 24 22-CC 00 23 04 00 B0 89 00
22 C6 10 16 03 80 0D 24-22 03 00 20 C4 00 80 89
00 22 06 10 16 03 80 0D-24 22 03 00 20 C4 00 80
89 00 22 06 10 16 03 80-0D 24 22 03 00 20 C4 00
80 89 00 22 06 10 16 03-80 0D 24 22 03 00 20 C4
00 80 89 00 22 06 10 16-03 80 0D 38 F1 CE 00 F3
83 00 73 C9 00 21 C9 0C-16 03 80 0D 38 F1 CE 00
F3 83 00 73 C9 00 21 C9-0C 16 03 80 0D 38 F1 CE
00 F3 83 00 73 C9 00 21-C9 0C 16 03 80 0D 38 F1
CE 00 F3 83 00 73 C9 00-21 C9 0C 16 00 00 FF 05
26 26 26 26 17 80 01 38-0E 17 80 01 38 0E 17 80
01 38 0E 17 80 01 38 0E-17 80 01 44 0E 17 80 01
44 0E 17 80 01 44 0E 17-80 01 44 0E 16 80 02 03
82 04 80 02 0F 80 08 16-80 02 03 82 04 80 02 0F
80 08 16 80 02 03 82 04-80 02 0F 80 08 16 80 02
    ....
    ....
00 00 FF 03 10 80 01 01-00 04 FF 3F 80 01 E0 0C
    ....
    ....
00 07 55 55 1F 1E 07 80-01 1F 1E 07 80 01 1F 1E
07 80 01 1F 1E 08 80 01-F0 1D
```

Header of a Vertical Replication Count record with 5 repeats

Vertical Replication Count record header with 3 repeats

Bit String Record

Solid run

Pattern Run Record (Pattern = 2 Byte)

Figure 23.12 Hex dump of an IMG file (*cont.*)

Graphics

24

GEM Metafile format (GEM)

In addition to the IMG format, there is another method for describing image data in GEM. This format does not store image data directly; it describes the objects of an image (circle, rectangle, line, text, and so on) together with their attributes (color, font style, line width, and so on). In this way, the output device is responsible for preparing the image. This has the advantage of creating a representation of the image description which is adapted to the output device. Metafile Format is used by the GEM program DRAW and also by many DTP programs such as Pagemaker and Ventura Publisher, which now also support this format.

24.1 Structure of the GEM Metafile header

A GEM Metafile contains a header *n* bytes long, followed by the records describing the graphic objects. The header data consists of 15 fields of 2 bytes each. These are interpreted as shown in Table 24.1

Offset	Bytes	Remarks
00H	2	Signature FFFFH for GEM Metafiles
02H	2	Header length in words
04H	2	GEM version
06H	2	Coordinate system (RC or NDC)
08H	2	X-Minimum
0AH	2	X-Maximum
0CH	2	Y-Minimum

Table 24.1 GEM Metafile header *(continues over...)*

Offset	Bytes	Remarks
0EH	2	Y-Maximum
10H	2	Page size X-axis
12H	2	Page size Y-axis
14H	2	X-Minimum
16H	2	X-Maximum
18H	2	Y-Minimum
1AH	2	Y-Maximum
1CH	2	Bit image opcode flag
1EH	18	Reserved

Table 24.1 GEM Metafile header (*con..*)

The first word contains the signature FFFFH. This is followed by the header length field. At present, this field contains 0018H; later versions may have different values. The version of GEM that created the file is stored in the third word, with the main version in the upper byte and the sub-version in the lower byte (0210H = 2.1).

The entry at offset 06H, which specifies the coordinate system used, is of particular interest. In GEM, the following variants are used:

Value	**Coordinate system**
0	NDC (Normalized Device Coordinates)
2	RC (Raster Coordinates)

Table 24.2 GEM coordinate systems

Figure 24.1 shows the origin of each of these coordinate systems:

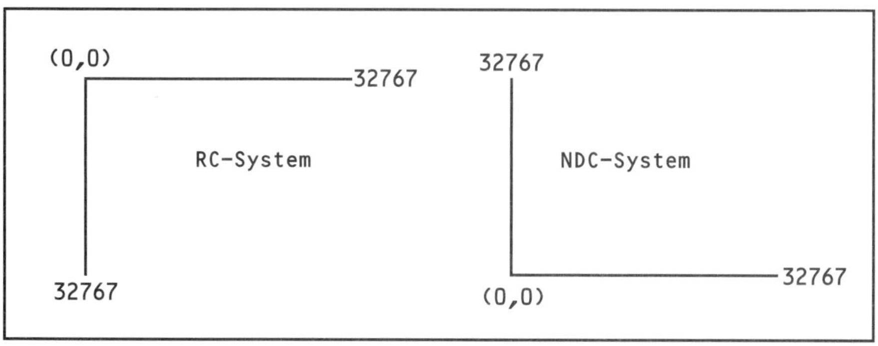

Figure 24.1 RC and NDC coordinate systems

The origin for the two coordinate systems is different. In the NDC system, resolution is related to a virtual coordinate system, whereas in the RC system resolution is determined by the output device used. While a virtual device has a resolution of 0–32767 dots, the resolution is reduced to 640 × 200 dots with a CGA card.

The following four fields specify the image area in which graphic objects may be represented. However, this information is not absolutely necessary, and the value 0 is often found in these fields.

The page size of an image in 1/10 millimeters is indicated at offset 10H. The first field specifies the image width and the second the image height. These dimensions can be used for rescaling the picture if the output device has different dimensions.

The following four words define a window within the metafile. These fields generally contain 0.

The next word is interpreted as a 16 bit flag, in which GEM notes whether bit image data is stored in the later metafile definitions. The coding is as follows:

Bit 0	Coding
0	No bit image opcode in file
1	Bit image opcode in file

Table 24.2 Data storage coding

The remaining bits of the flag have not so far been defined, and the remaining 9 words in the header are reserved.

24.2 Format of Metafile objects

The header is followed by the records containing the object descriptions. Each object description is structured as shown in Table 24.3.

Word	Remark
00H	Object opcode
01H	Number of XY-data pairs (vertices)
02H	Number of other integer values
03H	Object sub-opcode
04H	1st XY-values
...	....
	*n*th XY-values
...	1st integer value
...	....
	*n*th integer value

Table 24.3 Structure of an object description

The record begins with the opcode for the relevant graphic object. Word 1 defines the number of XY pairs. These values start at word 4. In the case of a rectangle, for example, they indicate the corners. Two words are available in the record for each pair. Word 2 contains the number of other integers relating to the object; the actual values are stored after the XY pairs. If words 1 or 2 are set to 0, the relevant fields (XY pairs or integer values) are not defined. The information stored in these fields depends on the object involved.

Table 24.4 lists the opcodes defined, and the corresponding graphic objects.

Type	Subtype	Object
03H	–	Clear Workstation
04H	–	Update Workstation
05H	02H	Exit Alphanumeric Mode
	03H	Enter Alphanumeric Mode
	14H	Form Advance
	15H	Output Window
	16H	Clear Display List
	17H	Output Bit Image File
	19H	Output Printer Alphanumeric Text
	63H	Set Bezier Quality (GEM/3)
06H	–	Polyline
07H	–	Polymarker
08H	–	Text
09H	–	Fill Area
0BH	–	Generalized Drawing Primitives (GDP)
	01H	Bar GDP
	02H	ARC GDP
	03H	PIE GDP
	04H	Circle GDP
	05H	Ellipse GDP
	06H	Elliptical Arc GDP
	07H	Elliptical Pie GDP
	08H	Rounded Rectangle
	09H	Filled Rounded Rectangle
	0AH	Justified graphics Text
	13H	Enter Alphanumeric Mode
	14H	Form Advance
	17H	Output Bit Image File
	19H	Output Printer Alphanumeric Text
0CH	–	Set Character Height
0DH	–	Set Character Baseline Vector
0EH	–	Set Color Representation
0FH	–	Set Polyline Line Type
10H	–	Set Polyline Line Width
11H	–	Set Polyline Color Index

Table 24.4 Opcodes for meta-objects (*continues over...*)

Type	Subtype	Object
12H	–	Set Polymarker Type
13H	–	Set Polymarker Height
14H	–	Set Polymarker Color Index
15H	–	Set Text Font
16H	–	Set Text Color Index
17H	–	Set Fill Interior Style
18H	–	Set Fill Style Index
19H	–	Set Fill Color Index
20H	–	Set Writing Mode
27H	–	Set Graphic Text Alignment
68H	–	Set Fill Parameter Visibility
6AH	–	Set Graphics Text Special Effects
6BH	–	Set Character Height (Points Mode)
6CH	–	Set Polyline End Styles
70H	–	Set User-defined Fill Pattern
71H	–	Set User-defined Line Style Pattern
73H	–	Fill Rectangle
81H	–	Set Clipping Rectangle

Table 24.4 Opcodes for meta-objects (*cont.*)

The parameters of the most important objects are described below:

24.2.1 Poly Line (Opcode 06H)

This object describes a line drawn between several points. The record structure is shown in Table 24.5:

Word	Remark
00H	Opcode 06H
01H	Vertex (X,Y) count
02H	Integer parameter count (0)
03H	Sub-opcode (0)
04H	X-coordinate 1st point
05H	Y-coordinate 1st point
...	...
...	X-coordinate *n*th point
...	Y-coordinate *n*th point

Table 24.5 Record format object 06H

This object has no integer values, and the XY coordinates of n points are stored from word 4 onwards. The number of parameters is stored in word 1.

In GEM/3, the function `Output Bezier` has been introduced as subcode 13.

24.2.2 Poly Marker (Opcode 07H)

This object enables several points to be marked. The object has no integer values, and the XY coordinates of n points are stored from word 4 onwards. The number of parameters is stored in word 1.

Word	Remark
00H	Opcode 07H
01H	Vertex (X,Y) count
02H	Integer parameter count (0)
03H	Sub-opcode (0)
04H	X-Coordinate 1st point
05H	Y-Coordinate 1st point
...	...
...	X-Coordinate nth point
...	Y-Coordinate nth point

Table 24.6 Record format object 07H

24.2.3 Text (Opcode 08H)

This object enables an ASCII text to be displayed at a given position. The format is as follows:

Word	Remark
00H	Opcode 08H
01H	Vertex (X,Y) count (1)
02H	Integer parameter count (x)
03H	Sub-opcode (0)
04H	X-Coordinate first character
05H	Y-Coordinate first character
06H	ASCII string
...	...

Table 24.7 Record format object 08H

The start coordinates for the text and the actual text string are stored in this record. The length of the text is stored in the integer parameter count word.

24.2.4 Fill Area (Opcode 09H)

This object specifies a filled area. The XY coordinates for the area to be filled are stored in the record.

Word	Remark
00H	Opcode 09H
01H	Vertex (X,Y) count (x)
02H	Integer parameter count
03H	Sub-opcode (0)
04H	X-Coordinate 1st point
05H	Y-Coordinate 1st point
...	...
...	X-Coordinate *n*th point
...	Y-Coordinate *n*th point

Table 24.8 Record format object 09H!

! In GEM/3, the sub-function 13 (output filled Bezier) has been added.

24.2.5 Generalized Drawing Primitives (GDP Opcode 0BH)

A number of basic graphic elements (circle, rectangle, and so on) are combined under this opcode. The sub-opcode is used to distinguish between elements. Angles are given in 1/10 degree and calculated counterclockwise.

24.2.5.1 Bar GDP (Opcode 0BH Subcode 01H)

Word	Remark
00H	Opcode 0BH
01H	Vertex (X,Y) count (2)
02H	Integer parameter count (0)
03H	Sub-opcode (01H)
04H	X-Coordinate corner 1 of bar
05H	Y-Coordinate corner 1 (diagonal)
06H	X-Coordinate corner 2
07H	Y-Coordinate corner 2 (diagonal)

Table 24.9
Record format
object 0BH, 01H

This object draws a rectangle and fills it with a selected *area* attribute. The record contains the XY coordinates for two diagonal corners of the rectangle to be filled.

24.2.5.2 Arc GDP (Opcode 0BH Subcode 02H)

This object uses the current *polyline* attribute and the selected drawing mode to produce an arc.

Word	Remark
00H	Opcode 0BH
01H	Vertex (X,Y) count (4)
02H	Integer parameter count (2)
03H	Sub-opcode (02H)
04H	X-Coordinate arc center point
05H	Y-Coordinate arc center point
06H	0
07H	0
08H	0
09H	0
0AH	Radius of arc (in axis units)
0BH	0
0CH	Start angle in ⅒ of degree (0–3600)
0DH	End angle in ⅒ of degree (0–3600)

Table 24.10
Record format
object 0BH, 02H

In the record, the start and end angles of the arc are defined in *angular degrees* × *10*. The XY coordinates and the radius of the arc are also defined. The scaling of the X axis is used for the radius.

24.2.5.3 Pie GDP (Opcode 0BH Subcode 03H)

This object creates a segment of a circle in the current write mode and fills the area with the pattern selected.

Word	Remark
00H	Opcode 0BH
01H	Vertex (X,Y) count (4)
02H	Integer parameter count (2)
03H	Sub-opcode (03H)
04H	X-Coordinate arc center point
05H	Y-Coordinate arc center point
06H	0
07H	0
08H	0
09H	0
0AH	Radius of arc
0BH	0
0CH	Start arc (1/10 degree, 0–3600)
0DH	End arc (1/10 degree, 0–3600)

Table 24.11 Record format object 0BH, 03H

In this record, the start and end angles of the arc are defined in *angular degrees* × *10*. The angle is indicated in the counterclockwise direction. The XY coordinates and the radius of the arc, which is based on the scaling of the X axis, are also defined. The fill attribute for the area can be selected using the meta-object 25H.

24.2.5.4 Circle GDP (Opcode 0BH Subcode 04H)

This object draws a circle in the current drawing mode and fills the area with the color selected.

Word	Remark
00H	Opcode 0BH
01H	Vertex (X,Y) count (3)

Table 24.12 Record format object 0BH, 04H (*continues over...*)

Word	Remark
02H	Integer parameter count
03H	Sub-opcode (04H)
04H	X-Coordinate arc center point
05H	Y-Coordinate arc center point
06H	0
07H	0
08H	Arc radius
09H	0

Table 24.12 Record format object 0BH, 04H (*cont.*)

The coordinates for the center and the radius of the circle are stored in the record. The fill attribute can be set via the meta-object 25H.

24.2.5.5 Ellipse GDP (Opcode 0BH Subcode 05H)

This object uses the selected drawing mode to display an ellipse, which is filled with the current pattern. The center of the ellipse and the radii in the relevant scaling are also stored in this record.

Word	**Remark**
00H	Opcode 0BH
01H	Vertex (X,Y) count (2)
02H	Integer parameter count
03H	Sub-opcode (05H)
04H	X-Coordinate ellipse center point
05H	Y-Coordinate ellipse center point
06H	Radius in X-axis units
07H	Radius in Y-axis units

Table 24.13 Record format object 0BH, 05H

24.2.5.6 Elliptical Arc GDP (Opcode 0BH Subcode 06H)

This object uses the selected drawing mode and displays an elliptical arc.

Word	Remark
00H	Opcode 0BH
01H	Vertex (X,Y) count (4)
02H	Integer parameter count (2)
03H	Sub-opcode (06H)
04H	X-Coordinate elliptic arc center point
05H	Y-Coordinate elliptic arc center point
06H	Radius in X-units
07H	Radius in Y-units
08H	Start angle (1/10 degree, 0–3600)
09H	End angle (1/10 degree, 0–3600)

Table 24.14 Record format object 0BH, 06H

The center point of the ellipse and the radii in the relevant scaling are stored in this record, together with the angles in *degrees* × *10*.

24.2.5.7 Elliptical Pie GDP (Opcode 0BH Subcode 07H)

This object uses the selected drawing mode and displays an elliptical pie, which is filled with the current pattern.

Word	Remark
00H	Opcode 0BH
01H	Vertex (X,Y) count (2)
02H	Integer parameter count (2)
03H	Sub-opcode (07H)
04H	X-Coordinate elliptic arc center point
05H	Y-Coordinate elliptic arc center point
06H	Radius in X-axis units
07H	Radius in Y-axis units
08H	Start angle (1/10 degree, (0–3600)
09H	End angle (1/10 degree, (0–3600)

Table 24.15 Record format object 0BH, 07H

The center point of the ellipse and the radii in the relevant axis scaling are stored in this record, which also contains the angles in *degrees* × *10*.

24.2.5.8 Rounded Rectangle GDP (Opcode 0BH Subcode 08H)

This object draws a rectangle with rounded corners in the type of line selected. The record contains the XY coordinates for two diagonal corners of the rectangle to be displayed. The object uses the line selected via code 23H to draw the shape.

Word	Remark
00H	Opcode 0BH
01H	Vertex (X,Y) count (2)
02H	Integer parameter count (0)
03H	Sub-opcode (08H)
04H	X-Coordinate corner 1
05H	Y-Coordinate corner 1
06H	X-Coordinate corner 2
07H	Y-Coordinate corner 2

Table 24.16
Record format object 0BH, 08H

24.2.5.9 Filled Rounded Rectangle GDP (Opcode 0BH Subcode 09H)

This object draws a rectangle with rounded corners and fills it with the selected color pattern.

Word	Remark
00H	Opcode 0BH
01H	Vertex (X,Y) count (2)
02H	Integer parameter count (0)
03H	Sub-opcode (09H)
04H	X-Coordinate corner 1
05H	Y-Coordinate corner 1
06H	X-Coordinate corner 2
07H	Y-Coordinate corner 2

Table 24.17
Record format object 0BH, 09H

The XY coordinates of two diagonal corners of the rectangle to be filled are stored in the record. The object uses the color attributes selected via code 25H for filling the shape.

24.2.5.10 Justified Graphics Text GDP (Opcode 0BH Subcode 0AH)

This object describes a string, which is left and right justified between two points. The current write mode and attributes selected are used.

Word	Remark
00H	Opcode 0BH
01H	Vertex (X,Y) count (2)
02H	Integer parameter count (*n*+2)
03H	Sub-opcode (0AH)
04H	X-Coordinate text alignment point
05H	Y-Coordinate text alignment point
06H	String length in X-axis units
07H	0
08H	Word spacing flag (modify if not 0)
09H	Char spacing flag (modify if not 0)
0AH	ASCII string

Table 24.18 Record format object 0BH, 0AH

The record contains the XY coordinates for the beginning of the string and the length of the string, in the units of the X scale. The *Word spacing flag* specifies whether the space between words in the string may be altered. If the flag is set to 0, the spacing must not be altered. The *Char spacing flag* fulfils the same function for the spacing between individual characters. From word 0AH the ASCII string is stored as integer parameter. The length of the string +2 is stored in word 02H (integer parameter count).

! In GEM/3, the sub-opcode 0DH (Enable/Disable Bezier capabilities) has been added.

24.2.6 Set Character Height (Opcode 0CH)

This object defines the character size for text displays.

Word	Remark
00H	Opcode 0CH
01H	Vertex (X,Y) count (1)
02H	Integer parameter count
03H	Sub-opcode
04H	0
05H	Character height

Table 24.19 Record format object 0CH

The height of the character is indicated in the units of the current coordinate system (NDC, RC).

24.2.7 Set Character Baseline Vector (Opcode 0DH)

This object defines the angle through which the base line of a character set may be rotated.

Word	Remark
00H	Opcode 0DH
01H	Vertex (X,Y) count
02H	Integer parameter count (1)
03H	Sub-opcode
04H	Angle (1/10 degree, 0–3600)

Table 24.20 Record format object 0DH

The angle is indicated in *degrees* × *10*.

24.2.8 Set Color Mode (Opcode 0EH)

This object defines a color index for the display.

Word	Remark
00H	Opcode 0EH
01H	Vertex (X,Y) count (0)
02H	Integer parameter count (4)
03H	Sub-opcode
04H	Color index
05H	Red color intensity (1/10%, 0–1000)
06H	Green color intensity (1/10%, 0–1000)
07H	Blue color intensity (1/10%, 0–1000)

Table 24.21 Record format object 0EH

For the given index, a color pattern based on the three primary colors is defined. The color intensities are indicated in parts per thousand.

24.2.9 Set Polyline Type (Opcode 0FH)

This object defines the line type for multiple lines.

Word	Remark
00H	Opcode 0FH
01H	Vertex (X,Y) count (0)
02H	Integer parameter count (1)
03H	Sub-opcode
04H	Line type

Table 24.22 Record format object 0FH

The line type is coded as follows:

Code	Line type
FFFFH	Solid
FFF0H	Long dash
E0E0H	Dot
FE38H	Dash-dot
FF00H	Dashed
F198H	Dash-dot-dot

Table 24.23 Line types

Additional user-specific codes can be defined via the object code 71H.

24.2.10 Set Polyline Width (Opcode 10H)

This object defines the line width for polylines.

Word	Remark
00H	Opcode 10H
01H	Vertex (X,Y) count (1)
02H	Integer parameter count
03H	Sub-opcode
04H	Line width
05H	0

Table 24.24 Record format object 10H

The line width indicates the thickness of the line in units of the X axis (NDC/RC units). The value is an odd number and begins with 1.

24.2.11 Set Polyline Color Index (Opcode 11H)

This object defines the color of a polyline. The color index in the record will have been previously defined via object 20H.

Word	Remark
00H	Opcode 11H
01H	Vertex (X,Y) count (0)
02H	Integer parameter count (1)
03H	Sub-opcode
04H	Color index

Table 24.25 Record format object 11H

24.2.12 Set Polymarker Type (Opcode 12H)

This object defines the symbol the *Polymarker* function uses to mark an object.

Word	Remark
00H	Opcode 12H
01H	Vertex (X,Y) count
02H	Integer parameter count (1)
03H	Sub-opcode
04H	Polymarker type

Table 24.26a Record format object 12H

The polymarker type is coded as follows:

Code	Marker type
01H	Point
02H	Plus
03H	Asterisk (default)
04H	Square
05H	Diagonal cross
06H	Diamond

Table 24.26b Polymarker type coding

Values greater than 6 are reserved for user-specific markers.

24.2.13 Set Polymarker Height (Opcode 13H)

This object defines the height of a Polymarker.

Word	Remark
00H	Opcode 13H
01H	Vertex (X,Y) count (1)
02H	Integer parameter count
03H	Sub-opcode
04H	0
05H	Height

Table 24.27 Record format object 13H

The `Height` parameter indicates the height in Y axis units (NDC/RC units).

24.2.14 Set Polymarker Color Index (Opcode 14H)

This object defines the color of a marker.

Word	Remark
00H	Opcode 14H
01H	Vertex (X,Y) count
02H	Integer parameter count (1)
03H	Sub-opcode
04H	Color index

Table 24.28 Record format object 14H

A predefined color index value is stored in this record.

24.2.15 Set Text Font (Opcode 15)

This object selects the font for the text to be displayed.

Word	Remark
00H	Opcode 15H
01H	Vertex (X,Y) count
02H	Integer parameter count (1)
03H	Sub-opcode
04H	Font index

Table 24.29 Record format object 15H

Code	Font Face
01	System Face
02	Swiss 721
03	Swiss 721 Thin
04	Swiss 721 Thin italic
05	Swiss 721 Light
06	Swiss 721 Light italic
07	Swiss 721 Italic
08	Swiss 721 Bold

Table 24.30 Font index (*continues over...*)

Code	Font Face
09	Swiss 721 Bold italic
10	Swiss 721 Heavy
11	Swiss 721 Heavy italic
12	Swiss 721 Black
13	Swiss 721 Black italic
14	Dutch 801 Roman
15	Dutch 801 Italic
16	Dutch 801 Bold
17	Dutch 801 Bold italic

Table 24.30 Font index (*cont.*)

Font numbers 1 to 13 relate to *Swiss* fonts; numbers 14 to 17 define the *Dutch* fonts. Further details are given in the GEM documentation.

24.2.16 Set Text Color Index (Opcode 16H)

This object defines the color of a font.

Word	Remark
00H	Opcode 16H
01H	Vertex (X,Y) count
02H	Integer parameter count (1)
03H	Sub-opcode
04H	Color index

Table 24.31 Record format object 16H

A predefined color index value is stored in this record. The colors are coded as shown in Table 24.32.

Code	Color
0	White
1	Black
2	Red
3	Green
4	Blue
5	Cyan
6	Yellow
7	Magenta
8	White
9	Black
10	Dark red
11	Dark green
12	Dark blue
13	Dark cyan
14	Dark yellow
15	Dark magenta
16-n	Device-dependent

Table 24.32 Standard color index

Color 0 is defined as the standard background color.

24.2.17 Set Fill Interior Style (Opcode 17H)

This object defines the fill pattern. Code 4 is reserved for user-defined fill patterns.

Word	Remark
00H	Opcode 17H
01H	Vertex (X,Y) count
02H	Integer parameter count (1)
03H	Sub-opcode
04H	Fill index

Table 24.33 Record format object 17H

The fill index is coded as follows:

Index	Remark
00H	Hollow
01H	Solid
02H	Pattern
03H	Hatch

Table 24.34
Fill index

24.2.18 Set Fill Style Index (Opcode 18H)

This object defines the index of the pattern filling an area.

Word	Remark
00H	Opcode 18H
01H	Vertex (X,Y) count
02H	Integer parameter count (1)
03H	Sub-opcode
04H	Pattern index

Table 24.35
Record format
object 18H

The index for the fill pattern is interpreted together with the index object 17H. It applies to patterns and hatching in GEM. Fill index 0 produces a hollow area for all pattern index values. Fill index 1 creates a solid area for all pattern index values. Fill index 2 can be used with pattern index values 0–8 to produce a grayscale (8 = black). Pattern index values 9–24 define several fill patterns (brick wall, and so on). Fill index 3 is defined with the pattern indices for hatch patterns. Additional information is given in the GEM reference manuals.

24.2.19 Set Fill Color Index (Opcode 19H)

This object defines the color to be used to fill areas.

Word	Remark
00H	Opcode 19H
01H	Vertex (X,Y) count
02H	Integer parameter count (1)
03H	Sub-opcode
04H	Color index

Table 24.36
Record format
object 19H

A predefined color index value is stored in this record (*see* Table 24.32).

24.2.20 Set Writing Mode (Opcode 20H)

This object defines the current writing mode. The values permitted for this parameter mode are listed in Table 24.37. The mode selected then determines how a displayed object is to be presented against an existing background.

Word	Remark
00H	Opcode 20H
01H	Vertex (X,Y) count (0)
02H	Integer parameter count (1)
03H	Sub-opcode
04H	Mode
	1 Replace
	2 Transparent
	3 XOR
	4 Reverse transparent

Table 24.37 Record format object 20H

24.2.21 Set Graphic Text Alignment (Opcode 27H)

This object defines the alignment of texts in graphics mode.

Word	Remark
00H	Opcode 27H
01H	Vertex (X,Y) count (0)
02H	Integer parameter count (2)
03H	Sub-opcode
04H	Horizontal justify (X)
05H	Vertical justify (Y)

Table 24.38 Record format object 27H

The two integer parameters in words 4 and 5 indicate the alignment of the text in the X and Y directions. The following codes apply to horizontal justification:

X-value	Alignment
0	Left (standard)
1	Centered
2	Right

Table 24.39 Alignment codes (X)

The values shown in the next table apply to vertical alignment. The *half line* (or x-height) of a font defines the top edge of the small letters a, c, v, x, and so on, the *descend line* defines the bottom edge of small letters such as y, g, q, and so on, and the *ascend line* defines the top edge of large letters and many small letters (according to font) such as d, t, b. The *base line* is the line upon which characters without descenders, such as a, c, v, sit. The *bottom line* and *top line* mark the upper and lower edge of the character field. Most fonts adhere to these definitions.

Y-value	Alignment
0	Base line
1	Half line
2	Ascend line
3	Descend line
4	Bottom line
5	Top line

Table 24.40 Alignment codes (Y)

The following values are permitted for this parameter mode.

Code	Remark
1	Replace
2	Transparent
3	XOR
4	Reverse transparent

Table 24.41 Background mode

The mode selected determines how a displayed object is to be represented against the existing background.

24.2.22 Set Fill Parameter Visibility (Opcode 68H)

This object switches the function for drawing a frame around areas on or off.

Word	Remark
00H	Opcode 68H
01H	Vertex (X,Y) count (0)
02H	Integer parameter count (1)
03H	Sub-opcode
04H	Flag

Table 24.42 Record format object 68H

If the flag contains the value 0, the outline of a figure will not be drawn. Any value not equal to 0 will produce an outline around the figure in a continuous line, drawn in the selected color.

24.2.23 Set Graphic Text Special Effects (Opcode 6AH)

This object enables the text display to be modified (bold, underline, italic, and so on).

Word	Remark
00H	Opcode 6AH
01H	Vertex (X,Y) count (0)
02H	Integer parameter count (1)
03H	Sub-opcode
04H	Effect flag

Table 24.43 Record format object 6AH

The flag in word 4 specifies the font display mode (Figure 24.2). If the relevant bit is set to 0, this font effect function is switched off. Combinations of bits enable combined font functions (such as italic, bold).

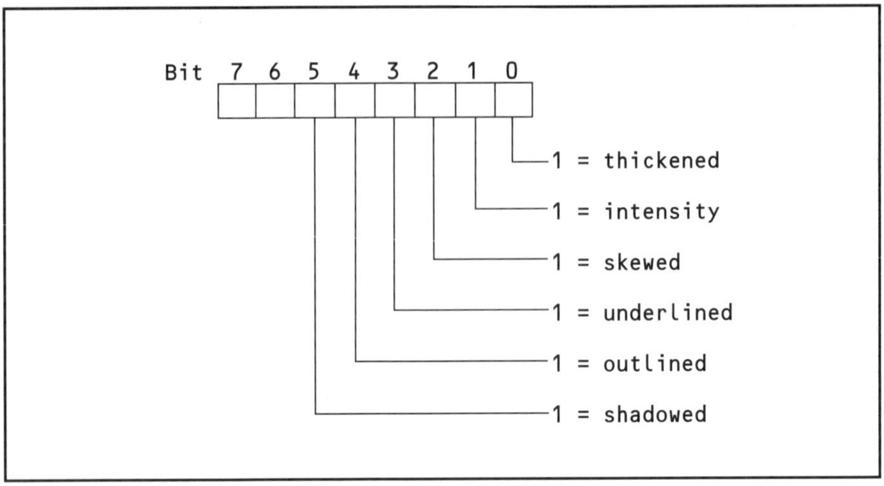

Figure 24.2 Coding font effects

24.2.24 Set Character Height (Opcode 6BH)

This object defines the height of the character to be displayed as a multiple of a point (*printer point*). The character height in points is stored as an integer parameter.

Word	Remark
00H	Opcode 6BH
01H	Vertex (X,Y) count (0)
02H	Integer parameter count (1)
03H	Sub-opcode
04H	Character cell height in points

Table 24.44 Record format object 6BH

24.2.25 Set Polyline End Style (Opcode 6CH)

This object defines the form of the start and end points of a line (polyline).

Word	Remark
00H	Opcode 6CH
01H	Vertex (X,Y) count (0)
02H	Integer parameter count (2)
03H	Sub-opcode
04H	End style of start point
05H	End style of end point

Table 24.45 Record format object 6CH

The parameter for the form may have the values 0 (squared), 1 (arrow) and 2 (rounded). Using these parameters it is possible for a line to have two different forms of end point.

24.2.26 Set User Defined Fill Pattern (Opcode 70H)

This object defines a user-defined fill pattern. For each color plane, 16 words containing the relevant bit pattern are stored. In the case of monochrome graphics, only one plane is needed (16 words). Coded bits indicate that the pixel is to be drawn in the foreground color. The pattern defined can be used for filling areas.

Word	Remark
00H	Opcode 70H
01H	Vertex (X,Y) count (0)
02H	Integer parameter count (x)
03H	Sub-opcode
04H	Fill pattern color planes
...	...

Table 24.46 Record format object 70H

Graphics

24.2.27 Set User Defined Linestyle Pattern (Opcode 71H)

This object enables the line style pattern to be defined by the user (*see* object 0FH). The pattern for a line is defined in one word in the integer parameter. For each bit set, one pixel is displayed in the line drawn.

Word	Remark
00H	Opcode 71H
01H	Vertex (X,Y) count (0)
02H	Integer parameter count (1)
03H	Sub-opcode
04H	Line style pattern

Table 24.47 Record format object 71H

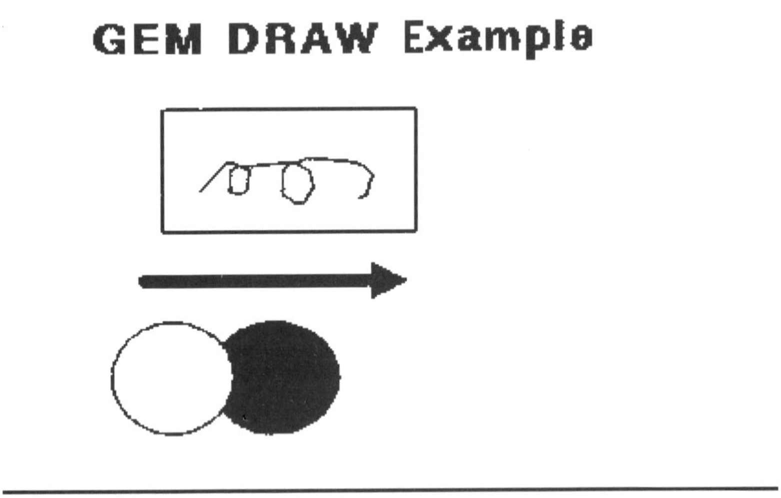

Figure 24.3 Example of a GEM Metafile

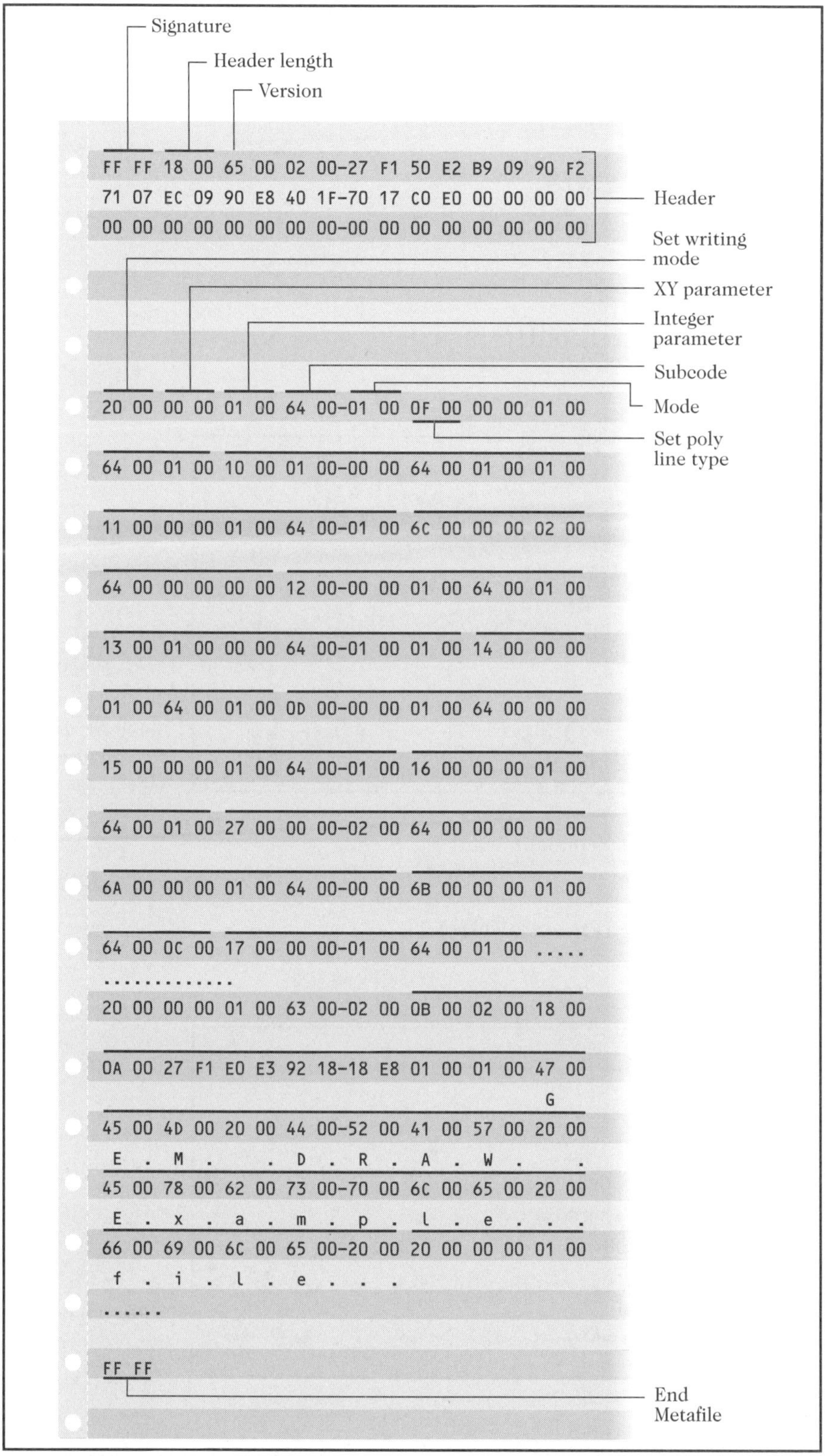

Figure 24.4 Part of a GEM Metafile hex dump

The end of a metafile is marked with the code FFFFH. Figure 24.3 presents a sample image, and the metafile for this image is shown in Figure 24.4 as a hex dump. Further information on the structure of GEM Metafiles is given in the second volume of the GEM Programmer's Toolkit[1].

24.2.28 Extensions for GEM/3

GEM/3 defines the following extensions.

24.2.28.1 Output Bezier (Opcode 06H)

This object draws a hollow Bezier curve.

Word	Remark
00H	Opcode 06H
01H	Vertex (X,Y) count
02H	Integer parameter count (x)
03H	Sub-opcode (0DH)
04H	Coordinates (n)
...	Point types (m)

Table 24.48 Record format object 06H

The number of coordinate points is defined in word 1.

24.2.28.2 Output filled Bezier (Opcode 09H)

This object draws a filled Bezier curve.

Word	Remark
00H	Opcode 09H
01H	Vertex (X,Y) count
02H	Integer parameter count (x)
03H	Sub-opcode (0DH)
04H	Coordinates (n)
...	Point types (m)

Table 24.49 Record format object 09H

The number of coordinate points is defined in word 1.

1 *GEM Programmer's Toolkit* Volume 2, Digital Research, 1986

24.2.28.3 Disable/Enable Bezier Capabilities (Opcode 0BH)

This object switches the Bezier capabilities on and off.

Word	Remark
00H	Opcode (0BH)
01H	Vertex (X,Y) count (0)
02H	Integer parameter count (0)
03H	Sub-opcode (0DH)
04H	Flag
	0 Bezier capabilities off
	1 Bezier capabilities on
05H	0 (Integer)

Table 24.50 Record format object 0BH

24.2.28.4 Set Bezier Quality (Opcode 05BH)

This object defines the quality of Bezier curves.

Word	Remark
00H	Opcode (05H)
01H	Vertex (X,Y) count (0)
02H	Integer parameter count (0)
03H	Sub-opcode (63H)
04H	32 = Bezier quality
05H	1
06H	Quality in percent

Table 24.51 Record format object 05H

25

Interchange File Format (IFF)

***This** standard was introduced by Electronic Arts for the storage of graphics and sounds in files. Originally, IFF files were used on Amiga computers. However, since the appearance of the DeLuxe Paint and DeLuxe Paint II programs, this format is also available to PCs.*

IFF files generally have the extension `.LBM` and are similar to GIF or TIFF files in terms of their block oriented structure (Figure 25.1).

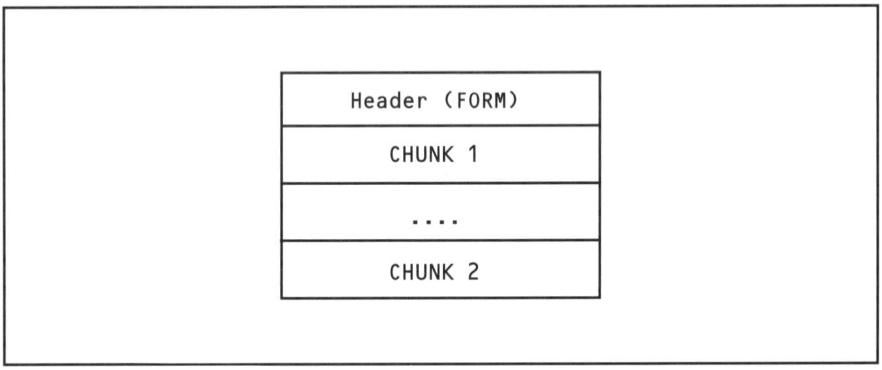

Figure 25.1
Structure
of an IFF file

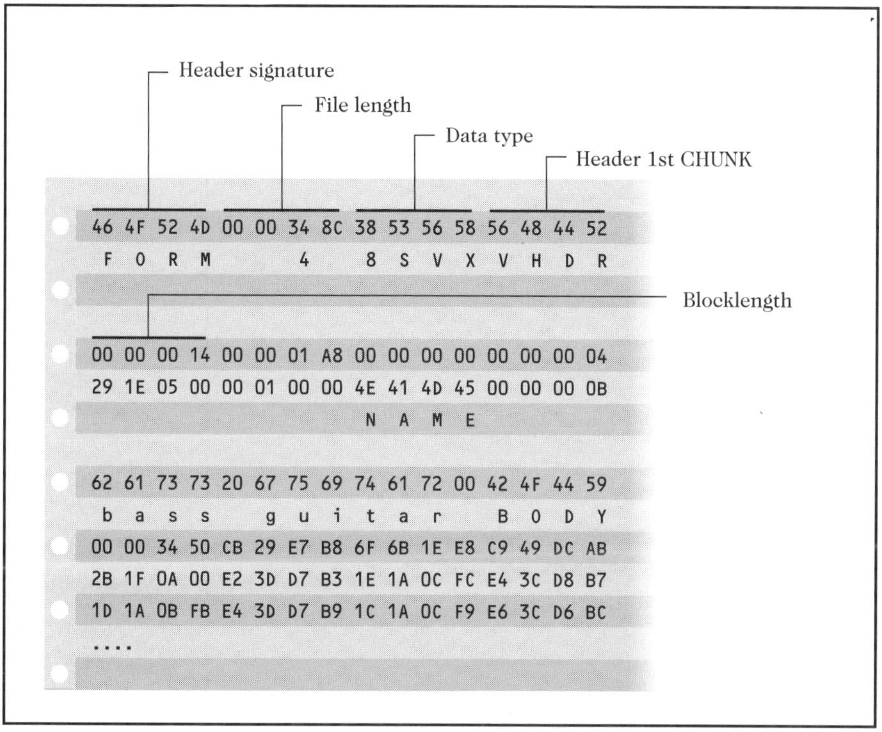

Figure 25.2 Part of an IFF file as a hex dump

The first block of an IFF file contains the header, in which information on the file length and type of data is stored. This is followed by one or more blocks of variable length, which are referred to as CHUNKs. These CHUNKs contain the specifications for data decoding, as well as the actual data. An extract from an IFF file is shown in Figure 25.2. The data is in AMIGA format, that is, high and low bytes are exchanged. The exact structure of the records is described below:

25.1 IFF header

At the start of the file, there is a 12 byte header containing the file length and two signatures. The structure of this header is shown in Table 25.1:

Offset	Bytes	Remarks
00H	4	Signature 1 IFF header (example: 'FORM')
04H	4	File length in bytes (Motorola format)
08H	4	Data type as ASCII string (example: 'ILBM')

Table 25.1 Structure of an IFF header

The first 4 bytes of the header (and also of the IFF file) always contain a signature as a 4-byte ASCII string, which enables valid IFF files to be identified. If an IFF file contains only one image, the signature '`FORM`' is used. In this case the CHUNKs with the image description follow the header.

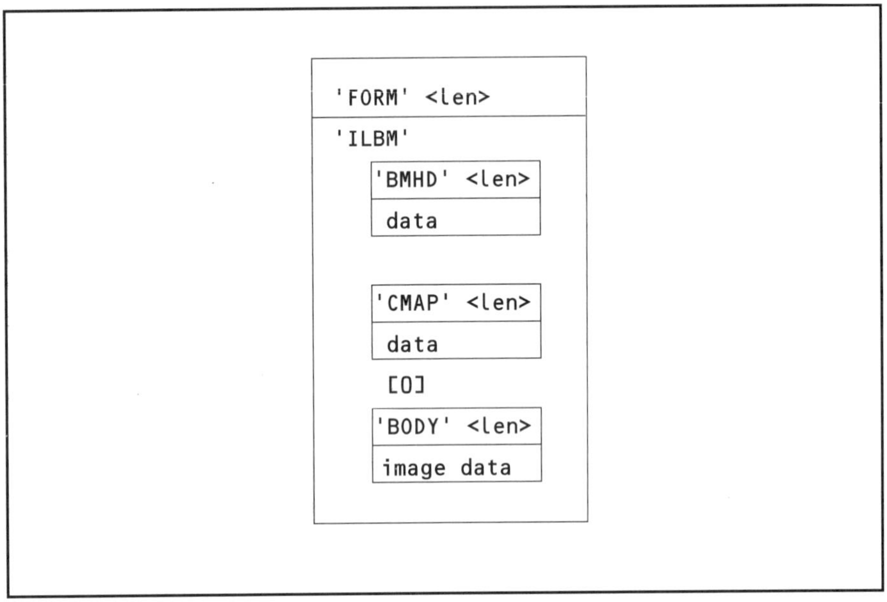

Figure 25.3 Structure of a FORM file

Sometimes it is necessary to merge several images into one IFF file (for example, a picture library). In this case, the CAT (ConcATenate) structure is used. The structure of this file is shown in Figure 25.4.

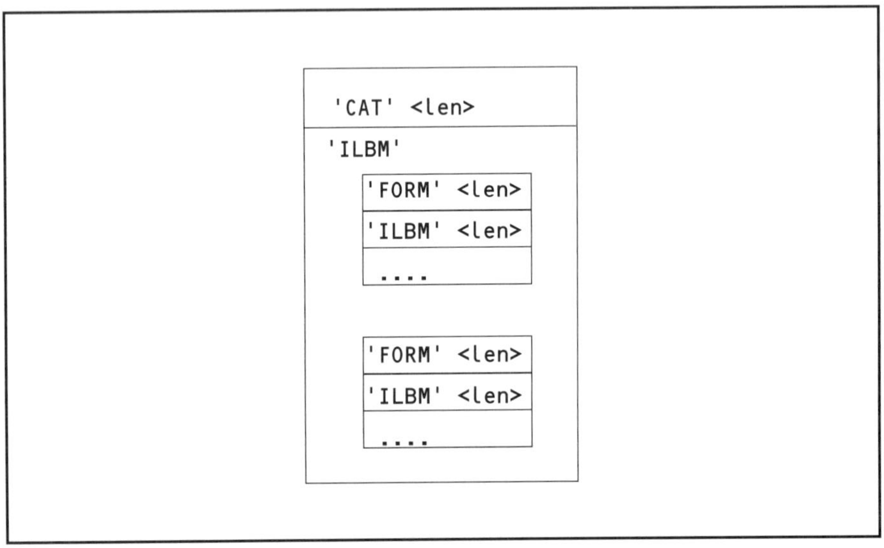

Figure 25.4 Structure of a CAT file

A CAT file may hold several `ILBM`s.

The signature ‘`LIST`’ in the file header indicates a file with several pictures. A CAT file contains just several objects (pictures). The LIST structure with the ‘`PROP`’ block makes it possible to share default properties in the file. With a LIST structure it is possible to share the same color map across many pictures. The structure of a LIST file is shown in Figure 25.5.

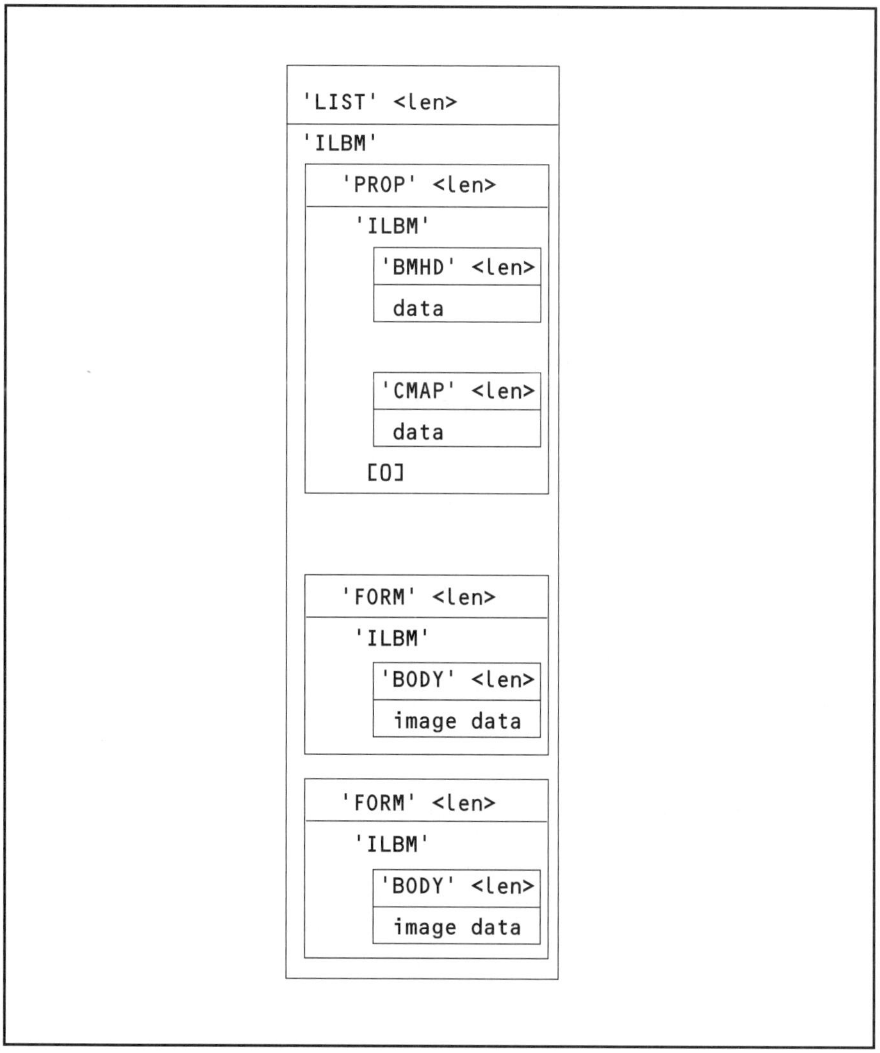

Figure 25.5 Structure of a LIST file

The signatures ‘`LIST`’ and ‘`CAT`’ are rarely used, so an IFF reader may skip this and process only ‘`FORM`’ structures.

This signature (`FORM`, `CAT`, `LIST`) is followed by a 32 bit value at offset `04H`, which specifies the file length in bytes. (Counting starts from 1, and the bytes are stored in *little endian* format – Motorola convention.) This value is required in order to determine the end of the last CHUNK. It should, however, be borne in mind that a file may contain several FORMs.

Signature	Data type
'WORD'	Word data (text file)
'ILBM'	Interleaved bitmap
'PBM'	Graphic like 'ILBM'
'FTXT'	Text file (IFF format)
'AIFF'	Audio IFF (Mac Sound manager)
'SMUS'	Sample music
'8SVX'	8 bit sample voice

Table 25.2 IFF header signatures

The IFF header is terminated at offset `08H` with another 4 byte signature. This is an ASCII string, specifying the type of data (graphics, text, music) contained in the following blocks. Table 25.2 gives a list of valid signatures. It should also be pointed out that there are a number of manufacturer-specific extensions (around 50), which are often inadequately documented. Only the options shown in Table 25.2 are described below.

The above information enables the storage of texts, graphics and sounds in an IFF file. For example, if the header contains the signature '`WORD`', one of the following CHUNKs contains text data. However, the signature '`ILBM`' generally occurs for graphics, as in the case of Deluxe Paint, because this package stores only graphics. Music data and sounds are prefixed with the signatures '`SMUS`' and '`8SVX`'.

Normally, an IFF file contains only one FORM header and the associated CHUNKs, but it is possible to combine graphics, text and sounds in one file. In this case, the file will contain several sets of FORMs and CHUNKs (*see* Figures 25.4 and 25.5).

25.2 IFF Block structure (CHUNK)

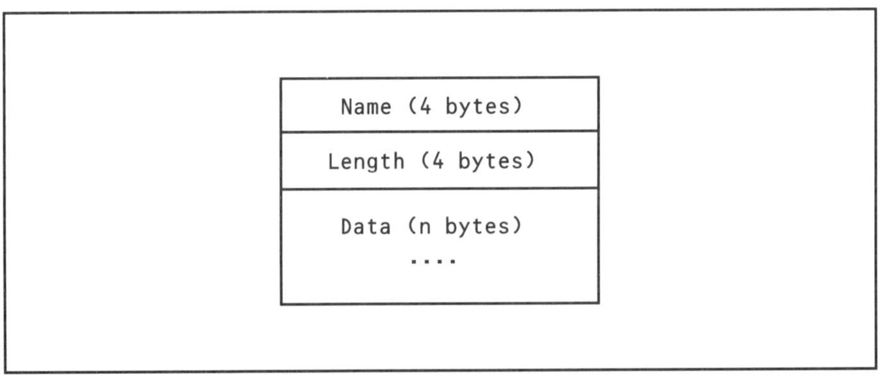

Figure 25.6 Structure of IFF CHUNKs

The header is followed by several blocks (CHUNKs) containing information on the graphics mode, color tables and image data. These CHUNKs have a schematic structure as shown in Figure 25.6.

The first entry contains a 4 byte signature in the form of an ASCII string indicating the type of the relevant CHUNK (block). Table 25.3 gives a list of valid block names for graphic and music data.

Name	Remarks
	Graphic (`ILBM`)
BMHD	Bitmap Header
CMAP	Color Map
CRNG	Color Cycle CHUNK (DPaint)
CCRT	Color Cycle CHUNK (Graphicraft)
GRAB	Hotspot in a graphic
SPRT	Sprite image
CAMG	Amiga specific
BODY	Bitmap data of the image
	Music (`8SVX`)
VHDR	Voice-data (tempo, octave and so on)
NAME	Voice name
(c)	Copyright
AUTH	Author's name
ANNO	Date
BODY	Sound-data
ATAK	Attack (envelope)
RLSE	Release (envelope)

Table 25.3 IFF CHUNK signatures

Depending on the program that created the file, other blocks with different names may also occur, and the overall concept enables new block types to be defined in future. Each block (CHUNK) always begins at an even address in the file. If the preceding block contains an odd number of bytes, a null byte will be appended, but this will not be included in the length field for the block. The first entry in the following block contains the 4 byte ASCII signature. The next entry in the block contains a 4 byte pointer indicating the current block length in bytes. This is followed by the data area, whose length can be calculated as the *block length minus 8*. If an unknown block appears, this may be ignored by the reader program. *DeLuxe Paint*, for example, creates additional blocks containing the areas for color processes.

The color areas in the palette menu can be adjusted, but this information is not needed for the display of image data and can thus be skipped. The structure of the individual CHUNKs is described below.

25.3 CHUNKs: ILBM FORM

To store graphic data, an ILBM FORM is used with various CHUNKs. The structure of the most common CHUNKs is outlined below.

25.3.1 Bitmap Header CHUNK (BMHD)

This CHUNK contains information on graphic mode, image size and so on, and must precede all other CHUNKs. Table 25.4 shows the structure of this block.

Offset	Bytes	Remarks
00H	4	Block name 'BMHD' as an ASCII string
04H	4	Block length in bytes (00H 00H 00H 14H)
08H	2	Image width in pixels
0AH	2	Image height in pixels
0CH	2	X-coordinate upper left corner (in DeLuxe Paint always 0)
0EH	2	Y-coordinate upper left corner (in DeLuxe Paint always 0)
10H	1	Number of bitplanes (for EGA always 4)
11H	1	Reserved (Masking)
12H	1	Image storing 0 = uncompressed 1 = compressed
13H	1	Reserved (Flags)
14H	2	Reserved (Transparency color number)
16H	1	X-aspect ratio
17H	1	Y-aspect ratio
18H	2	X-maximum (image width)
1AH	2	Y-maximum (image height)

Table 25.4 Structure of a bitmap header CHUNK

The CHUNK begins with the ASCII string 'BMHD' as a signature. This is followed by a 4-byte pointer indicating the block length in bytes. This entry should have the value 00H 00H 00H 14H. It is also important to note that the pointer is stored in Motorola format (little endian).

The next two 2-byte vectors describe the current image dimensions using the pixel as the unit of measurement. The coordinates of the top left corner of the image are stored at offset 0CH as 2-byte values (X,Y). The maximum dimensions possible are stored at offset 18H. In DeLuxe Paint, the value (0,0) is always stored in this position. When storing extracts of images, other coordinates may be stored here, under certain circumstances.

IFF files with ILBM CHUNKs are used principally for transferring color images. At offset 10H, there is a byte giving the number of color planes (*bitplanes*). With black and white pictures, this value is 1. As a standard for EGA cards, 16 different colors are provided, and the value is therefore set to 4 bitplanes. The value FFH thus corresponds to 256 color levels. This information is important for decoding the color map.

The byte at offset 17 (11H) is reserved for internal purposes. It defines what type of masking (0 = none, 1 = has mask, 2 = has transparent color, 3 = lasso mask) is to be used for this image. But, I suppose, this byte is never used.

At offset 12H, there is a byte flag specifying the image data compression. The value 0 indicates that the uncompressed data is stored in the BODY block. Since 640 × 350 pixels and 4 bits per color produce 112,000 bytes per image, there is a simple method of compressing the data. Values greater than 0 indicate that the data in the BODY CHUNK is in compressed form. However, only the codes 0 (*uncompressed*) and 1 (*compressed*) are defined at present. The compression algorithm is described below in Section 25.3.5.

The byte at offset 19 (13H) is reserved to store the Amiga CMAP flag. This byte must be set to 0 for consistency.

The next word (offset 14H) is also reserved. Some software packages store the number of the transparency color here. The value is only relevant if the lasso mask is used, but I have never seen a specification for the lasso mask, so the word should always be 0.

The bytes at offset 20 (16H) define the pixel aspect ratio for the X and Y axes. This is important for conversion to new image dimensions. The last two entries contain the width and height of an image in pixels.

25.3.2 Color Map CHUNK (CMAP)

With standard applications, images are built up from 16 colors. In the case of EGA/VGA cards, however, these colors can be derived from 16 million color combinations. Information on the current color palette is stored in a separate table in the optional CMAP CHUNK block, which follows the BMHD CHUNK and is structured as follows:

Offset	Bytes	Remarks
00H	4	Block name 'CMAP' as ASCII string
04H	4	Block length in bytes ($3 \times n$)
08H	$3 \times n$	Image table with n entries of 3 bytes each for the colors red, green, blue

Table 25.5 Structure of the Color Map CHUNK

! Amiga computers support 16 and 256 color graphic chips. In order to distinguish older CMAPs with 4-bit values from newer CMAP CHUNKs with full 8-bit values, the BMHD flag field is used. If bit 7 is set to 1, the CMAP uses full 8-bit values.

The first 4 bytes contain the name CMAP to indicate the CHUNK type. They are followed by the block length in bytes. At offset 08H, there is a table containing the color definitions. Three bytes are allocated to each color to define the proportion of red, green and blue, between 0 and 255. With 24 bits, 16 million color shades can be produced. With 16 selected colors, the table contains $16 \times 3 = 48$ bytes. In this case, each pixel is represented by 4 bits. In future versions of IFF files, the table may contain 256 entries of 3 bytes each. The block length enables the number of entries to be calculated. When evaluating the colors, it may be necessary to adapt or convert the colors, depending on the screen mode.

25.3.3 CRNG CHUNK (DeLuxe Paint)

CRNG is the abbreviation for color register change.

Offset	Bytes	Remarks
00H	4	Block name 'CRNG' (Color Cycle)
04H	4	CHUNK length in bytes
08H	2	Reserved (00H 00H)
0AH	2	Color Cycle Rate
0CH	2	Flag: active/not active
0EH	1	Lower color value (color register)
0FH	1	Upper color value (color register)

Table 25.6 Structure of a CRNG CHUNK

The CRNG CHUNK is used by Electronic Arts DeLuxe Paint program. The CHUNK identifies a contiguous range of color registers for shade and color cycling. This CHUNK is optional and must appear before the BODY CHUNK. DeLuxe Paint normally stores 4 CRNG CHUNKs in an ILBM.

If the low bit in the flag (offset 0CH) is set to 1, then the cycle is active. The colors move to the next higher position in the cycle. If the second bit in the flag is set, the color cycles move in the opposite direction.

The fields at offset 14 (0EH) and 15 (0FH) indicate the range of color registers (color numbers).

The color cycle rate (offset 0AH) determines the speed at which the colors will change. A rate of 60 steps per second is represented as 16384. Slower rates can be obtained with smaller values (8192 = 30 steps per second).

25.3.4 CCRT CHUNK (Graphicraft)

Commodore's Graphicraft program has a similar Color Cycle CHUNK. This, however, contains the signature CCRT and is structured as shown in Table 25.7:

Offset	Bytes	Remarks
00H	4	Block name 'CCRT' (Color Cycle)
04H	4	CHUNK length in bytes
08H	2	Direction
		0 no cycling
		1 forward
		-1 backward
0AH	1	Start color (color register low)
0BH	1	End color (color register high)
0CH	4	Delay (in seconds) for change
10H	4	Delay (in microseconds)
14H	2	Unused (00H 00H)

Table 25.7 CCRT CHUNK structure

The precise meaning of these fields was not available at the time of writing.

25.3.5 BODY CHUNK containing data

The actual image data is stored in the BODY CHUNK. The signature is followed by a 4 byte pointer giving the block length, as shown in Table 25.8:

Offset	Bytes	Remarks
00H	4	Block name 'BODY' as ASCII string
04H	4	Block length in bytes
08H	n	Image data

Table 25.8 BODY CHUNK structure (data block)

The image data follows at offset 08H. The entry 0 at offset 12H in the BMHD CHUNK indicates that the data is uncompressed; values greater than 0 indicate compressed data, but only the value 1 is used at present. The image data of one bitplane is stored row by row, in accordance with the following record structure:

1st Byte = Control byte

2nd Byte = Data byte

...

nth Byte = "

The first byte is interpreted as a control byte.

- If it contains a value less than 128 (80H), it is followed by n different data bytes, where n is the value of the control byte + 1.
- With values greater than 128 (80H), the following byte contains the compressed image sequence which is to be decoded. This byte should then be duplicated n times. The number n is calculated from the value of the control byte according to the following formula:

  n = 100H – value of the control byte

  The entry FDH in the control byte produces a repetition factor of 100H – FDH + 1 = 3. This enables efficient storage of uniform areas of the image (for example filled areas).
- A value of 80H in the control byte means that the byte will be skipped, and the following byte will be interpreted as a control byte.

The pixels in the data area are stored row by row.

25.3.6 GRAB CHUNK

This CHUNK is optional. It is used very rarely and describes a 'hot spot' (for example, mouse pointer). The CHUNK is structured as follows:

Offset	Bytes	Remarks
00H	4	Block name 'GRAB' as ASCII-string
04H	4	Block length in bytes
08H	2	X-coordinate in pixels (relative)
0AH	2	Y-coordinate in pixels (relative)

Table 25.9 GRAB CHUNK structure

25.3.7 DEST CHUNK

This CHUNK is also optional. It describes how to scatter source bitplanes into a destination bitmap. The CHUNK is structured as follows:

Offset	Bytes	Remarks
00H	4	Block name 'DEST' as ASCII string
04H	4	Block length in bytes
08H	1	Number of bitplanes in the source
09H	1	Reserved (00H)
0AH	2	Bits for destination bitplane (planePick)
0CH	2	Bitplane flag (planeOnOff)
0EH	2	Mask destination bitplane (planeMask)

Table 25.10 DEST CHUNK structure

The low order bits in *planePick, planeOnOff* and *planeMask* correspond one-to-one (bit 0 with bitplane 0, and so on) with the destination bitplanes. The higher bits should be ignored.

A bit set to 1 in *planePick* means to put the next source bitplane into the destination bitplane. The number of 1 bits must be equal to the number of bitplanes. If the bit in *planePick* is set to 0, the corresponding bit in *planeOnOff* must be inserted in the destination bitplane.

The last entry, *planeMask*, controls the writing to the destination bitmap. If a bit is set to 1, writing to the corresponding destination bitplane is allowed. Otherwise, the bitplane is left unmodified.

25.3.8 SPRT CHUNK

The optional SPRT CHUNK defines the priority of a Sprite. The CHUNK is structured as follows:

Offset	Bytes	Remarks
00H	4	Block name 'SPRT' as ASCII string
04H	4	Block length in bytes
08H	2	Sprite priority (0–7)

Table 25.11 SPRT CHUNK structure

The value 0 indicates the maximum priority, that is, the sprite supersedes all other sprites.

25.3.9 CAMG CHUNK

The CAMG CHUNK is specific to the AMIGA and indicates the graphic mode:

Offset	Bytes	Remarks
00H	4	Block name 'CAMG' as ASCII string
04H	4	Block length in bytes
08H	4	View mode register

Table 25.12 CAMG CHUNK structure

25.3.10 CLUT CHUNK

The CLUT CHUNK defines a Color Look Up Table:

Offset	Bytes	Remarks
00H	4	Block name 'CLUT' as ASCII string
04H	4	Block length in bytes
08H	4	Table type
0CH	4	Reserved
10H	256	Color table (8 Bit)

Table 25.13 CLUT CHUNK structure

The type of table (mono, RGB, and so on) is indicated at offset 08H. The following bytes are reserved. At offset 10H, there is a table containing 256 entries for the 8-bit color definitions. There are other CHUNK names reserved for the ILBM FORM, but these tend to be either very specifically coded or inadequately documented. For example, DPaint II uses the DPPV CHUNK to store information on the perspective of individual rotating objects. The PC version of DeLuxe Paint II Enhanced also contains a TINY CHUNK which can store partial images. (According to various sources, the length indicator in the CHUNK is said to be 1 too low in some cases.)

The program DeLuxe Paint II expects the CHUNKs in a fixed sequence: BMHD (offset 0CH), CMAP (offset 28H), BODY. If this sequence is not adhered to, the image cannot be read. But if the IFF specification says that the CHUNKs may occur in any order, only the the BODY CHUNK should be the last.

A third obstacle is that a new FORM ('PBM') has been defined for storing VGA pictures with 256 colors. The CHUNKs correspond to the structure of BMHD CHUNKs, but the bits stored are interpreted differently. With the ILBM FORM, the individual bits making up a pixel are divided into color planes. With 256 colors, this produces 8 (bit) color planes. The image is then stored bit by bit. In the first scan, bit 1 of each byte from the first row is collated and stored. In the next scan, bit 2 of each byte is read and stored by row. As soon as all 8 bits of a line have been stored in this way, the processing of line 2 of the image begins. This is a very laborious process. The PBM FORM indicates that the data (8 bits) for each pixel is to be stored directly as bytes. In this way, each pixel can be processed directly from the graphic memory, which is considerably faster and simpler. The data is stored in the BODY block and compressed as described above.

25.4 CHUNKs: 8SVX FORM

As with graphics, it is also possible to store digitized sounds (sampled data) in 8-bit format, in IFF files. The 8SVX CHUNK is provided for this purpose. The structure of the header is identical to the ILBM FORM except that, at offset 08H, there is a 4 byte string 8SVX as a signature. The associated CHUNKs are described below.

25.4.1 Voice Header CHUNK (VHDR)

This block contains information on the storage of digitized sounds in the BODY CHUNK. The VHDR CHUNK is structured as shown in Table 25.14:

Offset	Bytes	Remarks
00H	4	Signature 'VHDR' (Voice Header)
04H	4	CHUNK length in bytes
08H	4	OneShotHiSamples
0CH	4	RepeatHiSamples

Table 25.14 Structure of a VHDR CHUNK (*continues over...*)

Offset	Bytes	Remarks
10H	4	Samples per HiCycle (Bytes per wave, even number)
14H	2	Samples per second
16H	1	Octaves in BODY CHUNK
17H	1	Coding 0 = unpacked 1 = packed
18H	4	Volume

Table 25.14 Structure of a VHDR CHUNK (*cont.*)

To interpret the BODY CHUNK, these values must be evaluated. At offset 17H, there is a flag specifying how data is stored in the BODY CHUNK. The value 1 indicates that the data is packed (Fibonacci delta). For the volume setting at offset 18H, the standard value is 0001H 0000H.

25.4.2 NAME CHUNK (Name)

In this CHUNK, a text can be stored to indicate the instrument creating the sound. The record structure is shown in Table 25.15.

Offset	Bytes	Remarks
00H	4	Signature 'NAME' (Name)
04H	4	CHUNK length in bytes
08H	4	String containing the name of the instrument

Table 25.15 NAME CHUNK structure

Any string may be stored in the text field because it will be treated as a comment text. If the string occupies an odd number of bytes, a null byte (00H) must be added to the CHUNK, but this is not included in the length field for the CHUNK. The null byte enables the following CHUNK to begin at an even-numbered offset address.

25.4.3 BODY CHUNK (Data)

This CHUNK contains the digitized data. The structure is the same as for the ILBM BODY CHUNK (Table 25.8). There are two possible ways of using the stored voice data:

25.4.3.1 One Shot Sound

In this case, a unique sound (*effect*) has been digitized and stored. The Voice Header CHUNK contains information on the change rate in *Samples per second*, *OneShotHiSamples* and *RepeatHiSamples* for the number of data. If the value *SamplesperHiCycle* is not known, zero is used. The number of octaves is always set to 1.

25.4.3.2 Musical Instrument

The second use is for sampling and storing the sound of an instrument. The following digitization strategy is adopted: first, the sound of the instrument is recorded as a *OneShotHiSample*. The next stage is to store the duration of the sound in *RepeatHiSamples*. In order to reproduce the sound authentically, the sounds are stored over several octaves. The data in the Voice Header always relates to the highest octave stored. If the number of octaves in this header is greater than 1, the sound data is stored one octave after another in the BODY CHUNK. It should be noted that for each octave, *n* bytes are stored for *OneShotSamples* and *n* bytes for *RepeatHiSamples*. This means that the memory requirement is doubled from octave to octave. In the *SamplesperHiCycle* field in the Voice Header, the number of bytes is indicated per vibration, for a sound in the highest octave.

In general, the data is uncompressed, in order to avoid distortion. If the value 1 is stored at offset 17H in the Voice Header, the data is packed according to the Fibonacci-delta algorithm.

As described, the data is ordered sequentially by octave in the data block. For each sample, the amplitude is stored, signed and coded in 8 bits. With negative values only the uppermost bit is inverted. The smallest amplitude can be represented by 1000 0000B, while the largest amplitude has the value 0111 1111B.

25.4.4 ATAK CHUNK

This CHUNK is optional and describes a rising envelope curve (attack). The chunk contains 6 data bytes with the following structure:

Offset	Bytes	Remarks
00H	4	Block name 'ATAK' as ASCII string
04H	4	Block length in bytes
08H	2	Volume delay time
0AH	4	Volume factor

Table 25.16 ATAK CHUNK structure

The exact meaning of this data is not documented.

Graphics

25.4.5 RLSE CHUNK

This Chunk defines a falling envelope curve (release). The data area corresponds to the coding for the ATAK CHUNK. This CHUNK is also optional.

25.5 CHUNKs: AIFF FORM

This is a manufacturer-specific FORM for the Apple Macintosh Sound Manager. It is used for sampling music and language and offers many more options than the 8SVX form. Since the data structure is documented, this format is only briefly described here.

25.5.1 COMM CHUNK

The COMM CHUNK describes the samples and is structured as follows:

Offset	Bytes	Remarks
00H	4	Block name 'COMM' as ASCII string
04H	4	Block length in bytes
08H	2	Number of channels
0AH	4	Number of FRAMES (in SNDD)
0EH	2	Bits in samples
10H	10	Sample rate (frames/sec)

Table 25.17 COMM CHUNK structure

The Sample Rate value is entered as a 10 byte floating point number in Macintosh-Pascal format.

25.5.2 SNDD CHUNK

The SNDD CHUNK describes the sound data of the individual sections:

Offset	Bytes	Remarks
00H	4	Block name 'SNDD' as ASCII string
04H	4	Block length in bytes
08H	4	Offset to beginning of first FRAME
0CH	4	Block size in first FRAME
12H	*x*	Data

Table 25.18
SNDD CHUNK structure

The coding for this data is not included in the documentation.

25.5.3 INST CHUNK

The INST CHUNK specifies the instruments to be played for the MIDI interface.

Offset	Bytes	Remarks
00H	4	Block name 'INST' as ASCII string
04H	4	Block length in bytes
08H	1	Note base
09H	1	Pitch
0AH	1	Lowest musical note in range
0BH	1	Highest musical note in range
0CH	1	Smallest velocity
0DH	1	Highest velocity
0EH	2	Sound variation (in db)
10H	6	Sustain Loop
16H	6	Release Loop

Table 25.19
INST CHUNK structure

The FORM contains other CHUNKs (MIDI, AESD, APPL, COMT), but these will not be discussed further, since some of the codings are not known.

25.6 CHUNKs: SMUS FORM

This FORM (SMUS = Simple Musical Score) also stores data for music and sound which has been produced using MIDI tools. The FORM contains the following CHUNKs:

25.6.1 SHDR CHUNK

This CHUNK describes the SCORE header and is structured as follows:

Offset	Bytes	Remarks
00H	4	Block name 'SHDR' as ASCII string
04H	4	Block length in bytes
08H	2	Tempo (1/4 note per 128 minutes)
0AH	1	Volume (0..127)
0BH	1	Voices following track

Table 25.20 SHDR CHUNK structure

The exact coding of this data is not documented.

25.6.2 INS1 CHUNK

This CHUNK contains information on the instrument used for the following tracks. It is structured as follows:

Offset	Bytes	Remarks
00H	4	Block name 'INS1' as ASCII string
04H	4	Block length in bytes
08H	1	Register number instrument (0–255)
09H	1	Instrument selection flag 0 Selection per name 1 Selection in following bytes
0AH	1	MIDI channel (if flag = 0)
0BH	1	MIDI preset (if flag = 0)
0CH	*x*	Instrument name

Table 25.21 INS1 CHUNK structure

The exact coding of this data is not documented.

25.6.3 TRAK CHUNK

The TRAK CHUNK contains the music data for a MIDI track. It is structured as follows:

Offset	Bytes	Remarks
00H	4	Block name 'TRAK' as ASCII string
04H	4	Block length in bytes
08H	*n*	Data area
		1 Byte interpretation
		n Byte music notes

Table 25.22 TRAK CHUNK structure

Two bytes are stored for each note. The first byte defines how the note stored in the following byte is to be interpreted. The exact coding for this data is not currently available.

25.7 CHUNKs: FTXT FORM

The FTXT FORM was defined for formatted texts. However, this FORM has so far been used only by the program TextCraft, which is not very widely distributed. There are two CHUNKs for this FORM:

25.7.1 FONS CHUNK

The FONS CHUNK describes the font used in the text:

Offset	Bytes	Remarks
00H	4	Block name 'FONS' as ASCII string
04H	4	Block length in bytes
08H	1	Font number
09H	1	Reserved
0AH	1	Flag proportional font
0BH	1	Serif flag
		0 = unknown
		1 = serif font
		2 = font without serif
0CH	*x*	Font name

Table 25.23 FONS CHUNK structure (*continues over...*)

The exact coding of this data is not currently available.

Graphics

25.7.2 CHRS CHUNK

This CHUNK contains the text. It is structured as follows:

Offset	Bytes	Remarks
00H	4	Block name 'CHRS' as ASCII string
04H	4	Block length in bytes
08H	x	Text

Table 25.24 CHRS CHUNK structure

The exact coding of the text formatting is not currently available.

25.8 CHUNKs: WORD FORM

The WORD FORM was defined for formatted texts. However, this FORM has so far only been used in the program ProWrite from Horizon Software. By contrast with the FTXT format, formatting instructions can also be stored. There are two CHUNKs for this FORM:

25.8.1 FONT CHUNK

The FONT CHUNK is optional and describes the font used in the text:

Offset	Bytes	Remarks
00H	4	Block name 'FONT' as ASCII string
04H	4	Block length in bytes
08H	1	Font number (0–255)
09H	2	Font size
0BH	x	Font name

Table 25.25 FONT CHUNK structure

For every font used, a CHUNK of this kind should precede the data. However, the precise coding of the data is not currently available.

25.8.2 COLR CHUNK

This CHUNK describes the translation table for ISO colors. There are 8 entries altogether in the table. However, the coding of these entries is not currently available.

25.9 Other text CHUNKs

Other CHUNKs are defined to store and format text in an IFF file.

25.9.1 DOC CHUNK

This CHUNK introduces the start of a DOCUMENT section. The instructions for formatting the text follow this CHUNK.

Offset	Bytes	Remarks
00H	4	Block name 'DOC' as ASCII string
04H	4	Block length in bytes
08H	2	First page number
0AH	1	Type of page numbering
0BH	5	Reserved

Table 25.26 DOC CHUNK structure

Pages can be numbered with figures (1, 2) or letters (i, I, A, a). This option is indicated in the field *Type of page numbering*.

25.9.2 FOOT/HEAD CHUNK

The structure of both of these CHUNKs is identical. They describe the header and footer lines of a document.

Offset	Bytes	Remarks
00H	4	Block name 'FOOT' or 'HEAD'
04H	4	Block length in byte
08H	1	Position of header or footer
09H	1	1st page (0 = not page 1)
0AH	4	Reserved

Table 25.27 FOOT/HEAD CHUNK structure

If the value at offset 09H is 0, the header and footer texts on the first page of the document will not be displayed. The text for header and footer lines applies until the next CHUNK of type DOC, HEAD, FOOT or PCTS is encountered.

25.9.3 PARA CHUNK

This CHUNK describes the formatting of the following paragraph.

Offset	Bytes	Remarks
00H	4	Block name 'PARA' as ASCII string
04H	4	Block length in bytes
08H	2	Indent (in 1/10 point)
0AH	2	Left margin
0CH	2	Right margin
0EH	1	Spacing
0FH	1	Line justify
10H	1	Font number
11H	1	Flag font style
12H	1	Normal, sub- or superscript
13H	1	Internal color number
14H	4	Reserved

Table 25.28 PARA CHUNK structure

The exact coding of the individual entries is not currently available.

25.9.4 TABS CHUNK

This CHUNK describes the position of the tabulators.

Offset	Bytes	Remarks
00H	4	Block name 'TABS' as ASCII string
04H	4	Block length in bytes
08H	2	TAB position in 1/10 point
0AH	1	Alignment (left, center...)
0BH	1	Reserved

Table 25.29 TABS CHUNK structure

The precise coding of the individual entries is not currently available.

25.9.5 PAGE CHUNK

This page describes a page break in the text.

Offset	Bytes	Remarks
00H	4	Block name 'PAGE' as ASCII string
04H	4	Block length in bytes

Table 25.30 PAGE CHUNK structure

The CHUNK has no content; it merely defines a marker.

25.9.6 TEXT CHUNK

This CHUNK contains the text for a paragraph. It is structured as follows:

Offset	Bytes	Remarks
00H	4	Block name 'TEXT' as ASCII string
04H	4	Block length in bytes
08H	*x*	Text

Table 25.31 TEXT CHUNK structure

The text should contain no carriage returns or LF characters.

25.9.7 FSCC CHUNK

This CHUNK defines the parameters FONT, STYLE and COLOR for the preceding text:

Offset	Bytes	Remarks
00H	4	Block name 'FSCC' as ASCII string
04H	4	Block length in bytes
08H	2	Character position in paragraph
0AH	1	Font number
0BH	1	Flags for font style
0CH	1	Normal, subscript, superscript
0DH	1	Internal color number
0EH	1	Reserved

Table 25.32 FSCC CHUNK structure

Further details are not currently available.

25.9.8 PCTS CHUNK

This CHUNK specifies that a picture is to be merged with the text:

Offset	Bytes	Remarks
00H	4	Block name 'PCTS' as ASCII string
04H	4	Block length in bytes
08H	1	Number of bitplanes
09H	1	Reserved

Table 25.33 PCTS CHUNK structure

The CHUNK is followed by the definition of the image data (*see below*).

25.9.9 PINF CHUNK

This CHUNK defines further information about the picture which is to be merged with the text:

Offset	Bytes	Remarks
00H	4	Block name 'PINF' as ASCII string
04H	4	Block length in bytes
08H	2	Width in pixels
0AH	2	Height in pixels
0CH	2	Page number of image
0EH	2	X-position of image
10H	2	Y-position of image
12H	1	Mask (*see* ILBM BMHD)
13H	1	Compression
14H	1	Transparent
15H	1	Reserved

Table 25.34 PINF CHUNK structure

This CHUNK is followed by the definition of the image data. The image data is stored in a BODY CHUNK which corresponds to the coding of the ILBM FORM.

25.10 Miscellaneous CHUNKs

A number of additional CHUNKs have been defined which may appear in all FORMS. They define commentaries and additional information on the data. The following table shows the name and the structure of these CHUNKs.

Offset	Bytes	Remarks
00H	4	Block name CHUNK as ASCII string
		'(c)' copyright
		'ANNO' annotations
		'AUTH' author's name
		'CHRS' text
		'NAME' name for graphic, music, and so on
		'TEXT' unformatted text
08H	x	n bytes containing text

Table 25.35 Miscellaneous CHUNK structure

This ends the description of IFF formats. Further details can be obtained from the literature under references 3 and 4 below.

3 Morrison, Jery, EA IFF 85 **Standard for Interchange Format Files**, *Electronic Arts, January 14, 1985.*
4 Morrison, Jery, ILBM IFF, **Interleaved Bitmap**, *Electronic Arts, January 17, 1986.*

Graphics

26

Graphics Interchange format (GIF)

In 1987, CompuServe defined a protocol for exchanging graphic data via e-mail. The associated GIF format enables several pictures to be stored in one file. Decoding and compression guarantee good data compression and rapid reproduction of images. The graphics format is hardware-independent and enables pictures with up to 16000 × 16000 pixels composed of up to 256 colors to be stored in Intel format (Big endian).
The GIF specification published in 1987 is referred to as GIF87a. An extended version of the GIF standard (GIF89a) was published in 1989.

A GIF file consists of several blocks containing the graphics and additional data. As with the TIFF format, *tag* fields are also used. The blocks can be divided into three groups:

- Control blocks
- Graphic Rendering blocks
- Special Purpose blocks

The *Control* blocks (for example, Header, Logical Screen Descriptor, Graphics Control Extension, Trailer) contain information on the control of the image representation. *Graphic Rendering* blocks (for example, Image Descriptor, Plain Text Extension) contain the actual graphics data. The *Special Purpose* blocks (for example, Comment Extension, Application Extension) are manufacturer-specific and should be skipped by the decoder.

With the exception of the sub-blocks used for storing data, the block size is fixed. If the block contains a *Block Size* field, this field indicates the number of following bytes in the block. This size does not take into account any terminator that may be present.

Figure 26.1 shows the structure of a GIF file.

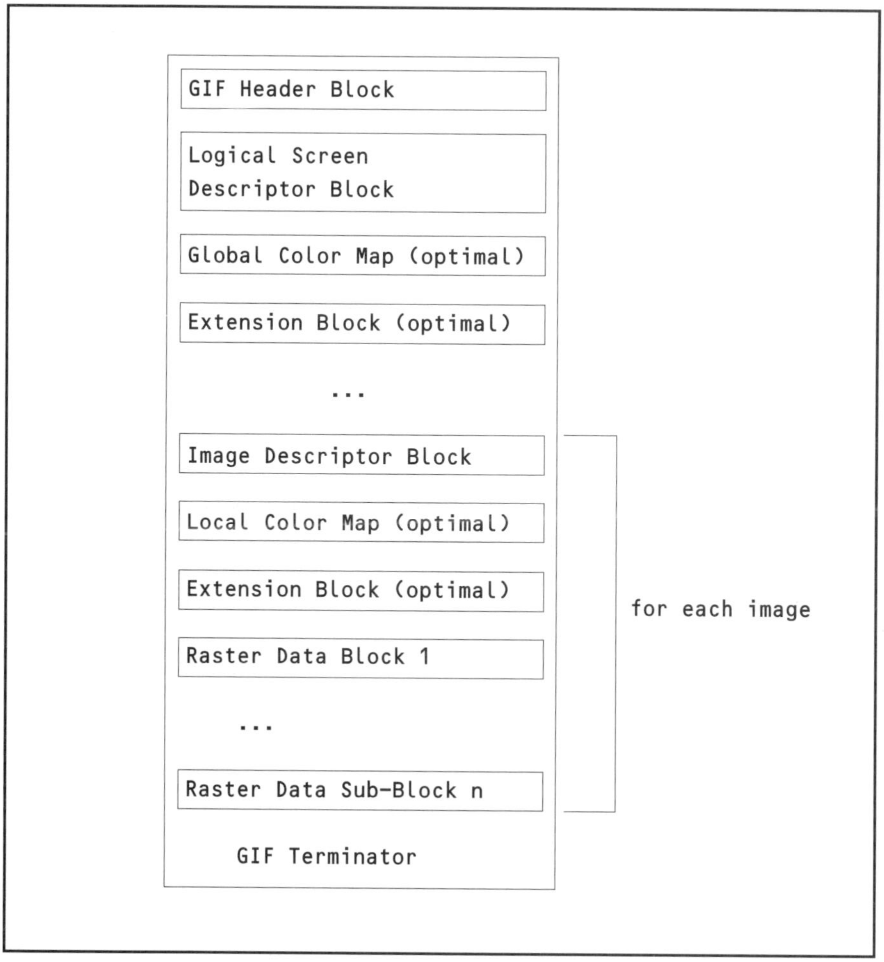

Figure 26.1 Structure of a GIF file

For every picture in the GIF file, an *Image Descriptor* and one or more *Raster Data* blocks are created. An optional *Local Color Map* block may also be present. Within this block structure, there may be sub-blocks (for example, blocks containing image data). The sub-blocks consist of a length byte, which defines the number of following bytes in the block (0–255), followed by the data area.

26.1 GIF header

A GIF file must always begin with a header. This header consists of 6 bytes and is structured as shown in Table 26.1.

Offset	Bytes	Field
00H	3	Signature 'GIF'
03H	3	Version '87a' or '89a'

Table 26.1
GIF header

The first three bytes contain a signature ('GIF'); these are followed by three bytes indicating the version of GIF. The following versions are currently defined:

- 87a GIF Definition May 1987
- 89a GIF Definition July 1989

The header may occur only once in a GIF file and it must be the first block in the file. The subsequent block structure is the same for GIF87a and GIF89a, but additional block types are defined in GIF89a. A number of the flags in the GIF89a version have also been modified. Reference will be made to these alterations at the relevant point in the description. Older GIF87a decoders can also process a GIF89a file, but the extended block types are skipped and information may therefore be lost.

26.2 Logical Screen Descriptor block

The header must be followed (at offset 06H) by the 7 byte *Logical Screen Descriptor* block containing data relating to the logical screen. This block is used in both GIF87a and GIF89a. The data applies to the whole GIF file and is structured as follows:

Bytes	Field
2	Logical Screen Width
2	Logical Screen Height
1	Resolution Flag
1	Background Color Index
1	Pixel Aspect Ratio

Table 26.2
Structure of a Logical Screen Descriptor block

The first entry contains a 16 bit value indicating the width of the logical screen in pixels. Intel notation (low byte first) is used for storage. The next field contains the screen height, also a 16 bit value. Both values relate to a virtual screen, the origin of which is located in the top left corner. At offset 04H, there is a bit field (*Resolution Flag*) coded as shown in Figure 26.2.

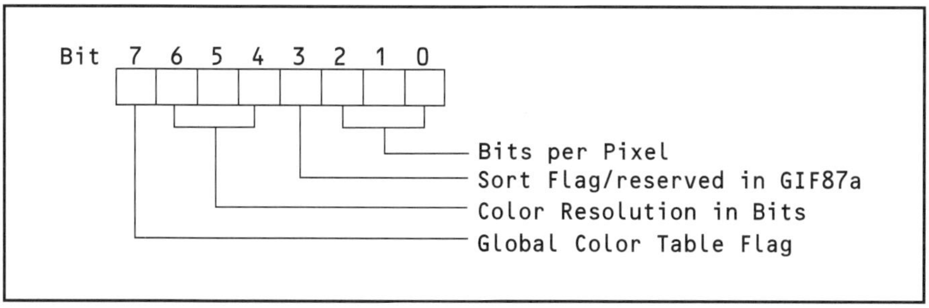

Figure 26.2 Coding Resolution flag

Bit 7 indicates whether there is a *Global Color Map*. If bit 7 is set to 1, the *Logical Screen Descriptor* block is followed by the *Global Color Map*. If this bit is set to 0, the *Global Color Map* is missing and the bits relating to the *Background Color Index* have no meaning.

Bits 4 to 6 determine how many bits are available in the color table for the RGB representation of a primary color (*Color Resolution*). The value in the bits should be increased by 1 in each case. The value 3 indicates that 4 bits are used per primary color in the corresponding palette.

In the GIF87a specification, bit 3 is marked as reserved and must be set to 0. In the GIF89a specification, this bit contains the *Sort Flag*. The value 1 indicates that the *Global Color Table* has been sorted. This sorting is carried out in descending order of importance, that is, the more frequently used colors are located at the start of the palette. This is useful for decoders that support only a few colors. The value 0 indicates that the *Global Color Map* has not been sorted.

In GIF87a, bits 0 to 2 indicate the number of bits per pixel. This value should be increased by 1. The maximum value of 7 means that 8 bits per pixel are available. 256 different colors can be used in one image. If the *Color Table Flag* is set in the GIF89a specification, these three bits define the size of the global color palette (*Global Color Table Size*) in bytes. Ultimately, this represents the same value (bits per pixel) because the size of the color table can be calculated as follows:

Color Table Size = 2 ** (value + 1)

This value should be set even if the GIF file does not contain a *Global Color Map* as it enables the decoder to select the corresponding graphic mode.

At offset 05H there is a byte indicating the background color (*Background Color Index*). This color is selected from the 256 possible colors. The background color is used for those sections of the screen not defined by the bitmap (for example, margins). If the *Global Color Flag* is unset (0), the byte should be set to 0 and skipped by the decoder.

The byte at offset 06H defines the *Pixel Aspect Ratio*. This byte is treated differently in GIF87a and GIF89a. The coding for GIF87a is shown in Figure 26.3:

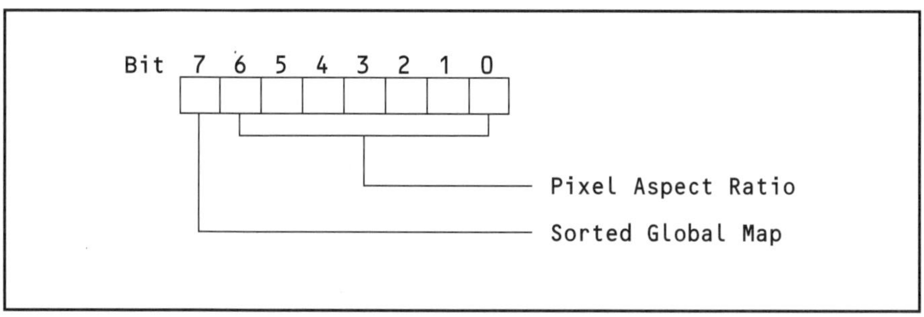

Figure 26.3 Coding Pixel Aspect Ratio flag (GIF87a)

In GIF87a, bit 7 is used as a *Sorted Global Color Map Flag*. The remaining bits indicate the *Pixel Aspect Ratio* of the original picture.

In GIF89a, the *Sorted Global Color Map* Flag is integrated into the *Resolution Flag* (see Figure 26.2) and all bits of the *Pixel Aspect Ratio* field are used. If the value of the field is not 0, the ratio of the image dimensions can be calculated as follows:

Aspect Ratio = (Pixel Aspect Ratio + 15) / 64

The *Pixel Aspect Ratio* is defined as the quotient of the image width divided by the image height. This specification allows a range between 4:1 and 1:4 in steps of 1/64.

26.3 Global Color Map block

Immediately after the *Logical Screen Descriptor* block, there may be an optional block containing the *Global Color Map*. This is always the case if bit 7 of the *Resolution Flag* in the *Logical Screen Descriptor* is set. The global color table is specified in the *Color Map* block and is used if a picture does not have a local palette.

A maximum of 8 bits are provided for each pixel, which enables only 256 colors or levels of gray to be represented. True Color Representation is not provided. The *Global Color Map* contains one triple (3 bytes), giving the primary colors red, green and blue, for each of the 256 colors (Figure 26.4).

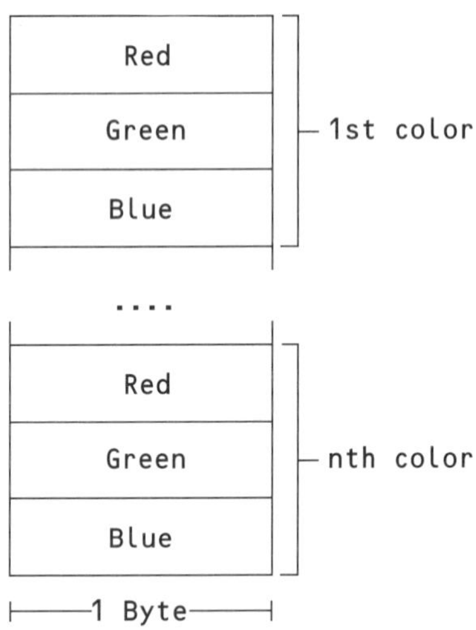

Figure 26.4
Structure of a Global Color Map

One byte is allocated to each of these three primary colors. The value in the byte determines the *intensity* of each primary color in the combined color. With three bytes per color, it is possible to represent 16 million colors, but via the palette, only 256 colors can be used for the picture. The value of a pixel is interpreted as an offset in the color table, and the graphics card then generates the associated color value. The size of the color table and the number of bits per color are also specified in the *Resolution Flag* (Palette size = 3 bytes * 2** bits per pixel).

26.4 Image Descriptor block

Every picture in the GIF file must be introduced by a 10 byte *Image Descriptor* block. This block is used in both GIF versions. Its structure is shown in Table 26.3.

Bytes	Field
1	Image Separator Header (ASCII `2CH` = `','`)
2	Coordinate Left Border
2	Coordinate Top Border
2	Image Width
2	Image Height
1	Flags

Table 26.3 Structure of an Image Descriptor block

This block contains the most important key data relating to a picture, such as its dimensions, and the coordinates of the top left corner.

The first byte contains the separator (`','` `2CH`). The two following fields contain the picture coordinates for the top left corner of the image in pixels and occupy 16 bits each (unsigned word). This data relates to the logical screen, that is, in window environments the coordinates refer to a window.

The image width is given in pixels in the fourth field (offset `05H` in the block) and the image height in pixels in the fifth field. Both values are defined as unsigned words.

The last byte is used for various flags, which are coded as shown in Figure 26.5:

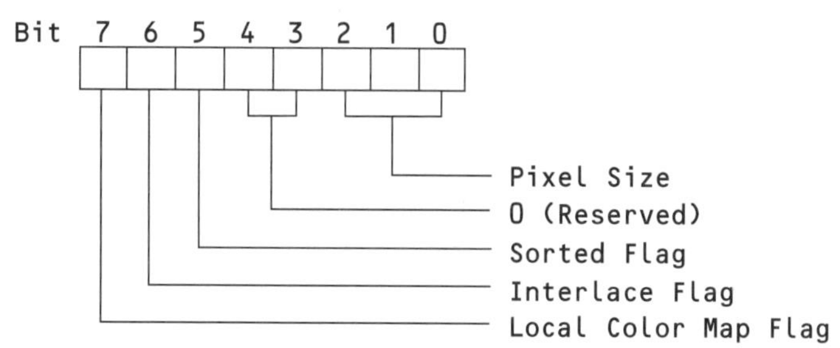

Figure 26.5 Coding of flags in the Image Descriptor block (IDB)

Graphics

If bit 7 = 1, the *Image Descriptor Map* is followed by a *Local Color Map*. In this case, the data will be used for the color table of the following part of the image and a decoder must save the *Global Color Map* and use the new data. After the image has been processed, the *Global Color Map* is restored.

Bit 6 defines the *Interlaced Flag*, that is, the graphic image can be stored in *sequential mode* (bit 6 = 0) or *interlaced mode* (bit 6 = 1). In sequential mode, the image is output line by line. Interlaced mode was created in order to enable the fastest possible transmission of a rough picture via telephone communication. In this mode, only every eighth line is transferred and output per scan. After the first scan only lines 0, 8, 16, and so on will be present. The missing lines are then completed in subsequent scans in the sequence 4, 2, 1, 3, 5, 7. After the second scan, lines 4, 12, 20, and so on, will be produced and lines 2, 10, 18, and so on, after the third scan.

In GIF89a, bit 5 indicates whether the local color table is sorted. If the bit is set, the most important colors are stored first in order of frequency of use. If the flag = 0, the colors in the table are not sorted. However, bit 5 is used only in very few applications because the official GIF87a documentation does not refer to this bit and sets it to 0.

Bits 3–5 in GIF87a are marked as reserved and must be set to 0.

The lower bits 0–2 define the number of bits per pixel (in GIF87a and GIF89a). The value of the bits should be increased by 1; thus the value 7 indicates that 8 bits are used per pixel. The number of entries in the color table (2**n) and therefore also its size (entries*3 bytes) can be calculated from this value. If no Local Color Map follows, the value of these three bits should be set to 0.

26.5 Local Color Map block

In addition to the global color table, local color tables can also be defined *before* the Raster Image blocks of a partial image. If the *Local Color Table Flag* in the *Image Descriptor* block is set, this block will be followed by the *Local Color Map* block. The decoder must then save the data from the *Global Color Map* and restore it after the image data has been processed. The structure of the *Local Color Map* is the same as that of the *Global Color Map* (*see* Figure 26.4). A GIF file may contain several *Local Color Map* blocks. *Local Color Map* blocks are defined in both GIF specifications.

26.6 Extension block

The block containing the *Local Color Map* may be followed by an optional *Extension* block. In GIF87a, these *Extension* blocks provided a means of implementing future extensions and were used for storing information about the device that produced the image, the software used, the scanner, and so on. The *Extension* blocks are structured as shown in Table 26.4.

Bytes	Field
1	Extension Block Header (ASCII 21H = '!')
1	Function code (0 .. 255)
1	Length of data block 1 (in bytes)
n	Data block 1
1	Length of data block 2
n	Data block 2
...	...
1	Length of data block *n*
n	Data block *n*
1	00H as terminator

Table 26.4 Structure of an Extension block (GIF87a)

The first byte of the *Extension* block contains the character ! as a signature. This is followed by one byte containing the function code, which defines the type of the following data.

These bytes are followed by the data area, which may contain several records of the same structure. The first byte of each of these records indicates the number of following data bytes. The maximum number of data bytes in a data area is 255.

With longer sequences of data, several sub-blocks are stored. The end of the *Extension* blocks is marked by a null byte (00H).

In GIF87a, the function codes are not defined, and the internal structure is also left to the developer of the encoder. In GIF89a, the situation is somewhat different because the specification describes various *Extension* blocks. The structure of these GIF89a *Extension* blocks is described in Sections 26.12, 26.13, 26.14 and 26.15.

26.7 Raster Data block

The actual image data is stored in one or more *Raster Data* blocks. If the *Local Color Map Flag* is set in the *Image Descriptor Flag* (Figure 26.5), the image data will follow after the color table. If there is no *Local Color Map*, the data will follow the *Image Descriptor* block or an *Extension* block. The first *Raster Data* block is structured as shown in Table 26.5:

Bytes	Field
1	Code size
1	Number of bytes in data block
n	Data bytes

Table 26.5 Structure of a Raster Data block

In the first byte of the first block, there is a byte referred to as the *Code Size*. This value defines the minimum code length required for the representation of the pixels in LZW (Lempel-Ziv and Welch) compression. This byte is used to initialize the decoder. The value is generally the same as the number of color bits per pixel. Code size = `2` is used only for black and white images (bits per pixel = 1).

The second byte defines the number of bytes in the following data block. This value is between `0` and `255`.

The compressed image data starts in the third byte. If the image data requires more than 255 bytes, additional sub-blocks are used (*see* Section 26.10). After decoding, the picture is built up starting in the top left corner and working from left to right and from top to bottom. A slightly modified form of the LZW algorithm is used for compression (*see* Section 26.8). This algorithm constructs a table from the characters read. These characters are collated into strings wherever possible and compared with patterns in the table. In the output file, only the *Index* to the position of the pattern in the coding table is stored. Newly occurring patterns are constantly added to this table. In the case of GIF files, the code sequences may be between 3 and 12 bits long. When the table is full, a reset code is stored and the process of constructing the table is restarted.

26.8 LZW Compression

In programs and GIF graphics files, the LZW method is used. This algorithm breaks the stream of characters into partial strings and stores these in a table. Only the indices into the relevant table are stored as output codes. The original character stream is subsequently regenerated on the basis of these output codes. Figure 26.6 shows the basic structure.

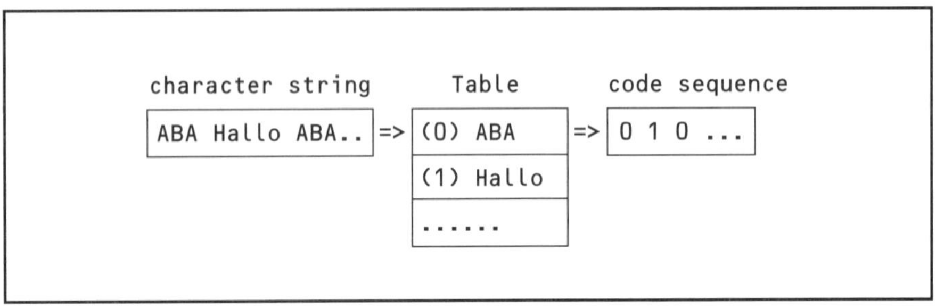

Figure 26.6
LZW Encoding

The character sequence in Figure 26.6 is broken down into partial strings (`ABA`, `Hallo`, and so on). These character sequences also occur in the coding table, but instead of the partial strings, the associated table index is output. The original character string of 11 characters (`ABAHalloABA`) becomes a code sequence of 3 characters. This very simple principle enables the compression of any character sequence.

There are, however, still two problems to solve. Firstly, the code table can only be determined *a priori* in very few cases; it is not stored with the code and it is not available for decompression. As a result, the algorithm must reconstruct the code itself at the compression and decompression stages. The second difficulty relates to the size of the table. In theory, the table must be infinitely large in order to accommodate all possible character combinations. However, for practical reasons, the size of the table is limited. These problems are overcome when applying the LZW algorithm to GIF files.

Before discussing the process, it is important to mention some of the terms involved:

`<new>`	Memory cell containing the last character read
`<old>`	Memory cell containing the penultimate character read
`[..]`	Character buffer for building the table
`[..]K`	Character buffer with appended character K

The buffer `[..]` is important for the construction of the table. It may contain individual characters or complete character strings. The aim of the algorithm is to store complete character strings that have not already been stored in the table. Each time this occurs, the relevant partial string is appended to the table and a code is output for the last partial string. In this way, the coding table is built up and can be reconstructed using the output code at any time during decompression.

The next question is the initialization of the table at the start of the compression process. The size must be established arbitrarily. For example, 12 bits enable 4096 entries to be encoded.

Each entry later stores a character sequence, but only the 12 bit indices for the table are stored as output codes. This achieves the desired compression. With a little knowledge of the possible characters in the input code, the table can be partly initialized with starting values. If, for example, the input characters are taken from the alphabet of upper case letters, the first 26 entries in the table can be assigned the codes for the characters (0 = A, 1 = B, 2 = C, and so on).

The LZW compression algorithm can then be described with the following pseudo-code instructions:

```
initialize table
   clear buffer [..]
   WHILE Not EOF DO
      read code in K
         IF [..]K in table?
         [..] < - [..]K
      ELSE
         add [..]K in table
         write table index of [..]
         [..] < - K
      ENDIF
WEND
write table index of [..]
```

First, the table should be initialized and the buffer [..] should be cleared. The sequence of input codes is then read in line by line. The character of the input sequence that has just been read is placed to the right of the buffer as a post-fix ([..]K). A check must now be carried out to see if the partial string [..]K already occurs in the table. If so, the algorithm processes the next character. If the string is not yet in the table, the next step begins. The new string [..]K is appended to the first free position in the table. Then the table index for the partial string [..] (not [..]K) is stored as an output code. The old buffer content is then replaced by the last read character K. The next character is read and the process is repeated. After reading all input characters, the buffer code with the remaining string from the table can be determined and sent to the output stream.

This process can be explained with a further example. From the set of letters A, B, C, D, the character string ABACABA is to be formed. The table can be initialized with the letters A, B, C, D in the first four entries. The following figure shows the individual stages of the compression process.

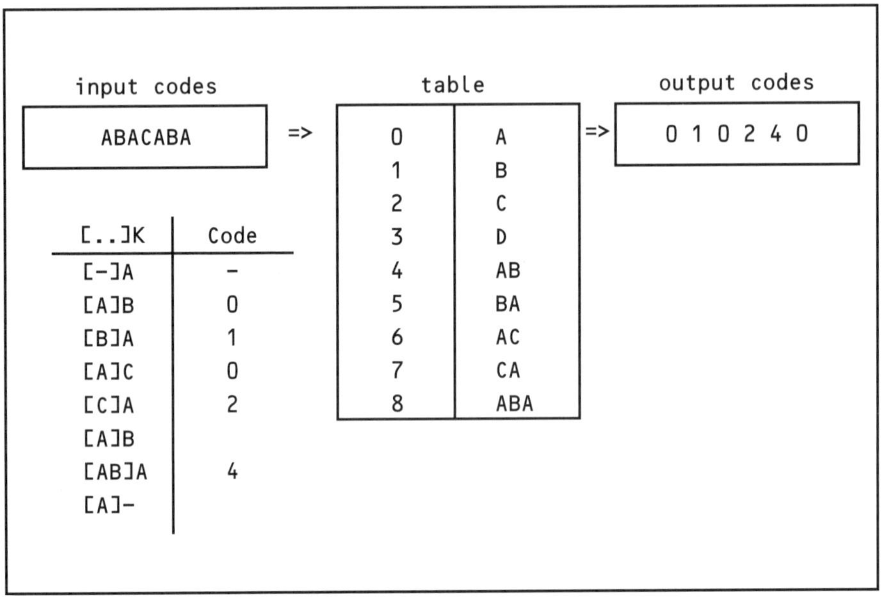

Figure 26.7 LZW compression

The character sequence ABACABA produces the code sequence 010240. This sequence only requires 6 codes, while the original string contains 7 characters. With longer character strings, considerably improved compression rates can be achieved.

At the decompression stage, the code sequence must be transformed into the output string. An algorithm described by the following pseudo-code instructions is used:

```
initialize string table
<code> := 1st code byte
table[code] - > output string
<old> := <code>
WHILE NOT EOF DO
   <code> := next code byte
   IF table[code] used?
      table[code] - > output string
      [..] < - table[old]
      K    < - 1st character (table[code])
      write [..]K in table
      <old> := <code>
   ELSE
      [..] < - table[old]
      K    < - 1st character (..)
      [..]K - > in output string
      [..]K - > table
      <old> := <code>
   END IF
WEND
```

`<old>` and `<code>` are two variables representing the penultimate character and the last character read. `[..]` defines a character buffer containing strings from the string table. The string table is referred to as `table[..]`. The instruction `-> output string` indicates that strings are to be written to the output unit.

The algorithm begins by initializing the string table with basic values. The first element of the code sequence is then read. This value acts as an index to the string table. The relevant string (the index points to the initialized section of the table) is written to the output stream. Next, the code read is stored in the variable `<old>`. The WHILE loop ensures that all elements in the code sequence are processed. As soon as a code element has been read, the algorithm checks whether the index points to a table entry that is already coded. If it does, the string is appended to the output stream. The string is then passed from `table[old]` into a character buffer, and the first character of the entry `table[code]` is appended (`[..]K`). The new partial string `[..]K` is entered in the table at the first free position. The last character read is then simply copied from `<code>` to `<old>`.

If the position in the table for `<code>` is still not occupied, the associated string must be generated. This is achieved by copying the existing string from `table[old]` to the buffer `[..]`. The first character of the buffer `[..]` is then copied to the variable `K` and appended to the buffer `[..]K`. This new string is entered in the table and also copied to the output stream. Finally, the content of `<code>` is saved in `<old>`. This process is repeated until all input codes have been read. The original character sequence is then in the output stream.

The following figure shows the individual stages of the decompression process:

```
      Code sequence           table          output codes
     ┌─────────────┐       ┌───┬──────┐     ┌─────────┐
     │ 0 1 0 2 4 0 │       │ 0 │  A   │     │ ABACABA │
     └─────────────┘       │ 1 │  B   │     └─────────┘
                           │ 2 │  C   │
 <code> <old> [..]K        │ 3 │  D   │
   0      -     -          ├───┼──────┤
   1      0   [A]B         │ 4 │  AB  │
   0      1   [B]A         │ 5 │  BA  │
   2      0   [A]C         │ 6 │  AC  │
   4      2   [C]A         │ 7 │  CA  │
   0      4   [AB]A        │ 8 │  ABA │
   -      0                └───┴──────┘
```

Figure 26.8
LZW decoding

The original character sequence `ABACABA` has been generated from the code sequence `010240`. At the start of the decompression process, the string table is initialized with the characters A, B, C, D. These were the original initialization characters in the compression table. During the processing of the input code, the complete character table is reconstructed. At the end of the process, the complete table containing all the entries from the original compression table has been created (compare the two examples).

26.9 Modified LZW Process for GIF Files

When compressing GIF files, the process described above is used with certain minor modifications. Since the codes are bit sequences, the number of bits per read-access must be defined. However, there is no point in reading just one bit (pixel). Even reading 8 bits per read-access is not without problems. Therefore, in GIF compression, a variable *code length*, which may be between 3 and 12 bits, is used. The first byte of the *Raster Data* block contains the value *Code size*, which corresponds to the number of bits per pixel, but is interpreted as a starting value for the *code length*. At four bits per pixel, the number $N = 3$ will be stored in the relevant field. This means that every time the input data is accessed, there will always be $N + 1 = 4$ bits to read. During processing, the *code length* per access may be extended to 12 bits. As soon as this length is reached, the table containing the output patterns is full, and must be reset.

The GIF compressor must therefore create a table with 4096 entries. At the start of the process, this table is initialized with a few codes. The size of this initialization area is defined by the value *code size*. At 1 bit per pixel, N must be set to $N = 2$. The entries #0 and #1 in the table are then initialized. At positions 2**N and 2**N + 1, two special codes are stored. With $N = 2$, these are the positions #4 and #5. The first entry at position #4 is referred to as a clear code `<CC>`. If this entry is recognized during decompression, the table must be re-initialized. The compressor will always output this code when the table is full. This code may also occur as the first character of an output stream, in order to activate a reset in the decompressor. The second entry is referred to as *end of information* `<EOI>`. It signals to the decompressor that the end of the code stream has been reached and no more data follows.

During compression/decompression, new strings should be stored from the position `<CC>` + 2. The code `<CC>` is written to the output stream at the start of compression and each time the table overflows. The reader must then re-initialize the table. The variable *code length* of the data to be read should present no major problems. Compression starts with the value indicated in the *code length*, *code size* + 1. Whenever a code from the table position (2**(*code length*) – 1) is output, the code length should be increased by 1. This is continued until a *code length* of 12 bits is reached. Then the table has to be re-initialized. Decompression also starts with the *code length code size* + 1. The *code length* should always be increased by 1, while the table entry (2**(*code length*) –1) is written into the output. It should also be pointed out that the bits in the code sequence correspond to the bits of the string code in the table.

26.10 Sub-blocks with Raster Data

Since an image generally requires more than 255 data bytes, the compressed data is subdivided into a *Raster Data* block and several (Raster Data) *Sub-blocks*. The sub-blocks are structured as shown in Table 26.5, but the first byte (*Code size*) is missing. Each sub-block begins with a length byte which defines the number of following bytes in the block (0–255). The maximum number of bytes in a sub-block is 256.

26.11 Block Terminator

The end of the image data area is indicated by a *Terminator* block (`00H`). This is simply a sub-block in which the length byte is set to `0`. The block contains only the length byte.

The *Image Descriptor, Local Color Map* and *Raster Data* blocks can be created several times in one file. This enables several pictures to be stored in one file.

26.12 Graphic Control Extension block (GIF89a)

This block was defined in GIF89a and contains additional parameters relating to the image. The block is optional and must be positioned after the *Image Descriptor* block, but before the *Raster Data* blocks. The data applies only to the following (partial) image. The block is structured as shown in Table 26.6:

Bytes	Remarks
1	Extension Block Signature (21H)
1	Graphic Control Label (F9H)
1	Block Size (4)
1	Flags
2	Delay Time
1	Transparent Color Index
1	Block Terminator (00H)

Table 26.6 Structure of the Graphic Control Extension block (GIF89A)

The first byte contains the signature for the *Extension* block and contains the fixed value 21H (='!').

Byte 2 contains the *Graphic Control Label*. This is simply the signature for a *Graphic Extension* block and contains the fixed value F9H.

The field block *Size* indicates the number of following data bytes in the block. The block terminator is not included in this calculation. In a *Graphic Control Extension* block, this field always contains the value 4.

The flag byte (offset 03H) is structured as shown in Figure 26.9.

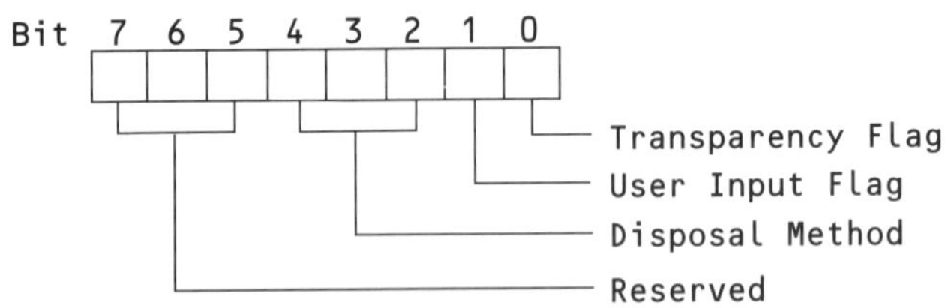

Figure 26.9 Coding of flags in the Graphics Control Extension block

The *Transparency Flag* indicates whether the *Transparency Index Field* is defined or not. If it is, the flag is set to 1. If the flag is set to 0, the *Transparency Index Field* does not contain a valid value.

The *User Input Flag* defines whether the program will wait for a user input after the output of the image. If the flag is set to 1, processing will not be continued until a user input is made. The type of user input (return, mouse click, and so on) is defined by the application. If a delay time is defined, processing will be continued after this time, even without a user input.

The *Disposal Method* defines what happens to the graphic after output, according to the following options:

0 No disposal specified.

1 Do not dispose of the graphic. It is left in place.

2 Restore to background color. The area covered by the graphic must be restored to the background color.

3 Restore to previous. The decoder must restore the previous screen image.

No other codes have yet been defined.

The *Delay Time field* is defined as an unsigned word. If the *User Flag* is set, this field will define the waiting time, after which processing of the data sequence will be resumed, in 1/100 seconds. This waiting time can be interrupted by a user input and begins immediately after the output of the graphic.

The *Transparency Index field* contains one byte value. If this byte value occurs in the data stream for the graphic, the pixel in question is not displayed. The decoder can go on to the next pixel. The screen background is retained during this process. The index is only valid if the *Transparency Flag* is set.

The last byte acts as a block *Terminator* and has the value `00H`. This byte is not included in the length of the *Extension* block. It is, in effect, an empty block which generally defines the end of several sub-blocks.

26.13 Comment Extension block (GIF89a)

This optional block was defined in GIF89a. It can contain comments on the GIF file (for example, author, credits). It is advisable to insert the block at the start or end of the GIF file. The contents of the block have no influence on GIF images. Table 26.7 shows the structure of this block:

Bytes	Remarks
1	Extension Block Signature (`21H`)
1	Comment Label (`FEH`)
1	Block Size
n	Comment string as sub-blocks with
	1 Length of sub-block
	n Data Area of sub-block
1	Block Terminator (`00H`)

Table 26.7 Structure of the Comment Extension block (GIF89A)

The first byte contains the signature for the *Extension* block. The byte has the fixed value of `21H` (=' ! ').

The second byte contains the signature for the *Comment Extension* block and is always `FEH`.

This signature is followed by a sequence of sub-blocks containing the actual comment text. Each sub-block contains the number of following bytes in its initial byte, which may be followed by between 0 and 255 data bytes. If the data string is longer than one block, it will be divided into several sub-blocks. The end of the *Comment Extension* blocks is marked by a terminator. This is a sub-block of one byte, containing the value 00H.

The comment string should be produced using 7 bit ASCII characters. It is not possible to represent multilingual characters (ä, ö, ü and so on). The contents of the block should not be used for storing decoding information, so that the decoder may skip the block.

26.14 Plain Text Extension block (GIF89a)

This optional block was also defined in GIF89a. The block may contain texts and parameters for the graphic representation of these texts. Table 26.8 indicates the structure of the block.

Bytes	Remarks
1	Extension Block Signature (21H)
1	Plain Text (01H)
1	Block Size
2	Text Grid Left Position
2	Text Grid Top Position
2	Text Grid Width
2	Text Grid Height
1	Character Cell Width
1	Character Cell Height
1	Text Foreground Color
1	Text Background Color
n	Sequence of Plain Text Sub-blocks with
	1 Byte Length Sub-block
	n Byte Sub-block with Plain Text
1	Block Terminator (00H)

Table 26.8 Structure of the Plain Text Extension block (GIF89A)

The first byte contains the signature for the *Extension* block. This byte has the fixed value 21H (='!').

The second byte contains the signature for the *Plain Text Extension* block and is always 01H.

The third byte contains the length indicator for the following data area. With the *Plain Text Extension* block, this value is fixed at 12 (0CH). The text is then stored in sub-blocks each with their own length indicator.

A sequence of fields, which are interpreted as unsigned words, begins at offset 03H from the start of the block. The first field defines the left margin (column number) for the text output grid. The position is defined in pixels from the left edge of the logical screen.

The following field establishes the upper grid position (row number) for the text output in pixels. It also relates to the logical screen.

The field *Character Cell Width* defines the width of a grid cell in pixels. This cell is then used to accommodate a character. The height of a grid cell is defined in *Character Cell Height*. This value is also indicated in a byte. The decoder must convert these values to the dimensions of the virtual screen. The result of this conversion must be an integer value.

The last two fields require only one byte each. They indicate the color value (index in the color table) for the foreground and background color of the text.

The actual text is stored in a sequence of sub-blocks which follow immediately after the structure described above. Each sub-block contains the number of following bytes in its first byte. This byte is followed by between 0 and 255 data bytes containing the text to be output. If the text is longer than one block, it is divided into sub-blocks. The end of the *Plain Text Extension* block is marked by a terminator, which is a one-byte sub-block containing the value 00H.

A grid of character cells is defined for the output of the text. Each cell accommodates a single character. The parameters for the grid of character cells are indicated in the *Text Extension* block in the *Text Grid* fields. The decoder must convert these parameters in such a way that the grid dimensions represent integers. Any value after the decimal point should be removed (truncated). For reasons of compatibility, the cell dimensions 8×8 or 8×16 (width $\times$ height) should be selected.

The individual characters are read sequentially and entered into the individual cells line by line, beginning at the top left corner of the grid. The best *monospace* font with a size appropriate for the decoder should be used for the display. The text to be displayed must be coded in 7 bit ASCII characters. It is not possible to represent multilingual characters (ä, ö, ü and so on). If character codes below 20H and above 7FH appear, the decoder will output a space (20H).

26.15 Application Extension Block (GIF89a)

This optional block was defined in GIF89a. The block is used for application-specific information. Table 26.9 shows the structure of the block:

Bytes	Remarks
1	Extension Block Signature (21H)
1	Application Extension (FFH)
1	Block Size 11
8	Application Identifier
3	Application Authentication Code
n	Sequence of Sub-blocks
	1 Byte Length Sub-block
	n Byte Sub-block with Data
1	Block Terminator (00H)

Table 26.9 Structure of the Application Extension Block (GIF89A)

The first byte contains the signature for the *Extension* block. This byte has the fixed value 21H (='!').

The second byte contains the signature for the *Application Extension* block and is always FFH.

The third byte contains the length of the following data area. In the *Application Extension* block this value is fixed at 11 (0BH). The actual parameters are stored in sub-blocks each with its own length indicator.

At offset 03H, there are 8 bytes containing the *Application Identifier*. This must consist of printable ASCII characters and is used for naming the application that created the data.

These 8 bytes are followed by three bytes for the *Application Authentication Code*. A binary code calculated by the application can be stored here, to ensure the unequivocal identification of the original application.

This field is followed by the sub-blocks containing the application-specific data. Each sub-block begins with a length byte, followed by up to 255 data bytes. The last block contains only the length byte which is set to 00H and acts as a terminator.

26.16 GIF Terminator

The end of a GIF file is marked by a *Terminator* block. This is a one-byte block containing a semicolon (code 3BH) as the terminator.

27

Tag Image File Format (TIFF)

***Aldus**, the developer of the desktop publisher Pagemaker, defined a format for storing graphic data (TIFF) some time ago, and this format is now supported by a number of manufacturers such as Hewlett Packard, Microsoft, Data Copy and Microtek. TIFF files are rapidly becoming the standard on both Apple Macintosh and IBM-PC compatibles, and this format is also used by scanner manufacturers.*

TIFF enables several levels of representation (*Bilevel*, *Graylevel*, *Color...*) and uses various compression processes. A number of the functions of the standard version have subsequently been extended. The information in this chapter relates exclusively to version 6.0.

A TIFF file consists of a header and a variable number of data blocks of differing lengths, which are addressed by a pointer (Figure 27.1):

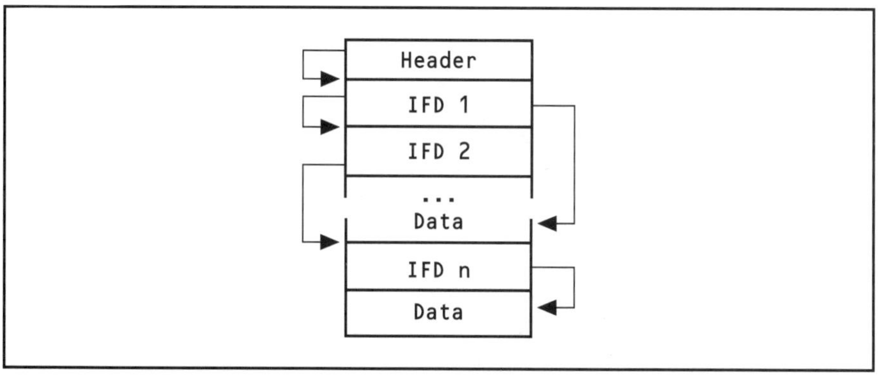

Figure 27.1 Structure of a TIFF file

The structure of the file is essentially based on blocks known as the *Image File Directory* (IFD). The IFDs form an interconnected list within the file and contain information on the data types stored, the image data, the graphic mode, and so on. Pointers from these IFDs may also indicate the actual data blocks. Image data is stored between the IFDs, in free areas within the file. As a result, the structure of TIFF files is very flexible, but it is also more complex than, for example,

PCX files. More images or different variations of an image can be stored within a single file. Figure 27.2 shows an extract from a TIFF file as a hex dump.

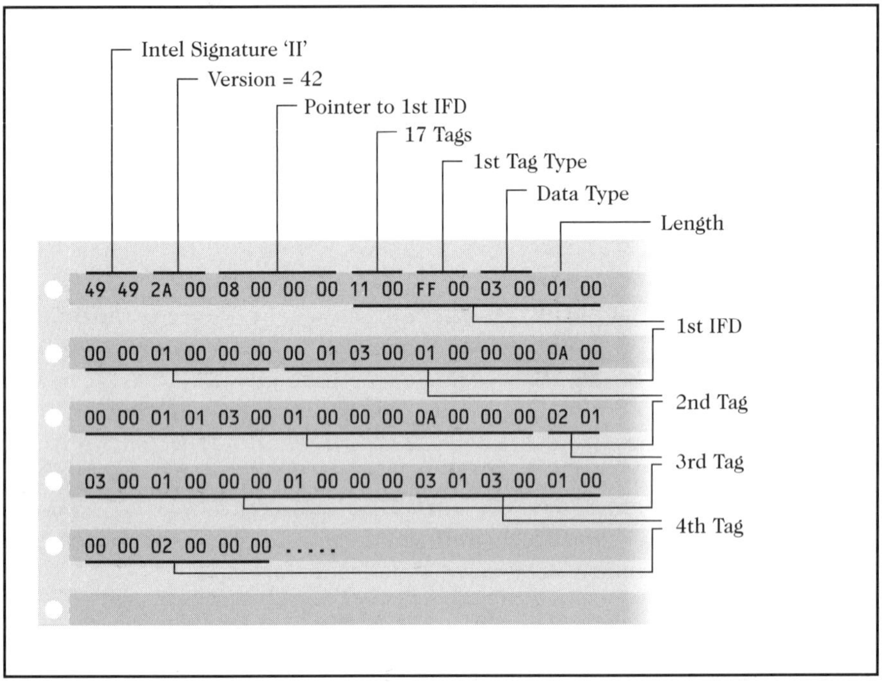

Figure 27.2 Part of a TIFF file hex dump

27.1 TIFF header

The format of the header, which occupies the first 8 bytes of the file, is fixed. The structure is shown in Table 27.1.

Offset	Bytes	Remarks
00H	2	Byte Order 'II' = Intel 'MM'= Motorola
02H	2	Version number
04H	4	Pointer to first IFD

Table 27.1 TIFF header structure

TIFF format is used both with Motorola processors (Macintosh) and Intel processors (IBM-PC). Unfortunately, there are two methods of storing individual bytes (Table 27.2).

Processor	Word	1st Byte	2nd Byte
Intel	3F55H	55H	3FH
Motorola	3F55H	3FH	55H

Table 27.2 Storing words in Intel and Motorola formats

In the case of Intel, the low byte is stored at the lower address (Big endian). This means that the lower values are on the left in the output. With Motorola, the high byte is stored first (Little endian), therefore low byte values appear on the right in the output.

The first two bytes contain a signature which specifies the byte order used. To avoid unnecessary calculations, both bytes have the same signature. For Intel format, both bytes contain the signature 'II' (4949H). The signature for Motorola is 'MM' (4D4DH). Both signatures are therefore defined by ASCII strings. All other data within the file will be interpreted in the format selected.

At offset 02H, there is a 16 bit value indicating the version number of the TIFF file. In all versions up to and including TIFF 6.0, this value is always set to 42 (2AH). The value is likely to remain 2AH in future unless the TIFF structure is changed.

The last 4 bytes of the header contain a pointer to the beginning of the first *Image File Directory* (IFD). The value of the pointer is the offset from the start of the file to the first IFD byte. In Figure 27.2, the first IFD begins at offset 08H. The pointer chain is continued within the IFDs.

27.2 Structure of the Image File Directory (IFD)

Data within a TIFF file may be arranged in any number of ways. Reference to this data is made via the IFDs. An IFD therefore functions as an index and as a header to the actual data areas. Starting with the header, all IFDs are linked by pointers (Figure 27.3).

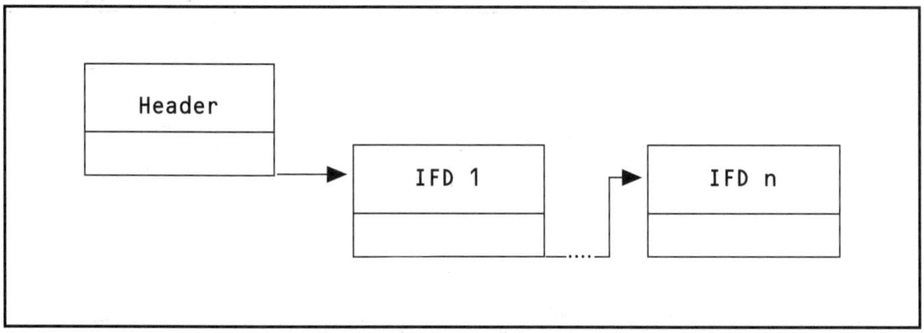

Figure 27.3 IFD chain

The second and subsequent pointers are located within the IFD data structure, which can be divided into three parts (count, tag field, pointer), as shown in Table 27.3:

Offset	Bytes	Remarks
00H	2	Number of entries
02H	12	Tag 0 (12 bytes)
0EH	12	Tag 1 (12 bytes)
	....	
...	12	Tag *n* (12 bytes)
...	4	Pointer to next IFD or 0, if no next IFD

Table 27.3 IFD block structure

The length of an IFD is variable. It is determined by the number of *tag* entries. A tag is a 12-byte data structure used to store information on the image data. (The structure of a tag is described below.) The number of tag entries is stored in the first word of the IFD. After the last tag, there is a 4-byte pointer to the following IFD. If there is no other IFD, the pointer contains the value 0.

27.2.1 Structure of a tag

At offset 02H in an IFD, there is a list of tags. These are data structures with a fixed length of 12 bytes. They are used to store data relating to image dimensions, pixel resolution, and so on. If the data does not fit into the tag structure, it will be stored in a free area elsewhere in the file, and the tag will contain a pointer (offset from start of file) to this data area (Figure 27.4).

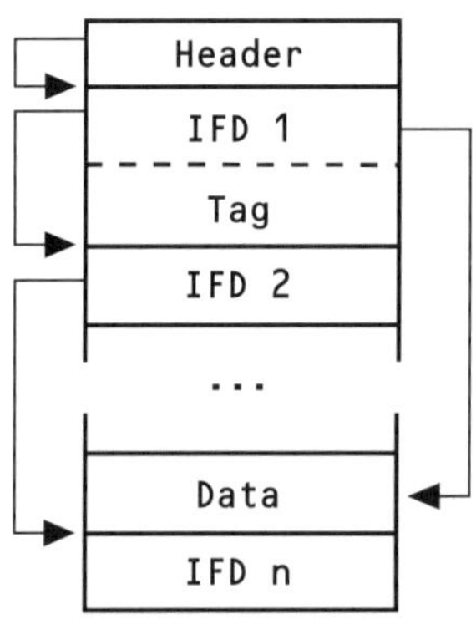

Figure 27.4 Pointer from a tag to the data area

Table 27.4 shows the structure of a tag:

Offset	Bytes	Remarks
00H	2	Tag type
02H	2	Data type
04H	4	Length of data area
08H	4	Pointer to data area, or a value if no area exists

Table 27.4
Tag structure

The first word in a tag indicates the tag type (the possible types are described below). The second word defines the data type of the values stored. At present, the definition is as shown in Table 27.5:

Code	Type	Remarks
01H	Byte	8 bit byte
02H	ASCII	8 bit ASCII code
03H	SHORT	16 bit unsigned integer
04H	LONG	32 bit unsigned integer
05H	RATIONAL	2 LONG numbers 1st LONG = number of a fraction 2nd LONG = denominator
06H	SBYTE	8 bit signed integer
07H	UNDEFINED	8 bit contain anything
08H	SSHORT	16 bit signed integer
09H	SLONG	32 bit signed integer
0AH	RATIONAL	2 SLONG numbers 1st SLONG = numerator of a fraction 2nd SLONG = denominator
0BH	FLOAT	4 byte single precision IEEE floating point
0CH	DOUBLET	8 byte double precision IEEE floating point

Table 27.5
Tag data types

The data types with codes 06H–0CH in Table 27.5 were defined in TIFF version 6.0.

At offset 04H, the length of the associated data area is stored. The unit used here depends on the data type. A data type defined as LONG, for example, with a length of 0AH occupies 10 × 4 bytes = 40 bytes. It should be noted that ASCII strings are always terminated with a null byte,

Graphics

which is not included in the length. If a string comprises an odd number of bytes, the next item of data to be stored must begin on an even address boundary.

The last 4 bytes of a tag, at offset 08H, are used to store the value. For example, the resolution of the X axis may be indicated here. If more than 4 bytes are required to store the data, the field will contain a 4-byte pointer to the actual data area. The data area may be located at any free position in the TIFF file.

For optimization reasons, the tags in an IFD must be arranged in ascending numerical sequence. In addition to the tag types described below (*public types*), company-defined (*private*) tag types may be used. For example, manufacturers may include additional information on special compression processes for picture data. These private tags cannot be evaluated by general-purpose read programs. When checking tag types, a program may stop as soon as it encounters a code higher than the highest valid tag number. The alternative is to skip the tag and continue with the interpretation of the file. The chances of success are particularly high if several images are stored.

27.2.2 Description of tag types

The tag definitions can be divided into several functional groups (Table 27.6). The TIFF version 6.0 specification also distinguishes between *Baseline* tags and *Extension* tags.

Code	TagGroup	Data type	Values
Image Organization Tags			
0FEH	NewSubfile	LONG	1
0FFH	SubfileType	SHORT	1
100H	ImageWidth	SHORT/LONG	1
101H	ImageLength	SHORT/LONG	1
112H	Orientation	SHORT	1
11AH	XResolution	RATIONAL	1
11BH	YResolution	RATIONAL	1
11CH	PlanarConfiguration	SHORT	1
128H	ResolutionUnit	SORT	1
Image Pointer Tags			
111H	StripOffsets	SHORT/LONG	StripPerImage
117H	StripByteCounts	SHORT/LONG	StripPerImage
116H	RowsPerStrip	SHORT/LONG	1
142H	TileWidth	SHORT/LONG	1
143H	TileLength	SHORT/LONG	1
144H	TileOffsets	SHORT/LONG	TilesPerImage

Table 27.6 Tag groups (*continues over...*)

Code	TagGroup	Data type	Values
145H	TileByteCounts	SHORT/LONG	TilesPerImage
Pixel Description Tags			
102H	BitsPerSample	SHORT	SamplesPerPixel
106H	Photometric Interpretation	SHORT	1
107H	Tresholding	SHORT	1
108H	CellWidth	SHORT	1
109H	CellLength	SHORT	1
115H	SamplesPerPixel	SHORT	1
118H	MinSampleValue	SHORT	SamplesPerPixel
119H	MaxSampleValue	SHORT	SamplesPerPixel
122H	GrayResponseUnit	SHORT	1
123H	GrayResponseCurve	SHORT	2**BitPerSample
12CH	ColorResponseUnit	SHORT	1
12DH	ColorResponseCurves	SHORT	1 or *n*
131H	Software	ASCII	
132H	DateTime	ASCII	
13BH	Artist	ASCII	
13CH	HostComputer	ASCII	
13DH	Predictor	SHORT	1
13EH	WhitePoint	RATIONAL	2
13FH	PrimaryChromatics	LONG	2*SamplesPerPixel
140H	ColorMap	SHORT	3*(2**BitsPerSamples)
Data Orientation Tags			
10AH	FillOrder	SHORT	1
Data Compression Tags			
103H	Compression	SHORT	1
124H	T4Options	SHORT	1
125H	T6Options	SHORT	1
152H	ExtraSamples	BYTE	*n*
153H	SampleFormat	SHORT	SamplesPerPixel
154H	SMinSampleValue	ANY	SamplesPerPixel
155H	SMaxSampleValue	ANY	SamplesPerPixel
156H	TransferRange	SHORT	6
Document & Scanner Description Tags			
10DH	DocumentName	ASCII	
10EH	ImageDescription	ASCII	
10FH	ScannerMake	ASCII	
110H	ScannerModel	ASCII	

Table 27.6
Tag groups
(*cont.*)

Graphics

Code	TagGroup	Data type	Values
11DH	PageName	ASCII	
11EH	XPosition	RATIONAL	
11FH	YPosition	RATIONAL	
129H	PageNumber	SHORT	2
8298H	Copyright	ASCII	
Storage Management Tags			
120H	FreeOffsets	LONG	
121H	FreeByteCounts	LONG	
Ink Management Tags			
14CH	InkSet	SHORT	1
14DH	InkNames	ASCII	
14EH	NumberOfInks	SHORT	1
150H	DotRange	BYTE/SHORT	*n*
151H	TargetPrinter	ASCII	
JPEG Management Tags			
200H	JPEGProc	SHORT	1
201H	JPEGInterchange-Format	LONG	1
203H	JPEGInterchange-FormatLength	LONG	1
204H	JPEGRestartInterval	SHORT	1
205H	JPEGLossLess-Predictors	SHORT	SamplesPerPixel
206H	JPEGPoint-Transforms	SHORT	SamplesPerPixel
207H	JPEGQTables	LONG	SamplesPerPixel
208H	JPEGDCTables	LONG	SamplesPerPixel
209H	JPEGACTables	LONG	SamplesPerPixel
YCbCr Management Tags			
211H	YCbCrCoefficients	RATIONAL	3
212H	YCbCrSubSampling	SHORT	2
213H	YCbCrPositioning	SHORT	1

Table 27.6
Tag groups
(con..)

The JPEG and YCbCr tags were introduced in TIFF version 6.0. The definitions of these tags are given below.

Graphics

27.2.2.1 NewSubFile tag (FEH)

This tag replaces the old *SubFile* tag, which was subject to too many limitations.

Tag type 254 (FEH)
Data type LONG
Length of data area = 1
Flag (Bitfield)

Table 27.7 NewSubfile tag

The data field contains individual flags with the following coding:

Bit 0: 1 picture has reduced resolution compared with another picture in the TIFF file.

1: 1 picture is a page of a multipage image

2: 1 Transparency Mask for other pictures in the TIFF file. Photometric Interpretation must then be equal to 4.

The remaining bits are not used and must be set to 0. The default setting for all bits is 0.

27.2.2.2 Subfile tag (FFH)

This tag contains the global description for the bitmap data used in the IFD. It is especially necessary when more than one image is stored in the file. In the TIFF definition, this tag is not compulsory. However, if it is used, the tags *ImageWidth*, *ImageLength* and *StripOffset* are also required. The *Subfile* tag is structured as shown in Table 27.8.

Tag type 255 (FFH)
Data type SHORT
Length of data area = 1
Subfile type (value 1, 2, 3)

Table 27.8 Subfile tag

In the value field, the following entries are defined:

Value	Remarks
1	Image with full resolution
2	Image with reduced resolution
3	Single page image

Table 27.9 Values in the Subfile tag

Value 1 indicates that the associated image was stored with full resolution. If the picture is stored again with reduced resolution, the associated tag will have the value 2. There must be a tag defining the image with full resolution. If the value 3 occurs, this represents an image page from an image comprising several pages. This necessitates a *PageNumber tag*, specifying the page number of the associated image. If the *Subfile tag* is missing from the TIFF file, the default setting is for full resolution.

27.2.2.3 ImageWidth tag (100H)

This tag describes the image width in pixels. The structure of the tag is as follows:

Tag type 256 (100H)
Data type SHORT or LONG
Length of data area = 1
ImageWidth (value 0...65535)

Table 27.10 ImageWidth tag

The image width is always measured in the direction of the X axis. This tag is mandatory in a TIFF file. The value can also be interpreted as the *number of image columns*.

27.2.2.4 ImageLength tag (101H)

This tag describes the image height (length) in pixels. It is structured as follows:

Tag type 257 (101H)
Data type SHORT or LONG
Length of data area = 1
ImageLength (value 0...65535)

Table 27.11 ImageLength tag

The image height is always measured in the direction of the Y axis. This tag is mandatory in a TIFF file. The value can also be interpreted as the *number of image lines*.

27.2.2.5 BitsPerSample tag (102H)

This tag indicates the number of bits that must be stored per pixel in one plane. The tag is structured as follows:

Tag type 258 (102H)
Data type SHORT
Length of data area = 1
BitsPerSample (value 1...65535)

Table 27.12 BitsPerSample tag

In black and white images, only one bit per pixel is needed. With 4 levels of gray, for example, 4 samples and therefore 4 bits per pixel are stored. For color images with 3 colors and 8 bits per color, 24 bits per pixel may be necessary. Since the colors are stored in three planes (red, green, blue), different bit numbers may be selected for each color (for example, red 8 bits, green 6 bits, blue 4 bits). The *BitsPerSample* values (here 864H) for the colors red, green and blue are stored in the first two bytes of the value field (offset 08H). 4 and 8 bits are permitted for *grayscale* images, while color images use 8 or 12 bits per pixel.

27.2.2.6 Compression tag (103H)

This tag describes the compression process used to store the data belonging to the relevant IFD.

Tag Type 259 (103H)
Data type SHORT
Length of data area = 1
Compression (value 1...65535) (Standard = 1)

Table 27.13 Compression tag

The compressed data is stored in a specific area and addressed via the *Strip Data Pointer*. The value in the *Compression tag* specifies the coding format.

1: The data is in uncompressed form, but the pixel information is partially packed by byte. The end of a data row is filled with empty bits, up to the byte limit.

If the number of bits per sample is greater than 8, TIFF will store the values in 16 or 32 bit blocks. The Intel and Motorola storage conventions should be taken into account here. With uncompressed image data, appropriate values should be set for *BitsPerSample*, *MinSampleValue* and *MaxSampleValue*. The value of *BitsPerSample* must always be the next suitable number $2n$. With 6 bits per sample, *BitsPerSample* is set to 8. *MinSampleValue* contains the value 0, and *MaxSampleValue* contains the value 64 (6 bits) to enable the TIFF reader to calculate the correct number of bits per pixel.

2: The data is compressed and stored using a modified CCITT/3 1-D process (Huffman RLE). By contrast with the normal CCITT/3 1-D process, no end characters are used and each new line is compressed independently of the preceding line.

The two following compression methods are used for the transfer of image data in FAX mode.

3: FAX CCITT Group 3-compatible storage. Each strip begins at a byte boundary and the data is stored by byte. End characters are used (T4 bi-level encoding).

4: FAX CCITT Group 4-compatible storage. Each strip begins at a byte boundary (T6 encoding).

StripOffset tags can be used with compression processes in accordance with CCITT/3, to increase efficiency.

5: LZW compression for monochrome, mapper color and color images.

6: JPEG compression (from TIFF version 6.0).

The values between 32768 and 65535 are reserved for manufacturer-defined (*private*) compression processes. So far, two of these coding methods have been made *public*:

32771: corresponds to type 1, but each line begins at the next free word boundary.

32773: uses PackBit compression.

For bi-level images, only compression methods 1, 2 and 32773 are permissible. Grayscale images can be stored using methods 1 and 32773. Information on the compression of image data is given in the description of the image data area.

27.2.2.7 PhotometricInterpretation tag (106H)

This tag is considered together with the *MaxSampleValue* and *MinSampleValue* tags. It indicates the way image data is interpreted.

Tag type 262 (106H) Data type SHORT Length of data area = 1 PhotometricInterpretation (value 0...8)

Table 27.14 PhotometricInterpretation tag

In the value field, the entries 0 to 8 are permitted to give the following modes:

0 For bi-level and grayscale images. The color level entered in *MinSampleValue* (for example, 0), is interpreted as white; the color level entered in *MaxSampleValue* (for example, FFH) is interpreted as black. In grayscale images, the image values are converted to the corresponding intermediate levels. This is the standard setting for compression type 2.

1 For bi-level and grayscale images. The color level entered in *MinSampleValue* is interpreted as black, and the value entered in *MaxSampleValue* is interpreted as white. In grayscale images, the image values are converted to the corresponding intermediate levels. If this value is pre-set for compression type 2, the image must be inverted in the output.

2 The data in the bitmap is coded according to the RGB system. The value entered in *MinSampleValue* represents the minimum color intensity. The value in *MaxSampleValue* the maximum.

3 *Palette Color*. In this mode a color is described by a value (1 sample). This value acts as an index to the *Color Response Curve* for the color intensity fields for red, green and blue. In this case, *SamplePerPixel* must be equal to 1, and the *Color Response Curve* must be supported.

4 *Transparency Mask*. This means that the image is interpreted as a mask (area) within another image in the same TIFF file. The values *SamplePerPixel* and *BitsPerSample* must be set to 1. Also, *PackBit* compression is required. If the bits of the mask are set (1), they define an inner section of an area, while unset (0) bits indicate the perimeter. In this way, it is possible to mark a partial image (region) within an image. The *TransparencyMask* image must have the same values in *ImageLength* and *ImageWidth* as the original image. A TIFF reader can evaluate the mask and display only the areas of the image located within the mask (bits = 1).

6 *YCbCr Color Space*. The image data is scaled according to the YCbCr color system. This mode has been adopted from version 6.0 of TIFF onwards.

8 *1976 CIEL*a*b Color System*. This value was also adopted in version 6.0 of TIFF.

There are no standard settings for this parameter. Information relating to the intensity of the RGB representation is interpreted in accordance with NTSC specifications. This tag should not appear if the data is coded according to the CCITT/3 method, since the coding already contains the interpretation of the image data. The scanner or reading device must support at least modes 0 and 1.

Graphics

27.2.2.8 Thresholding tag (107H)

This tag is used for image data that has been processed. With a grayscale image, for example, it indicates the method used.

Tag type 263 (107H)
Data type SHORT
Length of data area = 1
Thresholding (value 1, 2, 3)

Table 27.15 Thresholding tag

Three entries are permitted in the value field:

1. A *Bi-level* image (black and white picture) has been stored. The number of bits per pixel is set to 1.
2. A grayscale image has been transformed into a black and white picture (*dithered*). The bits per pixel are set to 1.
3. A grayscale image has been changed into a black and white picture using the Error-Diffusion Method.

With this type of image, it is not possible to carry out retrospective re-scaling, otherwise the image data would be altered.

27.2.2.9 CellWidth tag (108H)

Tag type 264 (108H)
Data type SHORT
Length of data area = 1
CellWidth (value 1, 2, 3)

Table 27.16 CellWidth tag

This tag describes the dimensions of the matrix in the *Dithering* or *Halftone* processes. It only occurs when the *Thresholding* tag (107H) specifies mode 2. The *CellWidth* tag indicates the width of the matrix and is supported by relatively few TIFF scanners.

27.2.2.10 CellLength tag (109H)

This tag describes the dimensions of a matrix in the *Dithering* or *Halftone* processes. It can be used with tag 107H, if mode 2 is specified.

Tag type 265 (109H)
Data type SHORT
Length of data area = 1
CellLength (value 1, 2 , 3)

Table 27.17
CellLength tag

The tag indicates the height of the matrix. It is used with relatively few scanners.

27.2.2.11 FillOrder tag (10AH)

This tag specifies how the data for a pixel is stored in bytes. The tag is structured as follows:

Tag type 266 (10AH)
Data type SHORT
Length of data area = 1
FillOrder (value 1, 2)

Table 27.18
FillOrder tag

The following modes apply to the entries in the value field:

1 The pixels are stored continuously in a byte. The first pixel to the left starts in the uppermost bit, and the following pixels are stored in the bits of lower value. This is the default mode.

2 The pixels are stored continuously in a byte. The first pixel to the right starts in the lowest bit, and the following pixels are stored in the bits of higher value.

27.2.2.12 DocumentName tag (10DH)

This tag specifies the name of the document from which the picture was created. It is structured as follows:

Tag type 269 (10DH)
Data type ASCII
Length of data area = n
Value: Pointer to the document name

Table 27.19 Document tag

The value field contains a pointer (offset from start of file) to the ASCII string containing the document name. The string is terminated with a null byte (00H) and may be stored anywhere in the file.

27.2.2.13 ImageDescriptor tag (10EH)

This tag contains various information on the currently stored image. It is structured as follows:

Tag type 270 (10EH)
Data type ASCII
Length of data area = n
Value: Pointer to document information

Table 27.20 ImageDescriptor tag

The value field contains a pointer (offset from start of file) to the ASCII string containing the information. The string is terminated with a null byte (00H). There is at present no specification for the coding of the information.

27.2.2.14 Make tag (10FH)

This tag defines the name of the manufacturer of the scanner.

Tag type 271 (10FH)
Data type ASCII
Length of data area = n
Value: Pointer to the make string

Table 27.21 Make tag

The value field contains a pointer (offset from start of file) to the ASCII string containing the manufacturer's name. The string is terminated with a null byte (00H).

27.2.2.15 Model tag (110H)

This tag defines the model and number of the scanner.

Tag Type 272 (110H)
Data type ASCII
Length of data area = *n*
Value: Pointer to the model string

Table 27.22
Model tag

The value field contains a pointer (offset from start of file) to the ASCII string containing the model name of the scanner. The string is terminated with a null byte (00H).

27.2.2.16 StripOffset tag (111H)

This tag specifies either the offset to the bitmap containing the image data or another pointer field. It always contains a 4-byte pointer (offset from start of file) to the start of a data field containing the *BitImage* data. Direct access to the data can be gained via this offset. At least one *StripOffset* pointer is needed to determine the position of the image data.

Tag type 273 (111H)
Data type SHORT or LONG
Length of data area = *n*
Pointer (value 0...(2**32) – 1)

Table 27.23
StripOffset tag

To increase the speed of the image output, it is possible to process only every *n* th line. For test purposes, a picture with a resolution of 300 dpi can be displayed at 75 dpi. Decoding of the remaining lines is not carried out during the first scan. This enables a rough image to be displayed very quickly. The missing lines can be added during subsequent scans. If this method is to be used, the starting position of all image lines in the *BitImage* data field must be known. Here, too, the *StripOffset* tag is useful, because the pointer in the value field need not refer directly to image data; it may indicate a table containing the actual *StripOffset* pointers. This table contains one such pointer for each image line.

The length field indicates which case applies. If the length field is 1, the pointer field contains a pointer to the first *StripOffset*. If the value in the length field is greater than 1, the pointer refers to a pointer table within the file. This table contains *n* entries, each pointing to the start of a strip area. The number n is stored in the length field of the tag. The default value for the pointer is LONG. SHORT data can only be stored in very small TIFF files in which this facility should not be used.

27.2.2.17 Orientation tag (112H)

Tag type 274 (112H)
Data type SHORT
Length of data area = 1
Orientation (value 1...8)

Table 27.24
Orientation tag

This tag specifies the orientation of a bitmap graphic in the X and Y directions. There are altogether 8 possible orientation directions for an image:

Code	1st bitmap row	1st column
1	Top border	Left border
2	Top border	Right border
3	Bottom border	Left border
4	Bottom border	Left border
5	Left border	Top border
6	Right border	Top border
7	Right border	Bottom border
8	Left border	Bottom border

Table 27.25
Image
Orientation tag

Value 1 is the default setting; the other values are, so far, rarely supported by scanners. A change of values rotates the image around the origin.

27.2.2.18 SamplesPerPixel tag (115H)

This tag indicates the number of samples per pixel. It is structured as follows:

Tag type 277 (115H)
Data type SHORT
Length of data area = 1
SamplesPerPixel (Value 1...65535)

Table 27.26
SamplesPerPixel
tag

With black and white images, the value is set to 1. For color pictures with three color planes, the setting is 3. Grayscale pictures with 4 or 6 levels still only contain one color plane, and are therefore set to value 1.

27.2.2.19 RowsPerStrip tag (116H)

This tag indicates the number of uncompressed lines in a strip.

Tag type 278 (116H)
Data type LONG or SHORT
Length of data area = 1
RowsPerStrip (value 0...(2**32)-1)

Table 27.27 RowsPerStrip tag

This tag is only valid if no data compression is used. The entry in the value field indicates the number of uncompressed lines in a strip (partial image). However, all strips (except for the last) must contain the same number of lines.

27.2.2.20 StripByteCounts tag (117H)

This tag is only used with data compression in accordance with the CCITT/3 method. It is used to check whether the correct amount of data has been read. The structure is as follows:

Tag type 279 (117H)
Data type SHORT or LONG
Length of data area = *n*
StripByteCounts (value 0...(2**32) -1)

Table 27.28 StripByteCounts tag

The tag is created for every compressed data record in the TIFF file to which a *StripOffsetPointer* is pointing. The value field contains the number of bytes in the associated strip.

27.2.2.21 MinSampleValue tag (118H)

In conjunction with the *MaxSampleValue* tag, this tag describes how the bitmap data should be interpreted as colors.

Tag type 280 (118H)
Data type SHORT
Length of data area = 1
MinSampleValue (Value 0...65535)

Table 27.29 MinSampleValue tag

The default value entered in the data field is 0 – the smallest possible value for a pixel. The tag is processed together with the *PhotometricInterpretation* tag.

27.2.2.22 MaxSampleValue tag (119H)

In conjunction with the *MinSampleValue* tag, this tag describes how the bitmap data should be interpreted as colors.

Tag type 281 (119H)
Data type SHORT
Length of data area = 1
MaxSampleValue (value 0...65535)

Table 27.30 MaxSampleValue tag

The default value in the data field is 65535 – the maximum value for a pixel. For black and white pictures, the minimum value is set to 0 and the maximum is defined as 1. In the case of a 4-bit grayscale image, the values are between 0 and 15. This tag is processed together with *PhotometricInterpretation*.

27.2.2.23 XResolution tag (11AH)

This tag specifies the image resolution in the X direction. It is structured as follows:

Tag type 282 (11AH)
Data type rational
Length of data area = 1
Value (1/((2**32) -1...(2**32) -1)

Table 27.31 XResolution tag

The resolution in pixels is particularly important for scanners that can operate with several degrees of resolution. This enables the scaling to be adapted to the features of the device. The range of resolution for normal devices is between 75 and 300 dpi (dots per inch). In the value field, a resolution of 300 dpi can be specified as 300/1 or a value of 75 dpi can be defined as 150/2 (*numerator/denominator*). The field can be stored anywhere in the file, and a pointer to the value is stored in the tag.

27.2.2.24 YResolution tag (11BH)

This tag specifies the image resolution in the Y direction. It is structured as shown in Table 4.124:

Tag type 283 (11BH)
Data type rational
Length of data area = 1
value (1/(2**32) -1...(2**32) -1)

Table 27.32
YResolution tag

The resolution in pixels is particularly important for scanners that can operate with several degrees of resolution. This enables the scaling to be adapted to the features of the device. The range of resolution for normal devices is between 75 and 300 dpi (dots per inch). In the value field, a resolution of 300 dpi can be specified as 300/1. The field can be stored anywhere in the file, and a pointer to the value is stored in the tag.

27.2.2.25 PlanarConfiguration tag (11CH)

This tag describes the organization of the data in color or grayscale images. The tag is not required for black and white images.

Tag type 284 (11CH)
Data type SHORT
Length of data area = 1
PlanarConfiguration (value 1, 2)

Table 27.33
Planar-Configuration tag

Image data for color or grayscale pictures can be stored in two different ways: All the information can be stored together in one pixel, that is, the color plane bits are positioned one after the other. Alternatively, it is possible to store the information on the pixels in several color planes or gray levels. In this case, all the pixels of one color plane are described before the next color plane is dealt with.

The value 1 specifies that all the data for one pixel are stored together. Value 2 indicates that the image data is subdivided into planes and stored by plane. The value of the *PhotometricInterpretation* tag must be taken into account in the evaluation.

27.2.2.26 PageName tag (11DH)

This tag specifies the name of the page from which the image was scanned. The tag is structured as follows:

Tag type 285 (11DH)
Data type ASCII
Length of data area = n
Pointer to document name

Table 27.34
PageName tag

The value field contains a pointer to the ASCII string containing the document name. The string is terminated with a null byte (00H).

27.2.2.27 XPosition tag (11EH)

This tag defines the X offset of an image extract.

Tag type 286 (11EH)
Data type RATIONAL
Length of data area = 1
Pointer to value

Table 27.35
XPosition tag

The value field contains a pointer to the actual value, which is stored as a rational number. This number specifies the X coordinate of the top left corner of the image in inches.

27.2.2.28 YPosition tag (11FH)

This tag defines the Y offset of an image extract. The value field contains a pointer to the actual value, which is stored as a rational number (numerator, denominator). The value 2.5 inches should be stored as 5/2. In Intel notation, this corresponds to 05H 00H 00H 00H 02H 00H 00H 00H. The number specifies the offset of the coordinate of the top left corner of the image in inches. In TIFF format, the positive axis points downwards.

Tag type 287 (11FH)
Data type RATIONAL
Length of data area = 1
Pointer to value

Table 27.36
YPosition tag

27.2.2.29 FreeOffsets tag (120H)

This tag contains a pointer to a table containing additional pointers. Each of these pointers refers to a free data area in the TIFF file. The tag is structured as shown below:

Tag type 288 (120H)
Data type LONG
Length of data area = n
Pointer to table

Table 27.37
FreeOffset tag

If only one free area exists, there will only be one pointer. The number of entries in the pointer table is indicated in the length field of the tag. This tag can be skipped.

27.2.2.30 FreeByteCount tag (121H)

This tag specifies the number of free bytes in a block. The tag is used in conjunction with the *FreeOffsets* tag.

Tag type 289 (121H)
Data type LONG
Length of data area = n
Pointer to data table

Table 27.38
FreeByteCount tag

The value field contains a pointer to a data table. This table contains n 4-byte entries, which each indicate the length of the associated free area. The position of these free areas can be determined via the *FreeOffsets* tag. The tag can be skipped.

27.2.2.31 GrayResponseUnit tag (122H)

In conjunction with the value for the *GrayResponseCurve*, this tag indicates how the image data should be interpreted. It is structured as follows:

Tag type 290 (122H)
Data type SHORT
Length of data area = 1
GrayResponseUnit (value 1...5)

Table 27.39 Gray-ResponseUnit tag

The entry in the value field specifies the value of the *GrayResponseCurve* tag. It is structured as follows:

Value	Present in units
1	1/10
2	1/100
3	1/1000
4	1/10000
5	1/100000

Table 27.40 GrayResponse Units

The grayscale can be determined via the relevant integer and scaling factor. If the value for the *GrayResponseUnit* is set to 3 and the entry in the *GrayResponseCurve* is set to 345, the result will be a grayscale of 0.345.

27.2.2.32 GrayResponseCurve tag (123H)

In conjunction with the value for the *GrayResponseUnit* this tag provides information on the interpretation of image data. It contains a vector to the actual data. For every sample plane of image data, there is an entry here which acts as the grayscale for interpreting the image data. The levels indicated represent the thresholds for calculating the gray tones between the minimum and maximum gray values.

Tag type 291 (123H)
Data type SHORT
Length of data area = 2**Bits/Sample
GrayResponseCurve (value 0...65535)

Table 27.41 Gray-ResponseCurve tag

27.2.2.33 T4Options tag (124H)

This tag is used for setting options when image data is coded according to the CCITT Group 3 method.

Tag type 292 (124H)
Data type LONG
Length of data area = 1
T4Options (value = 32-bit flag)

Table 27.42
T4Options tag

In the value field, the 4 bytes are interpreted as a 32-bit flag. All the unused bits are set to 0. The coding is as follows:

Bit 0: 0 for (standard) one-dimensional coding 1 for two-dimensional coding

Bit 1: 1 uncompressed mode used

Bit 2: 1 fill bits inserted to the end of a line

With a two-dimensional data coding, the first line of a strip must always be stored one-dimensionally. In TIFF 5.0, this tag was referred to as *Group3Options*.

27.2.2.34 T6Options tag (125H)

This tag is used for setting options when image data has been coded according to the CCITT Group 4 method. In the value field, the 4 bytes are interpreted as a 32-bit flag. Any unused bits are set to 0. The coding is as follows:

Tag type 293 (125H)
Data type LONG
Length of data area = 1
T6Options (value = 32-bit flag)

Table 27.43
T6Options tag

Only two bits in the 32-bit flag are used:

Bit 0: unused

Bit 1: 1 uncompressed mode used

In the current TIFF specifications, the remaining bits are unused. In TIFF 5.0, this tag was referred to as *Group4Options*.

27.2.2.35 ResolutionUnit tag (128H)

This tag specifies the unit used for the *XResolution* and *YResolution* tags. The value 2 indicates the default setting of dots per inch. The tag is structured as follows:

Tag type 296 (128H)
Data type SHORT
Length of data area = 1
Resolution unit (value 1, 2, 3)

Table 27.44 ResolutionUnit tag

The following values are permitted in the value field:

Value	Function
1	No absolute unit of measurement
2	Unit is inches
3	Unit is centimeters

Table 27.45 Resolution Unit

If the value is 0, any values that may be set in the *Resolution* tags are simply used to determine the ratio of the image dimensions. This tag is used very rarely.

27.2.2.36 PageNumber tag (129H)

This tag is used to indicate the (picture) page number for TIFF files consisting of several pictures. This is particularly important for FAX transmissions.

Tag type 297 (129H)
Data type SHORT
Length of data area = 2
PageNumber (value 1, value 2)

Table 27.46 PageNumber tag

The value field contains two 16-bit values. The first value indicates the current page number; the second value specifies the number of pages in the file. Individual pages do not need to be in order within the TIFF file.

27.2.2.37 ColorResponseUnit tag (12CH)

In conjunction with the value for the *ColorResponseCurve*, this tag provides information on the interpretation of image data. It is structured as follows:

Tag type 300 (12CH)
Data type SHORT
Length of data area = 1
ColorResponseUnit (value 1...5)

Table 27.47 Color-ResponseUnit tag

The entry specifies the value of the *ColorResponseCurve* tag. The following gradations are defined:

Value	Unit
1	1/10
2	1/100
...	
5	1/100000

Table 27.48 Unit Color Response Curve

The color scale can then be determined via the relevant integer number and the scaling factor. A value of 3 in the *ColorResponseUnit* field and an entry of 345 in the *ColorResponseCurve* produce an intensity level of 0.345.

27.2.2.38 TransferFunction tag (12DH)

In TIFF version 5, this tag was referred to as the *ColorResponseCurve*. In conjunction with the value for the *Color Response Unit*, it provides information on the interpretation of image data. The structure of the tag is as follows:

Tag type 301 (12DH)
Data type SHORT
Length of data area = {1 or 3}*(2**Bits/Sample)
TransferFunction (value 0...65535)

Table 27.49 TransferFunction tag

The tag contains a pointer to the actual data tables. Each entry in the table is of data type SHORT and therefore requires 16 bits. The table first contains all entries for the color red. This is followed by the entries for green and then the entries for blue. The number of entries per color can be calculated as:

2**BitsPerSample

With 4 bits, 16 entries are possible and with 8 bits 256 entries are possible. The value 0 in an entry represents the minimum intensity for the relevant color; the number 65535 stands for maximum intensity. The combination of values (0, 0, 0) describes the color black, while (255, 255, 255) represents white. The purpose of this *Color Response Curve* is to enable fine color gradation in an RGB image.

27.2.2.39 Software tag (131H)

This tag was introduced in TIFF version 5.0. It indicates the name of the software package that created the TIFF file.

Tag type 305 (131H)
Data type ASCII
Length of data area = 1
Pointer to a string

Table 27.50
Software tag

The data field contains a pointer to the relevant text. The reference number of the software that created the file may also be shown here.

27.2.2.40 DateTime tag (132H)

This tag indicates the date and time at which the TIFF file was created

Tag type 306 (132H)
Data type ASCII
Length of data area = 1
Pointer to a string

Table 27.51
DateTime tag

The string should have the format YYYY:MM:DD HH:MM:SS. The clock time is given in 24-hour mode. The ASCII string requires 20 bytes (including the terminating 00H).

27.2.2.41 Artist tag (13BH)

This tag indicates the name of the person who created the picture.

Tag type 315 (13BH)
Data type ASCII
Length of data area = 1
Pointer to a string

Table 27.52
Artist tag

The string can be used, for example, to display a copyright message. This tag may follow immediately after the header.

27.2.2.42 Host Computer tag (13CH)

This tag defines the name of the computer on which the TIFF file was created.

Tag type 316 (13CH)
Data type ASCII
Length of data area = 1
Pointer to a string

Table 27.53
Host Computer tag

The tag is optional and refers to a text indicating the name of the computer.

27.2.2.43 Predictor tag (13DH)

This tag is used if the value Compression = 5 (LZW compression) is used.

Tag type 317 (13DH)
Data type SHORT
Length of data area = 1
Value: 1, 2

Table 27.54
Predictor tag

This tag enables future compression of various images to be optimized using the LZW process. At present, the following values apply:

1	No prediction scheme used before coding
2	Horizontal differencing

If a TIFF reader finds an unknown value in this tag, the decoding of the image must be aborted.

27.2.2.44 White Point tag (13EH)

This tag defines a white point in the 1931 CIE xy color diagram (chromaticity diagram). Only the color (chromaticity) is specified and not the brightness (luminance).

Tag type 318 (13EH)
Data type RATIONAL
Length of data area = 2
Pointer to the xy-data

Table 27.55 White Point tag

The default setting for a white point is defined as follows:

D65: X = 0.313 X = 0.329

This value is used for calibrating a monitor or scanner.

27.2.2.45 PrimaryChromaticities tag (13FH)

This tag defines the chromaticities of primary colors.

Tag type 319 (13FH)
Data type RATIONAL
Length of data area = 6
Pointer to the data area

Table 27.56 Primary-Chromaticities tag

This value is defined in the 1931 CIE xy chromaticity diagram. The standard codings for the primary colors are as follows:

Red:	X = 0.635	Y = 0.340
Green:	X = 0.305	Y = 0.595
Blue:	X = 0.155	Y = 0.070

The value is used for calibrating a monitor or scanner.

27.2.2.46 ColorMap tag (140H)

This tag defines a specific color palette (color map)

Tag type 320 (140H)
Data type SHORT Length of data area = 3*(2**BitsPerSample) Pointer to the Color Map

Table 27.57
ColorMap tag

The value defines a pointer to the table containing the color map. This table begins with *n* entries indicating the intensity of the color red for each of the colors in the color map. These are followed by *n* entries for green, and then by *n* entries for blue. In this way, *n* colors can be defined for the associated image. The number *n* is calculated as follows:

2**BitsPerPixel

that is, with 4 bits per pixel, 16 colors can be represented. There will therefore be 16 consecutive entries in the table for each of the colors red, green and blue. The value for a color pixel is interpreted as an index to the relevant color table (palette). The actual color is mixed from the three entries in the table.

Each entry consists of 16 bits. The value `0` defines the minimum intensity of primary color, and the number `65535` indicates the maximum intensity of primary color. The combination `(0,0,0)` represents black, while `(65535, 65535,65535)` indicates white. The color table can be used with the *Color Response* curve to refine the color gradation. This tag must be used with all images that require a palette.

Graphics

27.2.2.47 HalftoneHints tag (141H, TIFF 6.0)

The purpose of the *HalftoneHints* field is to convey to the halftone function the range of graylevels within a colorimetrically specified image that is to retain tonal detail.

Tag type 321 (141H)
Data type SHORT
Length of data area = 2
HalftoneHints field

Table 27.58 HalftoneHints tag

The data field in the tag contains two 16 bit entries. The first word specifies the highlight gray level which should be halftoned at the lightest printable tint. The second word defines the shadow graylevel.

27.2.2.48 TileWidth tag (142H, TIFF 6.0)

The TIFF 6.0 specification provides for the division of an image into tiles instead of strips. This tag defines the width of a tile in pixels.

Tag type 322 (142H)
Data type SHORT or LONG
Length of data area = 1
Tile width in pixels

Table 27.59 TileWidth tag

27.2.2.49 TileLength tag (143H, TIFF 6.0)

This tag defines the height (length) of a tile in pixels.

Tag type 323 (143H)
Tile length in pixels
Data type SHORT or LONG
Length of data area = 1

Table 27.60 TileLength tag

The value for *TileLength* must be a multiple of 16 if JPEG compression is to be used.

27.2.2.50 TileOffsets tag (144H, TIFF 6.0)

For every tile containing an excerpt of an image, an offset to the data in the TIFF file is stored. This tag defines a table with the offsets in bytes.

Tag type 324 (144H)
Data type LONG
Length of data area = *n*
Pointer to offset table

Table 27.61
TileOffsets tag

This tag replaces the *StripOffset* tag. The offsets are arranged according to the associated tiles, from left to right and from top to bottom.

For *PlanarConfiguration = 1*, the number of *Tiles per Image* is stored in the length field. With *PlanarConfiguration = 2* the length field contains the value:

SamplesPerImage * TilesPerImage

With *PlanarConfiguration = 2*, the offsets of the first color plane are stored first.

27.2.2.51 TileByteCount tag (145H, TIFF 6.0)

This tag indicates the amount of compressed image data per tile, in bytes.

Tag type 325 (145H)
Data type SHORT or LONG
Length of data area = *n*
Pointer to offset table

Table 27.62
TileByteCounts tag

For *PlanarConfiguration = 1*, the number of *Tiles per Image* is stored in the *length field*. With *PlanarConfiguration = 2* the *length field* contains the value:

SamplesPerImage * TilesPerImage

With *PlanarConfiguration = 2*, the offsets of the first color plane are stored first.

27.2.2.52 InkSet tag (14CH, TIFF 6.0)

This tag defines the color model (ink set) in an image with color separation (Photometric-Interpretation = 5).

Tag type 332 (14CH)
Data type SHORT
Length of data area = 1
Ink set

Table 27.63
InkSet tag

The following values are permitted:

1 CMYK color system

2 not CMYK color system

The default entry is 1 for the CMYK color system. In this way, each color pixel in the image defines a color intensity (cyan, magenta, yellow, black).

27.2.2.53 InkNames tag (14DH, TIFF 6.0)

This tag is used in an image with color separation (PhotometricInterpretation = 5).

Tag type 333 (14DH)
Data type ASCII
Length of data area = 1
Pointer to string

Table 27.64
InkName tag

The names of the colors are defined as an ASCII character list. The number of entries must agree with the *NumberOfInks*.

27.2.2.54 NumberOfInks tag (14EH, TIFF 6.0)

The purpose of this tag is to indicate the number of colors (inks).

Tag type 334 (14EH)
Data type SHORT
Length of data area = 1
NumberOfInks

Table 27.65
NumberOfInks tag

The value generally corresponds to the value of *SamplesPerPixel*. The *ExtraSample* tag, which can define other values, is an exception. The standard setting for the number of inks is 4.

27.2.2.55 DOTRange tag (150H, TIFF 6.0)

This tag defines the range for the density of color dots.

Tag type 336 (150H)
Data type BYTE or SHORT
Length of data area = 2 or 2*SamplesPerPixel
DotRange[1]

Table 27.66
DotRange tag

DotRange[0] corresponds to a 0% dot and DotRange[1] corresponds to a 100% dot. If a DotRange pair for each component (cyan, and so on) is included, the values for a component are stored together.

27.2.2.56 TargetPrinter tag (151H, TIFF 6.0)

This tag defines the name of the output device.

Tag type 337 (151H)
Data type ASCII
Length of data area = any
Pointer to string

Table 27.67
TargetPrinter tag

The tag contains a pointer to the text containing the name of the output device.

27.2.2.57 Extra Samples tag (152H, TIFF 6.0)

This tag contains a description of supplementary data for an image.

Tag type 338 (152H)
Data type SHORT
Length of data area = m
Pointer to data

Table 27.68 Extra Samples tag

This tag refers to a data area, which holds m items of supplementary information for a pixel. In this case, there is more data present than can be accommodated in *PhotometricInterpretation*. For example, in an RGB image, more than three *SamplesPerPixel* may occur. The *ExtraSamples* tag then defines the meaning of the supplementary data. Possible values for each entry in the data area include:

0 Unspecified data

1 Associated alpha data (opacity information)

2 Unassociated alpha data (transparency information)

This extra information must be stored in the last bytes of the data area for a pixel. In the case of RGB values with 24 bits per pixel, for example, the alpha value can be stored in the 4th byte.

27.2.2.58 SampleFormat tag (153H, TIFF 6.0)

This tag defines how each data point of a pixel is to be interpreted.

Tag type 339 (153H)
Data type SHORT
Length of data area = SamplesPerPixel
Pointer to data

Table 27.69 SampleFormat tag

The following codes have been defined for these values:

1 unsigned integer data

2 signed integer data (two's complement)

3 IEEE floating point data

4 undefined data format

The default code is 1.

27.2.2.59 SMinSampleValue tag (154H, TIFF 6.0)

This tag defines how many image planes (samples) must be present for the picture.

Tag type 340 (154H)
Data type: best match for the data
Length of data area = SamplesPerPixel
Pointer to data

Table 27.70 SMinSample-Value tag

With 3 *SamplesPerPixel*, at least 3 values must be present for each pixel (for example, 3 bytes).

27.2.2.60 SMaxSampleValue tag (155H, TIFF 6.0)

This tag defines the maximum number of image planes (samples) that may be present for the picture.

Tag type 341 (155H)
Data type: best match for the data
Length of data area = SamplesPerPixel
Pointer to data

Table 27.71 SMaxSample-Value tag

With a value of 4, a maximum of 4 samples may be stored per pixel.

27.2.2.61 TransferRange tag (156H, TIFF 6.0)

This tag expands the range of the TransferFunction (*PhotometricInterpretation* tag).

Tag type 342 (156H)
Data type SHORT
Length of data area = 6
Pointer to data

Table 27.72 TransferRange tag

The first pair of values defines the *TransferBlack* and *TransferWhite* data. The arrangement of value pairs corresponds to the sequence in the *PhotometricInterpretation* tag. This may be followed by an RGB value as a real number.

27.2.2.62 YCbCrCoefficient tag (211H, TIFF 6.0)

This tag is used for transforming an RGB value into the YCbCr color system.

Tag type 529 (211H)
Data type RATIONAL
Length of data area = 3
Pointer to data

Table 27.73 YCbCrCoefficient tag

The value field contains three coefficients:

LumaRed

LumaGreen

LumaBlue

The YCbCr data can be determined from these coefficients:

Y = (LumaRed*R + LumaGreen*G + LumaBlue*B)

Cb = (B – Y)/(2 – 2*LumaBlue)

Cr = (R – Y)/(2 – 2*LumaRed)

Recalculation of the RGB values is carried out as follows:

R = Cr*(2 – 2*LumaRed) + Y

G = (Y – LumaBlue*B – LumaRed*R)/(LumaGreen)

B = Cb*(2 – 2*LumaBlue) + Y

The CCIR 601-1 values 299/1000, 587/1000 and 114/1000 are used as the standard setting for LumaRed, LumaGreen and LumaBlue.

27.2.2.63 YCbCrSubSampling tag (212H, TIFF 6.0)

This tag specifies subsampling factors for the chrominance components of a YCbCr image.

Tag type 530 (212H)
Data type SHORT
Length of data area = 2
Pointer to data

Table 27.74 YCbCrSub-Sampling tag

The value field contains the two factors *YCbCrSubsampleHoriz* and *YCbCrSubsampleVertic*. The first field (YCbCrSubsampleHoriz) may contain the following values:

1 ImageWidth of this chroma image is equal to the ImageWidth of the associated luma image.

2 ImageWidth of this chroma image is half the ImageWidth of the associated luma image.

4 ImageWidth of this chroma image is one quarter of the ImageWidth of the associated luma image.

The field *YCbCrSubsampleVertic* may contain the following values:

1 ImageLength of this chroma image is equal to the ImageLength of the associated luma image.

2 ImageLength of this chroma image is half the ImageLength of the associated luma image.

4 ImageLength of this chroma image is one quarter of the ImageLength of the associated luma image.

The standard setting for the field is 2,2.

27.2.2.64 YCbCrPositioning tag (213H, TIFF 6.0)

This tag specifies the position of the supplementary color components (subsampled chrominance components) relative to the luminance data.

Tag type 531 (213H)
Data type SHORT
Length of data area = 1
YCbCrPositioning

Table 27.75 YCbCrPositioning tag

The values for this field are:

1 centered

2 co-sited

The standard value for the field is 1.

27.2.2.65 ReferenceBlackWhite tag (214H, TIFF 6.0)

This tag specifies the distance (headroom and footroom) of the black and white color information from the maximum possible values. This technique is used in film and video technology.

Tag type 532 (214H)
Data type RATIONAL
Length of data area = 6
ReferenceBlackWhite

Table 27.76 Reference-BlackWhite tag

The value field contains value pairs for every color component. The first value defines the black; the second defines the white.

27.2.2.66 JPEGProc tag (200H, TIFF 6.0)

This tag specifies that a JPEG compression has been applied to the image.

Tag type 512 (200H)
Data type SHORT
Length of data area = 1
JPEGProc

Table 27.77 JPEGProc tag

The following codes are permitted in the value field.

1 Baseline sequential process

14 Lossless process with Huffman coding

Other values for the field will be defined in the future.

27.2.2.67 JPEGInterchangeFormat tag (201H, TIFF 6.0)

This tag specifies whether the JPEG data has been stored in Interchange Format in the TIFF file.

Tag type 513 (201H)
Data type LONG
Length of data area = 1
JPEGInterchangeFormat

Table 27.78 JPEGInter-changeFormat tag

If the data is in JPEG Interchange Format, the tag contains a pointer to the start of the data (Start of Image, (SOI marker code)). If the field is 0, the data is not in Interchange Format.

27.2.2.68 JPEGInterchangeFormatLength tag (202H, TIFF 6.0)

This tag indicates the length in bytes of the JPEG Interchange Format data area.

Tag type 514 (202H)
Data type LONG
Length of data area = 1
JPEGInterchangeFormat

Table 27.79 JPEGInterchangeFormatLength tag

The field is only relevant if the *JPEGInterchangeFormat* tag is present.

27.2.2.69 JPEGRestartInterval tag (203H, TIFF 6.0)

This tag defines the length of the restart interval used for data compression.

Tag type 515 (203H)
Data type SHORT
Length of data area = 1
JPEGRestartInterval

Table 27.80 JPEGRestartInterval tag

The interval is defined as the number of *Minimum Code Units* between restart markers. If the field is not present or set to 0, the data does not contain any restart markers.

27.2.2.70 JPEGLossLessPredictors tag (205H, TIFF 6.0)

This tag refers to a list of *Lossless Predictor Selection Values*. One entry is allocated to each component.

Tag type 517 (205H)
Data type SHORT
Length of data area = SamplesPerPixel
Pointer to table

Table 27.81 JPEGLossLess-Predictors tag

The values permitted as predictor factors are listed in Table 27.82:

Selection value	Prediction
1	A
2	B
3	C
4	A + B – C
5	A + (B – C) / 2
6	B + (A – C) / 2
7	(A + B) / 2

Table 27.82 Prediction values

A, B and C are sample values directly to the left of, above and diagonally to the left of the current point which has just been coded. Further details can be obtained in the JPEG Draft (ISO DIS 10918-1).

27.2.2.71 JPEGPointTransforms tag (206H, TIFF 6.0)

This tag refers to a list of *transformation points*. One entry is allocated to each component.

Tag type 518 (206H)
Data type SHORT
Length of data area = SamplesPerPixel
Pointer to table

Table 27.83 JPEGPoint-Transforms tag

This tag is only permissible for a lossless JPEG compression.

27.2.2.72 JPEGQTables tag (207H, TIFF 6.0)

This tag refers to a list of offsets for the *quantization tables*.

Tag type 519 (207H)
Data type LONG
Length of data area = SamplesPerPixel
Pointer to table

Table 27.84 JPEGQTables tag

Each table consists of 64 bytes. A description of the process is given in the JPEG specification (ISO DIS 10918-1).

27.2.2.73 JPEGDCTables tag (208H, TIFF 6.0)

This tag refers to a list of offsets to the DC Huffman table.

Tag type 520 (208H)
Data type LONG
Length of data area = SamplesPerPixel
Pointer to table

Table 27.85 JPEGDCTables tag

Each table consists of 16 bytes of code length 1...16, and up to 17 bytes containing values. A description of the process is given in the JPEG specification (ISO DIS 10918-1).

27.2.2.74 JPEGACTables tag (209H, TIFF 6.0)

This tag refers to a list of offsets to the Huffman AC tables

Tag type 521 (209H)
Data type LONG
Length of data area = SamplesPerPixel
Pointer to table

Table 27.86 JPEGACTables tag

Each table consists of 16 bytes of code length 1...16, and up to 256 bytes containing values. A description of the process is given in the JPEG specification (ISO DIS 10918-1).

27.2.2.75 Notes

From TIFF 5.0, four classes for the storage of image data have been defined (Table 27.87).

Class	Remark
TIFF-B	Bi-level images
TIFF-G	Grayscale images
TIFF-P	Color Map images
TIFF-R	Color RGB images

Table 27.87 TIFF classes (since version 5.0)

TIFF files contain the structural elements Header, Image File Directory and Image Raster Data. The IFD contains the tags giving extra information on the image data. The image data itself is stored in free areas of the TIFF file as *Image Raster Blocks*, and a complete image can be stored in one block. In addition to the problem of long processing times for decoding the data, the memory limitations of the evaluation device are often reached with larger images. A picture of 300 × 300 dpi requires 1 Mbyte of memory, which would overstretch a 640 Kbyte DOS computer. For this reason, the TIFF manual recommends that a picture should be split up into strips for processing. The *StripOffset* tags indicate the start of each strip in the *Image Raster Block*. Data in the individual strips may be stored in compressed or uncompressed form, as required. Each strip can be processed independently of the other image data.

With grayscale images, the pixel data is packed in bytes, one after the other. Color images can also be stored consecutively, that is, all the color information for one pixel is stored together sequentially. Alternatively, a color image can be divided into three planes: red, green and blue. Then, the image data for each plane can be stored together. The *SamplesPerPixel* tag indicates the number of color planes, and the *PlanarConfiguration* tag specifies the method of storage.

The entry in the value field of a tag requires 4 bytes and can be interpreted either as a pointer or as a value. If the data area is greater than 4 bytes, there is a pointer to this data in the value field. Otherwise, the values of the tag are stored directly in the last field. The length of the data area is stored in the tag.

A TIFF file may contain several images. The technique is used, for example, to store an image at various levels of resolution. This considerably speeds up the printing of sample copies, because fewer dots need to be processed at lower resolutions.

TIFF version 6.0 divides the TIFF tags into a *Baseline* group and *Extension* tags. Different tags are prescribed within the Baseline group for the individual groups (bi-level, grayscale, color, RGB color).

Tag Name	Code	Value
Bi-level Images		
ImageWidth	100H	
ImageLength	101H	
Compression	103H	1, 2, 32773
PhotometricInterpretation	106H	0, 1
StripOffsets	111H	
RowsPerStrip	116H	
StripByteCounts	117H	
XResolution	11AH	
YResolution	11BH	
ResolutionUnit	128H	1, 2, 3
Grayscale Images		
ImageWidth	100H	
ImageLength	101H	
BitsPerSample	102H	4, 8
Compression	103H	1, 32773
PhotometricInterpretation	106H	0, 1
StripOffsets	111H	
RowsPerStrip	116H	
StripByteCounts	117H	
XResolution	11AH	
YResolution	11BH	
ResolutionUnit	128H	1, 2, 3
Palette Color Images		
ImageWidth	100H	
ImageLength	101H	
BitsPerSample	102H	4, 8
Compression	103H	1, 32773
PhotometricInterpretation	106H	3
StripOffsets	111H	
RowsPerStrip	116H	
StripByteCounts	117H	
XResolution	11AH	
YResolution	11BH	
ResolutionUnit	128H	1, 2, 3
ColorMap	150H	
RGB Images		
ImageWidth	100H	
ImageLength	101H	

Table 27.88 Required tags for TIFF images *(continues over...)*

Graphics

Tag Name	Code	Value RGB Color
RGB Images		
BitsPerSample	102H	
8,8,8Compression	103H	1, 32773
PhotometricInterpretation	106H	2
StripOffsets	111H	
SamplesPerPixel	115H	>= 3
RowsPerStrip	116H	
StripByteCounts	117H	
XResolution	11AH	
YResolution	11BH	
ResolutionUnit	128H	1, 2, 3

Table 27.88 Required tags for TIFF images (*cont.*)

Every TIFF reader should be able to process these tags. In the case of the compression tag, only a small number of coding processes are defined for the baseline TIFF files.

27.3 TIFF Compression Processes

Since image data is often in compressed form, the TIFF specification provides various coding processes.

27.3.1 Uncompressed

All TIFF writers can store image data in uncompressed form. This generally guarantees that the data can be read by other TIFF readers. However, such files occupy a great deal of space.

27.3.2 PackBit Coding

With the code 32773, this process is one of the *private codings*. It originates from the Macintosh world. The image data is stored in records. The first byte of the records is the header, which indicates the number of following data bytes. Depending on the value of this byte, there are two different types of record:

Record	Description
Header 0-7FH	The record consists of a header and $n + 1$ data bytes, where n is the value of the header byte. The next $n + 1$ bytes of the input file will be read and copied to the output. The record contains uncompressed data.
Header 81H-FFH	The record consists of the header byte followed by one data byte. 80H is subtracted from the header byte value to give n. The data byte is then copied to the output $n + 1$ times.

Table 27.89 Packbit compression

The code 80H is not permitted in the header. If it is found, the byte will be skipped.

The TIFF 6.0 specification defines a number of supplementary requirements for Packbit compression:

- Each line of image data must be compressed separately. The packed data must not extend beyond one line.
- Uncompressed image data should be aligned to 16 bit boundaries. The number of uncompressed bytes per line is calculated as: (ImageWidth + 7) / 8.

The size of the record header means that sequences of data containing more than 128 identical data bytes must be divided into several records.

Graphics

27.3.3 FAX Compression (Modified Huffman Compression)

Some of the coding methods in the TIFF specification are based on the FAX CCITT/3 group compression. The scanner attempts to code continuous groups of white or black pixels wherever possible. Two tables have been defined: one containing codes for image runs between 0 and 63 consecutive white pixels and one containing codes for 0 to 63 consecutive black pixels. These tables also contain entries for discrete levels of black and white dot sequences with more than 63 dots. (The codes 64 to 2633 are provided for this purpose.) If a line is sampled, the scanner will store in the output file table codes corresponding to the number of white or black dots. In TIFF format, the following conditions apply:

- Each line within a bitmap is processed independently of the other lines.
- Fill bits at the edge of the image must not be compressed. The structure of the CCITT/3 tables is shown in Table 27.90 and in the corresponding ISO documentation.

- Every coded line must begin with a white bit pattern (for synchronization). In the case of images that begin with black dots, the code for a white pattern of 0 pixels is inserted.
- The EOL (end of line) markings designed for FAX CCITT/3 applications are not used in TIFF.

Using the code tables, the pixels of one row are analyzed. White and black image sequences are then assembled from the codes in the table. The resulting code sequences for these lines are of variable length. To synchronize the reader for color images, every line begins with a code number for a white pixel. If the original line begins with black pixels, the compression program will generate the code for a white pixel sequence containing 0 elements.

- Image sequences between 0 and 63 pixels are coded with a terminator code (word).
- Pixel sequences between 64 and 2623 (2560 + 63) are introduced with a make-up code (run length of the next smallest table entry). They are followed by the terminator code in which the difference is stored.
- Sequences longer than (or equal to) 2624 are introduced with the start code `2560`. If the remaining number of pixels is equal to or greater than 2560, additional sequences with this coding are generated. Only if the remaining number of pixels is less than `2560` will an additional code be generated with the number of remaining pixels.

If, at the decoding stage, the number of pixels read does not agree with the entry in *ImageWidth*, an insoluble error must have occurred.

No EOL codes are used in the compression process, and no fill bits are used at the right of the screen to complete the last byte of a row. The following table shows the code words (in binary values) for black and white pixel sequences.

Terminating codes

White & Black Run Length	Make-up Code Word	White & Black Run Length	Make-up Code Word
0	00110101	0	0000110111
1	000111	1	010
2	0111	2	11
3	1000	3	10
4	1011	4	011
5	1100	5	0011
6	1110	6	0010
7	1111	7	00011
8	10011	8	000101
9	10100	9	000100
10	00111	10	0000100
11	01000	11	0000101

Table 27.90 FAX coding tables (*continues over...*)

White & Black Run Length	Make-up Code Word	White & Black Run Length	Make-up Code Word
12	001000	12	0000111
13	000011	13	00000100
14	110100	14	00000111
15	110101	15	000011000
16	101010	16	0000010111
17	101011	17	0000011000
18	0100111	18	0000001000
19	0001100	19	00001100111
20	0001000	20	00001101000
21	0010111	21	00001101100
22	0000011	22	00000110111
23	0000100	23	00000101000
24	0101000	24	00000010111
25	0101011	25	00000011000
26	0010011	26	000011001010
27	0100100	27	000011001011
28	0011000	28	000011001100
29	00000010	29	000011001101
30	00000011	30	000001101000
31	00011010	31	000001101001
32	00011011	32	000001101010
33	00010010	33	000001101011
34	00010011	34	000011010010
35	00010100	35	000011010011
36	00010101	36	000011010100
37	00010110	37	000011010101
38	00010111	38	000011010110
39	00101000	39	000011010111
40	00101001	40	000001101100
41	00101010	41	000001101101
42	00101011	42	000011011010
43	00101100	43	000011011011
44	00101101	44	000001010100
45	00000100	45	000001010101
46	00000101	46	000001010110
47	00001010	47	000001010111
48	00001011	48	000001100100
49	01010010	49	000001100101
50	01010011	50	000001010010
51	01010100	51	000001010011

Table 27.90 FAX coding tables (*cont.*)

Graphics

White & Black Run Length	Make-up Code Word	White & Black Run Length	Make-up Code Word
52	01010101	52	000000100100
53	00100100	53	000000110111
54	00100101	54	000000111000
55	01011000	55	000000100111
56	01011001	56	000000101000
57	01011010	57	000001011000
58	01011011	58	000001011001
59	01001010	59	000000101011
60	01001011	60	000000101100
61	00110010	61	000001011010
62	00110011	62	000001100110
63	00110100	63	000001100111

Make-up codes

White & Black Run Length	Make-up Code Word	White & Black Run Length	Make-up Code Word
64	11011	64	0000001111
128	10010	128	000011001000
192	010111	192	000011001001
256	0110111	256	000001011011
320	00110110	320	000000110011
384	00110111	384	000000110100
448	01100100	448	000000110101
512	01100101	512	0000001101100
576	01101000	576	0000001101101
640	01100111	640	0000001001010
704	011001100	704	0000001001011
768	011001101	768	0000001001100
832	011010010	832	0000001001101
896	011010011	896	0000001110010
960	011010100	960	0000001110011
1024	011010101	1024	0000001110100
1088	011010110	1088	0000001110101
1152	011010111	1152	0000001110110

Table 27.90 FAX coding tables (*cont.*)

White & Black Run Length	Make-up Code Word	White & Black Run Length	Make-up Code Word
1216	011011000	1216	0000001110111
1280	011011001	1280	0000001010010
1344	011011010	1344	0000001010011
1408	011011011	1408	0000001010100
1472	010011000	1472	0000001010101
1536	010011001	1536	0000001011010
1600	010011010	1600	0000001011011
1664	011000	1664	0000001100100
1728	010011011	1728	0000001100101
EOL	000000000001	EOL	000000000001

Additional make-up codes

White & Black Run Length	Make-up Code Word
1792	00000001000
1856	00000001100
1920	00000001101
1984	000000010010
2048	000000010011
2112	000000010100
2176	000000010101
2240	000000010110
2304	000000010111
2368	000000011100
2432	000000011101
2496	000000011110
2560	000000011111

Table 27.90 FAX coding tables (*cont.*)

If a line is scanned, the scanner will store the table codes in the output file according to the number of white or black pixels. In TIFF format, the conditions described above apply.

Further information on the structure of the CCITT/3 tables is provided in the corresponding ISO documentation.

27.3.4 LZW Compression (Code 5)

This method of compression uses adaptive techniques to generate code tables. The algorithm itself has already been presented in the description of GIF (*see* Chapter 26). The following conditions apply to the TIFF compression process:

- With LZW, each strip must be compressed separately.
- A maximum of 8 Kbytes of uncompressed data may be contained in each strip
- The code length is variable, but must not exceed 12 bits. The table should be rebuilt for each strip.

If *BitsPerSample* = 4, each LZW code byte contains two (4-bit) pixels. At the start, the table can be initialized with the values 0 to 255. The first code issued is the *clear* code. Each strip should be terminated with an *EndOfInformation* code. LZW compressed strips must begin on byte boundaries. Alignment on word boundaries is not necessary. *FillOrder* is always taken to be 1. The compressed codes are stored byte-wise.

! **The Unisys Corporation holds a patent on the LZW compression process. Software developers who use this method for image compression require a license from this company.**

27.3.5 JPEG Compression

From TIFF version 6.0 onwards, JPEG compression is incorporated in the specification. The JPEG specification is an ISO standard and describes several compression variants. With *Baseline* compression, image information can be lost. The alternative provided is therefore referred to as the *Lossless* compression process. The prerequisite for the use of JPEG compression is that the image data contains 8 bit values for each component. Otherwise, the image data should be coded in bytes initially.

The compression variants are presented briefly in the TIFF 6.0 specification manual. A very good secondary reference is provided by W.B. Pennebaker and J.L Mitchell, *JPEG Still Image Compression Standard*, Van Nostrand Reinhold, ISBN 0-442-01272-1. The book contains the ISO specification for the JPEG process in the appendix.

28

Computer Graphic Metafile format (CGM)

***Computer** Graphic Metafile format enables the exchange of graphics between different computers. The definition of the metafile format was internationally standardized in 1987 (ISO 8662). Many American software manufacturers (for example, WordPerfect, Lotus) now support the CGM definition for the description of graphic data. This definition is closely related to the Graphic Kern System (GKS), and GKS Level 0 outputs are interchangeable with CGM. CGM files can also be interchanged with the recent ISO 8613 standard Office Document Architecture (ODA) and Interchange Format. CGM files can also be imported using the language SGML, as described in Chapter 20.*

From a practical viewpoint, CGM driver implementations are currently available for MS-DOS, OS/2, UNIX and VAX/VMS, the most well-known being the implementation by Graphic Software Systems. Certain sections of the CGM format are described below. There are three different methods of coding the CGM file:

- Coding in plain text as an ASCII file with embedded control sequences
- Binary coding of all data, parameters and commands
- Output using the 94 printable ISO 646 characters

Binary coding is ideal for storing and processing on computers, while plain text printout is more suitable for manual processing. The ISO character coding was specified for data exchange between computers.

28.1 Binary CGM Coding

Commands and parameters in this coding are stored in records. A record always begins on a word boundary. Records with an odd number of bytes are aligned with a word boundary by appending a null byte. Figure 28.1 shows the structure of a record:

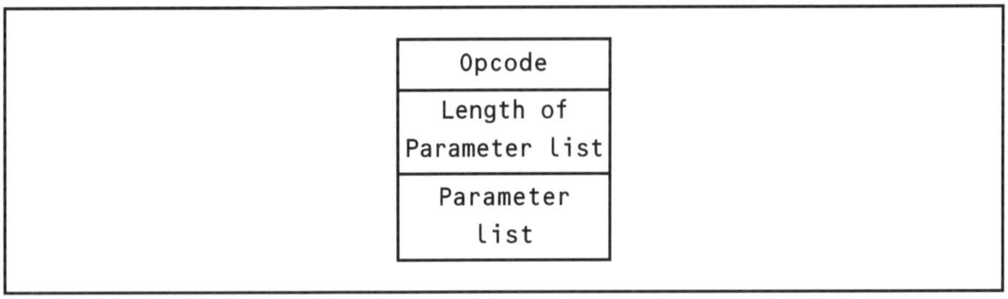

Figure 28.1 Structure of a CGM record

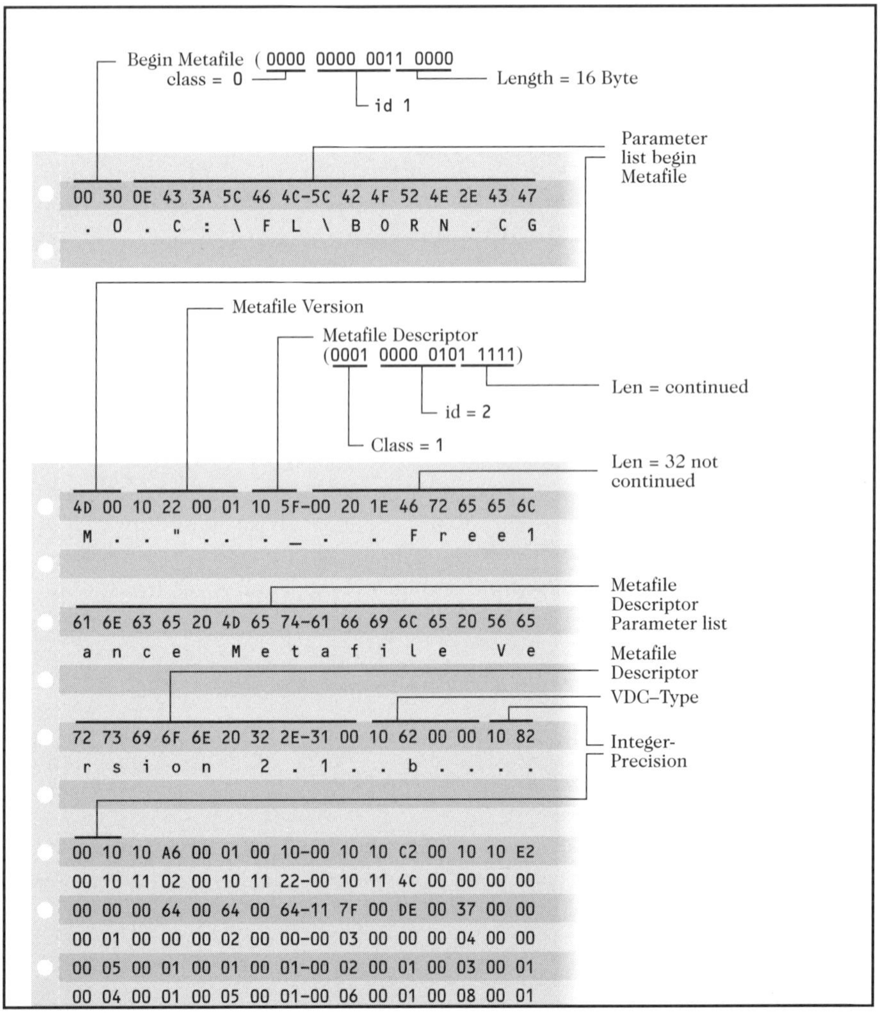

Figure 28.2 Hex dump of binary CGM records (*continues over...*)

```
00 04 00 01 00 05 00 01-00 06 00 01 00 08 00 01
00 09 00 01 00 0D 00 02-00 01 00 02 00 02 00 02
00 03 00 02 00 04 00 02-00 05 00 02 00 06 00 03
00 01 00 03 00 04 00 03-00 06 00 04 00 01 00 04
00 03 00 04 00 04 00 04-00 07 00 04 00 0B 00 04
00 0C 00 04 00 0F 00 04-00 10 00 04 00 11 00 04
00 12 00 04 00 13 00 05-00 02 00 05 00 03 00 05
00 04 00 05 00 06 00 05-00 07 00 05 00 08 00 05
00 0A 00 05 00 0E 00 05-00 0F 00 05 00 10 00 05
00 12 00 05 00 16 00 05-00 17 00 05 00 18 00 05
00 1B 00 05 00 1C 00 05-00 1D 00 05 00 1E 00 05
00 22 00 06 00 01 00 07-00 02 11 BF 00 60 11 53
 .  "  .  .  .  .  .  .  .  .  .  .  .  '  .  S
61 6E 73 2D 73 65 72 69-66 20 53 74 72 6F 6B 65
 a  n  s  -  s  e  r  i  f     S  t  r  o  k  e
11 53 61 6E 73 2D 73 65-72 69 66 20 53 74 72 6F
 .  S  a  n  s  -  s  e  r  i  f     S  t  r  o
6B 65 11 53 61 6E 73 2D-73 65 72 69 66 20 53 74
 k  e  .  S  a  n  s  -  s  e  r  i  f     S  t
72 6F 6B 65 11 53 61 6E-73 2D 73 65 72 69 66 20
 r  o  k  e  .  S  a  n  s  -  s  e  r  i  f
53 74 72 6F 6B 65 05 53-77 69 73 73 05 53 77 69
 S  t  r  o  k  e  .  S  w  i  s  s  .  S  w  i
73 73 05 53 77 69 73 73-05 53 77 69 73 73 70 44
 s  s  .  S  w  i  s  s  .  S  w  i  s  s  p  D
4C 42 01 01 00 6A 08 50-49 43 54 55 52 45 31 00
 L  B  .  .  .  j  .  P  I  C  T  U  R  E  1  .
20 26 00 00 00 00 00 00-20 42 00 00 20 62 00 00
20 82 00 00 20 A2 00 00-20 C8 00 00 00 00 7F FF
60 B8 00 80 54 5F 00 4A-00 01 00 00 00 00 00 00
00 00 00 00 00 3F 00 00-00 3F 00 00 00 57 00 00
00 00 00 64 00 2D 00 06-00 30 00 08 00 05 00 30
00 05 00 4C 00 05 00 5F-00 64 00 64 00 57 00 05
00 43 00 05 00 2D 00 00-00 00 00 00 00 00 00 00
00 3F 30 22 00 10 30 82-00 01 30 C2 00 00 51 C2
00 01 51 42 00 01 51 E2-02 AA 52 08 00 00 02 AA
02 AA 00 00 52 4C 00 01-00 02 00 00 00 00 00 00
00 00 40 98 28 F0 30 84-00 01 11 54 68 69 73 20
       @     (     0                T  h  i  s
69 73 20 61 20 54 65 78-74 20 20 20 20 20 00 01
 i  s     a     T  e  x  t
50 42 00 01 50 62 00 01-40 28 29 6F 3E 27 42 18
 P  B  .  .  P  b  .
3E 27 53 A2 00 01 53 C2-00 01 53 62 00 01 53 82
00 01 52 E2 00 01 52 C2-00 04 41 68 0E CC 27 F4
23 05 39 B7 41 86 36 80-4B 28 0A 5B 52 C2 00 01
40 F4 56 8F 4B 28 63 23-4D B2 63 23 42 97 53 1C


42 97 53 1C 49 91 00 A0-00 40
 B  .  S  .  I  .  .  .  .  @
```

End Metafile (class 0, Id 1, Len 0)

Figure 28.2 Hex dump of binary CGM records (*cont.*)

Graphics

Figure 28.2 shows part of a CGM file as a hex dump. With CGM files that have been created on PCs, it should be noted that the higher value byte of a word is stored first (lower address), contrary to the Intel convention. This is particularly clear in Figure 28.2.

The opcode and the length of the parameter list are stored in the record header as shown in Figure 28.3:

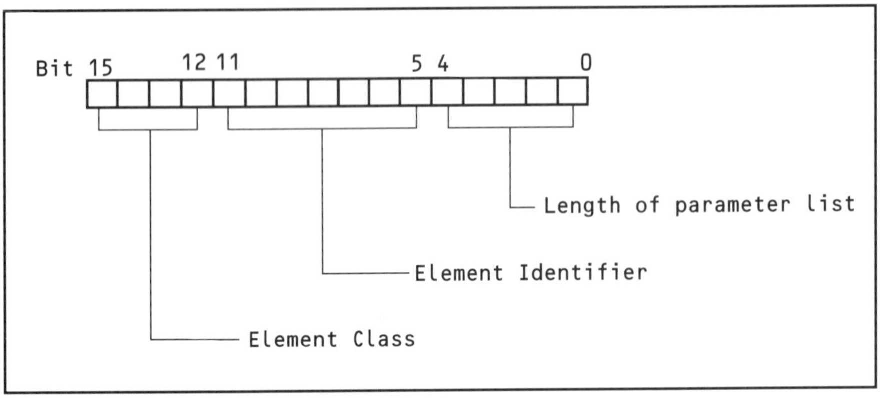

Figure 28.3 Short form of a record header

In the form shown in Figure 28.3, the header requires only one 16 bit word to store a CGM command. Bits 12–15 contain a code specifying the class of the metafile element. This is followed by the code (id) for the actual element in bits 5–11. These two entries function as an opcode within the header. Since a different number of parameters is defined for each opcode, these elements are followed by the length of the parameter list in bytes. For lists containing up to 30 bytes, the length is stored in bits 0–4 of the first word (Figure 28.3). To enable longer parameter lists to be stored, there is also an extended record header, as shown in Figure 28.4.

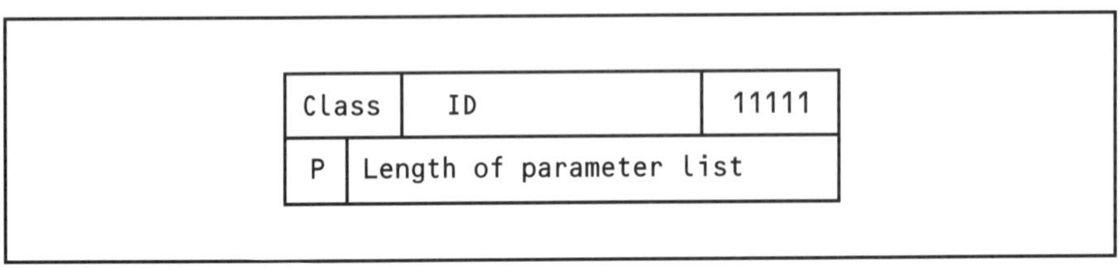

Figure 28.4 Extended record header

The extended record header occupies 2 words. As before, the first word contains the code of the metafile element. Bits 0 to 4 of the length field contain the binary signature 11111. This signifies that the following word is required by the header. The second word contains the length of the parameter list in bytes, in bits 0 to 14. The top bit acts as a flag (P). If the parameter list contains more than 127 bytes, its length cannot be accommodated in the length field. One solution to this problem is to split the parameter list into several *partial lists* each containing a maximum of 127 bytes. The P flag in the top bit of the second word indicates whether the parameter list is followed by an additional partial list. The chain of partial lists continues until the P flag contains the value 0 (Figure 28.5).

Negative values within the parameter list are stored in two's complement form and real numbers in IEEE floating point format. In the short form, a string may contain up to 254 characters, with its length being stored in the first byte of the ASCII string. In the long form, the string is stored as a series of partial strings. The first byte of a string contains the value `FFH`, and the length of the first partial string is stored in the following two bytes. The top bit of this word acts as an indicator for chained partial strings. If this bit is set to `1`, the remaining bits indicate the length of the partial string, and the string itself is followed by another string of the same structure. The last character string has the top bit in the string header set to `0`.

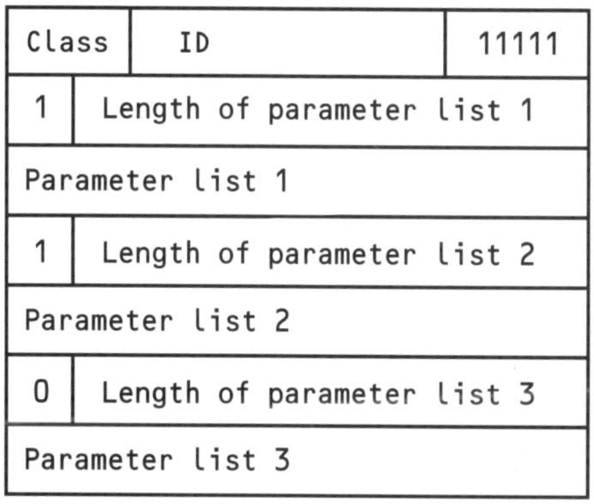

Figure 28.5 Chained parameter list

In binary coding, a metafile contains opcodes as shown in Table 28.1.

Class	ID	Element Name
0	1	Begin Metafile
0	2	End Metafile
0	3	Begin Picture
0	4	Begin Picture Body
0	5	End Picture
1	1	Metafile Version
1	2	Metafile Description
1	3	VDC Type
1	4	Integer Precision
1	5	Real Precision
1	6	Index Precision
1	7	Color Precision
1	8	Color Index Precision
1	9	Maximum Color Index
1	10	Color Value Extent
1	11	Metafile Element List
1	12	Metafile Defaults Replacements
1	13	Font List

Table 28.1 Metafile opcodes for binary encoding (*continues over...*)

Class	ID	Element Name
1	14	Character Set List
1	15	Character Coding Announcer
2	1	Scaling Mode
2	2	Color Selection Mode
2	3	Line Width Specification Mode
2	4	Marker Size Specification Mode
2	5	Edge Width Specification Mode
2	6	VDC Extent
2	7	Background Color
3	1	VDC Integer Precision
3	2	VDC Real Precision
3	3	Auxiliary Color
3	4	Transparency
3	5	Clip Rectangle
3	6	Clip Indicator
4	1	Polyline
4	2	Disjoint Polyline
4	3	Polymarker
4	4	Text
4	5	Restricted Text
4	6	Append Text
4	7	Polygon
4	8	Polygon Set
4	9	Cell Array
4	10	Generalized Drawing Primitive
4	11	Rectangle
4	12	Circle
4	13	Circular Arc 3 Point
4	14	Circular Arc 3 Point Close
4	15	Circular Arc Centre
4	16	Circular Arc Centre Close
4	17	Ellipse
4	18	Elliptical Arc
4	19	Elliptical Arc Close
5	1	Line Bundle Index
5	2	Line Type
5	3	Line Width
5	4	Line Color
5	5	Marker Bundle Index
5	6	Marker Type
5	7	Marker Size

Table 28.1 Metafile opcodes for binary encoding (*cont.*)

Class	ID	Element Name
5	8	Marker Color
5	9	Text Bundle Index
5	10	Text Font Index
5	11	Text Precision
5	12	Character Expansion Factor
5	13	Character Spacing
5	14	Text Color
5	15	Character Height
5	16	Character Orientation
5	17	Text Path
5	18	Text Alignment
5	19	Character Set Index
5	20	Alternate Character Set Index
5	21	Fill Bundle Index
5	22	Interior Style
5	23	Fill Color
5	24	Hatch Index
5	25	Pattern Index
5	26	Edge Bundle Index
5	27	Edge Type
5	28	Edge Width
5	29	Edge Color
5	30	Edge Visibility
5	31	Fill Reference Point
5	32	Pattern Table
5	33	Pattern Size
5	34	Color Table
5	35	Aspect Source Flags
6	1	Escape
7	1	Message
7	2	Application Data

Table 28.1 Metafile opcodes for binary encoding (*cont.*)

The following standard settings apply to the binary encoding mode:

- *Real Precision* values are represented as fixed point numbers in 32 bits (16 bit numerator, 16 bit denominator).
- *Integer Precision* values are represented in 16 bits.
- For *Color Precision*, one byte is used per color.
- *Index Precision* values require 16 bits; *Color Index Precision* values require 8 bits.

- The VDC EXTENT setting for REAL is (0.0,0.0), (0.999...,0.999...); for Integers the setting is (0,0),(32767,32767)
- The values for color extensions (*Color Extent*) are between (0,0,0) and (255,255,255).

The coding for the parameter lists can be found in the appropriate ISO documentation. A brief outline is given at the end of this chapter.

28.2 Coding as ASCII text

The ASCII plain text mode was defined to enable metafiles to be created, printed and tested using a text editor. The syntax for all commands is as follows:

Opcode <sep> Operand <sep> Operand...<term>

The end of each command is marked with a terminator <term>. Either a semicolon (;) or an oblique (/) may be used here. Spaces, tabs or commas can be used as separators <sep>. Operands are displayed in plain text and numbers can be enclosed in brackets to improve legibility. Real numbers are represented in the usual Fortran notation, with a decimal point in exponential or floating point notation (*Em.n* or *Fm.n*). Integer values may also be terminated with a decimal point. Numbers can be indicated in any numbering system with a base between 2 and 16. So-called zero characters (for example, the $ sign or an underline) can be included in the commands. These characters are ignored by the CGM parser, but they may enhance the legibility of the text.

Strings must be enclosed in single (') or double (") inverted commas. Two of these characters appearing consecutively indicate that one of them is an element of the string. There must be no separator between strings and other operators.

Comments can be included in the CGM file by enclosing them between percentage signs (%). They will be skipped by the parser. This type of comment may extend over several lines.

Table 28.2 lists the keywords in the ASCII coding:

Name	Element Name
BEGMF	Begin Metafile
ENDMF	End Metafile
BEGPIC	Begin Picture
BEGPICBODY	Begin Picture Body
ENDPIC	End Picture
MFVERSION	Metafile Version
MFDESC	Metafile Description
VDCTYPE	VDC Type
INTEGERPREC	Integer Precision
REALPREC	Real Precision
INDEXPREC	Index Precision
COLRPREC	Color Precision
COLRINDEXPREC	Color Index Precision
MAXCOLRINDEX	Maximum Color Index
COLRVALUEEXT	Color Value Extent
MFELEMLIST	Metafile Element List
BEGMFDEFAULTS	Metafile Defaults Replacements
ENDMFDEFAULTS	"
FONTLIST	Font List
CHARSETLIST	Character Set List
CHARCODING	Character Coding Announcer
SKALEMODE	Scaling Mode
COLRMODE	Color Selection Mode
LINEWIDTHMODE	Line Width Specification Mode
MARKERSIZEMODE	Marker Size Specification Mode
EDGEWIDTHMODE	Edge Width Specification Mode
VDCEXT	VDC Extent
BACKCOLR	Background Color
VDCINTEGERPREC	VDC Integer Precision
VDCREALPREC	VDC Real Precision
AUXCOLR	Auxiliary Color
TRANSPARENCY	Transparency
CLIPRECT	Clip Rectangle
CLIP	Clip Indicator

Table 28.2 Metafile opcodes for ASCII encoding *(continues over...)*

Name	Element Name
LINE	Polyline
INCRLINE	
DISJTLINE	Disjoint Polyline
INCRDISJTLINE	
MARKER	Polymarker
INCRMARKER	
TEXT	Text
RESTRTEXT	Restricted Text
APNDTEXT	Append Text
POLGON	Polygon
INCRPOLYGON	
POLGONSET	Polygon Set
INCRPOLGONSET	
CELLARRAY	Cell Array
GDP	Generalized Drawing Primitive
RECT	Rectangle
CIRCLE	Circle
ARC3PT	Circular Arc 3 Point
ARC3PTCLOSE	Circular Arc 3 Point Close
ARCCTR	Circular Arc Centre
ARCCTRCLOSE	Circular Arc Centre Close
ELLIPSE	Ellipse
ELLIPARC	Elliptical Arc
ELLIPARCCLOSE	Elliptical Arc Close
LINEINDEX	Line Bundle Index
LINETYPE	Line Type
LINEWIDTH	Line Width
LINECOLOR	Line Color
MARKERINDEX	Marker Bundle Index
MARKERTYPE	Marker Type
MARKERSIZE	Marker Size
MARKERCOLR	Marker Color
TEXTINDEX	Text Bundle Index
TEXTFONTINDEX	Text Font Index
TEXTPREC	Text Precision
CHAREXPAN	Character Expansion Factor
CHARSPACE	Character Spacing
TEXTCOLR	Text Color
CHARHEIGHT	Character Height
CHARORI	Character Orientation
TEXTPATH	Text Path

Table 28.2 Metafile opcodes for ASCII encoding (*cont.*)

Name	Element Name
TEXTALIGN	Text Alignment
CHARSETINDEX	Character Set Index
ALTCHARSETINDEX	Alternate Character Set Index
FILLINDEX	Fill Bundle Index
INTSTYLE	Interior Style
FILLCOLR	Fill Color
HATCHINDEX	Hatch Index
PATINDEX	Pattern Index
EDGEINDEX	Edge Bundle Index
EDGETYPE	Edge Type
EDGEWIDTH	Edge Width
EDGECOLR	Edge Color
EDGEVIS	Edge Visibility
FILLREFPT	Fill Reference Point
PATTABLE	Pattern Table
PATSIZE	Pattern Size
COLRTABLE	Color Table
ASF	Aspect Source Flags
ESCAPE	Escape
MESSAGE	Message
APPLDATA	Application Data

28.2
Metafile opcodes for ASCII encoding (*cont.*)

The following standard settings apply to the *Plain Text Encoding* method:

- *Real Precision* values lie between -32767 and 32767.
- *Integer Precision* values lie between -32767 and 32767.
- For *Color Precision*, the maximum value for a component is 255.
- *Index Precision* values lie between 0 and 127. The maximum integer value for *Color Index Precision* is 127.
- The VDC EXTENT setting for REAL is between 0.0 and 1.0, with 4 digits set. For integers, it is between -32767 and 32767.
- Values for color extensions (*Color Extent*) are between (0,0,0) for black and (255,255,255) for white.

The coding for the parameter lists is shown in the relevant ISO documentation.

28.3 Character coding with ISO characters

As a third option, closely related to the plain text coding described above, a metafile can be displayed using the ISO 646 7 or 8 bit ASCII codes. In this case, the opcode is specified by one or two characters from the relevant ISO 646 table. Table 28.3 lists the commands together with the ISO characters used:

Code1	Code2	Element Name
3/0	2/0	Begin Metafile
3/0	2/1	End Metafile
3/0	2/2	Begin Picture
3/0	2/3	Begin Picture Body
3/0	2/4	End Picture
3/1	2/0	Metafile Version
3/1	2/1	Metafile Description
3/1	2/2	VDC Type
3/1	2/3	Integer Precision
3/1	2/4	Real Precision
3/1	2/5	Index Precision
3/1	2/6	Color Precision
3/1	2/7	Color Index Precision
3/1	2/8	Maximum Color Index
3/1	2/9	Color Value Extent
3/1	2/10	Metafile Element List
3/1		Metafile Defaults Replacements
	2/11	Begin Metafile Defaults
	2/12	End Metafile Defaults
3/1	2/13	Font List
3/1	2/14	Character Set List
3/1	2/15	Character Coding Announcer
3/2	2/0	Scaling Mode
3/2	2/1	Color Selection Mode
3/2	2/2	Line Width Specification Mode
3/2	2/3	Marker Size Specification Mode
3/2	2/4	Edge Width Specification Mode
3/2	2/5	VDC Extent
3/2	2/6	Background Color
3/3	2/0	VDC Integer Precision
3/3	2/1	VDC Real Precision
3/3	2/2	Auxiliary Color
3/3	2/3	Transparency

Table 28.3 Metafile opcodes for ISO 646 encoding *(continues over...)*

Code1	Code2	Element Name
3/3	2/4	Clip Rectangle
3/3	2/5	Clip Indicator
2/0		Polyline
2/1		Disjoint Polyline
2/2		Polymarker
2/3		Text
2/4		Restricted Text
2/5		Append Text
2/6		Polygon
2/7		Polygon Set
2/8		Cell Array
2/9		Generalized Drawing Primitive
2/10		Rectangle
3/4	2/0	Circle
3/4	2/1	Circular Arc 3 Point
3/4	2/2	Circular Arc 3 Point Close
3/4	2/3	Circular Arc Center
3/4	2/4	Circular Arc Center Close
3/4	2/5	Ellipse
3/4	2/6	Elliptical Arc
3/4	2/7	Elliptical Arc Close
3/5	2/0	Line Bundle Index
3/5	2/1	Line Type
3/5	2/2	Line Width
3/5	2/3	Line Color
3/5	2/4	Marker Bundle Index
3/5	2/5	Marker Type
3/5	2/6	Marker Size
3/5	2/7	Marker Color
3/5	3/0	Text Bundle Index
3/5	3/1	Text Font Index
3/5	3/2	Text Precision
3/5	3/3	Character Expansion Factor
3/5	3/4	Character Spacing
3/5	3/5	Text Color
3/5	3/6	Character Height
3/5	3/7	Character Orientation
3/5	3/8	Text Path
3/5	3/9	Text Alignment
3/5	3/10	Character Set Index
3/5	3/11	Alternate Character Set Index

Table 28.3 Metafile opcodes for ISO 646 encoding (*cont.*)

Code1	Code2	Element Name
3/6	2/0	Fill Bundle Index
3/6	2/1	Interior Style
3/6	2/2	Fill Color
3/6	2/3	Hatch Index
3/6	2/4	Pattern Index
3/6	2/5	Edge Bundle Index
3/6	2/6	Edge Type
3/6	2/7	Edge Width
3/6	2/8	Edge Color
3/6	2/9	Edge Visibility
3/6	2/10	Fill Reference Point
3/6	2/11	Pattern Table
3/6	2/12	Pattern Size
3/6	3/0	Color Table
3/6	3/1	Aspect Source Flags
3/7	2/0	Escape
3/7	3/0	Domain Ring
3/7	2/1	Message
3/7	2/2	Application Data

Table 28.3 Metafile opcodes for ISO 646 encoding (*cont.*)

The ISO character coding was defined to enable the exchange of CGM files via communication lines. There are two methods of coding the parameters:

In *Basis Coding*, each byte of an operand contains the reserved bits, which indicate whether this is the last byte. In *Bitstream Format*, each parameter list is preceded by its length. Strings are enclosed between the characters ESCX and ESC[. Control characters, such as Space, Tilde or Delete, can be replaced by 2-character codes. This type of sequence always begins with the ISO code 7/14 [4, 5].

28.4 Metafile Commands

Several images can be stored in one metafile. Appropriate separators are used to distinguish between pictures in the file. All the details given below relate to *Plain Text Coding*. A metafile contains certain structural elements, which are placed at the beginning and end of the file and the image. Figure 28.6 gives an example of a minimal metafile:

4) D.B. Arnold/P.R. Bono: ***CGM and CGI, Metafiles and Interface Standards for Computer Graphics,*** Springer Verlag, Berlin, 1988, ISBN 0-387-18950-5

5) ***Computer Graphics Metafile for the Storage and Transfer of Picture Descrition Information.*** ISO 8632, Parts 1-4

```
BEGMF 'Metafile-Example';
MFVERSION 1;
MFELEMLIST drawingplus;
% first picture in the file %
BEGPIC 'Picture 1';
BEGPICBODY;
ENDPIC;
% second picture in the file %
BEGPIC 'Picture  2';
BEGPICBODY;
ENDPIC;
ENDMF;
```

Figure 28.6
Example of a Minimal Metafile

The file starts with a header containing the command BEGMF, the version number and the list of elements. This is followed by an image delimited by the separators BEGPIC and ENDPIC. The file contains two image areas. No image is displayed at this stage because the image description, which would have to be positioned between BEGPICBODY and ENDPIC, is missing. The commands MFVERSION and MFELEMENT are mandatory in every metafile. The individual instructions are described in more detail below.

Metafile Version

This command, which indicates the version of CGM, is mandatory. All CGM files that comply with the 1985 ISO 8632 standard must use version number 1.

Metafile Description

This command contains a string giving various additional items of information (for example, author, place) as an optional parameter. The content of the strings is not standardized.

VDC Type

This command is optional and indicates whether the *Virtual Device* coordinates are to be shown as real or integer values. The default setting is for integer values.

Integer Precision

This optional command is used to establish the resolution of operands of type *Integer*, for various coding processes.

Real Precision

This optional command is used to establish the resolution of operands of type *Real*, for various coding processes.

Index Precision

This optional command is used to establish the resolution of operands of type *Index*, for various coding processes.

Color Precision

This optional command is used to establish the resolution of operands of type *Color*, for various coding processes.

Color Index Precision

This optional command is used to establish the resolution of operands of type *Color Precision*, for various coding processes.

Maximum Color Index

This command indicates the upper limit of the index table for the metafile and enables the size of the color table to be defined. The standard maximum value for this index is limited to 63.

Color Value Extent

This optional command contains two parameters (*Minimum value, Maximum value*), which indicate the upper and lower limit for color values. The minimum value relates to the RGB setting (0,0,0), the maximum value to the setting (1,1,1).

Metafile Element List

This command is mandatory. It lists each of the elements contained in the file. The standard designators DRAWING SET (covers a number of elements) and DRAWING PLUS CONTROL SET cover all the metafile elements. If these designators are used, it is not necessary to list the elements explicitly.

Metafile Defaults Replacement

This command enables the transfer of a list of parameters which replace the default settings. The commands are enclosed between the separators BEGMFDEFAULTS and ENDMFDEFAULTS. The parameter LINEWIDTHxx, for example, enables the width of a line to be reset.

Font List

This optional command is used to indicate a list of fonts used. The list of font names is allocated sequentially from FONT INDEX1 to FONT INDEX n.

Character Set List

This optional command contains the parameters *Character Set Type* and *Designation Sequence Tail* and can be used in the *Character Set Index* and *Alternate Character Set Index* sequences. It is used for selecting character sets (for example, Japanese characters, German Umlaut).

Character Coding Announcer

This optional command signals to the interpreter that code extensions are to be used. The characters may be in the form of BASIC 7-bit, BASIC 8-bit, EXTENDED 7-bit or EXTENDED 8-bit.

Scaling Mode

This command contains the parameters *mode* and *scale factor*. The mode may be ABSTRACT or METRIC.

Color Selection Mode

This command selects the coding for the color of an image (direct or by index). The default setting is for just one color index to be indicated, so that the color has to be derived from a table, but it is also possible to indicate colors directly as triples (red, green, blue).

Line Width Specification Mode

The line width of an image is set via the *mode* parameter. The default setting is for the line width to be scaled by the interpreter.

Marker Size Specification Mode

The *mode* parameter is used to establish the size of markers in an image.

Edge Width Specification Mode

The *mode* parameter is used to determine the size of corners explicitly.

VDC Extent

This command enables the VDC coordinate system to be set via the two parameters *first corner* and *second corner*.

Background Color

This command contains the parameters *red*, *green*, *blue* and indicates the background color.

VDC Space and VDC Range

The *space* command indicates the coordinate system for the virtual metafile image space. *Range* describes the coordinate system for the real output device.

Precision Parameter Encoding

The commands REAL PRECISION and INTEGER PRECISION indicate the resolution of the relevant type of parameter.

Auxiliary Color

This command indicates an index or a color triple for the *auxiliary* color.

Transparency

This command switches the transparency function on or off. The function determines how lines and shapes are to be drawn.

Clip Rectangle

The command contains two parameters: *first corner* and *second corner*. These are used to determine the coordinates for the rectangle to which clipping operations refer.

Clip Indicator

This indicator enables the clipping function to be switched on and off.

Polyline

This command gives the XY coordinates for *n* points, through which a line is to be drawn.

Disjoint Polyline

This command contains a list of XY coordinates.

Polymarker

This command contains the XY coordinates of *n* marker points.

Text

The command contains the parameters *point, flag* and *string*. It enables the output of strings at the point indicated.

Restricted Text

The command contains the parameters *extent, point, flag* and *string*. It enables a text to be displayed.

Polygon

This command contains the XY coordinates of *n* points, through which a polygon is to be drawn.

Polygon Set

This command contains a list with one XY coordinate and a flag for each element.

Cell Array

This command contains the parameters *3 corner points, number of columns, number of rows, local color precision* and *cell color precision*.

Generalized Drawing Primitive

The command contains an identifier, a point list and a data record.

Rectangle

This command describes a rectangle in terms of the two parameters *corner-1* and *corner-2*.

Circle

Using the parameters *center point* and *radius*, this command describes a circle.

Circular ARC 3 Point

Using the parameters *start point, intermediate point* and *end point*, this command describes a circular arc.

Circular ARC 3 Point Close

Using the parameters *start point, intermediate point, end point* and *close type*, this command describes a filled segment of a circle.

Circular ARC Center

Using the parameters *center point, start point, end point* and *radius*, this command describes an arc.

Circular ARC Center Close

Using the parameters *center point, start point, end point, radius* and *close type*, this command describes a filled sector of a circle.

Ellipse

This command describes an ellipse in terms of *center point, 1st edge point and 2nd edge point.*

Elliptical Arc

Using the parameters *center point, 1st edge point, 2nd edge point, start point line* and *end point line*, this command describes an elliptical arc.

Elliptical Arc Close

Using the parameters *center point, 1st edge point, 2nd edge point, start point line, end point line* and *close type*, this command describes a sector of an arc.

Line Bundle Index

This command contains one parameter, with the default value of 1.

Line Type

This command determines the line type (*continuous, dotted,* and so on).

Line Width

This command contains one parameter specifying the line width.

Line Color

The command is used for determining the color of lines. Depending on the *Color Selection Mode*, the parameter is either a color index or a triple (red, green, blue).

Marker Bundle Index

The parameter is generally coded with the value 1.

Marker Type

The command establishes the type of a marker. Normally, a marker is indicated as a point.

Marker Size

This command establishes the size of a marker.

Marker Color

The command contains one parameter to establish the color of a marker either a color index value or a color triple.

Text Bundle Index

The default setting for the index is 1.

Text Font Index

The parameter of this command establishes the font used in the text.

Text Precision

One parameter determines how text attributes should be dealt with.

Character Expansion Factor

The geometry of a character can be varied via one parameter (standard 1.0).

Character Spacing

The spacing between two characters can be varied via one parameter (standard 0.0).

Text Color

This command is used to set the color of a text either as an index or as a color triple.

Character Height

Using one parameter, this command is used to set the height of a character.

Character Orientation

This command influences the direction of the character output via the parameters *up-vector-x, up-vector-y, base-vector-x* and *base-vector-y*. It is used for creating italic styles.

Text Path

The command enables the output direction to be indicated via a parameter. The default setting is *right*, corresponding to the normal direction of writing.

Text Alignment

Using four parameters, this command determines the alignment of texts.

Character Set Index

The command uses one parameter to select the character set used. The ISO 646 character set is selected via the index 1.

Alternate Character Set Index

This command sets the index of the alternate character set for ISO 2022 control characters.

Fill Bundle Index

The default setting for this parameter is 1.

Interior Style

The parameter of this command determines whether shapes are to be filled.

Fill Color

This command determines the fill color. The parameter is either an index or a color triple depending on the mode.

Hatch Index

This command specifies the pattern for hatched areas. Index 1 selects a horizontal, hatched pattern.

Pattern Index

The default setting for this value is 1. It is used for selecting the pattern.

Edge Bundle Index

The default setting for this value is 1.

Edge Type

The parameter of this command is used to determine the FORM of an edge around closed shapes. The default setting is solid.

Edge Width

This command establishes the line width for the edges of shapes.

Edge Color

This command determines the color for the edges around shapes.

Edge Visibility

This command switches the boundary line around a shape on and off.

Fill Reference Point

This command specifies a reference point for filling shapes. The point is normally in the bottom left corner.

Pattern Table

This command defines a pattern. The command contains the parameters *index, number of columns, number of rows, color resolution* and *n color patterns*. The color resolution determines the range of values for the following color pattern.

Pattern Size

This command contains four parameters. It determines the size of a pattern.

Color Table

This command defines the color table with *n* color triples. The number of color triples in the table is indicated in the first parameter.

Aspect Source Flags

The command parameters represent a list of ASF types and ASF values.

ESCAPE

This command enables the activation of device-specific features outside the CGM standard. The first parameter contains the code for the function to be called. This is followed by the parameters required by the function. The command should not be used.

Message

This command is used for displaying messages to the user. The first parameter contains a flag which can be set to action. The following text is then displayed by the CGM interpreter.

Application Data

This command enables application-specific data to be included in a metafile. The structure of the data area is not defined.

The above description of the structure of metafile elements is very brief. A comprehensive discussion would far exceed the scope of this book. Further information is contained in the reference books cited (*see references on page 768*).

29

WordPerfect Graphic format (WPG)

The WordPerfect Corporation has defined its own format for the storage of graphic files. This format can be read, for example, by the WordPerfect word-processing program and can be used in documents.

29.1 WPG header

This file format starts with a 16 byte header, whose structure is the same for all WP products (Table 29.1).

Offset	Bytes	Remarks
	File ID-Header for all WPCORP Products	
00H	4	WP signature -1, 'WPC'
04H	4	Pointer to start of graphic data
08H	1	Product type (1 for WordPerfect)
09H	1	File type (16H for WPG)
0AH	1	Major version number
0BH	1	Minor version number
0CH	2	Encryption flag (0 = unencrypted)
0EH	2	Reserved (0)

Table 29.1 Header Prefix of a WPG file

The first 4 bytes contain a signature, identifying the file as a WP file. This is followed by a 4 byte pointer, indicating the offset from the start of the file to the start of the graphic data. The next two bytes contain information on the type of product that created the file and the document type. In WordPerfect 5.0, the version numbers are always coded with the value 0.0 (1.0 in version 5.1). In the *Encryption* field, the value 0 indicates an unencrypted file.

29.2 WPG records

The 16 byte header is followed directly by the graphic data. WordPerfect stores this data in a kind of metafile format. The values are in records structured as shown in Table 29.2. The data is stored in byte format after the record length.

Bytes	Remarks
1	Record type
1	Record length (0-FEH)
n	Record data

Table 29.2 Record format up to 254 bytes

It is possible to have records longer than 254 bytes. In this case the record length field is extended to 2 or 4 bytes. Table 29.3 specifies the structure of records with a length of up to 7FFFH bytes.

Bytes	Remarks
1	Record type
1	0FFH
1	Record length least significant byte
1	Record length most significant byte (Value 0-7FH)
n	Record data

Table 29.3 Record format up to 32767 bytes

The value 0FFH in the second byte signals that the following 2 bytes are to be interpreted as a length field. The top bit of the higher value byte is always set to 0.

Bytes	Remarks
1	Record type
1	0FFH
1	Record length least significant byte High Word
1	Record length most significant byte High Word (bit 8 = 1)
1	Record length least significant byte Low Word
1	Record length least significant byte Low Word
n	Record data

Table 29.4 Record format longer than 32767 bytes.

If the record is longer than 32767 bytes, the length field is extended to 4 bytes (Table 29.4).

In this case, the second byte again contains the signature 0FFH and is followed by the length field. If the top bit of the most significant byte in the high word is set, the length field occupies 4 bytes. If this bit is set to 0, the record format is as shown in Table 29.3.

The following data field is structured as described below, depending on the record type. The tables show only the contents of the data area. The header is always structured as described above.

29.2.1 Fill Attributes (type 1)

Record type 1 defines the fill attributes and colors for rectangles, polygons and ellipses. The first data byte describes the pattern which is to fill the shapes. The color of the area to be filled is shown in the second byte as an index between 0 and 255. The record structure is as follows:

Offset	Bytes	Remark
00H	1	Fill pattern 0 = hollow 1 = solid 2 = narrow spaced +45 degree lines 3 = medium spaced +45 degree lines 4 = widely spaced +45 degree lines 5 = narrow spaced ±45 degree lines 6 = medium spaced ±45 degree lines 7 = widely spaced ±45 degree lines 8 = narrow spaced vertical lines 9 = medium spaced vertical lines 10 = widely spaced vertical lines

Table 29.5 Format record type 1 (*continues over...*)

Graphics

Offset	Bytes	Remark
		11 = inter-spaced dots or density
		12 = dots
		13 = dots
		14 = dots (medium density)
		15 = dots
		16 = dots
		17 = dots (maximum density)
		18 = medium-spaced dots
		19 = widely spaced dots
		20 = narrow-spaced horizontal lines
		21 = medium-spaced horizontal lines
		22 = widely spaced horizontal lines
		23 = narrow-spaced vert. & horiz. lines
		24 = medium-spaced vert. & horiz. lines
		25 = widely spaced vert. & horiz. lines
		26 = narrow-spaced 45-degree lines
		27 = medium-spaced 45-degree lines
		28 = widely spaced 45-degree lines
		29 = horizontal brick pattern
		30 = vertical brick pattern
		31 = –
		32 = interwoven pattern
		33, 34 = –
		35 = tiled roof pattern
		36 = thick 45-degree lines, widely spaced
		37 = checkerboard pattern
01H	1	Fill color (0–FFH)

Table 29.5 Format record type 1 (*cont.*)

Graphics

29.2.2 Line Attributes (type 2)

Record type 2 defines the attributes for lines to be drawn.

Offset	Bytes	Remarks
00H	1	Line type
		0 = no line
		1 = solid

Table 29.6 Format record type 2 (*continues over...*)

Offset	Bytes	Remarks
		2 = long dash
		3 = dotted
		4 = dash/dot
		5 = medium dash
		6 = dash/dot/dot
		7 = short dash
01H	1	Line color (0–FFH)
02H	2	Line width (wpu)

Table 29.6 Format record type 2 (*cont.*)

The first byte indicates the line type; the second defines the color. At offset 4, there is a word containing the line width in wpu.

29.2.3 Marker Attributes (type 3)

Offset	**Bytes**	**Remarks**
00H	1	Marker style
		0 = no markers
		1 = dot
		2 = +
		3 = *
		4 = circle
		5 = square
		6 = triangle
		7 = upside down triangle
		8 = diamond
		9 = X
01H	1	Marker color (0–FFH)
02H	2	Marker height (wpu)

Table 29.7 Format record type 3

Record type 3 defines the attributes for markers. The first byte indicates the form of the marker, while the second byte specifies the color. At offset 4, there is a word indicating the size of the marker in wpu.

29.2.4 Polymarker (type 4)

Record type 4 enables several markers to be defined. The structure of the record is shown below:

Offset	Bytes	Remarks
00H	2	Number of points
02H	2	X-coordinate of 1st point (in wpu)
04H	2	Y-coordinate of 1st point (in wpu)
...	2	...

Table 29.8 Format record type 4

The first word indicates the number of points marked. This is followed by a table containing *n* XY coordinate pairs. All coordinate data is given in wpu units, from the top left corner. A marker is drawn at each of the specified points with the attributes as selected.

29.2.5 Line (type 5)

This record type defines the lines drawn in a graphic image.

Offset	Bytes	Remarks
00H	2	X-coordinate of 1st end point (in wpu)
02H	2	Y-coordinate of 1st end point (in wpu)
04H	2	X-coordinate of 2nd end point (in wpu)
06H	2	Y-coordinate of 2nd end point (in wpu)

Table 29.9 Format record type 5

There are 4 words in the data area containing the XY coordinates for the two end points of the line. This line is drawn with the attributes as selected.

29.2.6 Polyline (type 6)

Record type 6 enables lines connecting a number of points to be drawn.

Offset	Bytes	Remarks
00H	2	Number of vertices
02H	2	X-coordinate of 1st point (in wpu)
04H	2	Y-coordinate of 1st point (in wpu)
...	2	...

Table 29.10 Format record type 6

The first data word indicates the number of points required. This is followed by a table containing *n* coordinate pairs. All coordinate data is given in wpu units, from the top left corner. The points are joined by a line, which is drawn according to the attributes set (color, width, pattern).

29.2.7 Rectangle (type 7)

Record type 7 defines rectangles within a graphic image.

Offset	Bytes	Remarks
00H	2	X-coordinate of lower left corner (in wpu)
02H	2	Y-coordinate of lower left corner (in wpu)
04H	2	Width of rectangle (in wpu)
06H	2	Height of rectangle (in wpu)

Table 29.11 Format record type 7

The first two data words indicate the coordinates of the lower left corner of the rectangle. The dimensions are given in the next two fields. The rectangle is drawn according to the attributes set (color, width, pattern).

29.2.8 Polygon (type 8)

Record type 8 enables a closed line (polygon) with up to 65,535 points to be drawn.

Offset	Bytes	Remarks
00H	2	Number of vertices
02H	2	X-coordinate of 1st point (in wpu)
04H	2	Y-coordinate of 1st point (in wpu)
...	2	...

Table 29.12 Format record type 8

The first data word indicates the number of points required. This is followed by a table containing *n* XY coordinate pairs. All coordinate data is given in wpu units, from the top left corner. The points are connected by a line drawn according to the attributes set (color, width, pattern). The result is an enclosed area.

29.2.9 Ellipse (type 9)

Record type 9 is used for drawing ellipses.

Offset	Bytes	Remarks
00H	2	X-coordinate of center point (wpu)
02H	2	Y-coordinate of center point (wpu)
04H	2	Radius of X axis (wpu)
06H	2	Radius of Y axis (wpu)
08H	2	Rotation angle (horizontal)
0AH	2	Start angle of arc (0–360 degrees)
0CH	2	End angle of arc (0–360 degrees)
0EH	2	Flags Bit 0: 1 = connect ends to center Bit 1: 1 = connect ends to each other

Table 29.13 Format record type 9

This meta-object enables ellipses, circles and segments of circles to be drawn. The attributes for drawing lines or for filling shapes will be used, depending on the element selected. The last data word contains two bits indicating whether segments or sectors of a circle are to be drawn. If both

Graphics

bits are set to 0, only circular arcs or elliptical arcs will be drawn. The length and position of an arc can be defined in terms of the angle. For an ellipse or a circle, the start angle should be set to 0 degrees and the end angle to 360 degrees.

Record type 10 is reserved for curved lines, but it is not currently used.

29.2.10 Bitmap (type 11)

Record type 11 (0BH) enables image data stored in bitmap format to be read.

Offset	Bytes	Remarks
00H	2	Image width in pixels
02H	2	Image height in pixels
04H	2	Number of bits per pixel (=colors) 1 = monochrome bitmap 2 = 4 color bitmap 4 = 16 color bitmap 8 = 256 color bitmap
06H	2	X resolution of source bitmap (pixel/inch)
08H	2	Y resolution of source (pixel/inch)
0AH	x	Bitmap data of image

Table 29.14 Format record type 11

The first two data fields indicate the image dimensions in pixels. The word at offset 04H defines how many bits per pixel are stored. The size of the bitmap data for the record can be calculated from this information. The data is stored by byte, starting at offset 0AH in the data area. To save space, it may be compressed as follows:

- If the value of the first byte is between 81H and FFH, the value 80H should be subtracted. The result (1–7FH) acts as a counter indicating how often the following data byte must be copied to the output.
- A value between 01H and 7FH in the first byte indicates the number of following data bytes which are to be transferred directly to the output.
- If the value of the first byte is 80H, there is a counter in the following data byte which indicates how often the value FFH should be copied to the output as a pattern.
- If the value of the first byte is 00H, there is a counter in the following data byte which specifies how often the last complete output line must be repeated.

This compression process enables the amount of memory needed for the image data to be reduced. However, this compression process is not supported by any other image format.

29.2.11 Graphic Text (type 12)

Record type 12 (0CH) enables texts to be displayed within a graphic image.

Offset	Bytes	Remarks
00H	2	Length of text (in bytes)
02H	2	X-coordinate of text position (in wpu)
04H	2	Y-coordinate of text position (in wpu)
06H	x	ASCII string for graphic text

Table 29.15 Format record type 12

The text attributes selected (size, color, and so on) are used for the text output.

29.2 12 Graphic Text Attributes (type 13)

Record type 13 (0DH) defines the attributes for texts to be displayed. The text attributes selected (size, color, font, and so on) are used for text output. Using the rotation angle, texts can be displayed in any direction required.

Offsets	Bytes	Remarks
00H	2	Nominal character cell width (in wpu)
02H	2	Character cell height (in wpu)
04H	10	Reserved
0EH	2	Font descriptor 0D50H = Courier font 1150H = Helvetica font (no serifs) 1950H = Times (serif) font
10H	1	Reserved
11H	1	Horizontal alignment 0 = left 1 = center 2 = right
12H	1	Vertical alignment 0 = base align 1 = center align 2 = cap align 3 = bottom align 4 = top align
13H	1	Text color (0-FFH)
14H	2	Rotation angle (0–360 degree)

Table 29.16 Format record type 13

Codes 0 and 2 for vertical alignment were not defined until version 5.1 and were reserved in earlier versions. The graphic text is displayed using vector fonts, which are supplied with WordPerfect. Proportionally spaced fonts are not currently supported.

29.2.13 Color Map (type 14)

This record type (0EH) defines a table containing the colors used. The table contains three bytes for each color, specifying the intensities of the primary colors red, green and blue. A triple of this kind must be defined for each color.

Offset	Bytes	Remarks
00H	2	Start index color (0–255)
02H	2	Number of entries in color map
04H	*xx*	Color map with 3 bytes for each color index (red, green, blue)

Table 29.17
Format record type 14

By varying the color intensities, it is possible to select around 16 million color gradations. The color is defined via an index to this table, and all color specifications for shapes, lines, and so on also relate to the table. If there is no color map record in a WPG file, WordPerfect will use the standard settings for the colors. These conform with the settings for IBM VGA cards:

Code	Color
0	Black
1	Blue
2	Green
3	Cyan
4	Red
5	Magenta
6	Brown
7	White

Table 29.18
Color indices

The color indices between 8 and 15 indicate the same colors with increased intensity (for example blue – light blue).

29.2.14 Start WPG Data (type 15)

This record type (0FH) signals the start of a data area. It also contains the version number of the WPG format and the image dimensions.

Offset	Bytes	Remarks
00H	1	WPG version number (current 1)
01H	1	WPG flags Bit 0 = 0 PostScript data included Bit 1 = 1 PostScript data only (no bitmap) Bit 2–7: Reserved
02H	2	Width of image space (in wpu)
04H	2	Height of image space (in wpu)

Table 29.19 Format record type 15

This record type is used in conjunction with record type 17 which enables PostScript data to be imported. If bit 0 = 1, the EPS file does not contain a bitmap to display. The origin of the image (0,0) is in the bottom left corner.

29.2.15 End WPG Data (type 16)

This record type (10H) terminates a data area within the WPG file. The record must occur at the end of a WPG file and has no data area.

29.2.16 PostScript Data (type 17)

This record type (11H) enables PostScript commands to be integrated into the graphics file.

Offset	Bytes	Remarks
00H	xx	Start of PostScript data

Table 29.20 Format record type 17

This record type can only be used if the output is to be via a PostScript printer.

29.2.17 Output Attributes (type 18)

Record type 12H defines foreground colors, background colors and the clipping area of an image in WPG version 5.0. In WPG version 5.1 the record type is reserved.

Offset	Bytes	Remarks
00H	1	Background color (0–255)
01H	1	Foreground color (0–255)
02H	2	X-coordinate of clipping window (in wpu)
04H	2	Y-coordinate of clipping window (in wpu)
06H	2	Width of clip window (in wpu)
08H	2	Height of clip window (in wpu)

Table 29.21 Format record type 18

The color values specify an index to the color table. The background table is used for black dots in black and white pictures and for transparent representations. If this record is missing, the entire image area is used as a *clip window*.

29.2.18 Curve (type 19, WPG version 5.1)

This record type (13H) is used for displaying curves. It uses the currently set (Bezier) line attributes and was not defined before WPG version 5.1.

Offset	Bytes	Remarks
00H	4	Size of equivalent WPG data
04H	2	Number of points
06H	2	X-coordinate (in wpu)
08H	2	Y-coordinate (in wpu)
0AH	2	Control point (X)
0CH	2	Control point (Y)
0EH	2	...

Table 29.22 Format record type 19

The first field defines the size of the equivalent WPG data area. It was introduced in WPG version 5.0 for reasons of compatibility.

29.2.19 Bitmap 2 (type 20, WPG version 5.1)

This record type (14H) is used to indicate bitmaps with shifted coordinates and rotation angle in WPG 5.1.

Offset	Bytes	Remarks
00H	2	Bitmap rotation angle (0–360 degree)
02H	2	Lower left x location (in wpu)
04H	2	Lower left y location (in wpu)
06H	2	Upper right x location (in wpu)
08H	2	Upper right y location (in wpu)
0AH	2	Image width (in pixel)
0CH	2	Image height (in pixel)
0EH	2	Bits per pixel 1 = mapped pixel array 8 = byte pixel array
10H	2	Resolution across (pixel/inch)
12H	2	Resolution up and down (pixel/inch)
14H	*n*	Bitmap data (compressed)

Table 29.23 Format record type 20

A header containing the rotation angle and the image coordinates precedes the data in this record. From offset 10H, the structure corresponds to that of record type 11 and the same compression method is used.

29.2.20 Start Figure (type 21, WPG version 5.1)

This record type (*15*H) is used for describing an image object in WPG 5.1.

Offset	Bytes	Remarks
00H	4	Figure length
04H	2	Rotation angle
06H	2	X1 coordinate of object
08H	2	Y1 coordinate of object
0AH	2	X2
0CH	2	Y2

Table 29.24 Format record type 21

The value in the *Figure length* field indicates the length of the object data area relative to the file position after reading the length field. The object data presumably follows at offset 0EH. However, information on coding is not currently available.

29.2.21 Start Chart (type 22, WPG version 5.1)

This record type (16H) is used for describing a diagram (chart) in WPG 5.1.

Offset	Bytes	Remarks
00H	4	Chart length
04H	2	X1 coordinate of object
06H	2	Y1 coordinate of object
08H	2	X2
0AH	2	Y2
0CH	2	Start of chart data

Table 29.25 Format record type 22

The value in the *Chart length* field indicates the length of the object data area relative to the file position after reading the length field. The data for structuring the diagram is stored as WPG commands from offset 0CH onwards.

Record type 23 is intended for *PlanPerfect* data. However, information on the record structure is not currently available.

29.2.22 Graphics text2 (type 24, WPG version 5.1)

In WPG 5.1, this record type (18H) is used to display a text as a graphic image.

Offset	Bytes	Remarks
00H	4	Size of equivalent WPG data
04H	2	Baseline rotation angle
06H	2	Text length (in bytes)
08H	2	X1 coordinate for text (in wpu)
0AH	2	Y1 coordinate for text (in wpu)
0CH	2	X2
0EH	2	Y2
10H	2	X scale factor (in wpu)
12H	2	Y scale factor (in wpu)
14H	1	Byte subtype (0–15) 0: window type 1: single line type 2: bullet text chart 3: simple text chart 4: free-format text chart
15H	*n*	Start of formatted string

Table 29.26 Format record type 24

A scaling factor of 100% means that the text will be displayed in the point size indicated. Functions may be embedded in the text.

29.2.23 Start WPG2 (type 25, WPG version 5.1)

Record type (19H) is used to introduce a WPG2 graphics file. The record type is defined from WPG 5.1 onwards.

Offset	Bytes	Remarks
00H	1	Subtype ID
01H	2	Subtype length
03H	*n*	Subtype data

Table 29.27 Format record type 25

This record only needs to be evaluated once. The foreground and background colors for a page are defined as subtypes.

30

AutoCAD Drawing Exchange format (DXF)

AutoCAD, *the most widely distributed CAD system in the PC sector, has been on the market since 1982. The DXF format for data exchange with external programs, which was introduced alongside it, is now supported by many other programs. A closer look at the Drawing Exchange format is clearly in order.*

30.1 Structure of a DXF file

A DXF file consists of a series of commands in ASCII format. Each command occupies two lines:

```
<Group code>
<Command>
```

The first line contains the *group code* which indicates the type of the following command. The group code may be in the range 0–999. Table 30.1 lists the AutoCAD group codes defined so far, up to version 10.0.

Group	Type	Remarks
0	String	Beginning of an element (LINE, BLOCK and so on)
1	String	Text value of a string (almost text)
2	String	Name of an element (LINE, BLOCK and so on)
3–4	String	...

Table 30.1 AutoCAD group codes up to version 10.0 (*continues over...*)

Group	Type	Remarks
5	String	Entity handle
6	String	Line type name
7	String	Text style name
8	String	Layer name
9	String	Name of header variable
10	Real	1st X-coordinate
11–18	Real	Other X-coordinates
20	Real	1st Y-coordinate (follows the 1st X-coordinate)
21–28	Real	Other Y-coordinates (follows the X-coordinates)
30	Real	1st Z-coordinate (version 9.x)
31–37	Real	Other Z-coordinates (since version 9.x)
38	Real	Element height (up to version 9.x)
39	Real	Object height/thickness
40–48	Real	Size factors (text height and so on)
49	..	(text and so on) An entry in groups 70–78 defines the number of the 49 groups
50–58	Real	Angles
62	Integer	Color number (7 = white, 256 = standard)
66	Integer	1 = other elements follow 0 = no elements follow
67	Integer	Entity is in model or paper space
68	Integer	Identify view port (On, Off, and so on)
69	Integer	Viewport ID number
70–78	Integer	Other flags, counter and so on
210	Real	X-component Z direction
220	Real	Y-component Z direction
230	Real	Z-component Z direction (version 10.0)
999	String	Comments (since version 9.x)
1000	String	Extended entity data
1001	String	Registered application name
1002	String	Extended entity data control string
1003	String	Extended entity data layer name
1004	Byte	Chunk of bytes in extended entity data

Table 30.1 AutoCAD group codes up to version 10.0 (*cont.*)

Group	Type	Remarks
1005	Integer	Extended entity data database handle
1010, 1020, 1030	Real	Extended entity data X, Y, Z,
1011, 1021, 1031	Real	Extended entity data X, Y, Z, coordinates of 3D world space position
1012, 1022, 1032	Real	Extended entity data X, Y, Z, coordinates of 3D world space displacement
1013, 1023, 1033	Real	Extended entity data X, Y, Z, coordinates of 3D world space direction
1040	Real	Extended entity data Floating-point value
1041	Real	Extended entity data distance value
1042	Real	Extended entity data scale factor
1070	Integer	Extended entity data 16-bit signed integer
1071	Integer	Extended entity data 32-bit signed long

Table 30.1 AutoCAD group codes up to version 10.0 (*cont.*)

The Z components in AutoCAD are only supported from version 10.0 onwards. The interpretation of commands 40–48, 50–58 and 70–78 depends on the element. (Further details are given in the relevant section.) A number of commands, such as the commands for comments, are only available from version 9.x. Command 38 (object height) is only supported up to version 9.x. The commands in the DXF file are subdivided into a maximum of four sections (header, tables, entities, blocks) and are terminated with the following command (group code `0` and ASCII string `EOF`):

```
0
EOF
```

The basic structure of the DXF file is shown in Figure 30.1.

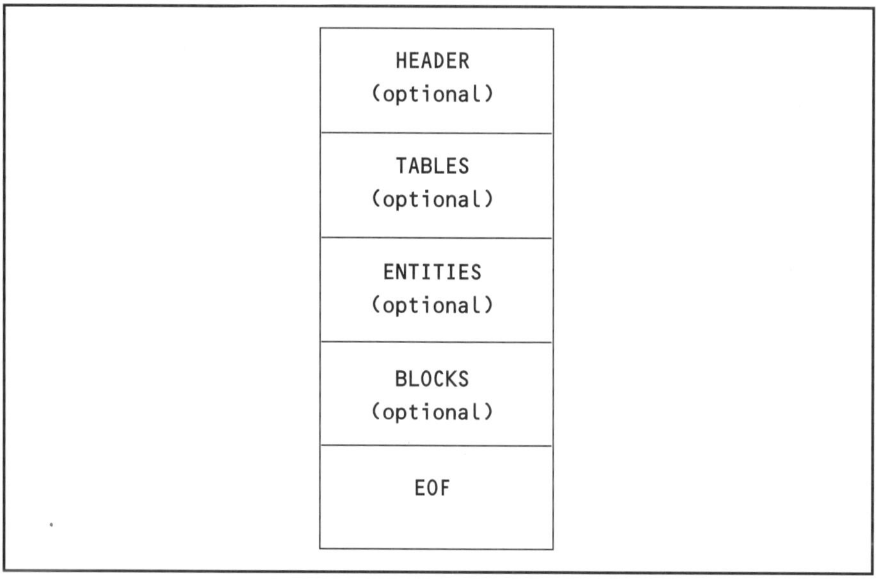

Figure 30.1 Structure of a DXF file

The **HEADER**, **TABLES**, **ENTITIES** and **BLOCKS** sections are optional and can be omitted from DXF files. They are used for storing the settings (color, pattern, and so on) for AutoCAD. The values contained here can only be adopted if the internal settings have not yet been set. This will be the case if no drawing operations have yet been carried out. Each of the sections **HEADER**, **TABLES**, **ENTITIES** and **BLOCKS** is enclosed between these two commands:

```
0
SECTION
.
.
0
ENDSEC
```

The **EOF**, **ENDSEC** and **SECTION** commands have the group code **0**. As shown in Table 30.1, all commands with this code are treated as elements. Figure 30.2 contains an extract from a valid DXF file.

```
  0        ]
SECTION    ]    Begin 1st section
  2        ]    ******************************
HEADER     ]    Section = HEADER
```

Figure 30.2 Extract from a DXF file (*continues over...*)

```
  9         ]
$ACADVER    ]   1st Header variable = Version
  1         ]
AC1003      ]   Text value element
  9
$INSBASE
 10
0.0
 20
0.0
  9
$EXTMIN
 10
0.805232
 20
0.525617
  9
$EXTMAX
 10
12.104994
 20
7.731443
  9
$LIMMIN
 10
0.0
 20
0.0
  9
$LIMMAX
 10
12.0
 20
9.0
  .
  .
  9
$ORTHOMODE
 70
      1
  9
```

Figure 30.2 Extract from a DXF file (*cont.*)

```
$REGENMODE
 70
      1
  9
$FILLMODE
 70
      1
  9
$QTEXTMODE
 70
      0
  9
$DRAGMODE
 70
      2
  .
  .
  9
$USERR4
 40          ]
0.0          ]     Size factor
  9
$USERR5
 40
0.0
  0          ]
ENDSEC       ]     HEADER end
  0          ]
SECTION      ]     Begin next section
2            ]     ******************************
TABLES       ]     Section = Table
  0          ]
TABLE        ]     Element = Table
  2          ]
LTYPE        ]     Type 1st element
 70          ]
      1      ]     Number of elements = 1
  0          ]
LTYPE        ]     Element LTYPE
  2          ]
```

Figure 30.2 Extract from a DXF file (*cont.*)

Graphics

```
EXTRACTED           Element name
 70          ]
       0     ]      Number of elements
  3          ]
Solid line   ]      Description line type
 72          ]
      65     ]      Justify code
 73          ]
       0     ]      Number of groups with code 49
 40          ]
0.0          ]      Length sum in group 49
  0          ]
ENDTAB       ]      End of table
  0          ]
TABLE        ]      Begin next table
  2          ]
LAYER        ]      Table name
 70          ]
       1     ]      Number of elements
  0          ]
LAYER        ]      Element
  2          ]
       0     ]      Element name
 70          ]
       0     ]      Flag
 62          ]
       7     ]      Color number
  6          ]
EXTRACTED    ]      Line type
  0          ]
ENDTAB       ]      Table end
 0           ]
TABLE        ]      Begin next table
  2          ]
STYLE        ]      Table name
 70          ]
       1     ]      Number of elements
  0          ]
STYLE        ]      Element type
  2          ]
STANDARD     ]      Element name
 70          ]
       0     ]      Flag
 40          ]
0.0          ]      Text height
 41          ]
1.0          ]      Text width
```

Figure 30.2 Extract from a DXF file (*cont.*)

```
  50         ]
0.0          ]  Text angle
 71          ]
        0    ]  Flags
 42          ]
0.2          ]  Last used height
  3          ]
txt          ]  Font name
  4          ]
             ]  Bigfont file name
  0          ]
ENDTAB       ]  End of table
  0          ]
TABLE        ]  Begin next table
  2          ]
VIEW         ]  Table name
 70          ]
        0    ]  Number of elements
  0          ]
ENDTAB       ]  End of table
  0          ]
ENDSEC       ]  End of section tables
  0          ]
SECTION      ]  Begin next section
  2          ]  ********************************
BLOCKS       ]  Section name = blocks
  0          ]
BLOCK        ]  Element type
  8          ]
        0    ]  Layer name
  2          ]
*X0          ]  Element name (unnamed)
 70          ]
        1    ]  Number of elements
 10          ]
0.0          ]  1st X-coordinate
 20          ]
0.0          ]  1st Y-coordinate
  0          ]
LINE         ]  Next element
  8          ]
  0          ]  Layer name
```

Figure 30.2 Extract from a DXF file (*cont.*)

```
INSERT          ]   Element type
  8
0               ]   Layer number
 62
         2      ]   Color number
  2
*X0             ]   Element name (unnamed)
 10
0.0
 20
0.0             ]   Coordinates
  0
TEXT            ]   Element type
  8
0               ]   Layer number
 10
0.987175
 20
3.401942        ]   Coordinates
 40
0.2             ]   Text height
  1
Hello !         ]   Text name (here Text)
  0
TEXT            ]   Other text
  8
0
 10
0.987175
 20
3.068609
 40
0.2
  1
This is a DXF file.
  0
CIRCLE          ]   Element type
  8
0               ]   Layer name
 62
         1      ]   Color
```

Figure 30.2 Extract from a DXF file (*cont.*)

```
  10
3.818549  ]
  20      ]     Center point
5.380913  ]
  40      ]
0.883144  ]     Radius
   0      ]
ENDSEC    ]     End of section
   0      ]
EOF       ]     End DXF file
```

Figure 30.2 Extract from a DXF file (*cont.*)

The image contains a text, a pentagon, a line and a circle. In its original form the DXF file is over 48 Kbytes long. The example has been shortened. The comments in Figure 30.2 have been added retrospectively and are not part of the DXF file. The only compulsory command in the file is `EOF`, which is necessary in order to create a defined end of file for AutoCAD.

30.2 DXF Header

The settings for the internal AutoCAD variables are stored in the Header section. However, AutoCAD only evaluates this data if no other settings have been defined, that is, if no drawing operations have yet been carried out. The section can therefore be omitted and for this reason is ignored by many external programs. Figure 30.3 illustrates the structure of the Header section:

```
   0      ]
SECTION   ]     Begin section
   2      ]
HEADER    ]     Section = HEADER
   9      ]
$ACADVER  ]     Header variable
   .
   .
   9
$USERR5
  40
0.0
   0      ]
ENDSEC    ]     Header end
```

Figure 30.3 Structure of a `HEADER` section

The section is framed by the two keywords `SECTION` and `ENDSEC`. The command following the start of the section identifies the section with this code:

```
2
HEADER
```

This is followed by the commands containing the variable definitions, each of which has the group code `9` followed by the relevant variable name. Each name begins with the character `$`. The following lines may contain parameters giving the variable settings. The command shown below, for example, defines the AutoCAD version that created the file:

```
9

$ACADVER

1

AC1003
```

30.3 DXF TABLE section

This section contains tables giving the definitions of line types, layers, text modes, and so on (the structure is shown in Figure 30.4). This information may be omitted from DXF files because AutoCAD only evaluates this data if no relevant internal definition is available. As soon as a drawing operation has been carried out, AutoCAD will ignore the `TABLE` section. This can cause problems because the attributes of the objects used in the `BLOCK` and `ENTITIES` sections (lines, and so on) are defined here.

```
  0       ]
SECTION   ]    Begin next section
  2       ]
TABLES    ]    Section = Table
  0       ]
TABLE     ]    Element = Table
  2       ]
LTYPE     ]    1st table part
  .
  .
  0       ]
ENDTAB    ]    Table end
  0       ]
TABLE     ]    Begin next table
  .
  .
  0       ]
ENDTAB    ]    Table end
  0       ]
ENDSEC    ]    End of the tables section
```

Figure 30.4 Structure of a `TABLE` section

The commands are enclosed between `SECTION` and `ENDSEC` commands. Several partial tables may be contained within the section. These must be enclosed between keywords such as `TABLE` and `ENDTAB`. After the word `TABLE`, the command indicating the name of the table appears:

```
2
Name
```

The group code is `2`, and the `Name` field may contain one of the key words shown in Table 30.2:

LAYER	VIEW
LTYPE	VPORT (Version 10.0)
STYLE	UCS (Version 10.0)

Table 30.2
Keywords in `SECTION` table

The name is generally followed by a command with the group code `70`, which indicates the number of table elements in the second line. Although the value entered here may not always be correct, the group code `70` must be entered.

30.3.1 LAYER

This table is structured as shown in Figure 30.5. It contains information on the color, line type and so on, of a layer.

```
  0          ]
TABLE        ]   Element = Table
  2          ]
LAYER        ]   Table name
 70          ]
        1    ]   Number of elements
  0          ]
LAYER        ]   Element
  2          ]
0            ]   Name of the element
 70          ]
        0    ]   Flags
 62          ]
        7    ]   Color number (white)
  6          ]
CONTIGUOUS   ]   Line type
  0          ]
ENDTAB       ]   End of table
```

Figure 30.5
Example of the `LAYER` table

The LAYER definition shown in Figure 30.5 consists of just one element, an extended line. The command with group code 62 defines the color. If this value is negative, the element in the layer is switched off and not drawn. The line type (group code 6) must first have been defined in LTYPE. Apart from this, the sequence of commands in the table may be in any order. The second command with group number 70 indicates the bit-coded status of the layer.

Bit	Function
0 = 1	Layer frozen
6 = 1	Layer contains elements

Table 30.3
LAYER status

Table 30.4 contains the definitions of the group codes for the LAYER table.

Group	Remarks
6	Name of line type
62	Color number (negative = Layer off)
70	Flag: Bit 0 = 1 : freeze

Table 30.4
Group codes for the LAYER table

The default setting for a layer provides the following values:

Color	White
Line type	CONTIGUOUS
Layer	On, not frozen

These values have been taken into account in Figure 30.5.

30.3.2 LTYPE

This table defines the appearance of lines within a layer. Figure 30.6 gives an example of an LTYPE table.

```
  0          ]
TABLE        ]    Element = Table
  2          ]
LTYPE        ]    Type of 1st element
 70          ]
        1    ]    Number of elements = 1
  0          ]
LTYPE        ]    Element LTYPE
  2          ]
EXTRACTED    ]    Name of element
 70          ]
        0    ]    Status
  3          ]
solid line   ]    Other text
 72          ]
       65    ]    Justify flag
 73          ]
        0    ]    Number of groups
 40          ]
0.0          ]    Sum of all lengths
  0          ]
ENDTAB       ]    End of table
```

Figure 30.6 Example of an LTYPE table

Table 30.5 shows the codes used in Figure 30.6:

Group	Remarks
3	Description of line type
40	Sum of all lengths in group 49
49	Line length negative = pen up positive = pen down 0 = dot
72	Justify code = 1 (align)
73	Number of groups with code 49

Table 30.5 Group codes for the LTYPE table

The group codes 72 and 73 define bit codes for the text alignment. The exact specification is not known.

Graphics

30.3.3 STYLE

Information on font styles is stored in this table. Figure 30.7 gives an example of a style definition within a table.

```
  0        ]
TABLE      ]    Begin table
  2        ]
STYLE      ]    Table name
 70        ]
        1  ]    Number of elements
  0        ]
STYLE      ]    Element type
  2        ]
STANDARD   ]    Element name
 70        ]
        0  ]    Flags
 40        ]
0.0        ]    Text height
 41        ]
1.0        ]    Text width
 50        ]
0.0        ]    Text angle (direction)
 71        ]
        0  ]    Flags
 42        ]
0.2        ]    Last used height
  3        ]
txt        ]    Font name
  4        ]
           ]    Bigfont file name
  0        ]
ENDTAB     ]    End of table
```

Figure 30.7 Example of a STYLE table

Table 30.6 lists the group codes available for STYLE.

Graphics

Group	Remarks
3	Name of character or symbol file
4	Bigfont file name
40	Text height defined (0 = not defined)
41	Factor width
42	Last used height
50	Slope angle (slope)
70	Flags
	Bit 1 = 1: symbol table
	Bit 3 = 1: vertical text
71	Text creation flags
	Bit 1 = 1: output backwards
	Bit 2 = 1: rotate 180 degrees

Table 30.6 Group codes of the STYLE table

Further details on the coding of the flags and fonts is not currently documented.

30.3.4 UCS

The UCS (*User Coordinate System*) is supported only from AutoCAD version 10.00. Table 30.7 lists the group codes permitted with UCS.

Group	Remarks
10,20,30	Origin (X,Y,Z) of coordinate system in world coordinates (since version 10.0)
11,21,31	Direction of X-axis in world coordinates
12,22,32	Direction of Y-axis in world coordinates

Table 30.7 Group codes of the UCS table

30.3.5 VIEW

This element enables various excerpts (regions) of a drawing to be selected. Table 30.8 lists the group codes that can be used in conjunction with VIEW.

Group	Remarks
10,20	Center (X,Y) of the view
11,21,31	View direction
12,22,32	Destination point in world coordinates (since version 10.0)
40	Height of view
41	Width of view
42	Lens length (since version 10.0)
43,44	Front and back plane (version 10.0)
50	Rotation angle
71	View mode (since version 10.0) Bit 0 = 1: Perspective view active Bit 1 = 1: Front plane active Bit 2 = 1: Back plane active Bit 3 = 1: 'UCS follow' mode active Bit 4 = 1: Front plane not in direction of vision

Table 30.8 Group code for VIEW table

In older versions of AutoCAD, the VIEW table does not contain any elements (Figure 30.2).

30.3.6 VPORT

This table is supported from AutoCAD version 10.0 onwards. Table 30.9 lists the group codes used:

Group	Remarks
10,20	Lower left corner viewport
11,21	Upper right corner viewport
12,22	Coordinates of view center
13,23	Catch point
14,24	Catch distance in X- and Y-direction
15,25	Raster width in X- and Y-direction
16,26,36	View direction from destination point
17,27,37	Coordinates of destination point
40	View height
41	Aspect rotation viewport

Table 30.9 Group codes for the VPORT table *(continues over...)*

Graphics

Group	Remarks
42	Lens length
43,44	Shift front and back plane from destination point
50	Catch rotation angle
51	Rotation angle view
71	View mode (since version 10.0) Bit 0 = 1: perspective view active Bit 1 = 1: front plane view active Bit 2 = 1: back plane view active Bit 3 = 1: 'UCS follow' mode active Bit 4 = 1: front plane not in direction of vision
72	Arc zoom percentage
73	Fast zoom factor
74	Coordinate system symbol
75	1 = SNAP on, 0 = SNAP off
76	1 = GRID on, 0 = GRID off
77	Catch style
78	Catch ISO pair

Table 30.9 Group codes for the VPORT table (*cont.*)

The exact coding is not currently documented.

30.4 BLOCK section of a DXF file

This table contains information on the elements used. In addition to AutoCAD blocks, other unknown blocks may also occur. For this reason, the name is prefixed with an asterisk. The command with group code 70 defines the *Block Flag* and is coded as shown in Figure 30.8:

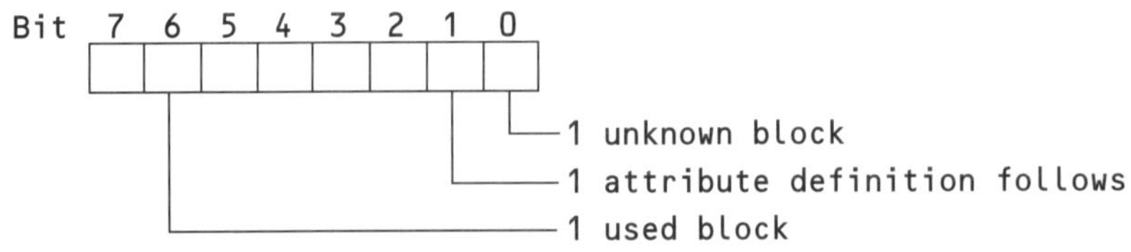

Figure 30.8 Coding block flags

As shown in Figure 30.9, a block is enclosed within a sequence of commands.

```
0
SECTION
2
BLOCKS
0
BLOCK
.
.
.
0
ENDBLK
8
0
0
ENDSEC
```

Figure 30.9 Example of a BLOCK section

The block consists of elements with group code 0: BLOCK, possibly ATTDEF and any number of objects (line, circle, and so on), which are used in ENTITIES. The definition is terminated by the element ENDBLK. Table 30.10 shows the allocation of group codes for BLOCK and ATTDEF:

Group	Remarks
	BLOCK
2	Block name
10,20,30	Coordinates (X,Y,Z) of base point
70	Block type flag
	Bit 0 = 1: Block is anonymous
	Bit 1 = 1: Attribute definitions follows
	ATTDEF
1	Predefined attribute value (for requests)
2	Attribute name
3	Text attribute begin
7	Name of text styles
10,20,30	Coordinates (X,Y,Z) of text start point

Table 30.10 Group code in BLOCKS (*continues over...*)

Graphics

Group	Remarks
11,21,31	Coordinate (x,y,z) of justification point (if group 72)
40	Text height
41	X-size factor (if <> 1)
50	Rotation angle (if <> 0)
51	Slope angle
70	Attribute flag
	Bit 0 = 1: invisible
	Bit 1 = 1: constant (without request)
	Bit 2 = 1: check request
	Bit 3 = 1: use default attribute
71	Text creation flag (if <> 0)
	Bit 1 = 1: backward
	Bit 2 = 1: rotate 180 degrees
72	Text justify type (if <> 0)
	Bit 0 = 1: left justified
	Bit 1 = 1: centered at base line
	Bit 2 = 1: right justified
	Bit 3 = 1: between two points
	Bit 4 = 1: centered
	Bit 5 = 1: aligned between two points
73	Field length (if <> 0)

Table 30.10 Group code in BLOCKS (*cont.*)

An attribute definition can be allocated to a BLOCK. In this case, bit 1 in the *Block Type* flag (group code 70) is set. The element ENDBLK may also appear as a terminator.

30.5 DXF ENTITIES Section

This section contains the actual image description. The objects described in the BLOCKS are used here. This section is framed by the sequence shown in Figure 30.10.

```
0
SECTION
2
ENTITIES
.
.
.
0
ENDSEC
```

Figure 30.10 Example of an ENTITIES Section

Various objects defined by group code 0 may appear within this section. Table 30.11 lists the objects in the ENTITIES section defined so far:

Object	Object	Object
LINE	SOLID	VERTEX
3DLINE	TEXT	SEQEND
POINT	SHAPE	3DFACE
CIRCLE	INSERT	DIMENSION
ARC	ATTRIB	
TRACE	POLYLINE	

Table 30.11 Elements in the ENTITIES section

The meaning of the group codes varies somewhat according to the object used.

30.5.1 LINE

This command is used to introduce the description of a line:

```
0
LINE
```

It is followed by additional commands which describe the line. Table 30.12 lists the relevant group codes:

Group	Remarks
0	Element = LINE
10,20,30	Start point (X,Y,Z) of line
11,21,31	End point (X,Y,Z) of line

Table 30.12 Group code for the LINE element

The line is described as a vector between two points. Z coordinates are permissible only after version 10.0. The line type, line width, and so on, are adopted from BLOCKS, but may also be set explicitly, using specifically defined commands. Only the start and end coordinates of the vector are contained in ENTITIES. The coordinates for one point are always stored consecutively (X,Y,Z) and then followed by the coordinates for the next point.

30.5.2 3DLINE

This command introduces the description of a three-dimensional line:

```
0
3DLINE
```

It is followed by other commands describing the line. Table 30.13 lists the relevant group codes:

Group	Remarks
0	Element = 3DLINE
10,20,30	Start point (X,Y,Z) of line
11,21,31	End point (X,Y,Z) of line

Table 30.13 Group code for the 3DLINE element

The line is described as a vector between two points. Z coordinates are permissible only after version 10.0. The line type, line width, and so on, are adopted from BLOCKS, but may also be set explicitly, using specifically defined commands. Only the start and end coordinates of the vector are contained in ENTITIES. The coordinates for one point are always stored consecutively (X,Y,Z) and then followed by the coordinates for the next point.

30.5.3 POINT

This command introduces the description of a point in the coordinate area:

```
0
POINT
```

Z components are supported from version 10.0 of AutoCAD onwards. Table 30.14 shows the group codes for the following commands:

Group	Remarks
0	Element = POINT
10,20,30	Point coordinates (X,Y,Z)
50	Angle of X-axis in world coordinates (UCS, since version 10.0)

Table 30.14 Group code for the POINT element

The command with group code 50 is supported from version 10.0 of AutoCAD onwards. It indicates the angle of the X axis in the user coordinate system compared with the zero axis.

30.5.4 CIRCLE

This command introduces the description of a circle:

```
0
CIRCLE
```

Z components are supported from version 10.0 of AutoCAD onwards. Table 30.15 shows the group codes for the following commands:

Group	Remarks
0	Element = CIRCLE
10,20,30	Arc center coordinates (X,Y,Z)
40	Arc radius

Table 30.15 Group code for the CIRCLE element

The command sequence may additionally contain commands for selecting the layer, the color, and so on.

30.5.5 ARC

This command describes an arc:

```
0
ARC
```

The element is followed by other commands, as listed in Table 30.16:

Group	Remarks
0	Element = ARC
10,20,30	Center coordinate (X,Y,Z)
40	Radius arc
50	Start angle of arc
51	End angle of arc

Table 30.16 Group code for the ARC element

The Z coordinates are supported from version 10.0 of AutoCAD onwards. Additional commands for the description of the color, the layer, and so on, may also be contained in the sequence.

30.5.6 TRACE

This element introduces the description of a closed line between four points (*band*), which in turn describes the outline of rectangles. The sequence begins with the element:

```
0
TRACE
```

This is followed by further commands describing the corner points, as shown in Table 30.17:

Group	Remarks
0	Element = TRACE
10,20,30	Coordinate (X,Y,Z) of 1st point
11,21,31	Coordinate (X,Y,Z) of 2nd point
12,22,32	Coordinate (X,Y,Z) of 3rd point
13,23,33	Coordinate (X,Y,Z) of 4th point

Table 30.17 Group code for TRACE

The Z coordinate is supported from version 10.0 of AutoCAD onwards. Additional commands for describing the color, the layer, and so on may also be contained in the sequence. In the case of triangles, two points contain the same coordinates.

30.5.7 SOLID

This element introduces the description of a closed area between four points, that is, a rectangle. The sequence begins with the element:

```
0
SOLID
```

This is followed by further commands describing the corner points, as shown in Table 30.18.

Group	Remarks
0	Element = SOLID
10,20,30	Coordinate (X,Y,Z) of 1st point
11,21,31	Coordinate (X,Y,Z) of 2nd point
12,22,32	Coordinate (X,Y,Z) of 3rd point
13,23,33	Coordinate (X,Y,Z) of 4th point

Table 30.18 Group code for the SOLID element

The Z coordinate is supported from version 10.0 of AutoCAD onwards. Additional commands for describing the color, the layer, the fill pattern and so on may also be contained in the sequence. In the case of triangles, the two last points contain the same coordinates.

30.5.8 TEXT

The following command is defined in order to incorporate text into AutoCAD DXF files:

```
0
TEXT
```

This is followed by a sequence of additional commands for describing the text (Table 30.19):

Group	Remarks
0	Element = TEXT
1	Text as ASCII string
7	Name of text style (standard = STANDARD)
10	Text insertion point X-coordinate
20	Text insertion point Y-coordinate
30	Text insertion point Z-coordinate
11	Text alignment point X-coordinate
21	Text alignment point Y-coordinate
31	Text alignment point Z-coordinate
40	Text height
41	Relative factor X-axis (standard = 1)
50	Rotation angle of text (standard = 0)
51	Character slope angle (standard = 0)
71	Generation flag (standard = 0) Bit 1 = 1: Text backward Bit 2 = 1: Rotate text 180 degrees
72	Justify 0: left 1: centered at baseline 2: right 3: aligned between 2 points 4: centered (between 2 points) 5: justified between 2 points (variable text width)

Table 30.19 Group code for the TEXT element

Graphics

The Z coordinate is supported from AutoCAD version 10.0 onwards. The commands for the coordinates of the alignment point appear only if the justification type (code 72) is not equal to 0. In AutoCAD, the text can be displayed at any angle required. If the angle is not equal to 0 degrees, a command with the group code 50 or 51 appears. Group code 51 defines the angle of inclination for letters (creation of italic script). Group code 7 is needed only if the text style deviates from STANDARD. Bits 1 and 2 of the generation flag (group code 71) specify the direction of the text display (backwards or upside down). The option for setting the alignment of the text can be selected using group code 72. This code also determines whether a second point is required for alignment. Further commands for describing the color, the layer, and so on may then follow.

30.5.9 SHAPE

This element is used in AutoCAD to define a symbol at the point indicated. The sequence begins with the command:

```
0
SHAPE
```

It may contain the additional commands shown in Table 30.20:

Group	Remarks
0	Element = SHAPE
2	Symbol name
10	Symbol insertion point X-coordinate
20	Symbol insertion point Y-coordinate
30	Symbol insertion point Z-coordinate
40	Symbol height
41	Relative scale factor (standard = 1)
50	Rotation angle (standard = 0)
51	Slope angle (standard = 0)

Table 30.20 Group code for the SHAPE element

The Z coordinate is supported from AutoCAD version 10.0 onwards. The commands for rotation angle, scaling factor and slope angle are listed only if values that do not correspond to the standard settings are used.

30.5.10 INSERT

This element is used to re-insert into the drawing an object from AutoCAD that has already been used. The start sequence may be followed by the commands shown in Table 30.21:

```
0
INSERT
```

The Z coordinate is supported from AutoCAD version 10.0 onwards. The commands for rotation angle, number of columns, and so on are only listed if the values used do not correspond to the standard settings. If bit `0` of the attribute flag (code `66`) is set, a sequence of `ATTRIB` elements, terminated with `SEQEND`, will follow the block commands. If an element from `LAYER 0` of the `BLOCK` section is described with `INSERT`, the attributes correspond to those of the insert layers.

Group	Remarks
0	Element = `INSERT`
2	Inserted block name
10	Block insertion point X-coordinate
20	Block insertion point Y-coordinate
30	Block insertion point Z-coordinate
41	Scale factor of X-axis (standard = 1)
42	Scale factor of Y-axis (standard = 1)
43	Scale factor of Z-axis (standard = 1)
44	Column distance
45	Row distance
50	Rotation angle (standard = 0)
66	Attribute flag
	Bit 0 = 1: `ATTRIB` follows the `BLOCK`
70	Columns (if multiple insertions, standard = 1)
71	Rows (if multiple insertions, standard = 1)

Table 30.21 Group codes for the `INSERT` element

Graphics

30.5.11 ATTRIB

This element follows an `INSERT` command if the attribute bit in this command is set. The table begins with the command:

```
0
ATTRIB
```

The Z coordinate is supported from AutoCAD version 10.0 onwards. The commands for field length, rotation angle, and so on are listed only if values that do not correspond to the standard settings are used. If the value of the element for group `72` is not equal to `0`, the coordinates of the second alignment point will be indicated. Table 30.22 lists all the other commands contained in this element:

Group	Remarks
0	Element = `ATTRIB`
1	Attribute text
2	Attribute name
7	Text style name (Standard = STANDARD)
10	Text insertion point X-coordinate
20	Text insertion point Y-coordinate
30	Text insertion point Z-coordinate
11	Alignment point X-axis if group 72 <> 0
21	Alignment point Y-axis if group 72 <> 0
31	Alignment point Z-axis if group 72 <> 0
50	Rotation angle of text (Standard = 0)
51	Slope angle of text (Standard = 0)
70	Attribute flag
	Bit 0 = 1: `BLOCK` is anonymous
	Bit 1 = 1: ATTDEF follows
71	Generation flag (Standard = 0)
	Bit 1 = 1: Text backward
	Bit 2 = 1: Rotate text 180 degrees
72	Justify
	0: left
	1: centered at baseline
	2: right
	3: aligned between 2 points
	4: centered (middle between 2 points)
	5: exact between 2 points (variable text width)
73	Field length (Standard = 0)

Table 30.22 Group codes for the `ATTRIB` element

30.5.12 POLYLINE

This element introduces the description of a connecting line between several points. The sequence begins with the command:

```
0
POLYLINE
```

Further commands are listed in Table 30.23:

Group	Remarks
0	Element = POLYLINE
40	Predefined start width
41	Predefined end width
66	Vertex point flag
	Value = 1: Vertex elements follow
70	Polyline flag
	Bit 0 = 1: closed polyline
	Bit 1 = 1: curve fitted in polyline
	Bit 2 = 1: curve fitted in polyline
	Bit 3 = 1: 3D-polyline (since version 10.0)
	Bit 4 = 1: polygon line (since version 10.0)
	Bit 5 = 1: polygon line close (version 10.0)
71,72	Counting polygon line maximum in 1st and 2nd direction (value > 0) since version 10.0
75	Flag, if bit 4 in group 70 = 1
	0: no plain curve
	5: quadratic curve
	6: cubic B-spline curve
	8: Bezier curve (since version 10.0)

Table 30.23 Group code for a POLYLINE element

Group codes 71, 72 and 75 are supported from AutoCAD version 10.0 onwards. The polygon line always consists of a sequence of point-specifying VERTEX elements. This sequence is terminated with SEQEND. Codes 40 and 41 are used for all elements in VERTEX that do not have their own group number 40 or 41.

30.5.13 VERTEX

This element introduces the definition of the points of a polyline. The sequence begins with the command:

```
0
POLYLINE
```

It is terminated with ENDSEQ. Several VERTEX elements with commands as shown in Table 30.24 may appear between these commands:

Group	Remarks		
0	Element = VERTEX		
10	Position vertex X-coordinate		
20	Position vertex Y-coordinate		
30	Position vertex Z-coordinate		
40	Predefined start width		
41	Predefined end width		
42	Bulge (0 = even, 1 = semi-arc)		
50	Direction of tangent, if bit 1 in group 70 is set		
70	Vertex flag		
		Bit 0 = 1:	additional vertex with curve fit
		Bit 1 = 1:	Vertex with tangent definition for curve fit
		Bit 3 = 1:	Curve vertext point created with curve fit
		Bit 4 = 1:	Control point for curve bounding box
		Bit 5 = 1:	3D-polyline vertex point (since version 10.0)
		Bit 6 = 1:	Polygon line vertex point (since version 10.0)

Table 30.24 Group codes for VERTEX elements

30.5.14 SEQEND

This sequence terminates ATTRIB and VERTEX definitions.

Graphics

30.5.15 3DFACE

This element introduces the description of three-dimensional surfaces. The sequence begins with the command:

```
0
3DFACE
```

The flags for invisible edges are supported from AutoCAD version 10.0 onwards. Table 30.25 lists the additional commands.

Group	Remarks
`0`	Element = `3DFACE`
`10,20,30`	Coordinate (X,Y,Z) of 3D-surface (1st point)
`11,21,31`	Coordinate (X,Y,Z) of 3D-surface (2nd point)
`12,22,32`	Coordinate (X,Y,Z) of 3D-surface (3rd point)
`13,23,33`	Coordinate (X,Y,Z) of 3D-surface (4th point)
`70`	Flags for invisible edges (since version 10.0)
	Bit 0 = 1: 1st invisible edge
	Bit 1 = 1: 2nd invisible edge
	Bit 2 = 1: 3rd invisible edge
	Bit 3 = 1: 4th invisible edge

Table 30.25 Group code for `3DFACE` elements

30.5.16 DIMENSION

This element is supported from version 9.0 onwards. It describes the dimensions of a drawing. The sequence begins with:

```
0
DIMENSION
```

and contains the commands shown in Table 30.26:

Group	Remarks
0	Element = DIMENSION
1	Dimension text
2	Name of an anonymous block
10,20,30	Definition point (X,Y,Z) dimension types
11,21,31	Center point (X,Y,Z) dimension text
12,22,32	Insertion point (X,Y,Z) dimension copy
13,23,33	Definition point Special point: 1st subsidiary line for linear dimension End point of subsidiary line for angle dimension
14,24,34	Definition point Special point: 2nd subsidiary line for linear dimension Start point of subsidiary line for angle dimension
15,25	Definition point for diameter and radius
35	1st point dimension line for radius and diameter Start point of 2nd subsidiary line for angle dimension
16,26,36	Specification point for arc and angle dimension
40	Direction length for radius and diameter dimension
50	Angle of rotated horizontal or vertical dimensions
51	Orientation dimension text (since version 10.0)
70	Dimension type 0: rotate 1: align 2: angle 3: diameter 4: radius Bit 7 = 1: Dimension position user-defined

Table 30.26 Group code for DIMENSION elements

Code 51 is used only from version 10.0 onwards. It indicates the direction of the dimension text.

30.6 AutoCAD Binary DXF

With version 10.0 of AutoCAD, a binary version of the DXF format was introduced. A binary DXF file begins with the signature:

```
AutoCAD Binary DXF<0DH><0AH><1AH>00H>
```

In DOS, the code `1AH` signals the end of a text file, that is, the binary DXF file cannot be processed by an editor or printed.

The format of a binary DXF file corresponds to the structure of ASCII DXF files, but numerical values are coded in binary notation.

- Group codes (2 bytes) are stored in Intel format (little endian).
- All floating point numbers are in 8-byte double-precision format.
- ASCII strings are terminated with a null byte `00H`.

As a result, binary DXF files are up to 30% shorter than the ASCII DXF files and can be loaded more quickly.

! **From AutoCAD 10.0 onwards, there are also Drawing Exchange Binary files (DXB), which begin with the signature:**

```
AutoCAD DXB<0DH><0AH><1AH>00H>
```

However, the structure of these files is not currently documented.
Further information about the DXF format is available from the Autodesk company.

31

Micrografx formats (PIC, DRW, GRF)

Micrografx *has developed several drawing tools. These tools use several Metafile formats (*`.PIC, .DRW, .GRF`*)*

This chapter describes the formats of the following file types:

Type	Product	
PIC	Windows Draw, In*a*Vision	Version 1
GRF	Windows Graph, Graph Plus	Version 2
DRW	Designer, Charisma and Draw Plus	

Table 31.1 Micrografx file formats

During the course of its development, the company has defined two different file formats (type 1 and type 2). This is reflected in the extensions `.PIC` on the one hand, and `.DRW` and `.GRF` on the other. All the records are structured in the same way:

```
<Length><Record Type><Data>
```

There are, however, a number of peculiarities concerning the length field. The data area can be longer than 255 bytes, so the format defines two methods of indicating length:

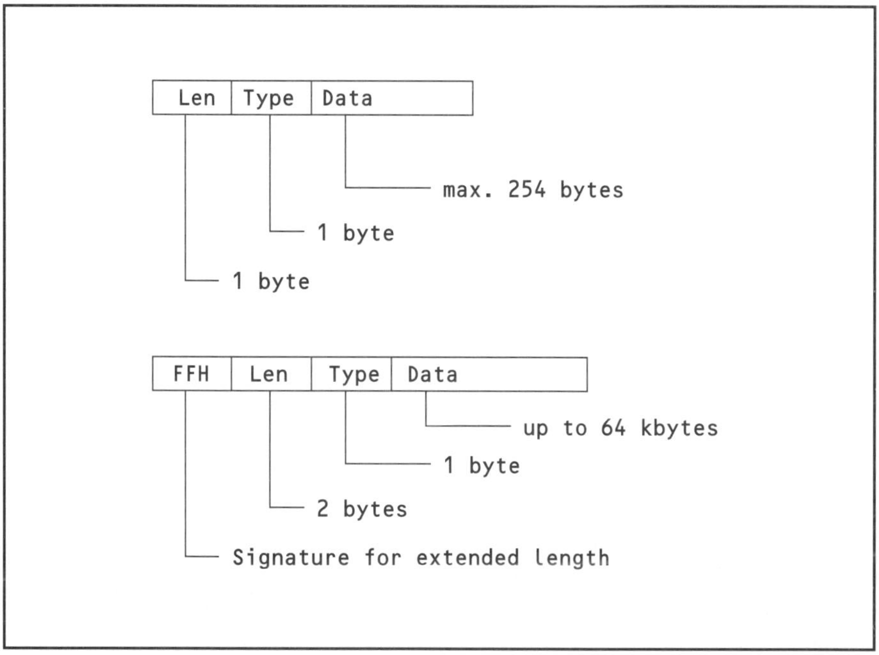

Figure 31.1 Structure for short and long records

Normally, the length field is one byte long and can accommodate values between 0 and 255 (FFH). This allows a maximum of 254 characters in the data record (FFH is reserved). With longer data records, the length field must be extended, which is why the value FFH was reserved to act as a signature. If the first byte contains FFH, it will be followed by another field containing the extended length. This field consists of 2 bytes, which are interpreted as an unsigned integer, thereby enabling the length of the data area to be up to 64 Kbytes. With values less than FFH in the first byte, this additional length field is not required.

As a result of a programming error in Windows Draw and In*a*Vision, four bytes are displayed for the length field of records that have a data area longer than 254 bytes. However, only the first two bytes contain a value. The following two bytes remain empty. In order to maintain compatibility, these two extra bytes are also displayed in all current Micrografx products.

The length field defines the number of bytes in the data area. This value does not include the bytes occupied by the length field and the record type.

The length field is followed by one byte specifying the record type. The record types are described below. These involve the description of both objects (circle, line, and so on) and operations (select color, and so on). All coordinate data refers to a device-independent, logical coordinate system with dimensions of 32,767 units in the X direction and 32,767 units in the Y direction. These coordinates are converted to the resolution of the output device. The default setting is for a conversion factor of 200 units per centimeter (or 480 units per inch). The remaining bytes in the record contain data for the record type concerned. The number of bytes is determined by the length field.

The files are structured in such a way that a given sequence of record types must be observed. For the version 1 format, the structure is as follows:

```
62          ]
       0        Color number
 10         ]
6.609264        1st X-coordinate
 20         ]
3.5             1st Y-coordinate
 11         ]
6.625           Other X-coordinates
 21         ]
3.5             Other Y-coordinates
  0         ]
LINE            Next element
 .
 .
  0         ]
ENDBLK          Block end
  8         ]
0               Layer name 0
  0         ]
ENDSEC          End of section
  0         ]
SECTION         Begin next section
  2         ]   ******************************
ENTITIES        Section name
  0         ]
LINE            Element name
  8         ]
0               Layer name
 10         ]
0.805232        1st X-coordinate
 20         ]
5.195401        1st Y-coordinate
 11         ]
3.091228        Other X-coordinate
 21         ]
7.731443        Other Y-coordinate
  0
LINE
  .
  .
  0
```

Figure 30.2
Extract from a DXF file (*cont.*)

Record	Position
Beginning of File	Must be 1st record
Version	Must be 2nd record
Background Color	Any position in file
Font Name	Any position in file
Color Flag	Any position in file
Grid Settings	Any position in file
Initial Value	Any position in file
Current Overlay	Any position in file
Overlay Header	Before SYMBOL definition
Overlay Color	After overlay header
Visible Overlay	Follows associated overlay header
Symbol ID	Must follow SYMBOL
Text	Must follow SYMBOL
Polygon Points	Must follow SYMBOL
End of File	Must be last record

Table 31.2 Record position (version 1)

The position of any other records in the file is arbitrary. The structure for the version 2 formats (DRW, GRF) is shown below:

Record	Position
Beginning of File	Must be 1st record
Version	Must be 2nd record
Background Color	Any position in file
Font Name	Any position in file
Initial View	Any position in file
Current Overlay	Any position in file
Resolution	Any position in file
Dimension	Any position in file
Ruler	Any position in file
Grid Settings	Any position in file
Page	Any position in file
Font	Any position in file
Pattern	Any position in file
Color Flag	Any position in file
File Annotation	Any position in file
Comment	Any position in file

Table 31.3 Record position (version 2) (*continues over...*)

Record	Position
Overlay Header	Before SYMBOL definition
Overlay Color	After overlay header
Visible Overlay	Follows associated overlay header
Locked Overlay	Follows associated overlay header
Overlay Name	Follows associated overlay header
Symbol	Follows associated overlay header
Symbol ID	Must follow a SYMBOL record
Text	Must follow a SYMBOL record
Polygon Points	Must follow a SYMBOL record
Bitmap	Must follow a SYMBOL record
End of File	Must be the last record

Table 31.3 Record position (version 2) (*cont.*)

The position of the other records in the file is arbitrary. In DRW and GRF files, the following records, at least, must appear:

Background Color
Color Flag
Current Overlay
Resolution
Dimensions
Version
Beginning of File

Version 2 files may contain record types which are unknown in version 1 (for example, bitmap). There is also an upgraded variant of the SYMBOL data structure.

Compression processes may be used in version 2 files, in the data area. However, compression is used only for data records that have more than 2 identical bytes and the run-length method is used. A compressed data record always consists of 3 bytes and begins with the value `FFH` (Figure 31.2).

FFH	Len	Data

Figure 31.2 Data compression

The second byte defines a counter indicating how often the following (data) byte is to be duplicated. The sequence:

```
FFH 05H 47H
```

thus becomes the byte sequence:

```
47H 47H 47H 47H 47H
```

If an uncompressed data byte contains the value FFH, it will be compressed according to the above notation (FFH 01H FFH). Uncompressed data is stored consecutively and may have values between 00H and FEH. Record types between 96 and 160 (60H to A0H) always contain uncompressed data areas. Data compression is used with all other records if possible.

Micrografx offers a toolkit for creating version 2 files, ensuring that compatibility with Version 1 is maintained.

31.1 Graphic File Record Types

The following record types may appear in PIC, DRW and GRF files:

31.1.1 CHART_SKIP_SYMBOLS (type 44, 2CH)

This record type is generated only by Charisma and Graph Plus. It is structured as follows:

Bytes	Remarks
1	Type 44 (2CH)
2	Number of symbols

Table 31.4 CHART_SKIP_SYMBOLS record

The two bytes in the data area define how many of the symbols following directly after the data record should be skipped, before additional symbol information is loaded from the file.

31.1.2 DRW_BACKGROUND (type 1, 01H)

This record type specifies the background color defined at the time the graphic image was saved:

Bytes	Remarks
1	Type 1 (01H)
4	Background color (R,G,B,I)

Table 31.5 DRW_BACKGROUND record

The background color is defined as a 4 byte value containing the (packed) intensities of the colors red, green and blue. One byte is used for each color proportion and the fourth byte is either unused or used for the intensity.

31.1.3 DRW_BAND (type 32, 20H)

This record type defines a rectangular area containing a pattern (bitmap).

Bytes	Remarks
1	Type 32 (20H)
1	Index
16	Pattern

Table 31.6 DRW_BAND record

The index is a one-byte value and specifies the index number by which the following pattern can be addressed. Other records can then call up the pattern using this index.

The pattern itself is defined in a 16-byte field, as a bitmap. The bitmap is often duplicated in order to fill given areas.

31.1.4 DRW_BITMAP (type 20, 14H)

This record defines a bitmap image.

Bytes	Remarks
1	Type 20 (14H)
n	Bitmap data

Table 31.7 DRW_BITMAP record

In the data area, the bitmap for a symbol is stored as a byte sequence. No compression is used in this record type.

31.1.5 DRW_COLOR (type 9, 09H)

This record type defines the color of the objects.

Bytes	Remarks
1	Type 9 (09H)
3	Color of following objects

Table 31.8 DRW_COLOR record

An entry containing three bytes for the primary colors red, green and blue is stored in the data area. The value indicates the color of the objects belonging to the relevant overlay. The record must be present if the DRW_COLOR_FLAG is set.

31.1.6 DRW_COLOR_FLAG (type 10, 0AH)

This record type defines whether an object group uses one color only.

Bytes	Remarks
1	Type 10 (0AH)
1	Flag

Table 31.9 DRW_COLOR _FLAG record

The flag is interpreted as a logical variable. If the byte is not set to 0, all objects in the following overlay will be displayed in one color.

31.1.7 DRW_COLOR_TABLE (type 35, 23H)

This record type defines a color table.

Bytes	Remarks
1	Type 35 (23H)
4	Color table

Table 31.10 DRW_COLOR _TABLE record

The record contains a color table for the Virtual Bitmap Manager (VBM) and influences the last bitmap loaded.

31.1.8 DRW_COMMENT (type 18, 12H)

This record type defines a comment text.

Bytes	Remarks
1	Type 18 (12H)
n	Comment

Table 31.11 DRW_COMMENT record

In the data field, there is an ASCII string containing the comment text. The file may have an unlimited number of comments.

31.1.9 DRW_CURR_OVERLAY (type 16, 10H)

This record type defines the number of overlays currently used to save the data.

Bytes	Remarks
1	Type 16 (10H)
2	Number of overlays

Table 31.12 DRW_CURR_OVERLAY record

Only one such record may appear in the file. Permitted values are between 0 and 63.

31.1.10 DRW_DIMENSIONS (type 24, 18H)

This record type defines the format of the dimension used for storing the data.

Bytes	Remarks
1	Type 24 (18H)
1	Format

Table 31.13 DRW_DIMENSIONS record

31.1.11 DRW_EOF (type 254, FEH)

This record defines the end of a file.

Bytes	Remarks
1	Type 254 (FEH)

Table 31.14 DRW_EOF record

The record has no data area.

31.1.12 DRW_FACENAME (type 2, 02H)

This record type defines the names of the fonts used.

Bytes	Remarks
1	Type 2 (02H)
n	Font name

Table 31.15 DRW_FACE-NAME record

The data area contains an ASCII string of length LF_FACESIZE. (This constant is defined in the WINDOWS.H file.) The name is used to select a valid font. Several font records may appear in one record. They are indexed from 0 to *n* in sequence. Texts indicate the font required using the relevant index.

31.1.13 DRW_FONT (type 21, 15H)

This record type defines a logical font which is used by several objects:

Bytes	Remarks
1	Type 21 (15H)
1	Index
1	PitchAndFamily
n	FaceName [LF_Facesize]

Table 31.16 DRW_FONT record

The index number by which other objects can refer to the logical font is specified in the index. The following byte defines the size (pitch) and the font type (font family) coded as follows:

Bits 0–1:	00	Default Pitch
	01	Fixed Pitch
	10	Variable Pitch
Bits 4–7:	0000	Unknown
	0001	Roman
	0010	Swiss
	0011	Modern
	0100	Script
	0101	Decorative

Table 31.17 Font size and font type

This is followed by a text field containing the names of the relevant fonts. Using this definition, a logical font can be defined from the family of fonts available.

31.1.14 DRW_GRADIENT (type 30, 1EH)

This record type defines how the symbols are to be filled using the `fill` function.

Bytes	Remarks
1	Type 30 (`1EH`)
1	Index
1	Flags
1	xPercent
1	yPercent
2	Angle

Table 31.18 DRW_GRADIENT record

The fill function enables the surfaces of objects (circles, rectangles, and so on) to be filled or hatched. This record describes the means by which an object is filled. The `Index` field specifies the index of the relevant definition. Using this index, another object can subsequently activate the fill function with the hatching required.

The following fields define the parameters for the gradients of the fill function. The `Flags` field defines whether the hatching is to be linear or radial. The coding is as follows:

00	radial
01	linear
02	square

Table 31.19
Flag coding

The two parameters `xPercent` and `yPercent` define the point of origin in the bounding box object from which the hatching starts. The `xPercent` parameter is not used in linear gradient mode, because shifts can only be made parallel to the `Y axis`. The `Angle` field indicates the angle of rotation in linear gradient mode, expressed in $\frac{1}{10}$ degree.

31.1.15 DRW_GRID (type 22, 16H)

This record type defines a grid within the drawing.

Bytes	Remarks
1	Type 22 (16H)
2	Horizontal grid
2	Vertical grid

Table 31.20
DRW_GRID
record

The parameters define the number of gridlines per unit in the drawing. The units refer to the ruler, which can be superimposed onto the image.

31.1.16 DRW_ID (type 4, 04H)

This record type defines a text string which is ascribed to a symbol in a Micrografx drawing.

Bytes	Remarks
1	Type 4 (04H)
n	ASCII string

Table 31.21
DRW_ID record

31.1.17 DRW_INFO (type 19, 13H)

This record type defines an ASCII string, which is interpreted as a global description of the file.

Bytes	Remarks
1	Type 19 (13H)
n	ASCII string

Table 31.22 DRW_INFO record

The string is terminated with a null byte. Only one record may appear in the file.

31.1.18 DRW_LOCKED (type 29, 1DH)

This record type contains a logical value indicating whether the last specified Overlay Record is locked.

Bytes	Remarks
1	Type 29 (1DH)
1	Locked Flag

Table 31.23 DRW_LOCKED record

If the value is not 0, the relevant overlay will be locked. For every overlay described in the file, one such record may appear.

31.1.19 DRW_MAX_LINK_ID (type 37, 25H)

This record is reserved for Micrografx products.

31.1.20 DRW_OLD_GRID (type 15, 0FH)

This record defines the start values for the grid, the ruler and the page.

Bytes	Remarks
1	Type 15 (0FH)
1	GridPosted
1	PagesPosted
1	RulersPosted
1	RulerType
1	SnapTo
2	HGridSize
2	HPageSize
2	HSnapSize
2	RulerIncrement
2	RulerSize
2	VGridSize
2	VPageSize
2	VSnapSize

Table 31.24 DRW_OLD_GRID record

The entries define the settings. The following conditions apply:

GridPosted is used as a logical flag defining whether the grid is displayed or suppressed. The same applies to the PagesPosted and RulersPosted fields, which influence the page display and the ruler. The PageType field is not currently defined.

The RulerType field defines the unit (0 = inch, 1 = cm). SnapTo switches the Snap function on and off. HGridSize defines the space between horizontal gridlines in the image area, while HPageSize indicates the horizontal size of the page in logical coordinates. The same principle applies to the fields beginning with V (vertical). The RulerIncrement field specifies the size of the steps used in the ruler.

31.1.21 DRW_OVERLAY (type 5, 05H)

This record type defines an overlay area.

Bytes	Remarks
1	Type 5 (05H)
2	Overlay number
2	Number of symbols

Table 31.25 DRW_OVERLAY record

The first entry defines the number of the overlay. Overlays introduce a sequence of records, which define a number of elements to be combined. For this reason the second parameter indicates the number of linked elements. Combined symbols can be created with this record. Only one such record may be used to introduce each overlay.

31.1.22 DRW_OVERLAY_NAME (type 23, 17H)

This record type defines the name of an overlay area.

Bytes	Remarks
1	Type 23 (17H)
n	Overlay name

Table 31.26 DRW_OVERLAY_NAME record

The entry defines the name of the overlay introduced in the previous record.

31.1.23 DRW_PAGE (type 27, 1BH)

This record type defines the application-specific size of a page in logical coordinates.

Bytes	Remarks
1	Type 27 (1BH)
2	PageWidth
2	PageHeight
2	Left Margin
2	Top Margin
2	Right Margin
2	Bottom Margin

Table 31.27 DRW_PAGE record

The values for page size do not include the margins.

31.1.24 DRW_PATTERN (type 28, 1CH)

This record type defines a pattern which is to be displayed.

Bytes	Remarks
1	Type 28 (1CH)
1	Index
16	Bit pattern

Table 31.28 DRW_PATTERN record

The first field contains the index with which the pattern is addressed. The following 16 bytes specify the actual pattern.

31.1.25 DRW_POLYGON (type 6, 06H)

This record type defines a polygon which is to be displayed.

Bytes	Remarks
1	Type 6 (06H)
*n** 4	X/Y-coordinates for polygon points

Table 31.29 DRW_POLYGON record

The polygon is defined by a number of X/Y coordinates which are linked by lines. The coordinates relate to the relative position of the previous symbol. This record only follows symbol records for polygons and connected lines.

31.1.26 DRW_RESOLUTION (type 25, 19H)

This record type defines the resolution of the logical coordinates of a unit on the ruler.

Bytes	Remarks
1	Type 25 (19H)
2	Resolution

Table 31.30 DRW_RESOLUTION record

31.1.27 DRW_RULER (type 26, 1AH)

This record type defines the type and the scale gradations of the ruler.

Bytes	Remarks
1	Type 26 (1AH)
1	Metric (Boolean)
2	nHorzSubdivisions
2	nVertSubdivisions
2	Increment

Table 31.31 DRW_RULER record

The `metric` field signals whether the ruler scale is to be metric (true) or in inches (false).

The `Subdivision` fields indicate the gradation of the ruler in X and Y directions, in units. The `Increment` field defines the gradation for the main markers (1,2,3 or 2,4,6, and so on).

31.1.28 DRW_SYMBOL (type 7, 07H)

This record type defines a symbol (circle, line, and so on).

Bytes	Remarks
1	Type 7 (07H)
x	Record structure for the symbol type

Table 31.32 DRW_SYMBOL record

Five different versions of this record type have been defined:

Version	Product
1	Windows Draw, In*a*Vision
2	Windows Graph, Graph Plus
3	Designer 2.x
4	Designer 3.x, Charisma 2.0x
5	Charisma 2.1, Designer 3.1

Table 31.33 Versions of the SYMBOL record type

The structure of each version of the record is described separately.

31.1.28.1 Record structure of version 1

This version of the SYMBOL record only occurs in PIC files. Its structure is relatively simple:

Bytes	Name	Remarks
1	`Type`	Object type
1	`Flags`	Line type, fonts, and so on
4	`Pos`	Position in logical coordinates (X,Y)
8	`Box`	Bounding box object (X,Y,dX,dY)
2	`Angle`	Rotation in 0.1 degree (counterclockwise)
2	`XScale`	Additive X-scaling
2	`YScale`	Additive Y-scaling
4	`Color`	Line, text, border color
2	`Handle`	Reserved
4	`Next`	Reserved (next symbol in list)
4	`Prev`	Reserved (previous symbol in list)
		Arc and pie slice
1	`Pattern`	Fill pattern
4	`FColor`	Fill color
4	`Start`	Start coordinates (X,Y)
4	`End`	End coordinates (X,Y)
8	`Frame`	Bounding box object
4	`Endp`	End point if single line (X,Y)
		Rectangle and ellipse
1	`Pattern`	Fill pattern
4	`FColor`	Fill color
8	`Frame`	Bounding box object

Table 31.34 Structure of a SYMBOL record type 1

The field for the type of symbol is coded as follows:

Code	Remarks
0	Elliptical arc
22	Monochrome bitmap
13	Closed ellipse, fillable
27	Clip path, single instance, closed

Table 31.35 Symbol types (*continues over...*)

Graphics

Code	Remarks
14	Elliptical arc, clockwise
24	Closed Bezier curve, fillable
15	Closed parabola, fillable
1	Closed polygon, fillable
16	Closed quadratic spline, fillable
17	Closed complex object, fillable
2	Collection of objects
29	Formatted text fitted along a curve
3	Circle, ellipse
5	Line with scalable text
6	Single line element
23	Open, not fillable Bezier curve
18	Parabola
20	Open, non-fillable complex polygon
8	Open, non-fillable simple polygon
19	Quadratic spline
9	Pie wedge
10	Rectangle
11	Rectangle with rounded corners
25	Rich text block
28	Closed clip path (tiled)
26	Virtual bitmap

Table 31.35
Symbol types (*cont.*)

The `Flag` field contains information on the object. The lower 4 bits define the line form or the font for the object. If bit 4 of the lower bits is set, the `winding fill` mode will be used; otherwise, the `alternate odd-even` mode will be used. For an object consisting of lines, the following applies to the lines:

Code	Style
00H	Solid
01H	Dashed
02H	Dotted
03H	Dash dotted
04H	Dash dot dash
05H	Invisible

Table 31.36
Line styles

With text objects, the lower 4 bits are logically linked with logical `OR`. They are coded as follows:

Bit	0:	Bold
	1:	Italic
	2:	Strikeout
	3:	Underline

Table 31.37
Text format

The mask for the 4 upper bits defines the following modes:

Bit	4:	No rotate
	5:	Proportional stretch
	6:	Static ID
	7:	Opaque

Table 31.38
Coding upper four bits

`Pos` contains the position of the logical coordinates (X,Y) for the relevant object. If the object is a component of a composed object, the coordinates are given in relative terms.

`Box` is the definition of the rectangle (X,Y,deltaX,deltaY) which can be drawn around the object. `Angle` defines the rotation of an object in 1/10 degree, counterclockwise.

`XScale` and `YScale` are used only with stretch in order to maintain the original size of the bounding box. `Color` is a 4-byte value, containing the color definition (RGB) of the original.

31.1.28.2 Record Structure of Version 2

This version of the SYMBOL record appears in DRW and GRF files. The structure is as follows:

Bytes	Name	Remarks
1	`Type`	Object type
1	`Flags`	Line type, fonts etc.
4	`Pos`	Position in logical coordinates (x,y)
8	`Box`	Bounding box object (X,Y,dX,dY)
2	`Angle`	Rotation in 0.1 degree counterclockwise

Table 31.39
Structure of a SYMBOL record type 2
(*continues over...*)

Bytes	Name	Remarks
2	XScale	Additive X-scale
2	YScale	Additive Y-scale
4	Color	Line, text, border color
2	Handle	Reserved
4	Next	Reserved (next symbol in list)
4	Prev	Reserved (previous Symbol in List)
		Arc, chord, pie
1	Pattern	Fill pattern
4	FColor	Fill color
4	Start	Start coordinates (X,Y)
4	End	End coordinates (X,Y)
8	Frame	Bounding box object
		Bitmap
2	HBitmap	Reserved
8	Rect	Clipping region
2	BitPxl	Bits per pixel
2	BytesL	Bytes per scanline
2	Planes	Number of color planes
2	Height	Bitmap height (in lines)
2	Width	Bitmap width (in pixels)
		Composed object
6	List	Symbol list
1	Flags	Reserved
8	Rect	Contracted bounding box
4	—	Reserved
2	Handle	Reserved
		Line segment
4	End	End point line
4	Start	Start point
1	Format	Line thickness
2	Increm	Increment
		Single line of text
2	Handle	Reserved
1	Font	Font index
2	Count	Character count
2	Height	Font height in logical units
2	Width	Font height in logical units
2	ESC	Escapement in 1/10 degrees (counterclockwise)
2	X	X-axis alignment

Table 31.39 Structure of a SYMBOL record type 2 (*cont.*)

Graphics

Bytes	Name	Remarks
2	Y	Y-axis alignment
	Space	Inter-character spacing (in logical units)
1	Align	Alignment horizontal and vertical
		Open or closed parabola
1	Pattern	Fill pattern
4	FColor	Fill color (RGB)
4	Start	Start point (X,Y)
4	Mid	Center point (X,Y)
4	End	End point (X,Y)
		Open or closed path
1	Pattern	Fill pattern
4	FColor	Fill color (RGB)
n	List	Symbol list
		Open or closed polygon or spline
1	Pattern	Fill pattern
4	FColor	Fill color (RGB)
2	Handle	Reserved
2	nPoints	Number of points (unsigned)
		Rectangle and ellipse
1	Pattern	Fill pattern
4	FColor	Fill color
8	Frame	Bounding box object
2	Round	Radius in logical coordinates for rounding
		Rich Text block
2	hBlock	Reserved
2	ESC	Escapement 0.1 degree counter-clockwise
2	x	x alignment point
2	y	y alignment point
1	AFlags	Application flags
4	BColor	Background color
2	Penw	Pen width
1	Style	Style line ends
1	Rad	Radius line end
4	Rotpt	Pivot point for symbol rotation (X,Y)
2	Penh	Pen height
2	Pena	Pen angle 0.1 degree (counterclockwise)
1	LineSt	Line type
8	Border	Bounding box (bordered)

Table 31.39 Structure of a SYMBOL record type 2 (*cont.*)

The same explanations apply as for version 1.

31.1.28.3 Record structure of version 3

This verion of the SYMBOL record appears in DRW and GRF files.

Bytes	Name	Remarks
1	Type	Object type
1	Flags	Line type, fonts and so on
4	Pos	Position in logical coordinates (X,Y)
8	Box	Bounding box object (X,Y,dX,dY)
2	Angle	Rotation in 0.1 degree (counterclockwise)
2	XScale	Additive X-scale
2	YScale	Additive Y-scale
4	Color	Line, text, border color
2	Handle	Reserved
4	Next	Reserved (next symbol in list)
4	Prev	Reserved (previous symbol in list)
		Arc, chord, pie
1	Pattern	Fill pattern
4	FColor	Fill color
4	Start	Start coordinates (X,Y)
4	End	End coordinates (X,Y)
8	Frame	Bounding box object
		Bitmap
2	HBitmap	Reserved
4	Rect	Clipping region
2	BitPxl	Bits per pixel
2	BytesL	Bytes per scanline
2	Planes	Number of color planes
2	Height	Bitmap height in lines
2	Width	Bitmap width in pixels
		Composed object
6	List	Symbol list
1	Flags	Reserved
8	Rect	Contracted bounding box
4	—	Reserved
2	Handle	Reserved

Table 31.40 Structure of a SYMBOL record type 3 *(continues over...)*

Bytes	Name	Remarks
		Single line of text
2	Handle	Reserved
1	Font	Font index
2	Count	Character count
2	Height	Font height in logical units
2	Width	Font width in logical units
2	ESC	Escapement in 1/10 degree (counterclockwise)
2	X	X-axis alignment
2	Y	Y-axis alignment
2	Space	Inter-character spacing
1	Align	Alignment (horizontal, vertical)
		Line segment
4	End	End point line
4	Start	Start point line
1	Format	Line thickness
2	Increm	Increment
		Open or closed parabola
1	Pattern	Fill pattern
4	FColor	Fill color (RGB)
4	Start	Start point (X,Y)
4	Mid	Center point (X,Y)
4	End	End point (X,Y)
		Open or closed path
1	Pattern	Fill pattern
4	FColor	Fill color (RGB)
n	List	Symbol list
		Open or closed polygon or spline
1	Pattern	Fill pattern
4	FColor	Fill color (RGB)
2	Handle	Reserved
2	nPoints	Number of points
		Rectangle and ellipse
1	Pattern	Fill pattern
4	FColor	Fill color
8	Frame	Bounding box object
2	Round	Radius rounding rectangle
1	AFlags	Application flags
4	BColor	Background color

Table 31.40 Structure of a SYMBOL record type 3 (*cont.*)

Bytes	Name	Remarks
2	Penw	Penwidth
1	Style	Style line ends
1	Rad	Radius rounded lines ends
4	Rotpt	Pivot point for symbol rotation (X,Y)

Table 31.40 Structure of a SYMBOL record type 3 (*cont.*)

The same explanations apply as for version 1.

31.1.28.4 Record structure of version 4

This version of the SYMBOL record appears in DRW and GRF files. The structure is as follows:

Bytes	Name	Remarks
1	Type	Object type
1	Flags	Line type, fonts and so on
4	Pos	Position in logical coordinates (X,Y)
8	Box	Bounding box object (X,Y,dX,dY)
2	Angle	Rotation in 0.1 degree (counterclockwise)
2	XScale	Additive X-scale
2	YScale	Additive Y-scale
4	Color	Line, text, border color
2	Handle	Reserved
4	Next	Reserved (next symbol in list)
4	Prev	Reserved (previous symbol in list)
		Arc, chord, pie
1	Pattern	Fill pattern
4	FColor	Fill color
4	Start	Start coordinates (X,Y)
4	End	End coordinates (X,Y)
8	Frame	Bounding box object
		Bitmap
2	HBitmap	Reserved

Table 31.41 Structure of a SYMBOL record Type 4 (*continues over...*)

Graphics

Bytes	Name	Remarks
8	`Rect`	Clipping region
2	`BitPxl`	Bits per pixel
2	`BytesL`	Bytes per scanline
2	`Planes`	Number of color planes
2	`Height`	Bitmap height in lines
2	`Width`	Bitmap width in pixel
		Composed object
6	`List`	Symbol list
1	`Flags`	Reserved
8	`Rect`	Contracted bounding box
4	—	Reserved
2	`Handle`	Reserved
		Single line of text
2	`Handle`	Reserved
1	`Font`	Font index
2	`Count`	Character count
2	`Height`	Font height in logical units
2	`Width`	Font width in logical units
2	`ESC`	Escapement in 1/10 degree (counterclockwise)
2	`X`	X-axis alignment
2	`Y`	Y-axis alignment
2	`Space`	Inter-character spacing
1	`Align`	Alignment (horizontal, vertical)
		Line segment
4	`End`	End point line
4	`Start`	Start point
1	`Format`	Line thickness
2	`Increm`	Increment
		Open or closed parabola
1	`Pattern`	Fill pattern
4	`FColor`	Fill color (RGB)
4	`Start`	Start point (X,Y)
4	`Mid`	Center point (X,Y)
4	`End`	End point (X,Y)
		Open or closed path
1	`Pattern`	Fill pattern
4	`FColor`	Fill color (RGB)

Table 31.41
Structure of a SYMBOL record Type 4 (*cont.*)

Graphics

Bytes	Name	Remarks
n	`List`	Symbol list
n	`Fsymb`	Fill symbol
		Open or closed polygon or spline
1	`Pattern`	Fill pattern
4	`FColor`	Fill color (RGB)
2	`Handle`	Reserved
2	`nPoints`	Number of points
		Rectangle and ellipse
1	`Pattern`	Fill pattern
4	`FColor`	Fill color
8	`Frame`	Bounding box object
2	`Round`	Radius rounded rectangle
		Rich Text block
2	`hBlock`	Reserved
2	`ESC`	Escapement in 0.1 degree
2	`x`	X alignment point
2	`y`	Y alignment point
1	`AFlags`	Application flags
4	`BColor`	Background color
2	`Penw`	Pen width
1	`Style`	Style line ends
1	`Rad`	End radius
4	`Rotpt`	Pivot point for symbol rotation (X,Y)
2	`Penh`	Pen height
2	`Pena`	Pen angle 0.1 degree (counter clockwise)
1	`LineSt`	Line style
8	`Border`	Bounding box (bordered)

Table 31.41 Structure of a SYMBOL record Type 4 (*cont.*)

The same explanations apply as for version 1.

31.1.28.5 Record structure of version 5

This version of the SYMBOL record appears in DRW and GRF files. The structure is as follows:

Bytes	Name	Remarks
1	Type	Object type
1	Flags	Line type, fonts and so on
4	Pos	Position in logical coordinates (X,Y)
8	Box	Bounding box object (X,Y,dX,dY)
2	Angle	Rotation in 0.1 degree (counterclockwise)
2	XScale	Additive X-scale
2	YScale	Additive Y-scale
4	Color	Line, text, border color
2	Handle	Reserved
4	Next	Reserved (next symbol in list)
4	Prev	Reserved (previous symbol in list)
		Arc, chord, pie
1	Pattern	Fill pattern
4	FColor	Fill color
4	Start	Start coordinates (X,Y)
4	End	End coordinates (X,Y)
8	Frame	Bounding box object
		Bitmap
2	HBitmap	Reserved
8	Rect	Clipping region
2	BitPxl	Bits per pixel
2	BytesL	Bytes per scanline
2	Planes	Number of color planes
2	Height	Bitmap height in lines
2	Width	Bitmap width in pixels
		Composed object
6	List	Symbol list
1	Flags	Reserved
8	Rect	Contracted bounding box
4	—	Reserved
2	Handle	Reserved
		Single line of text
2	Handle	Reserved
1	Font	Font index
2	Count	Character count
2	Height	Font height in logical units
2	Width	Font width in logical units
2	ESC	Escapement in 1/10 degree (counterclockwise)

Table 31.42 Structure of a SYMBOL record type 5 (*continues over...*)

Bytes	Name	Remarks
2	`X`	X-axis alignment
2	`Y`	Y-axis alignment
2	`Space`	Inter-character spacing
1	`Align`	Alignment (horizontal, vertical)
		Line segment
4	`End`	End point line
4	`Start`	Start point
1	`Format`	Line thickness
2	`Increm`	Increment
		Open or closed parabola
1	`Pattern`	Fill pattern
4	`FColor`	Fill color (RGB)
4	`Start`	Start point (X,Y)
4	`Mid`	Center point (X,Y)
4	`End`	End point (X,Y)
		Open or closed path
1	`Pattern`	Fill pattern
4	`FColor`	Fill color (RGB)
n	`List`	Symbol list
n	`Fsymb`	Fill symbol
		Open or closed polygon or spline
1	`Pattern`	Fill pattern
4	`FColor`	Fill color (RGB)
2	`Handle`	Reserved
2	`nPoints`	Number of points
		Rectangle and ellipse
1	`Pattern`	Fill pattern
4	`FColor`	Fill color
8	`Frame`	Bounding box object
2	`Round`	Radius rounded rectangle
		Rich Text block
2	`hBlock`	Reserved
2	`ESC`	Escapement in 0.1 degree
2	`x`	x alignment point
2	`y`	y alignment point
2	`Flags`	Reserved
2	`Handle`	Reserved
2	`nPoints`	Reserved

Table 31.42 Structure of a SYMBOL record type 5 (*cont.*)

Graphics

Bytes	Name	Remarks
1	AFlags	Application flags
4	BColor	Background color
2	Penw	Pen width
1	Style	Style line ends
1	Rad	End radius
4	Rotpt	Pivot point for symbol rotation (X,Y)
2	Penh	Pen height
2	Pena	Pen angle 0.1 degree (counter clockwise)
1	LineSt	Line style
8	Border	Bounding box (bordered)

Table 31.42 Structure of a SYMBOL record type 5 (*cont.*)

The same explanations apply as for version 1. Handles are used by Graph Plus, and the length is 2 bytes. Versions 1 to 4 are subsets of version 5. Patterns within an object are displayed according to the following codes:

Code	Pattern
C0H	Hatch
80H	Pattern
40H	Solid
00H	Unfilled

Table 31.43 Pattern codes

The hatching for a pattern is coded as follows:

Code	Hatch
00H	Horizontal
01H	Vertical
02H	Forward diagonal
03H	Backward diagonal
04H	Vertical-horizontal
05H	Diagonal crossed

Table 31.44 Hatch codes

The form of a line cap is coded as follows:

Code	Line cap
0	Rounded
1	Flat
2	Square

Table 31.45
Line cap codes

The form of line joins is coded as follows:

Code	Line join
0	Rounded
1	Beveled
2	Mitre

Table 31.46
Line join codes

31.1.29 DRW_SYMBOLVERSION (type 33, 21H)

This record type defines the version number used by the symbol definition.

Bytes	Remarks
1	Type 33 (21H)
2	Version number = 5

Table 31.47
DRW_
SYMBOL
VERSION
record

Only version number 5 is currently used.

31.1.30 DRW_TEXT (type 8, 08H)

This record type defines a text which is linked with the preceding symbol.

Bytes	Remarks
1	Type 8 (`08H`)
n	String

Table 31.48 DRW_TEXT record

31.1.31 DRW_TEXTEXTRA (type 36, 24H)

This record type is reserved for Micrografx.

31.1.32 DRW_TEXTHDR (type 31, 1FH)

This record defines a header for an S_TEXT symbol in the preceding DRW_SYMBOL record.

Bytes	Remarks
1	Type 31 (`1FH`)
1	Version
1	Vertical alignment
2	MemFlags
2	ESCAPE
x	DefFont
2	Number of parameters
x	Text parameter block

Table 31.49 DRW_TEXTHDR record

The `Version` field defines the version of the text. The vertical alignment is defined as follows:

Code	Vertical alignment
0	Top align
4	Middle align
8	Bottom align
16	Justify align

Table 31.50 Vertical alignment

The **MemFlags** field relates to the allocation of the text block. The **ESCAPE** field defines the escapement, in 1/10 degree, with which the text is to be displayed. The **DefFont** field contains a data structure defining the text fonts required. The structure contains the following entries:

Bytes	Remarks
1	Font index
1	Style
2	Font width
2	Font height

Table 31.51
Font description structure

The width and height of the font is in logical units and are stored as integers. The number of parameters refers to the number of paragraphs in the following field. The last entry is another data structure containing the text parameter block. This is structured as shown below:

Bytes	Remarks
2	Left margin
2	Right margin
2	Indent
1	Horizontal alignment
2	Extra leading
2	Maximum leading
2	Maximum ascending
2	Maximum height
8	Bounding box paragraph
2	Handle
2	Size (unsigned) *nBytes* of data record addressed by handle
2	Space before (short integer)
2	UserData (word)
2	Byte space after (short)
4	Paragraph offset relative to block origin

Table 31.52
Text parameter block data structure

The **Handle** field contains the address in memory at which the data records containing text are stored. The parameter **nBytes** indicates the size of this data area in bytes. The following fields define the formatting of the text. The last entry indicates the offset of the paragraph from the beginning of the block origin.

31.1.33 DRW_TEXTPARA (type 34, 22H)

This record defines a text parameter block, as described in the previous record (*see above*).

Bytes	Remarks
1	Type 34 (22H)
x	Parameter block

Table 31.53 DRW_TEXPARA record

31.1.34 DRW_VERSION (type 3, 03H)

This record defines various version numbers within the file.

Bytes	Remarks
1	Type 3 (03H)
2	Revision
1	Version
1	Application

Table 31.54 DRW_VERSION record

The first field `Revision` requires 2 bytes and contains the revision number of the application that created this file. The following byte defines the version number of the file, coded as follows:

1 In*a*Vision, Windows Draw, Graph
2 Charisma, Designer

The last byte contains an application-specific code:

0 = In*a*Vision, Windows Draw
1 = Windows Graph, Graph Plus, Charisma
2 = Designer

In the case of files with version number 1, the revision level is always set to 6 and the last byte to 0.

31.1.35 DRW_VIEW (type 14, 0EH)

This record defines the initialization values for the image origin and dimensions.

Bytes	Remarks
1	Type 14 (0EH)
4	WindowOrg
4	WindowExt

Table 31.55 DRW_VIEW record

The 4-byte field `WindowsOrg` defines the origin of the visible window (X,Y) in logical coordinates. The value corresponds to the setting at which the file was created. The X coordinate is stored in the lower word of the field.

In the following 4-byte field, the dimensions of the X and Y axes in logical coordinates are stored. The value for the X axis is always in the lower word.

31.1.36 DRW_VISIBLE (type 17, 11H)

This record contains a Boolean value indicating whether an overlay is to be visible.

Bytes	Remarks
1	Type 17 (11H)
1	Visible

Table 31.56 DRW_VISIBLE record

One VISIBLE record must be defined for every overlay record.

31.1.37 VERSION_REC (type 255, FFH)

This record marks the beginning of a file.

Bytes	Remark
1	Type 255 (FFH)
1	File version

Table 31.57 VERSION_REC record

The file version is coded as follows:

1 In*a*Vision, Windows Draw
2 Charisma, Designer, Windows Graph
Graph Plus, Draw Plus

This record may appear only once in the file.

References

1 Further information can be obtained from the Micrografx Developers Toolkits.

32

TARGA format (TGA)

The TARGA format was developed by TrueVision to enable the storage of True Color Images. Since the initial development of TARGA, a number of variants supporting different modes (monochrome, 256 colors, 24 bit, and so on) have appeared on the market.

All TARGA files contain a header followed by the image data, as shown in Figure 32.1.

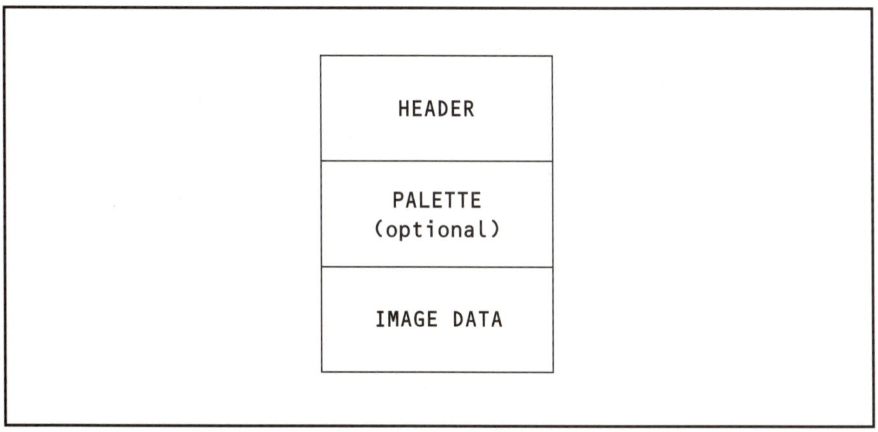

Figure 32.1 Structure of a TGA file

In the case of color map images (for example, pictures of 256 colors), the header may contain an optional color map. The pixels for 24-bit images are stored directly in the color required and the color map is therefore not needed. The header is followed by the area containing the image data, which may be either uncompressed or compressed using a range of compression processes.

32.1 TARGA header

The TARGA header has a fixed structure. It contains all the information necessary for evaluating an image file (for example, coding, image type, dimensions). However, there is no compulsory signature in the header of a TARGA file. Figure 32.2 shows a hex dump of part of a TARGA file.

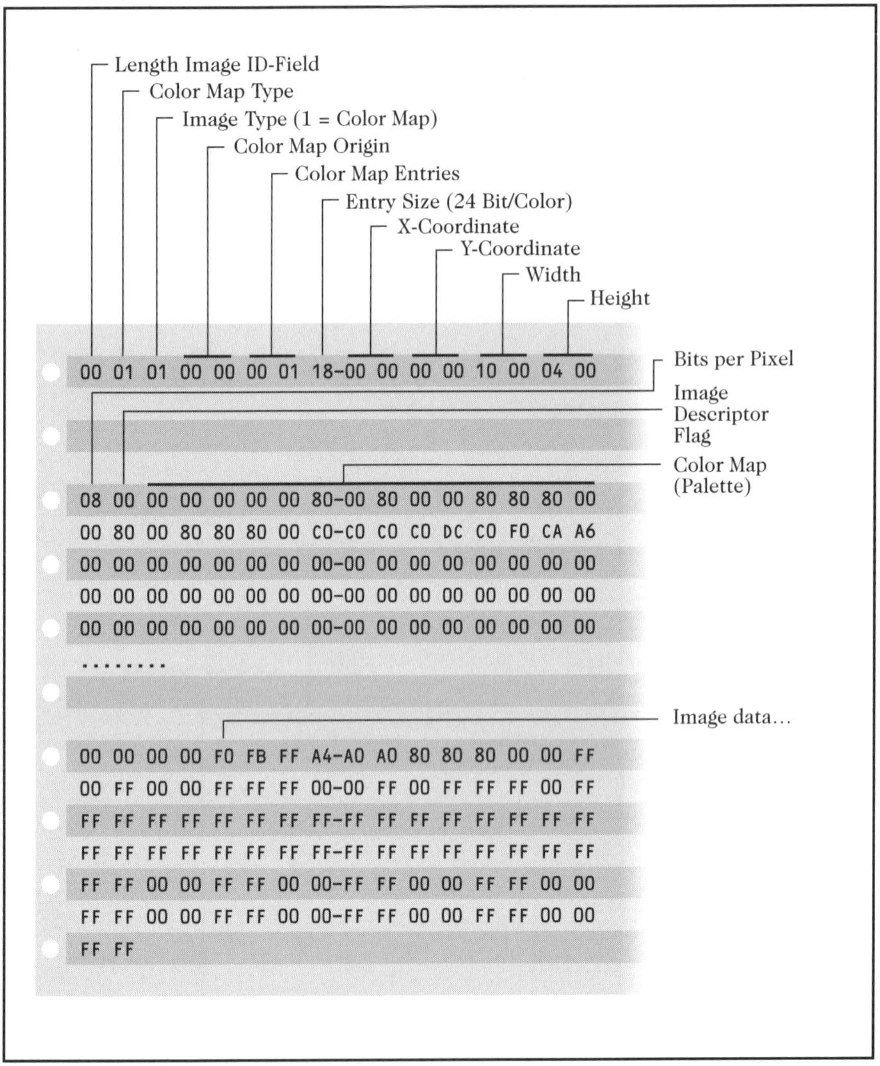

Figure 32.2 Hex dump of a TARGA file

TARGA format allows for various image types and coding variants. The individual fields are described below.

32.1.1 Color map images (type 1, 9, 32 and 33)

Color map images are color pictures in which a color index is stored for each individual pixel. The actual color is stored in a color map table. (This principle is used in other bitmap formats, such as PCX and TIFF.) The advantage of this form of storage is that the image data is significantly reduced, since only an index to the color table is required. The type of image is stored at offset `03H` in the header (`see` Table 32.1) are available. Various depths of color and methods of compression are available.

32.1.2 RGB images (type 2, 10)

With RGB images, 24 bits per pixel are stored in the file. This allows 8 bits for each color intensity and up to 16 million colors in the image. The process does not require a color map. Because of the range of colors available, 24-bit images are also described as true color images.

As well as the TARGA 24 files, there is the TARGA 32 format, in which 32 bits are stored for each pixel. Only the three lower bytes are used for coding the color. The upper byte contains attributes and the type of compression (type 2 = uncompressed, type 10 = RLE compression).

32.1.3 Monochrome images (type 3, 11)

Only two colors are required for black and white images, making the color map unnecessary. Pixels are stored sequentially in the file. Type 3 images are stored uncompressed, while type 11 uses RLE compression.

32.1.4 Structure of the header

Table 32.1 shows the structure of the header for all TARGA files. It should be noted that all data is stored in Intel format, that is, the lower value byte is stored at the lower address (low byte first).

Offset	Bytes	Remarks
00H	1	Length of image identification field, 0 to 255 bytes, 0 = no ID field
01H	1	Color map type 0 no color map 1 color map included

Table 32.1 Structure of a TGA header (*continues over...*)

Graphics

Offset	Bytes	Remarks
02H	1	TARGA image type 0: no image data in file 1: color map image, uncompressed 2: RGB image (24 bit), uncompressed 3: Monochrome image, uncompressed 9: Color map image, RLE-encoding 10: RGB image (24 bit), RLE encoding 11: Monochrome image, RLE encoding 32: Color map image with Huffman, Delta and RLE compression 33: Color map image with Huffman, Delta and RLE compression (4 Pass Quad Tree)
03H	2	Color map origin (integer)
05H	2	Color map length (integer)
07H	1	Color map entry size (16, 24, 32)
08H	2	X-coordinate origin
0AH	2	Y-coordinate origin
0CH	2	Image width in pixels
0EH	2	Image height in pixel
10H	1	Bits per pixel (1, 8, 24)
11H	1	Image descriptor byte
12H	*n*	Image identification field (optional)
..H	*n*	Color map (optional)

Table 32.1 Structure of a TGA header (*cont.*)

At offset 0 there is one byte indicating the length of the *Image Identification* Field. This field is optional and contains manufacturer-specific information. It begins at offset 12H. If the first byte is 0, the identification field is omitted and the color map begins at offset 12H.

The second byte indicates whether the file contains a color map. If it is 0, there is no color map. This normally applies to all RGB files (TARGA 24), but there are some programs that have a color map with an entry for the border color for RGB images. The entry in this field should be skipped for RGB images. If the second byte contains 1, there is a color map in the header. This applies to all color map images.

Since there are various types of TARBA file, the header also contains one byte indicating the type. This byte is always at offset 02H and is coded as shown in Table 32.1. The format descriptions for file types 1, 2, 3, 9, 10, and 11 are given below. Documentation on the remaining file types, especially regarding compression, was not available at the time of writing. At offset 03H, there are 5 bytes containing the specifications of the color map. The map itself follows the *Image Identification* Field. The word at offset 03H defines an index to the first valid entry in the color map. If there is a complete color map, the value of the field is set to 0. There is generally a complete color map, in which case, the value of the field is set to 0. At offset 05H, the length of the color map is stored, in terms of the number of entries (00H 01H = 100H = 256 entries). The byte at offset 07H defines the number of bits per pixel; 16 bits are defined for TARGA 16 files, 24 for TARGA 24 files and 32 for TARGA 32 files.

The image coordinates and dimensions are defined in a 10-byte field at offset 08H. Two byte values are interpreted as integer numbers. The X-coordinates for the origin of the image are stored at offset 08H and the Y-coordinates at offset 0AH. The alignment of the image (origin top left or bottom left) is specified in the flag at offset 11H. The image width in pixels is defined at offset 0CH, and the image height in pixels at offset 0EH.

The number of color planes (bits per pixel) is defined in the byte at offset 10H. Possible values are 1 (monochrome), 8 (256 colors) and 24 (16 million colors). In the case of 24-bit files, the image is a True Color picture, and the color map is omitted. There are also TARGA images in which the image data is written using 32 bits. The resolution of each pixel, however, is fixed at 24 bits. The remaining bits are used for attributes (alpha or transparency information).

The *Image Descriptor* Flag at offset 11H indicates whether attribute bits are used for the image data. Bits 4 and 5 define the position of the origin (bit 4 left, right, bit 5 top, bottom). Originally bit 4 was marked as reserved, so that the origin was positioned at bottom left or top left via bit 5. Bits 6 and 7 define the interleaving of individual image lines. Figure 32.3 shows the coding of the *Image Descriptor* Flag.

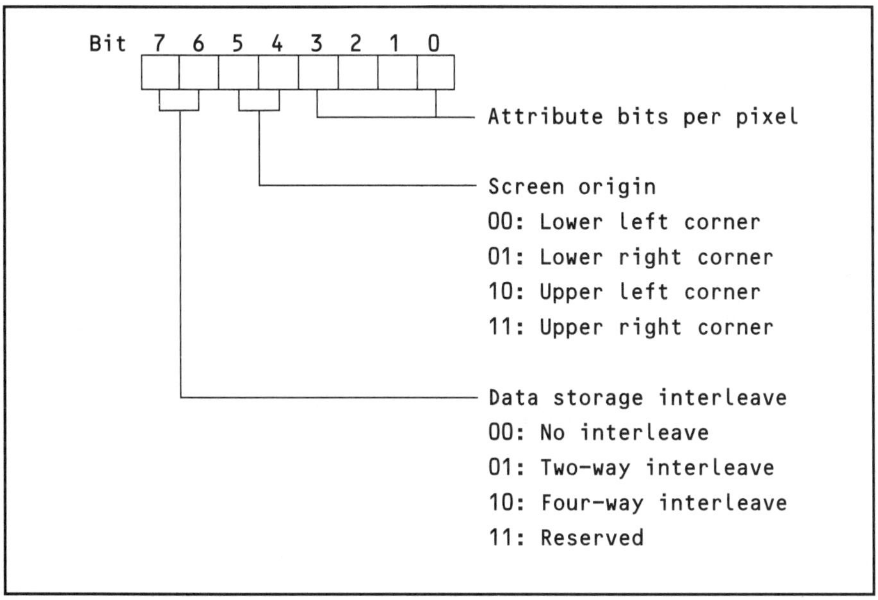

Figure 32.3 Coding of the Image Descriptor Flag

The value for the attribute bits in TARGA 16 files is set to 0 or 1. For TARGA 24 files, these bits should be set to 0, and for TARGA 32 files, 8 attribute bits are provided per pixel. The *Screen Origin* bit must be set to 0 for TrueVision images (origin in bottom left corner). For type 1 images, the whole *Image Descriptor* Flag should be set to 0.

An *Image Identification* Field may be stored at offset 12H. This field may contain up to 255 bytes and is used for manufacturer-specific information. The length of the field is indicated in the byte at offset 00H. If this byte contains the value 0, the *Image Identification* Field is omitted. If more than 255 bytes are required for this information, it may be stored after the image data. This happens, for example, with TARGA images processed using Image Alchemy.

32.1.5 Color map data

The optional table containing color map data may follow the image identification field (or be stored at offset `12H` if this field is omitted). If the color map type (offset `01H`) is set to `0`, the color map is not present. If the type is set to `1`, the position of the color map can be calculated, as follows:

Length of image identification field = `12H`

The number of entries in the color map table is stored at offset `05H`. The word at offset `03H` indicates the color value at which the color map begins. A value of `0` (default) means that the first entry in the color map is valid. The length of a table entry in bytes is stored at offset `07H` and may be 16, 24 or 32 bits. If an entry contains 32 bits, the first three bytes specify color data in the sequence blue, green, red. The fourth byte contains an attribute. Three-byte entries contain the color intensities (blue, green, red) with each color occupying one byte. With 16 bits, the colour information is coded as follows:

```
A RRRRR GGGGG BBBBB
```

The letters represent `A` = attribute, `R` = red, `G`, = green and `B` = blue. In all color map entries, surplus bits up to the byte limit are treated as attribute bytes.

32.2 The structure of the image data area

The color map is followed by the image data area. The start of this area can be calculated as follows:

`12H` = Length of image identification field + Length of color map

The image area contains the pixel data for an image of width * height. There are various depths of color (monochrome, 256 colors, 32767 colors, 16 million colors). In addition, image data can be stored either uncompressed or using various compression processes (see Table 32.1).

32.2.1 Uncompressed monochrome images (type 3)

Some programs permit the storage of uncompressed monochrome images. Figure 32.4 shows a hex dump of a 16 × 16 pixel monochrome image.

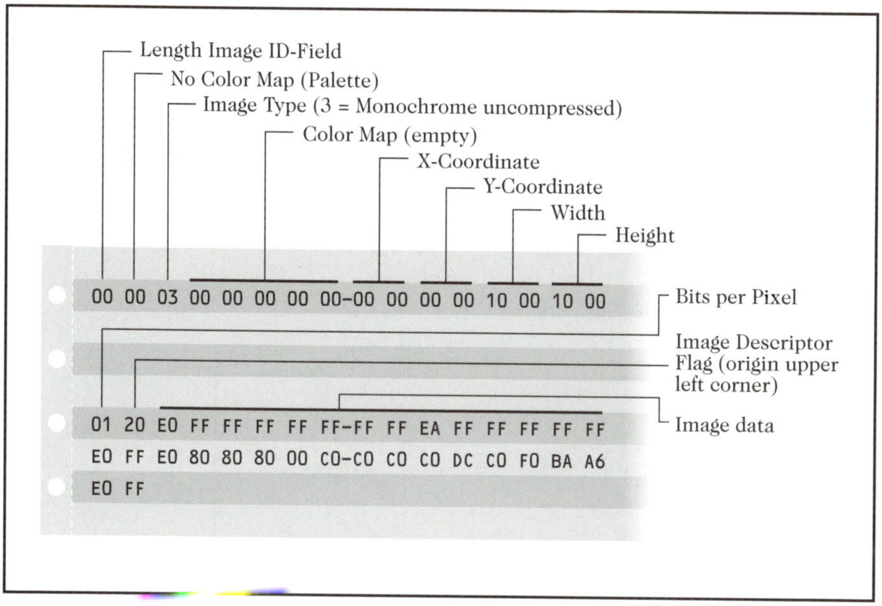

Figure 32.4 Hex dump of a 16 × 16 monochrome image (uncompressed)

An image of 16 × 16 pixels contains 256 pixels. The header indicates that only one bit is used per pixel. Eight pixels can therefore be stored in one byte, and the data area only requires 32 bytes.

32.2.2 Uncompressed color map images (type 1)

In the case of uncompressed color map images, *n* bits per pixel are stored. Each entry acts as an index to the color map, and the graphics card is responsible for the conversion. Figure 32.2 shows the structure of this kind of image file. The image data is stored as one byte per pixel.

It is interesting to note that although 256 entries are provided for the color map, only the first 16 entries have been given color values. The remaining values are initialized to `0` (black).

32.2.3 Uncompressed RGB images (type 2)

The image data in this case is also stored in a very simple way. The number of bits per pixel (16, 24, 32) is given in the header. With 16 bits per pixel, only 32767 colors can be represented. The image data is coded as follows:

```
A RRRRR GGGGG BBBBB
```

where `A` = attribute, `R` = red, `G` = green, `B` = blue. This means that 5 bits are available for each color (32767 colors).

With 24 bits per pixel, there are 8 bits for each color plane in the sequence red, green, blue, which allows for 16 million different colors (True Color representation). With 32 bits per pixel, the colors are coded three bytes in the sequence red, green, blue. The fourth byte contains an attribute (alpha and transparency information).

32.2.4 RLE-compressed color map images (type 9)

In order to save space, the TARGA format recognizes various compression processes. Only the frequently used RLE process will be described below (File Type 9).

Image data is compressed into records and coded as shown in Figure 32.5:

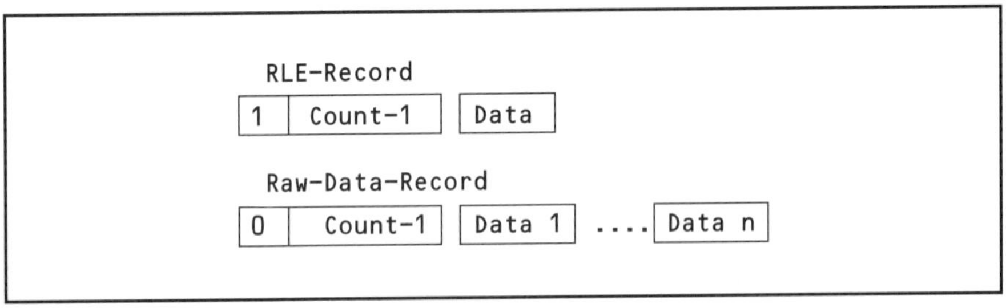

Figure 32.5 Record format for RLE coding

Each record comprises a header byte, followed by one or more data bytes. If the top bit of the header is set (1), the record is an RLE record in which several identical image data items have been compressed. The remaining 7 bits of the header byte contain a counter indicating the number of repetitions – 1. Repetition factors between 1 and 128 are possible using these 7 bits. The following byte contains the bit pattern to be copied. The hexadecimal sequence:

```
82H 02H
```

is thus expanded to:

```
02H 02H 02H
```

(82H = 3 repetitions). It should be noted that the image data of an expanded RLE record may extend beyond the current image line into the following line.

If image data bytes cannot be compressed, they should be stored in what is known as RAW format. In this case, the top bit of the header is set to 0. The remaining 7 bits contain a counter (n) indicating the number of following pixels – 1. The header is then followed by $n + 1$ pixels containing uncompressed data. Since each pixel corresponds to a byte, with 8 bits per pixel, the number of following pixels is the same as the number of following bytes. This data may also extend beyond the current image line.

The sequence:

```
8FH 0FH 07H 0FH 00H 0FH 0AH 0FH 09H 0FH 0CH 87H 0FH
```

is expanded as follows:

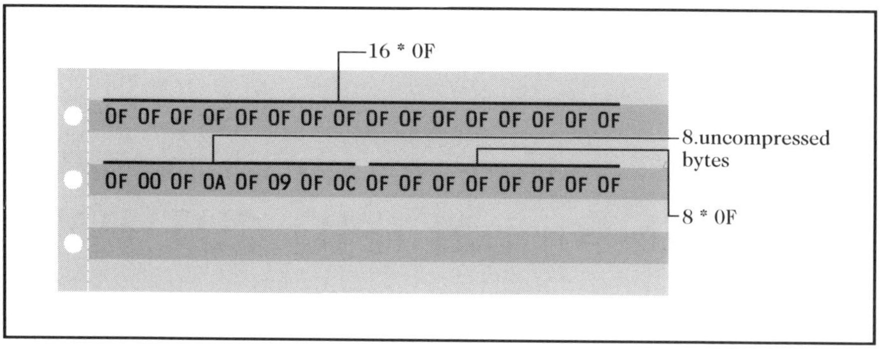

Figure 32.6 Expanded image data

The RLE process uses this technique to achieve a reduction in the amount of image data. The same coding procedure is also used for compressed monochrome images (type 11).

32.2.5 RLE-compressed RGB images (type 10)

The RLE process described above is also used for compressing RGB images. However, the actual treatment of image data is different in some cases.

A compressed record still begins with a header byte (see Figure 32.5). The top bit is set to `1` and the remaining bits define the repetition counter –1. The header is followed by a color value for the pixel to be copied. This color value requires not one byte, but several:

- With 16 bits per pixel, two bytes with the color coding `ARRRRRGGGGGBBBBB` (`A` = attribute, `R` = red, `G` = green, `B` = blue).
- With 24 bits per pixel, three bytes containing the color intensities for red, green and blue.
- With 32 bits per pixel, four bytes containing the color intensities for red, green, blue (one byte each) and an attribute (fourth byte).

The pixel should then be copied n times, where the value of n is the repetition counter + 1.

In the case of an image containing uncompressed data, the top bit in the header byte is set to `0` and the remaining bits define the repetition factor – 1. The header byte is followed by n pixels, where n is the repetition factor + 1. Each pixel consists of 16, 24 or 32 bits depending on the coding described above.

When actually analyzing various TGA files it became apparent that many programs use only the lowest four header bits as a counter. This leads to poorer compression, but does not adversely affect the reader program.

Graphics

33

Dr. Halo format (PIC, CUT, PAL)

***Dr. Halo** format is used for storing bitmap graphics. Mouse drivers from Genius are supplied with a program (Dr. Halo III or Dr. Genius) which supports images in PIC format. Various graphic conversion programs can also produce and convert CUT images.*

The PIC file format depends on the hardware used, that is, an image created with EGA cards cannot be displayed via VGA cards. There are therefore severe restrictions on practical usefulness. However, this does not apply to the CUT format which stores image excerpts from Dr. Halo pictures. The color map data is stored in a third file (PAL). Table 33.1 shows the file extensions for the various options:

Extension	Remarks
CUT	Cut of a Dr. Halo image
PIC	Dr. Halo Image file
PAL	Palette file for CUT and PIC images

Table 33.1
File extensions for Dr. Halo files

33.1 PIC format

A Dr. Halo image file consists of a header containing the identification marker and a number of image descriptor fields, followed by the actual image data. The image data is stored in 512-byte blocks. Table 33.2 shows the structure of the PIC header.

Offset	Bytes	Remarks
00H	2	Signature 'AH'
02H	2	Version number (integer) of the Dr. Halo driver library (almost always code E3H (¶))
04H	2	Unused (00H 00H)
06H	1	Image Flag (2 = Image File)
07H	1	Device Code
08H	2	Unused (00H 00H)
0AH	*n*	Adapter-specific data area for IBM EGA-Adapter 2 bytes Driver mode 0: 320 × 200, 4 colors 1: 640 × 200, 2 colors

Table 33.2
Structure of a PIC header

The third byte in the header normally contains the signature ¶. At offset 07H, there is a byte indicating the driver used, coded as shown in Table 33.3:

Code	Driver
1BH	HALODEBA, AT&T DEB
1CH	HALOINDA, AT&T Indigenous
15H	HALOIBME, Atronics Mega Graph, IBM EGA STB EGA Plus
49H	HALOHERC, Hercules Mono
01H	HALOIBM , IBM CGA
47H	HALOIBMV, Sigma VGA
36H	HALOIBMP, Sigma VGA
13H	HALOIBMP, STB VGA Extra

Table 33.3
Device codes

The driver modes are defined at offset 0AH together with the associated resolutions. Table 33.4 shows the values defined for the Dr. Halo drivers.

Driver	Number	Mode	Resolution	Colors	BIOS Mode
HALOIBM	01H	0	320 × 200	4	04H
		1	640 × 200	2	06H
HALOIBME	15H	0	320 × 200	4	04H
		1	640 × 200	2	06H
		2	320 × 200	16	0DH
		3	640 × 200	16	0EH
		4	640 × 350	16	10H
		5	640 × 800	16	-
		A	640 × 350	4	10H
HALOIBMG	1AH	0	320 × 200	4	04H
		1	640 × 200	2	06H
HALOIBMP	3CH	0	320 × 200	4	04H
		1	640 × 200	2	06H
		2	640 × 480	2	11H
		3	320 × 200	256	13H
HALOIBMV	47H	4	320 × 200	16	0DH
		5	640 × 200	16	06H
		6	640 × 350	16	10H
		7	640 × 480	16	12H
HALODEBA	1BH	2	640 × 200	8	-
		3	640 × 400	8	-
		4	640 × 400	16	-
		5	640 × 400	16	-

Table 33.3 Resolution and modes

The header is followed by the area containing the image data. In the case of EGA images, the image data begins at offset 12 (0CH). The image data area is written and read in blocks of 512 bytes.

The data within each 512-byte block is compressed according to the RLE process and stored in records within the block. Figure 33.1 shows the individual record structures.

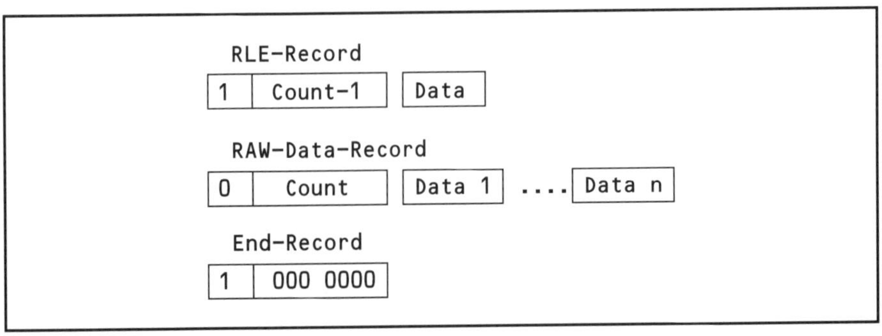

Figure 33.1 Record format for RLE encoding (PIC)

Each record consists of a header byte followed by one or more data bytes. In PIC format, identical data bytes in an image are stored in an RLE record. In this case the top bit of the header byte is set (1) and the remaining 7 bits define the number of repetitions. These 7 bits allow repetition factors between 1 and 127. The following byte contains the bit pattern to be copied. The hexadecimal sequence:

```
83H 02H
```

is expanded to:

```
02H 02H 02H
```

(83H = 3 repetitions).

If image data bytes cannot be compressed, they are stored in RAW format. In this case, the top bit of the header is set to 0 and the remaining 7 bits define the number of following bytes (n). The header will be followed by n bytes of uncompressed data.

The sequence:

```
90H 0FH 08H 0FH 00H 0FH 0AH 0FH 09H 0FH 0CH 88H 0FH
```

is expanded as follows:

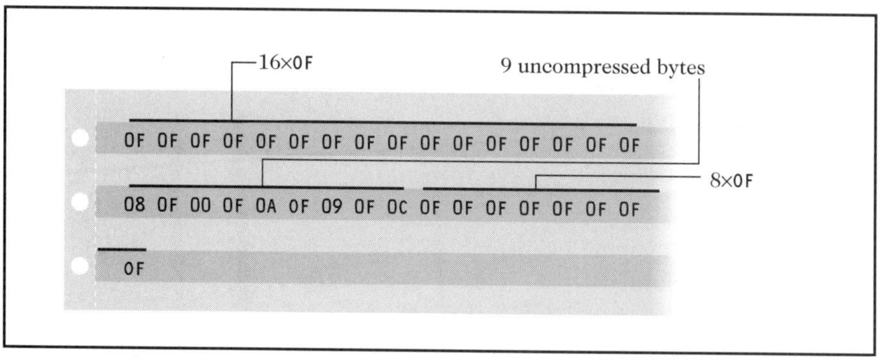

Figure 33.2 Expanded image data

Image data is always written or read in blocks of 512 bytes. RLE or RAW records must not extend beyond this 512-byte limit. For this reason, there are generally several unused bytes at the end of a block. The start of this unused area is marked with an end byte containing the value 80H, which must not appear elsewhere in RLE or RAW records. The next image data block begins in the following 512-byte block.

Because of its hardware dependence, a graphics file in PIC format cannot readily be transferred to other computers and can only be processed by the same Dr. Halo driver. This format has only been included here for the sake of completeness.

33.2 CUT format

In terms of exchanging images in Dr. Halo format, CUT files are of greater interest. These files are created in Dr. Halo III by cutting and saving an area of an image. The CUT format is hardware independent and is supported by various graphics programs. Each CUT file contains a 6-byte header followed by the image data. Table 33.4 specifies the structure of the CUT header.

Offset	Bytes	Remarks
00H	2	Image width in pixels
02H	2	Image height in pixels
04H	2	Unused (00H 00H)

Table 33.4 Structure of a CUT header

The remainder of the file contains the image data divided into records of the following structure:

Bytes	Remarks
2	Length data area in bytes
n	Data area with *n* bytes

Table 33.5 Structure of a CUT record

The data area in a CUT record is compressed using the RLE process, that is, the image data is stored in the same way as in the PIC format.

33.3 PAL format

PIC and CUT files do not contain information on the palette used. Instead, a separate palette file is used, with the extension PAL, but with the same file name as the CUT or PIC file. A PAL file consists of a 40-byte header, followed by the palette data, as shown in Table 33.6.

Offset	Bytes	Remarks
00H	2	Signature 'AH'
02H	2	Version number (integer) of the Dr. Halo driver library Code E3H (¶) is common
04H	2	File size –header length
06H	1	Signature for PAL files (0AH)
07H	1	Palette file subtype 0: generic 1: adapter-specific
08H	2	Adapter ID-Number (unused, if Palette file subtype = generic)
0AH	2	Graphic mode
0CH	2	Palette entries 15 = EGA, 255 = VGA
0EH	2	Maximum Red (only for EGA) 3 = 100%, 2 = 66%, 1 = 33%
10H	2	Maximum Green (only for EGA) 3 = 100%, 2 = 66%, 1 = 33%
12H	2	Maximum Blue (only for EGA) 3 = 100%, 2 = 66%, 1 = 33%
14H	19	Palette ID as ASCII text

Table 33.6 Structure of a PAL header

The first byte of the header is very similar to the CUT structure. Provided the value 0 (generic) is contained in the byte at offset 07H, device-specific information is not relevant. The palette ID string (offset 14H) generally contains the signature "Dr. Halo".

The header is followed by the table containing the palette information. The number of entries in the palette is stored at offset 0CH in the header. Each entry consists of three integer values giving the color intensities in the sequence red, green and blue. It should, however, be pointed out that only the lower byte is used, that is, the values are between 0 and 255 (0 to 100%). The color black is defined as 00H 00H, 00H 00H, 00H 00H and white as FFH 00H, FFH 00H, FFH 00H.

34

SUN Raster format (RAS)

A simple raster format for storing bitmap images has been defined by SUN. Monochrome and color images with 1, 8, 24 and 32 bits per pixel can be stored using these files. A number of conversion programs (for example, PaintShop) support this format and store the image data under DOS with the extension `.RAS`.

Figure 34.1 illustrates the structure of a RAS file:

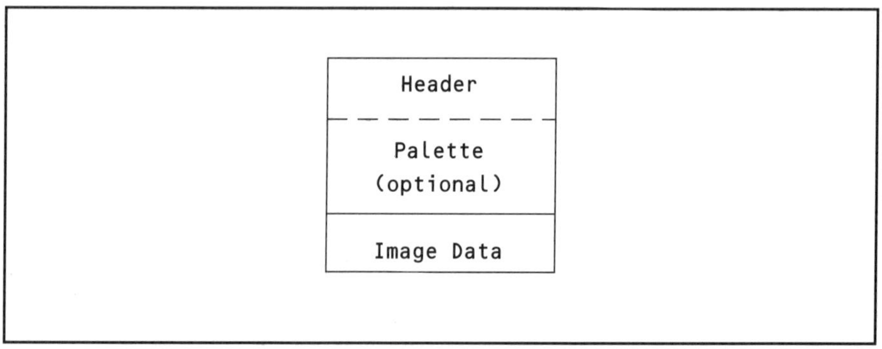

Figure 34.1 Structure of a RAS file

RAS files contain a 32-byte header, followed by a data area. This data area may contain either image data or optional palette data.

34.1 RAS header

The RAS header has a fixed length of 32 bytes, divided into 8 fields of 4 bytes each (DWORD). The data is stored in Motorola format (for example, 00H 00H 00H 01H = 1). The structure of the header is shown in Table 34.1:

Offset	Bytes	Remarks
00H	4	Signature (59H A6H 6AH 95H)
04H	4	Image width in pixels
08H	4	Image height in pixels
0CH	4	Bits per pixel
10H	4	Bytes in image data area
14H	4	RAW file type
18H	4	Palette flag 0: No color map 1: Color map 2: Raw color map
1CH	4	Length of color map

Table 34.1 Structure of a RAS header

The first four bytes contain a signature (59H A6H 6AH 95H). This signature is stored as a *magic number*, that is, the first word is mirrored in the second word. The image width in pixels is stored at offset 04H. An entry of 00H 00H 00H 10H indicates an image width of 16 pixels. The image height in pixels is stored at offset 08H. RAS files can store images of different bit depths, as shown in Table 34.2:

Bit/Pixel	Remarks
1	Monochrome
(4)	16 colors
8	256 colors
24	True color
32	True color

Table 34.2 Bits per pixel

The number of bits per pixel is specified at offset 0CH. With 32 bits per pixel, three bytes are used for color representation and one byte for additional information.

The DWORD at offset 10H defines the length of the image data area (without palette) in bytes. This value should be treated with caution, because in the original SUN format this field was temporarily used for the type of coding (00H = no coding). The length of the data area should therefore be calculated from the image data (width*height*bits per pixel).

SUN has defined a number of different types of raster file. The type is specified at offset 14H in the header. Table 34.3 lists the known RAS file types:

Code	Type
0	Old style
1	Standard style
2	Byte encoded
3	RGB format
4	TIFF format
5	IFF format
FFFFH	Experimental format

Table 34.3 SUN Raster file types

File types 0 and 1 define an identical memory format. If the value 2 is entered, the data is stored in RLE coding. In the case of RGB images, the image data for a pixel is stored as triples or quadruples (4 bytes) and the palette is generally omitted. If file types 4 (TIFF) or 5 (IFF) appear, this merely indicates that the raster file was originally converted from these formats. The code FFFFH is provided for the Experimental file type. This refers to an implementation-specific format. The following description relates to the standard format (Type 1).

The DWORD at offset 18H defines the type of color palette. This palette may be optionally stored after the header. If the value of the field is set to 0, the color palette is omitted and the image data will follow the header. If there is a color palette stored in the RAS file, the field will contain the value 1 (00H 00H 00H 01H). In this case the header is followed by the area containing the palette data. The value 2 (00H 00H 00H 02H) indicates a manufacturer-coded color palette (raw palette).

The length of the color palette in bytes is stored at offset 1CH. With 256 colors, the field will contain the entry 00H 00H 03H 00H, which corresponds to 256 colors of three bytes each.

34.2 Palette data area

If the field at offset 18H contains 00H 00H 00H 01H, the RAS file contains palette data at offset 20H. The length of this data area is specified in the header, at offset 1CH. A standard RAS palette consists of 256 colors, with 3 bytes for each color. However, the palette data for the 256 colors is stored differently from the normal conventions. At offset 20H, there are 256 data bytes containing the color intensities for red. At offset 120H, there are another 256 bytes containing the intensities for green, and at offset 210H, another 256 bytes containing the blue color intensities. Raster files with 24 or 32 bits have no palette and the image data in this case follows immediately after the header.

34.3 RAS data area

The image data area follows the header (unless there is a palette) or the palette. The number of bits per pixel is stored in the header at offset 0CH.

The number of image data bytes in an uncompressed file can be calculated from the image dimensions (height * width * bits per pixel).

34.3.1 Monochrome representation (1 bit per pixel)

With monochrome images, there is no palette and the image data is stored in one plane. One byte, in this context, represents 8 pixels.

34.3.2 Grayscales and color images (8 bits per pixel)

Pictures with 256 colors or grayscales require a palette, which follows the header. For grayscale images, this palette contains the corresponding definitions. For color images, the individual colors are described by three bytes (red, green, blue). Each (uncompressed) byte in the image data area describes one pixel.

34.3.3 True Color images (24/32 bits per pixel)

In these files, the palette is either omitted altogether or is stored as a manufacturer-specific (RAW Color) palette. With 24 bits per pixel, the image data is stored in 3 bytes per pixel; with 32 bits per pixel, the first three bytes contain the color information, and the fourth byte can be used for alpha values.

34.3.4 RLE coding in RAS files

If the header contains data type 2 at offset 14H the image data is in compressed format. The RAS format uses a simple RLE process for data compression. The image data should be read and decoded bytewise. If the value of the relevant byte is not equal to 80H or 00H, the image data byte is uncompressed. With monochrome images or images with 256 colors, the pixels can be displayed directly. In the case of 24-bit or 32-bit pictures, the value should be stored in an intermediate buffer until all the bytes for a pixel have been decoded. Only then can the pixel be displayed.

There is, however, the problem that an image data byte may contain the value 80H. In this case, a modified RLE record with the structure shown in Figure 34.2 will be used for coding.

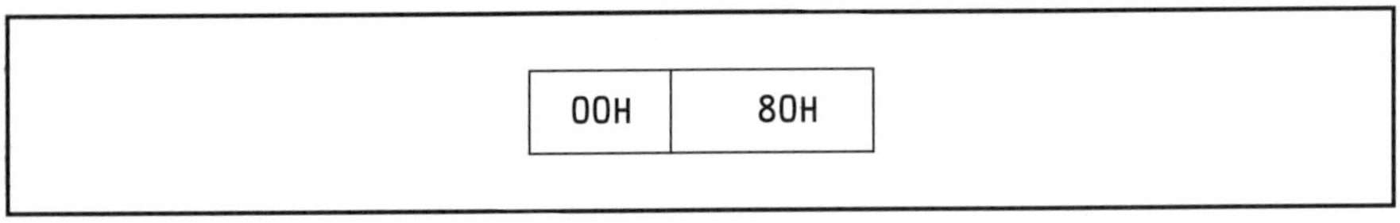

Figure 34.2 Storing 80H as a data byte

The first byte contains the value 00H, while the second byte, which is to be interpreted as an image data byte, is coded 80H.

Conversely, if the value 00H appears as an image data byte, this will be coded as an RLE record of length 1 (80H 01H 00H).

Compressed image data is stored as a byte stream, and the decoded data may therefore extend beyond the image line.

35

Adobe Photoshop format (PSD)

The Photoshop program from Adobe is available for both the Macintosh and Windows. It enables the creation, processing and storage of bitmap graphics with a maximum resolution of 30,000 × 30,000 pixels. In the PC environment, Photoshop images are stored in files with the extension `.PSD`.

These image files consist of a fixed-length header, a variable-length mode block, a variable-length image resource block, a reserved block and the actual image data (monochrome or color pictures).

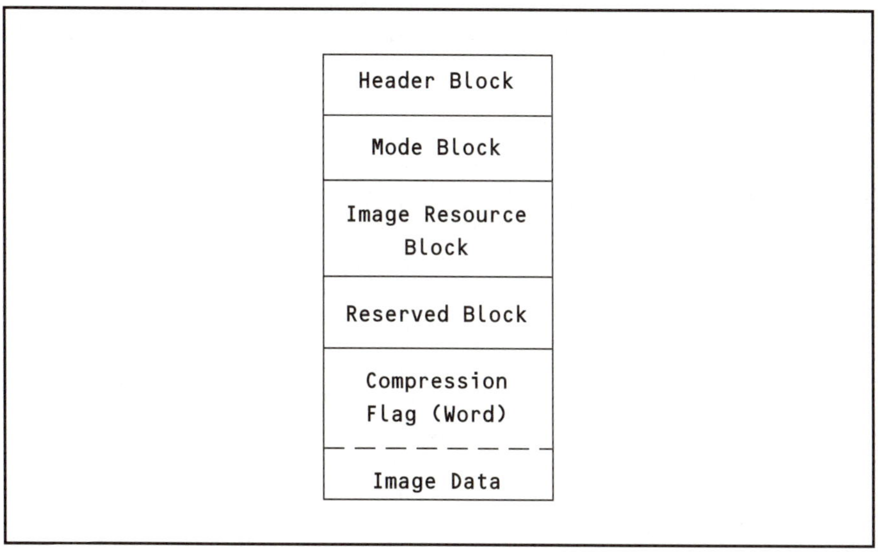

Figure 35.1 Structure of a Photoshop (PSD) file

The data in the PSD file is stored in Motorola format (big-endian).

35.1 Photoshop header

The header of a Photoshop file is of fixed length and contains the fields shown in Table 35.1:

Offset	Bytes	Remarks
00H	4	Signature '8BPS'
04H	2	Version number
06H	6	Reserved
0CH	2	Color channels
0EH	4	Y image size in pixels
12H	4	X image size in pixels
16H	2	Bits per channel
18H	2	Color mode

Table 35.1 Structure of a Photoshop header

At offset 0, there is a 4 character signature (8BPS). This signature is also used on Macintosh computers as an identification of the file type. The version number at offset 04H contains the value 1, at present. The following six bytes are reserved and should be set to 00H.

At offset 0CH, there is a word containing the number of color channels. In Photoshop 2.5, this value is between 1 and 16.

The image dimensions are stored in two fields (DWORD) at offset 0EH. The number of pixels permitted is 30,000 × 30,000. The number of bits per color channel is stored at offset 16H. In Photoshop 2.5, these values are between 1 and 8.

The *Mode* field contains two bytes and is stored at offset 18H. This defines the color mode of the file and is coded as shown in Table 35.2:

Mode	Remarks
0	Bitmap (monochrome)
1	Grayscale image
2	Color image with palette
3	RGB color image
4	CMYK color image
5	Multi-channel color image
6	Duotone image
7	Lab color image

Table 35.2 Modes in Photoshop

The meaning of the various mode values is not fully documented.

The header is followed by blocks containing additional information. All the blocks begin with a 4-byte length field, followed by a data area of variable length (see below).

35.2 Mode data block

The header is followed by a block in which data relating to the internal mode settings for Photoshop is stored. This block is structured as shown in Table 35.3.

Offset	Bytes	Remarks
00H	4	Block length
04H	*n*	Data area

Table 35.3 Structure of a mode block in Photoshop

The first field (DWORD) indicates the length of the *Mode* block. If the *Mode* field in the header (offset 18H) defines a palette color image, the *Mode* block is 768 bytes long and contains the 256 entries of the color palette. Each entry comprises 3 bytes giving the color intensities for red, green and blue.

If the *Mode* field in the header contains the value 6 (duotone image), Photoshop will store the corresponding specification data in the *Mode* block. The structure of this data is not currently available.

If the *Mode* field in the header defines another image type, the length field of the *Mode* block will contain the value 0. In this case, the data area of the *Mode* block is omitted, and the block is only 4 bytes long.

35.3 Resource data block

The *Mode* block is followed by a block containing the resource data. This block is structured as shown in Table 35.4:

Offset	Bytes	Remarks
00H	4	Block length
04H	*n*	Data area

Table 35.4 Structure of a resource data block in Photoshop

The first field (DWORD) indicates the length of the *Resource Data* block. This is followed by the data area containing information on the resources required for structuring the image. The documentation on the coding of this block is not available.

The *Resource* block is followed by another block which begins with a 4-byte field. The field defines the length of the data area. The length of the following data area (like that of the other blocks) is variable. Presumably this block has been provided for future extensions because the length field in Photoshop 2.5 is set to 0 and the data area is omitted.

35.4 Image Data Area

The reserved block is followed by a word specifying the type of compression.

Code	Compression type
0	Uncompressed image data
1	Image data RLE compressed

Table 35.5 Compression type

This word is followed by the actual image data area. The data is divided into individual planes and stored.

In the case of uncompressed image data, the data is stored by line. The compression method used is Mac Packbit. Image data areas are preceded by the lengths of the individual image lines in bytes. Each length occupies one word and the lengths are followed by the area containing the packed image data.

35.5 MAC Packbit Coding:

- The image data is compressed line-wise, that is, the decompressed data does not extend beyond an image line.
- During decompression one data byte is read at a time.
- If the top bit of this data byte is set (1), a packed record is present. The two's complement of the byte is calculated and this acts as a repetition counter for the following byte, which is copied *n* times.
- It the top bit contains the value 0, an uncompressed record is present. The value of the byte should then be increased by 1. This value indicates the number of uncompressed data bytes that follow.

The above steps should be repeated until all the bytes required for one image line have been read. These can then be displayed.

36

PCPAINT/Pictor format (PIC)

The program PCPAINT was developed for Mouse Systems in 1984. PC PAINT is available in various versions, the format having stabilized after version 2.0. The following description is therefore restricted to the format of PCPAINT 2.0 and Pictor 3.0/3.1.

The image files consist of a header, followed by an image data area for monochrome or color images (Figure 36.1).

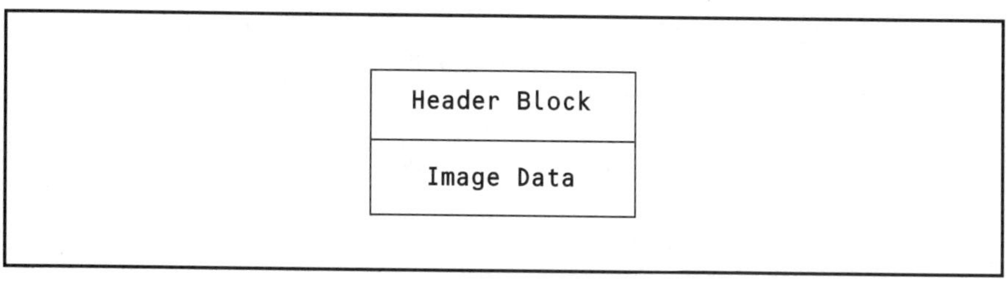

Figure 36.1 Structure of a PCPAINT/Pictor (PIC) file

The data within the PIC file is always stored in Intel format. The image is structured from bottom to top.

36.1 PCPAINT/Pictor header

The PIC header is of variable length and contains the fields shown in Table 36.1.

Offset	Bytes	Remarks
00H	2	Signature 1234H
02H	2	X image size in pixels
04H	2	Y image size in pixels
06H	2	X-coordinate lower left corner
08H	2	Y-coordinate lower left corner
0AH	1	Image flag Bit 0–3: bits per pixel and plane Bit 4–7: bitplanes
0BH	1	Reserved (FFH)
0CH	1	Video mode (0 default) 0: 40 column text 1: 80 column text 2: Text monochrome 3: 43 rows text A: 320 × 200 × 4 (CGA) B: 320 × 200 × 16 (Tandy 1000, etc.) C: 640 × 200 × 2 (CGA) D: 640 × 200 × 16 (EGA) E: 640 × 350 × 2 (EGA) F: 640 × 350 × 4 (EGA) G: 640 × 350 × 16 (EGA) H: 720 × 348 × 2 (Hercules) I: 320 × 200 × 16 (Plantronics) J: 320 × 200 × 16 (EGA) K: 640 × 400 × 2 (AT&T, Toshiba) L: 320 × 200 × 256 (VGA) M: 640 × 480 × 16 (EGA+, VGA) N: 720 × 384 × 16 (Hercules Incolor) O: 640 × 480 × 2 (VGA)
0DH	2	Extra info descriptor 0: nothing 1: palette (1 byte), border (1 byte) (CGA) 2: PCjr or non ECD 16 color register (0–15), 1 byte each 3: EGA with EDC 16 color register (0–63), 1 byte each 4: VGA 256 color info
0FH	2	Size of extra info field
17H	*n*	Extra info block (optional)
..H	2	Number of packed blocks

Table 36.1 Structure of a PCPAINT/Pictor PIC header

The signature 1234H for a PIC header is at offset 0. The next two bytes define the image width and image height in pixels. The origin of the image is stored at offset 06H as screen coordinates. The default setting for this value is 0,0. The image is built up from bottom to top.

The byte at offset 0AH is divided into two nibbles. The lower 4 bits define the number of bits per pixel and image plane. The upper 4 bits define the number of image planes. For CGA with 4 colors, the byte contains the value 02H; an EGA representation with 15 colors is coded 31H (3 levels, 1 bit per pixel and plane). The Plantronics 16 color mode is coded 12H.

As a special feature, PIC format stores the screen mode at offset 0CH. The word at offset 0DH defines whether a data area with *extra information* appears in the header. Palette data, for example, can be stored in this block. If the word is set to 00H, the *extra info* block is not present. The length of the *extra info* block in bytes is stored in the word at offset 0FH. If the length is 0, the block is not present.

The optional *extra info* block begins at offset 17H and contains palette data, whose structure is defined in Table 36.1 (offset 0DH). For example, with a CGA card, two bytes (palette, border) are needed. In mode 3, however, there are 64 bytes containing the register values.

The *extra info* block is followed by a word containing the number of packed image data blocks. If this number is 0, the file contains unpacked data.

36.2 PIC data area

The header is followed by the PIC data area containing packed or unpacked data. In PCPAINT 2.0, bitmaps are packed together, enabling the data to be displayed very simply on the PCjr (for example, 4 bits per pixel, 1 bit per plane). From Pictor 3.0 onwards, the bitplanes are separated before storage and stored plane-wise. A PIC file can contain image data with 1, 4 and 8 bits per pixel.

36.2.1 Monochrome Images (1 bit per pixel)

With 1 bit per pixel, data is stored in one plane. Each byte defines 8 pixels.

36.2.2 Color images (4 bits per pixel)

In this case, image data is divided into 4 planes. Each plane contains one bit per pixel, that is, a data byte describes 8 pixels in one color plane. For EGA and VGA cards, the image information must be assembled from the four color planes (red, green, blue, intensity).

36.2.3 Color images (8 bits per pixel)

Here, image data is stored either at 8 bits per pixel in one plane or at 1 bit per pixel in 8 planes. Color information for a pixel must then be assembled according to the coding.

36.2.4 Image data blocks (PIC file)

Image data is stored in individual blocks. The color information can be stored either in individual planes or collected together. The method of coding the planes is indicated in the header at offset 0AH. Both the number of bits per pixel and plane, and the number of planes are specified.

In the case of a packed PIC file (offset 17H > 0), image data is stored in blocks. When changing image plane, a new block must be created. The number of packed blocks is indicated in the header, after the *extra info* block.

36.2.5 Structure of a data block

Packed data is stored in individual packages (data blocks). These packages consist of a header, followed by the packed and unpacked image data. The block header is structured as shown in Table 36.2:

Bytes	Field
2	Blocksize (in bytes)
2	Unpacked data size (in bytes)
1	Marker for packed subrecords

Table 36.2 Structure of a block header

The block length and the length of the uncompressed data are stored as words. The block length includes these two length words.

At offset 05H, a code is defined as a *marker byte*. Within the block, this code is used to mark packed subrecords. The value stored in this byte either should not appear or appear only very seldom in the unpacked data area; otherwise the PIC file will be enlarged (*see below*).

This header is followed by the unpacked data and/or the subrecords containing the compressed data. The PIC format uses a very straightforward method of compression:

- If a data byte occurs several times consecutively, it is stored in a subrecord as a *Run Length*.
- Data bytes that are not identical are stored uncoded in a block.

The subrecords containing packed data are structured as shown in Table 36.3:

Bytes	Field
1	Marker (to mark a run)
1	Run count
	If run count = 0, 16-bit run count
1	Data byte for run

Table 36.3 Structure of a subrecord containing compressed data

The marker byte marks the packed subrecord. The chosen value is stored at offset 05H in the block header. The following byte contains the repetition counter for the next data byte. If the value is greater than 0, the data byte must be copied n times (maximum 255). An extended structure has been defined in order to create larger repetition factors. If the repetition counter = 0, a 16-bit repetition counter will follow. The last byte in the subrecord will then be repeated n times.

Unpacked data is stored as a simple byte sequence in the block. If a code with the value of the marker byte appears, this code must be stored in a compressed subrecord with the repetition counter 1. This explains why it is important for the marker code either not to appear or to appear only rarely in the image data; otherwise the image data byte will be stored in three bytes which significantly increases the length.

The data block can be read using the following algorithm:

```
Get block size
Get original size
Get marker byte
Repeat (for all bytes in block)
 Get next byte
 IF byte = marker code THEN
/* compressed subrecord
  Get run count byte
  IF run count = 0 THEN
   Get 16-bit run count
  ENDIF
  Get data byte
  Repeat run count
   write data byte
  END Repeat
 ELSE
/* uncompressed data byte
  write data byte
 ENDIF
END Repeat
```

Figure 36.2 Pseudo-code for PIC reader

Graphics

This storage structure is extremely economical if an image contains very little information, because there will be large areas containing the same image data which can be easily packed. In the case of images containing patterns, the image data is stored in uncompressed form.

37

JPEG/JFIF format (JPG)

***The** JPEG process only describes compression methods for images. In the JPEG Standard (ISO DIS 10918-1), Appendix B, the structure of the associated files is also described. However, this definition allows a great deal of freedom, which means that exchanging JPEG images between different applications and platforms is relatively problematic.*

The *JPEG File Interchange Format* therefore defines a minimum standard in order to ease the exchange of images using JPEG compression between various applications and platforms. The format is compatible with PCs, Macintosh and UNIX computers. For example, Macintosh Resource Forks are not used, thereby facilitating interchange with other platforms.

The JFIF format is based on the JPEG standard (ISO DIS 10918-1). The following description refers to version 1.02 of the JFIF specification. Files that correspond to the JPEG standard must be divided into individual blocks, also known as marker segments. Each marker segment consists of a marker, followed by optional parameters. If a marker segment requires more than one marker, the length of the segment is stored in the following field.

The JFIF format uses only a small number of the markers listed in Appendix B of the standard for the individual segments of the file. Figure 37.1 shows the structure of a JFIF file.

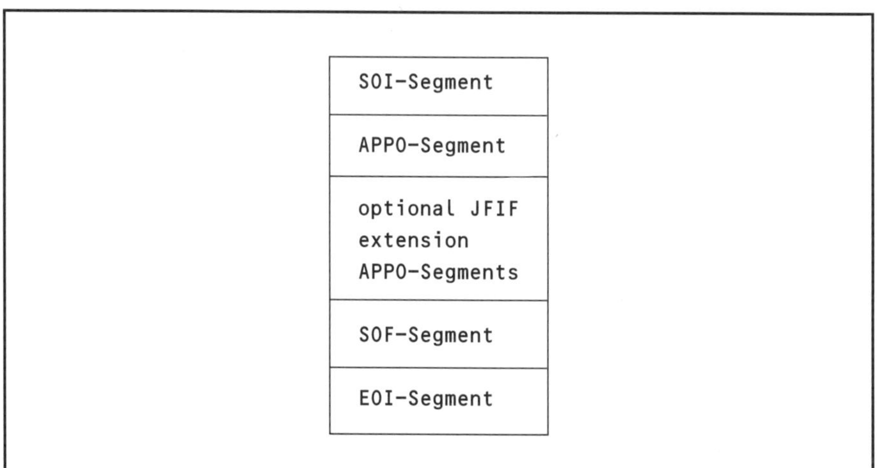

Figure 37.1 Structure of a JFIF file

The file always begins with a Start Of Image (SOI) marker segment. This is followed by an Application (APP0) marker segment, which contains additional information on the image data stored (for example, version, resolution). A JFIF file can also contain specially reduced images (thumbnails) to enable previewing. In this case, the first APP0 marker segment is followed by additional, optional extension APP0 marker segments. These are followed by the compressed image data in the Start Of Frame (SOF) marker segments. A JFIF file is always terminated with an End Of Image (EOI) marker segment.

The individual marker segments begin with a 2-byte marker which identifies the type.

The marker code consists of the value FFxxH, where xx represents a number between C0H and FEH. The marker codes are defined in Appendix B of the JPEG standard. All data in the JFIF file is stored in Motorola format. The structure of the individual marker segments of a JFIF file is described below.

! **The JPEG specification provides a series of additional marker segments describing the compression tables for the interchange format. These are also described below, but should not occur in JFIF files because these files require** Baseline DCT **compression.**

37.1 Start Of Image (SOI) marker segment

All JFIF files (and any other file conforming to the JPEG standard) must begin with an SOI marker segment. The structure of the segment is as follows:

Offset	Bytes	Remarks
00H	2	SOI signature (FFD8H)

Table 37.1 Structure of an SOI marker segment

The segment comprises only two bytes containing the signature. The signature is defined in the JPEG standard.

37.2 End Of Image (EOI) marker segment

All JFIF files (and any other file conforming to the JPEG standard) must be terminated with an EOI marker segment. The structure of the segment is as follows:

Offset	Bytes	Remarks
00H	2	EOI signature (FFD9H)

Table 37.2 Structure of an EOI marker segment

This segment also requires only two bytes for the signature.

37.3 Application (APP0) marker segment

The second segment of a JFIF file must be an APP0 marker segment. This segment indicates compatibility with the JFIF specification and is also used to identify the file.

Offset	Bytes	Remarks
00H	2	APP0 signature (FFE0H)
02H	2	Segment length
04H	5	ID = 'JFIF'
09H	2	Version (0102H)
0BH	1	Units
0CH	2	X density
0EH	2	Y density
10H	1	X Thumbnail
11H	1	Y Thumbnail
12H	3×*n*	RGB thumbnail values

Table 37.3 Structure the APP0 marker segment

This marker segment begins with the signature FFE0H. This is followed by a word containing the length of the block. The length includes all bytes within the block except the first two signature bytes. A 5-byte identification for the marker segment begins at offset 04H. In the case of a JFIF file, the signature 4AH 46H 49H 46H 00H must appear at this point. 'JFIF', corresponds to the ASCII string

The word at offset 09H contains the version number of the JFIF specification. The first byte contains the main version number. The current specification is version 0102H.

The fields beginning at offset 0BH define the resolution of the image. The byte at offset 0BH specifies the units used for the resolution and is coded as shown in Table 37.4:

Code	Unit
0	no units
1	X,Y are dots per inch
2	X,Y are dots per centimeter

Table 37.4 Units for resolution

If the unit code is set to 0, X and Y define the pixel aspect ratio. At offset 0CH, there is a word indicating the horizontal resolution (horizontal pixel density). The vertical resolution (vertical pixel density) is stored at offset 0EH.

The JFIF file may contain a specially reduced image (thumbnail) as an RGB bitmap. The width of this image in pixels is specified at offset 10H, and its height in pixels at offset 11H. If the file does not contain thumbnail images, both these fields should be set to 0. These fields are followed at offset 12H by the actual image data, which is stored as an RGB table with three bytes per entry (red, green, blue). The number of entries can be calculated from width * height.

! **Storing thumbnails in a JFIF APP0 marker is now discouraged. It is still supported only for backward compatibility.**

37.4 Extension APP0 (SOI) marker segment

From version 1.02 onwards, the APP0 marker segment may optionally be followed by another extension APP0 marker segment. The structure of an extension APP0 marker segment is described in Table 37.5.

Offset	Bytes	Remarks
00H	2	APP0 signature FFE0H
02H	2	Segment length
04H	5	ID = 'JFXX'
09H	1	Extension code
0AH	*n*	Data area

Table 37.5 Structure of an extension APP0

The extension APP0 marker segment also begins with the signature FFE0H. This is followed by a word containing the length of the block. This length includes all the bytes in the block except the first two signature bytes. A 5-byte identification field for the extension marker segment begins at offset 04H. In the case of a JFIF file, the signature 4AH 46H 58H 58H 00H, which corresponds to the ASCII string 'JFXX', must be shown here.

The 1-byte extension code, which specifies the type of the extension APP0 marker segment, follows at offset 09H. So far, the following codes have been defined:

Code	Remarks
10H	Thumbnail coded using JPEG
11H	Thumbnail stored using 1 byte/pixel
13H	Thumbnail stored using 3 bytes/pixel

Table 37.6 Coding of an extension APP0 marker segment

The data area follows at offset 0AH. This data area varies according to the extension used.

37.4.1 JFIF extension: Thumbnail coded using JPEG

This extension is used for storing thumbnails compressed using the JPEG process. The value 10H is stored as the extension code in the marker segment. The extension data field is structured as follows:

SOI Marker Segment
SOF Marker Segment
EOI Marker Segment

The structure of these segments is described below. In the data area, no marker segments containing the signatures 'JFIF' or 'JFXX' may appear.

37.4.2 JFIF extension: Thumbnail stored using 1 byte/pixel

With this extension, thumbnails are stored using one byte per pixel. The value 11H is stored as the extension code in the marker segment. The extension data field is structured as follows:

Bytes	Remarks
1	Thumbnail horizontal pixel count (X)
1	Thumbnail vertical pixel count (Y)
768	Palette containing 256 × 3 bytes (red, green, blue)
n	Data area containing 1 byte/pixel for the thumbnail image (*n* = X×Y)

Table 37.7 JFIF extension for Thumbnails (1 byte/pixel)

The data is stored in uncompressed form.

37.4.3 JFIF extension: Thumbnail stored using 3 bytes/pixel

With this extension, thumbnails are stored using three bytes per pixel. The value 13H is stored as the extension code in the marker segment. The extension data field is structured as follows:

Bytes	Remarks
1	Thumbnail horizontal pixel count (X)
1	Thumbnail vertical pixel count (Y)
n	Data area containing 3 bytes/pixel for the thumbnail image ($n = 3 \times X \times Y$)

Table 37.8 JFIF extension for Thumbnails (3 bytes/pixel)

The data is stored in uncompressed form.

37.5 Define Huffman Table (DHT) marker segment

The JPEG specification requires all tables containing definitions, which are needed during decoding, to be stored prior to their use in the data stream. The JPEG standard describes a series of marker segments containing tables for coding. The structure of the DHT marker is as follows:

Offset	Bytes	Remarks
00H	2	DHT Signature (FFC4H)
02H	2	Segment length
04H	1	Color component index
05H	16	Length of Huffman table
15H	n	Huffman table

Table 37.9 Structure of a DHT marker segment

The marker segment contains a two-byte signature, the segment length (excluding signature) and the index to the relevant color components. The length of the Huffman table is stored at offset 05H. This is followed by the actual table. Huffman tables are defined in the JPEG specification, but are not needed in JFIF files.

Graphics

37.6 Define Arithmetic Coding (DAC) marker segment

This marker segment contains information on the color components specified in the index. The DAC marker segment is structured as follows:

Offset	Bytes	Remarks
00H	2	DAC signature (FFCCH)
02H	2	Segment length
04H	1	Color component index
05H	1	Value

Table 37.10 Structure of a DAC marker segment

The marker segment contains a two byte signature and the segment length (excluding signature). After the index to the relevant color components, the arithmetic coding is stored as a byte. This marker segment is not used in JFIF files.

37.7 Define Quantization Table (DQT) marker segment

This marker segment defines a quantization table (DQT). The structure of the DQT marker segment is as follows:

Offset	Bytes	Remarks
00H	2	DQT signature (FFDBH)
02H	2	Segment length
04H	1	Index
05H	64	Quantization table

Table 37.11 Structure of a DQT Marker Segment

The marker segment begins with a 2-byte signature and the segment length (excluding signature). The index is coded as follows: bits 0 to 3 define the index to the quantization table, while bits 4 to 7 indicate the format of the entries. If the format value is 0, the entries are stored as bytes; value 1 defines entries stored as words. This marker segment should not be used in JFIF files.

37.8 Define Restart Interval (DRI) marker segment

Within the data blocks, it may be necessary to restart coding. The length of the restart interval is determined using a DRI marker segment.

Offset	Bytes	Remarks
00H	2	DRI Signature (FFDDH)
02H	2	Segment length
04H	2	Restart interval

Table 37.12 Structure of a DRI marker segment

This marker segment contains a two-byte signature and the segment length (excluding signature). The value of the restart interval is stored at offset 04H. After the minimum code units (MCU) indicated in the interval, the JPEG coding procedure is re-initialized. This marker segment should not appear in JFIF files (version 1.02).

37.9 Start of Frame (SOF) marker segment

SOF marker segments contain information on the image size and the allocation of quantization tables to the individual color components. There are various SOF marker segments, with identification codes 0, 1 .. 9, A, B, D, E and F. The JFIF specification provides only *Baseline* DCT coding, and the marker segments described above should not appear. Table 37.13 lists the various SOF marker segments:

Code	Marker Segments
	Non-differential Huffman coding
0	Baseline DCT
1	Extended sequential DCT
2	Progressive DCT
3	Spatial (sequential) lossless
	Differential Huffman coding
5	Differential sequential DCT
6	Differential progressive DCT
7	Differential spatial

Table 37.13 Coding SOF marker types (*continues over...*)

Graphics

Code	Marker Segments
	Non-differential arithmetic coding
8	Reserved
9	Extended sequential DCT
A	Progressive DCT
B	Spatial (sequential) lossless
	Differential arithmetic coding
D	Differential sequential DCT
E	Differential progressive DCT
F	Differential spatial

Table 37.13 Coding SOF marker types (*cont.*)

In the specification, the codes shown in Table 37.13 are referred to as Index SOFx. The code is also used as the last letter of the signature (for example, FFCAH = progressive DCT). An SOF marker segment is structured as shown in Table 37.14.

Offset	Bytes	Remarks
00H	2	SOFx signature (FFDxH)
02H	2	Segment length
04H	1	Data precision
05H	2	Image height in pixels
07H	2	Image width in pixels
09H	1	Number of components
0AH	1	ID of first component
0BH	1	Sample factor Bit 0–3: vertical Bit 4–7: horizontal
0CH	1	Quantization table number
0DH	1	ID of second component
0EH	1	Sample factor Bit 0–3: vertical Bit 4–7: horizontal
0FH	1	Quantization table number
10H	1	ID of third component
11H	1	Sample factor Bit 0–3: vertical Bit 4–7: horizontal
12H	1	Quantization table number
.....		

Table 37.14 Structure of a SOF marker segment

The marker segment has a 2-byte signature, where X is replaced by a value between `0` and `FH` in accordance with Table 37.13. Because of the baseline DCT compression, the signature `FFD0H` should appear. The segment length does not include the 2 bytes of the signature. The resolution value (data precision) is stored at offset `04H`. The words at offsets `05H` and `07H` define the image dimensions in pixels. The number of color components is stored at offset `09H`. For JFIF files, the values `1` or `3` are permitted.

The actual image data follows at offset `0AH` (ID, Sample factor, quantization number). The image data is divided into the number of components (1 or 3) coded according to the YCbCr color model.

37.10 Color coding

JPEG graphics are stored using the YCbCr color model. This color model enables a reduction of the information in the color plane (chrominance), while the brightness (luminance) remains unchanged. The standard YCbCr color space is determined in accordance with CCIR 601, that is, 256 color planes. RGB colors can be derived in a linear progression from the YCbCr color model. Gamma correction is not possible. If only one component is used, this should be the Y component. The coding for the YCbCr color system is shown below:

$$Y = 256 * E'y$$
$$Cb = 256 * [E'Cb] + 128$$
$$Cr = 256 * [E'Cr] + 128$$

The values E'y (0 .. 1.0), E'Cb (– 0.5 +0.5) and E'Cr (– 0.5 +0.5) are defined in CCIR 601. The 256 color levels of the YCbCr color system can be calculated directly from the RGB values:

$$Y = 0.299\ R + 0.578\ G + 0.114\ B$$
$$Cb = -0.1687\ R - 0.3313\ G + 0.5\ B + 128$$
$$Cr = 0.5\ R - 0.4187\ G - 0.0813\ B + 128$$

The values R, G, B represent the color intensities for red, green and blue. These may be between 0 and 255. Conversion from YCbCr color space to RGB color plane is carried out via the following formulae:

$$R = Y + 1.402\ (Cr - 128)$$
$$G = Y - 0.34414\ (Cb - 128) - 0.71414\ (Cr - 128)$$
$$B = Y + 1.772\ (Cb - 128)$$

The values Y, Cb and Cr may be between 0 and 255. In JFIF files, the image orientation is always from top to bottom. The image data is written from left to right.

For details of the coding and processing for individual data, reference should be made to the JPEG specification. The JPEG specification, the definition of data formats and a description of compression processes can be found in W. Pennebaker and J. Mitchell, JPEG: *Still Image Data Compression Standard*, Van Nostrand Reinhold, ISBN 0-442-01272-1.

37.11 Start Of Scan (SOS) marker segment

The SOS block introduces the start of a scan for many types of image. The structure is as follows:

Offset	Bytes	Remarks
00H	2	SOS signature (FFDAH)
02H	2	Segment length
04H	1	Number of components
05H	1	ID component
06H	1	Table index
		Bit 0–3: AC-table
		Bit 4–7: DC-table

Table 37.15 Structure of a SOS marker segment

This marker segment contains a 2-byte signature. The segment length does not include the two signature bytes. The byte containing the ID for the color components used is at offset 05H. The components are allocated to the tables via the byte at offset 06H. This marker segment should not appear in JFIF files.

! If unknown marker segments appear in a JFIF file, the JFIF reader can skip these without affecting the image decoding.

38

MAC-Paint format (MAC)

Apple *developed MAC-Paint Format for the Macintosh to enable the storage of monochrome images. The images have one bit per pixel and are stored with fixed dimensions of 576 × 720 pixels. The print resolution is 75 dpi. On Macintosh computers, MAC-Paint Files have the ending PNTG.*

Since a great many graphics are stored in this format, various conversion programs (for example, PaintShop) support the MAC-Paint Format when importing graphics to a PC. On a PC running MS-DOS, MAC-Paint files are given the extension `.MAC` (or, less often, `.PNT`).

Because of its Macintosh origins, this format exhibits a number of peculiarities. The first comes from the structure of the MAC file system, in which files are stored in what are known as *forks*. These forks represent data areas in which the operating system stores information. A Macintosh file always contains two forks. One fork is used for storing data, the second for resources (or program code). In physical terms, there are two files on the MAC, although the user only sees one.

With MAC-Paint files, the resource fork remains empty. When files are transferred from the Macintosh to other computers (for example, PCs), both forks are combined into one file. To enable this file to be read back onto the Macintosh and divided into two forks, an additional 128-byte header has been introduced. This header contains information for the Macintosh operating system, enabling it to reproduce the original fork structure. It is placed before the data to be exported.

If the data is not to be sent back to the Mac, the header can be removed. For this reason, there are two variants of MAC-Paint files:

- One variant has no header and corresponds to the original MAC format.
- The PC variant has a 128-byte header containing additional information.

Within the header, there are also two variants, corresponding to the original MacBinary and the MacBinary II Standard respectively. Both headers are 128 bytes long, but the MacBinary II header contains additional data.

Because of these characteristics, a MAC-Paint file on a PC is structured as shown in Figure 38.1:

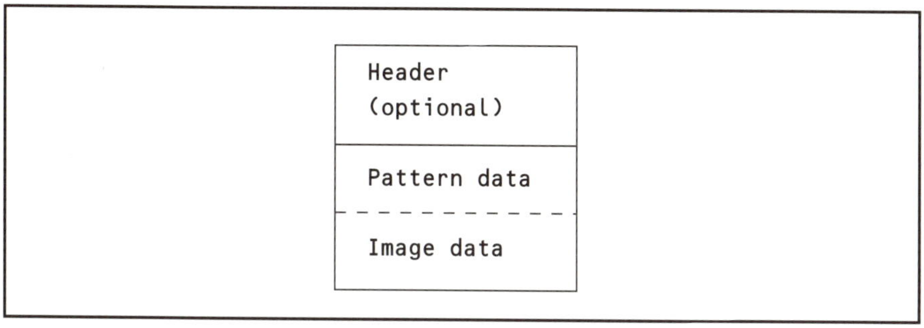

Figure 38.1 Structure of a MAC file

In the MAC file, the data is always stored in Motorola format. As a result of the peculiarities described above, a program has to determine whether the MAC file has a header. The following checks must be carried out:

- Check whether the bytes at offset `101` (`65H`) to `125` (`7DH`) have the value `00H`.
- The byte at offset 2 must be in the range `1–63`.
- The two DWORDS at offsets `83` (`53H`) and `87` (`57H`) should have values between `0` and `007FFFFFH`.

If the results of all these checks are positive, the MAC file has a 128 byte header. Another possible check is to determine whether the 4 bytes at offset `41H` have the signature '`PNTG`'. The Macintosh operating system uses this signature as the file type.

38.1 MAC header

The MAC header is 128 bytes long and contains the information required to import a file from other computers back to a Macintosh. The data is stored in Motorola format. Table 38.1 shows the structure of the header. The fields from offset `65H` onwards are defined in the MacBinary II Standard.

Offset	Bytes	Remarks
00H	1	Version (always 0)
01H	1	File name length
02H	63	File name
41H	4	File type
45H	4	File creator

Table 38.2 Structure of a MAC header (*continues over...*)

Offset	Bytes	Remarks
49H	1	File attribute flags
4AH	1	Reserved
4BH	2	File vertical position in window
4DH	2	File horizontal position in window
4FH	2	Window or folder ID
51H	1	File protection 1 = protected
52H	1	Reserved
53H	4	Data fork size in bytes
57H	4	Resource fork size in bytes
5BH	4	Creation time & date stamp
5FH	4	Modify time & date stamp
63H	2	GetInfo message length
	MacBinary II only	
65H	2	Finder Flags
67H	14*1	Reserved
75H	4	Unpacked file length
79H	2	Secondary header length
7BH	1	MacBinary version for upload
7CH	1	MacBinary version for read
7DH	1	CRC sum previous 124 byte
7EH	2	Reserved

Table 38.2 Structure of a MAC header (*cont.*)

At offset 0, there is always one byte coded with 00H. In the case of MAC Paint files without a header, the first byte is also 00H. If a file contains a value other than 00H, the file is not a MAC-Paint file.

This byte is followed by a second byte at offset 01H containing a length indicator (0–63) for the following file names. The file name begins at offset 02H and relates to the current file. Normally, the MAC operating system stores file names up to 63 bytes long, according to Macintosh conventions. When exporting to other platforms, the relevant naming conventions must be observed. In the case of UNIX, for example, 14 characters are allowed, while DOS accommodates 8 + 3 bytes for the file name. The file name is stored according to the Pascal convention, that is, the byte at offset 01H is the length byte for the string. The name is therefore not terminated with a null byte (as would be normal in C). Only bytes defined in the length indicator may be used as the file name.

The data type of the MAC application is indicated at offset 41H in the header. In the case of MAC-Paint files, the signature PNTG is used. The following four bytes are used for storing the name of the program which created the file. With MAC Paint, the string MPNT is used here.

The *File Attribute* flag at offset 49H is coded as shown in Table 38.3:

Bit	Remarks
0	Inited
1	Changed
2	Busy
3	Bozo
4	System
5	Bundle
6	Invisible
7	Locked

Table 38.3 Coding file attribute byte

This coding is specific to the MAC file system. The two words at offset 4BH define the X/Y position of the file on the (MAC) screen. The fields *Folder ID* and *File Protection* are designed specifically for the MAC file system.

The *SizeOfDataFork* field at offset 53H contains 4 bytes (DWORD) and indicates the length of the MAC data area. This is the file length minus the header length. The *SizeOfResourceFork* field is always set to 0 for MAC-Paint files.

The date and clock time of file creation and of the last modification (modify) are shown in the fields at offset 5BH. These values (DWORD) are stored as the number of seconds since 2 January 1904.

In MAC-Paint files, *GetInfoMessageLength* is always set to 0. The fields at offset 65H onwards are used only in the MacBinary II standard. Finder flags refer to the MAC operating system. The length of the uncompressed image file is stored at offset 75H. *SecondHeaderLength* is used for future extensions in which a second header is appended at offset 80H. The *Upload* and *Read* version numbers describe the internal software version of the transfer programs. The CRC sum for the previous 124 bytes is stored in the byte at offset 7DH. If this field contains the value 00H, the CRC sum should be ignored. The remaining bytes are used to pad out the header to 128 bytes.

38.2 MAC Data Area

The header is followed by the MAC data area. This always begins with the signature:

```
00H 00H 00H 02H
```

which indicates the start of the data area. At this stage another peculiarity of the MAC-Paint format becomes evident. When creating a new file, the MAC-Paint program displays 38 pre-defined bit patterns. These bit patterns can be changed and are saved with the file. After the 4-byte signature, the MAC-Paint file contains a 304-byte area in which these patterns are defined. This area is followed by 204 null bytes which are used to fill up the leader.

In a MAC-Paint file containing a header, the image data starts at offset 640 (280H). If the header is missing, the data starts at offset 512 (200H).

The image data is stored in a fixed raster of 576 × 760 pixels. One bit coded 0 or 1 is provided for each pixel, that is, one byte represents 8 pixels. An uncompressed file contains 51,840 bytes. The image data is read by line. Each uncompressed image line consists of 72 bytes. The data area contains 720 lines.

! **There are indications that the signature 00H 00H 00H 02H in the first four bytes of the data area represents modified patterns. If the first 512 bytes of the data area are set to 00H, MAC-Paint generates the 38 patterns with the initialization values.**

38.3 MAC Packbit coding

To save space in the memory when storing image data, the data is packed using a simple compression process known as MAC Packbit compression. A very good rate of compression is achieved because only monochrome images are involved. The data is decompressed using a very simple procedure:

- Image data is compressed by line. That means decompressed data does not extend beyond the end of an image line.
- During decompression, one data byte is read at a time.
- If the top bit of this data byte is set (1), a packed record is present. The two's complement of the byte is calculated and this acts as a repetition counter for the following byte. The following byte is then copied *n* times.
- If the top bit contains the value 0, the record is uncompressed. The value of the byte should then be increased by 1. This value indicates the number of uncompressed data bytes that follow.

The above steps should be repeated until 72 unpacked bytes have been obtained. These can then be displayed as an image line. It should be pointed out that on the Macintosh, black characters are displayed against a white background. This is not always the case with other systems (for example, DOS).

39

MAC-Picture format (PICT)

***The** MAC-Picture format (PICT) is a metafile format for the storing of images on Macintosh computers. The format was defined by Apple in order to store graphics using the program QuickDraw.*

There are two versions of the PICT format, which are designed for different versions of QuickDraw.

- The original format for QuickDraw 1 supports only monochrome bitmap images with a maximum size of 32 Kbytes. The image resolution of 72 dpi is based on the MAC screen.
- With QuickDraw (color) version 2.0, support was extended to include color images with 8-bit bitmaps. This format still allows monochrome images to be stored.

On a PC with MS-DOS, MAC-Paint files are given the extension `.PCT`. The data is stored in Motorola format (big-endian). Because of its Macintosh origins this format has a number of peculiarities.

The first comes from the structure of the MAC file system, in which files are stored in *forks*. These forks represent data areas in which the operating system stores information. A Macintosh file always contains two forks. One fork is used for storing data, the second for resources (or program code). In physical terms, there are two files on the MAC, although the user only sees one.

With MAC-QuickDraw files, the resource fork remains empty. The image data fork consists of a header and a sequence of metafile operators containing the associated binary data (Figure 39.1).

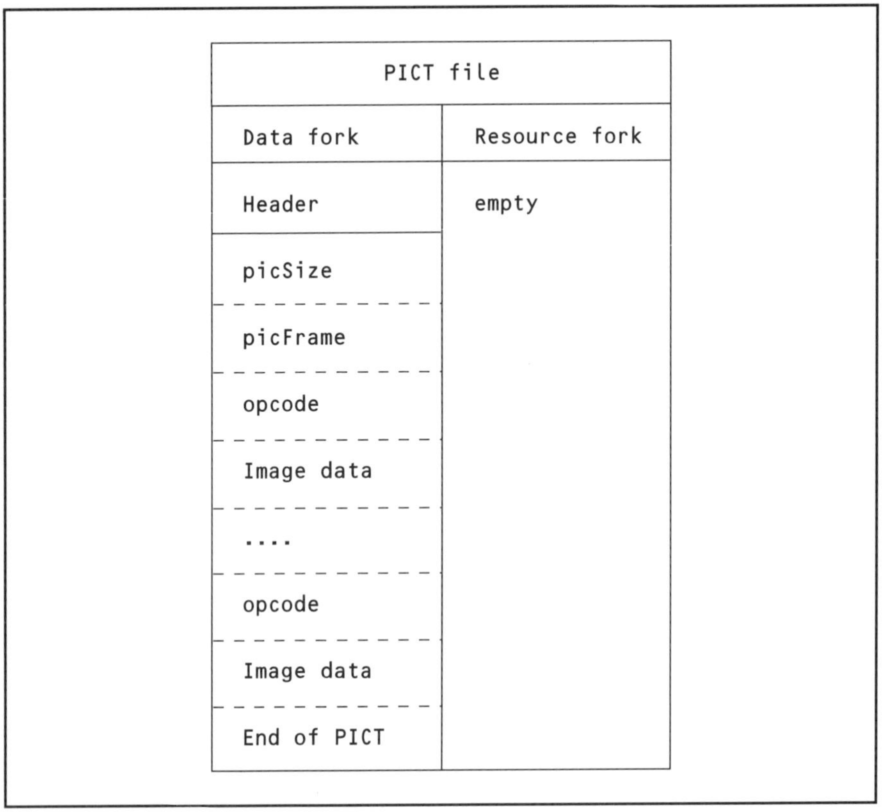

Figure 39.1 Structure of a PICT file

The Macintosh operating system provides a series of library routines for reading and writing PICT files. There are only small differences between the two versions of the PICT format:

- In PICT 1 format, an opcode occupies one byte. PICT 2 format always defines an opcode as a word (2 bytes). If PICT 1 opcodes are stored in PICT 2 format, they must be extended to 2 bytes.
- In version 1, data may begin on a byte boundary. In version 2, data and opcodes must always be aligned on a word boundary.

Furthermore, all unused opcodes in version 2 have a pre-defined number of data bytes, in order to ensure future compatibility with subsequent versions.

39.1 PICT header

The PICT header has a fixed length of 512 bytes and contains application-specific data (image size, scaling, version, and so on). The structure of this header has not been published, and the header should be skipped when importing data. The following data records contain all the information required to construct an image.

39.2 PICT data area

The 512-byte header is followed by the data area. This is divided as shown in Figure 39.1 into another header containing the elements *picSize* and *picFrame*, and other data records of varying length. The header is structured differently in versions 1 and 2.

39.2.1 PicSize record

The *PicSize* record follows the internal header at offset `200H`. This record defines the image dimensions and is structured as shown in Table 39.1.

Offset	Bytes	Remarks
00H	2	Picture size in bytes (integer)
02H	8	Picture frame

Table 39.1 Structure of the PicSize record

The first field is an integer specifying the file size (lower 16 bits) in bytes. The second field contains the image dimensions (bounding box) as a RECT structure. Four integer values are stored in the sequence (top, left, bottom, right).

39.2.2 PicFrame record (PICT 1)

The *PicFrame* record follows at offset `20AH`. This record enables the version of the PICT file to be determined. Because of the altered length of the opcode field, PICT files have a different structure in versions 1 and 2. The difference is also apparent in the *PicFrame* record. Table 39.2 defines the structure of the *PicFrame* record for PICT version 1:

Bytes	Remarks
1	Version operator (11H)
1	Picture version (01H)

Table 39.2 PicFrame record in PICT 1

In PICT 1 format, this record is followed by the image data.

39.2.3 PicFrame record (PICT 2)

The *PicFrame* record is also defined in PICT version 2. This record has the same fields, but each field is 2 bytes long (Table 39.3).

Bytes	Remarks
2	Version operator (0011H)
2	Picture version (02FFH)

Table 39.3 PicFrame record in PICT 2

If the signature 2FFH is recognized, a PICT 2 file is present, and all the following opcodes are coded as 2 bytes.

39.2.4 Reserved header record (PICT 2)

In PICT 2, the *PicFrame* record is followed by another header comprising 26 bytes. This record is already coded as a regular data record (opcode 0C00H). The structure of this header is shown in Table 39.4.

Bytes	Remarks
2	Reserved header opcode (0C00H)
24	Reserved data area

Table 39.4 Reserved header in PICT 2

In the MAC documentation, this header is marked as reserved for future versions of the PICT format. Table 39.5 shows the present coding of the 26 data bytes.

Bytes	Remarks
2	Header Opcode (0C00H)
4	Picture size in byte (-1 for version 2)
4	Original horizontal resolution (pixel/inch)
4	Original vertical resolution (pixel/inch)

Table 39.5 Contents of the reserved header (*continues over...*)

Bytes	Remarks
2	Upper left X corner
2	Upper left Y corner
2	Lower right X corner
2	Lower right Y corner
4	Reserved

Table 39.5 Contents of the reserved header (*cont.*)

39.3 Image data records (PICT 1,2)

In both versions of PICT, this preliminary section is followed by the actual image data, which is stored in records containing an opcode field, followed by the associated binary data.

- In PICT 1, each opcode field occupies one byte.
- In PICT 2, each opcode field occupies one word (2 bytes).

The end of the image data is indicated by the *End of Picture* record, which is represented by one byte (PICT 1) or one word (PICT 2), containing the value `FFH` or `00FFH` respectively. The structure of the image data can be described as follows:

opcode

data

opcode

data

opcode

data

...

`00FFH`

In PICT 2 format, the opcodes and data must always be aligned on 16 bit boundaries. The following table shows the opcodes defined in PICT 2:

Opcode	Size	Remarks
0000H	0	NOP
0001H	region	Clip area
0002H	8	Background pattern
0003H	2	Text font (word)
0004H	1	Text face (byte)
0005H	2	Text mode (word)
0006H	4	Extra space (fixed point)
0007H	4	Pen size (point)
0008H	2	Pen mode (word)
0009H	8	Pen pattern
000AH	8	Fill pattern
000BH	4	Oval size (point)
000CH	4	Origin (dhorz, dvert)
000DH	2	Text size (word)
000EH	4	Foreground color (long)
000FH	4	Background color (long)
0010H	8	Text ratio numerator (points) denominator (points)
0011H	1	Version
0012H	*n*	Color background pattern
0013H	*n*	Color pen pattern
0014H	*n*	Color fill pattern
0015H	2	Fractional pen position
0016H	2	Extra space for each char
0017H/ 0019H	0	Reserved opcodes
001AH	*n*	RGB foreground color
001BH	*n*	RGB background color
001CH	0	Highlight mode flag
001DH	*n*	RGB highlight color
001EH	0	Use default highlight color
001FH	*n*	RGB highlight color (arithmetic mode)
0020H	8	Line (x,y,x1,y1)
0021H	4	Line form (point)
0022H	6	Short line (x,y,dx,dy)
0023H	2	Short line from (dx,dy) (–128..127)
0024H/ 0027H	len+data	Reserved opcodes (len = 2 byte)

Table 39.6 PICT 2 opcodes (*continues over...*)

Opcode	Size	Remarks
0028H	5+*n*	Long text 4 location (x,y) 1 count (0..255) *n* text (0..255)
0029H	2+*n*	Draw horizontal text 1 dh (0..255) 1 count (0..255) *n* text
002AH	2+*n*	Draw vertical text 1 dv (0..255) 1 count (0..255) *n* text
002BH	3+*n*	Draw horizontal, vertical text 1 dh (0..255) 1 dv (0..255) 1 count (0..255) *n* text
002CH/ 002FH	len+data	Reserved opcodes (len = 2 byte)
0030H	8	Frame rectangle
0031H	8	Paint rectangle
0032H	8	Erase rectangle
0033H	8	Invert rectangle
0034H	8	Fill rectangle
0035H/ 0037H	8	Reserved opcodes
0038H	0	Frame same rectangle
0039H	0	Paint same rectangle
003AH	0	Erase same rectangle
003BH	0	Invert same rectangle
003CH	0	Fill same rectangle
003DH/ 003FH	0	Reserved opcode
0040H	8	Frame RoundRectangle
0041H	8	Paint RoundRectangle
0042H	8	Erase RoundRectangle
0043H	8	Invert RoundRectangle
0044H	8	Fill RoundRectangle
0045H/ 0047H	8	Reserved opcodes

Table 39.6 PICT 2 opcodes (*cont.*)

Opcode	Size	Remarks
0048H	0	Frame same RoundRectangle
0049H	0	Paint same RoundRectangle
004AH	0	Erase same RoundRectangle
004BH	0	Invert same RoundRectangle
004CH	0	Fill same RoundRectangle
004DH/ 004FH	0	Reserved opcodes
0050H	8	Frame oval
0051H	8	Paint oval
0052H	8	Erase oval
0053H	8	Invert oval
0054H	8	Fill oval
0055H/ 0057H	8	Reserved opcodes
0058H	0	Frame same oval
0059H	0	Paint same oval
005AH	0	Erase same oval
005BH	0	Invert same oval
005CH	0	Fill same oval
005DH/ 005FH	0	Reserved opcodes
0060H	12	Frame arc 4 Rect 4 Start angle 4 Arc angle
0061H	12	Paint arc
0062H	12	Erase arc
0063H	12	Invert arc
0064H	12	Fill arc
0065H/ 0067H	12	Reserved opcodes
0068H	4	Frame same arc
0069H	4	Paint same arc
006AH	4	Erase same arc
006BH	4	Invert same arc
006CH	4	Fill same arc
006DH/ 006FH	4	Reserved opcodes
0070H	poly	Frame polygon

Table 39.6
PICT 2 opcodes
(*cont.*)

Opcode	Size	Remarks
0071H	poly	Paint polygon
0072H	poly	Erase polygon
0073H	poly	Invert polygon
0074H	poly	Fill polygon
0075H/ 0077H	poly	Reserved opcodes
0078H	0	Frame same polygon
0079H	0	Paint same polygon
007AH	0	Erase same polygon
007BH	0	Invert same polygon
007CH	0	Fill same polygon
007DH/ 007FH	0	Reserved opcodes
0080H	region	Frame region
0081H	region	Paint region
0082H	region	Erase region
0083H	region	Invert region
0084H	region	Fill region
0085H/ 0087H	region	Reserved opcodes
0088H	0	Frame same region
0089H	0	Paint same region
008AH	0	Erase same region
008BH	0	Invert same region
008CH	0	Fill same region
008DH/ 008FH	0	Reserved opcodes
0090H	*n*	Copy bits, rect clipped
0091H	*n*	Copy bit, region clipped
0092H/ 0097H	len+data	Reserved opcodes (len = 2 byte)
0098H	*n*	Packed copy bits, rect clipped
0099H	*n*	Packed copy bits, region clipped
009AH/ 009FH	len+data	Reserved opcodes (len = 2 byte)
00A0H	2	Short comment
00A1H	4+*n*	Long comment 2 kind 2 size *n* data

Table 39.6 PICT 2 opcodes (*cont.*)

Graphics

Opcode	Size	Remarks
00A2H/ 00AFH	len+data	Reserved opcodes
00B0H/ 00CFH	0	Reserved opcodes
00D0H/ 00FEH	len+data	Reserved opcodes (len = 4 byte)
00FFH	0	End of picture
0100H/ 01FFH	2	Reserved opcodes
0200H/ 0BFFH	4	Reserved opcodes
0C00H	24	Header
0C01H/ 7EFFH	4	Reserved opcodes
7F00H/ 7FFFH	254	Reserved opcodes
8000H/ 80FFH	0	Reserved opcodes
8100H/ FFFFH	len+data	Reserved opcodes (len = 4 Byte)

Table 39.6 PICT 2 opcodes (*cont.*)

The size column in Table 39.6 indicates the record length, excluding the opcode bytes. The records are defined as Pascal structures in accordance with Table 39.7:

Bytes	Data type
1	Byte (unsigned)
1	SByte (signed –128..127)
2	Integer (signed)
2	Word (unsigned)
4	LongInteger (signed)
4	DWORD (unsigned)
4	Points (x,y: integer)
8	Rect (top, left, bottom, right: integer)

Table 39.7 Data types within PICT records (*continues over...*)

Bytes	Data type
n	Poly (10 bytes + data)
n	Region (10 bytes + data)
4	Fixed point
8	Pattern
2	Row bytes

Table 39.7 Data types within PICT records (*cont.*)

The records with opcodes 0040H to 0044H relate to rectangles with rounded corners. The radius of this rounding is defined via opcode 000BH (oval size).

A color pattern is defined for the records with opcodes 0012H, 0013H and 0014H. The structure is as follows:

Bytes	Field
2	Pattern type 0001H
8	Old pattern data
n	Pixel map
n	Color table
n	Pixel data
2	Pattern type 0002H
8	Old pattern data
n	RGB table

Table 39.8 Record structure opcodes 0012H–0014H

The *Color* table is a data structure which appears only with PICT 2 files. It is structured as follows:

Bytes	Field
4	ID-number color table (0)
2	Flags
2	Color table entries –1
(*n*+1)*8	Color table with 4-word entries: pixel value, red, green, blue

Table 39.9 Structure of a color table

However, if the *RGBColor* structure appears, this contains three integer values with the color intensities *red*, *green*, *blue*.

The *pixMap* structure used in the data records is shown in Table 39.10.

Type	Field
long	(unused)
word	RowBytes
rect	Bounds (Bounding box)
word	Version number (0)
word	Packing format (0)
long	Packet size (0)
fixed	Horizontal resolution (48000H)
fixed	Vertical resolution (48000H)
word	Pixel type (0)
word	Bits per pixel (1,2,4,8)
word	Components per pixel (1)
long	Offset to next plane (0)
long	Color table (0)
long	Reserved

Table 39.10 pixMap structure

The image data is stored in the *pixMap* structure and may be packed or unpacked. The following rules apply when decoding the data:

- If the field *RowBytes* < 8, the data is unpacked. The data area therefore contains RowBytes * (Bounds.bottom – Bounds.top) data bytes. The values for *Bounds* can be found in the bounding box.
- If the field *RowBytes* >= 8, a packed data area is involved. The individual lines are packed separately. The number of lines can be calculated as Bounds.bottom – Bounds.top. Each image line begins with the field *ByteCount* followed by the data. If *RowBytes* > 250, then *ByteCount* will be defined as a word. Otherwise, *ByteCount* is defined as a byte. The compressed image data follows *ByteCount*. This data is compressed according to the Packbit method (see MAC-Paint format, Chapter 38).

The data areas for the records 0090H and 0098H are structured as follows:

Type	Field
pixMap	Pixel map structure
rect	Source rectangle
rect	Destination rectangle
word	Transfer mode
PixData	Data area containing pixels

Table 39.11 Structure data area (opcode 0090H, 0098H)

The data areas for the records 0091H and 0099H are structured as follows:

Type	Field
pixMap	Pixel map structure
ColorTable	Color table structure
rect	Source rectangle
rect	Destination rectangle
word	Transfer mode
region	Mask region
PixData	Data area containing pixels

Table 39.12 Structure data area (opcode 0091H, 0099H)

! **Warning:** Opcodes 0090H to 0099H have been modified in PICT 2! The first word after the opcode is not the *BaseAddress* field; instead, the data area begins with the *RowBytes* field. If the top bit of *RowBytes* is set, a color image is present and each pixel will contain several bits. If the values for *RowBytes* are below 80H, the image is a monochrome image with one bit per pixel. The records with opcodes 0090H and 0091H contain unpacked bitmap data and may be used with data series of less than 8 bytes.

40

Atari NEOchrome format (NEO)

The *NEOchrome format is used for representing color images on the Atari. The file names have the extension* `.NEO`*. Because of the peculiarities of the Atari regarding reduced color representation, the format is restricted to Atari computers.*

The structure of a NEOchrome file is shown in Figure 40.1.

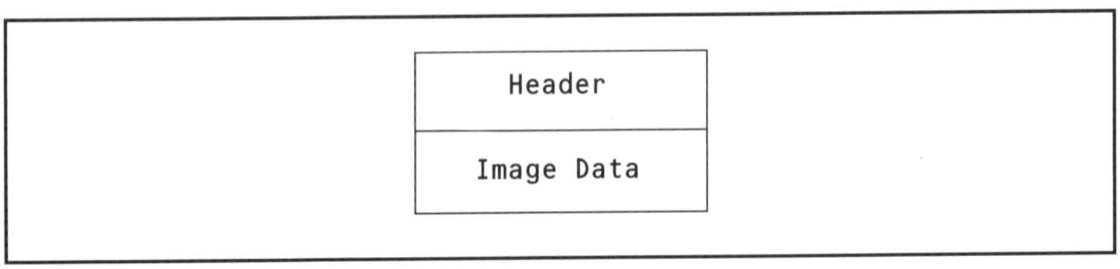

Figure 40.1 Structure of a NEOchrome (NEO) file

The format comprises a header with a fixed size of 140 bytes, followed by an image data area of 16,000 bytes. The data is stored in Motorola format (big-endian).

40.1 NEOchrome header

The header of a NEOchrome file is structured in words, as shown in Table 40.1.

Offset	Bytes	Remarks
00H	2	Flags (0)
02H	2	Image resolution
04H	16*2	Color palette
24H	12	Animation file name
30H	2	Color animation limits
32H	2	Color animation speed and direction
34H	2	Number of steps
36H	2	Image X offset (0)
38H	2	Image Y offset (0)
3AH	2	Image width
3BH	2	Image height
3CH	33*2	Reserved (00H)

Table 40.1 Structure of a NEO header

The first word contains a flag which is always set to 0. The second word defines the image resolution. With NEOchrome files, three resolutions are defined:

Code	Resolution
00H	Low resolution (320 × 200, 16 colors)
01H	Medium resolution (640 × 200, 4 colors)
02H	High resolution (640 × 200, 2 colors)

Table 40.2 Resolution of NEOchrome images

The number of high resolution colors is reduced because of the reduced options for color representation.

The color palette for the image is stored in the 16 words at offset 06. The color palette has three bits per color, as shown in Table 40.3.

Bit	Color
0-2	Blue
3	—
4-6	Green
7	—
8-10	Red
11-15	—

Table 40.3 Coding for Atari palette values

If this type of image is to be transferred to a PC, the color value shown should be multiplied by 32.

The palette is followed by the area containing the name of the file. This entry is generally filled with the space character ' '.

The word at offset 30H defines the limits (color animation limits) within which the colors of an image can vary:

Bits	Remarks
0-3	Right/upper color limit
4-7	Left/lower color limit
15	1: animation data valid

Table 40.4 Coding of limit values

This (color) animation limit is only valid if bit 15 of the word is set to 1. Otherwise the picture will be displayed with a fixed color combination.

The word at offset 32H defines the output speed for the image (animation speed) and the output direction. Table 40.5 indicates the coding for the individual bits of this word.

Bits	Remarks
0-7	Speed
15	Direction (0 normal, 1 reverse)

Table 40.5 Speed and direction coding

The playback speed defines the number of blank frames per animation frame. Bit 15 defines the direction of playback. The number of frames in an animation is stored at offset 34H.

The fields for the offset of the X and Y axes of the image are unused and are set to 0. The image width is always set to 320 pixels and the image height to 200 pixels. The remaining fields are used for filling out the header.

40.2 Data area of the NEOchrome file

The data area contains image data in uncoded form as a screen shot. Images are stored with 1, 2 or 4 bits per pixel.

With 1 bit per pixel, the data is in one plane, and one byte describes 8 pixels which must be played back in the given image raster.

At 2 bits per pixel, 4 colors can be represented, and the data is stored in two planes. The first byte contains 8 pixels on the first plane and the second byte contains 8 pixels on the second plane. If the file is to be transferred to a PC, the two bytes must be combined bitwise to form the color values.

With 4 bits per pixel, 16 colors are displayed. The data is stored in four planes. Each byte contains 8 pixels on the same plane. After the four bytes have been read, they must be combined bit by bit to give the color information for a pixel.

41

NEOchrome Animation format (ANI)

NEOchrome *Animation files have the extension* `.ANI` *and enable image sequences to be played back.*

The ANI files have a 22-byte header followed by one or more frames for the animation.

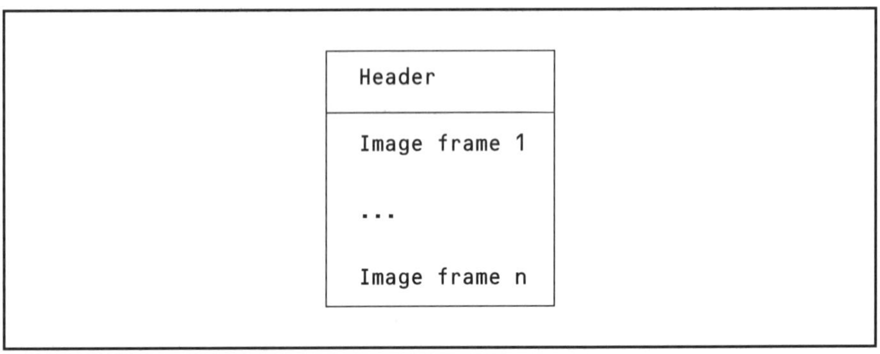

Figure 41.1 Structure of a NEOchrome (ANI) file

The data is stored in Motorola format (big-endian).

41.1 NEOchrome ANI header

The header of an ANI file is structured as shown in Table 41.1:

Offset	Bytes	Remarks
00H	4	Signature
04H	2	Image width
06H	2	Image height
08H	2	Image size + 10
0AH	2	Image X coordinate – 1
0CH	2	Image Y coordinate – 1
0EH	2	Number of frames
10H	2	Playback speed
12H	4	Reserved (00H)

Table 41.1 Structure of an ANI header

The first word contains a signature which is always coded BAH BEH EBH EAH. This is followed by the image width in bytes, which must be divisible by 8. The image height is stored at offset 06H and is defined in scan lines. The word at offset 08H defines the image size + 10 in bytes. The image coordinates, X,Y, are stored at offset 0AH. The value for the X coordinate defines the left image margin (in pixels – 1) and must be divisible by 16. The Y coordinate defines the top edge of the image in pixels – 1.

The word at 0EH defines the number of frames in the ANI file. The following field indicates the playback speed for the individual frames. This value defines the number of blank frames between two actual frames.

The last four bytes of the header are reserved and are set to 0.

The header is followed by the data area containing one or more images in the playback sequence. The method of storage is the same as described for the NEO format (*see* Chapter 40).

42

Animatic Film format (FLM)

The *Animatic Film format is used on the Atari to store image sequences with low resolution (320 × 200) and 16 colors.*

FLM files contain a 62-byte header, followed by one or more individual frames.

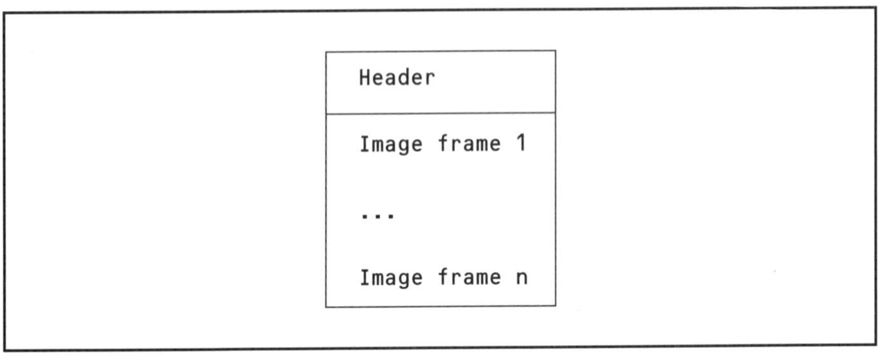

Figure 42.1 Structure of an Animatic Film file (FLM)

The data is stored in Motorola (big endian) format.

42.1 Animatic Film header (FLM)

The header of an FLM file is structured as shown in Table 42.1:

Offset	Bytes	Remarks
00H	2	Number of frames
02H	16*2	Color palette
22H	2	Film speed
24H	2	Play direction
26H	2	Action after last frame
28H	2	Frame width in pixels
2AH	2	Frame height in pixels
2CH	2	Major version number
2EH	2	Minor version number
30H	4	Signature
32H	3*4	Reserved (00H)

Table 42.1 Structure of an FLM header

The first word contains the number of frames in the file. This is followed by a palette containing 16 entries of two bytes each. The color intensities are stored with 3 bits each (*see* NEOchrome NEO format, Chapter 40).

The film speed is indicated at offset 22H. The value is in the range 0–99 and specifies the number of blank frames between two images.

The value 0 for play direction indicates that the image is to be played back in the sequence stored. If the value is 1, the images will be played in reverse sequence.

The word at offset 26H defines the action to be carried out after displaying the last image.

Value	Action
00H	Pause and then repeat from beginning
01H	Immediate repeat from beginning (loop)
02H	—
03H	Play back in reverse direction

Table 42.2 Action after last frame

The two words at offsets 28H and 2AH define the dimensions of the frame in pixels.

The following two words contain the version number of the Animatic software used to create the animation. The signature is stored at offset 30H and consists of four bytes with the values 27H 18H 28H 18H. The last 12 bytes are reserved and are set to 00H.

The header is followed by the data area containing the frames. The area contains a screen shot for each frame.

43

ComputerEyes Raw Data format (CE1,CE2)

ComputerEyes Raw Data format is only used on the Atari for storing graphics. The extension CE1 indicates images with low resolution (320 × 200), while CE2 stores images with medium resolution (640 × 200).

The data is stored in Motorola format (big-endian).

43.1 ComputerEyes Raw Data header (CEx)

The header of a `CEx` file is structured as shown in Table 43.1.

Offset	Bytes	Remarks
`00H`	4	Signature 'EYES'
`04H`	2	Resolution
`06H`	8*2	Reserved

Table 43.1 Structure of a `CEx` header

The first four bytes contain the signature `45H 49H 45H 53H` which corresponds to the string 'EYES'. This is followed by a word containing the resolution. The permitted entries are as follows:

`0`: Resolution 320 × 200

`1`: Resolution 640 × 200

The remaining 8 words of the header are reserved.

The header is followed by the image data area. With a resolution of 320 × 200 pixels, the data is stored in three planes:

64,000 bytes red plane, 1 pixel per byte

64,000 bytes green plane, 1 pixel per byte

64,000 bytes blue plane, 1 pixel per byte

If medium resolution is used, the image data area contains 128,000 bytes, arranged as 640 × 200 bytes. Each byte contains the value for one pixel.

44

Cyber Paint Sequence format (SEQ)

This *format was developed for Atari computers for the storing of image sequences with 16 colors and a low resolution (320 × 200).*

The data is stored in Motorola format (big-endian).

44.1 Cyber Paint Sequence header (SEQ)

The header of a SEQ file is structured as shown in Table 44.1:

Offset	Bytes	Remarks
00H	2	Signature (FEDBH or FEDCH)
02H	2	Version number
04H	4	Number of frames
08H	2	Display speed
0AH	118	Reserved
..H	n*4	Array of frame offsets

Table 44.1 Structure of a SEQ header

The first two bytes contain the signature FEDBH or FEDCH. This is followed by a version number. The number of frames in the file is indicated at offset 04H. The following word defines the delay between frames. The 128 bytes at offset 0AH are reserved and set to 00H. The header ends with an array of 4-byte entries, which contains the offsets of the individual images (frames).

44.2 Structure of the frame

Each frame consists of a header followed by the image data. This header is structured as shown in Table 44.2:

Offset	Bytes	Remarks
00H	2	Frame type
02H	2	Frame resolution
04H	16*2	Color palette
24H	12	File name
30H	2	Color animation limits
32H	2	Color animation speed and direction
34H	2	Number of color steps
36H	2	Frame x offset (0)
38H	2	Frame y offset (0)
3AH	2	Frame width
3CH	2	Frame height
3EH	1	Graphics operation
3FH	1	Compression
40H	4	Frame length in byte
44H	60	Reserved (00H)

Table 44.2 Structure of a frame header

The header is based closely on the NEOchrome header format. The first word identifies the type of frame. This is followed by a word containing the resolution code, which is set to 00H (320 × 200 pixels). The palette is stored in 16 words in Atari format (*see* NEOchrome format, Chapter 40). The file name is usually set to spaces. The *color animation speed* and *number of color steps* fields are not used.

The X-offset of the frame may be between 0 and 319 and the Y-offset between 0 and 199. The image dimensions may be set to 0, because the dimensions of the frame are fixed at 320 × 200 pixels. The *Operation* field describes how the data for a frame is written to the screen:

0: copy

1: exclusive OR

The *Compression* byte indicates a compressed data area if it is set to 1 and an uncompressed data area if it is set to 0.

Graphics

The length field relates to the data area and is always given in the case of compressed data. The last 60 bytes in the frame header are reserved. They are used to pad out the header to 128 bytes.

The data area follows the header and can store the data according to the *delta compression* method. In this case, only the differences from the preceding frame are stored.

A rectangle is placed around the image area containing the altered pixels. This rectangle is stored as a frame. The dimensions and position of the rectangle are indicated in the frame header.

- A delta frame of this type can be stored without being compressed. In this case, it is merged into the image area via the X,Y coordinates, using a simple copy operation.
- Alternatively, the image data can be merged into the image area using `XOR`. The operation field in the header indicates if this mode is to be used.
- With a compressed delta frame, the data must be decoded before being merged into the image area. A `copy` or an `XOR` operation is used, depending on the operation field in the header.
- A null frame has a height and width of 0 pixels, that is, the frame is identical to the preceding frame.

The image data is stored in the data area according to these criteria, thereby ensuring that the minimum amount of storage space is used.

44.3 Compression process

A simple process is used for compression:

- Initially, a word is read. This word then acts as a control element.
- If the value of this word is negative (bit `15 = 1`), the absolute value (`0 .. 32736`) defines the number of following words which are to be read uncompressed from the data area.
- With a value greater than `0`, the control word acts as a counter (`0 .. 32736`). The following word will be copied *n* times.

The value `00H` is theoretically possible, but has no meaning. The unpacked data is in four separate bitplanes, each of which is arranged vertically. The image data is then inserted into the image excerpt indicated (using `copy` or `XOR`).

45

Atari DEGAS format (PI*,PC*)

***The** Atari DEGAS format is used for representing animation with color images. There are several versions of this format, indicated by the endings* `.PI1`, `.PI2`, `.PI3`, `.PC1`, `.PC2` *and* `.PC3`*. The resolution is defined by the last digit of the extension (1 low, 2 medium, 3 high). The letter C in the extension means compressed image data, while PI* files are uncompressed.*

Each DEGAS file contains an individual image and consists of a header, followed by the image data area.

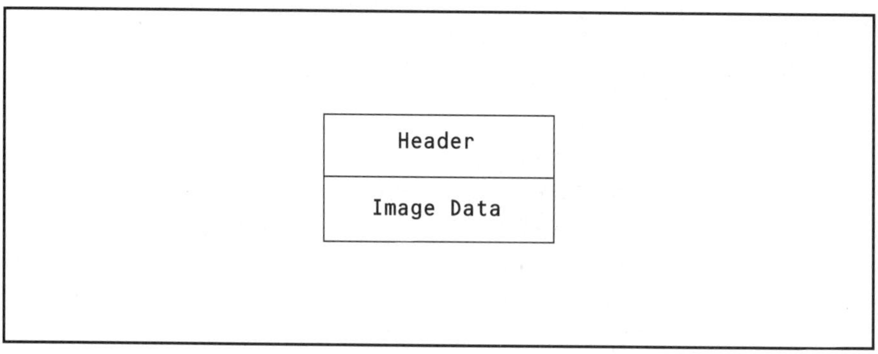

Figure 45.1 Structure of a DEGAS file

The header has a fixed length of 140 bytes and is followed by an image data area containing 32,000 bytes. The data is stored in Motorola format (big-endian).

45.1 DEGAS PI* files

The header of a PI* file is structured as shown in Table 45.1:

Offset	Bytes	Remarks
00H	2	Resolution 0 low 1 medium 2 high
02H	16*2	Color palette

Table 45.1 Structure of a DEGAS PI* header

The first word contains the resolution, in the lowest two bits. The levels of resolution are as described for the NEOchrome format (*see* Chapter 40).

Sixteen words containing the color palette for the image are stored at offset 02H, coded on the basis of three bits per color (*see* NEOchrome format).

In PI1, PI2 and PI3 files, the header is followed by the data area which contains uncompressed image data, and has a fixed length of 16,000 words. The data is stored as a screen extract.

45.2 DEGAS Elite PC* files

The DEGAS Elite PC1, PC2 and PC3 files are used for compressed image files. A PC* file is structured as shown in Table 45.2.

Offset	Bytes	Remarks
00H	2	Resolution 8000H low 8001H medium 8002H high
02H	16*2	Color palette
22H	*n*	Image data
..H	4*2	Starting color numbers
..H	4*2	Ending color numbers
..H	4*2	Direction
..H	4*2	Animation channel delay

Table 45.2 Structure of a DEGAS Elite PC* file

The file consists of a header, followed by the data area. An extension of the header data, containing information on animation, is located at the end of the file.

The first word contains the resolution, which is coded in the lowest two bits. Bit 15 is set to 1, to specify that the file is a DEGAS Elite file with compressed data. The levels of resolution are as described for the NEOchrome format (*see* Chapter 40).

Sixteen words containing the color palette for the image are stored at offset 02H, coded on the basis of three bits per color (*see* NEOchrome format).

In PC1, PC2 and PC3 files, the header is followed by the data area containing the uncompressed image data. This area contains a screen shot, compressed using the Packbit method.

- The data is compressed line by line.
- The first image line (0) begins at the top edge of the screen. Subsequent image lines are below this line.
- The data for each scan line is compressed plane by plane. The first scan line contains data for the lowest plane.
- The Packbit process stores the values in records. The first byte (n) acts as a control byte. If the value is less than 80H, it is followed by n uncompressed data bytes. If the control byte contains values greater than 80H, the following byte will define the compressed value, which will then be copied n times. The value n can be calculated from the control byte as follows: n = 100H – control byte + 1.

In DEGAS Elite images, the image data area is followed by additional information on animation, which is designed for four channels. The following information therefore relates to these four channels. Initially, there is a table of 4 words which contains the left color animation limit for these channels. The next table of 4 words contains the right color animation limit. The third 4-word table indicates the animation channel direction:

Code	Direction
00H	Left
01H	Off
02H	Right

Table 45.3 Direction of animation

The final 4-word field defines the delay times for the channels during animation. This value is given in 1/60 of a second and must be subtracted from 128. The color animation is specially designed for the graphics capabilities of Atari computers.

46

Atari Tiny format (TNY, TN*)

Tiny *Format was developed to store images on the Atari. There are several versions, distinguished from each other by extensions to their file names:*

The following extensions are defined to distinguish the versions:

`*.TNY`	any resolution
`*.TN1`	low resolution
`*.TN2`	medium resolution
`*.TN3`	high resolution

Tiny files comprise a header, followed by an image data area. The data is stored in Motorola format (big-endian). The structure of a Tiny file is shown in Table 46.1.

Offset	Bytes	Remarks
00H	1	Resolution 0 low 1 medium 2 high > 2 rotation information
01H	4	If resolution > 2

Table 46.1 Structure of a Tiny file (*continues over...*)

Offset	Bytes	Remarks
		1 byte left/right color limit
		1 byte direction/speed
		1 word rotation duration
..H	16*2	Color palette
..H	2	Number of control bytes
..H	2	Number of data words
..H	*n*	Control bytes
..H	*m*	Data area

Table 46.1 Structure of a Tiny file (*cont.*)

The first byte contains the resolution, in the two lowest bits. The levels of resolution are as described for the NEOchrome format (*see* Chapter 40).

If the value of this byte is greater than 2, the header contains additional information on color rotation, which appears immediately after the first byte. The byte at offset 01H defines the color animation limits. The top 4 bits indicate the left limit (start limit) and the 4 lowest bits the right limit (end limit). The following byte contains the code for the speed and direction of color animation. Negative values indicate that the direction is left, while positive values indicate right. The absolute value gives the animation speed in $\frac{1}{60}$ of a second. The last word defines the duration of the animation in steps (number of iterations).

The color rotation information (if present) is followed by a 16-word field containing the color palette, coded as described for the NEOchrome format. The palette is followed by a word indicating the number of control bytes. These (3 .. 10667) control bytes are located between the header and the data area and contain information on the decompression of the image data. The following word indicates the number of data words (1 .. 16000) used for the image data area.

The image data is compressed using Run-Length Encoding (RLE). One peculiarity is that the control bytes are separated from the compressed data. These control bytes are used for decoding the compressed image data. The following rules apply to every control byte read:

$x < 0$ If the value is negative (less than 80H), the absolute value indicates the number of words to be read from the data area.

$x = 0$ In this case, the next word in the control data area should be read. This word contains a repetition counter (128 .. 32767). The next word from the image data area will be repeated *n* times.

$x = 1$ The next word in the control data area should be read. This word contains the number of words to be read from the image data area (128 .. 32768).

$x > 1$ The control data byte contains a repetition counter (2 .. 127). The next word from the image data area should be repeated *n* times.

Graphics

The image data decoded in this way does not represent a screen shot; on the contrary, the screen data is divided into vertical columns. There are four areas for these columns:

1: columns 1, 5, 9 and so on

2: columns 2, 6, 10 and so on

3: columns 3, 7, 11 and so on

4: columns 4, 8, 12 and so on

Each column contains one word from the scan line. A word from the next column is then read. In this way the image is compressed line by line.

47

Atari Imagic Film/Picture format (IC*)

The *Imagic Film/Picture format was developed for storing images on the Atari. There are several variants which are distinguished by their file name extensions (*`.IC1`*,* `.IC2`*,* `.IC3`*). The last digit in the file extension indicates the resolution (1 low, 2 medium, 3 high).*

Imagic Film/Picture files consist of a header, followed by an image data area. The data is stored in Motorola format (big-endian). The header is structured as shown in Table 47.1:

Offset	Bytes	Remarks
00H	4	Signature 'IMDC'
02H	2	Resolution 0 low 1 medium 2 high
04H	2*16	Color palette
24H	2	Date stamp
26H	2	Time stamp
28H	8	File name
30H	2	Length of data area
32H	4	Registration number
34H	8	Reserved
3CH	1	Compression flag
3DH	3	IF compression = 01H 1 compression 1 — 1 escape byte

Table 47.1 Structure of an Imagic Film/Picture header

The first four bytes contain a signature which is followed by a word containing the resolution of the image. The color palette comprises 16 words, coded as described for the NEOchrome format (*see* Chapter 40).

The date and time at which the file was created are stored at offset `24H`, in GEMDOS format.

The file name is stored at offset `28H`. The word at offset `30H` defines the length of the data area. A compression flag is located at offset `3CH`. Data is uncompressed if the flag is set to `00H` and compressed if the flag is set to `01H`.

At offset `32H`, there is a registration number, which is of significance only to the program that created the file.

If the image data is compressed, there are three bytes at offset `3DH` giving further details. If the first byte is set to `FFH`, the data is stored in RLE compression format. Any other value indicates Delta Compression, that is, only the changes to individual frames have been stored.

Data compressed using RLE compression can be decoded using the following algorithm.

```
Escape byte
Read a byte
IF byte >= 2 THEN
 duplicate the next byte n times
ENDIF
IF byte = 1 THEN
 o = 0
 while n = 1 then
  o = o+1
  read byte n
 end
 k = n
 d = next byte
 duplicate d (256*o+k) times
ENDIF
Not (Escape byte)
```

Figure 47.1 Decoding RLE data

Data compressed using the Delta frame process can be decoded using the following algorithm.

```
Escape byte
Read a byte
IF byte >= 3 THEN
 duplicate the next byte n times
ENDIF
IF byte = 2 THEN
 n = next byte
 IF n = 0 THEN End of Picture
 IF N >= 2 THEN
  read n bytes from base picture
 ENDIF
 IF N = 1 THEN
  o = 0
  while n = 1 then
   o = o+1
   read byte n
  end
  k = n
  d = next byte
  duplicate d (256*o+k) times
 ENDIF
ENDIF
Not (Escape byte)
```

Figure 47.2 Decoding Delta Frame data

With the Delta Frame method, the file name of the base picture is indicated in the header. If this field is set to 00H, there is no base picture.

48

Atari STAD format (PAC)

***The** STAD format was developed for storing individual monochrome pictures with 640 × 400 pixels on the Atari. A PAC file contains a header and a data area compressed using the RLE method. The data is stored in Motorola format (big-endian).*

The header is structured as follows:

Offset	Bytes	Remarks
`00H`	4	Packing orientation
`04H`	1	RLE ID byte for pack-byte
`05H`	1	Pack-byte
`06H`	1	Special RLE ID byte

Table 48.1 Structure of a PAC file header

The first four bytes contain a signature indicating the packing direction. '`pM86`' indicates that the data has been packed in columns (vertical); with '`pM85`', the algorithm packs the data by line (horizontal).

The image data is stored after the 7-byte header, using the RLE process. Packed and unpacked records can therefore alternate. Packed records are introduced by one of the two RLE ID bytes.

The byte at offset `05H` in the header indicates the most frequently occurring byte. This byte does not need to be stored in the packed data area.

The data area can therefore contain three different types of record:

- The first record type contains two data bytes. The first byte corresponds to the RLE ID byte, which is stored at offset 04H in the header. The second byte contains a repetition counter, which defines how many times the pack-byte (stored at offset 05H in the header) is to be copied.
- The second record type comprises three data bytes. The first byte corresponds to the special RLE ID byte, which is stored in the header at offset 06H. The second byte contains a repetition counter and the third byte contains the actual image value. This third byte will be repeated *n* times.
- The third record type consists of a single byte, representing one uncompressed image value. This type of record occurs whenever the value of the byte read does not correspond to an RLE ID byte.

Compressed data is decoded either by row or by column and displayed in a 640 × 400 raster. Each unpacked data byte describes 8 pixels. The direction in which the pixels are to be displayed (horizontal, vertical) is indicated in the header.

49

Autodesk Animator format (FLI)

V arious *formats are used for storing moving pictures (animation). To a certain extent, the Autodesk Animator file format (FLI) represents a standard. In files of this type, image sequences can only be stored with a resolution of 300 × 200 pixels. An extended format (FLC) has been developed to overcome this limitation (see Chapter 50).*

An FLI file consists of a 128-byte header, followed by sections containing the individual frames. Figure 49.1 shows the structure of an FLI file.

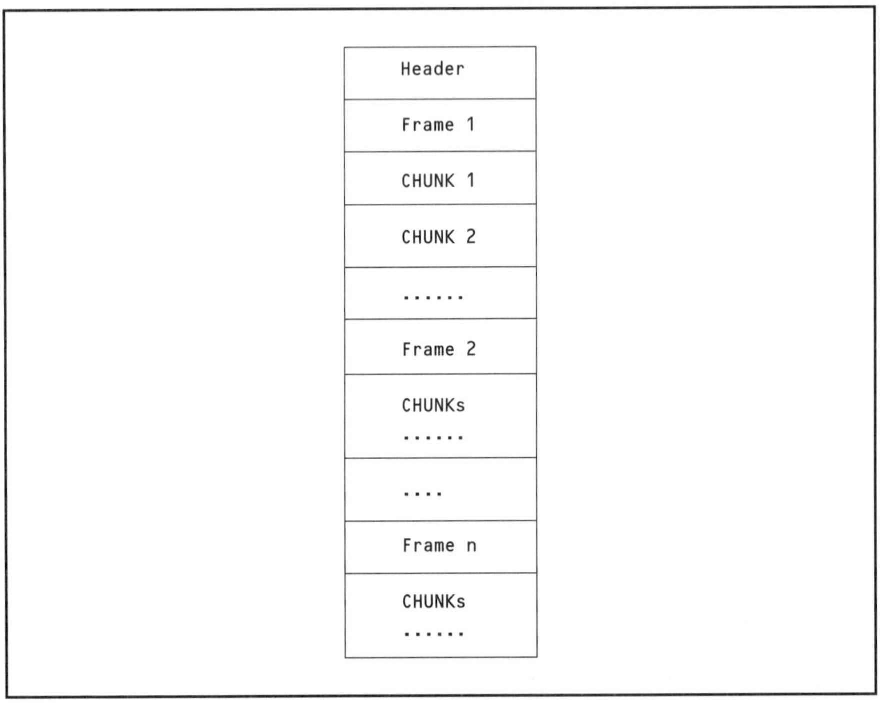

Figure 49.1 Structure of an Animator (FLI) file

Since the image data in an animation is very similar from one frame to the next, Animator stores only the changes between frames. The complete image need only be stored in the first frame. This requires different data structures and compression methods for the frames. These data structures are known as *CHUNKs*, as in the case of IFF files.

In the first frame, the complete picture (key frame) is stored using RLE compression. The following frames contain only the differences between images (delta frames). An additional frame at the end of the file indicates the differences between the first and last frames. All data in an FLI file is stored in Intel format.

49.1 FLI header

FLI files always begin with a 128-byte header. This header is structured as shown in Table 49.1:

Offset	Bytes	Remarks
00H	4	File size in bytes
04H	2	Signature AF11H
06H	2	Number of frames
08H	2	Screen width
0AH	2	Screen height
0CH	2	Bits per pixel
0EH	2	Flags
10H	4	Delay time
14H	2	Reserved (00H 00H)
16H	102	Fill bytes (00H)

Table 49.1 Structure of a FLI header

The first field defines the length of the FLI file. A 2 byte signature containing the values AF11H is stored at offset 04H. A different signature must be used if an image file with a resolution of less than 320 × 200 pixels is defined. This prevents other software from crashing when reading these files.

The word at offset 06H indicates the number of frames in the FLI file. Image sequences can be read and displayed on the basis of this value. The maximum number of frames in an FLI file is 4000.

The Screen width and Screen height fields define the resolution of the FLI images. With FLI files, this is limited to 320 × 200 pixels. However, this restriction does not apply to the FLC files described in the next chapter.

The number of bits per pixel is stored at offset 0CH. FLI files are restricted to a maximum of 8 bits per pixel; that is, images with up to 256 colors can be stored.

The flags at offset 0EH are reserved and must be set to the value 0003H. A certain speed must be observed when playing back the images. The delay time between two frames is indicated in units of 1/70 of a millisecond, in a 32-bit value at offset 10H. The remaining bytes of the header are reserved and set to 00H.

49.2 FLI frames

FLI files contain the image sequences for the animation in the data area which start at offset 80H. The individual images are stored in *frames*, and the number of frames (maximum 4000) is indicated in the header. Each frame has a 16-byte header, structured as shown in Table 49.2.

Offset	Bytes	Remarks
00H	4	Frame size in bytes
04H	2	Signature (F1FAH)
06H	2	Number of CHUNKs
08H	8	Reserved (0)

Table 49.2 Structure of a frame header

The first 4 bytes indicate the length of the frame in bytes, including the 16 bytes of the header. The signature F1FAH must follow at offset 04H; otherwise there is an error in the FLI file. The word at offset 06H indicates the number of CHUNKs in this frame.

CHUNKs are data structures containing the individual information for an image (for example, color palette, pixel data). Each CHUNK has a 6-byte header which contains a 4-byte length field and one word giving the CHUNK type. This is followed by the data, arranged in a CHUNK-specific structure. The CHUNK types defined in the FLI format are described below.

49.2.1 COLOR_64 CHUNK (type 11)

This CHUNK stores a *compressed color map*. The CHUNK always occurs if the color map has changed from that of the previous image. The CHUNK is structured as follows:

Offset	Bytes	Remarks
00H	4	CHUNK size in bytes
04H	2	CHUNK type (0BH)
06H	2	Number of packets
08H	*n*	Packets containing color map data

Table 49.3 Structure of a COLOR_64 CHUNK

The word at offset 06H defines the number of data packets in the CHUNK. These data packets contain the compressed color map.

The color map for a VGA card contains 256 entries of 3 bytes each, numbered from 0 to 255. The COLOR_64 CHUNK defines the entries in the color map which have changed since the preceding image. The first byte in a packet indicates the number of entries in the color map to be skipped. The following byte defines the number of entries to be changed. If this byte is set to 0, all 256 entries in the color map must be changed. This byte is followed by the color map data. Three bytes (red, green, blue) are stored for each color to be changed. In the COLOR_64 CHUNK the bytes for the color intensities may contain values between 0 and 63, that is, only 64 different colors can be represented. In the FLC format, a COLOR_256 CHUNK, which can define 256 colors, is used.

49.2.2 DELTA_FLI CHUNK (type 12)

This type of CHUNK contains compressed data (*byte oriented delta frame data*). The CHUNK describes the differences from the preceding frame.

Offset	Bytes	Remarks
00H	4	CHUNK size in bytes
04H	2	CHUNK type (0CH)
06H	2	Number of equal lines
08H	2	Number of changed lines
0AH	*n*	Data for changed lines

Table 49.4 Structure of a DELTA_FLI CHUNK

The word at offset 06H defines the number of image lines (with reference to the top edge of the image) which are the same as those in the previous image. These image lines do not need to be output.

The following word (offset 08H) contains the number of image lines which are different from the previous frame. These image lines are displayed from top to bottom.

The data for the changed image lines is stored in compressed form at offset 0AH. Each image line is compressed separately. The image data is compared byte by byte with the previous frame.

- The first byte in a compressed line indicates the number of following packets.
- If the relevant line of the previous frame has not changed, the value 0 is stored in the first byte. This is followed by the data for the next line.

The individual packets within each line are structured as follows:

1 byte skip count
1 byte size count
n bytes data

Table 49.5 Structure of a packet

The first byte (skip count) defines the number of pixels to be skipped in the line. These pixels have not changed since the previous frame. If there are more than 255 unchanged pixels, two packets must be used.

The `size count`, which also indicates whether compression has been used, is stored in the second byte.

- A positive value in the `size count` field acts as a counter. The following *n* bytes will be read and displayed as pixels.
- If the value in `size count` is negative (greater than `80H`), a compressed record is present. The following byte defines the value of the pixel which is to be displayed `size count` * (–1) times.

With this method of compression, only the image data areas that have changed since the preceding frame are stored. Under unfavourable conditions, it is possible for an FLI_LC CHUNK to grow to 70 kbytes in length (key frame: 7102 + width*height, delta frame: 802 + width * height). This may happen, for example, in video sequences, where 'image noise' usually occurs in the background. This length exceeds the 64-kbyte limit of the FLI definition. In this case, the Autodesk Animator stores the frame as an FLI_COPY CHUNK.

! This CHUNK was used by the original Animator. Animator PRO uses the FLC format which no longer uses this CHUNK. However, this type of CHUNK may occur in an Animator PRO file if the original animation was produced by Animator.

49.2.3 FLI_BLACK CHUNK (type 13)

This CHUNK has a very simple structure. It is used for producing a completely black frame, that is, all pixels are set to `00H`.

Offset	Bytes	Remarks
00H	4	CHUNK size in bytes
04H	2	CHUNK type (`0DH`)

Table 49.6 Structure of an FLI_BLACK CHUNK

The CHUNK does not have a data area. It is used in the first frame if the user has given the command `NEW` in the animator.

49.2.4 FLI_BYTE_RUN CHUNK (type 15)

This CHUNK stores the complete image in RLE format. It is similar to the FLI_LC CHUNK, except that the skip lines are not included; that is, the image description begins at the top line. This CHUNK is used in the first frame to store the complete image.

Offset	Bytes	Remarks
00H	4	CHUNK size in bytes
04H	2	CHUNK type (0FH)
06H	*n*	Data for changed lines

Table 49.7 Structure of an FLI_BRUN CHUNK

The data for the image lines is stored in compressed form at offset 06H. Each image line is compressed separately and stored in packets. The number of image lines is defined in the header.

- The first byte in a compressed line indicates the number of following packets.
- If the corresponding line in the previous image has not changed, the value 0 is stored in the first byte. This is followed by the data for the next line.

The individual packets within each line are structured as follows:

1 byte size count
n bytes data

Table 49.8 Structure of a packet

The first byte defines the `size count`, which also indicates whether compression has been used.

- A positive value in `size count` acts as a counter. The following *n* bytes will be read and displayed as pixels.
- A negative value (greater than 80H) in size count indicates a compressed record. The following byte defines the value of the pixel. This byte is displayed `size count` * (–1) times.

With this method of compression, all image data areas that have changed since the previous image are stored. Under unfavourable conditions, it is possible for FLI_BRUN CHUNK to grow to 70 kbytes in length, which exceeds the 64-kbyte limit of the FLI definition. In this case, Autodesk Animator stores the frame as an FLI_COPY CHUNK.

49.2.5 FLI_COPY CHUNK (type 16)

This CHUNK enables an image to be stored in uncompressed form.

Offset	Bytes	Remarks
00H	4	CHUNK size in bytes
04H	2	CHUNK type (10H)
06H	64000	Data bytes

Table 49.9 Structure of a FLI_COPY CHUNK

The CHUNK has a data area of 64,000 bytes which contains the image in uncompressed form. This CHUNK can be used in the first frame to display the image.

49.3 Animator CEL and PIC Format

Animator can store an image frame in a CEL file. The CEL file has a 32-byte header, which is followed by a palette (256*3 = 768 bytes) and an uncompressed color image. The file is structured as follows:

Offset	Bytes	Remarks
00H	2	Signature (9119H)
02H	2	Width of cel-image
04H	2	Height of cel-image
06H	2	X upper left corner
08H	2	Y upper left corner
0AH	1	Bits per pixel (8)
0BH	1	Compression (0 = none)
0CH	4	Image size in bytes
10H	16	Reserved (0)
1CH	256*3	Palette (red, green, blue)
31CH	*n*	Image data

Table 49.10 Structure of a CEL file

Animator can also store individual images in PIC files. These use the same format. Image data is set to width = 320, height = 200. The screen position is set to 0,0.

! **There is also a file known as a COL file in which Animator stores a 256*3 byte color palette. These bytes may contain values between 0 and 63.**

50

Autodesk 3D Studio format (FLC)

Animator *FLI files are restricted to a resolution of 320 × 200 pixels. With the 3D and Animator PRO programs, Autodesk introduced an extended format (FLC).*

FLC files consist of a 128-byte header, followed by various sections containing the frames. Figure 50.1 illustrates the structure of an FLC file:

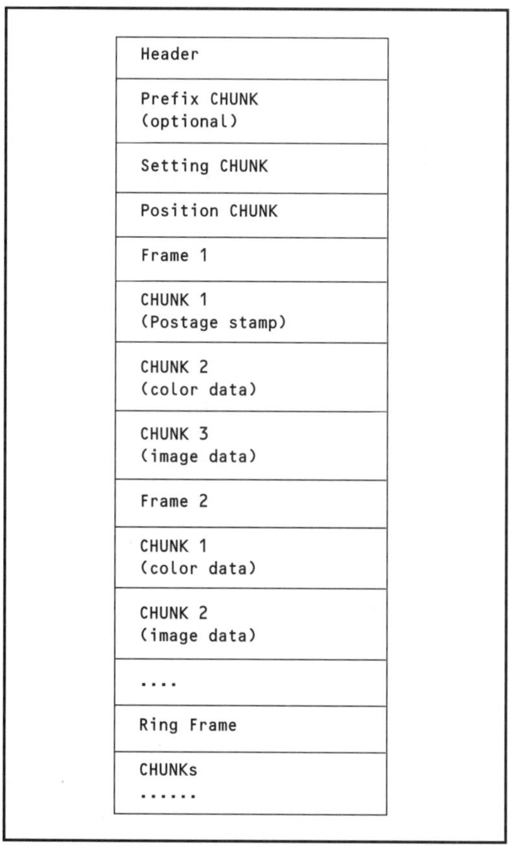

Figure 50.1
Structure of an FLC file

The structure of FLC files closely resembles that of FLI files. The first 16 bytes of the header are identical except for the signature. Many of the same CHUNKs are also used. However, FLC extends the image resolution.

Individual images are stored in frames in the FLC file. The first frame contains the palette and the complete image (RLE compressed). The following frames contain only Delta Frames and altered palettes if required. Data in FLC files is stored in Intel format.

50.1 FLC header

FLC files always begin with a 128-byte header, whose structure is shown in Table 50.1.

Offset	Bytes	Remarks
00H	4	File size in bytes
04H	2	Signature AF12H
06H	2	Number of frames
08H	2	Screen width in pixels
0AH	2	Screen height in pixels
0CH	2	Bits per pixel
0EH	2	Flags
10H	4	Delay time
14H	2	Reserved (00H 00H)
16H	4	Creation date and time
1AH	4	Serial number creator
1EH	4	Update date and time
22H	4	Update serial number
26H	2	X axis aspect ratio
28H	2	Y axis aspect ratio
2AH	38	Reserved (00H)
50H	4	Offset of 1st frame
54H	4	Offset of 2nd frame
58H	40	Fill bytes (00H)

Table 50.1 Structure of an FLC header

The first field defines the length of the complete FLC file. This is followed at offset 04H by a 2-byte signature containing the value AF12H.

A word indicating the number of frames in the FLC file follows at offset 06H. This value enables image sequences to be read and displayed.

The *Screen width* and *Screen height* fields define the resolution of the FLC images in pixels. The restriction to 320 × 200 pixels, found in FLI files, does not apply.

The number of bits per pixel is indicated at offset 0CH. In FLC files, this value is always set to 8 bits per pixel, that is, images with up to 256 colors can be stored.

The flags at offset 0EH are reserved and must be set to 0003H. This is presumably for controlling the playback procedure. If the value is 1, the animation is terminated after displaying the last frame. If the value is 2, the animation is repeated.

To play back the animation, a certain delay time must be observed between frames. This delay time is indicated in milliseconds as a 32-byte value at offset 10H.

The word at offset 14H is reserved. By contrast with FLI files, the fields from offset 16H are used. The first four bytes contain the MS-DOS date and time at which the file was created. The next four bytes are provided for the serial number of Animator PRO. These should be ignored and set to 0.

The 4 bytes at offset 1EH contain the date and time of the last modification. The following 4 bytes are used for the serial number of the program used to make the modifications. The value should be set to 0.

The two words at offsets 26H and 28H define the pixel aspect ratio of the X and Y axes. The default setting for this ratio is 1:1. With 320 × 200 images, the ratio should be set to 6:5.

At offsets 50H and 54H, there are 4-byte pointers to the first and second frames of the FLC file. These enable the optional prefix CHUNK to be skipped. The remaining bytes in the header are reserved and set to 00H.

50.2 FLC frames

The image sequences for the animation are stored in the data area, which starts at offset 80H. The individual pictures are stored as frames, and the number of frames is indicated in the header. Each frame comprises a 16 byte header, coded as shown in Table 50.2:

Offset	Bytes	Remarks
00H	4	Frame size in bytes
04H	2	Signature (F1FAH)
06H	2	Number of CHUNKs
08H	8	Reserved (00H)

Table 50.2 **Structure of a frame header**

The first four bytes indicate the length of the frame in bytes, including the 16 bytes of the header. The signature F1FAH must appear at offset 04H. Otherwise, there is an error in the FLC file. The word at offset 06H indicates the number of CHUNKs in this frame.

CHUNKs are data structures which contain the individual information on an image (for example, color palette, pixel data). Each CHUNK has a 6-byte header which contains a 4-byte length field and one word indicating the CHUNK type. This is followed by the data, in a CHUNK-specific structure. The CHUNK types defined in the FLC structure are described below.

50.2.1 PREFIX CHUNK (type F100H)

In FLC files, the first frame can be preceded by an optional prefix CHUNK. This enables Animator PRO to store private data. A prefix CHUNK is structured as follows:

Offset	Bytes	Remarks
00H	4	CHUNK size in bytes
04H	2	CHUNK type (F100H)
06H	2	Number of sub-CHUNKs
08H	8	Reserved (0)

Table 50.3 Structure of a prefix CHUNK

This prefix CHUNK may be followed by various sub-CHUNKs, whose structure is private. These CHUNKs should be skipped by external programs.

50.2.2 COLOR_256 CHUNK (type 4)

This CHUNK is used for storing a *compressed color map*. It occurs whenever the palette (color map) for the previous frame has changed. The structure of the CHUNK is as follows:

Offset	Bytes	Remarks
00H	4	CHUNK size in bytes
04H	2	CHUNK type (04H)
06H	2	Number of packets
08H	*n*	Packets containing color map data

Table 50.4 Structure of a COLOR_256 CHUNK

The word at offset 06H defines the number of data packets in the CHUNK. These data packets contain the compressed color map.

The color map for a VGA card contains 256 entries of 3 bytes each, numbered from 0 to 255. The COLOR_256 CHUNK defines entries in the palette that have changed since the previous frame. The first byte in a packet indicates the number of entries in the color map to be skipped. The following byte defines the number of colors to be changed. If this byte is set to 0, all 256 colors in the color map must be changed. The byte is followed by the actual color map data. Three bytes (red, green, blue) are stored for each color to be changed. In the COLOR_256 CHUNK the bytes for these color intensities contain values between 0 and 255, that is, 256 colors can be represented.

50.2.3 DELTA_FLC CHUNK (type 7)

This CHUNK contains compressed data (*word oriented frame data*). The CHUNK describes the differences by comparison with the preceding frame.

Offset	Bytes	Remarks
00H	4	CHUNK size in bytes
04H	2	CHUNK type (07H)
06H	2	Number of lines in CHUNK
08H	2	Data area

Table 50.5 Structure of a DELTA_FLC CHUNK

The word at offset 06H defines the number of image lines in the CHUNK. This is followed by an image area.

The image data is compressed line by line and stored in packets. Preceding these data packets, the image line may contain a number of optional words containing various information. Bits 14 and 15 indicate whether a packet value or an item of optional information is involved.

00 If bits 14, 15 are set to 0, the word defines the number of packets following for this line.

10 If bit 15 = 1 and bit 14 = 0, the lower byte of the word contains the value for the last pixel of the line. This is necessary for lines with odd numbers of pixels, because the data is stored by a word. The following word contains the number of packets for the line.

11 If both bits are set, the word contains a line skip count. This means that *n* lines should be skipped without changes. This word may be followed by additional, optional words (skip count, and so on).

The word containing the number of packets per pixel is followed by the compressed image data packets. The image lines always relate to the top edge. Before compression, image data is compared word by word with the preceding frame. The individual packets within a line are structured as follows:

1 byte skip count
1 byte size count
n bytes data

Table 50.6 Structure of a packet (FLC)

The first byte (skip count) defines the number of pixels in the line to be skipped. These pixels have not changed from the previous frame. If there are more than 255 unchanged pixels, two packets must be used.

The next byte contains the `size count`, which also indicates whether compression has been used.

- A positive value in `size count` acts as a counter. The following n bytes will be read and displayed as pixels.
- A negative value (greater than `80H`) in `size count` indicates a compressed record. The following byte defines the value of the pixel. This byte is displayed `size count` * (–1) times.

With this method of compression, all image data areas that have changed since the previous image are stored.

50.2.4 FLC_BLACK CHUNK (type 13)

This CHUNK has a very simple structure. It is used for producing a completely black frame, that is, all pixels are set to `00H`.

Offset	Bytes	Remarks
00H	4	CHUNK size in bytes
04H	2	CHUNK type (0DH)

Table 50.7 Structure of an FLC_BLACK CHUNK

The CHUNK does not have a data area. It is used in the first frame if the user has given the command `NEW` in the animator.

50.2.5 FLC_BYTE_RUN CHUNK (type 15)

This CHUNK stores the complete image in RLE format. It is similar to the FLI_LC CHUNK, except that the skip lines are not included; that is, the image description begins at the top line. This CHUNK is used in the first frame to store the complete image.

Offset	Bytes	Remarks
00H	4	CHUNK size in bytes
04H	2	CHUNK type (0FH)
06H	*n*	Data for changed lines

Table 50.8 Structure of an FLC_BYTE_RUN CHUNK

The data for the image lines is stored in compressed form at offset 06H. Each image line is compressed separately and stored in packets. The number of image lines is defined in the header.

- The first byte in a compressed line indicates the number of following packets. This byte was adopted from the Animator FLI format for reasons of compatibility. It should be skipped, because a line can accommodate more than 255 packets. The number of uncompressed bytes can be determined from the image width.
- If the corresponding line in the previous image has not changed, the value 0 is stored in the first byte. This is followed by the data for the next line.

The individual packets within each line are structured as follows:

1 byte	size count
n bytes	data

Table 50.9 Structure of a packet

The first byte defines the `size count`, which also indicates whether compression has been used.

- A positive value in `size count` acts as a counter. The following *n* bytes will be read and displayed as pixels.
- A negative value (greater than 80H) in `size count` indicates a compressed record. The following byte defines the value of the pixel. This byte is displayed `size count` * (–1) times.

With this method of compression, all image data areas that have changed since the previous image are stored.

50.2.6 LITERAL CHUNK (type 16)

This CHUNK enables an image to be stored in uncompressed form.

Offset	Bytes	Remarks
00H	4	CHUNK size in bytes
04H	2	CHUNK Type (10H)
06H	64000	Data bytes

Table 50.10 Structure of a LITERAL CHUNK

The CHUNK has a data area of width * height bytes which contains the image in uncompressed form. This CHUNK can be used in the first frame to display the image.

Graphics

50.2.7 PSTAMP CHUNK (Type 18)

This CHUNK contains an image of reduced size (100 × 63 pixels). It occurs only in the first frame. The structure of the CHUNK is shown in Table 50.11, but it can be skipped without difficulties.

Offset	Bytes	Remarks
00H	4	CHUNK size in bytes
04H	2	CHUNK type (12H)
06H	2	Height
08H	2	Width
0AH	2	Color type
0CH	*n*	Pixel data

Table 50.11 Structure of a PSTAMP CHUNK

The color type is always 01H, but the coding is currently not available.

51

Amiga Animation format (ANI)

On the Amiga, an extended IFF format is used to represent animations. The file contains a header and several CHUNKs, as shown in Figure 51.1:

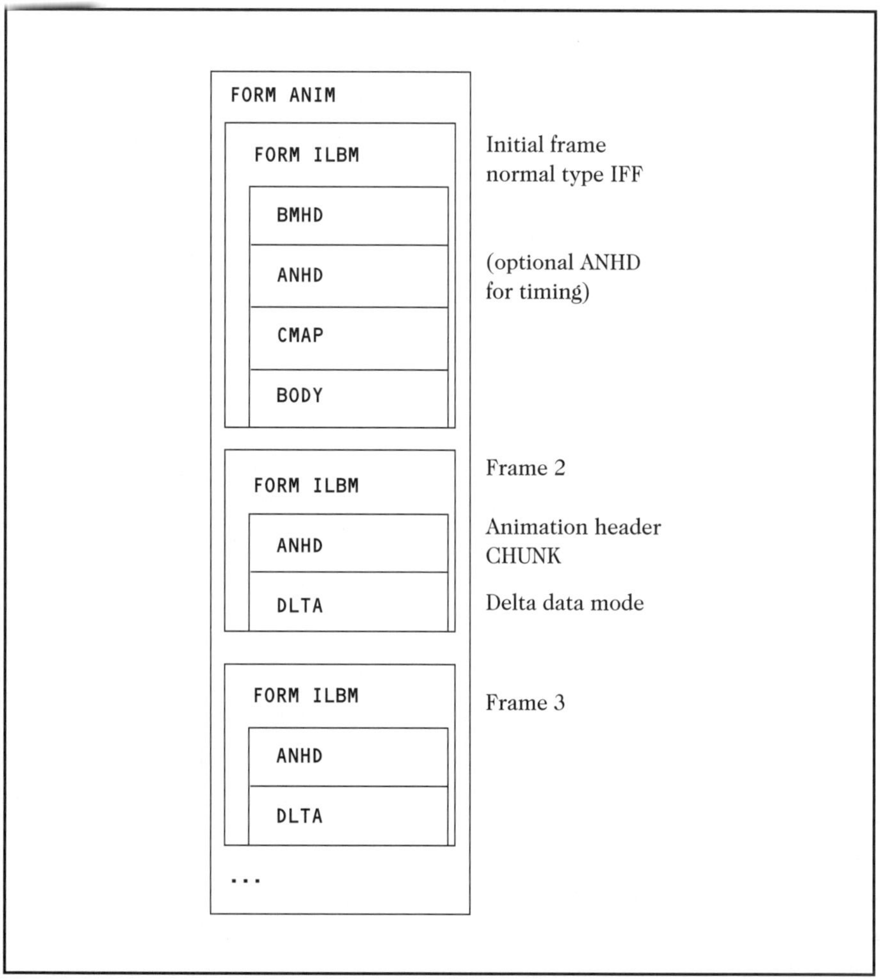

Figure 51.1
Structure of an Amiga (ANI) file

The data in ANI files is stored in Motorola format.

The aim of an ANIM file is to present the initial frame as a normal RLE coded IFF picture. Subsequent frames are described by their differences from a previous frame. The normal playback mode is to use two screens (A and B). The initial frame is loaded to screen A and B. After this, screen A is displayed and the first delta frame is used to alter screen B. If screen B is displayed, screen A will be altered by the next frame. Frame 2 is stored as differences from frame 1. All other frames are stored as differences from two frames back.

51.1 ANI header

An ANI file contains a header which is structured according to the IFF conventions, as shown in Table 51.1:

Offset	Bytes	Remarks
00H	4	Signature (46H 4FH 52H 4DH)
04H	4	File length in bytes
08H	4	IFF type 'ANIM'

Table 51.1 Structure of an ANI header

The first field contains the signature for IFF files ('FORM'). This is followed at offset 04H by the file length in bytes. The last four bytes contain the ID for the file type. In ANI files, the signature is 'ANIM'.

51.2 ANI CHUNKs

The header is followed by the CHUNKs of the ANI file. The initial FORM ILBM can contain all the normal ILBM CHUNKs. These are valid IFF CHUNKs which have already been described in the chapter on the IFF format (Chapter 25).

Signature	CHUNK type
BMHD	Bitmap header
CMAP	Color map
BODY	BODY data block
CAMG	Graphic mode
CRNG	Graphic mode

Table 51.2 IFF CHUNKs in an ANI file

Three new types of CHUNK have been defined in addition to those already described.

51.2.1 CPAN CHUNK

This CHUNK defines the length of an animation sequence. It is structured as follows:

Offset	Bytes	Remarks
00H	4	Signature (43H 50H 41H 4EH)
04H	4	Block length in bytes
08H	2	Version number
0AH	2	Number of images
0CH	4	Reserved

Table 51.3 Structure of a CPAN CHUNK

The first four bytes contain the signature 'CPAN'. This is followed by the block length in bytes. At offset 08H, there is a word for the processing program to store its version number. This value should be ignored by external software. The word at offset 0AH indicates the number of frames in the following sequence. The last four bytes are reserved.

51.2.2 ANHD CHUNK

This CHUNK acts as the header of the animation sequence. Its structure is as follows:

Offset	Bytes	Remarks
00H	4	Signature (41H 4EH 48H 44H)
04H	4	Block length in bytes
08H	1	Compression method 0: Set directly (ILBM BODY) 1: XOR ILBM mode 2: Long Delta mode 3: Short Delta mode 4: Generalized Short/Long Delta mode 5: Byte Vertical Delta mode 6: Stereo op 5 (third party) 74: ASCII J (reserved)

Table 51.4 Structure of an ANHD CHUNK (*continues over...*)

Graphics

Offset	Bytes	Remarks
09H	1	Mask
0AH	2	Width of view area
0CH	2	Height of view area
0EH	2	X-position of view area
10H	2	Y-position of view area
12H	4	Delay time 1
16H	4	Delay time 2
1AH	1	Frame count
1BH	1	Fill byte (0)
1CH	4	Compression flag
20H	16	Reserved (0)

Table 51.4 Structure of an ANHD CHUNK (*cont.*)

This CHUNK is used in subsequent FORM ILBMs in place of the 'BMHD' CHUNK. It begins with the signature 'ANHD', followed by the block length of the CHUNK.

The byte at offset 08H specifies the compression method used.

0: If this value occurs, an ILBM BODY with no compression is used for the initial frame.

1: The XOR mode is only of historical interest. This mode performs a simple bitwise XOR operation between the new frame and the two frames back.

2: The Long Delta mode stores in the actual new frame only long-words with different image parts. The long-words are stored together with an offset value in the bitmap. Each plane is handled separately. No data will be saved, if nothing is changed.

3: The Short Delta mode is identical to the Long Delta mode, except that only short-words are saved.

4: In the Generalized Delta mode, both the Long Delta mode and the Short Delta mode are put together.

5: The Byte Vertical Compression mode was defined by Jim Kent.

6: This mode is used by third party.

74: This mode is reserved for Eric Graham's compression technique. Details about this technique are not known.

The DWORD at offset 1CH presumably contains flags for compression methods 4 and 5. Only the six low bits are used.

Bit	
0	0: short data is used 1: long data is used
1	0: set data 1: XOR operation
2	0: separate info list for each plane 1: one info list for all planes
3	0: not run length coded 1: run length coded
4	0: horizontal compression 1: vertical compression
5	0: short info offsets 1: long info offsets

Table 51.5 Coding of the Compression flag

However, the significance of these compression methods is not currently documented. The byte at offset 09H contains a mask for the bits in image planes containing changes. This mask is only used for the XOR compression mode. The mask contains bits set to 1, if there is data in the plane. If the bits are set to 0, there is no data to be modified in the plane.

The two words at offsets 0AH and 0CH define a frame (width * height). The position of this frame is defined in the two words at offset 0EH and 10H. The fields from offset 0AH to 10H are only valid if the XOR compression is used.

Frames are played back with a certain delay between frames. The DWORD at offset 12H defines the delay relative to the first frame in units of 1/50 of a second. The DWORD at offset 16H defines the delay from the preceding frame. The byte at offset 1AH defines the number of preceding images to which a change applies. This technique enables the speed of animation to be varied. These fields are mostly unused and reserved for special applications.

Graphics

51.2.3 DLTA CHUNK

This CHUNK holds the data of the compressed frames. The format varies from the usual compression method.

The first image in an animation is generally stored as a bitmap, compressed using the RLE method. If the first byte is less than 80H, $n + 1$ following bytes are transferred as uncompressed image data. In the case of negative values (>80H) the following byte is repeated $n + 1$ times. No operation is carried out if the value is 80H.

The DLTA CHUNK copies the Delta Frames of the animation sequence. The structure is as follows:

Offset	Bytes	Remarks
00H	4	Signature (44H 4CH 54H 41H)
04H	4	Block length in bytes
08H	*n*	Graphic data area

Table 51.6 Structure of a DLTA CHUNK

The CHUNK is introduced with the signature 'DLTA'. This is followed by a DWORD containing the block length. The image data is compressed using various compression techniques.

Methods 2 and 3

This is the basic data CHUNK, used to hold the Delta compression data. The CHUNK starts with 8 long-words (32 bytes). The first 8 long-words are byte pointers into the data CHUNK for each bitplane (up to 8 bitplanes).

If there are modifications in a plane, the pointers for the plane data follow immediately at offset 32 (20H). The data for a given plane consists of groups of data words. In Long Delta mode, short words are for offsets/numbers and long words for the actual data are used. In Short Delta mode, all data is stored in short words. Each group consists of a starting word which is interpreted as an offset.

If the offset is positive, the value must be added to the pointer into the bitplane. The following data word would be placed at this position in the bitplane. Then the next offset would be added to the pointer and the data word must be placed into the bitplane. If the offset into the bitplane reaches 0FFFFH, the process terminates.

If the offset of the starting word is negative, the absolute value is the offset + 2.

The following short-word counts the number of words that follow. These words must be placed in contiguous locations in the bitplane. If there are no changed words in a given bitplane, the pointer in the first 32 bytes of the CHUNK is set to 0.

Method 4

This DLTA CHUNK is modified to have 16 long pointers at the start. The first 8 pointers define the start of the data for each of the 8 bitplanes. The next 8 pointers are offsets to the start of the offset/numbers data list. If there is only one data list for all 8 planes, all 8 pointers contain the same value. The first entry acts as a counter. If the counter is negative, the following data word is copied multiple times into the destination plane. Detailed information about the compression scheme is not available.

Method 5

This DLTA CHUNK uses the same 16 pointers as for method 4. The first 8 entries are pointers to the planes. The next 8 entries are unused. Detailed information about the compression scheme is not yet available.

Other methods use private compression schemes, which are not documented.

52

Audio/Video Interleaved format (AVI)

With *Video for Windows Microsoft introduced a new format (AVI) for representing images and sounds. This format is based on the Microsoft RIFF specification.*

52.1 Resource Interchange File Format (RIFF) specification

The *Resource Interchange File Format* was defined by Microsoft for Windows multimedia applications. The RIFF files represent a container in which the formats of other specifications can be stored, as shown in Table 52.1:

.AVI	Video data (Video for Windows)
.WAV	Audio wave data (Windows Wave files)
.RDI	Bitmap data
.RMI	MIDI data
.BND	Bundle of other RIFF files

Table 52.1 Examples of RIFF files

A description of the AVI format is given below. The WAV format is dealt with in Chapter 79. The structure of RIFF files is based on the IFF definition. RIFF files are divided into individual CHUNKs containing the data. A RIFF file begins with a header, structured as shown in Table 52.2:

Offset	Bytes	Remarks
00H	4	Signature 'RIFF'
04H	4	File size in bytes
08H	4	RIFF type

Table 52.2 Structure of a RIFF header

The first four bytes contain the signature of the RIFF file. If the data has been stored in Intel format (little-endian), the signature will be 'RIFF'. This is the default setting for RIFF files. However, it is also possible to store data in Motorola format (big-endian). In this case, the first four bytes will contain the signature 'RIFX'.

At offset 04H, there is a DWORD containing the length of the file. This length does not include the signature and the length field itself.

The last four bytes contain the signature for the RIFF type. If this string is shorter than 4 characters, the following bytes should be filled with spaces (20H). In the case of AVI files, for example, the signature stored here is 'AVI'.

52.2 Structure of a RIFF CHUNK

A RIFF CHUNK is structured as shown in Table 52.3:

Offset	Bytes	Remarks
00H	4	CHUNK signature
04H	4	CHUNK size in bytes
08H	*n*	CHUNK data

Table 52.3 Structure of a CHUNK

The first four bytes contain the signature of the CHUNK type. If this string is shorter than 4 characters, the following bytes should be filled with spaces (20H).

The DWORD at offset 04H indicates the number of following data bytes. In RIFF files, the CHUNKs always begin on word boundaries. A fill byte is appended if the length is an odd number, but the length field does not include this fill byte. The first 8 bytes of the CHUNK are not included in the length indication either, so that the value defines the actual number of following data bytes.

The area containing the data bytes can be divided into further sub-CHUNKs, which have the same structure as the CHUNKs and are used for various data.

52.3 AVI structure

AVI files are used by Video for Windows to store audio and video data. The AVI file begins with a RIFF header (`'RIFF' xx xx xx xx 'AVI'`), followed by several CHUNKs. These CHUNKs are divided into two LIST CHUNKs, which contain information on data decoding (first LIST CHUNK, `'hdrl'`) and the actual data (second LIST CHUNK, `'movi'`), as shown in Figure 52.1:

```
RIFF ('AVI '
 LIST ('hdrl'
        ....
      )
 LIST ('movi'
        ...
      )
 ['idx1' <optional AVI index>]
   ...
    )
```

Figure 52.1 Structure of an AVI file

Each LIST CHUNK is followed by further sub-CHUNKs containing the actual data.

```
RIFF ('AVI '
 LIST ('hdrl'
        'avih' <main AVI header>
    LIST ('strl' <stream line>
          'strh' <stream header>
          'strf' <stream format>
          'strd' <stream data>
           ....
         )
      )
 LIST ('movi'
        subchunk or
    LIST ('rec' <data>
          subchunk 1
           ....
          subchunk n
         )
      )
 ['idx1' <optional AVI index>]
   ....
    )
```

Figure 52.2 Sub-CHUNK structure in an AVI file

After the first `LIST` signature, an AVI reader must read the sub-CHUNKs containing the definition of the data format. As soon as another LIST CHUNK occurs, its type must be checked. It may be either another list in the header or the video data stream. The start of the video data is marked with the signature '`movi`'. This is followed by the sub-CHUNKs containing the actual video data.

If the signature '`idx1`' appears in a CHUNK, it indicates that the video data area is finished. This may be followed by optional AVI index definitions. The structure of the individual CHUNKs is described below:

52.3.1 AVI header CHUNK (hdrl)

The first LIST CHUNK contains the main AVI header sub-CHUNK, which has the CHUNK type '`hdrl`'.

Offset	Bytes	Remarks
00H	4	CHUNK signature ('LIST')
04H	4	Length of sub-CHUNK
08H	4	CHUNK type ('hdrl')
0CH	*n*	Sub-CHUNKs

Table 52.4 Structure of the hdrl CHUNK

The information in the header sub-CHUNK defines the format of the complete AVI CHUNK.

52.3.1.1 avih sub-CHUNK

This sub-CHUNK contains global data for the AVI CHUNK. The data area of the avih sub-CHUNK is structured as follows:

Offset	Bytes	Remarks
00H	4	Signature 'avih'
04H	4	CHUNK length (38H)
08H	4	Time delay between frames
0CH	4	AVI data rate
10H	4	Reserved
14H	4	Flags
18H	4	Number of frames

Table 52.5 Structure of an avih sub-CHUNK *(continues over...)*

Offset	Bytes	Remarks
1CH	4	Initial frames
20H	4	Number of data streams
24H	4	Suggested playback buffer size
28H	4	Video frame width (pixel)
2CH	4	Video frame height (pixel)
30H	4	Time scale unit
34H	4	Playback data rate
38H	4	Starting time
3CH	4	AVI data CHUNK size

Table 52.5 Structure of an avih sub-CHUNK (*cont.*)

The first field contains the signature 'avih'. This is followed at offset 04H by the data area of the sub-CHUNK, which is divided into 4-byte fields (DWORD). The first field keeps the CHUNK length. The next field contains the maximum data rate in bytes per second. This value indicates how many bytes per second the system must read from the AVI file in order to play back the images at the correct speed. If the system fails to reach this data rate (depending on the image size), the sequence will be played back with a delay.

The field at offset 10H is reserved and defines the *padding granularity*. This value is usually set to 2048.

The flags at offset 14H contain information on the following data. The following flags are currently defined:

10H	AVIF_HASINDEX: The AVI file has an idx1 CHUNK.
20H	AVIF_MUSTUSEINDEX: Index CHUNK must be used to determine the order of frames.
100H	AVIF_ISINTERLEAVED: Indicates that the AVI-file is interleaved. This is used to read data from a CD-ROM more efficiently.
10000H	AVIF_WASCAPTUREFILE: The AVI file is used for capturing real-time video.
20000H	AVIF_COPYRIGHTED: The AVI file contains copyrighted data.

These flag constants are defined in the header files of the AVI library.

The value at offset 18H defines the number of frames in the AVI file. The field containing the initial frames is used only with interleave images. The value indicates the number of frames positioned before the initial frame in the AVI file.

The field at offset 20H defines the number of streams in the AVI file. An AVI file with audio and video data has two streams.

The field at offset 24H indicates the minimum size of the playback buffer.

At offset 28H, there are two fields indicating the dimensions of the frame for the video sequence.

The time scale unit is stored at offset 30H. The following field indicates the playback data rate (frames). The rate in samples per second can be calculated as follows:

Data rate / Time scale

The *Start* field defines the start of the video and should be set to 0. The last field indicates the length (playing time) of the AVI file. The units are defined via the preceding fields (time unit and data rate).

52.3.2 Stream Line header CHUNK (strl)

The AVI header CHUNK is followed by one or more Stream Line header CHUNKs (strl). For every stream, there is an strl CHUNK. These CHUNKs contain information on the individual streams of the AVI file. The information in these streams relates to the corresponding data stream in the movi CHUNK of the same number.

The CHUNK is structured as shown in Table 52.5, but the signature 'strl' is entered as the CHUNK type.

Each of these strl CHUNKs must contain a *stream header* (strh) and a *stream format* (strf) sub-CHUNK. These may be followed by *stream data* sub-CHUNKs.

52.3.2.1 strh Sub-CHUNK

This header contains information on the associated stream. It is structured as follows:

Offset	Bytes	Remarks
00H	4	Signature ('strh')
04H	4	Length of sub-CHUNK (38H)
08H	4	Type (4 char)
0CH	4	Handler (4 char)
10H	4	Flags
14H	4	Reserved
18H	4	Initial frame
1CH	4	Scale
20H	4	Rate
24H	4	Start
28H	4	Length
2CH	4	Buffer size
30H	4	Quality
34H	4	Sample size

Table 52.6 strh sub-CHUNK in an AVI file

The first four bytes contain the signature '`strh`', followed by the length (in bytes) for the data area. The four bytes at offset `08H` define the type of stream. The string '`vids`' (video stream) or '`auds`' (audio stream) is stored here.

This area is followed by the stream header fields. The four bytes at offset `0CH` define the type of handler for data compression/decompression. The type is defined with 4 characters (for example, '`msvc`'). The DWORD at offset `10H` contains flags for the *data stream*:

`AVISF_DISABLED`	The stream data should be rendered only when explicitly enabled.
`AVISF_VIDEO_PALCHANGES`	Indicates that a palette change is included in the AVI file.

The bits for the individual flags are defined in the header files of the AVI library.

The DWORD at offset `18H` defines the number of frames that appear before the initial frame. This field is used only with Interleaved AVI files.

The remaining fields describe the playback characteristics of the AVI file. The `scale` field defines the time unit for the playback. The fields `scale`, `rate`, `start`, `length` and `buffer size` have the same meaning as the fields in the `hdrl` CHUNK.

In the `quality` field, there is an integer value between `0` and `10000` which indicates the quality to be used when encoding the data.

The `SampleSize` field indicates the size of an individual frame (*sample*). If the value is `0`, the frames are not all of the same size and are stored in sub-CHUNKs. If a non-zero value is stored here, all entries (*samples*) are the same size.

Some fields also appear in the Stream Line header. In this case, the data in the Stream Line header applies to all the data, while the data in the `strl` structure relates only to the following stream.

52.3.2.2 stream format CHUNK (strf)

This sub-CHUNK must appear in every Stream header CHUNK after the Stream header (`strh`) CHUNK itself. The CHUNK describes the format of the data in the associated stream.

If the stream contains video data, the stream format CHUNK is defined as a BITMAPINFO header structure.

Offset	Bytes	Remarks
00H	4	Header size
04H	4	Image width (in pixels)
08H	4	Image height (in pixels)
0CH	2	Number of planes
0EH	2	Bits per pixel
10H	4	Compression type
14H	4	Image size in bytes
18H	4	X pels per meter

Table 52.7 BITMAPINFO header structure (*continues over...*)

Graphics

Offset	Bytes	Remarks
1CH	4	Y pels per meter
20H	4	Colors used
24H	4	Colors important
28H	*n**4	RGB quad structure
		1 byte blue
		1 byte green
		1 byte red
		1 byte reserved

Table 52.7 BITMAPINFO header structure (*cont.*)

This structure is also used in Windows BMP files. The first DWORD indicates the length of the header (including the RGB quad records).

The following two fields define the image dimensions. The number of color planes in which the data is stored is specified at offset 0CH. This should be set to 1. The following word defines the number of bits per pixel.

A flag (DWORD) follows at offset 10H, indicating the compression of the image data.

0: RGB, uncompressed data as a bitmap

1: RLE8, 8 bits are compressed using the RLE process

2: RLE4, 4 bits are compressed using the RLE process

A description of the compression methods can be found in Chapter 60 which describes the Windows BMP format.

The DWORD at offset 14H indicates the image size in bytes. This is followed by two 4-byte fields for the horizontal and vertical resolution, which is indicated in *Picture Elements (pels)* per meter.

The last two fields are used for the management of color information. The number of colors used and the number of important colors are defined.

With *Audio data* the sub-CHUNK contains a PCMWAVEFORMAT or a WAVEFORMATEX structure. The WAVEFORMATEX structure is an extension of the PCMWAVEFORMAT structure.

Offset	Bytes	Remarks
00H	2	Format type
02H	2	Number of channels
04H	4	Sample rate
08H	4	Bytes per seconds

Table 52.8 Structure of a WAVEFORMATEX structure (*continues over...*)

Offset	Bytes	Remarks
0CH	2	Block size of data
10H	2	Bits per sample
12H	2	Byte count extend data

Table 52.8
Structure of a WAVEFOR-MATEX structure
(*cont.*)

The first field indicates the format type (WAVE_FORMAT_PCM) or (WAVE_FORMAT_EX). The number of audio channels is specified at offset 02H (1 = mono, 2 = stereo).

The DWORD at offset 04H indicates the sample rate of the audio channel in samples per second. The following field contains the average data transfer rate in bytes per second and is used to determine the size of the buffer.

The block size in which the data is stored is indicated at offset 0CH. This is necessary for Interleaved data (CD-ROM), because 2-Kbyte blocks are formed.

The WAVE_FORMAT_PCM structure is followed by the definition of *Bits per sample*. The last field appears only in WAVE_FORMAT_EX structure. It specifies the length of the following extra information.

52.3.2.3 Stream Data CHUNK (strd)

The *stream format* CHUNK may be followed by a *stream data* CHUNK. The format of this CHUNK is determined by the compression or decompression driver. The data block generally contains information on the configuration of the driver.

52.3.3 movi CHUNK

A movi CHUNK structure containing the actual data follows the CHUNKs of the first LIST structure. This data may be contained in one block or in several sub-CHUNKs (rec CHUNKs). The rec CHUNKs are used with CD-ROM to store interleaved data. In this case the data is stored in 2-Kbyte blocks, and the driver should read the complete data structure. The movi CHUNK is structured as follows:

Offset	**Bytes**	**Remarks**
00H	4	Signature 'LIST'
04H	4	CHUNK length in bytes
08H	4	CHUNK type 'movi'
0CH	*n*	Data area or sub-CHUNKs

Table 52.9
Structure of a movi CHUNK

The CHUNK begins with a 4-byte LIST signature. This is followed by the length of the following data area. The last four bytes contain the string 'movi' as the CHUNK type.

Graphics

52.3.3.1 rec CHUNK

If the data has been structured in rec sub-CHUNKs, the header is followed by the structure shown below:

Offset	Bytes	Remarks
00H	4	Signature 'LIST'
04H	4	Length of data area
08H	4	Sub-CHUNK type 'rec'
0CH	*n*	Data area

Table 52.10 Structure of a rec CHUNK

The sub-CHUNK is again introduced with the signature LIST. The following length relates to the data area of the sub-CHUNK. The DWORD at offset 08H defines the CHUNK-type (rec). The data follows at 0CH. If the space required by the data area is not a multiple of 2 Kbytes, it may be followed by a JUNK CHUNK as a filler (*see below*).

52.3.3.2 Structure of the data record

If the data in the movi CHUNK is in a block, this area will be structured as follows:

Offset	Bytes	Remarks
00H	4	Signature
04H	*n*	Data area

Table 52.11 Format of the data area

Since the format information is in the header stream, the data area contains only a 4-byte signature to identify the data. The coding is as follows:

xxwb Wave data follows.

xxdb DIB bitmap data (uncompressed) follows.

xxdc DIB bitmap data (compressed) follows.

The characters xx are used to identify the stream. A bitmap image is stored uncompressed or as a compressed DIB structure, that is, the data for a pixel is contained in one byte (with 8 bits per pixel).

52.3.4 AVI_PALCHANGE CHUNK

Within an AVI file, the palette (color map) may be changed between frames. This CHUNK is structured as follows:

Offset	Bytes	Remarks
00H	2	Signature 'xxpc'
02H	1	First palette to change
03H	1	Number of entries
04H	2	Flags
06H	*n**4	Palette entries

Table 52.12 Format of an AVI_PALCHANGE CHUNK

The CHUNK is introduced by a 2-byte string. The signature pc stands for *palette change*. The next byte defines the index to the first changed palette entry (0 to 255). This is followed by a byte containing the number of palette entries in the CHUNK. The coding for the flags at offset 04H is not documented. At offset 06H, there are *n* entries containing the palette data (green, blue, red, reserved).

! If AVI_PALCHANGE CHUNKs appear in the data stream, the VIDEO_PALCHANGE flag in the stream header (Table 52.6) must be set.

52.3.5 idx1 CHUNK

An AVI file may contain several optional idx CHUNKs appended to a movi CHUNK. These CHUNKs contain pointers to the individual data CHUNKs which define the sequence and also enable direct access to the data without having to analyze the complete AVI file. The CHUNK is structured as follows:

Offset	Bytes	Remarks
00H	4	Signature ('idx1')
04H	4	Flags
08H	4	CHUNK offset
0CH	4	CHUNK length

Table 52.13 Structure of an idx1 CHUNK

Graphics

The first four bytes contain the signature (idx1). This is followed by a DWORD containing flags.

AVIIF_KEYFRAME	The flag indicates key frames in the video sequence.
AVIIF_NOTIME	The CHUNK does not influence the video timing (for example, a palette change CHUNK).
AVIIF_LIST	Marks a LIST CHUNK.

The offset (relative to the movi CHUNK) to the relevant CHUNK is indicated at offset 08H, followed by the length of the CHUNK (not including the 8 byte header).

The above idx CHUNK can be repeated several times. If the movi CHUNK contains data in rec sub-CHUNKs, an idx CHUNK is defined for every record.

52.4 Other data CHUNKs

The RIFF definition enables the definition of certain other CHUNKs which are registered by Microsoft and published periodically. The following CHUNK is used as a filler for data areas:

52.4.1 JUNK CHUNK

The purpose of this CHUNK is merely to fill up the data structure to the block limit (for example, with CD-ROM files). The structure is as follows:

Offset	Bytes	Remarks
00H	4	Signature 'JUNK'
04H	*n*	Data

Table 52.14 Structure of a JUNK CHUNK

As an alternative, the signature 'PAD' may also occur. This is also used for filling data areas. The JUNK CHUNK was registered by IBM, while the PAD CHUNK was proposed by Microsoft.

! **More information about the AVI-format is available in the Microsoft Multimedia Developer's Kit.**

53

Intel Digital Video format (DVI)

With *the introduction of DVI, Intel created a hardware solution to the problem of representing digital videos on the PC. Software drivers, which can read files in DVI format, are supplied with the hardware.*

There are several different varieties of DVI files. Images without audio data are stored in files with various extensions:

Extension	Remarks
`.IMR`	Red channel video data (8 bit)
`.IMG`	Green channel video data (8 bit)
`.IMB`	Blue channel video data (8 bit)
`.IMY`	Y luminance channel video data (8 bit)
`.IMI`	I color channel video data (8 bit)
`.IMQ`	Q color channel video data (8 bit)
`.IMA`	Alpha channel video data (8 bit)
`.IMM`	Monochrome or grayscale video data (8 bit)
`.IMC`	Color map video data (8 bit)
`.CMY`	Compressed Y luminance channel video data (8 bit)
`.CMI`	Compressed I color channel video data (8 bit)
`.CMQ`	Compressed Q color channel video data (8 bit)
`.I8`	Device-dependent data (8 bit)
`.I16`	Device-dependent (16 bit)
`.C16`	Compressed device-dependent (16 bit)

Table 53.1 Intel formats for DVI hardware

Uncompressed 8-bit data is stored in individual files according to the color system used in each case. With the RGB system, the extensions `.IMR`, `.IMG`, `.IMB` apply respectively to data from each color channel. The letters R, G, and B stand for red, green and blue and signify the relevant color channel. The first letter I identifies uncompressed data. The letter C is used for compressed data.

53.1 AVSS format

The AVSS format (referred to below as DVI format) was developed for video sequences with audio data. This format is based on the AVI structure described in the previous chapter. An AVSS file consists of a header followed by additional structures as shown in Figure 53.1:

```
DVI-Header
 AVL-Header
  Stream Header
   Audio Substream Header
   Video Substream Header
  Frames
```

Figure 53.1 Structure of a DVI file

The DVI header is followed by an AVL header containing the description of the video and audio stream. The frames are stored after this header.

53.2 DVI header

A DVI file always begins with a 12-byte header structured as shown below:

Offset	Bytes	Remarks
00H	4	File ID 'VDVI'
04H	2	Header size
06H	2	Version
08H	4	Pointer to annotation

Table 53.2 Structure of a DVI header

The first four bytes contain the signature '`VDVI`' for a valid DVI file with audio and video data. If the audio data is missing, the signature '`VIM`' should be entered. This is followed by a word containing the header length in bytes (0CH). In some older versions, this value was set to 1. This should be ignored.

The version number of the header is currently set to 1. At offset 08H there is a pointer to a data area containing notes (annotation). The data area is generally appended to the end of the file. The entry 0 indicates that there are no notes.

53.3 AVL header

The DVI header is followed by the AVL header which is 120 bytes long. This introduces the structure describing the stream. Its format is shown below:

Offset	Bytes	Remarks
00H	4	Header ID 'AVSS'
04H	2	Header size
06H	2	Header version
08H	2	Number of stream groups
0AH	2	Stream group size
0CH	4	1st stream group location
10H	2	Stream group version
12H	2	Stream header size
14H	2	Stream header version
16H	2	Number of stream headers
18H	4	Offset of stream structure array
1CH	4	Header pool offset
20H	4	Number of labels in file
24H	4	Offset of 1st label
28H	2	Label size
2AH	2	Label format (version)
2CH	4	Offset of video sequence header
30H	2	Size of video sequence header
32H	2	Frame header version
34H	4	Number of frame headers
38H	4	Size of frame header + data
3CH	4	Offset of 1st frame
42H	4	Offset of last frame byte +1
46H	2	Size of frame header
48H	2	Size of frame directory
4AH	4	Offset of frame directory
4EH	2	Frame directory version
50H	2	Frames per second
52H	4	Update flag
56H	4	Unused (free block offset)
5AH	32	Fill bytes

Table 53.3 Structure of the AVL header

The first field identifies the header as an AVL file (AVSS). The field at offset 04H defines the length of the header (120). The version number of the header (offset 06H) defines the structure. The present structure is identified with the signature 03H.

A DVI file can be divided into several stream groups. The field at offset 08H defines the number of stream groups. This is followed by the length of each stream group. The next entry defines a pointer to the first entry in the group. The format of this group is determined by the version number. If there is no stream group, these fields are set to 0.

At offset 12H, there are four fields containing the description of the stream header. This is an array stored in the DVI file. The first field defines the size of each stream structure (44 bytes). The next field specifies a version number for the structure (currently 3). The third entry contains the number of entries in the array. The last field defines the offset of the first entry in the array.

The entry at offset 1CH points to the first sub-stream header. If the value 0 is shown here, there are no sub-streams.

If a DVI file contains labels, the fields at offset 20H define the number of labels, the offset to the first label, the size of a label and the version number of the label structure. A value of 00H in the field containing the number of labels indicates that no labels appear in the file.

The two fields at offset 2CH indicate the offset and the length of the (optional) video-sequence header.

The data format of the frame data is defined via the version indicator in the field at offset 32H. This is followed by fields containing information on the number of frames, the frame length (including the header) and the offset of the first frame header. The following field defines the size of all frame headers. The size of the frame directory is 4. The offset defines the position of the frame directory.

The number of frames per second in the playback is defined in the field at offset 50H (playback rate). The value 00H at offset 52H indicates an unmodified file. The remaining bytes are used to pad out the structure to 120 bytes.

53.4 Stream header

DVI files may contain one or more data streams. Each stream is preceded by its own header, structured as shown below:

Offset	Bytes	Remarks
00H	4	Signature 'STRM'
04H	2	Type
06H	2	Subtype
08H	2	Number of sub-stream headers
0AH	2	ID next stream
0CH	2	Group ID current stream

Table 53.4 Structure of a stream header (*continues over...*)

Offset	Bytes	Remarks
0EH	2	Unused
10H	4	Flags
14H	4	Frame size
18H	4	Offset of 1st sub-stream header
1CH	16	Stream name

Table 53.4 Structure of a stream header (*cont.*)

The first field contains the signature 'STRM'. This is followed by two words containing the type and the sub-type of the stream. The coding for the type is shown below:

Type	Remarks
02H	Compressed audio stream
03H	Compressed image stream
05H	Associated per frame data
06H	Uncompressed image stream
07H	Pad stream

Table 53.5 Stream types

The sub-type defines variations within the data.

Subtype	**Remarks**
00H	No subtype for audio data
01H	Y-channel data only
0BH	U-channel data only
0CH	V-channel data only
0DH	YVU data
0EH	YUV data

Table 53.6 Stream sub-types

There are no sub-types for audio data, so the value is set to 0. With video data, the sub-type defines the channel coding.

The word at offset 08H defines the number of sub-streams. The following field is not used and is set to FFFFH (–1). This is followed by an ID number for the current stream.

When set to the value 04H, the flags at offset 10H indicate that the size of the frames is to be changed.

The Frame size field (offset 14H) defines the size of a frame in the stream, in bytes. This is followed by the offset of the first sub-stream header. The stream name is stored as an ASCII string.

53.5 Audio stream header

Each stream header is followed by a sub-stream header. With audio data, the stream header contains the entry 02H as the type (*see above*). At the same time, the entry in the sub-type field is set to 00H. The header contains 168 bytes and is structured as follows:

Offset	Bytes	Remarks
00H	4	Signature ('AUDI')
04H	2	Header size
06H	2	Header version
08H	80	Filename
58H	4	ID of original frame
5CH	2	ID of original stream
5EH	2	Unused
60H	4	Frame count
64H	4	Offset of next header
68H	16	Library name
78H	16	Compression algorithm
88H	4	Data rate (bits/sec)
8CH	2	Filter cut off frequency
8EH	2	Unused
90H	2	Volume of left channel
92H	2	Volume of right channel
94H	4	Unused
98H	4	ID of start frame
9CH	4	Flags (mono, stereo)
A0H	2	Playback rate
A2H	2	Unused
A4H	4	Compression facility ID

Table 53.7 Audio stream header structure

The first four bytes contain the signature 'AUDI', followed by the length of the header (in bytes). The following word defines the version number (5) for the header structure. This is followed by a file name of 80 bytes. The name defines the file from which the data stream was taken. The string should be terminated with a null byte.

The next three fields are not used and are set to 0. The Frame count field (offset 60H) defines the number of audio frames in this stream. The field containing the offset of the next sub-stream is always set to 0. The same applies to the library names. The name of the compression algorithm is defined as an ASCII string (for example, 'apdcm4e' or 'pcm8').

The data transfer rate for the audio channel follows at offset 88H, in bits per second. The next word defines the maximum frequency in the audio channel. Higher frequencies are filtered out during the recording.

The volume of the audio channel is indicated as a percentage. The start frame is set to 0 and the flag defines mono (4000H) or stereo (8000H) operation. The remaining bytes are unused, or are set to 00H or FFH.

53.6 Video stream header

If a stream contains video data, the stream header is followed by a video stream header (136 bytes). This is structured as follows:

Offset	Bytes	Remarks
00H	4	Signature ('CMIG')
04H	2	Header size
06H	2	Header version
08H	80	Filename
58H	4	ID of original frame
5CH	2	ID of original stream
5EH	2	Unused
60H	4	Frame count
64H	4	Offset of next substream header
68H	2	X coordinate of top left corner
6AH	2	Y coordinate of top left corner
6CH	2	Image width in pixels
6EH	2	Image height in pixels
70H	2	X cropping coordinate
72H	2	Y cropping coordinate
74H	4	Unused
78H	4	Still period
7CH	2	Buffer minimum
7EH	2	Buffer maximum
80H	2	ID decompression algorithm
82H	2	Unused
84H	4	Compression facility I

Table 53.8 Structure of a video stream header

The first four bytes contain the signature 'CMIG', followed by the length of the header (in bytes). The following word defines the version number (4) of the header structure. This is followed by a data name consisting of 80 bytes. The name defines the file from which the data stream was taken. This string should be terminated with a null byte. The next three fields are not used and are set to 0. The Frame count field (offset 60H) defines the number of video frames in this stream. The field containing the offset of the next sub-stream is always set to 0.

The coordinates for the top left corner of the image, the frame dimensions and possibly information on the image crop follow in the fields from offset 68H.

The Still Period field defines the interval at which *intraframe encoding* is carried out. This field and the remaining field are set to 0 or FFH.

53.7 Frame structure

Each frame in the data area (audio and video) is preceded by its own header.

Offset	Bytes	Remarks
00H	4	Sequence number of frame
04H	4	Offset of previous frame
08H	4	Checksum
0CH	n*4	Array of all frame sizes

Table 53.9 Structure of a frame header

The header begins with the sequence number of the frame. This is followed by a pointer to the preceding frame. For the first frame, this pointer contains the value 0.

The checksum relates to the header. The field at offset 0CH contains n 4-byte entries, each containing the number of bytes of the frames which are stored in this stream.

The position of each frame is stored in a directory. For each frame, a frame-directory structure is stored in the stream. This contains a 4-byte pointer giving the offset of the frame.

! **More information about the DVI format is available from the Intel DVI Developer's Toolkit.**

54

MPEG Specification

The *MPEG specification, created by the Motion Pixture Expert Group represents a standard for the transfer of motion pictures. This standard is described in the (draft) ISO standard CD 11172. No file formats have been defined for MPEG data, at present.*

55

Apple QuickTime format (QTM)

A format for storing video sequences with audio data has been defined by Apple. QTM format (Quick Time Movie Resource) is used by the Quick Time product and is available for Macintosh or Windows.

On the Mac, these files are stored as type 'moov'; for Windows, the extension .QTM is used. The data is stored in Motorola format (big-endian).

Several tracks of audio and video data can be stored in a QTM file. Apple provides a Movie Toolbox for processing QTM files. In this toolbox, six different compression processes are defined. However, except for the JPEG process, these are all used exclusively by Apple. Audio data is stored in AIFF format.

QTM files are divided into separate blocks of information, rather like the CHUNKs in the AVI and DVI formats. In the Apple context, these blocks are known as *atoms*. The structure of an atom is shown below:

Offset	Bytes	Remarks
00H	4	Atom size
04H	4	Atom type
08H	*n*	Atom structure
..H	*n*	Atom data

Table 55.1 Structure of a QTM atom

The field containing the size of the atom includes the header and the type field for the atom. The type field is a 4-byte string which specifies the type of atom and the format of the data stored. This is followed by data structures, of which there are two types.

- A *container atom* can contain other atoms (including other container atoms).
- A *leaf atom* contains only data.

Figure 55.1 shows the structure of a QuickTime file.

- Movie Directory
  - Movie Header Atom
    - Clipping Atom
      - Clipping Region Atom
  - Track Directory
    - Track Header Atom
    - Clipping Atom
      - Clipping Region Atom
    - Edits Atom
      - Edits List Atom
    - Media Directory
      - Media Header Atom
      - Media Handler Atom
      - Media Info Atom
        - Video Media Info Atom
        - Sound Media Info Atom
          - Sound Media Info Header Atom
        - Handler Atom
          - Data Reference Atom
          - Sample Table Atom
    - User Data Atom
  - Movies User Data

Figure 55.1 Structure of a QuickTime file

Atoms can be nested to a depth of 5. Any unknown atoms should be skipped.

55.1 Movie Directory atom

A QTM file always begins with a Movie Directory Atom, which has the following structure:

Offset	Bytes	Remarks
00H	4	Atom size in bytes
04H	4	Atom type 'moov'
08H	*n*	Movie header atom
..H	*n*	Clipping atom
..H	*n*	Track atoms
..H	*n*	User data atom

Table 55.2 Structure of a Movie Directory atom

The first field defines the length of the atom and is followed by a signature indicating the type of the file. This is followed by various atom structures. In the Movie Header atom, information on the video sequence is stored. The Movie Clipping atom contains information on the visibility of the images. The Track atom contains an array for each track in the sequence. There is one track for each data stream. Additional information, such as copyright notices, can be stored in the User Data atom.

55.2 Movie Header atom

The structure of this atom, which contains global information on the QTM file, is shown below.

Offset	Bytes	Remarks
00H	4	Atom size
04H	4	Atom type 'mvhd'
08H	4	Version and flags
0CH	4	Creation time
10H	4	Modification time
14H	4	Time scale
18H	4	Duration of movie
1CH	4	Data rate to play
20H	2	Audio data volume
22H	2	Reserved

Table 55.3 Structure of a Movie Header atom (*continues over...*)

Graphics

Offset	Bytes	Remarks
24H	2*4	Reserved
2CH	3*3*4	Transform matrix
60H	4	Preview time
64H	4	Preview duration
68H	4	Poster time
6CH	4	Selection time
70H	4	Selection duration
74H	4	Current time
78H	4	Next value for track ID

Table 55.3 Structure of a Movie Header atom (*cont.*)

The header begins with a length field and a 4-byte signature. Only the first byte of the flag is used for the version number. On the Mac, date and time references (creation, modification) relate to 2 January 1904.

Time scale (offset 14H) defines the units per second. The *Duration* field indicates the length of a sequence in Time Scale units.

The data rate represents the number of bytes per second required for correct playback. The volume of the audio channel is indicated at offset 20H.

The Transform matrix (offset 2CH) is a two dimensional array of integer values. These values are used to transfer the visual coordinates system. A QTM file may contain a preview. Information on the preview sequence (time after which the preview begins, duration, and so on) is given in the fields *Preview time* and *Preview duration*. The field *Poster time* (offset 68H) defines the time when the movie poster appears in the track. The time and duration of the currently selected area in the sequence are shown in *Selection time* and *Selection duration*. QTM files enable the user to intervene interactively in the process. The field *Current time* (offset 74H) defines the time when the current selection appears in the movie. The ID of the next movie track is stored in the last field of the header.

55.3 Track Directory atom

Each data stream is introduced by a Track Directory atom. These atoms are stored in an array in the 'moov' atom.

Offset	Bytes	Remarks
00H	4	Atom size
04H	4	Atom type 'trak'
08H	*n*	Track header atom
..H	*n*	Clipping atom
..H	*n*	Edits atom
..H	*n*	Media atom
..H	*n*	User data atom

Table 55.4 Structure of a Track Directory atom

The first two words define the length and type ('trak') of the atom. This is followed by other atoms.

55.4 Track Header atom

This atom contains information on the associated track. It is structured as follows:

Offset	Bytes	Remarks
00H	4	Atom size
04H	4	Atom type 'tkhd'
08H	4	Version and flags
0CH	4	Creation time
10H	4	Modification time
14H	4	Track ID number
18H	4	Reserved
1CH	4	Duration
20H	4	Reserved
24H	4	Reserved
28H	2	Layer
2AH	2	Track group ID

Table 55.5 Structure of a Track Header atom (*continues over...*)

Offset	Bytes	Remarks
2CH	2	Volume
2EH	2	Reserved
30H	3*3*4	Transform matrix
64H	4	Track width
68H	4	Track height

Table 55.5 Structure of a Track Header atom (*cont.*)

The first two fields define the length and type of the atom. In the flag, only the first byte is used for the version number. The date and time of creation and last modification are defined in Mac format. This is followed by the track ID number.

The *Duration* field defines the length of the track in time units. In the layer field, the priority of the track (layer level) for playback is defined. The volume for the playback of audio data is specified in *Volume*. The Matrix contains data required for converting the pixels between various coordinate systems. The last two fields define the track for the sequence.

55.5 Media atom

This atom describes the media used in this track. It is structured as shown below:

Offset	Bytes	Remarks
00H	4	Atom size
04H	4	Signature 'mdia'
08H	*n*	Media header atom
..H	*n*	Handle atom
..H	*n*	Media info atom

Table 55.6 Structure of a Media atom

The first two fields define the length and type of the atom. This is followed by other atoms.

55.6 Media Header atom

The structure of this atom is shown in Table 55.7 below:

Offset	Bytes	Remarks
00H	4	Atom size
04H	4	Signature ('mdhd')
08H	4	Flags and version
0CH	4	Creation time
10H	4	Modification time
14H	4	Time scale
18H	4	Duration
1CH	4	Language
20H	4	Quality

Table 55.7 Media Header atom structure

The first two fields define the length and type of the atom. Only the first byte of the flag is used for the version number.

The creation time and modification time are stored in Mac time and date format.

Time scale defines the units in seconds, and the length of the track during playback is indicated in *Duration* time. The *language* field contains a code for the language version used in this track. The last field contains information on the quality of the information stored.

! Further information on QuickTime format can be obtained from the Reference Manual supplied with the QuickTime Developers Kit.

56

CAS Fax format (DCX)

The *CAS Fax format (DCX format) was defined for the storage of fax documents. The format is based on PCX and is capable of storing monochrome images. To achieve this, the PCX format has been somewhat extended.*

The structure of a DCX file is shown in Figure 56.1:

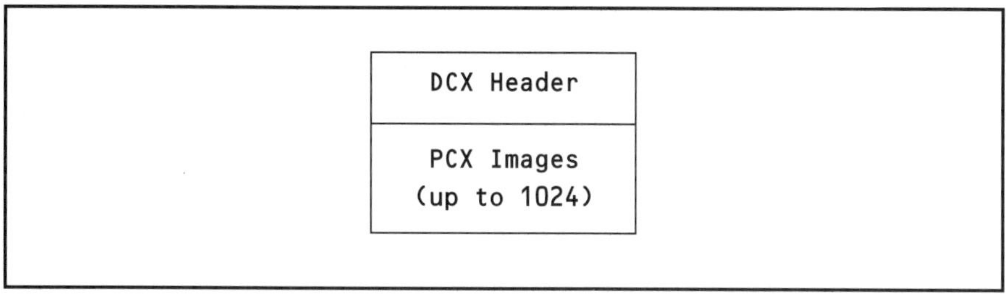

Figure 56.1
DCX Fax file structure

A DCX file contains a header, and up to 1024 frames, which are stored as monochrome images in PCX format.

56.1 DCX header

The structure of the DCX header, which is used for addressing the following images, is very simple.

Offset	Bytes	Remarks
00H	4	Signature
04H	1024*4	Image pointer array

Table 56.1 Structure of a DCX header

The first four bytes contain the signature values 3AH DEH 68H B1H. This is followed by 1024 4-byte entries containing (offset) pointers to the image frames. The value 00H in an entry indicates that there are no more images in the file.

The images are stored in PCX format. Each area begins with a header, followed by the data area (*see* PCX description in Chapter 22).

! There is another series of fax formats, which stores some of the data in compressed form using the CCITT Group 3 compression methods. The data is stored either directly in a file or appended to a header. The structure of this header varies from manufacturer to manufacturer. Generally, only 4 bytes are used for the signature.

57

Adobe Illustrator format (AI)

A dobe *Illustrator is available for Windows and for Macintosh. The program stores graphics in a modified PostScript format. The AI file consists of a Prolog, followed by the actual script data.*

Figure 57.1 shows the structure of an AI file.

```
%!PS-Adobe-3.0 EPSF-3.0
< Header comments >
%%EndComments
<Procedure settings>
%%EndProlog
Script <Setup>
<Objects>
<Page trailer>
<Document trailer>
%%EOF
```

Figure 57.1 Structure of an Illustrator (AI) file

The header comments always begin with %% and a keyword. They contain various items of information on the file.

57.1 AI header comments

The header of an AI file contains EPS commands for the reader. These are formatted as %% comments.

```
%!PS-Adobe-3.0 EPSF-3.0
%%BeginProlog
%%Creator: Adobe Illustrator (TM) 3.0.1
%%For: (user) (organization)
%%Title: (illustration title)
%%CreationDate: (date) (time)
%%BoundingBox: llx lly urx ury
%%DocumentProcessColors: keyword
%%DocumentFonts: font...
%%+font....
%%DocumentFiles: filename
%%+filename....
%%DocumentSuppliedResources: proset packarray version
%%+ procset Adobe_cmykcolor version revision
....
%%EndComments
```

Figure 57.2 Structure of an AI header

The meaning of these commands is described briefly below. The commands need not appear in every header. With Windows, certain commands, which are only of significance to the Mac, are omitted.

%!PS-Adobe-3.0 EPSF-3.0

This string introduces a valid EPS file and therefore also an AI file.

%%BeginProlog

Introduces the Prolog within the AI file.

%%EndProlog

Ends the Prolog of an AI file and introduces the Script section.

%%EndComments

Signals the end of the comment section in the Prolog.

%%Creator

This command indicates the name and version of the program that created the file.

%%For: (username) (organization)

Defines the user name and organization that created the document. Both parameters must be defined as valid PostScript strings (*see* description of PostScript in Chapter 84). Escape characters (for example, \230) may be used to represent foreign characters.

%%Title: (title)

Defines the title of the illustration. The title must be a valid PostScript string.

%%CreationDate: (date) (time)

This comment indicates the time and date at which the document was created. The parameters must be valid PostScript strings.

%%BoundingBox: llx lly urx ury

This command must appear in the AI header. It defines the bounding box of the image in integer coordinates (`llx`=lower left x, `lly`=lower left y, `urx` = upper right x, `ury` = upper right y).

%%DocumentProcessColors: keyword

The *keyword* contains strings giving the names of the colors used (for example, cyan, magenta, yellow, black). This information is useful for color separation.

%%DocumentCustomColors: (customcolorname)

This comment gives the name of special color systems (for example, PANTONE 156 CV) which have been used. The command can specify several colors, in which case the following line contains the character combination `%%+color`.

`%%CMYKCustomColors: cyan magenta yellow black (customcolorname)`

This comment specifies the color as an approximation to the color combination *cyan*, *magenta*, *yellow* and *black*. The command may refer to several colors, in which case the following line contains the character combination `%%+color`.

`%%DocumentFonts: font`

The font names used in the document are defined here. The fonts must be PostScript fonts, and the command may contain several font definitions, in which case the following line contains the character combination `%%+font`. This command is omitted if no fonts are used.

`%%DocumentFiles: filename`

If files must be imported in order to display a graphic, these should be specified here. The command may apply to several files, in which case the following line contains the character combination `%%+filename`.

`%%DocumentSuppliedResources: procset .. version revision`

This comment is used only after version 3 of Illustrator. It defines the versions of resources supplied for *Adobe_packedarray*, *Adobe_cmykcolor*, *Adobe_cshow*, *Adobe_customcolor*, *Adobe_pattern_AI3*, *Adobe_typography_AI3* and *Adobe_IllustratorA_AI3*. A line has the format: `%%DocumentSuppliedResources: procset .. version revision`, where the version number and revision number should be inserted in the .. space. The command may apply to several lines, in which case the following line contains the character combination `%%+procset...`

`%%DocumentNeededResources:`

This command appears in Adobe Illustrator 3 [AI3] and defines the resources needed in the document.

`%%IncludeResource`

This command appears in Adobe Illustrator 3 [AI3] and defines the resources included in the document.

`%%AI3_ColorUsage: keyword`

This command defines whether the document is to be displayed in black and white or in color. The keyword is set to `Black&White` or `Color`.

%%AI3_TemplateBox: lly lly urx ury

Defines `Bounding box`, which includes all the elements in a document template. The coordinates may be integers or real numbers. An element is taken to be 1/72 of an inch square. If a document is defined as a template, the bounding box must be set to `0`. In Illustrator 88, in version 4.0 for Windows and in the Japanese version, the command is referred to as `%%TemplateBox`.

%%AI3_TemplateFile: filename

Defines the name of the template file in the format `volume::directory id:filename`.

%%AI3_TileBox: llx lly urx ury

On the Mac, defines a bounding box around the visible image excerpt (tile). In Illustrator 88, in version 4.0 for Windows and in the Japanese version, the command is referred to as `%%TileBox`.

57.2 Script Setup

The header is followed by a Script Setup area. This consists of a sequence of parameters, followed by a keyword (in PostScript notation).

```
<script>::=    <setup>
               {<objects>]
               {<page trailer>}
               {<document trailer>}
               %%EOF
<setup> ::=    %%BeginSetup
               {%%IncludeFont:font}
               {<proc set init>}
               <font encoding>
               <pattern defs>
               %%EndSetup
<page trailer> ::=  %%PageTrailer
               gsave annotatepage grestore showpage
<document trailer> ::=  %%Trailer
               {<proc set termination>}
```

Figure 57.3 Structure of a Script Setup

The comment `%%IncludeFont` is used to indicate special fonts used in the document. If the font is missing, Illustrator will use a substitute font. The script is also used for initializing resources. The *Font Encoding* section is structured as follows:

```
<font encoding>::=    [
                      {re-encoding pairs}
                      <Te>
                      {<re-encoding pair>}
<re-encoding> ::=   %AI3_BeginEncoding
                      newFontName oldFontname
                      %AI3_EndEncoding <font type>
<font type> ::=       AdobeType | TrueType
```

Figure 57.4 Structure of a Font Encoding section

57.2.1 TE operator

The `TE` operator defines the platform for font encoding and is structured as shown below:

```
[encoding pair TE
```


57.2.2 TZ operator

The `TZ` operator creates a new font from an existing font. The `encoding pair` parameters represent a list of codes:

```
[encoding pair... TZ
For a Times-Roman font, this command might be defined as
follows:
%%BeginEndcoding: _Times-Roman Times-Roman
  [    /_Times-Roman/Times-Roman 0 0 1 TZ
%%EndEncoding
```

Figure 57.5 Font encoding

57.2.3 Pattern definition

Patterns used in the Illustrator should be defined in the Script Setup segment.

57.2.4 E operator

This operator defines a pattern in the following format:

```
(patternname) lly lly ury ury [<layerlist>]E
```

The patterns are allocated to different layers. This *layerlist* contains two definitions:

57.2.4.1 (colordefinition)@

This command defines the *Color* and *Overprinting* style. The Overprint style is defined with the `O` and `R` operators.

57.2.4.2 (tiledefinition)&

This operator defines the tile for the pattern. A pattern definition might be structured as follows:

```
%%BeginPattern: (sun)
 (sun) 100 200 120 300 [
 (0 0 0 R 0.03 0.05 0.15 0 (PANTONE 468 CV) ...
 _&
 (0 0 0 R 0.03 0.05 0.15 0 (PANTONE 468 CV) ...
(0 i 0 J 0 j 1 w 4 M [] 0 d
%%Note
105 115.3 m
105 120.3 L
...
s
) &
] E
%%EndPattern
```

Figure 57.6 Structure of a pattern definition

The pattern is constructed with `m` (moveto) and `l` (lineto) using the paramenters from the definition. The `s` stroke command is responsible for the output.

57.3 Script body

An Illustrator image consists of a sequence of graphic elements. These are referred to as objects and specified by the following object description:

```
<object>::={<A>}(object locking)
              <path object>|
              <path mask>|
              <composite object>|
              <text object>|
              <placed art object>|
              <subscriber object>|
              <graph object>|
              <PostScript document>
<path object>::=<paint style>
              <path geometry>
              <path render> |
              <guide operator>
<path mask>::=<paint style>
              <path geometry>
              <h> | <H>
              <W>
              <path render>
<composite object>::=<group object> |
              <group with mask> |
              <compound path> |
              <compound path mask> |
              <wraparound group>
<group object> ::=<u>
              <object>+<U>
<group with mask> ::=<q>
              {<object>}
              {<masked object>}
              <Q>
<masked object> ::=<mask> | <object>
<mask> ::=<path mask> | <compound path mask>
<compound path> ::=<*u>
              <compound path element>+<*U>
<compound path element> ::=
              <path object>+<compound group>
<compound group> ::=     <u>
              <compound path element>+<U>
```

Figure 57.7 Structure of an object description (*continues over...*)

```
<compound path mask> ::= <*u>
             <compound path mask element>+<*U>
<compound path mask element> ::=
             <path mask>+<compound mask group>
<compound mask group> ::=
             <compound mask bottom group> | <compound
mask non-bottom group>
<compound mask bottom group> ::=
             {<A>}
             <q>
             <path mask>+<Q>
<compound mask non-bottom group>::=
             {<A>}
             <u>
             <compound mask group>+<U>
```

Figure 57.7 Structure of an object description (*cont.*)

The individual operators in the Script region are briefly described below. In essence these operators are abbreviated PostScript commands, which are defined in the header.

57.3.1 Locked Object operator

This group contains only one command.

`flag A`

The flag accepts values of `0` and `1`. Value `0` enables the selection of an object for editing in the Illustrator. If `flag = 1` the object is locked.

57.3.2 Graphic State operators

These operators describe the graphic state.

`[array] phase d`

The `d` operator corresponds to the `setdash` operator in PostScript. `array` contains the definition of the line pattern and `phase` determines the phase of the pattern at the start of the path.

`flatness i`

The operator corresponds to the `setflat` operator in PostScript. Values must be in the range 0–100.

`flag D`

The `D` operator describes the direction (winding order) of an object when filling an area. If `flag = 0` the path will be filled clockwise.

`linejoin j`

This operator functions like the PostScript `linejoin` command. `0` = mitered joins, `1` = round joins, `2` = beveled joins. The initialization value is `0`.

`linecap J`

This operator functions like the PostScript `linecap` command. `0` = butt end caps, `1` = round end caps, `2` = square end caps. The initialization value is `0`.

`miterlimit M`

This operator functions like the PostScript `setmiterlimit` operator. The initialization value is `4`.

`linewidth w`

This operator corresponds to the `setlinewidth` command in PostScript. The initialization sets the line width to `1.0` (in user space). The value `0` is interpreted as the thinnest possible line.

57.3.3 Color operators

These operators determine the colors or grayscales for the following objects.

`gray g`

Defines the grayscale (`0.0` = black, `1.0` = white) used to fill paths. In PostScript, this function is fulfilled by the `setgrayscale` operator.

`gray G`

The `(stroke)` operator functions like the `gray g` command, but it acts on the paths which are filled with stroke.

`cyan magenta yellow black k`

This operator `(fill)` corresponds to the PostScript `setcmykcolor` command. It defines the colors for the path to be filled. Each of the operands must lie between `0.0` (minimum) and `1.0` (maximum).

`cyan magenta yellow black K`

Corresponds to the `..k` operator, but is used on paths with stroke `(stroke set cmykcolors)`.

`cyan magenta yellow black (name) gray x`

Defines a user-specific color (`fill custom color`) for filling paths.

`cyan magenta yellow black (name) gray X`

Corresponds to `..X`, but is used on stroke paths `(stroke custom color)`.

`(patternname) px py sx  sy angle rf r k ka [a b c d tx ty]p`

The `p` operator defines a pattern for fill operations (`fill pattern`). `px` and `py` define the distance (in points) from the origin of the ruler to the point at which the rectangle containing the pattern appears. `sx` and `sy` define the scaling factor. `angle` defines the rotational angle (in counter-clockwise direction) in which the pattern appears. `rf` (reflection flag) defines whether a reflection is applied to the pattern (`0` = true, `1` = false). `r` defines the angle through which the pattern is reflected. `k` specifies the shear angle and `ka` defines the shear axis. `[abcd tx ty]` defines the initialization matrix for the transformation of the pattern.

`(patternname) px py sx  sy angle rf r k ka [a b c d tx ty]p`

Corresponds to `...p`, but acts on a stroke pattern (`stroke pattern`).

`flag O`

Overprint flag (1 = `fill overprinting`).

`flag R`

Functions like the `O` operator, but is used on paths via the stroke command (stroke overprinting).

57.3.4 Group operators

These two commands are used for collating graphic objects into a single object (group).

`-u`

Marks the beginning of a sequence containing object descriptions for the group.

`-U`

Marks the end of the sequence containing object descriptions for the group.

57.3.5 Path definition commands

This group contains operators for the construction of paths. When drawing in PostScript, a path is constructed and then filled with color.

`x y m`

Corresponds to the PostScript operator `moveto` and defines the starting point. The commands must appear before every path description.

`x y l`

Draws a straight line from the current position to the position indicated as `x,y`. The new point acts as a smooth point for a line.

`x y L`

Functions like `x y l`, but the new point defines a corner.

`x1 y1 y2 y2 x3 y3 c`

Appends a Bézier curve to a path. The end point is indicated with `x3,y3` and forms a smooth point. `x1,y1 x2,y2` defines the Bézier coordinates.

`x1 y1 d2 y2 x3 y3 C`

Functions like `...c`, but uses `x3,y3` to define a corner.

`x2 y2 x3 y3 v`

Adds a segment of a Bézier curve to the current path (`x0,y0`). The new point `x3,y3` is used as a smooth point. `x0,y0` and `x2,y2` define the Bézier coordinates.

`x2 y2 x3 y3 V`

Functions like `...v`, but `x3,y3` define a corner.

`x1 y1 x3 y3 y`

Adds a segment of a Bézier curve to the current path. The new point `x3,y3` is used as a smooth point. `x1,y1` and `x3,y3` define the Bézier coordinates.

`x2 y2 x3 y3 Y`

Functions like `...y`, but `x3,y3` define a corner.

57.3.6 Path painting commands

These operators reset the current path to blank.

`-N`

This operator leaves the current path open (newpath is used for invisible paths).

`-n`

Closes the path but otherwise operates like `-N`.

`-F`

Fills the area enclosed by the path with the currently set color and the current fill pattern (fill path). The path remains open.

`-f`

Functions like `-F`, but closes the path (fill and close path).

`-S`

Draws (stroke path) the current path using the current color (stroking color) or pattern. The line width is set with `w`, the line shape with `j` and `d`.

`-s`

Functions like `-S`, but closes the path before carrying out the stroke command (stroke closed path).

-B

Functions like -F, but fills the path and carries out a stroke command. The path remains open (fill and stroke path).

-b

Functions like -B, but closes the path at the end of the operation (close, fill and stroke path).

57.3.7 Compound path commands

These commands operate like other PostScript commands in putting together paths (for example, for letter characters). The structure is defined in Figure 57.6.

-u

Introduces a compound path (group).

-U

Closes the compound path (ungroup).

57.3.8 Clipping operators

These commands mask the visible area. The q operator is used here. The structure of this operator is defined in Figure 57.6.

-q

Introduces a clipping operator (clipping group) with the description of the mask. The group objects define a mask (clip path). The mask encloses various objects. When the image is displayed (rendered), only these objects are visible.

-Q

Marks the end of a sequence with (mask) clipping operators.

-H

Is used for the path when producing a mask (closepath).

-h

Functions like -H, but closes the path.

-W

Interrupts the clip path and sets a new, reduced clip path.

Texts can also be used as masks, in which case the Tr operator should be used.

57.3.9 Text

The Illustrator can display texts in either revisable or final format. Texts are divided into three groups: *point text, area text and text on path*. The syntax of text objects is shown in Figure 57.8.

```
<text object> ::=
                        <To>
                        <text at a point>|
                        <text area>|
                        <text along a path>
                        <TO>
<text at a point> ::=
                        <Tp>
                        <TP>+
                        <text run>
<text area> ::=
                        <text area element>+
                        {<overflow text>}
<text area element> ::=
                        <Tp>
                        <path object>
                        <TP>
                        <text run>+
<text along a path> ::=
                        <Tp>
                        <path object>
                        <TP>
                        <text run>+
                        {<overflow text>}
<text run> ::=
                        {<text style>|
                        <paint style>|
                        <text position>|
                        <Tk>*}
                        <text body>
<text style> ::=
                        <Tr>|(render mode)
                        <Tf>|(font&size)
                        <Ts>|(rise&fall)
                        <Tz>|(horizontal scaling)
                        <Tt>|(tracking)
                        <TA>|(automatic kerning)
```

Figure 57.8 Text syntax *(continues over...)*

```
                         <TC>|(inter-character spacing)
                         <TW>|(inter-word spacing)
                         <Ti>|(indents)
                         <Ta>|(alignment)
                         <Tq>|(hanging indent)
                         <Tl>(leading)
<text position> ::=
                         <Tc>|(computed inter-character
spacing)
                         <Tw>|(computed inter-word spacing)
                         <Tm>|(text matrix)
                         <Td>|(translate)
                         <T*>|(translate down)
                         <TR>|(reset matrix)
<text body> ::=
                         <Tx>|<Tj>|<T+>|<T->
<overflow text> ::=
                         {<text style>|
                         <paint style>|
                         <TK>}*
                         <Tx>|<T+>
```

Figure 57.8 Text syntax (*cont.*)

The following commands are used for the output of texts:

`*w`

Marks a text sequence with word break (wrap around) at the end of a line.

`*W`

Marks the end of a wrap around sequence. Text objects appear within the sequence.

`type To`

Begins a text object (begin text object). `type` defines the type of text (`0` point text, `1` area text, `2` path text).

`TO`

Ends a text object.

`a b c d tx ty start Tp`

Begins a text path in a text object (begin text path). `(abcd tx ty)` defines the grid. `start` indicates the starting point of the text in the grid.

`TP`

Ends a text path in a text object (end text path).

`Tr`

Sets the text output mode (text rendering mode). The following operators apply:

0	Fill text
1	Stroke text
2	Fill and stroke text
3	Invisible text
4	Mask and fill text
5	Mask and stroke text
6	Mask, fill and stroke text
7	Mask only text
8	Filled text followed by type 9
9	Stroked text preceded by type 8

Table 57.1 Text rendering modes

`user tracking Tt`

Defines *Track kerning* (manual kerning).

`autokern TA`

Activates *Automatic kerning*. The setting from the header is used here. If `autokern = 0`, pair kerning will not be used.

`autokern kernvalue Tk`

Switches kerning on (*pairwise kerning*). If `autokern = 0`, manual kerning is used; `autokern = 1` activates automatic kerning.

`autokern kernvalue TK`

Switches kerning from *Overflow text* on; otherwise operates like `Tk`.

`min opt max TW`

Defines *word spacing* (minimum, optimum and maximum) as a percentage of the character width.

`wordspace Tw`

Defines *computed word spacing*.

`min opt max TC`

Defines *Character spacing* (minimum, optimum, maximum) as a percentage of the character width.

`charspace Tc`

Defines *computed character spacing*.

`leading paragraphLeading Tl`

Defines *line and paragraph leading* in 1/1000 square.

`rise Ts`

Defines subscripting (`-xxx Ts`) and superscripting (`+xxx Ts`). Positive and negative parameters indicate the shift in points.

`T+`

Defines a hyphen (discretionary hyphen).

`T-`

Defines a hyphen which is to be printed (printable hyphen).

`textstring Tx`

Defines non-justified text.

`textstring TX`

Defines non-justified text, that overflows beyond the visible area.

`textstring Tj`

Defines justified text.

`align Ta`

Defines alignment: `0` = left, `1` = centered, `2` = right, `3` = justified (right, left), `4` = justified (including last line).

`para 1st right Ti`

Controls the indentation of a paragraph. The parameters define the left indent (`para`), first-line left indent (`1st`) and right indentation (`right`).

`scale% Tz`

Condenses or expands the horizontal scaling of a character as a percentage of the font size.

`type To`

This operator introduces a text. `type` may be `0` = point text, `1` = area text or `2` = path text.

`[a b c d tx ty] startpt Tp`

The operator encloses the text path in brackets.

`[a b c d tx ty] Tm`

The operator sets the text matrix for the text.

`tx ty Td`

Translates the text matrix to the start of the following line, using `tx` and `ty`.

`T*`

Translates the text matrix to the start of the next line (final form).

`[a b c d tx ty] TR`

Resets the pattern matrix (for pattern prototype only).

`fontname size Tf`

Defines the re-encoded font names and font sizes in points.

! **The operands ^! # $ define Kanji bitmap strings.**

57.3.10 Graph operators

These operators define graphs within the document.

`Gs`

Introduces a graph.

`GS`

Ends the definition of a graph.

`left top right bottom Gb`

Defines the dimensions of a graph (bounds). Axes, labels, and so on are located outside the rectangle.

`a b c d e f g h i j [k l]Gy`

Defines the structure (style) of the graph.

`a`

Represents the type of graph:

5	Grouped column graph
6	Stacked column graph
7	Line graph
8	Pie chart
9	Scatter graph
10	Area graph

Table 57.2
Graph types

`b`

Defines hatching (1 = hatching).

`c`

Defines the data point order; that is, if `c = 0`, the lower points of a graph cover the points of the top row.

`d`

Defines the legend for pie charts:

14	Same as bar/line graphs
15	Legend in wedges
16	No legend

Table 57.3
Pie chart legend type

`e = 1`

Specifies draw marks, that is, marks are displayed at the points in scattered graphs.

`f = 1`

Specifies that individual points are to be joined by lines.

`g = 1`

Enables wider lines (shaped lines) to be drawn between points.

`h = 1`

Specifies draw legend across the top.

`i`

Defines the line shape width between 0 and 100.0 (default = 6).

`j`

Defines which axis is to be used for plotting the data (44 use left axis, 45 use right axis).

`k`

Specifies that the percentage values in a pie chart are to be displayed in the segments.

`l`

Defines the number of decimal places for the percentage values. This option is only available for Windows (Illustrator 4.x).

`a b c d e f g h i Gd`

Defines some of the values in a *Graph Style* dialog box and is specifically designed for the Illustrator.

Graphics

`a b c d x Gj`

Occurs only with the Mac and is part of the publish and subscribe facility for System 7 routines.

`x z Ga`

Introduces a graph-axis specification. `x` defines the axis (`1` bottom axis, `2` left axis, `3` right axis). `z` defines a string, which is appended to the label text.

`a b c d e f g h GA`

Describes the axis.

`a = 1`

Uses manual values for axis scaling.

`b`

Defines the type of tick marks. (`13` no tick marks, `14` short tick marks, `15` long tick marks).

`c`

Defines the minimum scale value of the axis.

`d`

Defines the maximum scale value of the axis.

`e`

Indicates the difference between two scaling ticks for manual scaling.

`f`

Defines small ticks per value.

`g`

Draws marks between the labels.

`h`

This string is appended to the axis label.

`rows columns 1st_row 1st_col Gz`

Shows the size of a table containing cells.

`x1, x2, .. xn Gc`

Reads in cell values.

`col width1... num Gw`

Overwrites the column width. The first parameter indicates the starting column. The last parameter defines the number of parameters.

`GC`

Concludes the definition of a table.

`version Gt`

Marks the start of a customized graph. Version is set to `2`.

`target customgraph Gx`

Defines a customized graph.

`x Gp`

Defines a customized graph with Illustrator operators.

`flag G+`

Resets if `flag = 0`.

`send G1`

As with `Gp`, if `send = 0 ->` send to back.

`a b c d e Gf`

Sets the paint style (`a = 1` fill graph, `b = 1` do stroke, `c` fill style, `d` stroke style, `e = 1` object has a fill mask).

`col GI`

Column index for data points.

`row Gr`

Index to table row.

`axis Gi`

Defines which axis is inside the object.

`a b c d e f g h i j Gm`

Used for customized graphs that use adaptation matrices.

`repeat Ge`

Used for customized graphs.

`tickvalue Gv`

Defines the value of a scaling tick.

Depending on the version of Illustrator, not all of the operators described are necessarily used. A more detailed description of the individual operands can be found in the AI file format specification.

58

Initial Graphics Exchange Language (IGES)

***IGES** represents a standardized format (NBSIR 88-3813) for the exchange of CAD data. The following description is based on IGES version 4.0. IGES files may be in ASCII or binary format. The ASCII format described here is particularly suitable for exchanging graphics between different platforms.*

In the ASCII format, a distinction can be made between compressed format and 80-characters-per-line format. The structure of IGES files is line-oriented. The illustration below shows a dump from an 80-character IGES file:

```
translator comments                                    S0000001
,,1HA,5HA.IGS,...                                      S0000002
....                                                   G0000001
4HINCH,32767,3.2767D1,....                             G0000002
110       1     1     1                         ..     D0000001
110       2     1     1                         ..     D0000002
...
110,6.80,5.0...                                        P0000001
110,20.3,4.5,6.3...                                    P0000002
....
S0000002G0000003D0000026P0000013                       T0000001
```

Figure 58.1 Structure of an ASCII-IGES file

Starting in column 74, each line contains a continuous sequence number for identification. These numbers are seven-digit numbers, to which leading zeros or spaces can be added.

Within each line, various rules must be observed:

- A separator must be defined to separate the parameters, (for example, comma). If two separators follow each other (,,), the relevant parameter is set to 0.
- A separator must also be defined for the lines within the parameter section. A semicolon (;) is generally used for this purpose. If this separator appears in a line before all the parameters have been read, the missing parameters will be set to 0.
- Separators must not appear within a text string.
- Numeric values must not extend beyond a line break.

At column 73, there is a letter defining the section of the IGES file. IGES files are divided into various sections containing different information (parameters, flags, and so on).

ID	Section
S	Start section
G	Global section
D	Directory entry section
P	Parameter data section
T	Terminate section
B	Flag section (only binary)
C	Flag section (only compressed ASCII)

Table 58.1 Section ID for IGES lines

The sections are described below.

58.1 Start section

The *Start* section contains comments for the user. An IGES file must contain at least one such line. The letters used for the comment must belong to the ASCII character set (codes up to 127).

58.2 Global section

The *Global* section contains formatting information (for example, definition of parameter separators). Each definition is effective immediately. The following table shows the entries in the Global section:

Index	Type	Remarks
1	String	Parameter separator (,)
2	String	End of line separator (;)
3	String	ID IGES sender
4	String	IGES filename
5	String	ID IGES writer
6	String	Preprocessor version
7	Integer	Maximum integer size
8	Integer	Maximum exponent size single precision
9	Integer	Decimals fraction Single precision
10	Integer	Maximum exponent size double precision
11	Integer	Decimals fraction Double precision
12	String	Product ID receiver
13	Real	Scale factor (.125)
14	Integer	Unit 1 = inch 2 = millimeter 3 = index reference 4 = foot 5 = mile 6 = meter 7 = kilometer 8 = mils (0.001 inch) 9 = micrometer 10 = centimeter 11 = micro inch
15	String	Unit name: `2HIN` or `4HINCH` = inch `2HMM` = millimeter `2HFt` = foot `2HMI` = mile

Table 58.2 Entries in a Global section (*continues over...*)

Graphics

Index	Type	Remarks
		2HM = meter
		2HKM = kilometer
		2HMIL = mile
		2HUM = micron
		2HCM = centimeter
		3HUIN = micro inch
		MIL12
		or IEEE260 = index
16	Integer	Maximum steps line width (*see* index 12 in directory section)
17	Real	Maximum line width (in units) (*see* index 12 in directory section)
18	String	Date and time
		(13HYYMMDD.HHNNSS
		YY = year
		MM = month
		DD = day
		HH = hour
		NN = minutes
		SS = seconds)
19	Real	Maximum resolution (in units of index 15)
20	Real	Maximum coordinate size
21	String	Author name
22	String	Company name
23	Integer	IGES version number
		1 = version 1.0
		2 = ANSI Y14.26M-1981
		3 = version 2.0
		4 = version 3.0
		5 = ANSI Y14.26M-1987
		6 = version 4.0
24	Integer	Reference to standard
		0 = no standard
		1 = ISO
		2 = AFNOR
		3 = ANSI
		4 = BSI
		5 = CSA
		6 = DIN
		7 = JIS

Table 58.2
Entries in a Global section (*cont.*)

Texts are always stored in the form nHxxxxx, where *n* represents the number of following characters (xxxx).

58.3 Directory Entry section

The Global section is followed by the *Directory Entry* section. This contains a directory entry for every description in the IGES file. Each of these directory entries uses two lines of 80 characters each, with 10 fields defined in each line. Fields 1 to 9 and 11 to 19 are used for definitions. Fields 10 and 20 (starting from column 73) contain the record numbers (for example, D0000001).

All data (integers or pointers) is displayed right justified and with leading zeros or spaces. Default values are used for any entries missing from a column.

Some individual fields contain only integer values; other fields contain only pointer constants, and there are also fields containing both integers and pointers. In this case, the fields must not have any blank entries (zero entries). Positive values describe an integer value; negative values describe pointers.

The following table contains an overview of the index record entries in a Directory Entry section.

Index	Remarks
1	Type of entry (100 = arc, 110 = line, and so on)
2	Pointer to 1st data line of this type
3	Structure with negative value, defines the schema for this type
4	Defines the line style (1 = solid, 2 = dashed 3 = phantom, 4 = centerline, 5 = dotted)
5	Defines the level number for the element
6	Defines the views of a element
7	Defines a transformation matrix
8	Label display, defines the element descriptions in different views
9	Status flag "aabbccdd" aa blank status: 00 visible 01 invisible bb subordinate entity switch 00 independent 01 physical dependent 02 logical dependent 03 both (1 and 2) cc entity use flag 00 geometry 01 annotation 02 definition 03 other

Table 58.3 Entries in a Directory Entry section (*continues over...*)

Index	Remarks		
		04	logical (position oriented)
		05	depends on 2D parameter
			dd hierarchy
		00	top down
		01	stepwise
		02	other
10	Line number (starts with D0000001)		
11	Type number entry (same as index 1)		
12	Line width for view		
13	Color		
		0	colorless
		1	black
		2	red
		3	green
		4	blue
		5	yellow
		6	magenta
		7	cyan
		8	white
14	Lines in Parameter Data section for element		
15	Number of form in Parameter Data section		
16	Empty		
17	Empty		
18	Entity label (up to 8 characterss)		
19	Entity number (for label)		
20	Line number (same as in 10)		

Table 58.3 Entries in a Directory Entry section (*cont.*)

The sequence for the indices in the Directory Entry section is arbitrary.

58.4 Parameter Data section

The *Parameter Data* section contains the actual parameters for the IGES entries. This means that the type of command is shown in the Directory Entry section. The associated commands are located in the record with the same number in the Parameter Data section. The data is defined in a free format. The first entry determines the type (for example, 124 = matrix definition). The individual parameters follow, up to column 63. These parameters are separated by separator characters (usually a comma). Column 65 contains a blank, followed by a pointer (columns 66 to 72) to the first line of the associated entry in the Directory Entry section. The character P is placed in column 73 as a signature for the Parameter Data section. The remaining columns are assigned the running seven digit number (starting with 1).

The meaning of the individual parameters depends on the element type (*see below*). The list of parameters is terminated with a separator (usually a semicolon).

58.5 Termination section

An IGES file must end with a *Termination section*. This section is reduced to one line containing six fields. The first four fields contain the number of records per section (Start section, Global section, Directory Entry section, Parameter Data section). Each field is 8 characters long, and the first letter indicates the type of the section (S, G, D, P). The fifth field, from columns 33 to 72, is not used and remains empty. The remaining columns are numbered T0000001.

58.6 Elements of an IGES file

The elements (line, circle, and so on) of an IGES file are defined in the Directory Entry section and the parameters in the Parameter Data section. All the elements are positioned in a 3D-coordinate system (model space). An additional coordinate system (definition space) can be defined for each element. This has no fixed origin. The origin is determined by means of a matrix and a reference vector in each case. Both coordinate systems are defined in element type 124 (matrix). Angles are defined in a clockwise direction. The geometrical elements are listed in the table below:

Index	Remarks	
100	CIRCULAR ARC with:	
	P1	ZT-reference point
	P2	X-value centre
	P3	Y-value centre
	P4	X coordinate start point arc
	P5	Y coordinate start point arc
	P6	X coordinate end point arc
	P7	Y coordinate end point arc
102	COMPOSITE CURVE with:	
	P1	number of elements
	P2-Pn	pointer to directory entry section containing element description

Table 58.4 Entries for geometric elements in Parameter Data section (*continues over...*)

Graphics

Index	Remarks	
104	CONIC ARC	
	P1-P6	coefficient to calculate ellipse
	P7	ZT reference point
	P8	X coordinate start point
	P9	Y coordinate start point
	P10	X coordinate end point
	P11	Y coordinate end point
	P12-Pn	Pointer to directory entry section
106	COPIOUS DATA, stores construction points	
	P1	interpretation flag (1 xy-coordinates, 2 xyz-coordinates, 3 xyz-coordinates + 3 definition vectors)
	P2	number of copious data
	P3	(interpretation flag = 1 -> fixed Z)
	P4-Pn	data points (abscissa, ordinate, if interpretation flag = 2)
108	PLANE	
	P1-P4	transfer coefficients
	P5	pointer to directory entry section
	P6	XT coordinate symbol point
	P7	YT coordinate
	P8	ZT coordinate
	P9	symbol size
	P10-Pn	pointer
110	LINE	
	P1	X coordinate start point
	P2	Y coordinate start point
	P3	Z coordinate start point
	P4	X coordinate end point
	P5	Y coordinate end point
	P6	Z coordinate end point
	P7-Fn	pointers
112	SPLINE CURVE	
	P1	spline type (1 linear, 2 quadratic, 3 cubic, 4 Wilson Fowler, 5 modified Wilson Fowler, 6 B-spline)
	P2	continuity
	P3	dimensions
	P4	number of segments
	P5-Pn	vertex points (first all x, then all y, then all z coordinates, then transformation coefficients and vectors)

Table 58.4 Entries for geometric elements in Parameter Data section (*cont.*)

Graphics

Index	Remarks	
114	SPLINE SURFACE	
	P1	surface type (*see* type 112)
	P2	type (1 Cartesian, 2 undefined)
	P3	number of lines
	P4	number of columns
	P5–Pn	vertex points (first all coordinates x,y,z for all rows, then for all columns, then transformation coefficients and vectors)
116	POINT	
	P1	X coordinate
	P2	Y coordinate
	P3	Z coordinate
	P4	Pointer
118	RULED SURFACE (arc area)	
	P1	pointer to 1st curve
	P2	pointer to 2nd curve
	P3	direction
120	SURFACE OF REVOLUTION	
	P1	pointer to surface line
	P2	pointer to surface vector
	P3	start angle
	P4	end angle
122	TABULATED CYLINDER	
	P1	pointer to surface line
	P2–P4	coordinates vertex surface vector
124	MATRIX, transformation matrix between model space and definition space	
125	FLASH, localization point for a closed area	
	P1	X coordinate reference point
	P2	Y coordinate reference point
	P3	1st size parameter
	P4	2nd size parameter
	P5	rotation angle
	P6	pointer to directory entry section
126	B-SPLINE CURVE	
	P1,P2	coefficients B-spline curve
	P3	proportion 1: 0 non planar, 1 planar
	P4	proportion 2: 0 open curve
128	B-SPLINE SURFACE	
	P1–P4	coefficients
	P5–P9	proportion
	P10–Pn	vertex points, widths, control points, pointers

Table 58.4 Entries for geometric elements in Parameter Data section (*cont.*)

Graphics

Index	Remarks	
130	OFFSET CURVE	
	P1	pointer to base curve
	P2	distance (1 unique, 2 varying in a linear function, 3 varying with a definable function)
	P3	pointer to curve (only if P2 = 3)
	P4	pointer to coordinate of P3 curve
	P5	offset type (1 arc, 2 parameter)
132	CONNECT POINT (simplifies curves)	
	P1	X coordinate
	P2	Y coordinate
	P3	Z coordinate
	P4-Pn	pointer
134	NODE for finite elements	
	P1	X coordinate
	P2	Y coordinate
	P3	Z coordinate
	P4	pointer to transformation matrix
136	FINITE ELEMENT	
	P1	type (one of 33)
	P2	nodes
	P3-Px	pointer to nodes
	Pn	element name
138	NODAL DISPLACEMENT AND ROTATION	
	data for finite elements	
	P1	number analyze
	P2-Pa	pointer to general nodes
	Pb	number of nodes
	Pc	number 1st node
	Pd	pointer to node directory entry
	Pe-Pz	n*3 entries (x,y,z) translation, then x,y,z rotation
140	OFFSET SURFACE	
	P1-P3	x,y,z coordinates (offset)
	P4	distance to original surface projection
	P5	pointer to original surface
142	CURVE ON PARAMETER SURFACE	
	P1	curve to surface projection (0 not specified, 1 curve to surface, 2 curve surfaces, 3 isoparametric curve)
	P2	pointer to surface
	P3	pointer to curve type B entry
	P4	pointer to curve type C entry
	P5	definition type (0 not defined, 1 surface above curve B, 2 curve type C, 3 all possibilities)

Table 58.4 Entries for geometric elements in Parameter Data section (*cont.*)

Index	Remarks	
144	TRIMMED SURFACE simple closed curve in a Euclidian surface	
	P1	pointer to surface, which should be trimmed
	P2	0, if curve includes surface 1, if surface includes curve
	P3	number of closed curves
	P4	pointer to closed border curve
	P5–Pn	pointer to other curves
146	NODAL RESULTS relation between node and physical interpretation (reserved)	
148	ELEMENT RESULTS (reserved)	
150	BLOCK	
	P1	length X
	P2	length Y
	P3	length Z
	P4–P6	coordinate corner
	P7–P9	vector for local x axis
	P10–P12	vector for local z axis
152	RECTANGULAR WEDGE	
	P1–P3	length x,y,z
	P4	distance to local x axis
	P5–P7	coordinate point
	P8–P10	vector for local x axis
	P11–P13	vector for local z axis
154	CIRCULAR CYLINDER	
	P1	cylinder height
	P2	base radius
	P3–P5	coordinate base center
	P6–P8	unit vector in direction of axis
156	CIRCULAR CONE	
	P1	height
	P2	base radius
	P3	top radius
	P4–P6	coordinate base center
	P7–P9	unit vector in direction of axis
158	SPHERE	
	P1	radius
	P2–P4	coordinate center
160	TORUS	
	P1	radius torus (from torus axis to center ring arc)
	P2	radius ring arc
	P3–P5	coordinate torus center
	P6–P8	unit vector in direction of axis

Table 58.4 Entries for geometric elements in Parameter Data Section (*continues over...*)

Index	Remarks		
162	SOLID OF REVOLUTION		
		P1	pointer to element
		P2	rotation angle
		P3-P5	coordinate of a point in the rotation axis
164	SOLID OF LINEAR EXTRUSION		
		P1	pointer to element
		P2	length of projection
		P3-P5	vector projection direction
168	ELLIPSOID		
		P1	length local x axis
		P2	length local y axis
		P3	length local z axis
		P4-P6	coordinates center
		P7-P9	vector for local x axis
		P10-12	vector for local z axis
180	BOOLEAN TREE		
		P1	length notation
		P2-Pn	negative value = pointer to operands or positive integer value of operation
184	SOLID ASSEMBLY		
		P1	number of entries
		P2-Pa	pointers to elements
		Pb-Pz	pointers to transformation matrices
430	SOLID INSTANCE		
		P1	index to solid art primitive

Table 58.4 Entries for geometric elements in Parameter Data section (*cont.*)

The index is entered in the Directory Entry section. The associated parameters P1 to Pn are located in the Parameter Data section in accordance with the above specification.

In addition to the geometrical elements from Table 58.4, the IGES specification provides annotation elements and structure elements. The annotation elements describe dimensioning, artificial lines, and so on. If an annotation element refers to a two-dimensional space (not in the definition space), a connection is set up using element 404. This element contains the two-dimensional matrix for converting coordinates. The following table lists the annotation elements.

Index	Remarks	
202	ANGULAR DIMENSION	
	P1	pointer to text node
	P2	pointer to WITNESS LINE 1
	P3	pointer to WITNESS LINE 2
	P4–P5	coordinate reference point
	P6	radius angular line
	P7–P8	pointer to arrow definition
206	DIAMETER DIMENSION	
	P1–P3	pointer to directory entry section
	P4–P5	coordinate arc center
208	FLAG NOTE	
	P1–P3	coordinate lower left corner flag
	P4	rotation angle
	P5–Pn	pointer to reference points
210	GENERAL LABEL	
	P1	pointer to GENERAL NOTE
	P2	number of reference points
	P3–Pn	pointer to reference points
212	GENERAL NOTE	
	P1–Pn	pointers and definitions
214	LEADER ARROW	
	P1	number of segments
	P2	height arrow head
	P3	width arrow head
	P4	length in z direction
	P5–P6	coordinate arrow head
	P7–Pn	coordinate pairs for segments
216	LINEAR DIMENSION	
	P1–Pn	pointers to text node, 1st arrow, 2nd arrow, two auxiliary lines
218	ORDINATE DIMENSION	
	P1	pointer to GENERAL NOTE
	P2	pointer to WITNESS LINE DIRECTORY
220	POINT DIMENSION	
	P1	pointer to text node
	P2	pointer to arrow
	P3	pointer to geometric element

Table 58.5 Entries for annotation elements in Parameter Data section *(continues over...)*

Graphics

Index	Remarks	
222	RADIUS DIMENSION	
	P1	pointer to text node
	P2	pointer to arrow
	P3–P4	coordinate arc center
228	GENERAL SYMBOL	
	P1	pointer to GENERAL NOTE
	P2	number of pointers to figures
	P3	number of associations
	P4–Pn	pointer to associations
230	SECTIONED AREA	
	P1	pointer to area shape
	P2	hatch code
	P3	x coordinate for pattern
	P4	y coordinate for pattern
	P5	z-line depth
	P6	line distance
	P7	pattern direction (in radius)
	P8	number of incorporated areas
	P9–Pn	pointer to area curves
106	SECTION defines a repeat value for a pattern, defined as COPIOUS DATA entry 31–38	
108	WITNESS LINE, defined as COPIOUS DATA entry 40	

Table 58.5 Entries for annotation elements in Parameter Data section (*cont.*)

The IGES definition also permits structure elements. These are listed briefly in the table below:

Index	**Remarks**
302	ASSOCIATIVITY DEFINITION defines order classes for the IGES file
304	LINE FONT DEFINITION defines a pattern for lines
306	MACRO DEFINITION defines a macro
308	SUBFIGURE DEFINITION defines a reference to a figure

Table 58.6 Entries for structure elements in Parameter Data section (*continues over...*)

Index	Remarks
310	TEXT FONT DEFINITION defines a text font (name, size, and so on)
312	TEXT DISPLAY TEMPLATE defines a template for text
314	COLOR DEFINITION contains the translate values for RGB values to CMY or HLS systems
320	NETWORK SUBFIGURE DEFINITION defines a figure which is used several times
402	ASSOCIATIVITY INSTANCE defines the relationship of groups
404	DRAWING collects a series of annotation elements
408	SINGULAR SUBFIGURE INSTANCE defines a single subfigure
410	VIEW defines the view to the modes space coordinate system
416	EXTERNAL REFERENCE contains pointer to external graphic files
600–699	USER DEFINED MACRO INSTANCE used to include macros

Table 58.6 **Entries for structure elements in Parameter Data Section** (*cont.*)

Structure elements can be evaluated by only a very few IGES readers. A detailed description of the IGES commands containing all the background information is given in the *Initial Graphic Exchange Specification* (NBSIR 88-3813).

PART 5

Windows and OS/2 file formats

File formats discussed in Part 5

With *the rapid spread of Windows 3.x, understanding the file formats of the individual applications programs is becoming an ever more pressing priority for an increasing number of users. Windows can exchange data via DDE, OLE and the clipboard, but for certain applications it is important to be able to access the files of Write, Cardfile, and so on directly. The same applies to the BMP files of OS/2, which can be partially read in Windows, but whose structure has so far remained largely unknown. These various output formats will therefore be the focus of our attention in this part.*

59

Windows 2.0 Paint format (MSP)

In Windows up to version 2.x, this format was used for storing bitmap graphics. With Windows 3.0/3.1, it is no longer used, but can be read with PaintBrush. I should like to present this format briefly because it has acquired a certain degree of importance in the exchange of images.

An MSP file is structured as follows:

- Header
- Index table
- Image data

The relevant structures are presented below.

59.1 The MSP header

The MSP header describes the content of image data. It contains 32 bytes and is structured as follows:

Offset	Bytes	Remark
00H	2	Signature 1 (6144H or 694CH)
02H	2	Signature 2 (4D6EH or 536EH)
04H	2	Width (bitmap) in pixels (X)
06H	2	Height (bitmap) in pixels (Y)
08H	2	ScreenAspect ratio X-axis
0AH	2	ScreenAspect ratio Y-axis
0CH	2	PrintAspect ratio X-axis
0EH	2	PrintAspect ratio Y-axis
10H	2	Printer resolution x in pixels (dxPrint)
12H	2	Printer resolution y in pixels (dyPrint)
14H	2	Reserved (0)
16H	2	Reserved (0)
18H	2	Checksum field
1AH	2	Reserved (0)
1CH	2	Reserved (0)
1EH	2	Reserved (0)

Table 59.1 MSP header

The first 4 bytes contain the signature for valid MSP files. There appear to have been several versions here. The Microsoft documentation available to me indicates the signature 44H 61H 6EH 4DH (in hex numbers), but I have also found references to another signature (4CH 69H 53H 6EH).

The two words at offset 04H indicate the dimensions of the bitmap (width * height) in pixels. The two words at offset 08H define the resolution (X,Y) of the screen in pixels. At offset 0CH, there are another two words, whose meaning is not clear to me. The entries indicate the resolution of the printer for which the image was produced, in X and Y directions. This presumably relates to print density (dots per inch). However, it is not clear to me why these values should be stored in an image file. At offset 10H, the printer resolution is again indicated in pixels for the X and Y axes, relating to the image to be printed. I interpret these values as the number of points in the relevant print direction, so that this value depends on the paper format.

At offset 18H, there is a checksum for the file, provided to ensure that the file is a valid MSP file. However, I do not have any information on the method of calculating the checksum.

59.2 The index table

At offset 20H, there is an index table of *n* words which contains the length of each image data line. The data in an MSP file is compressed according to the Run Length method. Each line of the image is indexed separately, the length of each image line depending on the bitmap. The length of each compressed line (in bytes) is stored in the corresponding entry in the index table as an unsigned integer (2 bytes). The number of entries is derived from the number of image lines (dyPrint, offset 12H). However, the extent to which the printer resolution is used still remains unclear to me.

59.3 The data area

The index table is followed by the data area containing the compressed image data. Its position is calculated by adding the lengths of the header and the index table:

= 32 Byte (header) + length of an index entry * number of lines (`dyPrint`)

= 32 + 2 * `dyPrint`

Two bytes are required for each index entry and two different processes are used for compression.

If the first byte = `0`, this byte is followed by a counter and a pattern (Figure 59.1).

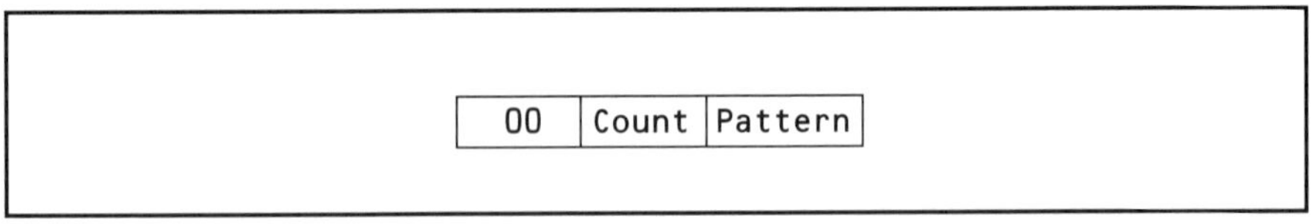

Figure 59.1
MSP data record (type 1)

The counter contains one byte and indicates how often the following byte containing the pattern is to be repeated. The following entry:

```
00H 80H 3FH
```

indicates that the pattern `3FH` is to be repeated 128 times (`80H`). If the value of the first byte is in the range `1–255`, the first byte contains a counter indicating the number of data bytes following (Figure 59.2). These data bytes contain an uncompressed bitmap, that is, the bits can be converted directly into pixels.

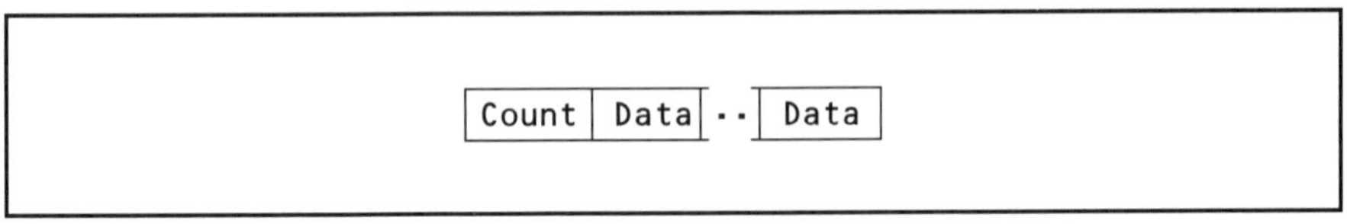

Figure 59.2
MSP data record (type 2)

The sequence:

```
03H 3FH 44H 00H
```

indicates that the following three bytes (`3FH 44H 00H`) have been stored directly as a pattern. Data bytes are read using these rules until an image line has been decoded. The number of bytes to be read is stored in the associated entry in the index table. As another example, the sequence:

```
00H 40H FFH
```

indicates that 64 bytes with the value `FFH` are to be output. This will produce a line consisting of 512 white pixels.

However, the value:

```
01H 01H
```

as a pattern produces a sequence of 7 black pixels and one white pixel.

The length calculation (bytes per line) for the index table entries is quite simple. If, for example, a line comprises 520 pixels (512 = 8), a length calculation involving the following values:

00H 40H FFH	→	3 data bytes for 512 white pixels
01H 01H	→	2 data bytes for 7 black and 1 white pixel

will produce the result 5 (bytes), which will be stored in the index table. This coding enables each image line to have a different length. To calculate the position (offset from start of file) of the data for an image line, the lengths of the index table entries for the preceding image lines must be summed. Then add the length of the header (32 bytes) and the length of the index table itself. The result is the position at which the *n* bytes of the image line required can be read.

60

Windows 3.x BMP and RLE format

From *Windows 3.0 onwards, the PaintBrush program is included in the package supplied. This program enables graphics to be produced and stored. In addition to importing graphics in MSP format, PaintBrush also supports the PCX and BMP formats. The BMP format is described in this chapter. The PCX format is described in Chapter 22.*

60.1 Windows 3.x Bitmap format (BMP)

Windows uses the BMP format for storing raster pictures. This format is device-independent and can store monochrome and color pictures. The PaintBrush program, supplied with Windows, is the most popular tool to read and write BMP files. A BMP file is composed of several data blocks (Figure 60.1).

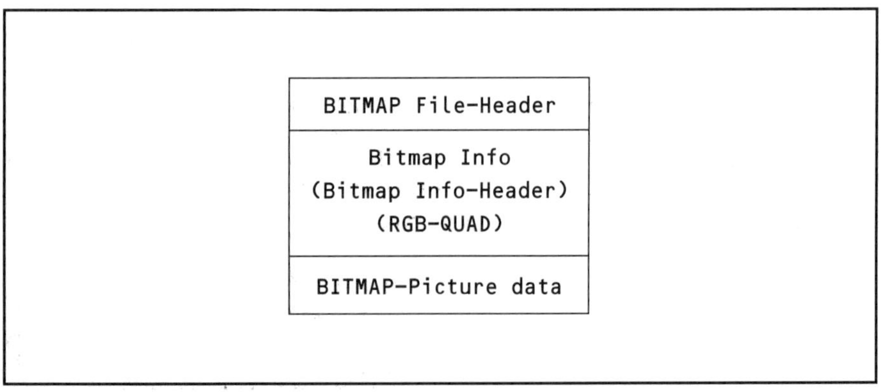

Figure 60.1 BMP format structure (Windows 3.x)

The BITMAP_FILE header is structured as shown below:

Offset	Bytes	Name	Meaning
00H	2	bfType	File ID ('BM')
02H	4	bfSize	File length in byte
06H	2	–	reserved (must be set to 0)
08H	2	–	reserved (must be set to 0)
0AH	4	bfOffs	Offset data area

Table 60.1 Structure of a Windows BMP header

The first word of the header must contain the signature BM to identify a valid BMP file. This is followed by a double word containing the file length in bytes. The header is terminated at offset 0AH with a 4-byte pointer specifying the offset from the start of the file to the first data byte of the picture.

However, the header merely describes the file and does not contain any details of the picture. For this reason, the file header is followed by the BITMAP_INFO block. This also contains a header (the BITMAP_INFO header), which describes the picture data. The BITMAP_INFO block is structured as shown in Table 60.2.

The field biSize (offset 0EH) indicates the length of the BITMAP_INFO header in bytes. This header is followed by a table containing the definitions of the color palette (RGB_QUAD).

Offset	Bytes	Name	Remark
			BITMAP_INFO Header
0EH	4	biSize	Length of BITMAP_INFO-Header in bytes
12H	4	biWidth	Width of bitmap in pixels
16H	4	biHeight	Height of bitmap in pixels
1AH	2	biPlanes	Color planes (must be set to 1)
1CH	2	biBitCount	Bits per pixel
1EH	4	biCompression	Compression type
22H	4	biSizeImage	Picture size in bytes
26H	4	biXPelsPerMetre	Horizontal resolution
2AH	4	biYPelsPerMetre	Vertical resolution
2EH	4	biClrUsed	Number of colors used

Table 60.2 Structure of a BITMAP_INFO block (*continues over...*)

Offset	Bytes	Name	Remark
32H	4	biClrImportant	Number of important colors
			RGB_QUAD
36H	n*4		Color definition with:
		rgbBlue	1 byte blue intensity
		rgbGreen	1 byte green intensity
		rgbRed	1 byte red intensity
		rgbres	1 byte reserved
			....

Table 60.2 Structure of a BITMAP_INFO block (*cont.*)

The two fields `biWidth` and `biHeight` indicate the width and height of the bitmap picture in pixels. This is significant for re-creating the picture.

The field `biPlanes` (offset `1AH`) defines the number of bit levels (planes) in the output device. At present, this entry should be set to `1`.

The field `biBitCount`, which defines the number of bits per pixel and also determines the number of colors in the picture, is of particular importance. The following values are permitted:

`1` Defines 1 bit per pixel, which indicates a monochrome picture. If the bit is set, the first color from the color table will be used. If the bit is unset, the second color from the color table will be used.

`4` Enables a picture containing 16 colors to be built up. The color palette contains 16 entries of 4 bytes each. Each pixel consists of 4 bits; that is, one byte contains the colors for 2 pixels. The value `1FH` thus represents the 2nd and 16th colors from the color table.

`8` This bitmap can contain up to 256 colors, each pixel being represented by 8 bits. These values serve as an index to the color table, which contains 256 elements. The value `00H` defines a pixel using the first color in the table.

`24` This value defines a picture with 2**24 (16 million) colors, that is, every pixel is represented by 24 bits. Since the color table in this case would be excessively large, the colors are coded directly in the picture data area. The 24 bits per pixel represent 3 bytes defining the intensity of the colors red, green and blue in the range `0-255`. Mixed colors are generated from these values by the output device. This enables the creation of very authentic color pictures. The index table containing the color definitions is omitted when this 24-bit presentation is used.

The compression method used for picture data is indicated in the `biCompression` field (offset `1EH`) as a 4-byte value. The following values are used:

`BI_RGB` Bitmap data not compressed.
`BI_RLE8` A run-length encoding process (RLE) is used for bitmaps with 8 bits per pixel.
`BI_RLE4` A run-length encoding process (RLE) is used for bitmaps with 4 bits per pixel.

These constants are coded in the earlier versions of Windows 3.x as follows:

```
BI_RGB   = 0

BI_RLE8  = 1

BI_RLE4  = 2
```

This compression process is described below.

! In my experience, PaintBrush stores picture data in uncompressed form in all modes.

The 4-byte `biSizeImage` field at offset `22H` indicates the length of the (compressed) bitmap data area in bytes. The two following fields `biXPelsPerMeter` and `biYPelsPerMeter` define the resolution of the target unit in pels (pels = picture elements) per meter for the X and Y axes. As a result, an application may select from a resource the most suitable bitmap for the relevant device.

The `biClrUsed` field (offset `2EH`) specifies how many colors from the color table the current picture actually uses. A picture can therefore contain fewer colors than are possible according to the color table. The most important colors should be stored at the start of the index table. If the value of the field = `0`, all colors will be used. However, this only applies if fewer than 24 bits are stored for each picture point. If the `biCount` field (offset `1CH`) is set to `24`, `biClrUsed` indicates the size of the reference table containing the colors. With 24-bit representation, a color table is not normally required. However, one may be provided for optimization reasons. If the area containing the bitmap data follows directly after the BITMAP_INFO header, the field must be set to `0`.

The last field, `biClrImportant` (offset `32H`), defines the number of colors which are important for the display. If the value is `0`, all colors in the reference table are important.

The table containing color definitions begins at offset `36H`. Each color is defined in terms of its proportion of blue, green and red. This definition contains 4 bytes; the last byte remains empty. The length of the table is determined by the number of colors (bits per pixel).

60.1.1 The data area

The header data is followed by a data area containing bitmap data. The picture is scanned line by line and stored. The data may be compressed at this stage (but this does not occur with PaintBrush). A distinction is made between the compression of pictures with:

4 bits per pixel (`RLE4`)

8 bits per pixel (`RLE8`)

A picture line is always stored contiguously. If necessary, missing pixels at the right margin can be added, up to a limit of 32 bits, and set to `0`. The origin of the picture is at the bottom left corner.

60.1.2 8-bit RLE compression

Provided 8 bits per pixel are used in the bitmap, Windows will use 8-bit RLE coding, in which picture data is represented as follows.

Identical consecutive bytes are compressed into 2 bytes, as follows:

Count	Color

Figure 60.2 RLE coding (type 1)

The first byte specifies how often the following byte is to be duplicated. This second byte defines an index into the color table from which the color is reconstructed. The sequence:

03H 44H

thus generates the sequence:

04H 04H 04H

which creates three pixels with color number 5 (counting begins at 0). The counter may contain values between 1 and 255.

However, if the first byte of a sequence contains 00H, type 2 coding (absolute mode) will be used. The coding is as follows:

00H	Count	Data	..	Data

Figure 60.3 RLE coding (type 2)

If the second byte contains a value between 3 and FFH, the record is a data record and the value indicates the number of data bytes to follow. Each of these bytes contains an index into the color table, which codes one pixel per byte. The sequence:

00H 04H 3FH 66H 01H 07H

defines 4 pixels of different colors. However, if the second byte contains values between 0 and 2, the record is an ESCAPE record. This record is used to mark the end of a line or a bitmap. The following coding is used:

Byte 2	Remark
0	End of a line
1	End of a bitmap
2	Delta record

Table 60.4 Coding of ESCAPE mode

The sequence 00H 00H thus marks the end of a line and the next byte therefore belongs to the next record. 00 01 marks the end of the bitmap.

A delta record consists of 4 bytes structured as follows:

```
00H 02H xxH yyH
```

The numbers xx and yy define a relative offset in pixels from the current position, at which the next pixel is to be displayed. Bitmaps containing only a few pixels can thus be stored very efficiently. The hexadecimal byte sequence:

```
03H 44H 04H 11H 00H 03H 01H 33H FFH 00H 02H 05H 01H
```

is converted into the hex values

```
44H 44H 44H
11H 11H 11H 11H
01H 33H FFH
```

5 pixels right, 1 pixel up.

60.1.3 4-bit RLE compression

This compression is essentially the same as the 8-bit RLE coding. If the first byte contains a value between 1 and 255, it is a repetition counter indicating how many pixels are to be constructed from the following byte. With 4 bits per pixel, the following byte always contains two color indices (or pixels). The first color value is determined and displayed on the basis of the top 4 bits. The lower 4 bits are then used to display the next color pixel. The third pixel is constructed from the 4 upper bits. This alternating method is repeated until the number of pixels indicated has been created.

If the first byte is 00H, the absolute coding (type 2) of 8-bit RLE compression is used, that is, the second byte must contain a value between 3 and FFH. This is followed by n databytes, each byte representing two pixels. In absolute mode the sequence of bytes must end at a word boundary. The same conditions apply to ESCAPE sequences (second byte = 0, 1 or 2 as for 8-bit RLE compression).

61

OS/2 Bitmap format (BMP, version 1.2)

***OS/2** uses a BMP format for storing raster pictures in the Presentation Manager in versions 1.1, 1.2 and 2.0. The data is stored as Device-Independent Bitmaps (DIB). This format can be read in Windows 3.x (at least up to OS/2, version 1.2). The internal structure must therefore rely significantly on the Windows BMP format.*

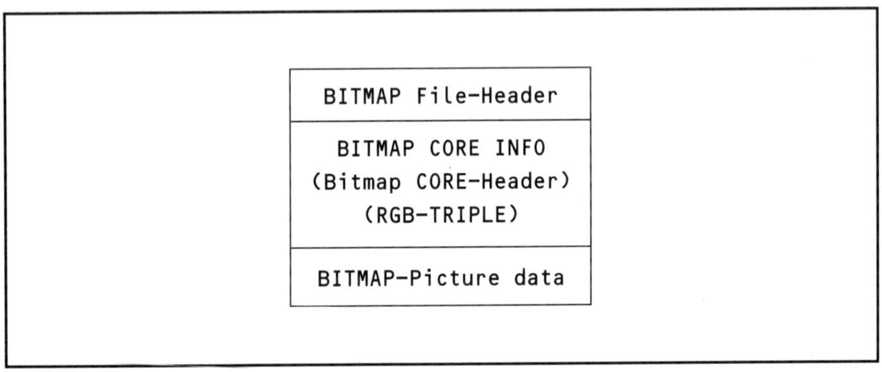

Figure 61.1 Structure of the BMP format (OS/2, up to version 1.2)

Figure 61.1 shows various deviations from this structure. The following description applies to the bitmap format of OS/2 up to version 1.2. The BITMAP_FILE header has the following data structure:

Offset	Bytes	Name	Remarks
00H	2	bfType	File ID ('BM')
02H	4	bfSize	File length in bytes
06H	2	-	Reserved (must be 0)
08H	2	-	Reserved (must be 0)
0AH	4	bfOffs	Offset data area

Table 61.1 Structure of an OS/2 BMP header (version 1.1/1.2)

The first word of the header must contain the signature BM to identify a valid BMP file. This is followed by a double word containing the file length in bytes. The header is terminated at offset 0AH with a 4-byte pointer specifying the offset from the start of the file to the first data byte of the picture.

The BITMAP_CORE_INFO block follows the file header and contains another header (BITMAP_CORE header), which describes the picture data. The second entry (RGB_TRIPLE) defines the color palette. The BITMAP_CORE_INFO block is structured as follows (Table 61.2):

Offset	Bytes	Name	Remarks
			BITMAP_CORE_INFO header
0EH	4	bcSize	Length of BITMAP_CORE_INFO header in bytes
12H	2	bcWidth	Width of bitmap in pixels
14H	2	bcHeight	Height of bitmap in pixels
16H	2	bcPlanes	Number of color planes (must be 1)
18H	2	bcBitCnt	Bits per pixel
			RGB_TRIPLE
1AH	*n**3		Color definition for *n* colors:
		rgbBlue	1 byte blue intensity
		rgbgreen	1 byte green intensity
		rgbRed	1 byte red intensity
			....

Table 61.2 Structure of a BITMAP_CORE_INFO block

The structure of this block differs somewhat from the Windows format. In particular, the header is shorter and a number of fields are reduced to 2-byte values.

The bcSize field (offset 0EH) indicates the length of the BITMAP_CORE_INFO header in bytes. The two fields biWidth and biHeight indicate the width and height of the bitmap picture in pixels.

The bcPlanes field (offset 16H) defines the number of bit levels (planes) in the output device. At present this value must be set to 1. The number of bits per pixel is indicated in a word at offset 18H. Here, the values 1 (monochrome), 4 (16 colors) and 24 (16 million colors) are allowed.

The table containing the definitions of the color palette follows at offset 1AH. By contrast with the Windows palette, each entry here contains only 3 bytes, in which the intensity of the primary colors blue, green and red is stored. One color is defined for each entry. The length of the color table depends on the number of bits per pixel (offset 18H). The following coding applies:

1 Defines 1 bit per pixel, which indicates a monochrome picture. If the bit is set, the first color from the color table will be used. If the bit is unset, the second color from the color table will be used.

4 Enables a picture containing 16 colors to be built up. The color palette contains 16 entries of 4 bytes each. Each pixel consists of 4 bits; that is, one byte stores the colors for 2 pixels. The value 1FH thus represents the 2nd and 16th color from the color table.

8 This bitmap can contain up to 256 colors, each pixel being represented by 8 bits. These values serve as an index into the color table, which has 256 elements. The value 00H defines a pixel using the first color from the index table.

24 This value defines a picture with 2**24 (16 million) colors, that is, every pixel is represented by 24 bits. Since the color table in this case would be excessively large, the colors are coded directly in the picture data area. The 24 bits per pixel represent 3 bytes defining the intensity of the colors red, green and blue in the range 0–255. Mixed colors are generated from these values by the output device. This enables the creation of very authentic color pictures. The index table containing the color definitions is omitted when this 24-bit representation is used.

! Please note that the colors in the table are ordered according to their importance.

61.1 The data area

The header data is followed by the data area containing the bitmap data. The picture is scanned line by line and stored. The data in a line may need to be padded out to the limit of 32 bits using null bits. The origin of the bitmap is in the bottom left corner. According to the information available to me so far, the data is uncompressed up to version 1.2 of OS/2.

! OS/2 version 1.3 uses the same coding as version 1.2. However, icons and other resources are stored as in version 2.0. Multiple version formats are also allowed (*see* Version 2.0, Chapter 62)

62

OS/2 Bitmap format (BMP, version 2.x)

OS/2 *version 2.x uses a BMP format for storing raster images. However, by comparison with earlier versions, this has been somewhat modified. The bitmap format is used for pictures, icons and pointers (cursor).*

The OS/2 bitmap format is a device-independent format which can store monochrome and color images. The resolution may be either 1, 4, 8 or 24 bits per pel (pel = picture element = pixel). The bitmap is stored in such a manner that the output device can process the data. The first pel appears in the bottom left corner (coordinate origin). The following pixels are displayed line by line from left to right. The individual lines are drawn from bottom to top. The highest value bit in a data byte indicates the first pel (that is, in monochrome presentation). The data within an output line is packed in bytes, each line ending at a 32-bit boundary. If necessary, individual pixels at the right margin of the screen can be filled with null bits. This technique has already been used in Windows. In version 2.0, an OS/2 BMP file is composed of several data blocks (Figure 62.1).

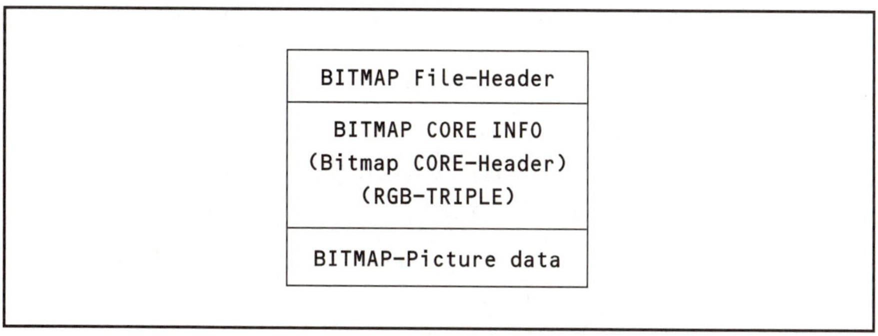

Figure 62.1
BMP structure
OS/2 version 2.0

The BITMAP_FILE header is structured as follows:

Offset	Bytes	Name	Remark
00H	2	usType	Type of resource file
02H	4	cbSize	BITMAP_FILE Header length in bytes
06H	2	xHotSpot	Only for icons and cursors
08H	2	yHotSpot	Only for icons and cursors
0AH	4	bfOffs	Offset data area

Table 62.1 **Structure of an OS/2 BMP header**

The first word of the header must contain the type of the bitmap file as a signature. The following signatures have been defined:

'BM' Bitmap file with picture

'IC' Icon file

'PT' Pointer (Cursor)

'CI' Color icon file

'CP' Color pointer

This is followed by a double word containing the length of the header in bytes. This information is necessary because, from version OS/2 onwards, the header may occur twice in the file. This is always the case if an icon or a pointer is stored in the file, which will then contain two bitmap pictures (XOR-mask and AND-mask. *See also* Windows Icon format, Chapter 63).

By contrast with the Windows header structure, the words at offsets 06H and 08H (xHotspot, yHotspot) are defined as coordinates of the 'hot spot' in the case of icons and pointers. With a bitmap picture, both entries are ignored. The header is terminated at offset 0AH with a 4-byte pointer specifying the offset from the start of the file to the first data byte of the picture. If this is followed by a second header, it will have the same data structure.

The header is followed by the BITMAP_INFO2 block. This also contains a header (BITMAP_INFO2 header) which describes the picture data. The second entry (RGB-TRIPLE2) is optional and defines the color palette. The BITMAP_INFO2 block is structured as shown in Table 62.2:

Offset	Bytes	Name	Remarks
			BITMAP_INFO header
0EH	4	cbFix	BITMAP_INFO2 header length in bytes

Table 62.2 **Structure of a BITMAP_INFO2 block** **(*continues over...*)**

Offset	Bytes	Name	Remarks
12H	4	cx	Width bitmap in pels
16H	4	cy	Height bitmap in pels
1AH	2	cPlanes	Number of color planes (set to 1)
1CH	2	cBitCount	Bits per pixel
1EH	4	ulCompression	Compression type
22H	4	cbImage	Bitmap length in bytes
26H	4	cxResolution	Horizontal resolution
2AH	4	cyResolution	Vertical resolution
2EH	4	cClrUsed	Colors used
32H	4	cClrImportant	Important colors
36H	2	usUnits	Units of measure
38H	2	-	Reserved
3AH	2	usRecording	Recording algorithm
3CH	2	usRendering	Rendering algorithm
3EH	4	cSize1	Size value 1
42H	4	cSize2	Size value 2
46H	4	ulClrEncoding	Color encoding
4AH	4	ulIdentify	Reserved for applications
			RGB_TRIPLE2
4EH	*n**4		Color definition for *n* colors:
		rgbRed	1 byte red intensity
		rgbGreen	1 byte green intensity
		rgbBlue	1 byte blue intensity
			....

Table 62.2 Structure of a BITMAP_INFO2 block (*cont.*)

All the entries in the offset column are based on the assumption that only one copy of the file header is used. The length of the header, however, is indicated in one field, so that the values in the offset column can be adjusted if necessary.

The `cbFix` field (offset `0EH`) indicates the length of the BITMAP_INFO2 header in bytes. This header is followed by an (optional) table containing the definitions for the color palette (RGB_TRIPLE2).

The two fields `cx` and `cy` indicate the width and the height of the bitmap pictures in pels. This is important for re-creating the picture.

The `cPlanes` field (offset `1AH`) defines the number of bit levels (planes) in the output device. At present the entry is set to 1 but it may have different values in future.

The `cBitCount` field at offset `1CH` is of particular importance. Its value defines the number of bits per pel at the output level and also establishes the number of colors in the picture. The following values are permitted:

1 Defines 1 bit per pixel, which corresponds to a monochrome picture. If the bit is set to 1, the first color from the color table will be used. If the bit is 0, the second color from the color table will be used.

4 Enables a picture containing 16 colors to be built up. The color palette contains 16 entries of 4 bytes each. Each pixel consists of 4 bits, that is, one byte stores the colors for 2 pixels. The value 1FH thus represents the 2nd and 16th color from the color table.

8 This bitmap can contain up to 256 colors, each pixel being represented by 8 bits. These values serve as an index into the color table, which has 256 elements. The value 00H defines a pixel using the first color from the index table.

24 This value defines a picture with 2**24 (16 million) colors, that is, every pixel is represented by 24 bits. Since the color table in this case would be excessively large, the colors are coded directly in the picture data area. The 24 bits per pixel represent 3 bytes defining the intensity of the colors red, green and blue in the range 0–255. Mixed colors are generated from these vaues by the output device. This enables the creation of very authentic color pictures. The index table containing the color definitions in the header is omitted when this 24-bit presentation is used.

The type of compression used for the picture data is indicated in the `ulCompression` field (offset 1EH) as a 4-byte value. Although I have no documentation on this area, it seems likely that the compression types for Windows 3.x bitmaps are used, as follows:

0 The bitmap data is in uncompressed form.

1 A run-length encoding process (RLE) is used for bitmaps with 8 bits per pixel.

2 A run-length encoding process (RLE) is used for bitmaps with 4 bits per pixel.

This compression process is described in Chapter 60 on the Windows Bitmap format.

! **In my experience, the bitmaps have to be stored in uncompressed form at present.**

The 4-byte `cbImage` field at offset 22H indicates the length of the (compressed) bitmap data area in bytes. The following fields `cxResolution` and `cyResolution` define the resolution of the target unit in pels (pels = picture elements) for the X and Y axes. In this way, an application can select from a resource the most suitable bitmap for the relevant device.

The `cClrUsed` field (offset 2EH) specifies how many colors from the color table are used in the current picture. A picture may contain fewer colors than are possible according to the color table. The most important colors should therefore be stored at the start of the index table. If the value of the field = 0, all colors will be used. However, this only applies if fewer than 24 bits per pixel are stored. If the `cBitCount` field (offset 1CH) is set to 24, `cClrUsed` indicates the size of the reference table containing the colors. With 24-bit representation, a color table is not normally required. However, one may be provided for optimization reasons. If the area containing the bitmap data follows immediately after the BITMAP_INFO header, the field must be set to 0.

The `cClrImportant` field (offset `32H`) defines the number of colors which are important for the display. The value `0` indicates that all colors in the reference table are important.

Up to offset `32H`, the data structure is the same as that used by Windows 3.x. At offset `36H`, the Windows data structure has been extended. The exact meaning of these values is not known. According to the information available, OS/2 does not evaluate these fields in version 2.0.

The header may optionally be followed by the table containing the color definitions. Each color is defined in terms of the proportion of blue, green and red, and requires 3 bytes per color. The length of the table is determined by the number of colors (bits per pixel). However, the sequence of individual bytes and the allocation of colors are not clear. While Windows opts for the usual sequence blue, green, red, the sequence in OS/2 version 2.0 seems to be inverted to red, green, blue.

62.1 The data area

The header data is followed by the data area containing the bitmap data. The picture is scanned line by line and stored. Data can be compressed if necessary. Each line of the picture is stored contiguously. If required, missing pixels at the right margin can be filled with null bits up to a limit of 32 bits. The origin of the picture is at the bottom left corner. Compression is presumably carried out according to the standard Windows method.

Since version 2.0 of OS/2 uses the same format for bitmap images, icons and pointers, the file structure has been extended. In the multiple-version format, the first section contains an array of BITMAP_ARRAY_HEADER structures:

```
BITMAP_ARRAY_FILE_HEADER
   BITMAP_FILE_HEADER
   Color Table
....
BITMAP_ARRAY_FILE_HEADER
   BITMAP_FILE_HEADER
   Color Table
....
```

The structure of the BITMAP_ARRAY_FILE_HEADER is shown below.

Offset	Bytes	Name	Meaning
00H	2	usType	Signature ('BA')
02H	4	cbSize	Length of BITMAP_ARRAY_FILE header (bytes)
06H	4	offNext	Offset of next header

Table 62.3 Structure of a BITMAP _ARRAY_FILE header (*continues over...*)

Offset	Bytes	Name	Meaning
0AH	2	cxDisplay	Resolution X-axis in pels
0CH	2	cyDisplay	Resolution Y-axis in pels
			Structure BITMAP_FILE header

Table 62.3 **Structure of a** BITMAP _ARRAY_FILE **header** (*cont.*)

The first word contains the signature 'BA' (BITMAP_ARRAY) to signal an extension to the header. The 4 bytes at offset 02H define the length of the BITMAP_ARRAY_FILE header in bytes. Since several bitmaps are generally stored in the structure, a 4-byte pointer to the beginning of the following BITMAP_ARRAY_FILE header is located at offset 06H. The cxDisplay and cyDisplay fields indicate the resolution provided by the output device (for example, VGA, 640 × 480). This header is then followed by the BITMAP_FILE header as already described.

In this case, the cy in BITMAP_INFO_HEADER contains double the value of the picture height. The reason for this is that two complete bitmaps need to be stored in order to display an icon or a pointer. The first bitmap defines the XOR-mask which contains the information for inverting a pixel (0 = do not invert; 1 = invert). The second bitmap contains the AND-mask, which determines whether a pixel is to be displayed (0 = black/white, 1 = screen/inverse screen). With color images, one bitmap contains the AND-mask and the XOR-mask and is stored as monochrome. The second bitmap then stores the color image. In the cy field of the BITMAP_INFO2 header, the value for the color bitmap must correspond to the actual size. However, in the black and white bitmap, the doubled value must be given. The same applies to the cx field. The definition of the color table is then followed by the data areas for the different bitmaps. The resolution for icons is defined in the following stages:

32 × 32	4 bit/pel	(16 colors, VGA)
40 × 40	4 bit/pel	(16 colors, 8514/A, XGA)
32 × 32	1 bit/pel	(monochrome)
20 × 20	1 bit/pel	(monochrome)
16 × 16	1 bit/pel	(monochrome)

Resolutions of 20 × 20 and 16 × 16 are provided for mini-icons.

Further information may be obtained from the IBM PM Programming Reference, Volume Two.

63

Windows Icon format (ICO)

***Windows** can store icons in EXE and DLL files or in separate ICO files. This chapter describes the format of the Windows 3.x ICO files.*

The icons used in Windows are stored as bitmaps of varying resolutions. The files have the `.ICO` extension and are stored in the following structure:

Offset	Bytes	Remarks
		Header
00H	2	Reserved (must be set to 0)
02H	2	Resource type (1 for icons)
04H	2	Number of pictures in file
		Resource directory
06H		Array with *n* entries:
	1	Icon width in pixels
	1	Icon height in pixels
	1	Color count
	1	Reserved
	2	Planes (Windows 3.1)
	2	Bits in the icon bitmap (Windows 3.1)

Table 63.1 Structure of a Windows Icon file (*continues over...*)

Offset	Bytes	Remarks
	4	Size of pixel array in bytes (icoDIBSize)
	4	Picture data offset in bytes
		... next entries
..	40	TBitMapInfoHeader
		16*4- TRGBQuad-color table
		Colors blue, green, red, intensity
..	512	Byte sequence with color bitmap (XOR)
..	128	Byte sequence with monochrome bitmap (AND)

Table 63.1 Structure of a Windows Icon file (*cont.*)

Windows determines the resolution of an output device and then converts the pixels of the icon accordingly. The first word in the icon file is reserved and must be set to `0`. This is followed by a word containing the type of the resource. For icons, the value `1` should be stored here. (Cursor images have the same header but the value `2` is stored as the resource type.) The word at offset `04H` indicates the number of pictures in the file. There is usually only one icon stored in an ICO file.

This header is followed by a field containing n entries which describe the icon. For each picture, this table contains the dimensions of the icon `width` × `height`. The permitted values are 16, 32 and 64 pixels. The `ColorCount` field contains the number of colors used (2, 8 or 16). The next 5 bytes are reserved in Windows 3.0. In Windows 3.1, only the first byte is reserved, and the next two words indicate the number of color levels (planes) and the number of bits in the icon map. The following 4 bytes indicate the size of the pixel array (in bytes) for the relevant icon. The double word following this contains the offset from the start of the file to the first image data (DIB).

The structure of the following 40 bytes is unknown. They are followed by the definition table for the color palette. Four bytes are allocated for the definition of each color. The data area follows the color table; its start address is defined in the header. Picture data is in uncompressed form, two bitmaps being stored for each icon. The first bitmap is the `XOR`-mask containing the color image for the icon. This bitmap contains 512 bytes. It is followed by the `AND`-mask containing the monochrome picture. This picture contains 128 bytes and is used for the transparent section of the icon.

! **The cursor format has the same structure. However, the coordinates (x,y) for the relevant hot-spot are indicated at offset `04H`, for every entry in the resource directory. In the icon format, the number of planes and the number of bitmap bits are shown here.**

64

Windows Metafile format (WMF)

***Bitmap** files can only portray point graphics. Windows enables the storage of graphics in the form of metafiles. A Windows metafile consists of a series of instructions for the Graphics Device Interface (GDI). The parameters of the meta-instructions are determined according to the call-up conventions of the individual GDI functions. The meta-instructions may be in memory or in a file. The following description refers to the file format (although a similar format is found in memory).*

The metafile consists of a header followed by a data section containing the actual meta-records.

64.1 The Metafile header

The header of a metafile is structured as shown below (Table 64.1):

Offset	Bytes	Name	Remarks
00H	2	mtType	Metafile type
02H	2	mtHeader	Header length in words
04H	2	mtVersion	Windows version
06H	4	mtSize	File length in words
0AH	2	mtNoObj	Maximum elements
0CH	4	mtMaxRec	Maximum record length
10H	2	mtnoPar	Unused

Table 64.1 Structure of a WMF header

It should be noted that all lengths in metafiles are indicated in words (2 bytes). The first word contains the type of the metafile:

0 Metafile is stored in the main memory
1 Metafile is stored in a file

The structure of meta-records is the same for both variants. The following word `mtHeaderSize` contains the size of the metafile header in words. At offset `04H`, there is a word containing the Windows version under which the metafile was created. This version is written as a BCD number (for example, `30H` corresponds to version 3.0 and later). At offset `06H`, there is a double word containing the length of the metafile in words. This is followed by the maximum number of objects that can be contained in the metafile at any one time. This is particularly important for metafiles that are to be stored in the computer memory. The `mtMaxRecord` field (offset `0CH`) defines the length (in words) of the largest metafile record in the file. The last word in the header is empty.

64.2 Placeable metafiles

In addition to standard metafiles, placeable metafiles (Aldus) have also been defined. These are standard metafiles which have been prefixed with a 22-byte header. The header contains additional information on the original size of the metafile and the aspect ratio of the image. The header is structured as follows:

Offset	Bytes	Remarks
00H	4	Binary key for file type (set to 9AC6CDD7H)
04H	2	Handle (set to 0)
06H	8	Bounding box in units 2-byte left margin 2-byte top margin 2-byte right margin 2-byte bottom margin
0EH	2	Metafile units per inch
10H	4	Reserved (must be 0)
14H	2	Checksum

Table 64.2 Placeable metafile header

Information on the bounding box around the image is indicated at offset `06H`. This is defined as a rect-structure (4 integer values) and indicates the coordinates of the top left and bottom right corner of the rectangle. This value must not exceed `32767`. The unit of measurement is defined in the word at offset 0EH and relates to n units per inch. This value should remain below 1440. The checksum is formed by XORing the first 10 words in the header. To read this type of metafile, a Windows application has to remove the 22-byte header and store a standard metafile.

64.3 Metafile records

The header is followed by the area containing the metafile records. These records are structured as follows:

Bytes	Remark
4	Size of metafile record (in words)
2	Record type
n*2	Array of words containing parameters

Table 64.3 Structure of a metafile record

The individual metafile record types for Windows 3.x are shown in Table 64.4.

Code	Record name
001EH	SAVEDC
0035H	REALIZEPALETTE
0037H	SETPALENTRIES
00F7H	CREATEPALETTE
00F8H	CREATEBRUSH
0102H	SETBKMODE
0103H	SETMAPMODE
0104H	SETROP2
0105H	SETRELABS
0106H	SETPOLYFILLMODE
0107H	SETSTRETCHBLTMODE
0108H	SETTEXTCHAREXTRA
0127H	RESTOREDC
012AH	INVERTREGION

Table 64.4 WMF record types (code order) (*continues over...*)

Code	Record name
012BH	PAINTREGION
012CH	SELECTCLIPREGION
012DH	SELECTOBJECT
012EH	SETTEXTALIGN
0139H	RESIZEPALETTE
0142H	DIBCREATEPATTERNBRUSH
01F0H	DELETEOBJECT
01F9H	CREATEPATTERNBRUSH
0201H	SETBKCOLOUR
0209H	SETTEXTCOLOUR
020AH	SETTEXTJUSTIFICATION
020BH	SETWINDOWORG
020CH	SETWINDOWEXT
020DH	SETVIEWPORTORG
020EH	SETVIEWPORTEXT
020FH	OFFSETWINDOWORG
0211H	OFFSETVIEWPORTORG
0213H	LINETO
0214H	MOVETO
0220H	OFFSETCLIPRGN
0228H	FILLREGION
0231H	SETMAPPERFLAGS
0234H	SELECTPALETTE
02FAH	CREATEPENINDIRECT
02FBH	CREATEFONTINDIRECT
02FCH	CREATEBRUSHINDIRECT
02FDH	CREATEBITMAPINDIRECT
0324H	POLYGON
0325H	POLYLINE
0400H	SCALEWINDOWEXT
0412H	SCALEVIEWPORTEXT
0415H	EXCLUDECLIPRECT
0416H	INTERSECTCLIPRECT
0418H	ELLIPSE
0419H	FLOODFILL
041BH	RECTANGLE
041FH	SETPIXEL
0429H	FRAMEREGION
0436H	ANIMATEPALETTE

Table 64.4 WMF record types (code order) (*cont.*)

Code	Record name
0521H	TEXTOUT
0538H	POLYPOLYGON
061CH	ROUNDRECT
061DH	PATBLT
0626H	ESCAPE
062FH	DRAWTEXT
06FEH	CREATEBITMAP
06FFH	CREATEREGION
0817H	ARC
081AH	PIE
0830H	CHORD
0922H	BITBLT
0940H	DIBBITBLT
0A32H	EXTTEXTOUT
0B23H	STRETCHBLT
0B41H	DIBSTRETCHBLT
0D33H	SETDIBTODEV
0F43H	STRETCHDIB

Table 64.4 WMF record types (code order) (*cont.*)

The data structures for these metafiles are described in the appropriate Windows manuals (for example, Windows SDK, Borland Pascal, C++). Extracts containing the structures of the relevant metafile records are shown below.

64.3.1 ANIMATEPALETTE

This is a function-specific metafile record.

Offset	Bytes	Remarks
00H	4	Record size (variable)
04H	2	Record type (0436H)
06H		Parameters
	2	First entry to be animated
	2	Number of entries (n) to be animated

Table 64.5 The ANIMATE PALETTE record (*continues over...*)

Offset	Bytes	Remarks
	*n**4	Palette entry array with: 1 byte red 1 byte green 1 byte blue 1 byte flag .....

Table 64.5 The ANIMATEPALETTE record (*cont.*)

The record replaces the entries in the logical palette.

64.3.2 ARC

This record defines an arc in a metafile.

Offset	Bytes	Remarks
00H	4	Record size (0EH)
04H	2	Record type (0817H)
06H		Parameters
	2	X1: X-coordinate upper left corner
	2	Y1: Y-coordinate upper left corner
	2	X2: X-coordinate lower right corner
	2	Y2: Y-coordinate lower right corner
	2	X3: logical X-coordinate arc starting point
	2	Y3: logical Y-coordinate arc starting point
	2	X4: logical X-coordinate arc endpoint
	2	Y4: logical Y-coordinate arc endpoint

Table 64.6 The ARC record

All parameters are defined as integers and the absolute value of X1 – X2 and Y2 – Y1 may not exceed 32,767 units.

64.3.3 BITBLT

This record exists in two versions. The record created by Windows versions earlier than 3.0 contains a device-dependent bitmap. After Windows 3.0 the record contains a device-independent bitmap. The `BITBLT` record stored by versions earlier than 3.0 contains the following structure:

Offset	Bytes	Remarks
00H	4	Record size (variable)
04H	2	Record type (0922H)
06H		Parameters
	2	High-order word of the raster operation
	2	Y-coordinate of source origin
	2	X-coordinate of source origin
	2	Destination of y-extend
	2	Destination of x-extend
	2	Y-coordinate of destination origin
	2	X-coordinate of destination origin
	2	Bitmap width in pixels
	2	Bitmap height in pixels
	2	Number of bytes per raster line
	2	Color planes in the bitmap
	2	Number of adjacent color bits
	n	Device dependent bitmap bits

Table 64.7 The `BITBLT` record (Windows 2.x)

In Windows 3.0 and higher the record uses the following structure:

Offset	Bytes	Remarks
00H	4	Record size (variable)
04H	2	Record type (0940H)
06H		Parameters
	2	High-order word of the raster operation

Table 64.8 The `BITBLT` record (Windows 3.x) *(continues over...)*

Offset	Bytes	Remarks
	2	Y-coordinate of source origin
	2	X-coordinate of source origin
	2	Destination of y-extend
	2	Destination of x-extend
	2	Y-coordinate of destination origin
	2	X-coordinate of destination origin
	n	BITMAPINFO structure
	n	Device independent bitmap bits

Table 64.8
The `BITBLT` record (Windows 3.x) (*cont.*)

For the BITMAPINFO structure *see* Chapter 60 on the Windows BMP format (Table 60.2).

64.3.4 CHORD

This function draws a chord. The X1,Y1 and X2,Y2 parameters specify the upper left and lower right corners of a rectangular bounding box for the ellipse.

Offset	**Bytes**	**Remarks**
`00H`	4	Record size (`0EH`)
`04H`	2	Record type (`0830H`)
`06H`		Parameters
	2	X1 coordinate of upper left corner rectangle
	2	Y1 coordinate of upper left corner rectangle
	2	X2 coordinate of lower right corner rectangle
	2	Y2 coordinate of lower right corner rectangle
	2	X3 coordinate of one end of line segment
	2	Y3 coordinate of one end of line segment
	2	X4 coordinate of one end of line segment
	2	Y4 coordinate of one end of line segment

Table 64.9
The `CHORD` record

The X3,Y3 and X4,Y4 parameters specify the endpoints of a line that intersects the ellipse. The chord is drawn by using the selected pen and filled by the selected brush.

64.3.5 CREATEBITMAP

This record creates a device-dependent bitmap.

Offset	Bytes	Remarks
00H	4	Record size (variable)
04H	2	Record type (06FEH)
06H		Parameters
	2	Bitmap width in pixels
	2	Bitmap height in pixels
	1	Color planes
	1	Bits per pixel
	*n**2	Array containing bitmap initialization string

Table 64.10 The CREATEBITMAP record

64.3.6 CREATEBITMAPINDIRECT

This record creates a device-dependent bitmap.

Offset	Bytes	Remarks
00H	4	Record size (variable)
04H	2	Record type (02FDH)
06H		Parameters
	2	Bitmap type (0)
	2	Bitmap width in pixels
	2	Bitmap height in pixels
	2	Bytes per raster line
	1	Color planes
	1	Bits per pixel
	*n**2	Array containing bitmap

Table 64.11 The CREATEBITMAP-INDIRECT record

64.3.7 CREATEBRUSH

The structure of this record (F8H) is unknown.

64.3.8 CREATEBRUSHINDIRECT

This record defines a logical brush which has a style, color and pattern.

Offset	Bytes	Remarks
00H	4	Record size (variable)
04H	2	Record type (02FCH)
06H		Parameters
	2	Style
	n	Color table
	2	Hatch

Table 64.12 The CREATEBRUSH-INDIRECT record

The brush style is is defined as a DIB bitmap, a hatched brush, a hollow brush, a pattern brush or a solid brush. The color table consists of an array of 16-bit indices into the current logical palette or a table containing literal RGB values.

64.3.9 CREATEFONTINDIRECT

This record defines a logical font.

Offset	Bytes	Remarks
00H	4	Record size (variable)
04H	2	Record type (02FBH)
06H		Parameters for font
	2	Height in logical units
	2	Width in logical units
	2	Escapement (angle 1/10 degree between base line and X-axis)
	2	Orientation (value ignored)

Table 64.13 The CREATEFONT record (*continues over...*)

Offset	Bytes	Remarks
	2	Weight for font
		0 do not care
		100 thin
		200 extra-light
		300 light
		400 normal
		500 medium
		600 semi-bold
		700 bold
		800 extra-bold
		900 heavy
	1	Italic (if not zero)
	1	Underline (if not zero)
	1	Strikeout (if not zero)
	1	Character set
		0 ANSI
		1 default
		2 symbol
		128 SHIFTJIS
		255 OEM
	1	Output precision
	1	Clip precision
	1	Quality
	1	Pitch and family
	n	Face name

Table 64.13 The `CREATEFONT` record (*cont.*)

64.3.10 CREATEPALLETTE

This function creates a logical palette.

Offset	**Bytes**	**Remarks**
00H	4	Record size (variable)
04H	2	Record type (0F7H)
06H		Parameters
	2	Version
	2	Entries (*n*)
	4**n*	Color palette
		1 byte for red, green, blue, flags

Table 64.14 The `CREATE-PALETTE` record

64.3.11 CREATEPATTERNBRUSH

In Windows 2.x, this function creates a logical brush which has a pattern defined in a bitmap.

Offset	Bytes	Remarks
00H	4	Record size (variable)
04H	2	Record type (01F9H)
06H		Parameters
	2	Bitmap width
	2	Bitmap height
	2	Bytes per raster line
	1	Color planes
	1	Bits per pixel
	4	Pointer to bit values
	n	Bit pattern

Table 64.15 The CREATE-PATTERNBRUSH record (Windows 2.x)

This function uses a modified structure in Windows 3.x.

Offset	Bytes	Remarks
00H	4	Record size (variable)
04H	2	Record type (0142H)
06H		Parameters
	2	Bitmap type
	2	Color table type
	n	BITMAPINFO structure
	n	Bitmap

Table 64.16 The CREATE-PATTERNBRUSH record (Windows 3.x)

For the BITMAPINFO structure see the BMP format description in Chapter 60 (Table 60.2).

64.3.12 CREATEPENINDIRECT

This record creates a logical pen which has a style, a width and a color.

Offset	Bytes	Remarks
00H	4	Record size
04H	2	Record type (02FAH)
06H		Parameters
	2	Style (solid, dash, dot, and so on)
	2	Pen width (x) in logical units
	2	Not used
	2	Color

Table 64.17 The CREATE-PENINDIRECT record

64.3.13 CREATEREGION

This record specifies a rectangular region.

Offset	Bytes	Remarks
00H	4	Record size
04H	2	Record type (06FFH)
06H		Parameters
	2	X upper left corner
	2	Y upper left corner
	2	X lower right corner
	2	Y lower right corner

Table 64.18 The CREATE-REGION record

The X – Y value must not exceed 32,767 units.

64.3.14 DELETEOBJECT

This record deletes an object. The record stores a handle as a parameter to the object table.

Offset	Bytes	Remarks
00H	4	Record size
04H	2	Record type (01F0H)
06H		Parameters
	2	Handle

Table 64.19 The DELETEOBJECT record

64.3.15 DRAWTEXT

This record draws a formatted text in a rectangle.

Offset	Bytes	Remarks
00H	4	Record size
04H	2	Record type (062FH)
06H		Parameters
	2	Format
	2	String length –1 (ASCIIZ string)
	8	Rectangle coordinates
	n	String

Table 64.20 The DRAWTEXT record

64.3.16 ELLIPSE

This record defines an ellipse.

Offset	Bytes	Remarks
00H	4	Record size
04H	2	Record type (0418H)
06H		Parameters
	2	X1 coordinate of upper left corner
	2	Y1 coordinate of upper left corner
	2	X2 coordinate of lower right corner
	2	Y2 coordinate of lower right corner

Table 64.21 The ELLIPSE record

The center of the ellipse is the center of the bounding rectangle.

64.3.17 ESCAPE

This record specifies an escape sequence to access the facilities of a particular device.

Offset	Bytes	Remarks
00H	4	Record size
04H	2	Record type (0626H)
06H		Parameters
	2	Escape number
	2	Number of following bytes
	n	Escape sequence

Table 64.22 The ESCAPE record

64.3.18 EXCLUDECLIPRECT

This record creates a new clipping region which consists of the existing clipping region minus the specified rectangle.

Offset	Bytes	Remarks
00H	4	Record size
04H	2	Record type (0415H)
06H		Parameters
	2	X1 coordinate of upper left corner
	2	Y1 coordinate of upper left corner
	2	X2 coordinate of lower right corner
	2	Y2 coordinate of lower right corner

Table 64.23 The EXCLUDE-CLIPRECT record

64.3.19 EXTTEXTOUT

This record writes a character string within a rectangular region using the current font.

Offset	Bytes	Remarks
00H	4	Record size
04H	2	Record type (0A32H)
06H		Parameters
	2	Y1 coordinate of first char
	2	X1 coordinate of first char
	2	String length
	2	Rectangular type
	8	Rectangle structure (X1,Y1,X2,Y2)
	n	String
	n	Word array containing inter-character distances

Table 64.24 The EXTTEXTOUT record

64.3.20 LINETO

This record defines a line from the current position to the specified point.

Offset	Bytes	Remarks
00H	4	Record size
04H	2	Record type (0213H)
06H		Parameters
	2	X coordinate of end point
	2	Y coordinate of end point

Table 64.25 The LINETO record

The end point is not included in the line.

64.3.21 MOVETO

This record moves the current position to the specified point.

Offset	Bytes	Remarks
00H	4	Record size
04H	2	Record type (0214H)
06H		Parameters
	2	X coordinate of new point
	2	Y coordinate of new point

Table 64.26 The MOVETO record

The end point is not included in the line.

64.3.22 OFFSETCLIPRGN

This record moves the clipping region of the given device by the specified offsets.

Offset	Bytes	Remarks
00H	4	Record size
04H	2	Record type (0220H)
06H		Parameters
	2	Move x units
	2	Move y units

Table 64.27 The OFFSET-CLIPRGN record

64.3.23 OFFSETVIEWPORTORG

This record (412H) modifies the viewport origin relative to the current values. The record uses the same structure as the OFFSETCLIPRGN record.

64.3.24 OFFSETWINDOWORG

This record (40FH) modifies the viewport origin relative to the current values. The record uses the same structure as the OFFSETCLIPRGN record.

64.3.25 PAINTREGION

This record fills the specified region with the selected brush.

Offset	**Bytes**	**Remarks**
00H	4	Record size
04H	2	Record type (012BH)
06H		Parameters
	n	Region to be filled

Table 64.28 The PAINTREGION record

64.3.26 PATBLT

This record creates a bit pattern on the specified device.

Offset	Bytes	Remarks
00H	4	Record size
04H	2	Record type (061DH)
06H		Parameters
	2	X coordinate of upper left corner
	2	Y coordinate of upper left corner
	2	Width
	2	Height
	8	Raster operation code

Table 64.29
The PATBLT record

The pattern is defined by a rectangle (in logical units) and a raster code. The raster code defines the function which is applicable to the destination bitmap (all black, all white, invert, copy, OR).

64.3.27 PIE

Defines a pie-shaped wedge by drawing an arc whose center and two end points are joined by lines. This record uses the same structure as the ellipse record. The opcode is 81AH.

64.3.28 POLYGON

This record defines a polygon consisting of two or more points (vertices).

Offset	Bytes	Remarks
00H	4	Record size
04H	2	Record type (0324H)
06H		Parameters
	2	Number of points n
	n*4	List of points (X,Y)

Table 64.30
The POLYGON record

64.3.29 POLYLINE

This record defines a polyline (series of line segments) and uses the following record structure:

Offset	Bytes	Remarks
00H	4	Record size
04H	2	Record type (0325H)
06H		Parameters
	2	Number of points *n*
	*n**4	List of points (X,Y)

Table 64.31 The POLYLINE record

64.3.30 POLYPOLYGON

This record defines several polygons and uses the following structure.

Offset	Bytes	Remarks
00H	4	Record size
04H	2	Record type (0538H)
06H		Parameters
	2	Number of polygons (*n*)
	*n**2	Number of points for each polygon
	*n**4	List of points (X,Y)

Table 64.32 The POLYPOLYGON record

64.3.31 RECTANGLE

This record defines a rectangle.

Offset	Bytes	Remarks
00H	4	Record size
04H	2	Record type (041BH)

Table 64.33 The RECTANGLE record (*continued over...*)

Offset	Bytes	Remarks
06H		Parameters
	2	X1 coordinate of upper left corner
	2	Y1 coordinate of upper left corner
	2	X2 coordinate of lower right corner
	2	Y2 coordinate of lower right corner

Table 64.33 The RECTANGLE record (*cont.*)

The rectangle is filled with the current brush and drawn with the selected pen.

64.3.32 RESIZEPALETTE

This record resizes the current palette.

Offset	**Bytes**	**Remarks**
00H	4	Record size
04H	2	Record type (0139H)
06H		Parameters
	2	New number of palette entries

Table 64.34 The RESIZEPALETTE record

64.3.33 ROUNDRECT

This record defines a rectangle with rounded corners.

Offset	**Bytes**	**Remarks**
00H	4	Record size
04H	2	Record type (061CH)
06H		Parameters

Table 64.35 The ROUNDRECT record (*continues over..*)

Offset	Bytes	Remarks
	2	X1 coordinate of upper left corner
	2	Y1 coordinate of upper left corner
	2	X2 coordinate of lower right corner
	2	Y2 coordinate of lower right corner
	2	Ellipse width for corners
	2	Ellipse height for corners

Table 64.35 The ROUNDRECT record (*cont.*)

The rectangle is filled with the current brush and drawn with the selected pen.

64.3.34 SCALEVIEWPORT

This record defines the viewport scale.

Offset	**Bytes**	**Remarks**
00H	4	Record size
04H	2	Record type (0412H)
06H		Parameters
	2	Current x multiplicator
	2	Current x divisor
	2	Current y multiplicator
	2	Current y divisor

Table 64.36 The SCALE-VIEWPORTEXT record

The new value is calculated by: new = old * multiplicator / divisor

64.3.35 SCALEWINDOWEXT

This record uses the same structure as the SCALEVIEWPORTEXT record and modifies the extension of the windows. The record type is 400H.

64.3.36 SETBKCOLOUR

This record defines a new background color. The opcode 201H is used. The record contains a color (4 bytes) as a parameter.

64.3.37 SETBKMODE

This record defines a new background mode. The opcode 102H is used. The record contains a word defining the new mode (opaque or transparent).

64.3.38 SETDIBITSTODEV

This record contains bits from a device-independent bitmap for a device.

Offset	Bytes	Remarks
00H	4	Record size
04H	2	Record type (0D33H)
06H		Parameters
	2	Flag for color palette
	2	Number of scan lines of the DIB
	2	First scan line in the DIB
	2	Y-coordinate of source in DIB
	2	X-coordinate of source in DIB
	2	Height of rectangle in DIB
	2	Width of rectangle in DIB
	2	Y-coordinate of origin destination rectangle in DIB
	2	X-coordinate of origin destination rectangle in DIB
	n	BITMAPINFO structure
	n	Bitmap

Table 64.37 The SETDIBITSTODEV record

For the BITMAPINFO see the BMP format description in Chapter 60 (Table 60.2).

64.3.39 SETPALETTEENTRIES

This record sets an RGB color value and flag in a range of entries in a logical palette.

Offset	Bytes	Remarks
00H	4	Record size
04H	2	Record type (0037H)
06H		Parameters
	2	First entry to be set in the palette
	2	Number of entries to be set (*n*)
	*n**4	1 byte for red, green, blue, flag

Table 64.38 The SETPALETTE-ENTRIES record

64.3.40 SETPIXEL

This record defines a pixel for the X,Y-point in a specified color.

Offset	Bytes	Remarks
00H	4	Record size
04H	2	Record type (041FH)
06H		Parameters
	2	X position
	4	Color for pixel (red, green, blue, flag)

Table 64.39 The SETPIXEL record

64.3.41 SETPOLYFILLMODE

This record defines the new fill mode for polygons. The record contains one parameter (word) defining the new fill mode. The record type is 106H.

64.3.42 SETROP2

This record defines the new drawing mode. The mode is stored as an integer (word) and the record type is 104H.

64.3.43 SETSTRETCHBLTMODE

This record sets the stretching mode (black on white, color on color, white on black). The mode is stored as an integer (word) and the record type is 107H.

64.3.44 SETTEXTALIGN

This record contains a (word) flag which sets the text alignment. The record type is 12EH.

64.3.45 SETTEXTCHAREXTRA

This record sets the amount of extra space (word parameter) in logical units to be added to each character. The record type is 108H.

64.3.46 SETTEXTCOLOR

This record (type 209H) defines the text color. The color is stored as a 4-byte parameter (red, green, blue, flag).

64.3.47 SETTEXTJUSTIFICATION

This record contains a parameter to justify a text.

Offset	Bytes	Remarks
00H	4	Record size
04H	2	Record type (020AH)
06H		Parameters
	2	Extra space
	2	Number of break characters

Table 64.40 The SETTEXT-JUSTIFICATION record

64.3.48 SETWINDOWEXT

This record defines the extension of the associated window.

Offset	Bytes	Remarks
00H	4	Record size
04H	2	Record type (020CH)
06H		Parameters
	2	X-extension in logical units
	2	Y-extension in logical units

Table 64.41 The SETWINDOWEXT record

64.3.49 SETWINDOWSORG

This record defines a new window origin for the associated window.

Offset	Bytes	Remarks
00H	4	Record size
04H	2	Record type (020BH)
06H		Parameters
	2	X-origin in logical units
	2	Y-origin in logical units

Table 64.42 The SETWINDOWSORG record

64.3.50 STRETCHBLT

This record contains a device-independent bitmap. There are two structures, one for early Windows 2.x versions (code B23H) and one for Windows 3.x versions (code B41H).

Offset	Bytes	Remarks
00H	4	Record size
04H	2	Record type (0B41H)
06H		Parameters
	2	Low-order word raster operation
	2	High-order word raster operation
	2	Source of Y-extend
	2	Source of X-extend
	2	Y-coordinate of source origin
	2	X-coordinate of source origin
	2	Destination of Y-extend
	2	Destination of X-extend
	2	Y-coordinate of destination origin
	2	X-coordinate of destination origin
	n	BITMAPINFO structure
	n	Bitmap

Table 64.43 The STRETCHBLT record

For the BITMAPINFO structure see the BMP format description in Chapter 60 (Table 60.2). In Windows 2.0 the BITMAPINFO structure is not applicable. The same structure is used as for the BITBLT record.

64.3.51 STRETCHDIB

This record contains a device-independent bitmap which is moved to a window.

Offset	Bytes	Remarks
00H	4	Record size
04H	2	Record type (0F43H)
06H		Parameters
	2	Raster operation performed

Table 64.44 The STRETCHDIBITS record (*continues over...*)

Offset	Bytes	Remarks
	2	Flag (color)
	2	Height source bitmap
	2	Width source bitmap
	2	Y-coordinate of source origin
	2	X-coordinate of source origin
	2	Height of destination rectangle
	2	Width of destination rectangle
	2	Y-coordinate of destination origin
	2	X-coordinate of destination origin
	n	BITMAPINFO structure
	n	Bitmap

Table 64.44 The `STRETCHDIBITS` record (*cont.*)

For the BITMAPINFO structure see the BMP format description Chapter 60 (Table 60.2).

64.3.52 TEXTOUT

This record contains a character string which must be displayed in the current font.

Offset	Bytes	Remarks
`00H`	4	Record size
`04H`	2	Record type (`0521H`)
`06H`		Parameters
	2	String length
	2	String
	2	Y-coordinate of start point
	2	X-coordinate of start point

Table 64.45 The `TEXTOUT` record

! A WMF reader or writer should use the Windows metafile functions to handle the data in the records. The data structures are described in the Windows SDK.

65

Write binary format (WRI)

***Windows** 3.0/3.1 comes with the word-processing program Write. Write uses a binary format to store its data. The format has much in common with Word, and WRI files can therefore be read by Word, although some of the format information is not handled correctly.*

Figure 65.1 shows an extract from a memory dump of a WRI file.

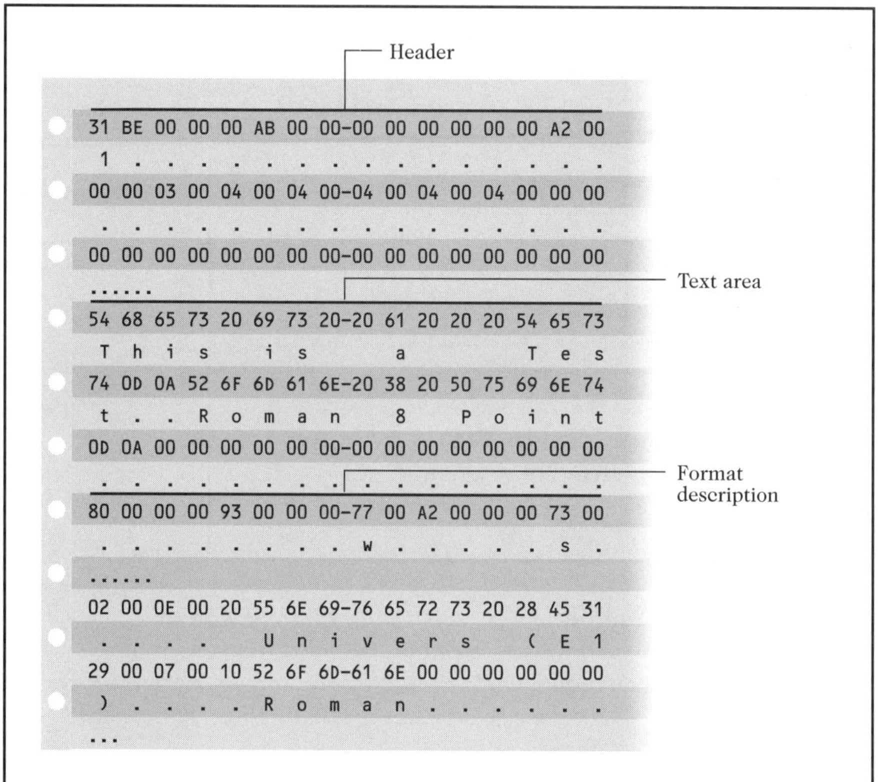

Figure 65.1
The Windows Write format

The data is stored in 128-byte blocks. These blocks are divided into three groups:

- Header
- Text area
- Formatting

A brief description of the structure of each of these groups is given below.

65.1 The Write header

The header contains 128 bytes and is based closely on the structure of the MS-Word header. It contains the signatures for valid WRI files and pointers to the text. Table 65.1 shows the header structure.

Offset	Bytes	Name	Remarks
00H	2	`wIdent`	Signature (must be `31H BEH` or `32H BEH`)
02H	2	`dty`	Signature (must be `00H 00H`)
04H	2	`wTool`	Signature (must be `00H ABH`)
06H	8		Reserved (`00H 00H 00H 00H 00H 00H 00H 00H`)
0EH	4	`fcMac`	Pointer to 1st byte after text area
12H	2	`pnPara`	Block number of paragraph formats
14H	2	`pnFntb`	Block number of footnote table
16H	2	`pnSep`	Block number of section formats
18H	2	`pnSetb`	Block number of section table
1AH	2	`pnPgtb`	Block number of page table
1CH	2	`pnFfntb`	Block number of font face-name table
20H	66	-----	Reserved (for Word)
60H	2	`pnMac`	Count of blocks in document
62H	2	-----	Reserved (`00H 00H`)
64H	28	-----	Unused (`00H 00H`)

Table 65.1
Write header

The first 14 bytes correspond to the Word signature and are always coded with the same values. If the file is a WRI file, the signature `31H BEH` will be stored in the first two bytes. If the signature `32H BEH` appears, the WRI file contains additional OLE objects (from Windows 3.1 onwards). The subsequent entries in the header relate to the text document. In `fcMac` (offset `0EH`), there is a 4-

byte pointer containing the offset of the character after the last valid character in the text. The number of text bytes can therefore be calculated as `fcMac - 128`.

The following entries contain block numbers. The absolute offset in bytes, from the start of the file to the start of a block, can thus be calculated as:

Block number * `128`

For example, with a block number of 10, the text will be located at offset `1280`. At offset `12H`, there is a pointer to the block containing the paragraph information. The block containing the character information is placed after the last text block (see also the description of Word format, Chapter 16). The block number can be calculated from the text length ((text length + `127`)/`128`).

The word at offset `14H` contains a pointer to the block containing the footnote information (`FNTB`). If this table is missing, the field will contain the value of `pnSep`. At offset `16H`, there is a pointer to the block containing the section information (section property, `SEP`). If the table is missing, this field points to `pnSetb`. The entry at offset `18H` defines the block number of the section table, `SetB`). If the table is missing, a pointer to `pnPgtb` is stored. Page breaks (page table, `PGTB`) are also stored in their own block, and the block number is stored at offset `1AH`. If this table is missing, Write stores a pointer to `pnFfntb` in the field. At offset `1CH`, Write stores the pointer to the font face-name table (`FFNTB`). If this pointer is missing, the entry points to `pnMac`.

The word at offset `60H` is then set to `0` and is used to distinguish between Word and Write files. If the word at offset `60H = 0` and the word at offset `62H` is non-zero, the file is a Word file. Otherwise, the text is stored in WRI format.

The remaining bytes in the header up to `7FH` are unused and set to `0`.

65.2 Text and image areas

The text area begins at offset `128` (`80H`). This area is also divided into 128-byte blocks. The end of the text (offset from start of file) is indicated by the pointer `fcMac`. Any unused bytes in the last block are filled with fill bytes.

It is important that the characters in the text area are ANSI characters and not (by contrast with Word) ASCII characters. Windows uses the ANSI character set, which largely agrees with the ASCII character set in the lower 128 characters. The only differences are in the codes above 128, for example, special characters such as Ä, Ö, Ü and so on.

The following format information in the text also needs to be taken into account:

- Paragraphs are terminated with a 'hard' RETURN (code `0DH`, `0AH`). This is the sequence created by pressing the RETURN key.
- All explicit page breaks are indicated in the text using the form feed character (code `0CH`).
- Line breaks and word breaks are not stored in the text; they are carried out by Write directly at the output stage.
- Tabulators in the text are indicated by the character `09H`.

Information on formatting the text is stored in the file trailer.

65.3 Pictures in the text area

Within the text, Write can store pictures and OLE objects (Windows 3.x) directly. A picture within the text is stored as a byte sequence, like a paragraph. The information that a picture is involved is contained in the format instructions. For each picture, a special bit is set in the paragraph formatting (PAP) (*see below*). The byte sequence for a picture is structured as follows:

Offset	Bytes	Remarks
00H	8	METAFILEPICT structure (hMF field undef.)
08H	2	Offset of picture left border (in twips = $^{1}/_{1440}$ inch)
0AH	2	Horizontal size in twips
0CH	2	Vertical size in twips
0EH	2	Number of following bytes (set to 0)
10H	14	Additional information for bitmaps only
1EH	2	Number of bytes in header (cbHeaderNumber)
20H	4	Number of following bytes (WMF or BMP)
24H	2	Scaling factor (X)
26H	2	Scaling factor (Y)
28H	x	Fill bytes (*see* cbHeaderNumber)
..H	x	Picture contents as bitmap or metafile

Table 65.2 Structure for pictures in Write

The picture is stored either as a Windows bitmap (BMP) or a Windows metafile (WMF). The length of the header is stored in the word at offset 1EH. The header is followed by the picture data. If the word at offset 00H is set to 99 (decimal), the picture data is in bitmap format. This setting in METAFILEPICT is only used by Write. If the value is not 99, the data is in metafile format. From Windows 3.1 onwards, however, the signature E3H is used for BMP data. The coding of these formats is described in the following sections.

The word at offset 0EH is not used from Windows 3.x onwards. It has been replaced by the length field at offset 20H. This field defines how many bytes the picture contains. Unless the picture has already been scaled, the entries at offset 24H and 26H have a scaling of 1000 (decimal) which corresponds to a 100% scaling.

65.4 OLE objects in the text area

From Windows 3.1 onwards, it is possible to merge OLE objects (pictures, sounds, videos and so on) into Write files as objects. In this case an OLE header is used instead of a picture header. The structure of the OLE header is as follows:

Offset	Bytes	Remarks
00H	2	OLE signature (0E4H)
02H	4	Unused
06H	2	Object type (1 = static, 2 = embedded, 3 = link)
08H	2	Offset of picture left margin (in twips = 1/1440 inch)
0AH	2	Horizontal size in twips
0CH	2	Vertical size in twips
0EH	2	Unused
10H	4	Number of bytes in the object data that follows the header
14H	4	Unused
18H	4	Hexadecimal number that, when converted to an 8-digit string, represents the unique name of the object
1CH	2	Unused
1EH	2	Number of bytes in this header
20H	4	Unused
24H	2	Scaling factor (X)
26H	2	Scaling factor (Y)
28H	*x*	Object contents

Table 65.3 Structure for OLE objects in Write

65.5 The format area

The text block is followed by various blocks containing text formatting information. The first format block always starts at a 128-byte boundary. The blocks containing character and paragraph information have an identical structure. Each block is stored in the following format:

Offset	Bytes	Remarks
00H	4	Byte number (offset) of first character covered by this page of format information
04H	*n**4	Array of format descriptors FOD (rgfod)
..H	*x*	Group of format properties FPROPs (grpfprop)
7FH	1	Number of format descriptors FODs on this page

Table 65.4 Block structure for character and paragraph formats

The individual blocks begin with a pointer to the first character in the text to which the formats apply. The pointers always contain the offset from the start of the file. This is followed (at offset 04H) by a field containing format descriptions. This field contains the following data structure for each entry:

Offset	Bytes	Remarks (FOD)
00H	4	Byte number after last character covered by this FOD
04H	2	Byte offset from beginning of FOD array to corresponding format properties (FPROP)

Table 65.5 Structure of a format descriptor entry (FOD) in the array

An item of format information relates to all characters (from the start pointer) until a new format definition is found. The start of the new definition is located in the FOD, in the first four bytes. The following word contains the offset from the start of the field containing the format descriptors to the format description (format property, FPRO) in the format block. The entry FFFFH indicates that there is no valid format description. This is a variable area which is built up dynamically during formatting. The first entry in the area containing the format description begins at the end of the block (offset 7EH). The last byte in the block (offset 7FH) contains a counter, in which the number of entries in the format-descriptor (FOD) table is stored. If the block is full, a new block with the above structure will be created. The area containing the format description is structured as follows:

Offset	Bytes	Remark (FPROP)
00H	1	Number of bytes in this FPROP
01H	*x*	Format description (CHP and PAP)

Table 65.6
Structure of a format property (FROP)

The entries in the format description field relate either to character properties (CHP) or to paragraph properties (PAP). One entry contains all the format bits required to describe the relevant format of the character or paragraph. The coding for character and paragraph formats is shown below.

65.6 Character property (CHP)

This block contains the format description for individual characters. It begins at a 128-byte boundary and is structured as follows:

Offset	Bytes	Remark
00H	1	Reserved (ignored by Write)
01H	1	Character format Bit 0: bold 1: italic 2..7: font code (low bits index in FFNTB)
02H	1	Font size in half points (default 24)
03H	1	Bit 0: underlined character 1-5: reserved 6: set for page only 7: reserved
04H	1	Bit 0-2: font code (high bits) 3-7: reserved
05H	1	Character position 0: normal 1..127: superscript 128..255: subscript

Table 65.7
Format description for characters (CHP)

The standard CHP has byte 0 = 1, byte 2 = 24 and all other bytes = 0. The format area (FPROP) contains a character counter with a value greater than 0.

65.7 Paragraph property (PAP)

The format description for paragraphs is structured as follows:

Offset	Bytes	Remark
00H	1	Reserved (must be set to 0)
01H	1	Bit 0–1: Justify 0 = left 1 = centered 2 = right 3 = both 2–7: reserved (must be set to 0)
02H	1	Reserved (must be set to 0)
03H	1	Reserved (must be set to 0)
04H	2	Right indent (1/20 point)
06H	2	Left indent (1/20 point)
08H	2	First line left indent (relative to left indent)
0AH	2	Interline spacing (default 240)
0CH	2	Reserved (0)
0EH	2	Reserved (0)
10H	1	Page flag Bit 0: 0 = header, 1 = footer 1–2: reserved (0 = paragraph, else header or footer 3: Start of printing 0 = do not print on first page 1 = print on first page 4: Paragraph type 0 = text 1 = picture 5–7: reserved (0)
11H	5	Reserved (must be set to 0)
16H	14*4	Up to 14 tab descriptors (TBD)

Table 65.8 Paragraph format (PAP)

The description of the tabulator position (tab descriptor) in the paragraph format is structured as follows:

Offset	Bytes	Remarks (TBD)
00H	2	Indent from left margin to tab stop (in 1/20 point)
02H	1	Tab type flag Bit 0-2: 0 normal tabs, 3 decimal tabs 3-5: reserved 6-7: reserved (must be 0)
03H	1	Reserved (ignored)

Table 65.9 Format of tab positions

The format description for a standard paragraph contains 61 in byte 0, 30 in byte 2 and 240 in bytes 10 to 11. All other bytes (12-78) are set to 0. Every FPROP must contain a value greater than 0 in the character counter.

One important difference between paragraph format and character format is that there must be a format description for every paragraph. With character formatting, a long text (including several paragraphs) may well be stored in the same format. In this case, one format description applies to all characters. There must be *no gaps* in the format description; that is, the format description begins with the first character at offset 128 and ends with the last valid character.

In Write files, all header and footer texts are stored at the beginning of the document. Texts are defined as paragraphs. If Write is reading files which have been produced by Word, Write can only recognize header and footer lines at the beginning of the text. If there are subsequent definitions in the text, these are described as normal text.

Footnotes and sections in Write are not managed via a footnote table. Write only creates one section per document and all header and footer texts are located at the beginning of the document before the first paragraph.

65.8 Section property

The format for a section property (SEP) is shown in the following table:

Offset	Bytes	Remark
00H	1	Count of bytes used (excluding this byte)
01H	2	Reserved (must be 0)
03H	2	Page length in 1/20 point (default is 11 × 1440 = 15840)
05H	2	Page width in 1/20 point (default is 8.5 × 1440 = 12240)

Table 65.10 Format of a section property (SEP) (*continues over...*)

Offset	Bytes	Remark
07H	2	Reserved (must be 0)
09H	2	Top margin in 1/20 point (default is 1440)
0BH	2	Text height in 1/20 point (default is 9 × 1440 = 12960)
0DH	2	Left margin in 1/20 point (default is 1.25 × 1440 = 1800)
0FH	2	Width of text area in 1/20 point (default is 6 × 1440 = 8640)

Table 65.10 Format of a section property (SEP) (*cont.*)

The lower and right margins can be calculated from the above information. Provided the above settings are adopted, there is no need for a section table (SETB) or a section property (SEP). If a section table is used, the first byte of the SEP must be set to a value between 1 and 16. The associated section table is structured as follows:

Offset	Bytes	Remark
00H	2	Number of sections (always 2 in Write)
02H	2	Undefined
04H		Array of section descriptors (SEDs):
	4	Offset of 1st character following section (cp)
	2	Undefined
	4	Offset of associated section property (fcSep)

Table 65.11 Structure of a section table

A Write document has only two section descriptors (SED). The rest of the table is occupied by fill-bytes up to the limit of 128 bytes. The first SED entry in the variable cp indicates that the SED will relate to all characters in the document. The fcSep field contains a pointer to the SEP block of the file. The second SEP entry in the table is a dummy and contains the value FFFFFFFFH in the fcSep field.

As an option, a `PGTB` section may follow in the block directly after the `SEP` section. This page table (`PGTB`) is structured as follows:

Offset	Bytes	Remarks
00H	1	Number of page descriptors `PGD` (`cpgd`) 1 to *n*
01H	1	Undefined
02H	*x*	Array containing `PGD`:
	2	Page number in printed document (`pgn`)
	4	Offset of first character in printed page (`cpMin`)

Table 65.12 Structure of a page table (`PGT`)

The field containing the page descriptions has *n* entries. The remaining area up to the end of the block is occupied by fill bytes.

65.9 Font table (FFNTB)

The `Font Face Name` table (`FFNTB`) can be stored in one block. The structure is as follows:

Offset	Bytes	Remark
00H	2	Number of font face names (`FFNs`)
02H	*x*	List of font face names (`FFN`) with:
	2	Number of bytes following in this `FFN`, Not including these 2 bytes (`cbFfn`)
	2	ID of font family (`ffid`)
	n	Font name as ASCIIZ text (`szFfn`)

Table 65.13 Structure of a font table (`FFNTB`)

If the value FFFFH is stored in the cbFfn field, the next entry in the table is stored in the following block. A value of 0 in this field indicates that there are no further entries. Permitted values for the font ID number are shown below:

FF_DONTCARE

FF_ROMAN

FF_SWISS

FF_MODERN

FF_SCRIPT

FF_DECORATIVE

Additional ID numbers can be defined in more recent versions of Windows.

66

Windows 3.x Calendar format (CAL)

The Windows Calendar program has its own format for storing data for appointments and notes. The following description relates to the version used with Windows 3.x.

66.1 The header

The header contains a signature indicating a valid calendar file, and information on the number of entries. Table 66.1 shows the structure of the header:

Offset	Bytes	Remarks
00H	...	Signature (B5H A2H B0H B3H B3H B0H A2H B5H)
08H	2	Count of dates (`cDateDescriptors`)
0AH	2	Alarm (in minutes)
0CH	2	Sound (Boolean)
0EH	2	Interval between appointments
10H	2	Interval in minutes
12H	2	Time format <>0 = 24-hour
14H	2	Start time
16H	50	Reserved

Table 66.1
The CAL header

The first 8 bytes contain the signature which identifies a valid calendar file. This sequence is constructed by adding the letter codes for the following character sequence:

'C' + 'r' = b5

'A' + 'a' = a2

'L' + 'd' = b0

'E' + 'n' = b3

'N' + 'e' = b3

'D' + 'l' = b0

'A' + 'a' = a2

'R' + 'c' = b5

The next word contains an integer counter with the number of dates in the file. The following 12 bytes are divided into six fields and contain global entries for the file. The first word defines the alarm time (early ring) in minutes. This is followed by a logical variable (`fSound`) which defines whether the alarm is to be audible. The word at offset `0CH` defines the breakdown of the appointment calendar:

0 = 15 minutes

1 = 30 minutes

2 = 60 minutes

The following word indicates the interval between appointments in minutes. When set to `true`, the variable (`f24HourFormat`) indicates that the clock time will be displayed in 24-hour format. If the value is `false` (0), a 12-hour display will be used. The last word used defines the earliest time used in the day display. This time appears in the first display for a day, and is stored as the number of minutes after midnight. The remaining bytes of the 64-byte header are reserved.

66.2 The data area

The header is followed by the data area containing the appointment entries. This data area consists of one field, in which each entry refers to one complete day. The number of entries in this array is described by the `cDateDescriptors` field in the header. Each element in the array consists of 12 bytes, with the following meanings:

Offset	Bytes	Remarks
00H	2	Date in days since 1.1.1980
02H	2	Date mark 128 : rectangle 256 : parentheses 512 : circle 1024 : cross 2048 : underscore
04H	2	Alarms set for the day
06H	2	Offset of 64-byte block containing information on the day
08H	2	Reserved (FFFFH)
0AH	2	Reserved (FFFFH)

Table 66.2 Structure of the data area

The first word contains the number of the day as an integer value, indicating the number of days since 1.1.1980. This is followed by a flag specifying how the date should be displayed. At offset 04H, the number of entries per day at which an alarm is to be set off is stored. The last word at offset 06H contains a pointer to a 64-byte block containing information on the day. Only the lower 15 bits in this word are used. The highest bit is always set to 0. As an example, if the value 6 is stored in the word, the offset to the block containing the daily information is calculated as 6*64 (bytes). The remaining two bytes are reserved and coded FFFFH.

66.3 Day-specific information area

All the information on a given day is stored at 64-byte boundaries after the array containing the description of the date. The structure of this information is as follows:

Offset	Bytes	Remarks
00H	2	Reserved (must be 0)
02H	2	Days since 1.1.1980
04H	2	Reserved (must be 1)
06H	2	Length of note text in bytes
08H	2	Number of appointments
0AH	x	Text of note
..H	$n*x$	Block of appointments

Table 66.3 Day-specific information

The word at offset 06H contains the length of the text information, which is followed by a field containing details of the appointments. The number of appointments is stored at offset 08H. Each entry in the block (array) of appointments is structured as follows:

Offset	Bytes	Remarks
00H	1	Size of the appointment, in entry bytes
01H	1	Flags Bit 0 = 1 alarm 1 = 1 special time
02H	2	Time (in minutes from 00:00)
04H	*x*	ASCIIZ string associated with the appointment

Table 66.4 Appointment block

The first value indicates the number of following bytes. Thus, the position of the following entry can always be determined. The text field contains the user's description of the appointment.

67

Windows Cardfile format (CRD)

The structure of the Windows 3.x Cardfile format is particularly simple. The header comprises 5 bytes, as follows:

Offset	Bytes	Remarks
00H	3	Signature ('MGC')
03H	2	Number of entries (cards)

Table 67.1
CRD file header

This header is followed by a text area (index line) containing the header texts (index lines) for the individual cards. The first entry begins at offset 05H. The following entries are then always 34 bytes from the start of the previous entry. Each entry in the area has the following format:

Offset	Bytes	Remarks
00H	6	Nullbytes (00H 00H 00H 00H 00H 00H)
06H	4	Offset of data area for card
0AH	1	Flag byte (00H)
0BH	22	Card header (index line text)
21H	1	End byte (00H)

Table 67.2
Index area
(CRD file)

The pointer indicates the offset from the start of the file to the first byte of the card data area. This data area is located after the index area containing the header texts for the cards.

The data area for a card can contain text and graphics. The following distinctions are therefore made:

Text

Text and graphics

Graphics

Blank card

The data structure of the card depends on these distinctions.

Graphics and Text	Text	Graphic	Remarks
0-1	0-1#	0-1	Bitmap length
2-3	*	2-3	Graphic width(*)
4-5	*	4-5	Graphic height (*)
6-7	*	6-7	X-coordinate graphic (*)
8-9	*	8-9	Y-coordinate graphic (*)
A-x	*	A-x	Bitmap (*)
x + 1/x + 2	2-3	x + 1/x + 2	Length of text entry (#)
x + 3 - y	4-z	*	Text (*)

Table 67.3 Structure of a cardfile data area

The bytes marked with the character (#) are 00H unless a graphic or text is present. The value of x is calculated as the length of the bitmap graphic + 9 bytes. The value for y is calculated as x + 2 + length of the text entry. The bytes marked with the character (*) do not exist unless a text or bitmap is stored. The value for z is calculated as 3 + length of the text entry.

The address (offset) of the first byte of a card is stored in the corresponding index table entry. The end of a card is not indicated by null bytes or in any other way.

Texts in the card are stored in ASCII format. An LF character is added to every CR character. In Windows 3.1, the Cardfile format has been extended somewhat to accommodate OLE information. However, the format description is not known to me at present.

68

Clipboard format (CLP)

The Windows Clipboard stores the contents of complete screens or of individual windows and marked areas. The contents of the clipboard can be pasted into other Windows programs or saved in a CLP file. Unfortunately, I know of no external program that can read CLP files directly. The information given in this chapter describes the clipboard format, as I understand it so far.

The file begins with a 4-byte header which identifies the file as a clipboard.

Offset	Byte	Remarks
00H	2	File ID signature (50H C3H)
02H	2	Format count
04H	2	Format ID
06H	4	Length of data area (Clipboard)
0AH	4	Offset of data block (in bytes)
0EH	79	Format name (private text)
...	..	Data structure in offset 04H–0EH repeated
...	..	Clipboard data areas

Table 68.1 Clipboard format

The first word contains the signature which marks a valid CLP file. This is followed by a word defining the number of data blocks in the clipboard. Several blocks with different formats can be stored in one file. The header is followed by n blocks (n = the number in the format count) containing information on the data areas. The first word of each such block contains a code describing the format of the data block. So far, the following data formats have been defined:

```
CF_TEXT                 1
CF_BITMAP               2
CF_METAFILEPICT         3
CF_SYLK                 4
CF_DIF                  5
CF_TIFF                 6
CF_OEMTEXT              7
CF_DIB                  8
CF_PALETTE              9
CF_OWNERDISPLAY         80H
CF_DSPTEXT              81H
CF_DSPBITMAP            82H
CF_DSPMETAFILEPICT      83H
```

Some of these formats have been described in the preceding chapters of this book. The next field contains the length in bytes of the associated data area. This is followed by a field containing a 4-bit offset from the start of the file to the first byte of the associated data area. The last entry in the block contains a 79-byte area for the names of private clipboard formats. Figure 68.1 shows an extract from a CLP file.

```
50 C3 01 00 02 00 CE 06-02 00 5D 00 00 00 42 69
 P  .  .  .  .  .  .  .  .  .  ]  .  .  .  B  i
74 26 6D 61 70 00 60 03-00 00 BD 00 9D 09 92 11
 t  &  m  a  p  .  '  .  .  .  .  .  .  .  .  .
07 3C 9D 09 00 00 9B 3B-B4 07 9E 09 00 00 05 00
 .  <  .  .  .  .  .  ;  .  .  .  .  .  .  .  .
00 00 3D 09 3D 09 C7 11-B0 25 35 09 9E 09 05 00
 .  .  =  .  =  .  .  .  .  %  5  .  .  .  .  .
......
```

Figure 68.1 Dump of a CLP file

This illustration contains a bitmap, as can be seen from the entry in the name field. This area is followed by the data areas for the clipboard. The coding for these areas is unknown to me (except for those formats already described above).

69

Windows 3.x group files (GRP)

***The** Windows 3.x program manager maintains information describing which programs belong to a group in separate files with the extension* `.GRP`*. The structure of a GRP file (as far as I can determine it) is described below. It should, however, be pointed out that all this information has been acquired through reverse engineering, and there may therefore be inaccuracies.*

Table 69.1 defines the structure of a Windows 3.x group file.

Offset	Bytes	Remarks
00H	4	File ID signature 'PMCC'
04H	2	Checksum
06H	2	Group file size in bytes
08H	2	CmdShow flag
0AH	8	Group window coordinates
12H	4	Lower left corner group window
16H	2	Pointer to group name
18H	2	Horizontal display resolution
1AH	2	Vertical display resolution
1CH	2	Bits per pixel
1EH	2	Planes
20H	2	Number of programs in the group
22H	*n**2	Array of program entries

Table 69.1 Header of a GRP file

The header of a group file begins with a 4-byte signature ('PMCC'). This is followed by a 2-byte checksum. The checksum is derived from the difference of all words (2 bytes) within the file. The exception here is the word containing the checksum (offset 04H), which is not counted. The last byte of the GRP file is also ignored if the length is an odd number (because a word cannot be formed from the last byte by itself). The checksum calculation can be described as follows:

csum = 0

csum = csum – *1st word*

csum = csum – *2nd word*

; Warning: skip 3rd word

csum = csum – *4th word*

.....

The size of the group file in bytes is stored at offset 06H. The following word (CmdShow) defines how the program manager is to display the group:

Value	Flag
00H	Hide
01H	Show normal
02H	Show minimized
03H	Show maximized
04H	Show no activate
05H	Show
06H	Minimize
07H	Show minimized and no activate
08H	Show no activate
09H	Restore

Table 69.2
CmdShow values

The coordinates for the group window (RECT-structure: X1, Y1, X2, Y2) are stored at offset 0AH. The following field contains the coordinate point (POINT structure) of the lower left corner of the group window relative to the parent window.

Offset 16H contains a pointer to the null-terminated string containing the name of the group. The following two fields define the image resolution to which the group icon has been set. The number of bits per pixel for the icon bitmap is stored at offset 1CH. This is followed by the number of color levels in the icon.

A word containing the number of entries in the following data structure is stored at offset 20H. This data structure begins at offset 22H and contains the entries for the programs of the relevant group. The following data structure is defined for each entry:

Bytes	Remarks
4	Coordinate (X,Y) of lower left corner of the icon in the group
2	Index value for the icon
2	Count of bytes in the icon resource
2	AND-mask count (in bytes) for the icon
2	XOR-mask count (in bytes) for the icon
2	Header offset
2	AND-pointer
2	XOR-pointer
2	Offset to program name
2	Offset to the command string
2	Offset to the icon path

Table 69.3
Group file data structure

The index value defines the icon number in an EXE file. This is followed by the number of bytes of the icon in the resource file. The fields containing the AND and XOR masks contain the number of bytes in the relevant masks. The header offset defines the offset from the start of the group file to the resource header for the icon. This is followed by two words containing pointers to the AND and XOR masks. The next word defines the offset from the start of the group file to a string with the item name. The following word contains the offset from the start of the group file to the string with the executable program name. The last entry specifies an offset from the start of the group file to a string that specifies the path where the icon file is located. The GRP file has one such data area for each entry in the program group.

PART 6

Sound formats

File formats discussed in Part 6

A great many formats are available for sound representation. They include IFF files (Chapter 25), which can also register sounds, and manufacturer-specific sound files. MIDI formats defined by the MIDI Association set the standard in this field. Part 6 describes the most important file formats for the storage of music and sounds.

70

Creative Music Format (CMF)

*C***reative** *Labs has defined its own format for the storage of sound data, based on the MIDI specifications. CMF files contain information on the instruments used in addition to the actual musical data.*

A CMF file is divided into several blocks as shown in Figure 70.1:

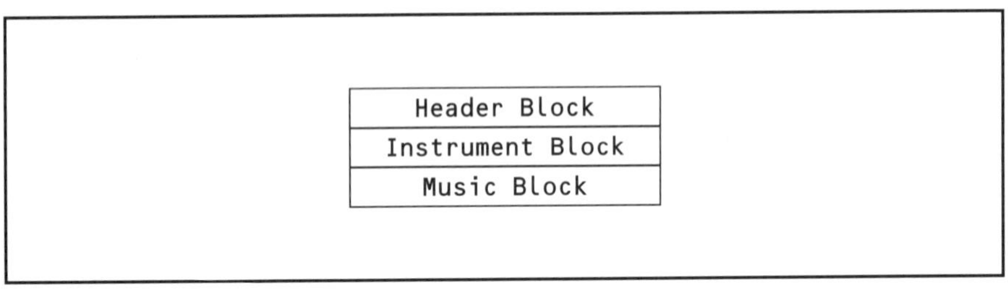

Figure 70.1 Structure of a CMF file

The data can be read sequentially and is stored in Intel format. Sounds are classified according to pitch and instrument. This differs from the approach used in other formats, which are generally based on digitized values and feedback systems. Only sounds defined for the instrument can be represented. However, the advantage is that the amount of data to be stored can be very significantly reduced.

70.1 CMF header

The header has a fixed structure as shown in Table 70.1:

Offset	Bytes	Remarks
00H	4	File ID (43H 54H 4DH 46H)
04H	2	Version
06H	2	Offset of instrument block
08H	2	Offset of music block
0AH	2	Cycles per quarter note
0CH	2	Cycles per second
0EH	2	Offset of music title
10H	2	Offset of composer's name
12H	2	Offset of comment
14H	16	Used channel table
24H	2	Number of instruments
26H	2	Basic speed
28H	*n*	Space for title, comments, and so on.

Table 70.1 Structure of a CMF header

The first four bytes of a CMF file contain the signature 'CTMF'. A BCD-coded version number is stored at offset 04H (for example, 010AH = 1.10).

At offset 06H, there are two (word) offset pointers to the following blocks. The pointer at offset 06H defines the start of the instrument block, relative to the start of the file. The second pointer indicates the start of the music block.

The number of rhythmic cycles per quarter note is stored at offset 0AH. The following word (offset 0CH) defines the number of rhythmic cycles per second. In this context, cycles are not equivalent to musical beats; this value establishes the speed of the output. In CMF format, the output is divided into rhythmic cycles. Each cycle represents the smallest unit of time within which output data can be presented. The cycles per second field contains values between 20 and 150. The cycles per quarter note field at offset 0AH defines the duration of each quarter note, calculated in rhythmic cycles. This word is only significant when calculating the length of a sound (duration = cycles per quarter note/cycles per second).

At offset 0EH, there are three words containing pointers to comment fields. These comment fields, if present, are stored in the area provided at offset 28H. The first word points to a string containing the title of the music. Each CMF file can contain one music title, which is stored as an ASCIIZ string at the specified offset in the header. If the pointer contains the value 0, there is no music title in the file. The second pointer defines the offset of the ASCIIZ string containing the name of the composer. Here too, the value 0 indicates that there is no corresponding string. The field at offset 12H contains a pointer to an optional comment, stored as an ASCIIZ string. If this pointer contains the value 0, the comment string is not present.

CMF format uses up to 16 channels (regardless of how many channels are on the Soundblaster card). At offset 14H, the header contains a table of 16 bytes. Each byte is allocated to one of these (1 to 16) channels. If a byte contains the value 0, the corresponding channel is not used in the CMF file. The value 1 indicates that the channel is used.

The word at offset 24H indicates how many instruments are used in the CMF file. This data also determines the size of the instrument block.

The word at offset 26H defines the basic speed of a musical composition. However, this parameter does not appear to be generally used and is (presumably) defined in the header for reasons of compatibility.

Space is provided at offset 28H to accommodate various ASCIIZ strings (music title, composer, comments). If no text is stored, the instrument block will begin here.

70.2 Instrument block

The *Instrument* block follows immediately after the header. The position of the instrument block is indicated in the header at offset 06H. All instruments used in the CMF file are defined in this instrument block. The block contains 16 bytes for each instrument, structured as follows:

Offset	Bytes	Remarks
00H	1	Modulator characteristic
01H	1	Carrier characteristic
02H	1	Modulator amplitude
03H	1	Carrier amplitude
04H	1	Modulator attack/decay
05H	1	Carrier attack/decay
06H	1	Modulator sustain/release
07H	1	Carrier sustain/release
08H	1	Modulator wave form
09H	1	Carrier wave form
0AH	1	Feedback/link
0BH	5	Reserved for future use

Table 70.2 Structure of an instrument entry

The number of instruments and therefore the number of stored 16-byte entries in the instrument block is at offset 24H in the header of the CMF file. The first byte defines the characteristic of the modulator and is structured as shown in Table 70.3:

Bits	Remarks
0-3	Multiplication factor
4	Envelope shortening
5	Envelope type
6	Vibrato effect
7	Tremolo effect

Table 70.3 Coding of the modulator characteristic

The second byte describes the characteristic of the carrier signal, coded in the same way (*see* Table 70.3). The byte at offset `02H` defines the amplitude of the modulator. This byte contains the attenuation factor and the parameter for amplitude attenuation:

Bits	Remarks
0-5	Attenuation factor
6-7	Amplitude attenuation

Table 70.4 Coding of the modulator amplitude

The byte at offset `03H` describes the carrier amplitude, coded as shown in Table 70.4. The modulator attack/decay value is stored at offset `04H`:

Bits	Remarks
0-3	Decay
4-7	Attack

Table 70.5 Coding of the attack/decay byte

The same information for the carrier is stored at offset `05H`. The byte at offset `06H` contains the modulator sustain/release value. This value describes two values of an ADSR envelope curve:

Bits	Remarks
0-3	Release
4-7	Sustain

Table 70.6 Coding of the sustain/release byte

Sound

The byte at offset 07H contains the sustain/release value for the carrier. The coding shown in Table 70.6 also applies to this byte. Offsets 08H and 09H contain one byte each indicating the wave form of the modulator and the carrier. The wave form is only coded in the two lowest bits 0 and 1. Bits 2 to 7 must be set to 0. Information relating to feedback/link is stored in the byte at offset 0AH, coded as shown in Table 70.7:

Bits	Remarks
0	Link
1-2	Feedback modulator
4-7	Reserved (must be set to 0)

Table 70.7 Coding of the feedback/link byte

The remaining 5 bytes are reserved for future extensions.

70.3 Music block

The *Music* block contains the actual data for the musical composition in the file. The development team from Creative Labs drew on the MIDI definition and also adopted certain sections of this structure.

The music block consists of a sequence of commands for the output of sounds and for control functions. These commands are named, in accordance with the MIDI specifications, as *events*. One interesting feature is that only the pitch and the duration are needed to enable an output to be made. An instrument channel defines whether a listener hears a trumpet, a guitar, and so on.

Each event must be preceded by a pause (rest) command, that is, commands for the output of sounds, control commands and pauses (rests) are interspersed. If no pause is needed between two events, the pause time is set to 0.

70.4 Structure of a Pause command

A `Pause` (rest) command consists of a record of variable length. The bytes in the record are coded as shown in Figure 70.2.

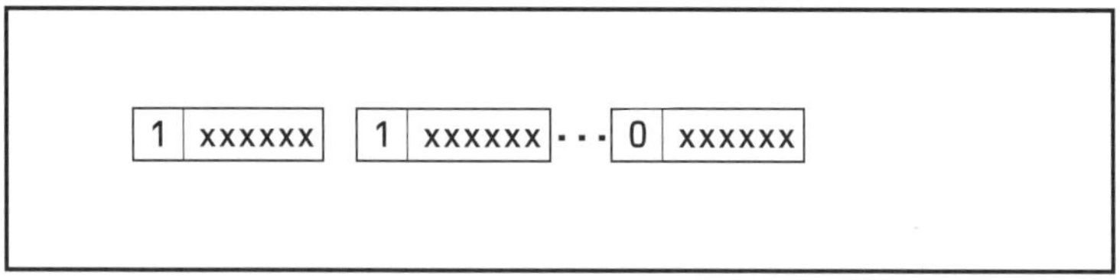

Figure 70.2
Structure of a `Pause` command

The individual bytes contain the length of the pause in rhythmic cycles, in bits `0-6`. If bit `7` is set to `1`, there is a following byte. In the last byte, bit `7` is set to `0`. To determine the value, the uppermost bit of each byte read must be ignored; that is, the remaining bits of the individual bytes are closed up.

The value determined in this way indicates the duration of the pause in rhythmic cycles. The duration of the pause in seconds can then be calculated as follows:

Duration = Length of pause (in rhythmic cycles) / rhythmic cycles per second.

The number of *rhythmic cycles per second* is stored at offset `0CH` in the header. The length of a pause can generally be coded in one byte (`0` .. `127`). The first pause record occurs at the start of the music block.

70.5 Commands within the music block

Each `Pause` (rest) command is followed by an event recorded in the music block. On the basis of the MIDI specifications, the CMF format recognizes the commands defined in Table 70.8.

Code	Remark
`9xH`	Sound on
`8xH`	Sound off
`BxH`	Control command
`CxH`	Program command

Table 70.8
CMF music block commands

For example, commands beginning with a code in the range `90H`–`9FH` switch on a sound. This sound will continue until switched off again by a command with a code in the range `80H`–`8FH`. Since there must be a pause between events, this pause generally specifies the length of the sound.

At this stage, the sound has not been allocated to an instrument. This allocation is achieved by the 4 lowest bits in the command byte indicated in Table 70.8 by the character `x` The values `0` to `0FH` represent the instrument channels 1 to 16, the actual instrument involved being decided in the instrument block. Code `90H`, for example, switches on a sound in instrument channel 1.

70.5.1 The Sound on command

The `Sound on` command contains three bytes with the following structure:

1 byte event code (`9xH`)
1 byte note (sound) number (`0..127`)
1 byte dynamics (`0..127`)

Table 70.9 Structure of a `Sound on` command

The first byte is used for the event code `9xH` and contains the number of the instrument channel in the lower 4 bits (for example, `90H` = instrument channel 1).

The second byte contains the code for the pitch. The range of values is between `0` and `127`. The individual notes (frequencies) are coded in accordance with the MIDI specification (see following sections). Concert pitch `a'`, for example, is represented by the value `45H`. Each semitone step upwards or downwards alters this value by `1`.

The third byte defines the (attack) dynamics of the instrument and is only relevant to instruments that support such dynamics. In CMF format, dynamics are represented simply as a volume value in the range `0` (quiet) to `127` (maximum volume). As soon as the command is recognized, the sound will be emitted. The sound can only be switched off by a `Sound off` command.

70.5.2 The Sound off command

The `Sound off` command contains 3 bytes structured as follows:

1 byte event code (`8xH`)
1 byte note (sound) number (`0..127`)
1 byte dynamic parameter (`0..127`)

Table 70.10 Structure of a `Sound off` command

The first byte is used for the event code and contains the number of the instrument channel in the lower 4 bits. The second byte defines the sound to be switched off. With polyphonic instruments, individual notes in the synthesizer can be switched off separately. The third parameter is not interpreted in terms of volume; it indicates the dynamics of the decay of the sound.

70.5.3 Control commands

In addition to the two events for switching a sound on or off, CMF format also recognizes additional control instructions. It is possible, for example, to set distortion factors.

A control command is introduced with the code `BxH`, where `x` represents the desired channel number. However, this channel number has no effect on some commands.

The second byte in the control record defines one of the four sub-commands and is followed by the data bytes. The structure of the record depends on the type of command. The sub-commands are described below.

70.5.3.1 CMF marker command

Markers are used for highlighting certain points in a CMF file. The command is structured as follows:

1 byte event code (`BxH`)
1 byte subcode (`66H`)
1 byte marker number (`0..127`)

Table 70.11 Structure of a marker event

The event code `BxH` introduces the marker. The channel number has no significance here. In the second byte, the value `66H` appears as a subcode. The third byte defines a marker number between `0` and `127`. A CMF file can therefore contain up to 128 sections. This is useful, for example, when synchronizing pictures and music.

70.5.3.2 CMF mode command

When playing music, it is possible to switch between melody and rhythm in CMF files. The relevant record is 3 bytes long and has the following format:

1 byte event code (BxH)
1 byte subcode (67H)
1 byte mode flag (0: melody, 1: rhythm)

Table 70.12 Structure of a mode event

A mode record is introduced by the event code BxH, where x represents the channel number in the lower 4 bits. Thus, mode switching relates to a defined instrument channel. In the CMF file, certain channels are allocated to given rhythmic instruments:

Channel	Instrument
12	Bass drum
13	Snare drum
14	Tom-tom
15	Top cymbal
16	High-hat cymbal

Table 70.13 Rhythm instruments in CMF channels

The channel number from Table 70.3 is reduced by one and added to the first code byte. For example, BFH will switch the instrument in channel 16.

The third byte defines the direction of switching; 0 switches the instrument to melody; and 1 activates the rhythm section.

70.5.3.3 CMF Increase frequency event

The sub-command *Increase frequency* is used to modify the tone color (distortion). The command has the following format:

1 byte event code (BxH)
1 byte subcode (68H)
1 byte frequency shift (0..127)

Table 70.14 Structure of an Increase frequency event

This control record is introduced by the event code BxH, where x represents the channel number in the lower 4 bits. The value 68H appears as a subcode in the second byte. The third byte defines the increase in pitch in steps of 1/128 of a semitone. The pitch then increases by the relevant frequency. The value entered may be between 0 and 127. A value of 32 will increase the frequency by $^{32}/_{128} = ^{1}/_{4}$ semitone.

70.5.3.4 CMF Decrease frequency

To lower the pitch of a sound, a sub-command with the following structure is used:

1 byte event code (BCxH)
1 byte subcode (66H)
1 byte marker number (0..127)

Table 70.15 Structure of a Decrease frequency event

This control record is introduced by the event code BxH, where x represents the channel number in the lower 4 bits. The value 69H appears as a subcode in the second byte. The third byte defines the decrease in pitch in steps of $^{1}/_{128}$ of a semitone.

70.5.4 CMF Program instrument channel command

The CMF format provides its own command for setting a channel to a specific instrument. This command is structured as follows:

1 byte event code (CxH)
1 byte instrument (0..15)

Table 70.16 Structure of a Program instrument channel event

This command is introduced by the event code CxH, where x represents the channel number. The second byte is used for the instrument number. Here again, values between 0 and 0FH can be entered. The driver can then read the instrument definition in the instrument block and allocate this to the relevant channel. In theory, any number of instruments can be described in a CMF file, with 16 instruments active at any one time. Changes are initiated by a Program instrument event.

70.5.5 CMF End of track command

The end of the *CMF music range* is introduced by the End of track command. The record is structured as follows:

1 byte event code (FFH) 1 byte subcode (2FH) 1 byte endcode (00H)

Table 70.17 Structure of an End of track event

In a CMF file, the End of track record always contains the byte sequence FFH 2FH 00H.

70.6 Data repetition in the music block

In the music block of a CMF file, data is stored in uncompressed form. The length of the file is limited to 64 Kbytes because the pointers only occupy 16 bits. However, a CMF file can accommodate larger musical compositions. This is achieved by the way in which sounds are listed (rather than by means of digitized data, as used in other sound formats). Periods of silence and periods without sound changes are defined by pause times. No data needs to be stored for these periods, which keeps the CMF files compact.

It is possible to compress the command code. Whenever two successive events have the same command code (for example, C9H), the second command code can be omitted. For example, if two notes with the codes 45H and 30H are to be output on channel 3, this can be achieved with the *Sound on* record, which contains 3 bytes.

92H 45H 7FH	set tone + volume
00H	pause time 0
92H 30H 50H	set new tone + volume

The sequence therefore contains 7 bytes and the opcode for event 92H (set tone) occurs twice. This sequence can be shortened to:

92H 45H 7FH	set tone + volume
00H	pause time 0
30H 50H	set new tone + volume

The opcode 92H after the pause time is simply omitted. If the CMF reader finds another byte with a value less than 80H after a pause command, this indicates new parameters for the last event. The required bytes should then be read in and executed with the last event code. This compression works because, in the music block, pause commands must alternate with events, and all event codes are greater than 80H.

71

Soundblaster Instrument format (SBI)

Creative Labs has developed additional file formats for the storage of musical data, which extend the CMF format. One problem lies in the adaptation of the instrument definitions to the sound card. If CMF files are involved, please refer to the instrument definitions in the Instrument block (see Chapter 70). These parameters can be varied in order to optimize the sound quality of an instrument. However, once you have found the optimum setting for your requirements, you are faced with a problem. You have to process every CMF file, changing the instrument definitions in the header.

Creative Labs defined the Soundblaster Instrument file format (SBI) in order to avoid this problem. Only the data for one instrument is stored in the file. A program can therefore read in this data before it reads a CMF file. If the CMF file uses the instrument, the instrument specifications from the SBI file will be used.

The structure of an SBI file is particularly simple. It contains only the data for one instrument and is limited to a fixed length of 52 bytes (Table 71.1). The data is stored in Intel format.

Offset	Bytes	Remarks
00H	4	File ID (53H 42H 49H 1AH)
04H	30	Instrument name
24H	1	Modulator characteristic
25H	1	Carrier characteristic
26H	1	Modulator amplitude
27H	1	Carrier amplitude
28H	1	Modulator attack/decay

Table 71.1 Structure of an instrument file (SBI) (*continues over...*)

Offset	Bytes	Remarks
29H	1	Carrier attack/decay
2AH	1	Modulator sustain/release
2BH	1	Carrier sustain/release
2CH	1	Modulator wave form
2DH	1	Carrier wave form
2EH	1	Feedback/link
2FH	5	Reserved for future use

Table 71.1 Structure of an instrument file (SBI) (*cont.*)

The first four bytes contain the signature 'SBI', followed by the character 1AH. This prevents the file from being displayed as a DOS text file. This signature is followed by the name of the instrument as an ASCIIZ string. Every byte need not be used, but standard names for identification should be entered.

The following byte contains the characteristic for the modulator. This byte is structured as shown in Table 71.2:

Bits	**Remarks**
0-3	Multiplication factor
4	Envelope shortening
5	Envelope type
6	Vibrato effect
7	Tremolo effect

Table 71.2 Coding of the modulator characteristic

The next byte describes the characteristic of the carrier signal, coded as for the modulator (*see* Table 71.2).

The byte at offset 26H defines the modulator amplitude. This byte contains the attenuation factor and the parameter for amplitude attenuation:

Bits	Remarks
0-5	Attenuation factor
6-7	Amplitude attenuation

Table 71.3 Coding of the modulator amplitude

The attenuation factor may contain values between 0 and 63, where 0 represents no attenuation and 63 represents maximum attenuation with minimum volume.

The byte at offset 27H describes the carrier amplitude, coded as for the modulator amplitude (Table 71.3). Offset 28H indicates the *Modulator attack/decay* value, as follows:

Bits	Remarks
0-3	Decay
4-7	Attack

Table 71.4 Coding of the attack/decay byte

The corresponding information for the carrier is stored at offset 29H. The byte at offset 2AH contains the *Modulator sustain/release* value. The byte describes two values of an ADSR envelope curve:

Bits	Remarks
0-3	Release
4-7	Sustain

Table 71.5 Coding of the sustain/release byte

The byte at offset 2BH contains the *sustain/release* value for the carrier, coded as shown in Table 71.5.

Offsets 2CH and 2DH contain one byte each defining the wave form of the modulator and the carrier. The wave form occupies only the lowest two bits 0 and 1. Bits 2 to 7 must be set to 0. Data on feedback/link is stored in the byte at offset 2EH, coded as shown in Table 71.6.

Bits	Remarks
0	Link
1–2	Feedback modulator
4–7	Reserved (must be set to 0)

Table 71.6 Coding feedback/link byte

The remaining 5 bytes are reserved for future extensions. If changes need to be made to an instrument, simply correct the relevant SBI file. The disadvantage of this format is that a separate file has to be loaded for each instrument.

72

Soundblaster Instrument Bank format (IBK)

To overcome the disadvantages of the SBI file, Creative Labs defined the Soundblaster Instrument Bank (IBK). This represents an extension to the SBI format and is capable of storing the data for several instruments.

An IBK file must always be 3204 bytes long and can define up to 128 instruments. The data is stored in Intel format.

Offset	Bytes	Remarks
00H	4	File ID (49H 42H 3BH 1AH)
04H	128*16	Instrument bank
804H	128*9	Instrument name

Table 72.1 Structure of a soundblaster instrument bank (IBK)

The first four bytes contain the signature 'IBK', followed by the character 1AH. This is followed by an area containing 128 blocks of 16 bytes each. These blocks contain the definitions of the instruments. The coding is the same as for the CMF *Instrument* block (*see* Chapter 70).

At offset 804H, there is an area for indexing the instrument names as ASCIIZ strings. Nine bytes are provided for each instrument. The names should be terminated with a null byte.

73

Creative Voice format (VOC)

As well as the CMF specification, Creative Labs, the developer of the Soundblaster cards, has defined other sound formats. One of the most widely distributed formats is the Creative voice format (VOC). While CMF files store the data in unpacked form, sound data can be packed in VOC format. This is possible because the Soundblaster cards can directly decode and output packed data.

A VOC file is used with the PC and contains the data in Intel format. The file consists of a header and a data area. The data area is divided into sub-blocks (CHUNKs) (Figure 73.1).

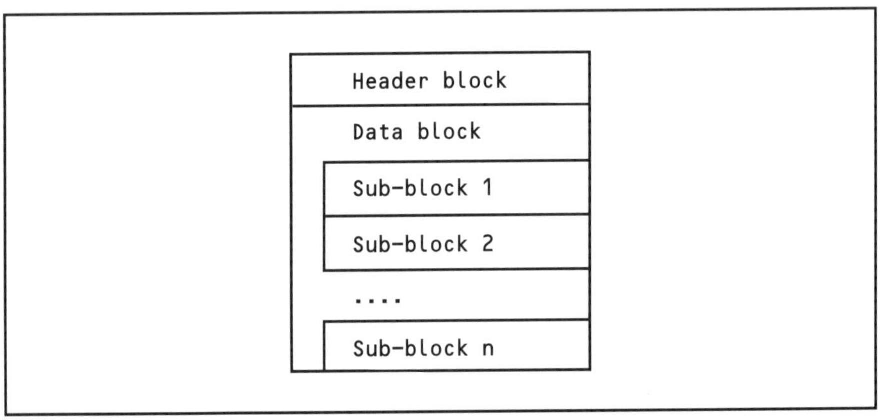

Figure 73.1 Structure of a VOC file

The header contains the identification code and the version number. The following data area is divided into sub-blocks with 9 different sub-types and contains the data in either coded or uncoded form.

73.1 VOC header

The header of a VOC file always contains 26 bytes and is structured as shown in Table 73.1:

Offset	Bytes	Remarks
00H	20	File ID
14H	2	Offset of sound data
16H	2	VOC version
18H	2	ID code version

Table 73.1 Structure of a VOC header

The first 20 bytes contain a signature. This is the string `Creative Voice File` to which the character `1AH` is appended. (The character `1AH` is used to denote the end of a file in MS-DOS.) There is a pointer at offset `14H`, indicating the beginning of the sound area. The value `1AH` is entered here because so far the header is of fixed size.

The two words at offsets `16H` and `18H` define the version number of the VOC format. The version is stored in BCD format at offset `16H`. For example, the entry `0AH 01H` (Intel format) indicates version 1.10. The word at offset `18H` contains the version number again in coded form, as an identification code. The two's complement of the preceding version number is added to the value `1233H`. In the case of version `010AH`, the ID code is calculated as `1233H – 010AH = 1129H`. The original version number can then be derived from: `1233H – 1129H`.

73.2 VOC data area

The header is followed by the data area of the VOC file. This data area is divided into various sub-blocks. There are 9 sub-blocks, each with a different structure. As far as I can determine, the 9th block has been defined as an extension block for future use.

The first byte of a sub-block contains the block type. With most blocks, this is followed by a 3-byte field containing the block length. The length of a block can be calculated from the three bytes as follows:

```
Len = Byte1 + 256*Byte2 + 65536*Byte3
```

The length of the block therefore relates to the length of the data area, that is, the first four bytes containing the block code and the block length are not included.

The actual data follows this length field. The VOC file always ends with a terminator block (type 0). The structure of the individual blocks is described below.

73.2.1 Terminator block (type 0)

This sub-block closes the VOC file. The length of a terminator block is just one byte. The block type is 00H.

73.2.2 Voice Data block (type 1)

This sub-block contains the sound data in the VOC file. The block is structured as shown in Table 73.2:

Offset	Bytes	Remarks
00H	1	Block type (01H)
01H	3	Block length
04H	1	Encoded sample rate
05H	1	Compression flag
06H	*n*	Sample data

Table 73.2 Structure of a Voice Data block (01H)

The byte containing the block type is followed by three bytes containing the block length. The sample rate is stored at offset 04H in coded form. This is necessary because only values from 0 to 255 can be represented in one byte. The byte at offset 04H therefore contains a time constant, which can be calculated from the sample rate as follows:

Time constant = 256 – (1000000/sample rate)

The sample rate can be expressed as:

Sample rate = 1000000/(256 – time constant)

A *Voice Data* block may contain packed or unpacked sample data. The byte at offset 05H contains compression information:

Code	Remarks
0	Unpacked 8 bits
1	Packed to 4 bits
2	Packed to 2.6 bits
3	Packed to 2 bits

Table 73.3 Packing code for VOC data

Code 0 indicates that the data is unpacked in 8 bits. Code 1 indicates 8 bits packed into 4 bits (2:1). With code 2, 8 bits are packed into 2.6 bits (3:1). With code 3, 8 bits are packed into 2 bits (4:1). The compression algorithm is designed in such a way that it filters out certain bits from the original sound data, which normally has to be sampled at 8 bits per sample. This results in a reduction in the number of bits, which leads to a loss in quality, because unpacking does not produce 8 bits. Unpacking is carried out by the Soundblaster chip. The actual voice data is stored at offset 06H in the format indicated.

73.2.3 Voice Continuation block (type 2)

Large-scale sound data cannot be stored in a *Voice Data* block because it is of limited length. For this reason, the *Voice Continuation* block was introduced. This block also contains sound data and is structured as follows:

Offset	Bytes	Remarks
00H	1	Block type (02H)
01H	3	Block length
04H	*n*	Sample data

Table 73.4 Structure of a Voice Continuation block (02H)

The byte containing the block type is followed by three bytes containing the length of the block. These are followed by the sample data. The coding is based on the preceding *Voice Data* block.

73.2.4 Silence block (type 3)

Rests in a piece of music are stored in the VOC file in a *Silence* block. This block is structured as shown in Table 73.5:

Offset	Bytes	Remarks
00H	1	Block type (03H)
01H	3	Block length
04H	2	Silence duration
06H	2	Sample rate

Table 73.5 Structure of a Silence block (03H)

The byte containing the block type is followed by three bytes containing the length of the block. These are followed by the value for the silence duration. The sample rate is indicated at offset 06H and stored in coded form as a time constant, as in the *Voice Data* block, except that the value is reduced by 1.

73.2.5 Marker block (type 4)

This sub-block is used for subdividing VOC files and is structured as follows:

Offset	Bytes	Remarks
00H	1	Block type (04H)
01H	3	Block length (02H)
04H	2	Marker number

Table 73.6 Structure of a Marker block (04H)

The byte containing the block type is followed by three bytes indicating the length of the block. In a *Marker* block, the block length is always set to 02H. The following word contains a number for the marker in the range between 1 and FFFEH. The values 0 and FFFFH are reserved. *Marker* blocks can be used for synchronization in the VOC file.

73.2.6 ASCII Text block (type 5)

This sub-block enables comment to be saved in VOC files as ASCII text. It is structured as shown below:

Offset	Bytes	Remarks
00H	1	Block type (05H)
01H	3	Block length
04H	*n*	ASCII string

Table 73.7 Structure of an ASCII Text block (05H)

The byte containing the block type is followed by three bytes containing the length of the block. The actual text, which should be terminated with a null byte 00H, is located at offset 04H.

73.2.7 Repeat Loop block (type 6)

This sub-block enables sequences of repetitions to be stored in the VOC file. A repetition sequence is introduced by a *Repeat Loop* block and terminated by an *End Repeat Loop* block. The blocks within this loop will then be repeated *n* + 1 times. The factor *n* is indicated in the *Repeat Loop* block.

Offset	Bytes	Remarks
00H	1	Block type (06H)
01H	3	Block length (02H)
04H	2	Repeat value – 1

Table 73.8 Structure of a Repeat Loop block (06H)

The byte containing the block type is followed by three bytes containing the length of the block. This is fixed at 02H. A word containing the repetition counter, which may be between 0 and 65,535, is located at offset 04H. Before starting a repetition sequence, this value should be increased by 1.

73.2.8 End Repeat Loop block (type 7)

This sub-block terminates a repetition sequence and is structured as follows:

Offset	Bytes	Remarks
00H	1	Block type (07H)
01H	3	Block length (00H)

Table 73.9 Structure of a End Repeat Loop block (07H)

The byte specifying the block type is followed by three bytes containing the length of the block. This is fixed at 00H.

73.2.9 Extended block (type 8)

This sub-block is not mentioned in most of the available documentation. It represents an extension of the type 1 sub-block. The purpose of the block is to declare a stereo sample. The

Extended block is therefore positioned immediately before the *Voice Data* block and is structured as follows:

Offset	Bytes	Remarks
00H	1	Block type (08H)
01H	3	Block length (04H)
04H	2	Time constant
06H	1	Compression code
07H	1	Mode (0: mono, 1: stereo)

Table 73.10 Structure of an Extended block (08H)

The byte specifying the block type is followed by three bytes indicating the length of the block. This is permanently set at 04H. A word containing the time constant is located at offset 04H. This constant occupies 2 bytes and in the case of mono-samples is generally derived from the sample rate on the basis of the following formula:

Mono time constant = 65532 – (256E**6/sample rate)

For stereo samples the frequency is halved:

Stereo time constant = (65532 – (256E**6/sample rate))/2

The sample rate can be calculated from the above data. The byte containing the compression factor is stored at offset 06H, coded as for sub-block 01H (*Voice Data*). The last byte in the extended block defines the mode of the following *Voice Data* block. The value 0 indicates mono-data, while stereo data is indicated by 1.

The *Voice Data* block, which necessarily follows the *Extended* block, contains the actual data. Here, the two fields for *Sample rate* and *Compression type* are ignored. With stereo data, the first value in the *Voice Data* block is used alternately for the left channel, the following value being used for the right channel.

74

Adlib Music format (ROL)

The company Adlib has defined its own format for storing sounds for Adlib cards. This file contains a header followed by blocks containing the descriptions of the music events. The data is stored in Intel format.

Figure 74.1 shows the structure of a ROL file.

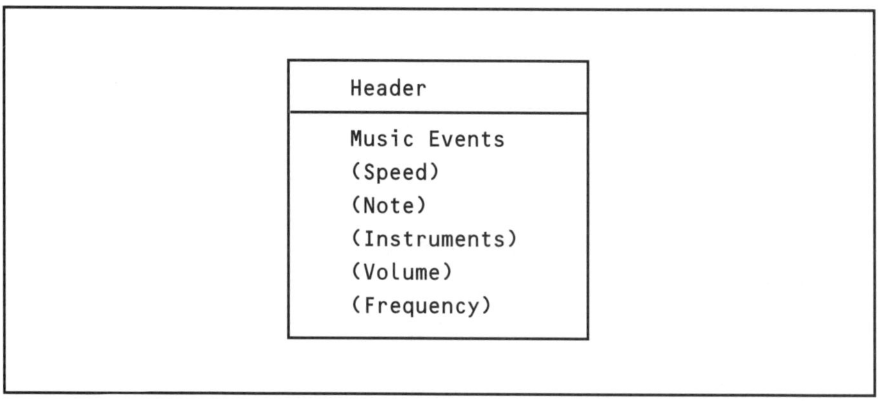

Figure 74.1 Structure of a ROL file

The header contains the identification code and the version number. The data area which follows is subdivided into events containing the description of the sound data.

74.1 ROL header

The header of a ROL file always contains `C9H` bytes and is structured according to Table 74.1.

Offset	Bytes	Remarks
00H	4	Format version
04H	40	Internal use
2CH	2	Timer ticks per 1/4 note
2EH	7	Used for visual composer
35H	1	Play mode 0: rhythm, 1: melody
36H	143	Internal use
C5H	4	Speed

Table 74.1 Structure of a ROL header

Most of the bytes of the header are used for internal purposes. The number of timer ticks per quarter note is defined at offset 2CH. The play mode is indicated at offset 35H. The last value (offset C5H) indicates the basic speed as a 4-byte floating point number.

74.2 ROL data area

The header is followed by the data area of the ROL file. This data area is divided into various sub-blocks, which are described below.

74.2.1 Tempo block

The initial block contains the tempo definitions in the data area. This block is of variable length and is structured as follows:

Offset	Bytes	Remarks
00H	2	Number of tempo events
02H	2	Length of tempo event
04H	4	Tempo multiplier
...	...	repeat last 2 fields

Table 74.2 Structure of the Tempo area

The first word indicates the number of *Tempo* events in this area. For each *Tempo* event, the area contains two fields containing the length (offset 02H) and the tempo, respectively. The length of an event is given in timer ticks. The tempo is defined as a 4-byte floating point number. This value is multiplied by the basic tempo setting to produce the tempo for the associated event.

74.2.2 Note block

The *Tempo* block is followed by the *Note* block, which is structured as follows:

Offset	Bytes	Remarks
00H	15	Internal use
0FH	2	Length of all notes
11H	2	Note
13H	2	Note length
...	...	repeat last 2 fields

Table 74.3 Structure of a Note area

The first 15 bytes of this block are reserved for internal use. The byte at offset 0FH defines the length of all notes in timer ticks. At offset 11H there is a word containing the value of the note. Before output to the driver, this value must be reduced by 60. The value 0 represents silence. The word at offset 13H indicates the length of the note in timer ticks. The two fields for the note and the length are repeated until the total length for all notes is reached.

74.2.3 Instrument block

The *Note* area is followed by a block containing the instrument definitions. This block is structured as shown below:

Offset	Bytes	Remarks
00H	15	Internal use
0FH	2	Number of instrument events
11H	2	Length of instrument event
13H	9	Instrument name
1CH	3	Internal use
...	...	repeat last 3 fields

Table 74.4 Structure of an Instrument area

The first 15 bytes are reserved for internal purposes. They are followed by a word indicating the number of following entries (number of instrument events). Three fields are stored for each instrument event. The first field (word) defines the length of the instrument event in timer ticks. The following 9 bytes contain the name of the instrument as a string, which should be terminated with a null byte. The last three bytes are reserved for internal use. This structure is repeated *n* times.

74.2.4 Volume block

This block defines the volume. It is structured as follows:

Offset	Bytes	Remarks
00H	15	Internal use
0FH	2	Number of volume events
11H	2	Length of volume event
13H	4	Volume shift
...	...	repeat last 2 fields

Table 74.5 Structure of a Volume area

The first 15 bytes are reserved. They are followed by a word containing the number of events entered. Each event comprises 6 bytes. The first byte indicates the length of the volume event in timer ticks. The following four bytes contain a floating point number indicating the change in volume. These fields are repeated for every event.

74.2.5 Frequency block

The last block in the ROL file defines the pitch (frequency) and is structured as follows:

Offset	Bytes	Remarks
00H	15	Internal use
0FH	2	Number of frequency events
11H	2	Length of frequency event
13H	4	Frequency shift
...	...	repeat last 2 fields

Table 74.6 Structure of a Frequency block

The first 15 bytes are reserved for internal purposes. They are followed by a word containing the number of frequency events. The individual events each contain 6 bytes: a word indicating the length of the pitch event in timer ticks and a 4-byte floating point number indicating the change in frequency (pitch). These two fields are repeated for every event.

75

Adlib Instrument Bank format (BNK)

In *addition to the ROL format, another format can be used for storing instrument descriptions. The BNK files store the instrument descriptions in a similar manner to Soundblaster files.*

The format of a BNK file is shown below:

Offset	Bytes	Remarks
00H	2	Format version
02H	6	Signature 'ADLIB'
08H	2	Number of instruments used
0AH	2	Number of instruments stored
0CH	4	Start of address instrument names
10H	4	Start of address instrument data
14H	8	Reserved
1AH	n*18	Instrument name list
..H	n*33	Instrument data list

Table 75.1 Structure of a BNK file

The first word contains the version number followed by the signature 'ADLIB'. The number of instruments used is given at offset 08H. This is followed by a word indicating the number of instruments defined. This value is important for calculating the lengths of the instrument tables. The following two 4-byte fields contain pointers to the start of the instrument name and instrument data tables.

75.1 Instrument name list

The list of instrument names contains *n* entries of 18 bytes each structured as follows:

Bytes	Remarks
2	Instrument index
1	Instrument data exists (0 no, 1 yes)
14+1	Instrument name

Table 75.2
Entry in Instrument name list

The first word contains the index for the instrument. The start of the associated data area in the data table can be calculated from this:

Offset = Start address + 28 * Index

The following byte indicates whether the data table contains values for the instrument (1 = yes). The instrument name should be entered as an ASCIIZ string and may occupy up to 14 characters.

75.2 Instrument data list

The list containing instrument data contains *n* entries of 33 bytes each, structured as follows:

Bytes	Remarks
1	Instrument type (0 melody, 1 rhythm)
1	Instrument number if rhythm
29	Instrument data
1	Modulator type sine wave
1	Carrier type sine wave

Table 75.3
Entry in Instrument data list

The first byte contains the instrument type (0 melodic, 1 rhythmic). In the case of rhythmic instruments, the instrument number is indicated in the next byte. The area containing the instrument data is 29 bytes long, but its structure is not documented. The last two bytes of an entry define the type of the modulator and the carrier.

76

AMIGA MOD format

***This** format was originally defined by Commodore for the Amiga computer. It has subsequently been adopted for other platforms, including the PC.*

The MOD format stores both digital data and notes, and belongs to the group of Soundtracker formats. The individual notes of an instrument are listed digitally and the musical composition is described in terms of individual notes and their duration. This enables an extremely good approximation to the sound of an instrument, but also keeps the files compact. The structure of a MOD file is divided into three blocks (Figure 76.1):

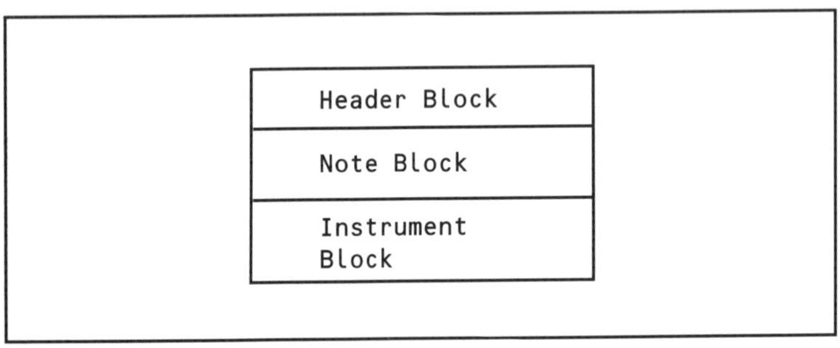

Figure 76.1
Structure of a MOD file

The header contains general information such as the name of the composition or the name of the instrument. The header is followed by the notes of the musical composition. The third block contains the digitized instrument data.

Unfortunately, a number of variants have begun to appear, each exhibiting minor structural differences. The older versions of MOD operate with up to 15 instruments. In one extended version, up to 31 instruments can be used.

In MOD format, the data is always stored in Motorola format. Length data in the MOD format is indicated in words, that is, a length in bytes is always double the value indicated.

76.1 MOD header

The header is structured as shown in Table 76.1:

Offset	Bytes	Remarks
00H	20	Sound track name
14H	22	Name of first instrument
2AH	2	Length of first instrument data area
2CH	1	Instrument calibration
2DH	1	Instrument volume
2EH	2	Instrument echo
30H	2	Echo length
..H		Next instrument

Table 76.1 Structure of a MOD header

The first 20 bytes of a MOD file contain the name of the musical composition. This name must be terminated with a null byte.

At offset 14H, the definitions of individual instruments begin. Each definition contains 30 bytes. The first 22 bytes contain the name of the instrument as an ASCII string. These are followed by a word which defines the length of the instrument data area. This area contains the digitized instrument data and is located at the end of the file. The length is indicated in words, that is, the value should be doubled to derive the length in bytes. In the following byte, only the lower 4 bits are used. This value is interpreted as a signed number (-8 .. 7) and is used for tuning the instrument. The next byte defines the volume in the lowest 6 bits. The MOD format can repeat sections of the digitized format as often as required in order to create effects such as reverberation and echo. The next word indicates the offset from the beginning of the instrument data at which the repetition begins. The word following this defines the length of the loop (in words).

This 30-byte area is repeated for every instrument. MOD may define 15 or 31 instruments. The distinction can only be determined by analyzing the area from byte ..470(1D6H). If there is an instrument name (ASCIIZ string) here, 31 instruments are present. Otherwise, the note area begins from this offset.

76.2 Note block

The header is followed by the area containing the notes. In the case of MOD files with 31 instruments, the first byte begins at offset 3B6H. With files containing 15 instruments, the offset is 1D6H. The structure of the note area is shown in Table 76.2.

Offset	Bytes	Remarks
00H	1	Pattern number
01H	1	(internal use by Amiga)
02H	128	Pattern area
..H	4	MOD file ID
..H	1024	Note area
..H	..	Next pattern area

Table 76.2 Structure of the Note area

The first byte indicates the number of the pattern used in this musical composition. At offset 02H, there is a 128-byte long area (pattern area) which contains the performance sequence of the following pattern of notes. Each entry can represent values between 0 and 63. The next four bytes specify an identification code for the MOD file. This can contain various values (for example, 'M.K.' or 'FLT4').

This initial section is followed by several 1024-byte areas containing the actual notes. The sequence in which these notes are performed is specified in the 128-byte pattern area. The number of areas is defined in the first byte of the note area.

The individual notes are coded in 4 bytes (32 bits) in a 1024-byte area. This gives 256 notes per block, which is subdivided into 64 blocks of 4 notes each. Since MOD files recognize four channels, each block contains the relevant notes for these channels. The first entry relates to channel 1 and is followed by the notes for channels 2, 3 and 4. The next block then begins with the note for channel 1.

76.3 Instrument data area

The music area is followed by the area containing digitized instrument data. This section contains the uncompressed, sequentially listed data for each instrument.

The length of this area may vary from instrument to instrument. The relevant lengths are indicated in the header of the MOD file.

The notes in the music area have a special coding: originally, only the lowest 4 of the 32 bits were used for specifying the instrument. However, after the MOD file structure was extended to 31 instruments, these 4 bits were no longer adequate. There are consequently two different structures for the notes in the two MOD file variants.

Bits	Remarks
0-3	Pitch
4-15	—
16-19	Instrument number
20-23	Adjective (effect)
24-31	Parameter for adjective

Table 76.3 Structure of a note in MOD files with 15 instruments

A somewhat modified structure is used for coding note values in MOD files with 31 instruments.

Bits	Remarks
0-3	Upper half byte instrument number
4-15	Pitch
16-19	Lower half byte instrument number
20-23	Adjective (effect)
24-31	Parameter for adjective

Table 76.4 Structure of a note in MOD files with 31 instruments

An adjective for the creation of an effect can be allocated to each note via bits 20-23. Up to 16 different adjectives are possible. Bits 24 to 31 are used for parameters. In the case of adjectives with two parameters, the lower four bits define the first parameter, and the upper four bits define the second parameter. With a single parameter, the adjective uses all 8 bits. The structure for adjectives is as follows:

0 **Arpeggio**: This adjective creates a three note chord (arpeggio) and has two parameters. The first parameter (bits 24-27) indicates the leap to the second pitch in semitone steps. The second parameter defines the leap to the third pitch in semitone steps.

1 **Portamento Up**: This adjective increases the frequency of a note while it is being played. The increase is defined by one parameter.

2 **Portamento Down**: This adjective lowers the frequency of a note while it is being played, at the speed indicated in the parameter.

3 **Portamento to Note**: Drags the pitch towards a given note. The parameter indicates the number of semitone steps to the desired note.

4 **Vibrato**: This adjective has two parameters which set the speed and strength of the vibrato effect. The vibrato effect alters the frequency while maintaining a constant

amplitude. The first parameter defines how quickly the pitch is to change (duration of each vibration). The second parameter defines the variation in pitch (frequency).

10 **Tremolo**: This adjective also has two parameters which make the note louder or softer. The amplitude of the note is increased or decreased. If the first parameter is 0, the amplitude will be decreased (softer) as parameter 2 increases; if the second parameter is 0, the amplitude increases at the rate defined in parameter 1.

11 **Jump**: Interrupts the current note and branches to another pattern. The target of the jump is indicated in parameter 1, in the range 0–127.

12 **Volume Note**: This adjective has one parameter which indicates the volume of the note, in the range 0–63.

13 **Next Pattern**: Ends the current note and branches to the next pattern. The parameter must be set to 0.

15 **Speed**: This attribute contains one parameter giving the speed of performance, in the range 0–31.

The MOD files can be processed using the above definitions.

77

AMIGA IFF format

This *format was also defined for the Amiga Computer; however, its use on other platforms is rare.*

On such computers, the IFF format is used for the storage of graphics, texts and sound. On the PC, it is essentially the graphics section which has been adopted.

The IFF format comprises a header, followed by individual CHUNKs describing the data. 8SVX CHUNKs are used for storing sounds. A description of the IFF format with the relevant CHUNKs can be found in Chapter 25, Interchange file format.

78

Audio IFF format (AIFF)

This *is a variant of the IFF format which is used on Apple computers. The AIFC specification (also known as AIFF-C) is an extended variant which is capable of storing compressed data. A description of AIFF CHUNKs is given in Chapter 25, Interchange file format.*

79

Windows WAV format

***This** format represents one of the realizations of the Resource Interchange Format (RIFF) proposed by Microsoft. The RIFF format is a format container, in which various data such as graphics, sound, and so on, can be packed. The RIFF files are divided into CHUNKs as in the IFF format. These CHUNKs determine the content of the data.*

Figure 79.1 shows the structure of a RIFF file:

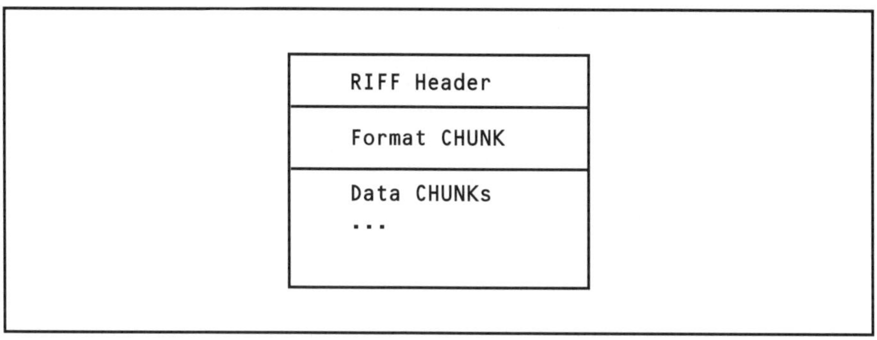

Figure 79.1
Structure of a WAV file

Each CHUNK is introduced by a 4-byte identification which is followed by a 4-byte field containing the length of the CHUNK. This is followed by a variable number of parameters. Since the RIFF format organizes data by word, a CHUNK containing an odd number of bytes must be padded with a null byte (pad byte). However, it should be noted that this pad byte is not included in the length. RIFF files store the data in (little-endian) Intel format.

79.1 WAV header

The header of a WAV file begins with a RIFF CHUNK structured as shown below:

Offset	Bytes	Remarks
00H	4	CHUNK name 'RIFF'
04H	4	CHUNK length
08H	4	RIFF type 'WAVE'

Table 79.1 Structure of a WAV header

The first four bytes of the WAV file contain the RIFF signature, which is simply the four letters 'RIFF'. This is followed by a 4-byte field containing the length of the header. The header is terminated with another 4-byte field, indicating the type of the file. For WAV files, the entry here is 'WAVE', thereby establishing the following CHUNKs as WAV CHUNKs.

79.2 FMT CHUNK

The header is followed by the format CHUNK, which is structured as follows:

Offset	Bytes	Remarks
00H	4	CHUNK name 'FMT'
04H	4	CHUNK length (10H)
08H	2	Format type 0: Mono 1: Stereo
0AH	2	Channel numbers
0CH	4	Sample rate (in Hertz)
10H	4	Bytes per second
14H	2	Bytes per sample 1 = 8 bit mono 2 = 8 bit stereo or 16 bit mono 4 = 16 bit stereo
16H	2	Bits per sample

Table 79.2 Structure of an FMT CHUNK

The first 4 bytes of the FMT CHUNK contain the signature 'FMT'. This is followed by a 4-byte field indicating the length of the CHUNK. The following word defines the sampling format (1 = mono, 2 = stereo).

The next fields define the number of channels used, the sampling rate in Hertz and the number of bytes per second required. The number of bytes per sample can vary between 1 (mono) and 4 (16 bit stereo). The last field defines the number of bits per sample (8, 12 or 16).

The following data CHUNK can be read on the basis of this information.

79.3 DATA CHUNK

The actual sound data follows the FMT CHUNK and is stored in a DATA CHUNK which is structured as follows:

Offset	Bytes	Remarks
00H	4	CHUNK name 'data'
04H	4	CHUNK length
08H	*n*	Data area

Table 79.3 Structure of a DATA CHUNK

The first 4 bytes of the DATA CHUNK contain the signature 'data'. This is followed by a 4-byte field indicating the length of the data area. In RIFF files, the DATA CHUNKs always have the same structure, that is, the data area always follows the length data. Interpretation of the data is governed by the preceding FMT CHUNK. With sound files, the data is indexed sequentially. For each sample, *n* bits have to be read. With an 8-bit mono sample, the data should be read and output byte by byte. With stereo samples, the values are stored alternately for the left and right channels.

! **With WAV files, there is generally only one DATA CHUNK. However, it is possible to arrange several CHUNKs one after the other, in which case several DATA CHUNKs may occur.**

80

Standard MIDI format (SMF)

The *development of the MIDI file format is due to the efforts of the two major keyboard manufacturers Roland and Sequential Circuit, who defined a standard for synthesizer interfaces in 1984. This standard is currently in general use for linking devices and is known as the MIDI interface. In order to exchange data sampled with these devices between different systems, a file format was also defined. The Standard MIDI file format (SMF) is now available for various platforms and MIDI files can be exchanged without conversion. Under Windows, for example, this format is used in MIDI files.*

The format is based to a considerable extent on the MIDI commands for communication with other devices, and data is stored in the form of events. The structure of MIDI files is based on the IFF format. A MIDI file consists of several blocks called CHUNKs (Figure 80.1).

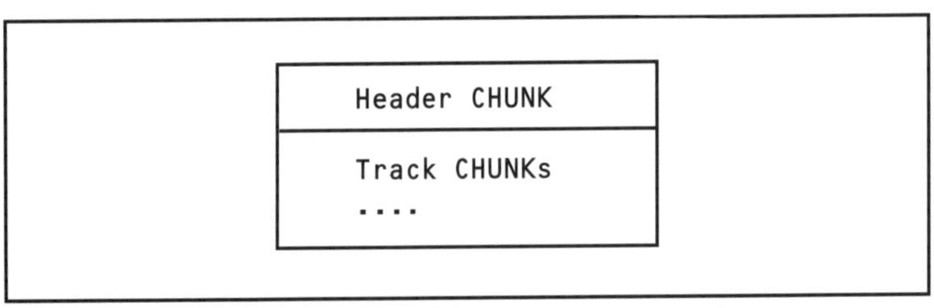

Figure 80.1
Structure of a MIDI file

These CHUNKs are read and interpreted sequentially. The data in MIDI files is stored in (big-endian) Motorola format. There are currently only two CHUNKs for MIDI files, a header CHUNK and the track CHUNK which contains the sound data.

80.1 MIDI Header CHUNK

The header CHUNK of a `MIDI` file has a fixed structure as shown in Table 80.1:

Offset	Bytes	Remarks
00H	4	File ID (4DH 54H 68H 64H)
04H	4	CHUNK length
08H	2	SMF type (0,1,2)
0AH	2	Number of tracks
0CH	2	Time format

Table 80.1 Structure of a MIDI header CHUNK

The first four bytes of a MIDI file contain the signature 'MThd', a certain indication that a file is a MIDI file. At offset 04H, there is a four-byte value indicating the length of the header. In MIDI version 1.0, this length is fixed at 00H 00H 00H 06H, that is, the data area of the header contains 6 bytes.

The next two bytes indicate the type of the `MIDI` file. In version 1.0, three different MIDI types are defined.

0 The Type 0 MIDI file contains only the data from one sound track. This MIDI type can be used if, for example, only one instrument is being sampled.

1 Type 1 is the most commonly used MIDI variant. It enables several independent tracks to be stored. Different instruments can be sampled in different tracks, which considerably simplifies follow-up processing. The number of tracks is indicated in the header.

2 Type 2 is another MIDI variant with several tracks. These tracks, however, do not represent separate instrument channels. They contain complete sections of a musical composition. These sections do not necessarily belong to the same piece of music.

The number of tracks (and also the number of data blocks) is stored at offset 0AH. With type 0 files, the value is always set to 1. The last word in the header CHUNK defines the time format used in the track CHUNK. Here, there are two options:

- The output speed can be defined in ticks per quarter note. This measurement is usual with sequencers that subdivide a quarter note (crotchet) into ticks. The more ticks per quarter note used, the better the time resolution will be.
- The other alternative is used for dubbing in film and video technology. In this context, the sounds relate to particular images or sequences. One frame indicates the number of pictures per second. A subframe defines $^1/_{100}$ frames. An SMPTE time code is used as the time format.

The distinction between the time systems used is made via bit 15 of the last word in the header. If this bit is set to 1, the MIDI format is based on the SMPTE time code. This format subdivides time from the start of a picture sequence into:

Hours:minutes:seconds:frames:subframes

The number of frames (pictures per second) is dependent on the video standard used (24, 25, 30 and 30-drop frames). Drop frames enable synchronization with the US NTSC standard, which uses exactly 29.97 pictures per second. At the beginning of each minute, the SMPTE system simply omits two frames, thereby compensating for the extra lines of the US standard.

If bit 15 is set, bits 8 to 14 indicate the frame number of the Time System. The value -29 corresponds to the correction value of 30-drop frames. Bits 0 to 7 define the number of subframes ($^1/_{100}$ pictures per second).

If bit 15 is unset, the tick method will be used. The tempo or the rate of rhythmic cycles is stored not in the header but in the tracks. If this information is not entered, the default settings are tempo = 120 and rhythm = 4/4.

80.2 Track CHUNK

The header CHUNK is followed by the track CHUNKs. These exhibit the usual structure for CHUNKs (Table 80.2).

Offset	Bytes	Remarks
00H	4	CHUNK ID (4DH 54H 72H 6BH)
04H	4	CHUNK length
08H	*n*	Data area

Table 80.2 Structure of a Track CHUNK

The first four bytes of a track CHUNK contain the signature 'MTrk'. This is followed by the 4-byte field indicating the length of the parameter area. This area is of variable length and contains the data for one track.

This data consists of a sequence of commands for the output of sounds and for control purposes. In accordance with MIDI specifications, the commands are called events. In addition to MIDI events, meta-events may also occur in this area.

Before each event, there must be a *Delta time* value, defining the time interval until the execution of the next event. If there is to be no waiting time, *Delta time* should be set to 0.

80.3 Structure of a Delta time command

A *Delta time* entry consists of a record of variable length, coded as shown in Figure 80.2:

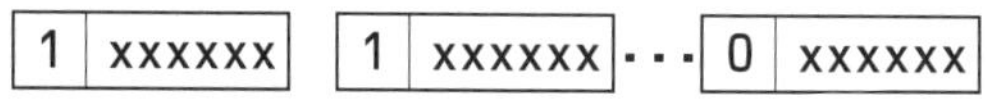

Figure 80.2 Structure of a Delta time value

The delay time is divided into 7-bit parcels and stored in individual bytes. Since the length varies with the size of the *Delta time* value, bit 7 is used as an end marker. In the first bytes, bit 7 is set to 1. Only in the last byte of the value is bit 7 = 0. In this way, the *Delta time* can be built up from several bytes and decoded without difficulty. The uppermost bit of the bytes read must be ignored, that is, the remaining bits of the individual bytes should be closed up.

The value determined in this way indicates the duration of the pause (rest) in the time format. If the time format used is *Ticks per second*, the *Delta time* should be divided by *Ticks per quarter*. With the SMPTE time system, the *Delta time* is related to the *Delta frames* of the time code.

80.4 Commands of the Track CHUNK

The data area of the Track CHUNK contains *Delta time* entries and event records alternately. A distinction is made here between MIDI events, system-exclusive events and meta-events. The structure of these event records is described below. The MIDI specification recognizes the MIDI events defined in Table 80.3:

Code	Data bytes	Remarks
Channel Mode messages		
8xH	2	Note off
9xH	2	Note on
AxH	2	Aftertouch (polyphonic)
BxH	2	Controller
CxH	1	Program change
DxH	1	Aftertouch (monophonic)
ExH	2	Pitch wheel

Table 80.3 MIDI commands (*continues over...*)

Code	Data bytes	Remarks
System Mode messages		
F8H	0	Timer
FAH	0	Start
FBH	0	Songstart continue
FCH	0	Stop
FEH	0	Active sensing
FFH	0	System reset
F2H	2	Song pointer
F3H	1	Song select
F6H	0	Tune
F0H		System exclusive
F7H	0	End of exclusive

Table 80.3 MIDI commands (*cont.*)

The value x in the command codes represents the channel number. For example, commands that begin with the codes 90H to 9FH switch on a note. This note will continue until it is switched off again with codes in the range 80H–8FH. Since there must be a pause between events, this generally indicates the length of the note. The channel associated with the note is indicated in the lower four bits of the code. 92H, for instance, switches on the note in channel 3. The values 0 to 0FH represent the instrument channels 1 to 16.

80.5 MIDI events

This group includes the individual MIDI commands for communication between devices. These commands are stored in the file in a 1:1 relationship with their parameters.

80.5.1 Note on

The Note on command contains 3 bytes with the following structure:

1 byte event code (9xH)
1 byte note number (0..127)
1 byte dynamics (0..127)

Table 80.4 Structure of a Note on command

The first byte is used for the event code 9xH and contains the number of the MIDI channel in the lower 4 bits (for example, 90H = MIDI channel 1).

The code for the note (pitch) is indicated in the second byte, where the range of values is 0–127. The individual notes are coded as shown in Table 80.5:

Code	Frequency(Hz)	Note	Octave
15H	27.500	A”	Subcontra-octave
16H	29.135	A sharp”	
17H	30.868	B”	
18H	32.703	C’	Contra-octave
19H	34.648	C sharp’	
1AH	36.708	D’	
1BH	38.891	D sharp’	
1CH	41.203	E’	
1DH	43.654	F’	
1EH	46.249	F sharp’	
1FH	48.999	G’	
20H	51.913	G sharp’	
21H	55.000	A’	
22H	58.270	A sharp’	
23H	61.735	B’	
24H	65.406	C	Great octave
25H	69.296	C sharp	
26H	73.416	D	
27H	77.782	D sharp	
28H	82.407	E	
29H	87.307	F	
2AH	92.499	F sharp	
2BH	97.999	G	
2CH	103.826	G sharp	
2DH	110.000	A	
2EH	116.541	A sharp	
2FH	123.471	B	
30H	130.813	c	Small octave
31H	138.591	c sharp	
32H	146.832	d	
33H	155.536	d sharp	
34H	164.814	e	
35H	174.614	f	
36H	184.997	f sharp	
37H	195.998	g	

Table 80.5
MIDI Note codes
(continues over...)

Sound

Sound

Code	Frequency(Hz)	Note	Octave
38H	207.652	g sharp	
39H	220.000	a	
3AH	233.082	a sharp	
3BH	246.942	b	
3CH	261.626	c'	One line octave
3DH	277.183	c sharp'	
3EH	293.665	d'	
3FH	311.127	d sharp'	
40H	329.628	e'	
41H	349.228	f'	
42H	369.994	f sharp'	
43H	391.995	g'	
44H	415.305	g sharp'	
45H	440.000	a'	
46H	466.164	a sharp'	
47H	493.883	b'	
48H	523.251	c"	Two line octave
49H	554.365	c sharp"	
4AH	587.330	d"	
4BH	622.254	d sharp"	
4CH	659.255	e"	
4DH	698.456	f"	
4EH	739.989	f sharp"	
4FH	783.991	g"	
50H	830.609	g sharp"	
51H	880.000	a"	
52H	932.328	a sharp"	
53H	987.767	b"	
54H	1046.502	c3	Three line octave
55H	1108.731	c sharp3	
56H	1174.659	d3	
57H	1244.508	d sharp3	
58H	1318.510	e3	
59H	1396.913	f3	
5AH	1479.978	f sharp3	
5BH	1567.982	g3	
5CH	1661.219	g sharp3	
5DH	1760.000	a3	
5EH	1864.655	a sharp3	
5FH	1975.533	b3	

Table 80.5
MIDI Note codes (*cont.*)

Code	Frequency(Hz)	Note	Octave
60H	2093.005	c4	Four line octave
61H	2217.461	c sharp4	
62H	2349.318	d4	
63H	2489.016	d sharp4	
64H	2637.020	e4	
65H	2793.826	f4	
66H	2959.955	f sharp4	
67H	3135.963	g4	
68H	3322.438	g sharp4	
69H	3520.000	a4	
6AH	3729.310	a sharp4	
6BH	3951.066	b4	

Table 80.5
MIDI Note codes (*cont.*)

The third byte defines the volume (amplitude) and the rise in the envelope curve (velocity or dynamics) of the note. The way in which this information is used depends on the device. This value can also be interpreted as the speed of attack of the instrument (for example, the piano). Synthesizers that do not support this function have the value `64` in this byte. The value `0` indicates that the note has no dynamics, that is, it is played but cannot be heard. In practical terms, this corresponds to the following command `Note off`.

80.5.2 Note off

The `Note off` command contains 3 bytes with the following structure:

1 byte event code (`8xH`)
1 byte note number (`0..127`)
1 byte dynamic parameter (`0..127`)

Table 80.6
Structure of a `Note off` command

The first byte is used for the event code, where `x` represents the number of the MIDI channel in the lower four bits. The second byte defines the note to be switched off. With polyphonic instruments, individual notes on the synthesizer can be switched off. The third parameter indicates the dynamics at the end of the note.

80.5.3 Polyphonic Key Pressure Aftertouch

This command can be used for Master Keyboards and with certain synthesizers that support this instruction. The command contains 3 bytes and is structured as follows:

1 byte event code (`AxH`)
1 byte key number (`0..127`)
1 byte pressure (`0..127`)

Table 80.7 Structure of a `Polyphonic Key Pressure Aftertouch` command

The first byte is used for the event code, where `x` represents the number of the MIDI channel in the lower 4 bits. The second byte defines the key pressed and the third parameter represents the pressure on the key pressed.

80.5.4 Channel Pressure Aftertouch

This command has the same function as `Polyphonic Key Pressure`. It is structured as follows.

1 byte event code (`DxH`)
1 byte pressure (`0..127`)

Table 80.8 Structure of a `Channel Pressure Aftertouch` command

The first byte is used for the event code, where `x` represents the number of the MIDI channel in the lower 4 bits. The second byte defines the pressure. Since there is no reference to the keys, this command applies to all keys pressed.

80.5.5 Control commands

In addition to the events described, the MIDI format also supports control commands, with which, for example, distortion factors can be set.

80.5.5.1 Pitch Wheel Change

This command alters the control of the pitch wheel. It is structured as follows:

1 byte event code (`ExH`)
1 byte wheel fine pitch (`0..127`)
1 byte wheel coarse pitch (`0..127`)

Table 80.9 Structure of a `Pitch Wheel Change` command

The first byte is used for the event code, where `x` represents the number of the MIDI channel in the lower bits. The two bytes containing the parameters each contain 7 bits and are combined to form a 14-bit value. The first parameter defines the fine setting (wheel fine) the lower part of the number. The second parameter contains the coarse setting (wheel coarse). The alteration of pitch relates to the average value, that is, the first parameter is set to `0` and the second parameter to `64`.

80.5.5.2 Control Change

This command is used for changing various control functions. It is structured as follows:

1 byte event code (`BxH`)
1 byte control (`0..127`)
1 byte value (`0..127`)

Table 80.10 Structure of a `Control Change` command

The first byte is used for the event code, where `x` represents the number of the MIDI channel in the lower bits. The next two bytes contain the code for the controller and the setting for this controller. Table 80.11 shows the definition of these codes:

Coarse-tune	Fine-tune	Controller
1	33	Modulation wheel
2	34	Breath controller
4	36	Foot pedal controller
5	37	Portamento time
6	38	Data entry
7	39	Main volume
64	—	Hold pedal
65	—	Portamento
66	—	Sustain pedal
67	—	Soft pedal
96	—	Data increment
97	—	Data decrement

Table 80.11 MIDI controller numbers

The first column (coarse-tune) indicates the usual controller number for coarse-tuning the controller. The second column contains the controller number for fine tuning. The value for the setting is given by the second parameter of the command.

The adjustment of pitch was formerly carried out via the codes 0 and 32. This function is now controlled by the pitch wheel.

The coarse-tuning of the controller is always implemented via codes 0 to 31, and the fine-tuning via codes 32 to 63. The codes 64 to 93 relate to switches. The codes from 96 to 121 have so far not been allocated to any device. Codes 122 to 127 contain information on operating modes.

80.5.6 MIDI Operating Mode commands

Codes 122 to 127 enable various modes to be set. The possible commands are summarized below.

80.5.6.1 Local control

This command is used for altering various control functions. Its structure is shown in Table 80.12:

1 byte event code (BxH)
1 byte code (7AH)
1 byte value (0: remote, 127: local)

Table 80.12 Local control command

The device control can be switched to the MIDI interface with the hex code sequence Bx7Azz (value zz = 0). This setting can be reversed with value zz = 127.

80.5.6.2 All notes off

This command switches off all notes in an active channel.

1 byte event code (BxH)
1 byte code (7BH)
1 byte value (0)

Table 80.13 All notes off command

The second data byte must be set to 0.

80.5.6.3 Omni mode off

This command is used for switching off the *Omni mode* of a device.

1 byte event code (BxH)
1 byte code (7CH)
1 byte value (0)

Table 80.14 Omni mode off command

80.5.6.4 Omni mode on

This command is used for switching on the *Omni mode* of a device.

1 byte event code (BxH)
1 byte code (7DH)
1 byte value (0)

Table 80.15 Omni mode on command

80.5.6.5 Monomode on, Polymode off

This command is used for switching on the *Monomode* of a device. The *Polymode* is automatically switched off.

1 byte event code (BxH)
1 byte code (7EH)
1 byte value (0yH)

Table 80.16 Monomode on command

The number of channels used is stored in the lowest four bits (y) of the third byte. The value 0 switches all channels.

Sound

80.5.6.6 Monomode off, Polymode on

This command is used for switching off the *Monomode* of a device. The *Polymode* is automatically switched on.

1 byte event code (BxH)
1 byte code (7FH)
1 byte value (00H)

Table 80.17 Monomode off command

The third byte is always likely to contain the value 00H.

80.5.7 MIDI Program commands

The MIDI format provides various commands for programming synthesizer channels. This enables different tone colours to be specified, depending on the allocation of a channel to a given instrument. The command is structured as follows:

1 byte event code (CxH)
1 byte program (0..127)

Table 80.18 Structure of a Program Instrument event

The command is introduced with the event code CxH. The character x represents the channel number. The second byte is used for the program number. Values between 0 and 7FH can be entered here.

80.5.8 MIDI Timing commands

These commands are used for the real-time control of MIDI devices. They consist of one byte containing the command code.

F8H Timing Clock: This command may occur directly after another command and is used for time synchronization of various MIDI devices.

FAH Start: This command is used for returning the *Song Position Pointer* to the current sequence.

FCH Stop: The current sequence is interrupted via this command, but the *Song Position Pointer* retains its position.

`FBH` `Continue`: When this command appears, the sequence is continued after the `Timing clock` command has been issued.

`FEH` `Active Sensing`: This command is used for monitoring the link to the MIDI system.

`FFH` `System Reset`: This command resets the instruments to their basic settings.

Codes `F9H` and `FDH` are not currently used.

80.5.9 MIDI System Common Commands

This group of commands enables the *Song Position Pointer*, the selection of songs, and so on, to be changed. The following commands have been defined.

80.5.9.1 Song Position Pointer

Switches the *Song Position Pointer* to another device. The record is structured as follows:

1 byte event code (`F2H`)
1 byte 1st data byte (`0..127`)
1 byte 2nd data byte (`0..127`)

Table 80.19 Song Position Pointer structure

The first data byte contains the lower 7 bits of the pointer; the second data byte contains the upper 7 bits.

80.5.9.2 Song Select

This command defines the sequences to be played and is structured as shown below:

1 byte event code (`F3H`)
1 byte data byte (`0..127`)

Table 80.20 Song Select structure

The data byte defines one of the 127 available sequences.

80.5.9.3 Tune Request

This command enables the re-calibration of analog synthesizers. It consists of one byte with the value F6H.

80.5.10 End Of System Exclusive (EOX)

This command also has only one command byte (F7H). The command indicates the end of a *System exclusive* sequence.

80.5.11 System Exclusive Commands (SOX)

This command enables new functions which are not covered by the MIDI definition to be integrated into a device. The sequence is structured as follows:

1 byte event code (F0H)
n byte length
n byte data byte sequence (0..127)
1 byte EOX command

Table 80.21 System Exclusive structure

The sequence begins with the event code F0H. As an extension to the MIDI commands, a length indication (1 to *n* bytes) is added. The length coding is carried out in a similar way to the Delta time procedure, that is, in the first length bytes, bit 7 = 1. The last length byte contains the value 0 in bit 7. Only 7 bits of each length byte are therefore used for the length.

The length is followed by *n* data bytes, whose meaning is determined by the relevant manufacturer. The values may be between 0 and 127.

The end of a *System Exclusive* sequence is defined by the EOX command (*see above*). The only exception is when time codes are inserted into the sequence for synchronization. In this case, the first part of the sequence does not end with the EOX command. Only the last part is terminated with EOX.

80.5.12 Real Time System Exclusive Command

The command enables the transfer of special formats within the *System Exclusive* commands. For example, the information is used for transferring SMPTE time codes. The command has two possible formats.

80.5.12.1 Long Format

This command consists of 7 data bytes and the EOX code (F7H) in the last byte. The coding is as follows:

1 byte event code (F0H)
n byte length
1 byte status (7FH)
1 byte long (02H)
1 byte hours (0..23)
1 byte minutes (0..59)
1 byte seconds (0..59)
1 byte type and frame
1 byte EOX code (F7H)

Table 80.22 Long Format structure

The last data byte contains the frame number in bits 0 to 4. Bits 5 and 6 define the frame type:

Value	Frame Type
0	24 frames/s
1	25 frames/s
2	30 frames/s, drop frame
3	30 frames/s, non-drop frame

Table 80.23 Frame type

80.5.12.2 Short Format

This command consists of 5 data bytes and the EOX code (F7H) in the last byte. The coding is as follows:

1 byte event code (F0H)
n byte length
1 byte status (7FH)
1 byte short (01H)
1 byte seconds (0..59)
1 byte type and frame
1 byte EOX code (F7H)

Table 80.24 Short Format structure

The last data byte contains the frame number in bits 0 to 4. Bits 5 and 6 define the frame type according to Table 80.23.

80.5.13 Universal System Exclusive

This command enables communication between MIDI devices. The command consists of a variable number of bytes (F0 <len> 7E xx xx...), which are terminated with an EOX command (F7H). The first data byte contains the channel number and the following byte contains the ID number of the device (01H Dump Header, 02H Data Packet, 03H Dump Request, 7CH Wait, 7DH Cancel, 7EH NAK, 7FH ACK). However, the transfer of data is device-specific and the structure will not be presented here.

80.6 Meta events

In addition to the MIDI commands described above, the MIDI format also recognizes a number of supplementary records. These are known as meta-events. All meta-events begin with the command code FFH, followed by an event ID code.

1 byte meta event (FFH)
1 byte event ID
n byte length
n byte data

Table 80.25 Meta-event structure

The length is coded according to the *Delta time* procedure, that is, the first length bytes contain bit 7 = 1. The last length byte has bit 7 = 0. The lower 7 bits of the length bytes are concentrated to give the length. Meta-events are described below.

80.6.1 Sequence number (00)

This event enables Patterns or Tracks to be numbered. The following code sequence applies:

```
FFH 00H 02H <number>
```

The number is coded as a word. This event is useful with SMF type 2 in order to bring the tracks into the correct sequence. The Sequence number must occupy the first position in the track; the preceding *Delta time* contains the value 00H.

80.6.2 Text (01)

This event is used for storing text. It is formatted as follows:

```
FFH 01H <len> <text>
```

The text length field 'len' is stored in the time code format. Thus the field may have a variable length.

80.6.3 Copyright note (02)

This event is used for copyright text, and is structured as shown below:

```
FFH 02H <len> <text>
```

The text contains the manufacturer's or composer's copyright notice and the date.

80.6.4 Sequence/Track name (03)

This event enables a name to be allocated to a sequence or track. The following code sequence applies:

```
FFH 03H <len> <text>
```

It should be remembered that many sequencers process only 8-character track names.

80.6.5 Instrument Name (04)

This meta-event is used to specify an instrument name. The following code sequence applies:

```
FFH 04H <len> <text>
```

The instrument type of the relevant track is defined as a string. The name should be limited to 8 characters.

80.6.6 Lyric (05)

The text of the song can be stored in this meta-event. The code sequence is:

```
FFH 05H <len> <text>
```

The length is indicated in bytes. Texts are normally allocated to music by syllable.

80.6.7 Marker (06)

This meta-event enables certain places in the MIDI file to be marked. The code sequence is:

```
FFH 06H <len> <text>
```

The text can be displayed during the processing of the MIDI file.

80.6.8 Cue point (07)

This meta-event is used in dubbing videos and films. The code sequence is:

```
FFH 07H <len> <text>
```

The text can indicate the relationship between important visual action and a given sound. Using this meta-event it is a simple matter to cue a certain region when dubbing.

80.6.9 Channel prefix (32)

This meta-event establishes the channel to which subsequent meta-events refer. The code sequence is shown below:

```
FFH 20H 01H <channel>
```

The channel number (`channel`) comprises one byte and its value must be in the range `0-15`. The command is useful in conjunction with meta-events 03 and 04. The channel allocation remains valid until the next meta-event 32 or until the next MIDI event.

80.6.10 End of track (47)

This event marks the end of a track. The following code sequence applies:

```
FFH 2FH 00H
```

This event must occur at the end of every track.

80.6.11 Set Tempo (81)

This meta-event indicates a new tempo. The code sequence is:

```
FFH 51H 03H <tempo>
```

The tempo field comprises three bytes. The value is interpreted as the duration of a quarter note in micro-seconds. The sequence:

bpm = (1000/tempo) * 60

enables the value of *Beats per minute* to be calculated.

80.6.12 SMPTE offset (84)

This meta-event defines an offset for an SMPTE time indication:

```
FFH 54H 05H <hour> <minutes> <seconds> <frames> <subframes>
```

The event determines the time at which a track is to be played. It must be positioned before the first MIDI event in the track. The *Delta time* indication before this event is always set to `0`.

80.6.13 Time signature (88)

This event establishes the type of rhythm.

```
FFH 58H 04H <nominator> <denominator> <clock> <count>
```

The `nominator` contains a value relating to the fraction of the number of beats. The `denominator` is defined as an exponent on base 2 (for example, 7/3 = 7/8 time). The clock field indicates the number of clock ticks per quarter note. The beat (for example, metronome) is set according to this time. The count field indicates how many 1/32 notes are to follow each quarter note. The standard entry here is 8 (1/4 note).

80.6.14 Key signature (89)

This meta-event indicates the key of the song.

```
FFH 59H 02H <sign> <key>
```

If the sign is positive (bit 7 = `0`), a sharp key is indicated, while bit 7 = `1` indicates a flat key. The lower 4 bits in the sign field indicate the number of key signs (`0` major, `1` minor). The sequence `FFH 59H 02H F3H 00H` therefore specifies a major key with three key signs (flats, in this case): three flats = E flat major.

80.6.15 Sequencer specific (127)

This meta-event is used for the transfer of system specific information. The code sequence is:

```
FFH 7FH <len> <events>
```

The `len` field is coded according to the time code, that is, the first bytes contain bit `7 = 1` and the last byte bit `7 = 0`. The events are then coded specifically.

The complete specifications of the MIDI format have been published by the MIDI Association (5316 W 57th Street, Los Angeles, California 90056, USA) in the book *MIDI File Specification*.

81

NeXt/Sun Audio format

The *NeXt Audio File Format is used in the UNIX context. This format begins with a header which is followed by a Sound structure.*

The header is structured as follows:

Offset	Bytes	Remarks
00H	4	Signature '.snd'
04H	4	Data location
08H	4	Data size
0CH	4	Data format
10H	4	Sampling rate
14H	4	Channel count
18H	n	Char info

Table 81.1 NeXt/Sun Audio File Header

The header consists of 4-byte fields in Motorola format. The first field contains the signature 2EH 73H 6EH 64H, which corresponds to '.snd'. This is followed by a pointer to the region containing the audio data. The length of the data area in bytes is defined at offset 08H. The 32-bit field at offset 0CH defines the format in which the audio data is stored. Table 81.2 contains the format codes for the audio data.

Format	Remarks
1	8 bit mu-law
2	8 bit linear
3	16 bit linear
4	24 bit linear
5	32 bit linear
6	Floating point
7	Double precision
8	Fragmented sampled data
9	—
10	DSP program
11	8 bit fixed point
12	16 bit fixed point
13	24 bit fixed point
14	32 bit fixed point
15	—
16	Non-audio display data
17	—
18	16 bit linear with emphasis
19	16 bit linear with compression
20	Combine 18 and 19
21	Music kit DSP commands
22	—

Table 81.2 Codes for data format

If code `10` occurs, the data area contains loadable program codes for the Digital Signal Processor (DSP loadable code).

It is standard for the audio data to be filed as a linear sequence in the data area. When processing audio data, sections can be removed, that is, the sequence is no longer continuous (fragmented). This is indicated with format code `8`. Fragmented areas are divided into blocks with their own header (as shown in Table 81.1). The block is terminated with the code `00H`.

PART 7

Page description languages

File formats discussed in Part 7

In *addition to file formats, a number of page description languages have been developed as "quasi-standard....." for output devices (printers and plotters). The Hewlett Packard Graphic Language (HP-GL) for plotters had already achieved significant distribution by 1976. Since HP defined HP-GL/2 as its successor, more and more manufacturers have come to support this format for exchanging graphic data. Part 7 describes language definitions for the well-established PostScript, PCL and HP-GL/2 languages .*

82

Hewlett Packard Graphic Language (HP-GL/2)

***The** language uses ASCII characters for the description of character operations. Each command begins with what is known as a mnemo-technical character (mnemonic), consisting of two upper- or lower-case letters, followed by several parameters. Separators (commas and/or blanks) are used between these parameters. A separator between the command and the first parameter is not absolutely necessary, but can be inserted to improve readability. A number of parameters are optional, but if one of the optional parameters is omitted, the following parameters must also be omitted.*

Figure 82.1 shows several valid commands together with their basic structure:

```
XX<param.>...<sep.><param>;

PDPU10,20  or  PD;PU10,20;   or  PD PU 10 20;
```

Figure 82.1 HP-GL/2 commands

Each instruction is terminated with a semicolon or the next keyword. When using an HP-IB interface, LF is also accepted as a terminator. However, for reasons of legibility, it is advisable always to use the semicolon as a terminator. Optional CR/LF characters inserted for text formatting are ignored. To keep the length of HP-GL/2 commands to a minimum, all superfluous characters are removed in the specification. With a few exceptions, a semicolon is no longer necessary as a terminator and even the separators between mnemonics and the first parameter can be omitted.

Numeric values in the command should be transferred as an ASCII string, and various number formats for parameters have been defined. Integer values must be in the range -2^{23} till + $(2^{23}-1)$.

There is also the *clamped integer type*, for integers in the range –32,767 to +32,767. In the case of decimal numbers, the whole number part must be in the integer range, and 5 places are permitted after the decimal point. The decimal point may be omitted if there are no decimal places in the number. By contrast, with *clamped real format*, values must be in the range –32767.9999 to +32767.9999. If there is no sign before a number, it will be interpreted as positive. Character strings are also permitted as parameters.

As a result of this notation, HP-GL/2 files can be readily transferred between computers and stored in files. In the command descriptions below, command parameters enclosed in round brackets ( ) are optional.

The language comprises various commands divided into groups. The HP-GL/2 kernel, the core of the language, contains 55 commands, which must be supported by all devices (Table 82.1). Additional groups of commands (*Technical Graphics Extension*, *Palette Extension*, *Dual Context Extension*, *Digitizing Extension*) are device-specific and are not supported by all units.

Configuration and Status Group
Set Default Values
Initialize
Input P1 and P2
Input Relative
Input Window
Advance Full Page
Rotate Coordinate System
Replot
Scale
Vector Group
Arc Absolute
Arc Relative
Absolute Arc Tree Point
Circle
Plot Absolute
Pen Down
Polyline Encoded
Plot Relative
Pen Up
Relative Arc Tree Point
Polygon Group
Edge Rectangle Absolute
Edge Rectangle Relative
Edge Wedge
Edge Polygon

Table 82.1 Breakdown of HP-GL/2 command groups (*continues over...*)

Fill Polygon
Polygon Mode
Fill Rectangle Absolute
Fill Rectangle Relative
Fill Wedge
Line and Fill Attributes Group
Anchor Corner
Fill Type
Line Attributes
Line Type
Pen Width
Raster Fill
Symbol Mode
Select Pen
User-Defined Line Type
Pen Width Unit Selection
Character Group
Alternate Font Definition
Character Fill Mode
Character Plot
Absolute Direction
Relative Direction
Define Label Terminator
Define Variable Text Path
Extra Space
Label
Label Origin
Select Alternate Font
Standard Font Definition
Absolute Character Size
Character Slant
Relative Character Size
Select Standard Font
Transparent Data
Technical Graphics Group
Begin Plot
Chord Tolerance Mode
Download Character
Enable Cutter
Frame Advance

Table 82.1 Breakdown of HP-GL/2 command groups (*cont.*)

Merge Control
Message
Media Type
Not Ready
Output Error
Output Hard-Clip Limits
Output Identification
Output P1 and P2
Output Status
Plot Size
Quality Level
Sort
Velocity Select
Palette Extension
Set Color Range for Relative Color Data
Number of Pens
Pen Color Assignment
Screened Vectors
Transparency Mode
Dual Context Extension
Enter PCL Mode
Reset
Primary Font Selection by ID
Secondary Font Selection by ID
Scalable or Bitmap Fonts
Digitizing Extensions
Digitize Clear
Digitize Point
Output Digitized Position and Pen Status

Table 82.1 Breakdown of HP-GL/2 command groups (*cont.*)

As can be seen from Table 82.1, the kernel is divided into groups. These are described below.

82.1 Configuration and Status Group

This group includes all kernel commands for implementing the basic setting of the output device.

82.1.1 Set Default Values

Command Set Default Values

Format `DF(;)`

Function Resets the values for `SC`, `AD`, `CF`, `DI`, `DT`, `DV`, `ES`, `FT`, `IW`, `LA`, `LO1`, `LT`, `PA`, `PM`, `RF`, `SC`, `SD`, `SI`, `SL`, `SM`, `SS`, `TD`, `UL` to the default values. The position of the scaling points `P1` and `P2`, the current pen, plotting size and rotation are not altered. The error status is also retained. The semicolon as separator in this command can be omitted if it is followed by another command.

82.1.2 Initialize

Command Initialize

Format `IN (n;)`

Function Initializes all programmable plot functions to their standard values. The error status is deleted. The command may optionally have the value `1`, which will initialize the factory-set values. The separator is also optional.

82.1.3 Input P1 and P2

Command Input P1 and P2

Format `IP P1x, P1y (,P2x, P2y;)`

Function Enables activation or resetting of the scaling points set. The parameters should be given as integers. Plotters have two scaling points (`P1` bottom left corner, `P2` top right corner). It is standard for these to be predetermined by the hardware. If these parameters are not entered, the points defined by the hardware will be used. The points are adapted accordingly in the case of a rotated output. The commands `IW`, `RO`, `SC`, `FT`, `LT`, `PW`, `WU`, `DR`, `LB` and `SR` relate to the input points `P1` and `P2`.

82.1.4 Input Relative

Command Input Relative

Format `IR P1x, P1y (,P2x, P2y;)`

Function Activates new scaling points or the values set. The parameters should be given as integers and they indicate the position of the points relative to the *hard-clip limits* pre-set by the device. The coordinate data for point 2 is optional. The commands `IW`, `RO`, `SC`, `FT`, `LT`, `PW`, `WU`, `DR`, `LB` and `SR` relate to the input points `P1` and `P2`.

82.1.5 Input Window

Command Input Window

Format `IW x1, y1, x2, y2(;)`

Function Sets a rectangular window for the output. The pen can then only draw inside the window (*soft clipping*). The coordinates for the two diagonally positioned points should be given as integers. If the parameters are omitted, the *hard-clip limits* determined by the hardware will be adopted. If the window is outside the character area of the device, no output will be made.

82.1.6 Advance Full Page

Command Advance Full Page

Format `PG (n);`

Function Implements a page-feed. The command must be terminated with a semicolon unless it is followed by an `RP` instruction. Optionally, a parameter `n` can be entered, specifying the page number after which the command will be carried out. With no parameter, a page feed will only be activated if the current page has just been drawn on. This command does not operate on devices with a PCL interface; an `FF` should be entered in PCL mode. The command affects the `PS`, `RP` and `BP` instructions.

82.1.7 Rotate Coordinate System

Command Rotate Coordinate System

Format `RO (angle;)`

Function Causes the coordinate system of the output unit to rotate through 90, 180 or 270 degrees, counterclockwise. The values `0`, `90`, `180` and `270` are thus permitted for the `angle` parameter. If the parameter is omitted, the output device will restore the angle of rotation to 0 degrees. Several requests using the same angle do not alter the angle of rotation because the values are not cumulative. The scaling points `P1` and `P2` are rotated together with the coordinate system.

82.1.8 Replot

Command Replot

Format `RP (n);`

Function Enables several copies of a plot to be made. The optional parameter `n` determines the number of copies. If this parameter is not entered, only one copy will be produced. However, the plotting instructions must still be in the buffer. The instruction must be terminated with a semicolon.

82.1.9 Scale

Command Scale

Format `SC Xmin, Xmax, Ymin, Ymax (, type, left, bottom;)`

Function Defines a user-specific coordinate system for the graphic output. The scaling is related to the points `P1` and `P2`. The `Xmin`, `Xmax`, `Ymin` and `Ymax` parameters should be transferred as floating point values. They represent the scaling of the X- and Y-axes. The optional `type` parameter can be used to determine whether the scaling is to be carried out *isotropically* or *anisotropically*. With anisotropic scaling (`type = 0`), the X- and Y-axes may have different scales. With isotropic scaling (`type = 1`), the X- and Y-axes have the same dimensions. The third setting (`type = 2`) is used for transferring the user-specific scaling to the output device. In this case, the `Xmax` and `Ymax` parameters contain the scaling factors for the corresponding axes. The optional `left` and `bottom` parameters indicate the size of the proportion of unused character area at the left and bottom margin, in the case of isotropic scaling. The values must be transferred as floating point numbers (0.01...1.00 for 0–100%)

82.2 Vector Group

This group contains the kernel commands for drawing vector graphics.

82.2.1 Arc Absolute

Command Arc Absolute

Format `AA x,y,arc(,chord angle;)`

Function This command is used for drawing an arc around a given *center point* `x`, `y`. The radius is calculated from the distance of the current point from the given center. The `arc` parameter indicates the angle of the arc. The sign of the parameter determines the direction in which the arc will be drawn: counterclockwise with positive values; clockwise with negative values. The optional `chord angle` parameter is used to indicate the resolution of the circle (the default is 5 degrees). This parameter determines how accurately a circle is to be drawn by joining together short straight-line sections (vectors). All parameters should be transferred as *clamped real values*. The coordinates are interpreted in the current scaling.

82.2.2 Arc Relative

Command Arc Relative

Format `AR dx,dy,arc(,chord angle;)`

Function This command is used for drawing an arc around a *center point* whose distance from the current coordinates is given by `dx`, `dy`. The radius is calculated from the distance `dx`, `dy`. The `arc` parameter indicates the angle of the arc. As with the arc absolute command, the sign of the parameter determines the direction in which the arc will be drawn. The optional `chord angle` parameter is used to indicate the resolution of the circle. All parameters should be entered as *clamped real values*.

82.2.3 Absolute Arc Tree Point

Command Absolute Arc Tree Point

Format `AT Xint, Yint, Xend, Yend(, chord angle;)`

Function Enables the output of a segment of a circle with absolute coordinate data. The arc is drawn from the current *pen position* around the *intermediate* point indicated by `Xint`, `Yint`. The end-point of the arc should be entered in absolute coordinates with the `Xend` and `Yend` parameters. The optional `chord angle` parameter determines the resolution of the arc.

82.2.4 Circle

Command Circle

Format `CI r (,chord angle;)`

Function Draw a circle with radius `r` around the current point. The optional `chord angle` parameter defines the resolution at which the circle will be constructed from straight vectors. The default setting for this value is 5 degrees. The parameters should be entered as *clamped real values*.

82.2.5 Plot Absolute

Command Plot Absolute

Format `PA X, Y (,...;)`

Function Causes the pen to move to the position indicated. If the `X` and `Y` parameters are missing, the command will relate to the following instructions. It is possible to enter more than one coordinate point. In this case, all points are approached consecutively, thereby enabling more complex line drawings to be achieved very simply.

82.2.6 Pen Down

Command Pen Down

Format `PD X, Y (,...;)`

Function Ensures that the pen begins drawing when operating with the plotter. If *XY*-coordinates are entered as parameters, the pen will move to these points. The command interprets the coordinate data as either absolute or relative, depending on whether it has been preceded by a `PA` or a `PR` command. The default setting assumes absolute coordinate data.

82.2.7 Polyline Encoded

Command Polyline Encoded

Format `PE (flag)(value)/(X,Y)...(flag)(value)/(X,Y);`

Function Draws a line in the current mode between the points entered. If no parameters are entered, the carriage return point is set. The parameter `flag` contains ASCII characters and specifies the mode in which the plotter is to interpret the following values:

Mode	Meaning
:	Select Pen
<	Pen Up
>	Fractional Data
=	Absolute Data
7	7-Bit Mode

Optional values can be transferred after the flag. `Flag = :` is followed by the number of the color pen to be selected. `Flag = <` lifts the pen and moves it to the next point indicated. The value `flag = >` signals that the following parameter indicates the number of binary places after the decimal point in the coordinates. `Flag = =` indicates absolute coordinates. In 7-bit mode, all coordinates are transferred as 7-bit characters. The coordinates are transferred as binary numbers based on 64 or 32.

82.2.8 Plot Relative

Command Plot Relative

Format `PR X, Y(,...;)`

Function Moves the pen from the current point to the coordinates. If the parameters are missing, the coordinate data in the following command is interpreted as relative values. If *X,Y* parameters are entered, the pen is moved to these coordinate points. Several points can be entered in one command.

82.2.9 Pen Up

Command Pen Up

Format `PU X,Y(,...;)`

Function Lifts the pen and – if coordinates are entered at the same time – moves it to the points indicated. Several points may be specified. If *symbol mode* (SM) is set, the symbol specified will be displayed at each point in the output.

82.2.10 Relative Arc Tree Point

Command Relative Arc Tree Point

Format `RT Xint, Yint, Xinc, Yinc(, chord angle;)`

Function Enables the output of a segment of a circle with relative coordinate data. The arc is drawn from the current *pen position* around the *intermediate* point given by `Xint` and `Yint`. The end-point of the arc should be given as relative coordinates using the *Xinc* and *Yinc* parameters. The optional `chord angle` parameter determines the resolution of the arc.

82.3 Polygon Group

These kernel commands affect the polygon buffer of the HP-GL/2 output device which is responsible for drawing polygons.

82.3.1 Edge Rectangle Absolute

Command Edge Rectangle Absolute

Format `EA X, Y(;)`

Function Defines a rectangle in terms of two opposite, absolute corner coordinates. One corner point is at the current coordinates, while the diagonally opposite corner point is indicated by the *X*, *Y* coordinates.

82.3.2 Edge Rectangle Relative

Command Edge Rectangle Relative

Format `ER X, Y(;)`

Function Defines a rectangle in terms of two opposite, relative corner coordinates. One corner point is at the current coordinates, while the diagonally opposite corner point is indicated by the *X*, *Y* coordinates, relative to the current point.

82.3.3 Edge Wedge

Command Edge Wedge

Format `EW radius, start angle, sweep angle (, chord tol.;)`

Function This command is used for the creation of pie-graphs. The parameters, which must be transferred as decimal numbers, indicate the radius of the circle and the segment via the two angles.

82.3.4 Edge Polygon

Command Edge Polygon

Format `EP(;)`

Function This command enables polygons to be drawn; their coordinates will have been written to the polygon buffer via `PM`, `RA`, `RR` and `WG`.

82.3.5 Fill Polygon

Command Fill Polygon

Format `FP(;)`

Function Fills a polygon in the polygon buffer with a pattern or a color.

82.3.6 Polygon Mode

Command Polygon Mode

Format `PM poly def(;)`

Function Enables the definition of a polygon. If the parameter is not present, the polygon buffer will be deleted. The values `0`, `1` and `2` which determine the following polygon mode can be used for the `poly def` parameter. The value `0` deletes the polygon buffer and sets polygon mode. The polygon buffer can then be filled using instructions such as `AA`, `AR`, `AT`, `PA`, `PD`, `PE`, `PR`, `PU` or `RT`. The polygon buffer is closed using the value `1` and is then ready for output. The value `2` terminates the current polygon and ends polygon mode.

82.3.7 Fill Rectangle Absolute

Command Fill Rectangle Absolute

Format `RA X, Y(;)`

Function Defines a filled rectangle with absolute coordinates. One corner is in the current output position, while the diagonally opposite corner is defined by the coordinates *X*, *Y*. By contrast with the `EA` instruction, this `RA` instruction produces a filled rectangle.

82.3.8 Fill Rectangle Relative

Command Fill Rectangle Relative

Format `RR X, Y(;)`

Function Defines a filled rectangle with relative coordinates. One corner is at the current output position; the diagonally opposite corner is defined by the coordinates X,Y.

82.3.9 Fill Wedge

Command Fill Wedge

Format `WG radius, start angle, end angle(,chord angle;)`

Function Enables the output of a filled segment of a circle. The radius, start and end angles should be entered as parameters. The center is at the current output position. The resolution of the curve can be indicated using the optional `chord angle` parameter. This command is used for printing pie-graphs.

82.4 Line and Fill Attributes Group

This group of kernel commands is used to select various types of line attribute and patterns for filling enclosed shapes.

82.4.1 Anchor Corner

Command Anchor Corner

Format `AC X,Y(;)`

Function Defines the start point from which a fill attribute begins. If the parameters are not entered, the start point is set at (0,0).

82.4.2 Fill Type

Command Fill Type

Format `FT type (,option1, option2;)`

Function Selects the shading pattern used to fill polygons (six variants are defined for the fill type):

Variant	Fill attribute	Option 1	Option 2
1	Solid bidirectional	-	-
2	Solid unidirectional	-	-
3	Parallel lines (hatched)	spacing	angle
4	Cross-hatching	spacing	angle
10	Shading	shading level	-
11	User-defined	raster fill index	pen

The optional parameters enable the angle, the spacing for hatching and the degree of shading to be adjusted. For fill types 3 and 4, option 1 specifies the distance between the lines in the fill. This distance is measured in the current units measured along the X-axis (default 1% of the diagonal distance between P1 to P2).

PDLs

82.4.3 Line Attributes

Command Line Attributes

Format `LA kind, value(,kind, value...;)`

Function Establishes the appearance of line ends, line joins and miters. The `kind` parameter defines the mode to which the following value relates:

`kind = 1`	line ends
`2`	line joins
`3`	miter limit

`Value` determines the appearance of the line. Further details of relevant forms can be obtained from the appropriate plotter manuals.

82.4.4 Line Type

Command Line Type

Format `LT pattern number (,pattern length, mode;)`

Function Defines the appearance of lines in terms of 8 adaptable and 8 fixed line types. If the (integer) value of `pattern number` is negative an adaptable line type will be selected. The optional length should be entered as a floating point number. The `mode` parameter enables the user to select whether the line attribute is to be given in absolute terms in millimeters (`mode = 1`) or in relative terms as a percentage (`mode = 0`).

82.4.5 Pen Width

Command Pen Width

Format `PW width(, pen;)`

Function Establishes the drawing width of the current pen or the pen indicated.

82.4.6 Raster Fill

Command Raster Fill

Format `RF index(,width, height, pen number,...;)`

Function Defines a rectangular pattern which can be used when filling enclosed shapes. If the parameter is not entered, a default fill attribute will be used. Customized patterns can be defined using this command. The `index` parameter allocates a number to the pattern so that only the index is required in future to call up the pattern. The optional `width` and `height` parameters specify the dimensions of the pattern in pixels. These values should be entered as multiples of 2 in the range 8–64. The `pen number` parameter enables the pattern to be allocated to one or more pens.

82.4.7 Symbol Mode

Command Symbol Mode

Format `SM char(;)`

Function Displays the given `char` symbol at every XY-point indicated, if the commands `PA`, `PD`, `PE`, `PR` and `PU` are used next. If the parameter is not entered, the last symbol is deleted.

82.4.8 Select Pen

Command Select Pen

Format `SP pen number(;)`

Function Selects the pen according to the number indicated. If no parameter is entered, pen number `0` will be selected.

82.4.9 User-Defined Line Type

Command User-Defined Line Type

Format `UL index(,gap1,...,gapn;)`

Function Enables the definition of user-specific line types. The `index` parameter allocates a number to each type. The line can be called up at a later stage using this index. The optional `gapx` parameters specify the pattern. The even parameters (`gap2`, `gap4`, ...) denote intervals with no line drawn. Up to 20 of these gaps can be defined.

82.4.10 Pen Width Unit Selection

Command Pen Width Unit Selection

Format `WU type(;)`

Function Specifies how the `PW` (*pen width*) parameter is to be interpreted. With `type = 0`, the `PW` parameter is interpreted in millimeters; `type = 1` indicates a relative percentage.

82.5 Character Group

This group of kernel commands enables various character sets to be selected, displayed in various directions, and so on.

82.5.1 Alternate Font Definition

Command Alternate Font Definition

Format `AD kind, value...(,kind, value;)`

Function Enables the definition of alternative fonts, including *font spacing*, *pitch*, *height*, *stroke weight* and *type face*. If no parameters are entered, the command will set the default font. The `kind` parameter specifies the attributes and should be entered as a *clamped integer* (1...7). Depending on the value of `kind`, the corresponding attribute is set according to the floating point value parameter. Further details can be obtained from the documentation for the relevant output device.

82.5.2 Character Fill Mode

Command Character Fill Mode

Format `CF fill mode(,edge pen;)`

Function Specifies how *outline fonts* are to be framed and defines the fill attribute for bitmap and stick fonts. A request without parameters will set the default font with filled characters. The `fill mode` parameter defines the way in which a character is to be displayed:

Mode	Fill Attribute
0	Solid fill with current pen
1	Outline font
2	Use current fill attribute but do not draw outline
3	Use current fill attribute and draw outline

The `edge pen` parameter specifies the pen number with which the outlines of the letters are to be drawn. If the integer parameter is missing, the current pen will be used.

82.5.3 Character Plot

Command Character Plot

Format `CP (c, l;)`

Function Shifts the pen to the *return point*, if no parameter is specified. The optional `c` parameter enables the pen to be shifted by *n* characters within the line. The pen is shifted by *n* lines with the `l` parameter.

82.5.4 Absolute Direction

Command Absolute Direction

Format `DI dx,dy(;)`

Function Defines the slope at which labels (text) are drawn, starting from the current point in the direction of the vector given by `dx`, `dy`. The default setting for horizontal display direction is (1,0). Values are indicated as absolute coordinates. The direction must be defined by a `DI` command.

82.5.5 Relative Direction

Command Relative Direction

Format `DR dx,dy(;)`

Function Defines the slope and direction for a label (text) to be displayed, in terms of `dx` and `dy`. The parameters refer to a point relative to the current position. The values `dx` and `dy` are therefore given as a percentage of `P2X` and `P2Y`.

82.5.6 Define Label Terminator

Command Define Label Terminator

Format `DT label terminator(,mode);`

Function Specifies the end marker for texts. All characters are allowed except `0`, `LF`, `ESC` and `;` (the semicolon is needed as a terminator for the command). A request with no parameters will set `ETX` as the terminator. The optional `mode` parameter enables the user to specify whether the terminator is to be displayed (`mode = 0`) or suppressed (`mode = 1`).

82.5.7 Define Variable Text Path

Command Define Variable Text Path

Format `DV path(,line;)`

Function Specifies the direction of a text path and the direction in which a `CR/LF` is to be implemented. The integer parameter `path` contains one of the following output angles, at which the text will be displayed:

Path	Angle
0	0 degrees
1	–90 degrees
2	–180 degrees
3	–270 degrees .

PDLs

A `CR/LF` will then be carried out in the direction indicated. The optional `line` parameter specifies the position of a character in terms of the preceding character. The same values apply as in the case of `path`.

82.5.8 Extra Space

Command	Extra Space
Format	`ES spaces(,lines;)`
Function	Adjusts the spacing between characters and lines in the output of text, without influencing the size of the characters. The `spaces` parameter determines the distance between two characters in a line, while the optional `lines` parameter defines the space between lines.

82.5.9 Label

Command	Label
Format	`LB string<term>;`
Function	Displays a text which is terminated with the terminator `<term>`, defined via `DT`. The parameters set for font, size and color are adopted; the text may contain up to 256 characters (including the terminator). The text output begins at the current position in the output direction set.

82.5.10 Label Origin

Command	Label Origin
Format	`LO position number(;)`
Function	Indicates the text position relative to the current position of the pen. Nineteen positions are defined.

82.5.11 Select Alternate Font

Command	Select Alternate Font
Format	`SA(;)`
Function	Selects an alternative font defined by the command `AD`. The default setting is *Roman 8*.

82.5.12 Standard Font Definition

Command	Standard Font Definition
Format	`SD kind, value...(,kind, value;)`
Function	Enables the definition of the standard font, including *font spacing*, *pitch*, *height*, *stroke weight* and *type face*. If there are no parameters, the command sets the default font. The kind parameter specifies the attributes and should be entered as a

clamped integer (1...7). Depending on the value of `kind`, the corresponding attribute is set according to the floating point value parameter. Further details can be obtained from the documentation for the relevant output device.

82.5.13 Absolute Character Size

Command Absolute Character Size

Format `SI width, height(;)`

Function Specifies the size of a character to be displayed, in centimeters. The parameters should be entered as integers. If the parameters are missing, the default setting will be adopted. The width in centimeters is indicated in the `width` parameter and the height in centimeters in the `height` parameter.

82.5.14 Character Slant

Command Character Slant

Format `SL tangent of angle(;)`

Function Defines the angle (*slant*) through which a letter is rotated in the output. This enables italic fonts to be created. A request with no parameters restores the angle to 0. Positive and negative gradients can be indicated as floating point values.

82.5.15 Relative Character Size

Command Relative Character Size

Format `SR width, height(;)`

Function Specifies the size of a character to be displayed as a percentage related to the points `P1` and `P2`. The parameters must be entered as integers. With no specified parameters, the default setting (0.75%, 1.5%) is adopted. `Width` defines the character width, `height` the character height; each value is specified as a percentage.

82.5.16 Select Standard Font

Command Select Standard Font

Format `SS(;)`

Function Exchanges the currently set font for the character set defined as the Standard Font.

82.5.17 Transparent Data

Command Transparent Data

Format `TD (mode;)`

Function Specifies the treatment of control characters in texts. The optional `mode` parameter selects the normal mode (value = `0`) in which the control characters will be interpreted. The value `mode = 1` sets the *Transparent Mode* in which the characters will be displayed. A request with no parameters will set the normal mode.

82.6 Technical Graphics Extension

In addition to the 55 commands of the HP-GL/2 core, there are machine-specific extensions which are not always available. One such extension is the *Technical Graphics Extension* which contains the following commands:

82.6.1 Begin Plot

Command	Begin Plot
Format	`BP (kind, value,...;)`
Function	Switches the plotter on, enabling it to begin a new printout. The optional `kind` parameter should be an integer in the range `1–4`. Further information can be obtained from the documentation for the relevant device.

82.6.2 Chord Tolerance Mode

Command	Chord Tolerance Mode
Format	`CT mode(;)`
Function	Selects the *chord tolerance* for the commands `AA`, `AR`, `CI`, `EW` and `WG`. Circles and curved areas are produced by the output device in the form of short straight vectors. The chord tolerance determines how many vectors will be used, for example, to create a circle. The fewer vectors used, the more angular the circle will appear. The standard setting for *chord tolerance mode* is 5 degrees. A request with no parameter will reset this default value of 5 degrees. The `mode` parameter enables the user to select whether the values occurring in subsequent commands are to be interpreted in degrees (`mode = 0`) or as deviations from circularity (`mode = 1`).

82.6.3 Download Character

Command	Download Character
Format	`DL n(,count, x, y,...;)`
Function	Defines a new character for the plotter. The `n` parameter specifies the ASCII character with which the new symbol is to be addressed in future. The count parameter indicates how many XY-parameters are to follow. These describe the new character in terms of pen movements and *pen up/down* instructions. Further information can be obtained from the documentation for the specific output device.

82.6.4 Enable Cutter

Command Enable Cutter

Format `EC (n;)`

Function Switches the automatic cutter function of the plotter on or off. A request with no parameter will switch this function off, while an integer parameter will switch it on.

82.6.5 Frame Advance

Command Frame Advance

Format `FR (;)`

Function Shifts the output medium in order to align the frame.

82.6.6 Merge Control

Command Merge Control

Format `MC mode(;)`

Function Controls the production of raster graphics. The parameter `mode = 0` switches the control off; `mode = 1` switches it on.

82.6.7 Message

Command Message

Format `MG (message;)`

Function Enables plotter messages to be displayed on screen. A request with no parameter will delete the message.

82.6.8 Media Type

Command Media Type

Format `MT type(;)`

Function Establishes the type of output medium. Type `0` indicates paper; `1` indicates transparencies. Further information is given in device documentation.

82.6.9 Not Ready

Command Not Ready

Format `FNR;`

Function Unloads the paper and sets the plotter in wait mode.

82.6.10 Output Error

Command Output Error

Format `FOE;`

Function Enables error status enquiries to be made. These will be answered with an integer value in ASCII.

82.6.11 Output Hard-Clip Limits

Command Output Hard-Clip Limits

Format `OH;`

Function Requests details of the *clipping limits* as ASCII integer values `X1`, `Y1`, `X2`, `Y2`. The coordinates of the top left and bottom right corners are used.

82.6.12 Output Identification

Command Output Identification

Format `OI;`

Function Requests the plotter identification number.

82.6.13 Output P1 and P2

Command Output `P1` and `P2`

Format `OP;`

Function Requests the coordinates for points `P1` and `P2`.

82.6.14 Output Status

Command Output Status

Format `OS;`

Function Requests the output status of the output device.

82.6.15 Plot Size

Command Plot Size

Format `PS (length, width;)`

Function Sets the *hard-clip limits* to the parameters indicated (`length`, `width`).

82.6.16 Quality Level

Command Quality Level

Format `QL (Quality;)`

Function Sets the output mode to *draft* (`quality = 0`) or *final* (`quality = 1`).

82.6.17 Sort

Command Sort

Format `ST (switches;)`

Function Specifies the manner in which the plotter sorts vectors before printing.

82.6.18 Velocity Select

Command Velocity Select

Format `VS (pen velocity, pen;)`

Function Specifies the output velocity for a selected pen.

82.7 Palette Extension

This group of extended commands enables the re-definition of the character color produced by the output device.

82.7.1 Set Color Range for Relative Color Data

Command Set Color Range for Relative Color Data

Format `CR (black-ref red, white-ref red,`
`black-ref green, white-ref green,`
`black-ref blue, white-ref blue;)`

Function Sets the red-green-blue range of the color scale. Optional parameters enable the intensity of the primary colors to be adjusted between black and white.

82.7.2 Number of Pens

Command Number of Pens

Format `NP n(;)`

Function Sets the number of colors for a color palette.

82.7.3 Pen Color Assignment

Command Pen Color Assignment

Format `PC (pen, red, green, blue;)`

Function Allocates a color to a given pen.

82.7.4 Screened Vectors

Command Screened Vectors

Format `SV screen type(,option1, option2;)`

Function Selects the type of fill attribute for screen displays.

82.7.5 Transparency Mode

Command Transparency Mode

Format `TR (N);`

Function Determines how white spaces are to printed on the plotter (transparent or opaque).

82.8 Dual Context Extension

These commands support mode-switching between HP-GL/2 and PCL. The group comprises the following commands:

82.8.1 Enter PCL Mode

Command Enter PCL Mode

Format `ESC%#A`

Function Ends HP-GL/2 mode and returns to PCL mode. The character `#` is used as a space-marker for a parameter `0` ... `3`, which defines the PCL mode. The character `ESC` represents the value `1BH`. Further details can be obtained from the documentation for the particular device.

82.8.2 Reset

Command Reset

Format `ESC E`

Function Returns the device to the currently set mode (HP-GL/2 or PCL).

82.8.3 Primary Font Selection by ID

Command Primary Font Selection by ID

Format `FI fontID`

Function Allocates an identification number between `0` and `32767` to a font. These ID numbers are used in PCL mode.

82.8.4 Secondary Font Selection by ID

Command Secondary Font Selection by ID

Format `N fontID`

Function Defines a character set with an identification number as a secondary font.

82.8.5 Scalable or Bitmap Fonts

Command Scalable or Bitmap Fonts

Format `SB (n);`

Function Specifies the type of a font (scalable or bitmap).

82.9 Digitizing Extensions

This group of commands is supported only by pen plotters that permit image digitization. The following commands are available:

82.9.1 Digitize Clear

Command Digitize Clear

Format `DC;`

Function Cancels the digitization mode.

82.9.2 Digitize Point

Command Digitize Point

Format `DP;`

Function Switches the plotter into digitization mode.

82.9.3 Output Digitized Position and Pen Status

Command Output Digitized Position and Pen Status

Format `OD;`

Function Enables a request for the current position during digitization. The XY-position and pen are displayed in the form of an ASCII string.

This brings the description of HP-GL/2 to a close. Further information can be obtained from the relevant plotter manuals.

83

Hewlett Packard Printer Communication Language (PCL)

With the introduction of LaserJet II, Hewlett Packard defined a new language for communication with a new generation of printers. This Printer Communication Language (PCL) established itself rapidly and has subsequently been emulated by many other printers. The commands of this language – like those of PostScript – enable the output of graphics and various fonts. Version PCL 4 was still in use with LaserJet II; however, the introduction of LaserJet III was accompanied by version PCL 5. The control sequences described below relate to this newer version of the language.

PCL commands are divided into several different groups. Each command begins with an ESC character (1BH) followed by several parameters. This character will be represented below as Esc. The numbers enclosed in square brackets [] represent the same sequence in hexadecimal notation.

83.1 Print Commands

These sequences process the complete printing operation.

83.1.1 Reset Printer

Command Reset Printer

Format	`EscE [1B 45]`
Function	Resets the printer to the standard setting.

83.1.2 Number of copies

Command	Number of copies
Format	`Esc&l#X [1B 26 6C #...# 58]`
Function	Specifies the number of copies to be printed on one page. The character # is a placeholder and defines the number of copies.

83.1.3 Landscape positioning of logical page

Command	Landscape positioning of logical page
Format	`Esc&l#U [1B 26 6C #...# 55]`
Function	Rotates the printed output so that the X-axis is in landscape format. The place holder # contains the number of points (1/720 inch) by which the printed image is to be shifted.

83.1.4 Portrait positioning of the logical page

Command	Portrait positioning of the logical page
Format	`Esc&l#Z [1B 26 6C #...# 5A]`
Function	Rotates the printed output so that the Y-axis is in portrait format. The placeholder # contains the number of points (1/720 inch) by which the printed image is to be shifted.

83.2 Page Description Commands

This group comprises commands for the definition of the output of a page.

83.2.1 Print (page) format

Command	Print (page) format
Format	`Esc&l#A [1B 26 6C #...# 41]`
Function	Indicates the page format and paper size. The space-marker # represents the code for the page format. The correct paper cassette must be used for the codes defined:

Code	Page format
	Paper format
1	Executive (7 1/4 × 10 1/2 inch)
2	Letter (8 1/2 × 11 inch)

(continues over...)

Code	Page format
	Envelope format
3	Legal ($8\,^{1}/_{2} \times 14$ inch)
26	DIN A4 (210×297 mm)
80	Monarch ($3\,^{7}/_{8} \times 7\,^{1}/_{2}$ inch)
81	COM-10 ($4\,^{1}/_{8} \times 9\,^{1}/_{2}$ inch)
90	International DL (110 mm × 220 mm)
91	International C5 (162 mm × 229 mm)

27 = A3

(cont.)

PDLs

83.2.2 Paper source

Command Paper source

Format `Esc&l#H [1B 26 6C #...# 48]`

Function Indicates the source of paper for the paper feed. The # parameter represents the code for the source. The following codes are defined:

Code	Source
0	Print current page
1	Take up paper from multi-purpose cassette
2	Feed paper manually
3	Take up envelope

83.2.3 Page length

Command Page length

Format `Esc&l#P [1B 26 6C #...# 50]`

Function Indicates the length of a page in lines. The # parameter represents the number of lines.

83.2.4 Print alignment

Command Print alignment

Format `Esc&l#O [1B 26 6C #...# 4F]`

Function Indicates the print alignment via the # parameter. The codes defined are shown in the following table:

Code	Print direction
0	Portrait
1	Landscape
2	Inverted portrait
3	Inverted landscape

83.2.5 Print direction

Command Print direction

Format `Esc&a#P [1B 26 61 #...# 50]`

Function Indicates the direction of print relative to the X-axis. The # parameter specifies the angle in 90-degree steps so that vertical fonts can be printed.

83.2.6 Top margin

Command Top margin

Format `Esc&l#Esc [1B 26 6C #...# 45]`

Function Establishes the top margin in the # parameter; the parameter defines the number of lines left blank.

83.2.7 Text length

Command Text length

Format `Esc&l#F [1B 26 6C #...# 46]`

Function Establishes the length in lines of the text to be printed in the # parameter.

83.2.8 Left margin

Command Left margin

Format `Esc&a#L [1B 26 61 #...# 4C]`

Function Establishes the left margin in the # parameter; the parameter indicates the number of columns to be left blank.

83.2.9 Right margin

Command Right margin

Format `Esc&a#M [1B 26 61 #...# 4D]`

Function Establishes the right margin in the # parameter; the parameter indicates the column number at which the text is to stop.

83.2.10 Delete side margins

Command Delete side margins

Format `Esc9 [1B 39]`

Function Restores the margin setting to the standard values.

83.2.11 Skip perforation

Command Skip perforation

Format `Esc&l#L [1B 26 6C #...# 4C]`

Function The # parameter establishes whether printing is to be interrupted at the bottom of the page and continued on the next page. If the # parameter is set to 0, this mode is active, and printing will be carried out over page boundaries. The value 1 switches this mode off.

83.2.12 Horizontal column spacing

Command Horizontal column spacing

Format `Esc&k#H [1B 26 6B #...# 4B]`

Function Establishes the horizontal spacing between two columns via the # parameter. The parameter indicates the spacing in 1/120 inch. Four positions are allowed.

83.2.13 Vertical line spacing

Command Vertical line spacing

Format `Esc&l#C [1B 26 6C #...# 43]`

Function Establishes the vertical spacing between two columns via the # parameter. The parameter indicates the spacing in 1/48 inch. Four positions are allowed.

83.2.14 Lines per inch

Command Lines per inch

Format `Esc&l#D [1B 26 6C #...# 44]`

Function Establishes the number of lines per inch via the # parameter. The values 1, 2, 3, 4, 6, 8, 12, 16, 24 and 48 are permitted for this parameter.

83.3 Cursor Commands

This group contains the commands controlling the position of the output cursor.

83.3.1 Vertical

Command Vertical

Format `Esc&a#R  [1B 26 61 #...# 52]`

Function Moves the cursor to line #. If movement is to be indicated in points (1/300 inch), the following sequence applies:

`Esc*p#Y  [1B 2A 70 #...# 59]`

Here, the # parameter indicates the number of points. The sequence:

`Esc&a#V  [1B 26 61 #...# 56]`

indicates the movement in decimal points (1/720 inch).

83.3.2 Horizontal

Command Horizontal

Format `Esc&a#C  [1B 26 61 #...# 43]`

Function Moves the cursor to column #. If the movement is to be indicated in points (1/300 inch), the following sequence applies:

`Esc*p#X  [1B 2A 70 #...# 58]`

Here, the # parameter indicates the number of points. The sequence:

`Esc&a#H  [1B 26 61 #...# 48]`

indicates the movement in decimal points (1/720 inch).

83.3.3 Half-line feed

Command Half-line feed

Format `Esc=  [1B 3D]`

Function Implements a line feed of one half-line. The control commands `CR`, `LF`, `Space`, `Tab`, `BS` and `FF` also cause cursor movements by line or by column.

83.3.4 Cursor position

Command Cursor position

Format `Esc&f#S  [1B 26 66 # 53]`

Function The # parameter establishes whether the cursor is to be read (# = 1) or saved (# = 0).

PDLs

83.4 Font Selection

This group enables the selection of individual fonts.

83.4.1 Font style

Command Font style

Format `Esc(##   [1B 28 #...#]`

Function Establishes the font style via the ## parameter which stands for ASCII characters. The PCL mode currently defines the following font styles:

Code	Font style
0D	ISO 60: Norway 1
1D	ISO 61: Norway 2 (*)
1E	ISO 4: Britain
0F	ISO 25: France (*)
1F	ISO 69: France
0G	HP Germany (*)
1G	ISO 21: Germany
0I	ISO 15:
0K	ISO 14: JIS ASCII (*)
2K	ISO 57: China (*)
0N	ECMA 94: Latin
0S	ISO 11: Sweden
1S	HP Spain (*)
2S	ISO 17: Spain
3S	ISO 10: Sweden (*)
4S	ISO 16: Portugal (*)
5S	ISO 84: Portugal (*)
6S	ISO 85: Spain (*)
0U	ISO 6: ASCII
2U	ISO 2: IRV (*)
8U	HP Roman8
10U	PC 8
11U	PC 8 (D/N)
12U	PC 850

The font styles marked with an asterisk (*) should no longer be used because their importance is declining.

PDLs

83.4.2 Primary spacing

Command Primary spacing

Format `Esc(s#P [1B 28 73 #..# 50]`

Function Establishes the spacing between characters using the # parameter:
= 0 fixed
= 1 proportional

83.4.3 Primary character density

Command Primary character density

Format `Esc(s#H [1B 28 73 #...# 48]`

Function Establishes the number of characters per inch using the # parameter.

83.4.4 Set character density

Command Set character density

Format `Esc&k#S [1B 26 6B #...# 53]`

Function Sets the character density using the # parameter. The following values are permitted:

Code	Density
0	10.0
2	Compressed (16,5)
4	Elite (12,0)

83.4.5 Primary character size

Command Primary character size

Format `Esc(s#V [1B 28 73 #...# 56]`

Function Establishes the size of a character in pica points, using the # parameter.

83.4.6 Font orientation

Command Font orientation

Format `Esc(s#S[1B 28 73 #...# 53]`

Function Establishes the orientation of the font via the # parameter. The following values are permitted:

= 0 upright

= 1 italic

PDLs

83.4.7 Primary font line thickness

Command Primary font line thickness

Format `Esc(s#B [1B 28 73 #...# 42]`

Function The command establishes the line thickness using the # parameter, for which the codes listed above are defined. The minus sign for thin fonts should be entered as part of the code.

Code	Line thickness
-7	Ultra-fine
-6	Extra-fine
-5	Fine
-4	Extra-thin
-3	Thin
-1	Three-quarter thin
-2	Half-thin
0	Normal
1	Half-bold
2	Three-quarter bold
3	Bold
4	Extra-bold
5	Black
6	Extra-black
7	Ultra-black

83.4.8 Font type

Command Font type

Format `Esc(s#T [1B 28 73 #...# 54]`

Function Establishes the font type via the # parameter. The following codes are permitted for #:

Code	Font type
0	Line printer
1	Pica
2	Elite
3	Courier
4	Helvetica

(continues over...)

PDLs

Code	Font type
5	Times Roman
6	Gothic
7	Script
8	Prestige

(cont.)

83.4.9 Standard font

Command Standard font

Format `Esc(s#@  [1B 28 33 40]`

Function The command in this format establishes the primary font; the secondary font is determined by:

`Esc)s#@  [1B 29 33 40]`

83.4.10 Transparent print data

Command Transparent print data

Format `Esc&p#X[data]   [1B 26 70 #...# 58 ...]`

Function Establishes the characters to be interpreted by the printer. The `#` parameter indicates the number of characters in the `[data]` field.

83.4.11 Underline on/off

Command Underline on/off

Format `Esc&d0D  [1B 26 64 30 44]`

Function The format establishes the underline on mode. The following format is provided for underline on adapted:

`Esc&d3D  [1B 26 64 33 44]`

In this mode, blank characters are not underlined. The following sequence:

`Esc&d@   [1B 26 64 40]`

is used to switch the underline mode off.

83.5 Font Management

This group contains the various commands required for loading and deleting fonts.

83.5.1 Allocate font code

Command Allocate font code

Format `Esc*c#D [1B 2A 63 #...# 44]`

Function The # parameter indicates the code number, which may be between 0 and 32767. All subsequent font management commands relate to this code number.

83.5.2 Control of font characters

Command Control of font characters

Format `Esc*c#F [1B 2A 63 #...# 46]`

Function The # parameter stands for one of the codes listed below:

Code	Meaning
0	Delete all fonts
1	Delete all temporary fonts
2	Delete the font with the last code allocated
3	Delete last character entered
4	Set temporary font
5	Set permanent font
6	Allocate/copy current font as temporary

83.5.3 Select font

Command Select font

Format `Esc(#X [1B 28 #...# 58]`

Function This format selects the font with the code number # as the primary font. The following format is used to set the secondary font:

`Esc)#X [1B 29 #...# 58]`

83.6 Creating Loadable Fonts

This command group can be used for the creation of customized fonts.

83.6.1 Font descriptor

Command Font descriptor

Format `Esc)s#W[data]` `[1B 29 73 #...# 57 Data]`

Function The # parameter establishes the length of the following font descriptor. *n* bytes containing the font description follow this command.

83.6.2 Character code

Command Character code

Format `Esc*c#Esc` `[1B 2A 63 #...# 45]`

Function The # parameter establishes the code of the ASCII character which is to be allocated to the next character.

83.6.3 Load characters

Command Load characters

Format `Esc(s#W[data]` `[1B 28 73 #...# 57 Data]`

Function The # parameter establishes the length of the following character descriptor. This command is followed by *n* bytes containing the character descriptor.

83.7 Graphics Commands

This group contains the commands used for the output of graphics in raster and vector format; the HP-GL/2 character set is supported.

83.7.1 HP-GL/2 Mode

Command HP-GL/2 Mode

Format `Esc%0B` `[1B 25 30 42]`

Function Establishes that the last pen position of the HP-GL/2 mode is being used. In the following format, this command determines that the graphics output is to begin at the current PCL position:

`E%1B` `[1B 25 31 42]`

83.7.2 HP-GL/2 Plot width

Command HP-GL/2 Plot width

Format `Esc*c#K` `[1B 2A 63 #...# 4B]`

Function The # parameter sets the width of the line in inches.

83.7.3 HP-GL/2 Plot length

Command HP-GL/2 Plot length

Format `Esc*c#L [1B 2A 63 #...# 4C]`

Function The # parameter sets the length of the plot line in inches.

83.7.4 Reference point in graphic area

Command Reference point in graphic area

Format `Esc*c0T [1B 2A 63 30 54]`

Function Establishes the current position as the reference position.

83.7.5 Width of graphic area

Command Width of graphic area

Format `Esc*c#X [1B 2A 63 #...# 58]`

Function The # parameter sets the width of the graphic area in decimal points.

83.7.6 Height of graphic area

Command Height of graphic area

Format `Esc*c#Y [1B 2A 63 #...# 59]`

Function The # parameter sets the height of the graphic area in decimal points.

83.7.7 Resolution of raster graphics

Command Resolution of raster graphics

Format `Esc*t###R [1B 2A 74 #...# 52]`

Function Establishes the resolution for raster graphics. The following codes take the place of the space-markers, depending on the resolution required:

Codes (in hex)	Resolution
37 35	75 points per inch
31 30 30	100 points per inch
31 35 30	150 points per inch
33 30 30	300 points per inch

These values are entered in hexadecimal notation and are inserted into the sequence as appropriate (for example, 75 points per inch = `Esc*t75R`).

83.7.8 Orientation of raster graphics

Command Orientation of raster graphics

Format `Esc*r0F [1B 2A 72 30 46]`

Function In this format, the image is rotated in the display, while the following sequence is used to print it in landscape format:

`Esc*r3F [1B 2A 72 30 46]`

83.7.9 Start raster graphics

Command Start raster graphics

Format `Esc*r0A [1B 2A 72 30 41]`

Function In this format, the left margin is established at column 0, while the following sequence fixes the left margin at the current position:

`Esc*r1A [1B 2A 72 31 41]`

83.7.10 Data compression

Command Data compression

Format `Esc*b#M [1B 2A 62 #...# 4D]`

Function Compresses the data according to the type of compression indicated by the value of the # parameter:

Code	Compression
0	Uncoded
1	Run-length coding
2	TIFF coding
3	Delta row

83.7.11 Transmission

Command Transmission

Format `Esc*b#W[data] [1B 2A 62 #...# 57 data]`

Function Transmits the data for a raster graphic. The # parameter indicates the number of data items that follow the command.

83.7.12 End of raster graphic

Command End of raster graphic

Format `Esc*rB [1B 2A 72 42]`

Function Marks the end of the raster graphic.

83.7.13 Raster height

Command Raster height

Format `Esc*r#T [1B 2A 72 #...# 54]`

Function The # parameter indicates the number of raster rows.

83.7.14 Raster width

Command Raster width

Format `Esc*r#S [1B 2A 72 #...# 53]`

Function The # parameter indicates the number of raster pixels per row.

83.8 Print Mode

This command group contains instructions for setting the relevant print mode (shading, transparency).

83.8.1 Select pattern

Command Select pattern

Format `Esc*v#T [1B 2A 76 #...# 54]`

Function The # parameter determines the print color as follows:

Code	Allocation
0	Full-tone black
1	Full-tone white
2	Gray toning pattern
3	Cross-hatching

83.8.2 Select source

Command Select source

Format `Esc*v#N [1B 2A 76 #...# 4E]`

Function The # parameter determines the mode of shading as follows:

Code	Allocation
0	Transparent
1	Opaque

83.8.3 Select pattern

Command Select pattern

Format `Esc*v#O [1B 2A 76 #...# 4F]`

Function The # parameter determines the mode of shading for the pattern as follows:

Code	Allocation
0	Transparent
1	Opaque

83.8.4 Width of rectangular shape

Command Width of rectangular shape

Format `Esc*c#A [1B 2A 63 #...# 41]`

Function Indicates the width in points of a rectangular shape to be filled. The following command is used to indicate the width in decimal points:

`Esc*c#H [1B 2A 63 #...# 48]`

83.8.5 Height of rectangular shape

Command Height of rectangular shape

Format `Esc*c#B [1B 2A 63 #...# 42]`

Function Indicates the height in points of a rectangular shape to be filled. The following format is used to indicate the height in decimal points:

`Esc*c#V [1B 2A 63 #...# 56]`

83.8.6 Fill rectangular shape

Command Fill rectangular shape

Format `Esc*c#P [1B 2A 63 #...# 50]`

Function The # parameter indicates the fill attribute for the rectangular shape:

Code	Fill attribute
0	Full-tone black
1	Full-tone
2	Gray shading
3	Hatching
4	Customized pattern
5	Current pattern

83.8.7 Pattern code number

Command Pattern code number

Format `Esc*c#G [1B 2A 63 #...# 47]`

Function The # parameter allocates a pattern type to the pattern or indicates the shading as a percentage. The following coding applies to the level of gray shading:

Code	Gray shading
2	2%
10	10%
15	15%
30	30%
45	45%
70	70%
90	90%
100	100%

These values should be entered as numbers (for example, 100% = 1B 2A 63 31 30 30 47). The pattern is coded as follows:

Code	Pattern
1	Horizontal lines
2	Vertical lines
3	Diagonal lines
4	Grid
5	Diagonal grid

83.9 Macros

This group contains the commands required for the definition of macros.

83.9.1 Macro coding

Command Macro coding

Format `Esc&f#Y [1B 26 66 #...# 59]`

Function Defines a code number for macros. The # parameter is a number between 0 and 32,767.

83.9.2 Macro control

Command Macro control

Format `Esc&f#X [1B 26 66 #...# 58]`

Function Defines the control of macros. The # parameter indicates one of the following control modes:

Code	Mode
0	Begin macro definition
1	End macro definition
2	Execute macro
3	Call up macro
4	Activate superimpose
5	Deactivate superimpose
6	Delete macro
7	Delete all temporary macros
8	Delete macro with last code allocated
9	Set temporary macro
10	Set permanent macro

The code is entered as a hex value for each digit (for example, code 10 = `31H 30H`).

83.10 Programming References

This group contains additional commands for the control of the printer display and line breaks. The commands can be used for fault finding.

83.10.1 Display function

Command Display function

Format `EscY [1B 59]`

`EscZ [1B 5A]`

Function The first command sequence switches off the display; the second switches it on again.

83.10.2 Automatic line break

Command Automatic line break

Format `Esc&s0C [1B 26 73 30 43]`

`Esc&s1C [1B 26 73 31 43]`

Function These two sequences are used for switching the automatic line break function on and off.

83.11 PCL-Access Expansion

The commands in this group enable PCL commands to be activated in HP-GL/2 mode. These commands are described in Chapter 82 on HP-GL/2 commands, in Section 82.8 *Dual Context Extension*. The HP-GL/2 mode can be activated via the sequence `Esc%0B`.

84

Encapsulated PostScript format (EPS) version 3.0

In defining PostScript, Adobe created a printer-independent page description language which is becoming established as the standard. Many software products therefore import images and text coded in PostScript. To facilitate exchange between various systems, Adobe defined Encapsulated PostScript Format (EPSF). This product includes PostScript programs which must comply with certain structural conventions (Document Specific Conditions (DSC)).

Figure 84.1 shows a file (EPS version 1.2) produced with the Lotus product Freelance.

```
%!PS-Adobe-2.0 EPSF-1.2
%%Title: born1.EPS
%%Creator: Freelance Plus 3.01
%%CreationDate: 8/1/1990
%%Pages: 1
%%DocumentFonts: (atend)
%%BoundingBox: 0 0 648 468
%%EndComments
%%BeginProcSet: Freelance Plus
/Freelance_Plus dup 100 dict def load begin
[ ] {bind} stopped { (patching the bind operator...) = flush
/*bind /bind load def /bind { dup xcheck { *bind } if } *bind def }
if pop /bdf {bind def} bind def /ldf {load def} bdf
/mt /moveto ldf /rt /rmoveto ldf /l2 /lineto ldf /c2 /curveto ldf
/sg /setgray ldf /gs /gsave ldf /ef /eofill ldf /rl2 /rlineto ldf
/st /stroke ldf /gr /grestore ldf /np /newpath ldf
/sv /save ldf /su /statusdict ldf /rs /restore ldf
/sw /setlinewidth ldf /sd /setdash ldf /cp /closepath ldf /ed
```

Figure 84.1 EPS file, produced with Freelance Plus (*continues over...*)

```
{exch def } bdf /cfnt {findfont exch makefont setfont} bdf
/itr {transform round exch round exch itransform} bdf
/fres 72 0 matrix currentmatrix dtransform
exch dup mul exch dup mul add sqrt def
/res fres def /mcm matrix currentmatrix bdf
%%EndProcSet
end
%%EndProlog
%%BeginSetup
Freelance_Plus begin
save newpath
.1 .1 scale
/ecm matrix currentmatrix bdf
/sem {ecm setmatrix} bdf
-720 -720 translate
0 setlinecap
0 setlinejoin
1.42 setmiterlimit%%EndSetup
Figure 84.1a - EPS file, produced with Freelance Plus
/Ich 256 array def StandardEncoding Ich copy pop /bullet
/paragraph/section/dieresis/tilde/ring
/circumflex/grave/acute/quotedblleft/quotesingle
/ellipsis/endash/emdash/guilsinglleft/guilsinglright
/quotedblbase/quotesinglbase/quotedblright/OE/oe
/Ydieresis/fi/fl/dagger/daggerdbl/Ccedilla/udieresis
/eacute/acircumflex/adieresis/agrave/aring/ccedilla
/ecircumflex/edieresis/egrave/idieresis/icircumflex
/igrave/Adieresis/Aring/Eacute/ae/AE/ocircumflex
/odieresis/ograve/ucircumflex/ugrave/ydieresis
/Odieresis/Udieresis/oslash/sterling/Oslash/florin
/aacute/iacute/oacute/uacute/ntilde/Ntilde/ordfeminine
/ordmasculine/questiondown/exclamdown/guillemetleft
/guillemetright/Aacute/Acircumflex/Agrave/cent/yen
/atilde/Atilde/currency/Ecircumflex/Edieresis/Egrave
/dotlessi/Iacute/Icircumflex/Idieresis/Igrave/Oacute
/germandbls/Ocircumflex/Ograve/otilde/Otilde/Uacute
/Ucircumflex/Ugrave/macron/cedilla/periodcentered
Ich 127 97 getinterval astore pop
/Ienc { /ncs Ich def /nfn ed /bfn ed /bfd bfn findfont def
/nf bfd maxlength dict def bfd{exch dup dup /FID ne exch
/Encoding ne and {exch nf 3 1 roll put}{pop pop} ifelse }
forall nf/FontName nfn put nf/Encoding ncs put nfn nf
definefont pop}bdf
```

Figure 84.1 EPS file, produced with Freelance Plus (*cont.*)

PDLs

```
/Ienc0 { /ncs Ich def /nfn ed /bfn ed /lnw ed /bfd bfn
findfont def /nf bfd maxlength 4 add dict def bfd{exch
dupdup /FID ne exch /Encoding ne and
{exch nf 3 1 roll put}{pop pop} ifelse }forall
nf/FontName nfn put nf/Encoding ncs put
nf/PaintType 2 put nf/StrokeWidth lnw put
nfn nf definefont pop}bdf
/IencS0 { /nfn ed /bfn ed /lnw ed /bfd bfn findfont def
/nf bfd maxlength 4 add dict def bfd{exch dup
/FID ne { exch nf 3 1 roll put}{pop pop} ifelse }forall
nf/FontName nfn put nf/PaintType 2 put
nf/StrokeWidth lnw put nfn nf definefont pop}bdf
/Helvetica /Flfon1 Ienc
[191 0 0.00 191 -18 -142]  /Flfon1 cfnt
0.000 sg
2737 3026 itr mt
(This is a text)
show
6 sw
sv np [] 0 sd
2764 3749 itr mt
4071 3749 itr l2
st rs
sv np
1352 2572 itr mt
2424 2572 itr l2
2424 3513 itr l2
1352 3513 itr l2
1352 2572 itr l2
cp
Figure 84.1b - EPS file, produced with Freelance Plus
st rs
sv np
3456 4438 itr mt
currentpoint translate
np 1.000 1.000 scale
0 0 549 0.000 360.000 arc sem
st rs
sv np
5156 4438 itr mt
5823 4573 itr l2
5823 3984 itr l2
```

Figure 84.1 EPS file, produced with Freelance Plus (*cont.*)

PDLs

```
4973 3984 itr l2
4973 4354 itr l2
5156 4438 itr l2
gs 0.000 sg
ef gr
cp
st rs
rs end
%%Trailer
%%DocumentFonts: Helvetica
```

Figure 84.1 EPS file, produced with Freelance Plus (*cont.*)

The EPS file consists of the actual PostScript instructions and the structural conventions (DCS) for program control. It is important that the EPS file describes a maximum of one page. Typically, the content of an EPS file is incorporated into another document as an image. The EPS file may therefore contain pictures, text and graphs and must correspond to the following structural conventions.

84.1 EPS structural conventions

The EPS structural conventions provide a *prolog* and a *script* for each EPS file. The prolog contains application-specific definitions, while the script contains the actual PostScript instructions. These sections are described by various items of structural information which are introduced as PostScript comments using the % character. The PostScript interpreter ignores the line, while a pre-processor evaluates the information contained in the line. In order to distinguish structural information from other comment lines, this information begins with the following characters:

```
%!
%%
```

followed by any ASCII string required. There must be no spaces between the two percentage characters and the keyword. If a keyword is terminated with a colon, it will be followed by additional parameters (for example, `%% Bounding Box: xx xx xx xx`). Figure 84.2 shows the structure of an EPS file with prolog and script.

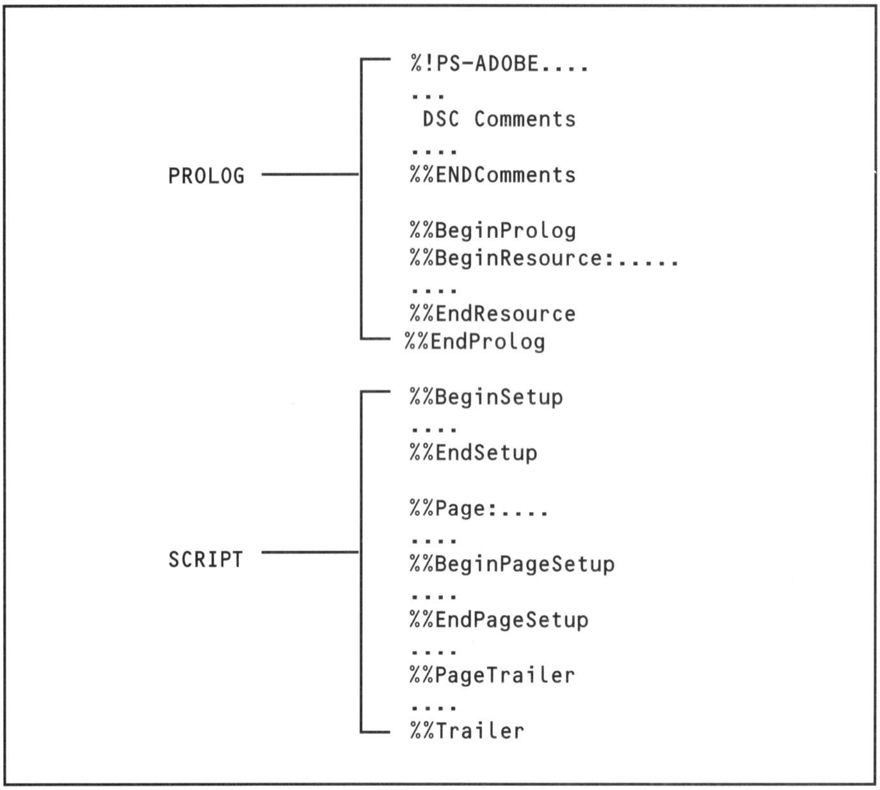

Figure 84.2 The structure of an EPS file

Please note that the individual sections may contain both DSC comments and PostScript instructions. Not all DSC comments need appear (*see below*).

84.2 Necessary DSC header comments

An EPS file must contain at least two DSC comment lines in the header.

84.2.1 %!PS-Adobe-3.0 EPSF-3.0

An EPS file always begins with the `!%PS` line, which marks the file as a PostScript file in accordance with the Adobe conventions. This line indicates the signature:

```
!PS-Adobe-
```

and may also contain the version number (here EPSF-3.0).

84.2.2 %%BoundingBox: llx lly urx ury

The second DSC instruction to appear in an EPS file, from EPSF 2.0 onwards, is the definition of the bounding box. (In earlier versions this instruction could appear anywhere in the header.) The bounding box defines a rectangle which encloses all the elements of an EPS file. The instruction is needed by the reader program to determine and possibly also to scale the size of the image. The instruction contains four integer values as parameters (`llx`, `lly`, `urx`, `ury`) which indicate the corners of the bounding box according to the initial coordinate system:

```
%%BoundingBox: 0 0 648 468
```

The arguments (`llx`, `lly`) describe the lower left corner, while the arguments (`urx`, `ury`) define the upper right corner.

84.3 Optional header comments

The header of the EPS file may contain additional comments giving further information.

84.3.1 %%DocumentFonts: Font1, Font2 ...

This comment enables names to be given to the fonts used. However, the instruction may be moved to the end of the file, in which case the following line must appear in the header:

```
%%DocumentFonts: (atend)
```

84.3.2 %%Title:, %%Creator:, %%CreationDate:

The following three instructions should, if possible, appear in an EPS file. They establish the document title and further information:

```
%%Title: title

%%Creator: text

%%CreationDate: date
```

The file name is also often stored in the title line. The program or the person responsible for creating the file should be noted in the following line (`Creator`) together with the date of creation. The time can also be included as a string in the date line.

84.3.3 %%Copyright:

With `%%Copyright:text`, a copyright text can be stored in the EPS file.

PDLs

84.3.4 %%DocumentData:

The instruction `%%DocumentData:Options` defines the type of data in the EPS file. The data is enclosed between `%%BeginData:` and `%%EndData` instructions. The following options are available:

`Clean7Bit`	If the page description contains only codes in the range `1BH–7FH` and `0AH` (`LF`), `0DH` (`CR`), and `09H` (`TAB`). The character combination `0DH,0AH` is used at the end of a line. An EPS line should never contain more than 255 characters.
`Clean8Bit`	Defines codes as for `Clean7Bit`, but includes the range `80H–FFH`.
`Binary`	Indicates EPS binary data. Values between `00H` and `FFH` may appear in the data.

Please note that the header must always be coded with `Clean7Bit` up to the instruction `%%EndComments`. With `Clean7Bit` and `Clean8Bit` EPS files, data outside the defined range is indicated with `ESCAPE` codes (for example, `05H = \005`).

84.3.5 %%EndComments

This instruction defines the end of the EPS header.

84.3.6 %%For:

This instruction names a recipient of the document:

```
%%For: text
```

where the recipient name is indicated as text.

84.3.7 %%LanguageLevel:

This command defines the language level (Level 1 or Level 2) used in the document.

84.3.8 %%Orientation:

This option defines the orientation of the output (portrait or landscape) and can be used for previewing the document.

84.3.9 %%Pages

The number of (virtual) pages is set with the sequence:

```
%%Pages: xx
```

The value `xx` should be a non-negative decimal number. This value has nothing to do with the number of physical pages to be output (in EPS, this is always 1). If the program creates no pages, a `0` should be entered. The option `atend` is also permitted.

84.3.10 %%PageOrder:

This option defines the order of pages to be output (ascending, descending, special).

84.3.11 %%Routing:

This comment line defines the (text) reply address of the document to be output.

84.3.12 %%Version:

This command can be used to indicate a version or revision number in the document.

84.4 Body Comments

These comments are essentially used for marking various subdivisions in the actual program section.

The line length in EPS files should not exceed 255 characters. Continuation lines are therefore necessary for some instructions. These are introduced as follows:

```
%%+...
```

This section also contains various keywords which always occur in pairs. A summary of possible comments is shown below.

84.4.1 %%BeginBinary:bytes, %%EndBinary

This sequence defines the beginning and end of an area containing binary data. The number of data bytes is indicated as a parameter after `%%BeginBinary`. However, this instruction has only been retained for compatibility reasons. In future versions, it will be possible to replace this instruction with the sequence `%%BeginData:–%%EndData`.

84.4.2 %%BeginData:bytes, %%EndData

This sequence defines the beginning and end of a data area. `%%BeginData:` is followed by the length in lines or in bytes, the data type (hex, binary or ASCII) and the orientation of the data (bytes or lines). The entry:

```
%%BeginData: 13 Hex Byte

image

4c4f0011...

%EndData
```

defines an image composed of hexadecimal data. A hexadecimal number always consists of two bytes (for example, `0A`).

84.4.3 %%BeginDefaults, %%EndDefaults

This sequence encloses an area in which default instructions appear. The area can appear only in the header, after `%%EndComments` and after any review section (`%%BeginPreview` ... `%EndPreview`) that may be present. Within the range, the following comments may appear: `%%PageBoundingBox:`, `%%PageCustomColors:`, `%%PageMedia:`, `%%PageOrientation:` `%%PageProcessColors:` `%%PageRequirements:`, `%%PageResources:`.

84.4.4 %%BeginPreview:, %%EndPreview

These two comments describe a preview image.

```
%%BeginPreview: width height depth lines
```

The `width` parameter indicates the width of the image in the preview. `Height` defines the height of the image and `depth` the number of bits per pixel (1,2,4 or 8). The `lines` parameter indicates how many data lines containing image data the image covers.

The image for the preview is stored as a bitmap in the file. The instruction `%%BeginPreview` should be placed after the `%%EndComment` instruction, but before the line `%%BeginDefaults`.

84.4.5 %%BeginProlog,%%EndProlog

These two instructions enclose the document prolog. The `%%EndProlog` instruction is positioned before the script section of the document.

84.4.6 %%BeginSetup,%%EndSetup

These comment lines enclose an area containing the settings for the output. The instructions `%%BeginPageSetup` and `%%EndPageSetup` are also available.

The prolog is terminated with an appropriate comment (`EndProlog`). The beginning of a page description can be indicated by the following sequence:

```
%%Page: label ordial
```

The relevant numbers are entered in `label` and `ordial`. Fonts for individual pages, which can be evaluated by a read program, can be specified as follows:

```
%%PageFonts: font1, font2 ...
```

84.5 Trailer comments

The trailer appears at the end of an EPS file, and is introduced by the comment:

%%Trailer

If the instruction `%%DocumentFonts: (atend)` occurred in the header, the character sets used in the document can be listed in the trailer as follows:

```
%%DocumentFonts: font1, font2 ...
```

An example is shown in Figure 84.1. The EPS file trailer can also contain comment lines giving resource requirements such as `%%DocumentNeededResources:` or `%%DocumentNeededFonts:`.

84.5.1 %%EOF

The end of an EPS file is indicated by the instruction `%%EOF`.

PDLs

84.6 Platform-specific formats for preview images

The contents of EPS files cannot be processed or displayed while they are being imported. The only means of displaying them is by printing them out. To simplify the positioning of an EPS file while it is being imported, the file may contain an additional preview image. On the Macintosh, these images are generally PICT image data stored under resource number 256 in a resource fork of the EPS file. On the PC, TIFF images or WMF images are used. In this case the file contains a binary header.

Offset	Bytes	Description
00H	4	Signature C5H D0H D3H C6H (byte 0 = C5H)
04H	4	Offset PostScript code range
08H	4	Length of PostScript range
0CH	4	Offset Metafile image
10H	4	Length of metafile range
14H	4	TIFF image offset
18H	4	Length of TIFF range
1CH	2	Header checksum

Table 84.1 Binary header for EPS files

The header contains the offset and the length of the image data ranges. One range (metafile or TIFF) must always be set to `0`, because only one image format is stored as a preview. The checksum is the result of an `XOR` operation on the first 28 bytes of the header. The checksum

FFFFH should be ignored. The format of the image data is described in Chapter 27 (TIFF) and Chapter 64 (Metafile).

84.7 Platform-independent formats for preview images

Alternatively, an EPS file can contain a preview image in a platform-independent format. In this case the image is stored as a bitmap in ASCII format. The ASCII data is bound into the file in the following sequence:

```
%%BeginPreview: Width Height Depth Lines
....
....
%%EndPreview
```

The sequence of bytes is the same as for the PostScript image-operator (zero-point at bottom left).

An EPS file containing integrated preview image data used under DOS should have the EPI extension. However, the section containing the preview data is placed after the header-comment section but before the document prolog. A bit value of 0 defines a white dot; the value 1 defines a black image dot. A line containing hexadecimal numbers must never contain more than 255 characters. Any characters that do not correspond to hexadecimal characters in the data range must be skipped. Every line containing hex-values begins with the % character so that the PostScript interpreter skips them. The data within an image line should always be multiples of 8 bits. If necessary the data line should be padded with 0-bytes.

84.8 PostScript instructions

PostScript instructions describing the output page are stored in an EPS file. All valid PostScript commands are allowed, with the exception of those listed in Table 84.2.

banddevice	clear	cleardictstack
copypage	erasepage	exitserver
framedevice	grestoreall	initclip
initgraphics	initmatrix	quit
renderbands	setglobal	setpagedevice
setshared	startjob	

Table 84.2 Illegal EPS commands

1. Adobe Systems Inc.: ***PostScript Language Tutorial Reference Manual***, First Edition
2. Adobe Systems Inc.: ***PostScript Language Tutorial and Cookbook***
3. Adobe Systems Inc.: ***PostScript Language Program Design***
4. Adobe Systems Inc.: ***PostScript Language Program Design***, Second Edition

Those intending to use this language are advised to consult the relevant Adobe manuals[1,2,3,4]. The most important PostScript instructions (Level1) are described briefly below.

84.8.1 abs

Command abs
Format `num abs`
Function Converts `num` into an absolute number and stores the result on the stack.

84.8.2 add

Command add
Format `num1 num2 add`
Function Adds `num1` and `num2` and stores the result on the stack.

84.8.3 and

Command and
Format `bool1 bool2 and`
Function `AND`s the two logical values `bool1` and `bool2` and stores the result on the stack.

84.8.4 arc

Command arc
Format `x y r ang1 ang2 arc`
Function Draws an arc of radius `r` at the point `x,y`. The `ang1` and `ang2` parameters indicate the angle of the arc.

84.8.5 arcn

Command arcn
Format `x y r ang1 ang2 arcn`
Function Draws an arc of radius `r` in clockwise direction at the point `x,y`. The `ang1` and `ang2` parameters indicate the angle of the arc.

84.8.6 arcto

Command arcto
Format `x1 y1 x2 y2 arcto`
Function Draws a straight line from the current point `x0,y0` to the point `x1,y1` and from there an arc to the point `x2,y2`. After execution, there are four parameters on the stack, indicating the tangent points.

84.8.7 ashow

Command ashow

Format `ax ay string ashow`

Function Displays a text string. The `type` widths can be corrected using `ax` and `ay`.

84.8.8 atan

Command atan

Format `num den atan`

Function Calculates the angle in degrees from the parameters `num` and `den`, and stores the result on the stack.

84.8.9 awidthshow

Command awidthshow

Format `cx cy char ax ay string awidthshow`

Function Displays a text string. The `type` widths are corrected using `ax` and `ay`. In addition, every `char` character in the text is corrected using `cx` and `cy`.

84.8.10 bind

Command bind

Format `proc bind`

Function Replaces the operator name for a procedure by its values and stores them on the stack.

84.8.11 bitshift

Command bitshift

Format `int1 shift bitshift`

Function Shifts the value of `int1` by shift to the left. If the value of `shift` is negative, the bits are shifted to the right. The result is placed on the stack.

84.8.12 ceiling

Command ceiling

Format `num ceiling`

Function Returns the least integer value, greater than or equal to `num`.

84.8.13 charpath

Command charpath

Format `string bool charpath`

Function Obtains a character path outline, that would result if `string` were shown using the `show` command.

84.8.14 clip

Command clip

Format `clip`

Function Clips the interior of a clip path.

84.8.15 clippath

Command clippath

Format `clippath`

Function Defines the current clip path.

84.8.16 closepath

Command closepath

Format `closepath`

Function Closes the current sub-path by means of a straight line segment from the current point to the start point.

84.8.17 copypage

Command copypage

Format `copypage`

Function Prints the contents of the current page without re-initializing the page, thereby enabling a sample of part of an image to be printed.

84.8.18 cos

Command cos

Format `angle cos`

Function Calculates the cosine value of the angle and stores the value on the stack.

84.8.19 currentpoint

Command currentpoint
Format `currentpoint`
Function Stores the current XY coordinates on the stack.

84.8.20 curveto

Command curveto
Format `x1 y1 x2 y2 x3 y3 curveto`
Function Draws a *Bezier curve* using the three points indicated.

84.8.21 cvi

Command cvi
Format `num cvi`
Function Converts `num` into an integer value and stores it on the stack.

84.8.22 cvn

Command cvn
Format `string cvn`
Function Converts a number in the form of a string into an integer value and stores it on the stack.

84.8.23 cvt

Command cvt
Format `string cvt`
Function Converts `num` into a floating point value and stores it on the stack.

84.8.24 cvrs

Command cvrs
Format `num string radix cvrs`
Function Converts a number `num` into a string using the base `radix` and stores the result on the stack.

84.8.25 cvs

Command cvs
Format `num string cvs`

Function Converts the value of any element in a text and returns a real value on the stack.

84.8.26 div

Command div

Format `num1 num2 div`

Function Divides `num1` by `num2` and stores the result on the stack.

84.8.27 dup

Command dup

Format `element dup`

Function Duplicates the uppermost element on the stack.

84.8.28 eoclip

Command eoclip

Format `eoclip`

Function Clips the interior of the current clipping path with the interior of the current path.

84.8.29 eofill

Command eofill

Format `eofill`

Function Fills the interior of the current path with the current color.

84.8.30 eq

Command eq

Format `elem1 elem2 eq`

Function Compares any two elements with each other and stores the result *true* or *false* on the stack.

84.8.31 exch

Command exch

Format `elem1 elem2 exch`

Function Exchanges the two uppermost elements on the stack.

84.8.32 exec

Command exec

Format `oper exec`

Function Places the operand on the stack and executes it directly.

84.8.33 exit

Command exit

Format `exit`

Function Ends the execution of a loop (`for`, `loop`, `repeat`, `forall`).

84.8.34 exp

Command exp

Format `base exp exp`

Function Calculates a floating point value from the `base` and the exponent (`exp`).

84.8.35 fill

Command fill

Format `fill`

Function Fills the interior of the current path with the current color.

84.8.36 findfont

Command findfont

Format `font findfont`

Function Searches for a name described by `font` in the font dictionary.

84.8.37 for

Command for

Format `start step end { proc } for`

Function Constructs a loop which begins with the value `start`. The loop index will be augmented by the interval `step` until the final value `end` is reached. The instructions enclosed in braces (`{}`) are executed for each iteration of the loop.

84.8.38 ge

Command ge

Format `num1 num2 ge`

Function Carries out a greater than or equal to comparison on `num1` and `num2` and stores the result as a Boolean value on the stack.

84.8.39 grestore

Command grestore

Format `grestore`

Function Restores the graphic status saved under `gsave`.

84.8.40 gsave

Command gsave

Format `gsave`

Function Saves the graphic status.

84.8.41 gt

Command gt

Format `num1 num2 gt`

Function Carries out a *greater than* comparison on `num1` and `num2` and stores the result as a Boolean value on the stack.

84.8.42 idiv

Command idiv

Format `int1 int2 idiv`

Function Carries out an integer division of `int1/int2` and stores the result on the stack.

84.8.43 if

Command if

Format `bool { proc } if`

Function Processes the instructions enclosed in brackets if `bool` is equal to true.

84.8.44 ifelse

Command ifelse

Format `bool { proc1 } { proc2 } ifelse`

Function Processes the `proc1` instructions if `bool` = true.

Otherwise the `proc2` instructions are implemented.

84.8.45 image

Command image

Format `width height bits_per_sample matrix proc image`

Function Transfers a raster image to the current page. The `width` and `height` parameters specify the dimensions of the image. The image is read in using `proc`.

84.8.46 imagemask

Command imagemask

Format `width height invert matrix proc imagemask`

Function Transfers a raster image to the current page. The `width` and `height` parameters specify the dimensions of the image. The image data is read in using `proc`. The logical value `invert` defines whether the bits are drawn directly or inverted (if inverted = false, 0 bits are drawn).

84.8.47 index

Command index

Format `a1 a2...ax n index`

Function Copies the *n*th stack element to the top of the stack, counting from the uppermost element (`0`).

84.8.48 le

Command le

Format `num1 num2 le`

Function Carries out a *less than or equal to* comparison on `num1` and `num2` and stores the result as a Boolean value on the stack.

84.8.49 lineto

Command lineto

Format `x y lineto`

Function Appends a straight line segment to the current path from the current position to the point x,y.

84.8.50 ln

Command ln

Format `num1 ln`

Function Stores the floating point value of `ln(num1)` on the stack.

84.8.51 log

Command log

Format `num1 log`

Function Stores the floating point value of `log(num1)` on the stack.

84.8.52 loop

Command loop

Format `{ proc } loop`

Function Continues executing the instructions of the `loop { proc }` until an exit operator is loaded.

84.8.53 lt

Command lt

Format `num1 num2 lt`

Function Carries out a less than comparison on `num1` and `num2` and stores the result as a Boolean value on the stack.

84.8.54 mod

Command mod

Format `int1 int2 mod`

Function Stores the result of the division `int1/int2` on the stack (modulus function).

84.8.55 moveto

Command moveto

Format `x y moveto`

Function Begins a new path and sets the current point to the coordinates indicated with `x,y`.

84.8.56 mul

Command mul

Format `num1 num2 mul`

Function Multiplies `num1` by `num2` and stores the product on the stack.

84.8.57 neg

Command neg
Format `num1 neg`
Function Inverts the value of `num1` and stores the result on the stack.

84.8.58 newpath

Command newpath
Format `newpath`
Function Creates a new path on the current page. The current point is then undefined.

84.8.59 not

Command not
Format `bool1 not`
Function Inverts the value of the logical variable and stores the result on the stack.

84.8.60 or

Command or
Format `bool1 bool2 or`
Function `OR`s the two operators and stores the result on the stack.

84.8.61 pop

Command pop
Format `pop`
Function Removes the uppermost element from the stack.

84.8.62 quit

Command quit
Format `quit`
Function Concludes the work of the interpreter.

84.8.63 rand

Command rand
Format `rand`
Function Stores a random number (integer) on the stack.

84.8.64 rcurveto

Command rcurveto

Format `dx1, dy1 dx2 dy2 dx3 dy3 rcurveto`

Function Draws a Bézier curve from the current path relative to the coordinate entries `dx`, `dy`.

84.8.65 repeat

Command repeat

Format `count { proc } repeat`

Function Executes the instructions in `proc` count-times.

84.8.66 rlinto

Command rlinto

Format `dx dy rlineto`

Function Creates a new sub-path through a relative shift by the distance `dx`,`dy`.

84.8.67 roll

Command roll

Format `elem1...elemx n j roll`

Function Shifts `n` elements of the stack by `j` positions round the circle.

84.8.68 round

Command round

Format `num1 round`

Function Rounds `num1` to the nearest integer value.

84.8.69 scale

Command scale

Format `x y scale`

Function Alters the scaling of the X and Y axes.

84.8.70 scalefont

Command scalefont

Format `font scale scalefont`

Function Scales the size of the font before output.

84.8.71 search

Command search
Format `string search`
Function Searches for string according to the string search and stores the result on the stack as:

`Reststring, search, start section, bool`

The uppermost value on the stack indicates whether the string has been found (`bool` = true).

84.8.72 setfont

Command setfont
Format `font setfont`
Function Activates the font indicated as the current font.

84.8.73 setgray

Command setgray
Format `num setgray`
Function Establishes the shading for drawing operations. The value of `num` can be between `0` (white) and `1` (black).

84.8.74 setlinewidth

Command setlinewidth
Format `num setlinewidth`
Function Sets the width of lines to a defined value.

84.8.75 show

Command show
Format `(text) show`
Function Displays the text from the stack in the current path.

84.8.76 showpage

Command showpage
Format `showpage`
Function Copies the current page to the output device.

84.8.77 sin

Command sin

Format `angle sin`

Function Calculates the sine of the `angle` indicated and stores the result on the stack as a floating point value.

84.8.78 sqrt

Command sqrt

Format `num sqrt`

Function Calculates the square root of `num` and stores the result on the stack as a floating point value.

84.8.79 string

Command string

Format `int string`

Function Creates a string object of length `int`.

84.8.80 stringwidth

Command stringwidth

Format `string stringwidth`

Function Returns the length of the string indicated.

84.8.81 stroke

Command stroke

Format `stroke`

Function Draws a line along the current path. Only after this operation will objects be drawn in the current color.

84.8.82 sub

Command sub

Format `num1 num2 sub`

Function Subtracts `num1` – `num2` and places the result on the stack.

84.8.83 truncate

Command truncate

Format `num truncate`

Function Removes the part of `num` after the decimal point and stores the result on the stack.

84.8.84 xor

Command xor

Format `bool1 bool2 xor`

Function `XOR`s the two values `bool1` and `bool2` and stores the result on the stack.

This concludes the description of the most important PostScript instructions. Further details are given in the references in Appendix C. This is particularly relevant in the case of Display PostScript and PostScript Level 2.

Appendices

A

Format conversion programs

A user who works with standard programs is often faced with the question of how to read existing files in external formats into the target program. In some cases, the program may be able to implement the required conversion. However, this approach is not always possible. This appendix briefly describes some of the products that explicitly carry out format conversions. The appendix begins with a summary of the file formats in use.

A.1 Summary of file formats

No matter how varied the software on the market may be, the file formats actually in use are equally if not more numerous. It is often a real problem even to identify the format used from the file name extension. The following section offers a brief summary, albeit incomplete, of the most common formats. The order in which the formats are presented is of no significance.

A.1.1 EPS

Encapsulated PostScript, used for describing text and graphics. Now supported by many programs as an output format; can generally be imported. However, very few programs are actually capable of displaying EPS images. A PostScript device is needed for this. The files are in text form and can be inspected with an editor.

A.1.2 DXF (File Extension DXF)

Graphic vector format, used by AutoCAD for exporting data. The format can be imported by a small number of programs. Files can be inspected and altered using an editor.

A.1.3 DHP (File Extension DHP)

Output format for the drawing program Dr. Halo II. A binary format, widely distributed in the USA.

A.1.4 CGM (File Extension CGM)

Computer Graphics Metafile format, an internationally standardized format for the output of graphics. Contains graphic elements in the form of meta-objects (circles, polygons, and so on). Now supported by many programs as an export/import format. Drivers are available from GSS.

A.1.5 IGES (File Extension IGE)

Graphic vector format, used by CAD programs for data export. The format can be imported by some programs. Files can be inspected and altered with an editor.

A.1.6 IMG (File Extension IMG)

Pixel graphic format for GEM programs (for example, GEM Paint). Can be imported by various programs.

A.1.7 GEM (File Extension GEM)

This is the vector format defined by the GEM user interface. It is another metafile format which describes the objects of the GEM VDI. Certain DTP programs can read GEM files. The GEM program DRAW creates images in this format.

A.1.8 HPGL

Graphics display format, defined to control the Hewlett Packard plotter. Basically, describes pen movements (vector operations). Now partially replaced by HPGL/2. Most programs can create HPGL/2 printouts. Many programs can read the data in again, enabling a computer-independent format.

A.1.9 TIFF (Extension TIF)

Tag Image File Format, a manufacturer-independent format defined by Aldus, HP and Microsoft. Now supported by many manufacturers, especially for scanners. Monochrome or color images can be stored as bitmaps.

A.1.10 PNTG (Extension MAC)

Also referred to as MAC format. Used on the Macintosh by the program MAC PAINT for storing graphics.

A.1.11 RIFF

Raster Image File Format, a compressed Macintosh variant of the TIFF format from Letraset. The Microsoft RIFF format can store multimedia data in various files (AVI, WAV).

A.1.12 PPIX (Extension PIX)

The graphics format of PC PaintBrush Plus.

A.1.13 PCX (Extension PCX)

Popular format for storing pixel graphics on the PC. Introduced by ZSOFT with PaintBrush. Can be imported by most programs.

A.1.14 WPG (Extension WPG)

Graphics format defined by the WordPerfect Corporation. A hardware-independent format for graphics.

A.1.15 PIC (Extension PIC)

Output format of LOTUS 1-2-3 for graphics files processed by Printgraph. The extension PIC is also used by other programs (for example Dr. Halo) for graphics. However, the structure of these formats is different, often giving cause for confusion.

A.1.16 DCA

This is the document format defined by IBM for the exchange of texts. The format is used on mainframes and can be read by a number of text programs. The Revisable Text variant (RTF) contains texts that can still be revised. In the Final Form Text variant (FFT), the texts are ready for printing.

A.1.17 MSP (Extension MSP)

Graphics format for the storage of monochrome or color bitmap graphics using Windows 2.x. Used by MS-PAINT. Can be read by a number of programs.

A.1.18 GIF (Extension GIF)

CompuServe format for the transfer of monochrome or color images in bitmap format. A hardware-independent format which can contain several images in each file.

A.1.19 RLE (Extension RLE)

Compressed bitmap files under Windows 3.x which are stored in BMP format. In Windows 3.x, the format is used for displaying start logos. Supported by programs such as WINGIF, Paintshop and Dodot.

A.1.20 BMP (Extension BMP)

Windows bitmap format for storing graphics. Used by PaintBrush. Images are stored in a device-independent form with the aim of ensuring compatibility between various graphics adapters.

OS/2 also uses a bitmap format. However, there are slight differences between this and the Windows BMP format (depending on the version).

A.1.21 WMF (Extension WMF)

Metafile format of Windows 3.x, used for storing graphics.

A.1.22 PCL

Printer description language developed for Hewlett Packard laser printers. Used by some programs as an import format.

A.1.23 GX2

Format of the program SHOW-Partner. Used for storing image sequences.

A.1.24 CLP (Extension CLP)

Format for the Windows Clipboard. Can contain texts and image data.

A.1.25 CAL (Extension CAL)

Format of the Windows calendar program for storing dates.

A.1.26 WRI (Extension WRI)

Used by the Windows program Write for storing texts. Similar structure to the Word format.

A.1.27 CRD (Extension CRD)

Format used by the Windows Cardfile to store index cards.

A.1.28 TXT (Extension TXT or DOC)

General format for storing texts. Used by many word processing programs. However, internal formats are different, and compatibility cannot be taken for granted.

A.1.29 IFF (Extension LBM)

Graphics format for the AMIGA. Used by the program Delux Paint on the PC.

A.1.30 CUT

Color map file for the program Dr. Halo.

A.1.31 FAX

Format used for FAX data transfer. A number of private formats are produced by various suppliers.

A.1.32 PIX (Extension PIX or IGF)

Format of the program Hijack. Used for storing internal images.

A.1.33 PCT

The program MAC Pict uses this format for storing graphics. This is the Macintosh metafile format.

A.1.34 TGA (Extension TGA)

Raster format (TARGA) for storing color images.

A.1.35 WKx (Extension WKx)

This extension is used by LOTUS 1-2-3 and SYMPHONY for storing spreadsheets. The letter x represents the version number.

A.1.36 BIFF (Extension XLS)

This format is used by EXCEL for storing spreadsheets.

A.1.37 DBF (Extension DBF)

Format used by dBASE for storing data banks. DBT (texts), NDX and NTX (index files), FRM and LBM (report and label files).

A.2 Text Formats

Text formats can be divided into two varieties:

- Text formats with ASCII and binary information
- Text formats with control commands in plain text

Typical representatives of the first group are the formats of Word, Write and WordPerfect. If this sort of file is displayed on screen via type commands, only a series of meaningless characters will appear. Without knowledge of the format, this kind of file cannot be read by an external program.

Files from the second group are different. Products such as WordStar or TEX create files which can be read in using a text editor if required. The format commands may be removed manually. As a result the texts can often be transferred even if automatic conversion is not possible. The Windows RTF format also belongs to this category.

Most manufacturers supply functions for text conversion in their software packages. Special programs capable of converting dozens of text formats are also available.

A.2.1 WordExchange

This program is offered by Microsoft for converting to Word. It can convert texts in both directions and supports a range of formats, including the following:

DEC WPS Plus
Display Writer
Multimate
Samna Word (up to version IV)
Wang PC (up to version 2.6)
WordPerfect
WordStar
Volkswriter 3
ASCII
DCA/RTF
DCA/FFT (only Word to FFT)
Navy DIF

The program runs on IBM PCs or compatibles and needs DOS 2.0 or later. At least 386 Kbytes of memory must be available.

A.2.2 Convert Perfect

This conversion program is offered by WordPerfect. The program converts 44 different programs to and from WPF. The format of the source file is automatically recognized. Convert Perfect supports a number of program formats, including the following:

Ami Pro 1.2 (Windows)
IBM-PC-Text
MS-Word
Multimate
Officewriter
WordStar
Euroscript

This program can be purchased directly from the manufacturer. It runs under MS-DOS on IBM PCs or compatibles.

The selection of these two programs does not represent a judgement of their value. There are many other programs capable of fulfilling the same functions.

A.3 Spreadsheet formats

In this context, LOTUS 1-2-3 represents a standard, and many programs are capable of importing this format.

Other formats, such as DIF and SYLK, have become established for exchanging data between different spreadsheet programs. There are also various less well-known programs for format conversion.

A.4 Graphics formats

This is, without doubt, the most extensive area. Many applications are involved. Indeed, many applications programs support a range of formats, and a number of conversion programs are available.

In terms of processing graphics, there are two distinct approaches.

A.4.1 Bitmap or Raster Image Graphics

Using this approach, the image is broken down dotwise into individual pixels and stored. The raster of pixels can be processed and compressed relatively simply. This approach is used by simple drawing programs, for producing screen shots and for scanners. This process is also suitable for processing photographs.

However, problems are encountered if these raster images need to be stretched or condensed. Only the pixels can be manipulated, which impairs the quality of the picture. Images can only be printed on devices that print using dots, so plotters cannot be used. Transfer between different machines causes various difficulties with resolution. Individual image elements cannot be processed separately. Typical representatives of this approach are PCX, TIF, IMG, GIF and IFF.

A.4.2 Vector or Metafile formats

These files contain a description of the image in terms of graphic objects (circles, lines, vectors, and so on). This approach is eminently suitable for representing technical drawings and is often used by CAD programs. The images can be scaled and manipulated as required.

However, vector-orientated devices (plotters) are required for printing. Alternatively, the image can be constructed in terms of objects and then converted to a dot pattern, thereby enabling a printer to be used. Vector graphics are not suitable for reproducing photographs or for scanning original graphics. Typical representatives of this approach are HPGL/2, GEM, WMF, DXF, IGES and CGM.

Conversion between vector and pixel formats is not generally possible. A number of programs for creating screen shots and converting formats will be considered in the following sections.

A.4.3 PIZAZZ Plus

This program is supplied by Turbo Power Software and is a powerful tool for producing screen shots. When the program is loaded in DOS in overlay mode, it occupies around 32 Kbytes of resident memory. The remaining sections of the program are not loaded until they are activated. The program stores screen shots in various graphic formats, and the screen shots can subsequently be processed using the following programs:

Word
WordPerfect
Ventura Publisher
Pagemaker
Publishers PaintBrush

PIZAZZ Plus stores the files either in the formats:

PCX
TIFF
IMG

or in an internal format. As an option, a text screen can also be dumped as an ASCII file. PIZAZZ Plus contains a set of printer drivers, which means that the screen shots can be printed using appropriate devices.

The only disadvantage is that PIZAZZ Plus cannot read in or store any graphics files. However, there is a way of carrying out this conversion, if necessary. In this case, a program for displaying the source format on screen is needed. PIZAZZ Plus can then be used to produce a screen shot in the desired output format.

It should also be mentioned that many word processing programs operating under DOS are supplied with their own screen-shot program. Typical examples are Capture (MS-Word) and Graf (WordPerfect). These programs are very suitable for simple applications. However, problems arise if the screen shots have to be converted into different formats, because the output format is specifically adapted to the relevant word processing program.

A.4.4 Hijack

Another very useful program is Hijack from Inset Systems. This program has an extensive range of functions. In addition to screen shots, it can also convert various graphics files into different output formats. The program occupies about 48 Kbytes of resident memory under DOS. In terms of format conversion, the program supports a range of possibilities:

File type	Extension	Remarks
AMIGA IFF	IFF, LBM	Source and Destination
ASCII Text	TXT	Only Source as Text file
AT Group 4	ATT	FAX-Format, only Source
AutoCAD	DXF	Source and Destination
CALS Rast.	CAL	US-Format (Source and Destination)
CompuServe	GIF	Source and Destination
Dr.Halo	CUT	Source and Destination
FAX Type	FAX	Source and Destination, Fax-Board
GEM Image	IMG	Source and Destination
GEM Meta	GEM	Source and Destination up to GEM/4
HP PCL	PCL	Source and Destination
HP-GL/2	PGL	Source and Destination
Inset PIX	PIX	Source and Destination (internal)
Inset IGF	IGF	Source and Destination (internal)
KoFAX Gr.4	KFX	Source and Destination
LOTUS PIC	PIC	Source and Destination
MacPaint	MAC	Source and Destination
Mac PICT	PCT	Source and Destination
MathCAD	MCS	Only Destination
Windows	WMF	Source and Destination (< 64 Kbyte)
Metafile	CGM	Source and Destination
MS-PAINT	MSP	Source and Destination
PC PBrush	PCX	Source and Destination
PM Bitmap	BMP	OS/2 only Destination
PostScript	EPS	Only Destination
TIFF	TIF	Source and Destination
TARGA	TGA	Source and Destination
Plot 10	P10	Only Source (Tektronix Format)
WordPerf.	WPG	Source and Destination

Table A.1
Hijack format conversion functions

There are a number of minor limitations which apply to various formats. The entry Source and Destination means that the relevant format can be read and written. In the case of graphics files, raster files cannot be converted into vector formats. However, it is possible to convert a vector file into a raster format. PCL outputs are interpreted exclusively as Sources and the output file must be in raster format.

A whole range of different FAX cards can now be supported. Reference should be made to the operating manuals, because the range of functions is constantly changing.

A.4.5 Graphic Workshop, PaintShop Pro, Image Alchemy

These programs are Shareware products which are registered for a very small sum. The programs operate under DOS or Windows and support a series of bitmap graphic formats. Graphic Workshop is also available in a DOS version.

A.5 Format Conversion using Windows

Converting between different formats is considerably simplified when using Windows. Links between various applications (word processing, spreadsheets, graphics) can be established via DDE and OLE. The data from each program is then available to the relevant application. The intermediate store also enables any screen graphics to be stored in BMP format. If a program for displaying the source file is available, it is possible to copy the screen to the intermediate store. The file can be saved via PaintBrush as a BMP or PCX file.

B

ISO 646 Character Set

The following tables show the coding for the 7-bit 646 character set of the International Standards Organization (ISO) alongside the corresponding hex values (left) and ASCII codes (right). It should be pointed out that the extended IBM character set (block graphics characters, and so on) represents a manufacturer-defined supplement to the ISO 646 character set and has not therefore been included in the table.

Hex	ISO	ASCII	Hex	ISO	ASCII
00	0/0	NUL	2B	2/11	+
01	0/1	TC1/SOH	2C	2/12	,
02	0/2	TC2/STX	2D	2/13	-
03	0/3	TC4/ETX	2E	2/14	.
04	0/4	TC4/EOT	2F	2/15	/
05	0/5	TC5/ENQ	30	3/0	
06	0/6	TC6/ACK	31	3/1	
07	0/7	BEL	32	3/2	
08	0/8	FE0/BS	33	3/3	
09	0/9	FE1/HT	34	3/4	
0A	0/10	FE2/LF	35	3/5	
0B	0/11	FE3/VT	36	3/6	
0C	0/12	FE4/FF	37	3/7	
0D	0/13	FE5/CR	38	3/8	
0E	0/14	SO	39	3/9	
0F	0/15	SI	3A	3/10	:
10	1/0	TC7/DLE	3B	3/11	;
11	1/1	DC1	3C	3/12	<
12	1/2	DC2	3D	3/13	=
13	1/3	DC3	3E	3/14	>
14	1/4	DC4	3F	3/15	?
15	1/5	TC8/NAK	40	4/0	@
16	1/6	TC9/SYN	41	4/1	A

Table B.1 ISO 646 character set (*continues over...*)

Hex	ISO	ASCII	Hex	ISO	ASCII
17	1/7	TC10/ETB	42	4/2	B
18	1/8	CAN	43	4/3	C
19	1/9	EM	44	4/4	D
1A	1/10	SUB	45	4/5	E
1B	1/11	ESC	46	4/6	F
1C	1/12	DT/FS/IS4	47	4/7	G
1D	1/13	PT/GS/IS3	48	4/8	H
1E	1/14	RS/IS2	49	4/9	I
1F	1/15	US/IS1	4A	4/10	J
20	2/0	SPACE	4B	4/11	K
21	2/1	!	4C	4/12	L
22	2/2	"	4D	4/13	M
23	2/3	#	4E	4/14	N
24	2/4	currency	4F	4/15	O
25	2/5	%	50	5/0	P
26	2/6	&	51	5/1	Q
27	2/7	'	52	5/2	R
28	2/8	(	53	5/3	S
29	2/9	)	54	5/4	T
2A	2/10	*	55	5/5	U
56	5/6	V	6B	6/12	k
57	5/7	W	6C	6/13	l
58	5/8	X	6D	6/14	m
59	5/9	Y	6E	6/15	n
5A	5/10	Z	6F	7/0	o
5B	5/11	[	70	7/0	p
5C	5/12	\	71	7/1	q
5D	5/13	]	72	7/2	r
5E	5/14	^	73	7/3	s
5F	5/15	_	74	7/4	t
60	6/0	'	75	7/5	u
61	6/1	a	76	7/6	v
62	6/2	b	77	7/7	w
63	6/3	c	78	7/8	x
64	6/4	d	79	7/9	y
65	6/5	e	7A	7/10	z
66	6/6	f	7B	7/11	{
67	6/7	g	7C	7/12	|
68	6/8	h	7D	7/13	}
69	6/9	i	7E	7/14	~
6A	6/10	j	7F	7/15	DEL

Table B.1
ISO 646 character set (*cont.*)

C

References

- Association of American Publishers : *Document Type Definitions and Short References (1987).*
- Adobe Systems, Inc.: *PostScript Language Program Design* (Addison-Wesley, Reading/Massachusetts, 1988).
- Adobe Systems, Inc.: PostScript Language Reference Manual (Addison-Wesley, Reading/Massachusetts, 1985).
- Adobe Systems, Inc.: PostScript Language Tutorial and Cookbook (Addison-Wesley, Reading/Massachusetts, 1985).
- Born, Günter: Dateiformate Programmierhandbuch (File Formats Programming Manual) (Addison-Wesley, Bonn, 1993).
- Computer Graphics Metafile for the Storage and Transfer of Picture Description Information (ISO 8632, Parts 1-4, 1987).
- D.B. Arnold, P.R. Bono: CGM and CGI, Metafiles and Interface Standards for Computer Graphics (Springer Verlag, Berlin/Heidelberg, 1988).
- EPSIG, Author's Guide to Electronic Manuscript Preparation and Markup, Association of American Publishers (Electronic Manuscript Series, 1989).
- Digital Research (Hg.): GEM Programmer's Toolkit, Vol. 2 (1986).
- Information processing – Text and Office Systems, (Standard Generalized Markup Language (SGML), ISO 8879, 1986).
- Martin Bryan: SGML: An Author's Guide to the Standard Generalized Markup Language (Addison-Wesley, Wokingham/England, 1988).
- T. Welch: A Technique for High-Performance Data Compression, IEEE Computer (Volume 17, Number 6, 1984).

Index

B

C

D

E

F

G

H

I

J

L

M

N

O

P

Q

R

S

T

V

W

Z